Interact with your textbook

→ **each book in the complete series offers free teaching and learning solutions online**

www.oxfordtextbooks.co.uk/orc/complete/

complete: law solution

 online resource centre
www.oxfordtextbooks.co.uk/orc/bogusz_sexton4e/

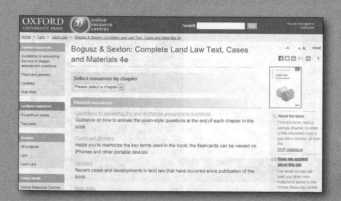

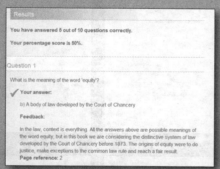

Visit the website for access to additional resources.

For lecturers

→ PowerPoint® slides containing figures from the book
→ a ready-made test bank containing 250 multiple-choice questions with answers and feedback

For students

→ updates
→ web links
→ guidance on answering the end-of-chapter questions
→ flashcard glossary

See the Guide to the Online Resource Centre on p. viii for full details.

complete: law solution

Reading and making sense of original case extracts is a vital part of understanding how law works. But how do you know which sections of which cases to read?

Books in the **complete** series combine extracts from a wide range of primary materials with clear explanatory text to provide students with a complete introductory resource.

Each author carefully unfolds the complexities of the subject, exposing the reader to relevant case extracts and supporting them with illuminating commentary. Helpful learning features are clearly presented and effectively employed, ensuring each **complete** title provides students with a stimulating introduction to the subject.

complete
series

complete

Land Law

Text, Cases, and Materials

Fourth Edition

Barbara Bogusz

Roger Sexton

OXFORD

UNIVERSITY PRESS

OXFORD
UNIVERSITY PRESS

Great Clarendon Street, Oxford, OX2 6DP,
United Kingdom

Oxford University Press is a department of the University of Oxford.
It furthers the University's objective of excellence in research, scholarship,
and education by publishing worldwide. Oxford is a registered trade mark of
Oxford University Press in the UK and in certain other countries

Published in the United States of America by Oxford University Press
198 Madison Avenue, New York, NY 10016, United States of America

British Library Cataloguing in Publication Data
Data available

Library of Congress Control Number: 2015933309

ISBN 978-0-19-872576-3

Printed in Italy by
L.E.G.O. S.p.A., Lavis (TN)

Preface

Land law has undergone several significant developments this century. In addition to the Land Registration Act 2002 which is intended to modernize the operation of land law and conveyancing, we have seen the courts developing the law. Notably, the Supreme Court, has recently considered the legal consequences of 'sale and lease back' schemes in *Scott v Southern Pacific Mortgages* and in *Coventry v Lawrence* [2014] the court adopted a less rigid approach to awarding damages in place of an injunction where the rights of a landowner have been infringed. For a subject that is generally recognized as developing slowly, the twenty-first century has shown that land law has a dynamism to it.

The aim of *Complete Land Law: Text, Cases, and Materials* is to provide the reader with a comprehensive and accessible book. As a cases and materials book the reader is given the benefit of access to key judgments and statutory materials which are supported by explanatory commentary and analysis.

Land law is a subject which necessitates the incremental development of the readers' knowledge and understanding. To achieve this we have organized the materials in a structured and logical manner. The opening chapters provide the reader with the foundations of land law. These provide a solid base through which the reader is equipped with the fundamental principles that are necessary to build a complete understanding of land law. It is our objective that this format will enrich your understanding of land law. To support the academic text the book uses diagrams, comprehension questions and case studies. Through this approach it is our intention that the book will provide an understandable and relevant explanation of land law in the twenty-first century.

We firmly believe that land law can be fun as well as challenging, and hope that our enthusiasm for this subject is apparent in the pages of this book. A lot of the enjoyment of any legal subject comes through discussion of the knottier points, and so we would like to thank all those colleagues and students (past and present) who, with their ideas and interest, have indirectly contributed to the content of this book.

We would like to express our gratitude to the anonymous OUP reviewers who have been extremely generous with their time reading the book and providing invaluable advice. Our thanks also go to Abbey Nelms for her patience, help, and support, and to Felicity Boughton, and the production and marketing team at Oxford University Press. Barbara would like to thank Ewa Żelazna for her research assistance. Barbara would like to give special thanks to Adam, Agnieszka, and Eugenia for their continued support.

B.B.
R.S.

Guide to Using the Book

Complete Land Law: Text, Cases, and Materials includes a number of different features that have been carefully designed to enrich your learning and help you along as you develop your understanding of land law.

> Law of Property Act 1925
>
> 199. Restrictions on constructive notice
>
> 1. A purchaser shall not be prejudicially aff
>
>   (ii) any other instrument or matter or a
>
>   (a) it is within his own knowledge

Key Cases and Materials

Extracts from key cases, legislation, and reports are reproduced and explained by the authors, providing you with access to the key materials you need to develop your understanding of land law.

> **periodic tenancy**
>
> this is a tenancy agreement which is chara
> intervals; these intervals could be weekly, r
> indefinitely until terminated by one or othe

Definitions

Key terms and principles are clearly defined throughout the text helping you to become familiar with the complex vocabulary used in land law.

> **cross reference**
> The impact of the 1925 legislation in relation to estates will be discussed in Chapter 5.

Following the major ref
law the owner of such ar

- 'Fee simple' means th
  perpetual.

- 'Absolute' means that
  of ownership of the pr
  of her lifetime, this w

Cross-references

Cross-reference boxes pinpoint related topics, helping you to build up a complete picture of land law.

> **REVIEW QUESTION** Paolo and Violetta cohab
> London. Paolo is unemployed, and spends tw
> Paolo now claims, 'I am part owner of the ho
> if Paolo and Violetta were married?
>
> (As part of your answer consider the type of

Review Questions

These questions enable you to check your understanding of key points as you move through each chapter.

Thinking Points

thinking point 1.5

Hans and Wendy wer
owner of the fee simp
Between sobs she ex
situation. She certain

Thinking points provide example scenarios,
enabling you to apply your learning and help
prepare for answering problem-based questions.

Pause for Thought

pause for thought

Why do you think it v
'heirs' and replaced t

Refer back to 2.5.1 a
statutory next of kin

These critical questions encourage you to reflect
on key case decisions or points of law and help
you to develop your analytical skills ready for
exams.

Summary

In the law which has existed since 1925, it
right in land.

Legal Estates

Summaries

At the end of each chapter a summary reiterates
the key topics covered in the chapter. You should
use these to check your understanding and return
to any areas that aren't yet completely clear.

Questions

1 Neema owns the legal fee simple estate (unregiste
ago she entered into a written agreement (not in th
to Markus for five years. The agreement specifically s
residential purposes only.

Questions

The exam-style questions at the end of each
chapter provide the ideal opportunity for you to
test your understanding of a topic. Guidance on
how to approach these questions can be found on
the Online Resource Centre.

Further Reading

Bogusz, B, 'Defining the scope of actual occupation under the La
recent judicial clarification' [2011] Conv 268
Considers judicial developments in the assessment of tr
occupation.

Cooke, E, *The New Law of Land Registration*, Oxford: H

Further Reading

These suggestions for additional reading have
been carefully selected to highlight key areas
and to help you deepen your knowledge of the
subject.

Guide to the Online Resource Centre

The Online Resource Centre that accompanies this book provides students and lecturers with ready-to-use learning resources. They are free of charge, and are designed to complement the book and maximize the teaching and learning experience.

www.oxfordtextbooks.co.uk/orc/bogusz_sexton4e/

For Students

These resources are available to all, enabling students to get the most from their textbook; no registration or password is required.

Regular Updates

The authors regularly update this section of the site to account for recent cases and developments in land law that have occurred since publication of the book.

Web Links

Links to useful websites enable you to click straight through to reliable sources of information, and efficiently direct your online study.

Guidelines to Answering the End-of-chapter Assessment Questions

The authors provide their advice on approaching the end-of-chapter assessment questions from the book, allowing you to check your own answers and develop your assessment skills ahead of exams.

Flashcard Glossary of Key Terms

Test your knowledge and understanding of the specialized terminology used in land law. This is a useful way of ensuring that you are using terms correctly in your assignments and exams.

For Lecturers

These resources are password protected for adopting lecturers to assist in their teaching. Registering is easy: click on the 'Lecturer resources' on the Online Resource Centre and complete a simple registration form which allows you to choose your own username and password.

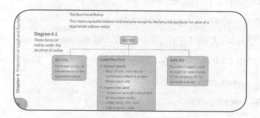

PowerPoint®Slides

A set of customizable PowerPoint® slides containing all the diagrams from the textbook for use in lectures and seminars.

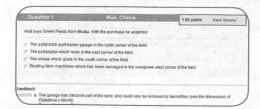

Test Bank

A fully customizable test bank containing 250 multiple-choice questions with answers and feedback to test your students.

New to this Edition

New cases and developments considered in this fourth edition include:

- *Bank of Ireland Home Mortgages Ltd v Bell* [2001] 2 FLR 809—application of s15 TOLATA 1996
- *Bank of Scotland Plc v Waugh* [2014] EWHC 2117—mortgages
- *Barca v Mears* [2004] EWHC 2170—insolvency and human rights
- *Best v Chief Land Registrar* [2014] EWHC 1370 (Admin)—adverse possession
- *Chaudhary v Chaudhary* [2013] EWCA Civ 758—actual occupation and easements
- *Re Citro (A Bankrupt)* [1991] Ch 142—co-ownership and bankruptcy
- *Coventry v Lawrence* [2014] UKSC 13—easements and remedies
- *Creasley v Sole* [2013] EWHC 1410—proprietary estoppel
- *Davies v Davies* [2014] EWCA Civ 568—proprietary estoppel
- *Donovan v Rana* [2014] EWCA Civ 99—intended easement
- *Dyer v Terry* [2013] EWHC 209—adverse possession
- *Edwards v Lloyds TSB* [2004] EWHC 1745—application of s15 TOLATA 1996
- *Elwood v Goodman* [2014] Ch 442—freehold covenants
- *Gold Harp Properties Ltd v Macleod* [2014] EWCA Civ 1084—rectification of the register
- *Holliday (A Bankrupt), Re* [1981] Ch 405—insolvency and co-ownership
- *Keay v Morris Homes* [2012] EWCA Civ 900—no part performance
- *Meah v GE Money Home Finance Ltd* [2013] EWHC 20—mortgages
- *Parshall v Hackney* [2013] EWCA Civ 240—rectification
- *Richall Holdings v Fitzwilliam* [2013] EWHC 86—conclusiveness of the register (s58)
- *Scott v Southern Pacific Mortgages* [2014] 3 WLR 1163—estate contract
- *Southwell v Blackburn* [2014] EWCA Civ 1347—proprietary estoppel
- *Swift 1st Ltd v Chief Land Registrar* [2014] All ER (D) 12 (February)—indemnity
- *Thamesmead Town Ltd v Allotey* (2000) 79 P & CR 557—covenants
- *Walby v Walby* [2012] EWHC 3089—easements
- *Walker v Burton* [2013] EWCA 1228—rectification
- *Wilkinson v Kerdene Ltd* [2013] EWCA Civ 44—freehold covenants
- *Wood v Waddington* [2014] EWHC 1358—s62 easements

Contents

Part 2 Unregistered Land

Part 3 Registered Land

Chapter 6 Minor Interests and Overriding Interests

Part 4 Acquisition of Interests in Land (I)

Chapter 7 Trusts of Land

Chapter 8   Co-Ownership of Land—The Basic Principles   216

Contents

Part 11 Mortgages

Acknowledgements

Extracts from unreported case reports, *Law Commission Reports*, Consultation papers; the Law Commission Papers 254 and 127 are Crown copyright material and are reproduced under Class Licence Number C2008002363 with the permission of the Controller of OPSI. Crown copyright material is reproduced with the permission of the Controller of HMSO and the Queen's Printer for Scotland.

HM Land Registry: The specimen title register, title plan, and form CH1 is Crown copyright and is reproduced with the permission of HM Land Registry under delegated authority from the Controller of HMSO.

Incorporated Council of Law Reporting for England and Wales, Megarry House, 119 Chancery Lane, London WC2A 1PP: extracts from *King's Bench Reports* (KB), *Queen's Bench Reports* (QB), *Appeal Court Reports* (AC), *Weekly Law Reports* (WLR), and *Chancery Reports* (Ch); www.lawreports.co.uk.

LexisNexis UK: from *All England Law Reports* (All ER) reproduced by permission of Reed Elsevier (UK) Limited trading as LexisNexis.

Sweet & Maxwell Ltd for extracts from *Planning and Compensation Reports*.

Every effort has been made to trace and contact copyright holders prior to publication but this has not been possible in every case. If notified, the publisher will undertake to rectify any errors or omissions at the earliest opportunity.

Table of Cases

Table of Cases

Table of Statutes

India

International

Table of Statutory Instruments

Part 1
Introduction: Estates and Interests in Land

Introduction to the Types of Property Rights in Land

Introduction

The aim of this chapter is to provide you with an introduction to certain basic concepts of land law. At this stage you are not expected to learn the detailed rules governing, for example, leases, easements, or restrictive covenants. Rather, the focus is on providing you with a broad overview of those property rights in land.

Before embarking on this broad overview, there is just one other preliminary point. In English law, 'land' includes not just the surface of the earth, but also buildings and things 'underground' as well. If you own an open site upon which a house is then built, the house becomes part of the land and is therefore yours.

> *Law of Property Act 1925*
>
> 205. General definitions
>
> (1)(ix) 'Land' includes land of any tenure, and mines and minerals, whether or not held apart from the surface, buildings or parts of buildings (whether the division is horizontal, vertical or made in any other way) and other corporeal hereditaments; also a manor, an advowson, and a rent and other incorporeal hereditaments, and an easement, right, privilege, or benefit in, over, or derived from land . . .

A number of points should be made about this complex statutory definition. First, there is the archaic language in the third and fourth lines. 'Manor' and 'advowson' are completely obsolete concepts, and can be safely ignored. 'Corporeal hereditament' is really another phrase for the physical land itself. **Hereditament** is a technical word for a property right that is capable of being inherited. **Incorporeal hereditament** is any right against land which is owned by someone else, such as the right ('profit') of one farmer to graze his sheep on land actually owned by a neighbouring farmer.

hereditament

property right that is capable of being inherited.

incorporeal hereditament

an intangible property right such as an easement, profit, or rentcharge, which is capable of being inherited.

Secondly, there is what may be termed the 'vertical extent' of land ownership. The owner of the surface of the land owns the subsoil and (in principle) any minerals under the land. In principle the owner of the surface also controls the air space immediately above his land, following the maxim *cuius est solum, eius est usque ad coelum et ad inferos* (the landowner owns everything up to the heavens and everything down to hell below). However, the court in *Bernstein v Skyviews and General Ltd* [1978] QB 479 limited the landowner's right to the airspace to the extent that it only extends 'to such a height as is necessary for the ordinary use and enjoyment of his land and the structures upon it' (per Griffiths J at 488). The airspace above land is now subject to all sorts of special legislation, for example s76(1) Civil Aviation Act 1982 which gives aircraft a general right to fly over land.

The extent of ownership of land below the surface was considered in *Bocardo SA v Star Energy UK Onshore Ltd* [2010] 3 WLR 654. The issue before the Supreme Court was whether the extent of land ownership was limited in the same way as in *Bernstein*, that is, land ownership only extends so far below the surface as is 'necessary for the ordinary use and enjoyment of' the land. The dispute arose over an oil field in Surrey, the apex of which was underneath a property owned by Bocardo. Star Energy drilled for oil from neighbouring land diagonally under Bocardo's land to access the oil. Bocardo sued for trespass. The Supreme Court did not apply the reasoning in *Bernstein*, and concluded that the landowner is 'the owner of the strata beneath it, including the minerals that are to be found there, unless there has been an alienation of by a conveyance, at common law or by statute to someone else' (per Lord Hope at para 27). Following this, Star Energy had committed a trespass, since the owner of the land below the surface was Bocardo.

Thirdly, we need to focus on the words 'buildings or parts of buildings (whether the division is horizontal or vertical or made in any other way)'. So the concept 'land' is not confined to open spaces such as fields, parks, and gardens, but extends to all manner of buildings such as houses, factories, and blocks of offices and flats. Moreover, it follows from the reference to division of buildings, whether horizontal or vertical, that an individual office or flat within a block is 'land'. Parts of buildings overhanging thin air, such as a modern balcony or the upper storey of a Tudor (16th century) house, are also undoubtedly 'land'.

Fourthly, and perhaps most importantly, there is the problem as to if and when 'chattels' such as bricks, stone blocks, and portakabins brought on to land legally become part of the land. The law relating to this problem was reviewed by the House of Lords in *Elitestone v Morris* [1997] 1 WLR 687. This case concerned the legal status of a wooden bungalow which rested by its own weight on concrete pillars embedded in the ground. Unlike a 'Portakabin', the bungalow could only be removed by demolition. The House of Lords therefore held that the bungalow had become part of the land. It followed that the lease which the defendant Morris had taken of the land included both the area upon which the bungalow stood and the bungalow itself. Morris was therefore protected from eviction.

Lord Lloyd of Berwick said:

> The nature of the structure is such that it could not be taken down and re-erected elsewhere. It could only be removed by a process of demolition. This, as will appear later, is a factor of great importance in the present case. If a structure can only be enjoyed in situ, and is such that it cannot be removed in whole or in sections to another site, there is at least a strong inference that the purpose of placing the structure on the original site was that it should form part of the realty at that site, and therefore cease to be a chattel . . .
>
> For my part I find it better in the present case to avoid the traditional twofold distinction between chattels and fixtures, and to adopt the three-fold classification set out in *Woodfall, Landlord and Tenant* (looseleaf ed.), vol. 1, para. 13.131:
>
>> 'An object which is brought onto land may be classified under one of three broad heads. It may be (a) a chattel; (b) a fixture; or (c) part and parcel of the land itself. Objects in categories (b) and (c) are treated as being part of the land.'
>
> So the question in the present appeal is whether, when the bungalow was built, it became part and parcel of the land itself. The materials out of which the bungalow was constructed, that is to say, the timber frame walls, the feather boarding, the suspended timber floors, the chipboard ceilings, and so on, were all, of course, chattels when they were brought onto the site. Did they cease to be chattels when they were built into the composite structure? The answer to the question, as Blackburn J. pointed out in *Holland v. Hodgson* (1872) L.R. 7 C.P. 328, *depends on the circumstances of each case, but mainly on two factors, the degree of annexation to the land, and the object of the annexation.* [Emphasis added]

Lord Lloyd then continued:

Degree of annexation

The importance of the degree of annexation will vary from object to object. In the case of a large object, such as a house, the question does not often arise. Annexation goes without saying. So there is little recent authority on the point, and I do not get much help from the early cases in which wooden structures have been held not to form part of the realty, such as the wooden mill in *Rex* v. *Otley* (1830) 1 B. & Ad. 161, the wooden barn in *Wansbrough* v. *Maton* (1836) 4 A. & E. 884 and the granary in *Wiltshear* v. *Cottrell* (1853) 1 E. & B. 674. But there is a more recent decision of the High Court of Australia which is of greater assistance. In *Reid* v. *Smith* (1905) 3 C.L.R. 656, 659 Griffith C.J. stated the question as follows:

> 'The short point raised in this case is whether an ordinary dwelling-house, erected upon an ordinary town allotment in a large town, but not fastened to the soil, remains a chattel or becomes part of the freehold.'

The Supreme Court of Queensland had held that the house remained a chattel. But the High Court reversed this decision, treating the answer as being almost a matter of common sense. The house in that case was made of wood, and rested by its own weight on brick piers. The house was not attached to the brick piers in any way. It was separated by iron plates placed on top of the piers, in order to prevent an invasion of white ants. There was an extensive citation of English and American authorities. It was held that the absence of any attachment did not prevent the house forming part of the realty. Two quotations, at p. 667, from the American authorities may suffice. In *Snedeker* v. *Warring* (1854) 12 N.Y. 170, 175 Parker J. said: 'A thing may be as firmly affixed to the land by gravitation as by clamps or cement. Its character may depend upon the object of its erection.' In *Goff* v. *O'Conner* (1855) 16 Ill. 421, 423, the court said:

> 'Houses, in common intendment of the law, are not fixtures to, but part of, the land . . . This does not depend, in the case of houses, so much upon the particular mode of attaching, or fixing and connecting them with the land upon which they stand or rest, as it does upon the uses and purposes for which they were erected and designed.'

Purpose of annexation

Many different tests have been suggested, such as whether the object which has been fixed to the property has been so fixed for the better enjoyment of the object as a chattel, or whether it has been fixed with a view to effecting a permanent improvement of the freehold. This and similar tests are useful when one is considering an object such as a tapestry, which may or may not be fixed to a house so as to become part of the freehold: see *Leigh* v. *Taylor* [1902] A.C. 157. These tests are less useful when one is considering the house itself. In the case of the house the answer is as much a matter of common sense as precise analysis. A house which is constructed in such a way so as to be removable, whether as a unit, or in sections, may well remain a chattel, even though it is connected temporarily to mains services such as water and electricity. But a house which is constructed in such a way that it cannot be removed at all, save by destruction, cannot have been intended to remain as a chattel. It must have been intended to form part of the realty. I know of no better analogy than the example given by Blackburn J. in *Holland* v. *Hodgson,* L.R. 7 C.P. 328, 335:

> 'Thus blocks of stone placed one on the top of another without any mortar or cement for the purpose of forming a dry stone wall would become part of the land, though the same stones, if deposited in a builder's yard and for convenience sake stacked on the top of each other in the form of a wall, would remain chattels.'

Applying that analogy to the present case, I do not doubt that when Mr. Morris's bungalow was built, and as each of the timber frame walls were placed in position, they all became part of the structure, which was itself part and parcel of the land. The object of bringing the individual bits of wood onto the site seems to be so clear that the absence of any attachment to the soil (save by gravity) becomes an irrelevance . . .

In *Deen v. Andrews* the question was whether a greenhouse was a building so as to pass to the purchaser under a contract for the sale of land 'together with the farmhouses and other buildings.' Hirst J. held that it was not. He followed an earlier decision in *H. E. Dibble Ltd. v. Moore* [1970] 2 Q.B. 181 in which the Court of Appeal , reversing the trial judge, held that a greenhouse was not an 'erection' within section 62(1) of the Law of Property Act 1925. I note that in the latter case Megaw L.J., at p. 187G, drew attention to some evidence 'that it was customary to move such greenhouses every few years to a fresh site.' It is obvious that a greenhouse which can be moved from site to site is a long way removed from a two bedroom bungalow which cannot be moved at all without being demolished.

Thus whether structures and chattels have become part of the land depends on a common-sense appraisal of:

- the degree of annexation; and
- the purposes (intentions) of the person(s) doing the attaching.

In *Leigh v Taylor* [1902] AC 157 heavy ornamental tapestries had been attached to the walls of a house so that residents and visitors could enjoy looking at them. The House of Lords held that the tapestries had not become part of the house. By contrast in *Holland v Hodgson* (1871–72) LR 7 CP 328 heavy machinery had been nailed to the factory floor. The Court of Common Pleas held that the machinery was part of the factory.

The wooden bungalow in *Elitestone* should be contrasted with the houseboat involved in *Chelsea Yacht and Boat Co v Pope* [2000] 1 WLR 1941. The houseboat was moored on a tidal stretch of the river Thames. It had connections to the shore for electricity, fresh water, and other services. The tidal nature of the Thames meant that it was actually floating for (on average) about half the day. The houseboat was held not to have become 'land'.

Tristmire Ltd v Mew [2011] EWCA Civ 912, [2012] 1 WLR 852 also involved houseboats. There were two houseboats which were once capable of floating, but now rested (above the water-line) on wooden platforms which were supported by wooden piles driven into the bed of a harbour.

Whatever condition they might now be in…they were structures which could have been removed without being dismantled or destroyed in the process. [Contrast the facts of *Elitestone*.] They also fall into a category of items such as caravans which, as designed, were moveable.

The Court of Appeal therefore held, distinguishing *Elitestone* and applying *Chelsea Yacht*, that the houseboats had not become part of the land.

REVIEW QUESTION In 1750 the first Duke of Bletchley purchased 'Spreadacres', a vast estate covering 10,000 acres. He laid out one small corner of the estate as an ornamental garden. This garden was expertly designed; the design included some carefully positioned heavy statues which rest on the ground by their own weight.

You have just purchased Spreadacres from the tenth Duke. Does the purchase include the statues?

(Consider the case law in this chapter's Introduction and the meaning of 'land'.)

1.1 Real Property and Personal Property

Most foreign legal systems divide property (and rights in property) into two types: moveable property and immovable property. The distinction is a perfectly logical one. All land (including buildings) is immovable; all other property is moveable. Unfortunately, English law (and other legal systems such as Australian law and Jamaican law which are derived from English law) draws a less logical distinction. English law distinguishes between real property and personal property.

1.1.1 Real Property

All property rights relating to land (fee simple estates, mortgages, easements, profits, etc) are real property, except leases.

1.1.2 Personal Property

This concept includes:

- rights in all types of property except land (so things as diverse as goods and chattels, money, stocks and shares, patents and copyrights are all personal property); and
- leases.

It will be immediately apparent that the big anomaly is leases. The reason for the anomaly is purely historical. In the Middle Ages a lease was regarded as a purely contractual right enforceable only against the landlord, not as a property right against the land itself.

intestacy (or 'to die intestate')
where a person dies without having made a will. His property (both real and personal) passes to his statutory next of kin.

Happily, the distinction between real property and personal property became much less important after 1925. Prior to 1926, if someone died **intestate** (without making a will) there was one set of rules governing the succession to his real property, and another different set of rules governing the succession to his personal property. After 1925, if someone dies intestate, the same rules of succession apply to both types of property.

There is one situation where the distinction between real property and personal property remains of some significance. This is where a legal document such as a will or trust is drawn up using the phrases 'real property' and 'personal property'. In interpreting the will or other document, these phrases must be given their technical legal meaning.

thinking point 1.1

Suppose that Charley Proper makes his own will, without getting any form of legal advice. The will reads: 'I leave my real property to my dear wife Florinda and my personal property to my son David.'

Charley was quite wealthy, and his assets included a 99-year lease over 'Greenroof', the former matrimonial home. Who will inherit the lease?

His son would inherit that lease, though that was probably not what Charley really intended.

1.2 Property Rights which Give Immediate Use and Enjoyment of Land

If somebody occupies land which they regard as 'theirs', this will almost certainly be because either:

- they own a fee simple estate in that land; or
- they hold a lease of that land.

(There are other possibilities which need not concern us yet.)

1.2.1 Fee Simple Estate

In everyday conversation we say things like, 'Farmer Giles owns all those fields over there'; 'Fiona Bloggs owns that cottage'; 'Big Company plc owns that hideous looking factory'. As a matter of strict legal theory such statements are incorrect. Ever since the Norman Conquest (1066), all English (and Welsh) land has been vested theoretically in the Crown (the monarch for the time being)!

The persons who are colloquially referred to as 'owners' of a piece of land (Giles, Fiona, Big Company) technically own not the land itself but a **fee simple** estate in the land. They hold this fee simple estate from the Crown under freehold tenure. (We might sometimes say in ordinary conversation things like, 'Fiona owns the freehold to her cottage' or 'Giles has got the freeholds to [of/in] those fields'.)

....

fee simple

the person who owns the fee simple is in practical reality the owner of the land. A fee simple can be freely bought and sold. In technical terms a fee simple is an 'estate' in land which (post 1925) gives its owner the right to enjoy the land for ever. If the owner of a fee simple dies, it passes according to the terms of his will, or the rules for intestacy.

....

Nowadays the idea that everybody holds 'their land' off the Crown is nothing more than an amusing historical relic. Since 1925 there has been no practical difference between ownership of a fee simple estate in land and ownership of all other types of property, such as furniture, jewellery, other types of goods, money, stocks and shares, bank accounts, etc. Ownership of a fee simple does not now involve performing any special obligations to the Crown.

Following the major reform of land law in 1925, for the fee simple estate to be recognized in law the owner of such an estate must have a 'fee simple absolute in possession'.

cross-reference
The impact of the 1925 legislation in relation to estates will be discussed in Chapter 3.

- 'Fee simple' means that the estate in land is inheritable and the duration of this estate is perpetual.
- 'Absolute' means that the estate is not restricted in any way. If a limitation is placed on right of ownership of the property, for example, Fiona can only live in the cottage for the duration of her lifetime, this would mean Fiona does not have absolute ownership of the property.
- 'In possession' means that the owner has an immediate right to enjoy and occupy the land.

bona vacantia

'ownerless property'. *Bona vacantia* arises if someone dies without making a will and without leaving any statutory next of kin (close relatives).

Ownership of a fee simple, just like ownership of goods and chattels, money, etc, is in principle perpetual. There is just one problem which occurs very occasionally. If an owner of property dies intestate (ie without having made a will), all his property passes (after debts etc have been paid) to his statutory next of kin. The deceased's widow(er) and children obviously qualify as 'statutory next of kin'. Failing them, other close blood relatives such as parents, siblings, uncles/aunts, and first cousins qualify as statutory next of kin. If, however, the deceased left no close relatives, his property is in effect now without an owner. The Latin phrase **bona vacantia** is used to describe such property. *Bona vacantia* (ownerless property) passes to the Crown.

thinking point 1.2

Jack owns the fee simple estate in a 5,000 acre farm, 'Bigtrees'. He is a bachelor and has no close relatives whatsoever. He is 30 years old and in excellent health. Why should he make a will?

Recent surveys show that two-thirds of people die intestate. For people who own very little property this perhaps does not matter. But if Jack dies intestate, the valuable fee simple in Bigtrees (together with all other property he owns) will pass to the Crown. Jack would probably prefer his wealth to go to his friends and/or his favourite charities.

lease

a lease is an estate in land where the tenant is granted exclusive possession of land for a fixed period.

1.2.2 Leases

If somebody has a **lease** over a piece of land then he has the right to use and enjoyment of that land for the duration of his lease. It must be stressed that a lease is itself a property right. Leases can (as a general rule) be bought and sold, given away, or left by will.

thinking point 1.3

If an owner of a lease died intestate, what would happen?

Like the rest of his property, the lease would pass to his statutory next of kin.

A lease may (depending on the circumstances) be extremely valuable. Suppose you owned a 999-year lease of a 5,000 acre farm; the rent payable is just £1 per year; there are no other obligations on you, the lessee. You would consider yourself quite a wealthy person!

Leases are basically of two types:

cross-reference
Leases are dealt with in more depth in Chapters 11 to 13.

- fixed term; and
- periodic tenancies.

Fixed Term Leases

A fixed term lease may be for any period of time, provided the maximum duration is fixed. Thus, for example, one could have a lease for one day, one week, five years, 21 years, 99 years, 999 years, or any other definite period. Very short fixed term leases are, however, unusual.

It is not possible to create a lease for an uncertain period such as 'so long as there is a Conservative/Liberal Democrat coalition government', or 'while Manchester United play in the Premier League'. However, a fixed term lease often includes a forfeiture clause entitling the lessor to terminate the lease prematurely if the lessee breaks any terms of the lease (eg fails to pay the rent). Such a clause does not infringe the rule that a lease must have a definite maximum duration.

Periodic Tenancies

A **periodic tenancy** is technically a lease for one period, which goes on extending itself automatically until either landlord or tenant gives notice to terminate the tenancy, for example weekly, monthly, quarterly, or yearly tenancies. The period of notice is usually one period.

. . . .

periodic tenancy

this is a tenancy agreement which is characterized by payment of rent at regular fixed intervals; these intervals could be weekly, monthly, or yearly. The periodic tenancy continues indefinitely until terminated by one or other side giving appropriate notice.

Suppose you have a monthly tenancy of the private lock-up garage in which you keep your car. As a matter of technical law you have a lease for one month, then another, then another... and so on, until either you or your landlord give one month's notice to terminate the arrangement. In practical terms, however, a periodic tenancy goes on indefinitely until one or other party gives notice.

. . . .

1.3 Property Rights against Land Owned by Other People

One of the factors which makes land law both interesting and complicated is the fact that while Bloggs may own the 'fee simple estate' in a piece of land, 'Blackacre', all sorts of other people may have rights against that fee simple, for example the leases mentioned earlier. But there are all sorts of other property rights which could affect the fee simple in Blackacre. One practical effect of the existence of a lot of 'third party' rights against a fee simple would be to reduce the value of that fee simple.

1.3.1 Mortgages

Mr and Mrs Average own the fee simple estate in their house. In order to finance their purchase they borrowed money from the building society. The moment they acquired the fee simple in the house the Averages granted to the building society a **mortgage**, that is, the Averages are the grantors of the mortgage; they are the mortgagors. The building society did not 'give' the mortgage. It lent the money, and was granted the mortgage. It is the mortgagee.

. . . .

mortgage
borrower (mortgagor) grants the lender (mortgagee) an interest in the property as security for a loan.

. . . .

The building society does not own the fee simple in the house; it owns its 'mortgage'. The mortgage gives the building society security. If the Averages fail to repay the loan the society can enforce its mortgage. This will usually involve taking possession and selling the house over the heads of the Averages.

Mortgages may of course exist with respect to all types of property, not just houses. Any person, not just building societies and banks, can be a mortgagee.

1.3.2 Restrictive Covenants

A restrictive **covenant** is another type of right in land which you may have already come across. Examples of a **restrictive covenant** could be: a farmer promises a neighbouring farmer not to develop his own land but to keep it for agricultural purposes only; or a shop owner promises a neighbouring house-owner that he will not sell takeaway food. In each of these two cases the land restricted is the servient land; the land benefited is the dominant land.

....

covenant

a promise between landowners regulating the use of the land.

restrictive covenant

a promise by one landowner in favour of a neighbouring landowner(s) that he will not do certain things upon his land.
....

A more complicated example is as follows. A developer sells off a new housing estate. Each house on the estate is subject to a set of similar restrictive covenants:

- houses shall not be used for any trade, profession, or business;
- front fences must not be more than one foot high;
- caravans and boats must not be kept on the properties; and
- there must be no outside TV aerials or satellite dishes.

Each purchaser is granted by the developer the right to enforce these covenants. Thus every house on the estate is both servient and dominant. This type of covenant is called a scheme of development or **building scheme**.

....

building scheme

(sometimes referred to as a scheme of development) a development (usually housing) where all the properties are subject to an organized system of restrictive covenants. Every property will be servient land, but every property will also be dominant land to the other properties on the development.
....

1.3.3 Easements

easement

a right of one landowner to make use of another nearby piece of land for the benefit of his own land.

This is a vague definition and a more precise one is not possible. The most commonly encountered kind of **easement**, and the one which is easiest to envisage, is the private right of way. For example, Andy, current owner of High Farm, has the right to use a track across Jack's Low Field in order to get from the public road to High Farm. We say that the easement is 'appurtenant' (ie attached) to High Farm: High Farm is the dominant land; Low Field is the servient land.

Another easement of considerable modern importance relates to drains. There may be a right 'appurtenant' to a building to run the drains from that building under neighbouring land (owned by someone else) to the public sewer. Similar easements can exist in relation to gas pipes, electric and telephone cables, etc.

thinking point 1.4

Reena owns two detached houses, next door to each other. She intends to sell West House, but retain East House. In discussion she mentions the following:

1 *That she cuts across the garden of West House to get to the local shop. She says 'I would like to continue to do so once I have sold West House'.*

2 *She is worried that a purchaser from her (or a later owner) might use West House for business purposes.*

Advise Reena.

(Refer to 1.3.2 and 1.3.3.)

1.3.4 Profits à Prendre

profit

a right to go on to somebody else's land and to remove from that land something which exists there naturally.

This loose definition of profits à prendre (**profits**) includes a quite extraordinary mixture of rights. The concept of a profit includes, for example:

- a right to extract minerals such as gravel or chalk;
- a right to cut peat;
- a right to go hunting or shooting over somebody else's land;
- a right to fish in someone's lake/river/pond; and
- a right of a farmer to graze sheep or other animals on land which does not belong to him.

In relation to easements and restrictive covenants, in addition to the servient land over which the right exists, there must also always be dominant land benefited by the right. A profit can and usually does exist **in gross**, that is, as a totally separate right not attached to any dominant land.

profit in gross

totally separate right not attached to any dominant land or any land at all.

A profit may, however, exist 'appurtenant' to dominant land, and one important example should be mentioned. The fee simple estates in the moorlands such as Dartmoor, the Northern Peak District, etc belong not to the government but usually to a private landowner. The sheep (and possibly other animals) which may be seen grazing on the moors do not (normally) belong to that private landowner. Rather, they belong to farmers who own farms on the edge of the moor.

1.3.5 Rentcharges

rentcharge

the right to receive payment of a regular (usually annual) sum of money. That sum of money is charged upon a fee simple estate in a piece of land.

This is a type of property right which many find difficult to understand. **Rentcharges**, for historical reasons, are very common in the Manchester and Bristol areas, but are relatively uncommon in all other parts of the country. If you are the owner of a rentcharge you are not landlord of the land. To explain this, it would be useful to explain what used to happen in the Bristol area from (about) 1950 to 1977 on the sale of new houses.

Imagine it is 1960. Bloggs is a builder of houses operating in the Bristol area. He builds new houses on land which he owns. He then sells each house for £10,000 and a perpetual rentcharge of £100 per annum. Smith buys one of these new houses from Bloggs. He pays £10,000 and acquires the fee simple estate in his house. Despite having the freehold, not a lease, Smith

13

must still pay £100 per annum to Bloggs. If Smith sells the house to Taylor, Taylor must now pay the £100 per annum.

Rentcharges have never been popular with the ordinary public. The Rentcharges Act 1977 did not abolish them, but:

- (subject to exceptions) it prohibited the creation of new ones; and
- it provided that existing rentcharges (which usually are perpetual, ie for ever) should terminate after a further 60 years.

1.3.6 Rights of Occupation: 'Home Rights'

This kind of property right was first created by Parliament by the Matrimonial Homes Act 1967. Sections 30 to 32 Family Law Act 1996 (as amended by the Civil Partnerships Act 2004) renamed these rights **home rights**. Viewed from a land law point of view, this is purely a change in terminology; there is no change in the nature of the right.

....

home rights

where one spouse or civil partner has sole title to the home (whether he/she has a fee simple or a lease), the other spouse or civil partner has a statutory right to occupy the home.

....

Home rights (formerly known as 'rights of occupation') have no application where the legal title to the home is in the joint names of both spouses or civil partners. Nor do home rights apply to cohabitees. They apply only to couples who have had a ceremonial marriage or civil partnership.

A further point of extreme importance is that home rights are entirely independent of any equitable share in the home which the spouse without legal title may have by virtue of a constructive or resulting trust.

cross-reference
See 8.8 for a discussion of implied trusts.

1.3.7 Interest Under a Resulting or Constructive Trust (Implied Trusts)

Detailed examination of resulting and constructive trusts forms part of the law of trusts. For present purposes you need only a basic understanding of resulting and constructive trusts which affect land law. This point is best explained by reference to an example.

Alex owns the fee simple in a house, Chenu. Beth makes substantial contributions to Chenu in one or more of the following ways:

1 Beth contributes directly towards the purchase price of Chenu.
2 Chenu is bought with the assistance of a mortgage, and Beth contributes substantially to the mortgage repayments.
3 Beth makes substantial improvements to Chenu, for example by personally renovating the house, or by paying for contractors to build an extension.

In this sort of situation the courts will normally infer that Beth was intended to have a share in the property approximately proportionate to her contributions. The court would presume that Beth's contribution was not intended to be a gift or loan. Suppose in situation (1) that the house cost was £180,000. Alex paid 'cash down', that is, he did not have to borrow. £60,000 was in fact provided by Beth. In principle Beth acquired a one-third (equitable) share in the property under a **resulting trust** because at the time when the property was purchased Beth made a direct financial contribution towards the purchase price.

In situations (2) and (3) Beth acquires a **constructive trust**. A constructive trust can be inferred from the conduct of the parties, through express or implied bargains, that is, both Alex and Beth have the common intention to share the beneficial (or equitable) ownership of the property. Equity will intervene to protect Beth's equitable entitlement through the imposition of a constructive trust if Alex, as the sole legal owner, endeavours to assert his legal rights contrary to what the parties had previously agreed to in their bargain(s).

. . . .

resulting trust

this arises where a party who is not the legal owner, contributes to the purchase price of the property at the time the property is acquired.

constructive trust

a constructive trust interest arises in favour of the party, who is not the legal owner, who either substantially contributes to the repayment of the mortgage or pays for or personally undertakes substantial improvements to the property.

. . . .

You may have noticed that we have not told you whether Alex and Beth are married. It does not matter. Nor would it matter if Beth had the legal title to the property and it was Alex who made substantial contributions. Nor would it matter if the property were not a house but some other kind, for example, a farm.

thinking point 1.5

Hans and Wendy were married in 1960. They have always lived in Grey House. Hans is sole owner of the fee simple in Grey House. Wendy has just come into your office in great distress. Between sobs she explains that Hans has just left her. Consider the land law aspects of this situation. She certainly has one, perhaps two, property rights against the home.

Wendy will automatically have home rights, and this will be so even if her role throughout the marriage has been purely as a housewife making no financial contributions to the family income. She may also have a constructive trust interest, but that would (normally) depend upon her having made a substantial contribution to the acquisition or improvement of the house.

REVIEW QUESTION Paolo and Violetta cohabit in Violetta's country house just west of London. Paolo is unemployed, and spends two years giving the house a complete renovation. Paolo now claims, 'I am part owner of the house.' Is he correct? Would it make any difference if Paolo and Violetta were married?

(As part of your answer consider the type of trust that exists.)

cross-reference
Proprietary estoppel is discussed further in Chapter 10.

1.3.8 Proprietary Estoppel

Proprietary estoppel arises where a landowner (L) encourages a third party (T) to expend money and/or effort on L's land, and T reasonably assumes that he will have some degree of permanence on the land. T acquires some sort of right with respect to the land. L is prevented (ie estopped) from revoking the right to use the land because T has relied upon L's encouragement to expend money or effort. This right is (in principle) binding on third parties.

. . . .

proprietary estoppel

this arises where the landowner has encouraged a third party to expend money or effort in reliance on the representation made that he will have some sort of right with respect to the land.

. . . .

REVIEW QUESTION Henry is an elderly widower, who is looked after by a highly skilled nurse, Sarah. Henry pays Sarah a wage well below the market rate. Sarah accepts the situation, as Henry has repeatedly reassured her that, on his death, he will leave her his house. When Henry dies, he leaves all his property to a close friend, Felicity. Advise Sarah.

1.3.9 Estate Contracts

As anyone who has bought a house or other land may well know, the purchase of a piece of land may be a long-drawn-out process. From a legal point of view, the purchase of a piece of land normally takes place in two stages (see Diagram 1.1):

1 The vendor and the purchaser enter into a contract under which it is agreed that the land should be sold by the vendor to the purchaser (the 'contract stage').

2 The vendor transfers the fee simple in the land to the purchaser by **conveyance** or land transfer (the 'completion stage').

Diagram 1.1
Buying property

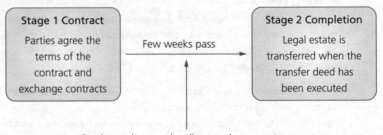

Stage 1 Contract — Parties agree the terms of the contract and exchange contracts — Few weeks pass → Stage 2 Completion — Legal estate is transferred when the transfer deed has been executed

Purchaser does not legally own the property but owns an interest in land: estate contract

. . . .

estate contract

a right which a purchaser of land acquires when he has agreed to buy, but ownership has not yet been transferred to him.

conveyance

the document (in the form of a deed) which transfers a legal estate in land from one person to another. It does not include a will or contract. A deed of gift can also act as a conveyance. A definition of a conveyance can be found in s205(1)(ii) Law of Property Act 1925.

. . . .

The time interval between stages (1) and (2) is normally only a few weeks. The important point to remember is that, during this time interval, the purchaser does not own the fee simple in the land. But he does own an interest in the land known as an **estate contract**. Using the previous example it is possible to say that an estate contract is a right which a person has once he has agreed to buy a parcel of land, but legal ownership has not yet been transferred to him.

1.3.10 Options

Suppose, during his travels, Andy comes across Purple House, a very attractive country residence. Andy immediately reacts, 'What a smashing place; one day I might want to buy it!' Andy approaches Valerie, the owner of Purple House, and they do the following deal.

Valerie grants to him an **option** exercisable at any time within the next ten years. He pays her £5,000 for the option. The option agreement includes a clause that should he exercise the option the price for Purple House itself is to be negotiated between them. If they cannot agree a figure, the price is to be fixed by an arbitrator appointed by the President of the Royal Institution of Chartered Surveyors.

option

a right under which the grantee (ie owner) of the option can at any time during a fixed period (not exceeding 21 years) exercise the option and insist that the land, the subject matter of the option, is sold or leased to him.

It is important to note the following points:

- If at any time in the next ten years Andy exercises the option, Valerie cannot turn round and say, 'But I don't want to sell.' Andy can sue if she refuses to comply.

- Valerie has in effect granted Andy a valuable right over Purple House. Hence the price of £5,000 which Andy paid for the option.

- An option should not be confused with a right of first refusal (sometimes called a **right of pre-emption**). A right of first refusal is much less valuable than an option. Suppose that Valerie had granted Andy a right of first refusal instead of an option. All that would mean is that if she decided to sell she would have to offer the property to Andy before she put it on the open market.

- The clause in the option agreement regarding the fixing of the price if Andy does exercise the option reflects standard modern practice.

pre-emption right
the holder of a right of first refusal can exercise their right should the owner of the property decide to sell.

1.3.11 The Trust

The Concept of the Trust

The concept of the trust is fundamental to English property law, and has been so for hundreds of years. You have probably already learnt that historically the common law had the biggest influence on the evolution of English law. But the system of rules known as equity, developed by the Court of Chancery, has also been and remains of profound importance. The concept of the trust is equity's biggest contribution to the English legal tradition:

A trust normally involves three parties or groups of parties:

- the settlor who creates the trust;

- the trustees who manage the trust property but do not keep any income (rents, interest, dividends, etc) derived from the property; and

- the beneficiaries who are entitled to the income from the trust property.

The structure of a trust is illustrated by Diagram 1.2.

The references in Diagram 1.2 to 'legal title' and 'equitable title' can be properly explained only by going back a long way in history to about 1300. The following story is typical of that era.

Diagram 1.2
Structure of a trust

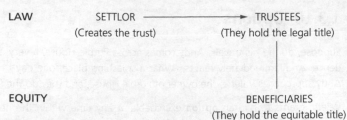

LAW   SETTLOR ──────────▶ TRUSTEES
       (Creates the trust)   (They hold the legal title)

EQUITY   BENEFICIARIES
                              (They hold the equitable title)

Sir Richard Goodbody is going abroad for a long period of time, quite probably on a crusade or some other warlike activity. He is concerned that, in his absence:

- his land ('Widetrees Manor') should be properly managed; and
- the income from the land should be used to support his wife and children.

He makes the following arrangement with Thomas and Terence, two old friends whom he thinks he can trust. He transfers the ownership (ie the 'fee simple') in Widetrees Manor to Thomas and Terence. They agree:

- to manage the land;
- to pay the income from the land to Lady Goodbody and the children;
- to transfer the land back to Sir Richard on his return; and
- should Sir Richard be killed, to transfer the land to Sir Richard's eldest son Stephen on his attaining the age of 21.

Now, with the vast majority of trusts created over the last 700 years, the trustees faithfully carry out their trust and the beneficiaries are perfectly happy. Thomas and Terence turn out to be a couple of rogues. They manage Widetrees Manor, but keep all the profits from the land for themselves. Lady Goodbody and the children (the 'beneficiaries') are left destitute. They resort to litigation.

Lady Goodbody first tries to bring proceedings against Terence and Thomas in one of the common law courts (the Court of King's Bench, Common Pleas, or Exchequer). These proceedings are dismissed. The court rules that, under the common law, Thomas and Terence are the legal owners of Widetrees Manor, and they can do what they like with the land. The claims of Lady Goodbody and the children are purely moral ones.

Lady Goodbody now goes to the Lord Chancellor, who until about 1550 was usually a distinguished clergyman rather than a lawyer. He is very concerned that Thomas and Terence carry out their moral obligations. He thus orders them to carry out the terms of the trust, and to pay the profits from the land to the Goodbody family. If they disobey his order, they are locked up for contempt of court, the 'court' being the Court of Chancery.

As a result of many cases similar to the example we have just considered, it became apparent that where a trust is created:

1 the trustees (Thomas and Terence in our example) are recognized by the common law as the owners of the property—they are the legal owners of the property; and

2 the beneficiaries (the Goodbody family in our example) are recognized by equity as the owners of the property—they are the equitable owners. Each beneficiary has a separate equitable interest in the trust property.

Until the reorganization of English courts in 1875, if trustees committed a breach of trust, the beneficiaries could not bring a successful claim in a common law court. They could only enforce their claim in the Court of Chancery. Although the courts were merged in 1875, the distinction between common law and equity has continued. In particular, it is still correct to refer to trustees as legal owners and to beneficiaries as equitable owners.

thinking point 1.6

Imagine that it is 1850. Tim and Tom hold a large farm, Blackacre, in trust for Anne, Betty, and Cath. Tim and Tom are in breach of trust by keeping the profits from Blackacre for themselves. In which court should the women commence proceedings?

Since the example occurred before 1875, they would of course sue in the Court of Chancery. If the example happened today, they would sue in the High Court. But note that the case would be allocated to the Chancery Division of the High Court.

Modern Trusts

The Trust Property

Any type of property can be subjected to a trust, even items such as antiques or valuable paintings. Land is still often subjected to a trust. However, in most modern trusts the trust property is stocks and shares, or other investment assets such as company debentures or government bonds. Usually trustees of investment assets have wide powers to vary the investments; see s3 Trustee Act 2000.

settlor

a person who creates a trust of land or other property.

The **settlor's** motivation in creating the trust may well even today be to benefit members of his family, or perhaps his friends or employees; or he may wish to benefit 'charity'. With a charitable trust the trust has charitable purposes; there are no human beneficiaries.

Trusts may be created '*inter vivos*', that is, while the settlor is still alive. Alternatively, a settlor may create a trust by his will, though it should be stressed that a will only takes effect when the testator (the person who has made the will) actually dies.

(It is usual to think of the settlor, trustees, and beneficiaries, as three distinct persons or groups of persons. This is not always the case. For example, a settlor may appoint himself as one of the trustees, or, rather paradoxically, some of the beneficiaries may also be trustees.)

19

Trusts of Land

This area of law has been subjected to major changes introduced by the Trusts of Land and Appointment of Trustees Act 1996 (TOLATA 1996). This Act came into force on 1 January 1997.

Prior to TOLATA 1996, trusts of land came in three basic forms:

* strict settlements;
* trusts for sale; and
* bare trusts.

Strict Settlement

This is a type of trust which could be applied only to land. Strict settlements used to be extremely important. It is estimated that even as late as the end of the nineteenth century, 50 per cent of all land in England was subject to a strict settlement! Nowadays strict settlements are rare but not unknown. For reasons which will emerge later in this text, modern lawyers discouraged their clients from creating strict settlements.

A strict settlement was usually created where the settlor hoped that the land would remain 'in the family' from generation to generation, for example land was granted to A for life, remainder to A's eldest son (B) for life, remainder to A's eldest grandson (C) in fee simple. Do not worry at this stage about the technical word 'remainder'.

What is important is to understand that:

- A, B, and C are the beneficiaries of a trust;
- A enjoys the benefits from the land for his lifetime;
- on A's death the right to enjoy the benefits from the land passes to B for his lifetime; and
- on B's death, C becomes entitled to the land outright, and can do what he likes with the land.

cross-reference
See 2.8.3 for a discussion of meaning of 'remainder'.

You may well be asking the question, 'If a strict settlement is a form of trust, and A, B, and C are the beneficiaries, who then are the trustees of the land?' Strangely, **strict settlements** are a big anomaly in this respect when compared to all other trusts. The life tenant, A in our example (and not independent trustees) acts as the trustee for himself and the other beneficiaries.

cross-reference
See also 7.1.2 for a discussion of strict settlements.

settlement

in modern law, another name for a trust.

strict settlement

a form of trust where the settlor's intention is that land should stay in the family from generation to generation. The legal title to the land is held by the life tenant, not by independent trustees.

Trust for Sale

Almost all trusts of land in existence immediately prior to 1997 were trusts for sale. For example, Hatherton House is conveyed by Xavier to Tanveer and Turi as trustees with a direction that they must sell the property and invest the proceeds; the investments are to be held in trust for Xavier's children. You will no doubt immediately realize that:

- Xavier is the settlor;
- Tanveer and Turi are the trustees; and
- Xavier's children are the beneficiaries.

What is rather more surprising is the fact that Tanveer and Turi do not in fact have to sell the land immediately. Trustees for sale nowadays invariably have 'a power to postpone sale'. This means that they can put off selling the property indefinitely. This is an important, if rather paradoxical, point which you will have to get used to.

One other point to make at this stage is that while a strict settlement could be applied only to land, any type of property can be made the subject of a **trust for sale**.

trust for sale

a form of trust under which the legal title was vested in trustees who were theoretically under a duty to sell the land and invest the proceeds for the benefit of the beneficiaries. In reality, the trustees often postponed the sale indefinitely.

pause for thought

In the previous example of a trust of Hatherton House, who holds the legal title to the land, and who owns equitable interests under the trust?

Bare Trust

This is also a form of trust which can be applied to any type of property. It is rare in practice. A bare trust is any trust where the legal ownership of the property is vested in trustees, but:

- there is only one beneficiary;
- he/she is of full age; and
- he/she is entitled to all the benefits from the trust property.

Trusts of Land post 1996

TOLATA 1996 governs:

- all trusts of land created after 1996; and
- all trusts of land existing on 1 January 1997, except strict settlements.

Except for the very few strict settlements which survive TOLATA 1996, there will be now just one type of trust, nowadays simply referred to as 'trusts of land'. Put in a slightly different way, all existing trusts for sale and bare trusts of land, and all new trusts affecting land, take effect as trusts of land. It is no longer possible to create a strict settlement.

Where a trust of land exists, the situation is like the old trust for sale, but with one difference. As with a trust for sale, the trustees hold the legal title and the beneficiaries own equitable interests. The difference is that with the trust of land, there is no longer the paradox of a duty to sell coupled with a power to postpone sale. Instead, the trust of land trustees have the power to sell at any time they choose.

REVIEW QUESTION If you are the owner of a property, that means you are responsible for the following:

- the day-to-day management of the property; and
- the benefits from the land (eg the profits from the farm; rent from the tenants).

In the light of this, where there is a trust of land, who 'owns' the land?

REVIEW QUESTION On being told that trustees are (traditionally) unpaid, a student remarked 'who would want to be a trustee?' Why did the student ask the question, and what might your answer be?

Proof of Title to Land

1.4.1 Importance of Proof of Title

As you probably already know, buying a piece of land (be it a house, field, factory, or anything else) can be a painfully slow process. One of the reasons for the slowness is that the purchaser needs to make all sorts of enquiries about the land he is intending to buy.

Above all, if you are buying a piece of land from Victor, you want to be absolutely sure that Victor does in fact own the land in question. In technical terms, you want to be sure that Victor has a 'good title' to the 'fee simple' in the land which you are buying. Think what a disaster it would be if you paid Victor £500,000 for the house of your dreams, only to find out later that Victor was a fraudster and the house really belonged to somebody else.

1.4.2 Methods of Proving that a Vendor has Good Title

In the English legal system it is up to the vendor to prove to the purchaser that he has got a 'good title' to the land being sold. All fee simple estates and leases in England and Wales are either unregistered title or registered title.

Until 1897 unregistered title was the only system operating in this country. It can be fairly described as the 'traditional system' for proving that a vendor has a title to his land.

1.4.3 Unregistered Title

Title Deeds

Where land is unregistered title, the vendor produces **title deeds** to the purchaser. The title deeds are simply those documents which have been used in the past to carry out transactions with the land. The popular conception of 'title deeds' is as a bundle or pile of old, perhaps even ancient, documents. Subject to the point about 'root of title', which will be explained later, this popular conception is correct.

· ·

title deeds

documentary records which the vendor shows to the purchaser as proof of ownership of the land. They are produced by the current owner of the land to show that his title to the land cannot be disputed.

· ·

When a vendor produces title deeds to a purchaser, the vendor is demonstrating that he and his predecessors in title have been in control of the land for such a long time that no one could possibly dispute their claim to ownership. 'Predecessors in title' means the person (let's call her Penny Predecessor) from whom the vendor obtained the property, the person from whom Penny obtained the property, and so on back in time.

Title deeds will include:

- conveyances, which is the name given to the formal document, which must be a deed, which is used to transfer a fee simple from one person to another, whether the transfer is a sale or gift;

- legal mortgages, even after the mortgage has been paid off;

- grants of probate to executors;

- grants of letters of administration to administrators; and

- assents from personal representatives.

Devolution of Ownership on Death

The matters mentioned in the last three categories have probably left you rather puzzled. They are all to do with what happens to a person's property on his/her death. After a person dies there will be a need for personal representatives (who may be either executors or administrators) to wind up the deceased's affairs. There are three possibilities:

1 The deceased has made a will (ie he has died 'testate'), and that will appoints executors who are able and willing to act. The executors will obtain from the court a grant of probate and then:

  (i) gather together all the deceased's property;

(ii) from that property pay any debts owed by the deceased;

(iii) pay any inheritance tax or other taxes which become payable on the deceased's death; and

(iv) (once they are sure that all debts and taxes have been paid) distribute the property according to the terms of the deceased's will.

2 The deceased died intestate, that is, without making a will. In such a case, close relative(s) of the deceased obtain letters of administration. The administrators (as they are called) then proceed as in point (1), except that when they get to stage (iv) they transfer the deceased's property to his statutory next of kin.

3 The deceased made a valid will, but that will either fails to appoint executors, or those appointed are either unable or unwilling to act. In such a case close relative(s) of the deceased obtain letters of administration with the will annexed. The administrators then proceed exactly as in point (1).

Assent

Here we have a rather awkward example of the law taking a perfectly ordinary little English word and giving it a technical meaning. In the context of documents relating to land, an **assent** is the document signed by executors or administrators transferring the land to the person entitled, either under the deceased's will or as statutory next of kin.

Investigating Title Deeds Back to the Root of Title

In investigating title deeds it is not necessary to wade through huge mountains of paper right back to the proverbial 'year dot'.

Normally the purchaser investigates only as far back as the **root of title** to discover the potential existence of estates, interests, and charges which may bind the purchaser. Usually the root of title is the most recent conveyance which is at least 15 years old (s23 Law of Property Act 1969).

1.4.4 Registered Title

The vendor proves his title to the purchaser by reference to a register kept by the government at various centres. Registered title is gradually taking over from unregistered title. Compulsory registration of title started in central London in 1897. It was extended to the rest of (modern) London in 1926. In the 1950s it was extended to parts of the south-east of England, south of the Thames. In the 1960s and 1970s it was extended to most of the heavily populated areas of the country. There was then a lull from 1978 to 1985. From 1985 to December 1990, new compulsory areas of registration were created every six months, with the result that, as from December 1990, the whole country is covered.

The Land Registry has had to be considerably expanded to meet the growth of registration of title. The registers are kept at over 20 District Registries scattered around England and Wales.

The fact that the whole country is now 'compulsory' does not mean that all titles to land are now in fact registered. When an area was designated 'compulsory' that did not mean that everybody had immediately to rush off to the District Registry and register the land they owned. That would have been hopelessly impractical. Ever since 1897 and until relatively recently the basic principle has been that a title to land must be registered the first time it is sold after the area in which it is situated is designated a compulsory area. For example, there is in central London ('compulsory' for about 115 years) a large amount of land where the fee simple titles have not been registered. The reason for this is that a lot of land in London is owned by long-established companies, the government, the Church, big charities, and family trusts of people such as the Duke of Westminster. Such people/organizations may own the fee simple estates for (literally) hundreds of years.

Under the Land Registration Act 1997, registration became compulsory where a fee simple passes by a gift, or by assent from personal representatives. This provision has now been replaced by s4 Land Registration Act 2002, which provides a complete list of those transactions with land which must be registered (ie 'triggering events').

thinking point 1.7

Will this extension of compulsory registration ensure that all fee simple estates are registered within (say) a hundred years?

Unfortunately not. It will not affect land owned by charities, companies, or government agencies (local or national). Such organizations 'never die'.

Voluntary Registrations

Prior to 1990, provided the land was situated within a compulsory area, it was always possible for somebody with an unregistered title to register that title voluntarily, thus not waiting for the next time the land was sold.

cross-reference
Adverse possession is discussed in Chapter 15.

With the whole country now a 'compulsory area', this general right to register voluntarily now extends throughout England and Wales. An existing owner with an unregistered title may wish to register voluntarily. Registration may make the land easier to sell, particularly if the owner intends to subdivide his land and sell it in lots of small units. The Land Registration Act 2002 created a new incentive to register a title voluntarily; a registered proprietor will under the 2002 Act have much greater protection against the claims of 'squatters' than an unregistered proprietor. Some charities, for example the Methodist Church, have decided to register all their properties voluntarily.

You may perhaps be surprised to learn that prior to 1990 it was not uncommon for registered titles to be found in non-compulsory areas. This was (usually) the result of voluntary registration by builders of new housing estates, such registrations being encouraged by the Land Registry.

Transactions with a Registered Title

Once a title has been registered, all subsequent transactions with that title must be registered. When registered land is sold a 'land transfer' is executed by the parties. This involves the completion of a TR1 form (available from the Land Registry). This completed form takes effect as a deed, and must be lodged for amendment of the Proprietorship Register at the Land Registry. Legal ownership of the land will pass to the purchaser once the Proprietorship Register has been amended.

REVIEW QUESTION It can be said that from everybody's point of view—sellers, buyers, estate agents, lawyers, mortgage lenders—it is better that a property is registered title rather than unregistered. Why?

Consider 1.4.3 and 1.4.4.

Concluding Remarks

If somebody is occupying a piece of land, his right to be there will (normally) stem from the fact that he either owns the fee simple ('freehold') in the land, or he has some form of lease (fixed term or periodic) over the land.

Fee simple estates and leases are not, however, the only property rights which can exist in land. There are a wide variety of property rights which people can enjoy over land which they do not themselves in any sense 'own'. Some of these rights, for example restrictive covenants and options, can come about only as a result of some formally agreed transaction. But others, notably interests under constructive trusts and proprietary estoppel, can arise informally as a result of a course of conduct. As you will see as you work through this text, much of the difficulty (but also the fascination) of land law lies in the rules governing rights against other people's land, whether those rights are created formally or informally, and whether they are capable of binding a purchaser will depend on how they are protected. The issue of how these rights can be protected will depend upon whether the land in dispute is registered or unregistered title.

Summary

Classification of Property Rights

- *Real property*—all property rights in land, except leases.
- *Personal property*—leases, and rights in all other types of property except land.

Property Rights Giving Immediate Enjoyment of Land

Diagram 1.3 illustrates the property rights which give immediate enjoyment of land.

Diagram 1.3
Property rights giving immediate enjoyment of land

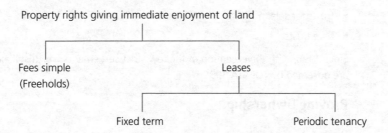

Property Rights against Land Owned by Someone Else

Diagrams 1.4 to 1.7 classify the property rights which can arise against land owned by someone else.

Diagram 1.4
Rights of a purely financial character

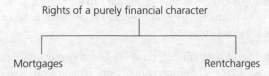

Rights of a purely financial character

Mortgages · Rentcharges

Diagram 1.5
Rights to purchase

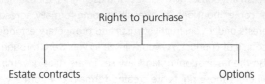

Rights to purchase

Estate contracts · Options

Diagram 1.6
Rights to use or restrict servient land

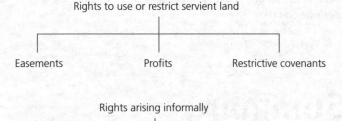

Rights to use or restrict servient land

Easements · Profits · Restrictive covenants

Diagram 1.7
Rights arising informally

Rights arising informally

Constructive trusts · Proprietary estoppel

Home Rights

Trusts of Land

Prior to 1997 there were three types of trust of land:

- strict settlements;
- trusts for sale;
- bare trusts.

Since 1996, with the exception of the few strict settlements which still exist, all trusts of land are governed by TOLATA 1996.

Proving Ownership

Unregistered land:

- Owner proves ownership by producing title deeds, that is, the past transactions with the land.
- The purchaser of land investigates title back to the 'root of title'.
- The root of title is the most recent transaction which is at least 15 years old.

Registered land:

- In effect the state keeps a register as to who owns which piece of land.

Further Reading

Bridge, S, 'Part and parcel: fixtures in the House of Lords' (1997) 56 CLJ 498
Case comment on *Elitestone v Morris*.

Gray, K, 'Property rights in thin air' (1991) 50 CLJ 252
See especially pp 292–294 for a discussion on 'vertical extent' of land ownership.

Gray, K, and Gray, SF, *Elements of Land Law*, 5th edn, Oxford: OUP, 2008
For an extended consideration of the question 'what is land?', see pp 8–55.

Haley, M, 'The law of fixtures: an unprincipled metamorphosis?' [1998] Conv 137
Case comment on *Botham v TSB Bank plc* where the Court of Appeal considered whether the contents of a flat, for example fitted carpets and bathroom accessories, were fixtures.

Thompson, MP, 'Must a house be land?' [2001] Conv 417
Case note which considers the Court of Appeal's decision in *Chelsea Yacht and Boat Club v Pope* on whether a houseboat could be viewed as part of land.

2

Tenures and Estates

Introduction

In medieval times, there were two legal concepts of fundamental importance to English land law. These concepts were 'tenures' and 'estates'. Where a person lawfully occupied a piece of land, he held that land under a tenure for the duration of an estate. Estates will be dealt with later in the chapter.

Originally there were many different types of tenure. Where a person occupied land his tenure indicated the type of conditions upon which he held his land. His estate indicated the length of time for which he held his land. Theoretically, this is still true today.

2.1 Feudal Tenures

We have already referred to the fact that in strict legal theory somebody who 'owns' a piece of land in fact holds a fee simple estate off the Crown under 'freehold tenure'. In the days of the feudal system (approx 1066–1300) there were lots of different tenures. As you may know, after the Norman Conquest, the king and other feudal lords granted land in fee simple to their supporters in return for the supporters rendering various types of services to the king or the other feudal lords. The supporter's tenure indicated the kind of services they had to perform. For example, if somebody held land under a 'military tenure', they had to supply troops for the army. If they held under 'socage' tenure, they had to help farm the feudal lord's land. If they held in 'frankalmoigne' tenure, they had to pray for the salvation of their feudal lord's soul!

This system of holding land in England in return for rendering physical services began to die out as early as the thirteenth century. By a statute called 'Quia Emptores' passed as early as 1290 (and still in force), Parliament banned further 'subinfeudation', that is, a fee simple can no longer be granted in return for the grantee rendering services.

Existing obligations on fee simple owners to perform services continued after 1290, but these obligations gradually disappeared as a result of a mixture of economic and historical factors. Many tenures also just disappeared, but some were abolished by Act of Parliament. In particular, the Tenures Abolition Act 1660 (part of the agreed compromise which led to the restoration of Charles II) abolished military tenure. **Copyhold** tenure (a form of tenure originally very important for small-scale farmers) was not abolished until 1925.

The result of all this is that today there is only one tenure left which has its origins in feudalism, namely freehold tenure. (Freehold tenure is actually the modern name for 'socage' tenure.) If somebody owns land, they (in technical terms) hold that land off the Crown under freehold tenure for a fee simple estate, there is no longer the requirement to render any services to the Crown.

copyhold
a form of tenure derived from medieval feudalism which existed until 1925. The 1925 legislation converted all copyholds into freeholds.

thinking point 2.1

Joe Bloggs has owned 'Greytrees' for a very long time. You are trying to explain basic land law to him. He suddenly interjects, 'Does this all mean that I don't really own Greytrees, but the Queen does and that I am merely her tenant and I have to do a lot of work for her?' How do you reassure Joe?

You should say something like this: 'You, Joe, are in the same position as every other landowner in England and Wales. You are technically a 'tenant' of Her Majesty, but you are not a lessee. You hold your land for a fee simple estate, a right to the land which goes on for ever. You hold that fee simple estate under a 'freehold' tenure. Once upon a time freehold tenure meant that a landowner had to work hard for his land, but nowadays the 'obligation to work for your land has disappeared'.

2.2 Leasehold Tenure

Leases did not exist under the feudal system of medieval times. The practice of granting land for a fixed period in return for a regular money payment (ie rent) only commenced in about 1450.

Where there is a lease the tenant holds the land from their landlord, and (normally) the tenant must pay for holding the land. The position of a tenant holding a lease from their landlord for a rent has been regarded as analogous to a medieval fee simple owner holding their land off the king or other feudal lord in return for rendering services.

The practical result of drawing this (somewhat strained) analogy between leases and feudal tenures is that 'leasehold' is today regarded by both textbook writers and Parliament as a form of tenure. For example, legislation sometimes refers to 'land of any tenure'.

2.3 Commonhold: A New Tenure for the Twenty-First Century

2.3.1 The Problem Commonhold is Designed to Solve

Consider the following scenario: Ralf owns a fee simple estate in Blue House, a four-storey building in Nottingham. The building is empty, and Ralf converts it into four one-storey flats. He wants to sell each of the flats, though he might retain ownership of 'the common parts' such as the hallway, stairs, and lift.

cross-reference
These rules regarding covenants in leases are discussed in depth in Chapter 13.

Under the law prior to the introduction of commonhold, Ralf would not 'sell' a fee simple estate to each of the four flat purchasers. Rather he would grant to each of them a long lease, probably for 99 years. Why?

Each 99-year lease would include promises ('positive covenants') by the lessee to keep the part of Blue House leased to the lessee in good repair. Such covenants were essential because otherwise Blue House might fall down because of possible neglect by the lessee on the ground floor. More important still, these positive covenants to repair would 'run with the land', that is, the landlord of Blue House for the time being (Ralf or his successors) would be able to enforce the promises to repair against the current owner of the 99-year lease.

cross-reference
For the discussion on
Rhone v Stephens
see Chapter 20.

Could not a fee simple in a flat be sold subject to a promise by the purchaser of the fee simple that they would keep the flat in good repair? In practice, the answer to this question was 'No!' Unfortunately, if a purchaser of a fee simple made a positive promise regarding the land, that promise was enforceable against the purchaser, but not against their successors in title (see *Rhone v Stephens* [1994] 2 AC 310).

For example, Ralf sold in fee simple the ground-floor flat in Blue House to Franco. Franco covenanted to keep the ground floor in good repair. Franco then sold the ground floor to Gareth. Ralf could not enforce the repairing covenant against Gareth. Now that could be potentially disastrous for the owners of the upper floors.

2.3.2 Commonhold Tenure to the Rescue

Parliament has used the ancient concept of tenure to try to solve this problem of the inability to sell flats in fee simple. The Commonhold and Leasehold Reform Act 2002 creates a new tenure, **commonhold** which allows residential flats to be owned in fee simple. The Act is not by its terms confined to flats. Commonhold could be applied, for example, to a block of offices. The Act came into force on 27 September 2004.

. . . .

commonhold

a form of land ownership—in effect a new form of tenure—which became available in 2004. It is envisaged that this new tenure will be used for blocks of flats. A special type of company, a 'commonhold association' will hold the block in fee simple. A flat-owner will hold his flat in fee simple off the association under commonhold tenure.

. . . .

The 2002 Act enables a person ('the developer') building a new block of flats (or creating a block of flats out of an existing building as in the Blue House example) to use the new commonhold system. Somewhat simplified, commonhold operates in the following way.

The developer of the flats creates a special form of limited company known as a 'commonhold association' or 'CA'. The CA is registered at the Land Registry as the owner of a normal fee simple in the building held off the Crown in freehold tenure. The CA is, in this respect, no different from any other landowner.

The big novelty is when somebody comes to buy a flat in the commonhold building. The purchaser of a flat buys, not a lease, but a fee simple held off the CA in commonhold tenure.

To illustrate what has been said so far. Ralf decides to organize Blue House as a commonhold. (The minimum size of a commonhold is just two flats.) Ralf will create the Blue House CA, which will be registered at the Land Registry as owner in fee simple of Blue House as a whole. Ralf would also register a 'Commonhold Community Statement' ('CCS'). This CCS will contain a detailed set of rules regarding the use and upkeep of the whole building. The CCS is likely to make the individual flat-owners liable for repair of their flats, but make the CA responsible for common parts such as the lifts, stairs, and corridors.

Suppose Ralf decides to sell the four flats in Blue House in 2011 to Phoebe, Qwara, Rita, and Steph. Ralf ceases to have any rights (or responsibilities) with respect to the building. The legal position will now be as follows:

- Each of the four purchasers will have a fee simple estate in their respective flats (called 'units' by the Act). Those estates will be held under commonhold tenure, and will be registered as separate titles at the Land Registry (there will therefore now be five files at the Registry regarding Blue House).

- All four purchasers (and only them) will be the members of the CA. When, for example, Rita sells her flat, the new purchaser will automatically become a member of the CA instead of Rita.

- The four purchasers will, of course, be subject to the detailed rules laid down in the CCS. The CA will remain owner of the common parts. The expenses of the CA will be met by its members applying the rules laid down in the CCS.

2.3.3 Common Parts in a Commonhold

When we talk of 'common parts' in a commonhold, we naturally think of the stairs, lifts, and corridors in a block of flats. However s25(1) Commonhold and Leasehold Reform Act 2002 defines 'common parts' simply as, 'every part of the commonhold which is not for the time being a commonhold unit in accordance with the commonhold community statement'. It is therefore perfectly possible to have commonholds where the common parts (in the direct ownership of the CA) includes 'communal areas' such as a garden, gym, or swimming pool. (Experience in jurisdictions such as Germany which already have the legal equivalent to commonhold suggests that there may be a demand for commonholds at the 'luxury' end of the property market.)

REVIEW QUESTION You are considering buying a flat in which you intend to live long term. You have located two similar properties. In one case the seller is offering a 50-year lease at a nominal rent. In the other case the seller is offering a fee simple commonhold. What are the legal advantages to you of buying the commonhold flat?

(Refer back to 2.3.2 and 2.3.3.)

Despite its apparent attractions, very few commonholds have been created. According to the Land Registry, only 14 commonholds had been registered as of 20 February 2008. (Law Commission Consultation Paper No 186, para 11.40.)

(2.4) Estates

We have already seen that in modern law the concept of tenures is of very limited significance. By contrast, the concept of estates remains of prime importance. If a person holds a piece of land, their 'estate' indicates the period of time over which they (and their successors) can continue to hold that land. Some of the basic rules regarding estates are easy to follow; but you must be warned that there are also some complex and confusing anachronisms.

Diagram 2.1
Estates in common law

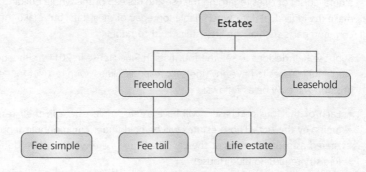

At common law there were four types of estates, and this is shown in Diagram 2.1. Under the generic category of freehold estate there are three estates, namely fee simple, life estate, and fee tail. The fourth type of estate is the leasehold estate.

The three 'estates of freehold' are far more ancient in origin than the leasehold estate, and they are discussed later.

2.5 Fee Simple

The fee simple estate in land has always been the most valuable and the most important of the estates. It has always been an 'estate of inheritance', that is, an estate which can pass on from generation to generation. Indeed, a fee simple has always been capable of lasting indefinitely.

Since the very early days, the owner of a fee simple has been able to sell it. He has also been able, on his death, to leave the fee simple by his will to whomever he chooses, even though that might mean that his 'heir' (who would have inherited the land on intestacy) was disappointed.

The 1925 legislation made quite important changes to the nature of a fee simple, and you still need to know the pre-1926 nature of a fee simple, as well as the modern position.

2.5.1 Fee Simple Estates before 1926

A fee simple estate continued indefinitely, subject only to the possibility of 'natural determination'. Natural determination occurred where the present owner of a fee simple died intestate without leaving any traceable heir. In the rare event of there being no traceable heir, there was an 'escheat'. The fee simple terminated and the Crown became entitled to the land.

Rules for Identifying the Heir

The following rules, which to us now may seem rather archaic, had to be applied if somebody died intestate owning a fee simple in land. As a general rule, the closest blood relative of the deceased was their heir. If the deceased left children, the eldest son was the heir. If the deceased left no son, but daughters, the daughters jointly constituted the heir. If the deceased left neither children nor remoter descendants (grandchildren, etc) then a collateral relative (such as a brother, an uncle, or a cousin) could inherit the fee simple as heir. The following points illustrate the rather antique nature of the rules for identifying heirs:

- the rules always preferred males over females;
- amongst males (only), the rules preferred the eldest over the others; and
- the deceased's surviving spouse could never be heir, even if the deceased had only very remote blood relatives, or no blood relatives at all.

thinking point 2.2

John died intestate in 1920. His main asset was a fee simple estate in Vastacres, worth £500,000. He left a widow with no financial resources of her own. He also left a sister aged 80, and two brothers aged 75 and 70. The brothers emigrated to Australia in 1900 and John never saw them again. Both became extremely prosperous. Who inherited the fee simple?

Applying the rules set out earlier, the widow cannot be heir, males are preferred over females, and between males the eldest takes. Thus the 75-year-old brother inherits the fee simple to Vastacres.

2.5.2 Fee Simple Estates after 1925

For purposes connected with fee simple estates (though not for certain other purposes, eg inheritance to fees tail) the old rules relating to heirs have been abandoned. The old concept of escheat for want of heirs was also abolished.

As you may remember from Chapter 1, a fee simple estate is now, in principle, eternal, and owning a fee simple is really no different from owning any other type of property. If a person dies intestate all their property passes to their statutory next of kin. The rules relating to next of kin give preference to surviving spouses, do not discriminate between the sexes, nor do they discriminate between elder and younger children. If someone dies intestate without statutory next of kin then all their property vests in the Crown as *bona vacantia* (ownerless property).

pause for thought

Why do you think it was that Parliament in 1925 (largely) abolished the rules regarding 'heirs' and replaced them with the rules regarding statutory next of kin?

Refer back to 2.5.1 and 2.5.2. Think about the reasoning behind the modern rules as to the statutory next of kin.

2.5.3 Modified Fee Simple Estates

cross-reference
See 2.6 for more information on fee tail estates.

So far, we have assumed that all fee simple estates are absolute, that is, that in principle they go on for ever and are unrestricted, subject to the (remote) possibility of the current owner dying intestate without any relatives capable of inheriting the estate. Now, in the twenty-first century, the overwhelming majority of fee simple estates are absolute. Unfortunately it is still just possible to come across 'modified fee simple estates'. No doubt you will quickly agree that modified fee simple estates should have been abolished in 1925. They are anachronisms, just like fee tail estates.

A fee simple is modified if it may come to a premature end for some specified reason other than lack of people to inherit. Just to confuse matters further, there are two types of modified fee simple, the determinable fee simple and the fee simple upon condition subsequent.

Determinable Fee Simple

This can be defined as a fee simple which terminates automatically on the occurrence of a specified event which may never happen. For example:

1 To John Smith in fee simple until he marries Fiona Bloggs.

2 To the X charity in fee simple while my grave remains in good condition.

3 To Ann Green in fee simple during the time that she remains a faithful Protestant.

Fee Simple upon Condition Subsequent

This can be defined as a fee simple where the grantee is given an apparently absolute fee simple, but a clause is then added to the effect that if a stated condition is broken, the estate shall be forfeit. For example:

1 To John Smith in fee simple provided that he never marries Fiona Bloggs.
2 To the X charity on condition that my grave remains in good condition.
3 To Ann Green in fee simple unless she forsakes the Protestant religion.
4 To David Brown in fee simple, but not if he marries a Roman Catholic.

thinking point 2.3

What do you think was the motivation of the grantor in example 1?

It is fairly obvious that the grantor (who is perhaps John's father) does not want John to marry Fiona. He is in effect saying to John, 'If you marry Fiona you lose your land!'

'It's All a Matter of Words'

It is very easy to identify a modified fee simple, but it is not always so easy to tell whether it is a determinable fee or a fee on condition subsequent. It depends on the kind of wording used by the grantor. If the grantor uses words of a temporal nature, such as 'until', 'during the time that', 'whilst', etc, then there is a determinable fee. If the grantor uses words of a conditional nature, such as 'provided that', 'on condition that', or 'unless', it is a fee simple upon condition subsequent.

The Differing Rights of the Grantor

With a determinable fee, the grantor retains a possibility of reverter. If the determining event takes place, the possibility of reverter automatically takes effect and revests an absolute fee simple in the grantor. Following the example given previously, if John marries Fiona then he loses the fee simple as soon as the marriage takes place. The grantor regains the fee simple without having to make any claim for it.

With a fee simple upon condition subsequent the grantor retains a right of entry. (The phrase 'right of entry' is really a euphemism for a 'right to forfeit'.) If the condition is broken the fee simple remains vested in the grantee until the grantor chooses to exercise the right of entry.

thinking point 2.4

If John marries Fiona, when (if at all) does he lose the land?

Now when the priest/registrar says 'I hereby pronounce you man and wife', John retains the fee simple until the grantor chooses to reclaim the land. (The grantor has got 12 years to get the fee simple back. He will, normally, get the fee simple back by repossessing the land. If the grantor allows 12 years to elapse without reclaiming the land, John can breathe again! He keeps the fee simple.)

One reason why modified fee simple estates should be abolished is that they are out of line with modern ideas of freedom, particularly religious freedom. Modified fee simple estates limiting freedom to marry and freedom of religion have been held valid by the House of Lords in *Blathwayt v Cawley (Baron)* [1976] AC 397. In this case, a clause of a testator's will provided that, in the event that one of the beneficiaries under his will should 'be or become a Roman

Catholic…the estate hereby limited to him shall cease and determine and be utterly void'. It later transpired that a life tenant did indeed become a Roman Catholic. The judge at first instance held that his estate should be forfeit. The case went to the House of Lords.

Lord Wilberforce said:

> …as to public policy. The argument under this heading was put in two alternative ways. First, it was said that the law of England was now set against discrimination on a number of grounds including religious grounds, and appeal was made to the Race Relations Act 1968 which does not refer to religion and to the European Convention of Human Rights of 1950 which refers to freedom of religion and to enjoyment of that freedom and other freedoms without discrimination on ground of religion. My Lords, I do not doubt that conceptions of public policy should move with the times and that widely accepted treaties and statutes may point the direction in which such conceptions, as applied by the courts, ought to move. It may well be that conditions such as this are, or at least are becoming, inconsistent with standards now widely accepted. But acceptance of this does not persuade me that we are justified, particularly in relation to a will which came into effect as long ago as 1936 and which has twice been the subject of judicial consideration, in introducing for the first time a rule of law which would go far beyond the mere avoidance of discrimination on religious grounds. To do so would bring about a substantial reduction of another freedom, firmly rooted in our law, namely that of testamentary disposition.
>
> Discrimination is not the same thing as choice: it operates over a larger and less personal area, and neither by express provision nor by implication has private selection yet become a matter of public policy.

The House of Lords unanimously upheld the condition subsequent which provided for forfeiture on the grantee becoming a Roman Catholic. The Law Lords stressed the freedom of landowners to give away their land on whatever conditions they saw fit. It is nevertheless submitted that *Blathwayt v Cawley (Baron) and Others* needs reconsideration in the light of the Human Rights Act 1998 and Article 9 of the European Convention on Human Rights guaranteeing freedom of religion.

On a few occasions (mainly in the nineteenth century) the courts have held a particular modified fee to infringe public policy. Notably, modified fee simple estates which discourage entry into the armed forces (eg to X provided he does not join the Navy) are ineffective. Modified fee simple estates are virtually obsolete.

REVIEW QUESTION Why do you think it is that Parliament has not abolished modified fee simple estates?

 ## 2.6 Fee Tail

Until the nineteenth century, land (particularly the large country estate) was often subject to a fee tail. Thankfully, very few fee tail estates exist today.

A fee tail is an 'estate of inheritance'; that is, it can pass on from generation to generation within the same family. It is an estate which lasts as long as the original grantee or any of his lineal descendants are still alive. Crucially, *if all the descendants of the original grantee die out the fee tail will terminate.* Unlike a pre- or post-1925 fee simple, a fee tail cannot pass to the collateral relatives (eg brother and sisters) of the original grantee.

Fees tail, which are a sort of 'cut down' version of a pre-1926 fee simple, were not abolished in 1925. However, since 1996 it is no longer possible to create a new fee tail. Where there is an attempt to create a fee tail interest this will take the effect of being a declaration that the land is held in trust absolutely for the grantee (Sch 1 para 5 Trusts of Land and Appointment of Trustees Act 1996 (TOLATA 1996)). This simply means that the grantee will hold a fee simple absolute in equity.

2.7 Life Estates

While fee tail estates are exceedingly rare today, property rights which last 'for life' are still quite common. The essential feature of a life estate is that its duration is governed by the length of the life of a named person or persons. A life estate is bound to come to an end sooner or later. Life estates can take various forms, for example:

1 Property is granted 'to Jessica Brown for life'.

This is the simplest and commonest form of life estate. Jessica enjoys the property for her own lifetime. Her rights terminate on her death, and she will have nothing which she can pass on by her will. Other forms of life estate can be a little more complex, for example:

2 Property is granted 'to Jessica and Jenson Brown for their lives', or

3 Property is granted 'to Jessica and Jenson Brown for their joint lives'.

The second example lasts as long as either Jessica or Jenson is alive. The third example is not so good; it lasts only as long as they are both alive.

The form of life estate which people sometimes find difficult is the estate 'pur autre vie', for example:

4 Property is granted to 'Ailsa Green for the life of Karen White'. This means that the estate comes to an end when Karen dies, not when Ailsa dies. If Ailsa dies before Karen the estate continues until Karen dies, and the right to enjoy the property until Karen's death will pass to Ailsa's successors under her will. If there is no will it will pass according to the normal intestacy rules.

There is one other complication with life estates. Go back to example 1. If Jessica decided to sell (or give) her life estate to Penny Pink, Penny would acquire the right to enjoy the property for Jessica's lifetime, not for her own. (Put another way, Penny would acquire an 'estate pur autre vie' lasting for Jessica's life.) If you stop and think for a moment, no doubt you will agree that this result is both logical and fair.

thinking point 2.5

In 1962 White House was granted 'to Tom, Dan, and Hanna for their joint lives'. Tom, Dan, and Hanna have just executed a deed transferring to you their rights in White House. Tom is on his death-bed. Is it worth your moving into White House?

Perhaps you had better start praying for a miracle to restore Tom to full health! You have acquired an estate pur autre vie which will terminate when the first of Tom, Dan, or Hanna dies.

2.8 Estates in Possession, Reversion, and Remainder

In the preceding discussion we have often assumed one thing which is not always true. We have assumed that all estates are 'in possession'. In fact, while most estates are 'in possession', estates in reversion and in remainder can also exist.

2.8.1 Estate in Possession

An estate in possession is one which confers on its owner an immediate right to occupy the relevant land.

2.8.2 Estate in Reversion

An estate in reversion arises where the owner of a greater estate (usually a fee simple) grants out of that estate a lesser estate. For example, Adam owns fee simple estates in Blueacre, Greenacre, and Redacre. He grants Blueacre 'to Brad for life'. He grants Greenacre 'to Charles in tail'. He grants Redacre 'to Dustin for 99 years'.

In each case, during the time that the life estate, fee tail, and lease are in possession, Adam retains an estate in reversion. When the life estate, fee tail, and lease expire, the right to actual enjoyment of the land returns to Adam. But what if, in the meantime, Adam has died? An estate in reversion (also an estate in remainder) can be inherited just like any other property. So it will be Adam's successors under the law of succession who will be able to claim possession of the land.

Two other points should be noted about reversions. First, sub-leases. If Dustin (in the example just considered) sub-leased Redacre to Enzo for 50 years, Dustin would also now have an estate in reversion. Secondly, unlike estates in remainder (see 2.8.3), an estate in reversion arises by implication. It arises whenever the owner of a greater estate creates a lesser estate but does not make express provision for what is to happen when the lesser estate expires.

2.8.3 Estate in Remainder

An estate in remainder arises where the owner of a fee simple grants a life estate (or possibly a fee tail) and then in the same document grants a further estate to follow on after the termination of the life estate or fee tail. For example:

- Felix owns the fee simple in Oaklands. He grants Oaklands 'to Gavin for life, remainder to Harry in fee simple'. This means that on Gavin's death the land will not revert to Felix. Rather it will pass on to Harry. If Harry died before Gavin, the land would pass on to Harry's successors under the law of succession.

It is possible to have a series of 'remainders', one after another. For example:

- Felix owns the fee simple estate in Grey Stones. Prior to 1997 he grants Grey Stones 'to Ian for life, remainder to John for life, remainder to Keith in fee simple'.

- Felix owns the fee simple estate in Brand Lodge. He grants Brand Lodge 'to Nala for life, remainder to Olivia for life, remainder to Philippa for life, remainder to Quirana for life... remainder to Wendy in fee simple'. This sort of thing is possible, but highly unlikely.

Note that one thing Felix cannot do is to grant land 'to Leonard in fee simple, remainder to Matthew in fee simple'. Having granted the fee simple to Leonard, he has given all his rights away. Matthew gets nothing.

thinking point 2.6

Felix owned Dower Gardens in fee simple. Prior to 1997 he executed a deed granting the land 'to Qian for life, remainder to Rafiq for life'. There are now three estates in Dower Gardens; what are they?

Applying the rules previously set out, you should conclude that Qian has a life estate in possession and Rafiq has a life estate in remainder. But Felix also still has an estate, as he retains a fee simple in reversion.

REVIEW QUESTION In 1975, High Farm was granted to Timothy (now aged 70) for life, remainder to Ursula (now aged 50) for life, remainder to you in fee simple.

1 Timothy has put his interest in the land up for sale. Do you think a buyer is likely to pay much for the interest?

2 Explain the nature of Ursula's rights.

3 Are your rights of any real value?

(Refer back to 2.7 and 2.8.3.)

39

2.9 Interests under Trusts

Equitable interests under a trust (of any type of property) may be in possession or in remainder. Consider the following example: Peter owns 10,000 shares in ICI:

- He transfers 6,000 of those shares 'to Tim and Tom as trustees, on trust for Oliver for life, remainder to Ranulf absolutely'. This means that during Oliver's lifetime he will get the (net) dividends from the shares. When Oliver dies, Ranulf (or if he is dead his successors) will have outright ownership of the shares.

- He transfers the other 4,000 shares 'to the National Westminster Bank plc, on trust for Steve for life, remainder to Tove for life'. The obvious question is, 'What happens to the shares after both Steve and Tove are dead?' The answer is that Peter retains an interest under a resulting trust. This resulting trust will take effect after the deaths of Steve and Tove, so that Peter (or his successors) will regain outright ownership of the shares.

One other point about the previous example: it is quite common nowadays to appoint as trustee a bank or, for example, accountants or solicitors. Why do you think this practice has become common?

Concluding Remarks

From 1926 until 2004, only two tenures were possible in modern land law, namely freehold and leasehold. But now there is a third tenure. Just as a 'freeholder' holds his land off the Crown, and a lessee holds his land off his landlord, so a commonholder, in effect, holds his flat off his commonhold association.

It remains to be seen how many commonholds will be created in practice. It is perhaps unfortunate that there is no compulsion on the developers of new blocks of flats to use the commonhold system. Developers are still in practice almost always choosing to build a block and then lease the flats to tenants. It would appear that, so far, very few commonholds have been registered with the Land Registry.

The cornerstone of English land law has been, for hundreds of years, the fee simple estate. The 1925 legislation changed (somewhat) the nature of the fee simple, but as we shall see from ensuing chapters, the cornerstone status of that estate was enhanced.

Life estates, and also life interests under trusts, have been important for hundreds of years. Though they occur less frequently than in the past, no one doubts their continued utility to property law generally. The same cannot be said regarding fee tail estates and modified fee simple estates. In 1989, the Law Commission produced a report which contained proposals for reform of 'Trusts of Land'. This topic included settled land and a wide variety of related issues, including fee tail estates and modified fee simple estates.

TOLATA 1996 is (largely) an enactment of the 1989 Law Commission report. The Act forbids the creation of new fee tail estates. Any attempt to create a fee tail will mean that the grantor declares himself to be a trustee for the grantee who will acquire an equitable fee simple (see Sch 1 para 5 TOLATA 1996).

The very few existing fee tail estates are unaffected by the 1996 Act. Disappointingly, the Act makes no provision banning modified fee simple estates.

# Summary

Tenures

The three types of tenure in land are shown in Diagram 2.2.

Diagram 2.2
Tenures

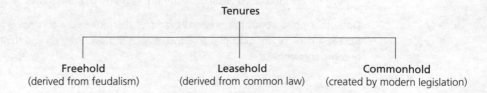

Tenures

Freehold
(derived from feudalism)

Leasehold
(derived from common law)

Commonhold
(created by modern legislation)

Freehold Estates

The three types of freehold estate in land in common law are shown in Diagram 2.3.

Diagram 2.3
Three types of freehold estate in land in common law

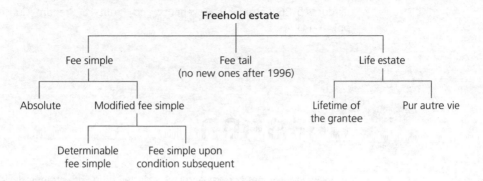

Any estate in land can exist:

- in possession;
- in remainder; and
- in reversion.

Further Reading

Clarke, D, 'The enactment of commonhold—problems, principles and perspectives' [2002] Conv 349
Discusses the rationale behind commonhold, and evaluates the type of commonhold enacted and whether a broader approach could have been adopted.

Grove, R, 'A developer's guide to commonhold' (2005) 155 NLJ 208–209
For more detail as to how commonholds can be set up.

Harpum, C, Bridge, S, and Dixon, M, *Megarry and Wade, The Law of Real Property*, 7th edn, London: Sweet & Maxwell, 2008
For a discussion of feudal tenures and estates of freehold, see Chapters 2 and 3.

Smith, P, 'The purity of commonholds' [2004] Conv 194
Considers the relationship and differences between commonholds and leaseholds.

Wong, SMJ, 'Potential pitfalls in the Commonhold Community Statement and the corporate mechanisms of the Commonhold Association' [2006] Conv 14
Evaluates the two organs in commonhold and draws upon experiences from other common law jurisdictions.

References

Law Commission, *Easements, Covenants and Profits à Prendre: A Consultation Paper* (Consultation Paper No 186, 2008). Available at http://lawcommission.justice.gov. uk/docs/cp186_Easements_Covenants_and_Profits_a_Prendre_Consultation.pdf, pp140–141.

Question

'As every law student knows, land law is cluttered up with strange devices such as fees tail, determinable fees, and fees upon condition subsequent. In 1989, the Law Commission merely proposed that no new entails should be created. This proposal, now enacted as part of the Trusts of Land and Appointment of Trustees Act 1996, does not go far enough.' Critically examine this statement.

Creation of Legal and Equitable Rights in Land

Introduction

This chapter begins by discussing changes made by the great reforming legislation of 1925 which had the effect of reducing the number of types of legal estates and legal interests. We then consider how legal and equitable property rights are created.

The rules of modern English land law are derived from three sources: common law, equity, and (increasingly in the twentieth and twenty-first centuries) statute. All three sources are represented in the discussion of the creation of property rights. You will see that the common law contributed a (relatively) straightforward set of rules, while the contribution of equity is altogether much more complex. You will also see that the Law of Property (Miscellaneous Provisions) Act 1989 (LP(MP)A 1989) has contributed to this area of law.

The differences in validity between legal and equitable property rights will be discussed in Chapter 4.

3.1 Legal and Equitable Property Rights

3.1.1 Legal Property Rights

As you saw from reading Chapter 1, there is a wide range of property rights which can exist with respect to land. Most (but not all) of these property rights were recognized by the common law. Property rights recognized by the common law were (and still are) classified as either legal estates (eg fee simple estates or leases) or legal interests (eg easements, profits, or rentcharges).

Prior to 1875, if somebody had a legal property right, he could protect that right by proceedings in either the common law courts or in the Court of Chancery. For example, in 1840, Harold, owner in fee simple of Westacre, executed a deed granting Ian, owner in fee simple of neighbouring Eastacre, a right of way across Westacre to get to Eastacre. Ian has a legal easement over Westacre.

In 1845 Kevin buys Westacre, and then blocks the right of way. Ian's legal property right binds everyone, not just Harold. Ian can sue Kevin in a common law court for the remedy of damages. He can also sue Kevin in the Court of Chancery for the equitable remedy of an injunction prohibiting the obstruction of the right of way.

3.1.2 Equitable Property Rights

From a very early stage in the history of the Court of Chancery, it became clear that it was possible to create property rights which were not recognized by the common law courts, but which were recognized and enforced by the Court of Chancery. These rights became known as equitable interests.

In Chapter 1 we have already briefly considered the most important type of equitable interest, namely the right of a beneficiary under a trust. We have also seen that if the beneficiaries of a trust tried to enforce their rights in a common law court they were sent away disappointed. If, however, they went to the Court of Chancery, their (equitable) property rights were enforced.

cross-reference
The concept of a trust was discussed at 1.3.11.

3.1.3 Legal and Equitable Property Rights after 1925

The two elements in the English legal system, common law and equity, have, ever since 1875, been administered by a unified court system. However, the 1875 court reform legislation did not abolish the distinction between legal property rights and equitable property rights. (Nor did the 1925 property reform legislation.) As we shall see (especially in Chapter 4), important consequences flow from whether property rights are 'legal' or 'equitable'.

3.2 Legal Estates and Interests and the 1925 Legislation

3.2.1 The Number of Types of Legal Estates and Interests prior to 1925

Prior to 1925 there was quite a wide variety of types of right in land recognized by the common law. But there was an even wider variety of types of right recognized by equity.

3.2.2 The Effect of the 1925 Legislation

As a result of the 1925 reform, the number of types of legal property rights was reduced, however, the number of types of equitable property rights remained the same. The 1925 legislators did not totally abolish any type of property right. Rather they (in effect) provided that certain types of right which previously were recognized by both law and equity are now recognized by equity alone. Property rights which were treated in this way include, for example, fees tail, determinable fees, life estates, and fees simple in remainder. You may well be wondering why this was done.

It was hoped that, by limiting the number of types of legal right, land law would be simplified, and that conveyancing transactions (buying and selling land, leasing, etc) would be made easier. It is debatable whether these ends have in fact been achieved.

3.2.3 Law of Property Act 1925, s1

Section 1(1) and (2) of the Law of Property Act 1925 (LPA 1925) sets out the types of property right which are capable of existing at law after 1925.

45

Law of Property Act 1925

1. Legal estates and equitable interests

(1) The only estates in land which are capable of subsisting or of being conveyed or created at law are—

(a) An estate in fee simple absolute in possession;

(b) A term of years absolute.

(2) The only interests or charges in or over land which are capable of subsisting or of being conveyed or created at law are—

(a) An easement, right, or privilege in or over land for an interest equivalent to an estate in fee simple absolute in possession or a term of years absolute;

(b) A rentcharge in possession issuing out of or charged on land being either perpetual or for a term of years absolute;

(c) A charge by way of legal mortgage;

(d) …and any other similar charge on land which is not created by an instrument;

(e) Rights of entry exercisable over or in respect of a legal term of years absolute, or annexed, for any purpose, to a legal rentcharge.

(3) All other estates, interests, and charges in or over land take effect as equitable interests.

cross-reference
For formalities of creating or transferring legal estates and interests, see 3.6.

cross-reference
See the summary at the end of this chapter for a list of equitable interests which come within s1(3) LPA 1925.

If a particular property right is one of the two 'estates' listed in s1(1), or falls into one of the five categories of legal interest listed in s1(2), then it can be a legal property right as long as the correct formalities have been complied with.

But if a particular property right falls outside all seven headings then, applying s1(3), it can only be an equitable interest, for example a restrictive covenant is not listed as capable of being a legal estate or a legal interest. It is, therefore, only recognized in equity under s1(3) LPA 1925.

thinking point 3.1

If you now look at s1(1) and (2) in the previous extract, you will find no reference to fee tail estates. What follows from the fact that these subsections do not mention fee tail estates?

It follows that any fee tail existing after 1925 exists only as an equitable interest.

3.3 Legal Estates Existing after 1925

Remember that an 'estate' is a right to enjoy possession of a piece of land for a period of time.

By s1(1) LPA 1925 there are now only two legal estates:

- fee simple absolute in possession; and
- term of years absolute.

3.3.1 Term of Years Absolute

term of years absolute

any estate which has a fixed maximum duration; this also includes any periodic tenancy, that is, a lease for one fixed period which goes on automatically renewing itself.

The statutory phrase **term of years absolute** is given a very elaborate definition by s205(1)(xxvii) LPA 1925:

> *Law of Property Act 1925*
>
> Section 205(1)(xxvii)
>
> 'Term of years absolute' means a term of years (taking effect either in possession or in reversion whether or not at a rent) with or without impeachment for waste, subject or not to another legal estate, and either certain or liable to determination by notice, re-entry, operation of law, or by a provision for cesser on redemption, or in any other event (other than the dropping of a life, or the determination of a determinable life interest); but does not include any term of years determinable with life or lives or with the cesser of a determinable life interest, nor, if created after the commencement of this Act, a term of years which is not expressed to take effect in possession within twenty-one years after the creation thereof where required by this Act to take effect within that period; and in this definition the expression 'term of years' includes a term for less than a year, or for a year or years and a fraction of a year or from year to year . . .

Term of years absolute can, however, be explained much more simply than is done in s205(1)(xxvii) LPA 1925. To all intents and purposes 'term of years absolute' is synonymous with 'lease'. The concept of a lease is explained at 1.2.2, and in particular it was stressed there that leases come in two forms, 'fixed term' and 'periodic tenancies'. All forms of lease (including a fixed term for, say, just six months, or a weekly periodic tenancy) are technically terms of years absolute.

3.3.2 Fee Simple Absolute in Possession

You may recall from Chapter 2 that fees simple, fees tail, and life estates were, at common law, 'estates of freehold'. Leases were not.

cross-reference
See 1.2.1 for an explanation of fee simple.

The basic plan underlying s1(1)(a) LPA 1925 and its concept 'fee simple absolute in possession' is easy to understand. The only freehold estate 'capable of subsisting or of being conveyed or created' at law is a fee simple absolute in possession which in principle goes on for ever and gives its owner an immediate right to enjoy the land. We have already considered the meaning of fee simple in 1.2.1 and now we must consider the 'absolute in possession' in greater detail.

'In Possession'

cross-reference
See 2.8 for a general discussion on 'estates in possession, remainder, and reversion'.

In Chapter 2 we considered 'estates in possession, remainder, and reversion'. It was said there that an estate in possession is one which confers on its owner an immediate right to occupy the relevant land. In the context of a general discussion on the nature of estates, that definition is perfectly sound; but in the context of the present discussion we need to add a qualification to this definition. First, though, an example:

Suppose Raashid owns a legal 'fee simple absolute in possession' in Hale Barns. He leases Hale Barns to Tamsin for six months at £10 per week rent. In a literal sense, Raashid will not be 'in possession' of Hale Barns for the next six months; Tamsin will be. Nevertheless, it would be very strange if, having had a legal estate in Hale Barns, Raashid should lose it, only to regain it after just six months. Moreover, if this were correct, nobody would seem to 'own' Hale Barns during the six months of the lease.

The answer to this puzzle is tucked away in s205(1)(xix) LPA 1925. This states that for the purposes of the 1925 Act, '"Possession" includes receipt of rents and profits or the right to receive the same, if any; . . .'

Now you may find this wording strange and archaic. What it really means is that a right to receive rent with respect to a piece of land (even a nominal rent or one which is not in fact collected) is deemed to be possession of that land. A slightly different way of putting it is to say that the right to receive rent from a piece of land is 'constructive possession' of that land. It follows that a fee simple in reversion to a lease counts as 'in possession' for the purposes of s1(1) LPA 1925. So, in our Hale Barns example Raashid retains a legal fee simple estate during the six months of the lease.

thinking point 3.2

Ning owns the legal fee simple absolute in possession with respect to Summerhill Gardens. She executes a deed leasing Summerhill Gardens to Seema for seven years. Almost immediately Seema executes a deed sub-leasing Summerhill Gardens to Amreena for five years. How many legal estates now exist with respect to Summerhill Gardens?

There are three. Ning, despite what has happened to Summerhill Gardens, retains her legal fee simple absolute in possession. Seema and Amreena both own terms of years absolute.

One other complication. You may well recall from 2.8.2 that a fee simple can exist in reversion, not just to a lease, but also to a life estate or fee tail. Now when somebody grants a life estate or fee tail, in practice he does so gratuitously. Unlike when he grants a lease, he does not charge a rent. A fee simple in reversion to a life estate or fee tail is therefore not, even under the wide statutory definition, 'in possession' and can exist only as an equitable interest. (Who owns the legal fee simple to the land in this situation will emerge later in 3.5.)

'Absolute'

Subject to minor exceptions which need not concern us, all modified fees simple are after 1925 only equitable interests.

3.4 # Legal Interests Existing after 1925

cross-reference
See 3.2.3 for an extract of s1 LPA 1925.

As already indicated, under s1(2) LPA 1925, there are five categories of legal interests. The categories are lettered (a) to (e).

3.4.1 (a) Easements and Profits

This category covers any easement or profit, provided its duration is equivalent to a fee simple absolute in possession or a term of years absolute. Thus rights such as private rights of way (an easement) and grazing rights (a profit) are normally going to be legal interests. However, carefully note the requirement regarding duration. If, for example, Sam granted his neighbour Charley a right 'for the rest of his life' to cross his land to get to his own house, Charley would have an easement for life. That right, even if granted by deed, could exist only as an equitable interest.

3.4.2 (b) Rentcharges

A rentcharge which in its duration is either 'perpetual' or for 'a term of years absolute' (ie lasts for a fixed period) is capable of being a legal interest. Again note the duration requirement. At one time rentcharges granted for the life of the recipient of the payments were quite common. If any such rights survive today, they must be equitable interests.

As we saw in 1.3.5, the Rentcharges Act 1977 prohibits (subject to exceptions) the creation of new rentcharges. It also provides that existing perpetual rentcharges can endure for only another 60 years (ie they will all expire in the year 2037). The 1977 Act, while it ensures the gradual decline in the number of rentcharges, does not affect the question whether a particular rentcharge is a legal interest or an equitable interest.

3.4.3 (c) 'A Charge by Way of Legal Mortgage'

The 'charge by way of legal mortgage' is the standard modern form of 'legal mortgage'. There must be literally several million of this type of legal interest in existence today.

3.4.4 (d) All Interests in Land which Arise by Operation of Statute

In this text we have so far assumed that all rights against a piece of land are created by action of the relevant parties. This is not entirely correct. Some rights arise against a piece of land by operation of an Act of Parliament. The owner of the rights will in practice be some form of government department.

In modern law, there are two (very contrasting) rights arising by statute which are sufficiently important for them to be mentioned as part of a land law course.

The Charge for Inheritance Tax

When a person dies owning a lot of property, the Revenue will claim what is often still loosely referred to as 'death duties'. With a very wealthy person, the bill for 'death duties' is substantial. 'Death duties' has, however, never been the official name for this tax. Prior to 1971 it was estate duty. From 1971 to 1984 it was capital transfer tax. Since 1984 it has been inheritance tax.

The important point for our purposes is that where inheritance tax is payable with respect to a piece of real property, that tax becomes a 'charge' on the land in favour of Her Majesty's Revenue and Customs. (The same used to be true of estate duty and capital transfer tax.) The Revenue has (in effect) a legal interest in the land.

Legal Aid Agency Charge—Usually Still Known as the 'Legal Aid Charge'

Where a legally aided litigant 'recovers or preserves' land, the costs of the litigation (in so far as they are not recovered from the other side) become a statutory charge on the land in favour of the Legal Aid Agency. This rule is particularly important where former spouses or cohabitees have been litigating about who owns their former home. The one who succeeds may find that she or he gets the house, but encumbered by a substantial charge (in effect a legal interest rather akin to a mortgage) in favour of the Legal Aid Agency.

3.4.5 (e) Rights of Entry

Section 1(2)(e) LPA 1925 covers 'Rights of entry exercisable over or in respect of a legal term of years absolute, or annexed, for any purpose, to a legal rentcharge'.

As explained earlier, 'right of entry' is synonymous with 'right to forfeit'. The practical effect of s1(2)(e) is that it applies where:

- a landlord has a right to forfeit a lease if the tenant breaks the terms of the lease; and
- a rentcharge owner has a right (if any) to reclaim the land if the money is not paid.

Both of these can be legal interests.

thinking point 3.3

Which of the following can exist as legal property rights after 1925:

- *an easement to last for ten years;*
- *a profit to last for the lifetime of the grantee;*
- *a determinable fee simple, 'to John in fee simple until he marries Fiona';*
- *a restrictive covenant; and*
- *a weekly periodic tenancy?*

Only the easement and weekly periodic tenancy come within s1(1) or (2), and they (alone) can be legal property rights. The easement comes within s1(2)(a); contrast this with the profit, which does not come within the same paragraph, as it lasts for a lifetime, not for a 'term of years'. The weekly periodic tenancy can be a legal property right because (paradoxically) it is a 'term of years absolute' within s1(1)(b).

3.5 Equitable Interests after 1925

The first point to remember is that if a property right falls within one of the seven headings in s1(1) and (2) LPA 1925, it can be a legal right; it does not follow that it must be a legal right. In particular, remember that in order to create or convey legal property rights a deed is required (s52 LPA 1925; see also s1 Law of Property (Miscellaneous Provisions) Act 1989). Thus, let us suppose that Len owns Willowmead House. He and Tom sign a document which is not a deed, under which Len leases Willowmead House to Tom for ten years. They have created a 'term of years absolute' within the meaning of s1(1)(b), but the transaction is only an equitable lease as it is not in the form of a deed and falls within the scope of s(1)3 LPA 1925.

cross-reference
See 3.6 on the formalities for the creation and transfer of legal property rights.

Section 1(3) LPA 1925 not only covers interests that have not complied with the formalities of creating a legal interest but also includes those interests which are only recognized in equity eg interests under an express trust and restrictive covenants.

3.5.1 The Status of Fees Tail, Fees Simple in Remainder, Determinable Fees, and Life Estates

Fee tail estates, fee simple estates in remainder, determinable fees, and life estates can now exist only as equitable interests. Any legal fee tail estates, legal life estates, etc existing on 1 January 1926 were automatically downgraded to equitable interests.

To illustrate the status of the estates over time let us suppose land had been granted by deed 'to Adrian for life, remainder to Bryan in fee tail, remainder to Craig in fee simple'.

Adrian	→	Bryan	→	Craig
for life		in fee tail		in remainder

If the land had been granted by deed in 1900, then until 1925, Adrian, Bryan, and Craig would each have a legal estate in the land. The legal ownership of the land was said to be divided up into 'temporal slices'. One legal estate followed on after another. Since 1925 it has been impossible to divide up the legal freehold ownership of land into 'temporal slices'. For every piece of land in the country there must now be just one legal freehold estate, a fee simple absolute in possession.

Suppose that at some time between 1997 and 2015 Croft Lodge was granted by deed, 'to Adrian for life, remainder to Bryan for life, remainder to Craig in fee simple'. Such a grant created a 'trust of land'. The life interests of Adrian and Bryan, and the interest of Craig, are equitable interests only.

3.6 Creation and Transfer of Legal Property Rights

The 1925 reform streamlined the number of legal estates and interests (see 3.4), but it would be incorrect to assume that a property right falling within the provisions of ss 1 (1) and (2) LPA 1925 would automatically be categorized as being 'legal'. Specifically the statute refers to those estates and interests which are 'capable of subsisting or of being conveyed or created at law. It is this latter prerequisite that requires the formalities to be complied with so that the property right would have attributes of being legal. Put simply, legal property rights require compliance with formalities.

To transfer an existing legal property right, or to create a new one, a deed is required. This rule is now embodied in s52(1) Law of Property Act 1925 (LPA 1925).

Law of Property Act 1925

52. Conveyances to be by deed

(1) All conveyances of land or of any interest therein are void for the purpose of conveying or creating a legal estate unless made by deed.

There are certain exceptions to this rule that a deed is required to create or transfer a legal estate or interest, for example leases not exceeding three years. These short term leases of three years or less can be created in writing or orally, provided they take effect in immediate possession at the best rent which can be reasonably obtained (s52(2)(d) and s54(4) LPA 1925) .

3.6.1 Formalities for a Deed: the Traditional Rule

The traditional rule is applicable to all deeds executed up to 30 July 1990. The traditional rule was that for a document to be a deed it must be signed, sealed, and delivered. A document is (normally) 'delivered' when it is handed over with the intention that it should take legal effect. As for sealing, special sealing wax used to be used, but in modern times almost everybody executing a deed 'sealed' it by attaching a small piece of adhesive red paper. Under the traditional rule there was no legal requirement for the signature(s) on the deed to be witnessed, though usually they were.

3.6.2 Formalities for a Deed: the Modern Rule

The modern rule is applicable to all deeds executed on or after 31 July 1990 and this is set out in s1 LP(MP)A 1989. Subsections 2 and 3 provide:

(2) An instrument shall not be a deed unless—

    (a) it makes clear on its face that it is intended to be a deed by the person making it or, as the case may be, by the parties to it ... and

    (b) it is validly executed as a deed by that person or, as the case may be, one or more of those parties,

(3) An instrument is validly executed as a deed by an individual if, and only if,—

    (a) it is signed—

        (i) by him in the presence of a witness who attests the signature; ...

    (b) it is delivered as a deed by him or a person authorised to do so on his behalf.

The effect of s1 is that as from 31 July 1990 to be a deed a document need not be sealed. But there is a requirement that the signature is witnessed.

Definition of a deed

s1 LP(MP)A 1989

- be 'clear on its face that it is intended to be a deed'; and
- be validly executed.

For a deed to be 'validly executed' by a person it must:

- be signed;
- that signature must be witnessed by one witness; and
- the deed must be 'delivered'.

Creation of Equitable Interests in Land

While, as we have just seen, legal estates and legal interests can normally be created only if a deed is used, equitable interests in land can be created in a wide variety of different ways:

- by express trust (s53 LPA 1925);
- by a contract to convey or create a legal estate or interest;
- by the granting of an estate or interest which is void at common law for want of the correct formalities;
- grant of an easement or profit which is not in duration equivalent to a fee simple absolute in possession or a term of years (s1(2) LPA 1925 specifically stipulates that a legal easement must be equivalent to a fee simple absolute in possession or a term of years);
- by a grant of an estate or interest by a person who owns only an equitable interest;
- by a grant of an interest which can exist only in equity;
- by constructive trust or proprietary estoppel.

Before we look at these headings in more detail, there is one other point which we must consider carefully.

3.7.1 'Equity Follows the Law' as to Types of Property Right

The system of rules known as equity was developed by the Lord Chancellors to correct some of the harsh injustices of the common law. We have already considered the concept of the trust (see 1.3.11). The rigid and inflexible common law refused to accept the trust as imposing legal duties on the trustees; but equity ruled otherwise and enforced trusts.

The maxim 'equity follows the law' simply means that equity copied the various types of property right recognized by the common law. Put another way, one can say that for every kind of legal estate or legal interest in land recognized by the common law there is an equivalent equitable interest capable of existing.

Thus, as legal fee simple estates can exist, so can equitable fee simple estates. As you can have legal leases, so also you can have equitable leases. There are legal mortgages, and so there are also equitable mortgages. There can be legal easements and legal profits, so therefore there can be equitable easements and equitable profits. And so on . . .

On the basis of what has just been said, you might conclude that the list of types of equitable property rights in land would be identical to the list of the types of legal property rights in land. This of course would be wrong, as there are certain types of equitable interests which have no legal equivalents. These include (as well as interests arising under an express trust):

- restrictive covenants;
- proprietary estoppel;
- constructive trusts; and
- estate contracts.

3.8 Creation of Equitable Interests in Land by Express Trust

Though express trusts of land are of enormous importance, there is only one point we need to note at this stage and this is s53(1)(b) LPA 1925.

> *Law of Property Act 1925*
>
> 53. Instruments required to be in writing
>
> 1. ...
>   (b) A declaration of trust respecting any land or any interest therein must be manifested and proved by some writing signed by some person who is able to declare such trust or by his will.

An express trust of land cannot be created simply by word of mouth. It can only be done by an *inter vivos* written document (which strictly speaking does not have to be a deed, though it is normal to use a deed) or by a will. Remember that a will takes effect only on the death of the testator.

3.9 Creation of Equitable Interests by a Contract to Convey or Create a Legal Estate or Interest

Before we can discuss this heading it is necessary for us to put this issue into context of when an equitable interest may arise and to consider the formalities for contracts to transfer land or create an interest.

3.9.1 Contracts for the Sale of Estates or Interests in Land

cross-reference
See 1.3.9 for a brief description of a land transaction.

If land is being bought or sold it is normal for the transaction to take place in two stages. There is first the 'contract stage', followed (normally a few weeks later) by the 'completion stage'. At the contract stage the interest of the purchaser is only equitable and does not have legal status. A deed of transfer is executed only at the completion stage, so it is only at completion that the ownership of the estate is transferred to the purchaser.

This two-stage process is not obligatory, but it is normal when purchasing a fee simple. It is also usual to have the two stages when a lessee is taking a new long-term lease, or where an existing long lease is being sold. It is also possible, though unusual, to have the two stages where other property rights such as easements, profits, or rentcharges are being created.

3.9.2 Formalities for Contracts to Sell Estates or Interests in Land

As you have probably already learnt from your studies of the law of contract, in English law, as a general rule, no special formalities are required for a valid contract. Contracts to sell property rights in land are the big exception to this general rule.

Old Rules: Contracts Created before 27 September 1989

Contracts entered into before 27 September 1989 were governed by s40 LPA 1925. Contracts entered into on or after 27 September 1989 are governed by s2 LP(MP)A 1989.

> *Law of Property Act 1925*
>
> 40. Contracts for sale, of land to be in writing etc
>
> (1) No action may be brought upon any contract for the sale or other disposition of land or any interest in land, unless the agreement upon which such action is brought, or some memorandum or note thereof, is in writing, and signed by the party to be charged or by some other person thereunto by him lawfully authorised.
>
> (2) This section . . . does not affect the law relating to part performance . . .

The practical effect of s40 was that if a contract relating to land was to be enforceable and so create rights, one of the following three conditions had to be satisfied:

1 The contract was in writing, signed by the person (usually the vendor) promising rights over his land, or by his agent.

2 The contract was purely oral, but subsequently a document came into existence evidencing the contract. This 'note or memorandum' had to be signed by the person promising rights over his land, or by his agent.

3 The contract was purely oral, but the person claiming rights under the contract (eg the purchaser or prospective tenant) did some act of 'part performance'. 'Part performance' meant some conduct which indicated the existence of a contract between the parties. For example, (in particular) if the contract envisaged transfer of possession of the land to (say) a tenant or even a purchaser, that tenant/purchaser taking possession of the land was considered an act of part performance (*Steadman v Steadman* [1974] 2 All ER 977).

It should be stressed that a contract which did not comply with s40 was not void, but merely unenforceable. If, with respect to such a contract, conditions (2) or (3) in the previous list were subsequently fulfilled, the contract became enforceable. (There is a sharp contrast with s2 LP(MP)A 1989, which will be discussed shortly.)

Current Rules: s2 Law of Property (Miscellaneous Provisions) Act 1989

Section 2 of the 1989 Act came into force on 27 September 1989. Section 2 LP(MP)A 1989 repealed s40 LPA 1925, and also abolished the rules about part performance. All contracts for the sale of estates and interests in land must now be in writing and signed by the parties. The first three subsections of s2 are crucial:

> (1) A contract for the sale or other disposition of an interest in land can only be made in writing and only by incorporating all the terms which the parties have expressly agreed in one document or, where contracts are exchanged, in each.

(2) The terms may be incorporated in a document either by being set out in it or by reference to some other document.

(3) The document incorporating the terms or, where contracts are exchanged, one of the documents incorporating them (but not necessarily the same one) must be signed by or on behalf of each party to the contract.

This provision is a strict one which must be complied with carefully. The crucial point about this provision is that the contract itself must be in writing and signed by the parties. Any contract which is oral, or in writing but not signed by all the parties, is void, and there are no obligations on the parties. Moreover, subsequent events such as the creation of a document recording the 'contract' or acts of 'part performance' cannot validate the void contract.

(Signature by an agent of a contracting party will satisfy s2, even if the agent has only been authorized orally. See *Mclaughlin v Duffield* [2009] 3 WLR 1139.)

thinking point 3.4

Vikram entered into a purely oral contract to sell Station Lodge to Peter in March 2012. At that stage the contract was void and Peter had no rights. Vikram never signed anything, but after the oral agreement he allowed Peter to take possession of Station Lodge. Can Peter claim any rights under the agreement?

The answer is no. The purely oral contract between Vikram and Peter is totally void, and nothing which happens subsequently can give Peter rights under the void agreement. If, however, Peter nevertheless took possession of the property and spent a lot of money and/or effort improving the property, that expenditure would create a constructive trust interest in his favour (Yaxley v Gotts [2000] Ch 162).

The terms of s2(5) LP(MP)A 1989 should be noted

nothing in this section affects the creation or operation of resulting, implied or constructive trusts.

The operation of this statutory provision was considered in *Yaxley v Gotts* [2000] Ch 162. In this case the second defendant offered to transfer to the claimant, a builder, ownership of the ground floor of a house which he was proposing to purchase, in return for which the claimant would convert the house into flats and manage the property on his behalf. The parties were friends and the offer was made and accepted orally. In the event it was the second defendant's son, the first defendant, who actually purchased the house. The claimant, believing the second defendant to be the owner, performed his side of the bargain, supplying labour, materials, and management services. The claimant and the defendants subsequently fell out and the first defendant refused to grant the claimant an interest in the property.

The Court of Appeal held that an oral agreement whereby the purchaser of a house promised to grant another, in exchange for materials and services supplied, an interest in the property, though void and unenforceable under s2 LP(MP)A 1989, was enforceable on the basis of a constructive trust under s2(5) in circumstances where, previously, the doctrines of part performance (or proprietary estoppel) might have been relied upon.

pause for thought

Why do you think it is that the common law recognized only one method (deed) of creating or transferring property rights in land, while equity recognizes several different methods of creating property rights?

3.9.3 Exchange of Contracts

Section 2 LP(MP)A 1989 leaves one hallowed land law tradition untouched. In both s2(1) and (3) reference is made to 'where contracts are exchanged'. It has always been possible for parties to contract to sell property rights in land by them both signing a single document setting out the agreed terms of the sale. However, solicitors have, on the sale of a fee simple, traditionally preferred to use an alternative method. Two identical documents are prepared, each setting out all the expressly agreed terms of the contract. The vendor signs one copy; the purchaser signs the other. Agreement is signified by 'exchanging contracts', that is, there is a swap. The purchaser gets the copy signed by the vendor and vice versa. Contracts in this form are still in widespread use and are perfectly valid.

We can now at last return to the discussion of how equitable interests are created.

3.9.4 Estate Contracts

Once a contract for the sale of a fee simple has been made, equity regards the purchaser as owning an equitable interest known as an estate contract. This equitable interest is normally of only short duration, as it comes to an end 'on completion', that is, when the legal estate is conveyed to the purchaser. Despite the short duration of estate contracts, the whole concept is important and we need to examine it in a little more depth.

We need first to consider the reasoning which gave rise to the concept of an 'estate contract'. The Lord Chancellors developed the broad maxim, 'Equity looks on that as done which ought to be done'. Applying this maxim to contracts to sell land, the Chancellors reasoned that the purchaser should be regarded as having a right to the land once the contract had been signed without having to wait for the conveyance of the legal estate. Moreover, the Chancellors backed up this argument with a weapon. Contracts for the sale of land, or rights in land, are always in principle enforceable by the decree of specific performance.

'Specific performance' is a remedy which prior to 1875 was available only in the Court of Chancery, and is therefore even today referred to as an 'equitable remedy'. As its name perhaps implies, it is an order of the court that the contract actually be carried out.

For most types of contract, the remedy of specific performance is not available. For example, Ishtar has contracted to purchase a ton of potatoes from Farmer Giles, and Farmer Giles fails to deliver. Ishtar can always get potatoes elsewhere, so for this breach of the contract the court would not grant specific performance. Ishtar would have to be content with the usual remedy for breach of contract, namely damages.

By contrast, Ross contracted to buy a field, Highacre, from Giles. Now each piece of land is unique, a fact which equity recognized. If Giles refuses to convey Highacre to him, Ross cannot buy Highacre from anyone else. Ross may well be able to buy a field of similar dimensions and value, but that replacement field will inevitably be in a different location. He may well not want that location. Ross will therefore seek a decree of specific performance compelling Giles to convey Highacre to him. In principle the court will grant him that decree.

The Consequences of an Estate Contract

During the period between contract and completion the vendor holds the legal title of the property until the property is transferred to the purchaser. The vendor, as a trustee, holds the property on a special type of trust for the purchaser. The purchaser becomes the equitable owner when the contract has been signed (effectively the beneficiary owning the equitable interest in the property). The purchaser acquires an equitable interest in the property, though it must be noted that the purchaser does not acquire a full proprietary right in the property until the legal estate has been transferred.

Between contract and completion the vendor retains the right to enjoy all benefits from the land, but there are a number of duties which the vendor has as trustee for the purchaser; these include: to keep the property in good condition and to take reasonable care of it; keep the farmland property in a proper state of cultivation; take care to prevent removal of soil by a trespasser; and not to abandon rubbish on the property. Lawrence Collins J in *Englewood Properties Ltd v Patel* [2005] 1 WLR 1961, said:

> ### The vendor as trustee
>
> 40. It has long been said that after contract, and until completion, the vendor becomes in equity a trustee for the purchaser...
>
> The principle has been restated in modern times [on several occasions], of which the following [is] perhaps the most helpful:
>
> ...
>
> (b) In *Heronsgate Enterprises Ltd v Harman (Chesham) Ltd* (unreported) 21 January 1993; Court of Appeal (Civil Division) Transcript No 38 of 1993, Sir Donald Nicholls V-C said:
>
>> 'It is well-established law that, subject always to the terms of the particular contract, a seller of property under a specifically enforceable contract is to be regarded after the contract has been made as holding the property as a trustee for the buyer. However, he is not a bare trustee. His trust obligations are limited in certain respects. For example, if, as is usually the case, he is entitled to remain in possession for the period after the contract has been made pending the date fixed for completion, he is entitled to keep and retain for his own benefit the rents and profits of the land arising during that period...The seller must take care not to damage the property or to prejudice the buyer's interest in the property of which, on completion, he will become the legal owner. But in general, *within those limits* he is entitled to the ordinary rents and profits, and for him to take steps to obtain them after contract and before the date fixed for completion, either by occupying and using the property himself or by permitting another to occupy and work the property in return for a rent, is not a breach of his duties as seller under a contract for sale.'

Lawrence Collins J concludes from this (and other passages) that a vendor of land under a specifically enforceable contract is only in a limited and narrow sense a trustee for the purchaser.

> ### thinking point 3.5
> *What if the land which has been contracted to be sold is currently leased to a tenant. Who is entitled to the rent?*
>
> *It is the vendor who is entitled to the rent up to the date the legal estate is conveyed to the purchaser, that is, 'the date of completion'.*

Lawrence Collins J in *Englewood Properties Ltd v Patel* also gives a detailed explanation of the consequences of the 'estate contract' trust:

> ### The consequences
>
> 44. Although there is some overlap, the cases can be divided into two broad categories. The first is where the existence of the trust, or the identification of the trust property, is in question....

46. In the well-known decision in *Rayner v Preston* 18 Ch D 1 the vendors agreed to sell a house which they had insured against fire risk. The house was damaged by fire after contract but before completion, and the issue was whether the purchaser was entitled to the benefit of the insurance. It was held by a majority that the purchaser was not entitled to the insurance proceeds. On the trust aspect, Cotton LJ held that the vendors were trustees in a qualified sense only, and only in respect of the property contracted to be sold, of which the policy was not a part. Brett LJ considered that it was a misnomer to describe the vendors as trustees of the house, but even if they were trustees the contract of insurance did not run with the land. James LJ, dissenting, considered that the vendors were trustees and held the insurance money for the purchaser because any benefit which accrued to a trustee by reason of his legal ownership was taken as trustee for the beneficial owner....

The remarks of Lord Walker of Gestingthorpe, in the tax case of *Jerome v Kelly* [2004] 1 WLR 1409 summarize the modern position:

It would be wrong to treat an incomplete contract for the sale of land as equivalent to an immediate, irrevocable declaration of trust (or assignment of beneficial interest) in the land. Neither the seller nor the buyer has unqualified beneficial ownership. Beneficial ownership of the land is in a sense split between the seller and the buyer on the provisional assumption that specific performance is available and that contract will in due course be completed, if necessary by the court ordering specific performance. In the meantime, the seller is entitled to the enjoyment of the land or its rental income.

Recently, the Supreme Court in *Scott v Southern Pacific Mortgages Ltd* [2014] UKSC 2014 discussed the nature of the estate contract once exchange of contracts has taken place. This case involved a leaseback scheme where the vendor, usually due to financial hardship, sells their property on the understanding that they will be able to continue to live in the property for an indefinite period at a low rent.

Mrs Scott had contracted to sell her home to North East Property Buyers Ltd (NEPB) on the understanding that she would be able to live in the property indefinitely as a tenant. The Supreme Court had to consider whether Mrs Scott had acquired a proprietary right based on that promise made on exchange of contracts.

Lord Collins acknowledged that the status of the vendor on exchange of contracts has been variously described to indicate that the vendor's trusteeship is limited in its scope. The duties and obligations that stem from the vendor as trustee were not disputed (discussed below) but it was the nature of the purchaser's equitable interest that arose from a specifically enforceable contract that called for further deliberation before the court.

Lord Collins noted:

65. ... It is true that the purchaser is given statutory rights to enforce the interests against third parties under a contract of sale by registration: the 2002 Act, sections 15(1)(b), 32, 34(1); Land Charges Act 1972, section 2(1), (4). But it does not follow that the purchaser has proprietary rights for all purposes.

...

66. In *Berkley v Poulett* [1976] EWCA Civ 1, [1977] 1 EGLR 86, 93 Stamp LJ said (at para 36) that the vendor 'is said to be a trustee because of the duties which he has, and the duties do not arise because he is a trustee but because he has agreed to sell the land to the purchaser and the purchaser on tendering the price is entitled to have the contract specifically performed according to its terms. Nor does the relationship in the meantime have all the incidents of the relationship of trustee and cestui que trust.'

The crucial point here is that when contracts have been exchanged, the estate contract merely has the status of an equitable interest and is not automatically to be viewed as having a proprietary status in every situation.

Mrs Scott claimed that she had an equitable proprietary interest, based on the promise of a tenancy made at the exchange of contracts, which took priority and was an overriding interest under Sch 3 para 2 LRA 2002.

The difficulty that arose in Mrs Scott's situation rested on the fact that NEPB, the company that promised Mrs Scott the tenancy for an indefinite period, did not have any grounds for making such a promise because NEPB did not own the legal estate in question (ie Mrs Scott's house) from which formed the basis of the promise.

Lord Collins succinctly stated:

> …even if the tenant had equitable rights as against the purchaser, those rights would only become proprietary and capable of taking priority over a mortgage when they were 'fed' by the purchaser's acquisition of the legal estate. That is because where the proprietary right is claimed to be derived from the rights of a person who does not have the legal estate, then the right needs to be 'fed' by the acquisition of the legal estate before it can be asserted otherwise than personally.

The Supreme Court has sought to clarify the status of an estate contract as being an equitable interest arising from a specifically enforceable contract. This interest is capable of protection through registration but what is apparent is that this equitable interest cannot always be assumed to have proprietary status.

Duties of the Vendor as a 'Trustee'

The scope of the vendor's duty has been explained succinctly by Lawrence Collins J in *Englewood Properties Ltd v Patel:*

> 47. But it remains clear that the nature of the trust is not of the kind which (in the absence of agreement to the contrary) requires the trustee to account for benefits received from the trust property. In *In re Hamilton-Snowball's Conveyance* [1959] Ch 308 the vendor had received, between contract and completion, compensation for the requisition of the premises. Upjohn J held that the vendor under a contract for sale is only a qualified trustee for the purchaser of the premises with vacant possession, together with any physical accretions thereto, and not of any right to compensation moneys payable to him under an Act of Parliament which did not, in the absence of express provision in the contract, form part of the subject matter of the sale. So also a vendor of a house was entitled to retain the benefits of payments from a tenant made between contract and completion, because the vendor had sold the house and not also the benefit of the lease: In *re Lyne-Stephens and Scott-Miller's Contract* [1920] 1 Ch 472, cf *Musselwhite* v *C H Musselwhite & Son Ltd* [1962] Ch 964, 987 (sale of shares).
>
> 48. The second category of cases, which is relevant to the question on this appeal, relates to the scope of the duty of the vendor as trustee. The following duties have been held to exist: (1) to keep the property in a proper state of cultivation, reasonable regard being had to incurring a liability on his part: *Earl of Egmont* v *Smith* 6 Ch D 469; (2) to use reasonable care to keep the property in a reasonable state of preservation, and, so far as may be, as it was when the contract was made: *Clarke* v *Ramuz* [1891] 2 QB 456, 459–460 and *Raffety* v *Schofield* [1897] 1 Ch 937, 944; (3) to take care to prevent removal of the soil by a trespasser: *Clarke* v *Ramuz* [1891] 2 QB 456, where Kay LJ also put the decision on the ground that the purchaser had not got the whole of what he had contracted to buy; (4) to keep the property in its then condition

and state, and at any rate, to take reasonable care of it and see that its condition did not deteriorate during that time: *Davron Estates Ltd* v *Turnshire Ltd* 133 NLJ 937 (failure to prevent
damage by squatters); (5) not to abandon rubbish on the property: *Cumberland Consolidated
Holdings Ltd* v *Ireland* [1946] KB 264; (6) in a case where there was a contract for the sale of
premises together with the goodwill of the business carried on from the premises, not to let
the business lapse, and to inform the purchaser with reasonable promptitude of what he was
doing: *Golden Bread Co Ltd* v *Hemmings* [1922] 1 Ch 162.

It is submitted that the 'consequences' identified by their lordships can be summarized into
two central points:

1 The vendor must take good care of the property and consult the purchaser before taking
   any managerial decisions regarding the property.
2 The risk of anything untoward happening to the property passes to the purchaser when the
   contract is signed.

The Crucial Consequences of an Estate Contract

The Vendor Must Take Good Care of the Property and Consult the Purchaser Before Taking Any Managerial Decisions Regarding the Property

Between contract and completion the vendor cannot (unless the purchaser agrees) demolish,
alter, or reconstruct the property. Other important decisions about the property can be taken
only with the agreement of the purchaser.

In *Abdullah v Shah* [1959] AC 124, the vendor owned a row of three shops. At the time the
contract of sale for the shops was signed, all three of them were leased to tenants. Between
contract and completion one of the tenants (unexpectedly) terminated his tenancy. The vendor without asking the purchaser, immediately relet the shop. The premises would have been
more valuable to the purchaser had they remained unlet. The purchaser claimed specific performance of the contract of sale and also claimed compensation for the financial loss arising
out of the sub-letting.

The Privy Council held that under both the Indian Transfer of Property Act 1882 and under
English law, the vendor should have consulted the purchaser about the proposed reletting.
Lord Somerville noted that the obligation under the Indian Trusts Act 1882, for the trustee
to deal with the trust property 'as carefully as a man of ordinary prudence would deal with
such property if it were his own; and in the absence of contract to the contrary a trustee
so dealing is not responsible for the loss, destruction, or deterioration of the trust property', was substantially the same position of the trustee under English law. Lord Somerville
commented:

> . . . it seems plain that the vendors had no right without consultation with the purchasers
> to diminish the value of the property as it was after the surrender by reletting . . .

Consequently, the purchaser was entitled to a reduction in the agreed completion price, by
way of compensation.

The Risk of Anything Untoward Happening to the Property Passes to the Purchaser When the Contract is Signed

In this context, the 'estate contract' concept usually works to the purchaser's disadvantage.
There are two kinds of 'disaster' which can befall a property between contract and completion. The first is actions taken by a public authority.

In *Hillingdon Estates Co v Stonefield Estate Ltd* [1952] 1 All ER 853 the local authority, after the contract was signed, made a compulsory purchase order on the property. The court held that the vendor was entitled to insist on completing the sale, even though the purchaser would then have to convey the land to the local authority. (The purchaser would of course get the compensation payable on compulsory purchase.)

Another example of a case where the purchaser had to take the land as it was and complete the purchase is *Amalgamated Investment & Property Co Ltd v John Walker & Sons Ltd* [1977] 1 WLR 164. The defendants contracted to buy an old building which they planned to demolish and replace with modern offices. The local authority then 'listed' the building as one of 'special architectural or historic interest', thus effectively preventing the development. The purchasers claimed rescission of the contract on the ground of 'mutual mistake', which is to say that both parties had thought, at the time of the contract, that the land would be suitable for development and would not be subject to a listing. On the other side, the vendors sought specific performance of the contract. The court held that the claimants must nevertheless complete the purchase.

Lawton LJ was of the opinion that:

> ...Anybody who buys property knows, and certainly those who buy property as property developers know, that there are all kinds of hazards which have to be taken into consideration. There is the obvious hazard of planning permission. There is the hazard of fiscal and legislative changes. There is the hazard of existing legislation being applied to the property under consideration—compulsory purchase, for example. Amongst the hazards are the provisions of section 54 of the Town and Country Planning Act 1971. That seems now to be a well-known hazard, as is shown by the form of inquiry before contract which was made by the purchasers in this case. They used a printed form. The printed form asked whether the property had been listed. Similarly, when they came to make a search in the local registry of land charges, once again they made specific inquiries as to whether there had been any listing of the premises. All that adds up, in my judgment, to indicating that those who deal in property nowadays appreciate the existence of these kind of risks. At common law anyone entering into a contract for the purchase of real property had to accept the risk of damage to the property after the contract had been made. Damage to the property nowadays can arise from causes other than fire and tempest. Financial loss can arise from government intervention. This is a risk which people have to suffer...

Sir John Pennycuick commented:

> In the present case, the contract was one of which, upon the date of its signature, specific performance would have been ordered. Consequently, the purchasers became in equity the owners of the property, subject, of course, to vendor's lien: see *Williams on Vendor and Purchasers*, 4th edn. (1936), p. 547. The listing struck down the value of the property as might a fire or a compulsory purchase order or a number of other events. It seems to me, however, that the listing did not in any respect prevent the contract from being carried to completion according to its terms; that is to say, by payment of the balance of the purchase price and by conveyance of the property. The property is none the less the same property by reason that listing imposed a fetter upon its use.... One cannot say that the circumstances in which performance, i.e., completion, will be called for would render that performance a thing radically different from that which was undertaken by the contract. On the contrary, completion, according to the terms of the contract, would be exactly what the purchasers promised to do, and of course the vendors.

In both *Hillingdon v Stonefield* and *Amalgamated Investment v John Walker* action by local government diminished the value of the property. Yet the transactions had to be completed, despite the losses suffered by the purchasers.

The second kind of 'disaster' which might occur is destruction of the property. The traditional position has been that, unless the parties agree otherwise, the purchaser of land must bear the risk of destruction once a contract of sale has been made. Suppose last week Beth contracted to buy a house. Yesterday the house was destroyed by fire (or hurricane or earthquake). Beth must still complete the deal at the agreed price even though Beth is now getting a bare site with perhaps some useless ruins on it.

It is advisable that a purchaser of a building (unless they intend to demolish) should insure the building immediately they agree the contract to purchase. The Law Society has published a set of 'Standard Conditions of Sale' which is intended to be used by solicitors when drafting contracts to sell land, though their use is not obligatory. Clause 5 reads:

> 5.1.1 The seller will transfer the property in the same physical state as it was at the date of the contract (except for fair wear and tear) which means that the seller retains the risk until completion.
>
> 5.1.2 If at any time before completion the physical state of the property makes it unusable for its purpose at the date of the contract: (a) The buyer may rescind the contract . . .

(The rest of Clause 5 does not really help the present discussion.)

Thus provided the contract is drafted using the Standard Conditions, the traditional rule that risk of physical destruction passes to the purchaser on the contract of sale being made, no longer applies. In practice, most contracts for sale of residential properties follow the Standard Conditions, but contracts for sale of commercial properties often do not use the Standard Conditions.

3.9.5 A Contract to Create Rights in Land Itself Creates an Equitable Interest in the Land

The preceding discussion has focused on contracts to transfer an existing fee simple estate in land. We must now consider the situation where an owner of a fee simple estate contracts to create out of that estate some property right such as a lease, mortgage, easement, or profit.

In practice the problem is most likely to arise in the context of leases, because, as indicated earlier, where a long-term lease is to be created the transaction often proceeds in two stages. The parties sign a contract for the lease, followed by a formal deed a few weeks later.

In *Walsh v Lonsdale* (1882) 21 Ch D 9 a landlord and tenant had entered into a contract for a seven-year lease and the tenant had gone into possession, but the parties had forgotten to execute the formal deed needed for a valid legal lease. The rent clause in the contract provided that under the lease the rent should be per year payable in advance at the beginning of each year (the precise figure would depend upon the number of looms run by the tenant for his business). Despite the absence of a deed granting a legal lease, the landlord demanded the rent in advance in accordance with the contractual term. Indeed, he attempted to recover the rent due by exercising his right of distress. The tenant claimed that as there was no deed and therefore no proper lease, any rent should be payable in arrear. He therefore claimed an injunction against the action for distress.

The Court of Appeal held that the landlord could claim rent in advance. The contract had created an equitable lease enforceable between the parties. The terms of this lease would correspond to the terms of the contract. Jessel MR said:

> . . . The question is one of some nicety. There is an agreement for a lease under which possession has been given. Now since the *Judicature Act* the possession is held under the agreement. There are not two estates as there were formerly, one estate at common law by reason

of the payment of the rent from year to year, and an estate in equity under the agreement. There is only one Court, and the equity rules prevail in it. The tenant holds under an agreement for a lease. He holds, therefore, under the same terms in equity as if a lease had been granted, it being a case in which both parties admit that relief is capable of being given by specific performance. That being so, he cannot complain of the exercise by the landlord of the same rights as the landlord would have had if a lease had been granted. On the other hand, he is protected in the same way as if a lease had been granted; he cannot be turned out by six months' notice as a tenant from year to year. He has a right to say, 'I have a lease in equity, and you can only re-enter if I have committed such a breach of covenant as would if a lease had been granted have entitled you to re-enter according to the terms of a proper proviso for re-entry.' That being so, it appears to me that being a lessee in equity he cannot complain of the exercise of the right of distress merely because the actual parchment has not been signed and sealed.

As a result of *Walsh v Lonsdale,* a contract for a lease creates an equitable lease. Similar reasoning can be applied to all other types of right in land. A contract for an easement will create an equitable easement. A contract for a profit will create an equitable profit.

thinking point 3.6

What will a contract for a mortgage create?

It will create an equitable mortgage. (But never lose sight of the fact that a contract relating to rights in land must now comply with s2 LP(MP)A 1989.)

3.10 An Informal Grant of Rights in Land May be Treated as a Contract and so Creates an Equitable Interest in Land

One thing may have struck you about the preceding discussion. There is in logic a difference between saying 'I promise to grant you this land' and 'I grant you this land'; between 'I promise to give you a lease' and 'I grant you this lease now'. Nevertheless, equity, with decisions such as *Walsh v Lonsdale,* has blurred over this logical distinction. The following discussion contributes further to this blurring.

In *Parker v Taswell* (1858) 2 De G & J 559, a landlord and tenant signed a document which purported to grant a lease to the tenant. The document did not bear a seal, and therefore could not constitute the grant of a legal lease by deed. The court held that a purported grant of land which lacked the necessary formality should be deemed to be a contract which could be enforced by a decree of specific performance. The Lord Chancellor in considering the purported grant of a lease said:

…the instrument now in question could not amount to a lease, because it was not signed by an agent lawfully authorised by writing, nor was it signed in the name of the principal, so as to render it a lease binding upon the lessor. Assuming, however, that it had been signed in the name of the lessor, and would therefore have amounted to a lease, as containing words of present demise, yet there is nothing, in the Act to prevent its being used as an agreement, though void as a lease because not under seal [note there is no longer a requirement for the document to be sealed, see s 1 LP(MP)A 1989].

The Legislature appears to have been very cautious and guarded in language, for it uses the expression 'shall be void at law'—that is as a lease. If the Legislature had intended to deprive such a document of all efficacy, it would have said that the instrument should be 'void to all intents and purposes.' There are no such words in the Act. I think it would be too strong to say that because it is void at law as a lease, it cannot be used as an agreement enforceable in equity, the intention of the parties having been that there should be a lease, and the aid of equity being only invoked to carry that intention into effect . . .

The Court of Chancery therefore held that a purported grant of property rights in land which lacked the necessary formality (ie a deed) to create a legal estate should be deemed to be a contract, which could be enforced by a decree of specific performance. The court indeed awarded the claimant specific performance of the transaction deemed to be a contract.

Although this may not have been realized in 1858 (when *Parker v Taswell* was decided), the effect of that decision is that if a grantor purports to create property rights informally (ie other than by deed) the informal grant creates an equitable interest. Put simply:

informal grant = deemed contract = equitable interest

A fairly modern example of this reasoning is the House of Lords decision in *Mason v Clarke* [1955] AC 778. SM Ltd granted a legal lease of a farm to Clarke. As is common in leases of agricultural holdings, the lease included a clause whereby the landlord retained the right to hunt and/or trap wild animals roaming over the leased land.

In 1950, the land in question (in common with much of the rest of England) was plagued by rabbits. In October 1950, SM Ltd granted to Mason (a specialist rabbit-catcher) the right for one year to catch all rabbits on the farm. This transaction was purely oral. Mason paid £100 for the right, and entered the land and set traps. Clarke interfered with the traps.

The House of Lords held that the oral grant of the right to catch rabbits was a specifically enforceable contract; that entering the land and setting the traps should be considered to be part performance (this case dealt with the pre-1989 rules, see 3.6.1) and that therefore Mason had an equitable profit that he could protect by an action for trespass.

3.10.1 Limits on the Principle that a Contract or Informal Grant Creates an Equitable Interest

There are two limitations to the broad principle that a contract or informal grant of rights creates an equitable interest. The first limitation is the formalities required for a contract to transfer or create rights in land. The second limitation on the principle that contracts/informal grants create equitable interests is that the right to treat a contract or an informal grant as creating an equitable interest depends on the availability of specific performance.

Formalities Required for a Contract to Transfer or Create Rights in Land

Contracts to create or transfer interests in land are governed by s2 LP(MP)A 1989. It follows from this that for a contract or informal grant to create an equitable interest in land the contract or informal grant must be in writing signed by both parties. A contract or other transaction with land which is oral, or which is unsigned writing, will be void. Moreover, subsequent events cannot validate the contract. This conclusion regarding s2 LP(MP)A 1989 is confirmed by the Court of Appeal decision in *United Bank of Kuwait plc v Sahib* [1997] Ch 107.

cross-reference
United Bank of Kuwait plc v Sahib *[1997] is discussed at 22.7 and 22.7.2.*

Right to Treat a Contract or an Informal Grant as Creating an Equitable Interest Depends on the Availability of Specific Performance

This second limitation is long-standing, and fortunately unaffected by modern statute. As we saw earlier in this chapter (at 3.9.4), all contracts (and transactions deemed to be contracts) for the transfer or creation of rights in land are in principle enforceable by the equitable remedy of specific performance. However, you may have already come across the maxim that 'All equitable remedies are discretionary', and also perhaps the quaintly worded maxim that 'He who comes to equity must come with clean hands'. It is not appropriate at this point to give you all the detailed ramifications of these two maxims. What matters now is their practical application in the context of the current discussion.

If somebody enters into a contract (or a transaction deemed to be a contract) to acquire rights in land, but he is then in substantial breach of his own obligations under that contract, he will be said to have 'unclean hands'. The court will consequently refuse to order specific performance of the contract. Moreover, because he is not entitled to the remedy of specific performance to compel completion of the transaction, the party with 'unclean hands' cannot claim that the contract or informal transaction has created an equitable interest in his favour.

This was shown in *Coatsworth v Johnson* [1886–90] All ER Rep 547. Johnson entered into an agreement to lease a farm to Coatsworth for 21 years. The agreement contained a clause to farm 'in good and husband-like manner'. Coatsworth took possession of the farm without a formal deed being executed in his favour. Within a few months of his taking possession he had allowed the condition of the land to deteriorate very badly. Johnson took the rather drastic step of evicting Coatsworth from the farm. Coatsworth sued for wrongful eviction, contending that the agreement created an equitable lease lasting 21 years.

Lord Esher MR said:

>...If there is a tenancy at will, how is the landlord to put an end to it? By giving notice to quit, and that is all. He has not to assign any reasons for giving that notice. Supposing there had been no breach of any covenant, he could have given that notice to quit so far as it is a tenancy at will. If it is a tenancy at will, the question of whether there is a breach of covenant or not is immaterial. But it is argued that it was not a tenancy at will, because, under the circumstances, the court of equity would have decreed specific performance of the lease; and it is said that now both sides of the court would consider that as done which the court of equity would have decreed to be done. That proposition is not to be denied.
>
>That raises this question: Would the court of equity in this case have decreed specific performance? If it would, then that is to be considered as done, and then there is a lease. But if it would not, then, there being no lease at common law, it being in the position that the court of equity would not decree specific performance for a lease, then it is no lease

at common law. But the proposition is this: It is admitted that, before the Conveyancing Act 1881, if there had been a breach of the contract as to cultivation, the court of equity would not have decreed specific performance. But it is said that, although the tenant has declined or neglected to cultivate in the way mentioned in the agreement, nevertheless the court of equity would decree specific performance, because it is said that the Conveyancing Act 1881, by s. 14, has altered the contract; and that now there is no breach of the contract to cultivate in a particular way, unless, besides the non-cultivation, there has been a demand by the landlord, or a notice by the landlord, not properly observed by the tenant. In other words, that s. 14 of the Conveyancing Act 1881, has altered the contract, and that it is not confined merely to relief in the case of breach of the contract.

It is clear to my mind that s. 14 of the Conveyancing Act 1881, has not altered the contract at all. It has merely dealt with relief, or non-relief, on the assumption that that particular stipulation of the contract has been broken. If the contract is not altered, then by the non-cultivation there is a breach of the contract. Would the court of equity then decree specific performance, there being in existence at the time this state of facts? The moment the plaintiff went into equity, and asked for specific performance, and it was proved that he himself was guilty of the breach of contract, which the defendant says he is by not cultivating, the court of equity would refuse to grant specific performance, and would leave the parties to their other rights. Then, if the court of equity would not grant specific performance, we are not to consider specific performance as granted. Then the case is at an end. It is a lease at will. . . .

The Court of Appeal held that Coatsworth's failure to take good care of the farm was a substantial breach of the contract which meant that he had 'unclean hands' in the sight of equity. He would therefore be denied the discretionary remedy of specific performance of the contract. He had no equitable lease and was therefore lawfully evicted.

67

thinking point 3.7

In 1990, Liam and Tyler signed a written contract (not a deed) under which Liam agreed to lease a corner shop to Tyler for 30 years. Liam is a fundamentalist Christian, and the contract therefore included a clause that Tyler must not open on Sundays. For the last year, Tyler has opened on a Sunday, and has done a roaring trade. Can Liam argue that, like the tenant in Coatsworth v Johnson, Tyler has lost his right to claim that he has an equitable lease?

You will probably agree that the answer is not clear-cut. Tyler will argue that in the light of the changes in the Sunday trading laws his breach of contract was trivial, and not such as to amount to 'unclean hands' depriving him of the right to specific performance, and therefore of his equitable lease. Liam will argue that although Tyler's conduct is no longer an offence, his activities still constitute, from Liam's point of view, a substantial breach of contract.

REVIEW QUESTION Leena and Tariq sign an agreement (not in the form of a deed) under which Leena leases her corner shop to Tariq for five years. One of the terms of the agreement is that Tariq keeps the shop open 8 a.m. to 8 p.m. seven days a week. In practice Tariq closes for a few hours every Friday so that he can go to the mosque for prayers. Has Tariq got a 'valid' lease?

(Consider 3.9.5, 3.10, and 3.10.1.)

3.11 Grant of an Estate or Interest by a Person Who Owns Only an Equitable Interest

Somebody who owns only an equitable interest in land has no rights recognized by the common law. Therefore, if he executes a deed purporting to create a right derived from his equitable interest, that right is itself only equitable. Etherton LJ, in *Re North East Property Buyers Litigation* [2012] EWCA Civ 17 at [59], confirmed the continued application of this rule stating 'an equitable owner of land cannot grant a legal interest. A person cannot grant a greater interest than he or she possesses'.

A brief example should suffice.

Suppose Leah owns the fee simple in Wrenwood. Last year she and Tanesha signed a document which is not a deed, under which Leah leases Wrenwood to Tanesha for ten years. The lease will, under the principles just discussed, be only an equitable lease. This year Tanesha executes a deed under which she sub-leases Wrenwood for five years to Stephen. Although a deed has been used, this sub-lease will also only be equitable. At common law Tanesha's lease does not exist, and of course it follows that she cannot create a legal right from something which does not exist.

3.12 Grants of Interests Which Can Exist Only in Equity

Restrictive covenants and express trusts are usually created by using a formal deed. Yet, as has already been mentioned, restrictive covenants and interests under trusts are recognized only by equity.

Concluding Remarks

We have seen that to create legal property rights in land a formal deed is required. Equitable property rights in land can (by contrast) arise in a number of different ways, even by conduct of the parties.

In the past many equitable interests arose as a result of contract (3.9.4) or 'informal grant' (3.10). But the limiting effect of s2 LP(MP)A 1989 must be carefully noted. A contract or 'informal' grant, to be valid and therefore create an equitable interest, must now (slightly paradoxically) have a degree of formality! While a deed is not required, the transaction must be in writing and signed by both parties.

Summary

In the law which has existed since 1925, it is possible to identify four 'families' of property right in land.

Legal Estates

This family has only two members:

- *a fee simple absolute in possession*—this estate goes on for ever and gives its owner either immediate personal enjoyment of the land or the right to collect rent from the land; and

- *term of years absolute*—this includes leases which are both fixed term leases and periodic tenancies.

Legal Interests

The most important members of this family are:

- easements which last for ever or for a fixed period;
- profits which last for ever or for a fixed period;
- charges by way of legal mortgage;
- 'legal aid' charges; and
- inheritance tax charges.

Equitable Interests which Arise by Agreement or by Conduct

The most important members of this family are:

- easements and profits which last for the lifetime of the grantee;
- easements and profits which are created by a signed agreement, rather than by a formal deed;
- restrictive covenants (even if created by deed);
- constructive trust interests; and
- proprietary estoppel.

Equitable Interests which Exist under Deliberately Created Express Trusts

The most important members of this family are:

- life estates/life interests;
- fee simple estates in remainder; and
- fee tail estates (but remember that there can be no new ones).

Creation of Legal Property Rights

To create or transfer legal estates or interests, a deed is required (see Diagram 3.1).

Diagram 3.1
Creation or transfer of legal property rights

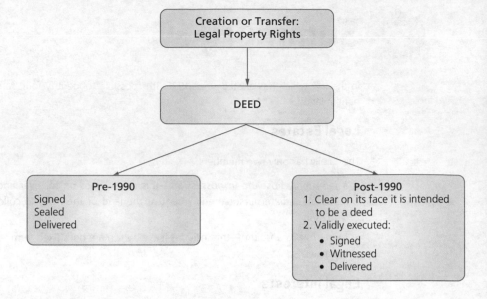

Creation or Transfer:
Legal Property Rights

DEED

Pre-1990
Signed
Sealed
Delivered

Post-1990
1. Clear on its face it is intended to be a deed
2. Validly executed:
   • Signed
   • Witnessed
   • Delivered

Creation of Equitable Property Rights

These can arise in a wide variety of ways:

• express trust;

• implied trusts: resulting trust or conduct giving rise to a constructive trust;

• contract to create a property right:
  – prior to 1989 this contract must comply with s40 LPA 1925;
  – after 1989 it must comply with s2 LP(MP)A 1989;

• informal grant void at common law:
  – but this 'informal' grant had prior to 1989 to comply with s40 LPA 1925;
  – after 1989 it must comply with s2 LP(MP)A 1989;

• grant of an easement or profit which is not in duration equivalent to a fee simple absolute in possession or a term of years;

• grant of an estate or interest created out of an equitable interest;

• creation of an interest (such as a restrictive covenant) which can only exist in equity;

• proprietary estoppel.

 # Further Reading

Critchley, P, 'Taking formalities seriously', in S Bright and JK Dewar (eds), *Land Law: Themes and Perspectives*, Oxford: OUP, 1998
This paper provides a useful general discussion of formalities in land law.

Dixon, M, 'Invalid contracts, estoppel and constructive trusts' [2005] Conv 247
Considers the ongoing debate on the relationship between proprietary estoppel and constructive trusts, and invalid contracts under s2 LP(MP)A 1989.

Gray, K and Gray, SF, *Elements of Land Law*, 5th edn, Oxford: OUP, 2008
See Chapter 8, pp 1058–1066, for an extended discussion of estate contracts.

Law Commission, *Transfer of Land—Formalities for Contracts for Sale Etc. of Land* (Report No 164, 1987)
For the reasoning behind the enactment of s2 LP(MP)A 1989.

Law Commission, *Transfer of Risk on Sale* (Report No 191, 1990)
For a discussion of the rule that the risk passes on signing a contract to sell land.

Moore, I, 'Proprietary estoppel, constructive trusts and s.2 of the Law of Property (Miscellaneous Provisions) Act 1989' (2000) 63 MLR 912
Case commentary on *Yaxley v Gotts*.

? Questions

1 Neema owns the legal fee simple estate (unregistered title) in 'Ramsey House'. Two months ago she entered into a written agreement (not in the form of a deed) to let Ramsey House to Markus for five years. The agreement specifically stated that the house should be used for residential purposes only.

Markus has just been made redundant, and is now considering using Ramsey House for a business repairing bicycles. He has heard rumours that Neema is about to sell the house.

Advise Markus, who is concerned that, as his lease is not in the form of a deed, he might be evicted by Neema.

2 Last week, by a written contract, Theo agreed to sell 'Taylor Cottage' to Umar, the sale to be completed in six weeks' time. Unfortunately, yesterday, a bus crashed into Taylor Cottage causing considerable damage.

This morning Theo demolished a small outhouse which stood at the bottom of the garden of Taylor Cottage.

Advise Umar, who wants either to rescind the contract or at least obtain a reduction in the previously agreed price.

Part 2

Unregistered Land

4

Protection of Legal and Equitable Property Rights in Unregistered Land

Introduction

We have already mentioned in Chapter 1 that there are two systems in land law, namely unregistered land and registered land. The land law reforms of 1925 marked the shift away from unregistered titles to a centrally held land register. Most land in England and Wales is now registered on the register of titles, and the unregistered land system has become less important. Despite this, there are still titles which are subject to the rules governing unregistered land. This chapter is dedicated to discussing how legal and equitable rights are protected under unregistered titles.

To understand this chapter there are a number of factors which need to be borne in mind which stem from the rules regulating unregistered titles.

From the point of view of somebody who owns a property right, it is better that the right should be legal rather than equitable. This is because legal property rights are good against the whole world.

Prior to 1926 almost all equitable interests were subject to the doctrine of notice. The 1925 legislators actually aimed to reduce the importance of the doctrine of notice. This policy aim is easy to understand. If somebody owns an equitable interest he can never be 100 per cent sure that his rights will remain enforceable against the land. There is always the risk that a purchaser of the land will come along who is a bona fide purchaser for value of a legal estate without notice of the equitable interest.

Since 1925 only a minority of equitable interests are subject to the doctrine. The 1925 legislation divides equitable interests which exist with respect to land which is unregistered title into three groups:

- equitable interests registrable as land charges;

- equitable interests which are 'overreachable'; and

- equitable interests which are neither registrable as land charges nor overreachable, and are therefore still subject to the doctrine of notice.

4.1 Legal and Equitable Property Rights: Case Study—High Chimneys

Before going any further, you must familiarize yourself with the facts of this case study designed to illustrate most of the points which we will encounter in this chapter.

Imagine that last winter Roger purchased the fee simple (unregistered title) in a large country house, High Chimneys, together with its quite extensive garden. Roger bought the house from Tatiana, a wealthy and elderly spinster. Before completing the purchase, Roger, his solicitor, and his surveyor made very careful enquiries regarding High Chimneys. There was a careful examination of the title deeds going back to a root of title in 1968, which was when Tatiana had bought the property from Amit. His surveyor and he himself made a very careful physical inspection of both the house and garden.

As a result of these careful enquiries and searching the Land Charges Register, Roger concluded that the land was not subject to any third party rights such as easements, profits, restrictive covenants, mortgages, etc. Roger therefore completed the purchase in March.

The last few months have been quite traumatic. First of all Roger had a visit from Olabode, owner of neighbouring Low Stacks. He produced a deed dated 1910. By that deed the then owner of High Chimneys granted to the then owner of Low Stacks a right of way across the garden of High Chimneys. This right of way was expressly granted for the benefit of Low Stacks, and was to last in perpetuity. Olabode explains that the right of way has not been used for five years (which is why Roger's surveyor did not detect any sign of a worn path or track), but that now he intends to use it every day as a short cut to the nearest station.

Soon after Olabode came Pierce, owner of Smokey Farm, which adjoins the foot of Roger's garden. He produced a written agreement (not a deed) dated 1950. By that written agreement the then owner of High Chimneys, Amit, agreed with the then owner of Smokey Farm a right to graze 15 sheep in the large garden. This right was expressly for the benefit of Smokey Farm, and was to last in perpetuity. Pierce explains that he has not owned any sheep for about the last eight years, but now he has acquired some and intends to graze them in Roger's garden. (Hopefully you have noted that Olabode owns a legal easement, while Pierce owns an equitable profit.)

Lastly, Gianluca arrives. He explains that from 1971 to 2011 he lived with Tatiana, but they have now split up. He further explains that he contributed a substantial amount of money to the original purchase of High Chimneys. He therefore has a resulting trust interest in the property. That interest is equitable. Gianluca claims that his equitable interest in the land binds Roger. He is very anxious to claim against Roger because Tatiana has taken the whole price paid to her and emigrated to Bolivia.

Do the rights of Olabode, Pierce, and Gianluca bind Roger?

4.2 Proof of Ownership—Title Deeds

cross-reference
See 1.4.3 for a discussion on title deeds.

As explained in Chapter 1, a purchaser should always investigate the vendor's title as this will provide proof of ownership of the estate. In this context, the predecessors in title will not only be identifiable from the title deeds but also indicate how the predecessors obtained title.

The deeds and other documents relating to the land must be inspected going back to the root of title, which is normally the most recent conveyance which is at least 15 years old (s23 Law of Property Act 1969), that is, the purchaser should inspect the root of title and all later documents. For example:

- In 1928 Alan conveyed Purpleacre to Barry
- In 1938 Barry conveyed Purpleacre to Clive ← Root of title
- In 1987 Clive conveyed Purpleacre to Dean
- In 1988 Dean conveyed Purpleacre to Edmund

Imagine that it is 2001 and Edmund is selling Purpleacre to Rishan. The 1938 conveyance from Barry to Clive will be the root of title. The purchaser through this process has documentary evidence of all the dealings in land which could affect the fee simple, dating from the root of title through to the most recent conveyance (in our example from 1938 to the 1988 conveyance).

thinking point 4.1

What if in the previous example the conveyance from Clive to Dean had been seven years earlier, in 1980?

That conveyance would be the root of title, as it is the most recent conveyance which is at least 15 years old.

The primary purpose of a conveyance is to transfer legal ownership from the vendor to the purchaser. But conveyances often do more than that. A conveyance will often also create third party rights such as easements, profits, and restrictive covenants. For example, Ella owned two adjoining fields, Woodbrook Field and Hill Top Field. She recently sold Woodbrook Field to Finley. As well as transferring ownership, the conveyance:

1 grants Finley a right of way (easement) over Hill Top Field to get to Woodbrook Field; and

2 contains a restrictive covenant entered into by Finley that he will use Woodbrook Field for agricultural purposes only.

Conveyances creating third party rights are commonplace. But a conveyance may also reveal existing third party rights. The point is really a simple one: where land is sold, that land may already be subject to third party rights such as easements or restrictive covenants. These may have been created some time ago, perhaps a hundred years or more. If land is sold subject to existing third party rights it is normal practice, though not absolutely obligatory, for the conveyance to mention ('recite') those existing rights.

Returning to our case study (4.1) Roger inspected the title deeds going back to the good root of title and he would have found out that Tatiana has purchased High Chimneys in 1968 from Amit. Roger as a prudent purchaser will need to ascertain if there are any third party rights which could potentially bind him and by obtaining the names of predecessors in title, this forms one part of the investigation that Roger would need to undertake to determine whether there are any potentially binding third party rights that could affect him. He will need to do the following:

• Identify any legal rights which will bind him automatically;

• Identify equitable interests which are neither registrable as land charges nor overreachable, and are therefore still subject to the doctrine of notice;

• Inspect the Land Charges Register;

• Identify interests which are 'overreachable'.

4.3 The Legal Property Rights of Olabode

Here the position is very simple. Roger is going to have to put up with Olabode tramping across his land because the easement is a legal property interest.

It is a fundamental principle that legal property rights are 'good against the whole world'. That means that, once a legal property right has been created with respect to a piece of land, that right binds everybody else who later acquires that land or other rights in that land.

Put another way, legal rights are in principle indestructible. It must be stressed that Roger is bound by Olabode's easement even though, at the time he bought High Chimneys, neither he nor his advisers knew or could have known of these rights. (Remember that they had all made careful enquiries. Incidentally, as Roger's solicitor and surveyor exercised all due care, there is no possibility of his suing them for professional negligence.)

thinking point 4.2

John owned the legal fee simple in Fairview Gardens. In September 2012, John granted a legal lease of Fairview Gardens to Karanjit for six years, but Karanjit has not as yet taken any steps to occupy Fairview Gardens. John has now sold the fee simple in Fairview Gardens to Leon, who knew nothing of Karanjit's lease. Is Leon bound by the lease?

Now it may well strike you that as a matter of simple moral justice Leon should not be bound by Karanjit's lease. Leon probably had no way of knowing that there was a lease, and Karanjit could not even be bothered to take possession of Fairview Gardens. Yet, where unregistered titles are concerned, the law is that Karanjit's lease does bind Leon. It is a legal property right, and (like Olabode's easement) will bind everybody who later acquires the relevant land or rights in that land. It is no good Leon saying, 'Karanjit was not in possession, so how could I know that there was a lease?'

(4.4) The Equitable Property Rights of Gianluca

equity's darling
bona fide purchaser for value of a legal estate or legal interest without notice.

doctrine of notice
equitable interests bind the whole world except the bona fide purchaser for value of a legal estate or legal interest without notice.

Equitable rights are not totally indestructible. An equitable interest is good against the whole world except a bona fide purchaser for value of a legal estate or legal interest who took without notice of the equitable interest (also known as **equity's darling**). Thus to be free of Gianluca's interest Roger must prove four things. He must prove that at the time he purchased High Chimneys:

1 he acted 'bona fide', that is, in good faith; and

2 he was a purchaser for value; and

3 he acquired a legal estate or legal interest; and

4 he had no notice of Gianluca's equitable interest.

Before examining the four elements of the **doctrine of notice** listed previously, we must recall a point made earlier: 'From the point of view of somebody who owns a property right, it is better that the right should be legal rather than equitable'. Put slightly differently, legal property rights are stronger than equitable property rights.

thinking point 4.3

Consider the case study of High Chimneys from the point of view of Olabode on the one hand, and Gianluca on the other. Olabode can sleep soundly in his bed, while Gianluca's position may not be so comfortable. Why is that?

The crucial point for Olabode is that he has a legal interest (as had Karanjit in thinking point 4.2). He can therefore relax. He can rest assured that whatever happens to High Chimneys, and whoever buys High Chimneys his right will still continue. It will continue even against Roger, who knew nothing of Olabode's right. His right is (in effect) indestructible.

Gianluca's position is not quite so comfortable. His right will bind somebody who is given or inherits the land. It will bind somebody who buys the land with notice of Gianluca's interest. But it has one weakness. It will not bind a bona fide purchaser for value of a legal estate or interest who took without notice of Gianluca's interest. If Roger is such a purchaser then Gianluca's rights will not bind Roger. His only claim will be against Tatiana for cash compensation. It will be his tough luck that she has just emigrated to Bolivia!

4.5 The Elements of the Doctrine of Notice

All four elements set out at 4.4 must be proved by a purchaser (Roger in the High Chimneys case study) if he is to take a piece of property free from an equitable interest affecting that property. James LJ in *Pilcher v Rawlins* (1872) 7 Ch App 259 explained:

> I propose simply to apply myself to the case of a purchaser for valuable consideration, without notice, obtaining, upon the occasion of his purchase, and by means of his purchase deed, some legal estate, some legal right, some legal advantage; and, according to my view of the established law of this Court, such a purchaser's plea of a purchase for valuable consideration without notice is an absolute, unqualified, unanswerable defence, and an unanswerable plea to the jurisdiction of this Court. Such a purchaser, when he has once put in that plea, may be interrogated and tested to any extent as to the valuable consideration which he has given in order to show the *bona fides* or *mala fides* of his purchase, and also the presence or the absence of notice; but when once he has gone through that ordeal, and has satisfied the terms of the plea of purchase for valuable consideration without notice, then, according to my judgment, this Court has no jurisdiction whatever to do anything more than to let him depart in possession of that legal estate, that legal right, that legal advantage which he has obtained, whatever it may be. In such a case a purchaser is entitled to hold that which, without breach of duty, he has had conveyed to him.

The crucial point that is made here is that where the purchaser buys the property for valuable consideration and has no notice of any third party interests, the purchaser has an 'absolute, unqualified, unanswerable defence'. If it transpires later on that a third party right existed but the purchaser was unaware of it, equity will not intervene.

4.5.1 Bona Fide

When talking about the doctrine of notice, lawyers usually use the Latin phrase 'bona fide'. This simply means 'good faith'. A person acts in good faith if he acts honestly and without any fraudulent intent.

Lord Wilberforce in *Midland Bank Trust Co Ltd v Green* [1981] 1 AC 513 noted that:

> ...the character in the law known as the bona fide (good faith) purchaser for value without notice was the creation of equity. In order to affect a purchaser for value of a legal estate with some equity or equitable interest, equity fastened upon his conscience and the composite expression was used to epitomise the circumstances in which equity would or rather would not do so. I think that it would generally be true to say that the words 'in good faith' related to the existence of notice. Equity, in other words, required not only absence of notice, but genuine and honest absence of notice.

In disputes which arise involving the doctrine of notice, it is usually easy for a purchaser to establish that the absence of notice is genuine and honest. (As we shall see at 4.5.4, it may be much more difficult for him to prove that he is 'without notice'.)

4.5.2 Purchaser for Value

If a person acquires a piece of land as a result of an *inter vivos* gift, or if they inherit it from somebody, that person is clearly not a purchaser for value, and so will always be bound by any equitable interests affecting the land.

thinking point 4.1

What would be the result if in the High Chimneys case study Tatiana had given Roger the property; or if she had died and left Roger the property by her will?

It is hoped you realized that in both cases Roger would always be bound by Gianluca's equitable interest. It would be no use his protesting that he had no 'notice' of Gianluca's interest. It would be wrong that Gianluca should lose his rights to somebody who has not had to do or pay anything for the property.

The Meaning of 'Value'

In the High Chimneys case study, Tatiana was so anxious to get a quick sale that she sold it to Roger at a bargain price which did not represent the real value of the land. Would Roger be a purchaser for value? The answer is 'yes'. What if Roger had paid only a nominal price of £1 for High Chimneys? Would Roger be a purchaser for value? The answer is still 'yes'!

In your studies of the law of contract you may have already encountered the 'doctrine of consideration'. In contract law even the smallest payment, or the most minimal 'detriment' may constitute consideration. As you have probably guessed, anything which constitutes 'consideration' in the law of contract will be 'value' for the purposes of the law of property.

Marriage as 'Value'

This may seem a rather obscure point, but it is of some significance to the historic development of property law. Until 1970, an engagement to marry was a legally enforceable contract. (You have probably heard of actions for breach of promise of marriage!) As a result of the Law Reform (Miscellaneous Provisions) Act 1970, engagements to marry are no longer legally enforceable. It follows that a promise to marry is no longer 'consideration'; nor is it 'value' for the purposes of the doctrine of notice.

Consider the following developments from the High Chimneys case study. Tatiana conveyed High Chimneys to Roger and in return, he did not pay a cash price, but he promised to marry her. She then disappeared to Bolivia before they could have a ceremony. Roger would not be a 'purchaser for value' of High Chimneys. Had the facts occurred before 1970 (say, in 1965), he would have been a purchaser for value.

thinking point 4.5

Change the case study in a slightly different way. Suppose Tatiana conveyed High Chimneys to Roger in March 2012 in return for his actually marrying her. Would Roger be a purchaser for value? (Put another way, is Roger's actually marrying her consideration?)

The crucial point in answering this question is to realize that the actual act of marrying is a 'detriment'
suffered by Roger (he has given up the freedom of his single status). It is 'consideration' and therefore it is
'value'; thus (on this version of the case study) Roger is, even today, a purchaser for value!

4.5.3 Purchaser of a Legal Estate or Legal Interest

This may strike you as a rather technical and arbitrary aspect of the doctrine of notice. Under this rule, a purchaser of an equitable interest cannot claim the benefit of the doctrine of notice. If you buy only an equitable interest in Blackacre, any existing equitable interest(s) in Blackacre is/are automatically binding on you.

To illustrate this, suppose in the High Chimneys case study Roger did not buy the legal fee simple; instead he entered into a contract with Tatiana under which she agreed to lease him the property for 99 years. Roger paid her an agreed 'premium' (capital lump sum) of £100,000, and took possession. Tatiana then ran off to Bolivia without executing a deed in his favour. On these facts Roger 'purchased' only an equitable lease. Roger will therefore be bound by Gianluca's equitable interest, even if he can establish that he had no notice of that interest.

What if, by contrast, Tatiana did execute a deed leasing the property to Roger before she disappeared westwards? Now on this version of the case study Roger is a purchaser of a legal estate. He therefore will not be bound by Gianluca's interest if he can prove the other elements of the doctrine of notice. (Note that this last illustration confirms the proposition that legal property rights are 'better' than equitable property rights.)

Another way of looking at the point made earlier is that if there are two or more equitable interests affecting the same piece of land the rule is 'first in time, first in right'. The first equitable interest to be created has the first claim, the second equitable interest has the second claim, and so on. For example, in 2010, Florian, the owner of Whitebarn, granted an equitable lease for ten years of Whitebarn to Yasuo. In 2011, while Yasuo was absent from Whitebarn because of a lengthy hospitalization, Florian granted an equitable lease for ten years of Whitebarn to Zak.

Yasuo has just come out of hospital, and we now have Yasuo and Zak arguing as to who can occupy Whitebarn. Yasuo will win the argument. His equitable interest was created first, therefore he has first claim to the land. His right has priority over any later created equitable interest(s).

Let us now add just one more twist to this Whitebarn example. In 2012, Yasuo has no more use for Whitebarn, so he assigns (ie transfers) his equitable lease to his friend Abu. Can Zak come along and say, 'I got my interest before Abu got his; I am first in time and should now be allowed to occupy Whitebarn!'?

Zak's claim to occupy Whitebarn will still fail. It is the order of creation of interests which matters, not the order of acquisition. Abu's interest was, of course, created before Zak's. It was created when, in 2010, it was granted to Yasuo. It would be very strange if, when Yasuo disposed of his equitable interest to Abu, that interest lost its priority.

thinking point 4.6

In 1992, Hayden acquired Oakmere House. In 2008, his partner, Letitia, acquired a constructive trust interest in Oakmere House. (She paid substantial sums to renovate the house.) Hayden has now left, and has just granted an equitable lease of Oakmere House to Martha for six years. Does Letitia's right bind Martha?

Would your answer be different if Martha's lease was a legal lease?

On the first version of the facts, we have two competing equitable interests with respect to the same piece of land. It follows that we must apply the 'first in time, first in right' rule. Letitia's right will have 'priority' and will bind Martha.

If, however, Martha's lease was a legal lease, she would be a purchaser of a legal estate. Thus, if she acted in good faith, gave value (eg agreed to pay rent) and was without notice of Letitia's right, Martha would not be bound by Letitia's interest.

REVIEW QUESTION Jacques owns Blue House. In May he agrees in a signed, but not witnessed, document to lease the house to Alfonse. Alfonse planned to move into the house in August.

In June, Jacques (not the most honest of men) agrees in a signed but unwitnessed document to lease the house to Bert. Bert moves in immediately.

In July Alfonse, having never moved into Blue House, transfers his rights over the house to Connor. Connor is claiming possession of the house. Is he in the right?

(Consider 3.9.5, 3.10, and this chapter up to 4.5.3.)

4.5.4 Without Notice of the Equitable Interest

In any dispute involving the equitable doctrine of notice, the most likely cause for arguments is the question of whether the purchaser has notice of the relevant equitable interests. In the High Chimneys case study, the crucial question will be, 'Did Roger, at the time the fee simple estate in High Chimneys was conveyed to him, have notice of Gianluca's equitable interest?'.

As purchaser Roger will have the task of proving that he was without any form of notice of Gianluca's interest. Notice comes in three forms:

- actual notice;
- constructive notice; and
- imputed notice.

This threefold division of notice is confirmed by s199(1)(ii) Law of Property Act 1925 (LPA 1925):

Law of Property Act 1925

199. Restrictions on constructive notice

1. A purchaser shall not be prejudicially affected by notice of—
    (ii) any other instrument or matter or any fact or thing unless—
        (a) it is within his own knowledge, or would have come to his knowledge if such inquiries and inspection had been made as ought reasonably to have been made by him; or
        (b) in the same transaction with respect to which a question of notice to the purchaser arises, it has come to the knowledge of his counsel, as such, or of his solicitor or other agent, as such or would have come to the knowledge of his solicitor or other agent, as such, if such inquiries and inspections had been made as ought reasonably to have been made by the solicitor or other agent.

Actual Notice

A purchaser has actual notice if, at the time of the purchase, they actually knew of the existence of the equitable interest. It does not matter how the purchaser acquired the information. It is unlikely that this will extend to casual conversations but that would depend on the facts of the case, for example where the purchaser 'has in some way been brought to an intelligent apprehension of the nature of the [equitable interest] which has come upon the property, so that a reasonable man, or an ordinary man of business, would act upon the information and would regulate his conduct by it...' (per Lord Cairns, *Lloyd v Banks* (1868) 3 Ch App 488 at 490–491), it would be fair to say that the purchaser has actual notice of the equitable interest. A vague rumour would not amount to actual notice (*Barnhart v Greenshields* (1853) 9 Moo PC 18).

Constructive Notice

A purchaser has constructive notice of any equitable interest which the purchaser would have discovered had they made those enquiries which a reasonable purchaser would make.

As you already know, when somebody buys a piece of land all sorts of careful enquiries must be made with respect to that land. Some of these enquiries may relate to the physical condition of the land (eg is it liable to subsidence or flooding?), but many of these enquiries relate (at least in part) to property law matters. When buying a piece of land the prudent purchaser always checks:

* whether the vendor has a good title to the land; and
* whether there are any third party rights (legal or equitable) such as easements, profits, or restrictive covenants affecting the land.

As you have probably already guessed the constructive notice rule in effect places a duty upon the purchaser to act wisely. The rule requires a purchaser to make those enquiries which a reasonable person, with competent legal advice, would make. (The rule makes no concessions to 'do-it-yourself' conveyancers who buy land without taking legal advice.)

Legal interests, you will recall, always bind the purchaser, whether they discover them or not. So a prudent or wise purchaser always looks very carefully for legal interests. Under the constructive notice rule the purchaser is expected to look just as carefully for equitable interests. In particular, there are two types of enquiry which every purchaser is expected to make:

1 inspect the land;
2 investigate the vendor's title.

Inspect the Land

rule in *Hunt v Luck* the purchaser must look for person(s) in possession, and if he finds anybody he must ask that person what interest he claims in the land.

When the prudent purchaser inspects the land, aspects of that inspection will relate to the physical condition of the land, for example is there evidence of subsidence? But the prudent purchaser will also be on the alert for matters such as worn tracks or grazing sheep. Their presence might indicate the existence of easements or profits. The purchaser will also want to establish whether anybody other than the vendor is occupying the whole or part of the land. Such a person might have a lease (perhaps legal, perhaps equitable), or might claim a constructive trust interest in the land or possibly some other right in the land.

If anyone (other than the vendor) is in possession of the land or part of it, the **rule in Hunt v Luck** [1902] 1 Ch 428 applies. Vaughan Williams LJ stated that:

> if a purchaser or a mortgagee has notice that the vendor or mortgagor is not in possession of the property, he must make inquiries of the person in possession—of the tenant who is in

possession—and find out from him what his rights are, and, if he does not choose to do that, then whatever title he acquires as purchaser or mortgagee will be subject to the title or right of the tenant in possession.

In this passage his Lordship is using the word 'tenant' in the loose sense of any person in actual control of the land.

If the purchaser fails to discover a person who is in possession, or fails to ask such a person whether they claim any interest in the land, the purchaser in this scenario has not made adequate enquiries. The purchaser is deemed to have constructive notice of any equitable interest owned by that person.

Put another way, a purchaser has notice of any equitable interest owned by a person in possession (of whole or part of the land) unless enquiry is made of that person and they do not reveal their interest.

There are additional facts in the High Chimneys case study that ought now to be considered. Darrell was living in the house last winter (when Roger bought it). Darrell moved into High Chimneys after Gianluca and Tatiana ended their relationship. Darrell made substantial contributions to the renovation of the property. He therefore has an interest in High Chimneys under a constructive trust.

When Roger visited High Chimneys, he somehow failed to realize that Darrell was there. (Or perhaps Roger saw him, but assumed that he was some kind of servant and so asked no questions.) Either way, Roger has not made proper enquiries. He will have constructive notice of Darrell's equitable interest.

Let us now assume that Roger did see Darrell, and he went up to him and said, 'Excuse me, do you claim any kind of right or lease over this house?' If he tells Roger that he has made substantial contributions to the house, or words to that effect, Roger has actual notice of his interest. But if Darrell replies, 'Mind your own business!', or something similar, Roger has sufficiently pursued this line of enquiry. He will not have notice of Darrell's interest.

thinking point 4.7

In 1980, Nicole bought The Ridings. In 2010, Josh started to cohabit with her in The Ridings. He acquired a constructive trust interest in The Ridings by paying off the bulk of the mortgage on the house.

The relationship has now broken up, and Josh is living alone in The Ridings. This morning a couple of surveyors called wanting to inspect the house. Josh told them to 'clear off!' and refused to let them in. The surveyors left saying, 'We will be back tomorrow'.

Advise Josh.

It is hoped you have concluded that Josh is a very lucky man, as he will get a second chance to tell the surveyors about his constructive trust interest. The surveyors are probably acting on behalf of a potential purchaser or mortgagee. Josh should tell them of his interest, so that the purchaser/mortgagee will have notice of his interest. If, on the other hand, Josh continues to be rude, then the purchaser/mortgagee will be able to say that he had made adequate enquiries and that he had no notice of Josh's interest.

Investigate the Title

As was explained in Chapter 1 and 4.2, a purchaser should always investigate the vendor's title.

There is no duty to inspect documents which are dated before the root of title. These documents are said to be 'behind' the root of title. If a purchaser fails to inspect a document which they should have inspected, then the purchaser has constructive notice of the contents of that document. In particular, the purchaser has constructive notice of all equitable interests created or revealed by that document.

Case Study—Brakenhill House

This case study provides an example of constructive notice through failure to investigate. The recent history of Brakenhill House is as follows:

- In 1929, Eric sold Brakenhill House to Norma
- In 1956, Norma sold Brakenhill House to Malcolm
- In 1973, Malcolm sold Brakenhill House to Leonard ← Root of title
- In 1989, Leonard sold Brakenhill House to Keith
- In 2001, Isobel purchased Brakenhill House from Keith

When Isobel bought the land in 2001, the correct root of title should have been the 1973 conveyance from Malcolm to Leonard. (It was the most recent document which was at least 15 years old.) Isobel should therefore have inspected both the 1973 and the 1989 conveyances. However, Isobel unfortunately only inspected the 1989 conveyance.

The 1973 conveyance, which Isobel did not inspect, revealed a restrictive covenant (not mentioned in the 1989 conveyance) in favour of a neighbouring property. That covenant, entered into as long ago as 1910, limited Brakenhill House to residential purposes only.

Isobel, who intended to convert Brakenhill House into offices, is bound by the restrictive covenant. She should have inspected the 1973 conveyance, and that would have revealed the 1910 covenant. She has constructive notice of that equitable interest.

What would be the position if the 1910 restrictive covenant was mentioned in the 1956 conveyance from Norma to Malcolm, but not in any later conveyances? Under the rule about 'root of title' Isobel did not have to investigate the 1956 conveyance. Therefore (whether or not she looked at the 1973 conveyance), she would not have had constructive notice of the covenant.

thinking point 4.8

In 1922, Peter sold Chorley Hall to Quentin. The 1922 conveyance contained a restrictive covenant under which Quentin promised to use the house for residential purposes only. In 1989, Quentin sold Chorley Hall to Richard. Scott bought Chorley Hall from Richard in 2002. Did he have notice of the restrictive covenant?

Would your answer be different if the conveyance from Quentin to Richard took place in 1980?

On the basis that the sale from Quentin to Richard took place in 1989, there can be no doubt that Scott would have notice of the restrictive covenant. The root of title, the most recent conveyance at least 15 years old, is that executed in 1922. If Scott looked at the 1922 conveyance he would have actual notice. If he did not bother to look at the 1922 conveyance, he would have constructive notice.

If the conveyance from Quentin to Richard took place in 1980, then that conveyance would be the root of title. If that (1980) conveyance recited the (1922) restrictive covenant, then Scott would still have notice of the restrictive covenant. But if the 1980 conveyance did not mention the restrictive covenant, then there would not be notice. The only mention of the covenant would be in a document 'behind the root of title', which Scott had no duty to investigate.

Imputed Notice

In most purchases of land, agents such as solicitors and/or surveyors are employed. The purchaser does not personally make the necessary enquiries. In view of this fact, a rule of **imputed notice** is essential if the doctrine of notice is to operate fairly. If an agent, while acting for a particular purchaser with respect to a particular transaction, receives actual or constructive notice of an equitable interest, that notice is ascribed to the purchaser himself (see s199(1)(ii)(b) LPA 1925, already quoted at 4.5.4). This rule applies to all forms of agent, and is not just confined to solicitors and surveyors.

....

imputed notice

if, at the time of the purchase, the purchaser's agent (solicitor, surveyor, etc) knew or ought to have known of the existence of the equitable interest, notice is ascribed to the purchaser.

....

To illustrate the point we have made we will use the facts from the Brakenhill House case study. Isobel employed a solicitor, Bloggs, to investigate the title to the house. Bloggs did look at the 1973 conveyance, noticed the 1910 restrictive covenant, but omitted to tell Isobel. Isobel will have imputed actual notice of the covenant.

What if Bloggs looked only at the 1989 conveyance, and failed to look at the 1973 conveyance? In that case Isobel would have imputed constructive notice of the restrictive covenant.

In either of these two situations Isobel would be justifiably annoyed with Bloggs! She would be bound by the restrictive covenant. But she would have one consolation. She could sue Bloggs for damages for professional negligence.

For a further example let us go back to one version of the High Chimneys case study. In one version of the case study (see 4.5.4 'Inspect the Land') Darrell, a friend of Tatiana's with a constructive trust interest in the property, is living in the property at the time of Roger's purchase.

Let us now assume that Roger did not visit High Chimneys prior to the purchase but left inspection of the property to his surveyor, Muggins. When Muggins visited the property, Darrell was out. Tatiana made no mention of Darrell, but there were male clothes lying around in some of the rooms. Muggins never reported this fact to Roger, nor did he take up with Tatiana the presence of the male clothing. It appears that Roger would have imputed constructive notice of Darrell's interest.

This last example is rather loosely based on *Kingsnorth Finance Ltd v Tizard* [1986] 1 WLR 783. Mr Tizard ('H') owned the legal title to the matrimonial home 'Willowdown', but Mrs Tizard ('W') had contributed substantially to the cost of acquisition and therefore had a constructive trust interest. The marriage broke down and W then spent most of her time with her sister nearby. However, W returned to Willowdown daily to help care for the couple's teenage children who still lived there. If H was away, W spent the night at Willowdown. W still kept personal clothes and belongings at Willowdown, shut up in a wardrobe.

H decided to remortgage Willowdown to Kingsnorth Finance. Kingsnorth (acting through local mortgage brokers) instructed a surveyor, Mr Marshall ('M'), to inspect the property. Because of his unusual family situation, H arranged for M to visit on a Sunday afternoon. H also cunningly arranged for W to take the children out for the day.

When M called, his suspicions were aroused when he spotted various items belonging to the children. H had described himself as single on the application form for the mortgage loan, but now admitted to M that he was 'separated'. M made no further enquiries, and M's report to

Kingsnorth did not mention his suspicions that there might be a wife/mother with some kind of claim on the house.

Kingsnorth lent H a large sum of money on the security of a mortgage of Willowdown; H later defaulted on the payments. Kingsnorth tried to enforce the mortgage, but the Deputy High Court Judge (Judge Finlay) held that W's constructive trust interest had priority over the mortgage. Judge John Finlay QC in his assessment of the case said:

> The plaintiffs were prejudicially affected by the knowledge of their agent, Mr Marshall, that Mr Tizard, contrary to what he had said in his application, was married: see section 199(1)(ii)(b). That put them on notice that further inquiries were necessary; the inquiries which in these circumstances ought reasonably to have been made by the plaintiffs would, in my judgment, have been such as to have apprised them of the fact that Mrs Tizard claimed a beneficial interest in the property; and accordingly, they would have had notice of such equitable rights as she had and the mortgage in these circumstances takes effect subject to these rights: see Section 199(1)(ii)(a).

I arrive at that conclusion without having considered the question: does the occupation of Mrs Tizard affect the mortgagees with notice of her rights, or are they only so affected if, as Mr Wigmore submits, they are aware of her occupation, that is, if they find her in occupation? On the balance of probabilities, I find that the reason Mr Marshall did not find Mrs Tizard in the house was that Mr Tizard had arranged matters to achieve that result. He told Mrs Tizard that on a particular Sunday, and I find in fact that it was the Sunday that Mr Marshall did inspect, he was going to entertain friends to lunch and would she take the children out for the day ...

I have already stated my finding that the wife was in occupation ... I conclude that had Mrs Tizard been found to be in occupation by the plaintiffs or their agent and so found in the context of what had been said by Mr Tizard to Mr Marshall and stated or implied in the forms he had signed, they, the plaintiffs, would clearly either have learned of her rights by inquiry of her or been fixed with notice of those rights had not inquiry of her been made.

In the light of my finding that Mr Marshall's information about Mr Tizard's wife is to be imputed to the plaintiffs and my conclusion that further inquiries should have been made by the plaintiffs because of that imputed knowledge, do I ask myself whether such an inspection as would have disclosed that Mrs Tizard was in the premises is one which ought reasonably to have been made by them, or is the proper question: can the plaintiffs show that no such inspection was reasonably necessary? The latter appears to me to be the proper way to put it. The plaintiffs did not make any further inquiries or inspections; had they done so it would have been open to them to contend that they had done all that was reasonably required and if they still had no knowledge of Mrs Tizard's rights or claims, that they were not fixed with notice of them. But in the absence of further inquiries or inspections, I do not think that it is open to the plaintiffs to say that if they had made a further inspection they would still not have found Mrs Tizard in occupation.

I would put it briefly thus. Mr Tizard appears to have been minded to conceal the true facts; he did not do so completely; the plaintiffs had, or are to be taken to have had, information which should have alerted them to the fact that the full facts were not in their possession and that they should make further inspections or inquiries; they did not do so; and in these circumstances I find that they are fixed with notice of the equitable interest of Mrs Tizard. ...

Here Mr. Marshall carried out his inspection on a Sunday afternoon at a time arranged with Mr. Tizard. If the only purpose of such an inspection was to ascertain the physical state of the property, the time at which the inspection is made and whether or not that time is one agreed in advance with the vendor or mortgagor appears to me to be immaterial. Where, however, the object of the inspection (or one of the objects) is to ascertain who is in occupation, I cannot see that an inspection at a time pre-arranged with the vendor will necessarily attain that object. Such a pre-arranged inspection may achieve no more than an inquiry of the vendor or mortgagor and his answer to it. In the case of residential property an appointment for inspection will, in most cases, be essential so far as inspection of the interior is concerned. How then is a purchaser or mortgagee to carry out such inspection as ought reasonably to have been made for the purpose of determining whether the possession and occupation of the property accords with the title offered? What is such an inspection as ought reasonably to be made must, I think, depend upon all the circumstances. In the circumstances of the present case I am not satisfied that the pre-arranged inspection on a Sunday afternoon fell within the category of 'such inspections which ought reasonably to have been made,' the words in the Law of Property Act 1925, section 199, which I have already read. The plaintiffs not having established that they made such an inspection, the conclusion that I have reached by another route is, in my view, fortified . . .

When confronted by the suspicious circumstances on the Sunday afternoon, M, as a reasonable man, should have carried out further enquiries independent of H. In particular, while it would have been wrong to have gone around opening up cupboards etc, M should perhaps have called around *unannounced* to determine exactly who was in occupation of the property. Kingsnorth therefore had imputed constructive notice of W's constructive trust interest.

REVIEW QUESTION 'If you have a constructive trust interest in a property, stay put, and make your presence obvious. If anyone asks why you are there, tell them!'

Why this advice? Is there any practical difference if the property is not a house, but a farm, shop, or factory?

(Consider 4.5.4 and the discussion on notice.)

REVIEW QUESTION In 2003, you bought Primrose Cottage (unregistered title) from Alicia. Alicia had bought the cottage in 1984 from Bethany, who had bought the cottage from Oscar way back in 1923.

When Oscar conveyed the cottage to Bethany, that conveyance contained a restrictive covenant in favour of neighbouring Daffodil House that Primrose Cottage should not be used for business or professional purposes.

You have only just heard about this restrictive covenant. You are converting the cottage into a small guest house, and the current owner of Daffodil House is threatening to seek an injunction. Consider your position.

What if the solicitor you employed in 2003 knew about the restrictive covenant, but forgot to tell you?

(Consider what you have understood about the doctrine of notice.)

4.6 Position of Successors in Title to a Purchaser without Notice

cross-reference
See 4.1 for the High Chimneys case study.

If a purchaser of a legal estate to which an equitable interest was subject takes the estate free from the equitable interest because of the doctrine of notice, all persons who derive title from that purchaser take free from the equitable interest as well.

To explain this point we must go back to the original version of the High Chimneys case study (where Gianluca left in 2011).

In Roger's dispute with Gianluca, Roger will contend that he is a bona fide purchaser for value of a legal estate without notice of Gianluca's interest. Gianluca does not accept this, and sues Roger in a court case. Roger will succeed if he proves the following:

1 he was acting bona fide;

2 he was a purchaser for value;

3 that he purchased a legal estate;

4 that he was without notice of Gianluca's interest. (Remember that in the original version of the case study both of Roger's agents and he himself made very careful enquiries which did not reveal even Gianluca's existence.)

Assuming that he has been successful in proving all of these points, let us now consider the following events. Roger wants to sell High Chimneys and decides to put it up for sale. Beatrice is the first prospective purchaser to visit the property. Luckily, she does not mind the sheep, nor does she mind Olabode cutting across the garden. But suddenly she says, 'Is this not the house there was that big court case about? A fellow called Gianluca came along and claimed he had some sort of share in it. I read all about it in the local paper.'

'Yes', Roger replies, 'but I won the case.'

'Congratulations', says Beatrice, 'but is there a risk that his claim will bind me? I seem to remember that you won because at the time you purchased you neither knew nor could have known of Gianluca's claim. I do know that Gianluca has a claim!'

thinking point 4.9

Why has Beatrice no need to worry?

Beatrice need not worry, for the reason given in the first paragraph of this section: once an equitable interest is void against a purchaser for value without notice, it is void against everybody else who derives title from that purchaser. This is so even if (like Beatrice) a successor in title has actual knowledge of the equitable interest (Wilkes v Spooner [1911] 2 KB 473).

This is both logical and fair. It would be illogical if an invalid equitable interest could in effect revive against a later purchaser. Such a revival would also be grossly unfair to somebody in Roger's position. He (personally) would not be bound by Gianluca's claim. But nobody would want to buy from Roger for fear that Gianluca would claim against them.

One final point. Reference has been made to 'persons who derive title' from the purchaser without notice. 'Persons who derive title' is not just confined to later purchasers. It extends to anyone whose rights are derived directly or indirectly from the original purchaser without notice. So if Beatrice does buy, all her successors are also protected from Gianluca's claim. If Roger decides not to sell, but to lease, or perhaps even to give away the property, the lessee or donee is not bound by Gianluca's claim.

4.7 Registration of Land Charges

The system of land charge registration was introduced in the Land Charges Act 1925 (now replaced by the Land Charges Act 1972) to reduce the importance of the doctrine of notice. The range of interests that require registration are listed within the Land Charges Act 1972 and are predominantly equitable in nature. The effect of registration of a land charge is provided in s198 LPA 1925:

> *Law of Property Act 1925*
>
> 198. Registration under the Land Charges Act 1925 [now 1972] to be notice
>
> (1) The registration of any instrument or matter [in any register kept under the Land Charges Act 1972 or any local land charges register] shall be deemed to constitute actual notice of such instrument or matter, and of the fact of such registration, to all persons and for all purposes connected with the land affected, as from the date of registration or other prescribed date and so long as the registration continues in force.

As we shall shortly see, a wide variety of equitable interests are registrable as land charges. A person who owns an equitable interest which is registrable as a land charge is well advised to register it. Why?

cross-reference
For further discussion on actual notice see 4.5.4.

1 If the interest is registered then s198(1) LPA 1925 provides that the registration shall constitute actual notice to the whole world of the equitable interest. Actual notice, as referred to in the statute, has been imported from the old doctrine of notice, and its effect on a registered land charge is that it is automatically binding on the purchaser. Thus if you register your right as a land charge, you can be sure that it will be binding on a purchaser.

2 If an interest is registrable as a land charge, but it is not registered, then by the Land Charges Acts 1925 (LCA 1925) and 1972 (LCA 1972), the interest is void against a purchaser for value (whatever the state of that purchaser's knowledge).

The important case of *Hollington Brothers Ltd v Rhodes* [1951] 2 All ER 578 is a dramatic illustration of the second principle. H 'leased' some offices to R for seven years by a document which was not a deed. R therefore acquired only an equitable lease. An equitable lease is (since 1925) registrable as a land charge. R took possession of the premises, but omitted to register his lease as a land charge.

cross-reference
For further discussion on the doctrine of notice see 4.5.

The equitable lease was valid against H, but H then sold its estate in reversion to D. This sale was expressly 'subject to and with the benefit of such tenancies as may affect the premises'. There can be no doubt that D had 'notice' of R's equitable lease. Nevertheless, D was not bound by it. The court emphasized that where an equitable interest is registrable as a land charge, the doctrine of notice is irrelevant. Harman J commented:

> After 1925 by virtue of the Land Charges Act, 1925 … this contract came within class C (iv) as a 'charge or obligation affecting land,' and, therefore, might be registered as a land charge in the register of land charges. Accordingly, by virtue of s 13(2) [now s4(6) LCA 1972], this being a land charge of class C, it is void
>
> > '… against a purchaser of the land charged therewith, or of any interest in such land, unless the land charge is registered in the appropriate register before the completion of the purchase …'
>
> Moreover, by the Law of Property Act, 1925, s 199(1)(i), a purchaser is not to be prejudicially affected by notice of any instrument or matter capable of registration under the Land Charges Act, 1925 [now LCA 1972], which is void against him by reason of non-registration. This land charge was not registered, and, accordingly, it is said that it was void against Daymar Estates Ltd notwithstanding their notice or knowledge, and, moreover, that there was no duty lying on the plaintiffs to register the contract to prevent this result …
>
> … The fact is that it was the policy of the framers of the legislation of 1925 to get rid of equitable rights of this kind unless registered … Finally, as under the Land Charges Act, 1925, s 13(2) [now s4(6)], an unregistered estate contract is void as against a purchaser of the land, and under the Law of Property Act, 1925, s 199(1), the purchaser is not to be prejudicially affected by it, I do not see how that which is void and which is not to prejudice the purchaser

can be validated by some equitable doctrine. There is, after all, no great hardship in this. The plaintiffs could, at any time until the completion of the assignment to Daymar Estates Ltd have preserved their rights by registration . . .

cross-reference
Midland Bank Trust Co Ltd v Green *is discussed at 4.7.5.*

The final sentence from this extract reinforces the importance of registration and so, the moral of this case (and the case of *Midland Bank Trust Co Ltd v Green* [1981] 1 AC 513) is clear. If you have an equitable interest which is registrable as a land charge, register it! If you do not, you will lose your rights if the land is sold. You will lose your rights even if the purchaser knew of your interest and/or could see you were occupying the land.

thinking point 4.10

In 1990, Lenny granted an equitable lease of his house 'Broomtrees' to Olaf for 50 years. Olaf lives in the house. The house is unregistered title. Recently Lenny sold the fee simple in the house to Raul. Raul knew of the equitable lease, because both Lenny and Olaf told him about it. Is Raul bound by Olaf's equitable lease?

Raul will be bound by Olaf's equitable lease only if Olaf had registered it as a land charge. If Olaf has not so registered, then his equitable lease will be void against a purchaser such as Raul. It is irrelevant that Raul knew of Olaf's lease.

4.7.1 The Operation of the Land Charges Register

Before examining this topic, remember that the Land Charges Register is relevant only where the title to land is unregistered. The Land Charges Register must not be confused with the Register of Title. As more and more titles are registered, the Land Charges Register is becoming less and less important.

The decline in importance of the Land Charges Register is very welcome, as it operates in a rather strange way. A person who owns a registrable interest registers it not against the land, but against the name of the owner (at the time the interest was created) of the legal estate out of which the interest is derived (s3 LCA 1972).

The Land Charges Register is basically an immensely long list of names of landowners. It used to be a gigantic card-index system kept in London (one name, one card). Critics predicted that the system would become unmanageable, and in the early 1970s those predictions came true. The situation was saved (in 1974) by transferring the Land Charges Register on to a computer kept at Plymouth. This computer system at Plymouth still operates, and serves the whole of England and Wales. One of the clear defects in the 1925 property legislation was (largely) solved not by legislation, but by a technology unheard of in 1925!

Computerization of the Land Charges Register has not altered the fact that registration must be against the name of the landowner as shown in the title deeds (*Standard Property Investment plc v British Plastics Federation* (1987) 53 P & CR 25). To illustrate this point Roger Sexton owns 5 Bankhall Close, and someone wishes to register a land charge against him. The conveyance of 5 Bankhall Close to him names him as 'Rodger Norman Sexton'. Registration must be against 'Rodger Norman Sexton', even though on his birth certificate and in everyday life he is 'Roger' without the 'd'. In the High Chimneys case study the equitable profit must be registered to bind Roger (s198 LPA 1925). Registration of the land charge must be against Amit's name as found on the title deeds.

Suppose, however, that you want to register a land charge, but you do not have access to the relevant title deed(s) to see how the name has been written. What do you do then? The answer (strange as it sounds) is that you register against all possible alternative versions of the name. This quite often happens with 'Class F' rights of occupation ('home rights').

thinking point 4.11

Wendy comes into your office in a flood of tears. She explains that her husband of nearly 50 years has just left her. She is still in the matrimonial home, which her husband bought in his sole name in 1960. The house is unregistered title. She is frightened that her husband will sell the house and she will be out on the street. She tells you, 'He usually called himself Stuart Pearse, but I am not sure that is the correct spelling. On the marriage certificate it says "Stewart Pierce".'

In this situation every good lawyer will 'drop everything' and immediately register a land charge. But what do you do about the names problem?

You would register against all possible versions of his name; for example, the two versions of the husband's first name multiplied by the three possible spellings of the surname (remember 'Pearce' is very common).

Registering against the estate owner's name where there is a sub-sale of land could give rise to complications. In *Barrett v Hilton Developments* (1975) 29 P & CR 300, B contracted to buy the land from C. Prior to the completion of the purchase B had contracted to sell the same piece of land to H. H registered the estate contract against B's name. The registration of the land charge against B's name was held to be ineffective. The court held that the land charge should have been registered against the name of C, as C was the owner of the legal estate at the time H's interest was created. (The 'estate owner's name' does not include a person entitled at the time of registration to have the legal estate conveyed to him.)

4.7.2 Searches of the Land Charges Register

As a result of s198 LPA 1925, all interests which have been correctly registered are automatically binding upon a purchaser; it is deemed to amount to actual notice of the registered Land Charge. As a purchaser buying land which is unregistered title, one enquiry they always should make is a 'search' of the Land Charges Register. The purchaser needs to know what (relevant) entries there are on the register.

When a purchaser is buying unregistered land they 'search' by supplying the Land Charges Department in Plymouth with a list of the names of the past owners of the land (if possible going back to 1925). In Chapter 1 and 4.2 in this chapter, we explained that the purchaser must inspect the relevant deeds for the property going back to the good root of title which is at least 15 years old (s23 Law of Property Act 1969 (LPA 1969)).

The Complexities of a Names-Based Register

The cases of *Oak Co-operative BS v Blackburn* [1968] and *Diligent Finance Co Ltd v Alleyne* (1972) illustrate just how awkward and cumbersome this system of registration against names can be.

In *Oak Co-operative BS v Blackburn* [1968] Ch 730, a man whose real name was Francis David Blackburn agreed to sell his house to Ms Caines. She registered her 'estate contract' land charge against the name Frank David Blackburn. Later, Blackburn mortgaged the house to the building society, which searched the Land Charges Register against the name of Francis Davis Blackburn. This search did not reveal Caines's estate contract. Blackburn defaulted on the mortgage repayments. So the courts had to decide whether Ms Caines's estate contract was binding on the building society. Russell LJ said:

...The question...is whether there was a valid registration of the estate contract. If it was such, then under section 198 (1) of the Law of Property Act, 1925, the plaintiffs had deemed actual notice of the estate contract and of its registration, whether or not they had on the facts actual or constructive notice of the third defendant's rights. If it was not such, then under section 199 (1) (*i*) of the Law of Property Act, 1925, it is provided that the plaintiffs should not be prejudicially affected by notice of the estate contract (even if they had it) and under section 13 (2) of the Land Charges Act, 1925 [now 4(6) LCA 1972], the estate contract was void as against the plaintiffs.

Section 10 (1) of the Land Charges Act, 1925 [now s2], provides that the following classes of charges on or obligations affecting land may be registered as land charges in the register, and Class (iv) is that now relevant...Section 10 (2) requires that 'a land charge shall be registered *in the name* of the estate owner whose estate is intended to be affected': and this really is the crux of the present case...Section 16 enables anyone to search in any register or index for himself. Section 17 provides for an official search. A proposing purchaser (for example) may lodge a requisition for such search and thereupon the registrar shall 'make the search required, and shall issue a certificate setting forth the result thereof.' Subsection (3) provides that in favour of the intending purchaser as against the person interested under the instrument (here the estate contract) 'the certificate, according to the tenor thereof, shall be conclusive, affirmatively or negatively, as the case may be.' Subsection (4) provides that every such requisition shall be in writing '*specifying the name against which* he desires search to be made, or in relation to which he requires a certificate of result of search, and other sufficient particulars.'

...

In the case of a request for an official search, which of course takes place before completion after title examined. We can only think that the name or names referred to in the request should be that or those appearing on the title. A nil certificate here as to Francis Davis *Blackburn* would not have served to override the third defendants land charge had it been registered in the name Francis David *Blackburn*, though it *could* have been issued.

In most cases of contracts to purchase land nowadays many of the formalities precede exchange of contracts, and indeed those acting for the vendor would have used in the contract the name of the proposed vendor as appearing on the title. But of course there are other cases, such as the present, where the contract is much less formally arrived at, and the purchaser has no ready means of ascertaining the 'title' names of the vendor. It would seem to be a great hardship on a purchaser registering in the name by which the vendor ordinarily passed that his registration should be entirely without operation, which is of course the submission of the plaintiffs in this case. We have said earlier that if in this case the search had been against 'Francis David Blackburn' and the certificate *had* referred to the fact that an estate contract was registered against 'Frank David Blackburn' in respect of this property, the proposed mortgage transaction would have been blown sky-high. But if the plaintiffs' contention is correct the registration would be no registration at all, and by force of sections 199 of the Law of Property Act, 1925, and 13 (2) of the Land Charges Act, 1925, the plaintiffs could have carried through the mortgage ignoring the estate contract though in fact aware of its existence. Indeed, if the plaintiffs had contracted to grant a mortgage loan subject to getting good title they would have been in breach of their contract by refusing to grant it.

We have come to the conclusion that the registration on this occasion ought not to be regarded as a nullity simply because the formal name of Blackburn was Francis and not Frank, and notwithstanding that Frank as a name is not merely an abbreviation or version of Francis but also a name in its own right, as are also for example Harry and Willie. We are not led to this conclusion by the fact that initials would seem to suffice for registration of a lis pendens: see *Dunn* v *Chapman* [1920] 2 Ch. 474—at least under the then legislation and rules: for presumably a request for search under a full name having the same initials should throw up all entries under those initials. We take a broader view that so far as possible the system should be made to work in favour of those who seek to make use of it in a sensible and practical way. If a proposing purchaser here had requested a search in the correct full names he would have got a clean certificate and a clear title under section 17 (3) of the Land Charges Act, 1925, and would have suffered no harm from the fact that the registration was not in such names: and a person registering who is not in a position to satisfy himself what are the correct full names runs that risk. But if there be registration in what may be fairly described as a version of the full names of the vendor, albeit not a version which is bound to be discovered on a search in the correct full names, we would not hold it a nullity against someone who does not search at all, or who (as here) searches in the wrong name.

The Court of Appeal therefore held in favour of Ms Caines. Despite the registration of the charge being registered in the wrong name, the court ruled that a registration against a version of the owner's name was valid and binding on anyone who searched against the wrong name, or who did not search at all. But Ms Caines's estate contract would not have been binding on the building society if it had an official search against the correct name as it appeared in the title deeds and Caines's interest had not been revealed.

In *Diligent Finance Co Ltd v Alleyne* (1972) 23 P & CR 346, the house was conveyed to 'Erskine Owen Alleyne', and used by himself and his wife as their matrimonial home. When the marriage broke down, Mrs Alleyne registered her 'Class F' matrimonial home rights against the name of Erskine Alleyne. Mr Alleyne later mortgaged the house to the claimants, who searched against the correct name of Erskine Owen Alleyne. Applying what had been said in *Oak Co-operative*, Mr Justice Foster held that the wife's land charge did not bind the claimants, and commented:

The question therefore is whether the court is entitled to assume from the conveyancing documents which I have mentioned that the first defendant's name Erskine Owen Alleyne is in fact his real and full name. It was pointed out on behalf of the plaintiff that no one was in a better position to know what the full name of her husband was than his wife, and further it was pointed out that the second defendant [Mrs Alleyne] must have known that the freehold property was mortgaged to the Greater London Council where one could find the name Erskine Owen Alleyne.

In my judgment, in the absence of any other evidence—and there is none—it is right for the court . . . to assume in the absence of evidence to the contrary that the proper name of a person is that in which the conveyancing documents have been taken. It is unfortunate, to say the least, that the Class F registration was not made against the proper name Erskine Owen Alleyne but only against Erskine Alleyne, but that is a mistake which I for my part cannot unfortunately rectify.

These cases demonstrate the problem that may be encountered by a person seeking to register a land charge who does not have the definitive version of the name as found on the title deeds. The problem is not alleviated simply because the Land Charges Register is held on a computer. Searches are only made according to the search terms provided by the person requesting the official search.

REVIEW QUESTION In what circumstances can a right be on the Land Charges Register but not bind a purchaser?

(Review your understanding in 4.7.2.)

4.7.3 Equitable Interests Registrable as Land Charges

The Land Charges Act 1925 (now replaced by the Land Charges Act 1972) introduced a system of classes of land charge. For our purposes these classes are discussed in the following sections in order of importance, rather than alphabetical order.

Class C(iv): Estate Contract

'Estate contract' was defined at 3.9.4 as the equitable interest which a purchaser of land acquires in the (usually fairly brief) period which elapses between the contract for sale and its completion by conveyance of the legal estate. This may be called the traditional definition. The definition of 'estate contract' contained in the LCA 1972 (see s2(4)(iv)) is far wider than the traditional definition. In consequence, quite a wide variety of rights are registrable under the general heading 'estate contract':

- any contract to create or convey a legal estate;
- equitable leases arising under contracts or informal grants (hence the need to register the lease in *Hollington v Rhodes*);
- options; and
- rights of pre-emption (ie first refusal).

Class D(ii): Restrictive Covenants

Any restrictive covenant entered into after 1925 (except one contained in a lease) is registrable as a land charge (s2(5)(ii) LCA 1972). Restrictive covenants entered into before 1926 (of which there is a tremendous number) are not registrable as land charges. They remain subject to the doctrine of notice.

thinking point 4.12

Pippa recently purchased Snooty House. Snooty House was unregistered title. When Pippa investigated title, the root of title was a conveyance dated 1983. That conveyance revealed a large number of restrictive covenants affecting Snooty House. Some were imposed on the house in 1910; others were imposed in 1940. When Pippa had a search made of the Land Charges Register, the official search certificate revealed no restrictive covenants. Is Pippa bound:

1 by the 1910 covenants?

2 by the 1940 covenants?

Provided she searched against the correct name(s) she will not be bound by the 1940 covenants, even though she knew about them. She will be bound by the 1910 covenants. The doctrine of notice applies to these 'old' covenants, and Pippa had notice of them because they were recited in the root of title.

Class F: Rights of Occupation; 'Home Rights'

Where one spouse (or civil partner) has the legal title to the matrimonial home in his/her sole name, the other spouse (or civil partner) automatically has a statutory right of occupation with respect to the home. This right of occupation, renamed 'home rights' by the Family Law Act 1996 (as amended by the Civil Partnerships Act 2004), is registrable as a land charge (s2(7) LCA 1972).

The Class F right is in addition to any right under a constructive trust which the spouse (or civil partner) who does not have the legal title may have by virtue of having contributed substantially to the cost of acquisition of the matrimonial home. Confusingly, a constructive trust interest is an equitable interest which is still subject to the doctrine of notice.

Class C(iii): General Equitable Charge

general equitable charge

an equitable charge for money where the owner of the charge does not take possession of the title deeds to the legal estate affected by the charge.

You may not find the definition of a **general equitable charge** particularly meaningful. What really matters is that there are two significant equitable interests covered by this concept:

- an equitable mortgage where the mortgagee does not take the title deeds to the property mortgaged; and
- an **unpaid vendor's lien**.

unpaid vendor's lien

this arises where a vendor of land conveys the land to a purchaser, but allows the purchaser to delay paying part or the whole of the price. It is a kind of equitable interest in the land which exists in favour of the vendor until he is paid in full.

Class D(iii): Equitable Easements and Profits

This class of land charge is relatively rare as most easements and profits are legal interests, and like legal interests generally they bind purchasers whatever the circumstances.

Equitable easements and equitable profits are registrable under Class D(iii) if created after 1925 (s2(5)(iii) LCA 1972). In the High Chimneys case study, Pierce produced a written agreement giving the then owner of Smokey Farm a profit. Since there is no mention of a deed the formalities of creating the interest in land, in this case a profit, have not been complied with (s52 LPA 1925, s1 LP(MP)A 1989). The equitable profit would need to be registered as a D(iii) land charge for it to bind Roger.

Equitable easements and equitable profits created pre-1926 are not registrable as land charges. They are still subject to the doctrine of notice.

Class C(ii): A 'Limited Owner's Charge'

This form of equitable interest is relatively rare nowadays. It arises in favour of a person who has only a life interest in a piece of land, but they pay off out of their own pocket a financial incumbrance burdening the fee simple, such as a mortgage, or a charge for inheritance tax, or the taxes now replaced by inheritance tax.

Class E: Annuities

This class is totally obsolete, and we need not bother with it.

4.7.4 Legal Interests Registrable as Land Charges

We now come to an anomaly in the law, actually the result of the 1925 reforms. The vast majority of property rights registrable as land charges are equitable interests which otherwise would have been subject to the doctrine of notice. Rather strangely, a few legal interests are also registrable as land charges.

The rights we are about to consider are called 'legal interests', as they fall within s1 LPA 1925. But ironically, as they are registrable as land charges, they are deprived of the all-important characteristic of legal interests, which is that they bind purchasers of the land whatever the circumstances. If an interest of one of the types discussed in the following sections is not registered as a land charge, it will be void against a purchaser in the usual way. It will even be void against a purchaser who actually knew of the unregistered interest (cf *Hollington Brothers v Rhodes*).

Class C(i): Puisne Mortgage

('Puisne' is pronounced 'puny'.) A puisne mortgage is a legal mortgage where the mortgagee does not take possession of the title deeds.

Where land is mortgaged, the mortgagee (ie the lender) normally takes possession of the title deeds relating to the land mortgaged. However, as you may already know, a piece of land may be mortgaged more than once, so that there are (simultaneously) two or more mortgages with respect to the same piece of land. Where this is the case, the first mortgagee (ie the lender whose mortgage was created first) will in practice have taken the deeds to the land. The later mortgagees (second, third, etc) will therefore not be able to take any deeds.

This in turn means that if a second or later mortgage is a legal mortgage, it will be a 'puisne' mortgage and registrable as a Class C(i) land charge (s2(4)(i) LCA 1972). (If a second or later mortgage is an equitable mortgage, it will constitute a general equitable charge registrable as a Class C(iii) land charge.)

Class D(i): Charge for Inheritance Tax

This charge was mentioned in Chapter 3 when discussing types of legal interest. The inheritance tax (in earlier days the capital transfer tax or estate duty) which may be payable with respect to a piece of real property is a charge on that real property. It is a legal interest, but it is registrable as a land charge, Class D(i) (s2(5)(i) LCA 1972). The charge can arise only in favour of Her Majesty's Revenue and Customs, and the taxpayer (the person who has inherited the land) is permitted to pay off the tax by annual instalments over ten years.

Strangely, it is the practice of the Revenue to register a Class D(i) charge only in exceptional cases where it anticipates having difficulty getting its money.

thinking point 4.13

Harold recently died. He owned, inter alia, Hugeacres (unregistered title), worth about £12 million. His will appointed the National Gloucester Bank to be his sole executor, and it (as it is entitled to) has put Hugeacres up for sale. Your wealthy friend Lance is thinking of buying, but in conversation he asks, 'Hugeacres must be subject to a whopping bill for inheritance tax. If I bought Hugeacres, could the taxman claim the money from me?' Advise Lance.

Although the inheritance tax is a 'legal' interest against Hugeacres, it is registrable as a land charge. It would bind a purchaser such as Lance only if the Revenue registered its claim on the Land Charges Register. The Revenue would be confident of getting its money from National Gloucester Bank, so it would not bother to register.

Classes A and B: Certain Types of Right Created by Act of Parliament

We need not bother with the details of these charges, which are nowadays mostly unimportant. There is, however, one very important type of Class B charge—the 'legal aid agency charge'—which was discussed briefly in Chapter 3. This arises in favour of the Legal Aid Agency for the costs of litigation involving a legally aided person in which a piece of land is 'recovered or preserved' for that person. It is the policy of the Legal Aid Agency (and was the policy of the Legal Services Commission which used to administer legal aid) to register all Class B charges arising in its favour.

4.7.5 Consequences of Failure to Register a Land Charge

We have been saying that an unregistered land charge is void against a purchaser for value of the land. This is something of an oversimplification. The exact consequences of failure to register a land charge depend on the type of charge involved.

Failure to Register an Estate Contract, Restrictive Covenant, Inheritance Tax Charge, or Equitable Easement/Profit

A failure to register as a land charge one of these types of interest will mean that it is void against a purchaser for money or money's worth of a legal estate or legal interest (s4(6) LCA 1972). The consequences of the non-registration of a land charge were illustrated in 4.7 in the discussion on *Hollington Brothers Ltd v Rhodes*. It must, however, be stressed that the interest will still be valid against the original grantor, donees from him, and people who inherit the land from him.

The case of *Midland Bank v Green* [1981] 1 AC 513 defined what was meant by a purchaser for 'money or money's worth'. In that case a father owned a farm. He granted his son an option to purchase the farm at any time in the next ten years. The son should have registered the option as an estate contract, but omitted to do so. Father and son later fell out. In order to spite the son, the father sold the farm (worth about £40,000) to his wife for just £500. The wife, of course, knew all about the option. Was she bound by it? The Court of Appeal, presided over by Lord Denning, found that the wife was bound by the option. That court said that 'money or money's worth' meant a fair price, which £500 clearly was not. Lord Denning offered no definition of the concept 'fair price'. To the great relief of property lawyers, the Court of Appeal decision was overturned by the House of Lords. Lord Wilberforce in the House of Lords said:

> My Lords, I can deal more shortly with the respondents' second argument. It relates to the consideration for the purchase. The argument is that the protection of section 13(2) of the Land Charges Act 1925 [now 4(6) LCA 1972] does not extend to a purchaser who has provided only a nominal consideration and that £500 is nominal. A variation of this was the argument accepted by the Court of Appeal that the consideration must be 'adequate'—an expression of transparent difficulty. The answer to both contentions lies in the language of the subsection. The word 'purchaser,' by definition (section 20(8) [LCA 1925]), means one who provides valuable consideration—a term of art which precludes any inquiry as to adequacy. This definition is, of course, subject to the context. Section 13(2), proviso, requires money or money's worth to be provided: the purpose of this being to exclude the consideration of marriage. There is nothing here which suggests, or admits of, the introduction of a further requirement that the money must not be nominal.

The argument for this requirement is based upon the Law of Property Act 1925 which, in section 205(1)(xxi) defining 'purchaser' provides that 'valuable consideration' includes marriage but does not include a 'nominal consideration in money.' The Land Charges Act 1925 contains no definition of 'valuable consideration,' so it is said to be necessary to have resort to the Law of Property Act definition: thus 'nominal consideration in money' is excluded. An indication that this is intended is said to be provided by section 199(1)(i). I cannot accept this. The fallacy lies in supposing that the Acts—either of them—set out to define 'valuable consideration'; they do not: they define 'purchaser,' and they define the word differently (see the first part of the argument). 'Valuable consideration' requires no definition: it is an expression denoting an advantage conferred or detriment suffered. What each Act does is, for its own purposes, to exclude some things from this general expression: the Law of Property Act includes marriage but not a nominal sum in money; the Land Charges Act excludes marriage but allows 'money or money's worth.' There is no coincidence between these two: no link by reference or necessary logic between them. Section 199(1)(i) by referring to the Land Charges Act 1925, necessarily incorporates—for the purposes of this provision the definition of 'purchaser' in the latter Act, for it is only against such a 'purchaser' that an instrument is void under that Act. It cannot be read as incorporating the Law of Property Act definition into the Land Charges Act. As I have pointed out the land charges legislation has contained its own definition since 1888, carried through, with the addition of the reference to 'money or money's worth' into 1925. To exclude a nominal sum of money from section 13(2) of the Land Charges Act would be to rewrite the section.

This conclusion makes it unnecessary to determine whether £500 is a nominal sum of money or not. But I must say that for my part I should have great difficulty in so holding. 'Nominal consideration' and a 'nominal sum' in the law appear to me, as terms of art, to refer to a sum or consideration which can be mentioned as consideration but is not necessarily paid. To equate 'nominal' with 'inadequate' or even 'grossly inadequate' would embark the law upon inquiries which I cannot think were contemplated by Parliament.

In summary, the House of Lords held that 'money or money's worth' was synonymous with the traditional concept of 'value', except that marriage does not count as money or money's worth. Thus Mrs Green was not bound by the option. Even if Mrs Green had paid just £1 or some other nominal consideration this would amount to 'value'.

The Court of Appeal in *Lloyds Bank v Carrick* [1996] 4 All ER 630, considered the effect of the non-registration of an estate contract. Mr Carrick contracted to sell a long lease of a maisonette to Mrs Carrick. A deed transferring the lease was never executed. However, Mrs Carrick paid the price, took possession, and (it appears) spent a lot of money upon the property. Mr Carrick later mortgaged the lease to the bank.

Mrs Carrick had never registered her 'estate contract' to purchase the lease as a Class C(iv) land charge. Her estate contract was therefore void as against the bank. However, Mrs Carrick claimed that, in addition to her estate contract, she also had a constructive trust or proprietary estoppel interest which would be binding on the bank under the doctrine of notice as it had not made adequate enquiries.

The Court of Appeal rejected Mrs Carrick's claim. It held that if a person acquires an estate contract to purchase a property, that person cannot avoid the consequences of non-registration by claiming in addition a constructive trust or proprietary estoppel interest, however much money and/or effort he/she has expended.

In contrast to *Lloyds Bank v Carrick* where the existence of an estate contract prevented Mrs Carrick from claiming either a proprietary estoppel or a constructive trust, the court in *Yaxley v Gotts* [2000] Ch 162 took a slightly different approach. In *Yaxley v Gotts* the claimant entered into a purely oral 'contract' to purchase a building. This contract was rendered void by s2 Law of Property (Miscellaneous Provisions) Act 1989, so the claimant had no estate contract interest in the land. Nevertheless, on the faith of the supposed 'contract', the claimant spent a lot of money and effort on reconstructing the building. The claimant was held to have acquired a constructive trust interest. Note that the claimant, who never had a valid contract to buy, ends up better off than Mrs Carrick in *Carrick*, who did have a contract.

Roger in the High Chimneys case study appears to have conducted a careful inspection of the Land Charges Register and has no notification of a registered D(iii) land charge (equitable profit). Since Roger is a purchaser for money or money's worth of a legal estate or legal interest, this land charge would be void for non-registration (s4(6) LCA 1972).

Failure to Register Other Land Charges

Midland Bank v Green demonstrates what may be described as a harsh rule; particularly on people who forget to register land charges such as estate contracts and restrictive covenants.

An even harsher rule applies where there is a failure to register land charges of a type not mentioned in the previous heading. The charges subject to this rule include Class F rights and general equitable charges, as well as less important matters such as limited owner's charges. A failure to register makes the interest in question void against a purchaser for value of any estate or interest in the land, legal or equitable (s4(2), (5), and (8) LCA 1972). A particular point should be made about the Class F home rights. In statistical terms, the number of Class F rights has been in decline ever since they were first invented in 1967. This is because nowadays almost all married couples or civil partners buy their homes in their joint names. However, there are still some marriages where the legal title to the home is in the husband's sole name. This is particularly true of marriages contracted in the 1940s and 1950s. In these cases the wife has Class F rights.

In practice, however, the wife probably has not registered her right. Class F rights are usually registered only when the marriage gets into difficulties and the wife goes to see a solicitor. The solicitor will immediately (while the wife is still in the office) register the Class F charge, but it may be too late. The husband may have already sold, leased, or mortgaged the home, or contracted to do so.

4.7.6 Other Registers Associated with the Land Charges Register

There are four specialized registers (one of them now obsolete, but the other three of some significance) which are closely associated with the Land Charges Register.

The Register of Pending Actions

If any court proceedings are brought which in any way relate to a piece of land, those proceedings should be registered as a 'pending action' (whether or not any proprietary rights are being claimed). This ensures that the outcome of the proceedings will bind any purchaser of the land.

You need not worry about the detailed law relating to 'pending actions', except that you do need to have a basic understanding of one point. This point involves another instance where land law and family law overlap. Where divorce proceedings are commenced, it is common for the less wealthy spouse (usually but not necessarily the wife) to claim a property adjustment order under ss23 to 25 Matrimonial Causes Act 1973. The divorce courts are given by these sections virtually unlimited powers to, in effect, redistribute property (of all kinds) belonging to one or other, or both, of the spouses. Inter alia, the court can order:

- property to be transferred from one spouse to the other;

- property solely owned by one spouse to be shared between the spouses;
- property jointly owned by the spouses to be transferred into the name of one spouse; and
- property jointly owned by the spouses to be sold and the proceeds divided as the court sees fit.

If an application for a property adjustment order does, or even may possibly, relate to a piece of land (the ex-matrimonial home or any other land), it should be registered as a pending action. In practice, in divorce proceedings where the legal title to the home is in the husband's name, the wife usually seeks a property adjustment order with respect to that home. This claim is in addition to:

- Class F home rights, which (anyway) cease on decree absolute of divorce; and
- any constructive trust interest she may have by virtue of having made a substantial contribution to the cost of the matrimonial home.

The issue of property adjustment orders will crop up again in later chapters of this book. The case of *Perez-Adamson v Perez-Rivas* [1987] 3 WLR 500 is instructive and shows the potential importance of a divorcing spouse registering a pending action. In that case the matrimonial home was in the sole name of the husband. The wife petitioned for a divorce, and in the petition requested a property adjustment order in her favour. She registered this application as a pending action. While the divorce proceedings were pending, the husband mortgaged the house to a bank. The Court of Appeal held (applying s198 LPA 1925) that the wife's claim had priority over the mortgage. Any property adjustment order made by the divorce court would therefore be binding on the bank.

The Register of Writs and Orders Affecting Land

Any judgment or court order which affects a piece of land should be placed in this register. Though there are others, two kinds of order are commonly found in this register:

- *An order charging land with a judgment debt.* A judgment debt arises where a court has awarded damages, but they have not been paid. Suppose you have successfully sued Charley Farnsbarn for damages for (say) breach of contract, and the court has awarded you £80,000 damages. He still refuses to pay, so you wish to enforce your judgment by 'execution' on Farnsbarn's property. Suppose Farnsbarn's most valuable asset is Highacre, worth £130,000. You should get a charging order against Highacre, and register it in the register of writs and orders. If Farnsbarn still does not pay the £80,000, you can force a sale of Highacre, and get your money out of the proceeds.
- *A receiving order in bankruptcy.* When somebody goes bankrupt all their property is vested, by court order, in their 'trustee in bankruptcy'.

Register of Deeds of Arrangement

Normally, an individual who is insolvent (ie unable to pay his/her debts) goes bankrupt. If, however, an insolvent person has a limited number of creditors, all of whom are willing to accept payment of only a percentage of their debts, a 'deed of arrangement' avoids the costs and stigma of bankruptcy. A deed of arrangement transfers most/all of the insolvent person's assets to a trustee who holds the property for the benefit of the creditors.

The Register of Annuities

This is now totally obsolete.

4.7.7 Searches of the Land Charges Register—The Importance of the Official Search Certificate

In Chapter 1 we gave an outline of the stages involved in buying a piece of land: contract stage where the parties enter into a contract under which the vendor agrees to sell the land to the purchaser; completion arises where the vendor executes a deed of transfer to the purchaser. During the period of time between these two stages, the purchaser will requisition a search of the Land Charges Register, having been given access to the title deeds by the vendor and obtained the names of the previous estate owners.

Provided the purchaser has searched against the correct names, if by some accident a correctly registered charge has been omitted from the search certificate, the purchaser will take free from the omitted charge. The search certificate is conclusive in favour of the purchaser.

> *Land Charges Act 1972*
>
> 10. Official searches
>
> (4) In favour of a purchaser or an intending purchaser, as against persons interested under or in respect of matters or documents entries of which are required or allowed as aforesaid, the certificate, according to its tenor, shall be conclusive, affirmatively or negatively, as the case may be.

Roger, when requisitioning a search of the Land Charges Register, must ensure that he provides the names of the owners as found on the title deeds. Remember the statutory requirement is to check as far back as the most recent conveyance which is 15 years old (good root of title). If Roger obtains a clear certificate from the Land Registry, then this is deemed to be in his favour and he is not affected by charges that have not been revealed.

The registry's error will (in effect) destroy the rights of the owner of the charge. Such errors are, fortunately, extremely rare, and it appears that the registry could be sued for negligence and made to pay compensation to the owner of the charge which they had accidentally destroyed (*Ministry of Housing and Local Government v Sharp* [1970] 2 QB 223).

Undiscoverable Land Charges

Earlier we mentioned that the purchaser must inspect the title deeds which are at least 15 years old and any later documents. There is no obligation to go 'behind' the root of title, that is, there is no obligation to examine documents which relate to earlier transactions. The problem that may arise is of a land charge which is registered against a name which is only in a document behind the root of title and which the purchaser has not discovered and, indeed, was not obliged to find. However, by virtue of s198(1) LPA 1925 registration of a land charge amounts to actual notice of the interest. Herein lies the problem. The purchaser is bound by a land charge which they have not discovered because there is no obligation to go behind the root of title.

To illustrate this, we will revisit the Brakenhill House case study and consider additional facts which have come to light.

- In 1929 Eric sold Brakenhill House to Norma
- In 1956 Norma sold Brakenhill House to Malcolm
- In 1973 Malcolm sold Brakenhill House to Leonard ← Root of title
- In 1989 Leonard sold Brakenhill House to Keith
- In 2001 Isobel purchased Brakenhill House from Keith

Norma in 1929 entered into a restrictive covenant, in favour of a neighbouring property, limiting Brakenhill House to residential purposes only. This was duly registered as a Class D(ii) land charge.

When Isobel purchased Brakenhill House in 2001 she should have inspected the following conveyances: the 1973 conveyance (the root of title) and the 1989 conveyance. Using the names found on the title deeds, the outcome of the searches of the Land Charges Register produced a clear search certificate. However, the restrictive covenant has been registered as a land charge and by virtue of s198(1) LPA 1925 Isobel has 'actual notice' of the interest. Isobel is bound by a restrictive covenant which she did not know about despite making all the appropriate searches. Furthermore, Isobel is under no obligation to go behind the root of title (ie look at the 1956 and 1929 conveyances) since the root of title is defined by statute as being the most recent document which is at least 15 years old. However, since Isobel did not have actual or imputed *knowledge* of the land charge at the date of contract she can rescind the contract (s24(1) LPA 1969).

cross-reference
See 4.5.4 for actual and imputed notice.

If Isobel sometime after completion finds out about the existence of a land charge which was behind the root of title she will be bound by this land charge by virtue of s198(1) LPA 1925. To alleviate the potential harshness of this outcome, statutory compensation is available to a purchaser who suffers loss by reason of a land charge being registered against the name of an owner of an estate in land who was not a party to any transaction, or concerned in any event, comprised in the relevant title (s25(1) LPA 1969). However, if Isobel actually knew about the restrictive covenant, for example Keith mentioned it to her when she was inspecting the property, the statutory compensation would not be payable.

The Official Certificate 'Priority Period'

When buying land, a purchaser needs in practice to search the register a few days before completing the purchase. The priority period rule (s11 LCA 1972) gives the purchaser protection against charges which are registered in the period between search and completion. A purchaser is not bound by a charge registered between search and completion provided that the purchase is completed within 15 working days from the date of the search certificate.

Priority Notices

A priority notice can be used by someone who contemplates a land charge being created in their favour in the near future, and they wish to ensure that their charge has priority over and is binding upon other transactions which happen to the relevant land.

For example, Valsamis is selling Glendale to Denise. It is envisaged that the conveyance will grant to Valsamis an option to repurchase Glendale. Valsamis knows that Denise intends to mortgage Glendale to Warren to secure funds for the purchase price. Valsamis wishes to ensure his option binds Warren. He therefore enters a priority notice.

For the priority notice device to work:

1 there must be an interval of at least 15 working days between the entry of the priority notice and the creation of the land charge;
   and

2 the charge must be created and registered within 30 working days of the entry of the priority notice.

If these conditions are satisfied then registration of the charge is deemed to have taken place at the moment the charge was created.

4.8 Overreachable Equitable Interests

Prior to the commencement of the Trusts of Land and Appointment of Trustees Act 1996 on 1 January 1997, those equitable interests which were overreachable fell into two related categories:

- interests under a trust for sale; and
- interests under a strict settlement.

After the commencement of the 1996 Act, equitable interests under all trusts of land are also overreachable.

4.8.1 The Essence of Overreaching

The essence of overreaching is that if the land is sold, the rights of the beneficiaries of a trust of land (or old trusts such as strict settlements and trusts for sale) cannot bind the purchaser. Provided the purchase price is paid to a minimum of two trustees or a trust corporation (s2(2) LPA 1925), the purchaser, irrespective of whether he had notice of the beneficiaries' rights, will take the land free from those rights ie those rights will not bind the purchaser (s27 LPA 1925).

The rights of the beneficiaries are not totally lost. These rights are transferred to the purchase price. This money will form a trust fund which must be invested. The beneficiaries will now have equitable interests in the trust fund.

For example, in 2006 Samuel conveys Heawood Park to Terry and Tammy, to hold on trust for Mina (his partner) for life, remainder to their child Lavinia. Under the trust of land which arises, Terry and Tammy have the power to sell the land at any time. Any purchaser of Heawood Park will buy the land from the trustees and pay the purchase price to the trustees. On paying the price to the trustees, the equitable interests of Mina and Lavinia will be overreached.

The leading case on this area is *City of London Building Society v Flegg* [1988] 1 AC 54. Mr and Mrs Flegg both contributed to the purchase of a house; the title to the house was registered in the names of their daughter and son-in-law (the Maxwell-Browns). The Fleggs, as a consequence of their contributions, each had a beneficial interest in the form of a constructive trust. The house was subsequently mortgaged to the building society by the Maxwell-Browns. The building society successfully argued in the House of Lords that the mortgage, being executed by two trustees, overreached the rights of Mr and Mrs Flegg.

cross-reference
See 9.2.2 for a discussion on Flegg and overreaching.

overreaching

the purchase price is paid to a minimum of two trustees, the purchaser, irrespective of whether he had notice of the beneficiaries' rights, will take the land free from those rights. The beneficiaries now have rights in the purchase money.

4.8.2 Overreaching on a Sale by Personal Representatives

This is a point where land law and succession law overlap, and it need be dealt with only briefly. As explained at 1.4.3, where a person dies their affairs are wound up by personal representatives, who will be either executors or administrators. Almost all deceased persons leave some debts (even if it is only the gas and electricity bills). Moreover, if the deceased was wealthy, there may be a huge taxation bill to pay. The personal representatives of the deceased have a completely free hand to sell whatever assets of the deceased they like so that they can pay the debts and/or taxes.

If the personal representatives sell any land owned by the deceased, the purchaser will always get a good title. The rights of people left property by the will are always overreached. Moreover, a purchaser from personal representatives is under no duty to check whether a sale is really necessary.

Suppose George (a fairly wealthy widower) has just died. His will appoints Eddie and Edwina to be his executors. He leaves his large house, 'High Manor', to his son Alan. The 'residue' (ie the rest) of his property he leaves to be divided equally between his three daughters, Betty, Cath, and Diana.

Eddie and Edwina need to sell something in order to pay debts/taxes. The 'residue' consists almost entirely of shares in small family private companies. Such shares are not easy to sell. They therefore sell High Manor. Alan cannot object to the sale. He will, however, be able to claim compensation (the value of High Manor) out of the residue.

Suppose, however, that the residue consists of shares in large public limited companies ('PLCs') quoted on the stock exchange. Such shares are very easy to sell. Eddie and Edwina still choose to sell High Manor. They are perfectly within their powers to do so. The purchaser (who, remember, need not check whether a sale is necessary) will get a good title and Alan will still have to claim compensation out of the residue.

4.8.3 Overreaching on a Sale by a Mortgagee of Mortgaged Land

This point can be left until we deal with the law of mortgages in Chapter 22.

4.9 Equitable Interests Still Subject to the Doctrine of Notice

Quite a few such interests remain, indeed rather more than was anticipated by the 1925 legislators:

- equitable fee simple under a bare trust;
- equitable mortgage where the mortgagee does take the title deeds (we will come back to this later; there will be very few, if any, of these rights created after 1989);
- a restrictive covenant created before 1926;
- a restrictive covenant contained in a lease;
- an equitable easement or equitable profit created before 1926;
- a right of entry for breach of a condition subsequent;
- proprietary estoppel (including a licence by estoppel); and
- a right under a constructive trust.

Concluding Remarks

In this chapter we have seen that, in an endeavour to reduce the importance of the equitable doctrine of notice, the 1925 legislators decreed that several important equitable interests should be registrable as land charges, and that other interests (especially interests under a trust of land) should be overreachable. But the doctrine of notice was not abolished.

Before you became a law student, you probably already knew that buying land (a house or any other type of land) was time-consuming. You now know one of the major reasons for the delays. It is essential that if you are buying land you make very careful enquiries regarding easements, profits, constructive trust interests, etc.

As we have just seen, there are quite a few rights still subject to the doctrine. It is particularly worth noting that (statistically) there are still a lot of 'old' (pre-1926) restrictive covenants in existence. However, it is the explosion of rights in the last two categories in the previous list (proprietary estoppel and constructive trusts) which accounts for the continued importance of the doctrine of notice. Indeed, constructive trust interests occur so frequently that they can be described as 'commonplace'. It should be added, though, that rights under a constructive trust can sometimes be overreached. How this can come about will have to wait until we consider the law of co-ownership.

Moreover, if you fail to discover a legal property right (eg a legal easement) you are stuck with it. You are bound by the right even though the most careful of enquiries would not have revealed its existence.

But if you fail to discover (say) a constructive trust interest, you may yet escape. You will not be bound by the interest if you are what old-fashioned lawyers sometimes call 'equity's darling', that is, a bona fide purchaser for value of a legal estate or interest without notice of the equitable interest.

Summary

Will a purchaser of land which is unregistered title be bound by third party property rights which exist against that land?

Proof of Title

The title deeds demonstrate that the predecessors in title have been in control of the land and no one can dispute their claim to ownership

- Good root of title—check the most recent conveyance which is at least 15 years old;
- Identify the names of the predecessors in title. This information will be used to search the Land Charges Register to determine whether any land charges have been registered.

Legal Property Rights

A legal property right 'is good against the whole world'. This means it will bind the purchaser even if the purchaser neither knew of the right nor had any means of finding out about the right.

Equitable Property Rights

The Doctrine of Notice

This means equitable interests bind everyone except for the bona fide purchaser for value of a legal estate without notice. The three types of notice under the doctrine of notice are set out in Diagram 4.1.

As *Kingsnorth Finance v Tizard* demonstrates, it is crucial that purchasers (and people acting on their behalf) carry out all enquiries which a reasonable person would make.

Diagram 4.1
Three forms of notice under the doctrine of notice

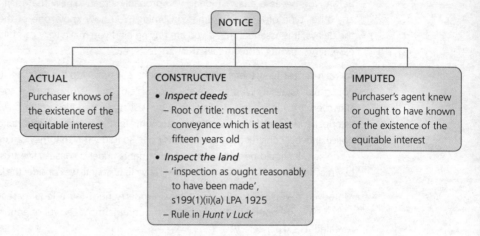

NOTICE

ACTUAL
Purchaser knows of the existence of the equitable interest

CONSTRUCTIVE
- *Inspect deeds*
  - Root of title: most recent conveyance which is at least fifteen years old
- *Inspect the land*
  - 'inspection as ought reasonably to have been made', s199(1)(ii)(a) LPA 1925
  - Rule in *Hunt v Luck*

IMPUTED
Purchaser's agent knew or ought to have known of the existence of the equitable interest

Third Party Rights which May Exist Against Land which is Unregistered Title

- *Legal interests which are good against the whole world.* The vast majority of legal interests still fall into this category.

- *Legal interests which are registrable as land charges*:

  - puisne mortgages;
  - legal aid charges;
  - charges for inheritance tax.

- *Equitable interests registrable as land charges.* The most important types of right in this category are:

  - post-1925 restrictive covenants;
  - home rights;
  - post-1925 equitable easements;
  - post-1925 equitable profits.

- *Equitable interests which are overreachable*:

  - rights of beneficiaries under trusts of land;
  - rights of beneficiaries under trusts for sale;
  - strict settlements.

- *Rights subject to the doctrine of notice*:
  - pre-1926 restrictive covenants;
  - constructive trust interests;
  - proprietary estoppel (licences by estoppel).
- *Registrable land charge*:
  - doctrine of notice does *not* apply;
  - right must be registered against the name of the estate owner (s3 LCA 1972)—the name can be found on the title deeds (*Standard Property Investment plc v British Plastics Federation*);
  - a correctly registered land charge will bind all purchasers, mortgagees etc (s4 LCA 1972);
  - a land charge that has not been correctly registered will be void against purchasers (and mortgagees), even though the purchaser may know of the right from some other source (*Midland Bank v Green*; s4 LCA 1972).

Further Reading

Gravells, NP, 'Land options: registration again …and again?' [1994] Conv 483
This article considers whether the registration of a land option should involve registration of both the grant of an option and the contract of sale following the exercise of the registered land option.

Howell, J, 'Notice: a broad view and a narrow view' [1996] Conv 34
Article considers the role of the doctrine of notice, and suggests that there are two types of 'notice' used in settling land disputes.

Howell, J, 'The doctrine of notice: an historical perspective' [1997] Conv 431
Article considers the role of the doctrine of notice in modern land law.

Neild, S, 'Imputed notice' [2000] Conv 196
This article evaluates what amounts to imputed notice and considers its application in the context of undue influence cases.

Thompson, MP, 'The purchaser a private detective' [1986] Conv 283
Critical case note on *Kingsnorth Finance v Tizard*.

Wade, HWR, 'Land charge registration reviewed' [1956] CLJ 216
A critical review of the land charges legislation 30 years after the 1925 land law reform.

❓ Question

In 1970, Ruth purchased the fee simple in Grand Villa, a large country house with two acres of grounds. The title was unregistered in an area which did not become an area of compulsory registration until 1988. Grand Villa was conveyed to Ruth in her sole name. Four weeks ago Les purchased Grand Villa from Ruth. Since the execution of the conveyance, the following matters have come to light.

- Martin, Ruth's husband, has returned from an extended business trip to Malaysia, and is alarmed to discover that Ruth has sold Grand Villa to Les. Martin claims that, since in 1985 he paid £200,000 for a total reconstruction of Grand Villa, he has 'rights' which bind Les.

- Dan has arrived at Grand Villa and has produced a document (not in the form of a deed) which Ruth and Dan signed six months ago. The document is a lease for 15 years of part of the grounds of Grand Villa.

- Harry, owner of neighbouring Fairways, has arrived at Grand Villa and produced a deed executed some time in the 1920s. (The exact date is difficult to read.) This deed was executed by the then owner of Grand Villa, and contains a restrictive covenant in favour of the owners of Fairways to the effect that Grand Villa is to be used for residential purposes only. Les plans to convert Grand Villa into a conference centre.

Advise Les as to whether any of these matters will affect him.

Part 3

Registered Land

5

Registration of Title—The Basic Principles

Introduction

The discussion in Chapter 4 focused exclusively on the legal principles which relate to land which is unregistered title. In view of the fact that the whole country is now an area of compulsory registration this may seem a rather artificial approach. However, you should always remember two things. First, there is still a lot of land which is unregistered title. Secondly, in order to understand the principles of registered land, some understanding of the principles governing unregistered land is essential. Unless there is further radical reform in English land law, it will never be possible for land lawyers to ignore the principles governing unregistered title.

The Land Registration Act 2002 (LRA 2002) certainly made major changes to the law, but did not make the principles governing unregistered title obsolete. The LRA 2002 received the royal assent in February 2002 but did not come into force until 13 October 2003.

The 2002 Act made major changes to the law which are dealt with in this chapter, and also impacts on Chapters 6, 15, 16, 18, and 19. The Act is meant to pave the way for the introduction of 'electronic conveyancing'. If and when this system becomes fully operational, land will no longer be bought and sold through paper documents such as contracts and deeds. Instead everything will be done electronically.

In this chapter we will be dealing with the basic principles which govern the substantive registration of estates in land.

The position of 'third party rights' (restrictive covenants, constructive trust interests, etc) will be discussed in Chapter 6.

 5.1 ## Registration of Title

There were inherent problems with the unregistered system of conveyancing. Proof of ownership was dependent on title deeds which could potentially be lost or damaged. From the discussion in Chapters 1 and 4 you would have noticed that the system of investigating the title by examining the deeds and searching the Land Charges Register can be cumbersome. The purchaser may run the risk of being subject to third party rights which were undiscoverable. Registration of title works on the basis that information relating to an estate in land is held centrally by the Land Registry; the need to rely on title deeds is eliminated. The purchaser should be able to locate all the relevant information relating to a property on the register of title. This should include both who owns the property and details of rights held by third parties.

Lord Wilberforce in *Williams and Glyn's Bank Ltd v Boland* [1981] AC 487 said:

> The system of land registration, as it exists in England, which long antedates the Land Registration Act 1925 [land registration was introduced in the mid-nineteenth century; early attempts which were based on voluntary registration completely failed. The Land Registration Act 1897 introduced

3. (10.07.2000) RESTRICTION: No disposition by a sole proprietor of the registered estate (except a trust corporation) under which capital money arises is to be registered unless authorised by the Court.

4. (05.10.2002) Caution in favour of Mary Gertrude Shelley of 18 Cambourne Street, Kerwick, Maradon, Cornshire PL14 7AR and of Messrs Swan & Co of 25 Trevisick Street, Kerwick, Maradon, Cornshire PL14 6RE.

5. (28.11.2003) RESTRICTION: No disposition of the registered estate by the proprietor of the registered estate is to be registered without a written consent signed by the proprietor for the time being of the Charge dated 12 November 2003 in favour of Fast and Furious Building Society referred to in the Charges register.

C: Charges register

This register contains any charges and other matters that affect the registered estate.

1. (19.12.1989) The passageway at the side is included in the title is subject to rights of way on foot only.

2. (10.07.2000) A Transfer of the land in this title dated 2 June 2000 made between (1) John Charles Brown and (2) Paul John Dawkins and Angela Mary Dawkins contains restrictive covenants.

    NOTE: Original filed.

3. (01.08.2002) REGISTERED CHARGE dated 15 July 2002 to secure the moneys including the further advances therein mentioned.

4. (01.08.2002) Proprietor: WEYFORD BUILDING SOCIETY of Society House, The Avenue, Weyford, Cornshire CN12 4BD.

5. (28.11.2003) REGISTERED CHARGE dated 12 November 2003.

6. (28.11.2003) Proprietor: FAST AND FURIOUS BUILDING SOCIETY of Fast Plaza, The Quadrangle, Weyford, Cornshire CN14 3NW.

7. (03.12.2003) The parts of the land affected thereby are subject to the leases set out in the schedule of leases hereto.

Schedule of notices of leases

	Registration date and Plan ref.	*Property description*	*Date of lease and Term*	*Lessee's Title*
1.	03.12.2003	13 Augustine Way, Kerwick	12.11.2003 999 years from 10.10.2003	CS385372

End of register

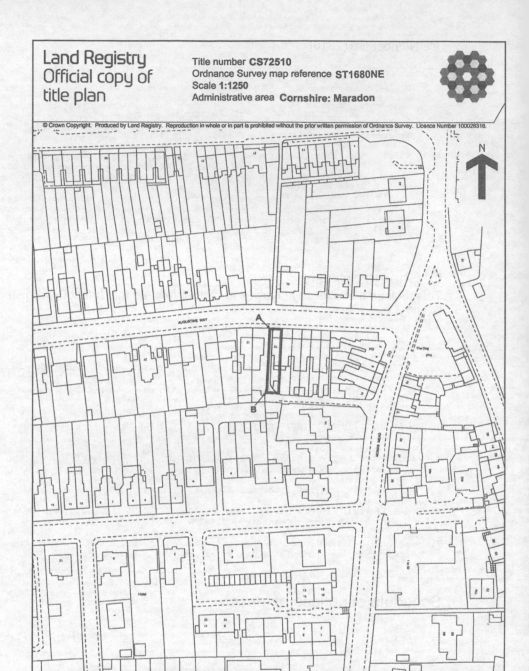

This official copy issued on 23 July 2007 shows the state of this title plan on 23 July 2007 at 11:39:46. It is admissible in evidence to the same extent as the original (s.67 Land Registration Act 2002).
This title plan shows the general position, not the exact line, of the boundaries. It may be subject to distortions in scale. Measurements scaled from this plan may not match measurements between the same points on the ground. See Land Registry Public Guide 19 – Title plans and boundaries.
This title is dealt with by Land Registry, Maradon Office.

Source: Reproduced with kind permission of the Land Registry

The current form of the Land Register is a file for each title (estate) registered. The file, which is nowadays held electronically, is divided into three parts, called:

- Property Register;
- Proprietorship Register; and
- Charges Register.

The use of the word 'Register' is in this context very unfortunate. One might think there were three files for each title registered. But in fact there is only one file, divided into three parts, which will be called the Property Part, the Proprietorship Part, and the Charges Part.

5.2.1 The Property Part

The property part indicates whether the estate registered is freehold or leasehold, and in the case of a lease the duration of the lease is provided. In the case of a lease created out of a registered reversion, it will contain a reference to the 'title' (ie file) number of that reversion (ie the freehold owned by the landlord).

If the land is 'dominant' with respect to any easements or restrictive covenants (ie benefited by such rights), the existence of such rights may be 'noted' in this section, but unfortunately this 'noting' is not mandatory. (Why 'unfortunately' will become apparent when we deal with the law of restrictive covenants.)

Most importantly, in this part of the Land Register there is a verbal description of the land, and a reference to the 'file plan'. The boundaries shown on this file plan are normally only 'general', that is, approximate. One feature of English land registration strange to foreign eyes is that our system does not normally fix the exact boundaries of each plot. The Land Registry suggests that their plans are in fact accurate to within a few centimetres. No doubt they usually are, but in *Lee v Barrey* [1957] Ch 251, there was a discrepancy of eight feet (2.5 m) between the plan and the actual boundary on the ground!

The discrepancy was even bigger in *Drake v Fripp* [2011] EWCA 1279. Two adjoining fields in Cornwall were originally in common ownership. In 1996 the defendant's predecessor in title sold one of the fields to the claimant's predecessor. A few years later a boundary dispute arose.

The Land Registry's plans for both properties showed the boundary as a 'Cornish hedge', 'a style of hedge found in Cornwall built of stone and earth'. The defendant, however, claimed that the legal boundary was a post-and-wire fence running parallel with the Cornish hedge and some '4 or 5 metres' into what the claimant said was his land.

After carefully examining the terms of the 1996 conveyance, the Court of Appeal held that the legal boundary was the post-and-wire fence. The practical result was that the claimant, despite the Land Registry plans, was not entitled to a strip of land totalling 1.5 acres out of a field of 153 acres. Moreover the claimant could not claim compensation from the Land Registry, *because their plans do not guarantee the position of the boundary.*

The Land Registry no doubt altered the plans to show the fence as the boundary. But note the following remarks of Lewison LJ in the Court of Appeal at [22]:

> The boundary currently shown on the title plan is a general boundary. If the title plan is altered so as to show the boundary running along the line of the fence it will still be a general boundary. In *Derbyshire County Council v Fallon* the deputy adjudicator Mr Michael Mark described this as producing 'another general boundary in a more accurate position than the current general boundary'.

A stark conclusion is to be drawn from *Drake v Fripp*. The general boundaries rule means that the Land Registry's plans will not settle boundary disputes.

cross-reference
*See Chapter 6.2.2
for a discussion on
'restrictions'.*

5.2.2 The Proprietorship Part

This part of the Land Register states the grade of title. It gives the name and address of the registered proprietor(s) and it indicates the 'restrictions' affecting the right to deal with the land.

5.2.3 The Charges Part

This part of the Land Register contains 'notices' of interests subject to registration (ie minor interests) such as restrictive covenants. It contains a note of any mortgage by registered charge created out of the estate registered and a note of any other registered estate (ie a lease) created out of the estate registered.

5.3 Categories of Rights in Registered Land

With registered land, the division of property rights into legal rights and equitable rights is (while not irrelevant) of less importance than with unregistered land. For most purposes rights in registered land divide into four categories:

1 *Estates and interests capable of substantive registration*

Each substantively registered estate has a separate file at the Land Registry with a separate title number (s27 LRA 2002).

 (i) Prior to 13 October 2003:

 • fee simple absolute in possession (freehold);

 • legal leases over 21 years;

 • rentcharge.

 (ii) After 12 October 2003:

 • fee simple absolute in possession (freehold);

 • legal lease of more than seven years;

 • expressly created profits in gross (this right is exercisable without reference to specific dominant land) whether or not the servient land is registered title; and

 • rentcharge.

2 *Unregistered interests which override registered dispositions (or 'overriding interests')*

These interests bind the registered proprietor and any purchaser from him irrespective of:

 (i) whether they are entered on the register in any way;

 (ii) whether the proprietor knew or ought to have known of them.

 (Cf legal interests in unregistered land.)

3 *Minor interests (or 'rights which need protection')*

These interests bind the purchaser of a registered title only if they are 'protected' in some way by an entry on the register of title. (Rather confusingly, overreachable equitable interests are also classified as 'minor' interests. They are, as with unregistered title, overreached provided the purchase price is paid to the correct trustees.)

4 *Mortgage by registered charge*

This is the standard form of registered land mortgage.

5.3.1 The Terminology Used by the Land Registration Act 2002

The fourfold classification of property rights just discussed existed under the LRA 1925, and continues to exist under the LRA 2002. However, the 2002 Act has made two changes in terminology.

With respect to the second category in the previous list, the 2002 Act does not talk of 'overriding interests', but rather of 'unregistered interests which override registered dispositions'. See, in particular, the heading to Sch 3 LRA 2002.

With respect to the third category, the terminology has also changed. The two-word phrase 'minor interests' does not appear in the LRA 2002. Officially, we should now talk of 'third party rights which need to be protected by an entry on the register'.

It is hoped readers will not be surprised to find that this book continues to use the old terminology. Apart from the obvious point, 'the old phrases are simpler', there is another strong argument for adhering to the old terminology. Most of the cases referred to in Chapter 6 were decided under the LRA 1925, and those cases use the old terminology.

First Registration of Title

5.4.1 Compulsory First Registration

Compulsory first registration of title arises where an event occurs which triggers the requirement for registration. This effectively means that an unregistered legal estate will now have to be entered into the register of title under its own independent title number. Since the introduction of the LRA 1925, the list of triggering events has been expanded over time by legislative changes: the Land Registration Act 1997 and the LRA 2002.

One of the most significant extensions to the principle of compulsory registration can be found in the LRA 2002, whereby leases granted for more than seven years, or the assignment of a lease with more than seven years to run, must be registered with its own individual title number. This is in contrast to the old law, where leases granted for more than 21 years or leases which had been assigned with more than 21 years to run had to be registered.

To understand this change, you must know the economic background. Leases of commercial premises such as shops, offices, and factories have always been a major feature of English commercial and industrial life. Until relatively recently, the typical commercial lease was for at least 25 years. However, particularly in the last 30 years, the length of commercial leases has reduced considerably. Neither business landlords nor business tenants want to commit themselves for long periods. The average length of a commercial lease is now only around ten years.

The Law Commission, the Land Registry, and the Government all felt that medium length commercial leases should be subject to compulsory registration.

These changes to registration of leases apply to all types of properties not just commercial properties. Two things should be noted. First, the business community may try to avoid the rules under the LRA 2002 by making new commercial lettings last exactly seven years. Secondly, except where a lease is assigned, existing leases for between seven and 21 years are not subject to compulsory registration.

Section 4 LRA 2002 provides a list of transactions which lead to compulsory first registration of title.

Land Registration Act 2002

4 When title must be registered

(1) The requirement of registration applies on the occurrence of any of the following events—

    (a) the transfer of a qualifying estate—

        (i) for valuable or other consideration, by way of gift or in pursuance of an order of any court,

        (ii) by means of an assent (including a vesting assent); or

        (iii) giving effect to a partition of land subject to a trust of land;

    (aa) the transfer of a qualifying estate—

        (i) by a deed that appoints, or by virtue of section 83 of the Charities Act 1993 has effect as if it appointed, a new trustee or is made in consequence of the appointment of a new trustee, or

        (ii) by a vesting order under section 44 of the Trustee Act 1925 that is consequential on the appointment of a new trustee;

    (b) the transfer of an unregistered legal estate in land in circumstances where section 171A of the Housing Act 1985 (c. 68) applies (disposal by landlord which leads to a person no longer being a secure tenant);

    (c) the grant out of a qualifying estate of an estate in land—

        (i) for a term of years absolute of more than seven years from the date of the grant, and

        (ii) for valuable or other consideration, by way of gift or in pursuance of an order of any court;

    (d) the grant out of a qualifying estate of an estate in land for a term of years absolute to take effect in possession after the end of the period of three months beginning with the date of the grant;

    (e) the grant of a lease in pursuance of Part 5 of the Housing Act 1985 (the right to buy) out of an unregistered legal estate in land;

    (f) the grant of a lease out of an unregistered legal estate in land in such circumstances as are mentioned in paragraph (b);

    (g) the creation of a protected first legal mortgage of a qualifying estate.

(2) For the purposes of subsection (1), a qualifying estate is an unregistered legal estate which is—

    (a) a freehold estate in land, or

    (b) a leasehold estate in land for a term which, at the time of the transfer, grant or creation, has more than seven years to run.

Arguably the most important triggers for first registration are:

- Transfer of an unregistered legal freehold estate made for valuable consideration, by deed of gift, by assent, or court order.
- Any grant of a new legal leasehold of more than seven years.
- Any assignment (or first legal mortgage) of an existing legal lease with more than seven years to run.
- Grant of a leasehold estate to take effect in possession more than three months after the date of the grant.
- First legal mortgage of a freehold estate.

The Land Registration Act 2002 (Amendment) Order 2008 provides for two additional events which 'trigger' compulsory first registration.

cross-reference
Appointment of trustees is discussed at 7.7.

Appointment of a New Trustee

If a new trustee is appointed to an existing trust of either a freehold estate or of a lease with more than seven years to run, the estate in question must be registered within two months of the deed of appointment. This extension to compulsory registration is important, because a considerable amount of English land is held on trust.

cross-reference
Partition is discussed at the end of 9.3.5.

Partition of Co-owned Land

Partition of co-owned land is not common amongst English landowners. However, if an unregistered freehold or lease with more than seven years to run is co-owned by two or more people, and the co-owners do decide to partition (ie split up) the land between them, the resulting estates must be registered within two months of the deed of partition.

5.4.2 Voluntary Registration

Section 3 LRA 2002 enables a land owner to voluntarily register freehold estates and leasehold estates which have more than seven years of the term to run. Since 1997, as an incentive the Land Registry has charged reduced fees for voluntary registrations and currently there is a discount of up to 25 per cent off the fee. It is hoped that landowners (especially those owning large tracts of land) will take advantage of this 'special offer', thus getting a lot of land on to the register sooner than otherwise would be the case. Moreover, as we saw in Chapter 1, voluntary registration may make the land easier to sell, particularly if the owner intends to subdivide their land and sell it in lots of small units.

cross-reference
See 5.6 for an outline of the first registration procedure.

Specifically voluntary registration is permitted for the following:

- freehold estate;
- lease granted with more than seven years to run;
- discontinuous lease (also known as timeshare lease) irrespective of the length of the term;
- rentcharges;
- franchise;
- profit à prendre in gross granted for an interest equivalent of a fee simple absolute in possession or a term of years with more than seven years to run.

5.5 Register of Estates Not Register of Plots

Most foreign systems of land registration (eg the much-admired German and Swedish systems) work on the basis that for each plot of land there will be just one file kept at the Registry. That file will show who owns the plot of land, and all third party rights affecting the plot.

The English system is not as efficient. There are very good geographical 'index maps', but each estate in a plot of land (except leases for not more than seven years which cannot be registered) has a separate file.

thinking point 5.1

Suppose Leonard owns the fee simple in Bloomsbury House, situated in central London. He grants a lease of Bloomsbury House to Teresa for 100 years. Teresa sub-leases Bloomsbury House to Susan for 50 years. How many files will there be in relation to Bloomsbury House?

Each of the three estates must be registered separately, and therefore there will be three files. Those files used to be 'hard copy', but nowadays are usually in electronic form.

Another curiosity of the English system of land registration is that one (quite commonly) encounters a situation where a lease is registered, but the fee simple out of which it is derived is not. You might be thinking 'How could this situation arise?' Under the LRA 2002 this situation arises whenever the owner of an unregistered freehold grants a lease for more than seven years.

Previously, this situation arose under the LRA 1925 where the landlord purchased their fee simple before the relevant area became compulsory, but granted a lease for more than 21 years after the area became compulsory. It could also arise where the landlord purchased their fee simple before the relevant area became compulsory, granted a long lease before the date set for compulsory registration, and then that lease was assigned with more than 21 years unexpired after the area became compulsory.

The general expansion in the registration of freehold titles will eventually mean that this situation of a registered lease created out of an unregistered freehold will become extremely rare. However, a side effect of the expansion of the registration of leases by the LRA 2002 is that, in the last few years, there has been an increase in the number of cases of a registered lease created out of an unregistered freehold.

REVIEW QUESTION Alfred owns the fee simple in 2 Clarendon Gardens; bought in 2005.

Basrat has a 99-year lease of 2 Clarendon Gardens granted in 2010; Carlos has a 50-year sub-lease of 2 Clarendon Gardens granted in 2011; Davinder has an eight-year 'sub-underlease' of 2 Clarendon Gardens granted in 2012.

How many files will there be at the Land Registry?

(Consider 5.4 and 5.5.)

5.6 Procedure Where a Sale or Lease Gives Rise to First Registration

The transaction goes through basically as an unregistered transaction, but with additional stages at the end (see Diagram 5.1):

1 The purchaser investigates the title deeds, inspects the land, and searches the Land Charges Register.

2 The legal title passes on the execution of the conveyance.

3 The purchaser must apply for first registration within two months of the execution of the conveyance (s6 LRA 2002).

4 If the purchaser fails to do so, the legal title revests in the vendor on trust for the purchaser. Consequently, the purchaser will only have an equitable estate.

5 The purchaser can then apply for late registration, but may have to pay a late fee.

Diagram 5.1
Procedure for first registration of title

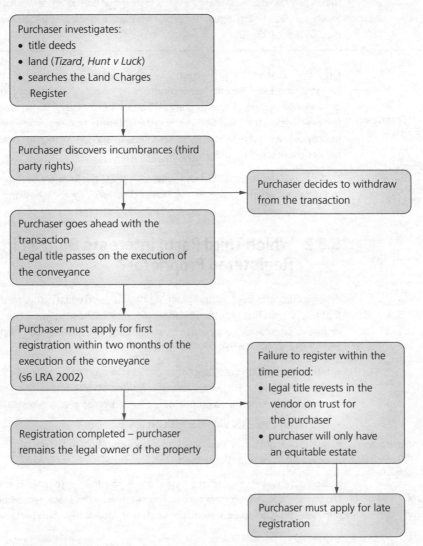

125

5.6.1 Applications for First Registration

Failure to register within two months is not that unusual. The sanctions for failure to register within two months (which are not changed by the 2002 Act; see s7 LRA 2002) may strike you as both strange and rather weak.

As we have just stated, the legal title revests in the vendor on trust for the purchaser. Yet the vendor has almost certainly moved away, and has no idea of their trustee status. Equally, when the purchaser does belatedly register, the legal title revests in the purchaser without the vendor ever knowing (or needing to know) that the vendor has lost their trustee status.

The only real sanction against late registration is that the Registry may charge a late fee.

> **thinking point 5.2**
>
> *Garside House is unregistered title. Joe now purchases Garside House. Joe does his own conveyancing. Garside House is conveyed to Joe, but he omits to register his title. Consider when (and by whom) the error is likely to be discovered.*
>
> *There are three possibilities. First, when Joe comes to sell Garside House, the new purchaser's solicitor will discover the error. Secondly, if Joe wants to mortgage Garside House, the potential lender will investigate Joe's title and discover the error. Thirdly, when Joe dies, his personal representatives will probably discover the error.*

On an application for first registration, the purchaser produces all the title deeds to the Registry. The Land Registry then conducts its own (very thorough) investigation of title. It decides what grade of title to grant. When in the course of its investigations it discovers (in the deeds or on the Land Charges Register) interests that require registration to protect their priority over a purchaser, that is, 'minor interests' such as restrictive covenants, the appropriate notices are entered onto the register.

cross-reference
See 5.7 for grades of title.

126

On first and later registrations under the LRA 1925, the Registry issued a land certificate to the registered proprietor. However, the LRA 2002 effectively abolishes land certificates.

5.6.2 Which Third Party Interests Bind a First Registered Proprietor?

When a purchaser buys an unregistered title and then registers that freehold or leasehold title, that title will, on first registration, be subject only to those third party interests (eg easements, restrictive covenants, constructive trust interests) still existing with respect to the land (ss 11 and 12 LRA 2002). These interests include:

- Interests which are the subject of an entry in the register in relation to the estate. This includes the entry of a 'notice' in respect of a burden affecting the registered estate. (Where the powers of the registered proprietor are limited in some way a 'restriction' will be entered.)

- Overriding interest(s) within Sch 1 LRA 2002.

cross-reference
'Notices' will be explained at 6.2.1.

- Interests acquired by squatters under the Limitation Act 1980 of which the proprietor has notice (ie adverse possession).

It should, however, be stressed that a purchase of an unregistered title which triggers first registration is an unregistered transaction with an extra stage tacked on the end. Suppose a purchaser buys an unregistered title which was subject to a third party right, but that right has become void against the purchaser either under the doctrine of notice (see 4.5) or under the Land Charges Act (see 4.7.5). That right cannot be revived (*Wilkes v Spooner* [1911] 2 KB 473). It will be void, even if either:

- the Registry erroneously enters a notice to 'protect' the right; or
- the right, were it still in existence, would be an overriding interest within Sch 1 LRA 2002.

5.7 Grades of Title

This is governed by ss 9 and 10 LRA 2002.

5.7.1 Freeholds

Once the Registry has investigated the title of an applicant for first registration, the Land Registry can grant the newly registered proprietor one of three grades of title. In almost all cases an absolute grade is granted. However, in a significant minority of cases (about 1 per cent of all titles) only a possessory grade is granted. A qualified grade is also possible, but they are extremely rare.

Absolute Title

This is the grade of title which is granted where the applicant's title is sound, that is, the title deeds are in order and it appears that nobody else could possibly claim the land. Where an absolute title is granted, the government (through the agency of the Land Registry) is in effect saying to the registered proprietor (and anybody who wants to buy the land from him) 'We guarantee that you own this land'.

Nevertheless, a fee simple registered with absolute title is subject to (s11 LRA 2002):

- overriding interests;
- minor interests protected by entry on the register;
- if the registered proprietor is a trustee, equitable interests under the trust of which the trustee has notice.

The registered freehold owner will not only be subject to burdens in relation to the land but will take the benefit of interests attached to the registered estate, such as an easement or a profit.

Possessory Title

This is the grade of title which is granted where the applicant for registration's claim to ownership is debatable. It particularly occurs where the title deeds produced by the applicant are inadequate, or if the applicant cannot produce any at all. The applicant may even admit that the land was not originally theirs, but claim that they now have a title by virtue of 'adverse possession'. (As we saw in 1.4.3 when discussing investigation of title, the adverse possession rule means that if somebody has been in control of a piece of land for 12 years, all rival claims are normally automatically destroyed by lapse of time.)

When it is first granted, a possessory title is of only limited comfort to the registered proprietor. The Registry is merely accepting that the proprietor is currently in control of the land; it does not guarantee that they are the owner. Any rival claimant to the land whose rights have not been time-barred under the adverse possession rule can still reclaim the land.

The great value of a possessory title is in the long term. If somebody is registered with a possessory title to a piece of land and remains in undisputed possession of that land for 12 years after registration, their title will normally be upgraded to 'absolute'. They then (just like any other proprietor with an absolute title) will have a clear guarantee that they are the undisputed owner of the land.

Qualified Title

This grade of title is extremely rare. It is granted where there is some minor question mark over an otherwise sound claim to ownership.

A qualified title is in effect 'absolute but for such-and-such'. A qualified title is the same as absolute, apart from a specified exception against which the proprietor is not guaranteed. This exception (qualification) can be either:

- with respect to claims arising before a certain date;

or

- with respect to claims arising under a specified instrument.

For example, if a document of title was only partly legible, the Registry might qualify a grant of title, saying that the proprietor is not protected from claims arising under the partially legible document.

(The paucity of qualified titles may perhaps be explained by the Land Registry's policy on technical defects of title. If there is an application for registration of a title, but there is some technical defect in the documents, for example documents going back 13 but not 15 years, the Registry usually deliberately ignores the technical defect and grants an absolute title.)

5.7.2 Leaseholds

There are four grades of title which may be granted to a lease: absolute, 'good leasehold', qualified, and possessory. Possessory leasehold is granted where the landlord's reversion to the lease is registered with a possessory title. Qualified leasehold is virtually unknown. That leaves absolute leasehold and good leasehold, both of which are common, though the percentage of good leasehold should gradually decline.

Good Leasehold

The existence of the good leasehold grade of title is really an unfortunate by-product of an outdated common law rule which ought to be abolished. That rule is that when a tenant takes a lease (even a very long lease) the tenant is not entitled to examine the landlord's title deeds; neither is the tenant entitled to insist that the deeds be produced to third parties such as the Land Registry. In effect, the tenant must take a chance that the landlord owns the land.

Where a lease for more than seven years is granted out of a reversion which is not registered, the lease must be registered. Normally, it can only be registered with good leasehold title, as neither the Registry nor the tenant will have access to the landlord's title deeds. The granting of a good leasehold title guarantees that the lease is valid and that the tenant is owner of that lease, but only on the assumption that the lessor's title to the reversion is sound. If it turns out that the landlord was leasing out land which the landlord did not own, there is no comeback against the Registry.

REVIEW QUESTION As a result of the LRA 2002, the proportion of registrable leases registered with good leasehold rather than absolute title may have actually temporarily increased. Why?

Will good leasehold eventually disappear completely?

Absolute Leasehold

This is an out-and-out guarantee that the lease is valid and that the tenant is owner of the lease. It is in practice granted where either:

- the landlord's reversion is already registered with absolute title; or
- (rare in practice) the tenant has been able to persuade the landlord to produce the freehold title deeds to the Land Registry. (This may happen if the tenant is some large organization which has made it clear that it will take a lease of the property only if it has access to the title deeds.)

thinking point 5.3

It was said at 5.7.2 that 'the percentage of good leasehold should gradually decline'. Why is this so?

Good leasehold is designed for the (currently still possible) situation where the lease is registered but the freehold from which it is derived is not registered, that is, it is unregistered land. As more and more freeholds are registered, there will be proportionately fewer registered leases created out of unregistered freeholds. (See also point (1) in the following section.)

129

Upgrading of Title

This area of law was simplified by the Land Registration Act 1986, and this simplified law has been carried forward into the LRA 2002 (see ss 62–64 LRA 2002). In appropriate cases the registered proprietor may apply for an upgrading of the registered title; but the registrar can (and often does) act without waiting for an application.

Of the following four situations listed, (1) and (2) occur frequently, while (3) and (4) are (in the nature of things) rare.

The registrar may upgrade a title in the following cases:

1 A good leasehold may be upgraded to absolute if the registrar 'is satisfied as to the title to the freehold and the title to any intermediate leasehold'. In practice, where a registered lease has been created out of an unregistered fee simple, and that fee simple is later registered with an absolute title, the lease will be immediately upgraded from good leasehold to absolute.

2 A possessory freehold may be upgraded to absolute if the title has been registered for 12 years, or the registrar is for some other reason satisfied that the proprietor's title is sound. As indicated earlier, if a possessory title has been registered without challenge for 12 years, it will be upgraded to absolute more or less automatically.

3 A possessory leasehold may be upgraded to good leasehold if the title has been registered for 12 years.

4 A qualified title may be upgraded to absolute (or good leasehold) if the registrar is now satisfied that the title is sound.

5.8 Land Certificates

Under the pre-2003 law, this was a copy of the relevant register file, which was issued whenever an estate was first registered or was subsequently transferred to a new owner. In principle it was issued to the registered proprietor, but if the estate was mortgaged by registered charge the land certificate was kept at the Registry. (In practice, as a result of the rule which operated when the land was mortgaged, an enormous number of certificates were kept at the Registry.)

The land certificate was not a 'title deed' or a 'document of title'. As a new certificate was created only when the estate in question was transferred, it might not accurately reflect the current state of the register. A wise purchaser would never therefore rely on the certificate, but would always search the register.

As already noted, the LRA 2002 makes no provision for land certificates.

5.9 Conclusiveness of the Register— and Does that Extend to Beneficial Ownership?

Section 58(1) LRA 2002 provides for the conclusive nature of the register of title as regards the legal estate.

> 1) If, on the entry of a person in the register as the proprietor of a legal estate, the legal estate would not otherwise be vested in him, it shall be deemed to be vested in him as a result of the registration

cross-reference
For further discussion on rectification see Chapter 16.

This provision applies not only in the case of where there has been some bona fide mistake as to who should be registered, but also where somebody has obtained registration as a result of a forged land transfer or some other fraudulent conduct. In these situations the registered proprietor of the legal estate will no doubt be subject to a claim for rectification of the register. (Rectification of the register is possible in limited circumstances.)

The meaning of the conclusiveness of the register has been questioned, in particular whether it extends to equitable ownership, following the recent decision in *Richall Holdings v Fitzwilliam* [2013] EWHC 86 which followed the reasoning of the court in *Malory v Cheshire Homes* [2002] 3 WLR 1, a case decided on the basis of the equivalent provisions in the LRA 1925.

In *Malory* a company had fraudulently sold and transferred a property to Cheshire Homes. Cheshire Homes was then registered as the legal owner of the property. The Court of Appeal held that due to the fraudulent transaction Cheshire Homes had upon registration only acquired legal title to the property and was subject to the beneficial rights of the original owner. The fraudulent transfer was according to Arden LJ 'void', and as a consequence the transfer did not constitute a 'disposition' under the LRA 1925. The result was that only a legal title transferred to Cheshire Homes on registration but the equitable title remained with the original owner of the property. Put another way, registration guaranteed legal ownership but not beneficial ownership.

The case of *Fitzwilliam* involved a forged power of attorney which empowered a third party to sell Fitzwilliam's property, without Fitzwilliam's knowledge. Richall purchased the property and was duly registered as the owner of the property. Fitzwilliam sought rectification of the register. This case was heard in the High Court Chancery Division and Newey J contended that he was bound by the decision in *Malory* and had to construe the provisions under the LRA 2002 in a similar manner unless the differences between the LRA 1925 and the 2002 Act were significantly different. Newey J concluded that the provisions were not sufficiently different. In applying *Malory*, the purported transfer based on the forged power of attorney was 'void' and did not constitute a 'disposition' under the LRA 2002. Fitzwilliam retained the equitable title in the property and when Richall became the registered proprietor he only acquired a bare legal title. The register was altered in Fitzwilliam's favour though this was done without a full discussion of the rectification or indemnity provisions in the LRA 2002.

It is possibly surprising that the High Court followed the reasoning in *Malory* since that case has been subject to considerable amount of criticism. Dixon commenting on *Fitzwilliam* stated:

> 'At the heart of the issue in *Fitzwilliam* was the effect of Richall's registration as proprietor of the property, bearing in mind that Richall were innocent of all wrongdoing and had done all they could to verify that they were purchasing a secure title. As Newey J. noted, had this dispute arisen under LRA 1925, he would have been bound to follow *Malory* and hold that registration as proprietor only transferred legal title because of the underlying fault in the conveyance—that it had been effected by fraud. This would have been so despite the criticism of *Malory* that, inter alia, it imported principles of unregistered conveyancing into the 1925 Act and severely comprised the principle of title guarantee by registration. However, what was much less certain was whether the decision in *Malory* applied to the equivalent provisions of the 2002 Act. Newey J. held that it did, and therefore that he must interpret the 2002 Act in the same manner as the 1925 Act. As a consequence, he held that the transfer to Richall was conclusive only as to legal title and that Fitzwilliam retained a beneficial interest in the property. Further, as a consequence, Fitzwilliam was entitled to have the register altered to reinstate him, presumably to correct a mistake within Sch.4 para.2 of the 2002 Act.
>
> . . .
>
> In short then, there are a number of reasons why *Malory* could have been distinguished, even working on the basis that it was a correct interpretation of the 1925 Act. That the judge in *Fitzwilliam* felt unable to do so is understandable, but it has serious consequences for title registration. If one thinks about Richall for a moment, what could they have done to ensure that they secured a good title? They sought and received assurances about the power of attorney and they checked the title register. Were they supposed to investigate root of title, make further and additional enquires and, inevitably, insure themselves in case the register did not provide title guarantee? The logic is that they, and future purchasers must do so, but that makes title registration a mere cipher for unregistered conveyancing. How could this have been avoided, with a workable and practical answer to the problem raised by *Fitzwilliam*?'

cross-reference
See Chapter 16 for rectification of the register of title.

Here Dixon argues that principles of unregistered conveyancing have crept into the Land Registration Act 2002 which, he argues, is clearly not the intention of the legislature. The outcome of *Fitzwilliam* calls into question the effect of s58. Dixon argues that *Fitzwilliam* undermines the principle of title guarantee by registration. Under *Fitzwilliam*, the register only guarantees legal title; it does not make any guarantee regarding equitable ownership.

5.10 Dispositions of Registered Titles

Once first registration of title has been completed, all subsequent dealings in land will be subject to the rules governing registered titles, that is, the Land Registration Act 2002 and Land Registration Rules 2003.

5.10.1 Powers of Disposition

In principle, the registered proprietor or a person who is entitled to be registered as the proprietor has unlimited powers of disposition of all kinds permitted by general law (ss 23 and 24 LRA 2002). The owner's powers are restricted only if an entry is made on the register to that effect, for example by a restriction (s26 LRA 2002).

The effect of these provisions provides transparency and certainty for the purchaser who relies on the information entered into the register. Protection is given to the purchaser ('disponee') whereby the purchaser's title will not be affected if it later transpires that the vendor ('disponor') did not have the power to dispose of the property.

5.10.2 Registrable Dispositions

To ensure the accuracy of the register both in terms of being up to date as well as complying with the mirror principle, all dealings in land are subject to registration requirements. These can be found in s27(1)–(2) LRA 2002.

> *Land Registration Act 2002*
>
> 27 Dispositions required to be registered
>
> (1) If a disposition of a registered estate or registered charge is required to be completed by registration, it does not operate at law until the relevant registration requirements are met.
>
> (2) In the case of a registered estate, the following are the dispositions which are required to be completed by registration—
>
> (a) a transfer,
>
> (b) where the registered estate is an estate in land, the grant of a term of years absolute—
>
> (i) for a term of more than seven years from the date of the grant,
>
> (ii) to take effect in possession after the end of the period of three months beginning with the date of the grant,
>
> (iii) under which the right to possession is discontinuous,
>
> (iv) in pursuance of Part 5 of the Housing Act 1985 (c. 68) (the right to buy), or
>
> (v) in circumstances where section 171A of that Act applies (disposal by landlord which leads to a person no longer being a secure tenant),
>
> (c) where the registered estate is a franchise or manor, the grant of a lease,
>
> (d) the express grant or reservation of an interest of a kind falling within section 1(2)(a) of the Law of Property Act 1925 (c. 20), other than one which is capable of being registered under the Commons Registration Act 1965 (c. 64),
>
> (e) the express grant or reservation of an interest of a kind falling within section 1(2)(b) or (e) of the Law of Property Act 1925, and
>
> (f) the grant of a legal charge.

According to s27(1), registration is all important where there is transfer of a registered estate in land or registered charge, otherwise it will not take effect in law.

For example, Alice, the registered proprietor of 3 The Ridings, recently sold the property to Nadia. Nadia must comply with the registration requirements under s27(1) to ensure that legal title will pass to her as the new owner of the property. If she does not, then Nadia will only have an equitable freehold estate in land. Consequently, Alice will hold the legal fee simple on bare trust for Nadia.

The various types of registrable dispositions which must be registered to operate at law are listed under s27(2). Apart from the transfer of the registered freehold estate, these include:

- grant of a lease with more than seven years to run from the date of the grant;
- grant of a lease to take effect in possession more than three months after the date of the grant;
- grant of a discontinuous lease;
- legal easements (express grant or reservation);
- legal mortgage charge.

For a transfer of a legal freehold the registration requirements are completed once the transferee has been entered in the register as proprietor (Sch 2 para 2 LRA 2002).

If there is the grant of a legal lease of more than seven years from the date of the grant and the landlord's freehold is itself registered title, the lease must be registered separately with its own independent title number. Reference is made in the landlord's title by way of a notice to show that the landlord's freehold is subject to a lease (Sch 2 para 3 LRA 2002).

Where the landlord's freehold is not registered and therefore subject to the rules relating to unregistered titles, registration of a new legal lease of more than seven years is subject to the registration requirements under s4 LRA 2002 (ie first registration).

Only expressly granted easements come within the scope of s27(2)(d). These easements do not have a separate title number, instead the registered estate which is burdened by the easement will be subject to an entry of a notice on the register (Sch 2 para 7 LRA 2002). Where the land which benefits from the new easement is registered, the existence of the new easement will also be noted on the register of that dominant estate.

Procedure on Transfer of a Registered Title

1 The transferor (vendor) proves title by reference to the register. The transferee (purchaser) will still have to check whether there are any overriding interests, as these will be binding even though they are not usually mentioned on the register of title.

2 The transferor (vendor) executes a document known as a 'land transfer', which requires the completion of the TR1 form from the Land Registry. This takes effect as a deed, and it is, for the purposes of the 1925 property legislation, a 'conveyance'. However, unlike a conveyance of unregistered land, a land transfer does not vest the legal title in the transferee (purchaser).

3 The transferee (purchaser) applies for registration, producing the completed TR1 form.

The changing of the files at the Registry passes the legal title, though the change in legal ownership is retrospective to the date when application for registration was made (s74 LRA 2002). The registration of the new proprietor ensures that the legal title passes to the transferee (purchaser) (s27(1) LRA 2002).

There is no time limit within which the application must be made unlike with first registration where there the owner has to apply for first registration within two months of the transfer. The transferee is still under an obligation to fulfil the registration requirements under the LRA 2002. Section 27(1) LRA 2002 provides that a registered disposition must be completed by registration otherwise it 'does not operate at law'. Registration confers legal title to the transferee (confirmed by s58 LRA 2002). Where the transferee has not applied to be registered as the new proprietor, the transferee will only have an equitable title until the registration requirements have been complied with and the transferor (vendor) will continue to hold the legal title to the property.

 # Concluding Remarks

In this chapter we have discussed the rules governing which estates must be registered, what grades of title can be granted, and the form of the register. These rules may be rather dull and mechanical, but they are extremely important. Perhaps the most crucial point is that to talk of 'registered land' is, strictly speaking, inaccurate. A piece of land (ie the physical area upon which you can walk) is never registered. It is the 'estate(s)' in that land which is or are capable of registration. The extension of compulsory registration to leases for more than seven years, and to express grants of easements and profits, makes this point of even greater importance.

 # Summary

The Form of the Register

Each registered *estate* has an independent title number. The register of title for an estate in land is divided into three parts:

- *Property Register* identifies the land and indicates the estate registered;
- *Proprietorship Register* indicates the name(s) of the registered proprietors; and
- *Charges Register* indicates mortgages and certain other property rights derived from the registered estate.

Compulsory First Registration of Title

- *Freeholds*—first registration is compulsory when an unregistered freehold is sold, given away, passes by an assent executed by personal representatives, or where there is a first legal mortgage.
- *Legal leases* must be registered if the duration is for more than seven years.
- *Existing lease* must be registered if it is assigned when there is more than seven years of the lease to run.

Grades of Title

A summary of the grades of title is set out in Diagram 5.2.

Diagram 5.2
Grades of title

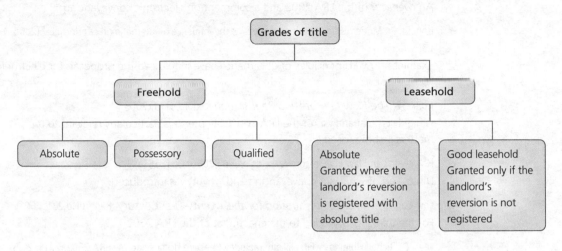

Upgrading of Titles

The two common cases of upgrading are:

- where a possessory freehold is upgraded to absolute freehold after the registered proprietor has been in possession for 12 years; and
- where a good leasehold is upgraded to absolute leasehold on the registration of the landlord's reversion with absolute freehold title.

Disposition of Registered Titles

- All dealings in registered land are governed by the Land Registration Act 2002.

Powers of Disposition

- Registered proprietor or person entitled to be registered as proprietor has unlimited powers of disposition (ss 23 and 24 LRA 2002);
- If the owner's powers are restricted, a restriction must be entered on to the register of title (s26 LRA 2002).

Registrable Dispositions

- Listed under s27(1)–(2) LRA;
- Transfer of a registered freehold;
- Legal leases;
- Legal easements; and
- Legal mortgage charge.

Further Reading

Bogusz, B, 'Bringing land registration into the twenty-first century—the Land Registration Act 2002' (2002) 65 MLR 556
An overview of the LRA 2002 and a comment on electronic conveyancing.

Bogusz, B, 'Modernising English property law: the influence of internal market principles' (2006) 17 EBLR 1395
Examines how EU principles of governance have influenced the proposals for electronic conveyancing.

Cooke, E, *The New Law of Land Registration*, Oxford: Hart, 2003
A highly critical analysis of the LRA 2002. Chapter 3 is particularly relevant to the matters just discussed.

Howell, J, 'Land law in an e-conveyancing world' [2006] Conv 553
Discussion of what is e-conveyancing and why it was introduced.

Law Commission, *Land Registration for the Twenty-First Century* (Report No 271, 2001)
For the thinking which led to the enactment of the LRA 2002.

Lees, E. 'Richall Holdings v Fitzwilliam: Malory v Cheshire Homes and the LRA 2002 (2013) 76(5) MLR 909
Critical appraisal of the two cases in light of their implications under the LRA 2002.

 # Questions

Jerry purchased Green Lodge in 1975 which was at the time unregistered title and not in an area of compulsory registration of title. Last month, Jerry granted a ten-year lease to Daniel.

Consider the following:

- Daniel is seeking your advice on the grade of title he acquires in Green Lodge.

- If in 1975 Green Lodge was in an area of compulsory registration of title, what should Jerry have done back in 1975?

- What would be the consequences if Jerry, back in 1975, had failed to take the appropriate action?

6

Minor Interests and Overriding Interests

Introduction

cross-reference
Mortgages will be discussed in more detail in Chapters 22–24.

In the previous chapter we saw that with the commencement of the Land Registration Act 2002 (LRA 2002), substantive registration now extends to leases for more than seven years and expressly granted profits in gross. What then is the position of short leases, and third party rights such as restrictive covenants, constructive trust interests, and home rights?

Leaving aside mortgages of a registered estate, all third party rights against a registered estate and all short term leases are either minor or overriding interests. If a third party right is a minor interest and has been entered onto the register of title, then it will be binding on purchasers of the estate affected (this is roughly comparable to a registrable land charge). If a right is a minor interest and has not been entered on the register, then it will be void against a purchaser. If, however, a third party right is an overriding interest, then it will still bind a purchaser, even though it does not appear on the register of title (this is roughly comparable to a legal interest against an unregistered title).

6.1 Minor Interests

Minor interests are all proprietary interests in registered land which are not:

- capable of substantive registration, that is, with a separate title number;

or

- overriding interests;

or

cross-reference
See 6.5.4 for a discussion on rights of persons in actual occupation.

- mortgages by registered charge.

Rights which are normally minor interests include:

- estate contracts, restrictive covenants, unpaid vendor's liens, and home rights (rights of occupation under the Family Law Act 1996), equitable easements and equitable profits created after the commencement of the LRA

- overreachable interests arising under a strict settlement, trust for sale, or trust of land.

It should be noted, though, that with the exception of home rights and interests under a strict settlement, most minor interests are capable of being promoted to 'overriding' by operation of Sch 3 para 2 LRA 2002, if the owner of the interest is in actual occupation.

cross-reference
Flegg's case and overreaching is discussed in more detail at 4.8.1 and 9.2.2.

This is even true of overreachable equitable interests arising under a trust for sale or trust of land. However, if an owner of an overreachable equitable interest is in actual occupation of the land, their rights can still be overreached provided the purchase price is paid by the purchaser to a minimum of two trustees or a trust corporation (ss 2 and 27 Law of Property Act 1925 (LPA 1925)). The House of Lords so decided in *City of London Building Society v Flegg* [1988] 1 AC 54.

Protection of Minor Interests

The owner of a minor interest should always protect it by entry on the register. This reinforces the application of the mirror principle. Registration of a third party interest not only protects the owner's interest, but in the case of a purchaser who checks the register of title they will know in advance about third party rights which can bind them if they decide to purchase the property.

Under the Land Registration Act 1925 (LRA 1925) there were effectively three types of entry which could be placed on the register to protect a minor interest; these were notices, cautions, and restrictions. The 2002 Act abolishes cautions as a means of protecting minor interests. However, all existing cautions on the register on 13 October 2003 will continue to be valid and governed by the old law (Sch 12 para 2(3) LRA 2002). As a matter of law the entry of a caution gave the person entering the caution only limited protection (see *Clarke v Chief Land Registrar* [1994] 4 All ER 96). But in practical reality, the presence of a caution entered against a registered title was effective to protect the minor interest. The presence of a caution on the register would put off all but the most foolhardy purchaser.

6.2.1 Notice

cross-reference
Compare this point
with the registration
of a land charge in
unregistered land,
discussed at 4.7.

Under the LRA 2002 the protection of minor interests is remarkably straightforward. Interests subject to registration, that is, minor interests, should normally be protected by the entry of a **notice** (s32 LRA 2002). From the point of view of the owner of a minor interest, the entry of a notice is the best method of protecting the priority of that interest against a purchaser (see s29(1), (2)(a)(i) LRA 2002).

. . . .

notice

'a notice is an entry in the register in respect of the burden of an interest affecting a registered estate or charge' (s32(1) LRA 2002).

. . . .

The Act does not provide a list of minor interests which require an entry in the form of a notice but s33 LRA 2002 provides a list of interests for which no notice may be entered in the register, for example an interest arising under a trust of land (expressly created or constructive). This will need to be protected by the entry of a restriction (s40 LRA 2002).

> *Land Registration Act 2002*
>
> 33. Excluded interests
>
> No notice may be entered in the register in respect of any of the following—
>
> (a) an interest under—
>
> (i) a trust of land, or
>
> (ii) a settlement under the Settled Land Act 1925 (c. 18),
>
> (b) a leasehold estate in land which—
>
> (i) is granted for a term of years of three years or less from the date of the grant, and
>
> (ii) is not required to be registered,
>
> (c) a restrictive covenant made between a lessor and lessee, so far as relating to the demised premises,
>
> . . .

The types of interest which will require an entry in the form of a notice on the register include:

- equitable lease due to a lack of formalities, for example contract in writing;
- equitable lease due to a failure to substantively register the lease;
- equitable lease created out of an equitable estate;
- equitable easements and equitable profits à prendre created after the commencement of the 2002 Act;
- freehold restrictive covenants;
- home rights (rights of occupation) for spouses or civil partners; and
- equitable mortgages.

Under the LRA 1925 there was one significant limitation which was put upon the entry of notices on to the register. For the owner of a minor interest to be able to enter a notice, the consent of the registered proprietor was required. It should be immediately added that proprietors often did agree to the entry of notices. However, under the LRA 1925, if the registered proprietor did not agree to the entry of a notice, the person claiming a minor interest could only enter a caution. The LRA 2002 permits both notices and restrictions to be entered without the consent of the registered proprietor.

So what now happens if a notice is entered to protect a claim to a minor interest, but that claim to an interest is disputed by the registered proprietor? In this situation, the registered proprietor should consider the following.

First, the entry of a notice to protect a claim to a minor interest does not guarantee that the minor interest actually exists. It merely ensures that the interest (if valid) binds a purchaser (s29(1), (2)(i)(a) LRA 2002).

Secondly, the registered proprietor can challenge the notice under the procedure sketched out in s36 LRA 2002. If the dispute as to the existence (or otherwise) of the minor interest cannot be settled by negotiation, the dispute will be referred to the Land Registration Section of the Property Chamber of the 'First Tier Tribunal'. If the First Tier Tribunal decides that the person who has entered the notice has a valid interest in the land, the Tribunal will order that the notice should remain on the register. If the Tribunal decides that the person who entered the notice does not have an interest, the notice will be deleted.

Thirdly, the registered proprietor could claim damages under s77(2) LRA 2002. A person who enters a notice 'without reasonable cause' (eg where they wrongly claim to have a minor interest) will be liable to pay damages to cover any loss suffered by the registered proprietor (eg the loss of a sale at good price).

6.2.2 Restrictions

A **restriction** is normally entered on the register where there is some special limit on the registered proprietor's freedom to dispose of the land. For example, a few 'corporate persons' (a corporate person is an artificial entity such as a limited company or local authority) do not have complete freedom to dispose of their land. If such a 'person' is a registered proprietor, an appropriate restriction should be entered.

cross-reference
See 4.8.1 for a
discussion on
overreaching.

restriction

ss 40–41 LRA 2002 provide a mechanism whereby an entry on the register can only be made if the terms of the restriction are complied with.

The important point for the purposes of this text is that a restriction should be used where registered land is subject to a strict settlement, trust for sale, or trust of land. Equitable interests under such trusts are technically minor interests, but they are overreachable as with unregistered land.

It follows that:

- where land is held under a trust for sale or trust of land, the trustee(s) are of course the registered proprietors. A restriction should be entered, however, requiring there to be at least two trustees for a valid disposition (the significance of this point will emerge in Chapters 8, and 9); and

- where land is subject to a strict settlement, the life tenant is owner of the fee simple and is therefore the registered proprietor. A restriction should be entered indicating that 'capital money' (eg in particular the purchase price when the land is sold) must be paid not to the registered proprietor but to the trustees of the settlement for the purposes of the Settled Land Act.

The decision of Briggs J in the fascinating case of *Republic of Croatia v Republic of Serbia* [2010] Ch 200 should also be noted. The case involved a claim by Croatia to part (or full) ownership of a long lease of a flat in London still registered in the name of the defunct Socialist Federal Republic of Yugoslavia. His lordship (in effect) held that any claim to part (or full) ownership by Croatia of a registered property can be protected by entering a restriction because protection of such a right or claim to ownership gave Croatia sufficient interest in doing so. (This decision is equally applicable to a dispute between private parties.)

Protecting Constructive Trust Interests under the 2002 Act

Under the LRA 1925, an owner of a constructive trust interest could protect his interest in the land by lodging a caution (see *Elias v Mitchell* [1972] 2 All ER 153). No new cautions can be created and the wording of s33(a) LRA 2002 explicitly excludes the protection of a constructive trust by a notice.

Land Registration Act 2002

33 Excluded interests

No notice may be entered in the register in respect of any of the following—

(a) an interest under
   (i) a trust of land

cross-reference
See 6.5.4 for a
discussion on actual
occupation.

Such a trust will have to be protected by a restriction (s40 LRA 2002). This change is of limited practical significance. The owner of a constructive trust interest is unlikely to know about the desirability of making an entry on the register. But he/she may well be in 'actual occupation' and therefore (in normal circumstances) the constructive trust interest will be overriding by virtue of Sch 3 para 2 LRA 2002.

Priorities of Interests in Registered Land

> *Land Registration Act 2002*
>
> 28 Basic rule
>
> (1) Except as provided by sections 29 and 30, the priority of an interest affecting a registered estate or charge is not affected by a disposition of the estate or charge.
>
> (2) It makes no difference for the purposes of this section whether the interest or disposition is registered.

Put simply, this section provides a basic rule that the priority of any interest in registered land is determined by the date of creation irrespective of whether the interest has been registered or not. The effect of this is that all pre-existing property rights are binding, whether or not they have been registered, on a transferee.

This is, crucially, subject to two exceptions found in s29 dealing with registered dispositions.

> *Land Registration Act 2002*
>
> 29. Effect of registered dispositions: estates
>
> (1) If a registrable disposition of a registered estate is made for valuable consideration, completion of the disposition by registration has the effect of postponing to the interest under the disposition any interest affecting the estate immediately before the disposition whose priority is not protected at the time of registration.
>
> (2) For the purposes of subsection (1), the priority of an interest is protected—
>
>   (a) in any case, if the interest—
>
>   (i) is a registered charge or the subject of a notice in the register,
>
>   (ii) falls within any of the paragraphs of Schedule 3, or
>
>   (iii) appears from the register to be excepted from the effect of registration, and
>
>   (b) in the case of a disposition of a leasehold estate, if the burden of the interest is incident to the estate.
>
> (3) Subsection (2)(a)(ii) does not apply to an interest which has been the subject of a notice in the register at any time since the coming into force of this section.
>
> (4) Where the grant of a leasehold estate in land out of a registered estate does not involve a registrable disposition, this section has effect as if—
>
>   (a) the grant involved such a disposition, and
>
>   (b) the disposition were registered at the time of the grant.

We shall begin this section with an explanation of a few of the terms and then consider the effect of s29 LRA 2002.

Section 27 LRA 2002 provides an explanation of what is a 'registrable disposition', for example the transfer of a registered estate, the grant of a leasehold estate of more than seven years, and the creation of a registered charge. The registered estate referred to in s29(1) includes the registered freehold and leasehold for more than seven years. It is worth noting that leases for less than seven years do not come within the scope of a registered estate, however, under s29(4) such leases are treated as though they are registrable dispositions. Valuable consideration as defined in s132(1) LRA 2002 does not include marriage consideration or nominal consideration in money.

Under s29 LRA 2002, the basic rule of priority (ie s28) does not apply where a purchaser for valuable consideration of a registered estate takes free from minor interests which have not been properly protected by a notice, or by a restriction where there is an interest under a trust (unless the interest is upgraded to overriding by the operation of Sch 3 para 2 LRA 2002). This will be so, even if the purchaser for valuable consideration knew of the unprotected minor interest. (Compare this point with the House of Lords decision in the unregistered land case of *Midland Bank v Green* [1981] 1 AC 513.) However, if the purchaser is not for value (eg they acquire by gift or will) and the interest has not been registered, the basic rule of priority applies, and the purchaser will be bound by pre-existing minor interests (*Halifax Plc v Popeck* [2009] 1 P & CR DG 3).

cross-reference
Midland Bank v Green *is discussed* at 4.7.5.

6.3.1 Fraud and Bad Faith

The purpose of registration is to ensure certainty and transparency of the register, and so reinforcing the 'mirror' principle. But in exceptional circumstances equity may intervene where there is bad faith or fraud. In this respect the decision in *Lyus v Prowsa Developments* [1982] 1 WLR 1044 is an example of an exception to the rule that an unprotected minor interest is void against a purchaser. Lyus entered into a contract to purchase a house from a property developer. However, the developer became insolvent and was wound up. The land owned by the developer was mortgaged to a bank which exercised its power of sale over the property. The property was purchased by Defendant One, who then sold it on to Defendant Two. These two sales were subject to an express understanding that the property was subject to Lyus's contract. When the land transfer was executed by the bank to Defendant One and subsequently from Defendant One to Two, it was expressly subject to a minor interest which had not been protected by entry on the register. The purchaser was held to be bound by the minor interest, because the purchaser had expressly undertaken to give effect to the unprotected minor interest.

Dillon J said:

> ...It has been pointed out by Lord Wilberforce in *Midland Bank Trust Co. Ltd v Green* [1981] AC 513, 531, that it is not fraud to rely on legal rights conferred by Act of Parliament. Under s. 20 [now s29 LRA 2002 but the wording of this section is different], the effect of the registration of the transferee of a freehold title is to confer an absolute title subject to entries on the register and overriding interests, but, 'free from all other estates and interests whatsoever, including estates and interests of His Majesty ...' In *Miles v Bull (No. 2)* [1969] 3 All ER 1585, Bridge J expressed the view that the words which I have quoted embraced, *prima facie*, not only all kinds of legal interests, but all kinds of equitable interests: see p. 1589. He therefore held, at p. 1590, as I read his judgment, that actual or constructive notice on the part of a purchaser of an unregistered interest would not have the effect of imposing a constructive trust on him. The interest in *Miles v Bull (No. 2)* was the interest in the matrimonial home of a deserted wife who had failed to protect her interest by registration under the Matrimonial Homes Act 1967. The contract for sale between the husband, who was the registered proprietor, and the purchaser provided that the house concerned was sold, subject to such rights of occupation as might subsist in favour of the wife, with a proviso that this was not to imply that the wife had, or would after completion have any such rights as against the purchaser. Plainly, therefore, the clause was only included in the contract for the protection of the husband who was the vendor. The wife was to get no fresh rights, and it was not in *Miles v Bull (No. 2)* a stipulation of the bargain between the vendor and the purchaser that the purchaser should give effect to the rights as against the vendor of the deserted wife. *Miles v Bull (No. 2)* is thus distinguishable from the facts of the present case as I interpret those facts.
>
> *It seems to me that the fraud on the part of the defendants in the present case lies not just in relying on the legal rights conferred by an Act of Parliament, but in the first defendant reneging*

> *on a positive stipulation in favour of the plaintiffs in the bargain under which the first defendant acquired the land.* That makes, as it seems to me, all the difference. It has long since been held, for instance, in *Rochefoucauld v Boustead* [1897] 1 Ch 196, that the provisions of the Statute of Frauds 1677 (29 Car, 2 c. 3), now incorporated in certain sections of the Law of Property Act 1925, cannot be used as an instrument of fraud, and that it is fraud for a person to whom land is agreed to be conveyed as trustee for another to deny the trust and relying on the terms of the statute to claim the land for himself. *Rochefoucauld v Boustead* was one of the authorities on which the judgment in *Bannister v Bannister* [1948] 2 All ER 133 was founded.
>
> It seems to me that the same considerations are applicable in relation to the Land Registration Act 1925 . . .
>
> [Emphasis added]

The court in this case imposed a constructive trust on the legal owner in favour of a claimant whose minor interest had not been protected by registration. The reasoning for this lies in the fact it would have been inequitable for the legal owner to renege on his express undertaking to respect Lyus's contract to buy the property.

The interaction between ss 28 and 29 LRA 2002, the concept of overriding interests, and the decision in *Lyus v Prowsa Developments* were considered at some length by the Court of Appeal in *Chaudhary v Yavuz* [2011] EWCA 1314.

Chaudhary owned number 37 Balaam Street. Vijay owned the neighbouring number 35 and the alleyway between the two (two-storey) buildings. In 2006, in pursuance of an informal agreement between the two neighbours, Chaudhary constructed a metal staircase in Vijay's alley so as to allow the tenants of his two first floor flats to gain easier access to their homes. This right was, in effect, an equitable easement of way which should have been protected by an entry of a notice on the Land Register. There was no entry on the Register.

In 2007 Vijay sold number 35, including the alley, to Yavuz. The contract of sale used the Standard Conditions of Sale, clause 3.1.2 of which reads:

> The incumbrances subject to which the property is sold are:-
>
> (a) those specified in the contract
>
> (b) those discoverable by inspection of the property before the contract . . .

The contract made absolutely no mention of any easement over the alley or staircase, though the presence of the staircase was obvious to anyone making an inspection of the property.

Was the equitable easement binding on Yavuz? It was not an overriding interest within Sch 3 para 3 as that provision is confined to legal easements. Nor could it fall within Sch 3 para 2, as Chaudhary's tenants using the staircase could not be regarded as 'actual occupation' of the alley.

The trial judge had, however, focused on clause 3.1.2(b) of the contract of sale, and had held, 'applying' *Lyus v Prowsa Developments*, that a constructive trust binding on Yavuz arose in favour of Chaudhary. This conclusion was overruled by the Court of Appeal.

The Court of Appeal regarded *Lyus* as correctly decided. But the constructive trust arose in that case because Prowsa Developments in their contract to purchase the land expressly undertook to recognize Lyus's right under the earlier contract of sale. There was no similar clause in Yavuz's contract expressly requiring him to recognize Chaudhary's easement.

The Court of Appeal in *Chaudhary* was highly critical of *Peffer v Rigg* [1977] 1 WLR 285. In *Peffer* the court (Graham, J) in effect held that a purchaser who has *actual* notice of an unprotected minor interest is not a purchaser in good faith, and for that reason is bound by the unprotected minor interest.

Title to the land was registered in *Peffer v Rigg*. Mr Peffer and Mr Rigg purchased a house as an investment and in order to accommodate a relative. The house was registered in Mr Rigg's sole name, but it was agreed that he would hold the legal title on trust for himself and Mr Peffer as tenants in common in equal shares. This arrangement was confirmed by an express deed of trust at a later date. On their divorce Mr Rigg transferred the house to Mrs Rigg for £1, as part of the divorce settlement. Mrs Rigg was, accordingly, registered as sole legal proprietor. She was fully aware, throughout, of the trust in favour of Mr Peffer. Unfortunately, Mr Peffer had failed to protect his interest on the register and so the question arose whether Mrs Rigg was bound by his interest.

The court held that even if the £1 consideration could be treated as valuable consideration, it was still necessary for the purchaser to show that she had purchased in good faith. This she had failed to do. Consequently, she could not take advantage of s59(6) LRA 1925 which provides that 'a purchaser acquiring title under a registered disposition' shall not be concerned with unprotected minor interests, apart from overriding interests. Her lack of 'good faith' meant that she was not to be regarded as a 'purchaser', at all, for the purposes of this section. In any event, the purchaser had known that the property she had received was trust property. She would therefore be liable as a constructive trustee, under normal trust principles, to account to the plaintiff for his share of the property.

Graham J said:

> On the evidence in this case I have found that the second defendant knew quite well that the first defendant held the property on trust for himself and the plaintiff in equal shares. The second defendant knew this was so and that the property was trust property when the transfer was made to her, and therefore she took the property on a constructive trust in accordance with general equitable principles: see *Snell's Principles of Equity*, 27th edn. (1973), pp. 98–99. This is a new trust imposed by equity and is distinct from the trust which bound the first defendant. Even if, therefore, I am wrong as to the proper construction of ss. 20 and 59, when read together, and even if section 20 strikes off the shackles of the express trust which bound the first defendant, this cannot invalidate the new trust imposed on the second defendant . . . .

The court imposed a constructive trust based on the fact that the purchaser had actual notice of the unprotected minor interest. *Peffer v Rigg* appeared to introduce the doctrine of notice into registered land; the general rule is that the doctrine does not apply to registered land.

The Court of Appeal in *Chaudhary* disapproved of *Peffer*. Lloyd LJ stated:

> 67. [Gray and Gray] note some isolated exceptions, including the decision of Graham J in *Peffer* v Rigg [1977] 1 WLR 285. In that case, concerned relevantly with the protection given by the Land Registration Act 1925 to a purchaser, defined as one taking in good faith for valuable consideration, the judge said that a purchaser 'cannot in my judgment be in good faith if he has in fact notice of something which affects his title'. That decision has been strongly criticised. It does not stand well with other authority, including the words of Sir Christopher Slade at paragraph 50 of *Lloyd v Dugdale*, introducing the passage about constructive trusts from which I have already quoted some passages:
>
> > 'There is no general principle which renders it unconscionable for a purchaser of land to rely on a want of registration of a claim against registered land, even though he took with express notice of it. A decision to the contrary would defeat the purpose of the legislature in introducing the system of registration embodied in the 1925 Act.'

cross-reference
See 6.5.5 for a
discussion of whether
the doctrine of notice
applies to registered
land.

68. In my judgment that approach is even more amply justified under the 2002 Act than it was before. It does not exclude the possibility that the court may find an obligation binding on the registered proprietor personally, by way of, for example, a constructive trust, as a result of which an obligation which is not protected on the register is nevertheless effective. *Lyus v Prowsa* is an example of that, and a rare one. The present case is not.

It is submitted that *Lyus,* as interpreted in *Chaudhary*, is correctly decided, but that *Peffer v Rigg*, which would fundamentally undermine the LRA 2002, is wrong.

REVIEW QUESTION Compare the registered land decisions in *Lyus v Prowsa Developments*, *Chaudhary v Yavuz*, and *Peffer v Rigg* with the unregistered land decisions in *Midland Bank v Green* and *Hollington Brothers v Rhodes*.

(Consider 4.7 and 6.3.1.)

6.4 Searches of the Register

The tradition of English land registration (to be contrasted with foreign systems) had been until 1990 one of privacy. The Registry was not open to the public, and to inspect a particular registered title you needed the permission of the registered proprietor. However, a person who had contracted to buy a registered title was automatically entitled to receive permission to inspect the register.

The Land Registration Act 1988 came into force in December 1990, and this Act allowed any person to inspect any registered title on the payment of an appropriate fee. This principle of a register freely open to public inspection is now set out in s66 LRA 2002. Nevertheless, the wise or prudent purchaser of a registered title will not rely on a personal inspection, but ask the Registry to make an 'official search' of the register.

In practice, a purchase of registered land is not completed on the day of the official search, but only after a few days have elapsed. Once an official search certificate is issued the purchaser has a priority period of 30 working days, though the length of this period may be altered by the Land Registration Rules. Provided the purchaser lodges the land transfer for registration within this priority period, the purchaser is not bound by entries, for example notices, restrictions, etc made on the register in the intervening period.

6.5 Overriding Interests (or Unregistered Interests Which Override Registered Dispositions)

It is extremely important to know whether a third party right (such as a constructive trust interest or easement) is minor or overriding. **Overriding interests** are a major hazard for any purchaser of a registered title. Such interests do not appear on the register, yet a purchaser is bound by overriding interests affecting the title purchased whether he knew about them or not.

....

overriding interest

an interest which binds the purchaser of a registered title, whether he knew about it or not, despite not being entered on the register of title.

....

The LRA 1925 listed out the 'old law' overriding interests in s70(1). Section 70(1) consisted of a number of lettered paragraphs. Many of the types of interest listed in s70(1) were unimportant; in practice there were five important categories of overriding interest.

One of the avowed purposes of the 2002 Act is to reduce the number of overriding interests which are binding upon the purchaser of a registered title. However, the 2002 Act achieves this purpose only to a very limited degree.

cross-reference
For a discussion on the limited practical significance of Sch 1, see 5.6.2.

Under the LRA 2002 overriding interests are provided for in two schedules: Sch 1 lists 'unregistered interests which override first registration', while Sch 3 lists 'unregistered interests which override registered dispositions'.

It is Sch 3 which is of overwhelming long-term importance, and we will focus our discussion on that schedule. The list of overriding interests set out in Sch 3 LRA 2002, consists of 14 numbered paragraphs. Schedule 3 is almost as long as s70(1) LRA 1925.

A number of unimportant overriding interests have been abolished. However, of the five important categories of overriding interests in the LRA 1925, only one was abolished. Of the remaining four important overriding interests, one, Local Land Charges, is retained unchanged (see Sch 3 para 6 LRA 2002). The other three categories are:

- easements and profits;
- short term legal leases; and
- property rights of a person in actual occupation.

These have all been reduced in their scope but continue to be of fundamental importance. The discussion in the following sections will be confined to the four (remaining) important categories of overriding interest.

6.5.1 Local Land Charges

(Previously s70(1)(i) LRA 1925, now Sch 3 para 6 LRA 2002.)

Local land charges have not been mentioned before, as they are a matter peripheral to a study of pure land law. Each District Council in England and Wales keeps a register of local land charges, and the system of local charges operates irrespective of whether title to the land is registered or unregistered. Thus, when buying land, the wise purchaser always 'does a local search'.

What sort of matters are local land charges? Basically they cover 'public law' rights such as the special charge which sometimes exists for the making up of a road; the 'listing' of a building as of historic interest; tree preservation orders; and many other matters connected with town and country planning.

6.5.2 Easements and Profits

Not all easements and profits are overriding interests under the LRA 2002. Those which are overriding fall into two categories:

1 existing easements and profits: created before 13 October 2003; and

2 legal easements and legal profits created by implied grant or prescription after 12 October 2003.

Existing Easements and Profits at the Commencement of the 2002 Act

Easements and profits already existing against a registered title will continue to be governed by s70(1)(a) LRA 1925 and the case law interpreting that provision (see Sch 12 para 9 LRA 2002).

Section 70(1)(a) LRA 1925 provided '...profits à prendre,...and easements not being equitable easements required to be protected by notice on the register' should be overriding.

The wording of s70(1)(a) was somewhat archaic, but certain consequences were clear:

- a legal profit was an overriding interest;
- an equitable profit was also an overriding interest (contrast unregistered land, where an equitable profit is registrable as a land charge); and
- a legal easement was an overriding interest.

That left equitable easements. Now on the wording of paragraph (a) you are probably thinking, as everybody used to think, that equitable easements were not overriding interests but minor interests, and that to be binding upon a purchaser they needed to be protected by an entry on the register. However, in *Thatcher v Douglas* (1996) 146 NLJ 282, the Court of Appeal, by some rather strained logic, managed to hold that an equitable easement was an overriding interest within s70(1)(a) LRA 1925 (see also, *Celsteel Ltd v Alton House Holdings Ltd* [1985] 1 WLR 204).

After 12 October 2003 all 'old' existing easements and profits, however they were created, and whether they are legal or equitable, continue to be overriding interests.

Legal Easements and Profits Created by Implied Grant or Prescription after the Commencement of the 2002 Act

As indicated in the previous chapter, easements may arise by implication—the creation of an easement is inferred from the circumstances of the sale (or lease) of what becomes the dominant property. Easements (and profits) can also arise by prescription—created by the conduct of the dominant owner.

Provisions for Easements and Profits Arising by Implied Grant or Prescription

A legal easement or profit arising by implied grant or prescription will only be overriding (Sch 3 para 3 LRA 2002) if any one of the following three conditions is fulfilled:

- the purchaser had 'actual knowledge' of the easement or profit on the date of the land transfer in his favour;

or

- the existence of the right would have been apparent 'on a reasonably careful inspection of the land over which the easement or profit is exercisable';

or

- if the easement or profit has been exercised at least once in the year prior to the land transfer.

thinking point 6.1

The rules under the LRA 2002 as to when easements and profits will be overriding interests are being trumpeted as a major reform 'which will make life easier for purchasers of registered land'. Frankly, that is not the case. Why?

First, surely you will agree that the rules under LRA 2002 are extremely complicated. Secondly, as a result of these rules, no pre-2003 easements and profits, and only a few post-2003 easements and profits arising by implied grant or prescription are excluded from being overriding. Such easements and profits even though not discovered by a purchaser, will be binding on him unless it has neither:

1 left physical evidence on the land of its existence;

nor

2 been exercised at least once in the year before the land transfer.

thinking point 6.2

Refer back to the High Chimneys case study at 4.1.

Assume that Roger purchased High Chimneys in 2014 from Tatiana, who was the registered proprietor of High Chimneys, but the facts regarding Olabode's easement and Pierce's profit are the same as before, in particular these rights were created before 2003. Will Roger be bound by their rights even though:

- *he had no knowledge of their rights; and*
- *he could not have possibly discovered those rights by inspecting the land; and*
- *those rights have not been exercised for several years?*

Roger will be bound by Olabode's legal easement and Pierce's equitable profit. The transitional provisions in Sch 12 para 9 allow all overriding easements and profits which existed before 13 October 2003 to retain their overriding status indefinitely.

What if Olabode's easement had arisen by either implied grant or prescription as recently as 2006, but in the last five years Olabode had not exercised his right regularly and there were no visible signs of those rights when Roger's surveyor inspected the land?

The easement, not discoverable by inspecting the land, would be binding on Roger if it had been exercised just once in the year before the land transfer in Roger's favour.

Easements and Profits Expressly Granted or Reserved after the Commencement of the 2002 Act

As already explained in the previous chapter, s27(2)(d) LRA 2002 requires all new express grants or reservations of easements and profits (created out of a registered title) to be registered to operate at law. If a dominant owner of an easement or profit fails to register their right, the easement or profit will take effect only as an equitable interest.

Suppose Roger from our High Chimneys case study in Chapter 4 had recently purchased High Chimneys. High Chimneys was unregistered title in the case study, but we are now assuming that High Chimneys is a registered property. Last week Olabode, owner of neighbouring Low Stacks, visited Roger and produced a deed dated 1 February 2004. By that deed Tatiana, the previous owner of High Chimneys, granted to Olabode a right of way across the garden of High Chimneys. This right of way was expressly granted for the benefit of Low Stacks, and was to last in perpetuity.

Roger would need to check the register of title to see if Olabode had protected his easement by registration. To protect the easement, a 'notice' should have been entered on to the register of title of the servient land (ie land which is burdened by the easement) (s38 LRA 2002). (The benefit of the easement should be registered on the dominant owner's register of title (s27(2)(d) LRA 2002).) If Olabode has protected his interest then Roger is bound. If Olabode has not protected his interest then the easement would only take effect as an equitable easement and would not bind Roger.

Equitable Easements and Equitable Profits Created after the Commencement of the 2002 Act are Always Minor Interests

Schedule 3 para 3 LRA 2002 refers only to legal easements and legal profits. So an equitable easement or an equitable profit which arises either:

- because there is an express grant of a profit in gross which the dominant owner fails to register;
  or
- because the easement or profit is to endure only for the life or lives of a person(s);
  or
- because a written contract not in the form of a deed creates the right;

cannot be an overriding interest.

It follows that all equitable easements created after the commencement of the 2002 Act will be minor interests, which will only bind a purchaser of the servient land if the burden of the easement has been registered as a notice against the servient land.

REVIEW QUESTION Summarize the rules relating to easements and profits as to when they must be registered and when they can be overriding.

6.5.3 Short Term Leases

All legal leases for a duration not exceeding seven years are overriding (Sch 3 para 1 LRA 2002). The short legal lease will be overriding irrespective of whether the tenant is occupying the property and irrespective of whether or not the tenant tells any enquirers that he has rights in the land.

Under the LRA 1925 leases over 21 years had to be registered. Any legal lease not exceeding 21 years was an overriding interest under s70(1)(k) LRA 1925. The reduction of the short lease period from 21 to seven years is the natural corollary of the decision to make all leases over seven years substantively registrable. But two special points should be noted. First, legal leases for between seven and 21 years already in existence on the day the 2002 Act commenced will continue to be overriding interests (Sch 12 para 12 LRA 2002). Put another way, on the commencement date (13 October 2003) there was no need for lessees with leases between seven and 21 years to rush off and substantively register.

Secondly, what happens if, after the commencement of the 2002 Act, a lease is granted by deed for ten years and the lessee takes possession but fails to substantively register the lease? The lease will not be totally void; it will take effect in equity, and it might well still be an overriding interest under Sch 3 para 2 LRA 2002 (property rights of a person in actual occupation).

REVIEW QUESTION You are negotiating a lease over 'High Rise', a block of offices which you need 'for the next few years' for your gradually expanding professional practice. From a legal point of view it is 'easier' to take a legal lease for seven years exactly. Why?

6.5.4 Property Rights of a Person in Actual Occupation

The aim of Sch 3 para 2 LRA 2002 is to protect the person who has a property right which has not been entered on to the register of title but who is in actual occupation. The protection afforded by the statute to the occupier provides a safeguard to those who have an unprotected property right and consequently the occupier is protected from losing their 'rights...in the welter of registration' (per Lord Denning MR, *Strand Securities Ltd v Caswell* [1965] Ch 958 at 979). Schedule 3 para 2 retains the majority of the protection provided for under s70(1)(g) LRA 1925: 'The rights of every person in actual occupation of the land...save where enquiry is made of such person and the rights are not disclosed'. However, Sch 3 para 2 is a more complex provision which cannot be understood without reference to the old law. In particular, a large amount of case law has developed around the old provision (s70(1)(g) LRA 1925) especially as to the meaning of 'actual occupation', and there can be no real doubt that (with one exception) this old case law will equally be applicable to Sch 3 para 2.

The important parts of Sch 3 para 2 read as follows:

> An interest belonging at the time of the disposition to a person in actual occupation, so far as relating to land of which he is in actual occupation, except for—
>
> (a) an interest under a settlement under the Settled Land Act 1925;
> (b) an interest of a person of whom inquiry was made before the disposition and who failed to disclose the right when he could reasonably have been expected to do so;
> (c) an interest—
>   (i) which belongs to a person *whose occupation would not have been obvious on a reasonably careful inspection of the land* at the time of the disposition, and
>   (ii) of which the person to whom the disposition is made does not have actual knowledge at that time;... [Emphasis added]

Rights which can be Overriding Interests

The LRA 2002 preserves the basic principle underlying s70(1)(g) LRA 1925, namely that a type of property right in land can be an overriding interest provided there is actual occupation on the date of disposition. It was the House of Lords in *Williams and Glyn's Bank Ltd v Boland* [1981] AC 487 that confirmed that where a proprietary interest, whose priority could be protected by an entry on the register (by notice, restriction, or caution), but has not been entered on the register, will nevertheless be an overriding interest if its owner is in actual occupation. Put simply:

Proprietary interest + Actual occupation = Overriding interest

The House in *Williams and Glyn's Bank Ltd v Boland* recognized that these proprietary interests which ought to be protected would normally be void (now s29(1) LRA 2002) but because the owner of the interest is in actual occupation that interest can become overriding. Actual occupation, in that sense, merely acts as a trigger to upgrade an unprotected right to an overriding one.

In *Williams and Glyn's Bank Ltd v Boland* [1981] AC 487 Mr Boland ('H') bought a house, registered title, in his sole name. His wife ('W') made substantial contributions to the cost of acquisition, and therefore acquired a constructive trust interest in the house. While H and W were living happily together in the house, H decided to borrow some more money. Without telling his wife, he borrowed it from the bank. He granted the bank a mortgage by registered charge. The bank did not bother to send an employee to the house, and certainly did not ask W any questions. H defaulted on repaying the loan, and the bank wished to enforce its mortgage by taking possession of the house and selling. Was W's interest binding on the bank? If it was, the bank was effectively prevented from enforcing its security.

The House of Lords unanimously held that W's constructive trust interest was an overriding interest by virtue of s70(1)(g) LRA 1925 and was therefore binding on the bank.

Lord Wilberforce said:

> This brings me to the second question which is whether such rights as a spouse has under a trust for sale are capable of recognition as overriding interests—a question to my mind of some difficulty. The argument against this is based upon the structure of the Land Registration Act 1925 and upon specific provisions in it.
>
> As to structure, it is said that the Act recognises three things: (a) legal estates, (b) minor interests, which take effect in equity, (c) overriding interests. These are mutually exclusive: an equitable interest, which is a minor interest, is incapable of being at the same time an overriding interest. The wife's interest, existing under or behind a trust for sale, is an equitable interest and nothing more. To give it the protection of an overriding interest would, moreover, contradict the principle according to which such an equitable interest can be overreached by an exercise of the trust for sale. As to the provisions of the Act, particular emphasis is placed on s. 3(xv) which, in defining 'minor interests' specifically includes in the case of land held on trust for sale 'all interests and powers which are under the Law of Property Act 1925 capable of being overridden by the trustees for sale' and excludes, expressly, overriding interests . . .
>
> My Lords, I find this argument formidable . . .
>
> How then are these various rights to be fitted into the scheme of the Land Registration Act 1925? It is clear, at least, that the interests of the co-owners under the 'statutory trusts' are minor interests—this fits with the definition in s. 3(xv). But I can see no reason why, if these interests, or that of any one of them, are or is protected by 'actual occupation' they should remain merely as 'minor interests.' On the contrary, I see every reason why, in that event, they should acquire the status of overriding interests. And, moreover, I find it easy to accept that they satisfy the opening, and governing, words of section 70, namely, interests subsisting in reference to the land . . .
>
> There are decisions, in relation to other equitable interests than those of tenants in common, which confirm this line of argument. In *Bridges v Mees* [1957] Ch 475 Harman J decided that a purchaser of land under a contract for sale, who had paid the price and so was entitled to the land in equity, could acquire an overriding interest by virtue of actual occupation, and a similar position was held by the Court of Appeal to arise in relation to a resulting trust: *Hodgson v Marks* [1971] Ch 892. These decisions . . . provide an answer to the argument that there is a

firm dividing line, or an unbridgeable gulf, between minor interests and overriding interests, and, on the contrary, confirm that the fact of occupation enables protection of the latter to extend to what without it would be the former. In my opinion, the wives' equitable interests, subsisting in reference to the land, were by the fact of occupation, made into overriding interests, and so protected by s 70(1)(g).

...I would only add, in conclusion, on the appeal as it concerns the wives a brief observation on the conveyancing consequences of dismissing the appeal...whereas the object of a land registration system is to reduce the risks to purchasers from anything not on the register, to extend (if it be an extension) the area of risk so as to include possible interests of spouses, and indeed, in theory, of other members of the family or even outside it, may add to the burdens of purchasers, and involve them in enquiries which in some cases may be troublesome.

But conceded, as it must be, that the Act, following established practice, gives protection to occupation, the extension of the risk area follows necessarily from the extension, beyond the paterfamilias [head of household], of rights of ownership, itself following from the diffusion of property and earning capacity. What is involved is a departure from an easygoing practice of dispensing with enquiries as to occupation beyond that of the vendor and accepting the risks of doing so. To substitute for this a practice of more careful enquiry as to the fact of occupation, and if necessary, as to the rights of occupiers can not, in my view of the matter, be considered as unacceptable except at the price of overlooking the widespread development of shared interests of ownership. In the light of s. 70 of the Act, I cannot believe that Parliament intended this, though it may be true that in 1925 it did not foresee the full extent of this development . . . .

Following previous case law the House of Lords confirmed that a purchaser may be bound by equitable interests (ie some minor interests) if the owner of these right(s) is in actual occupation.

The word 'rights' in s70(1)(g) LRA 1925 was construed to cover every proprietary interest in land (*National Provincial Bank Ltd v Hastings Car Mart* [1964] Ch 665). The courts have been flexible in their interpretation of proprietary right. For example, in *Williams and Glyn's Bank Ltd v Boland* the House of Lords confirmed that an equitable interest arising by way of constructive trust came within the scope of rights under s70(1)(g). Another example of a flexible interpretation of rights under s70(1)(g) can be found in *Webb v Pollmount* [1966] Ch 584. It is perhaps the most surprising of all the s70(1)(g) cases. It is, however, undoubtedly correct (and is equally applicable to Sch 3 para 2 LRA 2002). It is the clearest illustration of the proposition that 'Every type of property right in land can be an overriding interest provided there is actual occupation at the relevant time by its owner'.

In *Webb v Pollmount* [1966] Ch 584, L granted to Webb a legal lease to last for seven years. This lease was overriding under s70(1)(k). The lease also granted to Webb an option to purchase the fee simple reversion. Options to purchase land are normally 'minor interests', and therefore should be protected by entering a notice on the register. No notice was entered to protect Webb's option. The fee simple was sold to Pollmount Ltd, which claimed that the option was not binding on it. Section 70(1)(g) came to Webb's rescue. He was actually occupying the leased property at the time of the sale, therefore his option was an overriding interest within s70(1)(g).

Ungoed-Thomas J said:

> It was suggested for the defendant that 'the right of every person in actual occupation of the land' should be construed as the rights by virtue of which a person is in actual occupation of the land. The short answer to this, it seems to me, is that it does not say so; and the wording is in marked contrast with the wording in s. 14 of the Law of Property Act 1925, where reference is made to the interest of a person in possession or occupation of land 'to which he may be

cross-reference
See 6.5.3 for a discussion on short term leases as overriding interest.

153

entitled in right of such possession or occupation.' It is neither, in my view, consistent with the wording of s. 70(1)(g) of the Land Registration Act 1925, nor with the authorities from which I have quoted.

Although an option to purchase does not, like an option to renew, 'touch,' 'concern' or 'affect' 'the land demised and regarded as the subject matter of the lease' (so as, e.g., to bind the reversion under the Grantees of Reversions Act 1540), what we are concerned with here is not whether it so 'affects' 'the land demised' and is within the relationship of landlord and tenant as considered in the judgment of the Court of Appeal in *Woodall* v *Clifton* [1905] 2 Ch 257, but whether within s. 20(1)(b) it is an interest 'affecting the estate transferred' to the defendant. That it is capable of affecting the estate transferred to the defendant is not disputed; e.g., if the defendant had notice of it before transfer to him. So, it seems to me to fall within Russell LJ's test in *National Provincial Bank Ltd* v *Hastings Car Mart Ltd* [1964] Ch 665 of 'being capable of enduring through different ownerships of the land according to normal conceptions of title to real property.' And if it, thus, in the circumstances of this case, is a right 'affecting the estate transferred,' within the requirement of s. 20(1)(b), it seems to me that it is 'for the time being subsisting in reference to' registered land within the requirement of s. 70(1). My conclusion, therefore, is that subject to deciding the question as to the effect of s. 59, the option to purchase appears to be an overriding interest . . . .

Webb was of course occupying the property by virtue of his lease, but that was held not to matter. The option came within the scope of rights which could override the register. The court in this case held that 'rights of a person in actual occupation' were not to be confined to the right by virtue of which that person occupies the land (ie the lease) but would also extend to the option. The operation of s70(1)(g) LRA 1925 made all Webb's property rights in the land overriding. It is assumed that the same approach will be adopted under LRA 2002.

Interests which cannot be Overriding Interests under Sch 3 para 2

The LRA 2002 uses the term 'interests' instead of 'rights'. This reflects the broader range of proprietary interests which are capable of binding purchasers as provided for by the LRA 2002. It is now clear (ss 115 and 116 LRA 2002) that proprietary estoppel and rights of pre-emption are property rights and can therefore be upgraded to overriding under Sch 3 para 2 LRA 2002.

Personal rights are not capable of binding a purchaser. This was illustrated in the case *National Provincial Bank Ltd v Ainsworth* [1965] AC 1175 at 1261, where Lord Wilberforce in the House of Lords stated that 'purely personal rights including the wife's right to stay in the house . . . cannot affect purchasers . . .' Consequently, personal rights are not protected under Sch 3 para 2, and cannot become overriding interests.

That personal rights cannot be protected by Sch 3 para 2 is a key point in the recent Supreme Court decision in *Scott v Southern Pacific Mortgages* [2014] 3 WLR 1163 which considered whether a promise made to a vendor granting them a tenancy to live in the property indefinitely by the nominee purchaser could amount to a proprietary interest which could take priority. This case involved sale and lease back agreements where the owner of the property, in financial difficulty, sells their property to a nominee purchaser on the understanding that the vendor will continue to live in the property, having leased it back from the purchaser.

The Supreme Court held that the right would only become proprietary if the purchaser had been capable of creating a proprietary interest before completion. Put simply, the purchaser could not grant an equitable interest carved out of the vendor's land prior to the acquisition of the property. This is because the nominee purchaser had not acquired the legal estate which could then give effect to the promise as proprietary estoppel.

Added to this, the property was financed by way of a mortgage from a lender. The mortgage was used to pay for the purchase of the property and this takes place virtually simultaneously with the transfer of the property, and according to settled case law (*Abbey National v Cann*) there is no gap in time (known as *scintilla temporis*) where the vendor's rights can take priority over the lender's rights.

cross-reference
Strand Securities Ltd v Caswell *is discussed later in this section at 'Can an Agent or Employee be in Actual Occupation?'.*

'Matrimonial home rights' (now called 'home rights') were expressly excluded from the scope of the old provision (s70(1)(g) LRA 1925) and also excluded under Sch 3 para 2 (see Sch 11 para 34(2)(b) LRA s2(8)(b) Matrimonial Homes Act 1983; s31(10)(b) Family Law Act 1996). A licence is another example of a personal right which is not protected by Sch 3 para 2 (see *Strand Securities v Caswell*).

A further (unimportant) exception is created by Sch 3 para 2(a). An interest under a strict settlement (very few of these exist today) cannot be an overriding interest.

Actual Occupation

The LRA 2002 contains no definition of 'actual occupation'. Mummery LJ in the Court of Appeal in *Link Lending Ltd v Bustard* [2010] 2 P & CR DG15 noted that 'the trend of cases shows that the courts are reluctant to lay down, or even suggest, a single legal test for determining whether a person is in actual occupation'. This is undoubtedly the correct approach and allows the court to exercise a degree of flexibility in their interpretation in determining whether a person was in actual occupation or not. In the following sections we will discuss the cases dealing with 'actual occupation' and draw out the main features of this concept.

We have so far assumed that existing case law on the meaning of this phrase (in particular the decisions in *Boland* and in *Cann*) would apply to Sch 3 para 2 LRA 2002. Mummery LJ in *Link Lending* confirmed that the interpretation given to actual occupation under s70(1)(g) LRA 1925 is also applicable to Sch 3 para 2:

> The decisions on statutory construction identify the factors that have to be weighed by the judge on this issue. The degree of permanence and continuity of presence of the person concerned, the intentions and wishes of that person, the length of absence from the property and the reason for it and the nature of the property and personal circumstances of the person are among the relevant factors.

The Meaning of Actual Occupation

The House of Lords in *Williams and Glyn's Bank Ltd v Boland* [1981] AC 487 considered whether Mrs Boland, who was living with her husband, could establish actual occupation. Lord Wilberforce said:

> ...I now deal with the first question. Were the wives here in 'actual occupation'? These words are ordinary words of plain English, and should, in my opinion, be interpreted as such...The purpose for which [actual occupation] used [the court referred to *Barnhart v Greenshields* [1853] 9 Moo PCC 18] was evidently to distinguish the case of a person who was in some kind of legal possession, as by receipt of the rents and profits, from that of a person actually in occupation as tenant. Given occupation, i.e., presence on the land, I do not think that the word 'actual' was intended to introduce any additional qualification, certainly not to suggest that possession must be 'adverse': it merely emphasises that what is required is physical presence, not some entitlement in law. So even if it were necessary to look behind these plain words into history, I would find no reason for denying them their plain meaning.
>
> Then, were the wives in actual occupation? I ask: why not? There was physical presence, with all the rights that occupiers have, including the right to exclude all others except those

having similar rights. The house was a matrimonial home, intended to be occupied, and in fact occupied by both spouses, both of whom have an interest in it: it would require some special doctrine of law to avoid the result that each is in occupation.... There are observations which suggest the contrary in the unregistered land case of *Caunce* v *Caunce* [1969] 1 WLR 286, but I agree with the disapproval of these, and with the assertion of the proposition I have just stated by Russell LJ in *Hodgson* v *Marks* [1971] Ch 892, 934. Then it was suggested that the wife's occupation was nothing but the shadow of the husband's—a version I suppose of the doctrine of unity of husband and wife...This expression and the argument flowing from it was used by Templeman J in *Bird* v *Syme-Thomson* [1979] 1 WLR 440, 444, a decision preceding and which he followed in the present case. The argument was also inherent in the judgment in *Caunce* v *Caunce* [1969] 1 WLR 286 which influenced the decisions of Templeman J. It somewhat faded from the arguments in the present case and appears to me to be heavily obsolete....

From this extract we can say the following:

* the words 'actual occupation' must be construed literally and occupation should be treated as a matter of fact. The effect of this interpretation would lead the purchaser to be automatically bound by the interests of the person in actual occupation; and

* their Lordships very strongly disapproved *Caunce v Caunce* [1969] 1 WLR 286. The material facts of that case were identical to those in *Boland*, except that the title to the house was unregistered. The judge held that, for the purposes of the rule in *Hunt v Luck*, W was not in occupation of the home and that therefore the mortgagee did not have constructive notice of her equitable interest. *Caunce* has never been formally overruled, but it is assumed that it is wrong.

In *Abbey National Building Society v Cann* [1991] 1 AC 56 the House of Lords further clarified the meaning of 'actual occupation'. Mr Cann purchased a maisonette in his sole name. His mother, who lived with him, made a substantial contribution to the cost of acquisition and thus was entitled to a constructive trust interest.

At about 11.45 a.m. on 13 August ('the date of completion') furniture removers acting on behalf of Mrs Cann started laying carpets and bringing in her furniture. She was on holiday in the Netherlands at that time. At 12.20 p.m. the same day, a land transfer was executed in favour of Mr Cann. Mr Cann financed the purchase of the property by obtaining a mortgage loan.

Both the land transfer and the mortgage were registered on 13 September, by which time Mrs Cann was living in the maisonette with her son. Mr Cann defaulted in repaying the loan. Mrs Cann then claimed that her constructive trust interest was an overriding interest under s70(1)(g) binding on the building society.

Their Lordships considered the meaning of 'actual occupation' under s70(1)(g) LRA 1925. Lord Oliver, who delivered the only reasoned speech in *Abbey National v Cann*, elaborated on the issue of what constitutes 'actual occupation':

I have, up to this point, been content to assume that the facts of the instant case justify the proposition which found favour with Dillon L.J., that she was in actual occupation of the property at the material time. This is, of course, essentially a question of fact, but there is the serious question of what, in law, can amount to 'actual occupation' for the purposes of section 70(1)(g). In Williams & Glyn's Bank Ltd. v. Boland [1981] A.C. 487, 504, Lord Wilberforce observed that these words should be interpreted for what they are, that is to say, ordinary words of plain English. But even plain English may contain a variety of shades of meaning. At the date of completion Mrs. Cann was not personally even in England, leave alone in personal occupation of the property, and the trial judge held that the acts done by Mr. Abraham Cann and Mr. George Cann amounted to

> 'no more than the taking of preparatory steps leading to the assumption of actual residential occupation on or after completion, whatever the moment of the day when completion took place...'

For my part, I am content to accept this as a finding of fact...It is, perhaps, dangerous to suggest any test for what is essentially a question of fact, for 'occupation' is a concept which may have different connotations according to the nature and purpose of the property which is claimed to be occupied. It does not necessarily, I think, involve the personal presence of the person claiming to occupy. A caretaker or the representative of a company can occupy, I should have thought, on behalf of his employer. On the other hand, it does, in my judgment, involve some degree of permanence and continuity which would rule out mere fleeting presence.

The last paragraph of this quotation is of central importance, especially the points that actual occupation can be through an agent, and that it involves 'a degree of permanence'. Their Lordships concluded that Mrs Cann was not in actual occupation on 13 August (date of completion).

Does Actual Occupation have to be Continued and Uninterrupted Presence?

The simple answer to this question is 'no'. *Abbey National v Cann* (considered in the previous section) established that there must be 'some degree of permanence and continuity'. The claimant who is temporarily absent will also need to show that there is an intention to return to the property. It is not sufficient to simply argue that the mere presence of furniture in the property can amount to actual occupation (*Strand Securities v Caswell* [1965] Ch 958 at 985). In the case of *Chhokar v Chhokar* [1984] Fam Law 269, the husband was the sole legal owner of the matrimonial home who held the property on trust for both himself and his wife. He sold the property secretly to the purchaser while the wife was in hospital having a baby. When she returned she found that she was locked out of the house. The court held that because the wife's furniture was still in the property on the date of registration, this provided evidence of her continuing occupation and her intention to return to her home. This amounted to actual occupation despite the temporary absence.

A contrasting case is *Stockholm Finance Ltd v Garden Holdings Inc* [1995] NPC 162. The claimant, a Saudi Arabian princess, was absent from her home for a prolonged period, in this case 14 months, but had left belongings in the property. She was held not to be in actual occupation.

Robert Walker J said:

> Whether a person's intermittent presence at a house which is fully furnished, and ready for almost immediate use, should be seen as continuous occupation marked (but not interrupted) by occasional absences, or whether it should be seen as a pattern of alternating periods of presence and absence, is a matter of perception which defies deep analysis. Not only the length of any absence, but also the reason for it, may be material (a holiday or a business trip may be easier to reconcile with continuing and unbroken occupation than a move to a second home, even though the duration of the absence is the same in each case). But there must come a point at which a person's absence from his house is so prolonged that the notion of his continuing to be in actual occupation of it becomes insupportable.

Although, arguably the princess had the requisite intention to return, albeit periodically, as Robert Walker J suggests there comes a point at which the 'absence is so prolonged' that a person can no longer be considered in actual occupation.

The intention to return to the property was highlighted as an important factor for consideration by Mummery LJ in the Court of Appeal in *Link Lending Ltd v Bustard* [2010] 2 P & CR DG15.

Mrs Bustard suffered from a severe psychiatric condition for which she was treated for a number of years, which included receiving in-patient hospital treatment. She was a registered freehold owner of a property but in November 2004 she transferred the property to Mrs Hussain. After this transaction, Mrs Bustard continued to live in the property though on a number of occasions she was admitted into hospital for treatment. In January 2007, Mrs Bustard was sectioned under the Mental Health Act 1983 and was detained at a residential care home.

Mrs Hussain refinanced the property and a legal charge was granted to Link Lending in 2008. No interest payments were made and Link Lending initiated possession proceedings. Although Mrs Bustard was involuntarily detained elsewhere she continued to regularly visit the property and collect the post, and her possessions were still in the property.

The transfer to Mrs Hussain was open to challenge on grounds of undue influence, and an equity therefore arose in favour of Mrs Bustard. The issue before the Court of Appeal focused on whether that equity had established a priority over Link Lending's legal charge, applying Sch 3 para 2.

The court held that Mrs Bustard had an overriding interest. Her personal circumstances were such that although she was involuntarily detained, she had the requisite intention to return to the property despite living elsewhere for a long period of time. This manifested itself through frequent visits to the property and also medical evidence noted that she regularly expressed her wish to return to the property.

Can Children be in Actual Occupation?

The Court of Appeal in *Hypo-Mortgage Services Ltd v Robinson* [1997] 2 FLR 71 considered whether young children could be in actual occupation. Nourse LJ said:

> In *Bird and Another* v *Syme-Thomson and Another* [1979] 1 WLR 440 Templeman J, following *Caunce* v *Caunce and Others* [1969] 1 WLR 286 (a case on unregistered land), held that the spouse of a sole legal owner was not in actual occupation of the matrimonial home within s70(1)(g) ...
>
> Although both those decisions were effectively disapproved so far as spouses are concerned in *Williams & Glyn's Bank Ltd* v *Boland and Another* [1981] AC 487, I regard it as axiomatic that minor children of the legal owner are not in actual occupation within s 70(1)(g). That seems to have been assumed without discussion by Templeman J in *Bird* v *Syme-Thomson* ... The minor children are there because their parent is there. They have no right of occupation of their own. As Templeman J put it, they are only there as shadows of occupation of their parent. Moreover, as Mr Marks submits, it cannot have been intended that s 70(1)(g) should operate as the second defendant suggests. No inquiry can be made of minor children or consent obtained from them in the manner contemplated by that provision, especially when they are, as here, of tender years at the material date.

If, as Mummery LJ suggested in *Link Lending*, the established case law on actual occupation applies equally to Sch 3 para 2, this view that minor children cannot be 'in actual occupation' for the purposes of the old s70(1)(g) is still valid.

Can an Agent or Employee be in Actual Occupation?

Strand Securities v Caswell [1965] Ch 958 is a relatively old case which highlights how quirkish s70(1)(g) LRA 1925 could become. Caswell took a 39-year lease of a London flat. As the lease was for over 21 years, it should have been registered. Caswell did not register the lease. The practical effect of this failure to register the lease was that it took effect only as an equitable lease. The reversion was sold to Strand, who would be bound by Caswell's lease only if it was an overriding interest within s70(1)(g). Caswell did not personally live in the flat, but did drop in for the night from time to time when he was in London. The permanent occupant of the flat was his stepdaughter. He let her live there rent-free, as her marriage had broken down.

Lord Denning MR said:

> ...Even if [Mr Caswell] did not apply in time to register his sublease, he is not necessarily defeated. He may have an 'overriding interest' within s. 70(1)(g). This subsection expressly preserves 'the rights of every person in actual occupation of the land or in receipt of the rents and profits thereof.' [His Lordship stated the facts and continued]: Section 70(1)(g) is an important provision. Fundamentally its object is to protect a person in actual occupation of land from having his rights lost in the welter of registration. He can stay there and do nothing. Yet he will be protected. No one can buy the land over his head and thereby take away or diminish his rights. It is up to every purchaser before he buys to make inquiry on the premises. If he fails to do so, it is at his own risk. He must take subject to whatever rights the occupier may have. Such is the doctrine of *Hunt v Luck* [1902] 1 Ch 428 for unregistered land. Section 70(1)(g) carries the same doctrine forward into registered land but with this difference. Not only is the actual occupier protected, but also the person from whom he holds. It is up to the purchaser to inquire of the occupier, not only about the occupier's own rights, but also about the rights of his immediate superior. The purchaser must ask the occupier: 'To whom do you pay your rent?' And the purchaser must inquire what the rights of that person are. If he fails to do so, it is at his own risk for he takes subject to 'the rights of every person in actual occupation of the land or in receipt of the rents and profits thereof.'
>
> In this case it is clear that the [stepdaughter] was in actual occupation of the flat. The plaintiffs, therefore, took subject to her rights, whatever they were; see *National Provincial Bank Ltd v Hastings Car Mart Ltd* [1964] Ch 665. She was not a tenant but only a licensee...She had no contractual right to stay there. Her licence could be determined at any time and she would have to go in a reasonable time thereafter...So the plaintiffs could get her out, provided always that they could get rid of [Mr Caswell's] sublease.
>
> But although the [stepdaughter] was in actual occupation, it is said that [Mr Caswell] was also in actual occupation. We have had several cases lately in which we have held that 'possession in law is, of course, single and exclusive but occupation may be shared with others or had on behalf of others'...I would like to hold that [Mr Caswell] was sharing the occupation of the flat with [his stepdaughter]. But I cannot bring myself to this conclusion. The truth is that he allowed her to be in actual occupation, and that is all there is to it. She was a licensee rent free and I fear that it does not give him protection. It seems to be a very rare case—a case which the legislature did not think of. For it is quite clear that if the [stepdaughter] had paid a token sum as rent, or for use and occupation, to [Mr Caswell], he would be 'in receipt of the rents and profits' and his rights would be protected under s. 70(1)(g). Again if [Mr Caswell] put his servant or caretaker into the flat, rent free, he would be protected because his agent would have actual occupation on his behalf. It is odd that [Mr Caswell] is not protected simply because he let his stepdaughter in rent free. Odd as it is, however, I fear the words of the statute do not cover this case and [Mr Caswell] does not succeed on this point . . . .

The Court of Appeal held that Caswell was not in actual occupation and therefore he had no overriding interest within s70(1)(g). Later cases, especially *Abbey National v Cann*, underline the correctness of this conclusion. However, two startling points should be noticed:

- if Caswell had charged his stepdaughter a rent (even a nominal rent) he would have been 'in receipt of rents' and therefore would have had an overriding interest under s70(1)(g) LRA 1925;

- alternatively, if he had employed her as his caretaker, he would (as *Cann* confirms) have been through her agency 'in actual occupation' and therefore have an overriding interest under s70(1)(g) LRA 1925.

In summary, the person claiming to be in actual occupation may not necessarily involve their personal presence: a representative of a company, agent, builder or caretaker can occupy a property on behalf of their employer (see *Abbey National BS v Cann* [1991] 1 AC 56, *Lloyds Bank v Rosset* [1991] 1 AC 107).

Can the exercise of an easement amount to actual occupation?

The Court of Appeal in *Chaudhary v Yavuz* [2011] EWCA 1314 held that the use of an easement did not come within the ambit of actual occupation. Lloyd LJ explained:

> There was no indication that it was used otherwise than for passing and repassing between the street and the relevant flat or flats. In my judgment such use does not amount to actual occupation. I dare say that no-one else was in occupation of the metal structure either, but not every piece of land is occupied by someone, let alone in someone's actual occupation (as distinct from possession).
>
> . . .
>
> The first is that the Claimant, having put the metal structure in place, was in occupation of the relevant physical space (i.e. that taken up by the structure) by virtue of the presence of the structure itself. He drew an analogy with a person present on land by chattels which had been placed and left there, such as in *Malory Enterprises Ltd v Cheshire Homes (UK) Ltd* [2002] EWCA Civ 151, [2002] Ch 216 where using the land for storage was seen as relevant (see paragraph 82, [2002] Ch at 237C). He argued that if the presence of movable chattels can constitute actual occupation, so much the more would the presence of a large structure fixed to the land. I disagree. The metal structure became part of the land on any basis, regardless of whether any part of it, as a chattel, belonged (in any sense, for example as regards a right to remove it) to the owner of number 37, as opposed to his neighbour on whose land it was placed. It thus became part of what could be used or occupied. It makes no sense to say that its presence on the land of the Defendant was itself occupation of that land by the person who paid for it to be put up in the first place. Occupation must be, or be referable to, personal physical activity by some one or more individuals: see Lord Wilberforce in *Williams & Glyn's Bank v Boland* [1981] AC 487 at 505B-C—'physical presence, not some entitlement in law'. The only such activity in the present case was that of the Claimant's tenants and their visitors (and of course those of the Defendant) coming to and fro on the staircase and the level area at the top of the stairs. That is use, not occupation.

Lloyd LJ endorses Lord Wilberforce's view of occupation such that it must involve some 'personal physical activity' which is more than simply moving to and fro on a staircase.

Position Where There is a Sub-lease

Under s70(1)(g) LRA 1925 it was clear that if the owner of some property right such as an equitable lease did not occupy the land himself but sub-let that land to a third party, the owner of the property right could still claim the benefit of s70(1)(g) as a person 'in receipt of rents'. So if Caswell had sub-let to his stepdaughter his right would have been within s70(1)(g) LRA 1925. (See the end of the third paragraph of the quotation from Lord Denning in *Caswell*.)

Schedule 3 para 2 LRA 2002 is, by contrast to the old law, confined to the owners of property interests who are in 'actual occupation'. This provision cannot make the property interest overriding of somebody who is merely in receipt of rents.

Does Actual Occupation Apply to the Whole or Part of the Land?

Ferrishurst v Wallcite [1999] 1 All ER 977 pointed out yet another strange quirk of s70(1)(g) LRA 1925. The facts (slightly simplified) were that the plaintiffs had a lease of part of an office block, but the lease included an option to purchase the whole of the block. The Court of Appeal held that if a person had a right relating to the whole of a piece of registered land, then actual occupation of part of the land was sufficient to make the right an overriding interest with respect to the whole of the land.

The wording of Sch 3 para 2 LRA 2002 does not follow the generous interpretation found in *Ferrishurst v Wallcite*. If X has a property interest in the whole of Blackacre, but is in actual occupation of only part of Blackacre, then X's interest will be overriding only in relation to the part of the land X is occupying. The decision in *Ferrishurst v Wallcite* does not apply to the LRA 2002.

thinking point 6.3

In 2012 Stan was the registered (freehold) owner of two adjoining houses, Alpha House and Beta House. He granted an equitable lease of the two houses to Tai Yang. Tai Yang was going abroad, so he sub-let Alpha House to Susan and arranged for his friend Charley to live in Beta House as caretaker. Last month, Stan sold both houses to Reem. Is Reem bound by Tai Yang's equitable lease?

Tai Yang's equitable lease will be overriding with respect to Beta House, but not with respect to Alpha House.

How do you Actually Occupy Derelict Land?

In *Malory Enterprises v Cheshire Homes* [2002] Ch 216 the derelict land was part disused buildings, part open land. The crucial findings of the trial judge are summarized at para 10 of the Court of Appeal judgment. (The land under dispute is referred to as the 'rear land'.)

> Originally there was a concrete panel on the rear boundary and on the east boundary. The west boundary was open and there was no fence between the rear land and the front land on the boundary where they abutted. However, in September 1996 the openings on the west boundary were closed up by a Mr Neil Donald, a joiner [employed by the claimants]. In addition, in August 1996 Mr Donald boarded up the openings on the ground floor of the rear building and put up 'No trespassing' signs. In December 1996 he erected a low fence between the buildings: a post and rail fence with wooden uprights about three feet high. The rear land was, however, subject to vandalism and the wooden fence proved inadequate. Accordingly, in July 1997 Mrs Chang arranged for the erection of a high security steel fence in the gap between the buildings and in front of the low wooden fence. This was almost six feet high and was topped with razor wire. At a later stage, a gate was put into the fence held by a latch on the inside and locked in place by a padlock.

Both the trial judge and Court of Appeal found that the claimants (who had organized all these things) were in actual occupation of the derelict land (both open land and buildings) at the time of the land transfer in January 1999. Arden LJ continued:

> . . . That leaves the question whether the judge's finding that Malory BVI was in 'actual occupation' of the rear land is susceptible to review on appeal. The judge's finding involves questions of primary fact and the application of the correct principles to the facts. What constitutes actual occupation of property depends on the nature and state of the property in question, and the judge adopted that approach. If a site is uninhabitable, as the rear land was, residence is not required, but there must be some physical presence, with some degree of permanence and continuity: cf *Strand Securities Ltd v Caswell* [1965] Ch 958. As Lord Oliver of Aylmerton said in *Abbey National Building Society v Cann* [1991] 1 AC 56, 93:
>
> > It is, perhaps, dangerous to suggest any test for what is essentially a question of fact, for 'occupation' is a concept which may have different connotations according to the nature and purpose of the property which is claimed to be occupied. It does not necessarily, I think, involve the personal presence of the person claiming to occupy.

> A caretaker or the representative of a company can occupy, I should have thought, on behalf of his employer. On the other hand, it does, in my judgment, involve some degree of permanence and continuity which would rule out mere fleeting presence. A prospective tenant or purchaser who is allowed, as a matter of indulgence, to go into property in order to plan decorations or measure for furnishings would not, in ordinary parlance, be said to be occupying it, even though he might be there for hours at a time.
>
> 81 The requisite physical presence must, as it seems to me, in fairness be such as to put a person inspecting the land on notice that there was some person in occupation: see generally per Lord Oliver in *Cann's* case, at p 87. None of the authorities which we have been shown deal with completely derelict land.
>
> 82 For my own part, I am not persuaded by Mr Martin's arguments that the judge directed himself otherwise than in accordance with the principles which must be applied when determining 'actual occupation'. I do not consider that the judge confused actual occupation with possession or occupation of the front land with occupation of the rear land. Nor do I consider that he was wrong in the circumstances to attach significance to the fencing of the rear land. In this particular case, the fencing cannot be regarded as wholly separate from occupation of the rear land. The fencing was one of the factors relevant to be taken into account. The judge was also right in my judgment to attach significance to the access permitted from the front land. Even though there was another gate, the access from the front land supported the notion that some person connected with the front land claimed a right to be on the rear land. On that basis the question of whether applying those principles there was 'actual occupation' was essentially a question of fact for the judge. At the relevant time, there were derelict buildings on the rear land which meant that it was not possible to occupy it by living in those buildings or by cultivating the land or by using the land for recreation. The judge had to consider other acts denoting occupation, such as boarding up the windows of the building and fencing the site (in both cases) to keep vandals and trespassers out, and also using the land for storage. In my judgment, the judge was entitled to draw the conclusion that Malory BVI was in occupation from the facts as found by him and, accordingly, his conclusion cannot be disturbed by this court. Moreover, no one visiting the rear land at the time of the sale to Cheshire could have drawn the conclusion that the land and buildings on the rear land had been abandoned; the evidence of activity on the site clearly indicated that someone claimed to be entitled to be on it.

The court in this case noted that actual occupation is a factual issue which 'depends on the nature and state of the property in question'. In effect the court found that the increasingly strong security measures constituted 'actual occupation' of the derelict land.

At paragraph 81 Arden LJ says that the 'requisite physical presence must...be such as to put a person inspecting the land on notice that there was some person in occupation'. In this context this does not involve the incorporation of the equitable doctrine of notice into the law of registered land. Rather, anticipating Sch 3 para 2, it is pointing to the requirement that occupation needs to be 'obvious on a reasonably careful inspection' under that provision.

Date When There has to be Occupation

cross-reference
See 'The Meaning of Actual Occupation', earlier in this section for the facts of Abbey National Building Society v Cann.

In *Abbey National Building Society v Cann* [1991] 1 AC 56, as well as considering the meaning of actual occupation, what their Lordships had to decide was, on what date a person must be in 'actual occupation' to have an overriding interest under s70(1)(g) LRA 1925 binding upon a purchaser/mortgagee. Was it the date of completion of the sale or mortgage, or was it the (inevitably later) date of registration? Their Lordships held in favour of the 'date of completion'; on the facts of the case, 12.20 p.m. on 13 August. Lord Oliver said:

> In the Court of Appeal Mrs. Cann's claim failed because, in the view of all members of the court, she was aware that the balance of the purchase price of 7, Hillview, over and above the net amount to be produced by the sale of 30, Island Road, was going to be raised by George Cann

by mortgage of the premises. Having thus impliedly authorised him to raise this amount on mortgage she must necessarily have authorised him to that extent to create a charge to the society having priority to her interest and could not, as against the society, complain that George had exceeded a limitation on his authority of which the society was unaware. Dillon L.J., however, took the view that the events which took place between 11.45 a.m. and 12.20 p.m. on 13 August did constitute actual occupation of the property by Mrs. Cann sufficient to enable her to claim an overriding interest, a proposition which was doubted by Ralph Gibson and Woolf L.JJ . . . .

. . . the relevant date for determining the existence of overriding interests which will 'affect the estate transferred or created' is the date of registration. This does, of course, give rise to the theoretical difficulty that since a transferor remains the registered proprietor until registration of the transfer, it would be possible for him, in breach of trust, to create overriding interests, for instance, by grant of an easement or of a lease, which would be binding on the transferee and against which the transferee would not be protected by an official search. That would, of course, equally be the case in a purchase of unregistered land where the purchaser pays the price in advance of receiving a conveyance. I cannot, however, find in the theoretical possibility of so improbable an event a context for preferring the judge's construction.

The question remains, however, whether the date of registration is also the relevant date for determining whether a claimant to a right is in actual occupation. It is to be noted that it is not the actual occupation which gives rise to the right or determines its existence. Actual occupation merely operates as the trigger, as it were, for the treatment of the right, whatever it may be, as an overriding interest. Nor does the additional quality of the right as an overriding interest alter the nature or quality of the right itself. If it is an equitable right it remains an equitable right. As was observed in *Williams & Glyn's Bank Ltd.* v. *Boland* [1981] A.C. 487, 504, the purpose of section 70(1)(g) was to make applicable to registered land the same rule for the protection of persons in actual occupation as had been applied in the case of unregistered land in, for instance, *Hunt v. Luck* [1902] 1 Ch. 428. In relation to legal rights it does nothing, for it is not easy to conceive of a legal right in the land which would not already be an overriding interest under some other head as, for instance, paragraphs (a) or (k). Again, as regards equitable rights in an occupier which arise before completion and are supported by occupation at that date there is no difficulty. A chargee who advances money and so acquires an equitable charge prior to the creation of the occupier's right does not lose his priority because the occupier's right becomes an overriding interest. That interest remains what it always was, an interest subject to the prior equity of the chargee which, on registration, is fortified by the legal estate. Equally, a chargee advancing his money after the creation of the occupier's equitable right is, as one would expect, subject to such right.

The case which does give rise to difficulty if the date of registration is the relevant date for determining whether there is a claimant in actual occupation is one in which the sequence of events is that the right, unaccompanied by occupation, is created before completion and before the chargee has advanced his money and then subsequently the claimant enters into actual occupation after completion and remains in occupation up to the date when the registration of the charge is effected. The chargee in that event would have no possibility of discovering the existence of the claimant's interest before advancing his money and taking his charge, but would nevertheless be subject, on registration, to the claimant's prior equitable interest which, *ex hypothesi*, would not have been subject to the charge at its creation.

This does indeed produce a conveyancing absurdity and there is, as Nicholls L.J. observed [1989] Ch. 350, 374B–C, an internal context for supposing that the legislature, in enacting paragraph (g), must have been contemplating an occupation which preceded and existed at completion of a transfer or disposition. Not only was the paragraph clearly intended to reflect the rule discussed in *Hunt* v. *Luck* with regard to unregistered conveyancing, but the reference to inquiry and failure to disclose cannot make any sense unless it is related to a period in which such inquiry could be other than otiose. That absurdity can, I think, be avoided only by the route which the Court of Appeal adopted and by referring the 'actual occupation' in paragraph (g) to the date of completion of the transaction by transfer and payment of the purchase money...I agree, therefore, with the conclusion of the Court of Appeal in *Rosset* [1989] Ch. 350 that it is at that moment that it falls to be determined whether there is an actual occupation for the purposes of paragraph (g). I do not think that I can improve upon Nicholls L.J.'s analysis when he said, in the course of his judgment in Rosset, at p. 374:

> 'If this is right, the pieces of the jigsaw fit together reasonably well. A purchaser or mortgagee inspects and inquires before completion, in the established fashion. Or he fails to do so, at his own risk. He then completes the transaction, taking an executed transfer or mortgage. Whether or not an overriding interest under paragraph (g) subsists so far as his freehold or mortgage is concerned falls to be determined at that moment. If an overriding interest does subsist, then his estate when registered takes subject to that interest. If it does not, then subsequent entry of a person into occupation before the transfer or mortgage has been registered, and 'completed' for the purposes of section 19, does not have the consequence of creating an overriding interest under paragraph (g) in relation to that freehold or mortgage.' . . .

Following the House of Lords reasoning in *Cann*, both the High Court in *Thompson v Foy* [2010] 1 P & CR 16 and the Court of Appeal in *Link Lending v Bustard* [2010] 2 P & CR DG15 confirmed that the occupier had to be in actual occupation at the date of disposition (ie date of completion). This specific date which applied for the purposes of the old s70(1)(g) LRA 1925 is equally applicable to Sch 3 para 2.

Lewison J in *Thompson v Foy* considered whether actual occupation had to exist both at the time of disposition and at the time of registration. In his view the wording of the statute could potentially suggest that actual occupation needs to exist at both points in time. However, as Lewison J acknowledges, most academic commentators seem to be against this interpretation.

It has also become apparent from *Thompson v Foy* that actual occupation can be brought to an end by the person who was at one stage an actual occupier. Mrs Thompson was in actual occupation at the date of disposition, but decided to move out of the property before the date of registration. She removed her personal belongings from her bedroom and left her furniture giving the appearance of the property being fully furnished. The crucial factor in determining whether Mrs Thompson was in actual occupation was her decision not to return, that is, she no longer had the requisite intention to return to the property, consequently her actual occupation of the property ended before the date of registration.

The Owner of a Property Interest whose Occupation is Not Obvious on Reasonably Careful Inspection

Schedule 3 para 2(c) contains an important limitation on the 'actual occupation' overriding interest. Sub-paragraph (c) excludes from being overriding:

Land Registration Act 2002

Schedule 3 Unregistered interests which override registered dispositions

Interests of persons in actual occupation

2. . . .

(c) an interest—
   (i) which belongs to a person *whose occupation would not have been obvious on a reasonably careful inspection of the land* at the time of the disposition, and
   (ii) of which the person to whom the disposition is made does not have actual knowledge at that time; [Emphasis added]

Thus, the property interest of somebody whose occupation was not obvious on reasonably careful inspection will not be overriding, unless the purchaser of the registered title actually knew of the interest from some other source.

thinking point 6.4

Geraldine bought Grey House in 2010. She has lived there with her semi-literate 'boyfriend' Harold. Harold's one great talent was do-it-yourself. While Geraldine was out at work, Harold totally renovated Grey House, doubling its value. 'Constructive trust interest!' we all shout.

Geraldine recently sold Grey House to Keith. During the period Geraldine was negotiating and completing the sale to Keith, Harold was in hospital for lengthy treatment. Geraldine locked all Harold's belongings away in cupboards. Keith, very reasonably, assumed that Geraldine was the sole occupant of Grey House. Keith knew nothing of Harold, or of his constructive trust interest. Does Harold have an overriding interest binding on Keith?

The answer to this question is clear-cut. Harold's occupation was not obvious on reasonably careful inspection, so Harold does not have an overriding interest.

REVIEW QUESTION You have a constructive trust interest in Greenacre, and you do make use of Greenacre. Bearing in mind that the only entry you can make on the register is a 'restriction', how can you make reasonably sure that your interest will bind a purchaser (or mortgagee)?

Remember that 'Greenacre' might be:

- a house;
- a garden;
- offices;
- a factory; or
- any other type of land you can think of.

(Consider carefully Sch 3 para 2 LRA 2002.)

6.5.5 The Doctrine of Notice not Applicable to Registered Land

In *Williams and Glyn's Bank Ltd v Boland* Lord Wilberforce explained that actual occupation was a question of fact. In our discussion of this case we highlighted that this meant that a purchaser is automatically bound by the interests of the person who is in actual occupation. This would suggest that a physical presence by the person claiming the interest constitutes sufficient action to bind the purchaser. In *Strand Securities v Caswell* Lord Denning MR supported the passive nature of actual occupation when he stated that the person claiming the right of actual occupation can 'simply stay there and do nothing'.

An alternative analysis of when actual occupation will be present has been put forward by commentators such as Gravells (2010, at pp 212–213) and Hayton (1981, at p 87). This interpretation depends upon whether occupation could have been discovered through reasonable enquiries and inspections by the purchaser. The difference with this understanding, from that seen in *Boland*, is that the focus lies in the *discoverability* of occupation which places a positive burden upon the purchaser. The discovery of occupation through reasonable enquiries and inspections has been used in the Court of Appeal in *Lloyds Bank v Rosset* and *Abbey National v Cann*. The use of discoverability of occupation by the Court of Appeal would appear to overlap with the obligations a purchaser must satisfy when discharging the requirements of the doctrine of notice when title is unregistered.

Schedule 3 para 2 LRA 2002 places a positive obligation on the purchaser to make a 'reasonably careful inspection of the land' to discover actual occupation. While this will inevitably require the purchaser to make enquiries of persons present in the property, the policy behind Sch 3 para 2 is not to introduce the doctrine of notice to registered land.

Consider the wording of Sch 3 para 2 again:

Land Registration Act 2002

Schedule 3 Unregistered interests which override registered dispositions

Interests of persons in actual occupation

2. An interest belonging at the time of the disposition to a person in actual occupation, so far as relating to land of which he is in actual occupation, except for—

...

    (b) an interest of a person of whom inquiry was made before the disposition and who failed to disclose the right when he could reasonably have been expected to do so;

    (c) an interest—

        (i) which belongs to a person whose occupation would not have been obvious on a reasonably careful inspection of the land at the time of the disposition, and

        (ii) of which the person to whom the disposition is made does not have actual knowledge at that time;

The Law Commission in its report considering proposals for reforming the LRA 1925 was of the view that the doctrine of notice had no place in registered land (Law Commission, *Land Registration for the 21st Century: A Consultative Document* (Report No 254, 1988) at paras 3.44–3.47:

...we are concerned to emphasise what is generally assumed to be the case, namely that issues of good faith and notice are, subject to certain statutory exceptions, irrelevant in relation to registered land. The point is not wholly free from doubt because of the attempt to import doctrines of good faith and notice into registered conveyancing by the much-criticised decision in *Peffer v Rigg*. In that case, Graham J, applying the definition of 'purchaser' that is presently found in the Land Registration Act 1925, held that a purchaser could not be in good faith if he had notice of something which affected his title. It is generally assumed that this reasoning cannot be supported and our new definition of purchaser should preclude any possible repetition of it. However, we consider that the matter should be placed beyond doubt by a statement in the Act of the general principle that the doctrine of notice should have no application in dealings with registered land except where the Act expressly provides to the contrary.

...we have concluded—as the Law Commission has done on two previous occasions—that there should in general be no place for concepts of knowledge or notice in registered land. We have reached this conclusion for the following reasons—

(1) It was intended that the system of registration under the Land Registration Act 1925 should displace the doctrine of notice.

(2) There is little evidence of which we are aware that the absence of the doctrine of notice in dealings with registered land has been a cause of injustice in the seventy-two years in which the present system has been operative.

(3) The ethical argument is weaker than at first sight it appears to be if the issue is considered in relation to those principles which should in our view, guide the development of land registration. Registration should be regarded as an integral part of the process of creating or transferring interests in registered land, closely akin to the formal requirement of using a deed (or in some cases, writing) in unregistered conveyancing. Just as a deed is required to convey or create a legal estate or interest in unregistered conveyancing, a disposition of registered land must be completed by registration if it is to confer a legal estate or interest . . .

(4) In practice, if it were provided that unregistered rights in or over registered land were binding because a purchaser had *actual* knowledge of them, it would be very difficult to prevent the introduction by judicial interpretation of doctrines of *constructive* notice. If actual knowledge sufficed, the question would inevitably be asked: why not wilful blindness as well? In reality the boundary between actual knowledge and constructive notice is unclear and is, in our view, incapable of precise definition.

(5) The mere fact that a purchaser *could* be bound if he or she had actual knowledge of an unregistered right or interest would inevitably weaken the security of title that registered land at present provides . . .

We do however acknowledge that there is a need for some form of 'safety valve' in the registration system, for cases where parties cannot reasonably be expected to register their rights. This requirement is substantially met by the category of overriding interests . . .

Although the Law Commission wanted the LRA 2002 to categorically state that the doctrine of notice does not apply, no such statement can actually be found in the 2002 Act. At first glance Sch 3 para 2(c) appears to introduce the doctrine of notice by requiring a reasonably careful inspection or actual knowledge. This first impression would not be correct. The Law Commission clarified the origin of these requirements. These were not drawn from notice-based principles of priority applicable to unregistered land. These were, instead, derived by analogy from the rule of conveyancing law that a seller of land must disclose to the buyer prior to contract any irremovable latent incumbrances of which the buyer does not have actual knowledge (see Law Commission, *Land Registration for the 21st Century: A Conveyancing Revolution* (Report No 271, 2001) para 5.21.

The purpose of Sch 3 para 2 is to strike a fair balance between the requirement that a purchaser makes all appropriate enquiries to discover actual occupation with the obligation of the person in actual occupation to disclose any interest they may have. Consequently, it would appear that under Sch 3 para 2 the person who is in actual occupation can no longer remain a passive bystander.

When is it Reasonable to Expect that an Interest will be Revealed?

Under the old law (s70(1)(g) LRA 1925) an interest lost its overriding status—'where enquiry is made of such person [in actual occupation] and the rights are not disclosed'. For example, if:

- Charlie occupied Blackacre in which he had a property interest; and
- enquiry was made of Charlie about his interest; and
- Charlie did not reveal his interest;

the non-revelation automatically meant that Charlie's property right forfeited its overriding status. Contrast this very blunt old wording with para 2(b), which excludes from being overriding:

an interest of a person of whom inquiry was made before the disposition and who failed to disclose the right *when he could reasonably have been expected to do so*; [Emphasis added]

Under the LRA 2002, Charlie's property right will only forfeit overriding status if Charlie could reasonably have been expected to reveal his right. This approach envisages that there will be situations where it is not reasonable to expect someone to respond to an enquiry by revealing their right. Sub-paragraph (b) is likely to generate litigation.

thinking point 6.5

Mikaela bought Hathaway Court in 2010. She has lived there with her semi-literate partner Simon. Simon's one great talent was do-it-yourself. While Mikaela was out at work, Simon totally renovated Hathaway Court, doubling its value. 'Constructive trust interest!' we all shout.

Mikaela recently sold Hathaway Court to Khalid. When Khalid visited the house, he saw Simon, and Khalid asked Simon (both orally and in writing) 'Do you claim any share, interest or property right in this house?' Simon did not reply as he did not understand the question. Has Simon's constructive trust interest lost its overriding status?

Some readers may argue that 'It was not reasonable to expect Simon to reveal his interest'. Others, who think that purchasers like Khalid should be protected if they make proper enquiries will say, 'Simon's lack of education should be irrelevant. The reasonable partner would have answered Khalid's enquiry.'

At least, if the first interpretation of sub-para (b) is adopted, then this does potentially have the effect of actually increasing the number of overriding interests, and thus increasing the hazards for some purchasers of registered land. However, in some respects Sch 3 para 2 LRA 2002 is narrower in scope than its predecessor s70(1)(g) LRA 1925.

REVIEW QUESTION The large number of 'overriding interests' undermines the 'mirror principle'. Explain.

(Refer back to 5.1.1 and 6.5.)

Can an Overriding Interest be Overreached?

We have noted previously that following *Williams and Glyn's Bank Ltd v Boland* the effect of an overriding interest is that the purchaser takes the property subject to the interest. The bank paid the sole trustee of the property (Mr Boland) the mortgage money and overreaching would not have arisen.

In Chapter 4 we outlined the facts of *City of London Building Society v Flegg* [1988] 1 AC 54. In this case, Mr and Mrs Flegg both contributed to the purchase of a house; the title to the house was registered in the names of their daughter and son-in-law (the Maxwell-Browns). The Fleggs, as a consequence of their contributions, each had an interest as a tenant in common under a constructive trust. All four lived in the house, and were therefore in 'actual occupation'. The house was subsequently mortgaged to the building society.

The Court of Appeal had held that the mortgage did not overreach the rights of Mr and Mrs Flegg. It ruled that the decision in *Boland* meant that the Fleggs each had an overriding interest under s70(1)(g) LRA 1925 which could not be overreached even by a disposition made by two or more trustees.

cross-reference
For further discussion on Flegg see 4.8.1 and 9.2.2.

The House of Lords in *Flegg* unanimously overruled the Court of Appeal. The ruling in *Boland* that a non-trustee co-owner had an overriding interest if she/he was in actual occupation did not mean that such an interest could not be overreached by a disposition made by two or more trustees. It was an inherent characteristic of an interest under a trust for sale that it could be overreached by a disposition made by two trustees. The building society successfully argued (in the House of Lords) that the mortgage, being executed by two trustees, overreached the rights of Mr and Mrs Flegg. They could thus sell the house 'over the heads' of the Fleggs.

Concluding Remarks

When you read the Introduction to this chapter, you may well have thought, 'This is going to be easy. I learn the list of overriding interests; every right not on that list is a minor interest which you enter on the register much as you enter a land charge on the computer at Plymouth if the title to the land is unregistered.'

You now see that matters are not nearly as straightforward as that. In particular s70(1)(g) LRA 1925 created enormous problems (three House of Lords cases in the period 1978 to 1991) which have not been solved by Sch 3 para 2 LRA 2002.

The LRA 2002 does simplify matters by abolishing cautions and allowing notices and restrictions to be entered without the consent of the registered proprietor. But the 'rights of a person in actual occupation' problem has been made worse. The Society of Legal Scholars (the professional association for University Law Lecturers) recommended to the Law Commission that s70(1)(g) should be abolished without replacement. Instead, the devil we lecturers knew (and understood) has been replaced by an even worse devil, Sch 3 para 2.

# Summary

Interests Subject to an Entry on the Register (Minor Interests)

Notice

The following rights are interests subject to an entry on the register (ie minor interests) which should be protected by entry of a 'notice' on the register (s32(1) LRA 2002):

- equitable lease due to a lack of formalities, for example contract in writing;
- equitable lease due to a failure to substantively register the lease;
- equitable lease created out of an equitable estate;
- estate contracts;
- options to purchase;
- proprietary estoppel (licences by estoppel);
- equitable easements and profits à prendre;
- freehold restrictive covenants;
- rights of occupation for spouses or civil partners (home rights); and
- equitable mortgages.

Restriction

The following rights are minor interests which should be protected by an entry of a 'restriction' on the register (s40 LRA 2002):

- equitable interests arising under a strict settlement;
- equitable interests under a trust for sale;
- equitable interests under a trust of land; and
- constructive trust interests.

But with the exception of equitable interests under a strict settlement, all these interests could be 'upgraded' to overriding by operation of Sch 3 para 2 LRA 2002.

Overriding Interests

Under the LRA 2002, the following are (normally) overriding interests automatically binding on purchasers:

- easements and profits already existing on 12 October 2003;

- easements and profits created after 12 October 2003 by implied grant or by prescription;

- legal leases for a duration of not more than seven years (Sch 3 para 1 LRA 2002);

- local land charges; and

- property rights which are 'upgraded' by the operation of Sch 3 para 2 LRA 2002 (applies where title is registered).

The Operation of Sch 3 para 2 LRA 2002

First remember that home rights and interests under a strict settlement cannot be upgraded by the operation of this provision. All other property rights may be 'upgraded' by this provision. If you are considering whether somebody ('the claimant') has an overriding interest within Sch 3 para 2 LRA 2002, go through the multi-stage process in Diagram 6.1.

Diagram 6.1
Sch 3 para 2 LRA 2002—the multi-stage process

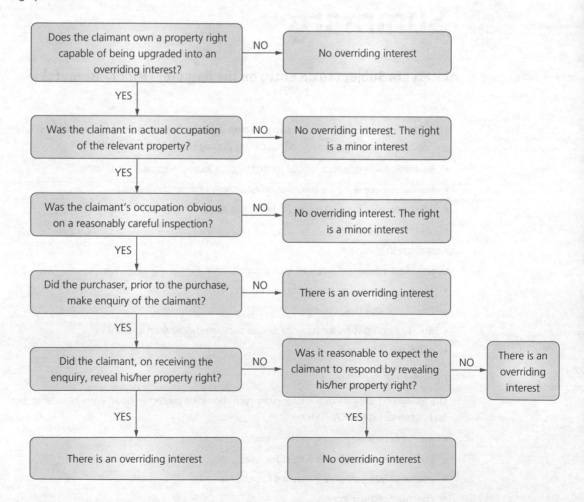

# Further Reading

Bogusz, B, 'Defining the scope of actual occupation under the Land Registration Act 2002: some recent judicial clarification' [2011] Conv 268
Considers judicial developments in the assessment of the factual matrix in actual occupation.

Cooke, E, *The New Law of Land Registration*, Oxford: Hart, 2003
A highly critical and stimulating analysis of the LRA 2002. See especially Chapter 5 which deals with overriding interests and related matters, and Chapter 9, which looks at foreign systems of land registration.

Dixon, M, 'The reform of property law and the Land Registration Act 2002: a risk assessment' [2003] Conv 136
Examines the changes introduced by the LRA 2002, useful discussion on overriding interests.

Dixon, M, 'Priorities under the Land Registration Act 2002' [2009] 125 LQR 401
Examines the rules of priority, ss28 and 29 LRA 2002, as applied by the court in *Halifax Plc v Curry Popeck* [2008] EWHC 1692.

Editor's note [2009] Conv 285
Discusses the High Court decision in *Thompson v Foy* [2010] EWHC 1076.

Gardner, S, *An Introduction to Land Law*, Oxford: Hart, 2007
A critical evaluation of the registered land regime, see pp 39–48.

Kenny, P, 'Children are spare ribs' [1997] Conv 84
A critical article on *Hypo-Mortgage Services v Robinson*.

Law Commission, *Land Registration for the Twenty-First Century* (Report No 271, 2001)
See in particular: Part IX on the operation of the register itself; Part VIII on overriding interests; Part VI on notices and restrictions.

McFarlane, B, 'Eastenders, Neighbours and Upstairs, Downstairs: *Chaudhary v Yavuz*' [2013] 1 Conv 74.
A case note on *Chaudhary v Yavuz* examining the impact on potentially wider interpretations of the overriding interest provisions under the LRA 2002.

References

Gravells, N, *Land Law: Text and Materials*, 4th edn, London: Sweet & Maxwell, 2010
Hayton, DJ, *Registered Land*, 2nd edn, London: Sweet & Maxwell, 1981

? Question

'Brecklands' is a detached house with garden situated in Derby. It has been registered title since 1989. Seema purchased Brecklands in November 2013, and became registered proprietor. In December 2013, she signed an agreement (not in the form of a deed) with her neighbour Ursula, allowing Ursula and her family to use the inside toilet in Brecklands. Ursula pays £10 per month for this right. In practice this right is 'exercised' about twice a day.

In February 2014, Seema signed another agreement (not in the form of a deed) with Ursula, under which she leased a part of Brecklands' garden to Ursula for six years. The agreement also granted to Ursula an option to purchase the whole of the garden for £12,000.

In April 2014, Seema married Pritesh, who moved into Brecklands. Pritesh had no income of his own, but he looked after the house, cooked the meals, and did very small do-it-yourself jobs.

In July 2014, Seema left Pritesh to go and live with Harun. Last week she sold Brecklands to Ahmed. Ahmed bought the property without taking any professional advice, and did not even visit the property. On arriving at Brecklands Ahmed finds Pritesh still living in the house, and refusing to move out. He also found Ursula digging the garden, and insisting that she has a right to use the toilet. Moreover, Ursula announces her intention of exercising the option to buy the whole of the garden.

Advise Ahmed.

Part 4

Acquisition of Interests in Land (I)

Trusts of Land

Introduction

In this chapter we first consider those aspects of the pre-1997 law relating to trusts of land which will aid your understanding of the modern law. We will explain the three types of express trusts which existed prior to the commencement of the Trusts of Land and Appointment of Trustees Act 1996 (TOLATA 1996). We set out the characteristics of each of the three 'old-style' trusts and discuss the problems associated with each of them.

We then turn to the modern post-1996 law. We endeavour to identify all those trusts and other dispositions which are caught by TOLATA 1996. We next consider certain basic principles regarding the appointment, retirement, and removal of trustees, and we follow that with an in-depth examination of the powers of trustees. There is, however, one important exception from this otherwise comprehensive coverage. This chapter does not consider co-ownership, which will be dealt with in Chapters 8 and 9.

pause for thought

Consider the following while reading this and ensuing chapters. Why do people create trusts of land?

7.1 The Three Types of Trust Under the Old Law

bare trust

a trust where there is only one beneficiary and he/she is of full age. The trustee is only under the obligation to hold the property on trust for that beneficiary.

Under the old law which operated prior to the commencement of the TOLATA 1996 there were three types of ('old-style') trusts which could exist: bare trust; strict settlement; and trust for sale.

7.1.1 The Bare Trust

In practice, such a trust of land is fairly rare. A **bare trust** exists where there is a trust, but there is only one beneficiary, and that beneficiary is of full age. For example, Blackacre is conveyed to Tim and Tom as trustees for Alain in (equitable) fee simple.

One special use of bare trusts—'purchase in the name of a nominee'—should be noted.

thinking point 7.1

Suppose Jack Bloggs is intending to buy a lot of land in Muddletown. He wants to conceal this fact, perhaps to avoid sending prices up when existing owners discover that there is somebody very keen to own property in the town. Consider how he goes about his plan of concealment, and how the 'bare trust' concept will assist him.

He employs a whole series of agents to act on his behalf. For example, with money provided by Jack, Akio buys Deene House, Bianca buys Lakeside Farm, Cian buys Olde Factory, and so on. By private arrangements known only to the trustee and beneficiary, Akio will hold Deene House on bare trust for Jack, Bianca will hold Lakeside Farm on bare trust for Jack, and Cian will hold Olde Factory on bare trust for Jack.

7.1.2 The Strict Settlement

strict settlement
this arose where the settlor wanted the land to be retained and enjoyed by successive beneficiaries.

Where there is a **strict settlement** the settlor envisages that the land will be retained and enjoyed as such by successive beneficiaries. The settlor wants the land to be kept, not to be sold. Such strict settlements were very common until about 1900, but nowadays are very rare.

For example, Fargate (a large country estate) was granted (prior to 1997), 'to X for life, remainder to Y in fee tail, remainder to Z in fee simple'.

Since 1925 all strict settlements must involve a succession of equitable interests and must involve a trust. (This is a consequence, of course, of s1 Law of Property Act 1925 (LPA 1925).) The Settled Land Act 1925 (SLA 1925) requires that the legal title to the land be held not by independent trustees but by the life tenant, acting as a trustee for himself/herself and the other beneficiaries. Thus in the Fargate example, X holds the legal fee simple in Fargate in trust for X, Y, and Z. To create a strict settlement a vesting deed and a trust instrument must be executed. The vesting deed provides information on who holds the legal title; in our example X the life tenant would hold the legal title. Details of the beneficial interests held by X, Y, and Z would be found in the trust instrument.

7.1.3 The Trust for Sale

trust for sale
this arises where the land is conveyed to trustees who are placed under a duty to sell the land.

The essence of a **trust for sale** is that land is conveyed to trustees who are placed under a 'duty' to sell the land. (If land was prior to 1997 conveyed to trustees who were given merely a power to sell the land, then a (highly irregular) strict settlement was created.)

For example, Pine House is conveyed to Tadeo and Tomasz as trustees for sale to sell Pine House and hold the proceeds in trust for Ella for life, remainder to her children in equal shares.

Where there is a trust for sale, the trustees have a power to postpone sale. In practice, this power to postpone sale is extremely important. If the power to postpone is exercised (and this often does happen) the beneficiaries (in the example, Ella, and after her death, her children) get the income or other benefits from the unsold land.

7.2 Criticism of the Old Law Governing Bare Trusts of Land

cross-reference
See 4.8 to 4.8.2 for a discussion on overreaching.

Where there is a trust for sale or strict settlement, the equitable interests of the beneficiaries are overreached on a sale or other disposition of the land, provided any 'capital money' (eg the price paid by the purchaser) is paid to at least two trustees.

Under the 'old' law operating prior to 1997, an equitable fee simple under a bare trust of land could not be overreached; if the land was unregistered the equitable fee simple was subject to the doctrine of notice.

Criticisms of Strict Settlements and the Settled Land Act 1925

7.3.1 An Anomalous Form of Trust

With every other type of trust, ancient or modern, the trustees hold the legal title to the trust property—the trustees are 'boss'. With a strict settlement, there is a big anomaly—the life tenant is 'boss'. In the Fargate example at 7.1.2, X, the life tenant, holds the legal title, and he decides whether the land should be sold, leased, etc.

With a strict settlement, there are independent 'trustees for the purposes of the Settled Land Act'. However, they have only limited functions. In particular, any 'capital money' arising on a sale or lease is paid to the SLA trustees, not to the life tenant. But the SLA trustees have no say in whether the land should be sold, leased, etc.

7.3.2 Limited Powers of Disposition of Life Tenants

The SLA 1925 gives the life tenant unlimited power to sell the land (s39 SLA 1925), but some of the other powers of the life tenant are limited by antiquated restrictions. For example, the life tenant cannot normally lease the land for more than 50 years (s41 SLA 1925). Nor can he grant options where the price on exercise of the option is to be fixed by an arbitrator, even though this is the only type of option which makes sense in modern economic conditions.

7.3.3 Complex Documentation

There had to be at least two documents to create a fully effective strict settlement: the 'vesting deed' transferring the legal estate to the life tenant, and the 'trust instrument' setting out the details of the equitable interests under the settlement. Mistakes were often made with the documentation. The situation when one life tenant died and was succeeded by another life tenant was particularly complex.

REVIEW QUESTION Back in 1965 Amandeep was a successful businessman who had invested most of his wealth in land. He was diagnosed as terminally ill. He decided to leave all his wealth to his wife and young children. On the advice of his solicitor, he executed a will creating a trust for sale of his land. Why do you think the solicitor advised a trust for sale of his land, not a strict settlement?

(Consider the differences between the two types of trusts.)

7.3.4 Accidental Strict Settlements

Modern competent lawyers never created strict settlements. But they could arise by accident.

Home-Made Wills

The testator said something like, 'I leave my house to my wife Betty for the rest of her life, and after her death it is to go to our daughter Andrea.' This created a strict settlement, with Betty as life tenant. (A testator who was properly advised would never create a strict settlement. Rather he would create a trust for sale similar to the one we will be setting out in thinking point 7.3.)

Conveying Land Subject to a Right to Reside

The problem here is slightly like that just discussed in that an accidental strict settlement may arise where a landowner has had poor (or no) legal advice. A landowner executes a deed taking effect immediately saying 'I convey my house, Greentrees, to Alicia on condition that Alicia allows Beate to live there for the rest of Beate's life.' Alicia is intended to be the outright owner of Greentrees, but is expected to allow Beate to live there for the rest of Beate's life. The leading case on this type of disposition is *Binions v Evans* [1972] 1 Ch 359.

In *Binions v Evans*, the trustees of the Tredegar Estate owned a cottage in which there resided rent-free Mrs Evans, the widow of an employee of the estate. The trustees sold the cottage to Binions, expressly on the condition that Mrs Evans should be allowed to live there for the rest of her life. Binions paid a reduced price because of this condition. Binions nevertheless tried to evict Mrs Evans; he claimed that she had no proprietary interest in the land. Not surprisingly, Binions found no sympathy in the Court of Appeal. The majority of the Court of Appeal (Megaw and John Stephenson LJJ) held that the conveyance to Binions created a life interest in favour of Mrs Evans. Therefore the land was 'settled land' within the meaning of the 1925 Act.

Megaw LJ said:

> …What was the effect in law of that agreement, as between the trustees and the defendant? In my view, Judge Bulger was right in holding that the effect was the same as the effect of the agreement considered by this court in *Bannister v Bannister* [1948] 2 All ER 133. In that case the defendant had orally agreed to sell two cottages to her brother-in-law, the plaintiff, in reliance on his statement: 'I do not want to take any rent, but will let you stay' in one of the cottages 'as long as you like rent free.' Troubles arose between the parties a few years later and the plaintiff sought to turn the defendant out, claiming that she was a mere tenant at will. The court (Scott LJ, Asquith LJ and Jenkins J) held, at p. 137:
>
> > '…the plaintiff holds no. 30 in trust during the life of the defendant to permit the defendant to occupy the same for so long as she may desire to do so and subject thereto in trust for the plaintiff. A trust in this form has the effect of making the beneficiary a tenant for life within the meaning of the Settled Land Act 1925, and, consequently, there is very little practical difference between such a trust and a trust for life simpliciter.'
>
> As was said by the court, at p. 136:
>
> > 'Similar words in deeds and wills have frequently been held to create a life interest determinable (apart from the special considerations introduced by the Settled Land Act 1925) on the beneficiary ceasing to occupy the premises:…'
>
> I confess that I have had difficulty in seeing precisely how the Settled Land Act of 1925 was applicable. But the court in *Bannister v Bannister* [1948] 2 All ER 133 so held, and I am certainly content, and we are probably bound, to follow that authority. I see no relevant distinction. The fact that the transaction—the creation of the trust—was there effected orally, whereas here there is an agreement in writing, surely cannot be a ground for saying that the principle is not here applicable. The fact that there is here express provision for determination by the beneficiary cannot provide a relevant distinction. The defendant in *Bannister v Bannister* [1948] 2 All ER 133 was free to give up occupation whenever she wished. The fact and nature of the obligations imposed upon the defendant by the agreement in the present case must tend in favour of, rather than adversely to, the creation of an interest in land, as compared with *Bannister's* case.
>
> I realise that the application of the Settled Land Act 1925 may produce some odd consequences; but no odder than those which were inherent in the decision in *Bannister v Bannister* [1948] 2 All ER 133. I do not find anything in the possible, theoretical, consequences to lead me to the conclusion that *Bannister's* case should not be followed.

> The plaintiffs took with express notice of the agreement which constitutes, or gives rise to, the trust. They cannot turn the defendant out of the house against her will; for that would be a breach of the trust which binds them . . .

As Megaw LJ says, the application of the SLA 1925 to the situation in *Binions v Evans* has some 'odd consequences'. In particular, Mrs Evans was a 'life tenant' and was entitled to have the freehold in the house transferred to her by **vesting deed**.

vesting deed
where land is 'settled land', the deed which vests the legal ownership of the land in the life tenant on trust for the beneficiaries under the strict settlement.

The majority view in *Binions v Evans* was applied in the case of *Ungurian v Lesnoff* [1990] Ch 206. In this case Mrs Lesnoff gave up her Polish nationality, secure home, and academic career, in order to take up residence with Mr Ungurian in Muswell Hill, London. They lived at 136 Muswell Hill Road as *de facto* husband and wife. Mrs Lesnoff made substantial improvements to the premises throughout the four years of their relationship and she remained in the premises after their separation. The home was registered in Mr Ungurian's sole name. He brought an action to recover possession of the premises.

Vinelott J found as a fact that this money was spent on the understanding that Mrs Lesnoff should be able to occupy the house for the rest of her life. The judge therefore held that Mrs Lesnoff had a life interest in the house (rather than a constructive trust share in the house) and that meant the house was settled land and Mrs Lesnoff was the life tenant of the strict settlement. The judge ordered a vesting deed to be executed transferring to her the legal freehold estate in trust for herself for life, remainder to Ungurian in fee simple.

Trusts with a Power to Sell the Land

Consider the following example:, Hillside House is conveyed to Tirath and Tajinder as trustees to hold the land in trust for Amrita for life, remainder to her son Vikram in fee simple. The trustees are given a power to sell the land, but are not placed under any duty to sell the land.

Under the 'old' law this disposition created a strict settlement. Amrita was the life tenant and was responsible for holding the legal estate and had the power to dispose of the land. That was not what the settlor intended.

Conveying Land to a Minor

A minor (ie a person under 18 years of age, formerly 21) cannot own a legal estate in land (s1(6) LPA 1925). Any attempt to grant a minor a legal estate is not, however, totally void. The minor will acquire an equitable interest equivalent to the legal estate intended to be granted. Thus, if Jamie conveys the fee simple in Vineyard House to his son Oscar, aged fifteen, Oscar acquires only an equitable fee simple. The legal fee simple remains with Jamie (see s19(1) LPA 1925 now replaced by Sch 1 para 1(3) TOLATA 1996).

Section 27(i) SLA 1925 provided that where there was an attempt to grant a minor a legal estate, the land was settled land, and thus governed by the complex provisions of the Act.

Criticisms of the Trust for Sale

7.4.1 The Artificial Nature of the *Duty* to Sell

For reasons which will become more apparent when we consider the law of co-ownership, there have been literally millions of trusts for sale of land created since 1925.

In all these trusts the trustees were under a notional duty to sell the land. In the vast majority of cases, trustees for sale exercised their power to postpone sale, and went on postponing sale for an indefinite period. Thus legal theory was out of touch with practical reality.

Prior to 1997 the power to postpone sale was given to trustees for sale by s25 LPA 1925.

> *Law of Property Act 1925*
>
> 25. Power to postpone sale
>
> (1) A power to postpone sale shall, in the case of every trust for sale of land, be implied unless a contrary intention appears.
>
> (2) Where there is a power to postpone the sale, then (subject to any express direction to the contrary in the instrument, if any, creating the trust for sale) the trustees for sale shall not be liable in any way for postponing the sale, in the exercise of their discretion, for any indefinite period; nor shall a purchaser of a legal estate be concerned in any case with any direction respecting the postponement of a sale.
>
> (3) The foregoing provisions of this section apply whether the trust for sale is created before or after the commencement or by virtue of this Act.
>
> (4) Where a disposition or settlement coming into operation after the commencement of this Act contains a trust either to retain or sell land the same shall be construed as a trust to sell the land with power to postpone the sale.

Section 25 has now been repealed, and replaced by the much more straightforward s4 TOLATA 1996, discussed later in this chapter.

7.4.2 The Archaic Doctrine of 'Conversion'

The Court of Chancery applied its maxim 'equity looks on as done that which ought to be done' to trusts for sale of land, and reasoned that 'the trustees should be deemed to have sold the land the moment the trust is set up'. The equitable interests of the beneficiaries of a trust for sale of land were personal property not real property. They were interests in money, not in land.

thinking point 7.2

In a case which arose shortly after 1925, a solicitor was the owner of an absolute ('fee simple') interest under a trust for sale of a piece of freehold land, that is, he was a beneficiary of the trust for sale. He made his own will, which in effect said, 'I leave my real estate to X and my personal property to Y.' Who received the interest under the trust for sale?

The answer is that Y was held entitled to the interest under the trust for sale.

The doctrine of conversion has been abolished (s3 TOLATA 1996).

7.4.3 Doubts as to Whether Beneficiaries Have a Right to Occupy the Land

This difficulty also stemmed from the doctrine of conversion. Traditionalist lawyers argued that the interests of beneficiaries under a trust for sale of land are interests in money not interests in land. So the beneficiaries had no right to occupy the trust land.

This argument was firmly rejected by the Court of Appeal in *Bull v Bull* [1955] 1 All ER 253. In that case S owned the legal title to the house in which S resided with his wife 'W', and his mother-in-law 'M'. M had paid 50 per cent of the cost of acquiring the house. It therefore followed (for reasons dealt with in Chapter 8) that S held the house on trust for sale for S and M in equal shares.

M and W fell out, and S took proceedings to evict M from the house. S argued that M's interest was only an interest in money, and gave her no right to live in the house. This argument was firmly rejected by the Court of Appeal (led by Denning LJ). The court held that where land subject to a trust for sale has in fact been acquired for personal occupation by the beneficiaries, then the beneficiaries do indeed have the right to occupy the land. This decision of Denning LJ in *Bull v Bull* gained almost universal support from his colleagues. The House of Lords in *Boland* expressly approved *Bull v Bull*.

7.4.4 Limited Powers of Trustees for Sale

Unless the trust provided otherwise, trustees for sale had the same limited and outdated powers of disposition as life tenants, for example they could not lease the land for more than 50 years.

cross-reference
See 7.10 for a discussion of s6 TOLATA 1996.

> *Law of Property Act 1925*
>
> 28. Powers of management, etc. conferred on trustees for sale
>
> (1) Trustees for sale shall, in relation to land or to manorial incidents and to the proceeds of sale, have all the powers of a tenant for life and the trustees of a settlement under the Settled Land Act 1925 including in relation to the land the powers of management conferred by that Act during a minority: and where by statute settled land is or becomes vested in the trustees of the settlement upon the statutory trusts, such trustees and their successors in office shall also have all the additional or larger powers (if any) conferred by the settlement on the tenant for life, statutory owner, or trustees of the settlement, and (subject to any express trust to the contrary) all capital money arising under the said powers shall, unless paid or applied for any purpose authorised by the Settled Land Act 1925 be applicable in the same manner as if the money represented proceeds of sale arising under the trust for sale.

You should compare s28 to the much simpler s6 TOLATA 1996. Section 28 has, of course, been repealed.

7.4.5 The Anomalous Concept of a Trust for Sale Subject to Consents

Under the old pre-1997 law, land could be conveyed to trustees for sale, but subject to a clause that the consent of named person(s) be obtained to the sale.

For example, land was conveyed, 'to Tobin and Tabor on trust for sale for X for life, remainder to Y. The sale shall only take place if W and X agree to it.' This was a valid trust for sale, even though Tobin and Tabor could not carry out their 'duty' to sell unless W and X agreed.

Although a trust for sale subject to consent was a paradoxical concept, much use has been made of such trusts.

thinking point 7.3

Assume that the TOLATA 1996 was never enacted. Luke owns a large house. He has a wife, Amelia, and a son Jake. Luke is in poor health, and wishes to make a will under which Amelia would have the right to occupy the house for the rest of her lifetime, but without any power to sell or lease the house. On Amelia's death the house would pass to Jake absolutely.

Why is it that Luke would be advised to create, not a strict settlement, but a trust for sale and what sort of provisions would that trust contain?

There are two reasons why Luke would not create a strict settlement. First, we would not want his family to get entangled in the highly complex law of strict settlements. Secondly, if a strict settlement were created, Amelia would be life tenant, and she would have a power to sell the house which could not be taken away from her.

Luke would create a trust for sale and appoint as trustees people who are sympathetic to his wishes; he would also include clauses:

- requiring that any sale be with the consent of both Amelia and Jake; and
- requiring the trustees to permit Amelia to live in the house pending sale.

In setting up the trust for sale, Luke's legal advisers would have also taken into account s26 LPA 1925.

Law of Property Act 1925

26. Consents to the execution of a trust for sale

(1) If the consent of more than two persons is by the disposition made requisite to the execution of a trust for sale of land, then, in favour of a purchaser, the consent of any two such persons to the execution of the trust or to the exercise of any statutory or other powers vested in the trustees for sale shall be deemed sufficient.

(2) Where the person whose consent to the execution of any such trust or power is expressed to be required in a disposition is not *sui juris* or becomes subject to disability, his consent shall not, in favour of a purchaser, be deemed to be requisite to the execution of the trust or the exercise of the power; but the trustees shall, in any such case, obtain the separate consent of the parent or testamentary or other guardian of an infant or of the . . . receiver (if any) of a person suffering from mental disorder . . .

cross-reference
For a discussion of TOLATA s10, see 7.12.5.

The practical effect of s26(1) LPA 1925 was that it was undesirable to create a trust for sale where the consent of more than two people was required. The consent of any two of the named persons would suffice for a valid sale. The practical effect of s26(2) LPA 1925 was that it was (possibly) undesirable to give the power of consenting to somebody who was underage (or mentally incapable). A parent or guardian could consent on their behalf.

Section 26 has now been repealed, but replaced by the (simpler) s10 TOLATA 1996, discussed later.

7.4.6 'Old Law'—Everybody Used Trusts for Sale

Arguably the most important part of this chapter so far is thinking point 7.3, and our suggested answer to it. The 'old' law of trusts of land was full of anachronisms and pitfalls for the unwary, but competent solicitors knew how to deal with that law. They avoided the creation of strict settlements and (by careful drafting), used the trust for sale to achieve their clients' wishes. Consent clauses were included where appropriate. As we shall see, the modern law gets rid of the anachronisms and the pitfalls but drafting of trusts of land may still require care.

7.5 The Definition of a Trust of Land

Section 1 of the 1996 Act contains a sweeping definition of the trust of land.

> *Trusts of Land and Appointment of Trustees Act 1996*
>
> (1) In this Act—
>
>   (a) 'trust of land' means (subject to subsection (3)) any trust of property which consists of or includes land, and
>
>   (b) 'trustees of land' means trustees of a trust of land.
>
> (2) The reference in subsection (1)(a) to a trust—
>
>   (a) is to any description of trust (whether express, implied, resulting or constructive), including a trust for sale and a bare trust, and
>
>   (b) includes a trust created, or arising, before the commencement of this Act.

trust of land
any trust of property that consists of or includes land.

Subsection (3) then excludes (existing) 'settled land' from the definition of **trust of land**.

Thus, right at the outset, the 1996 Act makes it clear that, with the exception of existing strict settlements, its legal regime is to apply to every conceivable type of trust of land, whether created before or after the commencement of the Act. It will be useful if we consider various possible types of trust, and how the all-embracing 1996 Act applies to them.

7.5.1 Existing Trusts for Sale

These are subject to TOLATA 1996, in particular:

cross-reference
Trusts for sale are discussed in 7.1.3.

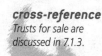

* implied trusts for sale (created by statute) have been automatically converted into trusts of land (s5(1) Sch 2 TOLATA 1996);

* existing express trusts for sale can exist under the 1996 Act but their use is limited due to the operation of s4(1) TOLATA 1996 (see the following extract and 7.5.2);

* the trustees have the unlimited powers of disposition granted by s6 TOLATA 1996. This effectively gives the trustees the power to sell rather than being under a duty to sell. You may recall that under a trust for sale the trustees were under a duty to sell;

* the (much improved) provisions for sorting out disputes contained in s14 are applicable.

Under the second point in the list it was noted that an express trust for sale can continue to exist after the implementation of the 1996 Act (1 January 1997), however if this trust includes any restriction on the trustees' power to postpone sale, that restriction is invalidated by s4(1) TOLATA 1996.

> *Trusts of Land and Appointment of Trustees Act 1996*
>
> 4. Express trusts for sale as trusts of land
>
> (1) In the case of every trust for sale of land created by a disposition there is to be implied, despite any provision to the contrary made by the disposition, a power for the trustees to

postpone sale of the land; and the trustees are not liable in any way for postponing sale of the land, in the exercise of their discretion, for an indefinite period.

(2) Subsection (1) applies to a trust whether it is created, or arises before or after the commencement of this Act.

(3) Subsection (1) does not affect any liability incurred by trustees before that commencement.

TOLATA 1996 has abolished the awkward doctrine of 'conversion' by virtue of which interests under a trust for sale were regarded as personal property not real property.

Trusts of Land and Appointment of Trustees Act 1996

3 Abolition of doctrine of conversion

(1) Where land is held by trustees subject to a trust for sale, the land is not to be regarded as personal property; and where personal property is subject to a trust for sale in order that the trustees may acquire land, the personal property is not to be regarded as land.

(2) Subsection (1) does not apply to a trust created by a will if the testator died before the commencement of this Act.

(3) Subject to that, subsection (1) applies to a trust whether it is created, or arises, before or after that commencement.

7.5.2 Trusts for Sale Arising after 1996

Any trust for sale created after the commencement of TOLATA 1996 is of course perfectly valid. However, it is governed by the legal regime under the 1996 Act and takes effect simply as a trust of land. Moreover, s4(1) TOLATA 1996 invalidates any provision which restricts or removes the trustees' power to postpone sale.

thinking point 7.4

In 1995, James owned a large farm, Spreadacres. He had five children, who were and are constantly quarrelling. He was diagnosed as terminally ill. He told his solicitor, 'I want to leave all my property to my children in equal shares. But to avoid them falling out over the management of Spreadacres, I want the farm sold within four years and the proceeds split between them.' 'Easy!' replied the solicitor, 'we will create a trust for sale, but include a clause restricting the power to postpone sale to four years from the date of your death.'

Consider this scenario on the assumption that:

1 James died shortly before the commencement of the 1996 Act.

2 James died shortly after the commencement of the 1996 Act.

If James died before the commencement of the 1996 Act, the restriction on the power to postpone would initially be valid. However (assuming the trustees have not been able to sell in the meantime), the restriction on the power to postpone sale would be invalidated by the commencement of the Act on 1 January 1997.

If James died after the commencement of the 1996 Act, his (undoubtedly well-meant) restriction on the power to postpone sale would be invalid from the outset.

7.5.3 Deliberately Created Trusts of Land after the Commencement of the 1996 Act

Note that in the second version of the scenario just considered, James made his will before 1 January 1997 but died after that date. In such a case, the 'trust for sale' which the testator intended simply takes effect as a trust of land.

It is perfectly possible for a post-1996 trust of land to be drafted as a trust for sale. But there seems to be no point in so doing. As the doctrine of conversion has been abolished by s3 TOLATA 1996, and as all trustees of land have a power to postpone sale indefinitely which cannot be excluded, a 'trust for sale of land' will be no different from any other trust of land.

In the past, numerous settlors creating trusts of land for the benefit of their families have employed the trust for sale. But they have done so, not because of any desire to see the land sold in the near future, but rather because the trust for sale was the only sensible way of achieving their wishes (see, eg, the answer to thinking point 7.3 at 7.4.5). The trust for sale, with its highly artificial 'duty to sell' was the lesser of two evils. The greater evil, to be avoided at all costs, was the strict settlement.

TOLATA 1996 eliminated the greater evil of the strict settlement and simultaneously rendered unnecessary the use of trusts for sale. Solicitors have quickly realized this and largely ceased employing trusts for sale. Instead, they simply convey the legal estate in the land to the chosen trustees, in trust for the chosen beneficiaries.

REVIEW QUESTION Why do you think that a trust for sale was regarded as the only sensible way of achieving the settlor's wishes?

(See thinking point 7.3 at 7.4.5.)

7.5.4 Bare Trusts after 1996

cross-reference
Re-read what was said about bare trusts at 1.3.11, 7.1.1, and 7.2.

A 'bare trust' of land is expressly brought within the definition of a trust of land (see s1(2)(a) TOLATA 1996). This is a point of some significance. Prior to the commencement of the 1996 Act, an equitable interest under a bare trust, unlike interests under a strict settlement or trust for sale, could not be overreached.

As a bare trust of land is now simply one form of trust of land, it is clear that the equitable interest of the sole beneficiary can now be overreached, provided the sale (or other disposition) is made by at least two trustees.

7.5.5 Constructive Trusts Affecting Land

cross-reference
Go back to 1.3.7, and refamiliarize yourself with the Chenu–Alex–Beth scenario set out in that section.

As we saw at 1.3.7, where somebody (Beth) makes a substantial contribution to the improvement of a piece of property (Chenu), that person (Beth) acquires a constructive trust interest in the property.

It follows from s1(2)(a) TOLATA 1996 that where land is subject to a constructive trust interest, a trust of land will automatically exist. The ramifications which flow from this are quite complex; we will consider the application of TOLATA 1996 to constructive trusts when we deal with co-ownership.

7.5.6 Treatment of Transactions Which Would Have Been Strict Settlements

As we have seen in 7.3.4, there are a number of situations where, prior to 1997, a strict settlement would arise 'by accident'. How are these situations dealt with by TOLATA 1996?

One Document Creating Equitable Interests

Consider the following: Joe owns 3 Madison Lane. He executes a single deed which purports to grant 3 Madison Lane, 'to Adam for life, remainder to Freya in fee simple'. Prior to 1926 this grant would have been a classic strict settlement, with Adam holding a legal life estate in possession, and Freya holding a legal fee simple in remainder.

If this grant took place at any time between 1926 and 1996 it would still be a valid strict settlement. However, Adam's life interest and Freya's fee simple in remainder were (and are) both equitable interests. More importantly, for reasons we need no longer consider, the use of a single deed was an error on Joe's part. The SLA 1925 provided a complicated rigmarole which had to be gone through before the land could be sold or dealt with in any other way. That rigmarole need not concern us.

If Joe executes his single deed after 1996 there is no great difficulty. He has (unwittingly) created a trust of land. This is because s2 TOLATA 1996 does not permit the creation of new strict settlements. Adam and Freya (as before) acquire equitable interests. Joe retains the legal estate in 3 Madison Lane; it therefore follows that he is the sole trustee of the trust of land.

> *Trusts of Land and Appointment of Trustees Act 1996*
>
> 2. Trusts in place of settlements
>
> (1) No settlement created after the commencement of this Act is a settlement for the purposes of the Settled Land Act 1925; and no settlement shall be deemed to be made under that Act after that commencement.
>
> . . .
>
> (6) Schedule 1 has effect to make provision consequential on this section (including provision to impose a trust in circumstances in which, apart from this section, there would be a settlement for the purposes of the Settled Land Act 1925 (and there would not otherwise be a trust)).

In brief, s2 means that any transaction which, prior to 1996, would have created a strict settlement (whether intended or not) now creates a trust of land.

Post-1996 Attempt to Create a Fee Tail

Although the 1996 Act does not abolish existing fee tail estates, it does provide that no new fee tail estates can be created. Schedule 1 para 5(1)(b) TOLATA 1996 provides that any document which purports to grant a fee tail 'operates instead as a declaration that the property is held in trust absolutely for the person to whom an entailed interest in the property was purportedly granted'.

For example, Daniel owns Redacre. After 1996 he executes a deed which purportedly conveys Redacre 'to my son Chad in fee tail'. This deed will create a (bare) trust of land, with Daniel as a sole trustee and Chad as the sole beneficiary.

Conveyance to a Minor

A minor (a person under 18 years of age) cannot own a legal estate in land (s1(6) LPA 1925). What then happens if someone purported to convey a legal estate to a minor or minors? Amazingly, under the old law the minor acquired an equitable interest and the land became settled land subject to all the complexities of the SLA 1925. Schedule 1 para 1(1) TOLATA 1996 now governs any attempted conveyance to a minor.

> *Trusts of Land and Appointment of Trustees Act 1996*
>
> Schedule 1
> Minors
> 1. (1) Where after the commencement of this Act a person purports to convey a legal estate in land to a minor, or two or more minors, alone, the conveyance—
>   (a) is not effective to pass the legal estate, but
>   (b) operates as a declaration that the land is held in trust for the minor or minors (or if he purports to convey it to the minor or minors in trust for any persons, for those persons).

thinking point 7.5

Aaron owns Spring Cottage. In 2013, he purports to convey Spring Cottage to his daughter Melissa, then aged 15. What is the effect of this conveyance?

Aaron has created a trust of land with himself as (sole) trustee of Spring Cottage and Melissa as the sole beneficiary. Technically this is not a 'bare' trust, as Melissa is underage. It will become a bare trust on her eighteenth birthday.

Schedule 1 para 1 was applied, with an arguably unfortunate result in *Hammersmith and Fulham BC v Alexander-David* [2010] Ch 272. The council purported to grant to the defendant, a homeless 16-year-old, a legal tenancy of a flat. Because of complaints from neighbours, the council sought to evict the defendant from the flat.

cross-reference
For a discussion on equitable leases see 3.9.5 and 3.10.

The Court of Appeal held that the legal tenancy on the flat was invalid. Instead, the council held the flat on trust for the defendant. The reasoning behind the decision was based on the statutory limits on a minor holding a legal estate. By virtue of s1(6) LPA 1925 and Sch 1 para (1) TOLATA 1996, a minor cannot hold a legal estate, only an equitable interest in land. Since the council had purportedly granted the tenant a legal tenancy (and had made no attempt to grant an equitable tenancy), that tenancy was held in trust by the council for the defendant. The council was subject to the normal trustee duty to preserve the trust property for the beneficiary, and therefore could not destroy it by giving notice to quit to the defendant.

Accidental Trusts of Land: Conveying Land Subject to a Right to Reside

thinking point 7.6

Re-read the cases of Binions v Evans *and* Ungurian v Lesnoff *at 7.3.4 and consider how these cases would be decided if the relevant events all occurred after the commencement of the TOLATA 1996.*

In Binions v Evans *the majority in effect ruled that there was a strict settlement with the effect that the cottage was granted by Tredegar Estates 'to Mrs Evans for life, remainder to Binions in fee simple'. Under the 1996 Act there is therefore a trust of land, with Tredegar Estates as the (sole) trustee and Mrs Evans and Binions as the beneficiaries.*

Compare this with the 3 Madison Lane example in 7.5.6.

In Ungurian v Lesnoff the judge in effect held that the house was subject to a strict settlement, 'to Lesnoff for life, remainder to Ungurian in fee simple'. Under the 1996 Act there is a trust of land, with Ungurian (he created the trust) as (sole) trustee of the legal estate, holding the house in trust for Lesnoff for life and then on 'resulting trust' to himself.

Accidental Trusts in Home-Made Wills

James thinks all solicitors charge extortionate fees, so he drafts his own will. He left his house, 'to my dear son Ewan, but on condition that he allows my beloved wife Caitlin to occupy the house for the rest of her life'. It appears that such a will under the old law would create a strict settlement, with Caitlin as the life tenant, and Ewan entitled to a fee simple in remainder.

thinking point 7.7

Consider what the outcome would be applying the TOLATA 1996 to James's will.

The will would create a trust of land, in effect, 'to Caitlin for life, remainder to Ewan in fee simple'. As James has not appointed any trustees, his personal representatives would act as the first trustees of the trust.

 ## 7.6 The Need for Two Trustees for a Trust of Land

We hope that you have noticed that in a number of the examples we have just been discussing there is only one trustee. It should be stressed that a trust of land (just like an 'old' trust for sale) is perfectly valid even though there is only one trustee. However, as we have already pointed out at 4.8.1, for a sale or other disposition by trustees to 'overreach' the equitable interests of beneficiaries, there must be at least two trustees.

This rule of minimum of two (s2 LPA 1925) has always applied to trusts for sale, and now applies to trusts of land. It follows that where there is a sole trustee of a trust of land, that trustee should appoint a colleague before selling the land or making any other disposition. What happens if he tries to sell (or mortgage or lease) the trust land acting on his own is a difficult question. It is best to delay considering that question until we reach 9.2.1.

 ## 7.7 Appointment, Retirement, and Removal of Trustees

What follows are certain basic principles you need to know for the purposes of land law.

7.7.1 The Original Trustees

The general rule is that the settlor appoints the original trustees by the document(s) setting up the trust. A person appointed at the outset can 'disclaim' the trust, that is, refuse to act. Equity has always ruled that, unless the trust instrument provides otherwise, trustees are not allowed to charge for their services, though they may claim the expenses of running the trust out of trust income. However, s29 Trustee Act 2000 now allows professional trustees (solicitors, accountants, banks, etc) to charge for their services even if the trust instrument says nothing about charges.

With a trust of land there is a maximum of four trustees (s34(2) LPA 1925). As we shall see in Chapters 8 and 9, this rule is important. If a document purports to appoint more than four trustees, the first four named are the trustees. For example, a deed conveys Valley House to Alistair, Bart, Curtis, David, and Ellis on trust. All the various beneficiaries are of full age. Ellis will not be a trustee. Suppose that Bart dies shortly after the trust is set up. Alistair, Curtis, and David continue as trustees, but Ellis does not become a trustee. As we shall see, Alistair, Curtis, and David can now appoint a colleague, who can be anybody they wish. There is no obligation on them to appoint Ellis.

A minor cannot be appointed to be a trustee, though an attempt to do so will not invalidate the trust. A settlor creates a trust of land, with Angela, Briony, and Cathy to be trustees, but Briony was only 17. Angela and Cathy will be the trustees. Briony would not become a trustee on her attaining 18. As you may have guessed, Angela and Cathy can appoint up to two colleagues, who can be whoever they wish. There is no obligation on them to appoint Briony after her eighteenth birthday.

7.7.2 Appointing Fresh Trustees to an Existing Trust

This is governed by s36 Trustee Act 1925, as amended. There are basically four rules:

- New appointments may be made by the person(s) nominated by the trust instrument as having the power to appoint new trustees. It is, however, relatively rare for a family trust to make provision for appointments by an 'outsider'. Such a provision is sometimes found in charitable trusts, and is normal in pension fund trusts.

- If there is no provision for appointment by an outsider(s), or the outsider(s) refuses to act, the existing trustee(s) appoints a new trustee(s). In practice this rule that existing trustees appoint new trustees is the rule which operates in the vast majority of cases. It is particularly important to realize that this rule operates even where (for whatever reason) there is currently only one trustee. That one trustee can appoint up to three colleagues.

- If all the trustees of a trust die, the rule then is that the personal representatives (executors or administrators) of the last trustee to die are automatically temporary trustees of the trust and have the power to appoint permanent trustees. It is perfectly permissible, indeed it is quite common, for the personal representatives to appoint themselves permanent trustees.

- The court may have to appoint trustees, though this will in practice happen only in cases of special difficulty, for example where all the trustees are incapacitated by mental illness.

7.7.3 When May New Appointments Be Made?

Additional Trustees

These may be appointed at any time provided the number of trustees is not increased above the maximum of four.

Replacement of Trustees

A new trustee may be appointed to replace an existing trustee if the existing trustee:

1 remains outside the United Kingdom for more than 12 months continuously;

2 desires to retire from the trust;

3 becomes unfit to act (due to bankruptcy, criminal conviction, etc);

4 becomes incapable of acting by reason of lunacy, old age, infirmity, or other reason; or

5 is removed under a power contained in the trust instrument.

(A trustee who is retiring may participate in the appointment of a replacement trustee.)

7.7.4 Removal of Trustees

A trustee may be removed:

- under heads (1), (3), (4), and (5) in the previous list;

- by the court; or

- where the beneficiaries, all being of full age and in agreement, desire the removal of a trustee.

The Rule in *Saunders v Vautier* and s19 TOLATA 1996

In order to explain the point made previously we need to explain the rule in *Saunders v Vautier* (1841) 10 LJ Ch 354. This rule remains of fundamental importance to both land law and the law of trusts. The rule is that if the beneficiaries of a trust (of any type of property) are all of full age and in unanimous agreement, they can in effect dictate what is to be done with the trust property.

For example, Tony and Troy are the trustees of a trust fund invested in stocks and shares. They hold the fund in trust for A for life, remainder to B absolutely. A and B are of full age. A would like to get his hands on some capital. B would also like some capital, but does not want to wait until A dies. They therefore agree to end the trust, and split the fund (say) 50–50. A and B have the right to do so under *Saunders v Vautier*.

The rule in *Saunders v Vautier* has now been reinforced by s19 TOLATA 1996. This section applies to all trusts of any type of property; it is not confined to trusts of land. Under s19, if the beneficiaries of a trust are all of full age and in unanimous agreement, they can by written direction:

- require a trustee or trustees to retire from the trust (ie sack the trustee(s)); and/or

- require the existing trustees to appoint a new trustee or trustees chosen by the beneficiaries.

> *Trusts of Land and Appointment of Trustees Act 1996*
>
> 19. Appointment and retirement of trustee at instance of beneficiaries
>
> (1) This section applies in the case of a trust where—
>
>   (a) there is no person nominated for the purpose of appointing new trustees by the instrument, if any, creating the trust, and
>
>   (b) the beneficiaries under the trust are of full age and capacity and (taken together) are absolutely entitled to the property subject to the trust.
>
> (2) The beneficiaries may give a direction or directions of either or both of the following descriptions—
>
>   (a) a written direction to a trustee or trustees to retire from the trust, and
>
>   (b) a written direction to the trustees or trustee for the time being (or, if there are none, to the personal representative of the last person who was a trustee) to appoint by writing to be a trustee or trustees the person or persons specified in the direction.
>
> (3) Where—
>
>   (a) a trustee has been given a direction under subsection (2)(a),
>
>   (b) reasonable arrangements have been made for the protection of any rights of his in connection with the trust,
>
>   (c) after he has retired there will be either a trust corporation or at least two persons to act as trustees to perform the trust, and
>
>   (d) either another person is to be appointed to be a new trustee on his retirement (whether in compliance with a direction under subsection (2)(b) or otherwise) or the continuing trustees by deed consent to his retirement, he shall make a deed declaring his retirement and shall be deemed to have retired and be discharged from the trust.
>
> (4) Where a trustee retires under subsection (3) he and the continuing trustees (together with any new trustee) shall (subject to any arrangements for the protection of his rights) do anything necessary to vest the trust property in the continuing trustees (or the continuing and new trustees).

In effect, the beneficiaries of a trust, provided they are adult and unanimous, can dismiss the existing trustees and replace them with people more to their liking.

thinking point 7.8

Suppose, in the imaginary trust discussed earlier, A and B are happy with their existing equitable interests under the trust, but do not like Tony and Troy as trustees. They would prefer Sadie and Sven. Advise A and B.

A and B should invoke s19. They will send Tony and Troy a written direction that they must execute a deed which appoints Sadie and Sven as trustees and then 'retires' Tony and Troy from the trust.

7.7.5 Retirement of Trustees

A trustee may retire:

- if another trustee is appointed in their place;
- if, after the trustee's retirement, there will be at least two persons continuing as trustees;
- by employing an express power to retire granted by the trust instrument;

- by getting the unanimous consent of all the beneficiaries; or
- by getting the court's consent.

7.7.6 Situations Where a Trustee is Also a Beneficiary

As we shall see more clearly in Chapters 8 and 9, there are certain situations where a trustee is also a beneficiary under the trust. Indeed, where there is co-ownership it is quite normal for a person to have dual roles as both trustee and beneficiary.

The point to get now is that if somebody is both trustee and beneficiary and they sell or give away their equitable interest, they nevertheless remain a trustee of the legal title. The disposal of their equitable interest is not to be treated as a resignation or retirement from the trust, nor is it as such grounds for removing them from the trusteeship.

7.8 Method of Appointment of Trustees

An appointment of a new trustee must be in writing; in practice it is normally made by deed in order to take advantage of s40(1) Trustee Act 1925. If the deed contains a declaration that the trust property shall vest in the new trustee(s), it conveys the legal title in the trust property from the existing trustees to the persons who will be the trustees after the appointment.

> *Trustee Act 1925*
>
> As amended by Trusts of Land and Appointment of Trustees Act 1996
>
> 40. Vesting of trust property in new or continuing trustees
>
> (1) Where by a deed a new trustee is appointed to perform any trust, then—
>
>   (a) if the deed contains a declaration by the appointor to the effect that any estate or interest in any land subject to the trust, or in any chattel so subject, or the right to recover or receive any debt or other thing in action so subject, shall vest in the persons who by virtue of the deed become or are the trustees for performing the trust, the deed shall operate, without any conveyance or assignment, to vest in those persons as joint tenants and for the purposes of the trust the estate interest or right to which the declaration relates; and
>
>   (b) if the deed is made after the commencement of this Act and does not contain such a declaration, the deed shall, subject to any express provision to the contrary therein contained, operate as if it had contained such a declaration by the appointor extending to all the estates interests and rights with respect to which a declaration could have been made.
>
> (2) Where by a deed a retiring trustee is discharged under [s39 of this Act or s19 TOLATA 1996] without a new trustee being appointed, then—
>
>   (a) if the deed contains such a declaration as aforesaid by the retiring and continuing trustees, and by the other person, if any, empowered to appoint trustees, the deed shall, without any conveyance or assignment, operate to vest in the continuing trustees alone, as joint tenants, and for the purposes of the trust, the estate, interest, or right to which the declaration relates; and

(b) if the deed is made after the commencement of this Act and does not contain such a declaration, the deed shall, subject to any express provision to the contrary therein contained, operate as if it had contained such a declaration by such persons as aforesaid extending to all the estates, interests and rights with respect to which a declaration could have been made.

(3) An express vesting declaration, whether made before or after the commencement of this Act, shall, notwithstanding that the estate, interest or right to be vested is not expressly referred to, and provided that the other statutory requirements were or are complied with, operate and be deemed always to have operated (but without prejudice to any express provision to the contrary contained in the deed of appointment or discharge) to vest in the persons respectively referred to in subsections (1) and (2) of this section, as the case may require, such estates, interests and rights as are capable and ought to be vested in those persons . . .

For example, A, B, and C are the existing trustees, and they appoint by deed D to replace C who is retiring from the trust, the declaration conveys the legal title from A, B, and C to A, B, and D.

thinking point 7.9

What has just been said rather assumes that any land involved is unregistered title. What do you think happens if (as is very likely) new trustees are appointed to a trust where the land involved is registered title?

The trustees prior to the new appointment(s) are the registered proprietors until the deed of appointment is presented to the Land Registry. The necessary change(s) are then made to the register.

7.9 Unanimity of Trustees

It is a general rule of the law of trusts that trustees can act only if there is unanimous agreement. Thus if there are four trustees of a trust for sale or trust of land, and the land is to be sold, all four trustees must sign both the contract and the conveyance. Likewise, if there are three trustees of a trust of land, all three must sign.

7.9.1 Exceptions to the Unanimity Rule

The exceptions are:

- if the trust instrument provides for decisions to be taken by a majority (such a provision is today not uncommon); and

- if land is held subject to a charitable trust. In the case of such a trust the law permits there to be more than four trustees but it also provides that decisions may be taken by a majority of the trustees of the charity.

7.10 The Powers of Disposition of Trustees of Land

Section 6 TOLATA 1996 is of central importance, and makes a radical departure from the previous law governing trusts for sale.

Trusts of Land and Appointment of Trustees Act 1996

6. General powers of trustees

(1) For the purpose of exercising their functions as trustees, the trustees of land have in relation to the land subject to the trust all the powers of an absolute owner.

(2) Where in the case of any land subject to a trust of land each of the beneficiaries interested in the land is a person of full age and capacity who is absolutely entitled to the land, the powers conferred on the trustees by subsection (1) include the power to convey the land to the beneficiaries even though they have not required the trustees to do so; and where land is conveyed by virtue of this subsection—

    (a) the beneficiaries shall do whatever is necessary to secure that it vests in them, and

    (b) if they fail to do so, the court may make an order requiring them to do so.

(3) The trustees of land have power to acquire land under the power conferred by section 8 of the Trustee Act 2000.

(5) In exercising the powers conferred by this section trustees shall have regard to the rights of the beneficiaries.

(6) The powers conferred by this section shall not be exercised in contravention of, or of any order made in pursuance of, any other enactment or any rule of law or equity.

(7) The reference in subsection (6) to an order includes an order of any court or of the Charity Commissioners.

(8) Where any enactment other than this section confers on trustees authority to act subject to any restriction, limitation or condition, trustees of land may not exercise the powers conferred by this section to do any act which they are prevented from doing under the other enactment by reason of the restriction, limitation or condition.

(9) The duty of care under section 1 of the Trustee Act 2000 applies to trustees of land when exercising the powers conferred by this section.

As you can see s6(1) TOLATA 1996 is very striking, it states, quite baldly:

For the purposes of exercising their functions as trustees, the trustees of land have in relation to the land subject to the trust *all the powers of an absolute owner*. [Emphasis added]

It should be stressed that this provision extends to all trusts of land, whether created before or after the commencement of the 1996 Act. (Regrettably, it has not been applied to life tenants under the few strict settlements which still exist.) The trustees of trusts of land can, unlike life tenants under a strict settlement, lease the trust land for any period they and the prospective tenant consider appropriate. Similarly, unlike life tenants, the trustees can grant an option to purchase the trust land at a price to be fixed by an arbitrator.

Life tenants of strict settlements do have power, under the SLA 1925, to mortgage the settled land to pay for improvements to the land, for example land drainage. However, the power under the SLA 1925 is subject to complex and antiquated restrictions which need not now concern us.

195

By contrast, trustees of land are, as a result of s6 TOLATA 1996, able to mortgage the trust land to raise funds for any purpose which benefits the land in the long term. In particular, the trustees are not subject to the outdated rules regarding improvements contained in Sch 3 SLA 1925.

The Trustees' Duties on Exercising their Powers

Ever since the Court of Chancery invented the concept of the trust in medieval times (remember 1.3.11 and Sir Richard Goodbody), trustees of all forms of trust have been under a duty to get the best financial return from the trust property obtainable by reasonable methods. This duty does of course apply to trustees of land.

This traditional duty on trustees to get the best return from the trust property is now both codified and amplified by s1 Trustee Act 2000, an Act which applies to all trustees of all types of trust when exercising their various powers and functions.

> *Trustee Act 2000*
>
> 1. The duty of care
>
> (1) Whenever the duty under this subsection applies to a trustee, he must exercise such care and skill as is reasonable in the circumstances, having regard in particular—
>   (a) to any special knowledge that he has or holds himself out as having, and
>   (b) if he acts as trustee in the course of a business or profession, to any special knowledge or experience that it is reasonable to expect of a person acting in the course of that kind of business or profession.

You should note that if a trustee has professional qualifications or business skills, a higher standard of care is expected of such a person (compare and contrast the tort of negligence). You should, however, also carefully note Sch 1 para 7 Trustee Act 2000:

> *Trustee Act 2000*
>
> Schedule 1 Application of duty of care
>
> (7) The duty of care does not apply if or in so far as it appears from the trust instrument that the duty is not meant to apply.

A trust deed can include a clause exempting trustees from liability for negligence in carrying out any or all of their powers and functions. The Unfair Contract Terms Act 1977 and similar legislation designed to protect consumers does not (unfortunately) apply to trusts. Schedule 1 para 7 Trustee Act 2000 is merely restating the existing law. In the alarming case of *Armitage v Nurse* [1998] Ch 241 the trustees had grossly mismanaged the trust property—a family farm—but they could not be sued for breach of trust as the deed included an exemption clause.

7.11.1 Specific Duties of Trustees of Land

If the trustees of land decide to sell all or part of the trust land, they are under a duty to get the best price reasonably obtainable. If trustees sell at less than the best price, then provided the purchaser has acted in good faith the sale will be valid and the purchaser cannot be sued. However, the trustees who sold at the cheap price will be in breach of trust, and the beneficiaries can insist that the trustees make up the shortfall.

Similarly, trustees who lease all or part of the trust land to a tenant must charge the full market rent. The trustees can, however, charge a premium on the grant of a lease, even though this has the effect of reducing the 'market' rent the tenant is willing to pay. If the trustees decide to grant an option over the trust land, it must be on terms similar to those which would be obtained by an outright owner acting in his own financial best interests.

Suppose, however, the trust land is farm land and the trustees decide to retain the land in their own possession. They will be under a duty to farm the land efficiently, so as to get the best financial return obtainable by reasonable farming methods.

cross-reference
Delegating trustees' powers is considered at 7.13 to 7.13.5.

thinking point 7.10

Darren and Sharon, two city-dwellers who know nothing about agriculture, are appointed trustees of Stonecroft, a large farm. Advise Darren and Sharon.

Clearly, they would be fools to try and run the farm themselves. They might well end up having to pay damages for breach of trust. On what has already been said, one hopes that you have spotted two possible courses of action. Darren and Sharon could lease Stonecroft to a tenant farmer who did have the requisite expertise. Alternatively, they could simply sell Stonecroft and invest the proceeds in stocks and shares, etc.

A rather different solution would be to appoint a person who is an expert in agriculture to manage the farm on their behalf. The manager's salary (and the wages of his employees) will be a legitimate expense of the trust which Darren and Sharon will be able to deduct from the gross revenue of the farm. The net income will be payable to the beneficiary(ies) with current equitable interest(s) under the trust. A yet further alternative may be to delegate their powers to a beneficiary under s9 TOLATA 1996.

7.11.2 Placing Trustees of Land Under a Duty to Consult the Beneficiaries

One of the criticisms often made of the SLA 1925 is that it makes the life tenant 'boss' of the settled land. Although a Settled Land Act life tenant is a (rather peculiar) type of trustee, subject to the general duty to get the best financial return for any disposition he makes, he is not under any duty to consult other beneficiaries about proposed dispositions.

Suppose Grey Stones is subject to a strict settlement, 'to John for life, remainder to [John's son] Keith for life, remainder to [Keith's son] Lloyd in fee simple'. John is life tenant and now wants to sell Grey Stones as he feels that he is getting too old to manage the land properly. Under the SLA 1925 John can sell Grey Stones without even consulting Keith and Lloyd, who may well be disappointed that they do not 'inherit' what they regard as the family estate.

Where there is a trust for sale, then normally independent trustees are 'bosses' of the trust land. It was possible, under the law operating prior to the TOLATA 1996, for a person creating a trust for sale to include an express clause that the trustees should consult the beneficiaries regarding the running of the trust, including the decision whether to carry out the 'duty' to sell. However, it seems that such a clause was included only in a minority of express trusts for sale.

Against this background of (usually) no duty to consult beneficiaries, s11 TOLATA 1996 does represent a small but not insignificant change in the law.

> *Trusts of Land and Appointment of Trustees Act 1996*
>
> 11. Consultation with beneficiaries
>
> (1) The trustees of land shall in the exercise of any function relating to land subject to the trust—
>
>   (a) so far as practicable, consult the beneficiaries of full age and beneficially entitled to an interest in possession in the land, and
>
>   (b) so far as consistent with the general interest of the trust, give effect to the wishes of those beneficiaries, or (in case of dispute) of the majority (according to the value of their combined interests).

A number of more detailed points should be made about this provision; all of these points tend to demonstrate that the duty created by s11(1) is somewhat restricted in character.

First, the duty is to consult the beneficiary or beneficiaries 'entitled to an interest in possession'. For example, in 2012, Acorn Lodge was conveyed, 'To Timmy and Tammy in trust for Mr and Mrs Smith for their lives, remainder to their [eight] children in equal shares'. Timmy and Tammy will be under a duty to consult Mr and Mrs Smith, not the children. This would be the case even if Mr and Mrs Smith were elderly and in poor health.

Secondly, it is a duty to consult not a duty to obey. Paragraph (b) talks of giving effect to the wishes of the beneficiaries, but only 'as far as consistent with the general interest of the trust'. It is the trustees who decide what is in the general interest of the trust.

Thirdly, unlike most of the TOLATA 1996, s11(1) only applies to trusts coming into effect after the commencement of the Act. Moreover, where a trust of land is created by a will, s11(1) only applies if the will was made after the commencement of the Act. A will is made when it is signed and witnessed. It takes effect when the testator dies, perhaps many years later.

thinking point 7.11

Jack made his will in 1996, but died in 2014. The will creates a trust which was phrased as a trust for sale but which will now take effect as a trust of land. Will the s11 duty to consult beneficiaries be applicable?

The answer is 'no', as the will was made before the Act commenced.

Finally, a purchaser of trust land is not under any duty to enquire whether the beneficiaries have been consulted. If beneficiaries have not been consulted when they should have been, the conveyance (or other transaction) is valid.

7.11.3 Personal Occupation of Trust Land by Beneficiaries

Prior to the coming into force of the TOLATA 1996 there were numerous trusts for sale displaying the following characteristics:

- the property involved was not some vast estate but a house, cottage, flat, or (occasionally) small business premises;
- it was the intention of the people creating the trust that the property should be used by beneficiaries of the trust as their home, or (where appropriate) their place of business; and
- despite the trust for sale, there was no intention that the property be sold in the foreseeable future. In technical terms, the trustees exercised their power to postpone sale.

These trusts for sale, numerous as they were, caused problems for traditionalist land lawyers. They pedantically and zealously applied the old doctrine of conversion: 'How can beneficiaries who have not got an interest in land but only an interest in proceeds of sale have a right to live on the land?'

Fortunately, these traditionalists lost the argument long before 1996. Back in 1955 Lord Denning in *Bull v Bull* held that where property subject to a trust for sale was acquired for occupation by the beneficiaries, the beneficiaries did have a right to occupy the land, notwithstanding the doctrine of conversion. This view was adhered to in later cases, and the House of Lords in *Williams and Glyn's Bank v Boland* [1981] AC 487 accepted that it was correct.

The 1996 Act sweeps away the doctrine of conversion and transforms all trusts for sale into trusts of land. Further, to make matters crystal clear regarding occupation of trust land by beneficiaries, it includes a specific provision on the issue, s12.

Section 12 of the Trusts of Land and Appointment of Trustees Act 1996

Trusts of Land and Appointment of Trustees Act 1996

12. The right to occupy

(1) A beneficiary who is beneficially entitled to an interest in possession in land subject to a trust of land is entitled by reason of his interest to occupy the land at any time if at that time—

   (a) the purposes of the trust include making the land available for his occupation (or for the occupation of beneficiaries of a class of which he is a member or of beneficiaries in general), or

   (b) the land is held by the trustees so as to be so available.

(2) Subsection (1) does not confer on a beneficiary a right to occupy land if it is either unavailable or unsuitable for occupation by him.

In short, a beneficiary (subject to s12(2)) has the right to occupy the trust land if either:

- the trust was set up to provide land for the beneficiary's occupation, either solely or jointly with others; or

- the trustees subsequent to the creation of the trust acquired the land for the beneficiary's occupation, either solely or jointly with others.

Three supplementary points should be made. First, if in pursuance to s12(1)(a) a beneficiary or beneficiaries exercise their right to occupy the trust land, the trustees are of course exempted from their normal duty to maximize the financial return from the land.

Secondly, for reasons which will emerge in Chapters 8 and 9, there will be numerous trusts where two or sometimes more beneficiaries have simultaneously the right to occupy the trust land. If the beneficiaries fall out with each other the extensive provisions in the 1996 Act for settling disputes will come in to play. These provisions (ss13, 14, and 15) are discussed in Chapter 9.

Thirdly, as a result of s12(2) TOLATA 1996, there is no right to occupy if the property is 'unavailable' (eg it has been leased to a long-term tenant) or 'unsuitable'. The issue of when a property is 'unsuitable' was discussed in *Chan Pui Chun v Leung Kam Ho* [2002] EWCA Civ 1075. The parties had been cohabitees. The defendant had bought Hill House 'a large 4 bedroom family property with a substantial garden, a swimming pool and a fish pond' (at [13]). The relationship broke down and, as a result, Miss Chan (the claimant) was living alone in the house. She proved that she had a constructive trust share in the house, and successfully argued that she had a right under s12 TOLATA 1996 to continue to live in the house for a short period. Parker LJ on the s12 issue in the Court of Appeal said:

> 100. Given the judge's finding that one of the purposes of the trust of Hill House was to provide a home for Miss Chan should her relationship with Mr Leung come to an end, the short issue on this aspect of the case is whether Hill House is 'unsuitable for occupation by [Miss Chan]' within the meaning of section 12(1) of the TLATA.
>
> 101. There is no statutory definition or guidance as to what is meant by 'unsuitable' in this context, and it would be rash indeed to attempt an exhaustive definition or explanation of its meaning. In the context of the present case it is, I think, enough to say that 'suitability' for this purpose must involve a consideration not only of the general nature and physical characteristics of the particular property but also a consideration of the personal characteristics, circumstances and requirements of the particular beneficiary. This much is, I think, clear from the fact that the statutory expression is not simply 'unsuitable for occupation' but 'unsuitable for occupation *by him*', that is to say by the particular beneficiary.
>
> 102. In the instant case Mr Leung's complaint, in substance, is that Hill House is too large for Miss Chan's needs and too expensive for her to maintain. However, taking into account that Miss Chan's requirement under the terms of the judge's order (which she has not cross-appealed) is for a right of occupation only until Summer 2003, I agree with the judge that Hill House is not 'unsuitable for occupation by [her]' within the meaning of section 12(1). In any event I would have taken some persuading that a property which was on any footing suitable for occupation by Miss Chan and Mr Leung whilst they lived together should be regarded as unsuitable for occupation by her alone once Mr Leung had left.

In brief, 'suitability' depends on:

- the size or the character of the premises;
- the characteristics of the person claiming to occupy; and
- the intentions of the other people involved.

thinking point 7.12

Gregory is a wealthy man who is seriously ill. He is making a new will. As well as many shareholdings, he owns two houses, Honeycomb Lodge and Dower House. He wants to leave both properties to his wife Hanna for life, reminder to their children in equal shares. He tells you that he envisages Hanna continuing to live in the family home Honeycomb Lodge, but that Dower House should be sold or leased. In the light of s12, what should he say in his will?

To avoid any doubt, he should say the purpose of the trust over Honeycomb Lodge is to provide a home for Hanna, and that the purpose of the trust over Dower House is investment, and it should not be regarded as available for occupation by Hanna.

7.11.4 Investment (or Other Use) of 'Capital Money' by Trustees of Land

If trustees of land sell all or part of the land, the sale will of course give rise to a payment of capital money (the price!). Capital money may also be generated by other transactions falling short of an outright sale, for example if a lease is granted at a premium, that premium is capital money. If an option is granted, the price paid for the option is capital money.

Any capital received by the trustees cannot just be left in a current bank account. It must be put to good use by the trustees for the benefit of the beneficiaries. To what sort of uses can trustees of land put capital which they have in their hands?

The trustees could, subject to the duty of care in s1 Trustee Act 2000, invest spare capital in any kind of investment, for example stocks and shares or government bonds (s3 Trustee Act 2000); or they could spend the money on improving any land which they retain; or they could exercise the very broad power originally granted by s6(3) and (4) TOLATA 1996 but now contained in s8 Trustee Act 2000.

> **Trustee Act 2000**
>
> 8. Power to acquire freehold and leasehold land
>
> (1) A trustee may acquire freehold or leasehold land in the United Kingdom—
>
>   (a) as an investment,
>
>   (b) for occupation by a beneficiary; or
>
>   (c) for any other reason.

The reference in s8(1) to 'freehold or leasehold land' means that trustees of land can buy a fee simple or a lease of any duration. Under the old law in force prior to the commencement of the 1996 Act, trustees for sale of land could purchase a fee simple or a lease with at least 60 years to run. Trustees of a trust of land can now invest in a short term lease. However, bearing in mind the duty of trustees to act in the interests of the trust as a whole, it would surely be a breach of trust for trustees of a trust expected to endure for many years to invest capital in buying short term leases.

The reference in s8(1)(c) to 'any other reason' may at first sight be puzzling. Again, we must read it against the background of the trustees' duty to act in the best interests of the trust. 'Any other reason' clearly must mean 'any other reason which benefits the trust or the beneficiaries'. For example, suppose the main trust land is North Meadow. Neighbouring East Meadow comes up for sale. The trustees fear that East Meadow will be purchased by someone who will use that land for an undesirable purpose which will depreciate the value of North Meadow. The trustees can use any spare capital they have to purchase East Meadow.

Sale of the Whole of the Trust Land Followed by Purchase of 'Replacement' Land

At the beginning of 7.11.3 the point was made that prior to the coming into force of the 1996 Act, there were numerous trusts for sale where the trust property consisted of just one house, cottage, or even flat. What if the trustees sold the house/cottage/flat—could the trustees then redeploy the proceeds on the purchase of a 'replacement'?

Amazingly, in *Re Wakeman* [1945] Ch 177, the court held that trustees for sale, once they had sold all the land they held, could not go out and buy replacement land. Instead, the money had to be put into investments such as stocks and shares. This highly inconvenient ruling could, however, be avoided by putting an express clause in the trust for sale authorizing the trustees to buy replacement land. Happily, the *Re Wakeman* principle has now been reversed by legislation, first by s17(1) TOLATA 1996 and now by s8(1) Trustee Act 2000.

7.12 Exclusion and Restriction on Trustees of Land Powers of Disposition

Section 8 TOLATA 1996 effectively allows settlors creating trusts of land to remove and/or restrict the wide powers of disposition conferred by s6. (Note that s7 referred to in s8 is a very minor provision not considered in this text.)

> *Trusts of Land and Appointment of Trustees Act 1996*
>
> 8. Exclusion and restriction of powers
>
> (1) Sections 6 and 7 do not apply in the case of a trust of land created by a disposition in so far as provision to the effect that they do not apply is made by the disposition.
>
> (2) If the disposition creating such a trust makes provision requiring any consent to be obtained to the exercise of any power conferred by section 6 or 7, the power may not be exercised without that consent.

Section 8(1) thus allows what can be called 'takeaway clauses', under which the settlor deprives the trustees of powers of disposition which they would otherwise have. The trustees' powers of disposition under this provision can either be removed totally or partially, depending on the settlor's wishes. Section 8(2) (less radically) provides for 'consent clauses', under which a disposition requires the consent of named person(s), consequently restricting the powers of the trustees.

7.12.1 Depriving the Trustees of Powers of Disposition

Section 8(1), unlike s8(2), represented a radical departure from the old law. Under the old and outmoded SLA 1925 the life tenant was given somewhat restricted powers of disposition, but those powers of disposition were then zealously guarded by s106 of the Act. Under s106 SLA 1925, any attempt to directly or indirectly limit the life tenant's statutory powers was void. Contrast this with TOLATA 1996. Section 6 of the 1996 Act gives the trustees unlimited powers of disposition, but s8 of the 1996 Act then tells settlors, 'you can take away any or all of the trustees' powers of disposition'. The powers of the trustees can be removed totally or partially.

A settlor could say, for example, 'the trustees shall have no power to lease the land for more than 50 years', or 'the trustees shall not grant any options to purchase with respect to the trust land'. Alternatively, there seems absolutely nothing to stop a settlor imposing a total removal of powers. He can now include in his trust of land a clause, 'The trustees shall have no power to create or convey any estate or interest in the land held in trust under this deed.'

7.12.2 The Problem Posed by Restricting the Powers of the Trustees

By using a clause like the one quoted in the previous paragraph, the settlor will have achieved, in the third millennium, the great ambition of generations of old-fashioned settlors of land. The settlor will have rendered the land in question (for the duration of the trust) inalienable.

It may be argued that no sensible settlor of a trust of land would ever, in modern economic conditions, create a trust which totally restricts the trustees' powers of disposition. That may be so. But the history of land law (and the law of trusts) is littered with eccentric settlors trying to impose their conditions for holding property on succeeding generations of their families. A lot of the thinking behind the Settled Land Acts 1882 and 1925 was to curb such eccentric settlors. By contrast, s8 TOLATA 1996 is an open invitation to such settlors to impose their eccentric wishes.

7.12.3 Dispositions Infringing s8(1) TOLATA 1996

What if the trustees attempt to make a disposition which exceeds their powers because the relevant power has been removed by the use of s8(1) TOLATA 1996? For example, what if the trustees 'sell' the fee simple despite the trust specifically stating that there shall be no power of sale?

Where the Land is Registered Title

cross-reference
Restrictions are explained in 6.2.2.

The limits on the trustees' powers will presumably be entered on the register in the form of a formal 'restriction' (ss40–41 Land Registration Act 2002). (The word 'restriction' is used in its technical land registration sense.) Any transaction in breach of the 'restriction' would be void, and the Registry would obviously refuse to register it.

If, for some reason, no 'restriction' has been entered on the register, then any sale in breach of the takeaway clause would (applying general principles of land registration law) be valid.

Where the Land is Unregistered Title

The problem of dispositions by trustees which exceed their powers is dealt with by s16(3) TOLATA 1996.

> *Trusts of Land and Appointment of Trustees Act 1996*
>
> 16. Protection of purchasers
>
> (3) Where the powers of trustees of land are limited by virtue of section 8—
>
> (a) the trustees shall take all reasonable steps to bring the limitation to the notice of any purchaser of the land from them, but
>
> (b) the limitation does not invalidate any conveyance by the trustees to a purchaser who has no actual notice of the limitation.

Thus a disposition in favour of a purchaser who has no actual notice of the use of s8 (limiting the trustees powers of disposition) will be valid.

---

thinking point 7.13

Consider whether a purchaser is likely to have actual notice of a restriction on the trustees' powers.

Almost all (potential) purchasers will have notice of restrictions on the trustees' powers. No faith should be placed in the trustees complying with s16(3)(a) TOLATA 1996. Rather, one should note that the limits on the trustees' powers will almost certainly be set out in the conveyance to the trustees. It follows that the only sort of purchaser who is likely to be 'protected' by s16(3)(b) is one who never even looked at the title deeds. Put a slightly different way, a conveyance in defiance of a clause which removes the powers of the trustees is likely to be valid in favour of a grossly negligent do-it-yourself purchaser who never even looked at the deeds. Vis-à-vis a purchaser who did look at the deeds, the conveyance will be void, as the purchaser is bound to have seen such a clause.

7.12.4 Are There Ways of Escaping from a Clause Removing the Powers of the Trustees?

In the light of the previous discussion, this is an important question. Suppose, for example, there is a clause partially removing the powers of the trustees which forbids them from leasing the land for more than 50 years. A potential tenant comes along, offering to take a lease for 99 years. The terms the potential tenant is offering to the trustees regarding premium, rent, tenants' covenants, etc are in economic terms absolutely irresistible. What can be done?

There are three possibilities which need to be considered, though perhaps only the first of these possibilities is of any help, and then only in limited situations.

Invoke the Rule in *Saunders v Vautier*

If all the beneficiaries of the trust are of full age and in total agreement, they can terminate the trust containing the takeaway clause, and set up another trust without the offending clause. Too much faith should not be placed in this solution to the problem which Parliament has created by s8 TOLATA 1996. In most trusts there is usually at least one non-adult beneficiary. Even when all the beneficiaries are adults, getting unanimity may not be easy.

Invoke the Statutory Disputes Jurisdiction of the Court

Section 14 TOLATA 1996 contains very wide powers for the courts to settle disputes arising regarding a trust of land. The details of this provision we will consider in Chapter 9. By s14(2)(a) the court is empowered to make an order:

> *Trusts of Land and Appointment of Trustees Act 1996*
>
> 14. Applications for order
>
> (2) . . .
>
>   (a) relating to the exercise by the trustees of any of their functions (including an order relieving them of any obligation to obtain the consent of, or to consult, any person in connection with the exercise of their functions) . . .

Ignoring for a moment the words in brackets, it is difficult to believe that the key phrase 'the exercise by the trustees of any of their functions' extends to cover 'functions' which the settlor has deliberately said the trustees shall not have.

Then, when we do look at the words in brackets we see that if a settlor has, pursuant to s8(2) TOLATA 1996, included a consent clause, then the need for consent(s) can be overridden by court order. The very presence of these words in brackets allowing a consent clause under s8(2) to be overridden by a s14 order strongly suggests that totally removing the trustees' powers of disposition under s8(1) cannot be overridden.

Invoke the Inherent Jurisdiction of the Court to Deal with 'Emergencies'

There is a line of cases in the law of trusts which say that if some 'emergency' arises in the administration of a trust, the court can authorize trustees to carry out transactions which would otherwise be beyond the trustees' powers. The leading (and seemingly most recent) case dates from 1901 (*Re New* [1901] 2 Ch 534 at 544). In that case the Court of Appeal stressed that the emergency must arise 'from some peculiar state of circumstances for which provision is not expressly made by the trust instrument'. The case must be one where 'it may reasonably be supposed to be one not foreseen or anticipated by the author of the trust'.

It is suggested that a clause which removes the trustees' power of disposition could not be overridden using this 'emergency' jurisdiction. A settlor who insists on inserting such a clause has presumably been advised by their solicitor of the risks involved, for example that by removing the trustees' powers of disposition that will prevent the trustees from seizing some golden economic opportunity to exploit the land. The 'emergency' can hardly be described as 'unforeseen'.

Nor has the settlor failed to expressly provide 'for some peculiar state of circumstances'. The settlor has made express provision. The settlor has, exercising the right under the 1996 Act, provided that the trustees shall have no power to deal with the situation.

7.12.5 Consent Clauses

While s8(1) TOLATA 1996 could be viewed as a radical departure in the law if contrasted with s106 SLA 1925, the same cannot be said for s8(2).

cross-reference
Re-read 7.4.5 and
thinking point 7.3.

Trusts of Land and Appointment of Trustees Act 1996

8. Exclusion and restriction of powers

[2] If the disposition creating such a trust [of land] makes provision requiring any consent to be obtained to the exercise of any power conferred by section 6 or 7, the power may not be exercised without that consent.

Under the old law we had the (somewhat paradoxical) concept of a trust for sale subject to consents. Under the 1996 Act we have the very similar concept of a trust of land subject to consents.

---

thinking point 7.14

At 7.4.5 we saw an example of a trust for sale:

To Tobin and Tabor on trust for sale for X for life, remainder to Y. The sale shall only take place if W and X agree to it.

Redraft this example so that it complies with the 1996 Act.

The land is conveyed, 'to Tobin and Tabor on trust for X for life, remainder to Y. If the trustees wish to create or convey any estate or interest in the land held in trust under this deed, they must obtain the consent of W and X.'

The close similarity of the trust of land subject to consents, to the trust for sale subject to consents, is further demonstrated by the following two points. The first point is s10(1) TOLATA 1996, equivalent to s26(1) LPA 1925.

> *Trusts of Land and Appointment of Trustees Act 1996*
>
> 10. Consents
>
> (1) If a disposition creating a trust of land requires the consent of more than two persons to the exercise by the trustees of any function relating to the land, the consent of any two of them to the exercise of the function is sufficient in favour of a purchaser.
>
> (2) Subsection (1) does not apply to the exercise of a function by trustees of land held on charitable, ecclesiastical or public trusts.
>
> (3) Where at any time a person whose consent is expressed by a disposition creating a trust of land to be required to the exercise by the trustees of any function relating to the land is not of full age—
>
> (a) his consent is not, in favour of a purchaser, required to the exercise of the function, but
>
> (b) the trustees shall obtain the consent of a parent who has parental responsibility for him (within the meaning of the Children Act 1989) or of a guardian of his.

Suppose land is conveyed to Tracey and Tania as trustees, 'Any sale or other disposition of the land to take place only with the consent of A, B, C, D, E, F, G, H, I, J, K, L, M, N, O, P, Q, R, S, T, U, V, W, X, Y, and Z.' The settlor has not been very smart. The consent of any two of A to Z will be sufficient to validate a sale or other disposition, for example a lease. By supplying a long list of names, rather than confining himself to two, the settlor has (ironically) made it easier to dispose of the land.

The second point has already been touched upon. Under the old law, where there was a trust for sale subject to consent, but a transaction was being blocked by a refusal of consent, the trustees (or beneficiaries) could invoke the court's jurisdiction under s30 LPA 1925. Under s30 the court could, inter alia, authorize a proposed transaction to go ahead despite the absence of consent(s).

The position is effectively the same under trusts of land subject to consents. At 7.12.4 reference was made to s14(2)(a) TOLATA 1996. While under this provision the court cannot (it seems) authorize a transaction in defiance of a clause which removes the powers of the trustees, it can authorize a transaction to go ahead without the consent(s) required by the trust deed.

A Likely Use for a Trust of Land Subject to Consents

thinking point 7.15

Using the facts from thinking point 7.3, but this time assuming that the 1996 Act applies to Luke's will. Here are the facts again:

Luke owns a large house. He has a wife, Amelia, and a son Jake. Luke is in poor health, and wishes to make a will under which Amelia would have the right to occupy the house for the rest of her lifetime, but without any power to sell or lease the house. On Amelia's death the house would pass to Jake absolutely.

Why is it that Luke would be advised to create, not a strict settlement, but a trust of land and what sort of provisions would that trust contain?

The answer is now more straightforward. Luke cannot, of course, create a strict settlement. His only option is to create a trust of land. He should appoint as trustees people who are sympathetic to his wishes. They will hold the large house in trust for Amelia for life, remainder to Jake. He should also include clauses:

- *requiring that any disposition affecting the land should be with the consent of both Amelia and Jake; and*
- *stating that a purpose of the trust is that the large house should be available for Amelia to live in. (The effect of this clause, will result in Luke conferring on Amelia a right to occupy the house under s12 TOLATA 1996.)*

7.13 Delegation of Trustees' Powers to Beneficiaries

7.13.1 The Old Law Background

Where a strict settlement exists (and there are still a few) the position regarding both ownership of the legal estate and powers of disposition is very anomalous when compared with every other type of trust, whether ancient or modern. One of the beneficiaries of the trust, the life tenant, is very much 'the boss'. The life tenant holds the legal title to the trust property. The life tenant also has wide (though not unlimited) powers of disposition over the settled land.

Where there is a strict settlement, there will be 'trustees for the purposes of the Settled Land Acts'. But 'SLA trustees' do not hold the legal title or indeed (speaking generally) have much to do until the land is sold. The most important role of SLA trustees is that when a transaction by the life tenant gives rise to a capital payment (eg the price on a sale or the premium on the grant of a long lease), the SLA trustees receive and invest that capital payment.

Where a trust for sale of land was created under the 'old' law, the trustees were 'boss'. They held the legal estate to the land and they had the powers of disposition over the trust land. The trustees (for sale) were in control, just like every other type of trust except the strict settlement.

Section 29 LPA 1925 constituted a relatively small exception to the rule that 'the trustees are "bosses" of a trust for sale of land'. Under the old s29, trustees for sale had power to delegate certain of their functions to a beneficiary currently entitled to the income from the land.

The following two points regarding the old s29 are worth noting:

- the power to delegate was confined to the day-to-day management of the land and the leasing of the land. Other functions of the trustees (eg sale!) could not be delegated; and
- if the trustees delegated management and/or leasing, and the beneficiary failed to exercise his (delegated) powers with proper care, it was the beneficiary, never the trustees, who was liable for any loss suffered.

....
power of attorney
a formal deed appointing the 'donee of the power' to act as an agent of the donor of the power.
....

7.13.2 Delegation by Trustees Under s9 TOLATA 1996

Section 9 TOLATA 1996 is a far-reaching provision, much wider in its scope than s29 LPA 1925, which it 'replaces'. However, in one material respect s9 is narrower than the old s29. Under the old s29, a delegation could be made by a simple written document. Under s9 TOLATA 1996 the trustees (acting jointly) must, in order to delegate their functions, use a **power of attorney**.

Trusts of Land and Appointment of Trustees Act 1996

As amended by Sch 2 Part II para 45 Trustee Act 2000

9. Delegation by trustees

(1) The trustees of land may, by power of attorney, delegate to any beneficiary or beneficiaries of full age and beneficially entitled to an interest in possession in land subject to the trust any of their functions as trustees which relate to the land.

(2) Where trustees purport to delegate to a person by a power of attorney under subsection (1) functions relating to any land and another person in good faith deals with him in relation to the land, he shall be presumed in favour of that other person to have been a person to whom the functions could be delegated unless that other person has knowledge at the time of the transaction that he was not such a person.

   And it shall be conclusively presumed in favour of any purchaser whose interest depends on the validity of that transaction that that other person dealt in good faith and did not have such knowledge if that other person makes a statutory declaration to that effect before or within three months after the completion of the purchase.

(3) A power of attorney under subsection (1) shall be given by all the trustees jointly and (unless expressed to be irrevocable and to be given by way of security) may be revoked by any one or more of them; and such a power is revoked by the appointment as a trustee of a person other than those by whom it is given (though not by any of those persons dying or otherwise ceasing to be a trustee).

(4) Where a beneficiary to whom functions are delegated by a power of attorney under subsection (1) ceases to be a person beneficially entitled to an interest in possession in land subject to the trust—

   (a) if the functions are delegated to him alone, the power is revoked,

   (b) if the functions are delegated to him and to other beneficiaries to be exercised by them jointly (but not separately), the power is revoked if each of the other beneficiaries ceases to be so entitled (but otherwise functions exercisable in accordance with the power are so exercisable by the remaining beneficiary or beneficiaries), and

   (c) if the functions are delegated to him and to other beneficiaries to be exercised by them separately (or either separately or jointly), the power is revoked in so far as it relates to him.

(5) A delegation under subsection (1) may be for any period or indefinite.

(6) A power of attorney under subsection (1) cannot be an enduring power within the meaning of the Enduring Powers of Attorney Act 1985.

(7) Beneficiaries to whom functions have been delegated under subsection (1) are, in relation to the exercise of the functions, in the same position as trustees (with the same duties and liabilities); but such beneficiaries shall not be regarded as trustees for any other purposes (including, in particular, the purposes of any enactment permitting the delegation of functions by trustees or imposing requirements relating to the payment of capital money).

   . . .

(9) Neither this section nor the repeal by this Act of section 29 of the Law of Property Act 1925 (which is superseded by this section) affects the operation after the commencement of this Act of any delegation effected before that commencement.

The far-reaching nature of s9 should be apparent if you study the terms of subss (1) and (5).

Suppose Travis, Tefo, and Tuan hold Manor Farm on trust for Lamar for life, remainder to Matthew in fee simple. At one extreme Travis, Tefo, and Tuan could simply delegate the management of the farm to Lamar for a short period, say one year. At the other extreme they could execute a power of attorney saying, 'We delegate all our functions in relation to Manor Farm to Lamar for an indefinite period.' This latter sort of delegation will be referred to as 'total delegation'. The trustees retain the legal estate to the land, but will have absolutely no functions in relation to the land. (Note that there cannot be any delegation to Matthew—he is not a beneficiary entitled to an interest in possession.)

7.13.3 The Revocation of a Section 9 Power of Attorney

First, note that it is a characteristic of a power of attorney that it ceases to be valid if the donee of the power (Lamar in the example just given) dies or becomes incapable of acting. Of greater importance is s9(3).

Trusts of Land and Appointment of Trustees Act 1996

9. Delegation by trustees

(3) A power of attorney under subsection (1) shall be given by all the trustees jointly and...may be revoked by any one or more of them; and such a power is revoked by the appointment as a trustee of a person other than those by whom it is given (though not by any of those dying or otherwise ceasing to be a trustee).

Two specific points should be carefully noted about this provision:

- while all trustees must sign a delegation, a revocation can be achieved by one trustee acting on their own. Suppose in the Manor Farm example, Travis, Tefo, and Tuan all sign a total delegation. Travis subsequently becomes concerned about the way Lamar is dealing with Manor Farm. He can unilaterally revoke the delegation, even though Tefo and Tuan still have complete confidence in Lamar; and
- if a trustee dies or resigns from the trust, that does not revoke a s9 delegation. However, if a new trustee is appointed, that does revoke the delegation. Suppose in the Manor Farm example, Travis, rather than force the issue regarding Lamar's competence, resigns from the trust. This resignation will not end the s9 delegation. But if Tefo and Tuan then appoint another trustee, Tod, that appointment will revoke the delegation.

7.13.4 Liability if a Delegatee Beneficiary Proves to be Incompetent

The Manor Farm example raises the perhaps obvious question, 'What if Lamar really is incompetent to run the farm? Who must compensate the trust for losses which it suffers because of Lamar's incompetence?'

Liability of the Delegatee(s)

This is governed by s9(7) TOLATA 1996.

Trusts of Land and Appointment of Trustees Act 1996

9. Delegation by trustees

(7) Beneficiaries to whom functions have been delegated under subsection (1) are, in relation to the exercise of the functions, in the same position as trustees (with the same duties and liabilities) . . .

Thus a delegatee under s9 becomes a kind of quasi-trustee. A delegatee will be under the usual duty of a trustee to take good care of the trust property and to get the best financial return from the land obtainable by reasonable methods. For example, if a delegatee with a 'total delegation' decides to sell the land, the delegatee must get the best price reasonably obtainable. If the delegatee fails to get that 'best price', the other beneficiaries (and presumably the real trustees) could sue to compel the delegatee to make up the difference.

Liability of the Trustees—The 1996 Rule

The original Trusts of Land and Appointments of Trustees Bill, as drafted by the Law Commission, provided that trustees who delegated their functions would (in principle) be liable for the acts and defaults of the delegatee(s). Sexton (1989, at p 68) suggested that 'under the new scheme trustees of land will not want to delegate their powers to a beneficiary whose competence is open to question. Moreover, once they have delegated powers to a beneficiary, they will need, in their own interests, to keep the beneficiary under close supervision.' However, Parliament in 1996 decided to enact a different rule, much more favourable to trustees than that proposed by the Law Commission, found in s9(8).

> *Trusts of Land and Appointment of Trustees Act 1996*
>
> 9. Delegation by trustees
>
> (8) Where any function has been delegated to a beneficiary or beneficiaries under subsection (1), the trustees are jointly and severally liable for any act or default of the beneficiary, or of any of the beneficiaries, in the exercise of the function if, and only if, the trustees did not exercise reasonable care in deciding to delegate the function to the beneficiary or beneficiaries.

Thus it was the decision to delegate which mattered. If that decision to delegate was taken with reasonable care, but the delegatee messed things up and caused a loss to the trust, the trustees were not liable.

Liability of the Trustees—The Stricter Rule in the Trustee Act 2000

The generous rule to trustees in s9(8) TOLATA 1996 did not survive very long. Any delegation under s9 made after the commencement date of the Trustee Act 2000 (1 February 2001) is governed by s9A TOLATA 1996 (inserted by Sch 2 Part II para 45 Trustee Act 2000).

> *Trusts of Land and Appointment of Trustees Act 1996*
>
> 9A. Duties of trustees in connection with delegation
>
> (1) The duty of care under section 1 of the Trustee Act 2000 applies to trustees of land in deciding whether to delegate any of their functions under section 9.
>
> (2) Subsection (3) applies if the trustees of land—
>
> (a) delegate any of their functions under section 9, and
>
> (b) the delegation is not irrevocable.
>
> (3) While the delegation continues, the trustees—
>
> (a) must keep the delegation under review,
>
> (b) if circumstances make it appropriate to do so, must consider whether there is a need to exercise any power of intervention that they have, and
>
> (c) if they consider that there is a need to exercise such a power, must do so.

(4) 'Power of intervention' includes—

    (a) a power to give directions to the beneficiary;

    (b) a power to revoke the delegation.

(5) The duty of care under section 1 of the 2000 Act applies to trustees in carrying out any duty under subsection (3).

(6) A trustee of land is not liable for any act or default of the beneficiary, or beneficiaries, unless the trustee fails to comply with the duty of care in deciding to delegate any of the trustees' functions under section 9 or in carrying out any duty under subsection (3).

(7) Neither this section nor the repeal of section 9(8) by the Trustee Act 2000 affects the operation after the commencement of this section of any delegation effected before that commencement.

Do not be confused by the reference to irrevocable delegations in s9A(2)(b). With the kinds of trusts we are concerned with in a land law course, a delegation is always revocable.

Under s9A the trustees are under a duty to take reasonable care to keep an active watch on the delegatee beneficiary, and to 'intervene' under subsection (4) if things appear to be going wrong. The trustees could 'intervene' by revoking (or at least threatening to revoke) the delegation or could give directions to the delegatee beneficiary. If trustees failed to keep a careful eye on the beneficiary, and/or failed to 'intervene' when things seemed to be going wrong, the trustees could be liable to compensate the other beneficiaries for any loss suffered.

cross-reference
See 7.11 for a discussion of Sch 1 para 7 Trustee Act 2000.

The practical effect of this s9A is that trustees of land may be less keen to delegate the running of the land to the relevant beneficiary(ies) for fear of incurring liability under this section. Suppose, then, that you are drafting a trust of land where the settlor is actually keen that the life beneficiary (Lamar in the Manor Farm example) should actually run the land. It is suggested that in drafting the trust, a clause should be inserted excluding the trustees' duty under s9A TOLATA 1996. This can be done under Sch 1 para 7 Trustee Act 2000 which allows trusts to include 'exemption clauses' limiting or excluding the trustees' liability for negligent acts.

211

7.13.5 Total Delegation Almost like Settled Land

You may find this heading puzzling, but where the trustees of land make a total delegation, the situation becomes somewhat analogous to 'old-fashioned' settled land. Why is this so?

There are two factors to consider. First, when there is a total delegation, the delegatee beneficiary, like a life tenant of settled land, becomes the effective 'boss' of the trust land. The second factor is an important point which has not been previously mentioned. The trustees can delegate those functions 'which relate to the land'. That phrase does not include the receiving and investing of any 'capital money' payable by a purchaser if the delegatee makes a disposition over the land. So if the delegatee beneficiary sells the land, the purchaser must pay the price to the trustees. If the purchaser pays the price to the delegatee, the equitable interests of the other beneficiaries will not be overreached. Similarly, if land is leased at a premium, the premium must be paid by the tenant to the trustees, not the delegatee who granted the lease.

There are, of course, significant differences between settled land and total delegation under a trust of land. In particular, even though there is a total delegation, the legal estate to the trust land remains with the trustees. When the delegatee sells, the delegatee is actually (validly) conveying a legal estate the delegatee has not got.

It should also be remembered that a total delegatee, unlike a life tenant, will have unlimited powers of disposition over the trust land. On the other hand, a life tenant cannot (normally) have their powers revoked. A delegatee's powers can be revoked by one trustee, perhaps acting in opposition to the other trustee(s) who wish the delegation to continue. Moreover, there is no duty to give any reason for the revocation.

thinking point 7.16

John is a farmer aged 65. He wishes to retire from farming. He wishes to create a trust over his farm, Widefields, with equitable interests 'to my daughter Linda [aged 35] for life, remainder in fee simple to her son Zak [aged 5]'. Linda has helped her father run the farm since graduating from agricultural college. John tells you proudly: 'She is a first-rate farmer, and with excellent business sense. I want her to have total control of Widefields. It is of course too early to say how Zak will turn out. He might not want to be a farmer. So when Linda in her turn retires, I want her to have the power to sell Widefields.' Advise John.

John cannot, of course, create a strict settlement. He would create a trust of land, appointing as trustees people who fully understand his intentions. (He should perhaps select younger members of 'our' firm of solicitors.) He should include in the trust the following three provisions:

- *a statement that a purpose of the trust is to allow Linda to occupy Widefields farm (he thus invokes s12 TOLATA 1996, which, it should be stressed, is not confined to residential premises);*

- *a paragraph setting out his views as to his daughter's capabilities as a farmer and businesswoman, and strongly recommending that the trustees make a 'total delegation' in her favour; and*

- *a clause exempting the trustees from the duty under s9A TOLATA 1996.*

(The trustees could make a total delegation confident that an accusation of negligence against them would get short shrift from a court.)

 # Concluding Remarks

In this chapter we have considered the various situations where a trust of land will exist and also certain rules which are common to all types of trust (including trusts of stocks and shares); these rules are not confined to trusts of land. This serves to underline a very important point. The trust for sale of land and the trust of land are merely two species of a very large family of 'animals', all of which are classified as 'trusts'. Remember that, as we said in Chapter 1, 'any type of property can be subjected to a trust'.

Land is, however, a very different type of asset from, say, shares or debentures. It cannot be moved, but it can be put to all sorts of uses and made subject to a wide range of transactions. It therefore necessarily follows that trustees of land need wide powers of disposition and management which will be irrelevant to trusts of abstract assets such as shares or debentures. It is these powers of disposition which we considered in some detail. Although this chapter covers most of the important provisions of the Trusts of Land and Appointment of Trustees Act 1996, we have not, however, considered ss 13, 14, and 15, though s14 has received a brief mention. These three sections provide for the settling of any disputes which may arise regarding a trust of land. While these sections are in principle applicable to all trusts of land, they are likely to be of particular importance where the trust of land exists in favour of co-owners. The law of co-ownership will be discussed in more detail in Chapters 8 and 9, and it will be sensible to deal with ss 13–15 of TOLATA in Chapter 9.

The provisions we have considered in this chapter are certainly not immune from criticism. The biggest problem is of course s8(1). This is a charter for eccentric settlors to saddle their families with unsaleable land. It seems to put the clock back to before 1882. Moreover, we should contrast eccentric settlors who impose total takeaway clauses with James in thinking point 7.4 at 7.5.2. He proposes an eminently sensible solution to the problems of his family but he is not allowed to adopt that solution because the power to postpone sale cannot be excluded. James cannot insist that the land be sold within a defined period.

# Summary

Trusts Prior to the TOLATA 1996

There were three types of trust of land:

Bare Trust

The equitable fee simple which existed under such a trust was still subject to the doctrine of notice. It was not overreachable.

Strict Settlement

This was an anachronism even in 1996. Where there is a strict settlement:

- the life tenant (not independent trustees) acts as trustee of the land, has the legal title to the land, and can even sell the land;
- if the life tenant sells the land, the price is paid by the purchaser to independent 'Trustees for the purposes of the Settled Land Act'; and
- strict settlements involved very complicated conveyancing documents.

Trust for Sale

- The trustees held the legal title and were theoretically under a duty to sell the land and invest the proceeds.
- In reality, most trustees for sale postponed the sale of the land, often indefinitely, and allowed the beneficiaries to enjoy the land.
- The (rather paradoxical) concept of trust for sale where the sale could only take place with the consent of named persons proved very useful, particularly when creating a trust of the family home.

Scope of the 1996 Act

With the sole exception of the relatively few strict settlements in existence on 1 January 1997, all trusts of land are now governed by the TOLATA 1996.

In particular the 1996 Act extends to:

- trusts for sale existing on 1 January 1997;
- trusts for sale created after 1996;
- all trusts of land deliberately created after 1996;
- all trusts of land accidentally created after 1996;
- all bare trusts of land, whenever created; and
- all attempts to convey land to a minor.

Appointment of Trustees

- The settlor should appoint the original trustees.
- A minor cannot be a trustee.
- As a general rule, the existing trustees appoint new or replacement trustees.
- Where a trustee is also a beneficiary, and that trustee disposes of his equitable interest under the trust, that disposal is not a resignation from the trust.

Saunders v Vautier and Section 19 TOLATA 1996

Where the beneficiaries of a trust are of full age and in total agreement, they can do what they like with the trust property. They can also dismiss the existing trustees and replace them with their own choices.

Right to Occupy Trust Land

Section 12 TOLATA 1996 gives the current beneficiary(ies) a right to occupy the land if either:

- the trust was set up with a view to personal occupation by the beneficiary(ies); or
- the land was acquired by the trustees with a view to personal occupation by the beneficiary(ies).

Trustees' Powers

In principle, trustees have all the powers of an outright owner of land (s6 TOLATA 1996), but those powers can be limited, either by:

- a partial or total takeaway clause restricting those powers (s8(1) TOLATA 1996);
- a consent clause allowing some or all powers to be only exercised if the consent of named person(s) is obtained (s8(2) TOLATA 1996).

Delegation of Trustees' Powers

Section 9 TOLATA 1996 allows the trustees to delegate any or all of their powers to the current beneficiary. But the trustees must be sure that the initial decision to delegate is a wise one. Furthermore, the trustees must now supervise the delegatee beneficiary, and intervene if things start going wrong (s9A TOLATA 1996).

 # Further Reading

Clements, L, 'The changing face of trusts: the Trusts of Land and Appointment of Trustees Act 1996' (1998) 61 MLR 56
Provides an overview of the TOLATA 1996.

Ferris, G and Bramley, E, 'The construction of sub-section 6(5) of the Trusts of Land and Appointment of Trustees Act 1996: when is a "right" not a "right"?' [2009] Conv 39
Considers the interpretation of s6(5) and its scope.

Law Commission, *Transfer of Land—Trusts of Land* (Report No 181, 1989)
For the thinking which led to the enactment of the 1996 Act and the reasoning behind the various provisions of the 1996 Act, see pp 1–25.

Pascoe, S, 'Right to occupy under a trust of land: muddled legislative logic' [2006] Conv 54
Article analyses the nature and scope of s12.

Sexton, R, 'The Law Commission's Report on Trusts of Land, at last a law for contemporary society' (1989) Trusts Law and Practice 65
A commentary on the report which led to the passage of TOLATA 1996.

Watt, G, 'Escaping s 8(1) provisions in "new style" trusts of land' (1997) 61 Conv 263
A discussion on the possible ways round the problems created by s8(1) TOLATA 1996.

? Questions

Gloria owns two houses, Hillside House and Mulberry House. She is critically ill and wishes to make a new will.

With respect to Hillside House, she wants to leave it to her son Ramon for life, remainder in fee simple to her grandsons Luis and Julio. 'I am very keen that Luis and Julio should inherit Hillside House after Ramon's death. I don't want the house disposed of during Ramon's lifetime.'

With respect to Mulberry House, she wants to leave it to her cousin Nicolas for life, remainder in fee simple to Nicolas's two children Phil and Philippa. 'Mulberry House is rather large and a long way from the shops. It may prove unsuitable for Nicolas. If that proves to be the case, would it be possible for him, or somebody on his behalf, to sell Mulberry House and buy (say) a lease of a smaller house on the edge of the town centre?'

Advise Gloria as to the drafting of her will.

8

Co-Ownership of Land—The Basic Principles

Introduction

pause for thought

Can you think of other examples of co-ownership of land?

The law of co-ownership is a topic which directly affects the private lives of many of the readers of this text. In the main, couples who are married, civil partners, or cohabitees co-own the fee simple of the house in which they live. Alternatively, they co-own a fixed term lease or periodic tenancy of the house or flat in which they are living. It should, however, be stressed that co-ownership is not confined to domestic/family situations. For example, business partners may well be co-owners of the premises from which they conduct their business.

This chapter will focus on certain basic principles. It has three main themes. The first is that there are two very distinct forms of co-ownership in modern English property law. The second is the way Parliament, in 1925, endeavoured to solve problems which existed at that time in relation to co-ownership. The third is how a joint tenancy may be severed and turned into a tenancy in common.

8.1 The Two Forms of Co-Ownership Existing Today

There were at common law four forms of co-ownership, but only two forms of co-ownership exist today:

- *Joint tenancy* Extremely common today; it is the usual (but not obligatory) form of co-ownership where the co-owners are members of the same 'family'.

- *Tenancy in common* This is common today. It is usual (but not obligatory) where the co-owners are in a business relationship. Sometimes found within a 'family'.

The words 'tenant' and 'tenancy' in this context are used in their older, broader, sense. The word 'tenant' connotes anybody who holds an estate in land, whether a fee simple, fee tail, life estate, or lease.

8.2 Joint Tenancy

Joint tenancy, at least in modern circumstances, is the simpler of the two forms of co-ownership. A joint tenancy indicates that the co-owners are holding the property concurrently.

Diagram 8.1
Joint tenancy

The co-owners are to be treated as a unit, whereby each co-owner is entitled to the whole of the property (per Lord Nicholls, *Burton v Camden LBC* (2000) 2 AC 399). This can be seen in Diagram 8.1.

A, B, and C hold the property as joint tenants and are treated as one complete entity. It is important to note that it is technically wrong to talk of joint tenants having 'shares' in land, one should rather talk of joint tenants having 'interests' or 'rights'. There are two crucial distinguishing features of a joint tenancy:

- right of survivorship; and
- 'four unities'.

8.2.1 Right of Survivorship (*Ius Accrescendi*)

On the death of a joint tenant his interest does not pass under the law of succession, but rather passes to the surviving joint tenant(s). Diagram 8.2 shows the position that initially A, B, and C are joint tenants. C dies. C's interest will pass to the surviving joint tenants.

Diagram 8.2
Right of survivorship

To illustrate how the right of survivorship operates consider the following example: Aidan, Ben, and Callum are joint tenants of Bramley Manor in fee simple. Callum dies. His will leaves 'all my property to my sister Donatella'. Donatella acquires no interest in Bramley Manor. Aidan and Ben are now joint tenants of Bramley Manor. This would even be true if Callum's will had said, 'I leave all my property including my interest in Bramley Manor to Donatella.'

Suppose that Ben now dies intestate, with his widow Elspeth as his sole 'statutory next of kin'. Elspeth acquires no interest in Bramley Manor. Aidan will be the sole outright owner in fee simple of Bramley Manor. When he dies normal succession laws will apply. To put the matter crudely, there is a sort of 'survival of the fittest'. Where there is a joint tenancy, the joint tenant who lives longest gets outright ownership.

This survivorship rule is the main reason why husband and wife co-owners, and other co-owners who are in a close family-type relationship, usually choose to be joint tenants rather than tenants in common. They genuinely wish the land to go to whoever lives longest. The survivorship rule also explains why people who are trustees of property (whether land or any other type of property) are always joint tenants of that property. There are no complications when a trustee dies. The legal title to the trust property automatically passes to the remaining trustee(s).

thinking point 8.1

Naresh and Indira, his wife, are joint tenants of The Copse, worth about £700,000. Naresh is killed in a road accident. He dies intestate. His assets (apart from The Copse) are worth £240,000. He leaves two children, Prakash and Reena. On intestacy a surviving spouse is always entitled to the first £250,000 of the deceased's assets. Above that figure and the children get a share.

Do the children inherit anything on their father's death intestate?

The children inherit nothing, and that would be true even if The Copse were worth not £700,000 but (say) £7,000,000. In working out who gets the deceased's assets on a death intestate, the fact that the deceased was a joint tenant of a (possibly valuable) piece of property must be totally ignored. Thus Indira is entitled to the £240,000 'other' assets left by her husband.

8.2.2 The 'Four Unities'

Wherever there is a joint tenancy, it necessarily follows that 'the four unities' exist between the co-owners:

- unity of possession;
- unity of interest;
- unity of title; and
- unity of time.

For co-owners to be joint tenants, the four unities: possession, interest, title, and time must be present. The unity of possession can be regarded as the cornerstone of co-ownership, without it co-ownership does not exist. What if one or more of the other unities listed were absent (ie interest, title, or time)? If any of these three unities is absent, the co-owners will be tenants in common.

Unity of Possession—The Cornerstone of Co-Ownership

Co-ownership exists with respect to a piece of land only if 'unity of possession' between two or more people exists with respect to that piece of land. There is unity of possession if two or more people have concurrent rights to enjoy the whole of the relevant piece of land. For example, Jack and Jill Smith own Dream House. They will each have rights to possess and enjoy the whole of the house. There is unity of possession and therefore co-ownership.

Contrast Dream House with Hollowtree Field. Farmers Dan and Gary 'own' Hollowtree Field. To the ordinary passer-by it appears to be a perfectly normal field. However, there is an imaginary line running north–south across the field. Dan and Gary know where this boundary line is. Everything to the east of that line belongs exclusively to Dan, and Gary has no rights. Everything to the west belongs to Gary, and Dan has no rights. Is there a joint tenancy in this situation? Of course not, there is no unity of possession and therefore no joint tenancy; indeed there is no co-ownership, but rather two separate individual ownerships.

Unity of Interest

For there to be unity of interest, each co-owner must have absolutely identical rights over the land in question. This subdivides into two separate points:

- *Each co-owner must have the same estate* It is of course possible for two or more people to be joint tenants. For example, A, B, and C are joint tenants of a ten-year lease. What is not possible is a joint tenancy between somebody with a ten-year lease and somebody with a 20-year lease.

- *Each co-owner must have an equal right to enjoy the land* Where there is a tenancy in common it is possible for the co-owners to have unequal shares. But where there is a joint tenancy, each joint tenant must have an equal interest in the land.

Assume Len, Mike, Ned, and Ossie are joint tenants in fee simple of Blue Field. They lease Blue Field to Terri. Each of the four joint landlords is entitled to 25 per cent of the rent.

It follows from unity of interest that transactions with the relevant land (eg conveyances or leases) require the agreement of all the joint tenants. However, where a periodic tenancy is held by joint tenants, one joint tenant can terminate the tenancy without the agreement of the other(s), *Hammersmith & Fulham LBC v Monk* [1992] 1 AC 478; *Sims v Dacorum BC* [2014] 3 WLR 1600).

Unity of Title

cross-reference
Severance is discussed at 8.11, 8.12, and 8.13.

This means that each joint tenant must have acquired his interest from the same document or transaction. As we shall see later when talking about 'severance', it is possible to have a situation where there is co-ownership but the co-owners have acquired their rights under different transactions. Such co-owners must necessarily be tenants in common.

Unity of Time

For there to be a joint tenancy, the rights of each joint tenant must 'vest in interest' at the same time. Put in more everyday language, the rights of each joint tenant must commence at the same moment.

It is relatively rare to come across situations where the rights of co-owners commence at different times. But sometimes land is left by will (or granted by deed) in terms such as 'to the children of X as each attains 21'. Now (unless all the children are twins/triplets/quads, etc) each child will attain 21 on a different date. There will be no unity of time. The children will therefore be tenants in common.

---

thinking point 8.2

What if land were granted 'to the children of X when the youngest attains 21'. Could the children in this example be joint tenants?

There would be unity of time, and the children therefore could be joint tenants.

8.3 Tenancy in Common

8.3.1 The Concept of Undivided Shares

Where a tenancy in common exists, the co-owners are said to own the property in 'undivided shares'. Each co-owner is regarded as having a distinct share in the property. The use of the adjective 'undivided' emphasizes that there is unity of possession. The land in question has not been physically divided up between the owners.

When a tenant in common dies there is no right of survivorship. The deceased tenant's share passes under the normal law of succession. Let us suppose that Aidan, Ben, and Callum, the same people mentioned at 8.2.1 as being joint tenants of Bramley Manor, are also tenants in common in equal shares of Lodge Farm. (See Diagram 8.3.)

Diagram 8.3
Aidan, Ben, and Callum are tenants in common of Lodge Farm

Aidan   Ben   Callum

When Aidan dies his one-third share in Lodge Farm passes according to the terms of his will to his sister Donatella. When Ben dies intestate his one-third share passes under the normal rules of intestacy to his widow Elspeth. (See Diagram 8.4.)

Diagram 8.4
Aidan dies and leaves his one-third share to Donatella. Ben dies intestate and his share passes to Elspeth

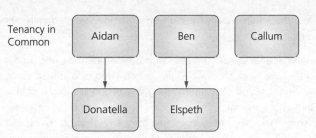

Tenancy in Common

Aidan — Donatella

Ben — Elspeth

Callum

thinking point 8.3

Naresh and Indira are tenants in common in equal shares of The Copse, worth about £700,000. Naresh is killed in a road accident. He dies intestate. His assets (apart from The Copse) are worth £240,000. He leaves two children, Prakash and Reena. On intestacy a surviving spouse is always entitled to the first £250,000 of the deceased's assets. Above that figure and the children get a share.

Do the children inherit anything on their father's death intestate?

This time, the answer is 'yes.' On his death, Naresh's assets are worth £590,000, his half share in The Copse plus his 'other' assets. Indira will be entitled outright to the first £250,000. The remaining £340,000 is split between her and the two children employing a rather complex formula the details of which we need not consider.

8.3.2 Unequal Tenancies in Common

As has already been stressed, unity of possession is an essential feature of a tenancy in common. The other three 'unities', namely interest, title, and time, may be present in a tenancy in common but are not essential.

It is particularly important to note that there can be a tenancy in common in unequal shares. For example, Len, Mike, Ned, and Ossie are tenants in common of Red Field, Len with a one-third share, Mike and Ned with a quarter share each, and Ossie with one-sixth. They must share the benefits of the field in the appropriate proportions.

thinking point 8.4

Len, Mike, Ned, and Ossie lease Red Field to Toni at £1,200 per annum rent. How should the rent be divided between them?

The rent should be divided £400 to Len, £300 each to Mike and Ned, and £200 to Ossie.

8.3.3 The Problems with Tenancies in Common in the Early Twentieth Century

At the beginning of the twentieth century joint tenancies were far less common than they are today. The idea (so prevalent today) of members of a family buying a home as joint tenants was almost unknown. On the other hand, there were a lot of tenancies in common, probably far more than exist today. In 1900, if a family 'owned' a farm, or a small business such as a shop, then usually the individual members of the family owned the land as tenants in common.

Nowadays, if a family 'owns' a farm or business premises, one usually finds on closer examination that the farm, shop, or whatever is owned by a limited company bearing some title such as 'Bloggs Brothers Limited'. Bloggs Brothers Limited is in law one person, therefore the land is not co-owned. The individual brothers will be shareholders in the company. They will also probably be directors of the company, though that is not essential. There is no legal limit on the maximum number of directors a company can have.

Reverting to talking about co-ownership of land, you may have already noticed a practical conclusion to be drawn from the 'Aidan, Ben, and Callum' examples at 8.2.1 and 8.3.1. Where there is a joint tenancy, the number of joint tenants will gradually decline by a process of natural wastage until the last survivor emerges as sole owner. Where there is a tenancy in common the fact that the shares of each co-owner pass according to the law of succession means that the number of co-owners is unlikely to decline, and the co-ownership is unlikely to come to an end.

We are at last getting to the problem which existed in the first part of the twentieth century. Suppose that in 1900 four brothers, Felix, Gerald, Harry, and Ian were tenants in common in equal shares of the fee simple in Streamfield Farm. In 1901, Jack, a neighbouring farmer, offered to buy a field which is inconveniently remote from the rest of Streamfield (see Diagram 8.5). The brothers accepted the offer and conveyed the field to Jack. For the conveyance to be valid all four brothers had to sign, as all four had a share in the legal fee simple in the field. (Getting four signatures on a document is not that difficult, particularly if the four people live in close proximity. But let us continue the story of Streamfield Farm.)

222

Diagram 8.5
Felix, Gerald, Harry, and Ian are tenants in common; Jack has bought a field from them

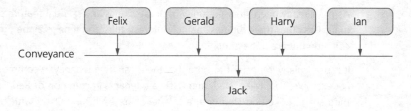

In 1905, Felix died. His will said 'My share in Streamfield is to be divided in equal shares between my three children.' In 1910, Gerald died. His will said 'My share in Streamfield is to be divided in equal shares between my four children'. In 1915, Harry died. His will said 'My share in Streamfield is to be divided in equal shares between my five children.' In 1920, Ian died. His will said 'My share in Streamfield is to be divided in equal shares between my six children.'

Thus in the early 1920s no fewer than 18 people were tenants in common of Streamfield Farm. This sort of situation was not uncommon. A whole host of people would be tenants in common of a piece of land. Some might have an extremely small share (see Diagram 8.6).

In 1921, Jack offered to buy the rest of Streamfield Farm at a price which all 14 tenants in common still in Britain thought was irresistible. The problem was the four who were abroad. Kate, Felix's daughter, had married and gone to Australia; Lance, one of Gerald's sons, was a sheep farmer in New Zealand; Morris, one of Harry's sons, was a 'Mountie' in remote north-west Canada; Nicola, one of Ian's children, had gone exploring in the Amazon jungle.

Diagram 8.6
Streamfield Farm in the early 1920s

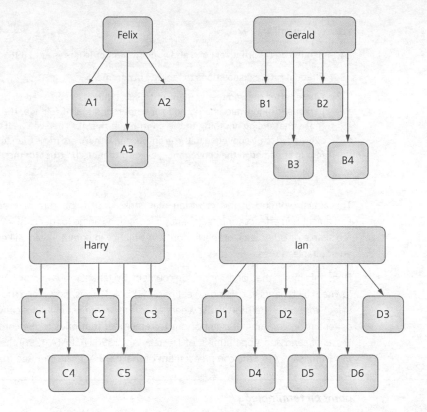

For a valid conveyance of the legal fee simple in Streamfield Farm, all 18 would have had to have signed. Some of the signatures could not be obtained. Reluctantly, Jack had to withdraw his offer. Effectively, Streamfield Farm was unsaleable. Stories like the one of Streamfield Farm were commonplace in 1925. Remember that 1925 was in an era of large families and the far-flung British Empire. Passenger planes and telecommunications were in their infancy. Parliament therefore decided that a drastic remedy was needed to solve the problem caused by tenancies in common. This remedy also affected joint tenancies.

8.4 The Reform of Co-Ownership in 1925—The Main Objective

cross-reference
Streamfield Farm is discussed at 8.3.3.

Parliament was desperate to ameliorate the problem illustrated by our Streamfield Farm example. It thus passed reforms (to be found in ss 34–36 Law of Property Act 1925 (LPA 1925)) which ensured that where land is co-owned a *maximum* of four signatures is required on any conveyance or other transaction affecting that land.

8.4.1 Drastic Treatment for Tenancies in Common

It would clearly have been impossible to completely abolish tenancies in common. Parliament did, however, enact s34 LPA 1925.

Law of Property Act 1925

As amended by the Trusts of Land and Appointment of Trustees Act 1996

34. Effect of future dispositions to tenants in common

(2) Where, after the commencement of this Act, land is expressed to be conveyed to any persons in undivided shares and those persons are of full age, the conveyance shall (notwithstanding anything to the contrary in this Act) operate as if the land had been expressed to be conveyed to the grantees, or, if there are more than four grantees, to the four first named in the conveyance, as joint tenants [in trust for the persons interested in the land] . . .

The actual wording of this provision may strike you as obscure or even intimidating. But Parliament is in effect saying, 'A tenancy in common can no longer exist with respect to a legal fee simple or other legal property rights. A tenancy in common can still exist with respect to an equitable interest.'

Does this mean that land cannot be 'owned' by tenants in common? No, land can still be 'owned' by tenants in common. Section 34(2) LPA 1925 is, however, crucial. This provision in effect imposes a 'statutory' trust where an estate or interest in land is conveyed to co-owners as tenants in common. It is important to remember that prior to the commencement of the Trusts of Land and Appointment of Trustees Act 1996 (TOLATA 1996) the imposed trust was a trust for sale. After the commencement of the 1996 Act, the imposed trust is a trust of land.

point on terminology

Whenever in Chapters 8 and 9 you read the phrase 'trust (for sale)', we are referring to a situation where prior to the commencement of the 1996 Act there was a trust for sale, but after its commencement there is a trust of land.

An example should explain how s34(2) LPA 1925 operates. In 1990 the fee simple in Stoneygate Farm was conveyed 'to Keith, Lars, Marc, and Nasser as tenants in common in equal shares'. This conveyance would, in 1990, have the following consequences:

- Stoneygate Farm is subject to a trust for sale;
- provided they were of full age at the time of the conveyance, Keith, Lars, Marc, and Nasser are the trustees of the trust for sale;
- like all other trustees, they hold the legal fee simple in Stoneygate Farm as *joint tenants*;
- Keith, Lars, Marc, and Nasser are also the beneficiaries of the trust (for sale). Each has a quarter share of the equitable interest under the trust as *tenants in common*. While the land remains unsold, each is entitled to a quarter of any income derived from the land. ('Income' includes profits from personal cultivation or rent from tenants.) When the land is sold, each will be entitled to a quarter of the proceeds of sale;
- like trustees for sale generally, Keith, Lars, Marc, and Nasser have the power to postpone the sale of land;
- in practical terms perhaps the most important point, the four 'trustees' will almost certainly not want to sell the land immediately. They will therefore exercise their power to postpone sale. Indeed, the four men may not know that there is a trust for sale. If that is the case, they will be subconsciously exercising the power to postpone; and

- from 1 January 1997, Stoneygate Farm is subject to a trust of land under the TOLATA 1996. It is no longer necessary to talk of the four men subconsciously exercising the power to postpone sale.

8.4.2 Why Impose Trusts on Tenants in Common?

Take our Stoneygate Farm example a little further. Let us suppose that Keith died in 2014. His will read, 'all my property I give to my four daughters Oliva, Penny, Querida, and Rita in equal shares'. The ownership position regarding the farm is as follows and as illustrated in Diagram 8.7:

- *The legal estate* This, of course, was held by the four men as trustees and as joint tenants. When Keith died there was a survivorship in the usual way. Thus Lars, Marc, and Nasser are now trustees of the legal title.

- *The equitable interests under the trust (of land)* Lars, Marc, Nasser, Oliva, Penny, Querida, and Rita are now all beneficiaries under the trust. The three men each have a quarter share. The four women each have a one-sixteenth share.

Diagram 8.7
Co-ownership of Stoneygate Farm following Keith's death in 2014

cross-reference
See 4.8.1 for a discussion on overreaching.

225

Suppose that Samir is now keen to buy Stoneygate Farm, and is willing to pay an attractive price. He should make his offer to the three trustees, since they hold the legal estate. If the trustees do decide to sell, they alone need sign the contract and conveyance. When the sale takes place the rights of all seven beneficiaries will be overreached.

---

thinking point 8.5

Just pause for a moment, think about this Stoneygate Farm example, and consider why the imposition of the trust (of land) on the tenants in common was a wise change in the law.

You should now see the advantage gained by imposing the trust (of land) upon the tenancy in common. The usual rule limiting the number of trustees of land to four applies (s34(2) LPA 1925); thus the number of owners of the legal title is strictly limited. Moreover it is the trustees who decide on whether the land should be sold, leased, etc. The 'overreaching' device ensures that the trustees' decisions bind the non-trustee beneficiaries. The usual rule that where there is a sale by trustees (of land) a minimum of two trustees is required to effect an overreaching also normally applies to imposed trusts (of land). However, as we shall see at 9.2.1, there is a significant exception to this 'minimum of two' rule. Under this exception a sale by a sole trustee will in certain circumstances be valid.

The usual rules for the appointment, retirement, and removal of trustees apply to imposed trusts (of land). If in the Stoneygate Farm example Lars, Marc, and Nasser wish to appoint one additional trustee they may do so. Moreover they can choose anybody. They are not obliged to pick from Oliva, Penny, Querida, and Rita.

cross-reference
See 7.7 on the rules for appointment, retirement, and removal of trustees.

It must also be stressed that if there are three trustees (of land) of a piece of land, all three must sign conveyances and other transactions with the land. If there are four trustees (of land), all four must sign conveyances and other transactions with the land.

8.4.3 What If There Are More Than Four Tenants in Common to Start With?

cross-reference
Conveyance to a minor is discussed at 'Conveying Land to a Minor' at 7.3.4.

Suppose land is conveyed 'to A, B, C, D, E, F, and G as tenants in common'. You may have already noticed that s34(2) LPA 1925 provides an answer to this problem. There is a somewhat arbitrary rule that the first four people, of full age, named in the conveyance will be the trustees.

Suppose that in this example C is only 17 at the date of the conveyance. A, B, D, and E will be the original trustees. C being 17 years old cannot hold a legal estate (Sch 1 para 1(1) TOLATA 1996). C's interest in the estate will be reflected in equity as a tenant in common. A, B, D, and E will of course remain the trustees when C attains 18 (see Diagram 8.8).

Diagram 8.8
Co-ownership of property where there are more than four tenants

LAW

EQUITY

If B dies, A, D, and E will continue as trustees. They may appoint a fourth trustee. If they do, they can appoint anybody. They are not obliged to pick C, F, or G.

8.5 Joint Tenancies in the Early Twentieth Century

Because of the convenience of the survivorship rule, trustees of property (land or any other property) have always been made joint tenants of the legal title to the property. Prior to 1925, joint tenancies of land were quite common. However, where such a joint tenancy existed with respect to a piece of land it usually transpired that the joint tenants held the land not for their own benefit but as trustees for other people.

In the early part of the twentieth century beneficial joint tenancies, that is, joint tenants holding land for their own personal enjoyment rather than as trustees, were relatively rare. This is in very marked contrast to the position today. There must be now several million 'beneficial' joint tenancies. Most, but not all, of these joint tenancies will exist where husband and wife, cohabitees, or civil partners jointly own their home.

8.5.1 Imposition of Trusts (for Sale) on Beneficial Joint Tenants

In 1925, Parliament (at a time when beneficial joint tenancies were rare) decided to impose a trust (for sale) on beneficial joint tenants (see s36(1) LPA 1925).

> *Law of Property Act 1925*
>
> 36. Joint tenancies.
>
> (1) Where a legal estate (not being settled land) is beneficially limited to or held in trust for any persons as joint tenants, the same shall be held in trust, in like manner as if the persons beneficially entitled were tenants in common, but not so as to sever their joint tenancy in equity.

As with tenancies in common the joint tenants are themselves the trustees (for sale). In the unusual event of there being more than four joint tenants, the first four named in the conveyance, of full age, will be the trustees.

Suppose David and Yvette Sidel decided in 1965 to buy 23 Eden Roc Avenue (a fee simple estate) as joint tenants, a kind of transaction which today is extremely commonplace. The fee simple in 23 Eden Roc Avenue is conveyed 'to David and Yvette Sidel as beneficial joint tenants'. A trust (for sale) was imposed upon David and Yvette, and the ownership position regarding 23 Eden Roc Avenue would have been as follows in Diagram 8.9:

Diagram 8.9
23 Eden Roc Avenue: co-ownership in law and in equity

LEGAL ESTATE

This is vested in David and Yvette as joint tenants and as trustees (for sale)

> David Yvette

EQUITY

David and Yvette are also joint tenants of the equitable interest under the trust (for sale)

> David Yvette

David and Yvette probably do not know that a trust (for sale) has been thrust upon them. There can be no doubt that David and Yvette would have been, prior to the commencement of the 1996 Act, subconsciously exercising 'the power to postpone sale' and enjoying the benefits of the trust by living in the house.

8.5.2 Why Impose a Trust (for Sale) on Joint Tenants?

Perhaps you have already been asking yourself this question. After all, we have already seen that, because of the survivorship rule, it is a natural characteristic of a joint tenancy that the number of joint tenants gradually dwindles to one. Moreover, although joint tenancies are far more common today than they were in 1925, modern joint tenancies usually start with only two joint tenants.

The answer to the question lies in the fact that Parliament in 1925 had to take into account the possibility of 'severance' of a joint tenancy. Every joint tenant has the right to 'sever' the joint tenancy. If a joint tenant does this, the joint tenant converts their interest as joint tenant into a share as tenant in common. That share becomes subject to the normal law of succession.

Prior to 1925 a joint tenant could sever their right in the legal estate. Since 1925 this has not been possible. Since 1925 any severance affects only the equitable interest under the trust (for sale). It is not necessary at this stage to explain how a severance is achieved (nowadays, as we shall see later on in this chapter, it is easy to achieve). What is needed is an example of the effects of severance.

Let us suppose that in 1990 three close friends, Rachel, Sally, and Tanya, decided to buy Quickthornes. The fee simple in Quickthornes was conveyed to them as joint tenants. They consciously chose to be joint tenants as they wished the survivorship rule to operate. The result of the 1990 conveyance was that there was a trust (for sale), but with the three women as both trustees of the legal title and joint tenants of the equitable interest under the trust (see Diagram 8.10).

Diagram 8.10
Quickthornes: co-ownership in law and in equity

LEGAL ESTATE

Rachel, Sally, and Tanya are joint tenants

> Rachel Sally Tanya

EQUITY

Rachel, Sally, and Tanya are joint tenants

> Rachel Sally Tanya

Now suppose that in 1994 Tanya quarrelled with Rachel and Sally. She consequently severed the joint tenancy. The position as to ownership of Quickthornes would now be as follows in Diagram 8.11:

Diagram 8.11
Quickthornes: Tanya's severance of the joint tenancy

LEGAL ESTATE

There would be no change. The three women remain trustees and joint tenants of the legal fee simple estate in Quickthornes

> Rachel Sally Tanya

EQUITY

Tanya now has a one-third share as tenant in common. Rachel and Sally own two-thirds as joint tenants

> Rachel Sally (2/3)

> Tanya (1/3)

Diagram 8.12
Quickthornes: co-ownership following Tanya's death

Tanya has just died. Her will leaves all her property 'to be divided in equal shares between my friends Vikram, Will, and Xavier'. The position as to ownership of Quickthornes is now as follows in Diagram 8.12:

LEGAL ESTATE

By virtue of survivorship, Rachel and Sally are the only trustees of the legal title

> Rachel Sally

Equitable interests

Rachel and Sally are still joint tenants of two-thirds. Vikram, Will, and Xavier each have a one-ninth share as tenant in common

> Rachel Sally (2/3)

> Vikram (1/9)

> Will (1/9)

> Xavier (1/9)

cross-reference
See 8.4.1 and 8.4.2 for the Stoneygate Farm example.

Hopefully, you have realized that this Quickthornes example has now reached a position rather similar to the Stoneygate Farm example. The number of co-owners of Quickthornes has grown, but the legal estate is vested in Rachel and Sally as trustees (of land). (Remember we now refer to the trust as a trust of land because of the operation of the TOLATA 1996.)

thinking point 8.6

You want to buy Quickthornes. To whom do you make the offer?

You make the offer to Rachel and Sally only. As trustees they can sell (or lease, etc) Quickthornes, and the rights of all five beneficiaries will be overreached.

8.6 The Current Conveyancing Practice to Create an Express Trust

All current property lawyers have been brought up knowing that wherever there is co-ownership of land there must be a trust. They know that there is no escaping the effects of ss 34–36 LPA 1925. (Remember that prior to the commencement of the 1996 Act, a trust for sale would have been created, but now these trusts for sale and newly created trusts are treated as trusts of land.)

Where land is conveyed to co-owners it is nowadays good conveyancing practice to create an express trust (of land). The formalities of creating an express trust are provided for in s53(1) LPA 1925:

> *Law of Property Act 1925*
>
> 53. Instruments required to be in writing
>
> (1) A declaration of trust respecting any land or any interest therein must be manifested and proved by some writing signed by some person who is able to declare such trust or by his will.

The co-owners will be made the trustees except in those cases where there are more than four. The 'express declaration of trust' will make it clear whether the equitable interests under the trust are held as joint tenants or as tenants in common. If the co-owners are tenants in common the size of the shares is spelt out. The express declaration of trust is usually contained in the conveyance or if the land is already registered title in the land transfer. Details of the express declaration of trust are not recorded on the register of title. The solicitor acting for the co-owners should therefore keep a copy of the conveyance or transfer.

By employing an express declaration of trust solicitors avoid the problems which we are about to discuss in the next section of this chapter. Moreover, the practice of having an express declaration of trust is a means of unambiguously demonstrating the intentions of the parties. In *Walker v Hall* (1984) 5 FLR 126, the Court of Appeal expressed the view that it might well be professional negligence for a solicitor acting for co-owners to fail to draw up an express declaration of trust. Dillon LJ said:

> The transfer of 33 Foxberry Road to Mr Hall and Mrs Walker is in the common form of a Land Registry Transfer. It transfers the property to Mr Hall and Mrs Walker as joint tenants but contains no statement of what their respective beneficial interests are to be. Ten years ago Bagnall J in *Cowcher v Cowcher* [1972] 1 WLR 425 at p. 442 drew attention to the desirability that solicitors should take steps to find out and declare what the beneficial interests are to be, when the legal estate in a house is acquired by two persons in their joint names. The

difficulties which otherwise arise, and which can so easily be avoided by a little care on the part of the solicitors, were emphasized recently by Griffiths LJ in *Bernard v Josephs* (1983) 4 FLR 178. I would wish to underline the point as strongly as I can and to suggest that the courts may soon have to consider whether a solicitor acting for joint purchasers is not guilty of negligence if he fails to find out and record what the joint purchasers' beneficial interests in the relevant property are to be . . .

The point his Lordship is making in this extract is that if there is an express declaration of trust, that declaration prevents later arguments between co-owners as to whether they are joint tenants or tenants in common, and if tenants in common, the size of their respective shares.

In *Goodman v Gallant* [1986] 2 WLR 236, a cohabiting couple acquired a house. The conveyance to them provided that the claimant and the defendant were to hold the property on trust for sale for themselves as joint tenants in equity. The defendant left and the claimant served a notice severing the joint tenancy. The claimant then issued a summons for a declaration as to their respective shares in the property, and claimed to be entitled to a three-quarters share. The registrar held that the express declaration of the joint tenancy in equity had established their respective beneficial shares, upon severance, as half and half. The judge at first instance upheld the registrar's conclusion, the claimant appealed to the Court of Appeal and the appeal was dismissed.

In a case where the legal estate in property is conveyed to two or more persons as joint tenants, but neither the conveyance nor any other written document contains any express declaration of trust concerning the beneficial interests in the property (as would be required for an express declaration of this nature by virtue of s. 53(1)(b) of the Law of Property Act 1925), the way is open for persons claiming a beneficial interest in it or its proceeds of sale to rely on the doctrine of 'resulting, implied or constructive trusts': see s. 53(2) of the Law of Property Act 1925. In particular, in a case such as that, a person who claims to have contributed to the purchase price of property which stands in the name of himself and another can rely on the well known presumption of equity that a person who has contributed a share of the purchase price of property is entitled to a corresponding proportionate beneficial interest in the property by way of implied or resulting trust: see, for example, *Pettitt v Pettitt* [1970] AC 777, 813–814, *per* Lord Upjohn. If, however, the relevant conveyance contains an express declaration of trust which comprehensively declares the beneficial interests in the property or its proceed of sale, there is no room for the application of the doctrine of resulting implied or constructive trusts. . . .

cross-reference
Severance is discussed at 8.11, 8.12, and 8.13.

The court confirmed that where there is an express declaration of trust in the conveyance that this is conclusive of how the parties wanted to hold the property. In this case, the express trust in the conveyance provided that the claimant and the defendant were to hold the property on trust for themselves as joint tenants. On severance of this joint tenancy the proceeds of sale were to be divided in equal shares.

cross-reference
See 8.9 and 8.10 for the discussion on Stack v Dowden.

In *Pankhania v Chandegra* [2012] EWCA 1438 a house had been conveyed to C and P on express trust for themselves as tenants in common in equity in equal shares. C (it appears) supplied all the finance for the purchase. The trial judge held C was sole owner of the house.

This conclusion was firmly overruled by the Court of Appeal. The modern court applied what had been said in *Goodman v Gallant* (over 25 years ago), and stressed that where there is an express declaration of trust, there is no room for applying the constructive trust principles laid down in *Stack v Dowden* [2007] 2 AC 432.

thinking point 8.7

Flawford House is conveyed to Anne and Bridget. There is an express declaration of a trust for themselves as joint tenants in equity. The price was £90,000. Anne contributed £60,000; Bridget contributed £30,000. Anne dies. Her will leaves all her property to Charles. Does Charles inherit any interest in Flawford House?

The answer is of course, 'no'. The express declaration of trust stating that Anne and Bridget are joint tenants in equity is conclusive. Thus when Anne dies, her equitable interest in Flawford House passes by survivorship to Bridget.

8.6.1 Declaration of Trusts Now Strongly Encouraged by Land Registry Rules

Land Registry Rules originally introduced on 1 April 1998 provided for standard forms of Land Transfer and application for first registration. The Land Registration Rules 2003 (in force from 13 October 2003) continued with these forms of Land Transfer (Form TR1) and application for first registration (Form FR1). These forms can be printed off from the Land Registry's website: www.landregistry.gov.uk.

Part 10 of Form TR1 asks that where the applicant for registration is more than one person, they put an X against one of three alternatives:

- they hold the property on trust for themselves as joint tenants;
- they hold the property on trust for themselves as tenants in common in equal shares;
- they hold the property on trust...

Part 9 of Form FR1 provides a similar three alternatives for joint applicants for first registration:

- they hold the property on trust for themselves as joint tenants;
- they hold the property on trust for themselves as tenants in common in equal shares;
- they hold the property on trust...

With both TR1 and FR1, the third alternative should be used:

- where the co-owners hold the property on trust for themselves in unequal shares;
- where there are co-owners who are not trustees of the legal title (eg because there are more than four co-owners);
- where the applicants/transferees are not beneficial co-owners but hold the land in trust for beneficiaries of a trust of land of the kind discussed in Chapter 7.

In all three cases, the applicants/transferees should fill in the blank in the third alternative with details of the equitable interests under the trust.

In effect, if the Land Registry Form Part 10 (TR1) is filled in by the co-owners, or their solicitor on their behalf, the form will act as a declaration of trust. Baroness Hale outlined this issue in *Stack v Dowden* [2007] 2 AC 432:

> The Land Registry form has since changed. Form TR1, in use from 1 April 1998, provides a box for the transferees to declare whether they are to hold the property on trust for themselves as joint tenants, or on trust for themselves as tenants in common in equal shares, or

> on some other trusts which are inserted on the form. If this is invariably complied with, the problem confronting us here will eventually disappear. Unfortunately, however, the transfer will be valid whether or not this part of the form is completed. The form itself states that the transferees are only required to execute it 'if the transfer contains transferee's covenants or declarations or contains an application by the transferee (eg for a restriction)'. So there may still be transfers of registered land into joint names in which there is no express declaration of the beneficial interests. However desirable such a declaration may be, it is unrealistic, in the consumer context, to expect that it will be executed independently of the forms required to acquire the legal estate. Not only do solicitors and licensed conveyancers compete on price, but more and more people are emboldened to do their own conveyancing. The Land Registry form which has been prescribed since 1998 is to be applauded. If its completion and execution by or on behalf of all joint proprietors were mandatory, the problem we now face would disappear. However, the form might then include an option for those who deliberately preferred not to commit themselves as to the beneficial interests at the outset and to rely on the principles discussed below.

Unfortunately, while the vast majority of applicants will in practice fill in Part 10, the Land Registry does still register applications where Part 10 TR1 is left blank. Moreover, while the vast majority of applicants will use TR1 or FR1 to give details of their trust, those details of the express declaration of trust are still not recorded on the register of title. To avoid possible arguments between co-owners, the solicitor acting for the co-owners should therefore still keep a copy of Form TR1 or FR1.

If joint owners have been registered after 12 October 2012 but have left Part 10 of TR1 (or Part 9 of FR1) blank, they can instead file a form JO expressly setting out the trusts on which the land is held.

It is difficult to see how this new (additional) procedure solves the problem which arose (in a very expensive way) in *Stack v Dowden*. Joint owners who have left Part 10 blank are unlikely to want to fill in a separate form giving details of their co-ownership trusts!

8.7 No Express Declaration of a Trust—Joint Tenants or Tenants in Common?

The rules which we are about to consider apply only where there is no express declaration of a trust. Where there is an express trust, that trust is conclusive as to whether the co-owners are joint tenants or tenants in common (see 8.6). Furthermore, where the beneficiaries hold their equitable interests as tenants in common, the express declaration is conclusive as to the size of their shares (*Stack v Dowden* [2007] 2 AC 432 confirms this point).

With a co-ownership where there is *no* express declaration of trust the following rules apply. There is an initial presumption that 'equity follows the law' and so the co-owners are joint tenants in law and in equity. This presumption in favour of joint tenancy can be rebutted in favour of a tenancy in common in the following situations:

- *Conveyance (or will) expressly describes the co-owners as tenants in common.*
- *Conveyance (or will) uses 'words of severance'*, for example 'I convey Blackacre to A, B, and C in equal shares', 'I grant Blackacre to be divided between my sons Tom, Dick, and

Harry'. Any words in a conveyance (or will) which indicate that the co-owners are to have distinct shares in the property, albeit those shares are geographically undivided, are 'words of severance'.

As you may have guessed, this rule about 'words of severance' is important only where lay people draft their own conveyances or wills. But you must not confuse 'words of severance' with the concept 'severance of a joint tenancy' which we shall be considering in the next chapter.

- *Where either unity of time, unity of title, or unity of interest is absent.* This of course follows from the very nature of joint tenancies and tenancies in common. Only unity of possession is required for a tenancy in common.

- *Where co-owned property is acquired for use by a business partnership.* For example, Anand, Bart, and Chetan buy High Tower for £300,000 to use as the office for their accountancy practice. They each contribute £100,000. High Tower is conveyed to them, but there is no express declaration of a trust. To save money, they do their own conveyancing. Anand, Bart, and Chetan will be tenants in common of the equitable interest under the trust imposed by s34 LPA 1925. Each will have a one-third share.

The reason behind this 'business partners are tenants in common' rule is as follows. Equity always considered that the very hit and miss 'survival of the fittest' survivorship rule which applies to joint tenancies is inappropriate in a commercial context. A businessman would (in most cases at least) want his interest in land held for use in the business to pass under his will. There is nothing, of course, to stop business partners making themselves joint tenants. Since 1925 they do so by creating an express trust with the partners as joint tenants of the equitable interests under the trust.

- *'Joint mortgage'.* Of the six rules under which a tenancy in common can arise, this rule is perhaps the least important. A joint mortgage can arise if there are joint lenders. A joint mortgage has the following features:
  - there is normally just one borrower;
  - there are two or more lenders who pool the money they are willing to lend;
  - they lend the pooled money as one loan;
  - the borrower grants the lenders a single mortgage;
  - the lenders are co-owners of the mortgage;
  - since 1925, the lenders hold their title to the mortgage on trust for themselves as tenants in common.

When in practice might there be a joint mortgage? Suppose Greg owns Bidworth Park, worth something over £1,000,000. He wants to borrow £1,000,000, and is offering Bidworth Park as security. He approaches Southern Sea Bank, which says, 'Sorry we would like to lend the full sum but we have only £500,000 available'. He approaches Central Bank, which gives a very similar reply. A joint mortgage will satisfy everyone. The two banks pool their respective half millions. Greg gets a single loan for £1,000,000 and grants a joint mortgage to the two banks.

- *Unequal contributions to the purchase of the property.* For example, two friends, Yulia and Zoya, buy Great House for £240,000. Great House is conveyed to Yulia and Zoya. There is no express declaration of a trust. Yulia contributed £180,000; Zoya £60,000. In this situation, it is presumed that both Yulia and Zoya will be tenants in common of the equitable interest under the trust. Their shares will be proportionate to their contributions: Yulia will have a three-quarters share and Zoya will have a one-quarter share. The example just given is a simple one, but rather unrealistic as Yulia and Zoya paid 'cash down'. This presumption can be rebutted if there is an express agreement or common intention between Yulia and Zoya to the contrary.

Resulting and Constructive Trusts: Introduction

So far we have considered the creation and the benefit of having an express trust where the legal title to the property is in joint names. Where an express trust declaration has not been made difficulties can arise in relation to the 'share' owned by each of the co-owners. The protracted litigation in *Stack v Dowden* is a classic illustration of this point. The trusts considered in the following sections are different, in that they arise where the legal title is in the sole name of one of the disputants.

8.8.1 Resulting Trusts

In 1.3.7, we used the example of Alex being the sole legal owner of Chenu. Beth had contributed £30,000 to the purchase price of Chenu. Her contribution to the purchase price is reflected as a beneficial interest in the form of a resulting trust. Alex is now a trustee. This is based on the classic approach adopted by the courts, that is, a *presumption* that Alex and Beth *intended* Beth to have a beneficial interest (the proportion of the shares would reflect the contributions made) in Chenu, rather than intending to give the money as a gift or a loan. This can be seen in Diagram 8.13:

Diagram 8.13
Legal and equitable co-ownership following Beth's contribution

LEGAL TITLE   Alex

EQUITABLE INTEREST   Alex   Beth

Beth has a beneficial
interest because of her
contributions

The case of *Dyer v Dyer* (1788) 2 Cox 92 clearly stated when a resulting trust would arise, Eyre CB said:

> The clear result of all the cases, without a single exception is, that the trust of a legal estate…whether taken in the names of the purchasers and other jointly, or in the names of others without that of the purchaser; whether in one name or several; whether jointly or successive, results to the man who advanced the purchase money. This is a general proposition supported by all cases…It is the established doctrine of a court of equity, that this resulting trust may be rebutted by circumstances in evidence.

This was reinforced in *Curley v Parkes* [2005] 1 P & CR DG15. In the Court of Appeal, Gibson LJ said that '…a resulting trust crystallises on the date that the property is acquired…On their face, [mortgage] payments commencing a month after the completion of the purchase are not payments of the purchase price.'

The main point to remember in relation to resulting trusts is that they are based on the presumed intention of the parties at the time the property is purchased. Put another way, the direct financial contributions made by the parties provide an indication of the presumed

cross-reference
See 8.9 for a discussion on joint legal owners of the property.

intention of the parties at the time of acquisition. Such contributions can be in the form of a sum of money towards the purchase price (eg cash contribution in the form of a lump sum or a deposit). Where a mortgage loan has been taken from the outset to finance a purchase of a property, and contributions are made to the mortgage repayments after the acquisition of the legal title, then a constructive trust would arise (see Gibson LJ, *Curley v Parkes* [2005] in the previous paragraph). See the discussion in 8.8.2.

Stack v Dowden [2007] has marked a significant change in the determination of resulting trusts in the family context, in particular where the home is held jointly and the contributions to the purchase of the property are unequal. This case has shifted the emphasis away from the presumption of a resulting trust based on financial contribution to focusing on the parties' intentions under a constructive trust. Baroness Hale stated that '[t]he presumption of resulting trust is not a rule of law' (at [60]) and that '[t]he law has indeed moved on in response to changing social and economic conditions. The search is to ascertain the parties' shared intentions, actual, inferred or imputed, with respect to the property in the light of their whole course of conduct in relation to it.' Lord Walker agreed with this view, however Lord Neuberger was not convinced by this approach and expressed reluctance to depart from well-established principles laid down by case law over the years.

In the Supreme Court in *Jones v Kernott* [2011] UKSC 53, Lord Walker and Lady Hale jointly stated obiter:

> 25. The time has come to make it clear, in line with *Stack v Dowden* . . . that in the case of the purchase of a house or flat in joint names for joint occupation by a married or unmarried couple, where both are responsible for any mortgage, there is no presumption of a resulting trust arising from their having contributed to the deposit (or indeed the rest of the purchase) in unequal shares. The presumption is that the parties intended a joint tenancy both in law and in equity. But that presumption can of course be rebutted by evidence of a contrary intention, which may more readily be shown where the parties did not share their financial resources.

The extract above suggests that resulting trusts would appear to be now limited in application. It continues to apply in the commercial context (*Laskar v Laskar* [2008] 1 WLR 2695). In the case of the family home, where the parties concerned are in an intimate relationship, Lord Walker and Lady Hale suggest that the basic presumption 'equity follows the law' is retained, such that where there are unequal contributions to the purchase price a joint tenancy will be presumed. Crucially this reasoning only applies where the property is purchased 'in joint names for joint occupation by a married or unmarried couples, where both are responsible for any mortgage' (see para 25 in the previous extract). Baroness Hale in *Stack v Dowden* indicated that the presumption of joint tenancy could be rebutted by considering a wide range of factors which would help to ascertain the parties' intentions.

Recently in *Chaudhary v Chaudhary* [2013] EWCA Civ 758, the court continued to recognize the existence of the resulting trust in the family context. In this case the grandmother had provided eight per cent of the purchase price. Her intention was not to gift the money to her son but that she would benefit from her contribution.

thinking point 8.8

Three friends, Rafiq, Sam, and Trev (all of full age), have just bought 14 Elliston Gardens for £240,000. Rafiq contributed £120,000, Sam £80,000, and Trev £40,000. The land has been conveyed to Rafiq alone. There is no mention of a trust. How do they hold the property in law and in equity?

In these circumstances Rafiq will be trustee of the legal estate. But the equitable interests under the resulting trust will be that Rafiq owns a half, Sam owns one-third, and Trev one-sixth.

cross-reference
It would be useful to refer back to the example used of a constructive trust in 1.3.7.

8.8.2 Constructive Trusts

In our discussion of constructive trusts in Chapter 1, Alex owned the fee simple in a house, Chenu. Beth made substantial contributions to Chenu in the following ways:

- Chenu is bought with the assistance of a mortgage, and Beth contributes substantially to the mortgage repayments; and/or

- Beth makes substantial improvements to Chenu, for example by personally renovating the house, or by paying for contractors to build an extension.

We said that in this sort of situation the courts will normally infer that Beth was intended to have a share in the property approximately proportionate to her contributions. In the situations noted here Beth acquires a constructive trust. A constructive trust can be inferred from the conduct of the parties, that is, both Alex and Beth have the common intention (or understanding) to share the beneficial (or equitable) ownership of the property. Unlike a resulting trust, a constructive trust arises where the financial contributions have been made after the property has been purchased. A constructive trust can be inferred by the courts irrespective of whether the parties are married or not.

Lord Bridge in the House of Lords in *Lloyds Bank v Rosset* [1991] 1 AC 107 considered how a constructive trust may arise. Mr Rosset received money from family trusts to buy a semi-derelict house on the understanding that the house should be in his sole name. The bulk of the renovation work was carried out by contractors employed and paid for by the husband. Mrs Rosset helped with the interior decoration, obtained necessary materials, and generally urged on the builders. Mr Rosset had obtained a mortgage loan from the bank (without Mrs Rosset's knowledge) to meet the costs of the renovation. Mrs Rosset did not make any financial contribution to the purchase of the property or to the cost of the renovation. Following matrimonial difficulties Mr Rosset left leaving his wife and children in the home. The loan taken out by Mr Rosset was not repaid. The bank brought proceedings for possession. The husband raised no defence to that claim. Mrs Rosset resisted the action by claiming to have a beneficial interest in the house under a constructive trust. She also claimed to have been in actual occupation of the property at the time of the completion of the loan (mortgage) from the bank. Accordingly, she claimed to have a beneficial interest in the property which would override the bank's right to enforce its security. (Section 70(1)(g) Land Registration Act 1925 (LRA 1925) provided that the rights of any person in actual occupation of land shall be 'overriding'.) The Court of Appeal allowed the wife's appeal. The bank appealed to the House of Lords. The appeal was allowed. The House of Lords held that the wife had not done enough to acquire a constructive trust interest. It followed that she had no overriding interest within s70(1)(g) LRA 1925.

Lord Bridge said:

> The first and fundamental question which must always be resolved is whether, independently of any inference to be drawn from the conduct of the parties in the course of sharing the house as their home and managing their joint affairs, there has at any time prior to acquisition, or exceptionally at some later date, been any agreement, arrangement or understanding reached between them that the property is to be shared beneficially. The finding of an agreement or arrangement to share in this sense can only, I think, be based on evidence of express discussions between the partners, however imperfectly remembered and however imprecise their terms may have been. Once a finding to this effect is made it will only be necessary for the partner asserting a claim to a beneficial interest against the partner entitled to the legal estate to show that he or she has acted to his or her detriment or significantly altered his or her position in reliance on the agreement in order to give rise to a constructive trust or a proprietary estoppel.

In sharp contrast with this situation is the very different one where there is no evidence to support a finding of an agreement or arrangement to share, however reasonable it might have been for the parties to reach such an arrangement if they had applied their minds to the question, and where the court must rely entirely on the conduct of the parties both as the basis from which to infer a common intention to share the property beneficially and as the conduct relied on to give rise to a constructive trust. In this situation direct contributions to the purchase price by the partner who is not the legal owner, whether initially or by payment of mortgage instalments, will readily justify the inference necessary to the creation of a constructive trust. But, as I read the authorities, it is at least extremely doubtful whether anything less will do.

From the extract you should have been able to identify the situations when the court may imply a constructive trust. The two possible routes which may lead to the creation of a constructive trust are:

- express agreement and in relying on the agreement a party acted to their detriment or altered their position;
- implied agreement through common intention and conduct.

Express Agreement and Detriment

According to Lord Bridge the express agreement between the parties to share the beneficial interest in the property is a clear indication of the parties' common intention. Lord Bridge provided examples of when such a trust could arise by referring to cases involving an express agreement.

Outstanding examples on the other hand of cases giving rise to situations in the first category are *Eves v. Eves* [1975] 1 W.L.R. 1338 and *Grant v. Edwards* [1986] Ch. 638. In both these cases, where the parties who had cohabited were unmarried, the female partner had been clearly led by the male partner to believe, when they set up home together, that the property would belong to them jointly. In *Eves v. Eves* the male partner had told the female partner that the only reason why the property was to be acquired in his name alone was because she was under 21 and that, but for her age, he would have had the house put into their joint names. He admitted in evidence that this was simply an 'excuse.' Similarly in *Grant v. Edwards* the female partner was told by the male partner that the only reason for not acquiring the property in joint names was because she was involved in divorce proceedings and that, if the property were acquired jointly, this might operate to her prejudice in those proceedings. As Nourse L.J. put it, at p. 649:

'Just as in *Eves v. Eves* [1975] 1 W.L.R. 1338, these facts appear to me to raise a clear inference that there was an understanding between the plaintiff and the defendant, or a common intention, that the plaintiff was to have some sort of proprietary interest in the house; otherwise no excuse for not putting her name on to the title would have been needed.'

The subsequent conduct of the female partner in each of these cases, which the court rightly held sufficient to give rise to a constructive trust or proprietary estoppel supporting her claim to an interest in the property, fell far short of such conduct as would by itself have supported the claim in the absence of an express representation by the male partner that she was to have such an interest.

The difficulty lies in providing evidence of conversations 'however imperfectly remembered and however imprecise their terms may have been', and leads to a haphazard approach to establishing the existence of such a trust. In *Midland Bank v Cook* [1995] Fam Law 675, Waite LJ was critical of this approach and noted that such evidence 'provides a vivid illustration of the difficulties which these cases pose for the honest recollections of witnesses and the barrenness of the terrain in which the judges and district judges who try them are required to search for the small evidential nuggets on which issues as to the existence—or the proportions—of beneficial interest are liable to depend'.

Apart from express agreement, Lord Bridge stated that there must be detrimental reliance whereby 'he or she has acted to his or her detriment or significantly altered his or her position in reliance on the agreement'. What would amount to detrimental reliance? It is clear in *Rosset* that it must be more than *de minimis*, Mrs Rosset was engaged in normal family activity and so had not acted to her detriment. Cases where detrimental reliance has been successfully argued include: extensive improvements to the property where the claimant uses a considerable amount of labour during the course of the improvements (the claimant in *Eves v Eves* [1975] 1 WLR 1338 wielded a 14 lb sledgehammer to demolish a large area of concrete); and substantial financial contributions to household expenses (*Grant v Edwards* [1986] Ch 638).

Implied Agreement Through Conduct and Detriment

Lord Bridge stated that an implied agreement (ie to infer the common intention of the parties to share the beneficial interest in the property) can be inferred from the conduct of the parties. Conduct according to Lord Bridge is specific and would arise in the form of direct contributions to the purchase price and payment of mortgage instalments. He adds that 'it is at least extremely doubtful whether anything less will do'. This statement seems to suggest that other contributions (indirect contributions) such as contribution to the general household expenses which are not related to the acquisition of the property would be outside the scope of inferring a constructive trust through conduct.

In *Le Foe v Le Foe* [2001] 2 FLR 970 the judge considered Lord Bridge's assessment of implied agreement contributions, and asserted that Lord Bridge's proposition was not made in absolute terms. The judge stated 'it will only be exceptionally that conduct other than direct contributions to the purchase price, either in cash to the deposit or by contribution to the mortgage instalments, will suffice to draw the necessary inference of a common intention to share the equity.' In this case, indirect contributions to the mortgage were sufficient to allow the court to infer that the parties intended to share the beneficial interest.

Lord Bridge's proposition that he doubts if 'anything less will do' has been criticized by academics and by Lord Walker in *Stack v Dowden* [2007] 2 AC 432:

> Lord Bridge's extreme doubt 'whether anything less will do' was certainly consistent with many first-instance and Court of Appeal decisions, but I respectfully doubt whether it took full account of the views (conflicting though they were) expressed in *Gissing v Gissing* [1971] AC 886 (see especially Lord Reid, at pp 896G–897B, and Lord Diplock, at p 909D–H). It has attracted some trenchant criticism from scholars as potentially productive of injustice: see *Gray & Gray, Elements of Land Law*, 4th ed, paras 10.132–10.137, the last paragraph being headed 'A More Optimistic Future'. Whether or not Lord Bridge's observation was justified in 1990, in my opinion the law has moved on, and your Lordships should move it a little more in the same direction . . .

Baroness Hale emphatically expressed the opinion (shared by the majority of their Lordships), 'The law has indeed moved on in response to changing social and economic conditions. The search is to ascertain the parties' shared intentions, actual, inferred or imputed, with respect to the property in the light of their whole course of conduct in relation to it.'

The extracts referred to by Lord Walker from *Gissing v Gissing* [1971] AC 886 provide a useful insight to the differing views put forward in relation to indirect contributions. These are set out in the following extracts.

Lord Reid stated (at 896G–897B):

> As I understand it, the competing view is that, when the wife makes direct contributions to the purchase by paying something either to the vendor or to the building society which is financing the purchase, she gets a beneficial interest in the house although nothing was ever said or agreed about this at the time: but that, when her contributions are only indirect by way of paying sums which the husband would otherwise have had to pay, she gets nothing unless at the time of the acquisition there was some agreement that she should get a share. I can see no good reason for this distinction and I think that in many cases it would be unworkable. Suppose the spouses have a joint bank account. In accordance with their arrangement she pays in enough money to meet the household bills and so there is enough to pay the purchase price instalments and their bills as well as their personal expenses. They never discuss whose money is to go to pay for the house and whose is to go to pay for other things. How can anyone tell whether she has made a direct or only an indirect contribution to paying for the house? It cannot surely depend on who signs which cheques. Is she to be deprived of a share if she says 'I can pay in enough to pay for the household bills,' but given a share if she says 'I can pay in £10 per week regularly.'

Lord Diplock stated (at 909D–H):

> Where this was the most likely inference from their conduct it would be for the court to give effect to that common intention of the parties by determining what in all the circumstances was a fair share.

> Difficult as they are to solve, however, these problems as to the amount of the share of a spouse in the beneficial interest in a matrimonial home where the legal estate is vested solely in the other spouse, only arise in cases where the court is satisfied by the words or conduct of the parties that it was their common intention that the beneficial interest was not to belong solely to the spouse in whom the legal estate was vested but was to be shared between them in some proportion or other.

> Where the wife has made no initial contribution to the cash deposit and legal charges and no direct contribution to the mortgage instalments nor any adjustment to her contribution to other expenses of the household which it can be inferred was referable to the acquisition of the house, there is in the absence of evidence of an express agreement between the parties no material to justify the court in inferring that it was the common intention of the parties that she should have any beneficial interest in a matrimonial home conveyed into the sole name of the husband, merely because she continued to contribute out of her own earnings or private income other expenses of the household. For such conduct is no less consistent; with a common intention to share the day-to-day expenses of the household, while each spouse retains a separate interest in capital assets acquired with their own moneys or obtained by inheritance or gift.

It would seem that in the light of what the Law Lords have said in *Stack v Dowden* [2007] and *Abbott v Abbott* [2007] UKPC 53, courts may be more willing to infer that parties in an intimate relationship have a common intention that the partner without legal ownership of the home should have a constructive trust interest in that home. In particular, where a house is acquired with the assistance of a mortgage, the partner without legal ownership may acquire an interest even though he/she does not directly contribute to the mortgage instalments.

A final point to note in this section. Both *Stack v Dowden* [2007] and *Jones v Kernott* [2011] were cases primarily dealing with the quantification of the beneficial interests of the parties, that is, what are the size of the shares in the property, rather than considering the acquisition of a beneficial interest. It is unclear at this stage whether much of the reasoning in these cases applies in determining the acquisition of a beneficial interest in a case where the property is owned by a sole name. Recently, the courts have been more willing to consider the whole range of conduct of the parties. For example, in *Geary v Rankine* [2012] EWCA Civ 555, Lewison LJ in the Court of Appeal summarized the factors to consider in a single name case following *Jones v Kernott* [2011]:

> 20. In a single name case of which this is one the first issue is whether it was intended that the claimant should have any beneficial interest in the property at all…There is no presumption of joint beneficial ownership. But the common intention has to be deduced objectively from their conduct.
>
> 21. …It is important to stress that the object of the search is a common intention; that is, an intention common to both parties. So Mrs Geary had to establish that despite the fact that the legal title to the property remained in Mr Rankine's sole name, he actually intended that she should have a beneficial interest in it. As I have said that actual intention may have been expressly manifested, or may be inferred from conduct; but actual intention it remains.

This, and cases such as *Ullah v Ullah* [2013] EWHC 2296, *Crown Prosecution Service v Piper* [2011] EWHC 3570 and *Re Ali* [2012] EWHC 2302 indicate the court's willingness to apply *Jones v Kernott* to a wide range of conduct. This approach could be viewed as a small step away from the more restrictive approach in *Rosset*, though, in principle, that case remains good law.

8.9 Joint Legal Owners of the Property

Consider now Abena and Barack. They decided to cohabit rather than get married. They bought 'Lovenest' (what may be called a 'quasi-matrimonial home') for £200,000, of which £180,000 was borrowed from Bloggs Bank. They granted a mortgage to the bank to secure the loan. The house was conveyed to them in their joint names but there was no express declaration of a trust. Abena paid the initial £20,000 deposit out of her savings, and she also paid some of the instalments. Barack paid the rest of the instalments. They did not keep a detailed record as to who paid what. The relationship has now broken down. In this kind of situation calculating the size of Abena's and Barack's shares as tenants in common will be very difficult, some would argue guesswork. However, if there had been an express declaration of trust, arguments as to who contributed what would not have arisen.

In *Stack v Dowden* [2007], the legal title to a house worth £770,000 was registered in the joint names of Mr Stack and Ms Dowden who had been cohabiting for 20 years. There was no express declaration of trust setting out the equitable ownership of the co-owners.

The House of Lords (led by Baroness Hale) first makes it clear that if there had been an express declaration of trust, that would have been conclusive and there would have been no litigation. Secondly, where there is no express declaration, there is nevertheless a strong presumption that the equitable ownership is the same as the legal ownership, that is, there is a strong presumption in favour of an equitable joint tenancy.

On the facts of the instant case the inference of unequal shares could unusually be drawn. It was clear that Ms Dowden had provided by far the greater share of the finance for the current house and its predecessor. The shares in the house were fixed at 65 per cent/35 per cent.

(Note that Mr Stack (who had been claiming 50 per cent) had to pay the considerable costs of the proceedings. It is thought that those costs exceeded the value of his share in the house. The whole house had been sold for £770,000.)

Baroness Hale said:

> Just as the starting point where there is sole legal ownership is sole beneficial ownership, the starting point where there is joint legal ownership is joint beneficial ownership. The onus is upon the person seeking to show that the beneficial ownership is different from the legal ownership . . . In joint ownership cases, it is upon the joint owner who claims to have other than a joint beneficial interest.

> The issue as it has been framed before us is whether a conveyance into joint names indicates only that each party is intended to have some beneficial interest but says nothing about the nature and extent of that beneficial interest, or whether a conveyance into joint names establishes a prima facie case of joint and equal beneficial interests until the contrary is shown. For the reasons already stated, at least in the domestic consumer context, a conveyance into joint names indicates both legal and beneficial joint tenancy, unless and until the contrary is proved.

Baroness Hale dismissed the approach of examining the parties' intention at the time of acquisition of the property. Had this not been the case, then the shares would have reflected the parties' initial contributions to the purchase price of the property but not later contributions such as mortgage repayments.

The starting point for Baroness Hale was based on the presumption of a joint beneficial tenancy where the parties are joint tenants in law. This approach was later endorsed by the Supreme Court in *Jones v Kernott* (see 8.8.1). Baroness Hale provided guidance on the factors that the court would take into consideration in rebutting that presumption:

> 68 The burden will therefore be on the person seeking to show that the parties did intend their beneficial interests to be different from their legal interests, and in what way . . .

> 69 In law, 'context is everything' and the domestic context is very different from the commercial world. Each case will turn on its own facts. Many more factors than financial contributions may be relevant to divining the parties' true intentions. These include: any advice or discussions at the time of the transfer which cast light upon their intentions then; the reasons why the home was acquired in their joint names; the reasons why (if it be the case) the survivor was authorised to give a receipt for the capital moneys; the purpose for which the home was acquired; the nature of the parties' relationship; whether they had children for whom they both had responsibility to provide a home; how the purchase was financed, both initially and subsequently; how the parties arranged their finances, whether separately or together or a bit of both; how they discharged the outgoings on the property and their other household expenses. When a couple are joint owners of the home and jointly liable for the mortgage, the inferences to be drawn from who pays for what may be very different from the inferences to be drawn when only one is owner of the home. The arithmetical calculation of how much was paid by each is also likely to be less important. It will be easier to draw the inference that they intended that each should contribute as much to the household as they reasonably could and that they would share the eventual benefit or burden equally. The parties' individual characters and personalities may also be a factor in deciding where their true intentions lay. In the cohabitation context, mercenary considerations may be more to the fore than they would be in marriage, but it should not be assumed that they always take pride of place over natural love and affection. At the end of the day, having taken all this into account, cases in which the joint legal owners are to be taken to have intended that their beneficial interests should be different from their legal interests will be very unusual.

> 70 This is not, of course, an exhaustive list. There may also be reason to conclude that, whatever the parties' intentions at the outset, these have now changed. An example might be where one party has financed (or constructed himself) an extension or substantial improvement to the property, so that what they have now is significantly different from what they had then.

At the end of para 69, Baroness Hale notes that these factors would only be considered where the circumstances are 'very unusual'. The presumption of a beneficial joint tenancy can be rebutted some time after the acquisition of the property, as Baroness Hale indicates in para 70.

8.10 Quantifying the Beneficial Interest Under a Constructive Trust

The quantification of a beneficial interest was the central issue in both *Stack v Dowden* [2007] and in *Jones v Kernott* [2011] UKSC 53. In both cases Mr Stack and Mr Kernott were legal owners of their respective properties and were questioning the size of their beneficial share. The problem arose because neither party had expressly stated the nature or size of their share, and in both cases the House of Lords and the Supreme Court had to consider this issue.

Baroness Hale, representing the majority opinion in the House of Lords in *Stack v Dowden*, considered the approach to be taken towards quantification in cases where the home is conveyed into joint names and adopted a flexible approach as shown by the following statement:

> The law has indeed moved on in response to changing social and economic conditions. The *search is to ascertain the parties' shared intentions, actual, inferred or imputed, with respect to the property in the light of their whole course of conduct in relation to it*. [Emphasis added]

In applying the tenet of this statement Baroness Hale continued:

> *Oxley v Hiscock* was, of course, a different case from this. The property had been conveyed into the sole name of one of the cohabitants. The claimant had first to surmount the hurdle of showing that she had any beneficial interest at all, before showing exactly what that interest was. The first could readily be inferred from the fact that each party had made some kind of financial contribution towards the purchase. As to the second, Chadwick LJ said, at para 69:
>
> > 'in many such cases, the answer will be provided by evidence of what they said and did at the time of the acquisition. But, in a case where there is no evidence of any discussion between them as to the amount of the share which each was to have—and even in a case where the evidence is that there was no discussion on that point—the question still requires an answer. It must now be accepted that (at least in this court and below) the answer is that *each is entitled to that share which the court considers fair having regard to the whole course of dealing between them in relation to the property*. And in that context, 'the whole course of dealing between them in relation to the property' includes the arrangements which they make from time to time in order to meet the outgoings (for example, mortgage contributions, council tax and utilities, repairs, insurance and housekeeping) which have to be met if they are to live in the property as their home.' [Emphasis supplied]
>
> *Oxley v Hiscock* has been hailed by *Gray & Gray, Elements of Land Law*, 4th ed, p 931, para 10.138, as 'an important breakthrough'. The passage quoted is very similar to the view of the Law Commission in Sharing Homes, A Discussion Paper, para 4.27 on the quantification of beneficial entitlement:
>
> > 'If the question really is one of the parties' 'common intention', we believe that there is much to be said for adopting what has been called a 'holistic approach' to quantification, undertaking a survey of the whole course of dealing between the parties and taking account of all conduct which throws light on the question what shares were intended.'

That may be the preferable way of expressing what is essentially the same thought, for two reasons. First, it emphasises that the search is still for the result which reflects what the parties must, in the light of their conduct, be taken to have intended. Second, therefore, it does not enable the court to abandon that search in favour of the result which the court itself considers fair. For the court to impose its own view of what is fair upon the situation in which the parties find themselves would be to return to the days before *Pettitt v Pettitt* [1970] AC 777 without even the fig leaf of section 17 of the 1882 Act.

Furthermore, although the parties' intentions may change over the course of time, producing what my noble and learned friend, Lord Hoffmann, referred to in the course of argument as an 'ambulatory' constructive trust, at any one time their interests must be the same for all purposes. They cannot at one and the same time intend, for example, a joint tenancy with survivorship should one of them die while they are still together, a tenancy in common in equal shares should they separate on amicable terms after the children have grown up, and a tenancy in common in unequal shares should they separate on acrimonious terms while the children are still with them.

We are not in this case concerned with the first hurdle. There is undoubtedly an argument for saying, as did the Law Commission in Sharing Homes, A Discussion Paper, para 4.23 that the observations, which were strictly obiter dicta, of Lord Bridge of Harwich in *Lloyds Bank plc v Rosset* [1991] 1 AC 107 have set that hurdle rather too high in certain respects. But that does not concern us now. It is common ground that a conveyance into joint names is sufficient, at least in the vast majority of cases, to surmount the first hurdle. The question is whether, that hurdle surmounted, the approach to quantification should be the same.

Baroness Hale did not adopt the same threshold as Lord Bridge in *Rosset*. The focus has shifted to examining the 'whole course of dealing' between the parties (following *Oxley v Hiscock*) to ascertain the intention of the parties over the course of time.

Baroness Hale concluded:

> ...a very unusual case. There cannot be many unmarried couples who have lived together for as long as this, who have had four children together, and whose affairs have been kept as rigidly separate as this couple's affairs were kept. This is all strongly indicative that they did not intend their shares, even in the property which was put into both their names, to be equal (still less that they intended a beneficial joint tenancy with the right of survivorship should one of them die before it was severed). Before the Court of Appeal, Ms Dowden contended for a 65% share and in my view she has made good her case for that.

8.10.1 Imputing or Inferring Intention

Both Lord Walker and Baroness Hale in *Stack v Dowden* [2007] suggested that intention may be imputed from the course of conduct by the parties in relation to the property. Lord Neuberger disagreed with this approach and considered the difference between inferred and imputed intention:

> 125   While an intention may be inferred as well as express, it may not, at least in my opinion, be imputed. That appears to me to be consistent both with normal principles and with the majority view of this House in *Pettitt v Pettitt* [1970] AC 777, as accepted by all but Lord Reid in *Gissing v Gissing* [1971] AC 886, 897 h, 898 b–d, 900 e–g, 901 b–d, 904 e–f, and reiterated by the Court of Appeal in *Grant v Edwards* [1986] Ch 638, 651 f–653 a. The distinction

between inference and imputation may appear a fine one (and in *Gissing v Gissing* [1971] AC 886, 902 g–h, Lord Pearson, who, on a fair reading I think rejected imputation, seems to have equated it with inference), but it is important.

126 An inferred intention is one which is objectively deduced to be the subjective actual intention of the parties, in the light of their actions and statements. An imputed intention is one which is attributed to the parties, even though no such actual intention can be deduced from their actions and statements, and even though they had no such intention. Imputation involves concluding what the parties would have intended, whereas inference involves concluding what they did intend.

Lord Neuberger considered that allowing the court to impute intention would be 'wrong in principle' and 'involve the judge in an exercise which is difficult, subjective and uncertain'. By imputing intention the court is inventing an intention where none had previously existed. In Lord Neuberger's view where the parties originally contributed unequal shares the original beneficial ownership cannot be altered by taking into account the parties' personal conduct and day-to-day financial affairs. Although this may be perceived as unfair, Lord Neuberger stated that 'fairness is not the guiding principle'. This view presented by Lord Neuberger was not followed by the majority of the House.

In *Jones v Kernott* [2011] UKSC 53 a cohabiting couple bought, in 1985, a house in their joint names but without an express declaration of trust. Ms Jones contributed £6,000 to the purchase of the property. Mr Kernott paid for and built an extension to the property increasing the value of the property by 50 per cent of the purchase price. Until they split up in 1993, they shared all the household expenses including the mortgage repayments. The parties split up in 1993, Mr Kernott leaving the house. After 1993 Ms Jones paid all the outgoings on the house.

It was eventually agreed between the parties that until 1993 the property had been owned in equity in equal shares. More than 12 years after their separation, Mr Kernott claimed his half share of the house that Ms Jones was still living in.

The judge in the county court held Ms Jones was entitled to a larger share of the property because of her investment in the property made over 14 years after the couple had separated. In assessing the division of shares between the couple based on what the court considered 'just and reasonable', the beneficial interests were divided 90 per cent for Ms Jones and 10 per cent for Mr Kernott.

Mr Kernott appealed to the High Court and his appeal was dismissed. The Court of Appeal concluded that each party had 50 per cent interest in the property. The Supreme Court reversed the Court of Appeal's decision.

On the issue of when intention could be imputed as opposed to inferred, Lord Walker and Lady Hale stated:

31 …we accept that the search is primarily to ascertain the parties' actual shared intentions, whether expressed or to be inferred from their conduct. However, there are at least two exceptions. The first, which is not this case, is where the classic resulting trust presumption applies. Indeed, this would be rare in a domestic context, but might perhaps arise where domestic partners were also business partners: see *Stack v Dowden*, para 32. The second, which for reasons which will appear later is in our view also not this case but will arise much more frequently, is where it is clear that the beneficial interests are to be shared, but it is impossible to divine a common intention as to the proportions in which they are to be shared. In those two situations, the court is driven to impute an intention to the parties which they may never have had.

From this, it is apparent that imputing intention is limited to specific circumstances such as those mentioned previously. The approach taken towards the determination of intention was explained by Lord Walker and Lady Hale:

> 47 ...where the parties already share the beneficial interest, and the question is what their interests are and whether their interests have changed, the court will try to deduce what their actual intentions were at the relevant time. It cannot impose a solution upon them which is contrary to what the evidence shows that they actually intended. But if it cannot deduce exactly what shares were intended, it may have no alternative but to ask what their intentions as reasonable and just people would have been had they thought about it at the time. This is a fallback position which some courts may not welcome, but the court has a duty to come to a conclusion on the dispute put before it.

Lord Kerr appeared to prefer a more dynamic approach towards imputing intention rather than simply using it as a last resort:

> 72. It is hardly controversial to suggest that the parties' intention should be given effect to where it can be ascertained and that, although discussions between them will always be the most reliable basis on which to draw an inference as to that intention, these are not the only circumstances in which that exercise will be possible. There is a natural inclination to prefer inferring an intention to imputing one. If the parties' intention can be inferred, the court is not imposing a solution. It is, instead, deciding what the parties must be taken to have intended and where that is possible it is obviously preferable to the court's enforcing a resolution. But the conscientious quest to discover the parties' actual intention should cease when it becomes clear either that this is simply not deducible from the evidence or that no common intention exists. It would be unfortunate if the concept of inferring were to be strained so as to avoid the less immediately attractive option of imputation. In summary, therefore, I believe that the court should anxiously examine the circumstances in order, where possible, to ascertain the parties' intention but it should not be reluctant to recognise, when it is appropriate to do so, that inference of an intention is not possible and that imputation of an intention is the only course to follow.
>
> 73. In this context, it is important to understand what is meant by 'imputing an intention'. There are reasons to question the appropriateness of the notion of imputation in this area but, if it is correct to use this as a concept, I strongly favour the way in which it was described by Lord Neuberger in *Stack v Dowden* [2007] 2 AC 432 para 126, where he said that an imputed intention was one which was attributed to the parties, even though no such actual intention could be deduced from their actions and statements, and even though they had no such intention. This exposition draws the necessary strong demarcation line between attributing an intention to the parties and inferring what their intention was in fact.
>
> 74. The reason that I question the aptness of the notion of imputing an intention is that, in the final analysis, the exercise is wholly unrelated to ascertainment of the parties' views. It involves the court deciding what is fair in light of the whole course of dealing with the property. That decision has nothing to do with what the parties intended, or what might be supposed would have been their intention had they addressed that question. In many ways, it would be preferable to have a stark choice between deciding whether it is possible to deduce what their intention was and, where it is not, deciding what is fair, without elliptical references to what their intention might have—or should have—been. But imputing intention has entered the lexicon of this area of law and it is probably impossible to discard it now.
>
> 75. While the dichotomy between inferring and imputing an intention remains, however, it seems to me that it is necessary that there be a well marked dividing line between the two. As soon as it is clear that inferring an intention is not possible, the focus of the court's attention should be squarely on what is fair and, as I have said, that is an obviously different examination than is involved in deciding what the parties actually intended.

Lord Walker and Lady Hale summarize the principles in the case:

51. In summary, therefore, the following are the principles applicable in a case such as this, where a family home is bought in the joint names of a cohabiting couple who are both responsible for any mortgage, but without any express declaration of their beneficial interests.

(1) The starting point is that equity follows the law and they are joint tenants both in law and in equity.

(2) That presumption can be displaced by showing (a) that the parties had a different common intention at the time when they acquired the home, or (b) that they later formed the common intention that their respective shares would change.

(3) Their common intention is to be deduced objectively from their conduct: 'the relevant intention of each party is the intention which was reasonably understood by the other party to be manifested by that party's words and conduct notwithstanding that he did not consciously formulate that intention in his own mind or even acted with some different intention which he did not communicate to the other party' (Lord Diplock in *Gissing v Gissing* [1971] AC 886, 906). Examples of the sort of evidence which might be relevant to drawing such inferences are given in *Stack v Dowden*, at para 69.

(4) In those cases where it is clear either (a) that the parties did not intend joint tenancy at the outset, or (b) had changed their original intention, but it is not possible to ascertain by direct evidence or by inference what their actual intention was as to the shares in which they would own the property, 'the answer is that each is entitled to that share which the court considers fair having regard to the whole course of dealing between them in relation to the property': Chadwick LJ in *Oxley v Hiscock* [2005] Fam 211, para 69. In our judgment, 'the whole course of dealing ... in relation to the property' should be given a broad meaning, enabling a similar range of factors to be taken into account as may be relevant to ascertaining the parties' actual intentions.

(5) Each case will turn on its own facts. Financial contributions are relevant but there are many other factors which may enable the court to decide what shares were either intended (as in case (3)) or fair (as in case (4)).

52. This case is not concerned with a family home which is put into the name of one party only. The starting point is different. The first issue is whether it was intended that the other party have any beneficial interest in the property at all. If he does, the second issue is what that interest is. There is no presumption of joint beneficial ownership. But their common intention has once again to be deduced objectively from their conduct. If the evidence shows a common intention to share beneficial ownership but does not show what shares were intended, the court will have to proceed as at para 51(4) and (5) above.

53. The assumptions as to human motivation, which led the courts to impute particular intentions by way of the resulting trust, are not appropriate to the ascertainment of beneficial interests in a family home. Whether they remain appropriate in other contexts is not the issue in this case.

54. It follows that we would allow this appeal and restore the order of the judge.

8.11 Severance of Joint Tenancies: Introduction

As you are probably aware, there has been over the last 60 years an enormous growth in the number of joint tenancies. This has come about as a result of two factors; first, the growth in owner occupation and, secondly, women's equality. Most but not all joint tenancies exist between married couples or between parties to a stable unmarried cohabitation.

The great attraction of a joint tenancy for married and unmarried couples is the automatic right of survivorship which operates on the death of one of the co-owners. But this advantage of a joint tenancy may disappear if the joint tenants fall out with each other. It is thus fortunate that the law provides for severance of joint tenancies, that is, a process whereby a joint tenancy is converted into a tenancy in common.

8.12 Severance of a Legal Joint Tenancy is Impossible

Since 1925, a legal joint tenancy cannot be severed (s36(2) LPA 1925). Any severance affects only the equitable interests under the trust. For example, Blackacre has been conveyed to A, B, and C as joint tenants on trust for themselves as joint tenants (see Diagram 8.14).

Diagram 8.14
A, B, and C are joint tenants in law and equity

cross-reference
Details of this method of severance can be found at 8.13.

LEGAL TITLE
A, B, and C are joint tenants

A B C

EQUITABLE INTEREST
A, B, and C are joint tenants

A B C

Later A severs the joint tenancy by sending a written notice of severance to B and C. The position will now be as illustrated in Diagram 8.15:

Diagram 8.15
A severs the joint tenancy

LEGAL TITLE
This will still be vested in A, B, and C
as joint tenants and as trustees

A B C

EQUITABLE INTEREST
A will have a one-third share as tenant in common; B and C will have the other two-thirds share as (between themselves) joint tenants.

A (1/3)   B C (2/3)

Suppose that C dies. What is the position now? (See Diagram 8.16.)

Diagram 8.16
C dies

LEGAL TITLE is vested in A and B as joint tenants
and as trustees

A B

EQUITABLE INTEREST
A has a one-third share as tenant in common while B
has a two-thirds share as tenant in common.

A (1/3)   B (2/3)

B will have a two-thirds share in equity because the rule of survivorship applies.

8.13 Methods of Severance

Severance of an equitable joint tenancy can be achieved in a number of ways.

> *Law of Property Act 1925*
>
> 36. Joint tenancies
>
> . . .
>
> (2) No severance of a joint tenancy of a legal estate, so as to create a tenancy in common in land, shall be permissible, whether by operation of law or otherwise, but this subsection does not affect the right of a joint tenant to release his interest to the other joint tenants, or the right to sever a joint tenancy in an equitable interest whether or not the legal estate is vested in the joint tenants: Provided that, where a legal estate (not being settled land) is vested in joint tenants beneficially, and any tenant desires to sever the joint tenancy in equity, he shall give to the other joint tenants a notice in writing of such desire or do such other acts or things as would, in the case of personal estate, have been effectual to sever the tenancy in equity, and thereupon [the land shall be held in trust on terms] which would have been requisite for giving effect to the beneficial interests if there had been an actual severance.
>
> [Nothing in this Act affects the right of a survivor of joint tenants, who is solely and beneficially interested, to deal with his legal estate as if it were not held [in trust].]

Stripped to its bare essentials, s36(2) provides:

> . . . where a legal estate . . . is vested in joint tenants beneficially, and any tenant desires to sever the joint tenancy in equity, he shall give to the other joint tenants a notice in writing of such desire
>
> or do such other acts or things as would, in the case of personal estate, have been effectual to sever the tenancy in equity, . . .

As well as leaving out non-essential words, we have split the paragraph into two parts. The first part relates to severance by written notice; the second part relates to informal severance and preserves the *Williams v Hensman* (1861) 1 Johns & Hem 546 modes of severance of a joint tenancy:

- 'an act of any one of the persons interested operating upon his own share', this includes total or partial alienation of the equitable interest;
- mutual agreement; and
- 'any course of dealing sufficient to intimate that the interests of all were mutually treated as constituting a tenancy in common'.

8.13.1 Severance by Written Notice

For a severance under this heading to be effective:

- the notice must be received by all the other joint tenant(s) or be deemed to have been received; *and*
- it must use the wording appropriate to effect a severance; *and*
- it must express a desire to sever the joint tenancy immediately.

Thus a joint tenant can sever by sending a written notice to each of the other joint tenants saying, 'I am severing our joint tenancy' or words to that effect. The notice of severance can be handed to the intended recipient. It is inadvisable to send the notice by ordinary post, as that may lead to disputes as to whether the notice has been received or not.

If the notice is sent through the post, registered post or recorded delivery should be used and the letter addressed to the recipient's residence or, where appropriate, place of business. This will take advantage of s196(4) LPA 1925. Under that provision a notice sent by recorded delivery or registered post to the correct address will be deemed to have been received by the addressee unless it is returned through the post office undelivered.

Law of Property Act 1925

196. Regulations respecting notices

(1) Any notice required or authorised to be served or given by this Act shall be in writing.

(2) Any notice required or authorised by this Act to be served on a lessee or mortgagor shall be sufficient, although only addressed to the lessee or mortgagor by that designation, without his name, or generally to the persons interested, without any name, and notwithstanding that any person to be affected by the notice is absent, under disability, unborn, or unascertained.

(3) Any notice required or authorised by this Act to be served shall be sufficiently served if it is left at the last known place of abode or business in the United Kingdom of the lessee, lessor, mortgagee, mortgagor, or other person to be served, or, in case of a notice required or authorised to be served on a lessee or mortgagor, is affixed or left for him on the land or any house or building comprised in the lease or mortgage, or, in case of a mining lease, is left for the lessee at the office or counting-house of the mine.

(4) Any notice required or authorised by this Act to be served shall also be sufficiently served, if it is sent by post in a registered letter addressed to the lessee, lessor, mortgagee, mortgagor, or other person to be served, by name, at the aforesaid place of abode or business, office, or counting-house, and if that letter is not returned [by the postal operator [within the meaning of [Part 3 of the Postal Services Act 2011]] concerned] undelivered; and that service shall be deemed to be made at the time at which the registered letter would in the ordinary course be delivered. . . .

The case of *Re 88 Berkeley Road* [1971] Ch 648 dramatically demonstrates the impact of s196(4) LPA 1925. Miss Eldridge and Miss Goodwin were elderly ladies who were joint tenants of their home, 88 Berkeley Road. Eldridge announced that she was getting married. Goodwin consulted solicitors, who advised her to sever the joint tenancy. The solicitors drafted a notice of severance and this was sent by recorded delivery to Eldridge at her 'residence', 88 Berkeley Road. When the postman called, Eldridge had already gone to work. Goodwin signed for the letter. Goodwin died soon afterwards. In the ensuing court case, Eldridge swore that she had never seen the letter. The question was whether there had been an effective severance of the joint tenancy.

Plowman J said:

Mr Bramall's second submission was, if he will allow me to say so, an ingenious one. He pointed to the words in s. 196(4)—and I quote: '. . . if that letter is not returned through the post office undelivered'—and he submitted that the facts of the present case showed that the letter was delivered into the hand of Miss Goodwin: in other words, it was really delivered to the sender, because the solicitors who sent it were Miss Goodwin's solicitors and her agents for this purpose, and that, since the letter was delivered into the hands of the sender, it was in effect returned through the Post Office undelivered.

Again, I do not feel able to accept that submission. In my view, the words '...if that letter is not returned through the post office undelivered' refer to the ordinary case of the Post Office being unable to effect delivery at the address on the letter for some reason or other, such as that the addressee has gone away or the house is shut or empty. It does not, in my judgment, apply to a case like the present where the letter has in fact been delivered by the postman at the address to which it was sent.

The third submission which Mr Bramall made was to this effect, that where a section in an Act of Parliament is potentially creating an unjust situation, as would be the case here if the notice is to be taken as having been received by the plaintiff although she never received it, then the Act ought to be construed strictly, and that that involves strict proof that the relevant document—the letter containing the notice of severance, in this case—was in fact served. And Mr Bramall pointed out that Mr Bender, who was an assistant solicitor in the firm of solicitors who were Miss Goodwin's solicitors at this time and who was responsible for dealing with this matter, could not actually prove putting the notice of severance in the envelope with the covering letter before it was sent. In my judgment, the onus of proof on the defendants here is no higher than proof that, on the balance of probabilities, that was done; and I feel no difficulty in reaching the conclusion that, on the balance of probabilities, it was in fact done.

For those reasons, I cannot accept Mr Bramall's submissions on s. 196(4) ...

In those circumstances, and with some regret having regard to my findings of fact, I feel bound to conclude that the notice of severance, even though never received by the plaintiff, was in fact sufficiently served for the purposes of s. 36(2) of the Law of Property Act 1925 with the consequence that the joint tenancy was severed during the lifetime of Miss Goodwin.

What if a Notice is Sent by Ordinary Post?

If a notice of severance is sent by ordinary post, then provided that it can be proved that the letter was actually put through the letterbox at the intended recipient's address, then it seems that the severance will be effective under s196(3) LPA 1925. Section 196(3) states 'any...notice shall be sufficiently served if it is left at the last known place of abode...of the person to be served'. In *Kinch v Bullard* [1999] 1 WLR 423 a letter of severance sent by ordinary post and which had undoubtedly arrived at the recipient's home was held to be effective as it had been 'left at' that home. In 1987, Mr and Mrs J purchased the freehold of a property in fee simple as beneficial joint tenants. They occupied the property as their matrimonial home. In June 1995, solicitors acting for Mrs J served a divorce petition on Mr J, and on 4 August they sent him a notice of severance of the joint tenancy by ordinary first class post, in an envelope addressed to him at the property. During the weekend of 5/6 August, Mr J suffered a serious heart attack and was admitted to hospital on 7 August. Meanwhile, either on 5 or 7 August, the postman put the notice through the letterbox at the property, whereupon Mrs J, who no longer desired to sever the joint tenancy, picked it up and destroyed it. Subsequently, Mr J died in hospital on 15 August and Mrs J died on 6 January 1996. The executors of Mr J, issued proceedings against the executors of Mrs J, claiming that Mrs J had given Mr J notice in writing of her desire to sever the joint tenancy, within the meaning of the proviso to s36(2) LPA 1925, since s196(3) of the Act provided that such a notice was 'sufficiently served if it is left at the last known place of abode or business in the United Kingdom' of the person to be served.

Neuberger J said:

...I consider that, if s. 196(3) is satisfied once it is shown that the relevant document was bona fide delivered to the last known place of abode or business of the addressee, then, although it might lead to an unfair result in an exceptional case, the law is at least simple and clear. On the other hand, if the court starts implying exceptions into the clear and simple statutory procedure, confusion and uncertainty could result.

...It is not so much that the facts of this case cause me concern: if the defendants, as the executors of Mrs Johnson, are effectively 'landed' with the consequences of Mrs Johnson having served the notice, that does not seem to me to be a particularly unfair result, particularly bearing in mind the extent to which equity tends to lean against joint tenancies (see the discussion in Megarry and Wade *The Law of Real Property* (5th edn, 1984) p.427). However, I am concerned that, if it could be said that the notice in the present case was validly served, unfair advantage could be taken of an addressee by the sender of a notice if the sender (or his agent) had some means of access to the notice after it was served in accordance with s.196, but before the addressee actually saw it, and this resulted in the notice being destroyed or hidden without the addressee ever becoming aware of it. Accordingly, I was at one time attracted by the proposition that some sort of qualification should be imposed on the provisions of s.196, so as to exclude from the concept of valid service a case where the sender has, in effect, intercepted the notice before it was received by the addressee, thereby somewhat extending the qualification or gloss laid down by Russell LJ in *Lord Newborough's case*. [*Newborough v Jones* [1975] Ch 90.]

On reflection, however, I think it neither appropriate nor desirable to impose such a further qualification on the plain words of s. 196(3). First, as a matter of general principle, the court should be slow to imply qualifications into a statutory provision, particularly when that provision is clear and simple in its effect and is intended to have practical consequences. Secondly, it does not seem to me that a conclusion in favour of the plaintiffs in the present case should lead to any unfair abuse. In the present case, it is Mr Johnson (or, more accurately, his executors) who wish to allege that the notice delivered by Mrs Johnson was validly served in light of s. 196(3). There is no potential for abuse in that context. If, however, it was the defendants, the executors of Mrs Johnson, who were seeking to allege that the notice was validly served, then it seems to me that it would be open to the plaintiffs, as executors of Mr Johnson, to contend successfully that, despite the apparent applicability of s. 196(3), valid service had not been effected...

To summarize, the court held that applying the natural meaning of s196(3) LPA 1925, a letter posted by ordinary post to the recipient's last known place of abode (or business) was a valid notice of severance provided it could be proved that the letter had arrived at the correct address. It did not matter whether the addressee had read the letter.

Furthermore, once a notice had been 'served' according to the terms of s193(3) or (4) it could not be withdrawn.

What Sort of Wording is Required in a Notice of Severance?

In the last 50 years or so there have been a number of cases where events have followed the next pattern:

- two people, usually but not always husband and wife, buy a house as joint tenants;
- the relationship breaks down;
- one of the two makes a statement, writes a letter, or commences divorce proceedings, or another form of litigation;
- before matters can be resolved, one of the parties suddenly dies; and
- there is litigation as to whether making a statement, writing a letter, or commencing divorce proceedings has brought about a severance.

cross-reference
Burgess v Rawnsley
is discussed at 8.13.3.

The surviving partner is of course arguing (as Miss Eldridge argued in *Re 88 Berkeley Road*) that there has been no severance. The personal representatives of the deceased argue that there has been a severance.

The Court of Appeal has in two modern decisions laid clear rules for resolving these cases. The cases are *Harris v Goddard* and *Burgess v Rawnsley*.

In *Harris v Goddard* [1983] 1 WLR 1203, the Court of Appeal ruled that any written statement by a joint tenant either expressly indicating or implying that he wishes *immediately* to end the joint tenancy relationship will sever that joint tenancy, provided the statement is received or is deemed to have been received under s196(4) or (3) LPA 1925.

The facts in the case involved a husband and wife who were beneficial joint tenants of the matrimonial home, from which the husband ran his retail business. The marriage broke down, and the wife petitioned for a divorce. The petition included an application for a property adjustment order under s24 Matrimonial Causes Act 1973. The application for the property adjustment order stated: 'That such order may be made by way of transfer of property and/or settlement of property and/or variation of settlement in respect of the former matrimonial home . . . as may be just.' (Applications in these broad general terms are very common. By 'variation of settlement' is meant, in this context, varying the terms of the existing trust for sale.)

cross-reference
For more information on Property Adjustment Orders, see 9.5.

While the divorce proceedings were pending, the husband was killed in a car crash. The husband's executors sought a declaration that the joint tenancy of the former matrimonial home had been effectively severed before the husband's death. The husband's executors argued the divorce petition, which included the property adjustment application, constituted valid notice of severance within the proviso to s36(2) LPA 1925.

Lawton LJ said:

> I start with s. 36. It dealt with beneficial tenancies, which must mean all joint tenancies, including those held by husbands and wives. The section makes no special provisions by way of giving extra rights or raising presumptions in favour of spouses. When severance is said to arise under s. 36(2), not from the giving of a notice in writing, but from '[doing] . . . other acts or things' which would, in the case of personal estate, have been effectual to sever a joint tenancy in equity, the fact that the parties were married may make the drawing of inferences easier. It is, in my judgment, only in this limited evidential context that the existence of the married state has any relevance. In reaching this conclusion I have followed what Russell LJ said in *Bedson v Bedson* [1965] 2 QB 666, 689–690 rather than the obiter statement of Lord Denning MR in the same case at p. 678. Lord Denning MR said that spouses holding as beneficial joint tenants cannot sever their interests so as to convert them into tenancies in common. The trial judge seems to have been influenced to some extent by what Lord Denning MR said. Since in this case severance is said to have come about by a notice in writing the sole question is whether that which is said to be the notice did show that Mrs Harris desired to sever the joint tenancy.

> In *Williams v Hensman* [1861] 1 Johns & Hem 546, 557, Page-Wood V-C said that a joint tenancy could be severed in three ways, that is, by disposal of one of the interests, by mutual agreement and 'by any course of dealing sufficient to intimate that the interests of all were mutually treated as constituting a tenancy in common.' The words in s. 36(2) 'do such other acts or things as would . . . have been effectual to sever the tenancy' put into statutory language the other ways of effecting severance to which Page Wood V-C referred in *Williams v Hensman*. The words 'and any tenant desires to sever the joint tenancy in equity, he shall give to the other joint tenants a notice in writing of such desire' operate to extend the mutual agreement concept of severance referred to in *Williams v Hensman*. Unilateral action to sever a joint tenancy is now possible. Before 1925 severance by unilateral action was only possible when one joint tenant disposed of his interest to a third party. When a

notice in writing of a desire to sever is served pursuant to s. 36(2) it takes effect forthwith. It follows that a desire to sever must evince an intention to bring about the wanted result immediately. A notice in writing which expresses a desire to bring about the wanted result at some time in the future is not, in my judgment, a notice in writing within s. 36(2). Further the notice must be one which allows an intent to bring about the consequences set out in s. 36(2), namely, that the net proceeds of the statutory trust for sale 'shall be held upon the trusts which would have been requisite for giving effect to the beneficial interests if there had been an actual severance.' I am unable to accept Mr Berry's submission that a notice in writing which shows no more than a desire to bring the existing interest to an end is a good notice. It must be a desire to sever which is intended to have the statutory consequences . . .

Perhaps this case should be a cautionary tale for those who draft divorce petitions when the spouses hold property as joint tenants in equity. The decision of Plowman J in *In re Draper's Conveyance* [1969] 1 Ch 486 is an example of how starting legal proceedings can sever a joint tenancy. In that case a wife, after a decree nisi but before a decree absolute, issued a summons under s. 17 of the Married Women's Property Act 1882 asking for an order that a house in the joint names of herself and her husband be sold and the proceeds of sale distributed in accordance with the parties' respective interests therein. An affidavit sworn by the wife in support of the summons contained this paragraph:

> In the premises I humbly ask that the said property may be sold and that the proceeds of sale thereof may be distributed equally; alternatively that the respondent pay me one half of the value of the said property with vacant possession . . .

Plowman J adjudged that the summons and the affidavit together effected a severance during the lifetime of the husband. I agree that it did; but it is not clear from the judgment whether the judge regarded the summons or the affidavit or both as notices in writing or whether the service of the summons and the filing of the affidavit were acts which were effectual to sever the joint tenancy. I do not share the doubts about the correctness of this judgment on this point which Walton J expressed in *Nielson-Jones v Fedden* [1975] Ch 222, 236 relying on *In Re Wilks* [1981] 3 Ch 59. The fact that the wife in *In re Draper's Conveyance* [1969] 1 Ch 486 could have withdrawn the summons is a factor which could have been taken into account in deciding whether what was done was effectual to sever the joint tenancy in equity. The weight of that factor would have depended upon all the other circumstances and was in that case clearly negligible.

I would dismiss the appeal.

The Court of Appeal held that severance had not been effected before the husband's death. A notice of severance within s36(2) LPA 1925 had to evince an intention to sever immediately. The application in the divorce petition had merely expressed the wife's desire to invite the court to exercise its jurisdiction to redistribute property as justice required.

cross-reference
Section 14 TOLATA 1996 is discussed at 9.3.3.

The Court of Appeal in *Harris v Goddard* expressly approved the decision in *Re Draper's Conveyance* [1969] 1 Ch 486, where a wife applied for an order for sale of the jointly owned matrimonial home. This application was held to have severed the joint tenancy. By demanding that the property be sold and the proceeds of sale split, the wife demonstrated that she wished an immediate end to the joint tenancy arrangement.

The remarks of Lawton LJ in *Harris v Goddard* approving *Re Draper* were applied in *Quigley v Masterson* [2011] EWHC 2529.

Mr Pilkington and Mrs Masterson cohabited for 16 years in a house in Coventry of which they were joint tenants in equity. The relationship broke down in 2001. Pilkington continued to live in the house until he became senile in early 2008. On the application of his daughter, Mrs Quigley, he was placed under the jurisdiction of the Court of Protection.

The house was now empty. Masterson applied to the Court of Protection for an order authorizing her to sell the house and divide the proceeds 50–50. This application was opposed by Quigley, who wanted sole charge of her father's financial affairs.

At a hearing in the Court of Protection on 3 February 2009, the district judge granted Masterson the necessary authority to sell the house, but also appointed Quigley to be her father's 'deputy' to manage all other aspects of his financial affairs. Pilkington died on 20 March 2009, and Masterson now contended that she was 100 per cent owner of the house by virtue of survivorship.

Henderson J held, first, that by analogy to *Re Draper*, Masterson's application to the Court of Protection was a notice of severance falling within the terms of the latter part of s36(2) LPA 1925.

Secondly, although Pilkington clearly never personally saw this 'notice', it was to be regarded as served on him on 3 February 2009, the day Quigley was appointed his 'deputy', that is, legal representative. As Henderson, J points out in para 34 of his judgment;

> It is important to remember at this point that the giving of a notice of severance is essentially a unilateral act, which does not depend in any way on the agreement of the recipient.

The joint tenancy had been severed on 3 February, and the proceeds of sale of the house were ordered to be divided 50–50.

A final observation: a direct application for an order of sale made under s14 TOLATA 1996 and served on the other co-owner(s) would undoubtedly sever any equitable joint tenancy in the relevant land.

8.13.2 'An Act of Any One of the Persons Interested Operating Upon His Own Share'

Total Alienation

If a joint tenant sells or gives away *inter vivos* his equitable interest, that effects a severance. The reason for this lies in the fact that one of the unities, that is the unity of title, has been destroyed and has led to severance of the joint tenancy. For example, Lodge Farm Barn was conveyed to Debbie, Electra, Fay, and Gena as joint tenants on express trust for themselves as joint tenants. Later, Gena sells her interest in Lodge Farm Barn to Hank. The position now is as follows in Diagram 8.17:

Diagram 8.17
Lodge Farm Barn, co-ownership following severance

LEGAL TITLE

This is unchanged. The four women remain joint tenants and trustees of the legal title. The fact that Gena has sold her equitable interest does not mean that she has resigned as a trustee. Gena cannot sever her legal joint tenancy (see s36(2) LPA 1925)

Debbie Electra Fay Gena

EQUITABLE INTEREST

Hank has a quarter share as tenant in common. The other three-quarters are held by Debbie, Electra, and Fay as joint tenants

Hank

Debbie Electra Fay

thinking point 8.9

Let us now suppose that Fay, Gena, and Hank all die. Hank's will leaves 'all my property to my old pal Keith'. What is the position now?

- *Legal title.* By virtue of survivorship, Debbie and Electra are the trustees. (Though there is no need for them to do so, they may appoint one or two additional trustees. Do you remember the discussion at 7.7.3?)
- *Equitable interest.* Keith has a quarter share as tenant in common. The other three-quarters belongs to Debbie and Electra as joint tenants.

Partial Alienation

A partial alienation would occur where a joint tenant mortgaged or leased his interest. If a joint tenant wished to sever the joint tenancy without his fellow joint tenant(s) knowing (see *First National Securities Ltd v Hergerty* [1985] QB 850), he could do so by mortgaging his interest to a friend to secure a loan of a nominal amount, for example £5. The equitable interest is severed but the legal estate remains the same.

Bankruptcy

cross-reference
For further discussion on a co-owner's bankruptcy see 9.4.

If a joint tenant goes bankrupt, his equitable interest vests in his trustee in bankruptcy (s306(1) Insolvency Act 1986) who holds it on trust for the benefit of all his creditors. The bankruptcy order automatically severs the joint tenancy (*Re Pavlou (A Bankrupt)* [1993] 1 WLR 1046). If Harry and Fran Brown are joint tenants of Highroofs, and Harry goes bankrupt. The position will now be as is shown in Diagram 8.18:

255

Diagram 8.18
Co-ownership and bankruptcy

LEGAL TITLE
This will still be held by Harry and Fran

> Harry Fran

EQUITABLE INTEREST
Fran and Harry's trustee in bankruptcy
will be tenants in common in equal shares

> Harry's trustee in bankrupcy

> Fran

Contract to Alienate

If a joint tenant contracts to sell, lease, or mortgage his interest, that will effect a severance.

8.13.3 Mutual Agreement

Page-Wood V-C in *Williams v Hensman* (1861) recognized that a joint tenancy could be severed by mutual agreement by all the joint tenants. A flexible approach is adopted towards mutual agreement whereby it can be express or inferred through the conduct of the parties.

The issue of severance by mutual agreement was considered in *Burgess v Rawnsley* [1975] 1 Ch 429. When you read this case, bear in mind that Lord Denning's judgment gives a graphic account of the facts, but his views as to the applicable law are not entirely correct. For the correct law, study Sir John Pennycuick's judgment noting his numbered propositions.

In *Burgess v Rawnsley* Mr Honick (a widower) and Mrs Rawnsley (a widow) met at a scripture rally in Trafalgar Square. They became close friends and bought as joint tenants the fee simple to the house of which Mr Honick had hitherto been a tenant. However, they later fell out. It was orally agreed that Honick should buy out Mrs Rawnsley's interest for £750. Before matters could finally be resolved, Honick died. The issue before the court was whether there had or had not been a severance. The court held that the oral agreement (though not an enforceable contract) had been sufficient to sever the joint tenancy.

Lord Denning MR said:

> Nowadays everyone starts with the judgment of Sir William Page Wood V-C in *Williams v Hensman* (1861) 1 Johns & Hem 546, 557, where he said:
>
> > A joint tenancy may be severed in three ways: in the first place, an act of any one of the persons interested operating upon his own share may create a severance as to that share....Secondly, a joint tenancy may be severed by mutual agreement. And, in the third place, there may be a severance by any course of dealing sufficient to intimate that the interests of all were mutually treated as constituting a tenancy in common. When the severance depends on an inference of this kind without any express act of severance, it will not suffice to rely on an intention, with respect to the particular share, declared only behind the backs of the other persons interested. You must find in this class of cases a course of dealing by which the shares of all the parties to the contest have been effected, as happened in the cases of *Wilson v Bell* (1843) 5 Ir Eq R 501 and *Jackson v Jackson* (1804) 9 Ves Jun 591.
>
> In that passage Page Wood V-C distinguished between severance 'by mutual agreement' and severance by a 'course of dealing.' That shows that a 'course of dealing' need not amount to an agreement, expressed or implied, for severance. It is sufficient if there is a course of dealing in which one party makes clear to the other that he desires that their shares should no longer be held jointly but be held in common. I emphasise that it must be made clear to the other party. That is implicit in the sentence in which Page Wood V-C says:
>
> > it will not suffice to rely on an intention, with respect to the particular share, declared only behind the backs of the other persons interested.
>
> Similarly it is sufficient if both parties enter on a course of dealing which evinces an intention by both of them that their shares shall henceforth be held in common and not jointly. As appears from the two cases to which Page Wood V-C referred of *Wilson v Bell* 5 Ir Eq R 501 and *Jackson v Jackson* 9 Ves Jun 591.
>
> I come now to the question of notice. Suppose that one party gives a notice in writing to the other saying that he desires to sever the joint tenancy. Is that sufficient to effect a severance? I think it is. It was certainly the view of Sir Benjamin Cherry when he drafted s. 36(2) of the Law of Property Act 1925. It says in relation to real estates:
>
> > ...where a legal estate (not being settled land) is vested in joint tenants beneficially, and any tenant desires to sever the joint tenancy in equity, he shall give to the other joint tenants *a notice in writing of such desire or do such other acts or things as would, in the case of personal estate, have been effectual* to sever the tenancy in equity, and thereupon under the trust for sale affecting the land the net proceeds of sale, and the net rents and profits until sale, shall be held upon the trusts which would have been requisite for giving effect to the beneficial interests if there had been an actual severance.
>
> I have underlined the important words. The word 'other' is most illuminating. It shows quite plainly that, in the case of personal estate one of the things which is effective in equity to sever a joint tenancy is 'a notice in writing' of a desire to sever. So also in regard to real estate.
>
> Taking this view, I find myself in agreement with Havers J in *Hawkesley v May* [1956] 1 QB 304, 313–314, and of Plowman J in *In re Draper's Conveyance* [1969] 1 Ch 486. I cannot agree with

Walton J [1975] Ch 222, 234–235, that those cases were wrongly decided. It would be absurd that there should be a difference between real estate and personal estate in this respect. Suppose real estate is held on a joint tenancy on a trust for sale and is sold and converted into personal property. Before sale, it is severable by notice in writing. It would be ridiculous if it could not be severed afterwards in like manner. I look upon s. 36(2) as declaratory of the law as to severance by notice and not a new provision confined to real estate. A joint tenancy in personal estate can be severed by notice just as a joint tenancy in real estate.

. . .

It remains to apply these principles to the present case. I think there was evidence that Mr Honick and Mrs Rawnsley did come to an agreement that he would buy her share for £750. That agreement was not in writing and it was not specifically enforceable. Yet it was sufficient to effect a severance. Even if there was not any firm agreement but only a course of dealing, it clearly evinced an intention by both parties that the property should henceforth be held in common and not jointly.

On these grounds I would dismiss the appeal.

Sir John Pennycuick said:

. . . It is not in dispute that an agreement for severance between joint tenants effects a severance. This is the rule 2 propounded by Sir William Page Wood V.-C. in *Williams* v. *Hensman,* 1 John. & Hem. 546, 557. The words he uses are contained in one sentence: 'Secondly, a joint tenancy may be severed by mutual agreement.' . . . In the present case the judge found as a fact that Mr. Honick and Mrs. Rawnsley at the beginning of July 1968 agreed upon the sale by her to him of her share at the price of £750 . . . The significance of an agreement [ie mutual agreement to sever] is not that it binds the parties; but that it serves as an indication of a common intention to sever, something which it was indisputably within their power to do. It will be observed that Page Wood V.-C. in his rule 2 makes no mention of specific enforceability. Contrast this position where severance is claimed under his rule 1 by reason of alienation by one joint tenant in favour of a third party. We were referred to a sentence in *Megarry and Wade, the Law of Real Property*, 3rd ed., p. 418, where, under the heading of 'Alienation in equity,' it is said:

'In equity, . . . a specifically enforceable contract to alienate creates an equitable interest in the property even though the legal act of alienation has not taken place.'

That statement has, I think, no application to an agreement between the two joint tenants themselves. . . .

Mr. Mummery advanced an alternative argument to the effect that even if there were no agreement by Mr. Honick to purchase Mrs. Rawnsley's share, nevertheless the mere proposal by Mr. Honick to purchase her share would operate as a severance under rule 3 in *Williams* v. *Hensman*, 1 John. & Hem. 546, 557. That rule is stated by Page Wood V.-C. in the following terms:

'And, in the third place, there may be a severance by any course of dealing sufficient to intimate that the interests of all were mutually treated as constituting a tenancy in common. When the severance depends on an inference of this kind without any express act of severance, it will not suffice to rely on intention, with respect to the particular share, declared only behind the backs of the other persons interested. You must find in this class of cases a course of dealing by which the shares of all the parties to the contest have been effected, as happened in the cases of *Wilson v. Bell*, 5 Ir.Eq.R. 501 and *Jackson* v. *Jackson,* 9 Ves.Jun. 591.'

I do not doubt myself that where one tenant negotiates with another for some rearrangement of interest, it may be possible to infer from the particular facts a common intention to sever even though the negotiations break down. Whether such an inference can be drawn must I think depend upon the particular facts. In the present case the negotiations between Mr. Honick and Mrs. Rawnsley, if they can be properly described as negotiations at all, fall, it seems to me, far short of warranting an inference. One could not ascribe to joint tenants an intention to sever merely because one offers to buy out the other for £X and the other makes a counter-offer of £Y.

...I think it may be helpful to state very shortly certain views which I have formed in the light of the authorities.

(1) I do not think rule 3 in Page Wood V-C's statement, 1 John & Hem 546, 557, is a mere sub-heading of rule 2. It covers only acts of the parties, including, it seems to me, negotiations which, although not otherwise resulting in any agreement, indicate a common intention that the joint tenancy should be regarded as severed.

I do not overlook the words which I have read from Page Wood V-C's statement, namely, that you must find a course of dealing by which the shares of all the parties to the contract have been affected. But I do not think those words are sufficient to import a binding agreement.

(2) Section 36(2) of the Law of Property Act 1925 has radically altered the law in respect of severance by introducing an entirely new method of severance as regards land, namely, notice in writing given by one joint tenant to the other.

(3) Pre-1925 judicial statements, in particular that of Stirling J in *In re Wilks, Child v Bulmer* [1891] 3 Ch 59, must be read in the light of this alteration in the law; and, in particular, I do not see why the commencement of legal proceedings by writ or originating summons or the swearing of an affidavit in those proceedings, should not in appropriate circumstances constitute notice in writing within the meaning of s. 36(2). The fact that the plaintiff is not obliged to prosecute the proceedings is I think irrelevant in regard to notice.

(4) Perhaps in parenthesis because the point does not arise, the language of s. 36(2) appears to contemplate that even under the existing law notice in writing would be effective to sever a joint tenancy in personalty; see the words 'such other act or thing.' The authorities to the contrary are rather meagre and I am not sure how far this point was ever really considered in relation to personalty before 1925. If this anomaly does exist, and I am afraid I am not prepared to say positively that it does not exist, the anomaly is quite indefensible and should be put right as soon as possible.

(6) An uncommunicated declaration by one party to the other or indeed a mere verbal notice by one party to another clearly cannot operate as a severance.

(7) The policy of the law as it stands today, having regard particularly to s. 36(2), is to facilitate severance at the instance of either party, and I do not think the court should be over zealous in drawing a fine distinction from the pre-1925 authorities.

(8) The foregoing statement of principles involves criticism of certain passages in the judgments of Plowman J and Walton J in the two cases cited. Those cases, like all other cases, depend on their own particular facts, and I do not myself wish to go on to apply these *obiter* statements of principle to the actual decisions in these cases.

To summarize: after analysing the older cases Sir John Pennycuick concluded that there were three forms of informal severance:

1 an oral agreement that the joint tenancy should be severed;

2 an oral agreement that one joint tenant should buy the other out; and

3 '[A]cts of the parties, including, it seems to me, negotiations which, although not otherwise resulting in any agreement, indicate a common intention that the joint tenancy should be regarded as severed'.

It is clear that where the parties have orally agreed to sever the joint tenancy this would amount to severance. It is important to remember that for there to be mutual agreement to sever the joint tenancy *all the joint tenants must agree to sever*. Where negotiations have taken place and the joint tenants are in agreement to sever then this too would amount to severance.

8.13.4 Course of Dealings

Apart from an oral agreement that one joint tenant should buy the other out, Sir John Pennycuick considered the status of negotiations. He suggested that 'negotiations . . . although not otherwise resulting in any agreement, indicate a common intention' to sever the joint tenancy rather than a binding agreement (see the extract of Sir John Pennycuick's judgment at point (1)). What is being suggested here is that the negotiations or mutual conduct between parties indicates a common intention to sever despite the lack of an agreement. An agreement in principle, whereby there is a possibility of re-opening negotiations or altering the provisional agreement would not amount to severance (*Gore and Snell v Carpenter* (1990) 60 P & CR 456).

8.13.5 Matters Which Are Not a Severance

Unilateral Oral Statements

Lord Denning in *Burgess v Rawnsley* took the view that even a unilateral oral statement by one joint tenant to the other(s) could amount to a severance (see previously). This view is not shared by any other judge and is clearly wrong.

> **thinking point 8.10**
> The view taken by Lord Denning in *Burgess v Rawnsley* is hopelessly impractical. Why? (There are two reasons.)
>
> First, if Lord Denning were correct, then angry unilateral statements made in haste during a family quarrel would be effective to sever the joint tenancy. Secondly, there would be problems proving what exactly had been said in the heat of argument.

Subsequent Use of Property for Business Purposes

In *Barton v Morris* [1985] 2 All ER 1032 a farm was conveyed to two cohabitees on express trust for themselves as joint tenants in equity. 'The property was run as a guest house and small farm on a partnership basis and Miss Barton kept partnership accounts which showed the farm as a partnership asset.' This use of the property for the purposes of a partnership was held not to sever the joint tenancy.

8.13.6 'Severance by Will'

You must always remember that you *cannot* sever a joint tenancy by will.

Concluding Remarks

At the beginning of this chapter we discussed the basic characteristics of joint tenancies and tenancies in common. This involved our considering very long-standing common law derived rules. One of the fundamental changes made by the 1925 property legislation was also dealt with, namely the imposition on co-owners of a trust. This cured one major problem thrown up by the common law—that of multiplicity of co-owners. But, it brought with it other problems, which, as we shall see in Chapter 9, have now been largely solved by the TOLATA 1996.

It is obviously extremely important for you to understand fully the various ways in which a joint tenancy can be severed. Some of these methods (eg written notice) are the result of the deliberate actions of the parties. Others (eg in particular severance by bankruptcy) come about automatically, irrespective of any intention. It is also very important to remember that certain matters do not constitute severance. The principle recognized in *Barton v Morris*, that subsequent business use of premises does not sever an expressly created joint tenancy, should always be kept very firmly in mind.

Summary

Co-Ownership

Whenever land is conveyed to co-owners, there must be a trust. English law recognizes two forms of co-ownership:

Joint tenancy

- The co-owners have equal interests in the land—each is entitled to the whole.
- If one joint tenant dies, his interest passes to the survivors (right of survivorship).
- A joint tenancy can exist in law and in equity.
- The co-owners are the trustees of the legal title, unless there are more than four, in which case the first four named will be the trustees.

Tenants in Common

- The tenants in common have shares in the land which may or may not be equal.
- When a tenant in common dies, his share passes according to the normal rules of succession.
- A tenancy in common cannot exist with respect to a legal estate.
- A tenancy in common can only exist with respect to equitable interests under a trust.

Determining whether Co-Owners are Joint Tenants or Tenants in Common

- *Express declaration of trust*—this would state how the property is to be held in equity, that is, as joint tenants or tenants in common.

- *No express declaration of trust*—there is presumption in favour of joint tenancy, but that presumption will be rebutted if:

  - the owners are described as tenants in common;
  - conveyance uses phrases such as 'in equal shares';
  - the owners, who are business partners, contributed unequal amounts to the costs of acquisition.

Implied Trust

Resulting trust—arises in favour of Y where X owns a piece of land ('Whiteacre') and Y contributes to the purchase price of Whiteacre.

Constructive trust—arises in favour of Y where X owns a piece of land ('Whiteacre') and Y substantially contributes to the repayment of the mortgage on Whiteacre, or pays for or personally undertakes substantial improvements to Whiteacre, or there are other circumstances from which an agreement to share the property can be inferred.

Severance

- A legal joint tenancy cannot be severed (s36(2) LPA 1925).
- A joint tenant in equity can sever the joint tenancy, whether or not he is a trustee of the legal title.
- Where one of three or more equitable joint tenants severs, his interest becomes a share as a tenant in common. The other parties remain equitable joint tenants vis-à-vis each other.

Methods of severance

- *Total alienation*—whether by sale, gift, or a bankruptcy.
- *Partial alienation*—by lease or mortgage.
- *A contract for total or partial alienation*.
- *Written notice* under s36(2) LPA 1925. The notice must demand an immediate end to the relationship, and must reach (or be deemed to have reached) the intended recipients.
- *Informal severance* by mutual agreement (*Burgess v Rawnsley*) or by a mutual course of conduct.

NOT severances

- Gift in a will.
- Unilateral oral statements.
- Subsequent use of premises for business purposes.

Further Reading

Brown, J, 'Interpreting "D.I.Y." documents: severance, release, trusts, certainty, vesting and undue influence' [2008] Conv 336
Case note commentary on *Wallbank v Price* where the court considered whether a 'home-made' document severing a joint tenancy was valid.

Crown, BC, 'Severance of joint tenancy of land by partial alienation' (2001) 117 LQR 477
This article considers the extent to which one joint tenant can sever by partial alienation.

Harding, M, 'Defending *Stack v Dowden*' [2009] Conv 309
An intellectually very deep analysis of *Stack v Dowden*.

Hopkins, N, 'Regulating trusts of the home: private law and social policy' (2009) 125 LQR 310
Considers the regulation of trusts of land in the context of the home as a means of achieving social policy objectives.

Hughes, D, Davis, M, and Jacklin, L, ' "Come live with me and be my love"—a consideration of the 2007 Law Commission proposals on cohabitation breakdown' [2008] Conv 197
A critical overview of the Law Commission's proposals on cohabitation.

Law Commission Report, *Cohabitation: The Financial Consequences of Relationship Breakdown* (Report No 307, 2007)
Proposal to provide a more structured approach towards the exercise of judicial discretion ordering property adjustment.

Lees, K, 'Geary v Rankine: money isn't everything' [2012] Conv 412
A case comment on *Geary v Rankine* following *Jones v Kernott*.

Pawlowski, M, 'Beneficial entitlement—no longer doing justice?' [2007] Conv 354
Case comment on *Stack v Dowden*.

Percival, M, 'Severance by written notice—a matter of delivery?' [1999] Conv 60
Case comment on *Kinch v Bullard*.

Piska, N, 'Intention, fairness and the presumption of resulting trust after *Stack v Dowden*' (2008) 71 MLR 120
An impact analysis of *Oxley v Hiscock* and *Stack v Dowden*.

Swadling, W, 'Explaining resulting trusts' (2008) 124 LQR 72
Academic analysis of resulting trusts.

Co-Ownership— The Resolution of Disputes

9

Introduction

By imposing a trust upon all co-owners, Parliament in 1925 solved the problem of the saleability of land belonging to a multiplicity of co-owners. But this 'solution' to the problems set out at 8.4 brought with it a whole crop of new difficulties. These difficulties related to the exact legal nature of the rights of co-owners (eg does a co-owner have the right personally to occupy the land?) and as to what happens if co-owners disagree regarding the fate of the property. Happily these problems are now largely solved by the Trusts of Land and Appointment of Trustees Act 1996 (TOLATA 1996).

The issues discussed in this chapter are of fundamental importance to contemporary England and Wales. This is because the amount of co-ownership has shown enormous growth since 1925. This growth is due not just to an increase in the number of expressly agreed co-ownerships but also to the growth in tenancies in common arising because someone has acquired a constructive trust 'share' in a piece of land.

9.1 The Effect of Imposing a Trust Upon Co-Owners

Before we launch in to perhaps the biggest problem created by the decision made in 1925 to impose a trust upon all co-owners, you need to remember two points:

1 A 'co-ownership trust', like any other trust, is subject to the 'maximum of four' limit on the number of trustees.

2 While a co-ownership trust can validly *exist* with only one trustee, a disposition (sale, lease, mortgage, etc) requires two trustees if it is to 'overreach' the rights of non-trustee co-owners. As we shall see in a moment, there is however an important exception to this 'minimum of two' rule.

9.2 Tenancy in Common Arising Because There is an Implied Trust

In the previous chapter we discussed how implied trusts may arise. You may recall that implied trusts arise because they are giving effect to the intentions of the parties. Neither a resulting nor a constructive trust will be apparent from the documents or the land register.

In 1.3.7 the 'Chenu' scenario was given to illustrate how a resulting or constructive trust may arise. You will recall that Alex owns the legal fee simple estate in Chenu. However, Beth, who may or may not be his wife, acquired a beneficial interest in the property. Beth acquired her share (the beneficial interest) in the form of a resulting trust by paying £30,000 towards the acquisition of the property. She would equally have acquired a share (under a constructive trust) if she had made substantial contributions to mortgage instalments, or had made a substantial contribution to the improvement of Chenu. As Beth acquires a share in Chenu, she and Alex become tenants in common! Consequently, as a result of ss 34–36 Law of Property Act 1925 (LPA 1925), there was a trust for sale, or after the commencement of the 1996 Act, trust of land. Alex will be a trustee, in trust for himself and Beth. This is illustrated in Diagram 9.1.

Diagram 9.1
Beth through her contributions becomes a tenant in common

Legal title — Alex

Equitable Interest — Alex — Beth

This trust will be irregular in two respects:

- there will be only one trustee; and

- the people involved (Alex, Beth, and later potential purchasers or mortgagees of Chenu) will probably not realize that a trust exists. They will, therefore, probably not realize that a second trustee should be appointed before any disposition takes place.

You will not be surprised to learn that this problem of an irregular ('undisclosed') trust is a frequent occurrence in contemporary legal practice. It arises frequently simply because cases of implied trusts, particularly constructive trusts often arise.

9.2.1 Dispositions by a Single Trustee

It will help your understanding if we continue to develop the 'Chenu' scenario. Suppose Alex sells, leases, or mortgages Chenu acting entirely on his own. Put in more technical language, he makes a disposition without appointing a second trustee. Will Beth's interest be overreached despite the absence of a second trustee? Or, and this is the only alternative, will it be binding upon the purchaser? 'Purchaser' in this context includes a mortgagee or lessee.

Unregistered Title

cross-reference
See 4.5.4 under 'Imputed Notice' for a discussion of Kingsnorth Finance Co Ltd v Tizard.

First, it should be stressed that where the relevant land is unregistered title, a constructive trust share is not registrable as a land charge. It is now well established that where a disposition is made by a sole trustee such as Alex, the doctrine of notice must be applied. This was the approach taken, for example, in *Kingsnorth Finance Co Ltd v Tizard* [1986] 2 All ER 64.

If a purchaser from Alex had notice (actual, constructive, or imputed) of Beth's interest (call it a 'share' if you like), he will be bound by Beth's interest. Beth's interest will not bind a purchaser only if that purchaser is a bona fide purchaser for value of a legal estate without notice of Beth's interest.

thinking point 9.1
Conrad is the owner in fee simple of Superhouse (unregistered title). His cohabitee, Daria, who moved into the property three years after Conrad had purchased the property, has contributed to the mortgage payments, and has therefore acquired a share under a constructive trust. The relationship has now

cross-reference
City of London Building Society v Flegg *is discussed at 4.8.1 and 9.2.2.*

broken down and Daria is contemplating the possibility of leaving. However she wants to be sure that her interest will bind a purchaser of Superhouse. Advise Daria.

First of all, there is no land charge which Daria can register. Rather, her constructive trust interest is subject to the equitable doctrine of notice. However, provided she stays put in Superhouse and reveals her interest to anybody who asks whether she has a share in the home, the rule in Hunt v Luck *will (normally) protect her. If Daria follows this advice, a purchaser from Alex will have notice of her equitable interest and be bound by it. It should be noted that we are temporarily ignoring the effect of the decision of the House of Lords in* City of London Building Society v Flegg [1988] 1 AC 54.*

cross-reference
Williams and Glyn's Bank Ltd v Boland [1981] AC 487 *was discussed at 6.5.4 under 'Rights which can be Overriding Interests', and you should re-read that text.*

Registered Title

Reverting to the 'Chenu' scenario, if the house is registered title then the decision of the House of Lords in *Williams and Glyn's Bank Ltd v Boland* will apply. It follows from *Boland* that if Chenu is registered title, Beth, provided she is in 'actual occupation' of Chenu at the relevant time, will have an overriding interest within Sch 3 para 2 Land Registration Act 2002 (LRA 2002), unless either her occupation is not obvious on a reasonably careful inspection or enquiry is made of her and she (unreasonably) fails to reveal her interest.

cross-reference
See 6.2.2 for a discussion on restrictions.

The owner of a constructive trust interest/share in a registered title who is not 'in actual occupation' (eg Beth has gone to live with another man) will have a minor interest. This minor interest can be protected by entering a restriction (s40 LRA 2002). Prior to the 2002 Act it could be protected by a caution.

In *Elias v Mitchell* [1972] Ch 652, two business partners had fallen out. One was the sole registered proprietor of their business premises, but both had 'shares' (as tenants in common) in the premises. The partner who was not the registered proprietor had left those premises. His interest was held to be a minor interest which could be protected by lodging a caution. There can be no doubt that this decision can be applied to 'domestic' situations such as our Chenu scenario; however, under s40 LRA 2002, a restriction will now have to be used.

thinking point 9.2

It is 2015, Conrad is owner in fee simple of Superhouse (registered title). His cohabitee, Daria, who moved into the property three years after Conrad had purchased the property, has contributed to the mortgage payments, and has therefore acquired a share under a constructive trust. The relationship has now broken down, and Daria is contemplating the possibility of leaving. However, she wants to be sure that her interest will bind a purchaser of Superhouse. Advise Daria.

cross-reference
City of London Building Society v Flegg *is discussed at 9.2.2.*

Provided she stays (visibly) put in Superhouse and reveals her interest to anybody who asks whether she has a share in the home, Daria's interest will be an overriding interest under Sch 3 para 2 LRA 2002 and a purchaser from Conrad will be bound by it.

If Daria moves out her position is better than if the house were unregistered. She should (cf the partner in Elias v Mitchell*) protect her minor interest by entering a restriction (s40 LRA 2002). Prior to 2003 she would have used a caution. (It should be added that we are temporarily ignoring the effect of the decision of the House of Lords in* City of London Building Society v Flegg [1988] 1 AC 54.*)*

9.2.2 What if Alex did Appoint a Second Trustee?

Suppose that in the Chenu scenario Alex does realize that there is a co-ownership and that therefore he is a lone trustee. If he wants to make a disposition (sale, lease, or mortgage) Alex can appoint a friend as co-trustee. The appointment of a second trustee changes the position dramatically:

- If the title to Chenu is *unregistered*, Beth's interest will be overreached in the usual way.
- If the title to Chenu is *registered*, a disposition by two trustees will similarly overreach Beth's interest, notwithstanding the operation of Sch 3 para 2 LRA 2002 or the entering of a restriction. This is because it is an inherent characteristic of Beth's interest (remember it is an interest under a trust) that it can be overreached by a disposition made by two trustees.

Overreaching in Action—*City of London Building Society v Flegg* [1988] 1 AC 54

You may recall that in Chapter 4 we discussed the essence of overreaching. To recap, if the land is sold the rights of the beneficiaries of a trust cannot bind the purchaser. Provided the purchase price is paid to the correct persons (minimum of two trustees or trust corporation, s2(2) LPA 1925, as amended), the purchaser, irrespective of whether he had notice of the beneficiaries' rights, will take the land free from those rights (see s27 LPA 1925 in the following extract).

> *Law of Property Act 1925*
>
> 27. Purchaser not to be concerned with the trusts of the proceeds of sale which are to be paid to two trustees or to a trust corporation
>
> (1) A purchaser of a legal estate from trustees of land shall not be concerned with the trusts affecting the land, the net income of the land or the proceeds of sale of the land whether or not those trusts are declared by the same instrument as that by which the trust of land is created.
>
> (2) Notwithstanding anything to the contrary in the instrument (if any) creating a [trust] of land or in [any trust affecting the net proceeds of sale of the land if it is sold], the proceeds for sale or other capital money shall not be paid to or applied by the direction of fewer than two persons as [trustees], except where the trustee is a trust corporation, but this subsection does not affect the right of a sole personal representative as such to give valid receipts for, or direct the application of, proceeds of sale or other capital money, nor, except where capital money arises on the transaction, render it necessary to have more than one trustee.

Where overreaching has taken place the rights of the beneficiaries are not totally lost. These rights are transferred to the purchase price. This money will form a trust fund which must be invested. The beneficiaries will now have equitable interests in the trust fund.

The leading case which illustrates the operation of overreaching is *City of London Building Society v Flegg* [1988] 1 AC 54. Mr and Mrs Flegg both contributed to the purchase of a house; the title to the house was registered in the names of their daughter and son-in-law (the Maxwell-Browns). The Fleggs, as a consequence of their contributions, each had a beneficial interest in the form of an implied trust. The Fleggs at all material times lived in the property. The house was subsequently mortgaged to the building society by the Maxwell-Browns, however the Maxwell-Browns defaulted on their mortgage. The Fleggs argued that they had by virtue of their contributions to the purchase price an equitable interest in the property, and that since they were in actual occupation they had an overriding interest under s70(1)(g) Land Registration Act 1925 (LRA 1925). The building society successfully argued in the House of Lords that the mortgage, being executed by two trustees, overreached the equitable rights of Mr and Mrs Flegg.

The House of Lords also held that s14 LPA 1925 which states: 'This Part of this Act shall not prejudicially affect the interest of any person in possession or in actual occupation of land to which he may be entitled in right of such possession or occupation', did not mean that the rights of co-owners in occupation could not be overreached.

Lord Templeman said:

> ...The respondents claim to be entitled to overriding interests because they were in actual occupation of Bleak House on the date of the legal charge. But the interests of the respondents cannot at one and the same time be overreached and overridden and at the same time be overriding interests. The appellants cannot at one and the same time take free from all the interests of the respondents yet at the same time be subject to some of those interests. The right of the respondents to be and remain in actual occupation of Bleak House ceased when the respondents' interests were overreached by the legal charge save in so far as their rights were transferred to the equity of redemption. As persons interested under the trust for sale the respondents had no right to possession as against the appellants and the fact that the respondents were in actual occupation at the date of the legal charge did not create a new right or transfer an old right so as to make the right enforceable against the appellants.
>
> One of the main objects of the legislation of 1925 was to effect a compromise between on the one hand the interests of the public in securing that land held in trust is freely marketable and, on the other hand, the interests of the beneficiaries in preserving their rights under the trusts. By the Settled Land Act 1925 a tenant for life may convey the settled land discharged from all the trusts powers and provisions of the settlement. By the Law of Property Act 1925 trustees for sale may convey land held on trust for sale discharged from the trusts affecting the proceeds of sale and rents and profits until sale. Under both forms of trust the protection and the only protection of the beneficiaries is that capital money must be paid to at least two trustees or a trust corporation. Section 14 of the Law of Property Act 1925 and section 70 of the Land Registration Act 1925 cannot have been intended to frustrate this compromise and to subject the purchaser to some beneficial interests but not others depending on the waywardness of actual occupation. The Court of Appeal took a different view, largely in reliance on the decision of this House in *Williams & Glyn's Bank Ltd.* v. *Boland* [1981] A.C. 487. In that case the sole proprietor of registered land held the land as sole trustee upon trust for sale and to stand possessed of the net proceeds of sale and rents and profits until sale upon trust for himself and his wife as tenants in common. This House held that the wife's beneficial interest coupled with actual possession by her constituted an overriding interest and that a mortgagee from the husband, despite the concluding words of section 20(1), took subject to the wife's overriding interest. But in that case the interest of the wife was not overreached or overridden because the mortgagee advanced capital moneys to a sole trustee. If the wife's interest had been overreached by the mortgagee advancing capital moneys to two trustees there would have been nothing to justify the wife in remaining in occupation as against the mortgagee. There must be a combination of an interest which justifies continuing occupation plus actual occupation to constitute an overriding interest. Actual occupation is not an interest in itself. For these reasons and for the reasons to be given by my noble and learned friend, Lord Oliver of Aylmerton, I would allow this appeal and restore the order of Judge Thomas who ordered the respondents to deliver up Bleak House to the appellants.

Lord Oliver of Aylmerton said:

> ...I turn to consider whether, in fact, the decision of this House in *Boland* [1981] AC 487 does lead to the conclusion that the occupying co-owner's interest under the statutory trusts is, by reason of his occupation, one which is incapable of being overreached. It has, I think, to

be borne in mind when reading both the judgments in the Court of Appeal in that case and the speeches in the House that they were prepared and delivered against a background of fact which precluded any argument that the interests of Mrs Boland and Mrs Brown had been over-reached under the provisions of the Law of Property Act 1925...

Considered in the context of a transaction complying with the statutory requirements of the Law of Property Act 1925 the question of the effect of s. 70(1)(g) of the Land Registration Act 1925 must, in my judgment, be approached by asking first what are the 'rights' of the person in occupation and whether they are, at the material time, subsisting in reference to the land. In the instant case the exercise by the registered proprietors of the powers con-ferred on trustees for sale by s. 28(1) of the Law of Property Act 1925 had the effect of over-reaching the interests of the respondents under the statutory trusts upon which depended their right to continue in occupation of the land. The appellants took free from those trusts (section 27) and were not, in any event, concerned to see that the respondents' consent to the transaction was obtained (section 26). If, then, one asks what were the subsisting rights of the respondents referable to their occupation, the answer must, in my judgment, be that they were rights which, vis-à-vis the appellants, were, eo instante with the creation of the charge, overreached and therefore subsisted only in relation to the equity of redemption. I do not, for my part, find in Boland's case [1981] AC 487 anything which compels a contrary conclusion. Granted that the interest of a co-owner pending the execution of the statutory trust for sale is, despite the equitable doctrine of conversion, an interest subsisting in reference to the land the subject matter of the trust and granted also that Boland's case establishes that such an interest, although falling within the definition of minor interest and so liable to be overridden by a registered disposition, will, so long as it subsists, be elevated to the status of an overrid-ing interest if there exists also the additional element of occupation by the co-owner, I cannot for my part accept that, once what I may call the parent interest, by which alone the occupa-tion can be justified, has been overreached and thus subordinated to a legal estate properly created by the trustees under their statutory powers, it can, in relation to the proprietor of the legal estate so created, be any longer said to be a right 'for the time being subsisting.' Section 70(1)(g) protects only the rights in reference to the land of the occupier whatever they are at the material time—in the instant case the right to enjoy in specie the rents and profits of the land held in trust for him. Once the beneficiary's rights have been shifted from the land to capital moneys in the hands of the trustees, there is no longer an interest in the land to which the occupation can be referred or which it can protect. *If the trustees sell in accord-ance with the statutory provisions and so overreach the beneficial interests in reference to the land, nothing remains to which a right of occupation can attach and the same result must, in my judgment, follow vis-à-vis a chargee by way of legal mortgage so long as the transac-tion is carried out in the manner prescribed by the Law of Property Act 1925, overreaching the beneficial interests by subordinating them to the estate of the chargee which is no longer 'affected' by them so as to become subject to them on registration pursuant to s. 20(1) of the Land Registration Act 1925.* [Emphasis added] In the instant case, therefore, I would, for my part, hold that the charge created in favour of the appellants overreached the beneficial inter-ests of the respondents and that there is nothing in s. 70(1)(g) of the Land Registration Act 1925 or in Boland's case which has the effect of preserving against the appellants any rights of the respondents to occupy the land by virtue of their beneficial interests in the equity of redemption which remains vested in the trustees.

The central point in *Flegg* is the sentence in Lord Oliver's speech which has been emphasized. Expressing the point more widely, it is an inherent characteristic of any equitable interest under any type of trust of land that it can be overreached by a disposition made by two trustees.

In *HSBC Bank Plc v Dyche* [2010] 2 P & CR 4 in order to determine whether overreaching had occurred, the court read the statutory requirements of overreaching under s2 LPA 1925 and the definition of a purchaser under s205(1)(xxi) LPA 1925 together. In this case the property was sold at an undervalue to the purchaser who was one of the trustees of the property. The court held that the purchaser intending to benefit from this transaction acted dishonestly in breach of trust. The purchaser was not 'in good faith' and the court concluded that overreaching did not occur.

thinking point 9.3

Conrad is owner in fee simple of Superhouse. His cohabitee, Daria, who moved into the property three years after Conrad had purchased the property, has contributed to the mortgage payments, and has therefore acquired a share under a constructive trust. The relationship has now broken down, and Daria is contemplating the possibility of leaving. However she wants to be sure that her interest will bind a purchaser of Superhouse. Conrad has just appointed his friend Gerard to be a second trustee of Superhouse. Advise Daria.

First, it is hoped you realized that with this question it makes no difference whether Superhouse is registered or unregistered title. Secondly, and this is the crucial point, as a result of Flegg there is nothing Daria can do 'to be sure that her interest will bind a purchaser of Superhouse'. If she gets the Land Registry to enter a restriction, that restriction will require the purchase price to be paid to two trustees. But there are two trustees, and therefore any sale (lease or mortgage) of Superhouse by the two trustees, Conrad and Gerard, will automatically overreach Daria's interest.

9.2.3 Other Trusts of Land Where There is Only a Single Trustee

This is a slight digression from the law of co-ownership, but it is appropriate to make it at this point. If you refer back to 7.5.6 to 7.6 you will see that in those sections we identified a number of situations where a trust of land may arise with only one trustee. These included:

- one document creating equitable interests;
- conveyance to a minor;
- accidental trusts of land: conveying land subject to a right to reside; and
- accidental trusts in home-made wills.

At 7.6 the point was made that where there is a sole trustee of a trust of land, that trustee should appoint a colleague before selling the land or making some other disposition.

thinking point 9.4

What would happen if a (sole) trustee tries to sell (or mortgage or lease) the trust land acting on his own?

It is hoped that you have realized that you apply to this question the discussion contained in 9.2.1. In summary, the position where there is a trust of land but a disposition is made by only one trustee is as follows.

Where the Trust Land is Unregistered Title

Apply the doctrine of notice. Where the purchaser from the sole trustee has no notice of the trust of land, then the purchaser is not bound by the rights of the beneficiary(ies) under the trust whose interest has in effect been overreached, notwithstanding there being only one trustee.

Where the purchaser has notice of the trust of land (eg under the rule in *Hunt v Luck* because a beneficiary is occupying the property) he will be bound by the equitable interests under that trust.

Where the Trust Land is Registered Title

Apply the usual rules about overriding and minor interests.

The only way an equitable interest under a trust of land can be an overriding interest is by virtue of Sch 3 para 2 LRA 2002. Thus the purchaser from a sole trustee will be bound by an equitable interest under a trust of land if the owner of that equitable interest is in actual occupation. If the owner of an equitable interest under a trust of land is not in actual occupation, his interest will be a minor interest, not normally binding on a purchaser from a sole trustee. The minor interest could however be 'protected' by entering a restriction.

9.2.4 Summary

For a summary of the issues discussed in the previous section, see Diagram 9.2.

Diagram 9.2
Does a trust share belonging to a claimant (C) bind a purchaser (A)?

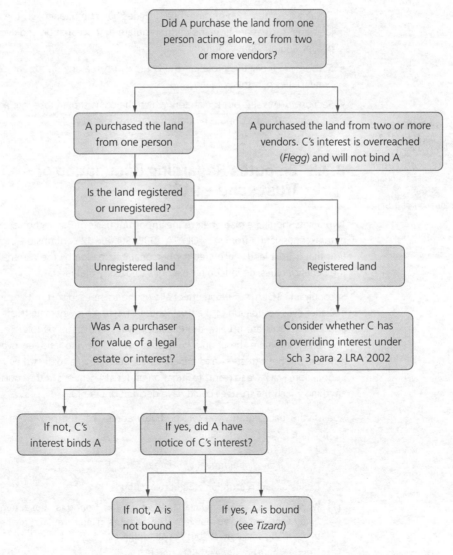

9.3 Sections 13 to 15 TOLATA 1996—Disputes Between Owners

Where a dispute has arisen regarding a trust of land, whether *'beneficiary v trustees'* or *'trustee v trustee'* or even *'beneficiary v beneficiary'* ss 13 to 15 TOLATA 1996 provide a procedure for the court to settle the dispute. These provisions replaced s30 LPA 1925 which also dealt with dispute resolution. Sections 13 to 15 TOLATA 1996 are not confined to co-ownership trusts, but there can be little doubt that most litigation invoking these sections involves co-owners who have fallen out with each other.

9.3.1 The Basic Pattern of ss13 to 15 TOLATA 1996

- *Section 13* Where two or more beneficiaries have simultaneously the right to occupy trust land, the trustees are given power to regulate that occupation and even to decide who can occupy and on what conditions.
- *Section 14* Under this provision the court can settle any dispute amongst trustees and/or beneficiaries of a trust of land.
- *Section 15* This sets out the factors which the court should take into account when making an order settling a dispute brought before it under s14.

cross-reference
Refer back to 7.11.2 and 7.11.3 for a discussion on the duty to consult beneficiaries and personal occupation of trust land.

9.3.2 Disputes Regarding Occupation of Trust Land—s13

Two points should be made before the important parts of this section are set out. First, s13 is a natural continuation from s12 TOLATA 1996. Section 12 confirms the commonsense proposition that if trust land is acquired for personal occupation by the current beneficiary(ies) then the beneficiary(ies) do indeed have a right to occupy that land.

Secondly, s13 TOLATA 1996 in effect allows the trustees to sort out arguments between beneficiaries over occupation of the trust land. But, with co-ownership trusts of land, the trustees and beneficiaries are usually, though not always, the same people. Section 13 is clearly of no direct use where the people in dispute over occupying land (eg over who should live in a house) are both trustees and beneficiaries. Such people, unless they can settle matters by negotiation, will have to resort to litigation under s14. Under s14 the court can (inter alia) order anything which the trustees could have decided under s13.

Against this background, you will probably agree that the provisions of s13, though quite lengthy, are largely self-explanatory.

Trusts of Land and Appointment of Trustees Act 1996

13. Exclusion and restriction of right to occupy

(1) Where two or more beneficiaries are (or apart from this subsection would be) entitled under section 12 to occupy land, the trustees of land may exclude or restrict the entitlement of any one or more (but not all) of them.

(2) Trustees may not under subsection (1)—

  (a) unreasonably exclude any beneficiary's entitlement to occupy the land, or

  (b) restrict such entitlement to an unreasonable extent.

(3) The trustees of land may from time to time impose reasonable conditions on any beneficiary in relation to his occupation of land by reason of his entitlement under section 12.

(4) The matters to which the trustees are to have regard in exercising the powers conferred by this section include—

(a) the intentions of the person or persons (if any) who created the trust,

(b) the purposes for which the land is held, and

(c) the circumstances and wishes of each of the beneficiaries who is (or apart from any previous exercise by the trustees of those powers would be) entitled to occupy the land under section 12.

(5) The conditions which may be imposed on a beneficiary under subsection (3) include, in particular, conditions requiring him—

(a) to pay any outgoings or expenses in respect of the land ...

(6) Where the entitlement of any beneficiary to occupy land under section 12 has been excluded or restricted, the conditions which may be imposed on any other beneficiary under subsection (3) include, in particular conditions requiring him to—

(a) make payments by way of compensation to the beneficiary whose entitlement has been excluded or restricted ...

(7) The powers conferred on trustees by this section may not be exercised—

(a) so as prevent any person who is in occupation of land (whether or not by reason of an entitlement under section 12) from continuing to occupy the land, or

(b) in a manner likely to result in any such person ceasing to occupy the land, unless he consents or the court has given approval.

thinking point 9.5

Tanner and Tyrone are trustees of 16 Clumber Road East in trust for three brothers, Albin, Boris, and Chaz in equal shares. The trust was created by the brothers' parents, 'to provide a home for our three boys'. Chaz has fallen out with his brothers. As the other two are constantly arguing with him, he has found a flat of his own. Advise Tanner and Tyrone.

They can make a decision under s13(1) excluding Chaz from 16 Clumber Road East. But under s13(5), they could require Albin and Boris to pay all the outgoings on the house. Under s13(6) they could also require Albin and Boris to make regular payments to Chaz (almost like a 'rent') for their exclusive use of the house. These payments, it is suggested, should not exceed one-third of the rent the house would fetch if it was leased out to a tenant.

Section 13(7) also needs to be considered:

Trusts of Land and Appointment of Trustees Act 1996

13. Exclusion and restriction of right to occupy

...

(7) The powers conferred on trustees by this section may not be exercised—

(a) so as to prevent any person who is in occupation of land (whether or not by reason of an entitlement under section 12) from continuing to occupy the land ... unless he consents or the court has given approval.

Suppose in our 16 Clumber Road East example Albin and Boris want Chaz to leave, but he resolutely refuses to go. Tanner and Tyrone cannot make a decision ordering him to vacate the house. If they want to 'evict' Chaz, they will have to get a court order authorizing his eviction.

Section 13(1) was an issue in the case of *Rodway v Landy* [2001] Ch 703. The claimants were GPs and co-owners of a purpose-built doctors' surgery. They fell out, and Dr Rodway sought a court order under s14 TOLATA 1996 (discussed in detail in the following section) that the premises should be sold and the proceeds of sale divided between them. The defendant counterclaimed for a court order which would (in effect) split ('partition') the premises between them.

The High Court and Court of Appeal both held that trustees of land (and if need be the court) have power under s13(1) to (in practical terms) physically divide up the land between beneficiaries. Gibson LJ said:

> The main argument of [counsel for Dr Rodway] related to section 13 of the 1996 Act. He submitted that the judge erred in concluding that he could make an order excluding or restricting each of the two doctors from a part of the property. This point turns on the construction of the words in parenthesis in section 13(1), '(but not all)' . . .
>
> [Counsel for Dr Landy] supported the reasoning and conclusion of the judge. He said that to construe the subsection literally, as [counsel for Dr Rodway] urged, would produce an irrational limitation on section 13(1) as it would mean that the trustees can exclude one of two beneficiaries entirely from the occupation of trust property but not limit each of them to occupation of only part of it. [Counsel for Dr Landy] urged that the words 'but not all' mean that the trustees may not exclude or restrict the entitlement of the beneficiaries collectively; after the trustees have exercised their powers the beneficiaries collectively must have rights which are as extensive as those which the beneficiaries collectively had previously. [Counsel for Dr Rodway] on the other hand submitted that the limitation on the power to exclude or restrict is in terms on the number of beneficiaries who may be excluded or restricted, and it is not related to the land which happens to be the subject of the restriction.
>
> I accept that the limitation on the power to exclude or restrict is expressed as a limitation on the number of beneficiaries who may be excluded or restricted. Plainly it would make no sense if there was no beneficiary left entitled to occupy land subject to a trust of land as a result of the exercise of the power under section 13. That is the force of the words '(but not all)'. But if an estate consisting of adjoining properties, Blackacre and Whiteacre, was held subject to a trust of land and A and B were entitled to occupy the estate, it would be very surprising if the trustees were not able under section 13 to exclude or restrict B's entitlement to occupy Blackacre and at the same time to exclude or restrict A's entitlement to occupy Whiteacre, thereby leaving A alone entitled to occupy Blackacre and B Whiteacre. So also I do not see why, in relation to a single building which lends itself to physical partition, the trustees could not exclude or restrict one beneficiary's entitlement to occupy one part and at the same time exclude or restrict the other beneficiary's entitlement to occupy the other part. *Each part is land subject to a trust of land and the beneficiaries are entitled to occupy that part until the entitlement of a beneficiary is excluded or restricted by the exercise of the power under section 13. So construed section 13(1) seems to me to make good sense and to provide a useful power which trustees might well wish to exercise in appropriate circumstances so as to be even-handed between beneficiaries*. In contrast, I can see no good reason why Parliament should want to confine the trustees to the all or nothing approach urged by [counsel for Dr Rodway]. I therefore agree with the conclusion of the judge on this point. [Emphasis added]

9.3.3 Courts Settling Disputes Regarding Trusts of Land—s14

Section 14 is a relatively short section, but of crucial importance. It is drafted in very straightforward language.

Trusts of Land and Appointment of Trustees Act 1996

14. Applications for order

(1) Any person who is a trustee of land or has an interest in property subject to a trust of land may make an application to the court for an order under this section.

(2) On an application for an order under this section the court may make any such order—

(a) relating to the exercise by the trustees of any of their functions (including an order relieving them of any obligation to obtain the consent of, or to consult, any person in connection with the exercise of any of their functions), or

(b) declaring the nature or extent of a person's interest in property subject to the trust, as the court thinks fit.

(3) The court may not under this section make any order as to the appointment or removal of trustees.

(4) The powers conferred on the court by this section are exercisable on an application whether it is made before or after the commencement of this Act.

The ambit of s14 permits anyone with an interest in the property (eg trustee, beneficiary, mortgagee of an equitable interest or trustee in bankruptcy of a beneficiary) to apply to the court for an order. Section 14 seems to cover almost every conceivable dispute which might arise regarding a trust of land. Most cases brought under s14 are likely to fall into one of four categories:

- disputes regarding size of co-ownership interests;
- disputes regarding occupation of the trust land;
- authorizing transactions without requisite consent(s);
- disputes as to whether co-owned land should be sold.

Disputes Regarding Size of Co-Ownership Interests

cross-reference
Refer back to the discussion at 8.7 to 8.10, especially the first paragraph of 8.7 and thinking point 8.8.

These disputes can be settled under s14(2)(b) TOLATA 1996. If a conveyance to co-owners does not contain an express declaration of trust, that omission leaves room for all sorts of arguments as to who owns what interests. Those arguments can be settled in proceedings brought under s14.

Disputes Regarding Occupation of the Trust Land

If the trustees cannot settle a dispute between beneficiaries regarding the occupation of trust land (s13 TOLATA 1996), then the court can do so under s14. Moreover, if the trustees have made a decision under s13 trying to settle an occupation dispute, then a beneficiary disgruntled with the trustees' decision could challenge that decision by proceedings under s14.

Authorizing Transactions without Requisite Consent(s)

This aspect of s14 has already been mentioned at 7.12.5. Where the trustees of land powers of disposition have been made subject to the consent of named person(s), then the withholding of consent can be overridden by court order.

275

Disputes as to Whether Co-Owned Land Should be Sold

This type of dispute may arise where two or more people buy a house or some other type of land. They fall out. One (or more) of the co-owners wants the land sold so that he can 'cash in his share'. The other(s) want to retain the land. We will return to consider how this type of dispute may be settled after we have considered s15 TOLATA 1996.

9.3.4 Factors to be Considered in Settling Disputes—s15

Trusts of Land and Appointment of Trustees Act 1996

15. Matters relevant in determining applications

(1) The matters to which the court is to have regard in determining an application for an order under section 14 include—

   (a) the intentions of the person or persons (if any) who created the trust,

   (b) the purposes for which the property subject to the trust is held,

   (c) the welfare of any minor who occupies or might reasonably be expected to occupy any land subject to the trust as his home, and

   (d) the interests of any secured creditor of any beneficiary. [Note: para (d) will apply in those relatively rare cases where a co-owner has mortgaged his *share* in the property.]

(2) In the case of an application relating to the exercise in relation to any land of the powers conferred on the trustees by section 13, the matters to which the court is to have regard also include the circumstances and wishes of each of the beneficiaries who is (or apart from any previous exercise by the trustees of those powers would be) entitled to occupy the land under section 12.

(3) In the case of any other application, other than one relating to the exercise of the power mentioned in section 6(2), the matters to which the court is to have regard also include the circumstances and wishes of any beneficiaries of full age and entitled to an interest in possession in property subject to the trust or (in case of dispute) of the majority (according to the value of their combined interests).

(4) This section does not apply to an application if section 335A of the Insolvency Act 1986 (which is inserted by Schedule 3 and relates to applications by a trustee of a bankrupt) applies to it.

Section 15 provides for a wide range of factors that the court should take into consideration in making a decision under s14 TOLATA 1996. These factors are neither in order of significance, nor do they form part of an exhaustive list as other factors may be taken into consideration by the court. In summary, the factors provided for under s15 are:

- intentions of the person(s) who created the trust;

- purpose(s) of the property which is subject to the trust;

- welfare of a minor;

- interests of any secured creditor.

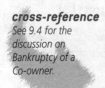

cross-reference
See 9.4 for the discussion on Bankruptcy of a Co-owner.

With regard to the last point, interests of any secured creditor, if an application for sale is brought before the court by the beneficiary's trustee in bankruptcy then the s15 factors are expressly excluded from consideration (s15(4) TOLATA 1996).

9.3.5 Settling Disputes as to Whether the Trust Property Should be Sold

In the situation where there is a dispute as to whether the co-owned land should be sold, the court has five types of order open to it:

- refuse a sale;
- refuse a sale but make an order regulating the right to occupy the property;
- order a sale;
- order a sale but suspend the order for a short period; and
- (only possible in exceptional cases) partition the co-owned property.

Whether the court will order sale will depend very much on the consideration given by the court to the specific facts of the case and to the various factors listed in s15 TOLATA 1996.

It is worth noting that the old s30 LPA 1925 gave rise to quite a lot of case law on the issue as to whether co-owned property should be sold when the co-owners fall out. This case law may be of assistance as we now consider how courts will settle similar disputes arising under s14 TOLATA 1996. The trusts under consideration under the old law were trusts for sale where there was an obligation to sell the property, but this is no longer the case with trusts of land. Commenting on the possible approach to be taken by the courts in determining the applicability of old case law, Neuberger J suggested in *Mortgage Corporation v Shaire* [2001] Ch 743 that despite the body of case law under s30 LPA 1925, a cautious approach should be adopted in considering their application in relation to the 1996 Act. This is because under the old law the courts had significantly less discretion compared to that permitted under s15 TOLATA 1996. Neuberger J noted:

The effect of the 1996 Act

To my mind, for a number of reasons, Mr. Asif is correct in his submission, on behalf of Mrs. Shaire that section 15 has changed the law. First, there is the rather trite point that if there was no intention to change the law, it is hard to see why Parliament has set out in section 15(2) and, indeed, on one view, section 15(3), the factors which have to be taken into account specifically, albeit not exclusively, when the court is asked to exercise its jurisdiction to order a sale.

Secondly, it is hard to reconcile the contention that Parliament intended to confirm the law as laid down in *Byrne* [*Lloyds Bank Plc v Byrne & Byrne* [1993] 1 FLR 369] with the fact that, while the interest of a chargee is one of the four specified factors to be taken into account in section 15(1)(d), there is no suggestion that it is to be given any more importance than the interests of the children residing in the house: see section 15(1)(c). As is clear from the passage I have quoted from the judgment of Nourse L.J. in *Citro* [*Re Citro (A Bankrupt)* [1991] Ch 142] as applied to a case such as this in light of *Byrne*, that would appear to represent a change in the law.

Thirdly, the very name 'trust for sale' and the law as it has been developed by the courts suggests that under the old law, in the absence of a strong reason to the contrary, the court should order sale. Nothing in the language of the new code as found in the 1996 Act supports that approach.

Fourthly, it is clear from the reasons in *Byrne* and indeed the later two first instance cases to which I have referred, that the law, as developed under section 30 of the Law of Property Act 1925, was that the court should adopt precisely the same approach in a case where one of the co–owners was bankrupt (*Citro*) and a case where one of the co–owners had charged his interest (*Byrne*). It is quite clear that Parliament now considers that a different approach is appropriate in the two cases – compare section 15(2) and section 15(3) of the 1996 Act with section 15(4) and the new section 335A of the Insolvency Act 1986.

Fifthly, an indication from the Court of Appeal that the 1996 Act was intended to change the law is to be found in (an albeit plainly obiter) sentence in the judgment of Peter Gibson L.J. in *Banker's Trust Co. v. Namdar* unreported, 17th February 1997. Having come to the conclusion that the wife's appeal against an order for sale had to be refused in light of the reasoning in *Citro* and *Byrne*, the learned Lord Justice said this:

> 'Unfortunately for Mrs. Namdar, the Appointment of Trustees Act was not in force at the time [i.e. at the time of the hearing at first instance].'

Of course it would be dangerous to build too much on that observation, but it is an indication from the Court of Appeal and indeed from a former Chairman of the Law Commission, as to the perceived effect of the 1996 Act.

Sixthly, the leading textbooks support the view that I have reached. In *Megarry & Wade*, already referred to, one finds this at para.9–064 on p.510:

> 'Although the authorities on the law prior to 1997 will therefore continue to provide guidance, the outcome will not in all cases be the same as it would have been under the previous law. This is because the legislature was much more specific as to the matters which a court is required to take into account.'

Emmet on Title, loose–leaf, 19th edition, January 1999 release, contains this at para.22–035:

> 'Cases decided on pre–1997 law may be disregarded as of little, if any, assistance because their starting point was necessarily a trust for sale implied or expressed as a conveyancing device enabling the convenient co–ownership of property.'

Seventhly, the Law Commission report which gave rise to the 1996 Act, *Transfer of Land, Trusts of Land, Law Com. No.181*, 1989 tends to support this view as well…In para.12.9 of the report the Law Commission describe the aim as being to 'consolidate *and rationalize*' (emphasis added) the current approach. When commenting on the proposed equivalents of what are now section 15(2) and section 15(3) the Law Commission said this in note 143:

> 'Clearly, the terms of these guidelines may influence the exercise of the discretion in some way. For example, it may be that the courts' approach to creditors' interests will be altered by the framing of the guideline as to the welfare of children. If the welfare of children is seen as a factor to be considered independently of the beneficiaries' holdings, the court may be less ready to order the sale of the home than they are at present.' …

Eighthly, to put it at its lowest, it does not seem to me unlikely that the legislature intended to relax the fetters on the way in which the court exercised its discretion in cases such as *Citro* and *Byrne*, and so as to tip the balance somewhat more in favour of families and against banks and other chargees. Although the law under section 30 was clear following *Citro* and *Byrne*, there were indications of judicial dissatisfaction with the state of the law at that time. Although Bingham L.J. agreed with Nourse L.J. in *Citro*, he expressed unhappiness with the result at p.161F, and Sir George Waller's dissatisfaction went so far as led him to dissent: see his judgment at p.161 to p.163. Furthermore, there is a decision of the Court of Appeal in *Abbey National Plc v. Moss* [1994] 1 F.L.R. 307, which suggests a desire for a new approach.

All these factors, to my mind, when taken together point very strongly to the conclusion that section 15 has changed the law. As a result of section 15, the court has greater flexibility than heretofore, as to how it exercises its jurisdiction on an application for an order for sale on facts such as those in *Citro* and *Byrne*. There are certain factors which must be taken into account – see section 15(1) and, subject to the next point, section 15(3). There may be other factors in a particular case which the court can, indeed should, take into account. Once the relevant factors to be taken into account have been identified, it is a matter for the court as to what weight to give to each factor in a particular case.

A difficult question, having arrived at this conclusion, is the extent to which the old authorities are of assistance, and it is no surprise to find differing views expressed in the two textbooks from which I have quoted. On the one hand, to throw over all the wealth of learning and thought given by so many eminent judges to the problem which is raised on an application for sale of a house where competing interests exist seems somewhat arrogant and possibly rash. On the other hand, where one has concluded that the law has changed in a significant respect so that the court's discretion is significantly less fettered than it was, there are obvious dangers in relying on authorities which proceeded on the basis that the court's discretion was more fettered than it now is. I think it would be wrong to throw over all the earlier cases without paying them any regard. However, they have to be treated with caution, in light of the change in the law, and in many cases they are unlikely to be of great, let alone decisive, assistance.

Refuse a Sale

The court in deciding whether an order for sale should be granted will take into account the factors listed under s15 TOLATA 1996. As mentioned previously, case law under s30 LPA 1925 provides useful guidance on the approach of the court in considering an application for an order for sale.

In *Re Buchanan-Wollaston's Conveyance* [1939] 1 Ch 738 there was a piece of open ground at Lowestoft in Suffolk separating four houses from the sea. This land was for sale, and the owners of the four houses clubbed together to buy it as tenants in common. They were anxious to preserve their view of the sea. One of the four subsequently sold his house and moved away. He then applied to the court for an order that the open ground should be sold and the proceeds divided. He argued that as the land was held on trust for sale it followed that if any of the four asked for a sale, a sale must take place. This argument was firmly rejected by the Court of Appeal.

Sir Wilfrid Green MR said:

…The statutory trust for sale is one which must be exercised and was intended by the Legislature to be exercised subject to the power of the Court to enforce it. That appears in s. 30. But the Legislature must be taken to have known the principles upon which the court of equity proceeds when asked by one of a body of trustees, or other persons who are not in agreement, to lend its assistance for the purpose of carrying out a trust; the Legislature must be taken to have known the principles upon which those powers are exercised, and the power of the Court to enforce the trust for sale must be exercised in regard to the statutory trust for sale according to well-known and ordinary principles. I am not going to enter into a discussion of the question whether or not the provisions of the Act in creating this trust for sale have the effect of overriding or nullifying any provisions in the instrument which in some way clog or fetter the trust for sale. That is a question which came into the discussion in the case of *In re Flint* [1927] 1 Ch 570, before Astbury J. If and when that particular question comes to be considered again, it will require perhaps some full examination, but what I am saying now is not affected by the decision in that case, because it seems to me that *the court of equity, when asked to enforce the trust for sale, whether one created by a settlement or a will or one created by the statute, must look into all the circumstances of the case and consider whether or not, at the particular moment and in the particular circumstances when the application is made to it, it is right and proper that such an order shall be made. In considering a question of that kind, in circumstances such as these, the Court is bound to look at the contract into which the parties have entered and to ask itself the question whether or not the person applying for execution of the trust for sale is a person whose voice should be allowed to prevail.* In the present case, Farwell J approached the matter from that angle and gave a perfectly definite and unhesitating answer to it, with which I entirely agree. He said in effect 'Here is a person who has contracted with others for a particular purpose, and the effect of the contract is to impose upon the power of the trustees to sell this land, certain restrictions.' Without going into the question which I mentioned a moment ago as to overriding or not overriding those things, he said: 'It is not right that the court of equity should in those circumstances, on the invitation of a person who has not acted in accordance with the contract, and is opposed by other persons interested, exercise the power of the Court and make an order for sale.' That, of course, does not mean that in other circumstances, at some future time, the Court will not lend its aid. Circumstances may change. If all the parties died and all their houses were sold, I apprehend, for example, that the Court, if asked to enforce a statutory trust for sale, would not be disposed to listen to arguments against such a sale adduced by people who had no real interest in keeping this land unsold. Questions of that kind can be decided if and when they arise . . . [Emphasis added]

In brief, where land was bought for a specific purpose and that purpose could still be fulfilled, the courts should normally refuse to order a sale. This decision was sensational back in 1939. Nowadays it appears as plain common sense. The Court of Appeal recognized (as most later courts have recognized) that the imposition of a trust for sale on co-owners was pure 'legal machinery' and it should not affect co-owners' substantive rights. The Court of Appeal emphasized that the court will take into account the circumstances of the case when exercising its discretion.

There can of course be absolutely no doubt that if a case similar to *Re Buchanan-Wollaston* arose under s14 TOLATA 1996, the courts would refuse a sale (see especially s15(1)(b) TOLATA 1996).

The facts of *Re Evers' Trust* [1980] 1 WLR 1327, are very different, but involve the same principle as in *Re Buchanan-Wollaston*. A cohabiting couple bought a house as joint tenants, in order to house themselves and the three children for whom they had responsibility. The relationship broke down, and the father left. The other four members of the family continued to live in the house. The father applied to court under s30 LPA 1925 for an order of sale. The application for sale was refused.

Ormrod LJ considered the application of s30 LPA 1925 (now ss14 and 15 TOLATA 1996) to the facts and said:

This approach to the exercise of the discretion given by section 30 has considerable advantages in these 'family' cases. It enables the court to deal with substance, that is reality, rather than form, that is, convenience of conveyancing . . .

The irresistible inference from [the facts of this case] . . . the judge found, they purchased this property as a family home for themselves and the three children. It is difficult to imagine that the mother, then wholly responsible for two children, and partly for the third, would have invested nearly all her capital in the purchase of this property if it was not to be available to her as a home for the children for the indefinite future. It is inconceivable that the father, when he agreed to this joint adventure, could have thought otherwise, or contemplated the possibility of an early sale without the consent of the mother. The underlying purpose of the trust was, therefore, to provide a home for all five of them for the indefinite future. Unfortunately, the relationship between the father and the mother broke down very soon, and the parties separated at the beginning of August 1979 in circumstances of great bitterness. This is clearly shown by two dates. On July 20, 1979, the mother issued her originating summons in the wardship proceedings; on August 2, 1979, the father issued his application under section 30 for an order for sale of the property . . .

It was further argued that the father ought to be allowed to 'take his money out' or 'to realise his investment.' In point of fact, his investment amounted to less than one-fifth of the purchase price of the property, and was smaller than the mother's investment. The major part of the purchase price was provided by the mortgagees, and the mother is prepared to accept full responsibility for paying the interest on the mortgage, and keeping up the capital re-payments. The father has a secure home with his mother. There is no evidence that he has any need to realise his investment. It is an excellent one, combining complete security with considerable capital appreciation in money terms. His share is now said to be worth about £5,000, i.e., it has more than doubled in value in two years. On the other hand, a sale of the property now would put the mother into a very difficult position because she cannot raise the finance to rehouse herself or meet the cost of borrowing money at present rates. So there is no justification for ordering a sale at the present time.

For these reasons the judge was right not to order an immediate sale but the form of his actual order is not satisfactory. Under s. 30 the primary question is whether the court should come to the aid of the applicant at the particular moment, and in the 'particular circumstances when the application is made to it . . .': see *Re Buchanan-Wollaston's Conveyance* [1939] 1 Ch 738 at 747. In the present case, at the present moment and in the existing circumstances, it would be wrong to order a sale. But circumstances may change unpredictably. It may not be appropriate to order a sale when the child reaches 16 years, a purely arbitrary date, or it may become appropriate to do so much sooner, for example on the mother's remarriage or on it becoming financially possible for her to buy the father out. In such circumstances it will probably be wiser simply to dismiss the application while indicating the sort of circumstances which would, *prima facie*, justify a further application. The ensuing uncertainty is unfortunate, but, under this section, the court has no power to adjust property rights or to redraft the terms of the trust. Ideally, the parties should now negotiate a settlement on the basis that neither of them is in a position to dictate terms. We would, therefore, dismiss the father's appeal, but would vary the order to dismiss the application on the mother's undertaking to discharge the liability under the mortgage, to pay the outgoings and maintain the property, and to indemnify the father so long as she is occupying the property.

Ormrod LJ noted that the greater part of the purpose of acquiring the house (housing the family of five) could still be fulfilled. The Court of Appeal did, however, indicate that if or when circumstances changed (eg the children grow up and leave home) a renewed application by the man would probably receive a sympathetic hearing.

Refuse a Sale but Make an Order Regulating the Right to Occupy the Property

Where a relationship has broken down and one party leaves the property, an issue concerning who pays rent or continues to pay for the mortgage instalments may arise. This was considered in *Dennis v McDonald* [1982] 2 WLR 275, a controversial decision under s30 LPA 1925.

In *Dennis v McDonald* [1982] 2 WLR 275, a cohabiting couple bought a house as tenants in common in equal shares. They eventually had five children. The relationship broke up because of the father's violence. The mother left home, but only had care of the two youngest children. The three older children continued to live with their father in the house. He continued to make the mortgage repayments. The mother made an application under s30 LPA 1925 for an order for sale of the property.

Purchas J said:

The main argument has revolved around the right or otherwise of the plaintiff to receive an occupation rent as a co-tenant who is excluded from the property. Mr Coningsby has referred me to a judgment of Lord Denning MR in *Jones (AE) v Jones (FW)* [1977] 1 WLR 438, 441:

'First the claim for rent. It is quite plain that these two people were in equity tenants in common having a three-quarter and one-quarter share respectively. One was in occupation of the house. The other not. Now the common law said clearly that one tenant

> in common is not entitled to rent from another tenant in common, even though that other occupies the whole…As between tenants in common, they are both equally entitled to occupation and one cannot claim rent from the other. Of course, if there was an ouster, that would be another matter: or if there was a letting to a stranger for rent that would be different, but there can be no claim for rent by one tenant in common against the other whether at law or in equity.'

In *Jones (AE)* v *Jones (FW)* the plaintiff failed not only on the ground that no occupation rent could be claimed by one tenant in common from another but also upon, the ground of equitable estoppel . . .

In the instant case the plaintiff is clearly not a free agent. She was caused to leave the family home as a result of the violence or threatened violence of the defendant. In any event, whatever might have been the cause of the breakdown of the association, it would be quite unreasonable to expect the plaintiff to exercise her rights as a tenant in common to occupy the property as she had done before the breakdown of her association with the defendant. In my judgment she falls into exactly the kind of category of person excluded from the property in the way envisaged by Lord Cottenham LC in *M'Mahon* v *Burchell* 2 Ph 127. Therefore, the basic principle that a tenant in common is not liable to pay an occupation rent by virtue merely of his being in sole occupation of the property does not apply in the case where an association similar to a matrimonial association has broken down and one party is, for practical purposes, excluded from the family home.

Arnold P said:

> …[it is said] there is that one should look, not at the detriment to the plaintiff, but at the advantage to the defendant and that he should be regarded as illicitly enjoying, and therefore accountable for, one-half of what he would have to pay for the property if he entered the property market as a willing tenant and found a willing landlord ready to let it to him.
>
> I am bound to say in the circumstances of this case that that is somewhat unrealistic. He occupies this property not because he has been able to negotiate in the market and obtain it but because he is a tenant in common. He occupies it in respect of, and by right of, his beneficial interest. He is not, therefore, subject to the vagaries of the market and starts off with a right of occupation. Something would have to be allowed in some way for that. Moreover, it is difficult to see what justification there is for charging a person in his position with such extra payment as a tenant would have to make by reason of the scarcity of relevant accommodation in the market. If one is setting out to achieve a fair solution in a situation in which plainly the defendant has to pay something, I can think of no better way of regulating that than by doing one's best to assess a fair rent for the property, with all its advantages and defects . . .
>
> [Note: compare s13(6)(a) TOLATA 1996.]

The order for sale was refused. One of the primary purposes of the trust as originally envisaged was to provide a home for the family, and this purpose was still subsisting. However, the father would have to pay an 'occupation rent' to the mother throughout the duration of his residence in the property. This rent was fixed at half a 'fair rent' for the premises.

thinking point 9.6

Study ss 13 to 15 TOLATA 1996 as set out in the previous section of this chapter, and consider how Dennis v McDonald *would be decided under the 1996 Act.*

The case would obviously be decided in a similar way to before. The court would refuse an order of sale, but make an order under s14 that the man make payments to the woman to compensate her for the fact that she is no longer occupying the home. (Note also s15(1)(c) TOLATA 1996.)

> *It is suggested that a similar solution (ie refuse a sale but order payments to compensate the co-owner(s) excluded from possession) should be adopted in every case where:*
>
> - *it is socially undesirable to order the property to be sold;*
>   *and*
> - *it is unfair that the co-owner(s) not in occupation should be excluded from all benefit from the property.*

Such a solution could be used, for example, where the co-owned property houses a flourishing business which might have to close if a sale were ordered. (An alternative compromise solution is that set out later in this section at 'Order a Sale but Suspend the Order for a Short Period', where we consider a suspended order for sale.)

In *Stack v Dowden* [2007] 2 AC 432 the House of Lords was mainly concerned with the equitable ownership of a home in the joint names of two cohabitees. It did, however, also briefly consider whether compensatory payment should be ordered to be paid to Mr Stack for the period of about two years during which he had been excluded from occupation of the home.

Baroness Hale said:

> There remains the question of the payment for Mr Stack's alternative accommodation. This matter is governed by the Trusts of Land and Appointment of Trustees Act 1996. Section 12(1) gives a beneficiary who is beneficially entitled to an interest in land the right to occupy the land if the purpose of the trust is to make the land available for his occupation. Thus both these parties have a right of occupation. Section 13(1) gives the trustees the power to exclude or restrict that entitlement, but under section 13(2) this power must be exercised reasonably. The trustees also have power under section 13(3) to impose conditions upon the occupier. These include, under section 13(5), paying any outgoings or expenses in respect of the land and under section 13(6) paying compensation to a person whose right to occupy has been excluded or restricted. Under section 14(2)(a), both trustees and beneficiaries can apply to the court for an order relating to the exercise of these functions. Under section 15(1), the matters to which the court must have regard in making its order include (a) the intentions of the person or persons who created the trust, (b) the purposes for which the property subject to the trust is held, (c) the welfare of any minor who occupies or might reasonably be expected to occupy the property as his home, and (d) the interests of any secured creditor of any beneficiary. Under section 15(2), in a case such as this, the court must also have regard to the circumstances and wishes of each of the beneficiaries who would otherwise be entitled to occupy the property.
>
> These statutory powers replaced the old doctrines of equitable accounting under which a beneficiary who remained in occupation might be required to pay an occupation rent to a beneficiary who was excluded from the property. The criteria laid down in the statute should be applied, rather than in the cases decided under the old law, although the results may often be the same. In this case, the judge applied neither. The property had been bought as a home for the parties and their children. By October 2004, three of the children were still minors. Both parties had the responsibility of providing them with a home. Ms Dowden remained responsible for the upkeep and outgoings on the home until it was sold. Mr Stack had to provide himself with alternative accommodation but had nothing to pay in respect of the upkeep of the family's home until he was able to realise his share in it upon sale. While, therefore, a case could be made for compensating him for his exclusion, it has to be borne in mind that he had agreed to go in the course of proceedings under the Family Law Act 1996. The reason given by the judge took no account, as he was required to do, of the statutory criteria. The fact that the house was to be sold as soon as possible, so that Mr Stack would not be kept out his money for long, was if anything a factor telling against the exercise of this discretion. I would therefore agree with the Court of Appeal on this point.

As that period of exclusion had been relatively short, and Ms Dowden had had to pay substantial outgoings on the home, the majority of their Lordships declined to order compensation.

Lord Neuberger dissented on this point. He would have awarded Mr Stack £900 per month compensation. Lord Neuberger said:

> The 1996 Act appears to me to apply here in this way. The trustees, Ms Dowden and Mr Stack, agreed pursuant to section 13(1) of the 1996 Act (through the consent order of 11 April 2003 and not seeking to disturb the status quo after it expired) that Mr Stack would be excluded from the house. Accordingly, they could have agreed pursuant to section 13(3) and (6)(a) that Ms Dowden would pay 'compensation' to Mr Stack for his exclusion. They initially agreed that in the order of 11 April 2003, but, once it expired, they could not agree whether to exercise that power. Accordingly, the decision whether to require compensation was a matter for the court under section 14.
>
> In my view the proper exercise of the court's power in the present case would have been to order compensation. First, both parties had the right in principle to occupy it, Ms Dowden was living there on her own as she wanted, she had excluded Mr Stack against his will, and he was incurring the cost of alternative accommodation: accordingly, such a payment seems appropriate in the absence of any good reason to the contrary. Secondly, the parties plainly thought it was right, when agreeing the order of 11 April 2003, that, as a quid pro quo for his exclusion from the house, Mr Stack should be paid (or credited) at the rate of £900 per month. The circumstances of the parties do not appear to have changed by (or after) 10 January 2004, when they effectively accepted that Mr Stack would remain excluded from the house.
>
> Thirdly, when exercising its power under section 14, the court is required to take into account four specific matters set out in section 15(1). In my view, those factors either favour ordering a payment in favour of Mr Stack, or they are neutral or irrelevant. Thus, paragraphs (a) and (b), the purpose for which the house was bought and the purpose for which it was held, favour the conclusion, as the house was bought as a home for Mr Stack (as well as Ms Dowden and the children), and, at any rate as far as he was concerned, that remained the position. Paragraph (c), the welfare of minors residing in the house, is neutral as there is no suggestion of prejudice to the four children whether or not he was paid. Paragraph (d), the interests of any secured creditor, is irrelevant for present purposes.
>
> It is true Ms Dowden had to pay all the outgoings in respect of the house, but Mr Stack had to pay all the outgoings, as well as the rent, in respect of his alternative accommodation.
>
> Further, if the compensation was calculated (as it often is) on the basis of the rental value of the trust property concerned, the outgoings would be taken into account when assessing its rental value.
>
> I accept that the judge's reason for ordering payment was weak, no doubt at least in part because of the brevity of the argument and because he was not referred to the 1996 Act. (However, it is only fair to the judge to say that, as the actual occupier of the house, Ms Dowden did have some control over the progress of its marketing and sale.) I also accept that the Court of Appeal was consequently entitled to reconsider the matter afresh. Nonetheless, I consider that the Court of Appeal went wrong in reversing the judge's decision on the point. The fact that the children needed a home is not in point. First, it does not meet the main ground for making a payment order, namely Mr Stack's exclusion from the house and having to find and pay for alternative accommodation. Secondly, Mr Stack was paying towards the children's maintenance, and, through his share of the beneficial ownership of the house, helping to house them. Thirdly, there was no evidence to suggest that ordering a payment to Mr Stack would have in any way harmed the children's interests. That Ms Dowden had agreed to pay £900 per month under the order of 11 April 2003 suggests that it would not have had that effect.
>
> The fact that the house might have been expected to be sold fairly soon after the hearing is a point which, in my view, is either irrelevant or cuts both ways. It did not alter the position: it merely rendered it more likely to come to an end sooner rather than later. Nor is it as if any

wrongful act by Mr Stack caused his exclusion: it was simply due to the relationship breaking down. The fact that, after the order of 11 April 2003 expired, Mr Stack accepted his exclusion should not count against him. To hold that a reasonable acceptance of exclusion would make it more difficult to claim compensation would put a premium on unreasonableness and encourage litigation.

I also disagree with the Court of Appeal on quantum. I can see no reason to depart from the figure which the parties originally agreed, and was not challenged before the judge, namely £900 per month. It is a figure which had a rational basis (namely the cost of Mr Stack's alternative accommodation). There is, in my view, a strong argument for saying that, on the basis of an analogy with trespass damages, that the court should be able to award compensation based either on the notional rental value of the house or the cost of the alternative accommodation.

In the last paragraph of the extract from Lord Neuberger's speech, his Lordship suggests awarding compensation for exclusion based either on what rent the property would fetch ('notional rental value') or on the cost of alternative accommodation, and this approach is, it is submitted, correct.

Order a Sale

Applying the old s30 LPA 1925, this solution is the one normally adopted where the purposes for which the property was acquired have clearly failed. For example, the property was acquired for use in a business, and that business has ceased. *Jones v Challenger* [1961] 1 QB 176 remains an instructive case. In this case a husband and wife bought their matrimonial home as joint tenants. The marriage broke down and the wife went to live with another man. The husband was left alone in the house. The wife applied for an order of sale under s30 LPA 1925.

Devlin LJ said:

In the case we have to consider, the house was acquired as the matrimonial home. That was the purpose of the joint tenancy and, for so long as that purpose was still alive, I think that the right test to be applied would be that in *In re Buchanan-Wollaston's Conveyance* [1939] 1 Ch 738. But with the end of the marriage, that purpose was dissolved and the primacy of the duty to sell was restored. No doubt there is still a discretion. If the husband wanted time to obtain alternative accommodation, the sale could be postponed for that purpose, but he has not asked for that. If he was prepared to buy out the wife's interest, it might be proper to allow it, but he has not accepted a suggestion that terms of that sort should be made. In these circumstances, there is no way in which the discretion can properly be exercised except by an order to sell, because, since they cannot now both enjoy occupation of the property, that is the only way whereby the beneficiaries can derive equal benefit from their investment, which is the primary object of the trust . . .

The Court of Appeal held that despite protests from the husband that the wife's adultery was being 'rewarded', the purpose of acquisition of the house had failed and a sale should be ordered. On a rather different point, it is submitted that a court would normally also order a sale if there were a large number of co-owners and a clear majority by value wanted a sale (see s15(3) TOLATA 1996).

Order a Sale but Suspend the Order for a Short Period

The possibility of making an order in this form was expressly recognized by the Court of Appeal in *Jones v Challenger*. The court can (under the old s30 LPA 1925 or s14 TOLATA 1996) suspend the order of sale for a few months so as to give a co-owner wishing to retain the property a chance to buy the other(s) out. He or she will have, of course, to pay the appropriate fraction of a fair value of the property.

thinking point 9.7

If co-owners fall out, what is a sensible compromise solution which can be achieved without litigation?

The parties agree that the co-owner(s) wanting to keep the property buy out the co-owner(s) who 'want the cash'. Arrangements will, of course, have to be made for the property to be valued.

Application for Sale made by the Mortgagee of a Co-owner

In *Mortgage Corporation v Shaire* [2001] Ch 743, already referred to at 9.3.5. Mr and Mrs Shaire purchased their matrimonial home. Their relationship broke down and Mr Shaire moved out of the house. Mr Fox moved in with Mrs Shaire, and they agreed to buy Mr Shaire's interest in the house. Mrs Shaire now had a 75 per cent interest in the property and Mr Fox a 25 per cent interest.

Sometime after Mr Fox died it transpired that he had forged Mrs Shaire's signature on a number of documents, which included two mortgages of the freehold of the house. The second mortgagee sought by possession proceedings to recover sums owed, which, as a result of the forgery, were charged not on the freehold but only on Fox's 25 per cent equitable interest in the property.

Neuberger J weighed up the various factors under s15 TOLATA 1996 such as Mrs Shaire not wanting to leave the house.

> [F]or Mrs. Shaire to have to leave her home of nearly a quarter of a century would be a real and significant hardship but not an enormous one. She would have a substantial sum that she could put towards a smaller home ... For TMC to be locked into a quarter of the equity in a property would be a significant disadvantage unless they had a proper return and a proper protection so far as insurance and repair is concerned.

Neuberger J concluded that rather than order the property to be sold, instead the mortgage money owed (ie 25 per cent) should be converted into a loan which Mrs Shaire could pay off over time. This case is illustrative of the wider discretion the courts are given under s15 TOLATA 1996 as compared to cases under the old s30 LPA 1925 which favoured the creditor at the outset.

There has been since *Mortgage Corporation v Shaire* a retreat from what can be perceived as a sympathetic approach adopted by Neuberger J in that case. In *Bank of Ireland Home Mortgages Ltd v Bell* [2001] 2 FLR 809 Mr and Mrs Bell jointly owned a property, and their respective shares were assessed to be 90 and 10 per cent. Mr Bell organized a mortgage of the property and forged Mrs Bell's signature on the documentation. The judge at first instance refused to order the sale of the property, taking into account the various factors under s15: the property was purchased as a family home, Mrs Bell and son (who was nearly 18) continued to occupy the property and she was in poor health. On appeal Peter Gibson LJ observed:

> ... a powerful consideration is and ought to be whether the creditor is receiving proper recompense for being kept out of his money, repayment of which is overdue (see *Mortgage Corporation v Shaire*, a decision of Neuberger J on 25th February 2000). In the present case it

> is plain that by refusing sale the judge has condemned the bank to go on waiting for its money with no prospect of recovery from Mr and Mrs Bell and with the debt increasing all the time, that debt already exceeding what could be realised on a sale. That seems to me to be very unfair to the bank.

In contrast to *Mortgage Corporation v Shaire*, the court took a pragmatic approach. Mrs Bell only had a small 10 per cent interest in the property, and with the debt increasing it would have been unrealistic for her to have a similar resolution to Mrs Shaire. In contrast, Mrs Shaire owned 75 per cent of the property and the debt only related to Mr Fox's 25 per cent share. The amount owed was not so big and it could be paid off.

Following the same lines as *Bell*, the court in *First National Bank Plc v Achampong* [2003] EWCA 487 had to balance the various factors in considering whether to order the sale of the property, Blackburne J considered the interests of the creditors as well as the potential impact upon the family. Mr and Mrs Achampong were joint owners of their home. A joint mortgage was obtained but had to be set aside because Mrs Achampong successfully claimed that it was procured by undue influence. Mr Achampong returned to Ghana and Mrs Achampong remained in occupation of the family home with her adult children, one of whom had a mental disability, and three grandchildren.

> …I regard it as plain that an order for sale should be made. Prominent among the considerations which lead to that conclusion is that, unless an order for sale is made, the bank will be kept waiting indefinitely for any payment out of what is, for all practical purposes, its own share of the property. While it is relevant to consider the interests of the infant grandchildren in occupation of the property, it is difficult to attach much if any weight to their position in the absence of any evidence as to how their welfare may be adversely affected if an order for sale is now made. It is for the person who resists an order for sale in reliance on section 15(1)(c) to adduce the relevant evidence. Insofar as the Achampongs' intention in creating the trust of the property was to provide themselves with a matrimonial home, and insofar as that was the purpose for which the property was held on trust, that consideration is now spent. Given the many years' absence of contact between Mr and Mrs Achampong, the fact that there has not yet been a divorce cannot disguise the reality that theirs is a marriage which has effectively come to an end. The possibility, therefore, that the property may yet serve again as the matrimonial home can be ignored. Insofar as the purpose of the trust—and the intention of the Achampongs in creating it—was to provide a family home and insofar as that is a purpose which goes wider than simply the provision of a matrimonial home, I am unpersuaded that it is a consideration to which much if any weight should be attached. The children of the marriage have long since reached adulthood. One of them is no longer in occupation. It is true that the elder daughter, Rosemary, is a person under mental disability and remains in occupation but to what extent that fact is material to her continued occupation of the property and therefore to the exercise of any discretion under section 14 is not apparent.

Though the purpose of the trust was considered together with the welfare of the grandchildren and Rosemary, yet here the interests of the creditors outweighed these factors.

The court took a slightly more sympathetic approach in *Edwards v Lloyds TSB* [2004] EWHC 1745. Mr and Mrs Edwards purchased their matrimonial home as joint owners. They separated and Mr Edwards moved out of the family home, Mrs Edwards continued to live at the property with their two children aged 13 and 15. It later transpired that Mr Edwards soon after their separation had obtained a mortgage loan, claiming he was the sole legal owner of the property, and forged Mrs Edwards signature as grantor of the mortgage. The bank sought an application for sale in relation to Mr Edwards 50 per cent share in the property. The court in this case refused an immediate order for sale. Having considered the earlier case law, namely *Mortgage Corporation v Shaire, Bank of Ireland*

Home Mortgages Ltd v Bell and *First National Bank plc v Achampong* and the factors in s15 TOLATA 1996, Park J concluded:

> I must weigh up the various factors which are relevant and do the best I can to reach a balanced conclusion. I mention now two particular points on the facts of this case which were (I believe) not present in any of the three cases to which I was referred. First, if the house was sold now it is hard to see how Mrs Edwards could find the money to buy another smaller one. In the other cases it appears to have been different. For example in *The Mortgage Corporation v Shaire* (supra) Neuberger J said that if the house was sold Mrs Shaire would still have a substantial sum which she could put towards a smaller home. In the present case, in contrast, the house is a two-bedroom house in which Mrs Edwards already has to share a bedroom with her daughter. The house is obviously at the lower end of the range of prices for houses in the area where she lives. If there was a sale and the husband's debt to the bank was taken out of half of the net proceeds before the balance was available to Mrs Edwards, I very much doubt that she would be able to find another house which she could afford to buy and which would be adequate to accommodate her and her children.
>
> 32. Second, whereas in the other three cases it appears that the debt owed to the bank already exceeded the value of the interest over which the bank had an equitable charge, in the present case that is not so. On the figures which I gave in paragraph 12 above the value of the bank's security (a 50% interest in the house) would be (if the entirety were sold) about £70,000. The husband's debt to the bank (£15,000 plus interest plus costs) is unlikely at present to be more than £40,000. It is true that interest is not currently being paid to the bank on the debt owed to it, but interest continues to accrue on the debt, and now and for some time to come the security will be sufficient to cover the increasing amount of the debt.
>
> 33. In the circumstances I do not want to order an immediate sale, because I believe that that would be unacceptably severe in its consequences upon Mrs Edwards and her children. But equally I believe that I should make some order which, admittedly later rather than sooner, should enable the bank to recover its debt with accrued interest upon it.

The postponement of the order for sale, granted for five years, was arguably influenced by the fact that the debt owed was not accruing in such a manner that it was greater than the security provided by the 50 per cent interest in the house, and also the court was amenable to acknowledging that the purpose of the trust was still ongoing.

Section 15 TOLATA 1996 gives the court discretion on the application of the various factors. From the case law it is apparent that the interests of secured creditors tend to prevail particularly where the debt is greater than the value of the debtor's share in the property.

The issue of whether a creditor's charging order forcing a sale under s14 TOLATA 1996 was compatible with Article 8 of the European Convention on Human Rights (this includes respect for private and family life and home and the enjoyment of possessions) was considered in *National Westminster Bank v Rushmer* [2010] EWHC 554, and the court concluded that it was compatible. Furthermore, Arnold J commented on the court's discretion under s15 in discharging its duties:

> ... section 15 has to be exercised compatibly with the Convention rights of those affected by an order for enforcement. In my judgment, it will ordinarily be sufficient for this purpose for the court to give due consideration to the factors specified in section 15 of TOLATA. That will ordinarily enable the court to balance the creditor's rights, which include its rights under Article 1 of the First Protocol, with the Article 8 rights of those affected by an order for sale. I would not rule out the possibility that there may be circumstances in which it is necessary for the court explicitly to consider whether an order for sale is a proportionate interference with the Article 8 rights of those affected, but I do not consider that this will always be necessary.

The court was satisfied that for the purposes of the European Convention rights, the discretion given to the court under s15 to take into account a range of factors when balancing the interests of the rights of a creditor with that of a person whose rights are affected was, 'ordinarily', sufficient.

Partition

Partition, that is, geographically splitting up co-owned property, is governed by s7 TOLATA 1996. Only in very rare cases is partition going to be a practical remedy. (Try partitioning an ordinary semi-detached house!) But in *Rodway v Landy* [2001] Ch 703, the Court of Appeal did (in effect) order the partition (rather than sale) of the doctors' surgery. It was capable of being split into two separate surgeries, each with its own consulting rooms, waiting areas, and toilets.

Gibson LJ said:

> [Counsel for Dr Rodway] also said that the judge failed to have regard to the purposes for which the property was held and the circumstances and wishes of Dr Rodway. I do not agree. The judge was well aware of the purpose that both doctors should occupy the property as medical practitioners. He was well aware that if either doctor had to leave the property there would be a loss of patients from his or her list and distress to the patients and that Dr Rodway would have preferred to be the purchaser of the property to try to fulfil her original vision. But he was entitled to have regard to the ages of the doctors [Dr Rodway is 66, Dr Landy 50], and to the fact that Dr Rodway will have to retire from National Health Service practice at 70, and that she gave evidence that she had no wish to retain ownership of a share of the property after she retired from that practice. In reaching the conclusion that there should be no sale but that on a scheme under section 13 each doctor should be excluded from the other's separate part of the property, the judge in my judgment can only be found to have erred in the one respect relating to GPFC [General Practice Finance Corporation, who were the mortgagees of the premises] being left in an invidious position. That, in my judgment is not so significant an error as to undermine the exercise of his discretion.

The purpose of the trust could be better fulfilled by ordering a division, not a sale, of the premises.

REVIEW QUESTION Can you think of any situation where physical partition of the land might be a practical solution for co-owners who have fallen out?

(Re-read the section on partition.)

 ## 9.4 Bankruptcy of a Co-Owner

Bankruptcy arises where a person can no longer pay their debts. The debts may arise from, for example, credit cards, personal or business loans or a mortgage.

It is possible for an individual to seek a court order to declare themselves bankrupt. In other situations creditors may apply to the court to seek a bankruptcy order against a debtor in order to recover at least part of the money owed. The most valuable asset held by a bankrupt debtor is usually the family home co-owned with a spouse or partner.

On a debtor being declared bankrupt, a trustee in bankruptcy is appointed to 'get in, realise and distribute the bankrupt's estate'. The trustee in bankruptcy will want to utilize the bankrupt's assets ('estate') to pay creditors at least a percentage of the debts owed. Where the bankrupt debtor is co-owner of a property, the trustee in bankruptcy will seek an order for sale from the court under s14 TOLATA.

In 9.3.4 it was noted that the s15 factors do not apply in cases involving bankruptcy. Instead s335A Insolvency Act 1986 provides various factors that the court may take into consideration, 'as it thinks just and reasonable' in granting an order for sale of land.

> 335A.—Rights under trusts of land
>
> (1) Any application by a trustee of a bankrupt's estate under section 14 of the Trusts of Land and Appointment of Trustees Act 1996 (powers of court in relation to trusts of land) for an order under that section for the sale of land shall be made to the court having jurisdiction in relation to the bankruptcy.
>
> (2) On such an application the court shall make such order as it thinks just and reasonable having regard to—
>
>   (a) the interests of the bankrupt's creditors,
>
>   (b) where the application is made in respect of land which includes a dwelling house which is or has been the home of the bankrupt or the [bankrupt's spouse or civil partner or former spouse or former civil partner]—
>
>   (i) the conduct of the [spouse, civil partner, former spouse or former civil partner], so far as contributing to the bankruptcy,
>
>   (ii) the needs and financial resources of the [spouse, civil partner, former spouse or former civil partner], and
>
>   (iii) the needs of any children; and
>
>   (c) all the circumstances of the case other than the needs of the bankrupt.
>
> (3) Where such an application is made after the end of the period of one year beginning with the first vesting under Chapter IV of this Part of the bankrupt's estate in a trustee, the court shall assume, unless the circumstances of the case are exceptional, that the interests of the bankrupt's creditors outweigh all other considerations.
>
> (4) The powers conferred on the court by this section are exercisable on an application whether it is made before or after the commencement of this section.

Although some of the factors listed in s335A are similar to those found in s15 TOLATA 1996, the court's discretion in taking into account the various factors in s335A(2) is significantly restricted. Section 335A(3) provides that where an application for sale is made by the trustee in bankruptcy more than one year after bankruptcy (ie from the time the bankrupt's estate was vested in a trustee), the interests of the creditors will outweigh all other considerations unless there are exceptional circumstances which will mean the order for sale will not be granted. Within the one year time frame the bankrupt has the opportunity to settle their financial affairs and if necessary to arrange alternative accommodation.

9.4.1 Exceptional Circumstances Justifying Refusal of an Order of Sale

Exceptional circumstances was liberally interpreted in *Re Holliday (A Bankrupt)* [1981] Ch 405. In this case the sale of the property was postponed for five years. The court took a sympathetic approach towards Mrs Holliday, who was not bankrupt and had to look after her three children, and there was no pressing need to settle the debt owed to the creditors. The court took into account that it would be difficult for Mrs Holliday to find comparable accommodation in the neighbourhood they were currently living in and, if the family had to move away, this could also impact on the children's education.

The court in *Re Citro (A Bankrupt)* [1991] Ch 142 was critical of *Re Holliday (A Bankrupt)* Nourse LJ explained:

> What then are exceptional circumstances? As the cases show, it is not uncommon for a wife with young children to be faced with eviction in circumstances where the realisation of her beneficial interest will not produce enough to buy a comparable home in the same neighbourhood, or indeed elsewhere; and, if she has to move elsewhere, there may be problems over schooling and so forth. Such circumstances, while engendering a natural sympathy in all who hear of them, cannot be described as exceptional. They are the melancholy consequences of debt and improvidence with which every civilised society has been familiar.

Nourse LJ although noting that the circumstances were 'melancholy' they were certainly not within what was perceived as 'exceptional circumstances'. From the extract above it can be noted that the fact that losing the family home and uprooting children from school does not come within the scope of exceptional circumstances. This then begs the question of what does come within its scope? The courts have tended to exercise their discretion where there is a grave illness, for example in *Claughton v Charalambous* [1999] 1 FLR 740 where an indefinite postponement of a sale was granted because the bankrupt's wife had a chronic illness and the home had to be adapted due to her disability. A 12-month postponement of a sale was granted in a case involving a paranoid schizophrenic (*Re Raval* [1998] 2 FLR 718).

Does the European Convention on Human Rights (ECHR) impact on s335A(3)?

The courts have had to consider whether the restrictive interpretation of 'exceptional circumstances' is compatible with the right to 'private and family life' under Article 8 of the ECHR or the right to 'peaceful enjoyment of possessions' under Protocol 1 ECHR. In *Barca v Mears* [2004] EWHC 2170 it was argued that a son's special educational needs came within the scope of exceptional circumstances which could postpone the order of sale of the property. However, the court held that the boy's problems were not extreme, and furthermore unlike in *Re Citro*, there was no question of the boy having to move school.

Strauss QC made the following observations in relation to the applicability of the ECHR:

> 37. Mr. Gibbon submitted, in my view correctly, that where a court considers that a statutory provision, as interpreted before the Convention became part of English law, is incompatible with the Convention, it should seek to re-interpret the relevant provisions so as to achieve compatibility: only if this is not possible should a court consider granting a declaration of incompatibility . . .
>
> 38. Mr. Gibbon made the following further submissions, which I also accept:—
>
> (1) The right to 'respect' for private and family life and the home is not absolute. The state must have regard 'to the fair balance that has to be struck between the general interest of the community and the interests of the individual, the search for which balance is inherent in the whole Convention': *Cossey v. U.K. (1990) 13 EHRR 622* para. 37.
>
> (2) What is 'necessary in a democratic society' requires an assessment of 'whether the interference complained of corresponded to a pressing social need, whether it was proportionate to the legitimate aim pursued, [and] whether the reasons given by the national authorities to justify it are relevant and sufficient': *Sunday Times v. U.K.* (1979) 2 EHRR 245 at 277–8.

(3) This proportionality test is satisfied if:

- the legislative objective is sufficiently important to justify the limitation on the fundamental right;
- the measures designed to meet the legislative objective are rationally connected with it; and
- the means used to impair the right or freedom are no more than is necessary to accomplish the legitimate objective.

See *Germany v. Council of the European Union* [1995] ECR-I-3723 at 3755–6 and *de Freitas v. Permanent Secretary of Ministry of Agriculture, Fisheries, Lands and Housing [1998] 3 W.L.R. 675*, a decision relating to the Constitution of Antigua and Barbuda.

39.   Clearly, in many or perhaps most cases, the sale of a bankrupt's property in accordance with bankruptcy law will be justifiable on the basis that it is necessary to protect the rights of others, namely the creditors, and will not be a breach of the Convention. Nevertheless, it does seem to me to be questionable whether the narrow approach as to what may be 'exceptional circumstances' adopted in *re Citro*, is consistent with the Convention. It requires the court to adopt an almost universal rule, which prefers the property rights of the bankrupt's creditors to the property and/or personal rights of third parties, members of his family, who owe the creditors nothing . . .

40.   In particular, it may be incompatible with Convention rights to follow the approach taken by the majority in *re Citro*, in drawing a distinction between what is exceptional, in the sense of being unusual, and what Nourse L.J. refers to as the 'usual melancholy consequences' of a bankruptcy. This approach leads to the conclusion that, however disastrous the consequences may be to family life, if they are of the usual *kind* then they cannot be relied on under section 335A; they will qualify as 'exceptional' only if they are of an unusual kind, for example where a terminal illness is involved.

41.   It seems to me that a shift in emphasis in the interpretation of the statute may be necessary to achieve compatibility with the Convention. There is nothing in the wording of section 335A, or the corresponding wording of sections 336 and 337, to require an interpretation which excludes from the ambit of 'exceptional circumstances' cases in which the consequences of the bankruptcy are of the usual kind, but exceptionally severe. Nor is there anything in the wording to require a court to say that a case may not be exceptional, if it is one of the rare cases in which, on the facts, relatively slight loss which the creditors will suffer as a result of the postponement of the sale would be outweighed by disruption, even if of the usual kind, which will be caused in the lives of the bankrupt and his family. Indeed, on one view, this is what the Court of Appeal decided in *Re Holliday*.

42.   Thus it may be that, on a reconsideration of the sections in the light of the Convention, they are to be regarded as recognising that, in the general run of cases, the creditors' interests will outweigh all other interests, but leaving it open to a court to find that, on a proper consideration of the facts of a particular case, it is one of the exceptional cases in which this proposition is not true. So interpreted, and without the possibly undue bias in favour of the creditors' property interests embodied in the pre-1998 case law, these sections would be compatible with the Convention.

43.   ...As was pointed out by Hoffmann J. in *Re Citro* it is difficult to balance the creditors' interests in obtaining payment and the bankrupt's family's personal interests, because they are different in kind. Nevertheless, even on the view of the law which is most favourable to Mr. Barca, and assuming in his favour that either 335A or section 337 applies, such an exercise would have to be undertaken, and on the facts of this case in my view the creditors' interests must prevail . . .

Strauss QC questioned whether the interpretation of the 'exceptional circumstances', the statutory test under s335A, was compatible with the ECHR, and he suggested that it may be necessary to have a 'shift in emphasis' in the interpretation of s335A to ensure compatibility with the ECHR. Strauss QC was of the opinion that in ordinary cases involving bankruptcy the creditor's interests will outweigh all other interests, whereas in those cases which involve exceptional circumstances the court can consider all the relevant facts without the pre-existing bias found in the pre-1998 case law which puts the creditor's interests first.

This approach has not been followed by the courts in subsequent cases. In *Nicholls v Lan* [2007] 1 FLR 744 the court did not find s335A to be inconsistent with the ECHR. Morgan QC stated that:

> the Court is required to perform a balancing exercise and to decide what is 'just and reasonable' and amongst the circumstances which are to be taken into account are the interests of the creditors and the needs of someone like [bankrupt's wife]. For my part, I do not see that the statutory test, leading to a balancing exercise, is inconsistent with the qualified nature of the rights enshrined in Article 8 and in Article 1 of the First Protocol. Indeed, it might be contended that section 335A precisely captures what is required by Article 8 and Article 1 of the First Protocol.

The court in *Ford v Alexander* [2012] EWHC 266 was satisfied that s335A did not infringe Article 8 of the ECHR, and in the court's view the provision is proportionate as it strikes a balance 'between the rights of creditors and the respect for privacy and the home of the debtor' [para 49].

9.5 The Modern Position of Husband and Wife Co-Owners on a Marriage Break-Up

The next few paragraphs arguably represent something of a digression into family law. It should be stressed that what follows is all you need to know for the purposes of a land law course. There is no need to learn the detailed 'property adjustment' rules in ss 23–25 Matrimonial Causes Act 1973 (MCA 1973).

Where husband and wife are co-owners of any property (usually it will be the matrimonial home) and the marriage has broken down, one spouse could still invoke s14 TOLATA 1996. Alternatively, a spouse could still invoke a special procedure available only for inter-spousal property disputes laid down in s17 Married Women's Property Act 1882.

Neither under s14 TOLATA 1996 nor under s17 of the 1882 Act do the courts have any power to *vary* the property rights of the spouses.

thinking point 9.8

How is this last point, in the context of s14 TOLATA 1996, relevant to cohabitees who co-own their home?

While under s14 the court can regulate the cohabitees' rights to occupy the property (as was done in Dennis v McDonald*), it could not order one (ex-)cohabitee to transfer part or all of his/her interest to the other (ex-)cohabitee.*

By contrast, as explained earlier when we considered the register of pending actions at 4.7.6, the divorce court does have nowadays very wide powers (under ss23–25 MCA 1973) to make 'property adjustment orders'. The co-owned property of divorcing couples is nowadays invariably dealt with under ss23–25. If a divorcing spouse tried to invoke s14 TOLATA 1996 (or s17 of the 1882 Act) the court should refuse the application and order that the matter be dealt with by the divorce court under ss23–25 MCA 1973. *Williams J v Williams M* [1977] 1 All ER 28 is a good example where a divorcing spouse attempted (unsuccessfully) to invoke the old s30 LPA 1925. In this case a married couple purchased a house in joint names, the husband providing the majority of the purchase price. The marriage was later dissolved and the wife remained in the house with the four sons of the family. She paid the mortgage instalments thereafter. The youngest son having reached the age of 12, the husband applied under s30 LPA 1925 for an order of sale. The judge at first instance granted the order of sale as requested. The wife appealed.

Lord Denning MR said:

> It seems to me that in this case the judge was in error in applying the old approach. He did not give proper effect to the modern view, which is to have regard to the needs of the family as a whole before a sale is ordered. We have here the wife and the four sons still in the house. The youngest son is only 13 years of age and still at school. It would not be proper at this stage to order the sale of the house, unless it were shown that alternative accommodation could be provided at a cheaper rate, and some capital released. That has not been shown here.
>
> The truth is that the approach to these cases has been transformed since the Matrimonial Proceedings and Property Act 1970 and the Matrimonial Causes Act 1973 (MCA 1973) which have given the power to the court after a divorce to order the transfer of property. In exercising any discretion under s. 30 of the Law of Property Act 1925, those Acts must be taken into account. The discretion should be exercised on the principles stated by this court in *Jackson v Jackson* [1971] 1 WLR 1539, 1543.
>
> I would add this: An application about a matrimonial home should not be restricted to s. 30 of the Law of Property Act 1925. In view of the wide powers of transfer and adjustment which are available under the new matrimonial property legislation it seems to me that the applications should be made to the Family Division under the relevant provisions. If taken out in another division, they should be transferred to a judge of the Family Division. In this very case it seems to me that the right course (which the wife's advisers ought to have taken before) is that they should now, and at once, take out the appropriate application under s. 24 of the Matrimonial Causes Act 1973 for any necessary orders and so on to be made with regard to the house and the property.
>
> That application should be brought on together with an application under s. 30.
>
> I would therefore be in favour of allowing the appeal, setting aside the order for sale made by Foster J and remitting the matter for further consideration by a judge of the Family Division when an application has been taken out under the matrimonial property legislation. I would allow the appeal accordingly. . . .

It is the third paragraph of this extract which is all-important. The court dismissed the s30 LPA 1925 application (nowadays that would be s14 TOLATA 1996) and required the dispute to be dealt with under ss23–25 MCA 1973.

Under ss23–25 MCA 1973 the divorce court is particularly careful where young children are still living in the ex-matrimonial home. Usually, of course, a parent is there with them. In such cases the divorce court is unlikely to order an immediate sale of the home. Rather, the normal practice is to refuse an order for immediate sale of the home and to make some kind of order which will ensure that the children can continue to live in the home until they have grown up: see *Mesher v Mesher* [1980] 1 All ER 126 (a case actually decided in 1973). Orders designed to protect children in this way are sometimes referred to as '*Mesher* orders'.

It is instructive to study the facts behind the case of *Thompson v Thompson* [1985] 2 All ER 243. The order of the divorce court, made in 1981, directed that the ex-husband and the ex-wife, who remained the trustees for sale, should postpone sale of the home 'until the youngest child of the family . . . reaches the age of seventeen years or finishes further education, whichever is later, or further order'. The ex-wife continued to live in the home with the two children, the youngest of which was (in 1985) aged 11. The ex-wife wanted to move from the home; ironically the ex-husband would not agree to a sale. She sought and obtained an order of sale, which was granted under s24A MCA 1973.

Another instructive divorce case is *Allen v Allen* [1974] 1 WLR 1171. There the matrimonial home had been in the husband's name alone. The Court of Appeal (varying the order of the divorce court judge) ordered:

> that the former matrimonial home should be transferred to the husband and the wife, to be held on trust for sale, with a direction that the sale should not take place until the younger child had attained the age of 17 years, or had finished his full-time education, whichever date should be the earlier, without either the consent of both the parents or under an order of the court, and that during that limited period the property should be held in trust for the wife to the exclusion of the husband for the purpose of her providing a home there for the children of the family, and, in particular, the two boys, and that at the expiration of that limited period it should then be held on trust for the two spouses in equal shares. [Per Buckley LJ]

Thompson, Allen, Harvey v Harvey [1982] 1 All ER 693 and many other divorce cases are striking for a number of reasons:

- The court continues as trustees (or, as in *Allen*, appoints as trustees) two people who are estranged from each other.
- The court inserted into the trust for sale provisions (such as that in *Thompson* and *Allen*) designed to ensure that the land would not be sold!
- These modern divorce cases demonstrated the highly artificial nature of the trust for sale which the 1925 legislation forced upon all co-owners. It thus underlined the good sense now embodied in the TOLATA 1996.

It is also worth noting that solutions such as those adopted in *Allen* and *Harvey* are often reached by divorcing couples by negotiation, without the need for the divorce court to impose an order. However, one unfortunate side effect of the Child Support Act 1992 is that it discourages divorcing spouses from settling their differences on the basis that the spouse with care of the children gets possession of the former matrimonial home.

9.6 Rights of Co-Owners in Equity—Are They Interests in Land?

At 7.4.2 we considered the 'archaic' doctrine of conversion. Under this doctrine, the equitable interests of beneficiaries under a trust for sale are personal property not real property. This 'conversion' doctrine gave rise to complex case law on the issue of whether equitable rights of co-owners were or were not 'interests in land'. The conclusion to be drawn from these cases was that for most (but not all) purposes equitable interests of co-owners, despite the doctrine of conversion, were interests in land. We need not now bother with this complex case law.

thinking point 9.9

Under the TOLATA 1996, are the equitable interests of co-owners interests in land?

The answer is of course 'yes', as s3 TOLATA 1996 abolishes the doctrine of conversion.

9.7 Law of Property (Joint Tenants) Act 1964

(This Act applies only to unregistered titles and is thus of declining importance.)

Where two or more people are joint tenants at law and in equity, the joint tenancy of course comes to an end the moment there is only one joint tenant left, that is, on the death of the 'penultimate' joint tenant. It follows that the moment there is only one owner, the trust (for sale) also ends. The sole survivor can deal with the land as an absolute owner and does not have to appoint another trustee to effect a sale, lease, etc.

Prior to 1964 there was, however, a practical difficulty if a last surviving joint tenant wanted to sell the land without appointing a second trustee. A purchaser from a last surviving joint tenant might well ask, 'How do I know that the joint tenancy has not been severed?' (If there has been a severance there will be a tenancy in common and the trust (for sale) will still continue and a second trustee is needed for a sale.)

Just think for a moment. It is now easy to sever a joint tenancy. Indeed it can be done without the knowledge of fellow joint tenants. Consequently, it is impossible for the 'last survivor' to prove objectively that there has been no severance and that the trust (for sale) is at an end.

Prior to 1964, purchasers therefore insisted that the last survivor appointed a co-trustee before selling the property. This was a source of annoyance to solicitors and their clients, and the 1964 Act is designed to end the annoyance. Under the 1964 Act a purchaser from the last surviving joint tenant can assume that there has been no severance unless either:

- a memorandum of severance has been endorsed upon the conveyance to the joint tenants; or
- a bankruptcy petition or receiving order has been registered as a pending action.

Thus, unless one or other of these conditions is fulfilled, a conveyance by a last surviving joint tenant acting on his/her own will convey a good title to a purchaser.

It should be noted that a 'memorandum of severance' is not another way of severing a joint tenancy. Rather it is something which can be endorsed on the conveyance to 'tell the world' that a severance has already taken place.

9.8 Co-Ownership of Registered Land

The co-owners are registered as joint proprietors, but as the register does not indicate any trusts affecting registered titles, the register will not indicate whether the co-owners are joint tenants or tenants in common; if the latter it will not indicate the size of the shares. Thus (as mentioned at 8.6) a solicitor acting for co-owners should retain in the files a document expressly declaring the equitable interests of the co-owners.

There is, however, one further point which should be noted. If the registered co-proprietors are tenants in common in equity or if they are trustees for other beneficiaries, then a 'restriction' should be entered in the proprietorship register in the following terms:

> No disposition by a sole proprietor of the land (not being a trust corporation) under which capital money arises is to be registered except under an order of the registrar or of the court.

If co-proprietors are registered without such a 'restriction' being entered, it is safe for a purchaser to deal with a last survivor, even if the purchaser suspects that there is now a tenancy in common.

A joint tenant who severs an equitable joint tenancy in a piece of registered land should also enter a restriction on the register.

Concluding Remarks

About 90 years have elapsed since the compulsory imposition of a trust for sale on co-owners and we have seen both an enormous increase in the amount of co-ownership and the realization that the 1925 legislators in solving one problem (multiplicity of co-owners) created several others.

Until 1996, Parliament's contribution to the solution of the problems had been minimal—the rather technical Law of Property (Joint Tenants) Act 1964, which despite its grandiose title tackled but one minor problem which is anyway confined to unregistered land.

In contrast, the judiciary have (usually) worked very hard to sort things out. The senior judiciary have brought an enormous amount of common sense into this socially important area of law. As long ago as 1939 the Court of Appeal (in *Re Buchanan-Wollaston*) refused to be blinded by the existence of the trust for sale imposed on all co-owners. It saw that the compulsory trust for sale was merely legal machinery which should not affect the substantive rights of the parties. Subsequent generations of judges, with minor exceptions, have endorsed that approach.

In 1996, common sense, at long last, reached the legislature. In the field of co-ownership the TOLATA 1996 in effect both adopts and adapts the common sense which shines through the pre-existing case law. For example, in 1955, Lord Denning held that where property is acquired by co-owners for personal occupation, then the co-owners do indeed (notwithstanding the existence of a trust) have the right to occupy the land. This was a sensation in 1955. However, Lord Denning's colleagues went along with him on this point (eg in *Boland*) and now we see the same point in s12 of the 1996 Act.

Judges also made great efforts to sort out the cumbersome s30 LPA 1925. These efforts are now reflected in ss14 and 15 TOLATA 1996. The factors listed in s15 are largely (though not completely) derived from existing case law. Section 13 is also very welcome; especially as, when read with ss14 and 15, it clearly vindicates the bold decision in *Dennis v McDonald*.

Finally, judges tried to circumvent (or simply ignore) the ridiculous doctrine of conversion. Section 3 TOLATA 1996 abolished the doctrine.

Summary

Does a constructive trust share belonging to a claimant (C) bind someone (A) who acquires the relevant land?

To answer this question go through the following multi-stage process found in Diagram 9.3.

Diagram 9.3
Constructive trust share

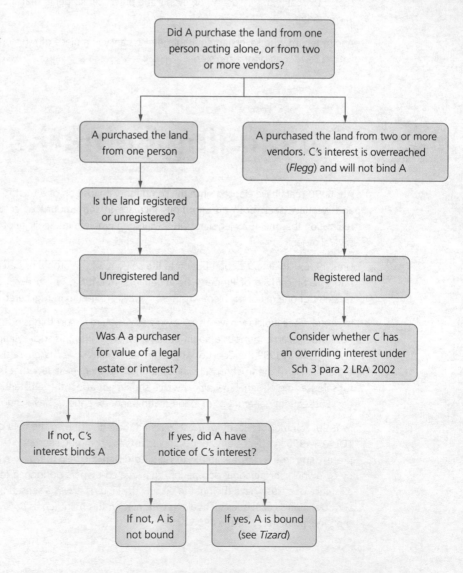

Five possible solutions where co-owners fall out

All five can be achieved either by negotiation or by court order (s14 TOLATA 1996):

- sell the property and divide the proceeds;
- those wanting to retain the land buy out the interest(s) of those wanting sale;
- as in *Buchanan-Wollaston* and *Evers* just let those who want to enjoy the land continue to enjoy the land;
- let those who want to enjoy the land continue to enjoy the land, but subject to conditions. Likely conditions are:
  - occupiers pay the outgoings (see s13(5)(a) TOLATA 1996);
  - occupiers pay 'rent' to those not in occupation (see s13(6)(a) TOLATA 1996);
- geographically divide ('partition') the land between the co-owners (only possible in a minority of cases).

Bankruptcy of a Co-owner

- Trustee in bankruptcy appointed to 'realise and distribute the bankrupt's estate':
  - application for order for sale under s14 TOLATA;
- Court considers various factors 'as it thinks just and reasonable' under s335A Insolvency Act 1986.

# Further Reading

Bright, S, 'Occupation rents and the Trusts of Land and Appointment of Trustees Act: from property to welfare' [2009] Conv 378
A detailed discussion of s13(6) TOLATA 1996, suggesting the courts should take a more flexible approach to this provision.

Dixon, M, Case comment on *HSBC Bank Plc v Dyche* [2010] 2 P & CR 4 [2010] Conv 1
Critical commentary on the reasoning of the court on overreaching.

Dixon, M, 'Trusts of Land, Bankruptcy and Human Rights' [2005] Conv 161
Comment on *Barca v Mears* 'exceptional circumstances' in relation to the ECHR.

Ferris, G and Battersby, G, 'The general principles of overreaching and the modern legislative reforms, 1996–2002' (2003) 119 LQR 94
This article considers overreaching within the framework of TOLATA 1996 and LRA 2002.

Gravells, N, '*HSBC Bank Plc v Dyche*: getting your priorities right' [2010] Conv 169
Reflective analysis of the case and critical commentary provided.

Harpum, C, 'Overreaching, trustees powers and the reform of the 1925 legislation' [1990] 49 CLJ 277
Article provides a modern view on overreaching.

Jackson, N, 'Overreaching in registered land law' (2006) 69 MLR 214
Critical review of the application of the overreaching mechanism in registered land.

Pascoe, S, 'Section 15 of the Trusts of Land and Appointment of Trustees Act 1996—a change in the law?' [2000] Conv 315

This article focuses on the application of s15(1)(d) and whether the secured creditor has primacy over other factors listed under s15.

Question

In 1988 four friends, Steven, Julia, Mark, and Tracey, purchased a cottage called 'The Retreat' for the purpose of a holiday home. The Retreat was unregistered title situated in an area which had not yet become an area of compulsory registration of title. The conveyance to them contained no express declaration of a trust for sale. The purchase money was provided equally and at the time of the purchase Tracey was only 17 years of age.

In January 2012, Julia became short of cash and therefore obtained a bank loan which was secured on her interest in The Retreat.

Some months later, Steven also found himself in financial difficulties. However, his solution to the problem was to create frequent arguments with the others in which he would demand that they 'buy him out'. These outbursts were ignored by the others and Steven eventually stopped using The Retreat.

In October 2012, Steven and Julia were killed in a car accident. By their wills Steven left all his property to his mother Violet, and Julia left all her property to her sister, Karen.

Mark is keen to sell The Retreat and has just found a purchaser who wants an early completion. Tracey vehemently opposes the proposed sale as since the deaths of Steven and Julia she has been living at The Retreat permanently. Violet is in agreement with Mark, but Karen is uncertain.

Advise Mark as to:

1 exactly who owns The Retreat and in what proportions; and

2 his prospects of forcing a sale.

Part 5

Acquisition of Interests in Land (II)

Licences and Proprietary Estoppel

## 10

Introduction

This chapter will consider both licences and proprietary estoppel. A licence affecting a piece of land may take a number of different forms. It is now settled that, unless a proprietary estoppel arises from a licence (as happened in *Inwards v Baker*), licences are not proprietary in character and cannot bind a third party who acquires the land over which the licence exists.

We have already discussed in Chapter 8 how an interest in land may be created by an implied trust, that is, a resulting or constructive trust. Proprietary estoppel also creates an informal interest in land. In Chapter 3 we highlighted the importance of having a deed when creating or transferring an interest in land, and where due to lack of formalities a written agreement would be recognized only in equity. Proprietary estoppel protects the person who has acted to their detriment on a promise (or oral agreement) that they will obtain an interest in land. Under these circumstances the courts have used equitable estoppel to provide a remedy for the person who has acted upon the promise by making some sort of sacrifice. It appears from a recent House of Lords decision that there could be a difference in how proprietary estoppel may be applied depending on whether the parties are in a domestic or commercial relationship.

This chapter will begin by considering the various licences that exist and then consider proprietary estoppel.

10.1 Licences

A licence is a personal permission to enter or occupy the property owned by the person giving the permission. The licence gives the person permission to do something legally, otherwise without which it would be illegal: this permission is personal. An often quoted passage from *Thomas v Sorrell* (1673) Vaughan 330 by Vaughan CJ states that 'a dispensation or license properly passeth no interest, nor alters or transfers property in anything, but only makes an action lawful, which without it had been unlawful'. This reinforces the fact that if the licensee obtains permission then he cannot be treated as a trespasser.

Furthermore, a licence does not equate to an estate or interest in land, it is simply a personal permission to do something and nothing more. Consequently, it cannot bind a third party nor can it be transferred. There was an attempt at one stage by the courts to elevate licences to have proprietary status, but since then there has been a return to the orthodox approach, and licences cannot normally bind successors in title. Equity, though, has intervened where the licensor's conduct is unconscionable, and has created the concept of a licence by estoppel, nowadays a form of proprietary estoppel. A licence by estoppel is capable of binding third parties.

There are four types of licences:

- bare licences;
- licences coupled with an interest;
- contractual licences;
- estoppel licences.

10.2 Bare Licences

A bare licence is the simplest form of licence and is often referred to as a gratuitous licence. This type of licence can be granted without payment. There are no formalities to comply with to create a licence. A bare licence can be created expressly, for example by an invitation to a party. An impliedly created licence can be created by words or conduct; for example, a postman delivering mail may have to cross the driveway to put the letters through the letterbox, likewise a milkman will have an implied licence to deliver milk to your doorstep.

The scope of the licence is limited to what it has been granted for. In *The Carlgarth* [1927] P 93, Scrutton LJ succinctly said that 'when you invite a person into your house to use the staircase, you do not invite him to slide down the banisters, you invite him to use the staircase in the ordinary way in which it is used'. Sliding down the banisters is beyond the scope of the permission given to use the stairs and so the person is now effectively treated as a trespasser!

A bare licence can be revoked on giving reasonable notice at any time and at the will of the licensor (*Wood v Leadbitter* (1845) 13 M & W 838). The licensee must be given reasonable time to leave the property. What amounts to reasonable notice and reasonable time depends on the circumstances of the case, that is, nature and purpose of the licence. Guests invited to a dinner party could be asked to leave immediately, however, whereas in a situation where the licensee has been asked to leave living accommodation, it may be more appropriate to allow the licensee time to pack up and find an alternative place to live.

thinking point 10.1

Friends invite you to come in and admire their garden. After half an hour, the friends decide that they want to go inside to play on the PlayStation. You are asked to leave, must you go?

The answer is 'yes', and in the circumstances you must go immediately.

10.3 Licences Coupled with an Interest

A licence may be coupled with an interest in land. The right to fish is a profit à prendre but closely associated with this proprietary right is the licence to enter the land and walk to the river. A profit on its own without the licence is of no use. In this situation both the licence and the proprietary interest are inseparable.

Formalities of creating a valid proprietary interest, such as a profit, must be complied with, for example granted by deed (though the profit could be created by prescription), and the licence is in addition to this grant. The interdependency of both the proprietary interest and licence means that the licence becomes irrevocable and assignable to a third party. It is capable of binding third parties.

REVIEW QUESTION What is a profit à prendre?

(Refer back to 1.3.4.)

10.4 Contractual Licences

A contractual licence is a licence which has been given for consideration; for example, parking a car in a commercial car park, a ticket to watch a film at the cinema, or an annual subscription to a health club. Similarly, a lodger (a licensee) has a contractual licence rather than a lease because of the absence of exclusive possession. In this situation there is a fine line between what is merely a personal right and what is a proprietary interest.

cross-reference
See 11.4.1 for the
distinction between
leases and licences.

Contractual licences are predominantly created expressly and are governed by principles of contract law. In certain circumstances the courts have shown a willingness to imply a licence. One area which can be viewed as being contentious is in the family context. Contractual licences provided an alternative approach to situations where a trust, such as a constructive trust, could not be implied.

In *Tanner v Tanner* [1975] 1 WLR 1346, Mr and Mrs Tanner were not married. She changed her name and became known as Mrs Tanner when she found out that she was pregnant. After she had given birth to twins, Mr and Mrs Tanner decided to buy a house. The house was purchased in Mr Tanner's name. The property was to provide a home for Mrs Tanner and her daughters. Mrs Tanner gave up a rent-protected tenancy and moved in with Mr Tanner. Mrs Tanner purchased a good deal of furniture and spent £150 on furnishings. The relationship deteriorated and Mr Tanner terminated her licence to live in the house. The Court of Appeal implied a contractual licence that Mrs Tanner could continue to live in the house with her children for as long as they were of school age. By the time of the hearing, Mrs Tanner had moved out of the house and the court felt that it would be appropriate to award her £2,000 in damages for breach of contract.

Lord Denning MR said:

> Nevertheless it seems to me plain on the evidence that the house was acquired in the contemplation and expectation that it would provide a home for the defendant and the twin daughters. The babies were only eight months old at the time. She gave up her flat in Steels Road (where she was protected by the Rent Acts) to move into this house. It was obviously provided for her as a house for herself and the twins for the foreseeable future.
>
> It is said that they were only licensees—bare licensees—under a licence revocable at will: and that the plaintiff was entitled in law to turn her and the twins out on a moment's notice. I cannot believe that this is the law. This man had a moral duty to provide for the babies of whom he was the father. I would go further. I think he had a legal duty towards them. Not only towards the babies. But also towards their mother. She was looking after them and bringing them up. In order to fulfil his duty towards the babies, he was under a duty to provide for the mother too. She had given up her flat where she was protected by the Rent Acts—at least in regard to rent and it may be in regard also to security of tenure. She had given it up at his instance so as to be able the better to bring up the children. It is impossible to suppose that in that situation she and the babies were bare licensees whom he could turn out at a moment's notice. The plaintiff recognised this when he offered to pay the defendant

£4,000 to get her out. What was then their legal position? She herself said in evidence: 'The house was supposed to be ours until the children left school.' It seems to me that enables an inference to be drawn, namely, that in all the circumstances it is to be implied that she had a licence—a contractual licence—to have accommodation in the house for herself and the children so long as they were of school age and the accommodation was reasonably required for her and the children. There was, it is true, no express contract to that effect, but the circumstances are such that the court should imply a contract by the plaintiff—or, if need be, impose the equivalent of a contract by him—whereby they were entitled to have the use of the house as their home until the girls had finished school. . . . It was a contractual licence of the kind which is specifically enforceable on her behalf: and which the plaintiff can be restrained from breaking; and he could not sell the house over her head so as to get her out in that way.

REVIEW QUESTION

- What are the essential elements of a contract?
- Apply these to the facts of *Tanner*.
- Do you think that there was a contract between Mr and Mrs Tanner?

In *Horrocks v Forray* [1976] 1 WLR 230, the deceased (Mr Sanford) was married but he formed a relationship with the defendant. The deceased maintained both the defendant and their daughter by providing living accommodation, clothing, holidays, and the day-to-day expenses for 13 years. A year before he was killed in an accident, he purchased a property for the defendant and their daughter. The claimants were the executors of the deceased's will. They claimed possession of the premises on the basis that the defendant's licence to occupy the property ended on the death of the deceased. Megaw LJ said:

I am quite unable to see, on the facts and circumstances of this case, that there was here any conceivable basis for an implication that any such binding promise had been made by Mr. Sanford as is suggested. The fact that he had it in mind to seek to provide some security for the defendant in the event of his death certainly does not go anything like far enough to bring into existence what is necessary to show a binding contract of this nature. There was here, in my judgment, simply nothing on the evidence that would have entitled the judge to come to the conclusion that there was any such contractual licence. I say that without going on to consider what I think might well be an extremely difficult further barrier in the way of the defendant. Supposing that she had established something which otherwise could be regarded as being a contract, where is the consideration for that contract to be found? In *Tanner* v. *Tanner* [1975] 1 WLR 1346 the consideration was perfectly clear: the lady had given up her rent-controlled flat as a part of the bargain that she would move into the other accommodation. There is no such consideration here. However, I do not wish to decide this case, as far as I am concerned, on any question relating to absence of consideration. But I am satisfied that the judge was completely right in his view that the defendant had wholly failed to show the existence of a contractual licence. I would accordingly dismiss the appeal.

The Court of Appeal was in this case reluctant to imply a contractual licence and distinguished it from *Tanner v Tanner* where Mrs Tanner had given up her rent-controlled flat. That, according to the court, amounted to consideration.

The defendant in *Horrocks v Forray* [1976] argued that there was a contractual licence based on the conduct of the parties. The court dismissed this argument. In considering the defendant's course of conduct, there was nothing to suggest an implied contractual licence.

In *Tanner v Tanner* [1975] the relationship had broken down and the parties were '[i]n a very real sense...making arrangements for the future at arm's length' (per Scarman LJ, *Horrocks v Forray* [1976]). According to Scarman LJ such conduct could perhaps provide a basis for a contractual licence. However, in the eyes of the court in *Horrocks*, the deceased was very generous over a number of years 'not because he was bound or was binding himself to be generous, but because he chose to be generous to the woman for whom there was a big place in his heart' (per Scarman LJ, *Horrocks v Forray* [1976]).

Since *Tanner v Tanner* there has been a move away from implying contractual licences. Hopefully, you will have seen that this is a very artificial approach to dealing with informal family arrangements. These types of cases are now evaluated on the basis of estoppel.

Where the contractual licence has a duration which is fixed, it will end at that time; for example, a lodger may have a licence to live in a designated room in a house for three months. There is no need to give notice, it simply expires. If no time period is specified for the duration of the contractual licence, then it could potentially last a number of years. In these circumstances reasonable notice must be given.

In principle, the licensor of a contractual licence can, as with bare licences, revoke the contractual licence at will. This is simply because, at common law, a contractual licence did not provide any interest in land and consequently there was no right for the licensee to remain in possession. There was a shift in the attitude by the courts towards such licences, whereby the courts have shown a willingness to use equitable remedies to prevent the licensor from revoking the licence. We shall consider revocation of licences both in common law and in equity. First, we shall discuss the relationship between the licensor and licensee, and then that of the licensee and a third party.

cross-reference
See 10.5 for a discussion of estoppel licences.

10.4.1 Revocation of a Licence by the Licensor

Common Law

The common law treated contractual licences in the same manner as bare licences; they were revocable at will. This may lead to a breach of contract because the licence was revoked before it was due to expire. The harshness of this approach is illustrated by *Wood v Leadbitter* (1845) 13 M & W 838. The claimant purchased a ticket which gave him access to the grandstand and enclosure at the Doncaster racecourse for four days. The claimant was asked to leave before the end of the meeting, but he refused to go. The claimant was removed, without using unnecessary violence, by the defendant. The claimant brought an action for assault and false imprisonment. He claimed that he had an irrevocable licence which entitled him to enter and remain in the enclosures during the races.

The Court of Exchequer drew a distinction between a bare licence and a licence coupled with an interest. The former was revocable whereas the latter was irrevocable. The court held the contractual licence to attend the races was revocable. As an alternative the court suggested the appropriate right of action lay in breach of contract and not in any right to remain on the land.

Equity

To alleviate the unfairness of the common law rule, aided by the fusion of law and equity in the Judicature Acts 1873 and 1875, the courts used equity to prevent the arbitrary end to a contractual licence. This was a significant development for the contractual licensee. There were two ways in which this was achieved by the courts:

• by implying a term into the contract which would prevent the licensor from revoking the contract; and

- by using equitable remedies, such as injunctions and specific performance, to prevent the licensor from revoking the contract.

In *Hurst v Picture Theatres Ltd* [1916] 1 KB 1, the claimant purchased a ticket to watch a film in the defendant's cinema. The defendant mistakenly thought that the claimant had not paid and asked him to leave. The claimant refused and he was forcibly removed from the cinema. A successful action for assault and false imprisonment was brought against the defendant.

Buckley LJ provided two reasons why the licensee should succeed in this case. First, he considered that a grant of an interest had been made to the claimant in the form of a right to enjoy watching the film. Following *Wood v Leadbitter* where there is a licence coupled with a grant, the licence cannot be revoked. However, Buckley LJ continued to provide a second alternative justification for finding in favour of the claimant:

> If there be a licence with an agreement not to revoke the licence, that, if given for value, is an enforceable right. If the facts here are, as I think they are, that the licence was a licence to enter the building and see the spectacle from its commencement until its termination, then there was included in that contract a contract not to revoke the licence until the play had run to its termination. It was then a breach of contract to revoke the obligation not to revoke the licence . . .

This second approach used equity as the basis for granting damages to the licensee. Although an injunction could not prevent the defendant from revoking the contractual licence (the claimant realistically would have had little time or opportunity to obtain one), the availability of the remedy of specific performance prevented the licensor from breaking his contract with the claimant. Put in another way, the licence permitted the licensee to enter the building and watch the film, and, implied into the contract was an irrevocable right to remain there until the film finished.

The first approach in *Hirst v Picture Theatres* of a licence coupled by a grant was criticized in *Cowell v Rosehill Racecourse Co Ltd* (1937) 56 CLR 605, where Latham CJ said 'the right to see a spectacle cannot, in the ordinary sense of legal language, be regarded as a proprietary interest. Fifty thousand people who pay to see a football match do not obtain fifty thousand interests in the football ground'. It is the second approach that is now followed by the courts.

Whether a term can be implied into a contract depends on the true construction of the contract between the parties, that is, did the parties intend the contractual licence to be irrevocable? This matter was considered in *Winter Garden Theatre (London) Ltd v Millennium Productions Ltd* [1946] 1 All ER 678. In this case a licence was granted to stage plays, ballets, or concerts for six months, with options to renew, at the licensor's theatre. Lord Greene MR, in the Court of Appeal, noted that equity will only intervene to grant an injunction where there is a term in the contract, either express or implied, that does not permit the licensor to revoke the contract. This reasoning was followed in the House of Lords, though the application of this to the facts was reversed. The House of Lords held that the licence was not perpetual, because it could be revoked on giving one month's notice, which in the circumstances was regarded as reasonable notice. According to their Lordships, where there is an express or implied term that the contractual licence is irrevocable, the sanctity of the contractual licence will be preserved by the courts of equity by granting an injunction.

thinking point 10.2

Do you think that the courts are more likely to imply that the contractual licence is irrevocable where the person remains on the land for a short period, compared to a longer period, for example six months or a year?

It seems that a short term licence, such as a ticket to a football match or the cinema, is irrevocable for the duration of the match, film, etc. But a long term licence, such as that to use the theatre in the Winter Gardens case, can be revoked by giving reasonable notice.

From the case law discussed so far we can conclude that a licensor can be prevented from revoking the contractual licence by an injunction. Can equitable remedies be used to enforce the performance of a contractual licence?

The Court of Appeal in *Verrall v Great Yarmouth Borough Council* [1981] QB 202 granted specific performance of a contractual licence in the interests of freedom of speech. The defendant council hired a hall for two days to the National Front (an extreme right wing political party). Following a change in the council's political control the contract was repudiated. The claimant brought an action for specific performance of the contract. The council argued that the contractual licence could be revoked at any time and the remedy to National Front would lie in damages. The court was of the view, irrespective of the political party involved, in the interests of fundamental freedoms, that is, speech and assembly, a decree of specific performance was granted, because under these circumstances damages would not be an appropriate remedy.

10.4.2 The Effect of Licences between the Licensee and a Third Party

Orthodox Approach

Does the contractual licence bind a third party purchaser? Under the rules in contract law a third party who is not party to the original contract is not bound by its terms. This reflects the orthodox approach in land law; the contractual licensee has only a personal right, and not a proprietary one.

This was confirmed in the House of Lords in *King v David Allen and Sons, Billposting, Ltd* [1916] 2 AC 54, where the claimant had been given permission to display posters and advertisements on the walls of a cinema. The cinema was then leased to a third party. The licence did not bind the third party; it was purely a personal obligation on the part of the defendants to permit the claimants to put posters on the walls.

Contractual Licences Allegedly as Equitable Interests

The Court of Appeal in *Errington v Errington and Woods* [1952] 1 KB 290 re-evaluated the status of contractual licences. A father purchased a house for his son and daughter-in-law to live in. The property remained in the father's name. He promised to convey the house to them if they continued to pay the mortgage repayments. The father died and left all his property to his wife, including the house. Up until the father's death, the son and the son's wife continued to pay the mortgage, but following his father's death, the son left his wife and moved in with his mother. The wife continued to pay the mortgage and occupied the house. The mother brought an action for possession. She did not succeed.

Denning LJ asserted that a contractual licence existed, and that licence bound the mother.

> The father's promise was a unilateral contract—a promise of the house in return for their act of paying the instalments. It could not be revoked by him once the couple entered on performance of the act, but it would cease to bind him if they left it incomplete and unperformed, which they have not done. If that was the position during the father's lifetime, so it must be after his death. If the daughter-in-law continues to pay all the building society instalments, the couple will be entitled to have the property transferred to them as soon as the mortgage is paid off; but if she does not do so, then the building society will claim the instalments from the father's estate and the estate will have to pay them. I cannot think that in those circumstances the estate would be bound to transfer the house to them, any more than the father himself would have been.

...the couple were licensees, having a permissive occupation short of a tenancy, but with a contractual right, or at any rate, an equitable right to remain so long as they paid the instalments, which would grow into a good equitable title to the house itself as soon as the mortgage was paid. This is, I think, the right view of the relationship of the parties....

...it seems to me that, although the couple had exclusive possession of the house, there was clearly no relationship of landlord and tenant. They were not tenants at will but licensees. They had a mere personal privilege to remain there, with no right to assign or sub-let. They were, however, not bare licensees. They were licensees with a contractual right to remain. As such they have no right at law to remain, but only in equity, and equitable rights now prevail. I confess, however, that it has taken the courts some time to reach this position. At common law a licence was always revocable at will, notwithstanding a contract to the contrary: *Wood* v. *Leadbitter* (1845) 13 M&W 838. The remedy for a breach of the contract was only in damages.... The rule has, however, been altered owing to the interposition of equity.

Accordingly, on the facts the court could only come to the conclusion that the son and his wife were licensees. Denning LJ then considered the effect of the contractual licence against a third party.

REVIEW QUESTION Before we consider the extract, it would be useful if you could answer this question: what is the doctrine of notice?

(Refer back to our earlier discussion of the doctrine in Chapter 4.)

Law and equity have been fused for nearly 80 years, and since 1948 it has been clear that, as a result of the fusion, a licensor will not be permitted to eject a licensee in breach of a contract to allow him to remain: see *Winter Garden Theatre, London* v. *Millenium Productions Ltd.* [1948] AC 173, 191, *per* Lord Greene, and in the House of Lords *per* Lord Simon; nor in breach of a promise on which the licensee has acted, even though he gave no value for it: see *Foster* v. *Robinson* [1951] 1 KB 149 where Sir Raymond Evershed M.R. said that as a result of the oral arrangement to let the man stay, he was entitled as licensee to occupy the premises without any payment of rent for the rest of his days. This infusion of equity means that contractual licences now have a force and validity of their own and cannot be revoked in breach of the contract. Neither the licensor nor anyone who claims through him can disregard the contract except a purchaser for value without notice.

In the present case it is clear that the father expressly promised the couple that the property should belong to them as soon as the mortgage was paid, and impliedly promised that so long as they paid the instalments to the building society they should be allowed to remain in possession. They were not purchasers because they never bound themselves to pay the instalments, but nevertheless they were in a position analogous to purchasers. They have acted on the promise, and neither the father nor his widow, his successor in title, can eject them in disregard of it. The result is that in my opinion the appeal should be dismissed and no order for possession should be made.

Contractual licences had been elevated to a higher status; crucially Denning LJ said '[n]either the licensor nor anyone who claims through him can disregard the contract except a purchaser for value without notice'. According to this statement, the widow was bound by the promise because she was not a purchaser within the scope of the doctrine of notice. She would only be able to take free of those rights if she was a purchaser without notice. The contractual licence was binding because it was categorized as an equitable interest.

The proprietary status of a contractual licence was maintained by Lord Denning in *Binions v Evans* [1972] Ch 359.

In *Binions v Evans* [1972] Ch 359, the majority of the Court of Appeal held that Mrs Evans had a life interest, and she was a life tenant under the Strict Settlement Act 1925.

cross-reference
For the facts of
Binions v Evans
see 7.3.4.

Aware of the consequences of awarding Mrs Evans a tenancy for life, where a life tenant can sell or lease the property and in his opinion contrary to the intention of the parties, Lord Denning MR continued to favour the contractual licence line of reasoning. In his judgment Lord Denning MR considered how the equitable interest in favour of Mrs Evans would arise. The purchasers bought the property expressly 'subject to' Mrs Evans' rights. This amounted to a contractual licence and, according to Lord Denning MR, a constructive trust would be imposed on the purchasers to allow Mrs Evans to continue to live there. This also applies in situations where the licensor impliedly takes subject to the licensee's rights. The licensee being in actual occupation of the land will have the benefit of a constructive trust. In this case the contractual licence, protected by the constructive trust, would take effect as an equitable interest.

The difficulty with this view is that it is not consistent with established case law such as *King v David Allen and Sons, Billposting, Ltd*, and *National Provincial Bank v Ainsworth*. Dissatisfaction was expressed at the lack of certainty in the approach to adopt in such cases.

In *Re Sharpe* [1980] 1 WLR 219, a nephew had purchased a property with the aid of a loan from his elderly aunt. By providing this loan, the nephew told his aunt that she could live there for as long as she liked. The nephew was later declared bankrupt. The court held that the elderly aunt had a contractual licence which was binding on the trustee in bankruptcy and could remain in the property until the loan had been repaid. (A trustee in bankruptcy is given control of the debtor's property on trust on behalf of the creditors. On obtaining the property, the trustee is still subject to third party property rights, both legal and equitable.)

The judgment given by Browne-Wilkinson J reflects the state of the law at the time. There was a clear lack of certainty in the correct approach to be used in such cases. The outcome of the case was clear to Browne-Wilkinson J where he states that 'in my judgment, whether it be called a contractual licence or an equitable licence or an interest under a constructive trust, Mrs. Johnson would be entitled as against the debtor to stay in the house'. The difficulty that faced Browne-Wilkinson J was how to get to the end result. The elderly aunt's claim was considered as:

> …the right to stay on the premises until the money she provided indirectly to acquire them has been repaid. This right is based upon the line of recent Court of Appeal decisions which has spelt out irrevocable licences from informal family arrangements, and in some cases characterised such licences as conferring some equity or equitable interest under a constructive trust. I do not think that the principles lying behind these decisions have yet been fully explored and on occasion it seems that such rights are found to exist simply on the ground that to hold otherwise would be a hardship to the plaintiff. …
>
> Are rights of the kind spelt out in the cases I have referred to merely contractual licences or do they fetter the property and create some right over it? On the authorities as they stand, I think I am bound to hold that the rights under such an irrevocable licence bind the property itself in the hands of the trustee in bankruptcy. Lord Denning M.R. has, on a number of occasions, said that these licences arise under a constructive trust and are binding on the third party's acquiring with notice. These statements are for the most part obiter dicta with which other members of the court have not associated themselves, preferring to rest their decision on there being a contractual licence.

Critical of this uncertainty that had arisen, Browne-Wilkinson J concluded:

> Accordingly, I hold that Mrs. Johnson is entitled as against the trustee in bankruptcy to remain in the property until she is repaid the sums she advanced. I reach this conclusion with some hesitation since I find the present state of the law very confused and difficult to fit in

with established equitable principles. I express the hope that in the near future the whole question can receive full consideration in the Court of Appeal, so that, in order to do justice to the many thousands of people who never come into court at all but who wish to know with certainty what their proprietary rights are, the extent to which these irrevocable licences bind third parties may be defined with certainty. Doing justice to the litigant who actually appears in the court by the invention of new principles of law ought not to involve injustice to the other persons who are not litigants before the court but whose rights are fundamentally affected by the new principles.

Contractual Licences Relegated to Orthodox Approach—Not Equitable Interests

The Court of Appeal in *Ashburn Anstalt v Arnold* [1989] Ch 1 answered Browne-Wilkinson J's pleas and undertook a comprehensive review of the case law in this area.

In this case, Arnold sold his leasehold interest in a shop subject to the condition that he could remain in the property rent-free until the redevelopment of the property took place. The court held that the agreement amounted to a lease and not a licence. (The decision of the court on this point has since been overruled by *Prudential Assurance Co Ltd v London Residuary Body* [1992] 2 AC 386, but this does not affect the *obiter dicta* statements made in the court in relation to contractual licences.)

Fox LJ giving judgment for the court considered the problem of a contractual licence having proprietary status. *Errington*, according to Fox LJ, was correctly decided though he noted that it was the analysis which conflicted with authorities in the area and said:

> Before *Errington* the law appears to have been clear and well understood. It rested on an important and intelligible distinction between contractual obligations which gave rise to no estate or interest in the land and proprietary rights which, by definition, did. The far-reaching statement of principle in *Errington* was not supported by authority, not necessary for the decision of the case and *per incuriam* in the sense that it was made without reference to authorities which, if they would not have compelled, would surely have persuaded the court to adopt a different ratio. Of course, the law must be free to develop. But as a response to problems which had arisen, the *Errington* rule (without more) was neither practically necessary nor theoretically convincing. By contrast, the finding on appropriate facts of a constructive trust may well be regarded as a beneficial adaptation of old rules to new situations.

Fox LJ concluded that 'a contractual licence does not create a property interest'. This is conclusive that contractual licences cannot bind successors in title; they are not proprietary in their nature. *Errington*, according to Fox LJ, may have been interpreted using estoppel and not as a binding contractual licence.

The last sentence of the passage above provides an insight into what the court viewed as a suitable alternative to the contractual licence reasoning which was not based on authorities. It was recognized that the constructive trust is very flexible and applies to a wide range of situations.

Fox LJ said:

> The test, for the present purposes, is whether the owner of the property has so conducted himself that it would be inequitable to allow him to deny the claimant an interest in the property . . .
>
> The court will not impose a constructive trust unless it is satisfied that the conscience of the estate owner is affected. The mere fact that that land is expressed to be conveyed 'subject to'

a contract does not necessarily imply that the grantee is to be under an obligation, not otherwise existing, to give effect to the provisions of the contract. The fact that the conveyance is expressed to be subject to the contract may often ... be at least as consistent with an intention merely to protect the grantor against claims by the grantee as an intention to impose an obligation on the grantee. The words 'subject to' will, of course, impose notice. But notice is not enough to impose on somebody an obligation to give effect to a contract into which he did not enter. Thus, mere notice of a restrictive covenant is not enough to impose upon the estate owner an obligation or equity to give effect to it. ...

In matters relating to the title to land, certainty is of prime importance. We do not think it desirable that constructive trusts of land should be imposed in reliance on inferences from slender materials. In our opinion the available evidence in the present case is insufficient.

Despite constructive trusts being flexible, they would only be applied in limited circumstances. The court agreed with Lord Denning MR in *Binions v Evans* where it was suggested the purchaser took the property subject to the defendant's constructive trust. This was because the purchaser had bought the property at a lower price subject to the agreement that the defendant could live in the property for the rest of her life. The constructive trust provided a mechanism by which the intention of the parties could be fulfilled. In contrast, in *Ashburn*, the property was not purchased at a lower price despite the condition that Arnold should remain in the property rent-free. The court concluded that a constructive trust will not be implied based on 'slender' evidence.

The binding effect of a contractual licence on a third party is limited:

- It will only bind a purchaser if a constructive trust is conferred to give effect to the agreement.
- The court will only impose such a trust where the conscience of the estate owner is affected.
- This is a question of fact; the evidence presented to the court must be more than 'slender'.

This return to orthodoxy in *Ashburn* has been approved in a number of cases in the Court of Appeal, for example *Lloyd v Dugdale* [2002] 2 P & CR 13 and *Haberman v Koehler* (1997) 73 P & CR 515.

The wealth of authorities has shown that contractual licences do not come within the scope of category of interests which bind successors in title. Lord Denning, progressive in his approach towards providing an equitable outcome for the party who potentially will lose out, did not provide sufficient authority for digressing from established precedent. The court was also arguably restricted in creating new equitable interests by s4(1) Law of Property Act 1925 (LPA 1925):

Law of Property Act 1925

4. Creation and disposition of equitable interests

(1) Interests in land validly created or arising after the commencement of this Act, which are not capable of subsisting as legal estates, shall take effect as equitable interests, and, save as otherwise expressly provided by statute, interests in land which under the Statute of Uses or otherwise could before the commencement of this Act have been created as legal interests, shall be capable of being created as equitable interests:

Provided that, after the commencement of this Act (and save as hereinafter expressly enacted), *an equitable interest in land shall only be capable of being validly created in any case in which an equivalent equitable interest in property real or personal could have been validly created before such commencement.*

[Emphasis added]

This emphasized proviso appears to place a restriction on new equitable interests. Smith (2014, at p 484) suggests 'it seems preferable to regard it as dealing with the effect of the 1925 legislation. In other words, it ensured that conventional rights alone were recognised in the immediate aftermath of the legislation, rather than inhibiting all development for the indefinite future.'

thinking point 10.3

What reasons exist for denying a licence proprietary status?

Perhaps the simplest answer is that licences are purely personal in character, and should operate exclusively between licensor and licensee. Moreover, the problem which arose in Errington *and* Sharpe *can be solved by using either constructive trust or proprietary estoppel.*

10.5 Estoppel Licences

The courts have used the doctrine of equitable estoppel to prevent a licensor from revoking the licence or to grant an interest in land. It has been applied to bare and contractual licences. Estoppel licences can be viewed as a form of proprietary estoppel. Proprietary estoppel arises where a representation has been made and a person relying on this has acted to their detriment. To prevent the representation being denied estoppel is invoked by the courts. To 'satisfy the estoppel' the courts can give the claimant a remedy using a range of alternatives, and one of which is to confer a licence for life (eg *Binions v Evans*). Nowadays 'estoppel licences' are usually regarded as a form of proprietary estoppel, a concept to which we now turn.

cross-reference
For a discussion on Binions v Evans *see 10.4.2.*

10.6 Proprietary Estoppel

In general terms proprietary estoppel protects a person who has done acts in reliance on an expectation that they will receive an interest in the landowner's land or an estate in fee simple. In such circumstances the doctrine of proprietary estoppel, which has its roots in equity, has been used by the courts to 'mitigate the rigours of strict law', and it will 'prevent a person from insisting on his strict legal rights—whether arising under a contract, or on his title deeds, or by statute—when it would be inequitable for him to do so having regard to the dealings which have taken place between the parties' (per Lord Denning MR, *Crabb v Arun District Council* [1976] Ch 179).

Lord Scott in *Cobbe v Yeoman's Row Management Ltd* [2008] 1 WLR 1752 explained the nature of proprietary estoppel:

An 'estoppel' bars the object of it from asserting some fact or facts, or, sometimes, something that is a mixture of fact and law, that stands in the way of some right claimed by the person entitled to the benefit of the estoppel. The estoppel becomes a 'proprietary' estoppel—a sub-species of a 'promissory' estoppel—if the right claimed is a proprietary right, usually a right to or over land but, in principle, equally available in relation to chattels or choses in action.

In effect, equity will intervene to prevent unconscionable denial of rights, and proprietary estoppel will usually come into existence if the right claimed is of a proprietary nature. The court in considering an appropriate remedy can either create or enforce property rights.

The facts (or mixture of fact and law) that may give rise to a claim in estoppel in these circumstances tend not to be formal ones, that is, in the form of a contract, rather informal ones where the intentions of the parties may not be clear. They could involve:

- a promise of gift in the form of an interest or an estate in land;
- both parties have a common expectation that one party will acquire an interest or land; and
- one party is mistaken as to their rights.

10.6.1 Promise of Gift

A good example to illustrate a promise of a gift is found in *Dillwyn v Llewelyn* (1862) 4 De GF & J 517. A father and son had signed an informal memorandum which provided that the son would have rights in the land so that the son could build a house. The son relied on this memorandum and built a house having spent a vast amount of money. The court upheld the son's claim to the land because he had relied upon the promise of the land as a gift and incurred expenditure as a result of relying on the promise.

10.6.2 Common Expectation

Lord Kingsdown (in his dissenting judgment) in *Ramsden v Dyson* (1866) LR 1 HL 129, explained how the doctrine of proprietary estoppel applies where the landowner has encouraged the expectation of an interest in land at some point (at the present time or some time in the future):

> If a man, under a verbal agreement with a landlord for a certain interest in land, or, what amounts to the same thing, under an expectation, created or encouraged by the landlord, that he shall have a certain interest, takes possession of such land, with the consent of the landlord, and upon the faith of such promise or expectation, with the knowledge of the landlord, and without objection by him, lays out money upon the land, a Court of equity will compel the landlord to give effect to such promise or expectation.

Although this is explained through the context of landlord and tenant, that was because the case involved a landlord and tenant, it has been accepted that it applies more generally. A good illustration of this can be found in *Inwards v Baker* [1965] 2 QB 29. In this case Baker junior was keen to build himself a bungalow, but he could not afford the price of an empty site. His father had some spare land. Baker senior said to his son, 'Why not put the bungalow on my land and make the bungalow a little bigger?' (This was an oral licence.) Baker junior did exactly that, and made the bungalow his permanent home. Baker senior retained ownership of the fee simple to the land, and so the house also became Baker senior's property. All was well while both senior and junior were still alive, but when Baker senior died his will (made long before the bungalow was built) left the land in question not to Baker junior but to Inwards. Inwards brought proceedings to recover possession of the bungalow. These proceedings failed.

The Court of Appeal held that since Baker junior had an expectation, which was induced and encouraged by his father, it would be unconscionable for Baker senior to deny his son his rights. The claimants were estopped (or prevented) from obtaining possession and Baker junior was conferred the right to remain in the property for the rest of his life.

10.6.3 Mistaken Belief

Mistaken belief arises where the claimant is acting under a misapprehension of their entitlement to their legal rights. The claimant then acts upon their mistaken belief to their detriment. The other party merely stands by and does nothing to rectify the mistaken belief held by the claimant. This is illustrated by an example given in *Ramsden v Dyson* (1866) where the Lord Chancellor said:

> If a stranger begins to build on my land supposing it to be his own, and I, perceiving his mistake, abstain from setting him right, and leave him to persevere in his error, a Court of equity will not allow me afterwards to assert my title to the land on which he had expended money on the supposition that the land was his own. It considers that, when I saw the mistake into which he had fallen, it was my duty to be active and to state my adverse title; and that it would be dishonest in me to remain wilfully passive on such an occasion, in order afterwards to profit by the mistake which I might have prevented.

In dealing with this type of claim Fry J in *Willmott v Barber* (1880) LR 15 Ch D 96, set out five criteria (known as *probanda*) that need to be satisfied for estoppel to apply. Fry J stated:

> A man is not to be deprived of his legal rights unless he has acted in such a way as would make it fraudulent for him to set up those rights. What, then, are the elements or requisites necessary to constitute fraud of that description? In the first place the plaintiff must have made a mistake as to his legal rights. Secondly, the plaintiff must have expended some money or must have done some act (not necessarily upon the defendant's land) on the faith of his mistaken belief. Thirdly, the defendant, the possessor of the legal right, must know of the existence of his own right which is inconsistent with the right claimed by the plaintiff. If he does not know of it he is in the same position as the plaintiff, and the doctrine of acquiescence is founded upon conduct with a knowledge of your legal rights. Fourthly, the defendant, the possessor of the legal right, must know of the plaintiff's mistaken belief of his rights. If he does not, there is nothing which calls upon him to assert his own rights. Lastly, the defendant, the possessor of the legal right, must have encouraged the plaintiff in his expenditure of money or in the other acts which he has done, either directly or by abstaining from asserting his legal right. Where all these elements exist, there is fraud of such a nature as will entitle the Court to restrain the possessor of the legal right from exercising it, but, in my judgment, nothing short of this will do.

cross-reference
See 10.6.2 for a discussion on Inwards v Baker.

According to Fry J, the five criteria apply to situations where there is a 'fraud'; one party knows that the other has made a mistake as to his legal rights (known as 'unilateral mistake').

However, the courts used these criteria and applied them not only to cases involving mistaken belief, but also to a wide range of estoppel claims. The courts tended to use the criteria in a prescriptive manner, which led to estoppel being restricted in its application and stifled development in this area.

10.6.4 A Less Restrictive Approach Towards Common Expectation Cases

Taylors Fashions Ltd v Liverpool Victoria Trustees Co Ltd [1982] QB 133 moved away from these five criteria. Liverpool Victoria Trustees had purchased properties which were all subject to leases. Both the tenants had an option to renew their lease (Taylors Fashions and Old & Campbell). These options were not registered under the Land Charges Act 1925 because the claimants did not believe that they were registrable. In evidence, Taylors Fashions had stated that they had undertaken extensive improvements to the property in the belief that the option was valid and enforceable. Taylors Fashions attempted to exercise their option to renew (as did the other claimant in this case) and the defendants refused to renew the lease. The question was whether Liverpool Victoria was estopped from denying the validity of the options to renew despite their non-registration as land charges. On the facts, Liverpool Victoria were not estopped as against Taylors Fashions, but were estopped against the other claimants, Old & Campbell Ltd. The court held that although options to renew were registrable land charges, estoppel could restrain the landlord from unconscionable denial of rights. In *Taylors Fashions*, the defendants had not acted unconscionably and the option to renew was not enforceable. Oliver J said:

> . . . certainly from the more recent authorities, which seem to me to support a much wider equitable jurisdiction to interfere in cases where the assertion of strict legal rights is found by the court to be unconscionable. It may well be (although I think that this must now be considered open to doubt) that the strict *Willmott* v. *Barber*, 15 Ch.D. 96 probanda are applicable as necessary requirements in those cases where all that has happened is that the party alleged to be estopped has stood by without protest while his rights have been infringed . . . in a case of mere passivity, it is readily intelligible that there must be shown a duty to speak, protest or interfere which cannot normally arise in the absence of knowledge or at least a suspicion of the true position. Thus for a landowner to stand by while a neighbour lays drains in land which the landowner does not believe that he owns (*Armstrong* v. *Sheppard & Short Ltd.* [1959] 2 Q.B. 384) or for a remainder man not to protest at a lease by a tenant for life which he believes he has no right to challenge (*Svenson* v. *Payne* (1945) 71 C.L.R. 531) does not create an estoppel. Again, where what is relied on is a waiver by acquiescence, as in *Willmott* v. *Barber* itself, the five probanda are no doubt appropriate. There is, however, no doubt that there are judicial pronouncements of high authority which appear to support as essential the application of all the five probanda over the broader field covering all cases generally classified as estoppel by 'encouragement' or 'acquiescence': see, for instance, the speech of Lord Diplock in *Kammins Ballrooms Co. Ltd.* v. *Zenith Investments (Torquay) Ltd* [1971] A.C. 850, 884.
>
> [Counsel for the claimants] submits, however, that it is historically wrong to treat these probanda as holy writ and to restrict equitable interference only to those cases which can be confined within the strait-jacket of some fixed rule governing the circumstances in which, and in which alone, the court will find that a party is behaving unconscionably. Whilst accepting that the five probanda may form an appropriate test in cases of silent acquiescence, he submits that the authorities do not support the absolute necessity for compliance with all five probanda, and, in particular, the requirement of knowledge on the part of the party estopped that the other party's belief is a mistaken belief, in cases where the conduct relied on has gone beyond mere silence and amounts to active encouragement. In Lord Kingsdown's example in *Ramsden* v. *Dyson, L.R.* 1 H.L. 129, for instance, there is no room for the literal application of the probanda, for the circumstances there postulated do not presuppose a 'mistake' on anybody's part, but merely the fostering of an expectation in the minds of *both* parties at the time but from which, once it has been acted upon, it would be unconscionable to permit the landlord to depart. As Scarman L.J. pointed out in *Crabb* v. *Arun District Council* [1976] Ch. 179, the 'fraud' in these cases is not to be found in the transaction itself but in the subsequent attempt to go back upon the basic assumptions which underlay it.
>
> . . .
>
> The fact is that acquiescence or encouragement may take a variety of forms. It may take the form of standing by in silence whilst one party unwittingly infringes another's legal rights. It may take the form of passive or active encouragement of expenditure or alteration of legal position upon the footing of some unilateral or shared legal or factual supposition. Or it may, for example, take the form of stimulating, or not objecting to, some change of legal position on the faith of a unilateral or a shared assumption as to the future conduct of one or other party. I am not at all convinced that it is desirable or possible to lay down hard and fast rules which seek to dictate, in every combination of circumstances, the considerations which will persuade the court that a departure by the acquiescing party from

the previously supposed state of law or fact is so unconscionable that a court of equity will interfere. Nor, in my judgment, do the authorities support so inflexible an approach, and that is particularly so in cases in which the decision has been based on the principle stated by Lord Kingsdown....

Furthermore the more recent cases indicate, in my judgment, that the application of the *Ramsden* v. *Dyson, L.R.* 1 H.L. 129 principle—whether you call it proprietary estoppel, estoppel by acquiescence or estoppel by encouragement is really immaterial—requires a very much broader approach which is directed rather at ascertaining whether, in particular individual circumstances, it would be unconscionable for a party to be permitted to deny that which, knowingly, or unknowingly, he has allowed or encouraged another to assume to his detriment than to inquiring whether the circumstances can be fitted within the confines of some preconceived formula serving as a universal yardstick for every form of unconscionable behaviour.

So regarded, knowledge of the true position by the party alleged to be estopped, becomes merely one of the relevant factors—it may even be a determining factor in certain cases—in the overall inquiry. This approach, so it seems to me, appears very clearly from the authorities to which I am about to refer. In *Inwards* v. *Baker* [1965] 2 Q.B. 29 there was no mistaken belief on either side. Each knew the state of the title, but the defendant had been led to expect that he would get an interest in the land on which he had built and, indeed, the overwhelming probability is that that was indeed the father's intention at the time. But it was not mere promissory estoppel, which could merely be used as a defence, for, as Lord Denning M.R. said, at p. 37, 'it is for the court to say in what way the equity can be satisfied.' The principle was expressed very broadly both by Lord Denning M.R. and by Danckwerts L.J. Lord Denning said at p. 37:

> 'But it seems to me, from *Plimmer's* case, 9 App.Cas. 699, 713–714 in particular, that the equity arising from the expenditure on land need not fail "merely on the ground that the interest to be secured has not been expressly indicated...the court must look at the circumstances in each case to decide in what way the equity can be satisfied."'

and a little further down he said:

> 'All that is necessary is that the licensee should, at the request or with the encouragement of the landlord, have spent the money in the expectation of being allowed to stay there. If so, the court will not allow that expectation to be defeated where it would be inequitable so to do.'

...

More nearly in point is *Crabb* v. *Arun District Council* [1976] Ch. 179 where the plaintiff had altered his legal position in the expectation, encouraged by the defendants, that he would have a certain access to a road. Now there was no mistake here. Each party knew that the road was vested in the defendants and each knew that no formal grant had been made. Indeed I cannot see why in considering whether the defendants were behaving unconscionably, it should have made the slightest difference to the result if, at the time when the plaintiff was encouraged to open his access to the road, the defendants had thought that they were bound to grant it. The fact was that he had been encouraged to alter his position irrevocably to his detriment on the faith of a belief, which was known to and encouraged by the defendants, that he was going to be given a particular right of access—a belief which, for all that appears, the defendants probably shared at that time.

The particularly interesting features of the case in the context of the present dispute are, first, the virtual equation of promissory estoppel and proprietary estoppel or estoppel by acquiescence as mere facets of the same principle and secondly the very broad approach of both Lord Denning M.R. [in *E. R. Ives Investment Ltd.* v *High* [1967] 2 Q.B. 379] and Scarman L.J., both of whom emphasised the flexibility of the equitable doctrine. It is, however, worth noting that Scarman L.J. adopted and applied the five probanda in *Willmott* v. *Barber*, 15 Ch.D.

96 which he described as 'a valuable guide.' He considered that those probanda were satisfied and it is particularly relevant here to note again the fourth one—namely that the defendant, the possessor of the legal right, must know of the plaintiff's mistaken belief. If Scarman L.J. had interpreted this as meaning…that the defendant must know not only of the plaintiff's belief but also that it was mistaken, then he could not, I think, have come to the conclusion that this probandum was satisfied…that, up to the critical moment when the plaintiff acted, *both* parties thought that there was a firm assurance of access. The defendants had, indeed, even erected a gate at their own expense to give effect to it. What gave rise to the necessity for the court to intervene was the defendants' attempt to go back on this subsequently when they fell out with the plaintiff. I infer therefore that Scarman L.J. must have construed this probandum in the sense…namely that the defendant must know merely of the plaintiff's belief which, in the event, turns out to be mistaken.

Finally, there ought to be mentioned the most recent reference to the five probanda which is to be found in *Shaw* v. *Applegate* [1977] 1 W.L.R. 970. That was a case where the plea of estoppel by acquiescence failed on appeal, but it is significant that two members of the court expressed serious doubt whether it was necessary in every case of acquiescence to satisfy the five probanda….So here, once again, is the Court of Appeal asserting the broad test of whether in the circumstances the conduct complained of is unconscionable without the necessity of forcing those incumbrances into a Procrustean bed constructed from some unalterable criteria…

The inquiry which I have to make therefore, as it seems to me, is simply whether, in all the circumstances of this case, it was unconscionable for the defendants to seek to take advantage of the mistake which, at the material time, everybody shared…

Doubt was expressed by Oliver J as to whether the five criteria set out in *Willmott v Barber* could still be applied in all cases involving proprietary estoppel. It was suggested those criteria should only be used in cases involving a mistaken belief where 'the party alleged to be estopped has stood by without protest while his rights have been infringed'. Instead, Oliver J stated the requirements of proprietary estoppel in the common expectation category:

if under an expectation created or encouraged by B that A shall have a certain interest in land, thereafter, on the faith of such expectation and with the knowledge of B and without objection by him, acts to his detriment in connection with such land, a Court of Equity will compel B to give effect to such expectation.

Oliver J also considered the role of unconscionability in cases involving expectation or encouragement, the issue for the court is 'whether, in particular individual circumstances, it would be unconscionable for a party to be permitted to deny that which, knowingly, or unknowingly, he has allowed or encouraged another to assume to his detriment'.

This modern approach has been followed in a number of cases in the Court of Appeal, for example *Gillett v Holt* [2001] Ch 210. However, there are a few cases which have shown allegiance to *Willmott v Barber*, such as *Matharu v Matharu* (1994) 68 P & CR 93 and *Coombes v Smith* [1986] 1 WLR 808.

an equity
simply means that the claimant has the right, having satisfied the requirements of proprietary estoppel, to obtain a remedy in equity, as the court thinks just.

10.6.5 Modern Approach Towards Proprietary Estoppel

The courts in determining whether there is a proprietary estoppel will consider: first, whether the equity has arisen that will prevent the landowner from enforcing their legal rights, and, secondly, the court may, if it is appropriate, 'satisfy the **equity**' (using the traditional terminology: *Crabb v Arun DC* [1976] Ch 179). In satisfying the equity, the court has had a wide discretion and may grant an interest in land or even an estate in land.

Cases involving mistake are rare, and the majority of cases involve 'common expectation'. For an equity to arise the following elements must exist:

- representation or expectation as to present or future rights in land;
- reliance; and
- detriment.

In considering these elements, the court will also consider whether the landowner has gone back on their representation, that is, whether their actions are unconscionable. The court in *Gillett v Holt* [2001] Ch 210 focused on unconscionability as an overarching principle through which it will determine whether the equity is established. Robert Walker LJ noted:

> it is important to note at the outset that the doctrine of proprietary estoppel cannot be treated as subdivided into three or four watertight compartments...it repeatedly became apparent that the quality of the relevant assurances may influence the issue of reliance, that reliance and detriment are often intertwined, and that whether there is a distinct need for a 'mutual understanding' may depend on how the other elements are formulated and understood. Moreover the fundamental principle that equity is concerned to prevent unconscionable conduct permeates all the elements of the doctrine. In the end the court must look at the matter in the round.

The court in this case warns that the aim is to prevent 'unconscionable conduct' and that it is necessary to take a holistic approach and look at the issue as a whole, rather than examining each element in isolation.

More recently, Lord Scott in the House of Lords in *Cobbe v Yeoman's Row Management Ltd* [2008] 1 WLR 1752, stated that:

> 16 ...unconscionability of conduct may well lead to a remedy but, in my opinion, proprietary estoppel cannot be the route to it unless the ingredients for a proprietary estoppel are present. These ingredients should include, in principle, a proprietary claim made by a claimant and an answer to that claim based on some fact, or some point of mixed fact and law, that the person against whom the claim is made can be estopped from asserting. To treat a 'proprietary estoppel equity' as requiring neither a proprietary claim by the claimant nor an estoppel against the defendant but simply unconscionable behaviour is, in my respectful opinion, a recipe for confusion...
>
> 18 Oliver J (as he then was) stated the requirements of proprietary estoppel in a 'common expectation' class of case in a well-known and often cited passage in *Taylors Fashions Ltd* v *Liverpool Victoria Trustees Co. Ltd* [1982] QB 133 at 144:
>
>> 'if A under an expectation created or encouraged by B that A shall have a certain interest in land, thereafter, on the faith of such expectation and with the knowledge of B and without objection by him, acts to his detriment in connection with such land, a Court of Equity will compel B to give effect to such expectation.'

Note the reference to 'a certain interest in land'. *Taylors Fashions* was a case where the 'certain interest' was an option to renew a lease. There was no lack of certainty; the terms of the new lease were spelled out in the option and the lessees' expectation was that on the exercise of the option the new lease would be granted. The problem was that the option had not been registered under the Land Charges Act 1925 and the question was whether the freeholders, successors in title to the original lessors who had granted the option, could be estopped from denying the right of the lessees to exercise the option. But what is the comparable expectation and the comparable 'certain interest' in the present case? Mr Cobbe's expectation, encouraged by Mrs Lisle-Mainwaring, was that upon the grant of planning permission there would be a successful negotiation of the outstanding terms of a contract for the sale of the property to him, or to some company of his, and that a formal contract, which would include the already agreed core terms of the second agreement as well as the additional new terms agreed upon, would be prepared and entered into. An expectation dependent upon the conclusion of a successful negotiation is not an expectation of an interest having any comparable certainty to the certainty of the terms of the lessees' interest under the *Taylors Fashions* option. In the *Taylors Fashions* case both the content of the estoppel, i.e. an estoppel barring the new freeholders from asserting that the option was unenforceable for want of registration, and the interest the estoppel was intended to protect, i.e. the option to have a renewal of the lease, were clear and certain. Not so here. The present case is one in which an unformulated estoppel is being asserted in order to protect Mr Cobbe's interest under an oral agreement for the purchase of land that lacked both the requisite statutory formalities (s.2 of the 1989 Act) and was, in a contractual sense, incomplete.

28 …Proprietary estoppel requires, in my opinion, clarity as to what it is that the object of the estoppel is to be estopped from denying, or asserting, and clarity as to the interest in the property in question that that denial, or assertion, would otherwise defeat. If these requirements are not recognised, proprietary estoppel will lose contact with its roots and risk becoming unprincipled and therefore unpredictable, if it has not already become so.

The House of Lords approved *Taylors Fashions* requirements for proprietary estoppel in common expectation cases. To bring a claim of proprietary estoppel it is important that the claim is based on a property interest. Unconscionability is a factor which is taken into consideration in a claim for proprietary estoppel, but such a claim will not succeed simply because the landowner has behaved unconscionably.

To summarize what we have said so far:

- A claim for proprietary estoppel is normally based on a property interest in land.
- Proprietary estoppel: representation or expectation as to present and future interest in land, reliance, and detriment; it must be unconscionable for the landowner to go back on his promise.

Representation or Expectation

There are two elements to consider under this section: first, what is the nature of the expectation which has arisen from the representation? Secondly, how has the expectation been created?

Nature of the Expectation

The landowner will normally make a representation to the claimant that they have or will acquire an interest in land. In *Cobbe v Yeoman's Row Management Ltd* [2008] 1 WLR 1752, Cobbe orally agreed in principle with Yeoman's Row to buy a site in central London. Both parties knew that this agreement was not a valid contract (it did not comply with s2 Law of Property (Miscellaneous Provisions) Act 1989). Nevertheless, Cobbe, with Yeoman's Row encouragement, spent a lot of time and trouble, spread over 18 months, obtaining planning permission to redevelop the site. This planning permission enhanced the value of the site by several million pounds. Yeoman's Row then refused to enter into a formal contract to sell the land to Cobbe.

The House of Lords held that, despite his efforts, Cobbe had not acquired a proprietary estoppel right. Lord Walker drew a distinction between commercial and domestic (or family) cases in respect of the nature of the expectation. Lord Walker said:

68 …In the commercial context, the claimant is typically a business person with access to legal advice and what he or she is expecting to get is a *contract*. In the domestic or family context, the typical claimant is not a business person and is not receiving legal advice. What

he or she wants and expects to get is an *interest* in immovable property, often for long-term occupation as a home. The focus is not on intangible legal rights but on the tangible property which he or she expects to get. The typical domestic claimant does not stop to reflect (until disappointed expectations lead to litigation) whether some further legal transaction (such as a grant by deed, or the making of a will or codicil) is necessary to complete the promised title.

The view of the House of Lords was that in a commercial context the expectation of an interest should not be vague. Lord Scott noted that case law refers to a requirement that there be an expectation of 'a certain interest in land' and that this presented a problem for the claimant, Lord Scott explains:

> [the] requirement that there be an expectation of 'a certain interest in land'... [created a] problem for Mr Cobbe's proprietary estoppel claim. The problem is that when he made the planning application his expectation was, for proprietary estoppel purposes, the wrong sort of expectation. It was not an expectation that he would, if the planning application succeeded, become entitled to 'a certain interest in land'. His expectation was that he and Mrs Lisle-Mainwaring, or their respective legal advisers, would sit down and agree the outstanding contractual terms to be incorporated into the formal written agreement, which he justifiably believed would include the already agreed core financial terms, and that his purchase, and subsequently his development of the property, in accordance with that written agreement would follow. This is not, in my opinion, the sort of expectation of 'a certain interest in land' that Oliver J in the *Taylors Fashions* case or Lord Kingsdown in *Ramsden v Dyson* had in mind.

The nature of expectation was the successful negotiation of a contract upon the grant of planning permission. This expectation was regarded as vague and did not correspond to 'a certain interest in land' (following the reasoning in *Taylors Fashions*).

In the domestic context Lord Walker notes that the expectation of the nature of the rights is not always specific. Previous case law has shown that as long as there is an interest or right in land, either at present or in the future, that would be sufficient to amount to an expectation. According to Lord Walker, in the domestic context cases it is not always apparent what exactly the expectation might be, and so where estoppel has been established it is sufficient that 'the claimant believed that the assurance on which he or she relied was binding and irrevocable' (examples of cases which Lord Walker referred to are: *Inwards v Baker; Gillett v Holt;* and *Jennings v Rice*).

Lord Walker took a slightly different approach in the later House of Lords case of *Thorner v Major* [2009] 1 WLR 776. In this case, David Thorner worked on a farm for over 30 years without payment. This farm was owned by his father's cousin, Peter Thorner. Between 1990 and 2005 Peter encouraged David to believe that he would inherit the farm and David acted in reliance upon this assurance. Peter died without leaving a will. David claimed that by reason of the assurance and reliance, Peter's estate was estopped from denying that he had acquired the beneficial interest in the farm.

The expectation, according to Lord Walker, does not necessarily need to be precise or specific, 'the relevant assurance must be clear enough. What amounts to sufficient clarity... is hugely dependent on the context'. The context itself is fact sensitive and Lord Walker appreciated that 'the meaning to be ascribed to words passing between parties will depend, often very much, on their factual context. This is particularly true in a case such as this, where a very taciturn farmer, given to indirect statements, made remarks obliquely referring to his intention with regard to his farm after his death.'

The crucial point to note from Lord Walker's opinion is that context becomes all important when considering an expectation or assurance, and the assurance must be 'clear enough'.

Lord Neuberger agreed with Lord Walker on this point saying:

> …there must be some sort of an assurance which is clear and unequivocal before it can be relied on to found an estoppel. However, that proposition must be read as subject to three qualifications. First, it does not detract from the normal principle, so well articulated in this case by Lord Walker, that the effect of words or actions must be assessed in their context. Just as a sentence can have one meaning in one context and a very different meaning in another context, so can a sentence, which would be ambiguous or unclear in one context, be a clear and unambiguous assurance in another context.

In this regard, arguably there is less emphasis placed on categorizing whether the assurance has been given in a commercial or domestic context.

On the issue of whether there had to be certainty as to the interest in land, Lord Walker seems to continue with a holistic approach in his assessment of whether there should be certainty as to the extent of the land in question. In doing so, Lord Walker observed that:

> …even where there was some uncertainty an equity could arise and could be satisfied, either by an interest in land or in some other way.

The expectation does not have to stipulate the precise property, rather it must be about or relate to some identifiable property. This approach can also be seen in Lord Neuberger's opinion:

> 93 In the context of a case such as *Cobbe's* case [2008] 1 WLR 1752, it is readily understandable why Lord Scott considered the question of certainty was so significant. The parties had intentionally not entered into any legally binding arrangement while Mr Cobbe sought to obtain planning permission: they had left matters on a speculative basis, each knowing full well that neither was legally bound—see para 27. There was not even an agreement to agree (which would have been unenforceable), but, as Lord Scott pointed out, merely an expectation that there would be negotiations. And, as he said, at para 18, an 'expectation dependent upon the conclusion of a successful negotiation is not an expectation of an interest having [sufficient] certainty'.
>
> 94 There are two fundamental differences between that case and this case. First, the nature of the uncertainty in the two cases is entirely different. It is well encapsulated by Lord Walker's distinction between 'intangible legal rights' and 'the tangible property which he or she expects to get', in *Cobbe's* case [2008] 1 WLR 1752, para 68. In that case, there was no doubt about the physical identity of the property. However, there was total uncertainty as to the nature or terms of any benefit (property interest, contractual right, or money), and, if a property interest, as to the nature of that interest (freehold, leasehold, or charge), to be accorded to Mr Cobbe.
>
> 95 In this case, the extent of the farm might change, but, on the deputy judge's analysis, there is, as I see it, no doubt as to what was the subject of the assurance, namely the farm as it existed from time to time. Accordingly, the nature of the interest to be received by David was clear: it was the farm as it existed on Peter's death. As in the case of a very different equitable concept, namely a floating charge, the property the subject of the equity could be conceptually identified from the moment the equity came into existence, but its precise extent fell to be determined when the equity crystallised, namely on Peter's death.
>
> 96 Secondly, the analysis of the law in *Cobbe's* case [2008] 1 WLR 1752 was against the background of very different facts. The relationship between the parties in that case was entirely arm's length and commercial, and the person raising the estoppel was a highly experienced businessman. The circumstances were such that the parties could well have been expected to enter into a contract, however, although they discussed contractual terms, they

had consciously chosen not to do so. They had intentionally left their legal relationship to be negotiated, and each of them knew that neither of them was legally bound. What Mr Cobbe then relied on was 'an unformulated estoppel...asserted in order to protect [his] interest under an oral agreement for the purchase of land that lacked both the requisite statutory formalities...and was, in a contractual sense, incomplete': para 18.

97 In this case, by contrast, the relationship between Peter and David was familial and personal, and neither of them, least of all David, had much commercial experience. Further, at no time had either of them even started to contemplate entering into a formal contract as to the ownership of the farm after Peter's death. Nor could such a contract have been reasonably expected even to be discussed between them. On the deputy judge's findings, it was a relatively straightforward case: Peter made what were, in the circumstances, clear and unambiguous assurances that he would leave his farm to David, and David reasonably relied on, and reasonably acted to his detriment on the basis of, those assurances, over a long period.

98 In these circumstances, I see nothing in the reasoning of Lord Scott in *Cobbe's* case [2008] 1 WLR 1752 which assists the defendants in this case. It would represent a regrettable and substantial emasculation of the beneficial principle of proprietary estoppel if it were artificially fettered so as to require the precise extent of the property the subject of the alleged estoppel to be strictly defined in every case. Concentrating on the perceived morality of the parties' behaviour can lead to an unacceptable degree of uncertainty of outcome, and hence I welcome the decision in *Cobbe's* case [2008] 1 WLR 1752 . However, it is equally true that focussing on technicalities can lead to a degree of strictness inconsistent with the fundamental aims of equity.

In *Southwell v Blackburn* [2014] EWCA Civ 1347 the assurance was made in relation to Ms Blackburn's rights of occupation in the house that her partner Mr Southwell had purchased for them to live in, and of which he was the sole named owner. Tomlinson LJ noted the key factual elements from the judgment in the lower court that indicated the strength of the assurance: 'she would always have a home and be secure in this one,' and that Mr Southwell was taking on a 'long term commitment to provide her with a secure home', and 'he led her to believe that she would have the sort of security that a wife would have, in terms of accommodation at the house, and income.' [at para 9] These were as far as Tomlinson LJ was concerned a clear indication that the assurance of accommodation went beyond the break up of the relationship.

thinking point 10.4

Grace, an elderly lady, requires assistance at home and Olivia has been looking after her for five years. Recently, Grace's health has deteriorated and she now needs 24-hour care. She asked Olivia to move in and said 'if you look after me, then when I am gone, all of this will be yours'. Olivia, an aspiring racing car test driver, gave up her job and moved in with Grace.

Do you think that the words 'all of this will be yours' is sufficient to identify the interest in land?

This statement may be sufficient to amount to determining the nature of the expectation. Even though Grace's promise was made on the condition that Olivia moves in, this does not prevent 'an equity' from arising.

A Promise of Inheritance: Property to be Left by Will

Another issue raised by the scenario in thinking point 10.4, is whether the promise of inheritance on the condition that Olivia moves into the property and looks after Grace is sufficient to amount to an expectation. A testamentary will can be changed at any time. This was recognized as an issue in *Gillett v Holt* [2001] Ch 210. In this case the claimant worked as a farm manager and was friends with a wealthy landowner (Mr Holt), who had repeatedly promised over a number of years that the claimant would inherit the farm business (including the farmhouse). After 1992 their friendship deteriorated. The claimant was dismissed in 1995. Mr Holt altered his will and did not make any provision for the claimant. The claimant bought an action based on proprietary estoppel and succeeded. The Court of Appeal held that repeated assurances over a long period would entitle him to inherit the property. Although the claimant was successful in this case, Robert Walker LJ noted in relation to wills:

> the inherent revocability of testamentary dispositions (even if well understood by the parties, as Mr Gillett candidly accepted that it was by him) is irrelevant to a promise or assurance that 'all this will be yours'...Even when the promise or assurance is in terms linked to the making of a will...the circumstances may make clear that the assurance is more than a mere statement of present (revocable) intention, and is tantamount to a promise. *Attorney General of Hong Kong* v *Humphreys Estate (Queen's Gardens) Ltd* [1987] AC 114...is essentially an example of a purchaser taking the risk, with his eyes open, of going into possession and spending money while his purchase remains expressly subject to contract. Carnwath J observed that the advice to the claimant in *Taylor* v *Dickens* 'not to count his chickens before they were hatched' is [1998] 3 All ER 917, 929:
>
>> 'an apt statement of how, in normal circumstances, and in the absence of a specific promise, any reasonable person would regard—and should be expected by the law to regard—a representation by a living person as to his intentions for his will.'
>
> In the generality of cases that is no doubt correct, and it is notorious that some elderly persons of means derive enjoyment from the possession of testamentary power, and from dropping hints as to their intentions, without any question of an estoppel arising. But in this case Mr Holt's assurances were repeated over a long period, usually before the assembled company on special family occasions, and some of them (such as 'it was all going to be ours anyway'...) were completely unambiguous.

In this case there was more than a mere statement; the repeated assurances over a long period of time were sufficient to indicate that Mr Holt had intended to fulfil his promise. Robert Walker LJ highlighted the inherent problem with wills, but the court will consider the surrounding circumstances and endeavour to ascertain the intention of the landowner in these situations.

In *Henry* v *Henry* [2010] 1 All ER 998, Geraldine, an increasingly frail old lady, owned a half share in a plot of agricultural land in St Lucia. She promised the claimant, Calixtus Henry, that she would leave him her half share if he cultivated the plot and cared for her until her death. This he did for more than 30 years.

Calixtus and his family, as well as Geraldine, lived off the produce of the plot, Calixtus having no other income. However, shortly before she died, Geraldine transferred her share in the plot to Theresa.

The trial judge rejected Calixtus's claim to a proprietary estoppel interest. He found that the claimant, although relying on Geraldine's promises, had, looked at overall, not suffered any detriment. He had looked after Geraldine for 30 years, but he had reaped the produce and lived on the property rent-free. There had been reliance but no detriment.

This conclusion that there was no detriment was decisively rejected by the Judicial Committee of the Privy Council, speaking through Sir Jonathan Parker.

The Board was in no doubt that by devoting his life to Geraldine and the plot rather than to other activities, Calixtus had acted to his detriment and thereby acquired a proprietary estoppel interest.

Sir Jonathan Parker stated:

> 51. In the judgment of the Board, the judge clearly misdirected himself in his approach to the issue of detriment. He said in paragraph 12 of his judgment that Calixtus Henry could not say that he had acted to his detriment and that, far from having suffered detriment

because of his reliance on the deceased's promises, he positively benefited. But he did not attempt to weigh the disadvantages suffered by Calixtus Henry by reason of his reliance on Geraldine Pierre's promises against the countervailing advantages which he enjoyed as a consequence of that reliance. That is a process which, on principle, he should have undertaken (see *Jennings v. Rice* (above)). Instead, in paragraph 12 of his judgment the judge merely listed three advantages which he considered that Calixtus Henry had enjoyed in consequence of his reliance on Geraldine Pierre's promises: viz. the fact that he had lived rent-free on the plot, the fact that the plot was the source of his livelihood in large measure, and the fact that he had reaped the produce of the plot and was able to sell any surplus and retain all the proceeds of such sales. The judge made no reference to the evidence contained in paragraphs 5, 6 and 7 of Calixtus Henry's witness statement (see paragraph 21 above), or to the evidence that Calixtus Henry had kept Geraldine Pierre supplied with produce from the plot and that he had cared for her.

52. In *Campbell v. Griffin* (2001) 82 P. & C. R. DG23, Lord Walker (Robert Walker LJ, as he then was), when considering the issue as to how the equity which had been found to have arisen in that case should be satisfied, described the court's approach to that issue as a cautious one. The court had to look at all the circumstances in order to achieve the minimum equity to do justice to the claimant. However, he went on to observe (as he also observed in his judgment in *Gillett v. Holt* (above)) that the court enjoys a wide discretion in satisfying an equity arising under the doctrine of proprietary estoppel. Lord Walker then went on to weigh the disadvantages which the claimant had suffered by reason of his reliance on the defendant's assurances against the countervailing advantages which he had enjoyed by reason of that reliance (including, in that case, rent-free occupation of the property in issue). Lord Walker concluded that the claimants' rent-free occupation of the property had not extinguished his equity, but that in all the circumstances the grant of a life-interest in the property would be disproportionate to his legal and moral claims over the property. In the result, exercising the wide discretion to which he had earlier referred, he concluded that the appropriate form of relief was an award of a fixed monetary sum charged on the property.

53. In the instant case the judge should have undertaken a similar weighing process to that undertaken by Lord Walker in *Campbell v. Griffin*; that is to say, he should have weighed any disadvantages which Calixtus Henry had suffered by reason of his reliance on Geraldine Pierre's promises against any countervailing advantages which he had enjoyed by reason of that reliance. Had he done so, he would have brought into account on, as it were, the debit side of the account the evidence contained in paragraphs 5, 6 and 7 of Calixtus Henry's witness statement (see paragraph 21 above), including the fact that other members of the family had not responded to Geraldine's offer of 'an opportunity to possess land on the mountain... if they would work the land and cared for her in her own country as she did not want to leave St Lucia to live abroad or to live in St Croix', but instead had moved to St Croix where they were able to live more comfortably.

54. It may be that the judge was led to address the question of detriment with such brevity by his belief that his second reason for dismissing the proprietary estoppel claim was indeed 'more compelling'. In truth, however, his second reason was unsustainable, given the terms of section 28 of the Land Registration Act (St Lucia). As the Court of Appeal recognised, any equity acquired by Calixtus Henry in respect of the plot is an overriding interest within the meaning of that section and is accordingly binding on Theresa Henry.

55. As to the relationship between reliance and detriment in the context of the doctrine of proprietary estoppel, just as the inquiry as to reliance falls to be made in the context of the nature and quality of the particular assurances which are said to form the basis of the estoppel, so the inquiry as to detriment falls to be made in the context of the nature and quality of the particular conduct or course of conduct adopted by the claimant in reliance on those assurances. Thus, notwithstanding that reliance and detriment may, in the abstract, be regarded as different concepts, in applying the principles of proprietary estoppel they are often intertwined (see the extract from Lord Walker's judgment in *Gillett v. Holt* quoted in paragraph 37 above). In the instant case, that is certainly so.

56. Nor, in the opinion of the Board, is there any substance in Miss Stacey's submission that the issue of proprietary estoppel has to be considered afresh in relation to the position of Theresa Henry as a third party purchaser. The Board does not rule out the possibility that cases may arise in which the particular circumstances surrounding a third party purchase may, notwithstanding the claimant's overriding interest, require the court to reassess the extent of the claimant's equity in the property. However, in the instant case that issue simply does not arise since the Defence of Theresa Henry and Marie Ann Mitchel contains no plea to that effect, nor was any such case pursued on their behalf at trial.

57. Accordingly, the Board concludes that the judge's finding that Calixtus Henry 'could not say that he has acted to his detriment' cannot stand; and that the Court of Appeal was entitled to revisit that issue.

58. However, the reason which the Court of Appeal gave for setting aside the judge's finding that no detriment had been suffered is, in the opinion of the Board, itself unsustainable.

59. In paragraph 11 of his judgment, Gordon JA concludes that the judge misled himself in attempting 'to compare the advantage with the detriment'. That, however, is precisely the process which the judge should have undertaken in this case but in the event failed to undertake. The Board concludes that the Court of Appeal's erroneous approach to the issue of detriment undermines its finding that Calixtus Henry 'did suffer a detriment in reliance on that promise'. Gordon JA's observation that '[o]ne does not buy the equity' amply demonstrates this. Whilst that statement is of course literally correct, at least in the context of the instant case, the existence and extent of any equity arising under the doctrine of proprietary estoppel is nevertheless dependent on all the circumstances of the particular case, including the nature and quality of any detriment suffered by the claimant in reliance on the defendant's assurances.

60. Accordingly, it falls to the Board to address the question of detriment afresh.

61. In the opinion of the Board, it is clear from the evidence, and in particular from paragraphs 5, 6 and 7 of Calixtus Henry's witness statement (see paragraph 21 above), which the judge must implicitly have accepted, that by remaining on the plot—and by doing so not only for his own benefit and that of his family but for Geraldine Pierre's benefit too in providing her with food and in caring for her—Calixtus Henry effectively deprived himself of the opportunity of a better life elsewhere. The Board concludes that that detriment is not outweighed by the advantages referred to in paragraph 12 of the judge's judgment.

62. Overall, the strong impression which the evidence conveys to the Board is that in reliance on Geraldine Pierre's promises Calixtus Henry has opted for a hard life, in which he has had to struggle to make ends meet and to provide for his family, in circumstances where more attractive prospects beckoned elsewhere.

63. Accordingly the Board concludes that in the instant case the requirement of detriment is met, and that an equity has arisen in Calixtus Henry's favour under the doctrine of proprietary estoppel in respect of Theresa Henry's half share in the plot.

64. It remains to consider how, in all the circumstances, that equity should be satisfied.

65. In paragraph 12 of his judgment, Gordon JA said this:

'As I have stated above [i.e. in the previous paragraph], there is no power in the court to say that the promise (and the resulting benefit) is disproportionate to the detriment.'

With respect to Gordon JA, the Board considers that that statement betrays a fundamental misconception as to the nature and purpose of the doctrine of proprietary estoppel, as set out in the authorities to which we have referred. Proportionality lies at the heart of the doctrine of proprietary estoppel and permeates its every application.

66. The Board concludes that, in all the circumstances of the case, the appropriate relief in order to achieve the minimum equity required to do justice to Calixtus Henry is to award him one half of Theresa Henry's undivided half share in the plot.

The Board followed *Gillett v Holt* by making a holistic assessment of the circumstances, this involved weighing up the advantages and disadvantages suffered by Calixtus due to his reliance on Geraldine's assurances.

The relationship between reliance and detriment was examined briefly. It was acknowledged that although these concepts may be viewed in abstract as being different, the Board in this case was of the view that in reality when applying the principles of proprietary estoppel these concepts are intertwined.

Assurance with No Link to an Interest in Land

If the assurance given by the landowner is general and does not have any link to an interest in land, then this will not be sufficient to give rise to a claim in equity. In *Coombes v Smith* [1986] 1 WLR 808, general assurances were given to the claimant that 'she would always have a roof over her head' was 'quite different from a legal right to remain' (per Deputy Judge Jonathan Parker QC).

Expecting a Later Contract Not Sufficient

So far we have considered the nature of the representations in the family context. Problems can arise where there is a 'gentleman's agreement' for the sale of some land. In *Cobbe v Yeoman's Row Management Ltd* [2008] 1 WLR 1752, you will recall that Cobbe orally agreed in principle with Yeoman's Row to buy a site in central London. Both parties knew that this agreement was not a valid contract (it did not comply with s2 Law of Property (Miscellaneous Provisions) Act 1989). Nevertheless, Cobbe, with Yeoman's Row encouragement, spent a lot of time and trouble, spread over 18 months, obtaining planning permission to redevelop the site. This planning permission enhanced the value of the site by several million pounds. Yeoman's Row then refused to enter into a formal contract to sell the land to Cobbe.

The House of Lords held that, despite his efforts, Cobbe had not acquired a proprietary estoppel right. Lord Scott followed the reasoning in *AG of Hong Kong v Humphreys Estate (Queen's Gardens) Ltd* [1987] 1 AC 114, where the Privy Council examined an agreement which was 'subject to contract'. This agreement did not preclude estoppel but the claimants to succeed should have indicated that they had given up the right to change their mind and withdraw. In that case they had not. Lord Scott went on to explain:

> The reason why, in a 'subject to contract' case, a proprietary estoppel cannot ordinarily arise is that the would-be purchaser's expectation of acquiring an interest in the property in question is subject to a contingency that is entirely under the control of the other party to the negotiations . . . The expectation is therefore speculative . . .
>
> My Lords, I can easily accept that a subject-to-contract reservation made in the course of negotiations for a contract relating to the acquisition of an interest in land could be withdrawn, whether expressly or by inference from conduct. But debate about subject-to-contract reservations has only a peripheral relevance in the present case, for such a reservation is pointless in the context of oral negotiations relating to the acquisition of an interest in land. It would be an unusually unsophisticated negotiator who was not well aware that oral agreements relating to such an acquisition are by statute unenforceable and that no express reservation to make them so is needed. Mr Cobbe was an experienced property developer and Mrs Lisle-Mainwaring [a director and shareholder of Yeoman's Row] gives every impression of knowing her way around the negotiating table. Mr Cobbe did not spend his money and time on the planning application in the mistaken belief that the agreement was legally enforceable. He spent his money and time well aware that it was not. Mrs Lisle-Mainwaring did not encourage in him a belief that the second agreement was enforceable. She encouraged in him a belief that she would abide by it although it was not. Mr Cobbe's belief, or expectation, was always speculative. He knew she was not legally bound. He regarded her as bound 'in honour' but that is an acknowledgement that she was not legally bound.

In *Cobbe v Yeoman's Row Management Ltd* their Lordships held that there was no proprietary estoppel because Cobbe had spent his money, etc not in the expectation or understanding that he had or would get an interest in the land, but rather on the assumption that the parties would be able to negotiate a binding contract of sale. The expectation was purely speculative. He was not encouraged to believe that Yeoman's Row would abide by the 'gentleman's agreement'.

thinking point 10.5

In Cobbe v Yeoman's Row, *what if Cobbe was a private individual dabbling in property development for the first time? And he did not realize that the oral contract was legally invalid?*

It is suggested that Cobbe would only succeed if he could prove that at the time he put in the effort getting planning permission, he thought that the contract gave him at least a share in the property.

How has the Expectation been Created?

The representation may be made by the landowner to the claimant by words, conduct, or in a passive manner. In this context, it must be recalled that according to Lord Walker in *Thorner v Major*, the assurance must be 'clear and unequivocal' such that the claimant would reasonably believe that the assurance by way of a statement or action could be relied upon. Where the evidence provided by the claimant simply reflects private conversations they had with the landowner which had not been mentioned to other family members or friends, it can be difficult to establish the necessary ingredients of the assurance or promise which are subsequently relied upon to their detriment (*Creasley v Sole* [2013] EWHC 1410).

Pascoe v Turner [1979] 1 WLR 431 provides a good illustration of a positive assurance that the claimant will acquire rights. In this case a housekeeper who became Mr Pascoe's lover was given an assurance on a number of occasions that '[t]he house is yours and everything in it'. The Court of Appeal held that because Mr Pascoe had encouraged or acquiesced in the housekeeper making improvements to the house in the belief that the property belonged to her, this gave rise to an estoppel and to do justice to the housekeeper the court ordered the transfer of the property to her.

The father in *Inwards v Baker* [1965] 2 QB 29 had made representations to his son to build a bungalow on his land. This had given rise to an expectation of rights in land.

Ramsden v Dyson (1866) LR 1 HL 129 illustrates the passive assurance which will arise when the landowner stands by and knowingly does nothing to rectify the claimant's mistake that they have an interest in land. Lord Wensleydale explained that '[i]f a stranger builds on my land, supposing it to be his own, and I, knowing it to be mine, do not interfere, but leave him to go on, equity considers it to be dishonest in me to remain passive and afterwards to interfere and take the profit'.

Reliance

Reliance acts as a causal link between the representation and the claimant acting to their detriment by altering their position. In *Amalgamated Investment & Property Co Ltd v Texas Commerce International Bank Ltd* [1982] QB 84 Goff J considered how this change in position could be determined:

> ...the question is not whether the representee acted, or desisted from acting, solely in reliance on the encouragement or representation of the other party; the question is rather whether his conduct was so *influenced* by the encouragement or representation...that it would be unconscionable for the representor thereafter to enforce his strict legal rights.

It is sufficient to show that the claimant was 'influenced', that is, induced by the representation, and relied on the landowner's representation to their detriment. Reliance cannot be viewed in isolation; 'reliance and detriment are intertwined' (per Robert Walker LJ, *Gillett v Holt* [2001] Ch 210). Issues which arise in this section will also be relevant in the section dealing with detriment.

The change in the claimant's position can be demonstrated by a positive act. The courts have adopted a flexible approach towards determining the types of actions that would come within the scope of reliance.

Expenditure of money or undertaking improvements to the property are clearly demonstrable means by which a change of position can be shown (*Inwards v Baker* [1965] 2 QB 29; *Dillwyn v Llewelyn* (1862) 4 De GF & J 517).

Alternative methods have also been accepted by the courts. In *Jones (AE) v Jones (FW)* [1977] 1 WLR 438, a son left his job and house, and moved his family into his father's house, and gave his father money amounting to a quarter of the purchase price of the house, on the understanding that the house was his. He was granted a life interest in the property and a quarter share in the house.

There are instances where the courts have upheld a claim for proprietary estoppel where there is a presumption that the claimant relied upon the assurances made. In *Greasley v Cooke* [1980] 1 WLR 1306, Miss Cooke, a maid, was assured by members of the family that she could stay in the property for the rest of her life. She cohabited with one of the members of the family, she continued to look after the house, and also cared for another member of the family who was mentally ill. Lord Denning MR in the Court of Appeal held the defendant did not need to prove that she had relied upon assurances given to her; it was presumed, based on her conduct:

> ...instead of looking for another job, she stayed on in the house looking after Kenneth and Clarice. There is a presumption that she did so, relying on the assurances given to her by Kenneth and Hedley. The burden is not on her, but on them, to prove that she did not rely on their assurances. They did not prove it, nor did their representatives. So she is presumed to have relied on them.

Once the presumption has arisen then the burden shifts to the other party to prove that the claimant did not rely on the promises.

In *Coombes v Smith* [1986] 1 WLR 808, Deputy Judge Jonathan Parker QC explained how presumption of reliance operates as found in *Greasley v Cooke* [1980]. He said:

> The statement of Lord Denning M.R., at p. 1311H, that 'There is no need for her to prove that she acted to her detriment or to her prejudice' must not be taken out of context. Read in context, I take it to mean merely that where, following assurances made by the other party, the claimant has adopted a course of conduct which is prejudicial or otherwise detrimental to her, there is a rebuttable presumption that she adopted that course of conduct in reliance on the assurances.

The presumption of reliance would apply when the claimant adopts a particular course of conduct which indicates detrimental reliance.

In *Coombes* both the parties were married when they became lovers. The defendant bought a house and when the claimant became pregnant by the defendant she left her husband. She moved into the defendant's house and gave up her job before she had the baby. The defendant did not move in with her but visited her regularly and paid her bills. The defendant purchased another house and the claimant moved in with him. The defendant assured her that he would always provide for her and that she would always have a roof over her head. The relationship ended. She sought to continue to occupy the property until her child was 17 years old. The court held that she did not have any rights in the property.

The court in Coombes considered the claimant's course of conduct based on the assurances given by the defendant: she became pregnant by the defendant, she left her husband and moved in with the defendant, she looked after the property and her child. This, according to the court, was not sufficient to raise the presumption of reliance by course of conduct. Deputy Judge Jonathan Parker QC added that 'it would be wholly unreal, to put it mildly, to find on the evidence adduced before me that the plaintiff allowed herself to become pregnant by the defendant in reliance on some mistaken belief as to her legal rights. She allowed herself to become pregnant because she wished to live with the defendant and to bear his child.'

Coombes can be contrasted with the more recent approach adopted by the courts towards personal sacrifice. In *Wayling v Jones* (1995) 69 P & CR 170 the court took a more liberal approach. A gay couple cohabited for over 16 years. The claimant worked for the defendant, and in return he received pocket money and all his living and clothing expenses. The defendant also promised to leave him his house and businesses on a number of occasions. When the claimant asked for his pocket money to be increased the defendant assured him that 'it'll all be yours one day'. The defendant never altered his will and died. The claimant brought a claim in proprietary estoppel.

The Court of Appeal focused on the conduct being 'of such a nature that inducement may be inferred' (per Balcombe LJ). At first instance in evidence the claimant admitted that he would have stayed with the defendant even if the promise had not been made. This was fatal to his claim. Balcombe LJ in the Court of Appeal found that taking in account the circumstances there was sufficient reliance on the promise made by the defendant. This was based on evidence in chief given by the claimant:

> Q. One question, Mr Wayling. Assuming you were in the Royal Hotel Bar, before Dan's death and Dan was there, if Dan had told you that he was not going to give the Royal Hotel to you but to somebody else after his death, what would you have done?
>
> A. I would have left.

Balcombe LJ concluded:

> I am satisfied that his answers in cross-examination do not relate to the only question that mattered: 'What would you have done if the deceased had told you that he was no longer prepared to implement his promises?' To that question the plaintiff had given his answer in chief as already mentioned.
>
> On the application of the principles set out above to the facts of this case I am satisfied: (a) that the promises were made; (b) that the plaintiff's conduct was of such a nature that inducement may be inferred; (c) that the defendants have not discharged the burden upon them of establishing that the plaintiff did not rely on the promises.

Coombes and *Wayling* provide a stark contrast in their approaches and are difficult to reconcile. Cooke (1995, at pp 390–391) commenting on these cases notes the discrepancy in the court's approach in *Coombes*:

> ...the Court of Appeal found in Wayling's favour. Summarising the law on reliance, Balcombe L.J. stated that there must be a sufficient link between the promises and the detriment, but that the promises do not have to be the sole inducement for the detriment, citing *Amalgamated Investment & Property Co. Ltd. v. Texas Commerce International Bank Ltd.* [1982] Q.B. 84 at pp. 104–105...Balcombe L.J. then considered the apparently fatal response to cross-examination. In his evidence in chief Wayling had said that if Jones, having made the promise, had revealed that he did not intend to keep it, he would have left.

Wayling would have acted in the same way if no promise had been made; but given that it had been made, he would have acted very differently if he had known it was not going to be kept. That, in Balcombe L.J.'s view, was sufficient to prevent the defendant from showing that the plaintiff had not relied upon the promise. Leggatt and Hoffmann L.JJ. agreed, and an order was made that the proceeds of sale of the hotel be paid to the plaintiff.

That this is an unusual interpretation of reliance is best seen by comparing a case where it was held that there was no reliance. In *Coombes v. Smith* [1986] 1 W.L.R. 809 the plaintiff left her husband, moved into the defendant's house and bore his child. She claimed an interest in the property on the basis of proprietary estoppel. She failed for a number of reasons, among them the fact that she acted as she did, not in reliance upon the defendant's assurance that he would provide for her, but simply because she wanted to. Imagine her reaction if she had heard her partner say that he was not going to provide for her, in spite of his promise. Surely she would have left, because that would have undermined her relationship with him. She would thus have met the *Wayling* test. But it was held that she did not rely upon the assurance, because the giving of that assurance, and her expectation of an entitlement to the property, did not influence her actions.

Cooke further comments that *Wayling* is 'unusually generous' and it may be limited to a 'family property case'.

The approach adopted in *Wayling* was followed in *Campbell v Griffin* [2001] EWCA Civ 990. Mr Campbell, aged 30, moved in with the Ascoughs (who were both in their late 70s) as a lodger. After five years of lodging with the Ascoughs their relationship had changed, the Ascoughs regarded Mr Campbell with affection and treated him as a son. As the Ascoughs became increasingly frail they depended on him for help in various ways. The Ascoughs made assurances to Mr Campbell that he had a home for life. After the couple died, it was apparent that there was no will in Mr Campbell's favour. Mr Campbell brought an action against the estate.

Robert Walker LJ said:

25. On the issue of reliance the judge's finding was that Mr Campbell acted 'out of friendship and a sense of responsibility'. The judge did not refer to the judgment of Balcombe LJ in *Wayling* v *Jones* (1993) 69 P&CR 170, 173, in which Balcombe LJ (with whom Hoffmann LJ, and probably also Leggatt LJ, agreed) stated as a principle:

'Once it has been established that promises were made, and that there has been conduct by the plaintiff of such a nature that inducement may be inferred then the burden of proof shifts to the defendants to establish that he did not rely on the promises— *Greasley* v *Cooke* [1980] 1 WLR 1306; *Grant* v *Edwards* [1986] Ch 638, 657.'

26. In his witness statement Mr Campbell said that if he had not had the assurances which he had received, he would have moved out of 26 St Botolph's Road. He said much the same (with some prompting) in his oral evidence in chief, stating as his reason, 'I think I want a home.' This evidence seems to have involved a step in Mr Campbell's process of thought which he spelled out only in cross-examination, that in common humanity he could not have stayed on as a lodger but ignored the Ascoughs' obvious human needs:

'Q That is right. They needed the help, whether or not they said anything to you about you being entitled to live there for the rest of your life.

A Yes.

Q So you would have done these things, would you not, even if they had said nothing to you about living there for the rest of your life.

A Yes, I would not have walked past them, if he had been lying on the floor, and had not eaten for two days, you have to do something.

Q Yes. Indeed, this was almost a family sort of relationship, was it not?

A It was a very close relationship, yes.'

27. Cases of this sort ought not to be decided by meticulous analysis of every single answer made during cross-examination by an honest but diffident witness who was (to his credit) not trying to exaggerate his claim. It is more difficult to differ from the judge on the issue of reliance, since he did see and hear the witnesses and he was able to observe Mr Campbell's demeanour when he was giving the evidence which is set out above. But just as this court reversed the trial judge in *Wayling v Jones*, I have after anxious consideration concluded that the judge overlooked the presumption of reliance and failed to address his mind to the different phases of the long history of this relationship. From 1978 to 1982 it was a very friendly relationship of elderly landlords and lodger, with both sides very contented with the relationship. By 1990 at latest there was a much closer, family-type relationship, with assurances of a home for life being given from about 1987. By 1990 Mr Campbell was doing much more for the Ascoughs than could be ascribed to even the most friendly lodger. He had become part of the family, and there was a strong presumption that the assurances given to him (to treat him, in effect, as a member of the family with moral claims on the Ascoughs) were influencing his conduct.

28. The fact that Mr Campbell agreed, under skilful cross-examination, that he would not in any event have ignored his elderly landlord

'...if he had been lying on the floor, and had not eaten for two days'

is not sufficient to rebut that presumption. In my judgment the judge was wrong on the issue of reliance also. In cases of this sort it is inevitable that claimants should be asked hypothetical questions of the 'what if' variety but the court is not bound to attach great importance to the answers to such hypothetical questions. As Lord Denning MR said in *Greasley v Cooke* [1980] 1 WLR 1306, 1311,

'No one can say what she [the claimant] would have done if Kenneth and Hedley [the two brothers who owned the property] had not made those statements.'

29. The court must of course pay close attention, and give due weight, to the oral evidence given by the witnesses who have lived through the events into which the court has to enquire. But it would do no credit to the law if an honest witness who admitted that he had mixed motives were to fail in a claim which might have succeeded if supported by less candid evidence. As Balcombe LJ said in *Wayling v Jones* (at p.173)

'The promises relied upon do not have to be the sole inducement for the conduct: it is sufficient if they are an inducement.'

In my judgment the assurances given by the Ascoughs were an inducement to Mr Campbell's conduct, from 1990 at latest. With respect to the judge, I consider that he erred (either in his evaluation of the evidence, or in his application of the legal presumption) in his conclusion that there was no sufficient causal connection between the assurances given by the Ascoughs and the detriment suffered by Mr Campbell.

Mr Campbell was successful in his claim. Following *Wayling*, the court recognized that Mr Campbell had mixed motives for staying and caring for the Ascoughs, and that should not be held against him. On the one hand, he had a great affection towards them, and on the other, there was an assurance that the property would be his. According to Robert Walker LJ the focus should be on the assurances given which were an inducement and this had a bearing on his conduct.

Detriment

Detriment arises when the claimant has changed their position relying on an assurance. The important factor here is the reliance on the promise to their detriment. It would at that stage be unconscionable for the landowner to deny the rights in land to the claimant.

Detriment may arise through expenditure of money which is perhaps the most obvious form. For example, in *Inwards v Baker* the son built a bungalow on his father's land; in *Pascoe v Turner* the claimant made improvements to the property.

In the vast majority of cases the courts have recognized that detriment can come in different forms. Robert Walker LJ in *Gillett v Holt* [2001] Ch 210 explained the modern approach towards detriment:

> The overwhelming weight of authority shows that detriment is required. But the authorities also show that it is not a narrow or technical concept. The detriment need not consist of the expenditure of money or other quantifiable financial detriment, so long as it is something substantial. The requirement must be approached as part of a broad inquiry as to whether repudiation of an assurance is or is not unconscionable in all the circumstances.
>
> There are some helpful observations about the requirement for detriment in the judgment of Slade LJ in *Jones v Watkins* 26 November 1987. There must be sufficient causal link between the assurance relied on and the detriment asserted. The issue of detriment must be judged at the moment when the person who has given the assurance seeks to go back on it. Whether the detriment is sufficiently substantial is to be tested by whether it would be unjust or inequitable to allow the assurance to be disregarded—that is, again, the essential test of unconscionability. The detriment alleged must be pleaded and proved.

This indicates that the courts are not willing to restrict themselves in interpreting detriment; it will depend on the circumstances but the detriment must be 'something substantial'. Merely moving into a property is not sufficient. In *Coombes v Smith*, the court rejected a claim for proprietary estoppel and viewed the move as a benefit. Contrast this with the facts of the case in *Tanner v Tanner* [1975] 1 WLR 1346, where Mrs Tanner gave up a secured tenancy to cohabit with Mr Tanner. This case was decided on the basis of a contractual licence, but if this was considered as a claim for proprietary estoppel, Mrs Tanner would have arguably given up 'something substantial'.

In *Southwell v Blackburn* [2014] which was decided on the basis of proprietary estoppel, Ms Blackburn had given up a secured tenancy on a house, on which she had spent between £15,000–£20,000 fitting out and furnishing the property, to move in with Mr Southwell. She had also given up her job and moved her children in with them, and contributed a small amount to the house Mr Southwell purchased. The property they lived in together was purchased by Mr Southwell in his sole name. There was an assurance that Ms Blackburn would 'always have a home' and 'be secure' in their house. The Court of Appeal viewed this as detrimental reliance and consequently that repudiation of the promise was unconscionable.

In *Davies v Davies* [2014] EWCA Civ 568 the court considered that in assessing detriment it should not to be undertaken in a manner which is similar to forensic accounting. The factual matrix of *Davies v Davies* was complicated by the relationship Ms Davies had with her parents in the period from 1989–2012. She worked on her parents' farm, initially for very little money. She was led to believe that she would inherit the farm. After falling out with her parents on numerous occasions, she moved in and out of the farm over a number of years, working and then ceasing to work on the farm and gaining employment elsewhere. The court confirmed that when assessing detriment, a wide range of factors are to be taken into account following the holistic approach in *Gillett v Holt* [2001].

In the following cases, the courts have recognized detriment which is of a personal nature:

cross-reference
See 10.4 for a discussion of Tanner v Tanner.

- worked as a gardener and handyman for nothing after an assurance of house and furniture: *Jennings v Rice* (2003) 1 P & CR 8;
- looked after family members without payment: *Greasley v Cooke* [1980] 1 WLR 1306;
- gave up accommodation and job: *Jones (AE) v Jones (FW)* [1977] 1 WLR 438;
- companion, chauffeur, substantial help in running the businesses, and in return received pocket money, living and clothing expenses: *Wayling v Jones* (1995) 69 P & CR 170;

- gave up the opportunity to continue education and had carried out duties beyond which an employee would normally be expected to do: *Gillett v Holt* [2001] Ch 210; and

- an aspiring actress gave up the opportunity to look for work to look after the landowner and assist him in his attempt to battle against alcoholism: *Ottey v Grundy* [2003] EWCA Civ 1176.

Unconscionability

The final element to be considered is unconscionability. This would arise where it is unconscionable for the land owner to enforce their strict legal rights where the claimant has relied to their detriment on a representation made by the land owner. Whether unconscionability is a separate element that needs to be satisfied in a claim for proprietary estoppel has been commented upon by Lord Walker in *Cobbe v Yeoman's Row Management Ltd*:

> 92 ... That argument raises the question whether 'unconscionability' is a separate element in making out a case of estoppel, or whether to regard it as a separate element would be what Professor Peter Birks once called 'a fifth wheel on the coach': *Birks & Pretto [eds], Breach of Trust* (2002), p 226. But Birks was there criticising the use of 'unconscionable' to describe a *state of mind* ... Here it is being used (as in my opinion it should always be used) as an objective value judgment on *behaviour* (regardless of the state of mind of the individual in question). As such it does in my opinion play a very important part in the doctrine of equitable estoppel, in unifying and confirming, as it were, the other elements. If the other elements appear to be present but the result does not shock the conscience of the court, the analysis needs to be looked at again.

One may well conclude that unconscionability is interlinked with the other elements of proprietary estoppel.

10.7 Satisfying the Equity

Once the three elements of proprietary estoppel have been fulfilled, the claimant is in a position to bring a claim for proprietary estoppel (ie an equity has arisen) against the landowner or his estate, and prevent him from asserting his rights. The court will consider how to satisfy the equity by awarding the appropriate remedy.

In determining the type of remedy to award, the underlying principle was expressed by the Privy Council in *Plimmer v Mayor etc, of Wellington* (1884) 9 App Cas 699 by Sir Arthur Hobhouse where he said '[t]he court must look at the circumstances in each case to decide in what way the equity can be satisfied'.

The courts have a wide discretion in the type of remedy, for example it may involve the transfer of property to the claimant (*Pascoe v Turner* [1979] 1 WLR 431); in *Campbell v Griffin* [2001] EWCA Civ 990 the court felt that it was inappropriate to award Mr Campbell the property since he was a lodger, and instead awarded him £35,000. Despite the wide discretion the courts must not use it in an arbitrary manner, 'the court must take a principled approach and cannot exercise a completely unfettered discretion according to the individual judge's notion of what is fair in any particular case' (per Robert Walker LJ, *Jennings v Rice* (2003) 1 P & CR 8).

In doing so, the court when considering the 'extent of the equity and the relief needed to satisfy it' would ask itself what is the 'minimum equity to do justice to the plaintiff'? (per Lord

Denning MR, *Crabb v Arun District Council* [1976] Ch 179). Implied in this, is that the court would seek to avoid greater relief than the claimant's expectation from the representation.

What remedy the claimant obtains can depend on the approach adopted by the court: first, this is based on the loss from having relied on the assurance, and, secondly, fulfilment of the claimant's expectations.

Reliance loss is based on the premise of compensating the claimant for the loss suffered as a consequence of relying on the assurance. The claimant would under these circumstances receive financial compensation covering the amount spent.

The second approach appears to have been favoured by the courts where the remedy gives effect to the claimant's expectations as far as possible. In *Pascoe v Turner* [1979] 1 WLR 431, the claimant's expectation was to obtain the house, and she acted to her detriment relying on the promise made by the landowner. The representation was specific and there was no doubt as to the interest in land involved. The court having taken into account the financial situation of both parties, the landowner was a wealthy businessman and the claimant was on a meagre income, awarded the claimant the property. The transfer of a property is seen as an exception, but the court's approach of taking into account the circumstances indicates that there is flexibility in the factors that will be considered.

In the majority of cases where the interest in land has not been specified this is where the courts may find difficulty in quantifying the remedy. The overall aim of conferring a remedy is not to provide for a greater remedy than the expectation (*Dodsworth v Dodsworth* (1973) 228 EC 1115).

In *Gillett v Holt* [2001] Ch 210, Robert Walker LJ said that the court would need to identify:

the maximum extent of the equity. The court's aim is, having identified the maximum, to form a view as to what is the minimum required to satisfy it and do justice between the parties. The court must look at all the circumstances, including the need to achieve a 'clean break' so far as possible and avoid or minimise future friction . . .

In *Sledmore v Dalby* (1996) 72 P & CR 196, Mr and Mrs Sledmore jointly purchased a house in 1962. In 1965, Mr Dalby married their daughter, and they moved into the Sledmores' house as tenants. The Sledmores accepted rent from them until 1976 when Mr Dalby became unemployed and the Sledmores' daughter had become ill. The Dalbys continued to pay their outgoings.

Between 1976 and 1979, Dalby carried out substantial improvements to the house, and was encouraged to do so by Mr Sledmore. Mrs Sledmore knew that her husband had formed the intention to give the property to the Dalbys and that he had told them of this. In 1979, Mr Sledmore conveyed his interest of the freehold of the house to Mrs Sledmore. Mrs Sledmore changed her will, so that only their daughter would inherit the property. Mr Sledmore died in 1980. Mr Dalby's wife died in 1983, and Dalby continued to occupy the house rent-free. He was asked to pay rent but refused.

Mrs Sledmore brought an action for possession against Mr Dalby in 1990. During this period of time Mr Dalby was employed and only spent a few nights a week in the house. Only one of Mr Dalby's daughters still lived at the house, and she was now aged 27 and employed. Mrs Sledmore's own house was in need of repair and she herself was now in financial difficulties. She was on income support and the Department of Social Security was paying the interest on her mortgage, which was in arrears. The Court of Appeal granted Mrs Sledmore possession of the property.

Despite the fact that Mr Dalby had shown that an equity had arisen in his favour, the court took into account the parties' circumstances. Mr Dalby was in employment and did not live in the property all the time, whereas Mrs Sledmore had a more pressing need. Roch LJ explained why Mr Dalby's claim in proprietary estoppel was defeated:

> The conclusion that I have reached is that it is no longer inequitable to allow the expectation created in the respondent's mind by Mr Sledmore's oral statements and by his encouragement of the respondent to carry out the improvements to the house which were carried out between 1976 and 1979 to be defeated. The respondent has lived rent free in this accommodation for over 18 years. During that time the insurance of the property has been paid for by the Sledmore family and the property has been re-roofed at their expense. The use made by the respondent of the house at the time of the trial was minimal and it is clear that there was accommodation for him elsewhere. He is a man in employment and therefore capable of paying for his accommodation. Whilst the respondent has lived in this house his elder daughter has married and left home and his younger daughter has reached the age of 27 and is able to maintain herself.
>
> On the other hand, the evidence indicates that the appellant is vulnerable in that she is liable to lose her present accommodation and that she has a pressing need for this house which is her property . . .
>
> I would allow this appeal and make an order for possession in the appellant's favour on the basis that the minimum equity to do justice to the respondent on the facts of this case was an equity which has now expired.

The assessment was based on the fact that Mr Dalby had the benefit of living in the property for over 18 years rent-free and that although he had spent money on the property, his equity had expired.

10.7.1 A Wide Interpretation of Satisfying the Equity

The Court of Appeal in *Jennings v Rice* (2003) 1 P & CR 8 did not confine themselves to a particular method in satisfying the equity. They chose a wide interpretation which took into account all the circumstances and ensures the remedy is proportionate.

In *Jennings v Rice*, Mrs Royle died intestate in 1997. Her estate was worth £1.285 million net with the house and furniture being valued at £435,000. Mr Jennings worked as a gardener for Mrs Royle. Initially he started to work for Mrs Royle on a part-time basis. The number of hours he worked increased and the demands made on him by Mrs Royle put a strain on his marriage because his wife disliked Mrs Royle.

Mrs Royle stopped paying Mr Jennings in the late 1980s. In the 1990s Mrs Royle became increasingly incapacitated and consequently dependent on Mr Jennings. Mr Jennings continued to look after Mrs Royle, though when he asked to be paid she told him 'he did not need to worry about that, he would be alright and she would 'see to it'. At all times she said to him 'this will all be yours one day' or words to that effect'.

In 1993 Mrs Royle was burgled. She persuaded Mr Jennings to stay overnight to provide her with security. Mr Jennings was reluctant at first, but eventually he did agree to do so and, from some time in 1994 until her death in 1997, he spent nearly every night on a sofa in a sitting room at her house.

The Court of Appeal upheld the £200,000 award at first instance (this award included the estimated cost of nursing care and the value of the house).

Lord Justice Robert Walker said:

> 42. This court was referred to two recent articles which contain a full and illuminating discussion of this area: Estoppel and the Protection of Expectations by Elizabeth Cooke [1997] 17 L.S. 258 and The Remedial Discretion in Proprietary Estoppel by Simon Gardner (1999)

115 LQR 438. Those articles could with advantage have been cited in *Gillett* v *Holt* [2001] Ch 210. Both are concerned with whether the fundamental aim of this form of estoppel is to fulfil the claimant's expectations, or to compensate him for his detrimental reliance on the defendant's non-contractual assurances, or is some intermediate objective; and (following on from the identification of the correct principle) the nature of the discretion which the court exercises in granting a remedy to the claimant. The articles amply demonstrate that the range of English authorities provides some support for both theories and for a variety of intermediate positions; and that recent Australian authority (especially the decision of the High Court in *Commonwealth* v *Verwayen* (1990) 170 CLR 394) has moved in favour of the reliance loss theory.

43. It cannot be doubted that in this as in every other area of the law, the court must take a principled approach, and cannot exercise a completely unfettered discretion according to the individual judge's notion of what is fair in any particular case....

44. The need to search for the right principles cannot be avoided. But it is unlikely to be a short or simple search, because (as appears from both the English and the Australian authorities) proprietary estoppel can apply in a wide variety of factual situations, and any summary formula is likely to prove to be an over-simplification. The cases show a wide range of variation in both of the main elements, that is the quality of the assurances which give rise to the claimant's expectations and the extent of the claimant's detrimental reliance on the assurances. The doctrine applies only if these elements, in combination, make it unconscionable for the person giving the assurances (whom I will call the benefactor, although that may not always be an appropriate label) to go back on them.

45. Sometimes the assurances, and the claimant's reliance on them, have a consensual character falling not far short of an enforceable contract (if the only bar to the formation of a contract is non-compliance with section 2 of the Law of Property (Miscellaneous Provisions) Act 1989, the proprietary estoppel may become indistinguishable from a constructive trust: *Yaxley* v *Gotts* [2000] Ch 162). In a case of that sort both the claimant's expectations and the element of detriment to the claimant will have been defined with reasonable clarity. A typical case would be an elderly benefactor who reaches a clear understanding with the claimant (who may be a relative, a friend, or a remunerated companion or carer) that if the claimant resides with and cares for the benefactor, the claimant will inherit the benefactor's house (or will have a home for life). In a case like that the consensual element of what has happened suggests that the claimant and the benefactor probably regarded the expected benefit and the accepted detriment as being (in a general, imprecise way) equivalent, or at any rate not obviously disproportionate ...

46. However the claimant's expectations may not be focused on any specific property. In *Re Basham* [1986] 1 WLR 1489 the deputy judge (Mr Edward Nugee QC) rejected the submission that there must be some clearly identified piece of property, and that decision has been approved more than once in this court. Moreover ... the claimant's expectations may have been formed on the basis of vague and inconsistent assurances. The judge said of Mrs Royle that she

> '... was prone to saying different things at different times and, perhaps deliberately, couched her promises in non-specific terms.'

He made that observation in relation to the failure of the contract claim, but it is relevant to the estoppel claim also.

47. If the claimant's expectations are uncertain (as will be the case with many honest claimants) then their specific vindication cannot be the appropriate test. A similar problem arises if the court, although satisfied that the claimant has a genuine claim, is not satisfied that the high level of the claimant's expectations is fairly derived from his deceased patron's assurances, which may have justified only a lower level of expectation. In such cases the court may still take the claimant's expectations (or the upper end of any range of expectations) as a starting point, but unless constrained by authority I would regard it as no more than a starting point.

48. I do not see that approach as being inconsistent with authority. On the contrary, I think it is supported by a substantial body of English authority. Scarman LJ's well-known reference to 'the minimum equity to do justice to the plaintiff' (*Crabb* v *Arun District Council* [1976] Ch 179, 198) must no doubt be read in the context of the rather unusual facts of that case, but it does not stand alone. As Scarman LJ recognised, the line of authority goes back to nineteenth-century cases such as *Duke of Beaufort* v *Patrick* (1853) 17 Beav 60 and *Plimmer* v *Wellington Corporation* (1884) 9 App Cas 699. A passage in the opinion of the Privy Council (delivered by Sir Arthur Hobhouse) in Plimmer's case at pp.713–4 is particularly instructive. The conclusion of the passage is that

> 'In fact the court must look at the circumstances in each case to decide in what way the equity can be satisfied'

Scarman LJ's reference to the minimum does not require the court to be constitutionally parsimonious, but it does implicitly recognise that the court must also do justice to the defendant.

49. It is no coincidence that these statements of principle refer to satisfying the equity (rather than satisfying, or vindicating, the claimant's expectations). The equity arises not from the claimant's expectations alone, but from the combination of expectations, detrimental reliance, and the unconscionableness of allowing the benefactor (or the deceased benefactor's estate) to go back on the assurances . . .

50. To recapitulate: there is a category of case in which the benefactor and the claimant have reached a mutual understanding which is in reasonably clear terms but does not amount to a contract. I have already referred to the typical case of a carer who has the expectation of coming into the benefactor's house, either outright or for life. In such a case the court's natural response is to fulfil the claimant's expectations. But if the claimant's expectations are uncertain, or extravagant, or out of all proportion to the detriment which the claimant has suffered, the court can and should recognise that the claimant's equity should be satisfied in another (and generally more limited) way.

51. But that does not mean that the court should in such a case abandon expectations completely, and look to the detriment suffered by the claimant as defining the appropriate measure of relief. Indeed in many cases the detriment may be even more difficult to quantify, in financial terms, than the claimant's expectations. Detriment can be quantified with reasonable precision if it consists solely of expenditure on improvements to another person's house, and in some cases of that sort an equitable charge for the expenditure may be sufficient to satisfy the equity . . . But the detriment of an ever-increasing burden of care for an elderly person, and of having to be subservient to his or her moods and wishes, is very difficult to quantify in money terms. Moreover the claimant may not be motivated solely by reliance on the benefactor's assurances, and may receive some countervailing benefits (such as free bed and board). In such circumstances the court has to exercise a wide judgmental discretion.

52. It would be unwise to attempt any comprehensive enumeration of the factors relevant to the exercise of the court's discretion, or to suggest any hierarchy of factors . . . To these can safely be added the court's recognition that it cannot compel people who have fallen out to live peaceably together, so that there may be a need for a clean break; alterations in the benefactor's assets and circumstances, especially where the benefactor's assurances have been given, and the claimant's detriment has been suffered, over a long period of years; the likely effect of taxation; and (to a limited degree) the other claims (legal or moral) on the benefactor or his or her estate. No doubt there are many other factors which it may be right for the court to take into account in particular factual situations.

53. The judge did in this case consider, although not in detail, what Mr Jennings might reasonably have earned in the way of arm's length remuneration for his services. He also considered what professional nursing care might have cost during the last eight years of Mrs Royle's life.

54. . . . In my view it would rarely if ever be appropriate to go into detailed inquiries as to hours and hourly rates where the claim was based on proprietary estoppel (rather than a restitutionary claim for services which were not gratuitous). But the going rate for live-in carers can provide a useful cross-check in the exercise of the court's discretion.

56. However I respectfully agree with the view expressed by Hobhouse LJ in *Sledmore* v *Dalby* (1996) 72 P&CR 196, that the principle of proportionality (between remedy and detriment), emphasised by Mason CJ in *Verwayen*, is relevant in England also. As Hobhouse LJ observed at p.209, to recognise the need for proportionality

'…is to say little more than that the end result must be a just one having regard to the assumption made by the party asserting the estoppel and the detriment which he has experienced.'

The essence of the doctrine of proprietary estoppel is to do what is necessary to avoid an unconscionable result, and a disproportionate remedy cannot be the right way of going about that.

The judgment highlights that an intermediate approach ought to be adopted in satisfying the equity, where elements of the expectation and reliance loss are taken into consideration.

The basis of the wider approach given by the Court of Appeal has as its basis *Crabbe*'s aim of doing justice when satisfying the equity. The difficulty the courts can be faced with is if the claimant's expectations are uncertain. Under those circumstances the court in *Jennings* did not think it appropriate to satisfy the claimant's expectations, though the expectation would simply be a useful starting point. In addressing how the equity would be satisfied under these circumstances it was suggested that 'the claimant's equity should be satisfied in another (and generally more limited) way' (per Robert Walker LJ). It was suggested that this would be achieved by taking into account all the circumstances (including expectation and detriment), and underlying this assessment is the requirement of proportionality. Proportionality in this situation is being used as a means of achieving a fair balance between an expectation and the detriment suffered by the claimant. If, for example, the expectation is vague, then it is unlikely that the claimant will receive a huge windfall, rather the courts will satisfy the equity in a way which avoids an unconscionable result.

The Board in *Henry v Henry* [2010] 1 All ER 998 (PC) confirmed that 'proportionality lies at the heart of the doctrine of proprietary estoppel and permeates its very application'. In *Suggitt v Suggitt* [2012] EWCA Civ 140 the court considered whether the relief granted by the judge had been disproportionate. Frank Suggitt owned 400 acres of farmland and a house (called Wellfield). During Frank Suggitt's lifetime his son, John, helped his father with jobs around the farm. Although John received no wage, his father paid for his accommodation, living expenses, and college fees. John was also given a share in the grain harvest and sheep sales. Frank decided that his son was not fit to run the farm and had entered into farming agreements with other local farmers. Frank left his entire estate to his daughter, Caroline, on the condition that if she was in the absolute opinion that John was capable of running and managing the farm she would transfer the farmland to him. Following Frank's death, Caroline did not effect the transfer. In the High Court the judge determined that Frank had made repeated unconditional assurances to John, his son, that led him to reasonably expect that the farmland would be his following his father's death. John had, according to the judge, acted to some measure to his detriment or changed his position in reliance on his father's promises in the expectation he would inherit. The High Court awarded John the farmland and the houses worth in total £3.3 million.

In the Court of Appeal, Arden LJ, in determining whether the relief was disproportionate, considered the suggested application of the principle of proportionality which Walker LJ had expressed in para 50 in *Jennings v Rice* (see previously):

44 …this principle does not mean that there has to be a relationship of proportionality between the level of detriment and the relief awarded. What Walker LJ holds in this paragraph is that if the expectations are extravagant or 'out of all proportion to the detriment which the claimant has suffered', the court can and should recognise that the claimant's equity should

be satisfied in another and generally more limited way. So the question is: was the relief that the judge granted 'out of all proportion to the detriment' suffered?

45. In my judgment, this particular question is again a question of evaluation and judgment. That judgment was exercised by the judge in favour of John in his award of the farmland and indeed of Wellfield...I do not, however, consider that in principle, we can interfere with the exercise by the judge of his evaluation of what was out of all proportion unless it is shown to have been clearly wrong. Since the promise was that John should have the farmland unconditionally, I do not consider that to grant him the farmland, whatever that means, could be said to be out of all proportion.

Even though the farmland and the house were valuable, Arden LJ stated 'the fact that, on the judge's findings, the assurances were made and the values only reflect the assurances.' The Court of Appeal upheld the High Court's decision.

10.8 Status of 'An Equity' Before it Has Been Satisfied

When the courts have satisfied the equity, the court may grant a proprietary interest in land. This proprietary right would be subject to the normal rules of protecting proprietary interests whether in registered or unregistered land.

What is unclear is the exact status of 'an equity' that has arisen but has not been satisfied by the court. This equitable right is called an inchoate equity. Does the inchoate equity bind a third party? Consider this example: a landowner has made a representation to the claimant that the property will be theirs. The claimant has in turn relied upon the expectation to their detriment. In the meantime the landowner sells the property. Under these circumstances an equity has arisen but there are questions which arise from this:

• What is the status of the equity that has arisen, is it a personal right or a proprietary right?

• Can the claimant enforce their 'inchoate equity' against the purchaser?

There are two views on this. First, the inchoate equity is not an interest in land, the courts have not as yet satisfied the equity as a proprietary right, nor does it come within the scope of rights or interests recognized under the LPA 1925.

The second view suggests that once the inchoate equity comes into existence then it is capable of binding a successor in title. It is this view which has been reflected in s116 Land Registration Act 2002 (LRA 2002).

Land Registration Act 2002

116. Proprietary estoppel and mere equities

It is hereby declared for the avoidance of doubt that, in relation to registered land, each of the following—

    (a) an equity by estoppel, and

    (b) a mere equity,

has effect from the time the equity arises as an interest capable of binding successors in title (subject to the rules about the effect of dispositions on priority).

[Emphasis added]

It is important to remember that where an inchoate equity has not yet been satisfied, it is still for the court to decide what is the appropriate remedy.

In the Privy Council case *Henry v Henry* [2010] 1 All ER 998, the Board affirmed that an equity acquired through proprietary estoppel would take effect as an inchoate equity, and could be an overriding interest which binds a third party subject.

Smith (2011, at p 166) explains the problem with the operation of s 116 LRA 2002:

> Why is it controversial as to whether estoppels should bind purchasers? The most obvious problem is that nobody knows exactly what C is entitled to. This may be because the nature of the assumption or expectation is unclear or because the remedy lies in the court's discretion. One might reply that the court's decision as to remedy is retrospective, but this fails to recognise the need of purchasers to know what is binding upon them. More difficulties arise if a monetary remedy is thought proper: how could that be treated as something that could bind a purchaser? A right to money is not by itself an interest in land. Section 116 is more understandable if we view the estoppel itself as binding the purchaser, rather than the interest eventually given. What binds the purchase is C's right to the exercise of the court's discretion. An order that money be paid would then be a direct order that the *purchaser* should pay. By way of contrast, McFarlane has argued that we should not distinguish between the position before and after the court order—a purchaser is bound by the remedy C is entitled to, provided that it is proprietary in nature. However, this underplays the role of discretion as regards the remedy and is difficult to reconcile with s.116.

In unregistered land, the binding nature of an inchoate equity is more problematic. It does not come within the scope of the land charges legislation, nor is it generally capable of being overreached (s2 LPA 1925). It has been held that where a purchaser has actual notice of the inchoate equity, it will bind them (*Lloyds Bank v Carrick* [1996] 4 All ER 630). If the purchaser only has constructive notice, then the authorities are divided as to whether the inchoate equity will bind the purchaser. See *Bristol and West Building Society v Henning* [1985] 1 WLR 778 at 781; see *Re Sharpe* [1980] 1 WLR 219 at 226.

Concluding Remarks

This chapter has outlined the difficulty that arises with informal transactions. The courts have sought to find an appropriate solution by restricting the proprietary scope of licences and also endeavouring to provide a remedy where there has been an unconscionable denial of rights. Equity has provided for flexibility in proprietary estoppel, but the consequence of this approach is that the remedies are not always certain from the outset.

Summary

Licence

Permission to do something legally, otherwise without which it would be illegal.

Bare Licences

- simplest form of licence;
- creation requires no formalities;
- scope is limited—only applies to what it has been granted for;
- revocation—the licence will end on giving reasonable notice.

Licences Coupled with an Interest

- Proprietary right has been granted and associated with this right is the licence to enter the land, for example profit.
- The grant of the proprietary right must comply with the formalities of creating a legal interest. The licence will be created in addition to this proprietary right.

Contractual Licence

- licence which has been given for consideration;
- creation—normally created expressly and governed by principles of contract law;
- a contractual licence does not bind a third party (*Ashburn Anstalt v Arnold; King v David Allen*);
- revocation:
  - *common law*: revocable at will (*Wood v Leadbitter*);
  - *equity*:
    - imply a term into the contract which prevents the licensor revoking the licence;
    - equitable remedies;
    - does a licence bind a third party? No (*King v David Allen; Ashburn Anstalt v Arnold*).

Estoppel Licences

Estoppel licences can arise where a representation has been made, for example permission to enter or occupy land, and the licensor will be prevented from revoking the licence because the licensee has relied on the representation to their detriment (*Inwards v Baker*). An estoppel licence is now regarded as a form of proprietary estoppel.

Proprietary Estoppel

Representation/Expectation

- Nature of the expectation:
  - *commercial context*: must be sufficiently certain, and the expectation should be a 'certain interest in land' (*Yeoman's Row v Cobbe*);
  - *domestic/family context*: nature of rights need not be specific as long as there is an interest or right in land (*Gillett v Holt; Jennings v Rice; Thorner v Major*).

Reliance

- Causal link between representation/expectation and detriment.
- Claimant must change their position, for example can be demonstrated by a positive act:
  - expenditure of money;
  - improvements to the property;
  - giving up a job opportunity;
  - caring for elderly persons.

Detriment

- What amounts to detriment depends on the circumstances but it must be 'something substantial' (*Gillett v Holt*). Examples include:
  - worked as a gardener and handyman for nothing after an assurance of house and furniture: *Jennings v Rice* [2003] 1 P & CR 8;
  - looked after family members without payment: *Greasley v Cooke* [1980] 1 WLR 1306;
  - gave up accommodation and job: *Jones (AE) v Jones (FW)* [1977] 1 WLR 438;
  - companion, chauffeur, substantial help in running the businesses, and in return received pocket money, living and clothing expenses: *Wayling v Jones* (1995) 69 P & CR 170;
  - gave up the opportunity to continue education and had carried out duties beyond which an employee would normally be expected to do: *Gillett v Holt* [2001] Ch 210;
  - an aspiring actress gave up the opportunity to look for work to look after the landowner and assist him in his attempt to battle against alcoholism: *Ottey v Grundy* [2003] EWCA Civ 1176;
  - working on a farm for no financial reward: *Thornton v Major* and *Henry v Henry*.

Unconscionability

This pervades each of the other elements of proprietary estoppel.

Satisfying the Equity

The courts exercise a wide discretion in awarding a remedy, though the courts will avoid granting greater relief than the claimant's expectation.

Examples of remedies awarded:

- transfer of property (*Pascoe v Turner*);
- the court in *Sledmore v Dalby* felt that the equity had already been satisfied whilst Mr Dalby lived in the property rent-free for 18 years;
- the court in *Jennings v Rice* awarded £200,000 rather than the whole estate which was worth £1.285 million. The court preferred to take into account all circumstances and avoided granting greater relief than the claimant's expectation.

📖 Further Reading

Bright, S and McFarlane, B, 'Proprietary estoppel and property rights' [2005] 64 CLJ 449
Considers when proprietary estoppel gives rise to a property right.

Cooke, E, 'Reliance and estoppel' (1995) 111 LQR 389
Examines the judgment in *Wayling v Jones*.

Dixon, M, 'Confining and defining proprietary estoppel: the role of unconscionability' (2010) 30 Legal Studies 408
Considers the role of unconscionability and its scope in proprietary estoppel.

McFarlane, B, 'Proprietary estoppel and third parties after the Land Registration Act 2002' (2003) 62 (3) CLJ 661
An analysis of whether proprietary estoppel gives rise to a proprietary interest or a personal one.

McFarlane, B and Robertson, A, 'The death of proprietary estoppel' [2008] LMCLQ 449
Critical article reviewing the House of Lords decisions in *Cobbe* and *Thorner*.

Mee, J, 'Proprietary Estoppel and Inheritance: Enough is Enough?' [2013] Conv 280
Article highly critical of the generosity of the remedy awarded to the claimant in *Suggitt v Suggitt*.

Neuberger, Lord, 'The stuffing of Minerva's owl? Taxonomy and taxidermy in equity' (2009) 68(3) CLJ 537
An overview of the doctrine of proprietary estoppel and examines recent developments in the area.

Pawlowski, M, 'Causal link and consensual arrangements in estoppel' [2008] Conv 253
Discussion on satisfying the equity where a promise of inheritance of property is made but the detriment has not been defined by the parties.

Smith, RJ, 'Licences and constructive trusts—"the law is what it ought to be" ' (1973) 32(1) CLJ 12
Article discusses contractual licences following *Binions v Evans*.

Wells, R, 'The element of detriment in proprietary estoppel' [2001] Conv 13
Discussion on what can amount to detriment.

References

Smith, R, *Property Law*, 8th edn, Harlow: Pearson Longman, 2014.

Part 6
Leases

Leases—The Basic Requirements

## 11

Introduction

As is obvious if you visit any law library, whole textbooks have been written on the law of leases, or 'landlord and tenant law' as it is often called. In this text we will spend some time covering the basic principles that you will need to know for your course. It should, therefore, in particular be stressed that the following legislation is outside the scope of this text.

- *The Rent Acts* These Acts (the history of which goes back to the First World War) grant special security to and control the rents of most residential tenants whose leases were granted before the Housing Act 1988.

- *Housing Acts 1988* and *1996* These Acts remove new residential leases from the scope of the Rent Acts.

- *Agricultural Holdings Acts* and the *Agricultural Tenancies Act 1995* which replaces those Acts. The Agricultural Holdings Acts gave special protection to tenant farmers. The 1995 Act removes most of that special statutory protection.

- *Landlord and Tenant Act 1954, Part II* This legislation grants special protection to lessees of business premises (eg shops, offices, and factories). In particular when the lease of a business tenant (eg a shopkeeper) runs out, he can usually insist that the lease be renewed.

- *Leasehold Reform Act 1967* and later similar legislation. This legislation allows long lessees of certain types of houses compulsorily to purchase the freehold reversions of their houses from private landlords.

- *Leasehold Reform, Housing and Urban Development Act 1993* This statute (inter alia) gives the lessees of long leases living in certain types of flats the right compulsorily to purchase the freehold reversion of their block of flats from private landlords.

- *The Commonhold and Leasehold Reform Act 2002* This Act, as well as creating the new commonhold tenure (briefly outlined in Chapter 2), gives further rights to lessees holding long leases of certain types of flats. Note that this Act does not give tenants of a block of flats the right to insist that the ownership of the block be converted to the commonhold system.

This chapter will cover a number of complex technical concepts. Much of the technicality stems from one simple fact: if the owner of a fee simple estate allows another person to make use of their land, that transaction may be a lease; alternatively it may be only a licence. Differentiating between leases and licences has given rise to a quite considerable amount of case law.

Other causes of the complexity of this chapter stem from matters we have already touched upon. In Chapter 1 we noted the differences between fixed term leases and periodic tenancies, while in Chapter 3 we considered *Walsh v Lonsdale* and noted that leases may be either legal leases or equitable leases. These matters must now be considered in greater depth.

11.1 The Essential Requirements for a Lease

There are three essential requirements:

1 the estate must be of a duration permitted for a leasehold estate;
2 the grant must give exclusive possession; and
3 the grant must have the correct formalities.

The first two of these requirements for a lease were confirmed by the House of Lords in *Street v Mountford* [1985] 1 AC 809. Lord Templeman said:

> There can be no tenancy unless the occupier enjoys exclusive possession; but an occupier who enjoys exclusive possession is not necessarily a tenant. He may be owner in fee simple, a trespasser, a mortgagee in possession, an object of charity or a service occupier. To constitute a tenancy the occupier must be granted exclusive possession for a fixed or periodic term certain in consideration of a premium or periodical payments.

The third requirement (correct formalities) is derived from statute, in particular ss 52 and 54 Law of Property Act 1925 (LPA 1925) and (in modern law) s2 Law of Property (Miscellaneous Provisions) Act 1989.

Lord Templeman, in the passage previously quoted says that for a valid lease there must be consideration of some kind; either a rent or premium. This view, which was not necessary for the actual decision in the case, is disputed, for example by the Court of Appeal in *Ashburn Anstalt v Arnold* [1989] Ch 1. It is submitted that the point is academic. In practice, if somebody wants to grant a leasehold estate as an act of generosity, they 'charge' a purely nominal rent of, say, one peppercorn a year.

11.2 Duration of Leases

Leases can either be for a fixed term, or they can be periodic tenancies.

11.2.1 Fixed Term Leases

Here we are talking of leases for periods such as one month, three years, 99 years, 999 years. The vital feature of a fixed term lease is that there is a fixed *maximum* duration. It is perfectly possible, indeed normal, for a lease to contain a forfeiture clause under which the landlord can terminate the lease prematurely if the tenant breaks any of the terms of the lease.

Some fixed term leases also contain a 'break clause', which can be invoked by the tenant. Under such a clause the tenant has a right unilaterally to terminate the lease before it has run its full course. For example, you will sometimes see '21-year leases with seven year breaks'.

The lease in principle lasts 21 years, but the tenant has the option to terminate the lease after seven or 14 years.

Leases for uncertain maximum periods are not permitted. In *Lace v Chantler* [1944] KB 368 leases 'for the duration of the war' were held to be invalid.

Lord Greene MR said:

> Normally there could be no question that this was an ordinary weekly tenancy, duly determinable by a week's notice, but the parties in the rent-book agreed to a term which appears there expressed by the words 'furnished for duration,' which must mean the duration of the war. The question immediately arises whether a tenancy for the duration of the war creates a good leasehold interest. In my opinion, it does not. A term created by a leasehold tenancy agreement must be expressed either with certainty and specifically or by reference to something which can, at the time when the lease takes effect, be looked to as a certain ascertainment of what the term is meant to be. In the present case, when this tenancy agreement took effect, the term was completely uncertain. It was impossible to say how long the tenancy would last. Mr Sturge in his argument has maintained that such a lease would be valid, and that, even if the term is uncertain at its beginning when the lease takes effect, the fact that at some future time it will be rendered certain is sufficient to make it a good lease. In my opinion, that argument is not to be sustained . . .

The decision in *Lace v Chantler* caused widespread panic, as 'leases' 'for the duration of the war' were (at the time) common. Parliament therefore rushed through an ingenious piece of legislation, the Validation of Wartime Leases Act 1944. This Act was retrospective, and converted grants 'for the duration of the war' into leases for a fixed term of ten years, with a proviso that either landlord or tenant could terminate the lease once the war ended by giving a month's notice.

The House of Lords applied the *Lace v Chantler* principle in *Prudential Assurance v London Residuary Body* [1992] 2 AC 386. In this case the former London County Council had, in 1930, granted a lease of property fronting the busy Walworth Road. The lease was on terms that 'the tenancy shall continue until the . . . land is required by the council for the purposes of the widening of [the road]'. The rent was £30 per annum. The road widening never took place. The issue was whether the tenancy might by now (1991) be determined. Lord Templeman said:

> Now it is said that when in the present case the tenant entered pursuant to the agreement and paid a yearly rent he became a tenant from year to year on the terms of the agreement including clause 6 which prevents the landlord from giving notice to quit until the land is required for road widening. This submission would make a nonsense of the rule that a grant for an uncertain term does not create a lease and would make nonsense of the concept of a tenancy from year to year because it is of the essence of a tenancy from year to year that both the landlord and the tenant shall be entitled to give notice determining the tenancy . . .
>
> My Lords, I consider that the principle in *Lace* v *Chantler* [1944] KB 368 reaffirming 500 years of judicial acceptance of the requirement that a term must be certain applies to all leases and tenancy agreements. A tenancy from year to year is saved from being uncertain because each party has power by notice to determine at the end of any year. The term continues until determined as if both parties made a new agreement at the end of each year for a new term for the ensuing year. A power for nobody to determine or for one party only to be able to determine is inconsistent with the concept of a term from year to year: see *Doe d Warner v Browne*, 8 East 165 and *Cheshire Lines Committee* v *Lewis & Co*. 50 LJQB 121. In *In re Midland Railway Co's Agreement* [1971] Ch 725 there was no 'clearly expressed bargain' that the term should continue until the crack of doom if the demised land was not required for the landlord's undertaking or if the undertaking ceased to exist. In the present case there was no 'clearly expressed bargain' that the tenant shall be entitled to enjoy his 'temporary structures' in perpetuity if

Walworth Road is never widened. In any event principle and precedent dictate that it is beyond the power of the landlord and the tenant to create a term which is uncertain.

A lease can be made for five years subject to the tenant's right to determine if the war ends before the expiry of five years. A lease can be made from year to year subject to a fetter on the right of the landlord to determine the lease before the expiry of five years unless the war ends. Both leases are valid because they create a determinable certain term of five years. A lease might purport to be made for the duration of the war subject to the tenant's right to determine before the end of the war. A lease might be made from year to year subject to a fetter on the right of the landlord to determine the lease before the war ends. Both leases would be invalid because each purported to create an uncertain term. A term must either be certain or uncertain. It cannot be partly certain because the tenant can determine it at any time and partly uncertain because the landlord cannot determine it for an uncertain period. If the landlord does not grant and the tenant does not take a certain term the grant does not create a lease.

The decision of the Court of Appeal in *In re Midland Railway Co.'s Agreement* [1971] Ch 725 was taken a little further in *Ashburn Anstalt v Arnold* [1989] Ch 1. That case, if it was correct, would make it unnecessary for a lease to be of a certain duration. In an agreement for the sale of land the vendor reserved the right to remain at the property after completion as licensee and to trade therefrom without payment of rent.

> 'save that it can be required by Matlodge [the purchaser] to give possession on not less than one quarter's notice in writing upon Matlodge certifying that it is ready at the expiration of such notice forthwith to proceed with the development of the property and the neighbouring property involving, *inter alia*, the demolition of the property.'

The Court of Appeal held that this reservation created a tenancy. The tenancy was not from year to year but for a term which would continue until Matlodge certified that it was ready to proceed with the development of the property. The Court of Appeal held that the term was not uncertain because the vendor could either give a quarter's notice or vacate the property without giving notice. But of course the same could be said of the situation in *Lace v Chantler* [1944] 1 KB 368. The cumulative result of the two Court of Appeal authorities in *In re Midland Railway Co's Agreement* [1971] Ch 725 and *Ashburn's* case [1989] Ch 1 would therefore destroy the need for any term to be certain.

In the present case the Court of Appeal were bound by the decisions in In re Midland Railway Co's Agreement and Ashburn's case. In my opinion both these cases were wrongly decided. A grant for an uncertain term does not create a lease. A grant for an uncertain term which takes the form of a yearly tenancy which cannot be determined by the landlord does not create a lease. [Emphasis added] I would allow the appeal.

cross-reference
For a discussion on periodic tenancies, see 11.2.2.

The House of Lords held that as all leases need by definition to be of a certain duration, it followed that the lease granted by the council was not a valid fixed term lease and it was void. However, the tenant's possession, and payment of a yearly rent, meant that the tenant had established an informal legal yearly tenancy. Such a tenancy could be determined on the giving of six months' notice.

The decision in the *Prudential Assurance* case was followed (somewhat reluctantly) by the Supreme Court in *Mexfield Housing Co-operative Ltd v Berrisford* [2011] UKSC 52. In that case the claimant 'mutual' housing association (of which the defendant Ms Berrisford was a member) purported to grant her a monthly tenancy of a house.

By clause 5 of the agreement she could terminate the arrangement by giving the usual one month's notice. By clause 6 the claimants restricted their right to terminate to situations where either the rent was 21 days in arrear, or the tenant was in breach of other obligations in the agreement, or the defendant ceased to be a member of the association. After many years, Mexfield purported, without relying on clause 6, to serve one month's notice to terminate the tenancy, even though none of the circumstances listed in clause 6 applied at the time. Mexfield claimed that Ms Berrisford had an implied periodic tenancy and that Mexfield was entitled to determine the tenancy by giving at least four weeks' notice.

Ms Berrisford did not challenge the traditional rule that the term of a lease or tenancy must be certain. Counsel for Ms Berrisford argued that the lease could only be determined by Mexfield under clause 5 or 6 of the agreement. This would mean that this agreement was not capable of taking effect as a lease because of its 'uncertain term'.

cross-reference
For a discussion on s149(6) see 11.2.3.

The Supreme Court confirmed that as a matter of contractual interpretation of the effect of clauses 5 and 6, the transaction could not take effect as a periodic tenancy. Prior to 1926, the agreement with an uncertain term would have been created as a tenancy for life with an uncertain term. It should be noted that this type of tenancy was a species of freehold estate and its term was uncertain. After 1926, s149(6) LPA 1925 effectively converted a tenancy for life of uncertain duration into a 90-year fixed term lease. The Supreme Court held that operation of s149(6) was not limited to converting tenancy for life at the time when the 1925 legislation came into effect, and the agreement between Ms Berrisford and Mexfield took effect as a 90-year fixed term lease determinable on Ms Berrisford's death or by the terms in the agreement.

---

thinking point 11.1

Arianit has just been appointed manager of Bruddersford Town Football Club. He knows that he is likely to be sacked if the team plays poorly. He wants to take a lease of a house in Bruddersford from Charley, a keen Bruddersford supporter. Arianit and Charley envisage that the lease will be for 'as long as Arianit remains manager'. What sort of lease would meet their requirements?

Arianit and Charley should agree on a fixed term lease for some very long period (eg 40 years), but include a clause that should Arianit cease to be manager either party can terminate the lease by (say) one month's notice.

11.2.2 Periodic Tenancies

Here we are talking of weekly, monthly, yearly, quarterly tenancies, etc. The practical effect of a **periodic tenancy** is that it continues indefinitely until terminated by one or other side giving the appropriate notice. Why, then, do periodic tenancies not infringe the rule that a leasehold estate must have a fixed maximum duration? At least three different explanations have been given:

1 a periodic tenancy is a lease for one period which goes on renewing itself automatically;

2 a periodic tenancy is a lease for one period which goes on extending itself automatically; and

3 a periodic tenancy is a lease because its maximum duration is 'capable of being rendered certain' by the giving of the appropriate period of notice.

cross-reference
Prudential Assurance v London Residuary Body *is discussed at 11.2.1.*

. . . .

periodic tenancy

a tenancy agreement which is characterized by payment of rent at regular fixed intervals, these intervals could be weekly, monthly, or yearly. The periodic tenancy continues indefinitely until terminated by one or other side giving appropriate notice.

. . . .

In *Prudential Assurance v London Residuary Body* the House of Lords clearly favoured explanation (1), so this must be regarded as the correct one. See the remarks of Lord Templeman in the second paragraph of our extract from *Prudential Assurance v London Residuary Body*.

The period of notice to terminate a periodic tenancy is prima facie one period, to expire at the end of a period. Thus, for example, on 1 January Les grants a monthly tenancy to Tom. Tom now decides he wants to leave. He must give, at least, one month's notice to expire on the last day of a calendar month.

thinking point 11.2

Assume today is 15 February. If Tom gives Les one month's notice that he is quitting the property, when will that notice expire?

The answer is that the notice will expire at midnight at the end of 31 March. You should note that in practical terms this means that if Tom in fact moves out on (say) 16 February, he must still pay the rent until the end of March.

The parties to a periodic tenancy can agree that the requisite notice should be less than one period, but not more, for example in a half-yearly tenancy they could agree to it being terminable on giving three months' notice. They could not agree to a year's notice.

A special rule operates for yearly tenancies. In the absence of contrary agreement, the period of notice is (anomalously) six months, though the parties can expressly agree to any period of notice up to one year.

It used to be thought that a party to a periodic tenancy could agree to conditions restricting his right to terminate the tenancy, in particular see *Re Midland Railway's Agreement* [1971] 1 All ER 1007. However, this case, and *Ashburn Anstalt v Arnold* [1989] Ch 1, were both overruled on this point by the House of Lords in the *Prudential Assurance* case. In *Prudential Assurance* the Court of Appeal had held that the tenants had a yearly tenancy, but subject to a condition that the tenancy could not be terminated until the land was required for the road-widening scheme. The House of Lords held that parties to a periodic tenancy cannot restrict their basic right to terminate the tenancy by giving the appropriate notice. See the remarks of Lord Templeman in the last two paragraphs of our extract from *Prudential Assurance v London Residuary Body*.

11.2.3 Special Problems Connected with the Duration of Leases

'Leases for Lives'

Traditionally life estates were created, for no consideration, as part of a strict settlement, and were governed by the Settled Land Act 1925 (SLA 1925), considered briefly in Chapter 7. If, after the commencement of the Trusts of Land and Appointment of Trustees Act 1996, a life estate is created for no consideration, a trust of land will automatically arise.

Back in 1925 the legislators had a problem with a practice which existed in some parts of the country. Landlords in some areas used to grant to tenant-farmers not fixed terms, but a life estate in return for the tenant paying a rent and/or **premium**. Clearly, it would have been totally wrong to bring such transactions within the SLA 1925.

premium
a capital sum paid for the grant of a lease.

Section 149(6) LPA 1925 is designed to convert such 'leases for life' transactions into fixed term leases, but unfortunately s149(6) is drafted in an unnecessarily wide way, and catches:

- a lease at a rent and/or premium granted for life or lives;
- a lease for a fixed period determinable on life or lives; and
- a lease for a fixed period determinable on marriage.

Law of Property Act 1925

149. Abolition of interesse termini, and as to reversionary leases and leases for lives

…

(6) Any lease or underlease, at a rent, or in consideration of a fine, for life or lives or for any term of years determinable with life or lives, or on the marriage of the lessee, [or on the formation of a civil partnership between the lessee and another person,] or any contract therefor, made before or after the commencement of this Act, or created by virtue of Part V of the Law of Property Act 1922, shall take effect as a lease, underlease or contract therefor, for a term of ninety years determinable [after the death or marriage (as the case may be) of the original lessee, or of the survivor of the original lessees,] by at least one month's notice in writing given to determine the same on one of the quarter days applicable to the tenancy, either by the lessor or the persons deriving title under him, to the person entitled to the leasehold interest, or if no such person is in existence by affixing the same to the premises, or by the lessee or other persons in whom the leasehold interest is vested to the lessor or the persons deriving title under him:

Provided that—

(a) this subsection shall not apply to any term taking effect in equity under a settlement or created out of an equitable interest under a settlement for mortgage, indemnity, or other like purposes;

(b) the person in whom the leasehold interest is vested by virtue of Part V of the Law of Property Act 1922, shall, for the purposes of this subsection, be deemed an original lessee;

(c) if the lease, underlease, or contract therefor is made determinable on the dropping of the lives of persons other than or besides the lessees, then the notice shall be capable of being served after the death of any person or of the survivor of any persons (whether or not including the lessees) on the cesser of whose life or lives the lease, underlease, or contract is made determinable, instead of after the death of the original lessee or of the survivor of the original lessees;

(d) if there are no quarter days specially applicable to the tenancy, notice may be given to determine the tenancy on one of the usual quarter days.

All the three types of transaction listed earlier are converted into leases for a fixed term of 90 years. However, once the relevant death or marriage has occurred either the landlord or the tenant (or their personal representatives) can terminate the lease by giving a month's notice to expire on one of the 'traditional quarter days'. The traditional quarter days are Lady Day (25 March), Midsummer (24 June), Michaelmas (29 September), and Christmas.

Section 149(6) works perfectly well when applied to transactions where a lease at a rent and/or premium is granted for life or lives.

However, the applicability of s149(6) to transactions where a lease is for a fixed period determinable on life or lives and a lease for a fixed period determinable on marriage creates a trap for the foolish landlord.

Suppose in 2009 Laurie leases Chestnut House to Terry at £500 per year rent, 'for ten years or until Terry's death, if earlier'. Terry is a healthy young man of 20. Laurie expects the lease to expire in 2019. But it is converted by s149(6) into a 90-year term, and Laurie will not be able to give notice to terminate the lease until Terry dies, which may not be for a very long time. The rent remains fixed at £500 per year.

thinking point 11.3

In 2012, Harry leased a house to Wassilla, a spinster aged 22, 'for five years or until her earlier marriage'. Harry is looking forward to getting the house back in 2017. Wassilla has just joined a religious group which required her to take a vow that she would never marry. Advise Harry.

Harry is caught by s149(6) LPA 1925. He will have to hope that Wassilla changes her religious views, as otherwise he (or his personal representatives) will not be able to terminate the lease until either Wassilla dies or she achieves the age of 112.

New Scope for Section 149(6)

The Supreme Court decision in *Mexfield Housing Cooperative Ltd v Berrisford* [2011] UKSC 52 has uncovered an application of s149(6) of possibly quite far-reaching importance. The Supreme Court first held, relying on old pre-1926 case law, that any lease (to a human being) for an uncertain term granted prior to 1926 was treated as a lease for life determinable either on the tenant's death or according to its other provisions.

cross-reference
Mexfield *is discussed at 11.2.1.*

The Supreme Court then applied this to the lease the relevant details of which are given earlier. It held that the parties' (modern) agreement should be interpreted as a 'lease for life' in the same way as the old pre-1926 agreements and was therefore caught by s149(6). The agreement between Ms Berrisford and Mexfield took effect as a 90-year fixed term, determinable on the defendant's death but also subject to the rights to terminate early under clauses 5 and 6 of the agreement.

Perpetually Renewable Leases

The essence of such a lease was that the tenant took a fixed term of X years, but every time X years expired the tenant had the option to renew the lease for a further X years. Thus, provided the tenant remembered to renew every time X years expired, they could keep the land indefinitely.

Prior to 1926 a perpetually renewable lease would be created by including in a fixed term lease a clause like the following: 'This lease shall be renewable by the tenant at his option on exactly the same terms and conditions, including this provision.' The crucial words are of course, 'including this provision'. Had they been omitted, the lease would have been renewable just once.

As a result of s145 Law of Property Act 1922 (LPA 1922), a perpetually renewable lease is not possible after 1926. Section 145 does not, however, invalidate leases containing the kind of clause just quoted. Far from it. Section 145 converts any purported grant of a perpetually renewable lease into a lease for 2,000 years (see also, Sch 15 para 1 LPA 1922). The tenant (not the landlord) has the option to terminate the lease by ten days' notice every time the lease would have been due for renewal had it been allowed to take effect as a perpetually renewable lease.

In *Caerphilly Concrete v Owen* [1972] 1 WLR 372 the landlords granted the tenant a lease stated to last for five years. However, the lease granted the tenant the option to renew the lease for a further five years 'at the same rent and containing the like covenants and provisos as are herein contained (including the option to renew such lease for a further term of five years at the expiration thereof)'. The words in brackets proved fatal for the landlords. Those words (prior to 1926) would have created a perpetually renewable lease. But the transaction took place in 1963, so the landlords discovered that they had leased their land for 2,000 years, and at a very low rent.

Tenancy at Will

A tenancy at will is a very insecure arrangement, because either side can terminate it at a moment's notice. It is particularly unattractive from the point of view of the tenant at will, as they can be thrown out without any prior warning.

In modern conditions, tenancies at will are relatively rare. One does, however, exist where a landlord has allowed somebody to take possession of their land intending them to be a tenant, but, probably because the execution of a formal lease has been forgotten, or the formal lease is for some reason invalid, no estate or interest has been granted to the tenant. It is, however, also possible to deliberately create a tenancy at will, as in *Manfield v Botchin* [1970] 2 QB 612.

If a tenant at will starts paying rent on a regular basis, the tenancy at will is automatically converted into a periodic tenancy. This rule, which we consider at 11.5.2 and which the House of Lords applied in the *Prudential Assurance* case, goes a long way to mitigating the extremely insecure position of tenants at will.

One other point. The Court of Appeal in *Heslop v Burns* [1974] 1 WLR 1241 had to consider whether a friendly arrangement to allow two friends to occupy a house rent-free created a tenancy at will. In this case a fairly wealthy person allowed two friends to occupy a house he owned rent-free. After his death, the friends remained in possession. They claimed that they had a tenancy at will, which, by s9 Limitation Act 1939, was deemed to have determined a year after its commencement. Thereafter, they claimed they had occupied the freehold as 'squatters' and now owned the freehold as of right. Stamp LJ said:

> On the facts of this case it is, in my judgment, abundantly clear that the parties did not enter into any arrangement, far less any arrangement intended to create a legal relationship, as to the terms on which the defendants should occupy the property. There was no contract, no arrangement, no statement by the deceased. The defendants, as I see it, were allowed to move into the property and occupy it simply as a result of the bounty of the deceased and without any arrangements as to the terms on which they should do so. There was no evidence of any discussion whatsoever taking place as to the terms of the occupation. It was by the effect of the bounty of the deceased or, if you will, because of his feelings of affection for Mrs Burns, that the home was provided, and it was, I think, for those reasons that the defendants remained there.

> The fact, which was relied on by counsel for the defendants, that the deceased had already said, in relation to each of the properties in Fowler Street and Love Walk, that he would leave it to the defendants, is no evidence that it was the intention of the deceased that the defendants should in the meantime be tenants at will rather than licensees. Counsel for the defendants submitted that, since the deceased intended to provide the defendants with a home, he must have intended to give them an interest in the property. But a tenancy at will was no more apt to achieve that purpose than a revocable personal licence to occupy the property; and if one asks the question what interest he intended them to have, it could only, consistently with counsel's submission, be an interest during the rest of the life of the deceased of such a nature as would exclude him from any right to turn them out. No such interest was created and I find it impossible to infer an intention on the part of the deceased to create such a situation. In my judgment the proper inference is that the defendants at the outset entered into occupation of the premises as licensees and not as tenants at will; not with a right to exclude the deceased from possession . . .

The Court of Appeal held that in effect such a friendly arrangement (made without intent to create legal relations) regarding the occupation of the house was to be treated as a licence, not as a tenancy at will. Accordingly, the 'friends' had no right to exclude the deceased (by his executors) from taking possession of the freehold.

Some Concepts Related to the Law of Leases

It is convenient to deal with certain miscellaneous points at this stage. It should be stressed that what follows is a bare outline of certain matters which you need to know to be able to understand the basic principles of the law of leases and also certain of the cases on the distinction between leases and licences.

11.3.1 Tenancy at Sufferance

This occurs where a tenant's lease has expired but the tenant (unlawfully) continues in possession without the landlord's express agreement or express disagreement. The tenant is said to 'hold over'. If the landlord expressly disagrees with the ex-tenant staying, the ex-tenant is simply a trespasser, who should leave immediately. If the landlord expressly agrees to the tenant staying in possession, there is a tenancy at will.

Like a tenancy at will, a tenancy at sufferance will automatically be converted into a periodic tenancy if the 'tenant' starts paying rent on a regular basis.

11.3.2 Protected Tenancy

This is a lease (granted prior to 15 January 1989) of a 'dwelling house' (which concept includes a flat) within the scope of the Rent Acts. If the lease terminates (even after 15 January 1989) then normally the tenant can lawfully stay in possession as a statutory tenant. They will not be a tenant at sufferance.

11.3.3 Statutory Tenancy

A statutory tenant technically has no estate or interest in the house or flat he/she is still occupying. He/she has a right given by the statute, a right which cannot be transferred, to continue to occupy the property notwithstanding the termination of the lease. Statutory tenancies are usually thought of as arising under the Rent Acts. It is worth noting that they could also arise under the Agricultural Holdings Acts, when a lease of a farm terminated but the tenant-farmer was allowed by the Acts to retain possession.

11.3.4 Secure Tenancies

Under the Housing Act 1980 public sector lettings such as council houses are secure tenancies; they are outside the Rent Acts and the Housing Act 1988, but the public sector secure tenant enjoys similar security of tenure to his private sector counterpart under the old Rent Acts. For lettings after 14 January 1989, the public sector tenant is better off.

11.3.5 Assured Tenancies

Under the Housing Act 1988, as a general rule, no new protected tenancies can arise. All private landlords of houses or flats were empowered by the 1988 Act to grant assured tenancies. The assured tenant has some degree of security of tenure, but there are no controls on the rent charged. Since the commencement of the Housing Act 1996 (February 1997), new assured tenancies are still possible, but rather unlikely because most tenancies created after this time tend to be assured shorthold tenancies.

11.3.6 Assured Shorthold Tenancies

Under the Housing Act 1988 a private landlord could grant an assured shorthold tenancy. Under the 1988 Act, an assured shorthold was a fixed term lease of a house or flat for at least six months. The tenant has no security of tenure once the fixed period expires; there are rather weak controls on the amount of rent. This form of letting has proved to be very popular with landlords.

Assured shorthold tenancies are now even more common. Subject to minor exceptions such as holiday lettings, the Housing Act 1996 provides that all private residential lettings are assured shortholds. It does not matter whether the residential letting is for a fixed term or is a periodic tenancy. If the letting is a periodic tenancy, then by way of exception to the usual common law rules about termination by notice, a landlord cannot terminate the tenancy before six months have elapsed from the date of the original grant. This six months rule is the only provision for security of tenure. There are still weak controls on the rent which can be charged.

11.4 The Distinction Between Leases and Licences

The distinction is very important because:

- As leases are property rights (an estate or interest in land), they are in principle freely alienable, that is, they can be sold, given away, or left by will. A licence is a right personal to the licensee and cannot be assigned. For example, suppose Roger was going away for a few weeks, and allowed a friend of his to occupy his flat rent-free in his absence. That would be a 'licence'. It would obviously be wrong for his friend to transfer his right to a third party.

- As leases are property rights, they in principle bind third party purchasers of the landlord's reversion. Licences generally do not bind purchasers of the land over which the licence is exercisable. Exceptionally, a licence could bind a purchaser if a licensee acquired by his activities on the land a proprietary estoppel or a constructive trust interest.

- Leases are usually subject to special legislation such as the (various) Landlord and Tenant Acts; licences are generally outside the scope of such legislation. Licences were also outside the scope of the old Rent Acts.

cross-reference
See 8.8.2 and 10.6 for a discussion of constructive trusts and proprietary estoppel.

As you will see if you quickly flip through the next few pages of this text, there have been many cases on the lease/licence distinction. Almost all of them relate to the last point mentioned, that is, leases are subject to security of tenure legislation. In almost all of them a landowner has granted a right to occupy his land, but tried to make the arrangement a **licence**, not a lease, so that the Rent Acts or other similar legislation are avoided.

cross-reference
For a discussion of licences, see 10.1 to 10.5.

....

licence

a licence is a personal agreement between the licensor (person who gives the permission) and licensee to enter/occupy the licensor's property. This right cannot be assigned.

....

11.4.1 Exclusive Possession as the Foundation of the Lease/Licence Distinction

The House of Lords decision in *Street v Mountford* [1985] 1 AC 809 both simplified and clarified the law. Most of the essential facts of this case are set out in the opening paragraph of Lord Templeman's speech:

> By an agreement dated 7 March 1983, the respondent Mr Street granted the appellant Mrs Mountford the right to occupy the furnished rooms numbers 5 and 6 at 5, St Clements Gardens, Boscombe, from 7 March 1983 for £37 per week, subject to termination by 14 days written notice and subject to [quite elaborate] conditions set forth in the agreement.

It should be added that the agreement was called a 'licence', but nevertheless undoubtedly granted Mrs Mountford exclusive possession. When the case was decided by the Court of Appeal, it held that as 'the [subjective] intention of the parties' was that there should be a licence, that was all Mrs Mountford had. She did not have any form of lease protected by the Rent Acts.

This decision of the Court of Appeal was blasted off the face of the earth, 'overruled' is too mild a word, by the unanimous decision of the House of Lords. Lord Templeman gave the only reasoned speech. The House held that whether a transaction is a lease or a licence depends (with minor exceptions) entirely on whether or not there is *exclusive possession*. The 'intent of the parties' and the label the parties attach to the transaction is irrelevant. As none of the minor exceptions was applicable, Mrs Mountford had a lease which was protected by the Rent Acts.

Lord Templeman said:

> ...My Lords, there is no doubt that the traditional distinction between a tenancy and a licence of land lay in the grant of land for a term at a rent with exclusive possession. In some cases it was not clear at first sight whether exclusive possession was in fact granted...
>
> In the case of residential accommodation there is no difficulty in deciding whether the grant confers exclusive possession. An occupier of residential accommodation at a rent for a term is either a lodger or a tenant. The occupier is a lodger if the landlord provides attendance or services which require the landlord or his servants to exercise unrestricted access to and use of the premises. A lodger is entitled to live in the premises but cannot call the place his own. In *Allan v Liverpool Overseers* (1874) LR9 QB 180, 191–192 Blackburn J said:
>
>> A lodger in a house, although he has the exclusive use of rooms in the house, in the sense that nobody else is to be there, and though his goods are stowed there, yet he is not in exclusive occupation in that sense, because the landlord is there for the purpose of being able, as landlords commonly do in the case of lodgings, to have his own servants to look after the house and the furniture, and has retained to himself the occupation, though he has agreed to give the exclusive enjoyment of the occupation to the lodger.
>
> If on the other hand residential accommodation is granted for a term at a rent with exclusive possession, the landlord providing neither attendance nor services, the grant is a tenancy;

any express reservation to the landlord of limited rights to enter and view the state of the premises and to repair and maintain the premises only serves to emphasise the fact that the grantee is entitled to exclusive possession and is a tenant. In the present case it is conceded that Mrs Mountford is entitled to exclusive possession and is not a lodger. Mr Street provided neither attendance nor services and only reserved the limited rights of inspection and maintenance and the like set forth in clause 3 of the agreement. On the traditional view of the matter, Mrs Mountford not being a lodger must be a tenant.

There can be no tenancy unless the occupier enjoys exclusive possession; but an occupier who enjoys exclusive possession is not necessarily a tenant. He may be owner in fee simple, a trespasser, a mortgagee in possession, an object of charity or a service occupier. To constitute a tenancy the occupier must be granted exclusive possession for a fixed or periodic term certain in consideration of a premium or periodical payments. The grant may be express, or may be inferred where the owner accepts weekly or other periodical payments from the occupier.

Occupation by service occupier may be eliminated. A service occupier is a servant who occupies his master's premises in order to perform his duties as a servant. In those circumstances the possession and occupation of the servant is treated as the possession and occupation of the master and the relationship of landlord and tenant is not created; . . .

In the present case, the agreement dated 7 March 1983 professed an intention by both parties to create a licence and their belief that they had in fact created a licence. It was submitted on behalf of Mr Street that the court cannot in these circumstances decide that the agreement created a tenancy without interfering with the freedom of contract enjoyed by both parties. My Lords, Mr Street enjoyed freedom to offer Mrs Mountford the right to occupy the rooms comprised in the agreement on such lawful terms as Mr Street pleased. Mrs Mountford enjoyed freedom to negotiate with Mr Street to obtain different terms. Both parties enjoyed freedom to contract or not to contract and both parties exercised that freedom by contracting on the terms set forth in the written agreement and on no other terms. But the consequences in law of the agreement, once concluded, can only be determined by consideration of the effect of the agreement. If the agreement satisfied all the requirements of a tenancy, then the agreement produced a tenancy and the parties cannot alter the effect of the agreement by insisting that they only created a licence.

The manufacture of a five-pronged implement for manual digging results in a fork even if the manufacturer, unfamiliar with the English language, insists that he intended to make and has made a spade.

It was also submitted that in deciding whether the agreement created a tenancy or a licence, the court should ignore the Rent Acts. If Mr Street has succeeded, where owners have failed these past 70 years, in driving a coach and horses through the Rent Acts, he must be left to enjoy the benefit of his ingenuity unless and until Parliament intervenes. I accept that the Rent Acts are irrelevant to the problem of determining the legal effect of the rights granted by the agreement. Like the professed intention of the parties, the Rent Acts cannot alter the effect of the agreement . . .

. . . in my opinion in order to ascertain the nature and quality of the occupancy and to see whether the occupier has or has not a stake in the room or only permission for himself personally to occupy, the court must decide whether upon its true construction the agreement confers on the occupier exclusive possession. If exclusive possession at a rent for a term does not constitute a tenancy then the distinction between a contractual tenancy and a contractual licence of land becomes wholly unidentifiable.

In *Somma* v *Hazelhurst* [1978] 1 WLR 1014, a young unmarried couple H and S occupied a double bedsitting room for which they paid a weekly rent. The landlord did not provide services or attendance and the couple were not lodgers but tenants enjoying exclusive possession. But the Court of Appeal did not ask themselves whether H and S were lodgers or tenants and did not draw the correct conclusion from the fact that H and S enjoyed exclusive possession. The Court of Appeal were diverted from the correct inquiries by the fact that the landlord obliged H and S to enter into separate agreements and reserved power to determine each agreement separately. The landlord also insisted that the room should not in form be let to either H or S or to both H and S but that each should sign an agreement to share the room in common with such other persons as the landlord might from time to time nominate. The sham nature of this obligation would have been only slightly more obvious if H and S had been married or if the room had been furnished with a double bed instead of two single beds. If the landlord had served notice on H to leave and had required S to share the room with a strange man, the notice would only have been a disguised notice to quit on both H and S. The room was let and taken as residential accommodation with exclusive possession in order that H and S might live together in undisturbed quasi-connubial bliss making weekly payments. The agreements signed by H and S constituted the grant to H and S jointly of exclusive possession at a rent for a term for the purposes for which the room was taken and the agreement therefore created a tenancy. Although the Rent Acts must not be allowed to alter or influence the construction of an agreement, the court should, in my opinion, be astute to detect and frustrate sham devices and artificial transactions whose only object is to disguise the grant of a tenancy and to evade the Rent Acts. I would disapprove of the decision in this case that H and S were only licensees and for the same reason would disapprove of the decision in *Aldrington Garages Ltd* v *Fielder* (1978) 37 P & CR 461 and *Sturolson & Co* v *Weniz* (1984) 272, EG 326.

In the present case the Court of Appeal, 49 P & CR 324 held that the agreement dated 7 March 1983 only created a licence. Slade LJ, at p. 329 accepted that the agreement and in particular clause 3 of the agreement 'shows that the right to occupy the premises conferred on the defendant was intended as an exclusive right of occupation, in that it was thought necessary to give a special and express power to the plaintiff to enter...' Before your Lordships it was conceded that the agreement conferred the right of exclusive possession on Mrs Mountford. Even without clause 3 the result would have been the same. By the agreement Mrs Mountford was granted the right to occupy residential accommodation. The landlord did not provide any services or attendance. It was plain that Mrs Mountford was not a lodger. Slade LJ proceeded to analyse all the provisions of the agreement, not for the purpose of deciding whether his finding of exclusive possession was correct, but for the purpose of assigning some of the provisions of the agreement to the category of terms which he thought are usually to be found in a tenancy agreement and of assigning other provisions to the category of terms which he thought are usually to be found in a licence. Slade LJ may or may not have been right that in a letting of a furnished room it was 'most unusual to find a provision in a tenancy agreement obliging the tenant to keep his rooms in a 'tidy condition' (p. 329). If Slade LJ was right about this and other provisions there is still no logical method of evaluating the results of his survey. Slade LJ reached the conclusion that 'the agreement bears all the hallmarks of a licence rather than a tenancy save for the one important feature of exclusive occupation': p. 329. But in addition to the hallmark of exclusive occupation of residential accommodation there were the hallmarks of weekly payments for a periodical term. Unless these three hallmarks are decisive, it really becomes impossible to distinguish a contractual tenancy from a contractual licence save by reference to the professed intention of the parties or by the judge awarding marks for drafting. Slade LJ was finally impressed by the statement at the foot of the agreement by Mrs Mountford 'I understand and accept that a licence in the above form does not and is not intended to give me a tenancy protected under the Rent Acts.' Slade LJ said, at p. 330:

> it seems to me that, if the defendant is to displace the express statement of intention embodied in the declaration, she must show that the declaration was either a deliberate sham or at least an inaccurate statement of what was the true substance of the real transaction agreed between the parties; ...

My Lords, the only intention which is relevant is the intention demonstrated by the agreement to grant exclusive possession for a term at a rent. Sometimes it may be difficult to discover whether, on the true construction of an agreement, exclusive possession is conferred. Sometimes it may appear from the surrounding circumstances that there was no intention to create legal relationships. Sometimes it may appear from the surrounding circumstances that the right to exclusive possession is referable to a legal relationship other than a tenancy. Legal relationships to which the grant of exclusive possession might be referable and which would or might negative the grant of an estate or interest in the land include occupancy under a contract for the sale of the land, occupancy pursuant to a contract of employment or occupancy referable to the holding of an office. But where as in the present case the only circumstances are that residential accommodation is offered and accepted with exclusive possession for a term at a rent, the result is a tenancy. The position was well summarised by Windeyer J sitting in the High Court of Australia in *Radaich* v *Smith* (1959) 101 CLR 209, 222, where he said:

> What then is the fundamental right which a tenant has that distinguishes his position from that of a licensee? It is an interest in land as distinct from a personal permission to enter the land and use it for some stipulated purpose or purposes.

> And how is it to be ascertained whether such an interest in land has been given? By seeing whether the grantee was given a legal right of exclusive possession of the land for a term or from year to year or for a life or lives. If he was, he is a tenant. And he cannot be other than a tenant, because a legal right of exclusive possession is a tenancy and the creation of such a right is a demise. To say that a man who has, by agreement with a landlord, a right of exclusive possession of land for a term is not a tenant is simply to contradict the first proposition by the second. A right of exclusive possession is secured by the right of a lessee to maintain ejectment and, after his entry, trespass. A reservation to the landlord, either by contract or statute, of a limited right of entry, as for example to view or repair, is, of course, not inconsistent with the grant of exclusive possession. Subject to such reservations, a tenant for a term or from year to year or for a life or lives can exclude his landlord as well as strangers from the demised premises. All this is long established law: see *Cole on Ejectment* (1857) pp. 72, 73, 287, 458.

My Lords, I gratefully adopt the logic and the language of Windeyer J. Henceforth the courts which deal with these problems will, save in exceptional circumstances, only be concerned to inquire whether as a result of an agreement relating to residential accommodation the occupier is a lodger or a tenant. In the present case I am satisfied that Mrs Mountford is a tenant, that the appeal should be allowed, that the order of the Court of Appeal should be set aside and that the respondent should be ordered to pay the costs of the appellant here and below.

In brief, the agreement was a tenancy, despite the use of the word 'licence'. The test to distinguish a lease from a licence was one of substance, not of form. The crucial question to ask was whether the agreement conferred 'exclusive possession'.

The House of Lords reaffirmed *Street v Mountford* in *Bruton v London and Quadrant Housing Trust* [2000] 1 AC 406. The London Borough of Lambeth owned a block of flats which they licenced to London and Quadrant Housing Trust to provide temporary accommodation for the homeless. Bruton had rented a flat from the defendant charitable housing trust. The agreement was described as a weekly licence which required him to allow access at all normal working hours to staff of the housing trust. Bruton claimed that the housing trust was in breach of its repair obligations under s11 Landlord and Tenant Act 1985. He based his claim on the fact that he had exclusive possession of a flat, and therefore he argued that he had a lease to which s11 applied. The transaction was described as a licence. Lord Hoffmann in considering the difference between a lease and licence said:

cross-reference
For a discussion on s11 Landlord and Tenant Act 1985 see 12.1.6.

> Did this agreement create a 'lease' or 'tenancy' within the meaning of the Landlord and Tenant Act 1985 or any other legislation which refers to a lease or tenancy? The decision of this House in *Street v. Mountford* [1985] A.C. 809 is authority for the proposition that a 'lease' or 'tenancy' is a contractually binding agreement, not referable to any other relationship between the parties, by which one person gives another the right to exclusive occupation of land for a fixed or renewable period or periods of time, usually in return for a periodic payment in money. An agreement having these characteristics creates a relationship of landlord and tenant to which the common law or statute may then attach various incidents. The fact that the parties use language more appropriate to a different kind of agreement, such as a licence, is irrelevant if upon its true construction it has the identifying characteristics of a lease. The meaning of the agreement, for example, as to the extent of the possession which it grants, depend upon the intention of the parties, objectively ascertained by reference to the language and relevant

background. The decision of your Lordships' House in *Westminster City Council v. Clarke* [1992] A.C. 288 is a good example of the importance of background in deciding whether the agreement grants exclusive possession or not. But the classification of the agreement as a lease does not depend upon any intention additional to that expressed in the choice of terms. It is simply a question of characterising the terms which the parties have agreed. This is a question of law.

In this case, it seems to me that the agreement, construed against the relevant background, plainly gave Mr. Bruton a right to exclusive possession. There is nothing to suggest that he was to share possession with the Trust, the council or anyone else. The Trust did not retain such control over the premises as was inconsistent with Mr. Bruton having exclusive possession, as was the case in *Westminster City Council v. Clarke* [1992] A.C. 288. The only rights which it reserved were for itself and the council to enter at certain times and for limited purposes. As Lord Templeman said in *Street v. Mountford* [1985] A.C. 809, 818, such an express reservation 'only serves to emphasise the fact that the grantee is entitled to exclusive possession and is a tenant.' Nor was there any other relationship between the parties to which Mr. Bruton's exclusive possession could be referable.

Mr. Henderson Q.C., who appeared for the Trust, submitted that there were 'special circumstances' in this case which enabled one to construe the agreement as a licence despite the presence of all the characteristics identified in *Street v. Mountford* [1985] A.C. 809. These circumstances were that the Trust was a responsible landlord performing socially valuable functions, it had agreed with the council not to grant tenancies, Mr. Bruton had agreed that he was not to have a tenancy and the Trust had no estate out of which it could grant one.

In my opinion none of these circumstances can make an agreement to grant exclusive possession something other than a tenancy. The character of the landlord is irrelevant because although the Rent Acts and other Landlord and Tenant Acts do make distinctions between different kinds of landlords, it is not by saying that what would be a tenancy if granted by one landlord will be something else if granted by another. The alleged breach of the Trust's licence is irrelevant because there is no suggestion that the grant of a tenancy would have been ultra vires either the Trust or the council: see section 32(3) of the Housing Act 1985. If it was a breach of a term of the licence from the council, that would have been because it was a tenancy. The licence could not have turned it into something else. Mr. Bruton's agreement is irrelevant because one cannot contract out of the statute. The trust's lack of title is also irrelevant, but I shall consider this point at a later stage. In *Family Housing Association v. Jones* [1990] 1 W.L.R. 779, where the facts were very similar to those in the present case, the Court of Appeal construed the 'licence' as a tenancy. Slade L.J. gave careful consideration to whether any exceptional ground existed for making an exception to the principle in *Street v. Mountford* [1985] A.C. 809 and came to the conclusion that there was not. I respectfully agree. For these reasons I consider that the agreement between the Trust and Mr. Bruton was a lease within the meaning of section 11 of the Landlord and Tenant Act 1985 . . .

. . . the term 'lease' or 'tenancy' describes a relationship between two parties who are designated landlord and tenant. It is not concerned with the question of whether the agreement creates an estate or other proprietary interest which may be binding upon third parties. A lease may, and usually does, create a proprietary interest called a leasehold estate or, technically, a 'term of years absolute.' This will depend upon whether the landlord had an interest out of which he could grant it. Nemo dat quod non habet. But it is the fact that the agreement is a lease which creates the proprietary interest. It is putting the cart before the horse to say that whether the agreement is a lease depends upon whether it creates a proprietary interest.

. . . In my opinion, the Trust plainly did purport to grant a tenancy. It entered into an agreement on terms which constituted a tenancy. It may have agreed with Mr. Bruton to say that it was not a tenancy. But the parties cannot contract out of the Rent Acts or other landlord and tenant statutes by such devices. Nor in my view can they be used by a landlord to avoid being estopped from denying that he entered into the agreement he actually made.

For these reasons I would allow the appeal and declare that Mr. Bruton was a tenant. I should add that I express no view on whether he was a secure tenant or on the rights of the council to recover possession of the flat.

In *Bruton* a tenancy not a licence had been created, as was also the case in *Addiscombe Gardens v Crabbe* [1958] 1 QB 513, a Court of Appeal decision which is clearly correct in the light of the later House of Lords decisions.

The judgment in *Bruton* is not quite as straightforward as one might assume. The House of Lords held that a tenancy existed between Mr Bruton and the housing trust, even though the housing trust did not have an estate from which they could confer a lease. As Lord Hoffmann notes above, the creation of a lease 'may' create a proprietary interest if the landlord has 'an interest out of which he could grant it'. But, according to Lord Hoffmann there could be instances, like in *Bruton* itself, where a lease has been created but it does not confer a proprietary interest. The significance of this decision is that the existence of a lease meant that the housing trust was subject to the implied repair covenants in the Landlord and Tenant Act 1985 s11.

11.4.2 The Meaning of Exclusive Possession

If there is no exclusive possession granted to the 'grantee' then the transaction is a licence. The test for exclusive possession is: 'Has the grantee been given the general control of the property?' This test stems from the nineteenth-century case of *Wells v Kingston upon Hull* (1875) LR 10 CP 402. In that case Hull Corporation owned a 'dry dock' used by shipowners to repair their ships. The corporation 'let' the dock to shipowners on terms which included provisions:

- that the corporation was responsible for opening and shutting the dock gates to allow ships to sail in and out; and

- that the shipowner should clean out the dock at the end of each day's work under the supervision of the corporation's employees.

In the following passage from Lord Coleridge CJ we have, to aid your reading, added additional paragraphing and emphasized what becomes the second paragraph.

> This case has been argued at considerable length, but it seems to me that it admits of decision on tolerably plain and simple grounds. The first point, viz. whether a contract in writing was essential, depends on whether, by the terms of the agreement between the parties, it was intended to confer an interest in land, or whether, apart from any intention, the effect of the agreement was such as necessarily to confer such an interest. Now prima facie it appears to me that such an agreement as this is not what would be generally understood as dealing with an interest in land. In ordinary language it is a contract for the use of a graving dock.
>
> *It is possible that in a contract for the use of such a dock such an exclusive right to the possession of the dock as to amount to an interest in land might be intended to be given, and then a written contract would be necessary. I cannot think that there was any such intention here. The terms of the regulations seem to me altogether inconsistent with the notion that the parties intended to give an interest in the land itself, or that the agreement between them amounted to the giving of such an interest. The mere use of the word 'let' in the first regulation, and the words 'occupiers of the dock' in some of the other regulations, is not of itself sufficient to create such an interest. It is obvious that they are not used as terms of art according to a strict unalterable legal signification, and they must be construed in connection with the whole of the document.* [Emphasis added]
>
> The provisions that priority is to be given according to the order of application only so far as possible, and that the borough treasurer is to decide all questions that may arise as to priority, and that his decision shall be final, do not seem very consistent with the notion that an absolute and exclusive interest in land was to be given as suggested. Down to the 7th regulation there is, at any rate, nothing inconsistent with the dock remaining in the possession and under the control of the corporation.
>
> The 7th regulation provides that the vessel may be prevented from leaving the dock if the dockage is not paid: in other words, the supposed tenant is not to be at liberty to walk out of

the tenement the exclusive possession of which is supposed to have been demised to him. The only way of preventing this would be by the corporation's locking the gates, for an injury to which it was suggested in argument trespass would lie by the shipowner. It seems to me that the right to do such an act is the strongest possible evidence of the intention to preserve the authority of the corporation over the dock.

By the 8th regulation again the corporation foreman is to open and shut the dock gates. So that the supposed tenant is not to have power to open and shut the doors of the tenement supposed to be demised to him. The provisions as to use of the blocks, shores, &c., and as to damage done to the property of the corporation, seem to point to the same conclusion, viz. that the intention is that the contract shall be for the use of the corporation's property, but not for the grant of the occupation or possession of the land.

The 11th regulation speaks of the corporation foreman or other person in charge of the dock. Judging of the intention from all these provisions taken together, I should say that the defendants plainly never meant to part with the possession of or control over the dock; the contract is merely for the use of the dock in a certain way and on certain terms while remaining in their possession and under their control. I can see nothing in any of the words of the regulations which, apart from the general intention apparent in the whole of them, necessitates our giving the agreement the effect contended for by the defendants.

It seems to me that the view we take is well within the authority of the decided cases. In the case of *Smith* v. *Overseers of St. Michael, Cambridge* [3 E & E 383], very strong words indeed were construed as not having the effect of taking the possession or property out of the party contracting.

It is true that that was a rating case, and, therefore, not precisely in point, but the principle laid down in the judgments seems applicable to the present case.

Hill, J., says:

> 'We must look not so much at the words as the substance of the agreement, and taking the whole together, we think it must be construed not as a demise of five rooms, but as an agreement by which the appellant, retaining possession of those rooms and keeping his servant there, bound himself to supply the other party there with fire, gas, and attendance. It is true exclusive enjoyment of the rooms is to be given, but that is the case where a guest in an inn or a lodger in a house has a separate apartment, or where a passenger in a ship has a separate cabin; in which case it is clear the possession remains in the innkeeper, lodging-house keeper, or shipowner.'

So here, looking to the substance of the agreement, I think there was no intention to pass an interest in land. The case of *Wright* v. *Stavert* [2 E & E 721] is also strongly in point. I adopt the words of Hill, J., in the case where he says:

> 'The defendant's position here is directly analogous to that of a domestic servant or a governess, or a person employed to build a house upon another's land; all of whom have a right incidental to their respective contracts to go upon land in order to carry out their contracts, but none of whom take under their contracts any interest in the land upon which they are entitled to go.'

These words seem exactly to hit the distinction between the cases within and those not within the statute. Here I think the defendants did not intend to confer any interest in land, though they did give plaintiff a right to go on to the land in order to carry out the contract. I do not think we are called on to discuss the nice question raised upon the effect of *Wood* v. *Leadbitter* [13 M & W 838] in Mr. Cave's ingenious argument, viz. as to whether the plaintiff was a licensee without an interest, and so must fail, because the licence had been revoked; or a licensee with an interest, and so the licence, being irrevocable, amounted to an interest in land. The dilemma suggested does not, as I think, arise. The contract did not relate to the possession or enjoyment of the land or any right over it, but only to the use of it under very stringent regulations, the defendants retaining themselves complete possession of and all rights over it.

The court concluded that the shipowner was not granted 'general control' of the dock. Therefore the 'letting' to the shipowner was in fact only a licence.

REVIEW QUESTION Try and change the terms of the agreement in *Wells* so that there would have been a lease.

(The changes will have to be drastic!)

Shell-Mex v Manchester Garages [1971] 1 WLR 612

In this case Shell granted the use of a filling station it owned to the garage company for one year. The agreement included a provision under which Shell retained control over the layout of the premises. It could move the pumps and the (extensive) underground storage tanks. The arrangement was held to be only a licence. Although this case and *Marchant v Charters*, discussed next, are still correct in their result, some of Lord Denning's remarks in them about 'intent of the parties' are clearly wrong in the light of *Street v Mountford*.

Marchant v Charters [1977] 1 WLR 1181

It has always been accepted that a 'lodger' does not have exclusive possession and therefore is only a licensee. In *Marchant v Charters* [1977] 1 WLR 1181, the 'grantee' was not a lodger in the traditional sense but occupied a 'service flat'. The grantor provided daily cleaning and regular changes of bedlinen. The question was whether the grantee was a licensee, or whether he was a tenant. Lord Denning MR said:

> ... Gathering the cases together, what does it come to? What is the test to see whether the occupier of one room in a house is a tenant or a licensee? ... It does not depend on whether the room is furnished or not. It does not depend on whether the occupation is permanent or temporary. It does not depend on the label which the parties put upon it. All these are factors which may influence the decision but none of them is conclusive. All the circumstances have to be worked out.
>
> Eventually the answer depends on the nature and quality of the occupancy. Was it intended that the occupier should have a stake in the room or did he have only permission for himself personally to occupy the room, whether under a contract or not? In which case he is a licensee.
>
> Looking at the position in this case, in my opinion Mr Charters was not a tenant of this one room. He was only a licensee. A contractual licensee, no doubt, but still only a licensee. So he does not have security of tenure under the Rent Acts. He is not protected against eviction. On this point I differ from the judge. It is sufficient for the deciding of this case. Mr Charters has no right to stay ...

The Court of Appeal held that Mr Charters was a licensee of his service flat, not a lessee.

11.4.3 Retention of Keys by the Grantor

The mere fact that a grantor retains keys to the premises does not as such negate the existence of a lease. In *Aslan v Murphy* [1990] 1 WLR 766, the claimant owned a basement room suitable for only one person and occupied exclusively by the defendant. The agreement under which the defendant held the premises provided that he had a mere 'licence' to occupy the room in common with other licensees, the claimant retained the keys to the room. The defendant was also required to vacate the room for 90 minutes each day. The judge at first instance held that the agreement created a 'licence'. The defendant appealed.

Lord Donaldson of Lymington MR said:

> In this court an attempt to uphold the judge's decision was made upon a different basis, namely, the landlord's right to retain the keys. The provisions relevant to this aspect of the agreement are:
>
>> 1 ... The licensor will retain the keys to the room and has absolute right of entry at all times for the purpose of exercising such control and (without prejudice to the generality of the foregoing) for the purpose of effecting any repairs or cleaning to the room or building or for the purpose of providing the attendance mentioned in clause 4 hereof or for the purpose of removing or substituting such articles of furniture from the room as the licensor might see fit. The said right of entry is exercisable by the licensor or his servants or agents with or without any other persons (including prospective future licensee of the room) ... 4. The licensor will provide the following attendance for the licensee: (1) housekeeping (2) lighting of common parts (3) cleaning of common parts (4) window cleaning (5) intercom (6) telephone coin box (7) cleaning of room (8) collection of rubbish (9) provision and laundering of bed linen (10) hot water (11) provision of household supplies.
>
> Provisions as to keys are often relied upon in support of the contention that an occupier is a lodger rather than a tenant. Thus in *Duke v Wynne* [1990] 1 WLR 766 ... the agreement required the occupier 'not to interfere with or change the locks on any part of the premises, [or] give the key to any other than an authorised occupier of the premises.' Provisions as to keys, if not a pretence which they often are, do not have any magic in themselves. It is not a requirement of a tenancy that the occupier shall have exclusive possession of the keys to the property. What matters is what underlies the provisions as to keys. Why does the owner want a key, want to prevent keys being issued to the friends of the occupier or want to prevent the lock being changed?
>
> A landlord may well need a key in order that he may be able to enter quickly in the event of emergency: fire, burst pipes or whatever. He may need a key to enable him or those authorised by him to read meters or to do repairs which are his responsibility. None of these underlying reasons would of themselves indicate that the true bargain between the parties was such that the occupier was in law a lodger. On the other hand, if the true bargain is that the owner will provide genuine services which can only be provided by having keys, such as frequent cleaning, daily bed-making, the provision of clean linen at regular intervals and the like, there are materials from which it is possible to infer that the occupier is a lodger rather than a tenant. But the inference arises not from the provisions as to keys, but from the reason why those provisions formed part of the bargain. On the facts of this case, the argument based upon the provisions as to keys must and does fail for the judge found that 'during the currency of the present agreement virtually 'no services' had been provided.' These provisions may or may not have been pretences, but they are without significance in the context of the question which we had to decide.

If the keys are retained for emergencies and routine inspections, that does not negate exclusive possession. But if the keys are required for the provision of (daily) services, then the grantee (as in *Marchant v Charters*) has only a licence.

11.4.4 Possessory Licences after *Street v Mountford*

The constantly recurring theme of the decision in *Street v Mountford* is that whether a transaction is a lease or a licence depends on whether exclusive possession is granted. However, almost at the end of his speech, Lord Templeman says this:

Sometimes it may be difficult to discover whether, on the true construction of an agreement, exclusive possession is conferred. Sometimes it may appear from the surrounding circumstances that there was no intention to create legal relationships. Sometimes it may appear from the surrounding circumstances that the right to exclusive possession is referable to a legal relationship other than a tenancy. Legal relationships to which the grant of exclusive possession might be referable and which would or might negative the grant of an estate or interest in the land include occupancy under a contract for the sale of the land, occupancy pursuant to a contract of employment or occupancy referable to the holding of an office. But where as in the present case the only circumstances are that residential accommodation is offered and accepted with exclusive possession for a term at a rent, the result is a tenancy.

In practice it therefore appears that there are, after *Street v Mountford*, four types of situation where somebody can have 'exclusive possession' of property but have only a licence. Put another way, there are four exceptions to the general rule laid down in *Street* that 'exclusive possession means that there is a lease'.

11.4.5 Acts of Generosity, Charity, or Friendship Where There is No Intent to Create Legal Relations

We have already noted *Heslop v Burns* [1974] 1 WLR 1241, where a licence was held to exist (see 'Tenancy at Will', 11.2.3). There is no reason to doubt that that decision is still correct after *Street*. Slightly more debatable is the decision of the Court of Appeal in *Rhodes v Dalby* [1971] 1 WLR 1325. Two men were long-standing friends. One owned a bungalow, but was going abroad for two years. The two men signed a document described as 'a gentleman's agreement' not intended to create legal relations. Under that agreement the friend staying in this country took possession of the bungalow during the two-year absence. He agreed to pay a quite high 'rent' for being able to live in the bungalow. Goff J in considering the 'gentleman's agreement' said:

...The plaintiff fastens on the word 'let', and on the payment of rent. But he cannot use it out of its context. What was admitted was that it was let on a gentleman's agreement. Counsel for the plaintiff very properly conceded that a gentleman's agreement normally means something which is not legally enforceable. I do not see how a letting on a gentleman's agreement, without further explanation, can be held sufficient evidence of a tenancy...

The decision that the agreement was a licence appears to be correct. The crucial fact was that the two men were friends *before* they signed the agreement.

The decision of the Court of Appeal in *Gray v Taylor* [1998] 4 All ER 17 is entirely consistent with *Street v Mountford*. The trustees of some almshouses granted Mrs Taylor exclusive possession of a flat within the almshouses. She did not pay rent, but was required to pay a (small) contribution towards the upkeep of the building. She was held to have only a licence.

11.4.6 Service Occupancies

It is perfectly possible for an employer to grant to an employee a formal lease over a house situated close to the place of work. However (and this is unaffected by *Street v Mountford*), if an employer, without executing a formal lease, allows an employee to live in the employer's accommodation so that they can readily be available for work at any time, the employee has a form of licence known as a 'service occupancy'. This is the case whether or not the employee is obliged by their contract of employment to live in the accommodation. This issue was considered in *Crane v Morris* [1965] 1 WLR 1104, where the defendant was employed as a farm worker and granted exclusive possession of a cottage on the farm upon condition that he remained in the employ of the claimant. The defendant did not pay rent. When the defendant left the claimant's employ and took up work in a factory, the claimant brought an action to regain possession of the premises.

Lord Denning MR said:

> …At one time it was said (as the judge said here) that, for there to be a service occupation and not a tenancy, the servant must be *required* to occupy the house in order to perform his duties, as distinct from being *permitted* to occupy it. It was also said that the difference between a licence and a tenancy was that, on a tenancy, the occupier had exclusive possession, but on a licence, he had not exclusive possession. We have got long past those days. It is now perfectly well settled that a man may be a licensee (and no tenant) even though he has exclusive possession; see *Errington v Errington* [1952] 1 KB 290. And a servant may be a licensee (and no tenant) even though he is not required to live in the house but only permitted to do so for the convenience of his work; see *Torbett v Faulkner* [1952] 2 TLR 659. *In this particular case I have no doubt whatever that the defendant was not a tenant. He was a licensee in the house, with permission to stay there rent free, so long as he remained in the employment of the farmer. Once he ceased to be in that employment, he could be turned out, being given, of course, a reasonable time to go.* It is not necessary to give a licensee notice to quit, any more than it is a tenant at will. A demand is sufficient: and a writ claiming possession is itself a sufficient demand … [Emphasis added]

The defendant was a service occupant (mere licensee), not a tenant.

thinking point 11.4

Can you think of types of workers who often have service occupancies?

Caretakers, agricultural workers, and members of the police, armed forces, and fire brigade often have 'service occupancies'. A rather more unusual case is Norris v Checksfield *[1991] 1 WLR 1241. In that case a coach mechanic had been granted the use of a bungalow close to the depot. The Court of Appeal held that he was a service occupier, not a tenant.*

11.4.7 Occupancy by Virtue of an Office

This point is most likely to affect clergymen, who (you may be surprised to learn) have traditionally not had contracts of employment. Clergymen are only licensees of their manses, vicarages, presbyteries, etc.

REVIEW QUESTION Can you think of other examples of occupancy by virtue of an office?

(There is a famous example in a street in London just off Whitehall!)

11.4.8 Occupancy Prior to the Completion of a Contract for Sale

From time to time a purchaser who has contracted to buy a piece of land is allowed by the vendor to take possession of the property even though the sale has not yet been completed by a conveyance or land transfer.

In the past, it was sometimes said that such a purchaser in possession 'ahead of completion' was a tenant at will. *Street v Mountford* confirms that this view is not correct. Rather, the purchaser is to be regarded as a licensee.

11.4.9 Flat-Sharing Agreements

In recent years there have been a number of cases where the facts have followed a similar sort of pattern. Two (or more) people are together looking for a flat or house to share. They find a 'landlord', who refuses to grant them a lease. Instead the 'landlord' grants each of them a separate 'non-exclusive' licence. Each licence includes a clause under which the grantor can introduce into the property other person(s).

Somma v Hazelhurst [1978] 1 WLR 1014

In this case H and S (a cohabiting couple) had each signed on the same day a separate agreement granting each the use of a bed-sitting room to be shared with a person 'to be introduced'. The Court of Appeal rejected the argument that the two transactions should be read together, and should be regarded as together granting exclusive possession and therefore creating a lease. In the view of the Court of Appeal, two licences had been created.

In the light of later cases, this decision is undoubtedly wrong. It was disapproved of in very strong terms by the House of Lords in *Street v Mountford*. Lord Templeman said of *Somma v Hazelhurst*, 'The agreements [sic] signed by H and S constituted the grant to H and S jointly of exclusive possession at a rent for a term for the purposes for which the room was taken and the agreement [sic] therefore created a tenancy.'

The 1988 Cases

In 1988 the House of Lords gave judgment on the same day in two cases raising the 'non-exclusive licence' issue. In *Antoniades v Villiers* [1988] 1 AC 417, Mr Villiers and Miss Bridger (a cohabiting couple) each signed on the same day an agreement giving them the right to use a small flat. Clause 16 of each agreement provided: 'The licensor shall be entitled at any time to use the rooms together with the licensee and permit other persons to use all of the rooms together with the licensee.'

Lord Oliver of Aylmerton said:

> *Antoniades v Villiers and another* The appellants in this appeal are a young couple who at all material times were living together as man and wife. In about November 1984 they learned from a letting agency that a flat was available in a house at 6, Whiteley Road, London SE19, owned by the respondent, Mr Antoniades. They inspected the flat together and were told that the rent would be £174 per month. They were given the choice of having the bedroom furnished with a double bed or two single beds and they chose a double bed. So, right from the inception, there was never any question but that the appellants were seeking to establish a joint home and they have, at all material times, been the sole occupants of the flat.
>
> There is equally no question but that the premises are not suitable for occupation by more than one couple, save on a very temporary basis. The small living-room contains a sofa capable of being converted into a double bed and also a bed-table capable of being opened out to form a narrow single bed. The appellants did in fact have a friend to stay with them for a time in what the trial judge found to be cramped conditions, but the size of the accommodation and the facilities available clearly do not make the flat suitable for multiple occupation. When it came to drawing up the contractual arrangements under which the appellants were

to be let into possession, each was asked to and did sign a separate licence agreement in the terms set out in the speech of my noble and learned friend, Lord Templeman, under which each assumed an individual, but not a joint, responsibility for payment of one half of the sum of £174 previously quoted as the rent.

There is an air of total unreality about these documents read as separate and individual licences in the light of the circumstance that the appellants were together seeking a flat as a quasi-matrimonial home. A separate licensee does not realistically assume responsibility for all repairs and all outgoings. Nor in the circumstances can any realistic significance be given to clauses 16 and 17 of the document. It cannot realistically have been contemplated that the respondent would either himself use or occupy any part of the flat or put some other person in to share accommodation specifically adapted for the occupation by a couple living together. These clauses cannot be considered as seriously intended to have any practical operation or to serve any purpose apart from the purely technical one of seeking to avoid the ordinary legal consequences attendant upon letting the appellants into possession at a monthly rent. The unreality is enhanced by the reservation of the right of eviction without court order, which cannot seriously have been thought to be effective, and by the accompanying agreement not to get married, which can only have been designed to prevent a situation arising in which it would be quite impossible to argue that the 'licensees' were enjoying separate rights of occupation.

The conclusion seems to me irresistible that these two so-called licences, executed contemporaneously and entered into in the circumstances already outlined, have to be read together as constituting in reality one single transaction under which the appellants became joint occupiers. That of course does not conclude the case because the question still remains, what is the effect? . . .

If the documents fall to be taken seriously at their face value and to be construed according to their terms, I see, for my part, no escape from the conclusion at which the Court of Appeal arrived. If it is once accepted that the respondent enjoyed the right—whether he exercised it or not—to share the accommodation with the appellants, either himself or by introducing one or more other persons to use the flat with them, it is, as it seems to me, incontestable that the appellants cannot claim to have had exclusive possession . . .

If the real transaction was, as the judge found, one under which the appellants became joint tenants with exclusive possession, on the footing that the two agreements are to be construed together, then it would follow that they were together jointly and severally responsible for the whole rent. It would equally follow that they could effectively exclude the respondent and his nominees.

Although the facts are not precisely on all fours with *Somma v Hazelhurst* [1978] 1 WLR 1014, they are strikingly similar and the judge was, in my judgment, entitled to conclude that the appellants had exclusive possession of the premises. I read his finding that, 'the licences are artificial transactions designed to evade the Rent Acts' as a finding that they were sham documents designed to conceal the true nature of the transaction. There was, in my judgment, material on which he could properly reach this conclusion and I, too, would allow the appeal.

Lord Templeman said:

. . . Parties to an agreement cannot contract out of the Rent Acts; if they were able to do so the Acts would be a dead letter because in a state of housing shortage a person seeking residential accommodation may agree to anything to obtain shelter. The Rent Acts protect a tenant but they do not protect a licensee. Since parties to an agreement cannot contract out of the Rent Acts, a document which expresses the intention, genuine or bogus, of both parties or of one party to create a licence will nevertheless create a tenancy if the rights and obligations enjoyed and imposed satisfy the legal requirements of a tenancy. A person seeking residential accommodation may concur in any expression of intention in order to obtain shelter. Since parties to an agreement cannot contract out of the Rent Acts, a document expressed in the language of a licence must nevertheless be examined and construed by the court in order to decide whether the rights and obligations enjoyed and imposed create a licence or a tenancy. A person seeking residential accommodation may sign a document couched in any language in order to obtain shelter. Since parties to an agreement cannot contract out of the Rent Acts, the grant of a tenancy to two persons jointly cannot be concealed, accidentally or by design, by the creation of two documents in the form of licences. Two persons seeking residential accommodation may sign any number of documents in order to obtain joint shelter. In considering one or more documents for the purpose of deciding whether a tenancy has been created, the court must consider the surrounding circumstances including any relationship between the prospective occupiers, the course of negotiations and the nature and extent of the accommodation and the intended and actual mode of occupation of the accommodation. If the owner of a one-bedroomed flat granted a licence to a husband to occupy the flat provided he shared the flat with his wife and nobody else and granted a similar licence to the wife provided she shared the flat with the husband and nobody else, the court would be bound to consider the effect of both documents together. If the licence to the husband required him to pay a licence fee of £50 per month and the licence to the wife required her to pay a further licence fee of £50 per month, the two documents read together in the light of the property to be occupied and the obvious intended mode of occupation would confer exclusive occupation on the husband and wife jointly and a tenancy at the rent of £100.

Landlords dislike the Rent Acts and wish to enjoy the benefits of letting property without the burden of the restrictions imposed by the Acts. Landlords believe that the Rent Acts unfairly interfere with freedom of contract and exacerbate the housing shortage. Tenants on the other hand believe that the Acts are a necessary protection against the exploitation of people who do not own the freehold or long leases of their homes. The court lacks the knowledge and the power to form any judgment on these arguments which fall to be considered and determined by Parliament. The duty of the court is to enforce the Acts and in so doing to observe on principle which is inherent in the Acts and has been long recognised, the principle that parties cannot contract out of the Acts.

The House of Lords, led by Lord Templeman, took a very robust approach. The practical realities had to be looked at. The two agreements were interdependent because both would have been signed or neither. In this situation, the two agreements had to be read together and was in reality a single transaction by Mr Villiers and Miss Bridger. In doing so, the House of Lords viewed the couple as joint tenants, who were granted exclusive possession and therefore they had a lease. For there to be a joint tenancy the four 'unities' must be present (ie title, interest, time, and possession), and in this case despite the fact that the agreements were signed separately, there was evidence of a joint tenancy: the agreements were identical and signed on the same date, and they moved in together.

Clause 16 should be ignored. It had been inserted by the grantor as a 'pretence', in an effort to show that Mr Villiers and Miss Bridger did not together have exclusive possession. Nobody would expect the grantor to exercise the 'right' conferred on him by clause 16. The purported 'licences' were a pretence intended to circumvent the Rent Acts.

Antoniades should be contrasted with *AG Securities v Vaughan* [1988] 1 AC 417. AGS owned a four-bedroomed flat. Each of the four occupiers had signed a non-exclusive licence. Each licence was signed on a different date, was for a different period, and was at a different rent. Was this one lease or four licences?

Lord Oliver of Aylmerton said:

AG Securities v Vaughan and others

The facts in this appeal are startlingly different from those in the case of *Antoniades*. To begin with the appeal concerns a substantial flat in a mansion block consisting of four bedrooms, a lounge, a sitting-room and usual offices. The trial judge found, as a fact, that the premises could without difficulty provide residential accommodation for four persons. There is no question but that the agreements with which the appeal is concerned reflect the true bargain between the parties. It is the purpose and intention of both parties to each agreement that it should confer an individual right on the licensee named, that he should be liable only for the payment which he had undertaken, and that his agreement should be capable of termination without reference to the agreements with other persons occupying the flat. The judge found that the agreements were not shams and that each of the four occupants had arrived independently of one another and not as a group. His finding was that there was never a group of persons coming to the flat altogether ... The only questions are those of the effect of each agreement vis-à-vis the individual licensee and whether the agreements collectively had the effect of creating a joint tenancy among the occupants of the premises for the time being by virtue of their having between them exclusive possession of the premises . . . .

But if the licence agreement is what it purports to be, that is to say, merely an agreement for permissive enjoyment as the invitee of the landlord, then each shares the use of the premises with other invitees of the same landlord. The landlord is not excluded for he continues to enjoy the premises through his invitees, even though he may for the time being have precluded himself by contract with each from withdrawing the invitation. Secondly, the fact that under each agreement an individual has the privilege of user and occupation for a term which overlaps the term of user and occupation of other persons in the premises, does not create a single indivisible term of occupation for all four consisting of an amalgam of the individual overlapping periods. Thirdly, there is no single sum of money payable in respect of use and occupation. Each person is individually liable for the amount which he has agreed, which may differ in practice from the amounts paid by all or some of the others.

... For my part, I agree with the dissenting judgment of Sir George Waller in finding no unity of interest, no unity of title, certainly no unity of time and, as I think, no unity of possession. I find it impossible to say that the agreements entered into with the respondents created either individually or collectively a single tenancy either of the entire flat or of any part of it. I agree that the appeal should be allowed.

The House of Lords held that a lease had not been created. There were four separate licences. There was no evidence of a joint tenancy where the occupiers had unity of title, interest, time, and possession. These agreements were independent and not interdependent as found in *Antoniades v Villiers*.

The Court of Appeal in *Mikeover v Brady* [1989] 3 All ER 618, reinforced the importance of the four unities being present for a joint tenancy. In this case, Mr Brady and Miss Guile (a couple) signed separate but identical licence agreements. They both paid £86.66 monthly rent. Two years later Miss Guile moved out of the property. Mr Brady continued to pay £86.66 per month in rent, but then fell into arrears. Mr Brady claimed that the two agreements were interdependent, which amounted to a lease. The Court of Appeal dismissed his claim and held that Mr Brady was a licensee.

Slade LJ stated:

It is, however, well settled that four unities must be present for the creation of a joint tenancy, namely the unities of possession, interest, title and time ... In the present case there is no dispute that the two agreements of 6 June 1984 operated to confer on the defendant and Miss Guile unity of possession and title. Likewise, there was unity of time in that each of their interests arose simultaneously and was expressed to endure for six months. The dispute concerns unity of interest. The general principle, as stated in Megarry and Wade p 240, is:

'The interest of each joint tenant is the same in extent, nature and duration, for in theory of law they hold but one estate.'

'Interest' in this context must, in our judgment, include the bundle of rights and obligations representing that interest. The difficulty, from the defendant's point of view, is that the two agreements, instead of imposing a joint liability on him and Miss Guile to pay a deposit of £80 and monthly payments of £173.32, on their face imposed on each of them individual and separate obligations to pay only a deposit of £40 and monthly payments of only £86.66. On the face of it, the absence of joint obligations of payment is inconsistent with the existence of a joint tenancy.

The absence of joint monetary obligations on the part of Mr Brady and Miss Guile led the court to conclude that there was no unity of interest, and therefore there was no joint tenancy.

thinking point 11.5

You own a house, the use of which you are willing to grant to full-time students. In mid-September you are approached by a group of four law students, who want accommodation for the forthcoming academic year. They want a lease to last to the following early July. You would rather give them 'non-exclusive licences'. How do you achieve your objective?

To achieve your objective you grant them four separate non-exclusive licences, to begin and end on different dates. For example:

- *Licence A would run from 20 September to 1 July;*
- *Licence B would run from 23 September to 4 July;*
- *Licence C would run from 18 September to 6 July; and*
- *Licence D would run from 25 September to 5 July.*

11.4.10 'Pretence' Clauses Designed to Negate Exclusive Possession

We have already seen that in *Antoniades v Villiers* (see 11.4.9) the grantor inserted the highly artificial clause 16 in an effort to fool the courts into thinking that Mr Villiers and Miss Bridger, even taken together, did not have exclusive possession. The preferred approach adopted by the House of Lords was to focus on the realities of the transaction, such that 'where the language of licence contradicts the reality of lease, the facts must prevail' (per Lord Templeman). The robust approach taken by Lords Templeman and Oliver in *Antoniades* was applied by the Court of Appeal in two cases it decided together in 1989, *Aslan v Murphy* [1990] 1 WLR 766 and *Duke v Wynne* [1990] 1 WLR 766.

In *Aslan v Murphy*, referred to at 11.4.3, A granted to M the use of a tiny basement room. The licence included a term that A could introduce another occupant. It also included another provision that M had no right to use the room between 10.30 and 12.00 hours. Both these clauses were found to be 'pretences', and M was held to be a tenant.

Lord Donaldson of Lymington MR said:

General principles

The status of a tenant is essentially different from that of a lodger and owners of property are free to make accommodation available on either basis. Which basis applies in any particular case depends upon what was the true bargain between the parties. It is the ascertainment of that true bargain which lies at the heart of the problem.

Labelling

The labels which parties agree to attach to themselves or to their agreements are never conclusive and in this particular field, in which there is enormous pressure on the homeless to agree to any label which will facilitate the obtaining of accommodation, they give no guidance at all. As Lord Templeman said in *Street v Mountford* [1985] 1 AC 809, 819:

> 'The manufacture of a five-pronged implement for manual digging results in a fork even if the manufacturer, unfamiliar with the English language, insists that he intended to make and has made a spade.'

Exclusive or non-exclusive occupation

This is the touchstone by which the 'spade' of tenancy falls to be distinguished from the 'fork' of lodging. In this context it is necessary to consider the rights and duties of the person making the accommodation available ('the owner') and the rights of other occupiers. The occupier has in the end to be a tenant or a lodger. He cannot be both. But there is a spectrum of exclusivity ranging from the occupier of a detached property under a full repairing lease, who is without doubt a tenant, to the overnight occupier of a hotel bedroom who, however upmarket the hotel, is without doubt a lodger. The dividing line—the sorting of the forks from the spades—will not necessarily or even usually depend upon a single factor, but upon a combination of factors.

Pretences

Quite apart from labelling, parties may succumb to the temptation to agree to pretend to have particular rights and duties which are not in fact any part of the true bargain. *Prima facie*, the parties must be taken to mean what they say, but given the pressures on both parties to pretend, albeit for different reasons, the courts would be acting unrealistically if they did not keep a weather eye open for pretences, taking due account of how the parties have acted in performance of their apparent bargain. This identification and exposure of such pretences does not necessarily lead to the conclusion that their agreement is a sham, but only to the conclusion that the terms of the true bargain are not wholly the same as those of the bargain appearing on the face of the agreement. It is the true rather than the apparent bargain which determines the question 'tenant or lodger?'

The effect of the Rent Acts

If an occupier would otherwise be protected by the Rent Acts, he does not lose that protection by agreeing that he will surrender it either immediately or in the future and whether directly and in terms or indirectly, e.g. by agreeing to substitute a shared for an exclusive right of occupation should the owner so require; *Antoniades v Villiers* [1990] 1 AC 417, 461 ...

The judge was, of course, quite right to approach the matter on this basis that it is not a crime, nor is it contrary to public policy, for a property owner to license occupiers to occupy a property on terms which do not give rise to a tenancy. Where he went wrong was in considering whether the whole agreement was a sham and, having concluded that it was not, giving effect to its terms, i.e. taking it throughout at face value. What he should have done, and I am sure would have done if he had known of the House of Lords approach to the problem, was to consider whether the whole agreement was a sham and, if it was not, whether in the light of the factual situation the provisions for sharing the room and those depriving the defendant of the right to occupy it for 90 minutes out of each 24 hours were part of the true bargain between the parties or were pretences. Both provisions were wholly unrealistic and were clearly pretences.

The Court of Appeal held that the two clauses regarding the use of the room had no legal significance, and should be ignored.

In *Duke v Wynne* [1990] 1 WLR 766, D granted to Mr and Mrs W (who had two children living with them) a three-bedroom house for two years. D again reserved the right to introduce other occupiers to the property. This clause was found to be a 'pretence'. D had no genuine intention of introducing other person(s) to the house. The Ws were held to have a lease.

11.5 Formalities for Leases

There are three kinds of formality possible for a lease:

1 legal leases arising by express grant;
2 legal leases arising by operation of law;
3 equitable leases arising by virtue of a contract or an informal grant.

11.5.1 Legal Leases by Express Grant

Normally to create a lease which is valid as a legal lease a deed is required (s52 LPA 1925). Moreover, under contemporary law, if a lease by deed for a period of more than seven years is to take effect as a legal lease it must be substantively registered (s4(1)(c)(i) and s27(1)–(2)(b) Land Registration Act 2002 (LRA 2002)).

An exception to the general rule in s52 that a deed is required for a legal lease is provided by s54(2) LPA 1925.

> *Law of Property Act 1925*
>
> 54. Creation of interests in land by parol
>
> (1) All interests in land created by parol and not put in writing and signed by the persons so creating the same, or by their agents thereunto lawfully authorised in writing, have, notwithstanding any consideration having been given for the same, the force and effect of interests at will only.
>
> (2) Nothing in the foregoing provisions of this Part of this Act shall affect the creation by parol of leases taking effect in possession for a term not exceeding three years (whether or not the lessee is given power to extend the term) at the best rent which can be reasonably obtained without taking a fine.

To summarize, under this provision no special formality is required to create a legal lease of three years or less if it satisfies *all* the following conditions (even an oral grant will suffice):

- The lease is for a period not exceeding three years. (This includes periodic tenancies.)
- The lease is at the best rent reasonably obtainable.
- No premium ('fine') is charged for the grant of the lease.
- The lease takes effect in possession immediately.

In *Fitzkriston LLP v Panayi* [2008] L & TR 26, the Court of Appeal confirmed that 'best rent reasonably obtainable' means 'the market rent'. In this case independent evidence had shown that the market value for the rental of the property was around £12,000, whereas the lease agreement referred to a rent of £4,000 per year and according to Rix LJ this was 'not a market rent or best rent'.

11.5.2 Legal Leases by Operation of Law

This applies only to periodic tenancies. A periodic tenancy will arise automatically where a tenant at will (or at sufferance) commences paying rent calculated on a periodic basis. It is in effect presumed that the parties intended a periodic tenancy; see, for example, the case of *Martin v Smith* (1874) LR 9 Ex 50.

cross-reference
See 11.2.1 for a discussion of Prudential Assurance v London Residuary Body.

What the 'period' (weekly, monthly, etc) is for the periodic tenancy depends on the period by reference to which the rent is calculated, looking at all the evidence available. Usually the period by reference to which the rent is calculated is also the period by reference to which it actually has to be paid: £x per week will mean a weekly tenancy; £y a month will mean a monthly tenancy, and so on. In *Prudential Assurance v London Residuary Body* [1992] 2 AC 306, the House of Lords held, applying the principle we are currently considering, that as the rent had been fixed at £30 per annum, a yearly tenancy had arisen.

A problem might seem to arise if, for example, the evidence shows that informally the parties had agreed to a rent of £600 per annum, payable in monthly instalments. As the rent is calculated on an annual basis, there would in this example be a yearly tenancy.

A periodic tenancy by operation of law will not arise if the parties have expressly agreed that the arrangement between them should remain a tenancy at will. Neither will one arise where a prospective lessee has been let into possession, starts paying rent, but continues to negotiate with the landlord for the grant of a fixed term lease: *Javad v Aqil* [1991] 1 All ER 243.

thinking point 11.6

Roger has never owned a car. He has therefore allowed Tom to keep his car in the garage attached to Roger's house. There is nothing in writing, but Tom pays him £100 per month rent. Roger has now bought a car, and therefore wants Tom out of his garage. How much notice must he give?

Assuming that Tom has had exclusive possession, he will have a monthly periodic tenancy. He will therefore be entitled to a month's notice to quit.

11.5.3 Equitable Leases

As a result of *Walsh v Lonsdale* it is sometimes said that 'an agreement for a lease is as good as a lease'. This is rather misleading, as there are in fact important differences between legal leases and equitable leases:

pause for thought

Re-read 3.9.5 and 3.10 regarding the creation of equitable leases. Note particularly the rulings in Walsh v Lonsdale *and* Parker v Taswell.

- A person's right to treat an agreement or an informal grant as an equitable lease depends on his being able to obtain specific performance. (Remember *Coatsworth v Johnson* at 3.10.1.)
- Where the reversion is unregistered title, the equitable lease is registrable as a land charge. (Class C(iv) estate contract.)
- Where the reversion is registered title, an equitable lease can be protected by entering a notice on the register of title (s32 LRA 2002). If the equitable lease is not protected by a

notice, could it become an overriding interest? It cannot be an overriding interest within Sch 3 para 1 LRA 2002 since this only applies to legal leases, but it could of course come within Sch 3 para 2 LRA 2002 if the person with the interest is in actual occupation.

- An equitable lessee is not a 'purchaser of a legal estate' for the purposes of the Land Charges Acts or the old doctrine of notice. Only a legal lessee is a 'purchaser of a legal estate'.

- An assignee of a pre-1996 equitable lease is apparently not directly bound by the obligations in the lease. It seems that the doctrine of 'privity of estate', does not apply to pre-1996 equitable leases.

- Section 62 LPA 1925 (which relates to the implied grant of easements and profits) does not apply to equitable leases.

11.5.4 Equitable Lease and Legal Periodic Tenancy Existing Concurrently

cross-reference
For further discussion on 'privity of estate', see Chapter 13.

As a result of a single informal transaction, a tenant may actually have simultaneously both a legal periodic tenancy and an equitable lease over the same piece of land.

Suppose L and T informally agree (in a document which does not amount to a deed) to a ten-year lease of Blackacre at £500 per annum rent. T takes possession and pays the rent. At *law*, T will have a yearly periodic tenancy by operation of law; *in equity*, T will have a ten-year lease. Applying the usual principle that where law and equity are in conflict, equity should prevail, it is the equitable lease which will govern the rights of the parties.

The legal periodic tenancy will not be totally invalid; rather it will lie dormant. If the equitable lease should fail for any reason such as 'unclean hands' (remember *Coatsworth v Johnson*) or non-registration as a land charge, the legal periodic tenancy will become operative.

thinking point 11.7

In 2010, Carolyn and Dinah entered into a written agreement (which was not in the form of a deed) whereby Carolyn agreed to let to Dinah a field in which Dinah proposed to keep rabbits. The agreement was to last for ten years. The rent was fixed at £60 per month. The field is unregistered title.

Dinah promised that she would not allow her rabbits to escape into neighbouring fields remaining in Carolyn's possession. Numerous rabbits have escaped into Carolyn's fields, causing damage to her crops of lettuces and carrots. Recently Carolyn sold all her fields, including the one occupied by Dinah, to Edwina. Advise Edwina, who wants Dinah to vacate the field immediately.

Dinah originally had an equitable lease, but it certainly will not be binding on Edwina. Even assuming that Dinah registered her equitable lease as a land charge, she clearly has 'unclean hands', and therefore has now lost her claim to an equitable lease. However, Dinah still has her monthly legal periodic tenancy. Edwina will therefore have to give her a month's notice before she can gain possession of the field.

⊙ Concluding Remarks

It is hoped that two things have been achieved in this chapter. First, you should now have enough understanding to be able to decide whether a particular transaction is a lease or whether it is something else. If it is a lease, you should be able to identify what type it is. Secondly, you should have a foundation of knowledge upon which we can build in the next three chapters.

 # Summary

Essential Characteristics of a Lease

- The grant must give exclusive possession.
- The estate must be of a duration permitted for a leasehold estate.
- The grant must have the correct formalities.

Types of Leases

The law recognizes two types of lease:

- fixed term lease; and
- periodic tenancy.

The following transactions *cannot*, in modern law, be valid leases:

1 a lease for an uncertain period (eg so long as Manchester United play in the Premier League) (but note the impact of *Mexfield v Berrisford*);

2 a 'lease for life'—this is converted into a 90-year fixed term; and

3 a perpetually renewable lease—this is converted into 2,000 years' fixed term.

'Tenancies at will' and 'tenancies at sufferance': the law does recognize but these arrangements are *not* leases.

Lease/Licence Distinction

Lease—Key Points to Note

- A lease is a property right which can be sold, given away, or inherited.
- A lease can bind third party purchasers of the reversion.
- A transaction which grants the grantee exclusive possession is (subject to exceptions) a lease.
- A grantee has exclusive possession if he has general overall control of the property.
- A grantee of a flat will normally have exclusive possession, even though the landlord retains a key for emergencies and/or so that he can inspect the property.

Licence—Key Points to Note

- A licence is purely personal to the licensee. It is a personal right.
- A licence cannot be sold or given away.
- A licence does not bind a third party purchaser, unless there is an estoppel.
- A 'lodger' (a common type of licensee) does not have exclusive possession.
- A licence can usually be revoked at will and at any time.

Possessory Licences

The following are licensees, *despite* having exclusive possession:

- a person who occupies land because of the generosity of (or friendship to) the land owner;
- a person who occupies his employer's house/flat so that he can be readily available for work; and
- a person who occupies a house/flat by virtue of his office (eg the Prime Minister's occupation of No 10).

Formalities for Leases

- *Legal lease of more than three years*—a deed is normally required (s52 LPA 1925).
- *Legal lease of more than seven years* must be substantively registered (s4(1)(c) and s27(1)–(2) LRA 2002).
- *Legal lease for not more than three years* at the full market rent can be created without any special formality (s54(2) LPA 1925).
- *Legal periodic tenancy*—can arise 'by operation of law'—this happens without formality if somebody possessing land starts paying a regular rent to the landowner.
- *Equitable lease*—can arise applying the principles in *Walsh v Lonsdale* and *Parker v Taswell*.

Further Reading

Bright, S, 'The uncertainty of certainty in leases' (2012) 128 LQR 337
Discusses the impact of *Mexfield v Berrisford*.

Brown, J and Pawlowski, M, 'Rethinking s 54(2) of the Law of Property Act 1925' [2010] Conv 146
A call for reform of this short but important provision governing formalities for leases lasting not more than three years.

Hill, J, 'Shared accommodation and exclusive possession' (1989) 52 MLR 408
For a discussion of flat-sharing agreements.

Hinojosa, J, 'On property, leases, licences, horses and carts: revisiting Bruton v London & Quadrant Housing Trust' [2005] Conv 114
A reply to Pawlowski's analysis of *Bruton*.

Pawlowski, M, 'The *Bruton* tenancy—clarity or more confusion' [2005] Conv 262
Case commentary on *Bruton v London & Quadrant Housing Trust*.

Waite, AJ, 'Leases and licences: the true distinguishing test' (1987) 50 MLR 226
An in-depth consideration of how to distinguish between leases and licences.

? Question

'Whether a transaction under which someone acquires the right to use another's property is a lease or a licence depends largely, but not exclusively, on whether the transaction grants "exclusive possession." '

Discuss.

12

Obligations in Leases

Introduction

Leases (particularly long leases of commercial properties such as shops, offices, and factories) are often very elaborate documents containing pages and pages of detailed obligations. In essence, a lease is a contract where the landlord and tenant have agreed to certain contractual obligations. These contractual obligations or terms in the contract are known as covenants. The landlord and tenant can expressly agree to certain terms in the lease, or certain obligations are implied by law.

12.1 Implied Landlord's Covenants

As mentioned previously, the lease represents an agreement between the landlord and tenant with regard to their corresponding obligations. Commonly found covenants, whether created expressly or impliedly include: allowing the tenant quiet enjoyment of the lease, prohibiting the landlord from derogating from the landlord's grant of the lease, and repair.

12.1.1 Quiet Enjoyment

Implied into every lease, unless there is an express covenant to the contrary, is a covenant whereby the landlord will not do anything which 'substantially interferes with the tenant's title to, or possession of, the demised premises or with the tenant's ordinary and lawful enjoyment of the demised premises. The interference need not be direct or physical' (per Lord Millett, *Southwark LBC v Mills* [2001] 1 AC 1). What amounts to an interference? Lord Hoffmann in *Southwark LBC v Mills* suggested that this could include 'regular excessive noise'. The House of Lords confirmed that operation of this covenant is purely prospective. According to the House of Lords, 'It is a covenant that the tenant's lawful possession *will* not be interfered with by the landlord or anyone claiming under him. The covenant does not apply to things done before the grant of the tenancy, even though they may have continuing consequences for the tenant' (per Lord Hoffmann).

The quiet enjoyment covenant does not simply deal with the issue of noise. This covenant also prevents the landlord behaving in a manner which is improper. For example, in *Lavender v Betts* [1942] 2 All ER 72 the landlord removed the tenant's doors and windows rendering the flat uninhabitable. The court held that the acts of the landlord were in breach of the covenant for quiet enjoyment.

REVIEW QUESTION Can you think of other examples of the breach of the covenant for 'quiet enjoyment' (perhaps not as extreme as the facts of *Lavender v Betts*)?

12.1.2 Non-Derogation from Grant

Non-derogation from grant means the landlord who has granted a lease to the tenant cannot engage in acts which would undermine the purpose of that lease. Lord Millett in *Southwark*

LBC v Mills noted that 'there seems to be little if any difference between the scope of the covenant [for quiet enjoyment] and that of the obligation which lies upon any grantor not to derogate from his grant. The principle is the same in each case: a man may not give with one hand and take away with the other.'

In *Harmer v Jumbil (Nigeria) Tin Areas Ltd* [1921] 1 Ch 200 the landlord leased the land to the tenant (T1) for the express purpose of storing explosives. The landlord entered into a covenant with the tenant for quiet enjoyment, but no other express covenant. Both parties were aware that storing explosives would require a government licence, and that such a licence was unlikely if there were buildings in the area. The landlord then leased an adjoining property on terms which permitted the re-opening of a mine. The tenants of this property (T2) reopened the mine and erected three buildings close to the explosives store.

Younger LJ said:

> ...the principle that a grantor shall not derogate from his grant, a principle which merely embodies in a legal maxim a rule of common honesty. 'A grantor having given a thing with one hand,' as Bowen L.J. put it in *Birmingham, Dudley and District Banking Co. v. Ross* (1887) 38 Ch. D. 295, 313, 'is not to take away the means of enjoying it with the other.' 'If A. lets a plot of land to B.,' as Lord Loreburn phrases it in *Lyttelton Times Co. v. Warners* [1907] A. C. 476, 481, 'he may not act so as to frustrate the purpose for which in the contemplation of both parties the land was hired.' The rule is clear but the difficulty is, as always, in its application. For the obligation laid upon the grantor is not unqualified. If it were, that which was imposed in the interest of fair dealing might, in unscrupulous hands, become a justification for oppression, or an instrument of extortion. The obligation therefore must in every case be construed fairly, even strictly, if not narrowly. It must be such as, in view of the surrounding circumstances, was within the reasonable contemplation of the parties at the time when the transaction was entered into, and was at that time within the grantor's power to fulfil. But so limited, the obligation imposed may, I think, be infinitely varied in kind, regard being had to the paramount purpose to serve which it is imposed. If, for instance, the purpose of a grant would in a particular case be frustrated by some act of the lessor on his own land which, while involving no physical interference with the enjoyment of the demised property, would yet be completely effective to stop or render unlawful its continued user for the purpose for which alone it was let, I can see no reason at all in principle why...that act should not be prohibited, just as clearly as an act which, though less completely effective in its result, achieved it by some physical interference.

The landlord was under an implied obligation not to do anything which would interfere with the purpose of the lease which was storing explosives. The leasing of adjoining land for mining was a breach of that obligation.

thinking point 12.1

What if in Harmer *the landlord had no idea of the purposes T1 had in mind for the land leased to him?*

There would have been no breach of an implied obligation. The tenant's purpose has to be in the contemplation of both parties.

12.1.3 Liability to Repair—General

Usually the lease itself will contain a clause, either:

• placing liability to repair the property on the landlord;

or

- placing liability to repair on the tenant (common in long leases);

  or

- dividing the responsibility between landlord and tenant. For example, it is quite common to see leases where the landlord promises to do 'external' repairs and the tenant promises to do 'internal' repairs.

The form of repair clause adopted is a matter for negotiation between the parties. This was echoed in the House of Lords in *Southwark LBC v Mills* [2001] 1 AC 1, where Lord Millett stated '[i]n the absence of statutory intervention, the parties are free to let and take a lease of poorly constructed premises and to allocate the cost of putting them in order between themselves as they see fit'. This quotation shows that the parties should decide who is responsible for what. Historically, the common law has generally avoided implying repairing obligations on either the landlord or tenant. However, more recently the courts have shown a willingness to imply a repairing covenant where necessary.

In *Barrett v Lounova (1982) Ltd* [1990] 1 QB 348, a lease of a dwelling house (dating from 1941) included a covenant, where the tenant had covenanted to carry out all the internal repairs on the premises. The question was, 'who should be responsible for carrying out the external repairs?'

Kerr LJ said:

> ...I turn to the issue whether or not there is to be implied a term to the effect that the landlord was bound to keep the outside in reasonable repair, as the recorder decided. In that regard it is common ground that he directed himself correctly when he said:
>
>> Clearly on the authorities the law does not permit the court to imply terms merely on the basis that implication would seem to be reasonable or fair. In essence, what is required before such implication is made is either a situation where the parties to the agreement, if asked about the suggested implied term would have said words such as 'Oh yes, of course we both agree. Is there any need to mention it?;' or where it is not merely desirable but necessary to imply such a term to give business efficacy or in other words necessary to make the contract workable, which amounts to the same thing.
>
> Those two ways of putting the test as to whether or not a term should be implied, sometimes referred to as 'the officious bystander test' and the 'business efficacy test,' are of course correct.
>
> But whether or not, on applying those tests, the implication falls to be made is not easy, and the authorities are of no direct assistance ... on the basis that an obligation to keep the outside in a proper state of repair must be imposed on someone, three answers are possible. First, that the tenant is obliged to keep the outside in repair as well as the inside, at any rate to such extent as may be necessary to enable him to perform his covenant. I would reject that as being unbusinesslike and unrealistic. In the case of a tenancy of this nature, which was to become a monthly tenancy after one year, the rent being paid weekly, it is clearly unrealistic to conclude that this could have been the common intention. In that context it is to be noted that in *Warren* v *Keen* [1954] 1 QB 15, this court held that a weekly tenant was under no implied obligation to do any repairs to the structure of the premises due to wear and tear or lapse of time or otherwise, and that it was doubtful whether he was even obliged to ensure that the premises remained wind and watertight. Any construction which casts upon the tenant the obligation to keep the outside in proper repair must in my view be rejected for these reasons; and also because there is an express tenant's covenant relating to the inside, so that it would be wrong, as a matter of elementary construction, to imply a covenant relating to the outside as well.
>
> The second solution would be the implication of a joint obligation on both parties to keep the outside in good repair. I reject that as being obviously unworkable and I do not think that Mr Pryor really suggested the contrary.

cross-reference
See 12.3 for the implied common law covenants on tenants.

cross-reference
For a more specific discussion on repair, see 12.1.5 and 12.1.6.

> That leaves one with the third solution, an implied obligation on the landlord. In my view this is the only solution which makes business sense. The recorder reached the same conclusion by following much the same route, and I agree with him.
>
> Accordingly I would dismiss this appeal.

In summary, in order to 'give business efficacy to the agreement' (ie to get things to work properly), there was an implied obligation on the landlord to do the external repairs.

It is still possible to have a situation where, because of the drafting of the lease, when a particular type of defect arises in the leased premises neither landlord nor tenant is under a duty to the other party to repair it. For example, in long fixed term leases you will often see a covenant under which the tenant agrees to do the repairs 'fair wear and tear excepted'. If a defect arises in the premises which *is* fair wear and tear, the tenant is not liable to repair the defect; but neither is the landlord liable to make good the defect.

Fitness for Habitation

A distinction is drawn between furnished and unfurnished property in this area. Where the property let is furnished there is an implied covenant that the property is in a fit state to be inhabited at the start of the lease (*Smith v Marrable* (1843) 11 M & W 5). The landlord is not liable if the property becomes unfit for habitation during the course of the tenancy (*Sarson v Roberts* [1895] 2 QB 395).

This duty does not apply to unfurnished property.

Contractual Duty of Care with Respect to Common Parts

The House of Lords in *Liverpool City Council v Irwin* [1977] AC 239 showed a willingness to imply a contractual duty to maintain the essential facilities enjoyed by the tenant where there are flats being rented out to various tenants. The obligation rests on the landlord to keep in reasonable repair common parts; for example, stairs, lifts, and rubbish chutes. If such an obligation were not implied then 'the whole transaction becomes inefficacious, futile and absurd' (per Lord Salmon, *Liverpool City Council v Irwin*).

12.1.4 Implied Covenants—The Landlord and Tenant Act 1985

The Housing Acts 1957 and 1961 imposed on landlords of 'dwelling houses' (ie houses and flats) obligations which applied notwithstanding any agreement to the contrary. These Acts have now been consolidated into the Landlord and Tenant Act 1985.

12.1.5 Sections 8 to 10 Landlord and Tenant Act 1985

Sections 8–10 of the 1985 Act are of extremely limited significance, because they apply *only* to lettings at not more than £52 per annum (£80 per annum within London). They do not apply to lettings for three or more years. The £52/£80 per annum rent limit was laid down in 1957.

Despite repeated criticism from courts, law reform bodies, and academics, the limit has never been raised.

Section 8 provides that the dwelling must be kept 'fit for human habitation'. The standards are strict, detailed matters being set out in the 1985 Act. However, as the rent limits for ss 8–10 are so absurdly low, these provisions have only limited relevance today.

Landlord and Tenant Act 1985

8. Implied terms as to fitness for human habitation

(1) In a contract to which this section applies for the letting of a house for human habitation there is implied, notwithstanding any stipulation to the contrary—

   (a) a condition that the house is fit for human habitation at the commencement of the tenancy, and

   (b) an undertaking that the house will be kept by the landlord fit for human habitation during the tenancy,

(2) The landlord or person authorised by him in writing, may at reasonable times of the day, on giving 24 hours' notice in writing to the tenant or occupier, enter premises to which this section applies for the purpose of viewing their state and condition.

(3) This section applies to a contract if—

   (a) the rent does not exceed the figure applicable in accordance with subsection (4), and

   (b) the letting is not on such terms as to the tenant's responsibility as are mentioned in subsection (5).

(4) . . .

(5) This section does not apply where a house is let for a term of three years or more (the lease not being determinable at the option of either party before the expiration of three years) upon terms that the tenant puts the premises into a condition reasonably fit for human habitation.

(6) In this section 'house' includes—

   (a) a part of a house, and

   (b) any yard, garden, outhouses and appurtenances belonging to the house or usually enjoyed with it.

(10) Fitness for human habitation

In determining for the purposes of this Act whether a house is unfit for human habitation, regard shall be had to its condition in respect of the following matters—

   repair,
   stability,
   freedom from damp,
   internal arrangement,
   natural lighting,
   ventilation,
   drainage and sanitary conveniences,
   facilities for preparation and cooking of food and for the disposal of waste water;

and the house shall be regarded as unfit for human habitation if, and only if, it is so far defective in one or more of those matters that it is not reasonably suitable for occupation in that condition.

The only practical significance of ss 8–10 is shown by the following thinking point.

thinking point 12.2

Martin owns a derelict house in Nottingham. Four students desperate for accommodation approach him. (As it happens, two are studying building, one is studying quantity surveying, and the other interior design.) They say, 'Lease your house to us for two years at one penny a week rent, and we will do it up for you. We can put up with the discomfort!' Advise Martin.

12.1.6 Sections 11 to 14 Landlord and Tenant Act 1985

Sections 11–14 of the 1985 Act repairing obligations apply to all lettings of dwellings for a term of less than seven years; also to lettings for more than seven years if the landlord has an option to terminate within the first seven years. This is subject to the exceptions listed in s14. It is possible for the parties to agree that ss 11–14 shall not apply, but only if the consent of the County Court is obtained in advance. Applications to the court for such consent are relatively rare (s12 Landlord and Tenant Act 1985).

Landlord and Tenant Act 1985

11. Repairing obligations in short leases

(1) In a lease to which this section applies (as to which, see sections 13 and 14) there is implied a covenant by the lessor—

   (a) to keep in repair the structure and exterior of the dwelling-house (including drains, gutters and external pipes),

   (b) to keep in repair and proper working order the installations in the dwelling-house for the supply of water, gas and electricity and for sanitation (including basins, sinks, baths and sanitary conveniences, but not other fixtures, fittings and appliances for making use of the supply of water, gas or electricity), and

   (c) to keep in repair and proper working order the installations in the dwelling-house for space heating and heating water.

(1A) If a lease to which this section applies is a lease of a dwelling-house which forms part only of a building, then, subject to subsection (1B), the covenant implied by subsection (1) shall have effect as if—

   (a) the reference in paragraph (a) of that subsection to the dwelling-house included a reference to any part of the building in which the lessor has an estate or interest; and

   (b) any reference in paragraphs (b) and (c) of that subsection to an installation in the dwelling house included a reference to an installation which, directly or indirectly, serves the dwelling house and which either—

      (i) forms part of any part of a building in which the lessor has an estate or interest; or

      (ii) is owned by the lessor or under his control.

(1B) Nothing in subsection (1A) shall be construed as requiring the lessor to carry out any works or repairs unless the disrepair (or failure to maintain in working order) is such as to affect the lessee's enjoyment of the dwelling-house or of any common parts, as defined in section 60(1) of the Landlord and Tenant Act 1987, which the lessee, as such, is entitled to use.

(2) The covenant implied by subsection (1) ('the lessor's repairing covenant') shall not be construed as requiring the lessor—

   (a) to carry out works or repairs for which the lessee is liable by virtue of his duty to use the premises in a tenant-like manner, or would be so liable but for an express covenant on his part,

   (b) to rebuild or reinstate the premises in the case of destruction or damage by fire, or by tempest, flood or other inevitable accident, or

    (c) to keep in repair or maintain anything which the lessee is entitled to remove from the dwelling-house.

(3)   In determining the standard of repair required by the lessor's repairing covenant, regard shall be had to the age, character and prospective life of the dwelling-house and the locality in which it is situated.

(3A) In any case where—

    (a) the lessor's repairing covenant has effect as mentioned in subsection (1A), and

    (b) in order to comply with the covenant the lessor needs to carry out works or repairs otherwise than in, or to an installation in, the dwelling-house, and

    (c) the lessor does not have a sufficient right in the part of the building or the installation concerned to enable him to carry out the required works or repairs, then, in any proceedings relating to a failure to comply with the lessor's repairing covenant, so far as it requires the lessor to carry out the works or repairs in question, it shall be a defence for the lessor to prove that he used all reasonable endeavours to obtain, but was unable to obtain, such rights as would be adequate to enable him to carry out the works or repairs.

(4)   A covenant by the lessee for the repair of the premises is of no effect so far as it relates to the matters mentioned in subsection (1)(a) to (c), except so far as it imposes on the lessee any of the requirements mentioned in subsection (2)(a) or (c).

(5)   The reference in subsection (4) to a covenant by the lessee for the repair of the premises includes a covenant—

    (a) to put in repair or deliver up in repair,

    (b) to paint, point or render,

    (c) to pay money in lieu of repairs by the lessee, or

    (d) to pay money on account of repairs by the lessor.

(6)   In a lease in which the lessor's repairing covenant is implied there is also implied a covenant by the lessee that the lessor, or any person authorised by him in writing, may at reasonable times of the day and on giving 24 hours' notice in writing to the occupier, enter the premises comprised in the lease for the purpose of viewing their condition and state of repair.

12. Restriction on contracting out of s. 11

(1)   A covenant or agreement, whether contained in a lease to which section 11 applies or in an agreement collateral to such a lease, is void in so far as it purports—

    (a) to exclude or limit the obligations of the lessor or the immunities of the lessee under that section, or

    (b) to authorise any forfeiture or impose on the lessee any penalty, disability or obligation in the event of his enforcing or relying upon those obligations or immunities, unless the inclusion of the provision was authorised by the county court.

(2)   The county court may, by order made with the consent of the parties, authorise the inclusion in a lease, or in an agreement collateral to a lease, of provisions excluding or modifying in relation to the lease, the provisions of section 11 with respect to the repairing obligations of the parties if it appears to the court that it is reasonable to do so, having regard to all the circumstances of the case, including the other terms and conditions of the lease.

13. Leases to which s. 11 applies: general rule

(1)   Section 11 (repairing obligations) applies to a lease of a dwelling-house granted on or after 24th October 1961 for a term of less than seven years.

(2)   In determining whether a lease is one to which section 11 applies—

    (a) any part of the term which falls before the grant shall be left out of account and the lease shall be treated as a lease for a term commencing with the grant,

(b) a lease which is determinable at the option of the lessor before the expiration of seven years from the commencement of the term shall be treated as a lease for a term of less than seven years, and

(c) a lease (other than a lease to which paragraph (b) applies) shall not be treated as a lease for a term of less than seven years if it confers on the lessee an option for renewal for a term which, together with the original term, amounts to seven years or more.

(3) This section has effect subject to—section 14 (leases to which section 11 applies: exceptions), and section 32(2) (provisions not applying to tenancies within Part II of the Landlord and Tenant Act 1954).

14. Leases to which s. 11 applies: exceptions

(1) Section 11 (repairing obligations) does not apply to a new lease granted to an existing tenant, or to a former tenant still in possession, if the previous lease was not a lease to which section 11 applied (and, in the case of a lease granted before 24th October 1961, would not have been if it had been granted on or after that date).

(2) In subsection (1)—

'existing tenant' means a person who is when, or immediately before, the new lease is granted, the lessee under another lease of the dwelling-house;'former tenant still in possession' means a person who—

(a) was the lessee under another lease of the dwelling-house which terminated at some time before the new lease was granted, and

(b) between the termination of that other lease and the grant of the new lease was continuously in possession of the dwelling-house or of the rents and profits of the dwelling-house; and 'the previous lease' means the other lease referred to in the above definitions.

(3) Section 11 does not apply to a lease of a dwelling-house which is a tenancy of an agricultural holding within the meaning of the Agricultural Holdings Act 1986.

(4) Section 11 does not apply to a lease granted on or after 3rd October 1980 to—

a local authority,

a new town corporation,

an urban development corporation,

the Development Board for Rural Wales,

a registered housing association,

a co-operative housing association, or

an educational institution or other body specified, or of a class specified, by regulations under section 8 of the Rent Act 1977 (bodies making student lettings) a housing action trust established under Part III of the Housing Act 1988.

(5) Section 11 does not apply to a lease granted on or after 3rd October 1980 to—

(a) Her Majesty in right of the Crown (unless the lease is under the management of the Crown Estate Commissioners), or

(b) a government department or a person holding in trust for Her Majesty for the purposes of a government department.

The key points to note under ss 11–14 are that the landlord must:

• keep in repair the structure and exterior of the house (including drains, gutters, and external pipes) (*Quick v Taff Ely BC* [1986] 1 QB 809 indicates complications which can arise);

• keep in repair and proper working order the installations in the home for the supply of water, gas, and electricity, for space heating and the heating of water; and

• in the case of blocks of flats, keep in repair 'common parts' such as lifts and staircases (added by s116 Housing Act 1988, thus codifying—for flats—the decision in *Liverpool City Council v Irwin* [1977] AC 239).

Structure and exterior

The landlord is under an implied obligation to keep in repair the structure and exterior of the house under s11(1) Landlord and Tenant Act 1985. The court in *Irvine's Estate v Moran* (1992) 24 HLR 1 provided guidance on what would come within the scope of 'structure' of a house. The court did not consider that structure should be limited to load-bearing parts only, rather it was broad enough to cover the essential appearance, stability, and shape of the house. To be considered as part of the structure it would have to be a material or significant element of the house. Although the court expressed reluctance in providing a specific definition of 'structure', the court was of the view that it does not extend to the various ways in which a house may be fitted out, equipped, decorated, and generally made to be habitable. The court held that windows including sashes, cords, and the window frames came within the scope of 'structure', whereas door furniture and the internal plaster, which was viewed as a decorative finish, did not form part of the structure of the property.

The Court of Appeal in *Grand v Gill* [2011] 1 WLR 2253, took a different view regarding plasterwork and concluded that 'plaster forming part of or applied to walls and ceilings is part of the structure' (per Lloyd and Thomas LJJ).

12.1.7 The Crucial Principle in *O'Brien v Robinson*

The principle in this case applies whenever a landlord is under an obligation to do repairs, whether that obligation is imposed by the terms of the lease or by the Landlord and Tenant Act 1985.

In *O'Brien v Robinson* [1973] AC 912, a tenant and his wife were injured when the ceiling of their flat suddenly and unexpectedly caved in upon them. Some years previously the tenants of the flat above had caused violent vibrations of the ceiling by prolonged 'dancing' and 'banging on the floors'. The tenant sued the landlord for damages for personal injuries.

Lord Morris said:

> ... In the case of *Morgan v Liverpool Corporation* [1927] 2 KB 131 one basis of claim was that there had been a failure to perform the statutory undertaking that the house would be 'kept in all respects reasonably fit for human habitation.' As I have shown, there was at that date a statutory right in a landlord to enter for the purposes of inspection. The accident which gave rise to the claim was that when the upper portion of a window was being opened one of the cords of the window sash broke with the result that the top part of the window slipped down and caught and injured the plaintiff's hand. In the argument on behalf of the plaintiff in the Court of Appeal it was admitted that the defect was a latent one (of which the plaintiff did not know and about which accordingly he could not give any notice) but it was contended that there was a statutory obligation on the landlord which was different from that contained in an ordinary covenant and that in the Act [Housing Act 1925], there were no words requiring that any notice should be given to the landlord. Furthermore, reliance was placed on the statutory right of the landlord to enter and inspect. Apart from any such statutory right the facts of the case showed that there was a notice posted up in the house containing certain conditions which included a reservation by the landlord of the right of entering the house at any time without previous notice in order to view the state of repair.

The Court of Appeal held that the landlord was not liable and that any liability was conditional upon his having been given notice of any defects even though they were latent ones and that this result was not affected by the fact that the landlord had a right to enter in order to inspect ... all three Lords Justices were of the opinion that the claim failed because the landlord did not have notice and because in such a case as that under consideration notice was required before the liability of the landlord to repair existed. Lord Hanworth MR said (at p. 141) that it had 'long been established law that where there is a covenant on the part of a landlord to keep the premises in repair, the tenant must give notice to the landlord of what is out of repair...' He held that notice was required whether or not the landlord had means of access: he said that the fact that the origin of a covenant was statutory did not give the covenant any higher authority than one inserted in a contract by the parties. Atkin LJ said that in ordinary circumstances the obligation of a landlord to do repairs does not come into existence until he has had notice of the defect which his contract to repair requires him to make good. He said, at p. 151:

> I think the power of access that is given, extensive though it may be, does not take the case away from the principle from which the courts have inferred the condition that the liability is not to arise except on notice. The position is quite a satisfactory one, because as soon as the tenant is aware of the defect he must then give notice, and if the landlord does not repair it, the landlord will be liable. If in fact the tenant is not able to ascertain the defect, there seems to be no reason why the landlord should be exposed to what remains still the same injustice of being required to repair a defect of which he does not know, which seems to me to be the real reason for the rule. This was a case in which notice was not given to the landlord. As I have said, it appears to me that, as soon as the defect became so known by the fall of the sash, the tenant was able to give notice to the landlord and did give notice. In my view the landlord then became under a liability to repair in the circumstances of this case, because if he did not, the house would be in a state not in all respects fit for human habitation; but as no notice was given, I think the landlord was not liable ...

In my view, these and other parts of the judgment of Atkin L.J. were based on the reasoning that it is only when defects (though previously latent or invisible) become patent and are made known to the landlord that his liability to repair arises. Furthermore, it seems to me that ... a landlord's obligation to take action only arises when he has notice of a defect. He will not have notice if no one knows that there is a defect.

The question does not now arise for express decision as to whether a landlord's obligation to repair will arise not only when he receives notice from his tenant of a defect but also if he receives such notice aliunde or if he has knowledge of it: but I observe that in *Griffin v. Pillet* [1926] 1 K.B. 17, where a lessee gave notice that steps to a dwelling house needed attention but where the lessee did not know that the steps were in fact actually dangerous, Wright J. held that a liability rested upon the lessor when subsequently he, though not his lessee, did acquire knowledge that the steps were actually dangerous. The purpose of a notice is to impart knowledge that the moment for action under a covenant to repair has or may have arisen. If a lessor who is under an obligation to keep premises in repair acquires knowledge that there is a state of disrepair which may be dangerous, then, even if such knowledge is not shared by the lessee, I would consider that there arises an obligation on the part of the lessor to take appropriate action.

It is clear that in *O'Brien v Robinson* [1973] AC 912 their Lordships held that a landlord can be liable for disrepair only if either:

- the landlord knows of the need for repair;

  or

- the landlord has 'had information about the existence of a defect ... such as would put him on enquiry as to whether works of repair were needed'.

thinking point 12.3

What is the moral of this case for tenants who are concerned about the condition of their premises?

If your landlord is liable to do the repairs, tell the landlord of any defect or possible defect the moment it arises. Until the landlord has been told of the defect, the landlord cannot be made liable for any damage suffered by the tenant as a result of the disrepair.

If a landlord is liable to do repairs the landlord will in practice expressly reserve a right to enter the premises to carry out the repairs. The House of Lords has assumed that such an express right entitles a landlord to take complete possession temporarily, if temporary complete possession is necessary to carry out the repairs: *Heath v Drown* [1973] AC 498.

12.1.8 Landlord's Covenant to Repair Common Parts

The Court of Appeal has held that where a landlord covenants with a tenant to repair property which the landlord retains *in the landlord's possession* (eg in particular the landlord promises to repair the common parts of a block of offices or flats) the principle in *O'Brien v Robinson* does not apply.

In *British Telecom v Sun Life Assurance* [1996] Ch 69 the Court of Appeal held that a landlord must make good defects in the property retained by the landlord, whether or not the landlord knew that there might be a defect and whether or not the tenant(s) have complained. In this case the claimant company was the tenant of premises on the sixth and seventh floors of a building under a lease which required the defendant company, as landlord, to keep the building as a whole, and not merely the demised premises, in 'complete good and substantial repair and condition'. In the summer of 1986 a bulge appeared in the brick cladding forming part of the external walls and main structure of the building at fifth-floor level. On 1 September 1986, the landlord was informed of the disrepair, which was caused by the fact that the external cladding had been badly fixed to the inner wall. The landlord immediately erected scaffolding and temporary protection and took steps preparatory to carrying out the necessary remedial work, which began in February 1988. In the meantime the tenant brought proceedings against the landlord, claiming damages for breach of its repairing covenant which, the tenant contended, occurred immediately the bulge in the cladding appeared. The judge ruled, on a preliminary issue of construction, that the landlord was in breach of its covenant to keep the other parts of the building, in which the demised premises were situated, in repair immediately a problem arose. The landlord appealed, contending that the breach, if any, occurred only on the expiration of a reasonable period for doing the repairs following the appearance of the defect.

Nourse LJ said:

> ... It is now established by a line of authority culminating in the decision of the House of Lords in *O'Brien* v *Robinson* [1973] AC 912 that, where a defect occurs in the demised premises themselves, a landlord is in breach of his obligation to keep them in repair only when he has information about the existence of the defect such as would put a reasonable landlord on inquiry as to whether works of repair to it are needed and he has failed to carry out the necessary works with reasonable expedition thereafter (see [1973] AC 912 at 928, 930 per Lord Diplock). It has come as something of a surprise to me to learn that there is no decision of comparable authority governing the case where the defect occurs in premises not comprised in the demised premises themselves.
>
> The basic submission of Mr Reynolds QC, for the defendant, is that to such a case the rule established by *O'Brien* v *Robinson* applies by analogy. He accepts that, since the premises affected by the defect are either in his possession or under his control, the landlord must be treated as having the necessary knowledge of it. But he submits that the landlord is in breach of his obligation to keep the premises in repair only when the defect occurs and he has failed to carry out the necessary repairs with reasonable expedition thereafter. In support of these submissions Mr Reynolds referred us at some length to the judgments in the Court of Appeal in Ireland in *Murphy* v *Hurly* [1921] 2 IR 335 and the speeches in the House of Lords (see [1922] 1 AC 369), but I did not find those references to be of any significant assistance.

For a reason which will appear in due course, I was for much of the argument inclined to the view that Mr Reynolds' submissions were, or at all events ought to be, correct. But a consideration of the authorities on which the rule established by *O'Brien* v *Robinson* is founded has satisfied me that it is in truth an exception from the general rule and, moreover, one which proves it . . . .

. . . The general rule is that a covenant to keep premises in repair obliges the covenantor to keep them in repair at all times, so that there is a breach of the obligation immediately a defect occurs. There is an exception where the obligation is the landlord's and the defect occurs in the demised premises themselves, in which case he is in breach of his obligation only when he has information about the existence of the defect such as would put a reasonable landlord on inquiry as to whether works of repair are needed and he has failed to carry out the necessary works with reasonable expedition thereafter.

I desire to make two further points. First, I express no concluded view as to the case where a defect is caused by an occurrence wholly outside the landlord's control. Suppose, for example, that the roof of the house in *Melles & Co.* v *Holme* [1918] 2 KB 100 had been damaged by a branch from a tree standing on neighbouring property not in the possession or control of the landlords and that the rainwater had found its way down into the plaintiff's rooms by that means. The stance adopted by Mr Gaunt QC, for the plaintiff, was that such a case would be covered by the general rule, and it was that which caused me to start by thinking that Mr Reynolds' submissions ought to be correct. On reflection and provisionally, I can see no reason why such a case should not, for reasons similar to those expressed in *Makin* v *Watkinson* (1870) LR 6 Exch 25, be made the subject of a further exception to the general rule. That point will have to be decided if and when it arises for decision.

Secondly, Mr Gaunt was disposed to accept that the position might be different in a case where the landlord's obligation was not to keep the premises in repair, but simply to repair them. Having confined myself to the former obligation, I say nothing about the latter, which is in any event, as I believe, a rarity in modern leases and tenancy agreements. I would dismiss this appeal.

A covenant in a lease to keep the demised premises in 'complete good and substantial repair and condition' which extended to the building as a whole obliged the landlord to keep the other parts of the building in which the demised premises were situated in repair at all times; consequently there was a breach of the repairing covenant immediately a defect occurred.

The landlord was therefore in breach of covenant as soon as the property ceased to be in a state of repair and not at the later time when the landlord had information about the existence of the defect and had failed to carry out the necessary works with reasonable expedition.

12.1.9 What does 'Repair' Mean?

The same principles apply whether it is a landlord's covenant or a tenant's covenant.

Leases often use phrases such as 'good tenantable repair', 'substantial repair', 'satisfactory repair', etc. However, it seems that the adjectives are superfluous, and add nothing to the basic meaning of 'repair'.

The duty to repair was expressed thus by *Cheshire*:

. . . after making due allowance for the locality, character and age of the premises at the time of the lease, he must keep them in the condition in which they would be kept by a reasonably minded owner. [*Cheshire and Burn*, 17th edn, p 246.]

The standard of repair is fixed at the commencement of the lease. An example of this can be found in *Anstruther-Gough-Calthorpe v McOscar* [1924] 1 KB 716. A 95-year lease was granted in 1825 of three houses. They were built in 1825, in a very pleasant position on the then edge of the built-up area of London. By the time the lease expired in 1920 the area (in the vicinity of King's Cross station) had become very 'run down'. The landlord brought an action against the tenant for breaking the covenant to repair. Scrutton LJ said:

> ...The question in dispute seems to be whether, as the purposes for which such a subject matter is ordinarily used may vary from time to time, the standard of repair is to vary from time to time, or remains as it was when the subject matter was demised. For instance, where a fashionable mansion let for a long term of years has fallen to the position of a tenement house for the poorer classes, is the standard of repair to become less onerous than when the house is let?
>
> To take an illustration of Bankes LJ, if the sub-tenants of a tenement house do not want a front door, is the tenant to be excused from keeping a properly repaired front door on the premises? In my view this question has been decided, as far as this Court is concerned, by the decision in *Morgan v Hardy* (1886) 17 QBD 770. In that case the referee had to decide between the claim that the premises must be properly repaired and the contention that, as the premises and the neighbourhood had deteriorated, and in consequence of such deterioration a great portion of the repairs required 'were not suited to the said premises and were unnecessary for their use and enjoyment', they need not be considered in awarding damages. This Court, affirming Denman J, said very summarily that it was a wholly untenable proposition to say that the depreciation of the neighbourhood ought to lower the amount of damages for breach of a covenant to repair. This can only mean that the fact that the class of persons who would use the house at the end of the term had deteriorated, so that their requirements in the way of repairs were less, was immaterial in ascertaining the repairs that the tenant was bound to execute. *Morgan v Hardy* was the case of a fifty years' lease.
>
> In *Proudfoot v Hart* (1890) 25 QBD 42 the lease was for three years only, and the covenant was to keep in good tenantable repair. There was no suggestion of any change in character of the house or its probable tenants between the beginning and the end of the term. Lopes LJ framed a definition which Lord Esher adopted as follows: 'Such repair, as having regard to the age, character, and locality of the house, would make it reasonably fit for the occupation of a reasonably minded tenant of the class who would be likely to take it.' I do not think there was any intention of suggesting that a deterioration in the class of tenants would lower the standard of repairs; the point was not before the Court, and had been decided the other way by the Court four years previously. Therefore in my view we are bound to look to the character of the house and its ordinary uses at the time of the demise. It must then be put in repair and kept in repair. An improvement of its tenants or its neighbourhood will not increase the standard of repair, nor will their deterioration lower that standard....

The tenant (even in 1920) should have maintained the property to the 1825 standard.

thinking point 12.4

Just pause for a few moments and consider the possible financial implications of Anstruther-Gough-Calthorpe v McOscar *for tenants who hold under long leases.*

The rule applied in that case is of course extremely harsh on tenants of long leases who have covenanted to repair. That is why a tenant's promise to repair is nowadays often subject to the proviso 'fair wear and tear excepted'. If such a proviso is included the tenant will not have to make good the natural ageing of the premises.

The 'fair wear and tear exception' may not be much protection for tenants in some kinds of situations, as Talbot J explained in *Haskell v Marlow* [1928] 2 KB 45:

> The tenant is bound to do such repairs as may be required to prevent the consequences flowing originally from wear and tear from producing others which wear and tear would not directly produce. For example, if a tile falls off the roof, the tenant is not liable for the immediate consequences, but if he does nothing and in the result more and more water gets in, the roof and walls decay and ultimately the top floor, or the whole house, becomes uninhabitable, he cannot say that it is due to reasonable wear and tear.

12.1.10 The Repair/Reconstruction Distinction

An obligation to 'repair' extends to replacing defective subsidiary parts of a building, but not to complete reconstruction of the building. In *Ravenseft Properties v Davstone Ltd* [1980] QB 12, Forbes J restated the test thus:

> ...it is always a question of degree whether that which the tenant[/landlord] is being asked to do can properly be described as repair, or whether on the contrary it would involve giving back to the landlord[/tenant] a wholly different thing from that which he [leased].

In *Ravenseft Properties Ltd v Davstone (Holdings) Ltd*, stone-cladding on a concrete block of flats began to bow away from the wall. In order to address the risk of stones falling, the landlord made full repairs. The tenant, a property development company, had covenanted to be liable for repairs and so the landlord company brought the present action to recover the cost of the works it had carried out.

Forbes J:

> The true test is...it is always a question of degree whether that which the tenant is being asked to do can properly be described as repair, or whether on the contrary it would involve giving back to the landlord a wholly different thing from that which he demised.

> In deciding this question, the proportion which the cost of the disputed work bears to the value or cost of the whole premises, may sometimes be helpful as a guide. In this case the figures have not been finally worked out in complete detail.... I accept Mr Clark's estimate that the cost would have been in the region of £5,000. The total cost of the remedial works was around £55,000, the balance of £50,000 being for re-fixing the stones and other ancillary works which was not, as I find, necessary to cure any defect of design, but to remedy what was originally defective workmanship. For comparison, the cost of building a structure of this kind in 1973 would have been in the region of £3 million, or rather more. I find myself wholly unable to accept that the cost of inserting these joints could possibly be regarded as a substantial part of the cost of the repairs, much less a substantial part of the value or cost of the building. Mr Colyer urges me not to consider cost and that may, perhaps, in some circumstances, be right. He argues that the result of carrying out this improvement is to give back to the landlord a safe building instead of a dangerous one and this means the premises now are of a wholly different character. Further, he argues that because they are of a wholly different character, the work on expansion joints, the work necessary to cure the inherent defect, is an improvement of a character which transforms the nature of the premises demised, and, therefore, cannot fall within the ambit of the covenant to repair. I cannot accept this. The expansion joints form but a trivial part of this whole building and looking at it as a question of degree, I do not consider that they amount to such a change in the character of the building as to take them out of the ambit of the covenant to repair. I pass to Mr Colyer's second point, namely, that the tenant is not liable under the repair covenant for that part of any work of repair necessary to remedy

an inherent defect. Again it seems to me that this must be a question of degree. I do not consider that they amount to such a change in the character of the building as to take them out of the ambit of the covenant to repair.

It was a question of degree whether the works carried out by the landlord were properly to be described as 'repairs' or 'improvements'. On the facts of *Ravenseft* the works were to be regarded as repairs, because at the end of the lease the tenant would return to the landlord substantially the same building that the landlord had originally leased out.

In *Lister v Lane* [1893] 2 QB 212 the tenant did not have to reconstruct the whole house when the foundations became unsafe. However, in *Lurcott v Wakely* [1911] 1 KB 905, the tenant had to replace the front wall of a house, and in *Ravenseft Properties v Davstone Ltd* [1980], as we have seen, a property company had to replace the external stone-cladding on the whole of a block of flats. 'Repair' includes painting only in so far as painting is necessary to prevent deterioration of woodwork.

12.1.11 Uncomfortable Living Conditions

In *Quick v Taff Ely Borough Council* [1986] 1 QB 809, the claimant was tenant of a council house. The tenant complained of condensation, created by the type of windows in the house, which caused damage to the woodwork and furniture. The tenant brought proceedings for an order of specific performance of the landlord's obligation to repair the 'structure and exterior' of the premises.

Dillon LJ:

> ...In my judgment, the key factor in the present case is that disrepair is related to the physical condition of whatever has to be repaired, and not to questions of lack of amenity or inefficiency. I find helpful the observation of Atkin LJ in *Anstruther-Gough-Calthorpe v McOscar* [1924] 1 KB 716, 734 that repair 'connotes the idea of making good damage so as to leave the subject so far as possible as though it had not been damaged.' Where decorative repair is in question one must look for damage to the decorations but where, as here, the obligation is merely to keep the structure and exterior of the house in repair, the covenant will only come into operation where there has been damage to the structure and exterior which requires to be made good.
>
> If there is such damage caused by an unsuspected inherent defect, then it may be necessary to cure the defect, and thus to some extent improve without wholly renewing the property as the only practicable way of making good the damage to the subject matter of the repairing covenant. That, as I read the case, was the basis of the decision in *Ravenseft v Davstone Ltd* [1980] QB 12. There was an inherent defect when the building, a relatively new one, was built in that no expansion joints had been included because it had not been realised that the different coefficients of expansion of the stone of the cladding and the concrete of the structure made it necessary to include such joints. There was, however, also physical damage to the subject matter of the covenant in that, because of the differing coefficients of expansion, the stones of the cladding had become bowed, detached from the structure, loose and in danger of falling. Forbes J in a very valuable judgment rejected the argument that no liability arose under a repairing covenant if it could be shown that the disrepair was due to an inherent defect in the building. He allowed in the damages under the repairing covenant the cost of putting in expansion joints, and in that respect improving the building, because, as he put it, at p. 22, on the evidence 'In no realistic sense...could it be said that there was any other possible way of reinstating this cladding than by providing the expansion joints which were, in fact, provided.'
>
> ...

In the present case the liability of the council was to keep the structure and exterior of the house in repair—not the decorations. Though there is ample evidence of damage to the decorations and to bedding, clothing and other fabrics, evidence of damage to the subject matter of the covenant, the structure and exterior of the house, is far to seek. Though the condensation comes about from the effect of the warm atmosphere in the rooms on the cold surfaces of the walls and windows, there is no evidence at all of physical damage to the walls—as opposed to the decorations—or the windows.

There is indeed evidence of physical damage in the way of rot in parts of the wooden surrounds of some of the windows but (a) that can be sufficiently cured by replacing the defective lengths of wood and (b) it was palpably not the rot in the wooden surrounds which caused damage to the bedding, clothes and fabrics in the house, and the rot in the wooden surrounds cannot have contributed very much to the general inconvenience of living in the house for which the judge awarded general damages.

Despite the miserable conditions described in the penultimate paragraph of the extract, the council was held not liable by the Court of Appeal. Evidence of lack of amenity was not evidence of a need for repair.

12.2 Remedies for Breach of the Landlord's Covenants to Repair

If a landlord is in breach of a covenant to repair, then the most usual remedy for the tenant is to sue for damages. However, in the last 40 years both the courts and Parliament have been busy expanding the remedies available to tenants against recalcitrant landlords who fail to do repairs which they know need doing.

12.2.1 No Rent-Strikes, *But ...*

pause for thought

Never forget the principle in O'Brien v Robinson that a landlord becomes liable only if the landlord knew or ought to have known of the defect: see 12.1.7.

A tenant cannot simply go on 'rent-strike'. The tenant cannot say to the landlord, 'I am not paying the rent until you do the repairs'. The tenant can, however, carry out the repairs himself (or herself) or employ contractors to do the work and deduct the cost from future instalments of rent: *Lee-Parker v Izzet* [1971] 1 WLR 1688. In this case, the tenants, having executed certain repairs on their own account, sought to withhold rent to cover the cost they had incurred. The landlord should have carried out the repairs himself. Goff J said:

> ...the third and fourth defendants further claim a lien for the cost of the repairs or alternatively for the value of any permanent improvement effected thereby, and they also claim a set off against rent in their capacity as tenants.
>
> First, they say that in so far as the first defendant was, as landlord, liable to do the repairs by the express or implied terms of the tenancy agreement, including the covenants imported by section 32(1) of the Housing Act 1961, they, having done them themselves, are entitled to treat the expenditure as a payment of rent, for which reliance is placed on *Taylor v Beal* [1591] Cro Eliz 222. That is dicta only and the actual decision must have been the other way, because one of the majority in opinion thought the point was not open on the pleadings. However, *Woodfall's Landlord and Tenant* says the case—that is, the *dicta*—would still seem to be the law: see 27th edn. (1968), vol. 1, p. 655 para. 1490. The case is dealt with in *Foa's General Law*

of Landlord & Tenant, 8th edn. (1957), on the question of distress only, at p. 559, citing also *Davies* v *Stacey* (1840) 12 Ad & El 506, where the point was left open. *Foa* states, at p. 559:

> 'Where the lessor covenants to repair and neglects to do so, and the repairs are thereupon executed by the lessee, a payment made by the lessee for the cost of such repairs is not (it is submitted) equivalent to payment of rent so as to reduce the amount for which the landlord may distrain.'

> ... I do not think this is bound up with technical rules of set off. It is an ancient common law right. I therefore declare that so far as the repairs are within the express or implied covenants of the landlord, the third and fourth defendants are entitled to recoup themselves out of future rents and defend any action for payment thereof. It does not follow however that the full amount expended by the third and fourth defendants on such repairs can properly be treated as payment of rent. It is a question of fact in every case whether and to what extent the expenditure was proper. ...

The tenants could withhold rent to cover the repairs. This was not by way of lien or set-off, but was an ancient common law right. The tenants would not have been able to withhold rent had they not executed the repairs themselves at their own cost.

thinking point 12.5

Suppose that the rent is £50 per week. The tenant spends £1,000 on repairs. If the tenant invokes Izzet's case, what does the tenant say to the landlord or the landlord's rent collector?

The tenant can say, 'See you in 20 weeks' time'.

We must, however, warn you that this 'do-it-yourself' remedy has its limitations. First, a tenant contemplating employing builders to do the repairs should ensure that the tenant gets several quotations before engaging contractors to do the repairs. Secondly, this remedy is not much good where a landlord has allowed a whole block of offices or flats, leased to individual tenants, to fall into a bad state of disrepair. Repairing the whole block is likely to be beyond the resources of an individual tenant, and even beyond the resources of the tenants acting jointly.

12.2.2 Specific Performance for Breach of a Repairing Obligation

Where the property is a dwelling house s17(1) Landlord and Tenant Act 1985 specifically authorizes the courts to award specific performance of the landlord's obligation to repair. This is notwithstanding the fact that the tenant is still in possession of the property to be repaired.

Landlord and Tenant Act 1985

17. Specific performance of landlord's repairing obligations

(1) In proceedings in which a tenant of a dwelling alleges a breach on the part of his landlord of a repairing covenant relating to any part of the premises in which the dwelling is comprised, the court may order specific performance of the covenant whether or not the breach relates to a part of the premises let to the tenant and notwithstanding any equitable rule restricting the scope of the remedy, whether on the basis of a lack of mutuality or otherwise.

If the facts of the instructive case *Jeune v Queen Cross Properties* [1974] Ch 97 were to recur today, the tenants would undoubtedly seek an order under s17(1) Landlord and Tenant Act 1985. The claimant tenants sought an order that the defendant landlord should reinstate a York stone balcony which had partially collapsed at the front of their house, spoiling the appearance of the whole of a Georgian terrace. Pennycuick V-C considered whether a tenant could obtain an order of specific performance against the landlord:

> Now, on the face of it, in common sense and justice, it seems perfectly clear that this is the appropriate relief [order for specific performance]. The defendant's repairing covenant requires it to maintain, repair and renew the structure, including the external walls. A mandatory order upon the defendant to reinstate the balcony is a much more convenient order than an award of damages leaving it to the individual plaintiffs to do the work. There is nothing burdensome or unfair in the order sought.
>
> My only pre-occupation in this matter has been in regard to a principle which I am told is stated in some textbooks to the effect that specific performance will never be ordered of repairing covenants in a lease. So far as the general law is concerned, apart from a repairing covenant in a lease, it appears perfectly clear that in an appropriate case the court will decree specific performance of an agreement to build if certain conditions are satisfied . . .
>
> Now [the decision in *Hill v Barclay*] is, I think, an authority laying down the principle that a landlord cannot obtain against his tenant an order for specific performance of a covenant to repair. It does not however apply to a landlord's covenant to repair, although it is said that there may be some other explanation for the words 'The difficulty upon this doctrine of a court of equity is, that there is no mutuality in it.'
>
> Counsel for the plaintiff has looked through various textbooks on the law of landlord and tenant and assures me that, although *Hill v Barclay* (1810) 16 Ves 402 is repeatedly cited, there is no other authority in point.
>
> It is worthwhile to refer to two passages in Halsbury's Laws of England. In the landlord and tenant volume it is stated:
>
> > 'Unless the lease contains a proviso empowering the landlord to re-enter for forfeiture on breach of the covenant to repair, the landlord's remedy is an action for damages; for specific performance of such a covenant will not ordinarily be granted'.
>
> Reference is made there to *Hill v Barclay* . . .
>
> In *Halsbury*, vol. 36 (1961)—on specific performance—there is this passage, at p. 267: 'In particular, the court does not, as a rule, order the specific performance of a contract to build or repair.' It then goes on to refer to the circumstances in which specific performance of a contract to build will be granted.
>
> There is nothing at all there inconsistent with a power in the court to make an order on a landlord to do specific work under a covenant to repair. I cannot myself see any reason in principle why, in an appropriate case, an order should not be made against a landlord to do some specific work pursuant to his covenant to repair. Obviously, it is a jurisdiction which should be carefully exercised. But in a case such as the present where there has been a plain breach of a covenant to repair and there is no doubt at all what is required to be done to remedy the breach, I cannot see why an order for specific performance should not be made against the landlord to do some specific work pursuant to his covenant to repair.

The court applying general principles of equity, decreed specific performance of the landlord's obligation to repair the balcony. In this case the landlord was plainly in breach of the covenant and there was no doubt as to what precisely was required to be done to remedy the breach.

REVIEW QUESTION Bearing in mind the facts of Jeune v Queens Cross, can you think of other situations where a tenant would be particularly keen to get specific performance?

12.2.3 Appointing a Receiver

cross-reference
For a discussion of the role of receivers in the law of mortgages, see 23.5.

In the last 30 years or so there have been increasing problems with recalcitrant private landlords of blocks of flats and blocks of offices failing to carry out their repairing obligations. Often the premises involved are 'up market'.

In 1983 somebody hit upon the bright idea of invoking s37 Supreme Court Act 1981 to appoint a receiver: *Hart v Emelkirk* [1983] 3 All ER 15. Mention of the word 'receiver' probably makes you think of insolvent companies; but 'receivers' have their uses in land law! We shall come across them again in the law of mortgages.

In the present context, 'appointing a receiver' works as follows:

* The court appoints a responsible professional person to act as receiver.
* The landlord must hand over management (though not of course ownership) of the block to the receiver.
* Rents are now payable to the receiver, not to the landlord.
* The receiver uses the money from the rents to pay for the repairs.

The remedy under s37 of the 1981 Act does unfortunately have its limitations as illustrated by the facts of *Evans v Clayhope Properties Ltd* [1987] 2 All ER 40. Suppose the block requires very extensive repairs, costing more than the total of several years' rent. Such a situation is far from unknown. Appointing a receiver under s37 is no good. The receiver cannot enter into long-term repair contracts binding on the landlord. Neither can the receiver mortgage the block to finance the repairs.

On a rather different point, s37 of the 1981 Act cannot be invoked against a local authority landlord which fails to repair its housing stock: *Parker v Camden LBC* [1985] 2 All ER 141. This is because s111 Housing Act 1957 unequivocally vests the management of local authority housing in the local authority.

12.2.4 Appointing a Receiver-Manager

The tenants of a privately owned block of flats (but not offices) were in 1987 given a new stronger 'receiver' remedy against landlords who fail to do repairs. They can apply for the appointment of a receiver-manager under ss 21–24 Landlord and Tenant Act 1987. This application for a receiver-manager used to be made to the County Court, but must now be made to the Property Chamber of the 'First Tier Tribunal'. It would appear that under s24 the tribunal could (unlike the courts under the Supreme Court Act 1981):

* authorize the receiver-manager to mortgage the block to pay for repairs; and/or
* require the landlord to pay repair bills incurred by the receiver-manager.

12.2.5 Local Authorities Taking Action against Private Landlords

Where a house, flat, or block of flats is in disrepair, the local district council can serve a notice on the landlord requiring specified repairs. If the landlord fails to comply, the council can enter the property, carry out the repairs, and charge them to the landlord (see the Housing Acts 1957–1988; Secure Tenants of Local Housing Authorities (Right to Repair) Regulations (SI 133/1994), (SI 844/1994) and (SI 73/1997)).

12.2.6 Measure of Damages Against Landlords

If a tenant sues the landlord for damages, the tenant can recover, in addition to the cost of repairs actually done by the tenant:

- compensation for any injury to health suffered; and
- the cost of alternative accommodation if the disrepair is such as to render the premises uninhabitable.

In *Calabar Properties v Stitcher* [1984] 1 WLR 287, the condition of the tenant's flat was so bad she became ill and had to rent alternative accommodation. The defects in the external parts of certain rented premises had resulted in the interior becoming damp. Consequently, the tenant withheld payment of ground rent and was sued by the landlords. The tenant counterclaimed for damages for breach of the landlord's covenant to keep external parts in good repair. After some time the dampness, which had resulted in ill health, forced the tenant to vacate the premises. The judge at first instance found for the tenant and awarded damages for the cost of repairing the flat and for disappointment, discomfort, loss of enjoyment, and ill health. However, the judge refused to award damages for loss of use and wasted rent, etc during the period for which the house was uninhabitable, as this had not been included in the tenant's counterclaim. The Court of Appeal affirmed the judge's conclusions. Griffiths LJ in considering the claim stated:

> ...The object of awarding damages against a landlord for breach of his covenant to repair is not to punish the landlord but, so far as money can, to restore the tenant to the position he would have been in had there been no breach. This object will not be achieved by applying one set of rules to all cases regardless of the particular circumstances of the case. The facts of each case must be looked at carefully to see what damage the tenant has suffered and how he may be fairly compensated by a monetary award.

> In this case on the findings of the judge the plaintiff landlords, after notice of the defect, neglected their obligation to repair for such a length of time that the flat eventually became uninhabitable. It was also clear that unless ordered to do so by an order of the court, the plaintiffs had no intention of carrying out the repairs. In these circumstances the defendant had two options that were reasonably open to her: either of selling the flat and moving elsewhere, or alternatively of moving into temporary accommodation and bringing an action against the plaintiffs to force them to carry out the repairs, and then returning to the flat after the repairs were done. If the defendant had chosen the first option then the measure of damages would indeed have been the difference in the price she received for the flat in its damaged condition and that which it would have fetched in the open market if the plaintiffs had observed their repairing covenant. If however the defendant did not wish to sell the flat but to continue to live in it after the plaintiffs had carried out the necessary structural repairs it was wholly artificial to award her damages on the basis of loss in market value, because once the plaintiffs had carried out the repairs and any consequential redecoration of the interior was completed there would be no loss in market value. *The defendant should be awarded the cost to which she was put in taking alternative accommodation, the cost of redecorating, and some award for all the unpleasantness of living in the flat as it deteriorated until it became uninhabitable. These three heads of damage will, so far as money can, compensate the defendant for the plaintiffs' breach.* [Emphasis added]

thinking point 12.6

Bearing in mind the two sentences of Griffiths LJ we have just emphasized, what would be the position if landlords were in breach of a covenant to repair a shop, with the result that (potential) customers considered the premises unsafe?

The tenant should be able to claim loss of profits. That is the equivalent to an 'award for all the unpleasantness of living in the flat'.

12.3 Tenant's Covenants—Express and Implied

There are certain terms within a lease that will be expressly decided upon by the parties which will deal with tenant's liabilities and obligations; for example, payment of rent, covenants regulating the tenant's ability to assign or sub-let the premises.

Apart from the express covenants, there are a number of implied covenants which affect the tenant, these include:

- payment of rent;
- a fixed term lessee is liable for 'permissive waste', that is, the tenant must maintain the property in the condition it was in at the commencement of the lease;
- a periodic tenant is under no liability to repair, but must use the property in a responsible manner; and
- where the landlord is not expressly liable for rates and taxes, these must be paid for by the tenant.

12.3.1 Rent—Form and Payment of Rent

Rent need not be in money, but could be in kind, such as 'five hundred bottles of champagne a year' (s205(1)(xxvii) Law of Property Act 1925 (LPA 1925)). In practice, the rent agreed upon at the commencement of a lease almost always takes the form of a regular money payment (£600 per year, £20 per week, etc). Unless the parties agree otherwise, rent is payable 'in arrear', that is, at the end of each year, week, etc. However, landlords almost always insist on payment in advance, at the beginning of each year, week, etc.

12.3.2 Rent Reviews

Whole encyclopaedias have been written on this topic! Ask anyone who is a surveyor. The first point to realize is that, unless the parties agree otherwise, the rent agreed on at the beginning of a lease remains the same throughout its duration. Nowadays, of course, long term leases usually contain a provision to protect landlords from the ravages of inflation. It is possible to put in a clause 'index-linking' the rent, but this is relatively rare.

> **thinking point 12.7**
>
> Consider why index-linking of rents has never really caught on.
>
> The value (and changes in value) of a property (and therefore the rent it will fetch) can vary widely according to the type of property and its location. Even in a recession, there may be local 'booms' for particular kinds of property. Imagine that Blogtown gains a reputation for small-scale, high-tech industry. There is, consequently, a shortage of small factory units. Rents for such units go up, even though elsewhere in Blogtown there are offices and shops standing empty.

Usually, in long fixed term leases, there is a 'rent review clause'. Most modern rent-review clauses provide for the landlord to claim a higher rent every five years, though there is no special magic in 'five' years; other periods, such as every seven years, are encountered.

Rent-review clauses usually operate in the following way:

- the landlord must serve notice on the tenant claiming a higher rent, and proposing what the new rent should be. The lease usually provides that this notice must be served some time (eg six months) before the new rent becomes payable;

- the tenant can accept the new rent, or make a counter-proposal; and

- if the parties cannot agree a new rent, the matter is referred to an arbitrator. Usually the lease provides for the arbitrator to be appointed by the president of the Royal Institution of Chartered Surveyors (RICS).

In the 1970s there was a lot of litigation involving landlords who had been late in claiming a rent review. In some cases landlords claimed a review even though the first date for payment of the new rent was past, and the tenants were continuing to pay the old rent.

The House of Lords ended the controversy with a very pro-landlord decision in *United Scientific Holdings Ltd v Burnley Borough Council* [1977] 2 All ER 62. A rent-review clause in a lease provided for the upwards-only variation of the rent at ten-year intervals. On the date for the first increase in rent the level of the reviewed rent had not been agreed between the parties. The tenant sought a declaration that, time was of the essence, and the landlord had lost its right to raise the rent for the second period of ten years. The House held that time was not of the essence. The new rent could still be determined in accordance with the formula set out in the lease.

Lord Diplock said:

My Lords, during the last two decades since inflation, particularly in the property market, has been rife, it has been usual to include in leases for a term of years, except when the term is very short, a clause providing for the annual rent to be reviewed at fixed intervals during the term and for the market rent current at each review date if it be higher, to be substituted for the rent previously payable. The wording of such clauses varies; there are several different ones now included in the books of precedents; but a feature common to nearly all of them is that not only do they specify a procedure for the determination of the revised rent by agreement between the parties or, failing that, by an independent valuer or arbitrator, but they also set out a time-table for taking some or all of the steps in that procedure which, if followed, would enable the revised rent to be settled not later than the review date.

The question in both of these appeals, which have been heard together, is whether a failure to keep strictly to the time-table laid down in the review clause deprives the landlord of his right to have the rent reviewed and consequently of his right to receive an increased rent during the period that will elapse until the next review date . . .

It is not disputed that the parties to a lease may provide expressly that time is or time is not of the essence of the contract in respect of all or any of the steps required to be taken by the landlord to obtain the determination of an increased rent, and that if they do so the court will give effect to their expressed intention. But many rent review cases that are now maturing do not contain express provision in these terms . . .

The rent review clauses that have given rise to the two instant appeals, as well as nearly all those which have been considered in the reported cases, if they result in any alteration of the rent previously payable can only have the effect of providing for the payment of a higher rent than would be payable by the tenant if the review clause had not been brought into operation. So the only party who can benefit from a review of rent under these clauses is the landlord. It is accordingly unlikely that the tenant would take the initiative in obtaining a review of the rent, even where the clause contains provision for his doing so—as it does in the second of the instant appeals.

It was this concentration of initiative and benefit in the landlord that led the Court of Appeal in the second appeal to regard the rent review clause as conferring upon the landlord a unilateral right to bring into existence a new contractual relationship between the parties. This they regarded as sufficiently analogous to an option, to make time of the essence of the occurrence of each one of the events in the time-table laid down in a review clause for the determination of the new rent. For my part, I consider the analogy to be misleading. The determination of the new rent under the procedure stipulated in the rent review clause neither brings into existence a fresh contract between the landlord and the tenant nor does it put an end to one that had existed previously. It is an event upon the occurrence of which the tenant has in his existing contract already accepted an obligation to pay to the landlord the rent so determined for the period to which the rent review relates. The tenant's acceptance of that obligation was an inseverable part of the whole consideration of the landlord's grant of a term of years of the length agreed. Without it, in a period during which inflation was anticipated, the landlord would either have been unwilling to grant a lease for a longer period than up to the first review date or would have demanded a higher rent to be paid throughout the term than that payable before the first review date. By the time of each review of rent the tenant will have already received a substantial part of the whole benefit which it was intended that he should obtain in return for his acceptance of the obligation to pay the higher rent for the succeeding period.

My Lords, I see no relevant difference between the obligation undertaken by a tenant under a rent review clause in a lease and any other obligation in a synallagmatic contract that is expressed to arise upon the occurrence of a described event, where a postponement of that event beyond the time stipulated in the contract is not so prolonged as to deprive the obligor of substantially the whole benefit that it was intended he should obtain by accepting the obligation.

So upon the question of principle which these two appeals were brought to settle, I would hold that in the absence of any contra-indications in the express words of the lease or in the inter-relation of the rent review clause itself and other clauses or in the surrounding circumstances the presumption is that the time-table specified in a rent review clause for completion of the various steps for determining the rent payable in respect of the period following the review date is not of the essence of the contract . . .

In *United Scientific Holdings Ltd v Burnley Borough Council* their Lordships held that 'time is not of the essence' with a rent-review clause. This means that if the landlord is late in claiming a rent review, prima facie that does not matter. The landlord can still insist on a higher rent, and if necessary have it fixed by the arbitrator, even though he forgetfully allowed the review date to slip by. Their Lordships reasoned that in modern economic conditions, tenants with long leases of shops, offices, factories, etc expect the rent to go up every few years. It would be wrong to allow tenants to benefit from landlords' forgetfulness. There are two exceptions to the general principle in *United Scientific Holdings Ltd v Burnley Borough Council*:

1 the parties can always expressly agree in the lease that 'time shall be of the essence'; if the landlord is late claiming the review, that is the landlord's hard luck. This point is illustrated by *Weller v Akehurst* [1981] 3 All ER 411; and

2 there could be an estoppel. If a landlord delayed a very long time in claiming a review and the tenant reasonably assumed that the old rent would remain in force and acted on that assumption, then the landlord could be estopped from claiming a review. But mere delay does not give rise to an estoppel.

Amherst v James Walker Goldsmith & Silversmith Ltd [1983] 1 Ch 305, provides an example of where the landlord exercised a rent-review clause after a lengthy delay. Amherst was the landlord of a shop and James Walker Ltd, the well-known 'high street chain', was the tenant. Amherst claimed a rent review four years late. Amherst succeeded in his claim. The crucial point was that the rent on one shop was a relatively insignificant matter for a big firm like James Walker.

Oliver LJ said:

Essentially, as it seems to me, the question is one of construction not of remedies and what one has to ask is whether, as a matter of construction of the contract, compliance with the time stipulation is so essential to the contract that any failure to comply with it entitles the other party, without more, to treat the contract as repudiated. Of course, that does not mean either that the contract is to be treated for all purposes as if the time had never been mentioned or that, when it comes to exerting any remedies for breach of contract, the ordinary rules of specific performance are suspended or abrogated. Thus, albeit the contract is not to be construed as if time were essential, damages may still be obtained for failure to comply with the fixed date for completion if damage can be shown: see *Raineri* v *Miles* [1981] AC 1050.

Equally where, as a matter of construction, time is not of the essence, it does not follow that the party in default may not, by extensive delay or other conduct, disentitle himself from having it specifically performed: see, e.g., *Cornwall* v *Henson* [1900] 2 Ch 298 and *MEPC Ltd* v *Christian-Edwards* [1978] Ch 281.

But the question of how the contract should be construed and the question of whether a party in default may have deprived himself of a right to rely on the contract must now, in my judgment, be treated as logically distinct and separate questions, whatever may be the historical origin of the rule of construction.

Mr Rich's submission treats the service of a renewal notice after the time stipulated as a submission to the court of the issue whether or not the contract should be performed. But the landlord, in serving notice, is not invoking the aid of the court to perform the contract. He is exercising the right which the contract, as properly construed, confers upon him. If it is to be construed in the sense that time is of the essence, he has no right to serve the notice. If it is not, then the right subsists, unless the tenant can show either that the contract, or that part of the contract, has been abrogated or that the landlord has precluded himself from exercising it. He may do that by showing that the contract has been repudiated—for instance, where he has served a notice calling upon the landlord to exercise his right within a reasonable time or not at all and such notice is ignored—or that some event has happened which estops the landlord from relying on his right. But I know of no ground for saying that mere delay, however lengthy, destroys the contractual right. It may put the other party in a position where, by taking the proper steps, he may become entitled to treat himself as discharged from his obligation; but that does not occur automatically and from the mere passage of time. I know of no authority for the proposition that the effect of construing a time stipulation as not being of the essence is to substitute a fresh implied term that the contract shall be performed within a reasonable time and even if such a term is to be substituted the passage of a reasonable time would not automatically abrogate the contract. It is, I think, important to distinguish between that which entitles a party to treat the contract as at an end and that which entitles the party not in default to enforce it. No one contests that, once the stipulated date is passed, proceedings may be instituted to enforce the agreement [see, e.g. *Woods* v *Mackenzie Hill Ltd* [1975] 1 WLR 613], but that is quite a different question . . .

In my judgment, therefore, the deputy judge was right in the conclusion at which he arrived, although I would in fact go further and suggest that, despite what Lord Salmon said in *United Scientific Holdings Ltd* v *Burnley Borough Council* [1978] AC 904, even delay plus hardship to the tenants would not disentitle the landlord to exercise the right which he has on the true construction of the contract unless the combination amounted to an estoppel. In my judgment, the contractual right continues to exist unless and until it is abrogated by mutual agreement or the contract is discharged by breach or, to adopt the example of Lord Diplock in the *United Scientific* case, by the obligor being substantially deprived of the whole benefit that it was intended that he should have (which I take to be a reference, in effect, to frustration or failure of consideration and which I cannot envisage as arising in this sort of case). Apart from these circumstances, the only way in which I can envisage the landlord as being precluded from relying upon the clause is by an estoppel . . .

Finally, I should add that I am not, for my part, persuaded that in fact the instant case is one where 'unreasonable' delay has occurred. The expression 'unreasonable delay' does, I think, require some definition. It must, I think, mean something more than 'prolonged delay' and it may, I suppose, be used to express the notion either of delay for which no acceptable reason can be advanced or delay which no reasonable man would incur acting in his own interest. But if this is its meaning then the absence of reason has no necessary relation to duration. If on the other hand, as I suspect, the phrase is used to describe such delay as it would not in the circumstances be reasonable to expect the other party to put up with, then it seems to me that it contains within it, by necessary implication, the notion of hardship or prejudice, for how otherwise is the other party harmed by it?

In the instant case certainly no prejudice is shown nor does it seem to me that there has been any substantial delay which is not perfectly rationally accounted for. The landlord's solicitors tried to rectify their omission within a month of the contract date and they can hardly be blamed, in the state of the law as it then stood, for not pursuing the matter further prior to 1978. If, thereafter, they had appreciated that their original letter did not, in fact, comply with the lease not only as to date but in point of form also, they could, no doubt, have issued a fresh notice before issuing the first originating summons, so that all matters could be dealt with in one set of proceedings. That they did not do so may be unfortunate, but it has been extremely beneficial to the tenants who got a further uncovenanted reprieve; but I cannot, speaking for myself, regard their failure to do so as 'unreasonable.' . . .

thinking point 12.8

Consider how you would alter the facts in Amherst v James Walker *to produce a situation where the court would hold that there was an estoppel preventing a late claim for a rent review.*

Suppose 'big' James Walker owns the freehold to a spare shop which they lease to 'little' Mr Amherst. Walker forgets to claim a rent review. After waiting two years Amherst reasonably concludes that the rent is not going to go up. So in fixing the prices Mr Amherst charges customers in his shop, he very reasonably assumes that his rent is going to stay the same until the next review date. This would estop Walker from presenting a late claim for a rent review.

12.4 Covenants Against Assigning, Sub-Letting, and Parting with Possession

A lease is of course a property right, an estate in land. It therefore follows that, prima facie, a lessee can:

- *assign* the lease, that is, transfer the lease to somebody else, retaining no rights whatsoever;
- *sub-lease* (when a person sub-lets they create a lease out of their lease—refer back to the Redacre example at 2.8.2);
- *part with possession* to a licensee, for example to a friend, or to an employee occupying the property under a 'service occupancy'.

cross-reference
See 11.4.6 for a discussion on service occupancy.

However, it should immediately be added that modern leases often restrict the lessee's right to assign, sub-let, or part with possession. As a generalization:

- short term leases and periodic tenancies (particularly of flats/houses) usually contain 'absolute covenants' under which the tenant is totally banned from assigning, sub-letting, or parting with possession;

- medium term lettings (eg ten to 50 years) usually contain a 'qualified covenant', under which the tenant can assign, sub-let, or part with possession (the whole or part of the premises) only if the landlord consents; and

- very long term leases (eg a 99-year lease of a flat) usually contain no restrictions on the right to assign, sub-let, or part with possession.

It must be stressed that 'qualified covenants' are particularly common where the premises are of a commercial nature, for example shops, offices, or factories. Landlords of commercial premises have found that it is not a good idea to insert into a commercial letting an 'absolute covenant'. The insertion of an absolute covenant into a commercial letting would substantially reduce the amount of rent the tenant was willing to pay.

12.4.1 Absolute Covenants

cross-reference
Forfeiture is discussed in more detail in 14.2.

The covenant creates an absolute ban on all transactions. However, an assignment or sub-letting in defiance of the ban *does* convey or create an estate in the land. Breach of the covenant will merely entitle the landlord to damages, and to forfeit the lease, assuming the lease contains a forfeiture clause: *Peabody Fund v Higgins* [1983] 3 All ER 122.

A landlord can waive observance of an absolute covenant so as to permit a transaction in favour of a person the landlord considers desirable. But a decision by a landlord to withhold the waiver cannot be challenged, however unreasonable, sexist, or racist the landlord is being. For example, in 2013 Louis leased a house to Andrew for five years. The lease contained an absolute covenant against assigning, sub-letting, or parting with possession. Andrew has now decided to buy a house. He comes to Louis with Agnes: 'Please can I assign my lease to Agnes?'

Now Louis can say 'Yes', and waive the absolute covenant. But if Louis says, 'No, I don't like the colour of her hair' or 'I don't like women as my tenants', Louis's decision to withhold his waiver cannot be challenged. As we will see in a moment, the position would be very different if Louis had inserted only a 'qualified covenant' into the five-year lease.

12.4.2 Qualified Covenants

Where there is a qualified covenant, a tenant can assign, sub-let, or part with possession only if the tenant gets the landlord's consent.

Landlord and Tenant Act 1927

19. Provisions as to covenants not to assign, etc, without licence or consent

(1) In all leases whether made before or after the commencement of this Act containing a covenant condition or agreement against assigning, underletting, charging or parting with the possession of demised premises or any part thereof without licence or consent, such covenant condition or agreement shall, notwithstanding any express provision to the contrary, be deemed to be subject—

   (a) to a proviso to the effect that such licence or consent is not to be unreasonably withheld, but this proviso does not preclude the right of the landlord to require payment of a reasonable sum in respect of any legal or other expenses incurred in connection with such licence or consent; . . .

Section 19(1)(a) Landlord and Tenant Act 1927 is applicable to qualified covenants but not to absolute covenants. Put more simply it provides:

> [A covenant against] assigning, underletting [ie sub-letting], charging or parting with possession of demised premises without licence or consent...shall...be subject to a proviso that such licence or consent is not to be unreasonably withheld.

Section 19(1)(a) operates 'notwithstanding any express provision to the contrary'. Thus, a landlord who wants to retain the freedom to veto assignments or sub-lettings on whatever grounds the landlord pleases (colour of hair, etc) should insert an absolute covenant. But always remember that tenants of commercial premises are unlikely to accept an 'absolute covenant', or do so only in return for a considerable reduction in rent.

When is Consent 'Unreasonably Withheld'?

There is not much statutory guidance on this issue. However:

- The Race Relations Act 1976, the Sex Discrimination Act 1975, the Equality Act 2006 (ss 45 and 47), and the Equality Act (Sexual Orientation) Regulations (SI 1263/2007, reg 5) provide that consent withheld on grounds of race, sex, religion or belief, or sexual orientation is unreasonably withheld.
- Section 144 LPA 1925 prohibits the charging of a premium for the giving of consent to an assignment or a sub-letting.
- The House of Lords in *Ashworth Frazer Ltd v Gloucester City Council* [2001] 1 WLR 2180, has held (clarifying earlier conflicting case law) that it is in principle reasonable for a landlord to prohibit an assignment where it reasonably believes that an assignee may break a covenant in the lease relating to the use of the property.

In this case, the tenant, Ashworth Frazer Ltd, wished to assign the lease to an assignee to use in a manner in breach of a user covenant in the lease and sought the consent of the landlord council to an assignment. The landlord refused its consent. The judge held that the council's ground of refusal was reasonable. The Court of Appeal upheld the judge's interpretation of the lease but concluded that they were constrained by authority to hold that it was unreasonable for the council to refuse consent solely on the ground that the intended use would be in breach of a user covenant in the lease. The appeal to the House of Lords was allowed.

The House of Lords considered that the court neither could nor should determine by strict rules the grounds on which a landlord might reasonably or unreasonably withhold consent. A landlord is not permitted to refuse consent on grounds which are wholly extraneous to the relationship of landlord and tenant with regard to the subject matter of the lease. The issue of whether the landlord's conduct was reasonable or unreasonable depends on the facts in each case.

Lord Bingham said:

> When a difference is to be resolved between landlord and tenant following the imposition of a condition (an event which need not be separately considered) or a withholding of consent, effect must be given to three overriding principles. The first, as expressed by Balcombe LJ in *International Drilling Fluids Ltd v Louisville Investments (Uxbridge) Ltd* [1986] Ch 513, 520 is that
>
> > 'a landlord is not entitled to refuse his consent to an assignment on grounds which have nothing whatever to do with the relationship of landlord and tenant in regard to the subject matter of the lease...'

The same principle was earlier expressed by Sargant LJ in *Houlder Bros & Co Ltd* v *Gibbs* [1925] Ch 575, 587:

> 'in a case of this kind the reason must be something affecting the subject matter of the contract which forms the relationship between the landlord and the tenant, and…it must not be something wholly extraneous and completely dissociated from the subject matter of the contract.'

While difficult borderline questions are bound to arise, the principle to be applied is clear. Secondly, in any case where the requirements of the first principle are met, the question whether the landlord's conduct was reasonable or unreasonable will be one of fact to be decided by the tribunal of fact. There are many reported cases. In some the landlord's withholding of consent has been held to be reasonable (as, for example, in *Pimms Ltd* v *Tallow Chandlers Company* [1964] 2 QB 547 and *Bickel* v *Duke of Westminster* [1977] QB 517), in others unreasonable (as, for example, in *Bates* v *Donaldson* [1896] 2 QB 241, *Houlder Bros* [1925] Ch 575 and *International Drilling* [1986] Ch 513). These cases are of illustrative value. But in each the decision rested on the facts of the particular case and care must be taken not to elevate a decision made on the facts of a particular case into a principle of law. The correct approach was very clearly laid down by Lord Denning MR in *Bickel* v *Duke of Westminster* [1977] QB 517, 524.

Thirdly, the landlord's obligation is to show that his conduct was reasonable, not that it was right or justifiable. As Danckwerts LJ held in *Pimms Ltd* v *Tallow Chandlers Company* [1964] 2 QB 547, 564: 'it is not necessary for the landlords to prove that the conclusions which led them to refuse consent were justified, if they were conclusions which might be reached by a reasonable man in the circumstances…' Subject always to the first principle outlined above, I would respectfully endorse the observation of Viscount Dunedin in *Viscount Tredegar* v *Harwood* [1929] AC 72, 78 that one 'should read reasonableness in the general sense'. There are few expressions more routinely used by British lawyers than 'reasonable', and the expression should be given a broad, common sense meaning in this context as in others.

The main points to note from this case:

- if the tenant has asked the landlord for consent to assign, the landlord cannot refuse to give consent on grounds which have nothing to do with the landlord and tenant relationship;
- whether the landlord's conduct is reasonable is a question of fact;
- the landlord only needs to show that his/her conduct was reasonable, and not that it was right or justifiable; and
- what is meant by 'reasonable'? 'The expression should be given a broad, common sense meaning in this context as in others' (per Lord Bingham, see the previous extract).

thinking point 12.9

What, then, if a landlord said to a tenant, 'I will agree to your proposed transaction if you give me £10,000', but the tenant says 'I will not pay'?

The landlord would be threatening to break s144, and therefore withholding consent because the £10,000 was not forthcoming would clearly be unreasonable.

Apart from the matters just discussed, whether or not the landlord's veto is reasonable is primarily a question of fact. That has not prevented an enormous amount of case law developing, the effect of which was summarized and clarified in *International Drilling Fluids Ltd* v *Louisville Investments (Uxbridge) Ltd* [1986] 1 Ch 513. Except in one (obvious) respect, this case appears unaffected by the Landlord and Tenant Act 1988 (an Act we will discuss after we have considered the case).

In *International Drilling Fluids Ltd v Louisville Investments (Uxbridge) Ltd* [1986] 1 Ch 513, a lease was granted for 30 years and provided that the demised premises should not be used 'for any purpose other than as offices'. The lease could not be assigned without the landlord's permission (known, somewhat confusingly, as the landlord's 'licence'), but such licence was not to be unreasonably withheld. The tenant requested the landlord's consent to an assignment. The landlord refused, on the ground, inter alia, that the proposed use of the premises as offices would reduce the value of the landlord's reversion and create parking problems. The judge held that the landlord's refusal to give consent to the assignment had been unreasonable. The landlord appealed unsuccessfully. Balcombe LJ:

From the authorities I deduce the following propositions of law.

(1) The purpose of a covenant against assignment without the consent of the landlord, such consent not to be unreasonably withheld, is to protect the lessor from having his premises used or occupied in an undesirable way, or by an undesirable tenant or assignee: *per* A L Smith LJ in *Bates v Donaldson* [1896] 2 QB 241, 247, approved by all the members of the Court of Appeal in *Houlder Brothers & Co. Ltd v Gibbs* [1925] Ch 575.

(2) As a corollary to the first proposition, a landlord is not entitled to refuse his consent to an assignment on grounds which have nothing whatever to do with the relationship of landlord and tenant in regard to the subject matter of the lease: see *Houlder Brothers & Co. Ltd v Gibbs*, a decision which (despite some criticism) is binding on this court: *Bickel v Duke of Westminster* [1977] QB 517. A recent example of a case where the landlord's consent was unreasonably withheld because the refusal was designed to achieve a collateral purpose unconnected with the terms of the lease is *Bromley Park Garden Estates Ltd v Moss* [1982] 1 WLR 1019.

(3) The onus of proving that consent has been unreasonably withheld is on the tenant: see *Shanly v Ward* (1913) 29 TLR 714 and *Pimms Ltd v Tallow Chandlers Company* [1964] 2 QB 547, 564. [Now see Landlord and Tenant Act 1988.]

(4) It is not necessary for the landlord to prove that the conclusions which led him to refuse consent were justified, if they were conclusions which might be reached by a reasonable man in the circumstances: *Pimms Ltd v Tallow Chandlers Company* [1964] 2 QB 547, 564.

(5) It may be reasonable for the landlord to refuse his consent to an assignment on the ground of the purpose for which the proposed assignee intends to use the premises, even though that purpose is not forbidden by the lease: see *Bates v Donaldson* [1896] 2 QB 241, 244.

(6) There is a divergence of authority on the question, in considering whether the landlord's refusal of consent is reasonable, whether it is permissible to have regard to the consequences to the tenant if consent to the proposed assignment is withheld. In an early case at first instance, *Sheppard v Hong Kong and Shanghai Banking Corporation* (1872) 20 WR 459, 460, Malins V-C said that by withholding their consent the lessors threw a very heavy burden on the lessees and they therefore ought to show good grounds for refusing it. In *Houlder Brothers & Co Ltd v Gibbs* [1925] Ch 575, 584, Warrington LJ said:

An act must be regarded as reasonable or unreasonable in reference to the circumstances under which it is committed, and when the question arises on the construction of a contract the outstanding circumstances to be considered are the nature of the contract to be construed, and the relations between the parties resulting from it.

In a recent decision of this court, *Leeward Securities Ltd v Lilyheath Properties Ltd* (1983) 271 EG 279 concerning a sub-letting which would attract the protection of the Rent Act, both Oliver LJ and O'Connor LJ made it clear in their judgments that they could envisage circumstances in which it might be unreasonable to refuse consent to an underletting, if the result would be that there was no way in which the tenant (the sub-landlord) could reasonably exploit the premises except by creating a tenancy to which the Rent Act protection would apply, and which inevitably would affect the value of the landlord's reversion. O'Connor LJ said, at p. 283:

It must not be thought that, because the introduction of a Rent Act tenant inevitably has an adverse effect upon the value of the reversion, that that is a sufficient ground for the landlords to say that they can withhold consent and that the court will hold that that is reasonable.

To the opposite effect are the *dicta, obiter* but nevertheless weighty, of Viscount Dunedin and Lord Phillimore in *Viscount Tredegar* v *Harwood* [1929] AC 72, 78, 82. There are numerous other dicta to the effect that a landlord need consider only his own interest: see, e.g., *West Layton Ltd* v *Ford* [1979] QB 593, 605, and *Bromley Park Garden Estates Ltd* v *Moss* [1982] 1 WLR 1019, 1027. Those *dicta* must be qualified, since a landlord's interests, collateral to the purposes of the lease, are in any event ineligible for consideration: see proposition (2) above. But in my judgment a proper reconciliation of those two streams of authority can be achieved by saying that while a landlord need usually only consider his own relevant interests, there may be cases where there is such a disproportion between the benefit to the landlord and the detriment to the tenant if the landlord withholds his consent to an assignment that it is unreasonable for the landlord to refuse consent.

(7) Subject to the propositions set out above, it is in each case a question of fact, depending upon all the circumstances, whether the landlord's consent to an assignment is being unreasonably withheld: see *Bickel* v *Duke of Westminster* [1977] QB 517, 524, and *West Layton Ltd* v *Ford* [1979] QB 593, 604, 606–607.

In the present case, the judge, having made the findings of specific fact set out above, carefully considered the relevant authorities. He then reached the conclusion that the views of the landlords' expert witnesses about the effect of the proposed assignment on the value of the reversion, although views which could be held by reasonable professional men, did not in the circumstances of this case, where there was no prospect of the landlords wishing to realise the reversion, constitute a ground for reasonable apprehension of damage to their interests. That was a decision on the facts to which the judge was entitled to come. He made no error of law in reaching his decision; he took into account nothing which he ought not to have considered, and he omitted nothing which he ought to have considered. In my judgment, this court ought not to interfere.

But in any event, in my judgment, the judge reached the right decision. Although he did not expressly mention the disproportionate harm to the tenants if the landlords were entitled to refuse consent to the assignment, compared with the minimum disadvantage which he clearly considered the landlords would suffer by a diminution in the paper value of the reversion—'paper value' because he was satisfied there was no prospect of the landlords wishing to realise the reversion—he clearly recognised the curious results to which the landlords' arguments, based solely upon a consideration of their own interests, could lead. As he said in his judgment:

'It seems to me that, if Mr Lewison is right, the more substantial the lessee, the more easily the landlord would be able to justify a refusal of consent to an assignment, since unless the proposed assignee's covenant was as strong as the assignor's, a reasonable man might form the view that the market would consider the reversion less attractive if the lease were vested in the assignor. To take the matter to extremes, if a lease was made in favour of a government department it would be unassignable except to another government department; for as Mr Matthews [one of the expert witnesses] accepted in cross-examination, the market would prefer to have the government as the lessee, whether the premises were being used as serviced offices or not, even if they were standing empty, rather than a company, however strong its covenant.'

In my judgment, the gross unfairness to the tenants of the example postulated by the judge strengthens the arguments in favour, in an appropriate case of which the instant case is one, of it being unreasonable for the landlord not to consider the detriment to the tenant if consent is refused, where the detriment is extreme and disproportionate to the benefit to the landlord.

The court devised seven numbered propositions. Our comments on the numbered propositions are as follows:

1 (a) It is clearly reasonable for a landlord to veto a proposed assignee/sub-tenant/licensee who is of bad character, for example one who has a criminal record.

(b) It is clearly reasonable for a landlord to object to a transaction which will depreciate the value of his reversion. The leading cases are *Norfolk Capital Group v Kitway Ltd* [1976] 3 All ER 787, and *Bickel v Duke of Westminster* [1975] 3 All ER 801. In both cases a long lease of a house was vested in a limited company. It was proposed to assign the lease to a human tenant who would be able to take advantage of various pieces of protective legislation not available to 'artificial persons'. This fact would have the effect of reducing the value of the landlords' fees simple in reversion. It was held that the landlords were reasonable in vetoing the assignments.

(c) It is clearly reasonable for the landlord to object where the proposed assignee/sub-tenant proposes using the premises for unsuitable purposes. For example, using a house in a narrow street for a business which will create a lot of parking problems. Refer also to the court's proposition (5).

2 For example, 'I don't want the lease assigned to him because he has just run off with my wife.' Such an attitude would clearly be unreasonable.

3 Overruled by the Landlord and Tenant Act 1988.

4 Refer back to note (c) under proposition (1).

5 A short but very important point. See also the following text.

6 There have been a lot of cases in recent years where a tenant of business premises has been anxious to sell the business. The lease of the premises is of course an important asset of the business. If a landlord is unwilling to approve a particular prospective purchaser of the business as assignee of the lease, the prospective purchaser is not going to buy the business.

With respect to Balcombe LJ's proposition (5), consider whether it would be reasonable for a landlord to object to a proposed assignee on the ground that the assignee would use the premises for a business which competes with a similar business carried on by the landlord. (For example, 'Your proposed assignee is a greengrocer; so am I'.) This point is controversial. The (first instance) case of *Premier Confectionery v London Commercial Sale Rooms* [1933] Ch 904, suggests that the landlord would be in the right. But it can be argued this case is wrong on this point, as the landlord's reason for the veto has nothing to do with the landlord and tenant relationship (see proposition (2) in *International Drilling*).

The defendants leased by separate leases a shop and a neighbouring kiosk. Both premises were tobacconists. The claimants were tenants under both leases. They sought the landlord's consent to assign the lease of the kiosk to Mrs Kramer. The defendants refused consent as they did not want competition between the two shops.

Bennett J:

> If the defendants have in law the right to consider the possible effect upon their property of the shop and the kiosk being in the occupation of different tenants, I have no doubt that in withholding their consent to the assignment of the kiosk to Mrs Kramer they did not act unreasonably. They acted as a reasonable man might have acted in the circumstances. The real question is whether as a matter of law the defendants, for the purpose of determining whether or not they would give their consent to the assignment, had the right to consider the effect upon their property, and in particular upon the shop which is a part of it, of the kiosk being occupied separately from the shop, and by a tenant bound to carry on there a trade which will compete with the trade for which the shop is best suited. In my judgment, they have.

In *Houlder Brothers & Co.* v *Gibbs* [1925] Ch 575 the Master of the Rolls, Warrington and Sargant LJJ all accepted and acted upon the reasoning of A. L. Smith LJ in *Bates* v *Donaldson* [1896] 2 QB 241. Sargant LJ in particular proceeded upon the footing that the statement of A. L. Smith LJ that the covenant in question in that case was inserted 'in order to protect the lessor from having his premises used or occupied in an undesirable way, or by an undesirable tenant or assignee,' was a statement which shows the limits which are to be put upon such a clause as the clause in question. If a reasonable man might think that the proposed user of the premises, or the proposed occupation of the premises will be undesirable, then, in my judgment, it is within the right of the landlord to withhold his consent to an assignment which will result in that undesirable use or occupation. The defendants in this case have withheld their consent because they in good faith think that in all the circumstances the occupation of the kiosk by Mrs Kramer is undesirable.

Mr Morton for the plaintiffs contended that the defendants are really seeking to consolidate the two agreements, and that if they had intended that the shop and the kiosk should always be in the occupation of one tenant they should have inserted a stipulation to that effect in the agreement of September 14, 1928. The argument (if I followed it rightly) was that it was not reasonable for a landlord to withhold his consent to a proposed assignment if the subject-matter with regard to which the proposed assignment was objected to might have been made the subject-matter of an express stipulation at the time the tenancy was created. In my judgment, this is not the law. It is, in my opinion, clear from the judgments delivered by the members of the Court of Appeal in *Bates* v *Donaldson* [1896] 2 QB 241 and in *Houlder Brothers & Co.* v *Gibbs* [1925] Ch 575 that a landlord may withhold his consent to an assignment because he objects to the use the proposed assignee intends to make of the premises proposed to be assigned, although that use is not forbidden by the terms of the tenancy or by any rule of law.

I decide this case in favour of the defendants for the following reasons: (a) Because the proposed assignment will result in the kiosk being occupied separately from the shop; (b) Because that is a matter which the defendants are entitled to consider in determining whether or not they will give their consent; (c) Because the defendants believe that the separation of the kiosk from the shop may injuriously affect their property; and (d) Because that opinion is one which may be entertained by reasonable persons and is not wholly unreasonable.

Back in 1933 it was thought reasonable to stifle competition between neighbouring shops. It is at least questionable whether the courts would support that view today.

12.4.3 Seeking the Landlord's Consent to a Proposed Transaction

The Landlord and Tenant Act 1988 represented a shift in the law in favour of tenants. Until 1988, the onus of proof that the landlord was withholding his consent unreasonably was on the tenant. Moreover, landlords frequently delayed their decisions for inordinate periods. Landlords who did eventually say 'yes' often imposed stringent conditions. The overall effect of the 1988 Act was:

- to put pressure on landlords to make a decision on the tenant's application without unreasonable delay;
- to ensure that landlords who veto transactions have really good grounds for doing so; and
- to ensure that landlords, if they impose conditions, impose only sensible ones.

If a tenant has a proposed transaction (assignment, sub-letting, or parting with possession), the tenant must always first ask the landlord for consent in writing, even if the tenant thinks that there could not possibly be any reasonable objection.

Landlord and Tenant Act 1988

1. Qualified duty to consent to assigning, underletting etc of premises

(1) This section applies in any case where—

    (a) a tenancy includes a covenant on the part of the tenant not to enter into one or more of the following transactions, that is—

        (i) assigning,

        (ii) underletting,

        (iii) charging, or

        (iv) parting with the possession of,

the premises comprised in the tenancy or any part of the premises without the consent of the landlord or some other person, but

    (b) the covenant is subject to the qualification that the consent is not to be unreasonably withheld (whether or not it is also subject to any other qualification).

(2) In this section and section 2 of this Act—

    (a) references to a proposed transaction are to any assignment, underletting, charging or parting with possession to which the covenant relates, and

    (b) references to the person who may consent to such a transaction are to the person who under the covenant may consent to the tenant entering into the proposed transaction.

(3) Where there is served on the person who may consent to a proposed transaction a written application by the tenant for consent to the transaction, he owes a duty to the tenant within a reasonable time—

    (a) to give consent, except in a case where it is reasonable not to give consent,

    (b) to serve on the tenant written notice of his decision whether or not to give consent specifying in addition—

        (i) if the consent is given subject to conditions, the conditions,

        (ii) if the consent is withheld, the reasons for withholding it.

(4) Giving consent subject to any condition that is not a reasonable condition does not satisfy the duty under subsection (3)(a) above.

(5) For the purposes of this Act it is reasonable for a person not to give consent to a proposed transaction only in a case where, if he withheld consent and the tenant completed the transaction, the tenant would be in breach of a covenant.

(6) It is for the person who owed any duty under subsection (3) above—

    (a) if he gave consent and the question arises whether he gave it within a reasonable time, to show that he did,

    (b) if he gave consent subject to any condition and the question arises whether the condition was a reasonable condition, to show that it was,

    (c) if he did not give consent and the question arises whether it was reasonable for him not to do so, to show that it was reasonable,

and, if the question arises whether he served notice under that subsection within a reasonable time, to show that he did.

Section 4 places further pressures on landlords. It makes a landlord who breaks any of the duties laid down in the Act liable in damages to the tenant. Thus, for example, a tenant who was unable to sell their business because of the landlord's delaying tactics in giving consent, might have a claim for hefty damages.

Landlord and Tenant Act 1988

4. Breach of duty

A claim that a person has broken any duty under this Act may be made the subject of civil proceedings in like manner as any other claim in tort for breach of statutory duty.

The courts have been very firm in implementing the policy behind the 1988 Act. In *Norwich Union v Shopmoor* [1998] 3 All ER 32, Sir Richard Scott V-C held that if a tenant's application for consent has not received a written reply within a reasonable time, then consent was deemed to be unreasonably withheld. This case was then followed by Neuberger J in *Footwear Corp v Amplight* [1998] 3 All ER 52, who added that any purely *oral* objections from the landlord must be ignored. Moreover, it is clear from the *Footwear* case and other cases that the courts are being strict with landlords on the issue of how long is a reasonable time for replying. It seems that, at most, landlords have three months in which to reply to a tenant's request for permission.

This strict approach of the lower courts was confirmed by the Court of Appeal in *Go West Ltd v Spigarolo* [2003] 2 WLR 986. Moreover, in that case the court held that if the landlord's refusal of consent is challenged by the tenant as being unreasonable, the landlord can rely only on reasons set out in the written reply to the tenant's request. Other reasons cannot be relied on when the dispute reaches court. In the *Go West* case, the landlord vetoed a proposed assignment on the grounds (in effect) that it was unsure of the financial soundness of the proposed assignee. In ensuing litigation, the landlord was not entitled to rely on the state of repair of the premises as grounds for withholding consent.

A further blow against recalcitrant landlords is the decision of Peter Smith J in *Design Progression Ltd v Thurloe Properties Ltd* [2005] 1 WLR 1. In that case the existing tenant (the claimants) wanted to assign the lease of a shop to a very successful businesswoman. There could be no possible reasonable objection to her being the tenant.

The landlords nevertheless withheld their consent, hoping that the claimants would, in desperation, surrender their lease to the landlords. The landlords would then be able to let to the successful businesswoman at a much increased rent. Put another way, the landlords unlawfully withheld their consent hoping to make a profit from their unreasonable and unlawful actions. Peter Smith J awarded the claimants not only £75,000 compensatory damages (the premium the businesswoman was willing to pay for the assignment), but also £25,000 exemplary ('punitive') damages.

If the landlord vetoes a proposed transaction (or fails to reply in writing within a reasonable time) there are four courses of action open to the tenant:

1 to concede that the landlord has a good argument and abandon the proposal;

2 to abandon the proposal, but claim damages under the Landlord and Tenant Act 1988 (this is what happened in *Design Progression Ltd v Thurloe Properties Ltd* [2005] 1 WLR 1);

3 to go ahead with the proposed transaction, risking proceedings for damages (and forfeiture if the lease contains a forfeiture clause); and

4 to seek a declaration from the court that the consent is being withheld unreasonably (the tenant may well add a claim for damages under the 1988 Act).

thinking point 12.10

Consider why the Landlord and Tenant Act 1988 makes it easier for tenants of business premises (eg a shop) to sell their businesses.

With shops and other small businesses, the (long) lease over the shop or other premises is often the business's most valuable asset. If a shopkeeper who wants to sell up and retire cannot sell (ie assign for consideration) their lease, the shopkeeper obviously will not be able to sell the business. The 1988 Act makes it easier to sell the lease.

12.4.4 Section 19(1A) Landlord and Tenant Act 1927

This provision is a pro-landlord provision, which applies to qualified covenants against assignment of leases of commercial properties (offices, shops, factories, etc) commencing *after* 1995. It has no application to sub-letting or parting with possession.

Landlord and Tenant Act 1927

As amended by s22 Landlord and Tenant Act 1995

19. Provisions as to covenants not to assign, etc. without licence or consent

. . .

(1A) Where the landlord and the tenant under a qualifying lease have entered into an agreement specifying for the purposes of this subsection—

(a) any circumstances in which the landlord may withhold his licence or consent to an assignment of the demised premises or any part of them, or

(b) any conditions subject to which any such licence or consent may be granted, then the landlord—

(i) shall not be regarded as unreasonably withholding his licence or consent to any such assignment if he withholds it on the ground (and it is the case) that any such circumstances exist, and

(ii) if he gives any such licence or consent subject to any such conditions, shall not be regarded as giving it subject to unreasonable conditions;

and section 1 of the Landlord and Tenant Act 1988 (qualified duty to consent to assignment etc.) shall have effect subject to the provisions of this subsection.

This provision was inserted into the 1927 Act at the insistence of big commercial landlords (property companies, institutional investors, etc) who were very concerned that leases should not be assigned to tenants who will be unable to pay rent, do repairs, etc. Where s19(1A) applies, a landlord can tighten his/her control over the assignment of a lease by including in the lease a specific clause stipulating that the landlord is entitled to withhold consent in given circumstances. A withholding of consent in those circumstances will not be unreasonable.

For example, the lease states 'The Landlord will not consent to an assignment if the assignee fails to provide a banker's reference that he will be able to pay the rent.' A potential assignee who is in fact financially very sound forgets to provide the reference. The landlord's veto will automatically be reasonable and not open to challenge under the 1927 and 1988 Acts.

However, there are limits on these types of clauses. The clause cannot leave the decision as to whether circumstances exist justifying a landlord's veto to the landlord's subjective opinion. For example, a clause 'The Landlord will not agree to an assignee unless he is satisfied that the assignee can pay the rent' is not allowed. However, it is permitted to have a clause which entrusts a decision to an independent third party, for example 'The landlord will not agree to an assignee unless the assignee can produce satisfactory evidence that he can pay the rent. In the event of a dispute as to whether the evidence is satisfactory, the matter shall be resolved by an arbitrator appointed by the president of the RICS.'

12.5 Remedies Against a Tenant in Breach of Repairing Obligations

12.5.1 Damages

You should remember that in some leases, particularly long term ones, the tenant undertakes to do the repairs. If the tenant fails to do repairs they have promised to do, then normally the landlord can recover from the tenant the cost of repairing the property. However, the landlord's right to damages may be limited or eliminated by s18 Landlord and Tenant Act 1927.

> *Landlord and Tenant Act 1927*
>
> 18. Provisions as to covenants to repair
>
> 1. Damages for a breach of a covenant to repair...shall in no case exceed the amount (if any) by which the value of the reversion in the premises is diminished...In particular no damage shall be recovered for a breach of covenant to repair if it is shown that the premises would at or shortly after the termination of the tenancy have been or be pulled down...

If, on the expiry of the lease the landlord is going to demolish the premises, or reconstruct the premises to such an extent that the state of repair is immaterial, the landlord will not be able to claim any damages from the tenant for his breach of the covenant to repair. The purpose of this provision is merely to put the landlord in the position he/she would have been if the tenant's breach had not occurred.

A rather disturbing situation faced the judge in *Hibernian Properties v Liverpool City Council* [1973] 2 All ER 1117. A tenant leased a row of houses in Liverpool from Hibernian. The tenant undertook to do the repairs. He failed so miserably in this task that Liverpool City Council public health officials came along, condemned the properties as unfit for human habitation, and made the houses the subject of a compulsory purchase order. The houses were then demolished.

Hibernian were paid compensation by Liverpool City Council limited to 'the site value'. That meant that they received no compensation for the buildings. They therefore sued the tenant for damages. He pleaded the second sentence of s18 of the 1927 Act as a defence: 'The property has been pulled down. Therefore no damages are payable.' The judge boldly rejected this defence, holding that the words 'by the landlords' must be implied into s18 after the words 'pulled down'.

cross-reference
Forfeiture of leases is discussed in 14.2.

The Leasehold Property Repairs Act 1938 is also relevant to cases where the tenant is liable to do repairs. It can be properly understood only after we have considered forfeiture of leases.

12.5.2 Specific Performance—Enforcing the Tenant's Repairing Obligation

An order for specific performance of a tenant's repairing obligation may be awarded by the court to a landlord. However, the court in *Rainbow Estates Ltd v Tokenhold Ltd* [1999] Ch 64 was of the view that specific performance would only be available where damages would not be an adequate remedy. Deputy High Court Judge Lawrence Collins QC said:

> In my judgment, a modern law of remedies requires specific performance of a tenant's repairing covenant to be available in appropriate circumstances, and there are no constraints of principle or binding authority against the availability of the remedy. First, even if want of

mutuality were any longer a decisive factor (which it is not) the availability of the remedy against the tenant would restore mutuality as against the landlord. Second, the problems of defining the work and the need for supervision can be overcome by ensuring that there is sufficient definition of what has to be done in order to comply with the order of the court. Third, the court should not be constrained by the supposed rule that the court will not enforce the defendant's obligation in part ... it is by no means clear that there is such a principle, ... it does not mean that the court cannot in an appropriate case enforce compliance with a particular obligation such as a repairing covenant.

Subject to the overriding need to avoid injustice or oppression, the remedy should be available when damages are not an adequate remedy or, in the more modern formulation, when specific performance is the appropriate remedy ...

It follows that not only is there a need for great caution in granting the remedy against a tenant, but also that it will be a rare case in which the remedy of specific performance will be the appropriate one: in the case of commercial leases, the landlord will normally have the right to forfeit or to enter and do the repairs at the expense of the tenant; in residential leases, the landlord will normally have the right to forfeit in appropriate cases.

REVIEW QUESTION Bearing in mind the facts of the case of *Jeune v Queen Cross Properties* [1974] Ch 97 where specific performance was granted of a landlord's covenant to repair, in what kind of situations would it be appropriate for the court to grant specific performance of the tenant's duty to repair?

Concluding Remarks

The law relating to obligations between landlord and tenant is often attacked as being too heavily biased in favour of landlords. Critics point to decisions such as *United Scientific Holdings*, *O'Brien v Robinson*, and *Anstruther-Gough-Calthorpe v McOscar*. They also cite the rule banning rent-strikes should the landlord fail to do the repairs, pointing out that in many American states such strikes are permitted.

The pro-landlord bias is gradually disappearing. Over the last 40 years, both the courts and Parliament have done a lot to redress the balance. See, for example, the Landlord and Tenant Act 1988, and the rigorous way in which it has been applied by the courts. And just look again at the sections in this chapter dealing with the greatly expanded remedies which tenants (particularly of residential properties) have if their landlords are in breach of a duty to repair. The decision in *Calabar Properties v Stitcher* is perhaps of particular importance (see 12.2.6).

The real problem with the law discussed in this chapter is the piecemeal way in which it has been developed. This produces anomalies. For example, why on earth should the 'receiver' remedy created by ss 21–24 Landlord and Tenant Act 1987 be confined to residential properties?

What is needed is a complete and organized statutory code of obligations between landlord and tenants. The Law Commission has been proposing something along these lines ever since 1975. But like many other proposals for major structural reform of land law, this proposal just gathers dust.

Express Covenants

Both parties are free to negotiate the terms of the lease.

Implied Landlord's Covenants

Quiet Enjoyment

The landlord impliedly covenants that he will not do anything which substantially interferes with the tenant's title or possession of the property and enjoyment of the property.

Non-Derogation from Grant

The landlord who has granted a lease to the tenant cannot engage in acts which would undermine the purpose of that lease.

Repairs

Common law implied covenants:

- fitness for habitation of furnished premises; and
- contractual duty of care with respect to common parts.

Implied Statutory Covenants

- Low rent (under £52 pa)—dwelling must be kept 'fit for human habitation' (ss8–10 Landlord and Tenant Act 1985).
- Lease for a term of less than seven years of a dwelling house, there is an obligation to keep in repair (s11 Landlord and Tenant Act 1985):
  - structure and exterior;
  - installations: water, gas, and electricity and for sanitation (there is also the obligation to keep these in proper working order); and
  - installations for space heating and heating water.
- The landlord is only liable to repair defects he either knows about or would have known about had he acted on information suggesting that there might be a need for repair (*O'Brien v Robinson*).

Remedies for Breach of the Landlord's Obligation to Repair

Tenant can:

- carry out repairs himself or employ contractors to do the work and deduct the cost from future instalments (*Lee-Parker v Izzet*);
- sue for specific performance (s17(1) Landlord and Tenant Act 1985);
- sue for damages, including (where appropriate) injuries to health and cost of alternative accommodation;
- seek appointment of a receiver under the general powers of the court (s37 Supreme Court Act 1981); and

- seek appointment of a receiver-manager from the Property Chamber of the 'First Tier Tribunal'. This applies to blocks of flats only (ss 21–24 Landlord and Tenant Act 1927).

Tenant's Express and Implied Covenants

Express Covenants

Certain terms in the lease will be agreed by the parties, for example payment of rent, covenants regulating the tenant's ability to assign, or sub-let the premises.

Qualified Covenants Against Assigning, Sub-letting, etc

These covenants are common in commercial lettings. The tenant normally needs consent to an assignment or sub-letting, but the landlord must have reasonable grounds if he withholds consent. Such reasonable grounds would normally relate to the assignee/sub-tenant's character or proposed use of the premises.

If the tenant wants to assign or sub-let he should seek permission in writing from the landlord.

If the landlord:

- does not reply within about three months; or
- gives consent but on unreasonable conditions; or
- unreasonably withholds consent;

then the tenant should either:

- go ahead and assign or sub-let; or
- sue the landlord for damages and/or a declaration.

In any litigation, the onus will be on the landlord to prove that his grounds for objection are reasonable. Moreover he can rely only on grounds which he advanced when first asked for permission.

Implied Covenants

These include:

- payment of rent;
- tenant must maintain the property in the condition it was in at the commencement of the lease; and
- rates and taxes, if the landlord has not agreed to be expressly liable for these.

Remedies Against a Tenant in Breach of Repairing Obligations

These are:

- damages; and
- specific performance.

 # Further Reading

Fancourt, T, 'Licences to assign: another turn of the screw' [2006] Conv 37
Article which considers whether the courts are taking a tougher stance towards landlords who refuse to permit an assignment or underletting of a lease.

Pawlowski, M and Brown, J, 'Liability of landlords for condensation dampness' [2001] Conv 184
Considers the courts' willingness to consider cases where tenants are forced to live in damp and unfit accommodation due to the difficulty in holding the landlord liable for dampness because there is no damage of the building.

Smith, PF, 'A case for abrogation: the no-liability for unfitness principle' [1998] Conv 189
Discussion on the lack of an implied covenant to require landlords to provide accommodation which is fit for human habitation.

References

Burn, EH and Cartwright, J, *Cheshire and Burn's Modern Law of Real Property*, 17th edn, Oxford: OUP, 2006.

? Question

Tricia has a five-year lease of a flat. She is always moaning to you about the state of repair of the whole block of flats. 'I sometimes think that the landlords don't know the dreadful conditions we tenants are living in.' Advise Tricia.

## 13

The Running of Covenants in a Lease

Introduction

As we saw at 12.4, a tenant who no longer wants to use the land they have leased can (subject to the terms of his lease) assign (ie transfer) that lease to a third party. Alternatively, the tenant can sub-let the whole or part of the property to a sub-tenant, provided the sub-tenancy is shorter in duration than the head lease. One day shorter will suffice. Equally a landlord is free to sell his/her fee simple reversion, though (except in unusual situations such as in *Hollington v Rhodes* [1951] 2 TLR 691) the purchaser will take the fee simple subject to the tenant's leasehold estate.

The issues discussed in this chapter can be summarized in the form of a question:

If a tenant assigns their lease, or sub-lets, and/or a landlord sells his/her fee simple, who is now entitled to enforce the various terms of the lease, and against whom can they be enforced?

Before addressing these questions be warned that the Landlord and Tenant (Covenants) Act 1995 (LTCA 1995) made important changes in the law. But, subject to one minor exception, the changes only apply to leases granted on or after the commencement date of the 1995 Act, which was 1 January 1996. We shall therefore start by considering the law relating to leases created before 1996 which will continue to govern all pre-1996 leases and then turn to consider the post-1995 leases under the 1995 Act.

13.1 Case Study—Kirby House

Before we explain the operation of the law to pre-1996 leases, we need to consider the case study of Kirby House. There are four stages in the recent history of Kirby House (see Diagram 13.1):

• In 1995, Lawrence leased the house to Teresa for 25 years.

• In 2000, Teresa assigned the lease to Anne.

• In 2005, Lawrence sold the fee simple reversion to Roger.

• In 2010, Anne sub-lets the house to Susan for nine years.

By the terms of the lease agreed back in 1995, Lawrence covenanted to keep the property in good repair.

Diagram 13.1
The letting of Kirby House

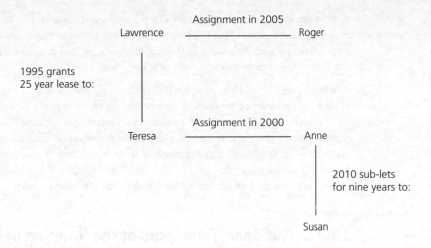

Teresa covenanted:

1 to pay £500 per annum rent;

2 to use the property only for residential purposes; and

3 to paint the landlord's portrait every five years.

In 2015, the following problems have arisen:

1 Roger is very vain and wants Teresa and/or Anne to paint his portrait.

2 The rent is a long way in arrears. Can Roger sue for that rent (logically the answer should be 'yes') and, if so, whom can he sue—Anne, Teresa, or Susan?

3 To the great annoyance of Anne and Susan, the property is in disrepair. Who can enforce the repairing covenant? Who can the covenant be enforced against?

4 Susan is using the house for business purposes. Can anyone stop her from doing so?

427

13.2 Pre-1996 Leases—Liability of Original Parties after Assignment

It is extremely important for you to realize that in all leases granted prior to 1996 the original contractual liability of a party to a lease lasts for the full duration of the lease. If the landlord and tenant are in privity of contract then all the covenants in the lease will be enforceable between them. However, only the original parties to a lease are in 'privity of contract'. If the landlord and tenant are not in privity of contract then we must consider whether the parties are in privity of estate.

Privity of estate governs relationships between a landlord and tenant in circumstances where either the original landlord or tenant have assigned their interest. Privity of estate is a means by which covenants in a lease may be enforced between individuals who do not have a direct contractual relationship. The phrase 'privity of estate' recognizes the existence of a relationship between the landlord and tenant which though not contractual nevertheless creates obligations arising from the tenure that has been granted. Establishing privity of estate is not sufficient on its own to enforce leasehold covenants. The covenants must 'touch and concern the land' and must not be personal in their nature. These covenants are attributable to the land or in this case to the lease.

In the Kirby House case study the original parties were Lawrence and Teresa. Between 1995 and 2000 all the terms of the lease were enforceable between them. However, privity of contract will not provide the answer to three of the four questions just posed, though Roger could sue Teresa, the original tenant, for the arrears of rent.

Where the lease is pre-1996 an original tenant of (say) a 50-year lease can be sued for arrears of rent run up by an assignee many years after the tenant has parted with the lease. Or the tenant can be sued for 'breaching' a repairing covenant, even though the tenant has now no control over the premises. This point is of particular concern to small traders who 'sell up and retire'. They sometimes find that a peaceful retirement is rudely interrupted by a hefty claim for damages. The reason for this lies in contract law which provides that contractual liability remains with the original parties for the full duration of the lease under privity of contract.

13.2.1 The Basic Principles of the Running of Covenants in Pre-1996 Leases

To summarize the previous issues, the following basic principles are points to bear in mind when considering liability of a tenant:

- If the landlord and tenant are in privity of contract then all the covenants in the lease will be enforceable between them. However, only the original parties to a lease are in 'privity of contract'. (In the Kirby House case study, the original parties were Lawrence and Teresa. Between 1995 and 2000 all the terms of the lease were enforceable between them. Since 2000 a lot has happened. Privity of contract will not provide the answer to three of the four questions just posed.)

- If the landlord and the tenant are not in privity of contract but are in privity of estate, then those covenants which 'touch and concern the land' (but only those covenants) are enforceable between them.

- Privity of estate exists where two persons are in a direct relationship of landlord and tenant.

Thus in the Kirby House case study (see Diagram 13.2):

- Between 2000 and 2005 there was privity of estate between Lawrence and Anne.

- Between 2005 and 2010 there was privity of estate between Roger and Anne.

- From 2010 onwards there is (still) privity of estate between Roger and Anne; in addition there is a separate privity of estate (and contract) between Anne and Susan.

Diagram 13.2
Kirby House: privity of estate and contract

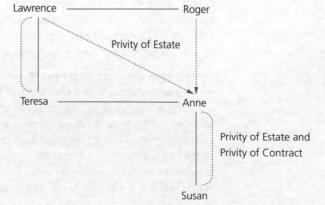

Privity of Estate and Privity of Contract

Lawrence ——————— Roger

Privity of Estate

Teresa ——————— Anne

Privity of Estate and Privity of Contract

Susan

thinking point 13.1

Why is there no privity of estate between Roger and Susan?

Roger and Susan are not in a direct landlord and tenant relationship. Remember Anne bought the lease from Teresa. The freehold owner is Roger and consequently Anne's landlord is Roger. The point illustrated by this thinking point is absolutely crucial.

13.2.2 Which Covenants Touch and Concern the Land?

The tests traditionally applied are:

'Does the covenant affect the landlord qua landlord or the tenant qua tenant?' ('Qua' means 'in his capacity as'.)

or

'Does the covenant have some direct connection with the landlord and tenant relationship?'

If you are thinking that these tests are somewhat vague and uncertain in their operation, then you are right. Moreover, the courts have not always been consistent in applying these tests. If confronted with some new covenant not covered by existing case law you should apply the tests, but you should also consider whether the covenant is analogous to a covenant on which there is already a court decision. The important court decisions are summarized in the following sections.

Covenants by Landlords which Do Touch and Concern

- a covenant to repair, also to reconstruct or repaint;
- a covenant granting the tenant an option to renew the lease;
- a covenant to supply the land with fresh water. (This decision should also apply to covenants to provide 'services' such as gas and electricity.)

Covenants by Landlords which Do Not Touch and Concern

- a covenant granting the tenant an option to purchase the freehold reversion;
- a covenant in the lease of a public house under which the landlord brewery promised not to supply beer to other pubs within a half-mile radius: *Thomas v Hayward* (1869) LR 4 Ex 311.

Covenants by Tenants which Do Touch and Concern

- covenants to pay rent;
- covenants to pay rates or other taxes payable with respect to the land leased;
- covenants to repair, repaint, etc;
- covenants relating to the use for which the premises may be put;
- 'tie clauses' under which the tenant of a pub or filling station can sell only the landlord's brand of beer or petrol. (See *Clegg v Hands* (1890) 44 Ch 503, which makes an ironic contrast with *Thomas v Hayward*.)

Covenants by Tenants which Do Not Touch and Concern

Interestingly, examples are hard to find. One which is noteworthy is *Gower v Postmaster-General* (1887) 57 LT 527. This was a covenant by a tenant to pay rates on land not comprised within the lease. This case could perhaps be extended by analogy to, say, a covenant to carry out building work on land other than that comprised in the lease.

13.2.3 Solution to Kirby House Case Study

thinking point 13.2

Try to apply the principles set out previously, that is, privity of contract and estate to the four problems (numbered 1 to 4) which have now arisen regarding the lease of Kirby House:

1

2

3

4

Your answers should be similar to what now follows:

1 *The portrait painting. The covenant to paint the portrait does not 'touch and concern the land'. A covenant which does not touch and concern is called 'a personal covenant'. Personal covenants which have been inserted into a lease normally remain enforceable only between the original parties. Thus Roger cannot insist on having his portrait painted. Assuming that Lawrence has remembered what was agreed 20 or so years ago, he could insist that Teresa paint his (Lawrence's) portrait.*

2 *The arrears of rent. A covenant to pay rent does touch and concern the land. It follows that as there is privity of estate between Roger and Anne, Roger can (and normally would) sue Anne for those arrears. For reasons mentioned earlier at 13.2, he could alternatively sue Teresa, assuming he can find her.*

3 *The repairing covenant. A repairing covenant also touches and concerns the land. At the current time it is Susan who is personally suffering from the disrepair of the house. However, there is no privity of estate between Susan and Roger. It is only Anne who can enforce the repairing covenant against Roger.*

cross-reference
see 13.5.2 for restrictive covenants in leases.

4 *The use of the house for business purposes. As there is privity of estate between Roger and Anne, but not between Roger and Susan, you are probably thinking that Roger can sue Anne, but not Susan, on the covenant to use the house for residential purposes only.*

On the basic principles of the law of leases, this would be correct. Unfortunately, there is an added complication which will work to Roger's advantage. Roger, although he cannot sue Susan under the basic law of leases, will have a case against her under the law of restrictive covenants.

13.2.4 Assignment of the Reversion to a Pre-1996 Lease

Where the reversion has been assigned, ss 141(1) and 142(1) Law of Property Act 1925 (LPA 1925) transmit the benefit and burden of the original covenants which touch and concern the land from the original to the new landlord. Using the Kirby House case study to illustrate this point, Roger will have the benefit and burden of the original covenants which touch and concern the land (see Diagram 13.3).

Diagram 13.3
*Lawrence sells
the fee simple
to Roger*

Privity of Estate and
Privity of Contract

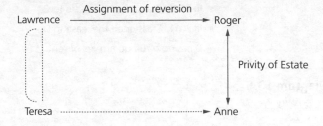

Assignment of reversion

Lawrence → Roger

Privity of Estate

Teresa ┄┄┄┄┄┄┄┄┄┄→ Anne

---

thinking point 13.3

What would happen if Lawrence was in breach of the repairing covenant when he assigned the reversion to Roger? Who should Anne sue?

Roger would not be liable for breaches which occurred before the reversion was assigned. Anne could sue Lawrence on the basis that liability for breaches that occurred before the assignment continue after the assignment.

13.2.5 Assignment of a Pre-1996 Lease

Following the principles outlined in 13.2.1, Teresa assigned the lease to Anne in 2000. Between Anne and Lawrence there was privity of estate (landlord and tenant relationship). Anne could only sue or be sued upon those covenants which touched and concerned the land. Under the privity of contract rules governing pre-1996 leases, Teresa remains liable for any breaches committed by Anne due to privity of contract between Lawrence and Teresa (see Diagram 13.4).

431

Diagram 13.4
*Teresa assigns the
lease to Anne in
2000*

Privity of Estate and
Privity of Contract

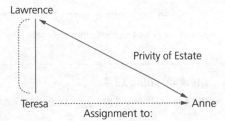

Lawrence

Privity of Estate

Teresa ┄┄┄┄┄┄┄┄┄┄→ Anne
Assignment to:

To alleviate the harshness of the outcome of the application of the privity of contract rule, Teresa (the original tenant) can obtain an indemnity, which is considered in the following section.

13.2.6 Indemnities between Assignees of a Lease

The rules about to be discussed go a little way towards mitigating the harshness on original tenants of the rules set out previously. In various contexts (including the present one) the law gives to a defendant to legal proceedings a 'right of indemnity'. This is a right, having paid damages to the claimant, to reclaim those damages from a third party.

Diagram 13.5 represents the following:

- In 1984, L granted a 99-year lease to A.

- In 1991, A assigned the lease to B.

- In 2001, B assigned the lease to C.
- In 2011, C assigned the lease to D.
- D has now run up arrears of rent.

Diagram 13.5
Indemnity

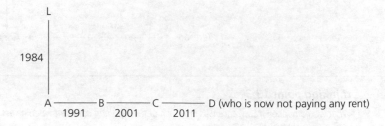

In this situation L has a choice of whether to sue A (on the original tenant's contractual liability) or D under the privity of estate rule. L can recover only one lot of compensation; he will choose to sue whoever has the most money. Consider the following scenarios:

- *L decides to sue A* A, having paid L, will have two alternative rights of indemnity:
  - at *common law* a right against the tenant in possession at the time of the breach (D in this case);

  or

  - under *s77(1) LPA 1925*, a right against the person to whom he assigned the lease (B in this case).

- *A decides to claim indemnity from B* B pays A:
  - B can then claim indemnity from C (s77(1) LPA 1925) or D (common law).
  - B decides to claim indemnity from C. C pays B.
  - C can then claim indemnity from D.
  - C decides to claim indemnity from D.

thinking point 13.4

Will it be worthwhile C taking proceedings against D?

Probably no! D is the one who is behind with the rent, and everyone else has avoided suing him, so it looks as though he has got little or no money. It follows from the answer just given that C will probably end up footing the bill. Do you think this is fair? Arguably, this is fair. It was C who brought the financially unsound party (D) into this scenario, so it is C who should bear the loss.

13.2.7 Position of Covenants which Do Not Touch and Concern

Toni is the tenant of the Spotted Cow. She holds the property on a 21-year lease granted in 1995 from Lovely Ales plc. The lease includes a covenant under which Lovely Ales promise not to supply their beer to other pubs within a quarter-mile radius. This type of covenant does not 'touch and concern' the land.

Alice is contemplating taking an assignment of the lease of the Spotted Cow. She wants to get the benefit of the 'local monopoly' in Lovely Ales beer. As the 'local monopoly' does not

cross-reference
Covenants touching and concerning the land are discussed at 13.2.2.

'touch and concern the land', it will not automatically pass to Alice on the assignment of the lease. But it will pass if the deed assigning the lease includes a special express clause assigning the benefit of the 'local monopoly' covenant. So Alice should ensure that such a special clause is inserted into the assignment.

Alice should, however, be warned of one thing. If Lovely Ales sell their business to another brewery, the successor brewery will not be bound by the 'local monopoly' covenant.

The point of this Spotted Cow example is this. The benefit of a covenant which does not touch and concern the land can be passed on to an assignee of a lease, but only if there is a separate express assignment of the benefit of the covenant. However, the burden of a covenant which does not touch and concern is enforceable only against the original covenantor, Lovely Ales plc in this example.

13.2.8 Position of Options to Purchase the Reversion

Anybody who is an assignee of a lease which contains an option to purchase the landlord's reversion is almost certainly going to want to obtain that option as well as the lease itself. A covenant by the landlord granting a tenant an option to purchase the reversion does *not*, however, touch and concern the land. Nevertheless, the assignee can get what the assignee wants, provided the assignee remembers that the option (as well as being a covenant) is an independent equitable interest in the land.

Consequently:

- If the reversion is unregistered title, the option should be registered as a land charge. It comes within the very broad definition of an 'estate contract', Class C(iv). Registering the option as a land charge will make the option binding on a purchaser of the reversion.
- If the reversion is registered title, then it will usually be an overriding interest, under Sch 3 para 2 Land Registration Act 2002 (LRA 2002) (*Webb v Pollmount* [1996] Ch 584).
- If you are purchasing a lease which includes an option to purchase the reversion, you should ensure that the deed assigning the lease also includes a separate clause assigning the option.

13.2.9 Position of Options to Renew the Lease

A covenant by a landlord giving a tenant an option to renew the lease *does* touch and concern the land. However, in *Phillips v Mobil Oil* [1989] 1 WLR 888, the Court of Appeal created a yet further complication by holding that, if the reversion is unregistered title, such an option is registrable as a Class C(iv) land charge. A tenant of a filling station who had not registered their option to renew as a land charge was thus not able to exercise it against a purchaser of the freehold reversion.

thinking point 13.5

What if the fee simple in reversion to Phillips's lease had been registered *title?*

If the reversion were registered, the tenant's option would normally be an overriding interest within Sch 3 para 2 LRA 2002, applying the principle in Webb v Pollmount. *Provided Phillips had been 'in actual occupation' there would be no need for him to enter a notice.*

thinking point 13.6

Lion Petrols plc owns the freehold in Blogford Garage. Its title is unregistered. In 1995, it granted a 21-year lease of the garage to Tony. The lease contains a clause giving the tenant a right to purchase the freehold. Ali now wants to take an assignment of the lease; he particularly wants to ensure that he will (if he can raise the finance) be able to exercise the option. Advise Ali. (There are two points you should make.)

First, Ali should ensure that the option has been registered as a land charge. Secondly, he should insist that the deed assigning him the lease includes a separate provision assigning to him the benefit of the option.

thinking point 13.7

The 1995 lease of Blogford Garage (predictably) includes a clause that the tenant must not sell brands of petrol other than Lion's. Will Ali be bound by this 'tie clause'?

Of course he will. There will be privity of estate between Lion and Ali, and courts consistently have held that 'tie clauses' touch and concern the land (see 13.2.2). (See also Regent Oil v Gregory (Hatch End) *[1965] 3 All ER 673.)*

13.3 The Landlord and Tenant (Covenants) Act 1995

It is only in the last few years that changes made by this Act have had large-scale impact, as the Act only applies to post-1995 leases ie those created on or after 1 January 1996. The Act applies equally to legal and equitable leases. In the years prior to 1996, the press (even the tabloids) were full of stories about former original tenants who have assigned their leases but who many years later have been sued for breach of covenant (eg arrears of rent) by the landlord under what has (perhaps misleadingly) been dubbed the 'privity of contract' rule. There were widespread calls for the law to be changed so that the original tenant would not be liable for breaches of covenant which happened after he had assigned the lease.

The LTCA 1995 was eventually passed against opposition from landlords. They argued that they carefully select original tenants, and let only to persons of sound financial standing who will be able to pay the rent for the full duration of the lease. An assignee of a lease is selected by the assignor. An assignee may not be of the same sound financial standing as the original tenant.

Landlords did, however, extract two important concessions from Parliament. The first was s19(1A) Landlord and Tenant Act 1927, already discussed in the previous chapter (see 12.4.4). The second is 'authorized guarantee agreements' (discussed later in 13.3.3).

13.3.1 All Covenants in a Lease Now 'Touch and Concern the Land'

Perhaps the most surprising change made by the 1995 Act is that s3 effectively transfers the benefit and burden of all covenants on assignment to the new landlord or tenant, except those covenants expressed to be personal. Any covenant entered into by a tenant actually written into a lease granted after 1995 will be enforceable by the current landlord against the current tenant under the doctrine of privity of estate, and similarly any covenant entered into by a landlord and written into the lease will be enforceable by the current tenant against the current landlord under the doctrine of privity of estate.

Landlord and Tenant (Covenants) Act 1995

3. Transmission of benefit and burden of covenants

(1) The benefit and burden of all landlord and tenant covenants of a tenancy—

    (a) shall be annexed and incident to the whole, and to each and every part, of the premises demised by the tenancy and of the reversion in them, and

    (b) shall in accordance with this section pass on an assignment of the whole or any part of those premises or of the reversion in them.

(2) Where the assignment is by the tenant under the tenancy, then as from the assignment the assignee—

    (a) becomes bound by the tenant covenants of the tenancy except to the extent that—

      (i) immediately before the assignment they did not bind the assignor, or

      (ii) they fall to be complied with in relation to any demised premises not comprised in the assignment; and

    (b) becomes entitled to the benefit of the landlord covenants of the tenancy except to the extent that they fall to be complied with in relation to any such premises.

(3) Where the assignment is by the landlord under the tenancy, then as from the assignment the assignee—

    (a) becomes bound by the landlord covenants of the tenancy except to the extent that—

      (i) immediately before the assignment they did not bind the assignor, or

      (ii) they fall to be complied with in relation to any demised premises not comprised in the assignment; and

    (b) becomes entitled to the benefit of the tenant covenants of the tenancy except to the extent that they fall to be complied with in relation to any such premises.

    ...

(6) Nothing in this section shall operate—

    (a) in the case of a covenant which (in whatever terms) is expressed to be personal to any person, to make the covenant enforceable by or (as the case may be) against any other person; or

    (b) to make a covenant enforceable against any person if, apart from this section, it would not be enforceable against him by reason of its not having been registered under the Land Registration Act [2002] or the Land Charges Act 1972.

(7) To the extent that there remains in force any rule of law by virtue of which the burden of a covenant whose subject matter is not in existence at the time when it is made does not run with the land affected unless the covenantor covenants on behalf of himself and his assigns, that rule of law is hereby abolished in relation to tenancies.

You should note that as a result of s3(6)(a) the original landlord and the original tenant can still expressly agree that a covenant is purely personal to them and only enforceable between them. You should have also noticed that the statute does not make any reference to covenants which 'touch and concern' the land, instead reference is made to landlord and tenant covenants. These are defined in s28(1) LTCA 1995.

Landlord and Tenant (Covenants) Act 1995

28. Interpretation

'landlord' and 'tenant', in relation to a tenancy, mean the person for the time being entitled to the reversion expectant on the term of the tenancy and the person so entitled to that term respectively;

'landlord covenant', in relation to a tenancy, means a covenant falling to be complied with by the landlord of premises demised by the tenancy;

'tenancy' means any lease or other tenancy and includes—

(a) a sub-tenancy, and

(b) an agreement for a tenancy,

but does not include a mortgage term;

'tenant covenant', in relation to a tenancy, means a covenant falling to be complied with by the tenant of premises demised by the tenancy.

thinking point 13.8

Reconsider the 'Spotted Cow' example given earlier in 13.2.7. This time assume that Toni's lease of the Spotted Cow was granted in 1999. What would be the position when Toni assigns the lease to Alice?

If Toni assigns the lease to Alice, Alice will now automatically get the benefit of the 'local monopoly' clause. A separate assignment of this clause is no longer required. More important still, if Lovely Ales sell their business to another brewery, the local monopoly will be enforceable against the successor brewery.

Reconsider also the situation in thinking point 13.6 on the assumption that the lease of Blogford Garage was granted in 1999. Ali need no longer insist that there be a special clause in the assignment transferring to him the option, but he should still ensure that it has been registered as a land charge (see s3(6)(b) LTCA 1995).

13.3.2 Original Tenant's Liability Ceases on Assignment

Section 5 is the key provision in the 1995 Act. It basically provides that an original tenant cannot be liable for breaches of covenant which occur after he has assigned the lease. However, an original tenant will still be liable if the assignment is itself in breach of covenant, or if the assignment occurs 'by operation of law' on death or bankruptcy of the original tenant (s11 LTCA 1995).

Landlord and Tenant (Covenants) Act 1995

5. Tenant released from covenants on assignment of tenancy

(1) This section applies where a tenant assigns premises demised to him under a tenancy.

(2) If the tenant assigns the whole of the premises demised to him, he—

(a) is released from the tenant covenants of the tenancy, and

(b) ceases to be entitled to the benefit of the landlord covenants of the tenancy, as from the assignment.

(3) If the tenant assigns part only of the premises demised to him, then as from the assignment he—

(a) is released from the tenant covenants of the tenancy, and

(b) ceases to be entitled to the benefit of the landlord covenants of the tenancy;

only to the extent that those covenants fall to be complied with in relation to that part of the demised premises.

(4) This section applies as mentioned in subsection (1) whether or not the tenant is tenant of the whole of the premises comprised in the tenancy.

Subsection (2)(a) is the central provision in the 1995 Act. Subject to the exceptions already mentioned, and an exception we are about to discuss, a tenant who has assigned their lease need no longer worry about future breaches of covenant.

13.3.3 Authorized Guarantee Agreements

cross-reference
See 12.4.4 for a discussion of s19(1A) Landlord and Tenant Act 1927.

Authorized guarantee agreements (commonly known as AGAs) are a major concession to landlords (s16 LTCA 1995). If a tenant needs a landlord's consent to assign the lease (whether under an absolute or qualified covenant against assigning) then the landlord can give his/her consent on condition that the tenant guarantees that the person to whom they are assigning will perform the tenant's covenants in the lease. If the tenant refused to agree to enter into an authorized guarantee agreement the landlord can refuse to allow the tenant to assign the lease. The landlord's refusal would come within the scope of s19(1A) Landlord and Tenant Act 1927, and would be deemed to be reasonable.

Landlord and Tenant (Covenants) Act 1995

16. Tenant guaranteeing performance of covenant by assignee

(1) Where on an assignment a tenant is to any extent released from a tenant covenant of a tenancy by virtue of this Act ('the relevant covenant'), nothing in this Act (and in particular section 25) shall preclude him from entering into an authorised guarantee agreement with respect to the performance of that covenant by the assignee.

(2) For the purposes of this section an agreement is an authorised guarantee agreement if—

(a) under it the tenant guarantees the performance of the relevant covenant to any extent by the assignee; and

(b) it is entered into in the circumstances set out in subsection (3); and

(c) its provisions conform with subsections (4) and (5).

(3) Those circumstances are as follows—

(a) by virtue of a covenant against assignment (whether absolute or qualified) the assignment cannot be effected without the consent of the landlord under the tenancy or some other person;

(b) any such consent is given subject to a condition (lawfully imposed) that the tenant is to enter into an agreement guaranteeing the performance of the covenant by the assignee; and

(c) the agreement is entered into by the tenant in pursuance of that condition.

(4) An agreement is not an authorised guarantee agreement to the extent that it purports—

(a) to impose on the tenant any requirement to guarantee in any way the performance of the relevant covenant by any person other than the assignee; or

(b) to impose on the tenant any liability, restriction or other requirement (of whatever nature) in relation to any time after the assignee is released from that covenant by virtue of this Act.

(5) Subject to subsection (4), an authorised guarantee agreement may—

(a) impose on the tenant any liability as sole or principal debtor in respect of any obligation owed by the assignee under the relevant covenant;

437

(b) impose on the tenant liabilities as guarantor in respect of the assignee's performance of that covenant which are no more onerous than those to which he would be subject in the event of his being liable as sole or principal debtor in respect of any obligation owed by the assignee under that covenant;

(c) require the tenant, in the event of the tenancy assigned by him being disclaimed, to enter into a new tenancy of the premises comprised in the assignment—

(i) whose term expires not later than the term of the tenancy assigned by the tenant, and

(ii) whose tenant covenants are no more onerous than those of that tenancy;

(d) make provision incidental or supplementary to any provision made by virtue of any of paragraphs (a) to (c).

(6) Where a person ('the former tenant') is to any extent released from a covenant of a tenancy by virtue of section 11(2) as from an assignment and the assignor under the assignment enters into an authorised guarantee agreement with the landlord with respect to the performance of that covenant by the assignee under the assignment—

(a) the landlord may require the former tenant to enter into an agreement under which he guarantees, on terms corresponding to those of that authorised guarantee agreement, the performance of that covenant by the assignee under the assignment; and

(b) if its provisions conform with subsections (4) and (5), any such agreement shall be an authorised guarantee agreement for the purposes of this section; and

(c) in the application of this section in relation to any such agreement—

(i) subsections (2)(b) and (c) and (3) shall be omitted, and

(ii) any reference to the tenant or to the assignee shall be read as a reference to the former tenant or to the assignee under the assignment.

(7) For the purposes of subsection (1) it is immaterial that—

(a) the tenant has already made an authorised guarantee agreement in respect of a previous assignment by him of the tenancy referred to in that subsection, it having been subsequently revested in him following a disclaimer on behalf of the previous assignee, or

(b) the tenancy referred to in that subsection is a new tenancy entered into by the tenant in pursuance of an authorised guarantee agreement;

and in any such case subsections (2) to (5) shall apply accordingly.

. . .

It must be stressed that this authorized guarantee agreement, when given by the assignor tenant, lasts only as long as the original assignee is the tenant of the property. Suppose:

- L in 2008 grants a 99-year lease to T.

- In 2010, T assigns the lease to U, with T entering into an authorized guarantee agreement.

- In 2012, U assigns to V, who in 2017 falls into arrears of rent or breaks some other kind of covenant.

T is not liable on the guarantee. His liability ceased in 2012, when U assigned to V.

The scope of s16 LTCA 1995 was considered by the High Court in *Good Harvest Partnership LLP v Centaur Services Ltd* [2010] EWHC 330. The defendant in this case acted as *guarantor* for the tenant. As a condition for assigning the lease, both the tenant and the *guarantor* were required to enter into an authorized guarantee agreement. The assignee failed to pay the rent, and the claimant brought an action against the defendant to recover rent due. The court held that where a lease was being assigned only the tenant could enter into an authorized guarantee agreement. The tenant's guarantor could not be required to act as guarantor for the assignee. The court was of the view that the Act clearly releases the *guarantor* from their obligations on assignment of a lease. The Court of Appeal in *K/S Victoria Street v House of Fraser (Stores Management) Ltd* [2011] 2 P & CR 15 confirmed that the landlord cannot require the guarantor to guarantee the liability of a future assignee.

13.3.4 Cessation of Original Landlord's Liability

A landlord of a post-1996 lease who disposes of his reversion still remains liable on the covenants he entered into (eg relating to repair). However, ss 6–8 LTCA 1995 provide a procedure under which he can be released from this continuing liability. The ex-landlord must serve notice on the tenant at the latest four weeks after he has assigned his reversion. The landlord is automatically released from his covenants once four weeks have elapsed from service of the notice, unless the tenant objects. If the tenant does object, the landlord is only released if a County Court decides that such a release would be reasonable.

13.3.5 Notice to Tenant or Guarantor of Arrears

Section 17 LTCA 1995 is the one significant provision which applies to pre-1996 leases as well as new leases. If a landlord wants to recover arrears of rent (or service charges) from an original tenant or somebody who has entered into an authorized guarantee agreement, then the landlord must serve a warning notice within six months of the arrears arising.

(13.4) # Position of Equitable Leases

13.4.1 Pre-1996 Equitable Leases

cross-reference
Remember
Coatsworth v
Johnson *discussed*
at 3.10.1.

A tenant under an equitable lease can assign the lease and the rights thereunder. However, the court in *Purchase v Lichfield Brewery* [1915] 1 KB 184 held that the doctrine of privity of estate did not apply to equitable leases. In consequence, an assignee of an equitable lease could not be sued by the landlord for rent or breach of other obligations in the lease. Liability for the rent and other obligations in the lease remained solely with the original tenant.

> **thinking point 13.9**
>
> *An assignee of an equitable lease was nevertheless well advised to ensure that the tenant's obligations in the equitable lease were carried out. Why?*
>
> *If there were any substantial breach of these obligations, the right to specific performance would be lost and consequently there would no longer be any equitable lease.*

13.4.2 Post-1995 Equitable Leases

As a result of a provision tucked away in the definition section of the LTCA 1995 (s28(1)), it appears that the 1995 Act does apply to equitable leases. It therefore follows that where a post-1995 equitable lease is assigned, the original tenant ceases to be liable on the obligations on the lease; the assignee is liable instead.

Landlord and Tenant (Covenants) Act 1995

28. Interpretation

(1) In this Act (unless the context otherwise requires)—

'assignment' includes equitable assignment and in addition (subject to section 11) assignment in breach of a covenant of a tenancy or by operation of law;

'authorised guarantee agreement' means an agreement which is an authorised guarantee agreement for the purposes of section 16;

'collateral agreement', in relation to a tenancy, means any agreement collateral to the tenancy, whether made before or after its creation;

'consent' includes licence;

'covenant' includes term, condition and obligation, and references to a covenant (or any description of covenant) of a tenancy include a covenant (or a covenant of that description) contained in a collateral agreement;

'landlord' and 'tenant', in relation to a tenancy, mean the person for the time being entitled to the reversion expectant on the term of the tenancy and the person so entitled to that term respectively;

'landlord covenant', in relation to a tenancy, means a covenant falling to be complied with by the landlord of premises demised by the tenancy;

'new tenancy' means a tenancy which is a new tenancy for the purposes of section 1;

'reversion' means the interest expectant on the termination of a tenancy;

'tenancy' means any lease or other tenancy and includes—

    (a) a sub-tenancy, and

    (b) an agreement for a tenancy,

but does not include a mortgage term;

'tenant covenant', in relation to a tenancy, means a covenant falling to be complied with by the tenant of premises demised by the tenancy.

 13.5   # Position of Sub-Tenants and Head Landlords

As we have already seen, there is no privity of estate between a head landlord and a sub-tenant. In the Kirby House case study at 13.1, there was no privity of estate between Roger and Susan. It follows that the terms of the head lease are not, as a general rule, enforceable by or against a sub-tenant. A sub-tenant should, however, be wary of the following two points.

13.5.1 Forfeiture Clauses

A sub-tenant should as far as possible ensure that all terms of the head lease which are enforceable by forfeiture are in fact observed. If the head lease is forfeited, any sub-lease derived from it is automatically destroyed as well. But you should note the possibility of the sub-tenant claiming relief under s146(4) LPA 1925. The operation of s146 LPA 1925 is discussed in Chapter 14.

13.5.2 Restrictive Covenants in the Head Lease

Here we have another awkward anomaly in the law. In the case study at 13.1 it was indicated that Roger will be able to enforce the 'residential purposes only' covenant against Susan under the law of restrictive covenants, the detailed principles of which are discussed in Chapters 20 and 21. (It should be noted that the landlord's reversionary estate counts as the 'dominant land'.)

If a head lease is granted after 1995, a restrictive covenant in that lease is automatically binding on a sub-tenant by virtue of s3(5) LTCA 1995. This provides:

> Any landlord or tenant covenant of a tenancy which is restrictive of the user of the land shall, as well as being capable of enforcement against an assignee, be capable of being enforced against any other person who is the owner or occupier of any demised premises to which the covenant relates even though there is no express provision in the tenancy to that effect.

In consequence, any restrictive covenant in a lease is binding (for the duration of the lease) on sub-tenants, licensees, and even squatters on the leased land!

⭕ Concluding Remarks

The best way of concluding this chapter is to return to the Kirby House case study at 13.1 and consider Diagram 13.6.

Diagram 13.6
The letting of Kirby House with assignment to Susan

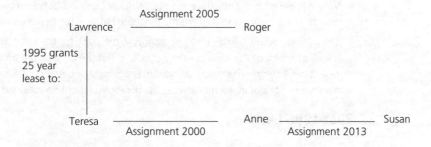

Lawrence —————— Assignment 2005 —————— Roger

1995 grants 25 year lease to:

Teresa —————— Assignment 2000 —————— Anne —————— Assignment 2013 —————— Susan

thinking point 13.10

What difference would it make to the four problems listed at 13.1 if, instead of sub-letting to Susan, Anne had assigned the lease to Susan?

1 *With respect to the 'purely personal' portrait painting covenant, the answer is as before. The covenant remains enforceable by Lawrence against Teresa.*

2 *Roger can sue either Teresa or Susan (but not Anne) for the arrears of rent. But you should note that if he chooses to sue Teresa, Teresa can claim an indemnity from Anne (s77(1) LPA 1925) or Susan (common law).*

3 *On the revised version of the case study, Susan is in privity of estate with Roger, and this will work to her advantage. Susan can sue Roger for the disrepairs.*

4 Roger can sue Susan invoking the privity of estate principle. There is no need for him to invoke the (rather technical) rule regarding restrictive covenants.

If you now compare the answers to the four problems with those following thinking point 13.2, you will see that a lot does turn on whether the transaction between Anne and Susan is a sub-letting (a lease created out of a lease) or an assignment (a transfer of the existing leasehold estate).

In answering examination problems in the area of law covered in this and/or the next chapter, some students often get confused between assignments and sub-lettings. This is fatal to their chances of getting good marks. To help avoid the confusion, here are two tips:

- as we did with Kirby House, always draw a diagram to illustrate the facts of the problem; and
- in that diagram always use vertical lines for leases and sub-leases, and horizontal lines for assignments and sales of freehold reversions.

Summary

Successors in title to the original landlord and to the original tenant may be liable to each other on the covenants in the lease if there is 'privity of estate'. Privity of estate exists between two parties if they are in a direct landlord and tenant relationship.

Pre-1996 Leases

- Where there is privity of estate but not privity of contract between two parties, only covenants which 'touch and concern the land' are enforceable between them.
- The original tenant is liable on all covenants in the lease for the full duration of the lease. If a later assignee of the lease breaks a covenant but the original tenant is sued, the original tenant has a common law right of indemnity against the person breaking the covenant, and a statutory right of indemnity against the person to whom he assigned the lease.

Post-1995 Leases

- Where there is privity of estate between two parties, all covenants in the lease are enforceable between them, except covenants expressed to be personal.
- When an original tenant assigns the lease he ceases to be liable on the covenants in the lease.

Authorized Guarantee Agreements

Where a post-1995 lease contains a qualified covenant against assignment, and the current tenant asks for permission to assign, the landlord may, if it is reasonable to do, ask the assignor to enter into an 'authorized guarantee agreement'. Under such a guarantee, the assignor (A1) guarantees that the assignee (A2) will perform the covenants. The guarantee only lasts so long as A2 remains owner of the lease.

Sub-tenants are generally not liable on covenants contained in the head lease. However, restrictive covenants are normally directly enforceable by the head landlord against the sub-tenant.

A sub-tenant should (where possible) ensure that covenants in the head lease which are enforceable by forfeiture are performed.

Further Reading

Davey, M, 'Privity of contract and leases—reform at last' (1996) 59 MLR 78
An academic commentary on the 1995 Act.

Law Commission, *Landlord and Tenant—Privity of Contract and Estate* (Report No 174, 1988)
This report provides the rationale which led to the Landlord and Tenant (Covenants) Act 1995.

Smith, RJ, 'The running of covenants in equitable leases and equitable assignments of legal leases' (1978) 37(1) CLJ 98
For the puzzling position of equitable leases prior to the 1995 Act.

Walter, P, 'The Landlord and Tenant (Covenants) Act 1995: a legislative folly' [1996] Conv 432
Highly critical view of the 1995 Act.

Questions

In 1990, Lisa leased (by deed) a house to Tommy for 40 years. The lease includes the following covenants:

1 the tenant should pay £2,000 per year rent;

2 the tenant should not use the house for any purpose other than as a private dwelling;

3 the tenant should not assign, sub-let, or part with possession except with the landlord's consent.

The lease does not contain a forfeiture clause.

Lisa believes that Tommy intends to assign or sub-let to Percy. She is alarmed at that prospect, as Percy uses a number of houses in the area as branches of his very extensive accountancy practice.

Advise Lisa:

• as to the possible legal consequences if she withheld her consent to an assignment or sub-letting to Percy; and

• as to her position if she gave her consent to an assignment or sub-letting, but subsequently wishes to enforce covenants (1) or (2).

14

Termination of Leases

Introduction

There are various ways in which a lease can come to an end (see 14.1). Most of the ways in which a lease can terminate (eg notice or expiry) are self-explanatory; only one of them, forfeiture, requires extended consideration.

As you have probably guessed, forfeiture of a lease occurs where the landlord cancels a lease because the tenant has broken a provision in that lease. If a long term lease is forfeit, that could be a disaster for the tenant, particularly if the rent is low relative to the value of the property. It is therefore not surprising that the law has placed quite severe restrictions on a landlord's right to forfeit a lease. However, as we shall see, those restrictions have become rather complex, and possibly too protective of tenants.

14.1 Ways in Which Leases May Terminate

14.1.1 Natural Expiry

This occurs where a fixed term lease runs out and requires no further explanation here.

14.1.2 Giving of Notice

A lease may be terminated:

- by either the landlord or the tenant giving notice to terminate a periodic tenancy; or
- by the tenant invoking a 'break clause' in a fixed term lease. A 'break clause' is in effect an option to terminate the lease early.

14.1.3 Merger

A merger occurs where the tenant buys the landlord's reversion. The former lease then comes to an end.

cross-reference
For a discussion on a lease being frustrated, see 14.1.5.

14.1.4 Surrender

A lease is surrendered where it is terminated by mutual agreement between landlord and tenant or possibly where the landlord is in serious breach and the tenant treats this conduct as a repudiation of the lease. It must be stressed that, except where there is a break clause or the lease has been 'frustrated', a tenant cannot unilaterally give up a fixed term lease he no longer wants.

If a tenant just walks away from leased premises he no longer needs, he remains liable for the rent for the full duration of the lease. Moreover, the landlord is under no duty to mitigate his loss by forfeiting the lease and then re-letting (*Reichman v Beveridge* [2006] EWCA Civ 1659).

REVIEW QUESTION In 2010, you took a 20-year lease of a small factory on the Blogtown Trading Estate. Your business is booming, and you are considering moving to larger premises. Consider your position under the 2010 lease. Can you 'get rid of it'?

14.1.5 Frustration

pause for thought

If you have not yet studied the doctrine of frustration, or are perhaps 'rusty' as to what it involves, read the relevant chapter in your contract textbook. Concentrate on the issue of what sorts of events do/do not constitute frustration. There is no need for you to consider the consequences of a contract being frustrated.

A contract is 'frustrated' when something unanticipated happens, the fault of neither party, which makes the performance of the contract radically different from that which was originally agreed.

In *National Carriers v Panalpina* [1981] AC 675, the House of Lords ended many years of controversy by holding that this law of contract rule of 'frustration' does apply to leases. In January 1974 the defendants took a ten-year lease of a warehouse. In May 1979, the local authority closed the only access road to the warehouse. The closure was likely to last 20 months. The tenants refused to pay any further rent, arguing that the lease was frustrated by the lack of any road access.

Lord Hailsham LC said:

> This discussion brings me to the central point at issue in this case which, in my view, is whether or not there is anything in the nature of an executed lease which prevents the doctrine of frustration, however formulated, applying to the subsisting relationship between the parties. That the point is open in this House is clear from the difference of opinion expressed in *Cricklewood Property and Investment Trust Ltd. v. Leighton's Investment Trust Ltd.* [1945] A.C. 221 between the second Lord Russell of Killowen and Lord Goddard on the one hand, who answered the question affirmatively, and Viscount Simon L.C. and Lord Wright on the other, who answered it negatively, with Lord Porter reserving his opinion until the point arose definitively for consideration. The point, though one of principle, is a narrow one. It is the difference immortalised in H.M.S. Pinafore between 'never' and 'hardly ever,' since both Viscount Simon and Lord Wright clearly conceded that, though they thought the doctrine applicable in principle to leases, the cases in which it could properly be applied must be extremely rare . . .

> . . . Is there anything in principle which ought to prevent a lease from ever being frustrated? I think there is not. In favour of the opposite opinion, the difference in principle between real and chattel property was strongly urged. But I find it difficult to accept this, once it has been decided, as has long been the case, that time and demise charters even of the largest ships and of considerable duration can in principle be frustrated . . . I accept of course that systems of developed land draw a vital distinction between land, which is relatively permanent, and other types of property, which are relatively perishable. But one can overdo the contrast.

> Coastal erosion as well as the 'vast convulsion of nature' postulated by Viscount Simon LC in the *Cricklewood case* [1945] 1 All ER 252 at 255–256, [1945] AC 221 at 229 can, even in this island, cause houses, gardens, even villages and their churches to fall into the North Sea . . . In the result, I come down on the side of the 'hardly ever' school of thought. No doubt the circumstances in which the doctrine can apply to leases are, to quote Viscount Simon L.C. in the *Cricklewood* case, at p. 231, 'exceedingly rare.' Lord Wright appears to have thought the same, whilst adhering to the view that there are cases in which frustration can apply, at p. 241. But, as he said in the same passage: ' . . . the doctrine of frustration is modern and flexible and is not subject to being constricted by an arbitrary formula'.

Their Lordships held that the doctrine of frustration did apply to leases, but that a 20-month interruption in the enjoyment of a ten-year lease was not such a drastic change in the rights of the parties as to amount to a frustration terminating the lease. Unfortunately, their Lordships did not indicate how long an interruption there would have to be to terminate the lease.

thinking point 14.1

Traditionalist land lawyers do not like Panalpina, and would have preferred the House of Lords to have followed old cases (going back to the seventeenth century) which held that leases cannot be frustrated. Consider why we think like this.

The Panalpina decision is productive of a lot of uncertainty. Suppose that the blockage of the access road had lasted several years. The lease would be frustrated, but exactly when? This question is important as the lease, and therefore the tenant's liability for rent, would terminate on the exact date of frustration.

14.1.6 Repudiatory Breach by the Landlord Accepted by the Tenant

It is of course trite contract law that if one party to a contract commits a serious breach of contract going to the root of the contract, the other party can accept that repudiation and regard that contract as terminated. It seems that this doctrine can also be applied to breaches of terms of leases committed by landlords, though currently there is only a very limited amount of case law on the point (see *Hussein v Mehlman* [1992] 2 EGLR 87; *Nynehead Developments v RH Fibreboard Containers Ltd* [1999] 1 EGLR 7). It can be argued that the introduction of this contract rule into the law of leases is highly unwelcome. It could generate a lot of disputes as to whether the landlords' conduct was sufficiently grave so as to justify the tenant treating the lease as terminated.

REVIEW QUESTION Using similar facts to those provided in the Review question at 14.1.4, consider the following:

In 2010, you took a 20-year lease of a small factory on the Blogtown Trading Estate. The landlord is in breach of covenant to keep the roads on the trading estate in good repair. Can you 'get rid' of the lease?

14.1.7 Forfeiture

This is discussed in more depth at 14.2.

Forfeiture of Leases

14.2.1 The Need for a Forfeiture Clause

Obligations in leases are usually phrased as covenants, for example T covenants to pay the rent or T promises to do the repairs. Where the tenant's obligations in a legal lease are phrased as covenants, the landlord has the right to **forfeit** for breach by the tenant of one of the tenant's obligations only if the lease contains an express forfeiture clause ('right of entry'). (If there is an equitable lease the forfeiture clause is implied into the lease as an equitable right of entry.) Moreover, that forfeiture clause must extend to the breach which has in fact occurred. The breach does not automatically end the lease, but the lease becomes voidable and consequently this gives the landlord the option to choose whether to terminate the lease or to waive forfeiture.

. . . .

forfeiture of a lease

where the landlord cancels a lease because the tenant has broken a provision in that lease. Forfeiture specifically provides for the landlord's right to re-enter the property and cancel the lease.

. . . .

Virtually every lease in existence today, except some very long term leases, includes a very widely drawn express forfeiture clause which can be invoked if the tenant breaks any of the tenant's obligations. In the case of non-payment of rent, it is usual for the forfeiture clause to allow a period of 'grace'. For example, it is common for a lease to provide that the landlord can forfeit for non-payment of rent, but only if the rent is 30 days or one month in arrears.

If, which nowadays is unlikely, an obligation in a lease is phrased as a condition rather than a covenant, for example 'I grant you this lease provided that the premises are kept in good repair', no forfeiture clause is necessary. The landlord automatically has a right of entry for breach of the condition (*Doe d Lockwood v Clarke* (1807) 8 East 185).

14.2.2 Modes of Forfeiture

Traditionally there have been two alternative ways in which a landlord can forfeit a lease:

- *Peaceable re-entry* This should be resorted to only if the property has been abandoned, or if it is absolutely clear that the tenant will leave of their own free will.

- *Court proceedings for forfeiture* Such proceedings are usually essential because ss 6–13 Criminal Law Act 1977 make it a crime to repossess property by force.

'Peaceable re-entry' is not often used to forfeit a lease. In giving the leading speech in the House of Lords in *Billson v Residential Apartments* [1992] 1 AC 494, Lord Templeman described peaceable re-entry as a 'dubious and dangerous method of determining [a] lease'. The decision of the House in this case further discourages the use of peaceable re-entry, except in cases of commercial premises abandoned by the tenant. For reasons which will emerge at 14.2.3, peaceable re-entry should never be used to forfeit a lease of an occupied dwelling house.

In *Billson v Residential Apartments Ltd* [1992] 1 AC 494, a tenant undertook major reconstruction works without their landlord's consent and in breach of covenant. The landlord served a s146(1) Law of Property Act 1925 (LPA 1925) notice forfeiting the lease. The tenants having failed to remedy the breach, the landlord early one morning peaceably re-entered the vacant premises and changed the locks. Only later did the tenant apply for relief from forfeiture.

Lord Templeman said:

> When a tenant receives a s. 146 notice he will not know whether the landlord can be persuaded that there is no breach or persuaded to accept in due course that any breach has been remedied and that he has been offered adequate and satisfactory compensation or whether the landlord will seek to determine the lease by issuing and serving a writ or will seek to determine the lease by re-entering the premises. The tenant will not wish to institute proceedings seeking relief from forfeiture if those proceedings will be aggressive and hostile and may be premature and unnecessary. Parliament cannot have intended that if the landlord employs the civilised method of determining the lease by issuing and serving a writ, then the tenant will be entitled to apply for relief, but if the landlord employs the dubious and dangerous method of determining the lease by re-entering the premises, then the tenant will be debarred from applying for relief . . .
>
> My Lords, I accept the conclusion that a landlord who serves a notice under s. 146(1) can be said, for the purposes of s. 146(2) to be proceeding to enforce his rights under the lease. A tenant authorised by s. 146(2) to apply to the court for relief against forfeiture if he fails to comply with a s. 146 notice may make that application after service of the notice for the purpose of elucidating the issues raised by the notice, ascertaining the intentions of the landlord, and setting in train the machinery by which the dispute between the landlord and the tenant can be determined by negotiation or by the court. But the fact that the tenant may apply to the court for relief after service of the s. 146 notice does not mean that if he does not do so he loses the right conferred on him by s. 146(2) to apply for relief if and when the landlord proceeds, not by action but 'otherwise' by exercising a right of re-entry. No absurdity follows from a construction which allows the tenant to apply for relief before and after a landlord re-enters without first obtaining a court order . . .
>
> The results of s. 146 and the authorities are as follows. A tenant may apply for appropriate declarations and for relief from forfeiture under s. 146(2) after the issue of a s. 146 notice but he is not prejudiced if he does not do so. A tenant cannot apply for relief after a landlord has forfeited a lease by issuing and serving a writ, has recovered judgment and has entered into possession pursuant to that judgment. If the judgment is set aside or successfully appealed the tenant will be able to apply for relief in the landlord's action but the court in deciding whether to grant relief will take into account any consequences of the original order and repossession and the delay of the tenant. A tenant may apply for relief after a landlord has forfeited by re-entry without first obtaining a court order for that purpose but the court in deciding whether to grant relief will take into account all the circumstances, including delay, on the part of the tenant. Any past judicial observations which might suggest that a tenant is debarred from applying for relief after the landlord has re-entered without first obtaining a court order for that purpose are not to be so construed. I would therefore allow the appeal and set aside the orders of the trial judge and the Court of Appeal.

cross-reference
Relief from forfeiture is discussed in detail at 14.4.

The House of Lords concluded that a tenant whose lease has been forfeited by peaceful re-entry without a court order can apply for relief from forfeiture, that is, restoration of the lease. The application for relief should be made as soon as possible, as 'the court in deciding whether to grant relief will take into account all the circumstances, including delay, on the part of the tenant'.

14.2.3 Forfeiture of a Lease of a Dwelling House

First, a little bit of a digression. In the last 60 or so years, there has been an enormous problem with landlords 'harassing' tenants (cutting off electricity, creating loud noises at night, etc) in an effort unlawfully to drive those tenants out of the houses or flats they have leased.

The 'harassment' of tenants is made criminal by s1 Protection from Eviction Act 1977, but that provision did not create a civil claim for damages or an injunction.

Protection from Eviction Act 1977

1. Unlawful eviction and harassment of occupier

(1)　In this section 'residential occupier', in relation to any premises, means a person occupying the premises as a residence, whether under a contract or by virtue of any enactment or rule of law giving him the right to remain in occupation or restricting the right of any other person to recover possession of the premises.

(2)　If any person unlawfully deprives the residential occupier of any premises of his occupation of the premises or any part thereof, or attempts to do so, he shall be guilty of an offence unless he proves that he believed, and had reasonable cause to believe, that the residential occupier had ceased to reside in the premises.

(3)　If any person with intent to cause the residential occupier of any premises—

(a)　to give up the occupation of the premises or any part thereof; or

(b)　to refrain from exercising any right or pursuing any remedy in respect of the premises or part thereof;

does acts [likely] to interfere with the peace or comfort of the residential occupier or members of his household, or persistently withdraws or withholds services reasonably required for the occupation of the premises as a residence, he shall be guilty of an offence.

(3A)　Subject to subsection (3B) below, the landlord of a residential occupier or an agent of the landlord shall be guilty of an offence if—

(a)　he does acts likely to interfere with the peace or comfort of the residential occupier or members of his household, or

(b)　he persistently withdraws or withholds services reasonably required for the occupation of the premises in question as a residence,

and (in either case) he knows, or has reasonable cause to believe, that that conduct is likely to cause the residential occupier to give up the occupation of the whole or part of the premises or to refrain from exercising any right or pursuing any remedy in respect of the whole or part of the premises.

(3B)　A person shall not be guilty of an offence under subsection (3A) above if he proves that he had reasonable grounds for doing the acts or withdrawing or withholding the services in question.

However, under ss27 and 28 Housing Act 1988, a statutory tort has been created of harassing a 'residential occupier'.

The central point, though, for our present purposes is s2 Protection from Eviction Act 1977.

Protection from Eviction Act 1977

2. Restriction on re-entry without due process of law

Where any premises are let as a dwelling on a lease which is subject to a right of re-entry or forfeiture it shall not be lawful to enforce that right otherwise than by proceedings in the court while any person is lawfully residing in the premises or part of them.

This section effectively renders it impossible to forfeit a lease of an occupied dwelling by peaceable re-entry. Section 2 also applies to prevent forfeiture by peaceful re-entry where a shop with living accommodation above the shop is leased as one unit (see *Patel v Pirabakaran* [2006] 1 WLR 3112).

14.3 Waiver of Forfeiture

Waiver of forfeiture must not be confused with relief from forfeiture.

The essence of 'waiver' is that the landlord, because of the landlord's conduct, is deemed to have forgiven the tenant, and the landlord has renounced their claim to forfeiture and concedes the continued existence of the lease. The landlord can still pursue a claim for damages.

cross-reference
See 14.4 for relief from forfeiture.

Relief from forfeiture occurs where the court decides that although the tenant has broken the terms of the lease, the tenant should be allowed to keep the lease. In effect the court shows mercy and forgives the erring tenant.

Waiver will occur where:

- the landlord knows of the breach;

    and

- with that knowledge, he does some unequivocal act, known to the tenant, which would indicate to a reasonable onlooker that the landlord regards the lease as still subsisting.

The most frequently occurring 'unequivocal acts' are where the landlord either demands or accepts rent for a period after the breach. If the landlord distrains, that is, seizes the tenant's goods to cover arrears of rent, that is an 'unequivocal act' irrespective of when the rent in question was due. Another example of an 'unequivocal act' would be where the landlord enters into negotiations to renew the lease on its expiry, or offers to vary the terms of the existing lease.

A landlord has knowledge of facts constituting a breach if they come to his attention, or to the attention of any of his agents. If Agent 1 has knowledge of a breach and Agent 2 sends out a rent demand, there is a waiver. The case of *Central Estates (Belgravia) v Woolgar (No 2)* [1972] 1 WLR 1048 illustrates many of the points just discussed. Woolgar, an OAP and a First World War veteran, was tenant of a long lease (due to expire in 1993) of a sizeable house in central London. He had a fall from grace, and was convicted of using the premises as a homosexual brothel. In view of his past exemplary record, he was granted a conditional discharge by the magistrates. The landlords, however, decided to forfeit the lease for breach of the covenant in the lease prohibiting illegal user, and served on Woolgar the warning notice required by s146 LPA 1925. The landlords decided to forfeit the lease as the property would be much more valuable to them with 'vacant possession'. A minor official of the landlords then made a crucial mistake, he sent a rent demand for a future instalment of rent to Woolgar.

Lord Denning MR stated:

> …The material question is whether the demand and acceptance of rent in September 1970 was a waiver of the forfeiture. If it was, the landlords were not entitled to issue this plaint for possession as they did in December 1970. The judge held there was not a waiver because, as he found, the tenant when he paid the rent knew full well that the landlords' intention to forfeit the lease remained unchanged… [I]f it is sought to say that an existing *lease continues in existence* by waiver of forfeiture, then the intention of the parties does not matter. It is sufficient if there is an unequivocal act done by the landlord which recognises the existence of the lease after having knowledge of the ground of forfeiture. The law was well stated by Parker J in *Matthews v Smallwood* [1910] 1 Ch 777, which was accepted by this court in *Oak Property Co. Ltd v Chapman* [1947] 2 All ER 1:
>
>> It is also, I think, reasonably clear upon the cases that whether the act, coupled with the knowledge, constitutes a waiver is a question which the law decides, and

therefore, it is not open to a lessor who has knowledge of the breach to say 'I will treat the tenancy as existing, and I will receive the rent, or I will take advantage of my power as landlord to distrain; but I tell you that all I shall do will be without prejudice to my right to re-enter, which I intend to reserve'. That is a position which he is not entitled to take up. If, knowing of the breach, he does distrain, or does receive the rent, then by law he waives the breach, and nothing which he can say by way of protest against the law will avail him anything.

...So we have simply to ask: was this rent demanded and accepted by the landlords' agents with knowledge of the breach? It does not matter that they did not intend to waive. The very fact that they accepted the rent with the knowledge constitutes the waiver. The position here is quite plain. The agents, who had full authority to manage these properties on behalf of the landlords, did demand and accept the rent with full knowledge. It may be that the instructions did not get down the chain of command from the partner to the subordinate clerk who issued the demands and gave the receipts for rent. That cannot affect, to my mind, the legal position. It comes within the general rule that the knowledge of the agent—and of his clerks—is the knowledge of the principal. A principal cannot escape the doctrine of waiver by saying that one clerk had the knowledge and the other received the rent. They must be regarded as one for this purpose. The landlords' agents knew the position and they accepted the rent with knowledge. That is a waiver...

Buckley LJ said:

...the effect in law of an act relied on as constituting a waiver of a right to forfeit a lease must be considered objectively, without regard to the motive or intention of the landlord or the understanding or belief of the tenant.

Applying this objective approach the rent demand waived the breach, even though it had been sent out in error. Woolgar had not been in any way misled by the demand; even after the demand was sent he still personally believed that he was going to be evicted from the premises. The court stressed that the test for an 'unequivocal act' was not what the tenant subjectively thought; rather it was an objective test of what a 'reasonable onlooker' would think. The reasonable onlooker always considers rent demands as indicating that the landlord intends to allow the lease to continue.

Osibanjo v Seahive Investments [2009] 2 P & CR 2 is an interesting case where the tenant, Mr Osibanjo, sent a cheque for £10,000 covering rent arrears of £3,414.80 which were the subject of a bankruptcy petition against him and in part payment of further arrears of rent.

Seahive's solicitors banked the cheque, but wrote to the defendant returning the balance of £6,585.20 covering the further arrears; the letter stated 'for the avoidance of doubt the clearance of your cheque...should not be regarded as a waiver by our client of his right to forfeit the lease'.

The Court of Appeal held that there was no waiver of breaches of user covenants which the landlords had only discovered after they had filed the bankruptcy petition. The parties in their correspondence had stipulated the division of the amount for which the cheque was drawn. According to Mummery LJ:

In those circumstances an objective observer would have had no ground for supposing that the amount re-paid by Seahive to Mr Osibanjo had been accepted by Seahive as rent...the processing of the cheque is not in itself conclusive of the question whether the payment was accepted as rent. The processing is evidence of payment to Seahive, but for waiver of forfeiture it must also be shown that the payment was *accepted* and that it was accepted *as rent* by the landlord.

In *Blackstones Ltd v Burnetts* [1973] 1 WLR 1487, Burnetts had a lease from Blackstones of premises in central London. There was a qualified covenant against sub-letting. Burnetts obtained Blackstones' consent to sub-let to two people, A and D, trading in partnership. However, Burnetts actually sub-let to a different person, Flat Finders Ltd (A and D were the directors of that company).

The landlord's solicitors heard of what had happened. The solicitors seem to have been ignorant of the very basic principle of company law that a company is a separate person from its shareholders and directors. They sought counsel's opinion as to whether there had been a breach of the qualified covenant against sub-letting. Clearly, there had been such a breach. While this opinion was awaited, a clerk in the landlords' office sent out a rent demand for the next quarter's rent. The rent demand was held to have waived the breach.

thinking point 14.2

What is the moral for landlords of the cases just discussed?

If you want to forfeit a lease, give clear instructions to all your agents (and not just to your specialist rent collectors) that they must neither send out rent demands nor accept rent paid without a demand being sent.

REVIEW QUESTION What if rent demands are sent out by an automated computer system?

What if the rent is paid by direct debit?

(Consider 14.3 and *Central Estates (Belgravia) v Woolgar.*)

14.4 Relief from Forfeiture

Where a tenant claims relief from forfeiture, he will normally do so by counterclaiming for relief in the landlord's proceedings to terminate the lease. The tenant could bring a separate action 'for relief', but that is unlikely as it would mean unnecessary additional costs.

14.4.1 Relief from Forfeiture for Non-Payment of Rent

Under a set of archaic common law rules, in order for the landlord to start forfeiture proceedings against the tenant for non-payment of rent, the landlord must make a formal demand for rent on the day the money is due to be paid before sunset. Nowadays, to avoid this procedure the lease will contain a clause enabling the landlord to forfeit for non-payment of rent, 'whether formally demanded or not'.

The tenant will be able to claim relief from forfeiture once the landlord has started forfeiture proceedings. Such relief from forfeiture was traditionally governed by equity, but has now been incorporated into statute (s38 Supreme Court Act 1981). Three conditions must be fulfilled for relief to be granted:

1 the tenant must pay all the arrears of rent;

2 the tenant must pay all the landlord's costs; and

3 it must appear just and equitable to grant relief.

You probably already know that it is a general rule of English litigation that the loser of court proceedings pays both sides' costs. Point (2) of the previous list is a perfectly sensible exception to this rule. The tenant 'wins' relief, but the tenant must pay the landlord's legal costs as part of the price of winning.

It is fair to say that if points (1) and (2) are satisfied the court will in normal circumstances automatically conclude that it is 'just and equitable' to grant relief. Point (3) really means that the court has a discretion to refuse relief even though the tenant pays off all the arrears of rent and the landlord's costs.

thinking point 14.3

Can you think of situations where a court might refuse relief despite the fact that the tenant has cleared the arrears and paid all the landlord's costs?

The court might well refuse relief if the circumstances are such that the tenant is very likely to fall into serious arrears of rent again. It might also refuse relief if the tenant is in serious breach of other obligations in the lease as well as rent, for example had broken covenants regarding the user of premises.

Another (related) aspect of 'condition (3)' in the previous list is that in exceptional cases the court can grant relief on conditions which do not relate to payment of rent. Suppose the tenant is rather neglecting the property. The court could grant relief on condition that the property be put into good repair: *Belgravia Insurance v Meah* [1964] 1 QB 436.

Relief against forfeiture for non-payment of rent has one further oddity. Unlike relief where court proceedings have been taken under s146 LPA 1925 the court has the power to grant relief to the tenant even *after* the landlord has repossessed the property! The tenant can claim this 'late relief' up to six months after the landlord's repossession. But it should be stressed that this late relief requires the expense of separate court proceedings brought by the tenant, and that the court would not grant this late relief if the landlord had already let the property to a new tenant.

In granting relief from forfeiture to the tenant, the tenant is allowed to keep the original lease.

14.4.2 Forfeiture for Breach of Covenant Other than Rent

This is governed by s146 LPA 1925.

Law of Property Act 1925

146. Restrictions on and relief against forfeiture of leases and underleases

(1) A right of re-entry or forfeiture under any proviso or stipulation in a lease for a breach of any covenant or condition in the lease shall not be enforceable, by action or otherwise, unless and until the lessor serves on the lessee a notice –

(a) specifying the particular breach complained of; and

(b) if the breach is capable of remedy, requiring the lessee to remedy the breach; and

(c) in any case, requiring the lessee to make compensation in money for the breach;

and the lessee fails, within a reasonable time thereafter, to remedy the breach, if it is capable of remedy, and to make reasonable compensation in money, to the satisfaction of the lessor, for the breach.

(2) Where a lessor is proceeding, by action or otherwise, to enforce such a right of re-entry or forfeiture, the lessee may, in the lessor's action, if any, or in any action brought by

himself, apply to the court for relief; and the court may grant or refuse relief, as the court, having regard to the proceedings and conduct of the parties under the foregoing provisions of this section, and to all the other circumstances, thinks fit; and in case of relief may grant it on such terms; if any, as to costs, expenses, damages, compensation, penalty, or otherwise, including the granting of an injunction to restrain any like breach in the future, as the court, in the circumstances of each case, thinks fit.

The procedure provided for by this provision enables the tenant to take the opportunity to remedy the breach. This was highlighted by Slade LJ in *Expert Clothing Service and Sales Ltd v Hillgate House Ltd* [1986] Ch 340, where he said that 'an important purpose of the section 146 procedure is to give even tenants who have hitherto lacked the will or the means to comply with their obligations one last chance to summon up that will or find the necessary means before the landlord re-enters'.

Section 146(2) provides that the court can, in its discretion (in the landlord's forfeiture proceedings or in separate proceedings commenced by the tenant), grant relief from forfeiture. The general rule under s146(2) is that a tenant cannot claim relief once a landlord has actually repossessed the property. But this general rule applies only if the landlord forfeits by court proceedings.

In *Billson v Residential Apartments* [1992] 1 AC 494, the defendant was lessee of an empty building. The defendant broke a covenant against altering the building without the landlord's consent. The landlord served a s146 notice. After waiting a reasonable time, the landlord, instead of commencing court proceedings for possession, peaceably re-entered the building early one morning, changed the locks, and assumed control of the building.

cross-reference
Refer back to 14.2.2 to the extract from Billson v Residential Apartments.

The Court of Appeal held that once a landlord had peaceably re-entered, the tenant had no right to claim relief. However, this decision was overruled by the House of Lords, which held that where the landlord forfeited a lease by peaceable re-entry, the tenant could, after the landlord has reoccupied the property, commence court proceedings to get the property back. Their Lordships stressed that there is no fixed time limit on such an application for relief after peaceable re-entry. However, if the tenant delayed a long time before claiming relief, that would be a factor to be considered by the court when exercising its discretion whether or not to grant relief.

> **thinking point 14.4**
>
> *Why does the decision in* Billson *further discourage the use of peaceable re-entry to forfeit leases?*
>
> *If a landlord forfeits by court proceedings under s146, the landlord knows that once he/she has taken possession under the court order there is no possibility of the tenant's lease being restored. If the landlord forfeits by peaceable re-entry, the landlord is subject to the risk that the court will give the lease back to the tenant.*

14.4.3 The Four Stages Required by s146 for Forfeiture by Court Proceedings

- The landlord must specify to the current tenant the particular breach complained of. The landlord must serve a carefully drafted warning notice on the *current* tenant: *Old Grovebury Estates v Seymour Plant Sales (No 2)* [1979] 3 All ER 504.
- The tenant is required to remedy the breach 'if the breach is capable of remedy'. If during this time the tenant 'remedies' the breach, the landlord cannot claim forfeiture. The landlord must then wait 'a reasonable time' before commencing forfeiture proceedings.

- Assuming (as is usually the case) the breach is not remedied within a 'reasonable time', the landlord can issue a claim form demanding forfeiture.
- When the landlord's forfeiture case reaches court, the tenant can admit the breach, but beg the court to grant him/her relief. The court is most likely to grant relief either where the breach (eg disrepair) has now at last been put right, or where the landlord has not been substantially harmed by an 'irremediable' breach. As a condition of relief, the tenant must compensate the landlord for any harm actually suffered.

14.4.4 The s146 Notice Must Be Drafted Correctly

The notice must spell out in detail what breaches the landlord is relying on. For example, it is not sufficient to say, 'the property is in disrepair'. If the breach is capable of remedy, the landlord must specifically include a clause in the notice demanding the breach be put right.

If the s146 'warning' notice has not been drafted correctly, any court proceedings commenced by the landlord will be abortive, even if the tenant is clearly a sinner who should be thrown out. In such a case the landlord would have to serve another (this time correctly drafted) s146 notice and start all over again. *Akici v LR Butlin* [2006] 1 WLR 201, is a good modern illustration of the importance of ensuring that the s146 notice is drafted correctly. In this case the claimant was a tenant of commercial premises which he used as a pizza takeaway. A company, Deka Ltd, was involved in this business, and the company (originally not owned by the claimant) paid the rent. The lease included a clause 'not to charge assign...underlet or part with possession of a part of the demised premises...nor to share possession of the whole or any part of the premises nor to part with possession of the whole of the...premises' except with landlord's consent.

The defendant landlords served a s146 notice alleging 'assignment or alternatively subletting or alternatively parting with possession of the premises without the landlord's consent'. The claimant bought all the shares in Deka Ltd, but the defendants continued with forfeiture proceedings. The claimant sought relief. The trial judge found as a fact that the claimant (Akici) had *not* parted with possession, but was merely sharing occupation with the company. On the basis of that finding, the Court of Appeal held that the s146 notice was not correctly drafted, and therefore invalid.

Neuberger LJ said:

> As explained above the judge found, rightly in my view, that Mr Akici had not parted with possession of the premises to the company, but that he had shared possession of the premises with the company. However, the section 146 notice upon which Butlins relied alleged that the particular breach complained of was assigning, underletting or parting with possession of the premises. There was no express allegation of sharing possession . . .
>
> *The simple point made on behalf of Mr Akici was that the section 146 notice in the present case does not 'specify . . . the particular breach complained of', in that the only breach (or at least the only relevant breach) which has been established against him is sharing possession, whereas the notice specifies assigning, subletting or parting with possession.* [Emphasis added]
>
> As I understand it, while he would have accepted that argument if he had been construing the notice simply by reference to its terms and the nature of the breach, the judge considered that, once one construed the notice in the context of the correspondence passing between the parties, it did specify, or at least should be read as if it specified, sharing possession as a breach.
>
> If one confines oneself to the contents of the notice, it is very difficult to see how it can fairly be construed as specifying the sharing of possession as a breach of covenant complained of. The notice quotes clause 4.18, which includes covenants not to assign, not to sublet, not to part with

possession, and not to share possession, and then goes on to allege the breach complained of, which is assigning, subletting or parting with possession. On any rational approach, it seems to me that a reasonable recipient of the notice would have understood that sharing of possession was not being complained of. Although included in the clause of the lease which was quoted, it was excluded from the list of breaches complained of. To put the point another way, clause 4.18 of the lease quite clearly distinguishes between parting with possession and sharing possession, and the relevant breach of covenant alleged in the notice was parting with possession, and no mention was made of sharing possession. In this connection it is not irrelevant that an alienation provision such as clause 4.18.1 is, when properly analysed, in fact a series of separate covenants wrapped up together in a single clause: see *Jackson* v *Simons* [1923] 1 Ch 383, 383, per Romer J and *Marks* v *Warren* [1979] 1 All ER 29, 31, per Browne-Wilkinson J.

I was at one time attracted by Mr Lloyd's point that this objection to the notice is unduly technical, because it would have been clear to the reasonable recipient that what was being complained of was the presence of the company on the premises. In those circumstances, it was argued, the notice made clear the nature of the lessors' complaint and, in so far as the breach was capable of remedy, it also made it clear what the lessee had to do to put matters right. In that connection Mr Lloyd relied on the approach to the construction of contractual notices under leases adopted by the majority of the House of Lords in *Mannai Investment Co Ltd* v *Eagle Star Life Assurance Co Ltd* [1997] AC 749.

I accept the submission that the approach of the majority of the House of Lords in *Mannai* to contractual notices would apply to section 146 notices, despite Mr Butler's submission to the contrary. However, I have none the less come to the conclusion that Mr Lloyd's defence of the notice cannot stand. Even applying the *Mannai* case the notice has to comply with the requirements of section 146(1) of the 1925 Act, and if, as appears pretty plainly to be the case, it does not specify the right breach, then nothing in the *Mannai* case can save it.

Quite apart from this, if, on its true construction, the section 146 notice did not specify sharing possession as a breach complained of, it can be said with considerable force that it neither informed the recipient of the breach complained of, nor indicated to him whether, and if so how, he must remedy any breach. On the basis that there was a sharing of possession, a reasonable recipient of the section 146 notice would have been entitled to take the view that he need do nothing, because the lessors were only complaining about the presence of the company if there was a parting with possession (or assigning or underletting) by Mr Akici to it.

Accordingly, a reasonable recipient in this case (and it is the understanding of such a hypothetical person by reference to which the validity of the notice is to be assessed according to the *Mannai* case [1997] AC 749) could, to put it at its lowest, reasonably have taken the view that the lessors were not objecting to any sharing of possession, and consequently that no steps need be taken, either with a view to remedying the breach or with a view to improving the prospects of obtaining relief from forfeiture.

We were referred to authorities relating to the validity of notices served under section 146 and its statutory predecessor. I do not consider that they provide much assistance on the point that we have to determine in the present case. It is, however, appropriate to mention the decision of the House of Lords in *Fox* v *Jolly* [1916] 1 AC 1, 23 where the last sentence of the speech of Lord Parmoor appears to me to encapsulate the proper approach to section 146 notices and, it may be said, to notices generally:

> 'I think that the notice should be construed as a whole in a common-sense way, and that no lessee could have any reasonable doubt as to the particular breaches which are specified.'

In this case I think it is impossible to say that no lessee would have been in any doubt but that the lessors were not contending that he was sharing possession of the premises . . .

In brief, the s146 notice must unambiguously identify the breach or breaches about which the landlord is complaining.

Despite the conclusions that the s146 notice was invalid, the Court of Appeal judgment in *Akici v LR Butlin Ltd* also contains a very valuable discussion of the distinction between breaches capable of remedy and those incapable of remedy. This will be considered in the next section.

14.4.5 Remediable or Irremediable Breaches?

There are a few initial observations to be made before the case law on this area is considered:

- The need to draft the s146 notice correctly (discussed previously). There have been a number of cases where the landlord has drafted his s146 notice on the assumption that the breach is irremediable, but the court has ruled that the breach was 'remediable'. The landlord's forfeiture proceedings were therefore dismissed (see *Glass v Kencakes* [1966] 1 QB 611).

- The length of the 'reasonable time' which must elapse between service of the s146 notice and the commencement of proceedings for possession:

  - where the breach is remediable, then the landlord must wait at least three months;

  - where the breach is irremediable, a fortnight's delay between service of notice and commencement of proceedings generally suffices. Two days was held to be insufficient in *Horsey Estates v Steiger* [1899] 2 QB 79 at 91.

- The court is more likely to grant relief where the breach is capable of remedy.

The wording of s146(1) LPA 1925 requires the tenant to remedy the breach 'if it is remediable'. It is apparent from the wording of the statute that some breaches are capable of remedy and some are not. In *Expert Clothing Service and Sales Ltd v Hillgate House Ltd* [1986] Ch 340, Slade LJ stated:

> In my judgment, on the remediability issue, the ultimate question for the court was this: if the section 146 notice had required the lessee to remedy the breach and the lessors had then allowed a reasonable time to elapse to enable the lessee fully to comply with the relevant covenant, would such compliance, coupled with the payment of any appropriate monetary compensation, have effectively remedied the harm which the lessors had suffered or were likely to suffer from the breach? If, but only if, the answer to this question was 'No,' would the failure of the section 146 notice to require remedy of the breach have been justifiable.

The issue of remediability rests on whether the harm suffered by the landlord can be effectively removed. The courts drew a distinction between positive and negative covenants.

Positive Covenants

Breaches of positive covenants, for example repairing and painting covenants, are generally capable of remedy. This is confirmed by the decision in *Expert Clothing v Hillgate House* [1986] Ch 340. In that case the tenant had breached a covenant to reconstruct the premises by an agreed date. The Court of Appeal held that the breach was 'remediable' by the tenant belatedly doing the reconstruction. The landlords served a notice under s146 LPA 1925 that the lease was forfeit due to an irremediable breach of covenant. The tenants claimed relief from forfeiture on the basis that the notice had been defective. They claimed that the breach was capable of remedy, and the notice had not given them an opportunity to effect that remedy.

Slade LJ said:

> I would, for my part, accept the submission of [counsel for the defendants] that the breach of a positive covenant (whether it be a continuing breach or a once and for all breach) will ordinarily be capable of remedy. As Bristow J pointed out in the course of argument, the concept

of capability of remedy for the purpose of s. 146 must surely be directed to the question *whether the harm that has been done to the landlord by the relevant breach is for practical purposes capable of being retrieved*. In the ordinary case, the breach of a promise to do something by a certain time can for practical purposes be remedied by the thing being done, even out of time. [Emphasis added]

The breach was 'remediable' by the tenant belatedly carrying out the works of reconstruction.

Negative Covenants

In the past, breaches of negative covenants have generally been regarded as incapable of remedy. In particular, it has long been accepted that breaches of covenants against assigning, sub-letting, and parting with possession are incapable of remedy (*Scala House v Forbes* [1973] 3 All ER 308).

However, the Court of Appeal in *Savva v Hussein* (1996) 73 P & CR 150, a case involving the breach of a covenant not to alter a building without consent, expressed the view that all breaches of negative covenants, except those within the *Scala House* principle (see later), were to be regarded as capable of remedy. The court in this case approved the remediability test (outlined previously) as applying to both positive and negative covenants. The application of this test focuses on the effect on remedying the harm. Staughton LJ in *Savva v Hussein* observed:

In my judgment, except in a case of breach of a covenant not to assign without consent, the question is: whether the remedy referred to is the process of restoring the situation to what it would have been if the covenant had never been broken, or whether it is sufficient that the mischief resulting from a breach of the covenant can be removed. When something has been done without consent, it is not possible to restore the matter wholly to the situation which it was in before the breach. The moving finger writes and cannot be recalled. That is not to my mind what is meant by a remedy, it is a remedy if the mischief caused by the breach can be removed. In the case of a covenant not to make alterations without consent or not to display signs without consent, if there is a breach of that, the mischief can be removed by removing the signs or restoring the property to the state it was in before the alterations.

From what you have read so far, you ought to have noticed that the courts have shown that a breach of either a positive or a negative covenant is to be treated as being remediable, though there are exceptions which will be dealt with in more detail in the following section.

Modern Treatment of Breaches which are Incapable of Remedy

Despite the courts showing a more flexible approach to breaches of positive and negative covenants and treating them as remediable, it has long been accepted that breaches of covenants against assigning, sub-letting, and parting with possession are incapable of remedy (see *Scala House v Forbes* [1973] 3 All ER 308).

The Court of Appeal in *Akici v LR Butlin Ltd* [2006] 1 WLR 201, held that a breach of a covenant against parting with possession or sharing of the leased premises is capable of remedy and was in fact remedied by the licensee giving back possession to the tenant. The court in *Akici* was of the view (confirming what had been said in *Savva v Hussein*) that in principle the breach of any covenant by a tenant should be regarded as capable of remedy. The only exceptions were (i) breach of a covenant against assigning and sub-letting, and (ii) breach of a covenant against illegal or immoral user where (unlike in *Glass v Kencakes*) the tenant is personally responsible for the illegality or immorality.

Neuberger LJ in *Akici v L R Butlin Ltd* [2006] 1 WLR 201, said:

Was the breach capable of remedy?

The judge was of the view that a breach of covenant against sharing possession was not capable of remedy within the meaning of section 146 in the light of the reasoning of the Court of Appeal in *Scala House and District Property Co Ltd v Forbes* [1974] QB 575 . . .

Considering the matter free of authority I would, like the judge, be firmly of the view that a covenant against sharing possession, indeed a covenant against parting with possession, should be capable of remedy. It seems to me that there are two principal purposes of section 146 in relation to forfeiture clauses in leases. The first is to enable a lessee in breach of covenant to have the opportunity to remedy the breach, where that is possible, and thereby to avoid the forfeiture altogether, provided the lessors are fully reimbursed with regard to damages and costs. The second principal purpose of the section, which only arises where the lessee fails to remedy the breach or where the breach is incapable of remedy, is to enable the court to accord the lessee relief from forfeiture, where the lessors enforce the forfeiture.

In those circumstances it seems to me that the proper approach to the question of whether or not a breach is capable of remedy should be practical rather than technical. In a sense it could be said that any breach of covenant is, strictly speaking, incapable of remedy. Thus, where a lessee has covenanted to paint the exterior of demised premises every five years, his failure to paint during the fifth year is incapable of remedy, because painting in the sixth year is not the same as painting in the fifth year, an argument rejected in *Hoffmann v Fineberg* [1949] Ch 245, 253, cited with approval by this court in *Expert Clothing Service and Sales Ltd v Hillgate House Ltd* [1986] Ch 340, 351c–d. Equally it might be said that where a covenant to use premises only for residential purpose is breached by use as a doctor's consulting room, there is an irremediable breach because even stopping the use will not, as it were, result in the premises having been unused as a doctor's consulting room during the period of breach. Such arguments, as I see it, are unrealistically technical.

In principle I would have thought that the great majority of breaches of covenant should be capable of remedy, in the same way as repairing or most user covenant breaches. Even where stopping, or putting right, the breach may leave the lessors out of pocket for some reason, it does not seem to me that there is any problem in concluding that the breach is remediable. That is because section 146(1) entitles the lessors to 'compensation in money . . . for the breach' and, indeed, appears to distinguish between remedying the breach and paying such compensation . . . .

There are three types of classification of covenants. They are (a) positive and negative (relevant to the transmission of the burden of freehold covenants, equitable in origin), (b) continuing and 'once and for all' (relevant to waiver of forfeiture, with a common law origin), and (c) remediable and irremediable (relevant for section 146, and thus statutory in origin). These three types of classification are thus for different purposes and have different origins. Attempting to equate one class of one type with one class of a different type is therefore likely to be worse than unhelpful.

Any idea that negative covenants are by their nature irremediable has been put to rest by the decision of this court in *Savva v Hussein* (1996) 73 P & CR 150. In that case the breach of covenant consisted of carrying out alterations in breach of a covenant not to do so. After quoting the passage I have just cited from the *Expert Clothing* case, Aldous LJ said, at p 157, that he could 'see no reason why similar reasoning should not apply to some negative covenants'. He went on to quote with approval of a subsequent passage in Slade LJ's judgment [1986] Ch 340, 358:

'if the section 146 notice had required the lessee to remedy the breach and the lessors had then allowed a reasonable time to elapse to enable the lessee fully to comply with the relevant covenant, would such compliance, coupled with the payment of any appropriate monetary compensation, have effectively remedied the harm which the lessors had suffered or were likely to suffer from the breach?'

As Aldous LJ, with whom Sir John May agreed, then went on to say 73 P & CR 150, 157: 'It is only if the answer to that question is "no" it can be said that the breach is not capable of being remedied.'

In these circumstances it appears to me that, unless there is some binding authority, which either calls into question the conclusion or renders it impermissible, both the plain purpose of section 146(1) and the general principles laid down in two relatively recent decisions in this court, namely the *Expert Clothing* [1986] Ch 340 and *Savva* 73 P & CR 150 cases, point strongly to the conclusion that, at least in the absence of special circumstances, a breach of covenant against parting with possession or sharing possession, falling short of creating or transferring of legal interest, are breaches of covenant which are capable of remedy within the meaning of section 146.

The only authority which could be cited to call that conclusion into question is the *Scala House* case [1974] QB 575 itself, but that does not deter me from my conclusion. First, it was only concerned with underletting; secondly, the reasoning of the leading judgment in the case is, at least in part, demonstrably fallacious and inconsistent with common sense and many other authorities; thirdly, it has been overtaken and marginalised by the *Expert Clothing* and *Savva* cases; fourthly, there is no reason of logic or principle why the reasoning or conclusion in the *Scala House* case should be extended to apply to a breach which falls short of creating a legal interest.

Neuberger LJ was frustrated that he was bound by a previous Court of Appeal decision (*Scala House*). Regarding that case he said 'the reasoning of the leading judgment in the case is, at least in part, demonstrably fallacious and inconsistent with common sense and many other authorities; thirdly, it has been overtaken and marginalised by the *Expert Clothing* and *Savva* cases'.

Immoral User

Where premises have been used for immoral purposes by the tenants themselves, established case law regards these breaches as irremediable due to the stigma attached to the property, which could not be removed once the activities had ceased (*Rugby School (Governors) v Tannahill* [1935] 1 KB 87; *Van Haarlam v Kasner* (1992) 64 P & CR 214).

The case of *Glass v Kencakes* [1966] 1 QB 611 involved a breach of covenant against illegal and/or immoral use by the sub-tenant where the original tenant was not aware of the breach. The issue was whether the breach was irremediable. The tenant of a lease containing a covenant against illegal/immoral user sub-let to a sub-tenant who used the premises for the purpose of prostitution. The original tenant was not aware of the breach. When the landlord became aware of the immoral user he served a notice on the tenant under s146 LPA 1925 alleging that the lease was forfeit because of an irremediable breach of covenant. The tenant, in turn, served a notice to the same effect on the sub-tenant.

Paull J said:

As I see it, the result of the agreement between counsel is that clause (2) [of the s146 notice] must be taken to read: 'The above-mentioned covenants have been broken and the particular breach complained of is that the first and third floors of the said premises have been used other than residential flats in that they have been used for a business purpose, that is for the purpose of prostitution, an immoral business.' … it is this breach which is said to be incapable of remedy. Upon the strict wording of the notice clearly the plaintiff fails. That is agreed by [Counsel for the claimant]. What follows in this judgment therefore must be read as based on a notice stating the words which I have set out …

The question before me therefore resolves itself into a question which can be simply stated, but which I have found very difficult to decide. I would state it in these words: Where the

461

covenant, the breach of which is complained of, is a covenant that premises shall only be used in a certain manner and that covenant is broken by a sub-tenant of the lessee, is it capable of remedy by the lessee where the user which constitutes the breach is in fact an immoral user but where the lessee does not know that there is any such or any breach and the circumstances are such that the lessee has no reason to suppose that any, and in particular any such, breach has been or is being committed by the sub-tenant? If the position is that in some circumstances such a breach is capable of remedy and in some circumstances not, is the breach in this case capable of remedy? . . .

While there can be no doubt but that [*Rugby School (Governors) v Tannahill* [1935] 1 KB 87] held that permitting the use of premises for immoral or illegal purposes is incapable of remedy, it does not follow that the court held that a mere breach of user carried out by a sub-tenant of the lessee, of which breach the lessee does not and cannot reasonably know, renders the lessee's breach incapable of remedy even if the breach involved immoral user of the premises. As [counsel for the defendants] pointed out, if such is the position it would follow that the freeholder of a large block of flats could terminate the long lease of a lessee of the whole block merely because, however careful the lessee had been, one of the large number of tenants did in fact use a flat for the purpose of prostitution for even one night and force the lessee to go to the expense of claiming relief, a claim which, on one argument of [counsel for the claimant], the court would not grant in fact once there had been immoral user of the premises.

It is necessary, therefore, to see precisely how far the courts have gone. In the *Rugby School* case [[1935] 1 KB 87] Greer L.J. said [at 90, 91]: 'This particular breach, however conducting the premises, or permitting them to be conducted, as a house of ill fame—is one which in my judgment was not remedied by merely stopping the user. I cannot conceive how a breach of this kind can be remedied. The result of committing a breach would be known all over the whole neighbourhood and seriously affect the value of the premises.' Maugham L.J. said [at 93, 94]: 'The use of the premises for a long period for an immoral purpose seriously tends to damage their value and give them a bad name . . . and merely ceasing for a reasonable time, perhaps a few weeks or a month, to use the premises for an immoral purpose would be no remedy for a breach of the covenant which had been committed over a long period.' These phrases seem to me not altogether applicable to a case such as the present. In the *Rugby School* case the remedy could not include terminating altogether the right to the premises of the persons who had so used the premises for that would involve forfeiture. That case must therefore be read subjectam materiam, it being reasonably clear that the judges never had in their mind a situation where the right to the premises of the person who permits the immoral use can be taken away.

On the other hand, it may be said that if one considers damage to premises it does not matter who has used the premises for the immoral purpose, although again it would seem to me that it may well be that both the Lord Justices had in mind a situation where it became known in the neighbourhood that the same person who had committed the breach was still going on in occupation and that the premises might well be so used again.

. . . I think that the following propositions may be stated: (1) The mere fact that the breach complained of is a breach of user by a sub-tenant contrary to a covenant in the lease does not render the breach incapable of remedy. If one of the tenants of these flats in Queensway had, unknown to the defendants, carried on a small business of dressmaking in the flats, I would hold without hesitation that the breach was capable of remedy so far as the defendants are concerned, but it may be that the remedy would have to consist not only of stopping the tenants from carrying on that business but of bringing an action for forfeiture—it being then left to the court to decide whether the particular tenants should be granted relief. (2) The fact that the business user involves immorality does not in itself render the breach incapable of remedy provided that the lessees neither knew nor had any reason to know of the fact that the flat was being so used. The remedy in such a case, however, must involve not only that immediate steps are taken to stop such a user so soon as the user is known, but that an action for a claim for forfeiture of the sub-tenant's lease must be started within a reasonable time. If therefore the lessee has known of such a breach for a reasonable time before the notice is served, the breach is incapable of remedy unless such steps have been taken. [3] It does not follow that such a breach is always capable of remedy. All the circumstances must be taken into consideration. For example, if the notice is not the first notice which has had to be served, or if there are particularly revolting circumstances attaching to the user, or great publicity, then it might well be that the slate could not be wiped clean, or, to use another phrase, the damage to the property might be so great as to render the breach incapable of remedy.

At first sight propositions (2) and (3) would seem to put the landlord in great difficulties as to the form of his notice, since a mistake would be fatal. However, Harman J, in *Hoffman's case* [*Hoffman v Fineberg* [1949] Ch 245] said that a form calling on the tenants to remedy the breach and adding the words 'if it is capable of remedy' probably is a good notice, and I would go further and say that I can see no reason why it should not be a good notice. If such a notice is served then the landlord, having allowed a reasonable time to elapse, can bring his action claiming (1) that the breach is incapable of remedy, or (2) if it is capable of remedy that it has not been remedied, and (3) in any event asking that the court should not permit the lease to continue.

Paull J forfeited the sub-lease—there was no possibility of relief. He then held that the tenant had (in effect) remedied (his arguably technical) breach of the head lease by evicting the sub-tenant before the property became tainted with a stigma.

Glass v Kencakes was decided before the Court of Appeal's decision in *Central Estates (Belgravia) v Woolgar (No 2).*

cross-reference
See 14.3 for the facts and the court's ruling on waiver in Central Estates (Belgravia) v Woolgar (No 2).

Woolgar also, in the alternative to arguing waiver, claimed relief from forfeiture. The Court of Appeal broke new ground by holding that relief could be granted even where the breach was irremediable. In *Central Estates (Belgravia) v Woolgar (No 2)*, all three judges of the Court of Appeal assumed that a breach of a covenant against illegal/immoral user was normally a breach incapable of remedy. A majority of the court (had it not already decided the waiver issue in Woolgar's favour) would have granted Woolgar relief. The majority was clearly impressed by three facts: (i) Woolgar's hitherto exemplary character; (ii) his genuine repentance; (iii) the fact that if there was a forfeiture the landlord's fee simple (now with 'vacant possesion') would substantially increase in value.

thinking point 14.5

If a case like Glass v Kencakes *recurred today (an innocent head tenant prejudiced by the nefarious activities of a sub-tenant) how do you think that the court would deal with the case?*

Even after Savva v Hussein *and* Akici, *the court would probably deal with the matter by granting relief from forfeiture, without worrying whether the breach was capable of remedy.*

More recently, in *Patel v K & J Restaurants Ltd* [2010] EWCA Civ 1211, the court considered whether the defendant had acted promptly on discovering the sub-tenant's immoral use of the property. This issue corresponds with proposition (2) in *Glass v Kencakes* (see previously). The tenant, K & J Restaurants, leased a building which had on the ground floor and basement a restaurant, and on floors one to three there were flats which were sub-let to a number of tenants. It transpired that one of the flats was used as a brothel. The police informed K & J Restaurants and stated that a letter would be sent to them confirming this.

No action was taken by K & J Restaurants, and three months later the police served notices to Patel and K & J Restaurants that the premises were being used as a brothel. The court held that because K & J Restaurants did not take appropriate steps with reasonable promptness when they were first alerted to the possibility of immoral use, this breach was no longer capable of remedy. However, relief from forfeiture was granted on the basis that there was no stigma affecting the property.

14.4.6 Relief to Sub-Tenants

If a head lease is forfeited, then all sub-leases created out of that head lease are destroyed as well. Situations thus arise from time to time where a sub-tenant who has faithfully fulfilled all the conditions of the sub-lease is nevertheless imperilled by the failure of the head tenant to perform an obligation in the head lease (contrast *Glass v Kencakes* at 14.4.5 'Immoral User').

A sub-tenant who is imperilled by the head tenant's failure to pay the rent under the head lease can (in theory) claim relief in equity. This remedy is unlikely to be invoked nowadays for two reasons:

- the lease of the (unsatisfactory) head tenant is preserved by the sub-tenant's efforts in paying off the arrears, yet the head tenant may well again fall into arrears; and
- if the sub-lease is of part of the property, relief cannot be confined to that part. In one old case the head lease consisted of 100 houses. Each house was sub-let to a separate individual tenant. The head tenant fell into arrears of rent. One of the sub-tenants applied to the Court of Chancery for relief. He was told he could have relief, but only if he paid off the arrears of rent under the head lease with respect to all 100 houses. That was, one would imagine, beyond his resources (see *Webber v Smith* (1689) 2 Vern 103).

Today, sub-tenants may seek relief under s146(4) LPA 1925. This provision applies to all breaches of covenants, including (unlike the rest of s146) non-payment of rent. Mortgagees of leases can also seek relief under s146(4) where a mortgaged lease is threatened with forfeiture, and in modern conditions this is very important.

Law of Property Act 1925

146. Restrictions on and relief against forfeiture of leases and underleases

...

(4) Where a lessor is proceeding by action or otherwise to enforce a right of re-entry or forfeiture under any covenant, proviso, or stipulation in a lease, or for non-payment of rent, the court may, on application by any person claiming as under-lessee any estate or interest in the property comprised in the lease or any part thereof, either in the lessor's action (if any) or in any action brought by such person for that purpose, make an order vesting, for the whole term of the lease or any less term, the property comprised in the lease or any part thereof in any person entitled as under-lessee to any estate or interest in such property upon such conditions as to execution of any deed or other document, payment of rent, costs, expenses, damages, compensation, giving security, or otherwise, as the court in the circumstances of each case may think fit, but in no case shall any such under-lessee be entitled to require a lease to be granted to him for any longer term than he had under his original sub-lease.

Section 146(4) works in the following way. The sub-tenant may apply for relief from the court if the landlord is seeking to enforce his right of re-entry or forfeiture. If the court decides that the head lease should be forfeited but that the sub-tenant should be protected, the head lease is destroyed by court order. The ex-sub-tenant is granted a new head lease for a period not exceeding that unexpired under the old sub-lease. If the old sub-lease was of part of the property, the new head lease will relate to that part only. The court has a discretion as to the detailed terms of the new head lease.

Where a mortgagee of a lease claims relief, and the court decides that the lessee himself does not deserve relief, and the court orders the old lease to be destroyed, a new (head) lease is granted in its place to the ex-mortgagee. The mortgagee now becomes a lessee.

You may have noticed that the drafting of s146(4) is somewhat obscure. However, the courts have managed to make sense of it. A good example of how s146(4) works is *Chatham Empire Theatre (1955) Ltd v Ultrans Ltd* [1961] 1 WLR 817. A head lease had been granted by the claimant to the first defendant's predecessor in title. The premises subject to the head lease included a theatre, a cinema, a car park, and a restaurant. The first defendant sub-let the cinema, car park, and restaurant to other parties but retained possession of the theatre. The defendant company failed to pay the rent due under the head lease and ultimately became insolvent. The claimant served a forfeiture notice on the first defendant company. The sub-tenants of the cinema applied for relief from forfeiture. Against the sub-tenant's application the claimant argued that relief should not be granted unless the sub-tenants were prepared to pay the full arrears of rent due under the head lease.

Salmon J said:

[Counsel for the claimants] argued that the defendants should be granted relief against forfeiture only if they pay the whole of the rent outstanding at the date of the issue of the writ in respect of the cinema, the theatre, the car park and the restaurant premises, that is to say, all the premises comprised in the head lease. He bases that contention on the well-known principle which is alluded to by Joyce J. in *London Bridge Buildings Co. v. Thomson* [1903] 89 LT 50 and by Lord Greene M.R. in *Egerton v. Jones* [1939] KB 702 that in a case of relief against forfeiture the plaintiffs are entitled to be put back into the position that they would have been in if the forfeiture had not occurred. There is no doubt about that principle, and no question arises where a tenant is applying for relief against forfeiture in an action by his landlord. In this case, however, the question is how that principle applies—and it does obviously apply—when a sub-lessee of a part of the premises is claiming relief against forfeiture; is the landlord entitled to be put back in the same position as he was in before the forfeiture qua the whole of the premises in the head lease or only in respect of the premises of which the sub-lessee is in possession?

…It seems to me quite plain that s. 146(4) LPA 1925 confers on the court the widest discretion as to the terms on which relief should be granted. [Counsel for the defendants] contends that the defendants should be required to pay only £195 per quarter for the three relevant quarters, that is to say, £585. The defendants had, of course, paid this sum to Ultrans, Ltd., who have not paid it to the plaintiffs. [Counsel] says that the defendants ought only to pay that part of the arrears attributable to their property, the property which was sub-let to them. [Counsel for the claimants] says that the whole of the arrears in respect of the whole property in the head lease ought to be paid by the defendants. That really is the chief issue between the parties.

In my judgment it is clearly equitable that the landlord should be put in the same position as he was in before the forfeiture *qua* that part of the property, namely, the cinema, let to the defendants. In my judgment the defendants ought to be required as a condition of obtaining relief, to pay £585 plus an element for the premium and not the whole of the £2,730. One can envisage a case in which a block of property comprising a large number of shops and other premises is let to one corporation for £30,000 a year. The corporation then sub-lets the separate shops to various small shopkeepers at perhaps £300 a year each. After some time the corporation goes into liquidation owing perhaps half a year's rent. It is quite plain that the legislature gives the right to the small shopkeeper to come and ask for relief. If [counsel for the claimants] contention is correct, the apparently wide discretion conferred by s. 146(4) is so limited that the court could not give relief to the small shopkeeper unless he paid the £15,000 rent in arrear in respect of the whole block. It is suggested that that would not work any hardship because he could recoup himself from the corporation. That does not really commend itself to me as a practical argument because, in the first place, he will not be able to find the £15,000, and in any event the insolvent corporation could not pay. I cannot believe that in circumstances such as those the court's discretion is fettered as contended on behalf of the plaintiffs. I should have thought that if the shopkeeper paid his proportion of the arrears, namely, £150, and it was otherwise just and equitable that there should be relief, he should obtain relief on that basis. I can certainly conceive of cases where it would be quite wrong to give a sub-lessee relief on this basis; great hardship could be caused to the head lessor if granting relief to one or two of many sub-tenants would make it impossible for him to deal with the premises as a whole. Every case must be considered on its own facts.

In effect, the sub-tenants of the cinema were held entitled to relief under s146(4) provided they paid off an appropriate portion of the rent (and other) arrears.

14.5 Leasehold Property (Repairs) Act 1938

This statute was passed because of a problem with 'shark' landlords in the 1930s who were inducing tenants to surrender long leases of poorly repaired property by threatening them with heavy claims for damages.

The landlord would first write to the tenant saying something like, 'Dear Tenant, Your house/ shop is in shocking repair. We are going to sue you for £X,000 damages.' This terrified the tenant. (Many of the tenants affected were small businesses suffering from the effects of the Depression.)

A few weeks later another letter would arrive, in terms, 'Dear Tenant, If you agree to surrender your lease we will forget about our claim for damages.' The tenants were usually only too glad to accept the invitation. The practical outcome was that the landlord had succeeded in terminating the lease while bypassing the elaborate procedure laid down in s146 LPA 1925.

The 1938 Act applies to all leases for more than seven years with at least three years to run. Where the Act applies, a landlord cannot enforce a repairing covenant by forfeiture or damages unless he first serves a s146 notice. In addition to the usual particulars, the warning notice must inform the tenant that he/she has 28 days in which to serve a 'counter-notice' claiming the protection of the Act. If this counter-notice is served, the landlord cannot take any further steps to enforce the repairing covenant unless the landlord first gets leave ('permission') of the court. This leave is generally given only if there is a pressing need for immediate repairs. Indeed the House of Lords has held that:

> ...save in special circumstances, the landlord must prove (on the balance of probabilities) that the immediate remedying of a breach of the repairing covenant is required in order to save the landlord from substantial loss or damage which the landlord would otherwise sustain. [per Lord Templeman in *Associated British Ports v CH Bailey plc* [1990] 2 AC 703]

(If you get a chance to read this case, read first the penultimate paragraph of Lord Templeman's speech. You will then understand the real reasons underlying this very protracted litigation.)

If the landlord completes the repairs, leave of the court cannot be granted retrospectively. This situation arose in *Sedac Investments v Tanner* [1982] 1 WLR 1342. In this case a local Conservative Club covenanted to do the repairs but allowed the building to get into a dangerous state. The landlords (under pressure from the local authority) did the repairs themselves. The landlords then sued, but found their claim for damages blocked by the 1938 Act. There was no longer any pressing need for repairs.

A somewhat similar situation arose in *Jervis v Harris* [1996] Ch 195, except that the lease expressly provided that if the landlord should carry out repairs the tenant would indemnify the landlord for the cost. It was held by the Court of Appeal that the 1938 Act did not prevent an action being brought on this indemnity clause.

thinking point 14.6

What is the moral for landlords of the decisions in Sedac Investments *and* Jervis v Harris?

When drafting new leases where the tenant will be liable to do the repairs, always include an indemnity clause similar to that in Jervis v Harris *[1996].*

 # Concluding Remarks

The Law Commission, in 1986, proposed radical reform of this complex area of law. Under the Law Commission's then proposals the existing law on forfeiture of leases for tenant's breach of covenant would be completely swept away. It would be replaced by a new statutory scheme under which if a tenant is in serious breach of covenant the landlord could apply to the court for an order terminating the lease. These proposals have since been updated in the Law Commission's Report No 303, published in 2006, *Termination of Tenancies for Tenant Default*.

thinking point 14.7

Refer back to what was said about Billson v Residential Apartments *at 14.2.2. In that case the House of Lords in December 1991 overruled a Court of Appeal decision made in February 1991. Also refer back to the remarks at 14.4.6 regarding s146(4) LPA 1925 and in particular to the question of relief for mortgagees. Then consider the following questions, bearing in mind that 1991 was the depths of a recession and that a General Election was expected in the spring of 1992:*

1   *What had less scrupulous landlords been doing from February to December 1991?*

2   *Which wealthy organizations were particularly upset by the activities of these less scrupulous landlords?*

3   *What would Parliament have been forced to do if the House of Lords had upheld the Court of Appeal decision in favour of the landlords?*

Here are some thoughts:

1   *Landlords were staging 'dawn raids'; that is, peaceably re-entering deserted buildings before the tenants arrived. The landlords thought that (courtesy of the Court of Appeal) they had thereby forfeited the lease(s) and deprived the tenants, sub-tenants, and mortgagees of their right to seek relief.*

2   *The answer to this question lies in the answer to (1). Financial institutions, especially the big banks, had lent money to tenants who were now in severe financial difficulties because of recession. The banks had taken mortgages of the tenants' leases to secure the loans, but these mortgages were being destroyed by the dawn raids.*

3   *Had the House of Lords ruled the other way in* Billson, *the big banks would have been screaming at the government for immediate reform. With an election pending, the government would have been forced to dust off the 1986 Law Commission Report and tell Parliament, 'We do not have time to argue the details. We must immediately enact these proposals.'*

Finally, we would draw your attention to an examination question asked about twenty years ago. Candidates were invited to discuss the following proposition:

> 'A landlord who wants to forfeit a lease is often faced with a long and tortuous process. During that process he dare not collect any rent. And the proceedings for forfeiture may well end with the court forgiving the erring tenant.'

The law is arguably too protective of tenants. It is certainly not surprising that when the Court of Appeal in *Billson* appeared to open a door to landlords to circumvent one of the protections for tenants, many landlords rushed through only to find that door slammed shut by the House of Lords. The House of Lords (led by Lord Templeman) took the heat off the government, but certainly did not eliminate the need for wholesale reform of this area of law.

 # Summary

Termination of Fixed Term Leases

This can come about through:

- natural expiry;
- giving notice under a break clause;
- merger;
- surrender;
- frustration;
- repudiatory breach by landlord accepted by tenant; and
- forfeiture.

Forfeiture

- The lease must contain a forfeiture clause.
- The landlord normally forfeits by court proceedings; peaceable re-entry is a risky process.
- The landlord must be careful not to waive the right to forfeit. In particular, once the landlord knows of the breach of covenant, the landlord must not demand or accept rent.

Forfeiture for Non-Payment of Rent

- No special statutory procedure.
- The tenant can claim relief from forfeiture (by offering the arrears and costs) at any time up to six months after the landlord has retaken possession.

Forfeiture for Breaches of Covenant Other than Non-Payment of Rent

- The landlord must follow the procedure laid down in s146 LPA 1925:
  - serve a notice; wait a reasonable time; then commence court proceedings;
  - tenant can claim relief at any time up to when the landlord repossesses; even after re-possession if the landlord re-enters without a court order;
  - the court can grant relief even though the breach is irremediable.

Position where Sub-Tenants' Activities makes Head Lease Liable to Forfeiture

The head tenant should get rid of the sub-tenant as soon as possible, and then claim relief with respect to the head lease.

Position where a Sub-Tenant (or Mortgagee) is Prejudiced by Head Tenant's Breach

The innocent party should claim relief under s146(4) LPA 1925. The court awards the ex-sub-tenant (or ex-mortgagee) a new head lease.

The Leasehold Property (Repairs) Act 1938

This restricts landlords who want to sue for damages (or forfeit) for disrepair. But only applies to leases for more than seven years with at least three years to run.

# Further Reading

Law Commission, *Forfeiture of Leases* (Report No 142, 1986)
The Law Commission's 1986 proposals regarding reform of forfeiture which are still very relevant today.

Bridge, S, 'Forfeiture: a long overdue reform?' (2007) 11 Landlord & Tenant Review 145
The Law Commission has further updated proposals in the area of terminating leases.

Pawlowski, M, 'Repudiatory breach in the leasehold context' [1999] Conv 150
Case note on *Nynehead Developments v Fireboard* on repudiatory breach by the landlord accepted by the tenant.

Pawlowski, M, 'Termination of tenancies for tenant default—Law Commission's draft bill' (2007) 11(1) Landlord & Tenant Review 9
Discusses proposals for reform of forfeiture of leases.

❓ Questions

In 2003, Letitia leased (by deed) a shop to Tajinder for 40 years. The lease includes a covenant under which the tenant undertakes to ensure that the shop is not used for illegal purposes. Rent is payable quarterly and in advance to Letitia's agent Rocky. The lease also includes a forfeiture clause which can be invoked if the tenant breaks any of the covenants.

In 2014, Tajinder lawfully assigned the lease to Androniki. In early 2015, Dandy, one of Androniki's shop assistants, took advantage of the fact that Androniki did not normally arrive at the shop until 9.30 a.m. He started an early morning 'side-line' selling cocaine. After only a month Androniki found out about the illegal trade. She immediately dismissed Dandy and reported his activities to the police. Last week Dandy was convicted of drug-trafficking.

Letitia has just read of Dandy's conviction in the local newspaper. She has decided to endeavour to forfeit the lease. She tells you, 'The rent under the existing lease is ridiculously low; if I can get Androniki out a new tenant would be willing to pay three times as much.'

Advise Letitia.

Part 7

Informal
Acquisition of
Legal Estates

## 15

Adverse Possession and the Limitation Acts

Introduction

Adverse possession is commonly associated with squatters' rights. You may have come across articles in newspapers highlighting a squatter's triumphant victory in acquiring land due to having lived in a property for more than 12 years. The properties that have been acquired in such a way can vary in value from £2 million for a house in South Kensington to a two-bedroom council-owned property. In a modern case *JA Pye v Graham (Oxford) Holdings* the dispute took ten years to resolve; the case was considered in the House of Lords and in the European Court of Human Rights. The widowed farmer, successful in her legal claim, obtained 25 hectares of prime building land worth £10 million. Such gains are not very common, in fact the most common type of case for applying the adverse possession rules involves a small encroachment between neighbours, for example where a boundary fence is moved perhaps a foot.

This chapter will initially consider the basic principles for adverse possession. These principles apply equally to unregistered and registered land. It will then move on to discuss adverse possession against land which is subject to a lease and, finally, the very complex rules applicable where adverse possession is taken against land which is registered title.

15.1 Rationale of Adverse Possession

point on terminology

Unfortunately the word traditionally used by lawyers for any person who takes adverse possession is 'squatter'. This word, used in its time-honoured legal sense, is both broader in meaning and less emotive than the present-day colloquial usage.

Title to the land is acquired by the squatter where the squatter has effectively been in possession of the land for a long period of time, and acquires the land in an informal manner. Adverse possession is a vital part of English land law. If the concept did not exist, then the English system of unregistered title would be impossible to operate.

Where land is unregistered title the vendor produces title deeds to the purchaser to prove their ownership. But the title deeds ('paper title') do not as such guarantee the title of the vendor. The title deeds produced by the vendor to a purchaser merely demonstrates to the purchaser that the vendor and their predecessors in title have been in control (or possession) of the land for such a long time that no one could possibly dispute their claim to ownership.

Why can no one dispute their claim to ownership? The answer to this lies in the Limitation Act 1980 (LA 1980) and its central concept of adverse possession. This ensures that all stale claims of ownership are 'time-barred' or, put more bluntly, destroyed by lapse of time. The 1980 Act provides the limitation period of 12 years for claims to recover unregistered land, and also registered land where the land was adversely possessed before the Land Registration Act 2002 (LRA 2002) came into force (13 October 2003). The rules relating to registered land after 13 October 2003 are governed by the LRA 2002.

Another justification of adverse possession is socio-economic. Some would argue that land is a very scarce commodity, and that if the landowner does nothing with their land, but a stranger then makes good use of the land over a long period of time, the original owner deserves to lose ownership to the stranger! However, adverse possession as a concept seems to conflict with the policy objectives of land registration, which include certainty and transparency. The very fact that adverse possession applies to registered land undermines the efficiency and accuracy of the system of land registration.

These issues were highlighted by the Law Commission when a review of the land registration system was undertaken in 2001. You should pay particularly careful attention to the following extract:

Law Commission (Law Com Report No 271) *Land Registration for the Twenty-First Century: A Conveyancing Revolution*

[The footnotes have been omitted.]

2.70 ...There are two main reasons why we consider that we should introduce a new system. First, at the practical level, there is a growing public disquiet about the present law. It is perceived to be too easy for squatters to acquire title. Perhaps precisely because it is so easy, adverse possession is also very common. Although the popular perception of a squatter is that of a homeless person who takes over an empty house (for whom there is understandable sympathy), the much more typical case in practice is the landowner with an eye to the main chance who encroaches on his or her neighbour's land. Secondly, as a matter of legal principle, it is difficult to justify the continuation of the present principles in relation to registered land. These two reasons are in fact interconnected.

Why do we have a doctrine of adverse possession?

2.71 The reasons why there is a doctrine of adverse possession are well known and often stated, but they need to be tested. For example, it is frequently said that the doctrine is an embodiment of the policy that defendants should be protected from stale claims and that claimants should not sleep on their rights. However, it is possible for a squatter to acquire title by adverse possession without the owner realising it. This may be because the adverse possession is either clandestine or not readily apparent. It may be because the owner has more land than he or she can realistically police. Many public bodies fall into this category. A local authority, for example, cannot in practice keep an eye on every single piece of land that it owns to ensure that no one is encroaching on it. But the owner may not even realise that a person is encroaching on his or her land. He or she may think that someone is there with permission and it may take an expensive journey to the Court of Appeal to discover whether or not this is so. In none of these examples is a person in any true sense sleeping on his or her rights. Furthermore, even if a landowner does realise that someone typically a neighbour is encroaching on his or her land, he or she may be reluctant to take issue over the incursion, particularly if it is comparatively slight. He or she may not wish to sour relations with the neighbour and is, perhaps, afraid of the consequences of so doing. It may not only affect relations with the neighbour but may also bring opprobrium upon him or her in the neighbourhood. In any event, even if the policy against allowing stale claims is sound, the consequences of it under the present law the loss for ever of a person's land can be extremely harsh and have been judicially described as disproportionate.

2.72 There are other grounds for the doctrine of adverse possession that have greater weight. Land is a precious resource and should be kept in use and in commerce. A person may be in adverse possession where the true owner has disappeared and there is no other claimant for the land. Or he or she may have acquired the land informally so that the legal ownership is not a reflection of the practical reality. A person may have innocently entered land, quite reasonably believing that he or she owned it, perhaps because of uncertainties as to the boundaries.

2.73 In relation to land with unregistered title, there are cogent legal reasons for the doctrine. The principles of adverse possession do in fact presuppose unregistered title and make sense in relation to it. This is because the basis of title to unregistered land is ultimately possession. The person best entitled to the land is the person with the best right to possession of it. As we explain below, the investigation of title to unregistered land is facilitated (and therefore costs less) because earlier rights to possess can be extinguished by adverse possession. However, where title is registered, the basis of title is primarily the fact of registration rather than possession. It is the fact of registration that vests the legal title in the registered proprietor. This is so, even if the transfer to the proprietor was a nullity as, for example, where it was a forgery. The ownership of land is therefore apparent from the register and only a change in the register can take that title away. It is noteworthy that, in many Commonwealth states which have systems of title registration, these considerations have led to changes in the law governing acquisition of title by adverse possession. In some states it has been abolished altogether. In others, it has been modified. As we have indicated above, the doctrine of adverse possession does have benefits and we do not therefore favour outright abolition in relation to registered land. However, we consider that the balance between landowner and squatter needs to be adjusted to overcome some of the deficiencies outlined above, while maintaining the advantages it can offer. We have therefore devised a modified scheme of adverse possession that attempts to achieve that balance and is at the same time appropriate to the principles of registered title.

15.1.1 Adverse Possession Human Rights Compliant

cross-reference
For the English cases defining adverse possession, see 15.5 and 15.6.

Some critics of adverse possession have argued that, at least when applied to registered land, adverse possession infringed the Human Rights Act 1998. The decision of the Grand Chamber of the European Court of Human Rights held that provisions on adverse possession in the Land Registration Act 1925 (LRA 1925) do not infringe the guarantee of 'free enjoyment of possessions' contained in Article 1 of the First Protocol of the European Convention on Human Rights (*Pye v United Kingdom* (Application No 44302/02)).

In *Ofulue v Bossert* [2008] 3 WLR 1253, the Court of Appeal confirmed that adverse possession as defined by the English cases is compliant with the Human Rights Act 1998. When *Ofolue v Bossert* reached the House of Lords, this conclusion was considered beyond argument both by the parties and by the Law Lords. (In the House of Lords the argument focused exclusively on whether there had been an acknowledgement of title (see later).)

15.2 Possession Gives a Right to Sue Trespassers

First consider the following propositions:

• ownership is often defined as 'the best right to possess'; and

- possession of land, or any other property, is itself evidence of ownership of that land or property. The longer the possession, the better the evidence of ownership.

We all have heard the phrase 'Possession is nine-tenths of the law.' In the context of land law, this cliché is correct! A person in possession of land, though they have no title to it, can nevertheless defend that possession by legal proceedings against anyone but the true owner.

thinking point 15.1

Anthea is the owner in fee simple of Flores Field. Bart seized possession of Flores Field nine years ago and has remained in possession ever since. Charlotte (a total stranger with no connections to Anthea) is trying to interfere with Bart's possession, or even to evict Bart from Flores Field. If Bart sues Charlotte for trespass, who will succeed?

Bart will be successful in his action. It will be no defence for Charlotte to say, 'But it is not Bart's land.' If Charlotte wants to defeat Bart's action then she would have to show that she has a better claim to the land. For example, she has been granted a lease by Anthea or she has inherited the property.

pause for thought

1   *Do you personally think that the rules discussed so far in this chapter are suited to our modern civilization?*

2   *Do you personally think these rules are compatible with the human rights of landowners?*

3   *What about 'squatters' who say, 'We have a fundamental human right to a roof over our heads'?*

In thinking about these issues consider carefully what has been said at 15.1 and 15.2, and think about how what you have learnt about in other subjects regarding human rights could be applied here.

(15.3) The Limitation Act 1980

Section 15(1) LA 1980 replaces legislation dating back many centuries. The practical effect of this provision (and its predecessors) is to declare that in appropriate circumstances possession shall be ten-tenths of the law! This Act applies to unregistered land. In the case of registered land this provision applies in the same manner and to the same extent as it does to unregistered land but only where adverse possession has been completed by 13 October 2003.

> *The Limitation Act 1980*
>
> 15. Time limit for actions to recover land.
>
> (1) No action shall be brought by any person to recover any land after the expiration of twelve years from the date on which the right of action accrued to him or, if it first accrued to some person through whom he claims, to that person.

Under a provision which is now tucked away in Sch 1 para 8(1) LA 1980, a 'right of action' accrues to the owner of a piece of land when a stranger takes 'adverse possession' of the land against him.

The Limitation Act 1980

Schedule 1

Right of action not to accrue or continue unless there is adverse possession

8. —(1) No right of action to recover land shall be treated as accruing unless the land is in the possession of some person in whose favour the period of limitation can run (referred to below in this paragraph as 'adverse possession'); and where under the preceding provisions of this Schedule any such right of action is treated as accruing on a certain date and no person is in adverse possession on that date, the right of action shall not be treated as accruing unless and until adverse possession is taken of the land.

The practical effect of what has been said so far is as follows:

1 Once adverse possession has started, the adverse possessor can defend their possession against all but the original owner.

2 Once adverse possession has continued for 12 years, the adverse possessor can defend their possession against all including the original owner.

Thinking point 15.1 has already illustrated proposition (1). Consider the following example: Anthea was the owner in fee simple (unregistered title) of Flores Field. In 1984 Bart seized possession of Flores Field and remained in possession until 1996. In 1996, because Bart was in continual possession for 12 years he can defend his possession against the whole world including the original owner (Anthea). The title will be based on his long possession of the land.

Looked at from another angle, the effect at the end of the 12 years' adverse possession was that the original owner's title is completely extinguished (s17 LA 1980). In the example given, Anthea's title to Flores Field would be extinguished. The adverse possessor (Bart) has a completely new (fee simple) title based on his long adverse possession. You should note, however, that it is not correct to say that in the year 1996 Anthea's title is transferred to Bart; there is simply no conveyance of land. Anthea may well, after 1996, retain title deeds to 'her' fee simple title to Flores Field, but those deeds will be worthless scraps of paper.

Commencement of Adverse Possession

15.4.1 Dispossession and Discontinuance

Adverse possession will commence either where the adverse possessor displaces the original owner (also known as the paper owner) or where the original owner has discontinued their possession and the squatter takes possession. Dispossession or discontinuance must take place so adverse possession can commence. This applies equally to unregistered land (Sch 1 para 1 LA 1980) and registered land.

The difference between dispossession and discontinuance was explained by Fry J in *Rains v Buxton* (1880) 14 Ch D 537 at 539–540, where he stated that 'the difference between the dispossession and the discontinuance of possession might be expressed in this way—the one is where a person comes in and drives out the others from possession, the other case is where the person in possession goes out and is followed into possession by other persons'.

It was acknowledged in the House of Lords in *JA Pye (Oxford) Ltd v Graham* [2003] 1 AC 419 that the difference between these two concepts can be difficult and 'a very fine one' (per Nourse LJ, *Buckinghamshire County Council v Moran* [1990] Ch 623 at 645). The House of Lords clarified the meaning of the word dispossession, the ordinary sense of the word is used where it simply means that the squatter assumes possession of the land. Lord Browne-Wilkinson said:

> Many of the difficulties...which I will have to consider are due to a conscious or subconscious feeling that in order for a squatter to gain title by lapse of time he has to act adversely to the paper title owner. It is said that he has to 'oust' the true owner in order to dispossess him; that he has to intend to exclude the whole world including the true owner; that the squatter's use of the land has to be inconsistent with any present or future use by the true owner. In my judgment much confusion and complication would be avoided if reference to adverse possession were to be avoided so far as possible and effect given to the clear words of the Acts. *The question is simply whether the defendant squatter has dispossessed the paper owner by going into ordinary possession of the land for the requisite period without the consent of the owner.* [Emphasis added]

> It is clearly established that the taking or continuation of possession by a squatter with the actual consent of the paper title owner does not constitute dispossession or possession by the squatter for the purposes of the Act. Beyond that, as Slade J said [in *Powell v McFarlane* [1977] 38 P & CR 452], the words possess and dispossess are to be given their ordinary meaning.

> It is sometimes said that ouster by the squatter is necessary to constitute dispossession: see for example *Rains v Buxton* [1880] 14 Ch D 537, 539 per Fry J. The word 'ouster' is derived from the old law of adverse possession and has overtones of confrontational, knowing removal of the true owner from possession. Such an approach is quite incorrect. There will be a 'dispossession' of the paper owner in any case where (there being no discontinuance of possession by the paper owner) a squatter assumes possession in the ordinary sense of the word. Except in the case of joint possessors, possession is single and exclusive. Therefore if the squatter is in possession the paper owner cannot be. If the paper owner was at one stage in possession of the land but the squatter's subsequent occupation of it in law constitutes possession the squatter must have 'dispossessed' the true owner for the purposes of Schedule 1, paragraph 1.

Discontinuance arises where the paper owner 'goes out of possession and is followed in by the squatter' (per Nourse LJ, *Buckinghamshire County Council v Moran* [1990] Ch 623 at 645). This simply means that the paper owner effectively abandons the property and the squatter then takes possession. Where the paper owner demonstrates some acts of control towards the property no matter how slight, this will be sufficient to negate discontinuance (*Powell v MacFarlane* (1979) 38 P & CR 452).

15.4.2 The 'Apparently Abandoned Plot' Problem

Apart from dispossession and discontinuance, there may be a situation where the land has been left for the time being. The paper owner may have plans to build on the land in the future but in its current state it is not being used.

The initial approach taken by the courts in a situation where a landowner had a piece of land which they left vacant but for which they had future plans was that a third party who occupied the land was not in adverse possession until either the owner abandoned their plans or the stranger did acts which rendered those plans impossible. The first case in the line appears to be *Leigh v Jack* (1879) 5 Ex Div 264. However, it was two mid-twentieth-century cases which caused considerable consternation.

In *Williams Brothers Ltd v Raftery* [1957] 3 All ER 593 the plaintiffs purchased in 1937 a piece of waste ground at the back of their factory. They hoped to expand their premises onto this ground, but they were prevented from doing so, first by the war, and then by the refusal of planning permission.

In 1940, the defendant came along, saw the waste ground, and started 'to dig for victory', that is he used the ground as a vegetable patch. Having helped to defeat Hitler, he then kept greyhounds on the land, erecting kennels and fencing. In 1957 the plaintiffs suddenly claimed possession of the ground. The defendant claimed he had gained a title to the ground by adverse possession.

A director of the plaintiffs testified that they had always retained their expansion 'plans', and that they had always hoped that the town planners would change their minds. (He did not produce any actual drawings, maps, or diagrams.) The Court of Appeal held that in view of the fact that the 'plans' for the ground had been 'retained' and that the defendant had done nothing to render them impossible, the defendant never had adverse possession of the land.

In *Wallis's Cayton Bay Holiday Camp v Shell-Mex* [1975] QB 94 the defendants acquired one and one-third acres of land in the middle of a field for the purposes of a new filling station. This one and one-third acres adjoined the site of a proposed new road, but neither the road nor the one and one-third acres were marked off by boundary markers. All a passer-by would see (looking from, say, the top of a double-decker bus) was an arable field no different from its neighbours. The field belonged to Wallis's, which farmed both it and adjoining fields through a subsidiary company.

For 11 and a half years Wallis's farming activities extended to the one and one-third acres. Then the local authority abandoned the scheme for the new road. Shell promptly wrote to Wallis's offering to sell the one and one-third acres. Wallis's did not reply. (Why they did not reply relates to another point of adverse possession law with which we will deal at 15.7.1.) Instead, they carried on their farming for eight more months, and then claimed that they had got title through adverse possession.

The Court of Appeal ruled that as Shell had only recently abandoned their plans, there had been only a few months, not 12 years' adverse possession. Shell therefore won.

Lord Denning further confused matters by holding that people like Wallis's and Raftery were 'by a legal fiction' deemed to have had an implied licence to occupy the land. As they were there 'by permission', they could not be adverse possessors.

thinking point 15.2

The decisions in Williams Brothers *and* Wallis's *cases were heavily criticized by many as undermining the whole concept (and utility) of adverse possession. Consider why this may be the case?*

The practical result of the Williams Brothers *and* Wallis's *cases was that whether or not there was adverse possession depended not upon the activities of the alleged adverse possessor, but upon the state of mind of the original owner.*

The following statutory provision was designed to overrule the *Williams Brothers* and *Wallis's* line of cases.

Limitation Act 1980

Schedule 1 Provisions with respect to actions to recover land

8(4) For the purpose of determining whether a person occupying any land is in adverse possession of the land it shall not be assumed by implication of law that his occupation is by permission of the person entitled to the land merely by virtue of the fact that his occupation is not inconsistent with the latter's present or future enjoyment of the land.

cross-reference
For a discussion of Pye v Graham, see 15.5.

This is not the clearest of statutory provisions, and it seems to aim only at Lord Denning's 'implied licence' idea. However, the Court of Appeal in *Buckinghamshire County Council v Moran* [1990] Ch 623 held that this provision did overrule the broader principle 'recognized' in *Williams Brothers and Wallis's*. This conclusion is now confirmed by the House of Lords decision in *JA Pye (Oxford) Ltd v Graham* [2003] 1 AC 419.

In *Buckinghamshire County Council v Moran* [1990] Ch 623, Moran extended his garden onto land which he knew was owned by the county council; he knew they intended to build a road on it. In giving a judgment holding that Moran was an adverse possessor and that the county council had lost their title, Slade LJ said:

...[it is] too broad a proposition to suggest that an owner who retains a piece of land with a view to its utilisation for a specific purpose in the future can never be treated as dispossessed, however firm and obvious the intention to dispossess, and however drastic the acts of dispossession of the person seeking to dispossess him may be. Furthermore, while it may well be correct to say that the implied licence doctrine (so long as it survived) itself involved the 'adaptation' of the literal application of the statutory provisions 'to meet one special type of case', I do not think it correct to suggest that the decisions in *Leigh* v. *Jack*, 5 Ex.D. 264, or *Williams Brothers Direct Supply Ltd*. v. *Raftery* [1958] 1 Q.B. 159 (or indeed any other decisions prior to *Wallis's case* [1975] Q.B. 94) authorise or justify an application of the statutory provisions otherwise than in accordance with their ordinary and natural meaning... If in any given case the land in dispute is unbuilt land and the squatter is aware that the owner, while having no present use for it, has a purpose in mind for its use in the future, the court is likely to require very clear evidence before it can be satisfied that the squatter who claims a possessory title has not only established factual possession of the land, but also the requisite intention to exclude the world at large, including the owner with the paper title, so far as is reasonably practicable and so far as the processes of the law will allow.

Nourse LJ stated:

Adopting the distinction between dispossession and discontinuance which was suggested by Fry J. in *Rains* v. *Buxton*, 14 Ch.D. 537, 539, I take the first case to be one where the squatter comes in and drives out the true owner from possession and the second to be one where the true owner goes out of possession and is followed in by the squatter. In the light of that distinction, a very fine one, it is sometimes said that the intention of the true owner may be material in this way. If he intends to use the land for a particular purpose at some future date, a discontinuance of possession can be prevented by the slightest acts of ownership on his part, even by none at all. That no doubt is perfectly correct, but nothing follows from it except that the case becomes one where the true owner must be dispossessed before his title can be lost. He can only be dispossessed if the squatter performs sufficient acts and has a sufficient intention to constitute adverse possession. Those acts and that intention are no different from those which are required in a case of discontinuance, there being no practical distinction between what is necessary to exclude all the world in a case where the true owner has retained possession and in one where he has discontinued it.

> By this route I have come to a belief that the intention of the true owner, although it may have some influence in theory, is irrelevant in practice. To that I would make one exception. If an intention on the part of the true owner to use the land for a particular purpose at some future date is known to the squatter, then his knowledge may affect the quality of his own intention, reducing it below that which is required to constitute adverse possession. To say that is only to emphasise that it is adverse possession on which everything depends. I think it very doubtful whether the distinction between dispossession and a discontinuance of possession can ever have decisive consequences, a consideration which is perhaps confirmed by the confusion between them which is found in some of the decided cases.

The approach of examining the intention of the original owner has been discredited. Thus, in cases where the owner of the original 'paper' title has retained plans for the land, it will be perfectly possible for his title to be destroyed by adverse possession. It will be a question of fact whether, despite the 'paper' owner retaining plans known to the alleged 'squatter', the latter has done sufficient to establish adverse possession.

15.5 Possession

Once the adverse possessor has control over the land either through dispossession or discontinuance then adverse possession has been triggered under the statutory regime of limitation. In unregistered land this is governed by the LA 1980. The LRA 2002 (post October 2003) regulates adverse possession in registered land.

Adverse possession has a specific meaning which the House of Lords in *JA Pye (Oxford) Ltd v Graham* [2003] 1 AC 419 confirmed. Lord Browne-Wilkinson said:

> . . . there are two elements necessary for legal possession: (1) a sufficient degree of physical custody and control ('factual possession'); (2) an intention to exercise such custody and control on one's own behalf and for one's own benefit ('intention to possess').

15.5.1 Factual Possession

The adverse possessor must take physical control of the land and must exclude everyone else from the land. As has already been said, the most common cases of adverse possession today are encroachments between neighbours, for example where a boundary fence is moved. However, every few years we do seem to get a (reported) case where an adverse possessor successfully 'annexes' to their own property a quite large chunk of land. For example, *Buckinghamshire County Council v Moran* where the defendant expanded his garden onto an area of land owned by the council intended to become part of a bypass. The defendant bought a new chain and lock for the gate, which he locked and kept the key. There was no other access to the plot except for climbing over fences or through hedges. This was sufficient to exclude the world and he succeeded in his case.

In *Powell v McFarlane* (1979) 38 P & CR 452, a 14-year-old boy decided to graze his cow on the defendant's land. The boy's grandmother wrote to the defendant seeking permission to do this. They did not receive a reply. The boy decided to enter the disputed land. He cut hay and used it to feed the family cow. He mended the fence. The boy organized a clay pigeon shoot on a few occasions. When the boy grew up he had set up a business felling and treating trees. A sign giving details of his business was put up on the land and could be seen from the road. Over a number of years the defendant's wife visited the disputed land and found nothing unusual.

Slade J said:

> The question what acts constitute a sufficient degree of exclusive physical control must depend on the circumstances, in particular the nature of the land and the manner in which land of that nature is commonly used or enjoyed. In the case of open land, absolute physical control is normally impracticable, if only because it is generally impossible to secure every part of a boundary so as to prevent intrusion. 'What is a sufficient degree of sole possession and user must be measured according to an objective standard, related no doubt to the nature and situation of the land involved but not subject to variation according to the resources or status of the claimants': *West Bank Estates Ltd.* v. *Arthur* [1967] AC 665, *per* Lord Wilberforce. It is clearly settled that acts of possession done on parts of land to which a possessory title is sought may be evidence of possession of the whole. *Whether or not acts of possession done on parts of an area establish title to the whole area must, however, be a matter of degree.* [Emphasis added] It is impossible to generalise with any precision as to what acts will or will not suffice to evidence factual possession. On the particular facts of *Cadija Umma* v. *S. Don Manis Appu* [1969] AC 136 PC the taking of a hay crop was held by the Privy Council to suffice for this purpose; but this was a decision which attached special weight to the opinion of the local courts in Ceylon owing to their familiarity with the conditions of life and the habits and ideas of the people [ibid, at pp. 141–142]. Likewise, on the particular facts of the Red House Farms case, mere shooting over the land in question was held by the Court of Appeal to suffice; but that was a case where the court regarded the only use that anybody could be expected to make of the land as being for shooting [(Unreported), Court of Appeal (Civil Division) Transcript No 411 of 1976, pp 6G, 12B, G]: *per* Cairns, Orr and Waller L.JJ. Everything must depend on the particular circumstances, but broadly, *I think what must be shown as constituting factual possession is that the alleged possessor has been dealing with the land in question as an occupying owner might have been expected to deal with it and that no-one else has done so.* [Emphasis added]

The occasional use of the land by the claimant as a teenager was held not to amount to possession.

The key point emphasized by Slade J is the manner in which the possessor deals with the land. Does the possessor treat the land as their own? Each case will have to consider the various circumstances to ascertain whether physical possession has taken effect. For example, in *Dyer v Terry* [2013] EWHC 209 mowing grass and picking up litter was insufficient to establish factual possession.Possession of the land by the squatter must be openly exercised. If the squatter conceals their presence from the paper owner then this would not amount to adverse possession. Where adverse possession is openly exercised, the paper owner has the opportunity to challenge the squatter's possession of the land.

Where there is a break in the period of adverse possession of the land, then this can be fatal to a claim for adverse possession (see Sch 1 para 8(2) LA 1980).

For a long period of possession to extinguish an original owner's title, the possession must be 'adverse' to the original (paper) owner's title. This means that the possessor's occupation of the land must be inconsistent with the title of the original owner. Permission to occupy the land by the owner would not amount to adverse possession. What would happen if permission had been granted to use the land, but the situation has changed where the permission has effectively lawfully been withdrawn?

The answer can be found in *JA Pye (Oxford) Ltd v Graham* [2003]. The dispute related to a field which originally belonged to Pye, but which Graham had been using for many years for grazing and hay-making. Until 1983, these activities had been carried on by Graham under a licence granted by Pye. At the end of 1983, Pye wanting to develop the land, refused to renew the licence, and told Graham to vacate the field. Graham did not vacate the field, but continued to use it for grazing and hay-making and similar activities until Pye started proceedings in 1997.

Local inhabitants thought that the field belonged to Graham, and that it was part of the farm he owned ('Manor Farm'). The House of Lords held that Graham had acquired title to the land by virtue of adverse possession. He had both factual possession of the land, and the necessary intent to exclude everyone from the land. Indeed Graham (or rather, his widow) won the case, even though it was clear that if Pye had at any time offered him a new lease or licence over the field, he would have gladly agreed to be a tenant or licensee.

Tenants and Trustees Cannot Be in Adverse Possession

During the running of a lease, a tenant cannot be in adverse possession against his landlord with respect to the land comprised in the lease. A tenant's possession is not in any way inconsistent with or in conflict with the landlord's ownership of the fee simple.

thinking point 15.3

What if a tenant fails to pay the rent? Does that make his possession 'adverse'?

Failure to pay rent does not make the tenant's possession 'adverse'. The tenant's lease is derived out of the landlord's freehold, and is not in conflict with that freehold, irrespective of whether or not the tenant pays rent. However, the right to an instalment of rent is time-barred after a six-year delay in collecting that instalment.

Trustees of land can never be in adverse possession against their beneficiaries. This is because there is no inconsistency between the trustees' legal title and the beneficiaries' equitable interests.

thinking point 15.4

A, B, C, D, and E are tenants in common of Highhouse, but only A and B are trustees of the legal title. A and B get nasty and lock C, D, and E out of the house. They keep C, D, and E locked out for more than 12 years. Are the rights of C, D, and E time-barred?

Even if the unhappy state of affairs continues for 50 years or more, C, D, and E will never be time-barred; their rights cannot be extinguished by the trustees' decision to keep possession of the house exclusively for themselves (see also Earnshaw v Hartley *[2000] Ch 155).*

One other significant point is that a purchaser of land who takes possession prior to completion of the contract of sale is not in adverse possession unless and until the contract of sale is rescinded. A purchaser's 'estate contract' equitable interest is in no way inconsistent with the vendor's ownership of the legal fee simple (*Hyde v Pearce* [1982] 1 All ER 1029).

Adverse Possession Where One Plot Has Two Registered Owners?

In *Parshall v Hackney* [2013] EWCA Civ 240, the land in dispute was a small triangular paved plot measuring only a few square metres. It was situated at the front of 29, Milner Street, Kensington. It had historically always been part of number 29. Number 29 had been registered title since 1904, and the original title plan included the disputed land.

The nearby number 31 was separated from number 29 by a private road (Lennox Garden Mews). Number 31 was first registered in 1980. 'The Land Registry included the disputed land in the title of No 31. That was a mistake on the part of the Land Registry, because the disputed land was already included in the registered title of No 29.' (per Mummery LJ at para 5)

The result of this mistake was that from 1980 to 2000 there were two completely separate registered owners for one piece of land!

The Hackney family acquired no. 31 in 1986. In July 1988 they took control of the disputed land. 'At that time the owners of No 31 fixed a chain and metal eye (or hook) into a concrete bollard to demarcate the disputed land as a parking space, which had been used, and was used thereafter, exclusively by the owners of No 31.' (per Mummery LJ at para 14)

'In October 2000, the Land Registry made another mistake. That mistake happened in the course of computerising the title plan to No 29. The Land Registry excluded the disputed land from No 29. Although that accidental slip eliminated, to the extent of the disputed land, the overlap between the two registered titles, it did not resolve the questions of either title or rectification.' (per Mummery LJ at para 10)

When the current owner of No 29 discovered the 2000 error, he brought proceedings for rectification of the register. (Such proceedings are not subject to any time limit.)

In defence to the claim, the defendant contended that she and her predecessors had been in adverse possession of the disputed land since 1988, and that therefore any title the claimant had was time barred by October 2003 (the coming into force of the Land Registration Act 2002). This argument was accepted by the Land Registry Deputy Adjudicator and (on an initial appeal) by a deputy High Court Judge.

The Court of Appeal overturned the lower court decisions and (in effect) ordered rectification of the register. It held that where a registered proprietor (the Hackneys in the instant case) take possession of land which is included within their title, that possession is lawful and can never be *adverse* possession.

> 87 There was no dispossession in July 1988, because the taking of possession of the disputed land was not unlawful. It was lawful for the owners of No 31 to take and remain in possession of the disputed land, because they had a registered title to it. As long as they remained registered proprietors of the disputed land, that possession would be lawful and could not be adverse to the owners of No 29.
>
> 88 It is now in the respondent's interest to ignore the concurrent registration of title to the disputed land during the relevant period and instead to rely on a possessory title to the disputed land. But, unless and until the land register is rectified by order, the legal position is that the owner of No 29 did not have a completed cause of action for recovery of the disputed land. They could neither have nor plead a better title to the disputed land than the owners of No 31. They both had registered title to it with all that entails under the 1925 Act.
>
> 89 This is a case of *equality* of registered titles, rather than the normal case of *relativity* of titles. The two registered titles co-exist on the register unless and until corrected by rectification. The determination of the question of rectification is logically prior to the determination of the question of possessory title. It has to be decided who was entitled to be registered as proprietor of the disputed land before it can be decided whether the right of the proprietor to recover the disputed land is statute-barred. (per Mummery LJ emphasis in the original.)

The upshot of *Parshall v Hackney* is that if, erroneously, there are two separate registrations over the same piece of land, neither of the registered proprietors can be in adverse possession against the other.

It is respectfully submitted that (at least on this point) *Parshall v Hackney* is wrongly decided. The essence of *adverse* possession is that the claim to the land by the 'squatter' by virtue of the Limitation Act is *inconsistent with* (ie in competition with) the claim of the original 'paper owner'.

It may well be correct to describe *Parshall v Hackney* as 'a case of *equality* of registered titles'. But that cannot hide the fact that the two titles were in direct conflict with each other. A tenant's title is not inconsistent with that of their landlord. Trustees' title is not inconsistent with that of the beneficiaries of the trust. But Hackney's title was most definitely inconsistent with that of Parshall. The behaviour of the Hackney family in annexing the disputed land was lawful vis-a-vis the world at large, but it was surely unlawful vis-a-vis the owner of No 29.

15.5.2 Intention to Possess (*Animus Possidendi*)

The adverse possessor must have control and exclusive possession of the land. Added to this the adverse possessor must have intention to possess the land. According to Slade J in *Powell v McFarlane* (1979) 38 P & CR 452 'intention, in one's own name and on one's own behalf, to exclude the world at large, including the owner with the paper title if he be not himself the possessor, so far as is reasonably practicable and so far as the processes of the law will allow.'

In applying this to the facts, Slade J considered that:

> There are a few acts which by their very nature are so drastic as to point unquestionably in the absence of evidence to the contrary, to an intention on the part of the doer to appropriate the land concerned. The ploughing up and cultivation of agricultural land is one such act: compare *Seddon* v. *Smith* [[1877] 36 LT 168, CA]. The enclosure of land by a newly constructed fence is another. As Cockburn C.J. said in *Seddon* v. *Smith* [[1877] 36 LT 168, CA] 'Enclosure is the strongest possible evidence of adverse possession,' though he went on to add that it was not indispensable. The placing of a notice on land warning intruders to keep out, coupled with the actual enforcement of such notice, is another such act. So too is the locking or blocking of the only means of access. The plaintiff however, did none of these things in 1956 or 1957. The acts done by him were of a far less drastic and irremediable nature. What he did, in effect, was to take various profits from the land, in the form of shooting and pasturage, hay and grass for the benefit of the family cow or cows and goat, and to effect rough repairs to the fencing, merely to the extent necessary to secure his profits by making the land stockproof. On many days of the year neither he nor the animals would have set foot on it. These activities, done, as they were, by a 14-year-old boy who himself owned no land in the neighbourhood, were in my judgment equivocal within the meaning of the authorities in the sense that they were not necessarily referable to an intention on the part of the plaintiff to dispossess Mr. McFarlane [the defendant] and to occupy the land wholly as his own property. At first, surely, any objective informed observer might probably have inferred that the plaintiff was using the land simply for the benefit of his family's cow or cows, during such periods as the absent owner took no steps to stop him, without any intention to appropriate the land as his own.
>
> …On the evidence it seems to me inherently possible, if not likely, that as at 1956–57 he entered it simply with the idea of taking what he needed from it by way of grazing, etc. until he was stopped, and with no real thought at that time of establishing a permanent dominion over it. Very probably by 1962, when he was older and had established his own business and had already been using the land for several years, his intentions had hardened, just as his activities (for example his parking of vehicles and lorries and the erecting of a sign board) had become more unequivocally those of a person asserting ownership. It is, I think, quite possible that he did effectively take possession of the land in 1962 by sufficient acts and manifestations of *animus possidendi*. However, this does not assist him for the purposes of the present proceedings.

In Mr Justice Slade's view the 14-year-old boy did not have the intention to possess the property and merely used the property for his benefit, but when he got older and had established his own business, he had then demonstrated through his activities unequivocal acts of a person asserting ownership, and consequently having the requisite intention to possess. The claimant was not, however, successful in his claim as he was not able to show 12 years' possession.

In the case of *JA Pye (Oxford) Ltd v Graham* [2003] 1 AC 419, the House of Lords considered whether Graham had the intention to possess the land. Lord Browne-Wilkinson considered the importance of evidence of physical control but noted that it is not always possible to conclude that there is an intention to possess.

Lord Browne-Wilkinson said:

> ...there has always, both in Roman law and in common law, been a requirement to show an intention to possess in addition to objective acts of physical possession. Such intention may be, and frequently is, deduced from the physical acts themselves. But there is no doubt in my judgment that there are two separate elements in legal possession. So far as English law is concerned intention as a separate element is obviously necessary. Suppose a case where A is found to be in occupation of a locked house. He may be there as a squatter, as an overnight trespasser, or as a friend looking after the house of the paper owner during his absence on holiday. The acts done by A in any given period do not tell you whether there is legal possession. If A is there as a squatter he intends to stay as long as he can for his own benefit: his intention is an intention to possess. But if he only intends to trespass for the night or has expressly agreed to look after the house for his friend he does not have possession. It is not the nature of the acts which A does but the intention with which he does them which determines whether or not he is in possession.

In *Buckinghamshire County Council v Moran* [1990] Ch 623, the Court of Appeal considered that placing a lock, chain, and gate were unequivocally acts of securing and enclosing the land, enabling the defendant to have exclusive physical control. This conduct enabled the court to infer that the defendant had the intention to possess the land.

What about somebody who takes possession of a parcel of land thinking it is theirs when in fact it belongs to somebody else?

In *Roberts v Swangrove Estates Ltd* [2008] 2 WLR 1111 the Crown Estates Commissioners took control of land they thought to be 'foreshore' (land between the high and low water marks) but to which the claimants had a paper title. Could the Commissioners claim a title by adverse possession? At para 87 Mummery LJ said:

> As for the broader ground it has not been demonstrated, in my judgment, that the judge was wrong in ruling in favour of the Commissioners. There was evidence that they believed that the Magor Land was foreshore and, as such, part of the Crown Estate. As Saville LJ explained in *Hughes v. Cork* (14 February 1994 unreported) it is obvious that it is possible for a person who (albeit mistakenly) believes himself to be the true owner to have the requisite intention to exclude others and to acquire title by adverse possession. Adverse possession is not confined only to those who think or know that they are trespassing on someone else's land. All that matters for limitation purposes is that the person claiming adverse possession is in factual possession together with an intention to exclude everyone else. There is no sensible reason why a person who mistakenly believes that he is the true owner of land and behaves accordingly should be denied the benefit of a limitation defence, which is available to a person who commits the wrong of taking and retaining possession of land which he knows belongs to another person.

In consequence, the Crown Estates, who always thought that the land was theirs, could claim title by adverse possession, just like Moran in *Buckinghamshire County Council v Moran* who well knew that the land originally belonged to the county council.

REVIEW QUESTIONS Is there adverse possession in the following situations?

1 In 1960 Letitia leased 24 High Street to Tatiana for 30 years. Tatiana has lived there ever since. Tatiana stopped paying rent in 1980. She tells everybody 'It's my house—heaven only knows what has happened to Letitia. I have not heard from her since 1981.'

(Refer back to 15.5.1.)

2 John and Jane own 142 Acacia Avenue. In 2002 they went on an extended holiday to their villa in the south of France. In their absence Trig and Troy broke into number 142 and made themselves at home. They dumped all of John and Jane's belongings out in the street. Meanwhile, John and Jane had a big win on the French lottery, so they never returned to number 142.

(Consider 15.2 and 15.5.)

3 The property title to Greyacre belongs to Smith. Greyacre is derelict open land of about a quarter of an acre. The Patel family are fitness fanatics and train on Greyacre for about one hour a day.

4 As question 3, but the Patel family:

(i) fences off Greyacre;

(ii) gain access through a gate to which they have the key; and

(iii) install fitness equipment all over Greyacre.

(In answering questions 3 and 4 consider 15.5 and the meaning of possession.)

15.6 Offence of Squatting in a Residential Building

The enactment of the Legal Aid, Sentencing and Punishment of Offenders Act (LASPOA) 2012 has criminalized squatting in residential buildings, and came into force on 1 September 2012. Under s144 an offence is committed if a) the person is in a residential building as a trespasser, and b) the person knows or ought to know that he or she is a trespasser, and c) the person is living in the building or intends to live there for any period.

The ambit of the provision, as it currently stands, makes it harder for a person to claim adverse possession of a residential building. What is apparent from the parliamentary debates is that the aim of this provision is to deter squatters from entering and occupying a residential building without permission. The difficulty that has subsequently arisen is that the Land Registry has been refusing adverse possession claims to residential buildings on the grounds that the claim is based on a criminal act (using the maxim *ex turpi causa*). This issue was considered in *Best v Chief Land Registrar* [2015] EWCA Civ 17.

Mr Best had been working for a client when he became aware of a residential property nearby which was empty and vandalized. He entered the property and made substantial improvements to the property over time with a view to making it his permanent residence. Mr Best had since 2001 treated the house as his own and he finally moved into the property in January 2012, and was living in the property as a trespasser from 1 September 2012, when the LASPOA

2012 came into effect. On 27 November 2012 Mr Best applied to register title to the property. Mr Best was subsequently informed by the Land Registry that his application would be cancelled because his claim for adverse possession was based on a criminal offence. The justification for this stance given by the Land Registry was that Schedule 6 of the LRA 2002 implicitly requires that the claimant's possession should not have constituted a criminal offence for any part of the ten year period relied upon.

The Court of Appeal at the outset acknowledged that there was no indication that Parliament would have enacted s144 if that meant the criminal law upsetting the normal operation of adverse possession rules. Further, the court sought to balance the conflict between squatting in criminal law and that of adverse possession in civil law, and in doing so Sales LJ stated:

> the Supreme Court confirmed the position arrived at in *Tinsley v Milligan* [1994] 1 AC 340: the law of illegality does not operate to confer a broad discretion on a court to take any illegal actions on the part of a claimant into account when deciding the extent to which such illegality has an impact upon the relief sought by the claimant. Rather, the task for the court is to identify in the specific context in question a particular rule which reflects in an appropriate way the relevant underlying policy in that area: see *Hounga*, paras. [42] et seq...Although in each case a rule is to be identified, rather than just taking a discretionary approach of a kind disapproved in *Tinsley v Milligan, Hounga* and *Les Laboratoires Servier*, there is not one single rule with blanket effect across all areas of the law. Instead, there are a number of rules which may be identified, each tailored to the particular context in which the illegality principle is said to apply: see *Gray v Thames Trains Ltd* [para. [30]: the *ex turpi causa* policy is based 'on a group of reasons, which vary in different situations'; and para. [32]: as between rules applicable in different contexts, 'the questions of fairness and policy are different and the content of the rule is different. One cannot simply extrapolate rules applicable to a different kind of situation'] and *Les Laboratoires Servier*, paras. [19] and [22].

The difficulty in this case arose out the conflict between those exercising their right under Schedule 6 para 1 LRA 2002, ie to register as the owner of the freehold having been in adverse possession for 10 years, and that of relying on behaviour which constitutes a criminal act. In Sales LJ view, to resolve this conflict it involves:

> ...balancing the public policy considerations which underlie and find expression in the provisions of the LRA governing acquisition of title by adverse possession against the public policy considerations which underlie and find expression in section 144 of LASPOA. Addressing that focused issue, I consider that it is clear that in enacting section 144 of LASPOA, Parliament did not intend that it should have any impact on the law of adverse possession set out in the LRA. The mischief which section 144 was intended to address and the objective it was intended to achieve had nothing to do with the operation of the law of adverse possession.
>
> ...
>
> In my judgment...Parliament did not intend that section 144 or the policy considerations which underlie it should have any bearing upon the operation of the law of adverse possession. Parliament is not lightly to be taken to have legislated with the intention of producing such capricious and arbitrary effects upon a carefully crafted and comprehensive statutory regime such as that contained in the LRA.

Sales LJ went on to note:

> ...The registered proprietor of a house can prevent a criminal offence under section 144 of LASPOA from occurring, by giving his consent for the squatter to be in the house and thus removing the squatter's status as a trespasser, which is one of the ingredients of the offence specified in section 144...this indicates that there is no overriding public policy concern

associated with section 144 which ought to be taken to affect the usual balance of interests between landowner and adverse possessor established by the law of adverse possession.

…

…contravention of section 144 of LASPOA does not have an impact upon the usual operation of the law of adverse possession. This is not a case where the provision of the criminal law reflects any discrete public policy interest in disturbing the usual distribution of rights between landowner and adverse possessor in private law, as set out in the LRA. The public policy concerns balanced and given expression in the adverse possession provisions of the LRA continue to apply with full force, and there is no significant countervailing public policy factor inherent or reflected in section 144 which supervenes to distort the balance of rights set out in the LRA. The 'interests of the state' and 'the public interest' are not engaged in a relevant way so far as the operation of the LRA is concerned.

The court held that claims for adverse possession were unaffected by s144 LASPOA 2012. That section gave rise to no public policy concern which should override the normal operation of the rules of adverse possession.

15.7 Preventing the Acquisition of Title by Adverse Possession

To prevent an adverse possessor from obtaining title in either unregistered land or applying for registration of proprietorship in registered land, the paper owner must prevent the limitation period from being completed.

15.7.1 Time Starts Running Afresh by Acknowledgement of Title

If an adverse possessor, with time running in their favour, acknowledges the original owner's title, time stops running in the adverse possessor's favour (s29 LA 1980). A new time period starts from the date of the acknowledgement of title.

By 'acknowledgement of title' is meant any direct or indirect recognition by the adverse possessor of the original owner's title, provided it is in writing and signed by the adverse possessor and addressed to the original owner (s30 LA 1980). An oral acknowledgement would not be sufficient to stop the time running.

In *Edginton v Clark* [1963] 3 WLR 721, the adverse possessor wrote to the original owner of the land offering to buy. The offer was accepted and a deposit paid, but the purchase was never completed. The adverse possessor was held, by making the offer, to have acknowledged title. The period of adverse possession would begin afresh from the date of that acknowledgement.

Upjohn LJ said:

…If a man makes an offer to purchase freehold property, even though it be subject to contract, he is quite clearly saying that as between himself and the person to whom he makes the offer, he realises that the offeree has a better title to the freehold land than himself, and that would seem to be the plainest possible form of acknowledgment.

[Counsel for the claimant], however, has ingeniously argued that when an intending purchaser makes an offer to purchase, he does not thereby acknowledge that the vendor can prove or establish the title which the purchaser is entitled to have on a sale and purchase of land, and he says that the letters properly understood merely mean: 'If you can prove your title which I am bound to accept, then I will buy', and accordingly, so the argument proceeds, there is no acknowledgment of the vendor's title.

We are quite unable to accept that argument. Of course an intending purchaser does not acknowledge that the vendor has a marketable title when he makes an offer to purchase. That is a matter for inspection of title and requisitions at a later stage; but what he does acknowledge is that as between the intending purchaser and the vendor, the vendor has the better title to the land and that seems to us all that is required.

...Whether or not a particular writing amounts to an acknowledgment must depend on the true construction of the document in all the surrounding circumstances, and it is quite plain that in [*Doe d Curzon v Edmonds* [1840] 6 M & W 295] there was no acknowledgment by the writing, for it challenges the ownership of the true owner, but offers by way of compromise to accept a tenancy. Had a bargain been concluded, then no doubt that would have been an acknowledgment because by agreeing to become a tenant, the writer could not deny his landlord's title, and that, we think, is the explanation of the concluding words at the end of the judgment.

The House of Lords in *Ofolue v Bossert* [2009] 2 WLR 746 approved the decision in *Edginton v Clark* (see para 76 of the leading speech of Lord Neuburger) but distinguished it on the facts.

In *Ofolue,* the claimants were registered proprietors of a house in Bow in which the defendant had been living since 1983. In 1987 the claimants commenced possession proceedings which dragged on and on...In January 1992 the defendant sent a letter marked 'without prejudice' offering to buy the house for £35,000. The claimants rejected this offer. The claimants did nothing to hurry along the 1987(!) proceedings and those proceedings were eventually stayed for want of prosecution in 2000. In September 2003 (less than 12 years since the January 1992 letter) the claimants commenced fresh proceedings for possession.

The House of Lords decided the case by applying the general principles regarding 'without prejudice' letters sent by a party to any type of litigation offering to settle the case. Such letters cannot be used against a party sending such a letter. It followed that the January 1992 letter was therefore not an acknowledgement within s29 LA 1980. Bossert's claim to title by adverse possession succeeded.

15.7.2 Acknowledgement of Title Made by Person in whose Favour Time has Already Run is of No Effect

thinking point 15.5

In 2000, Bernie took adverse possession of Daisy Farm, the original owner of which was Oleg. Bernie has maintained adverse possession ever since. In 2013, Oleg writes to Bernie offering to 'sell' Daisy Farm. Bernie immediately writes back, 'Dear Oleg, I am interested in buying Daisy Farm from you, I will go and see my solicitor.' What will the solicitor advise?

Bernie's solicitor will advise her that Oleg's title was time-barred in 2012. What about the letter? Fortunately for Bernie, it was sent too late!

Bernie's position must be contrasted with that of the defendant 'Tillson' in *Colchester Borough v Smith* [1992] 2 All ER 561. Tillson had been (apparently) in adverse possession of the plaintiff's land for well over 12 years. Despite that fact, the plaintiff began proceedings for possession against him. These earlier proceedings were compromised on the terms:

- that Tillson accepted that the plaintiff still owned the land; and
- that the plaintiff granted Tillson a lease of the land.

In later proceedings for possession brought on the expiry of the lease, Tillson claimed that he had a freehold title by virtue of adverse possession. The Court of Appeal ruled that Tillson was bound by the earlier compromise and therefore was estopped from disputing the plaintiff's title to the freehold.

15.8 The Effect of Adverse Possession

15.8.1 Unregistered Land

Freehold

When time runs out there is not an automatic 'statutory conveyance' of the original owner's title to the adverse possessor. In the Bernie–Oleg example in thinking point 15.5, Oleg's fee simple in Daisy Farm was destroyed in 2012 and his right to recover the property is time-barred. Bernie has a completely new fee simple based on her long possession of Daisy Farm. It is important to remember that the adverse possessor takes possession of the land as owner of the fee simple. Whilst the limitation period is running it is at this point the paper owner can defeat the adverse possessor's title.

An adverse possessor does, however, take 'his' or 'her' land subject to third party rights such as easements, profits, and restrictive covenants. This was made clear in *Re Nisbet and Potts' Contract* [1906] 1 Ch 386, which also held that an adverse possessor was not a 'purchaser' for the purposes of the doctrine of notice. Neither will an adverse possessor be a purchaser for the purposes of modern legislation such as the Land Charges Acts.

In *Re Nisbet and Potts' Contract* [1906] 1 Ch 386, a 'squatter' had extinguished the unregistered title of the original freeholder by adverse possession. The question was whether this had the effect of releasing the adverse possessor's new title from a restrictive covenant to which the original freehold had been subject. The Court of Appeal held the 'squatter' was bound by the restriction. The covenantee had not, as yet, had any cause to enforce the restriction, so it would be a nonsense to hold that the enforcement of the covenant in the future had been time-barred by the squatter's adverse possession. Nor could the squatter claim to be a 'purchaser' for value of the legal estate without notice of the restrictive covenant. Collins MR said:

> . . . the Statute of Limitations, as one would expect, does not purport to annul by lapse of time any rights other than those which persons might have, and ought to have, exercised during the period limited. The statute does not begin to run in any case against a person until that person has been put to what is generally called his 'right of entry.' Unless the circumstances have been such as to put the person who is to be barred by the lapse of time upon the assertion of his right, the time does not begin to run against him. All that the statute does is this. By s. 34 it says: 'At the determination of the period limited by this Act to any person for making

an entry or distress, or bringing any writ of quare impedit or other action or suit, the right and title of such person to the land, rent, or advowson, for the recovery whereof such entry, distress, action, or suit respectively might have been made or brought within such period, shall be extinguished.' That is the whole right the squatter acquires, namely, the extinguishment of a title adverse to his own. But how does that affect the question here? What machinery is there in the Statute of Limitations affecting the right of a covenantee who has the benefit of a restrictive covenant? *Nothing in the Act has been pointed out to us which touches that right at all. In fact, unless and until the right of the covenantee has been in some way infringed, so that it becomes necessary for him to enforce that right, there is no reason, either in principle or in fairness, why his right should be in any way affected.* [Emphasis added]

What if an Adverse Possessor Displaces a Tenant?

What, however, if the land in question has been leased to a tenant, and it is the tenant who is displaced by the adverse possessor? The principles applicable were restated by the House of Lords in *Fairweather v St Marylebone Property Co* [1963] AC 510.

Back in 1893, a landlord (L) owned the fee simple in a house and an adjoining shed. In that year he granted a 99-year lease of the house and shed to T. T left the shed derelict. In 1920, a neighbour (M) took adverse possession of the shed. M and his successor, Fairweather, maintained the adverse possession until the dispute arose in 1959.

In 1959, St Marylebone bought from L the fee simple to the house and shed. By agreement between St Marylebone and T, the 99-year lease was 'surrendered', that is, terminated by mutual agreement. This of course gave St Marylebone an immediate right to occupy the house. They then sued Fairweather, claiming possession of the shed.

Fairweather argued that because of the adverse possession he had acquired title to the rest of the term of the leasehold estate over the shed; the landlord (he said) could not claim the land until 1992! This neat, logical argument was not accepted by the House of Lords. Why not?

- A tenant's right to occupy land leased to him is lost after 12 years' adverse possession against him. Thus from 1932 onwards, T could not claim possession of the shed from M or (later) Fairweather.

- Where there has been 12 years' adverse possession it is wrong to say that the adverse possessor acquires the estate of the person they have displaced. Rather, the adverse possessor has a completely new title. Thus, Fairweather had not acquired T's leasehold estate over the shed lasting until 1992. The adverse possessor occupies the freehold; possession of this land can only be defeated by the owner of the land (landlord) who has a better right than the adverse possessor.

- Instead, Fairweather had a defective title to the land; defective in the sense that in certain circumstances he could be ousted by the landlord, for example by forfeiture.

- Where the tenant has lost the right to occupy the land to an adverse possessor, the lease is not totally destroyed. It continues to have a notional existence between landlord and tenant.

- When this 'notional lease' is terminated by agreement between the landlord and tenant, by forfeiture or by the expiry of the originally agreed period, the landlord gains an immediate right to claim possession of the land from the adverse possessor.

- The landlord will be time-barred only if they allow 12 years to elapse from the termination of the notional lease without bringing proceedings against the adverse possessor.

In the *St Marylebone* case the claimants sued almost immediately after the termination of the notional lease. Thus Fairweather, who thought he had got the shed until 1992, was evicted some 30 years earlier than he had anticipated.

Hopefully, you have already realized that anybody who (like Fairweather) maintains adverse possession against a tenant, even for well over 12 years, is going to be in a very insecure position. If the notional lease is terminated in any way, the adverse possessor can expect almost immediate eviction.

thinking point 15.6

Consider the following situation. In 1984, Larry, the owner in fee simple of Dull Shack, leased Dull Shack to Tan for 99 years at a nominal rent. In 1990, Tan became a permanent invalid, and forgot all about his lease of Dull Shack. Larry did not bother to collect the nominal rent.

In 1995, Nina, a neighbour, took adverse possession of Dull Shack, using it for general storage purposes. She has continued in adverse possession ever since. Tan has recently remembered his lease of Dull Shack, and he also is informed that Nina is in adverse possession. What can he do to get Dull Shack back? (There are two, alternative answers.)

1   *Tan should approach Larry, and suggest the following 'deal':*

   (i)   *Tan surrenders the lease to Larry.*

   (ii) *Larry sues Nina for possession.*

   (iii) *Having got possession Larry grants a fresh lease to Tan.*

Larry will probably charge a price for his cooperation.

2   *An alternative 'deal', which involves less trouble to Larry, is as follows:*

   (i)   *Tan buys Larry's fee simple in reversion.*

   (ii) *This (seemingly) brings about a termination of the 'notional lease' by 'merger'. (The same person cannot be both landlord and tenant!)*

   (iii) *In his new capacity as owner of a fee simple, Tan sues Nina for possession. As this fee simple has not been extinguished by adverse possession, Tan should win.*

Entering into one or other of these deals can be called 'pulling the St Marylebone trick'.

The Problem of a Tenant Encroaching on Adjoining Land

In 1997, Lakia leased Centreacre to Tom for 21 years. In 1999, Tom moved both the eastern and western fences of Centreacre a few feet so as to encroach upon Westacre and Eastacre. The original fee simple in Westacre belongs to Lakia. The original fee simple in Eastacre belongs to Nasser.

The fences have remained in their 1999 position. In effect Tom has for the last umpteen years maintained adverse possession of two strips of land. Since 2011, no one will have been able to claim those strips from him. But what happens in 2018, when his lease expires?

The principles applicable in this kind of situation were restated in *Smirk v Lyndale Developments Ltd* [1975] 1 All ER 690. The plaintiff, a British Railways employee, had a weekly service tenancy of a house owned by his employer. During the period of his occupation he took it upon himself to cultivate adjoining land ('the blue plot') which was also owned by his employer. His employer eventually sold the title to the house and 'the blue plot' to the defendant. The plaintiff claimed to have acquired title to 'the blue plot' by adverse possession. The court held that where a lessee encroaches upon other land, the encroachment is presumed to be an extension in the 'locus' of the lease. This means that the tenant is presumed merely to be expanding the area granted to him/her. The plaintiff failed, therefore, to show that he had acquired title to 'the blue plot' by adverse possession. This is so whether the land encroached upon belongs to a stranger or to the lessee's landlord.

thinking point 15.7

Consider, therefore, what the answer is to our Centreacre problem. Remember that there are two separate strips of land to think about.

Applying the law set out in Smirk v Lyndale *to our example of Centreacre, the outcome is not favourable to Tom! When his lease expires in 2018 he will not be able to retain either of the two strips. Lakia will regain the strip Tom 'pinched' from Westacre. She will also get the strip which Tom 'pinched' from Nasser's Eastacre.*

Tom's only hope of retaining one or both of the strips is if he can rebut the presumption that he is expanding the area of his lease. It seems that to rebut the presumption he would have to show that he was treating the land encroached upon as distinct from the land leased.

Suppose that Tom's lease of Centreacre contained a covenant that he cannot keep dogs on the land. Suppose that on the strip 'pinched' from Westacre he has since 1999 kept kennels full of Alsatians, Rottweilers, etc (or, if you like, Chihuahuas and Pekinese). Tom will be able to claim that he has a permanent title to the western strip. He will be able to tell Lakia that she cannot have this strip back. His dogs (of whatever breed) will not have to move to a new home!

Adverse Possession where Land is Held in Trust

The following rules apply whether land is held under a strict settlement, under a trust for sale, or under a trust of land. It is essential to consider the equitable interests under the trust separate from the legal estate.

1 An equitable interest in possession is time-barred after 12 years' adverse possession of the land.

2 An equitable interest in remainder or reversion is time-barred after:

   (i)   12 years from the adverse possession starting; or

   (ii) six years from the equitable interest coming into possession, whichever is later.

3 The legal estate is not time-barred until all equitable interests under the trust have been time-barred.

Mauveacre has since 1997 been held in trust for Isabella for life, remainder to Robert in fee simple. (It does not matter whether the trust is a strict settlement, a trust for sale, or trust of land. It does not matter whether the legal title is vested in Isabella as life tenant or in independent trustees.)

Ellis took adverse possession of Mauveacre in 2002 and has maintained adverse possession ever since. Isabella died in early 2016:

- Isabella's equitable life interest was 'time-barred' back in 2014. See rule (1) in the previous list.
- Robert's equitable fee simple will not be time-barred until 2022. See rule (2)(ii).
- The legal estate (whoever has got it) will also be time-barred in 2022. See rule (3).

thinking point 15.8

What would be the position if Isabella died in 2007, only five years after adverse possession had commenced?

- *In what year was Robert's equitable interest time-barred?*
- *In what year was the legal estate time-barred?*

Robert's equitable interest was time-barred in 2014, applying rule (2)(i). Applying rule (3), the legal estate was also time-barred in 2014.

15.8.2 Registered Land

It will be best to begin with three preliminary comments. First, you may well be surprised that the law relating to adverse possession applies where the land is registered land. Many foreign lawyers familiar with continental systems of land registration would share your surprise. The very fact that adverse possession applies to registered land undermines the efficiency and accuracy of our system of land registration.

Secondly, it is only in the last 45 years or so that there have been (outside London) large numbers of registered titles. This probably explains why there is relatively little case law on the impact of adverse possession on a registered title.

Thirdly, the LRA 2002 does *not* abolish adverse possession against registered titles, but it does introduce a radically different new set of rules which are compliant with the European Convention on Human Rights. However, for the foreseeable future it will be necessary to know the basic principles of the LRA 1925 rules.

Freehold

Land Registration Act 1925

75. Acquisition of title by possession

(1) The Limitation Acts shall apply to registered land in the same manner and to the same extent as those Acts apply to land not registered, except that where, if the land were not registered, the estate of the person registered as proprietor would be extinguished, such estate shall not be extinguished but shall be deemed to be held by the proprietor for the time being in trust for the person who, by virtue of the said Acts, has acquired title against any proprietor, but without prejudice to the estates and interests of any other person interested in the land whose estate or interest is not extinguished by those Acts.

(2) Any person claiming to have acquired a title under the Limitation Acts to a registered estate in the land may apply to be registered as proprietor thereof.

This provision applied where 12 years' adverse possession had already been completed by 12 October 2003. After that date adverse possession of registered land is governed by the 2002 Act.

The effect of s75(1) LRA 1925 is that the original owner in fee simple holds the fee simple under a 'bare trust' for the adverse possessor, who obtains a new equitable fee simple. This provision provided a practical solution to the problem which would have arisen if the unregistered land approach of extinguishing the title had been adopted. As you may recall, the register of title provides information on who owns the land and this information cannot be destroyed in the same way. The alternative solution provided for under this provision was to allow the adverse possessor to apply to be registered as proprietor and have the register rectified. Provided there was sufficient proof of the adverse possession, the registrar had to rectify the register. This rectification in effect transferred the legal fee simple from the original owner to the adverse possessor. The original owner was not compensated in any way.

thinking point 15.9

Daryl was the original owner in fee simple of Greystone House. In 1990 Sam took adverse possession and has maintained it ever since. Now if Daryl's fee simple in Greystone House was unregistered, that fee simple would have been destroyed in 2002. Sam gets a new fee simple based on her long possession. What if (ever since he acquired the land in 1980) Daryl was registered proprietor of Greystone House?

Applying s75(1) LRA 1925, if Daryl was registered proprietor in fee simple of Greystone House, his fee simple was not destroyed in 2002. Rather, he held that fee simple under a 'bare trust' in trust for Sam, who had a new equitable fee simple.

Section 70(1)(f) Land Registration Act 1925

This provision made the rights of an adverse possessor an overriding interest. Therefore Sam's equitable fee simple would automatically bind a purchaser of Daryl's legal title.

Rectification of the Register

Although s70(1)(f) LRA 1925 gave Sam considerable security, an adverse possessor in whose favour time had already run could apply for rectification of the register. Provided there was sufficient proof of the adverse possession, the registrar had to rectify the register. This rectification in effect transferred the legal fee simple from the original owner (Daryl) to the adverse possessor (Sam). The original owner (Daryl) was not compensated in any way.

Land Registration Act 2002

The LRA 2002 completely revolutionizes the way adverse possession operates where adverse possession is taken against a registered estate. As from the commencement date of the 2002 Act, s75 LRA 1925, the strange trust which arises under that section, and the s70(1)(f) overriding interest are all swept away. They are replaced by a (very different) set of rules which, as we shall see, considerably strengthen the position of registered proprietors who find that some or all of their land has been adversely possessed.

The LRA 2002 almost makes title to land sacrosanct where the registered proprietor cannot lose their estate to an adverse possessor, even if that adverse possession has lasted a very long time, say 50 years. Where an adverse possession claim in registered land is made after 12 October 2003, the adverse possessor is subject to the rules under the LRA 2002.

Under ss96–98 LRA 2002 the owner of the land, except a registered chargee, is no longer subject to the 12-year limitation period under s15 LA 1980 and consequently it is no longer possible for the adverse possessor to extinguish the (registered) title of any person. However, the adverse possessor who has occupied the land for ten years can apply for registration of the estate (s97 LRA 2002). Once this registration process has been triggered, the rules under Sch 6 LRA 2002 will apply.

Land Registration Act 2002

96. Disapplication of periods of limitation

(1) No period of limitation under section 15 of the Limitation Act 1980 [c. 58] [time limits in relation to recovery of land] shall run against any person, other than a chargee, in relation to an estate in land or rentcharge the title to which is registered.

(2) No period of limitation under section 16 of that Act [time limits in relation to redemption of land] shall run against any person in relation to such an estate in land or rentcharge.

(3) Accordingly, section 17 of that Act [extinction of title on expiry of time limit] does not operate to extinguish the title of any person where, by virtue of this section, a period of limitation does not run against him.

97. Registration of adverse possessor

Schedule 6 [which makes provision about the registration of an adverse possessor of an estate in land or rentcharge] has effect.

98. Defences

(1) A person has a defence to an action for possession of land if—

    (a) on the day immediately preceding that on which the action was brought he was entitled to make an application under paragraph 1 of Schedule 6 to be registered as the proprietor of an estate in the land, and

    (b) had he made such an application on that day, the condition in paragraph 5(4) of that Schedule would have been satisfied.

(2) A judgment for possession of land ceases to be enforceable at the end of the period of two years beginning with the date of the judgment if the proceedings in which the judgment is given were commenced against a person who was at that time entitled to make an application under paragraph 1 of Schedule 6.

(3) A person has a defence to an action for possession of land if on the day immediately preceding that on which the action was brought he was entitled to make an application under paragraph 6 of Schedule 6 to be registered as the proprietor of an estate in the land.

(4) A judgment for possession of land ceases to be enforceable at the end of the period of two years beginning with the date of the judgment if, at the end of that period, the person against whom the judgment was given is entitled to make an application under paragraph 6 of Schedule 6 to be registered as the proprietor of an estate in the land.

(5) Where in any proceedings a court determines that—

    (a) a person is entitled to a defence under this section, or

    (b) a judgment for possession has ceased to be enforceable against a person by virtue of subsection (4),

the court must order the registrar to register him as the proprietor of the estate in relation to which he is entitled to make an application under Schedule 6.

(6) The defences under this section are additional to any other defences a person may have.

(7) Rules may make provision to prohibit the recovery of rent due under a rentcharge from a person who has been in adverse possession of the rentcharge.

Before the rules on adverse possession under the LRA 2002 are considered in depth, the 'transitional' rules under the Act must be considered first.

Adverse Possessors Who Have Already Been 'Squatting' for More than 12 Years on 13 October 2003

First remember that most adverse possessions are not spectacular cases like *Buckinghamshire County Council v Moran* or *JA Pye (Oxford) Ltd v Graham* but rather are cases where one neighbour has encroached upon another neighbour's land. Such encroachments may go on for generations before the original (or current) registered proprietor of the strip encroached upon realizes that they may have 'lost' a piece of land which the register says belongs to them.

There can be no doubt that on 13 October 2003 (the commencement of the LRA 2002) there were many cases where an adverse possessor had already had at least 12 years' adverse possession against a registered proprietor—quite possibly a lot longer. In these cases, the following happened as the clock struck midnight on 13 October 2003 (see Sch 12 para 18 LRA 2002 in the following extract):

• the trust which existed under s75 LRA 1925 disappeared;

• the adverse possessor therefore lost their interest under the now non-existent trust; and

• the adverse possessor did *not* have an overriding interest under s70(1)(f) LRA 1925 (that provision has been repealed).

However:

- the adverse possessor is able to apply for the register to be rectified so as to make them the owner of the estate against which they have 'squatted'. The registered proprietor will have no defence to this application; and

- this right to have the register rectified is a property right against the relevant registered estate. It is not automatically an overriding interest, but will normally be converted into an overriding interest by virtue of 'actual occupation' under Sch 3 para 2.

Land Registration Act 2002

Schedule 12 Transition

Adverse possession

18 (1) Where a registered estate in land is held in trust for a person by virtue of section 75(1) of the Land Registration Act 1925 immediately before the coming into force of section 97, he is entitled to be registered as the proprietor of the estate.

(2) A person has a defence to any action for the possession of land (in addition to any other defence he may have) if he is entitled under this paragraph to be registered as the proprietor of an estate in the land.

(3) Where in an action for possession of land a court determines that a person is entitled to a defence under this paragraph, the court must order the registrar to register him as the proprietor of the estate in relation to which he is entitled under this paragraph to be registered.

(4) Entitlement under this paragraph shall be disregarded for the purposes of section 131(1).

(5) Rules may make transitional provision for cases where a rentcharge is held in trust under section 75(1) of the Land Registration Act 1925 immediately before the coming into force of section 97.

thinking point 15.10

John became registered freehold proprietor of Yellow House in 1980. Keith became registered freehold proprietor of neighbouring Brown House in 1985.

Between the gardens of the two houses there is Grey Strip, about a metre wide. The Land Registry has Grey Strip registered as part of Yellow House. However, in 1988, Keith erected a fence so that Grey Strip became part of the Brown House garden. Keith has cultivated Grey Strip ever since.

In 2012 John sells Yellow House to Laura. Laura, having looked closely at the Land Registry plan, claims that Grey Strip is hers, and sues to evict Keith. Keith counterclaims for rectification of the register.

What will the court decide?

Keith should succeed in the case. The legal analysis is as follows:

- *from 2000 to 12 October 2003 s75 LRA 1925 applied. John held Grey Strip in trust for Keith;*

- *on 13 October 2003, Keith lost his equitable interest under the trust, but still retained a 'property right' to have the register rectified;*

- *that property right will be an overriding interest under Sch 3 para 2 LRA 2002 binding on a purchaser such as Laura; and*

- *Laura's claim to evict Keith will therefore fail, and Keith will have the register rectified so that Grey Strip is now part of Brown House.*

(Though this is not expressly stated by any of the Law Lords, *Ofulue v Bossert* was in effect a 'transition' case governed by Sch 12 LRA 2002. The register was rectified in the defendant's (Bossert's) favour (see para 104 of Lord Neuburger's speech).)

The Fundamental (Post-2003) Principle Regarding Adverse Possession—The Almost Sacrosanct Title of the Registered Proprietor

This principle is that a registered proprietor cannot lose their estate to an adverse possessor (see ss 96–98 and Sch 6 LRA 2002). However, this principle that the registered title is sacrosanct from 'squatters' is subject to a number of exceptions, only two of which are significant. It is submitted that these exceptions are:

- the two years' inaction after application exception; and
- the reasonably believing encroacher exception.

Land Registration Act 2002

Schedule 6

Registration of the Adverse Possessor

Right to apply for registration

1 (1) A person may apply to the registrar to be registered as the proprietor of a registered estate in land if he has been in adverse possession of the estate for the period of ten years ending on the date of the application.

   (2) A person may also apply to the registrar to be registered as the proprietor of a registered estate in land if—

      (a) he has in the period of six months ending on the date of the application ceased to be in adverse possession of the estate because of eviction by the registered proprietor, or a person claiming under the registered proprietor,

      (b) on the day before his eviction he was entitled to make an application under sub-paragraph (1), and

      (c) the eviction was not pursuant to a judgment for possession.

   (3) However, a person may not make an application under this paragraph if—

      (a) he is a defendant in proceedings which involve asserting a right to possession of the land, or

      (b) judgment for possession of the land has been given against him in the last two years.

   (4) For the purposes of sub-paragraph (1), the estate need not have been registered throughout the period of adverse possession.

Notification of application

2 (1) The registrar must give notice of an application under paragraph 1 to—

      (a) the proprietor of the estate to which the application relates,

      (b) the proprietor of any registered charge on the estate,

      (c) where the estate is leasehold, the proprietor of any superior registered estate,

      (d) any person who is registered in accordance with rules as a person to be notified under this paragraph, and

      (e) such other persons as rules may provide.

   (2) Notice under this paragraph shall include notice of the effect of paragraph 4.

Treatment of application

3 (1) A person given notice under paragraph 2 may require that the application to which the notice relates be dealt with under paragraph 5.

(2) The right under this paragraph is exercisable by notice to the registrar given before the end of such period as rules may provide.

4 If an application under paragraph 1 is not required to be dealt with under paragraph 5, the applicant is entitled to be entered in the register as the new proprietor of the estate.

5 (1) If an application under paragraph 1 is required to be dealt with under this paragraph, the applicant is only entitled to be registered as the new proprietor of the estate if any of the following conditions is met.

(2) The first condition is that—

(a) it would be unconscionable because of an equity by estoppel for the registered proprietor to seek to dispossess the applicant, and

(b) the circumstances are such that the applicant ought to be registered as the proprietor.

(3) The second condition is that the applicant is for some other reason entitled to be registered as the proprietor of the estate.

(4) The third condition is that—

(a) the land to which the application relates is adjacent to land belonging to the applicant,

(b) the exact line of the boundary between the two has not been determined under rules under section 60,

(c) for at least ten years of the period of adverse possession ending on the date of the application, the applicant (or any predecessor in title) reasonably believed that the land to which the application relates belonged to him, and

(d) the estate to which the application relates was registered more than one year prior to the date of the application.

(5) In relation to an application under paragraph 1(2), this paragraph has effect as if the reference in sub-paragraph (4)(c) to the date of the application were to the day before the date of the applicant's eviction.

Right to make further application for registration

6 (1) Where a person's application under paragraph 1 is rejected, he may make a further application to be registered as the proprietor of the estate if he is in adverse possession of the estate from the date of the application until the last day of the period of two years beginning with the date of its rejection.

(2) However, a person may not make an application under this paragraph if—

(a) he is a defendant in proceedings which involve asserting a right to possession of the land,

(b) judgment for possession of the land has been given against him in the last two years, or

(c) he has been evicted from the land pursuant to a judgment for possession.

7 If a person makes an application under paragraph 6, he is entitled to be entered in the register as the new proprietor of the estate....

Effect of registration

9 (1) Where a person is registered as the proprietor of an estate in land in pursuance of an application under this Schedule, the title by virtue of adverse possession which he had at the time of the application is extinguished.

(2) Subject to sub-paragraph (3), the registration of a person under this Schedule as the proprietor of an estate in land does not affect the priority of any interest affecting the estate.

(3) Subject to sub-paragraph (4), where a person is registered under this Schedule as the proprietor of an estate, the estate is vested in him free of any registered charge affecting the estate immediately before his registration.

(4) Sub-paragraph (3) does not apply where registration as proprietor is in pursuance of an application determined by reference to whether any of the conditions in paragraph 5 applies.

. . .

Meaning of 'adverse possession'

11 (1) A person is in adverse possession of an estate in land for the purposes of this Schedule if, but for section 96, a period of limitation under section 15 of the Limitation Act 1980 (c. 58) would run in his favour in relation to the estate.

(2) A person is also to be regarded for those purposes as having been in adverse possession of an estate in land—

(a) where he is the successor in title to an estate in the land, during any period of adverse possession by a predecessor in title to that estate, or

(b) during any period of adverse possession by another person which comes between, and is continuous with, periods of adverse possession of his own.

(3) In determining whether for the purposes of this paragraph a period of limitation would run under section 15 of the Limitation Act 1980, there are to be disregarded—

(a) the commencement of any legal proceedings, and

(b) paragraph 6 of Schedule 1 to that Act.

Two Years' Inaction after Application—The Application Stage

It is worth considering Sch 6 para 1(1) LRA 2002, a provision which, at first sight, appears to totally contradict a statement made earlier, 'a registered proprietor cannot lose their estate to an adverse possessor, even if that adverse possession has lasted a very long time, say 50 years'.

Schedule 6 para 1(1) LRA 2002 reads:

A person may apply to the registrar to be registered as the proprietor of a registered estate in land if he has been in adverse possession of the estate for the period of ten years ending on the date of the application.

This appears to be saying, 'Ten years' adverse possession and the adverse possessor gains ownership by simply asking the Registry to change the register!' However, careful reading of the rest of Sch 6 shows that this conclusion would be totally wrong. Paragraph 2 requires that notice of the application be given to the registered proprietor, and para 5 in effect provides that if the registered proprietor objects then the application must automatically be rejected. The latter provision gives the registered proprietor an unequivocal opportunity to defeat an adverse possession claim where previously the title was obtained by the adverse possessor automatically. The outcome of these rules on adverse possession under the LRA 2002 has made the acquisition of property through this method very difficult for the adverse possessor.

thinking point 15.11

In 1999, Bloggshire County Council became registered proprietor of a strip of land on which it intended to build a new road. It left the land derelict. In 2000, Michael, whose garden backed onto the strip, incorporated the strip into his garden. Like Moran in the real case of Buckinghamshire County Council v Moran, *Michael knew that the land belonged to the council.*

In 2016, someone tells Michael about Sch 6 para 1 LRA 2002, so he applies to be registered as proprietor. What happens next?

- The Registry gives notice to the council of Michael's application.
- The council will of course object.
- The Registry must therefore reject the application.

But as we shall see in the next section, this is not necessarily the end of the story.

If, through some oversight, the council—or any other registered proprietor—were not to object to the application under para 1(1), the application by the adverse possessor would be granted; that is, the (former) registered proprietor would lose ownership immediately. However, no doubt almost all para 1 applications will meet with objection from the registered proprietor.

The 'Two Years to do Something' Stage

Once an adverse possessor's application under Sch 6 para 1 has been rejected, the registered proprietor cannot just sit and do nothing thinking, 'the register gives me permanent protection from losing my land to the adverse possessor'. An idle registered proprietor will eventually be caught out by Sch 6 paras 6 and 7 LRA 2002.

Schedule 6 para 6(1) LRA 2002 provides:

> Where a person's application under paragraph 1 is rejected, he may make a further application to be registered as the proprietor of the estate if he is in adverse possession of the estate from the date of the application until the last day of the period of two years beginning with the date of its rejection.

Schedule 6 para 7 LRA 2002 then bluntly states:

> If a person makes an application under para. 6, he is entitled to be entered into the register as the new proprietor of the estate.

What this means for the adverse possessor is that if, after having their first application rejected, the adverse possessor remains in adverse possession for a further two years, they can make a second application to be registered as owner and this time the adverse possessor's application must succeed. During this two-year period the original registered proprietor has time in which to do something about the adverse possessor. In practical terms the proprietor will have two choices, either:

- take eviction proceedings against the adverse possessor; or
- make an agreement with the adverse possessor so that they can continue to occupy the land as a lessee.

thinking point 15.12

In 1999, Bloggshire County Council became registered proprietor of a strip of land on which it intended to build a new road. It left the land derelict. In 2000 Michael, whose garden backed onto the strip, incorporated the strip into his garden. Like Moran in the real case of Buckinghamshire County Council v Moran, Michael knew that the land belonged to the council.

In 2016, Michael applies to be registered as proprietor. The Land Registry have just rejected Michael's application under Sch 6 para 1 LRA 2002. What should Bloggshire County Council do next?

It should sue Michael for possession of the strip. However, it could offer to compromise the proceedings by granting him a periodic tenancy, for example a monthly tenancy, of the strip. In that way Michael can keep the land until the planned road is actually built.

Summary of Two Years' Inaction after Application for Rectification

The adverse possessor will gain title if all six of the following steps are completed:

1 the adverse possessor has at least ten years' adverse possession of the land;

2 the adverse possessor applies under Sch 6 para 1 LRA 2002 to be registered as proprietor;

3 the registered proprietor is given notice of the application;

4 the registered proprietor objects to the application, and it is therefore rejected;

5 the adverse possessor remains in adverse possession for a further two years; and

6 the adverse possessor then makes a second application under Sch 6 para 6 LRA 2002.

Exceptionally, if the registered proprietor does not object to the para 1 application, the adverse possessor will gain title after step 3.

The 'Reasonably Believing Encroacher' Exception

This exception to the general rule that a registered title is sacrosanct as against an adverse possessor will be invoked (if it all) at step 4 in the previous analysis. The 'reasonably believing encroacher' rule is the one significant exception to the rule that if a registered proprietor objects to a para 1 application, that application must be rejected. Indeed, if the adverse possessor proves (if need be to a tribunal or to a judge) that they are a 'reasonably believing encroacher' they will 'win' the land, and the register will be immediately rectified in the adverse possessor's favour.

The 'reasonably believing encroacher' rule is to be found in subpara 4 of para 5. If the adverse possessor can prove:

• the land to which the [para 1] application relates is adjacent to land belonging to the applicant; and

• for at least ten years of the period of adverse possession ending on the date of the application, the applicant (or any predecesor in title) reasonably believed that the land to which the application relates belonged to them;

then the adverse possessor succeeds. So land which the adverse possessor reasonably thought was theirs (but was not) actually becomes theirs!

The explanation for including this strange 'reasonably believing encroacher' rule in the LRA 2002 lies in something mentioned back in 5.2.1. There, it was stated:

> One feature of English land registration strange to foreign eyes is that our system does not normally fix the exact boundaries of each plot. The Land Registry suggests that their plans are in fact accurate to within a few centimetres. No doubt they usually are, but in *Lee v Barrey* [1957] Ch 251, there was a discrepancy of eight feet (2.5 m) between the plan and the actual boundary on the ground!

In other words, the lines on the Registry's plans are only approximately correct. It follows that those plans will not be conclusive if a boundary dispute arises between neighbours. Moreover, it is implicit in the LRA 2002 that a landowner might reasonably think that a boundary is in a different place from that marked on the Registry's plans. How then does this 'reasonably believing encroacher' exception actually work?

thinking point 15.13

Maria became registered freehold proprietor of Red House in 2004. Natalie became registered freehold proprietor of neighbouring Pink House in 2007.

Between the gardens of the two houses there is Grey Sliver, a strip about a metre wide. The Land Registry has Grey Sliver registered as part of Red House. However, in 2008, Natalie erects a fence so that Grey Sliver becomes part of the Pink House garden. Natalie cultivates Grey Sliver as part of her garden.

In 2029, Maria sells Red House to Oliver. Oliver, having looked closely at the Land Registry plan, claims that Grey Sliver is his, and threatens Natalie with proceedings to evict her from Grey Sliver. Natalie applies under Sch 6 para 1, and when Oliver objects to her application, Natalie invokes the 'reasonably believing encroacher' exception. What will the tribunal or judge decide?

Surely the tribunal or judge will reject Natalie's claim. It was Natalie who put up the fence thus 'annexing' Grey Sliver. She cannot possibly say 'I reasonably believed this Grey Sliver strip was mine.'

thinking point 15.14

Same facts as in thinking point 15.13 except that Natalie sells Pink House to Querida in 2016. Querida, like most house purchasers, does not have a detailed survey of the property done for her. Neither she nor her solicitor compare the Land Registry plan with the situation 'on the ground'. (Even if they had, they may well have not spotted the discrepancy.) For 13 years Querida cultivates her garden never realizing that a dispute might arise regarding the ownership of one of the edges of that garden. Then, in 2029, Oliver buys Red House, and starts making threatening noises regarding the land he calls 'Grey Sliver'. Querida applies under Sch 6 para 1, and when Oliver objects to her application, Querida invokes the 'reasonably believing encroacher' exception. What will the tribunal or judge decide?

The tribunal or judge will probably rule in Querida's favour, and correct the register so that Grey Sliver appears as part of Pink House. It is possible that Oliver's lawyer will argue: 'A reasonable person would (in 2016) have had the garden measured up by a surveyor.'

Zarb v Parry—Buying Knowing that There Had Been a Boundary Dispute

As many anticipated, the 'reasonably believing encroacher' rule has generated quite a lot of litigation, and there are now two cases which have reached the Court of Appeal. The first was *Zarb v Parry* [2012] 1 WLR 1240 (see especially paras 45–59 and paras 77–80 of the judgment).

The facts of this case need to be carefully considered. In 1992 a Mr Little sold to his then neighbours Mr and Mrs Ceen a part of his garden. Both Little and the Ceens thought that the southern boundary of the plot conveyed was an already existing hedge. Little reinforced this belief by erecting a 'stock-proof' fence on his land just to the south of the hedge. However, as a result of a mistake in the plan annexed to the 1992 land transfer, the legal boundary was 12 feet to the north of the hedge! Little thus (unknowingly) retained a paper title to a strip of land which was in fact possessed by the Ceens, and then by their successors, the Parrys.

In 2000 Little sold his property to the Zarbs. In 2000, the Zarbs did query the boundary, but after repeated phone calls and correspondence from Mrs Ceen, the Zarbs did not at that time pursue the matter.

In 2002 the Parrys bought the Ceens' property, 'Fleet House'. *'Mr and Mrs Parry understood that there had been a boundary dispute with the Zarbs but that the dispute had been resolved prior to the completion of their purchase of Fleet House.'* (Para 6, emphasis added)

One fine morning in July 2007 the Parrys suddenly found the Zarbs starting to erect a boundary fence across their garden along the line of the 'paper title' boundary. After an altercation, the Zarbs removed the fence posts which they had banged into the ground.

The parties then took the (sensible) course of getting a jointly appointed surveyor (Mr Powell) to give his opinion on the boundary. Powell said that the boundary was the hedge. The Zarbs did not accept Powell's opinion, and in June 2009 commenced litigation claiming (in effect) possession of the disputed strip (to which they did have a paper title). The Parrys' defence was to rely on Sch 6 para 5(4) LRA 2002, the 'reasonably believing encroacher' rule. The Court of Appeal (affirming the trial judge) had no difficulty (on this point) in ruling in the Parrys' favour.

Little, the Ceens, and the Parrys had all believed that the long-existing hedge was the boundary, and the reasonableness of this belief was effectively confirmed by the opinion from the surveyor Powell. (Contrast this situation with that of Natalie in our thinking point 15.13 who created a *new* boundary fence *after* she had arrived on the scene.)

It is very important that when they bought the land in 2002, the Parrys thought that the boundary issue had been resolved. Arden LJ stated:

> 58 These proceedings have been costly and there is a cautionary story here for purchasers of land. No doubt those advising on transfers of land will consider what they need to do in future to protect their clients from costly disputes such as this one. Purchasers are not necessarily protected merely because the seller gives an assurance that the dispute with a neighbour has seemingly 'gone away'. Boundary disputes have a habit of reappearing until finally resolved. The neighbour or the neighbour's successor in title may, for whatever reason, resuscitate the dispute, unless something is done to prevent them from doing so. It may be that the purchaser will have to consider whether to ask the neighbour to confirm the boundaries and have the necessary deed of confirmation registered at the Land Registry in a manner capable of binding successors in title. That will involve extra costs and delay but the costs may be less than the undoubted cost of litigation of this kind. If the neighbour refuses to be bound by an agreement as to the boundary the purchaser will then know the risks that he is running by completing the purchase. Moreover, the purchaser on acquiring possession might himself be advised to bring matters to a head by himself applying for registration as owner of the land in question.

It is submitted that if somebody buys a piece of land knowing that a boundary dispute might flare up in the future, it will be difficult for them to rely on the 'reasonably believing encroacher' rule. (Note that Querida in our thinking point 15.14 did not know when she bought the land in 2016 that there might be a boundary dispute.)

IAM Group Plc v Chowdery—The Personal Beliefs of the Encroacher Decisive

IAM Group Plc v Chowdery [2012] EWCA Civ 505 involves startling facts, very different from those in *Zarb v Parry*. Numbers 26 and 26a Rye Lane were adjoining buildings. A deed, executed in 1928 by the then owners of the properties, set out a clear, straight, *vertical* boundary. The title plans at the Land Registry reflected this boundary, and the registers for both properties referred to the 1928 deed.

In 1990 Chowdery took a tenancy of number 26a. He took possession not only of 26a, but also of some rooms on the first and second floor of number 26. *These rooms were only accessible from 26a.* In 1993 Chowdery bought the freehold to number 26a. He thought that his purchase included the rooms in number 26 he was already using.

The claimants purchased number 26 in 2000, but only in 2009 did it (by letters from its solicitors) start questioning Chowdery's right to the rooms on the first and second floors. In August 2010 it commenced proceedings claiming possession of the rooms. Chowdery counterclaimed for a declaration that he was entitled to be registered as owner of the disputed rooms.

The trial judge ruled in Chowdery's favour, finding that at all relevant times he honestly and reasonably believed he was owner of the rooms.

On appeal, the claimants argued that when Chowdery bought number 26a in 1993, his solicitors (who had since gone out of business leaving no conveyancing records) would have looked at the Land Registry plan and the 1928 deed referred to in the register for number 26a, and would have realized that number 26a did not include the rooms Chowdery was already occupying on the upper floors of number 26. This knowledge should be imputed to Chowdery, thus (it was argued) destroying the reasonableness of his belief in his ownership of the disputed rooms.

This argument was very firmly rejected by the Court of Appeal. Etherton LJ stated:

> 26. I do not accept the central proposition, advanced skilfully by Mr Evans, that the issue of reasonableness turns on the knowledge which the respondent's solicitors in 1993 would or should have had if they had been reasonably competent. There was no evidence before the Judge as to what those solicitors did or thought about the matter. Before the Judge, and in the skeleton arguments for the purpose of this appeal, the appellant criticised the failure of the respondent to produce the conveyancing file. It appears, however, that the firm of solicitors acting on the 1993 transfer on the respondent's behalf no longer exists, and it is certainly almost impossible now to locate the conveyancing file. Accordingly, precisely what those solicitors asked and knew is not before the court as a matter of evidence.

> 27. In my judgment, the issue is not the knowledge of a reasonably competent solicitor acting for the respondent in 1993. We are not here concerned with knowledge in the context, which frequently arises, of imputing an agent's knowledge to the principal. We are here concerned with the requirement as to the reasonable belief of a particular person. In this case, it is the respondent, but generally it is the person who is seeking to apply for registration of title by virtue of adverse possession. What is in issue therefore is not imputed knowledge but rather whether that particular person—here the respondent—was reasonable in holding the belief that he or she did in all the circumstances. That can involve a question as to whether the respondent should have made enquiries of his solicitors or elsewhere as to whether, notwithstanding his purchase of the freehold of No. 26a in 1993, the disputed property was in fact comprised within his paper title.

> 28. On the basis of the facts found by the Judge there was nothing to put the respondent on notice in 1993 that he needed to raise with his solicitors whether his title to No. 26a included the disputed property, of which he had enjoyed exclusive possession without challenge or question from the time he first acquired an interest in 1990 and the access to which obtained solely from No. 26a. That, in my judgment, is the end to the ground of appeal based upon the respondent's inferred knowledge derived from the assumed conduct of what would have been hypothetically competent solicitors.

In brief, the Court of Appeal held that in applying the 'reasonably believing encroacher' rule, it is only the *personal* beliefs of the encroacher which matter. In this context imputed knowledge/notice is not applicable.

What about the solicitor's letters which Chowdery had received in 2009 and 2010 questioning his ownership of the rooms? The Court of Appeal ruled that these letters did not shake the reasonableness of his beliefs.

> 29. So far as concerns the letters from the appellant challenging the title of the respondent to the disputed property in 2009 and 2010, it is clear from *Zarb v Parry* that the mere fact that a paper title owner challenges the asserted ownership of land by the adverse possessor is not in every case sufficient to render unreasonable any continuing belief of ownership on the part of adverse possessor. On the facts in *Zarb v Parry* the adverse possessor satisfied the requirement of reasonable belief even though that the paper title owner had challenged the assertion of ownership by the adverse possessor.
>
> 30. The question in each case is what, in all the circumstances, is the proper conclusion as to the reasonableness or otherwise of the continued belief as to ownership by the adverse possessor. In the present case, by the time of the letters from the appellants challenging the respondent's asserted title of the disputed property, the respondent had enjoyed unchallenged exclusive occupation for some 18 years. During that period the respondent's exclusive occupation of the disputed property had never been challenged or questioned by anyone who had any interest in No. 26, and indeed the appellant's own tenants had seemingly acknowledged that the disputed land was not being used by them, and access was only obtained via No. 26a. In the light of those facts the Judge was not only entitled but right to conclude that the letters from the appellants did not result in the continuing belief of the respondent that he owned the disputed property ceasing to be a reasonable one.

REVIEW QUESTION In 1999, Anwen became registered proprietor of Yellow Field. She promptly forgot about her new asset. Since 2001, Huw has intensively cultivated Yellow Field as part of his farm, and everyone in the area assumes Yellow Field is Huw's.

Advise Huw as to the legal status of Yellow Field, and whether there is anything he can do to secure his long-term position.

(Consider in particular the process we set out at 'Summary of Two Years' Inaction after Application for Rectification')

Leasehold

What if an Adverse Possessor Displaces a Tenant? Land Registration Act 1925

Briefly, the position under the pre-2003 law if a 'squatter' maintained adverse possession against a registered lease for more than 12 years was as follows:

- Under s75(1) LRA 1925 the original registered lessee held the lease in trust for the squatter. This approach differed from the unregistered land situation where we said that the squatter extinguishes the tenant's estate after 12 years. In registered land title was only extinguished when the register of title had been altered.

- The squatter had the right to apply for the register to be rectified in their favour so that they became the registered lessee.

- Once the register was rectified the original lessee had no rights whatsoever in the land. Therefore, once the register was rectified, the original lessee could not defeat the (former) squatter's claim by 'pulling the St Marylebone trick' (ie entering into one of the 'deals' suggested at thinking point 15.6).

- In *Spectrum Investments v Holmes* [1981] 1 WLR 221, the freehold of the premises was registered in 1901 and a 99-year lease was granted to a lessee from Christmas Day, 1902. This lease was registered early in 1903. In 1939, the lessee granted an oral weekly tenancy to Mrs Holmes. The lessee then assigned the lease to Mrs David, who was duly registered as proprietor thereof. Mrs Holmes stopped paying rent in 1944. She died in 1951 and her daughter, Miss Holmes, took up possession as her successor. Miss Holmes was registered with possessory title to the lease in 1968 and Mrs David's registered proprietorship was removed by the rectification of the register in 1968. In April 1975, the freehold reversion was transferred to the claimant, Spectrum Investment Co. In May 1975, Mrs David purportedly surrendered her lease to the claimant. The claimant then brought proceedings for possession against Miss Holmes. The court held that the purported surrender by Mrs David had no effect. She ceased to have any interest capable of being surrendered from the moment that the register was rectified in 1968.

Browne-Wilkinson J said:

... It is clear from the references in section 75(3) that section 75 applies to a leasehold interest. Under section 75(3) the registrar is under a mandatory duty to register the squatter on the application made by the squatter under section 75(2) if the registrar is satisfied as to the squatter's title. For what does the squatter make application? I will read section 75(2) again: 'Any person claiming to have acquired a title under the Limitation Acts to a registered estate in the land may apply to be registered as proprietor thereof.'

To my mind the words are clear and unequivocal: the squatter claims to have acquired a title to 'a registered estate in the land' (i.e. the leasehold interest) and applies to be registered as a proprietor '*thereof*' (my emphasis). Therefore under section 75(2), references to the squatter having acquired title to a registered estate must include the rights which under the Limitation Act 1939 the squatter acquires in relation to leasehold interests. Section 75(2) then refers to the squatter applying to be registered as proprietor 'thereof.' This word can, in my judgment, only refer back to the registered estate in the land against which the squatter has acquired title under the Act of 1939, i.e. the leasehold interest. *The clear words of the Act therefore seem to require that, once the 12 years have run, the squatter is entitled to be registered as proprietor of the lease itself, and is bound to be so registered if he applies for registration. It follows that in my judgment the defendant (as the squatter) is correctly registered as proprietor of the lease itself in accordance with the clear requirements of section 75. If that is right, Mrs. David cannot be entitled to rectification of the register as against the defendant, and she can therefore never get into a position in which she is competent to surrender the lease to the plaintiff.* [Emphasis added]

I am conscious that in so deciding I am reaching a conclusion which produces at least a limited divergence between squatter's rights over registered and unregistered land. Once the squatter is rightly registered as proprietor under section 75(3) the documentary lessee and the freeholder can no longer defeat the squatter's rights by a surrender. But I am not deciding anything as to the position during the period between the date when the squatter obtains his title by adverse possession and the date on which he obtains registration of it. This is the period covered by section 75(1) which is the subsection on which Lord Radcliffe in *St. Marylebone Property Co. Ltd.* v. *Fairweather* [1963] A.C. 510 542, and Sir John Pennycuick in *Jessamine Investment Co.* v. *Schwartz* [1978] Q.B. 264 , 275, were commenting. It may well be, as their dicta suggest, that during the period preceding any registration of the squatter's rights, the documentary lessee (as registered proprietor of the lease) and the freeholder can deal with the legal estate without reference to a person whose rights are not recorded on the register. But once the Act provides for registration of the squatter's title, it must in my judgment follow that the squatter's rights (once registered) cannot be overridden. The difference between registered and unregistered land in this respect is an inevitable consequence of the fact that the Land Registration Act 1925 provides for registration of the squatter as proprietor and that registered proprietors have rights.

Adverse Possession against a Lease under the Land Registration Act 2002

The position under the new law is much simpler than under the old. It is clear from the wording of the legislation that where adverse possession is taken against a leasehold estate, any applications by the adverse possessor for registration under Sch 6 paras 1 and 6 will be with respect to that leasehold estate, not the freehold. This will have the drawback for the (former) adverse possessor that he becomes subject to the covenants in the lease.

thinking point 15.15

In January 2000 Lakia leased 45 Green Water Close to Tamsin for 25 years. In January 2012, Squidge takes adverse possession of 45 Green Water Close. In February 2022, Squidge applies under Sch 6 para 1, but Tamsin objects, so his application is rejected. Nevertheless, Tamsin makes absolutely no effort to evict Squidge. It is now late 2024. Is there any point in Squidge now making an application under Sch 6 para 6?

Not really. By the time the application has been processed, the lease will have expired.

Concluding Remarks

Hopefully, you now see why at the beginning of this chapter we indicated that adverse possession is basically a simple concept which has always brought with it complex ramifications. The LRA 2002 has added to the complications.

Should the concept of adverse possession simply be abolished? Many non-lawyers consider that adverse possession is absurd. 'It's legalized theft.' (Actually, land cannot be stolen.) What arguments are there in defence of the concept of adverse possession? As previously stated, the concept is essential to the proper operation of unregistered title. By destroying stale claims to ownership, the concept ensures that the person who (together with his predecessors in title) has been in control of unregistered land for a lengthy period is indeed the owner.

This argument cannot be applied to registered land. The only arguments which can justify applying adverse possession to registered land are socio-economic, and rather controversial. Some would argue that land is a scarce commodity, and 'people' like Williams Brothers Ltd, and Buckinghamshire County Council should not allow land to lie derelict. By contrast, people like Messrs Raftery, Moran, and even Graham should be rewarded for their efforts.

The LRA 2002, by strengthening the position of the registered proprietor as against the adverse possessor, has largely rejected the socio-economic arguments in favour of the concept of adverse possession. However:

- the 'two years' inaction after application' exception in effect allows the socio-economic arguments to prevail in favour of the adverse possessor where the registered proprietor, having received a clear warning of the adverse possessor's claim, cannot be bothered to take action against the adverse possessor;

- the 'reasonably believing encroacher' rule, as applied in *IAM Group v Chowdery*, can work against a 'sleeping' landowner who allows a neighbour to make long-term use of land which according to the register lies on the sleeper's side of the boundary.

# Summary

Adverse Possession Defined

There is adverse possession where somebody (the 'squatter'):

- takes control of the land, that is, factual possession;
- with intent to exclude everyone else from the land; and
- the squatter's claim to the land is inconsistent ('adverse to') the title of the original owner.

Adverse Possession and Unregistered Land

Freehold Title

Once the adverse possession has lasted 12 years, the 'squatter' gains a new title based on long possession and the title of the original freehold owner is destroyed.

Leasehold Title

Once the adverse possession has lasted 12 years, the squatter cannot be evicted by the lessee. But the lease remains valid between the lessee and the lessor, and time does not start to run against the lessor until this 'notional' lease has terminated.

Adverse Possession and Registered Land

Where the 12 Years Expired before 13 October 2003

The legal title remains with the registered proprietor, but the 'squatter' has a right to have the register rectified in their favour. This right to rectification is a property right, and (if Sch 3 para 2 LRA 2002 is satisfied) it will be an overriding interest binding on a purchaser of the registered estate.

Adverse Possession under the Land Registration Act 2002

- No matter how long the adverse possession lasts, the squatter does not gain a property right against the registered estate.
- After the 'squatter' (S) has been in possession for ten years, they can *apply* to be registered as proprietor. Notice is given to the current owner (C). If C does not object, S will be registered as owner in place of C.
- If C does object, then subject to the 'reasonably believing encroacher' exception, S's application must be rejected.
- If S's first application is rejected, then C has two years within which to evict S (or grant to S some form of lease). If C does not act within two years, S can reapply to be registered as proprietor. And this second application must be granted.

Reasonably Believing Encroacher

S will succeed in their first application, despite C's objections, if they can show:

- S owns land adjacent to that in dispute; and
- for at least ten years, S reasonably believed the land in dispute was theirs.

Further Reading

Cooke, E, *The New Law of Land Registration*, Oxford: Hart, 2003, Chapter 7
A critical analysis of the provisions in the LRA 2002 regarding adverse possession.

Dixon, M, 'Human rights and adverse possession: the final nail?' [2008] Conv 160
Discussion of *Ofulue v Bossert* and whether *Pye v Graham* had finally decided whether adverse possession is human rights compatible.

Dockray, M, 'Why do we need adverse possession?' [1985] Conv 272
Provides an explanation of the rationale behind adverse possession.

Harpum, C, and Radley-Gardner, O, 'Adverse possession and the intention to possess—a reply' [2001] Conv 155
A critical evaluation of Tee's conclusions In her article published in 2000 (see below).

Lees, K, '*Parshall v Hackney*: A tale of two cities' [2013] Conv 222
A case comment on Parshall v Hackney.

Tee, L, 'Adverse possession and the intention to possess' [2000] Conv 113
For an extended debate on adverse possession and the intention to possess.

Tee, L, 'Adverse possession and the intention to possess' [2002] Conv 50
Response to Harpum's reply to Tee's earlier article.

 # Questions

Ewa holds a freehold title to Redacre. She uses most of Redacre for her business as a scrap merchant. However, she left vacant part of Redacre; this part is called the 'Grey Land'.

In 1989, Fran, the owner of nearby Blue House, started to cultivate Grey Land as an ornamental garden. Fran admits that, 'I have known all along that Grey Land belongs to Ewa.' Indeed, in 2002, Fran wrote to Ewa offering to buy Grey Land. (Ewa did not reply to this letter.)

Advise Fran as to the legal position with respect to Grey Land:

1 on the assumption that Ewa's title to the land is unregistered;

2 on the assumption that Ewa has been registered proprietor of Redacre (including Grey Land) since 1970.

On the assumption that Ewa has been the registered proprietor since 1970, would your advice be different if Fran had not started to cultivate the Grey Land until 1998, but had never written to Ewa offering to buy the land?

Part 8

Protection for the Purchaser of Registered Land

Rectification of the Register of Title

Introduction

Rectification of the register is a short but not unimportant topic. It is natural to deal with it immediately after adverse possession. With adverse possession somebody with apparent title to a parcel of land loses that title. The same is true of where the register is rectified.

As indicated in the previous chapter, if somebody maintained adverse possession against a registered proprietor for the requisite period, usually 12 years under pre-2003 law, they could apply to have the register rectified. On the register being rectified, the original owner ceased to have a legal title and the (former) adverse possessor acquired a legal title. Under post-2003 law, adverse possessors (such as the Parrys in *Zarb v Parry* and Chowdery in *IAM Group v Chowdery*) will still in effect be able to obtain rectification of the register in certain circumstances under Sch 6 Land Registration Act 2002 (LRA 2002).

Rectification of the register is not, however, confined to adverse possession situations. There may be other reasons why the register would need to be altered, for example there could be an error on the register of title. Section 65 LRA 2002 permits the register of title to be altered. It is important to have such a provision because the government guarantees the accuracy of the register through the indemnity principle. The government may have to pay compensation to a person who has suffered a loss as a consequence of the inaccuracy of the register of title (Sch 8 LRA 2002).

16.1 Rectification of the Register (Other Than Adverse Possession)

Rectification of the register in situations other than adverse possession is governed by Sch 4 LRA 2002. This schedule is not intended to change the substantive law on rectification, and reference to old pre-2003 cases will still therefore be very helpful. Schedule 4 does, however, clarify the terminology we should use when discussing making changes to the register.

Schedule 4 distinguishes between 'alteration' and 'rectification'. 'Alteration' is very broad in meaning, and covers every change made to the register whatever the circumstances. The concept 'rectification' is confined, by Sch 4 para 1, to an alteration 'which prejudicially affects the title of a registered proprietor', for example this may arise where an 'owner' loses land even though it is registered in their name.

The power to alter the register of title has been granted to the registrar and to the courts. Alteration of the register may involve 'correcting a mistake', 'bringing the register up to date', or 'giving effect to any estate, right or interest excepted from the effect of registration' (Sch 4 paras 2 and 5 LRA 2002). Additionally the land registrar has the power to remove a superfluous entry (Sch 4 para 5(d) LRA 2002).

We now set out Sch 4 in full, but we should immediately stress that para 3, sub-para 2 is *the* provision of central importance.

Land Registration Act 2002

Schedule 4 Alteration of the Register

Introductory

1 In this Schedule, references to rectification, in relation to alteration of the register, are to alteration which—

(a) involves the correction of a mistake, and

(b) prejudicially affects the title of a registered proprietor.

Alteration pursuant to a court order

2 (1) The court may make an order for alteration of the register for the purpose of—

(a) correcting a mistake,

(b) bringing the register up to date, or

(c) giving effect to any estate, right or interest excepted from the effect of registration.

(2) An order under this paragraph has effect when served on the registrar to impose a duty on him to give effect to it.

3 (1) This paragraph applies to the power under paragraph 2, so far as relating to rectification.

(2) If alteration affects the title of the proprietor of a registered estate in land, no order may be made under paragraph 2 without the proprietor's consent in relation to land in his possession unless—

(a) he has by fraud or lack of proper care caused or substantially contributed to the mistake, or

(b) it would for any other reason be unjust for the alteration not to be made.

(3) If in any proceedings the court has power to make an order under paragraph 2, it must do so, unless there are exceptional circumstances which justify its not doing so.

(4) In sub-paragraph (2), the reference to the title of the proprietor of a registered estate in land includes his title to any registered estate which subsists for the benefit of the estate in land.

4 Rules may—

(a) make provision about the circumstances in which there is a duty to exercise the power under paragraph 2, so far as not relating to rectification;

(b) make provision about the form of an order under paragraph 2;

(c) make provision about service of such an order.

Alteration otherwise than pursuant to a court order

5 The registrar may alter the register for the purpose of—

(a) correcting a mistake,

(b) bringing the register up to date,

(c) giving effect to any estate, right or interest excepted from the effect of registration, or

(d) removing a superfluous entry.

6 (1) This paragraph applies to the power under paragraph 5, so far as relating to rectification.

(2) No alteration affecting the title of the proprietor of a registered estate in land may be made under paragraph 5 without the proprietor's consent in relation to land in his possession unless—

(a) he has by fraud or lack of proper care caused or substantially contributed to the mistake, or

(b) it would for any other reason be unjust for the alteration not to be made.

(3) If on an application for alteration under paragraph 5 the registrar has power to make the alteration, the application must be approved, unless there are exceptional circumstances which justify not making the alteration.

(4) In sub-paragraph (2), the reference to the title of the proprietor of a registered estate in land includes his title to any registered estate which subsists for the benefit of the estate in land.

7 Rules may—

(a) make provision about the circumstances in which there is a duty to exercise the power under paragraph 5, so far as not relating to rectification;

(b) make provision about how the register is to be altered in exercise of that power;

(c) make provision about applications for alteration under that paragraph, including provision requiring the making of such applications;

(d) make provision about procedure in relation to the exercise of that power, whether on application or otherwise.

Rectification and derivative interests

8 The powers under this Schedule to alter the register, so far as relating to rectification, extend to changing for the future the priority of any interest affecting the registered estate or charge concerned.

Costs in non-rectification cases

9 (1) If the register is altered under this Schedule in a case not involving rectification, the registrar may pay such amount as he thinks fit in respect of any costs or expenses reasonably incurred by a person in connection with the alteration which have been incurred with the consent of the registrar.

(2) The registrar may make a payment under sub-paragraph (1) notwithstanding the absence of consent if—

(a) it appears to him—

(i) that the costs or expenses had to be incurred urgently, and

(ii) that it was not reasonably practicable to apply for his consent, or

(b) he has subsequently approved the incurring of the costs or expenses.

The Situations Where Rectification of the Register May Be Appropriate

Put simply, rectification of the register (by order of the court or of the Registry) will be appropriate whenever a mistake has occurred which has resulted in somebody being registered as an owner when they should not really be entitled to the land. Experience indicates that these 'mistakes' usually fall into one of three categories:

- double conveyancing;
- some other mess-up which has resulted in the wrong person being registered as owner; and
- fraud and/or forgery.

16.2.1 'Double Conveyancing'

'Double conveyancing' occurs where somebody owns a piece of land, conveys that land to one person, and then later purports to convey the same land to somebody else.

thinking point 16.1

Consider the following example of 'double conveyancing' on the assumption that all the titles involved are unregistered. Xena owned the freehold to Greenfield; Greenfield included a small area known as Greypatch.

In 1980, Xena sold Greypatch to Yolanda; the legal estate to Greypatch was conveyed to Yolanda. It would be the normal practice for Yolanda to ensure that the fact of the sale of Greypatch was endorsed upon the title deeds to Greenfield. Yolanda (perhaps she was a 'do-it-yourself conveyancer') failed to do so. In 1987, Xena (purportedly) conveyed the whole of Greenfield, including Greypatch, to Zosia. Who owns Greypatch?

The answer is (of course) Yolanda. Xena, having already given up ownership of Greypatch to Yolanda, cannot convey it to Zosia.

thinking point 16.2

What if, in a case of double conveyancing, the area in which the land is situated becomes an area of compulsory registration between the dates of the two conveyances? Change (slightly) the facts of thinking point 16.1.

In 1985, the district in which Greenfield is situated became an area of compulsory registration of title, and in 1987 Zosia applied for registration as proprietor of the whole of Greenfield. Zosia presented to the Registry a perfect set of title deeds for the whole of Greenfield. What would the Registry do?

The Registry would of course grant Zosia an absolute title to Greenfield, including Greypatch. Zosia will therefore become legal owner of Greypatch. Yolanda will lose her title to Greypatch, but is likely to seek rectification. Whether she gets rectification will depend on the application of the rules discussed at 16.2.4.

thinking point 16.3

Will the problems caused by 'double conveyancing' ever completely disappear?

Only when there is no land left which is unregistered.

16.2.2 Other (Possibly Negligent) Mistakes

The facts of *Re 139 Deptford High Street* [1951] 1 Ch D 884 are instructive, even though, for reasons which will emerge later, the case would be decided differently today. Prior to 1948, number 139 was unregistered title. In 1948, V sold number 139 to P. The conveyance, which had no plan attached, described the land as 'all that shop and dwelling house situate and known as 139, High Street, Deptford in the County of London'. P applied for first registration.

It appears that V, P, their respective legal advisers, and the Land Registry all (reasonably) thought that number 139 included a small piece of disused land at the back next to the railway. P was registered as proprietor of the dwelling house/shop and the land at the back. In fact this land really 'belonged to' British Railways. The registration thus deprived the railway of that small piece of land. When the railway found out, it sought and obtained rectification of the register on the basis that P (albeit innocently) had caused the error at the Registry by submitting inaccurate documents.

A very different kind of 'mistake' to that in *Re 139 Deptford High Street* arose in *Baxter v Mannion* [2011] EWCA Civ 120, which involved the operation of the machinery of Sch 6 LRA 2002 discussed in the previous chapter (at 'The Fundamental (Post-2003) Principle Regarding Adverse Possession—The Almost Sacrosanct Title of the Registered Proprietor' under section 15.8.2). Mannion was registered as owner of a small field in which for some years Baxter (without permission) occasionally grazed horses. In May 2006 Baxter boldly (but not fraudulently) applied under Sch 6 to be registered as proprietor of the field. As a result of a mixture of personal illness and family problems Mannion did not respond to the notice informing him of the Sch 6 application. Baxter was therefore registered as owner of the field.

On an application for rectification of the register by Mannion, the Land Registry Adjudicator rejected Baxter's evidence that he had been in everyday occupation of the field. It followed that he had not been in adverse possession, and that the Registry should not have granted his Sch 6 application. The Adjudicator held that there had been a 'mistake' under Sch 4 para 5 LRA 2002, and ordered rectification of the register. On appeal, Henderson J and the Court of Appeal affirmed all these conclusions.

16.2.3 Registration Obtained through Fraud and/or Forgery

This is illustrated, first, by a story which happened at about the time of the First World War when there was a notorious criminal at work in London. He operated in the following way:

- He would find a wealthy spinster who owned her own house.
- He would marry her.
- He would forge a conveyance or land transfer of her house in his favour.
- On the strength of the forgery, he got himself registered as proprietor of the house.
- He would murder his wife by drowning her in the bath.

And so on . . .

When he was caught, the personal representatives of the unfortunate women sought and obtained rectification of the register against the criminal.

A second, very modern illustration is certain facts of a case which was discussed in Chapters 5 and 6, *Malory v Cheshire Homes* [2002] Ch 216. You may recall that the case involved a derelict piece of land which had belonged to the claimants, 'Malory Enterprises (BVI)'. How Cheshire Homes (the well-known charity for the severely disabled) came to be registered proprietors of the derelict land is explained in para 5 of the judgment:

> In 1996 a company was dishonestly set up in the United Kingdom with the name Malory Enterprises Ltd ['Malory UK']. By deception this company obtained from [the] Land Registry a new land certificate in which the name of the proprietor was stated to be 'Malory Enterprises Ltd' of a new address. It then sold and executed a transfer of the [disputed] rear land to Cheshire, which was then registered as proprietor . . .

In effect Malory UK had impersonated Malory BVI, and fooled both the Registry and Cheshire Homes. When Malory BVI discovered the fraud, they sought and obtained rectification of the register. (As we saw in Chapter 6, its claim to the derelict land was held to be an overriding interest by virtue of the fact that Malory BVI was still in actual occupation at the time of the 'transfer' to Cheshire.)

REVIEW QUESTION Bearing in mind the modern problem of 'identity theft', are we likely to get more cases where X gets registered as owner of land which really should belong to Y?

(See also what follows in 16.2.4.)

16.2.4 Rectification Against a Registered Proprietor in Possession

In the various situations like those discussed in 16.2.1 to 16.2.3, the parties who 'have lost their land' will claim rectification of the register, if need be, by litigation.

However, if a claim for rectification is brought against a registered proprietor who is in possession of the disputed land (and most defendants to a rectification claim will be in possession) then the claim is subject to restrictions set out in Sch 4 paras 3(2) and 6(2) LRA 2002.

> *Land Registration Act 2002*
>
> Schedule 4 Alteration of the Register
>
> Alteration pursuant to a court order
>
> 3 ...
>
> (2) If alteration affects the title of the proprietor of a registered estate in land, no order may be made under paragraph 2 without the proprietor's consent in relation to land in his possession unless—
>
> > (a) he has by fraud or lack of proper care caused or substantially contributed to the mistake, or
> >
> > (b) it would for any other reason be unjust for the alteration not to be made.
> >
> > ...
>
> (4) In sub-paragraph (2), the reference to the title of the proprietor of a registered estate in land includes his title to any registered estate which subsists for the benefit of the estate in land.
>
> ...
>
> Alteration otherwise than pursuant to a court order
>
> 6 ...
>
> (2) No alteration affecting the title of the proprietor of a registered estate in land may be made under paragraph 5 without the proprietor's consent in relation to land in his possession unless—
>
> > (a) he has by fraud or lack of proper care caused or substantially contributed to the mistake, or
> >
> > (b) it would for any other reason be unjust for the alteration not to be made.
> >
> > ...
>
> (4) In sub-paragraph (2), the reference to the title of the proprietor of a registered estate in land includes his title to any registered estate which subsists for the benefit of the estate in land.

These provisions, which reflect s82(3) Land Registration Act 1925 (LRA 1925) (as amended in 1977), puts a registered proprietor in possession in a strong position. The registered proprietor can only lose the land registered in their name if:

- they were fraudulent; or
- they were negligent; or
- it is for some other reason unjust not to rectify the register.

Clarification has been provided by the LRA 2002 with regards to who is included within the scope of a 'proprietor in possession'.

> *Land Registration Act 2002*
>
> 131. 'Proprietor in possession'
>
> (1) For the purposes of this Act, land is in the possession of the proprietor of a registered estate in land if it is physically in his possession, or in that of a person who is entitled to be registered as the proprietor of the registered estate.
>
> (2) In the case of the following relationships, land which is (or is treated as being) in the possession of the second-mentioned person is to be treated for the purposes of subsection (1) as in the possession of the first-mentioned person—
>
>   (a) landlord and tenant;
>   (b) mortgagor and mortgagee;
>   (c) licensor and licensee;
>   (d) trustee and beneficiary.
>
> (3) In subsection (1), the reference to entitlement does not include entitlement under Schedule 6.

Put simply, 'proprietor in possession' includes not only owners who are in actual physical possession, but also owners who have handed over actual possession to a tenant, licensee, or beneficiary of a trust of land (s131(2) LRA 2002). It even includes a mortgagor owner whose mortgagee has taken possession with a view to selling the property. The adverse possessor is not regarded as being in possession for the purposes of rectification of title (s131(3) LRA 2002).

Rectification Against a Fraudulent Proprietor in Possession

The murderer-cum-fraudster in the 'Brides in the Bath' case in 16.2.3 would clearly (even in modern law) have no defence to a claim for rectification.

Rectification Against a Negligent Proprietor in Possession

thinking point 16.4

What if a case like Re 139 Deptford High Street, *discussed in 16.2.2, were to occur today; would rectification be granted?*

Rectification of the register would be refused. A registered proprietor in possession who had obtained registration by putting forward inaccurate document(s) would now be caught under Sch 4 para 6(2) only if either:

- *the registered proprietor knew that the document(s) were inaccurate (that would be a case of fraud); or*

- *the registered proprietor ought to have known that the documents were inaccurate (that would be a case of 'lack of proper care').*

thinking point 16.5

Applying the modern law to the facts of Re 139 Deptford High Street, *would it make any difference if the documents submitted to the Land Registry had included a plan showing the small piece of land 'at the back' as part of number 139?*

Only if the person submitting the documents knew or ought to have known that the plan was inaccurate.

Rectification Where it Would be Unjust Not to Rectify

Two points should be made about the provision which is now Sch 4 para 6(2) LRA 2002 (formerly s82(3)(c) LRA 1925):

- It is clear from its context and wording (particularly the use of a double negative) that this provision should be used only in a case where it is absolutely clear that justice demands that the register be rectified.

- There has been only one case of real significance involving s82(3)(c) (*Epps v Esso* [1973] 1 WLR 1071). In that case, Templeman J, applying the no-nonsense approach for which he (as Lord Templeman) became famous, refused rectification. The approach adopted by Templeman J in *Epps* is very much in line with the approach adopted by Parliament in 2002 that rectification should only be granted in exceptional circumstances.

In *Epps v Esso*, from 1935 to 1955, C had owned the whole of the relevant area, situated in Gillingham, Kent (see Diagram 16.1).

Diagram 16.1
The land in dispute in Epps v Esso [1973]

R O A D	House
	Strip
	Garage

In 1955, C's personal representatives conveyed the house and strip to Edna Jones. She covenanted to erect a wall between the strip and the garage, but failed to do so. The existing fence between strip and house remained in situ. The strip therefore appeared to 'belong to' the garage.

In 1957, Gillingham became an area of compulsory registration.

In 1959, C's personal representatives conveyed the garage and strip to Ball. Ball applied for first registration, and was registered as proprietor of both garage and strip. There was thus a 'double conveyancing' situation (see 16.1.1). But as Ball, the second purchaser, had become registered proprietor of the strip, he had legal title, and not the first purchaser, Edna Jones. (This is the same as Greypatch in thinking point 16.2.)

Since 1959, the strip had been in use as part of the garage. In 1964, Ball sold the garage including the strip, to Esso; Esso became registered proprietor.

In 1968, Edna Jones's personal representatives sold the house and purported to sell the strip to Epps, but the Land Registry refused to register him as proprietor of the strip. He applied for rectification. Rectification was refused by the court. Templeman J said:

> In the confrontation envisaged...the registered proprietor, who is a victim of double conveyancing, and the first purchaser or his successors, deprived of the legal estate by registration, the court must first determine whether the registered proprietor is in possession. If the

registered proprietor is not in possession then s 82(3) [LRA 1925] does not apply, and the court will normally grant rectification: see *Chowood Ltd v Lyall* (No 2) [1930] 2 Ch 156. A fortiori if the registered proprietor is not in possession but the applicant has an overriding interest constituted by an equitable interest protected by actual occupation, the court will grant rectification: see *Bridges v Mees* [1957] Ch 475 at 486. However, the power of rectification given by s 82(1) never ceases to be discretionary, so that where s 82(3) does not apply there may still be circumstances which defeat the claim for rectification.

If the registered proprietor is in possession, the applicant for rectification will not normally be in actual occupation, and one of the conditions specified in s 82(3) must be satisfied if rectification is to be granted. If the registered proprietor is the first registered proprietor and has caused or contributed to the mistake in registration then s 82(3), condition (a) applies, and rectification will normally be granted: see *Re 139 High Street, Deptford* [1951] Ch 884. But where the applicant has, for example, allowed the registered proprietor to build on the land, then, even though the conditions in s 82(3)(a) have been satisfied, the court, taking the hint from s 82(3)(c) and exercising the discretion conferred by s 82(1), may refuse to rectify: see *Re Sea View Gardens, Claridge v Tingey* [1967] 1 WLR 134.

If the proprietor is not the first registered proprietor but is a subsequent transferee he will not normally be responsible for the mistake in registration in any way at all, so that the conditions specified in s 82(3)(a) will not be satisfied; to this limited extent a subsequent transferee is in a better position than the first registered proprietor. But whether the proprietor be the first registered proprietor or a subsequent transferee rectifications will still be granted under s 82(3)(c) if for any reason in any particular case it is considered that it would be unjust not to rectify the register against the registered proprietor.

It follows that the crucial questions in the present case are, first, whether Mr Jones was in actual occupation of the disputed strip when the defendants completed their purchase in 1964; secondly, whether the defendants were in possession at the date when the plaintiffs completed their purchase of 4 Darland Avenue in 1968; and if those questions are decided in favour of the defendants, thirdly, whether it would be unjust not to rectify against them . . .

In my judgment Mr Jones was not in actual occupation of the disputed strip when the defendants completed their purchase of Darland Garage, and was not thereafter in actual occupation.

Mr Jones gave evidence that every night he parked his car on the disputed strip, and sometimes the car was there during the day. Mr Jones's recollection, not unnaturally, was not very reliable, and I find that he sometimes parked his car on the disputed strip, but how often and when no one can now determine with any certainty. But even if Mr Jones regularly parked his car on the disputed strip I do not consider that this constituted actual occupation of the disputed strip in the circumstances of the present case. I reach this conclusion for the following reasons. First, the parking of a car on a strip 11 feet wide by 80 feet long does not actually occupy the whole, or a substantial, or any defined part of that disputed strip for the whole or any defined time. Secondly, the parking of a car on an unidentified piece of land, apparently comprised in garage premises, is not an assertion of actual occupation of anything.

In addition to these two reasons there are circumstances which show that, not only was Mr Jones not in actual occupation, but on the contrary the defendants were. First, there is no evidence that Mr Ball or the defendants were ever aware that Mr Jones parked his car on the disputed strip . . . Secondly, the brick wall four feet from the house, 4 Darland Avenue, was an assertion that the occupier of Darland Garage occupied land up to that wall, and was just as much in possession of the disputed strip as of any other part of the apparent Darland Garage premises. Thirdly, as appears from the defendants' photographs, there was no method of driving on to the strip from Darland Avenue without trespassing on to the garage premises unless the car in question was bounced up the kerb and steered between a stop-sign and a tree. These difficulties could, no doubt, be overcome, but they added force to the apparent assertion by all the indications on the ground that the disputed strip was part and parcel of Darland Garage and was occupied and possessed therewith, and that the claim and title of 4 Darland

Avenue ceased where the brick wall ceased. In the result Mr Jones and the plaintiffs were, in my judgment, never at any material time in actual occupation of the disputed strip, and the defendants were at all material times in possession of the disputed strip. The defendants claimed that they occupied the disputed strip by depositing waste materials on the strip as part of the garage land. Precise evidence of this was, not unnaturally, impossible to obtain. I accept, however, that they did treat the disputed strip just in the same way that they treated any other part of the garage land and premises.

In my judgment, therefore, s 82(3) does apply because Mr and Mrs Jones and the plaintiffs had no overriding interest protected by actual occupation and because the defendants were in possession. There remains the question, under s 82(2)(c), whether it would be unjust not to rectify against the defendants.

In my judgment, justice in the present case lies wholly with the defendants and not with the plaintiffs. There was nothing on the register or on the ground on or before the date when the defendants became the registered proprietors of the disputed strip which put them on enquiry. On the contrary, both the register and the appearance on the ground proclaimed that title to and possession of the disputed strip and the garage premises were one and indivisible. No reasonable requisition by the defendants from their vendor, Mr Ball, would in the circumstances have disclosed the existence of, let alone any claim to, the disputed strip. The absence of any indication on the ground was due to the default of the plaintiffs' predecessor in title in not complying with her covenant to build a boundary wall which would mark out the disputed strip. On the other hand, the plaintiffs, even without hindsight, were taking a gamble. The title disclosed to them showed the obligations of Mrs Jones to build a boundary wall. Inspection of the site disclosed that the only wall in existence was the original wall four feet from the side of the house. It was possible that the frontage of 39 feet mentioned in the 1955 conveyance was a mistake; whether it was a mistake or not it was possible that the true 1955 boundary between 4 Darland Avenue and Darland Garage was the line of the original wall. If the true 1955 boundary was not the existing wall but a new wall to be constructed on the northern boundary of the disputed strip it was possible that because of the failure to build the wall or to mark out the disputed strip, title to the disputed strip had been lost by adverse possession, or, as in fact happened, by a natural mistake on registration.

The plaintiffs must have realised that there might be some difficulty over the boundary between 4 Darland Avenue and Darland Garage; hence Mr Epps's letter dated 31st July 1968. The enquiries made in that letter after completion could have been made, and ought to have been made, before completion. The plaintiffs or their legal advisers, if properly instructed, ought to have required their vendor, Mr Jones, to prove that the boundary between 4 Darland Avenue and Darland Garage was 11 feet from the brick wall, and was known to and acknowledged by the owner of Darland Garage to be that unmarked boundary and not the apparent boundary constituted by the brick wall four feet from the side wall of the house. The plaintiffs or their legal advisers, if properly instructed, ought to have realised that, without further enquiries to their vendor, and enquiries by their vendor to the defendants, it had not been established that the vendor was in a position to give a good title or in a position to give possession of the disputed strip to the plaintiffs.

In my judgment, whereas the defendants bought the disputed strip, the plaintiffs bought a law suit, thanks to the default of their vendor in not taking steps to assert ownership and possession of the disputed strip, and thanks to the failure of the plaintiffs to make before completion the enquiries which they made immediately after completion. [Emphasis added]

Templeman J regarded as totally irrelevant the following two arguments:

• Epps was in an unequal bargaining position (ie 'little man') claiming rectification against a huge organization. A strip 11 feet by 80 feet was a lot of land for Epps; to a multinational like Esso it was tiny.

• That the rules governing the grant of 'indemnity' (ie compensation) were much more generous to Esso than to Epps. If rectification had been granted against Esso, it would have got full compensation at a 1973 valuation. If rectification was refused, Epps would seemingly have got no compensation (see 16.4.2).

Templeman J was of the view that, 'Justice in the present case lies wholly with the defendants.' He applied what we call 'a comparative conveyancing care' approach. When Esso purchased the garage, both the register and the physical layout of the site indicated that the strip was part of the garage. When Epps purchased the house the title deeds said that the strip was part of the house. But the fact that no brick wall had been erected, and the physical appearance of the site, should have warned him that there was a problem. He should have raised the question of the boundaries with Esso before going ahead with his purchase. Templeman J summarized the situation by saying: 'Whereas the defendants bought the disputed strip, the plaintiffs bought a law suit.'

thinking point 16.6

Consider again the sad situation of the 'Brides in the Bath' murderer/fraudster. If the murderer/fraudster had sold one of the houses to a purchaser, who had moved in, could the register be rectified, under modern law, against such a purchaser?

The personal representatives would succeed in getting rectification only if they could show that the purchaser knew or ought to have known that the murderer/fraudster had gained title by criminal activities. If the purchaser (like Esso in Epps v Esso) had bought an apparently sound title, the personal representatives should not get rectification under the 'unjust not to rectify' heading.

cross-reference
See Chapter 15.5.1 under Adverse Possession Where One Plot Has Two Registered Owners? for the facts of Parshall v Hackney.

'Justice' where the same plot is registered to two owners

In *Parshall v Hackney* [2013] EWCA Civ 240, almost the whole judgment of the Court of Appeal is devoted to the issue of whether the respondent was in adverse possession of the few square metres of disputed land which had been registered in the names of two separate owners. Having concluded that the respondent's undoubted possession of the land was not 'adverse', the Court of Appeal quickly concluded in just one sentence that *it was just* to rectify the register. Mummery, LJ at para 97 said:

> The points forcefully advanced by Mr Rodger [leading counsel for the respondent] against rectification could not disguise the plain unvarnished fact that his client is seeking to take the benefit of a mistake by the Land Registry, which had occurred through no fault on the appellants' side and which it would be unjust not to correct.

The inference to be drawn from this ruling is that where through a mistake at the Land Registry Y becomes registered proprietor of a plot which is already registered in the name of X, it will (at least normally) be just to rectify against Y even if Y (as was the case in *Parshall v Hackney*) has been in possession of the disputed land for a considerable period.

It is respectfully submitted that the Court of Appeal's ruling on this point is wrong. Justice should surely favour the competing proprietor who makes active use of the 'double registered' land.

Walker v Burton—Not Unjust to Leave a (Major) Mistake Unrectified

The situation in *Walker v Burton* [2013] EWCA 1228 was extremely different from that in *Parshall v Hackney*.

In 2000 the Burtons bought from Mr and Mrs Brown an old farm house 'Over Hall' in the tiny Pennine village of Ireby. The sale to them did not expressly refer to the Lordship of the Manor of Ireby, but the Burtons reasonably believed, on the basis of earlier documents (one as recent as 1995) that the Lordship passed to them on the sale of Over Hall.

A Lordship of the Manor is an **incorporeal hereditament** (see Introduction in Chapter 1) the title to which could be registered under the Land Registration Act 1925 but cannot now be under the Land Registration Act 2002. The Burtons took advice from a firm of solicitors specializing in manors, and on 10th October 2003 (three days before the 2002 Act came into force) registered their 'ownership' of the Lordship of the Manor.

More importantly, in economic terms, the Burtons reasonably believed, on the advice of the specialist solicitors, that by virtue of their ownership of the Lordship of the Manor they also owned the local 'manorial waste', poor quality land of about 300 acres called 'Ireby Fell'. In February 2005 they applied to be registered as (first) proprietors of the fell. Mr Burton made a statutory declaration that, to the best of his knowledge, 'Ireby Fell has always been in the ownership of the Lord of the Manor of Ireby'. (Para. 27 of the Court of Appeal judgment.) The Land Registry registered the Burtons as proprietors of Ireby Fell.

The applicants, a few villagers not actually claiming any rights over the Fell, sought rectification of the register. They sought closure of both files; the registration of the Lordship and the registration of the Fell. Before the Deputy Land Registry Adjudicator they succeeded regarding the Lordship of the Manor and that file was closed. But the Deputy adjudicator refused rectification with respect to Ireby Fell. These conclusions were affirmed by a Deputy High Court judge, and then by the Court of Appeal.

With respect to the (incorporeal) Lordship of the Manor, the deputy adjudicator found on the basis of historic evidence that, despite the modern documentation referring to the Lordship, the Lordship had actually been extinguished by (at the latest) the 17th century. Moreover, Sch 4 para 6(2) LRA 2002 could not protect the Burtons' claim to the Lordship. Mummery, LJ, giving the judgment of the Court of Appeal explains:

> 47 [as] regards the Lordship, the question of protecting the registered proprietor in possession of it could not arise, as possession refers to physical possession of 'land' as defined in the 2002 Act. That is not possible in the case of the Lordship: it is an incorporeal hereditament, not land as defined in s. 132 of the 2002 Act; cf the definition of land in s. 205(ix) of the Law of Property Act 1925, which included a manor or lordship. It follows that, as regards the registration of the Lordship, the issues of lack of care contributing to mistaken registration and the injustice of not correcting the mistake did not arise for consideration.

Sch 4 para 6(2) LRA 2002 was however crucial with respect to Ireby Fell. Registering the Burtons as owners of the Fell was undoubtedly a 'mistake' by the Land Registry. On the issue of whether the Burtons had contributed to the mistake by fraud or lack of proper care, the Court of Appeal at para 98 said:

> ... [T]he Deputy Adjudicator was entitled to reach the conclusion on the materials before him and the submissions that this was not a case of lack of care causing or contributing to the mistaken registration of the Fell. The Burtons had behaved reasonably and responsibly in engaging solicitors to advise them and to act for them. The standard to be applied to the solicitors was that of an ordinary competent solicitor undertaking work of that type. The position on the Fell registration was that the Lordship had been expressly conveyed to the Burtons by the sellers of Over Hall Farm. The declaration made by Mr Burton in 2005 was found to be in good faith and in the honest belief that it was true that the Lordship had

been registered and the Fell went with it as waste of the Manor. That belief of Mr Burton was reasonable having regard to what was known about the title to the Lordship, in particular the provisions of the 1836 Stinting Agreement [controlling grazing on the Fell]. It was unreasonable to expect him to go back beyond that in order to research the earlier origins of the Lordship.

Was it unjust not to rectify the register of the Fell? The applicants argued that as the registration of the Lordship was closed, the same must logically follow for the registration of the Fell.

94 I understand the basic logic of the argument that, as there was a mistake in the registration of the Fell, then it ought to be rectified, particularly when (a) the title to the Fell depended on the title to the Lordship; (b) the mistaken registration of the Fell was consequential on the mistaken registration of the title to the Lordship; and (c) the mistaken registration of the title to the Lordship has been ordered to be rectified by closing that title.

95 Though logical, I do not think that the Deputy Judge was wrong to reject that submission in the face of para. 6(2) which requires the court to take the specified factors into account in cases where there is a registered proprietor in possession of the land. That was not the case with the correction of the Lordship registration, because the Lordship does not fall within the definition of 'land', it being an incorporeal hereditament. *The consequential nature of the mistaken registration of the Fell does not result in the disapplication or downgrading of para 6(2).* [Emphasis added.]

There were two separate titles to be considered. The title to the 'incorporeal' Lordship was not protected by para 6(2), but the title to the Fell (physical land controlled by the Burtons) was.

Despite the unusual way in which the Burtons had gained ownership of the Fell, the Court of Appeal had no difficulty in holding that it was not unjust not to rectify the register against them. In deciding that it was fair to leave the Burtons as owners of 300 acres for which they had not paid, two factors seem to have been decisive.

102 ... [T]here was no prospect of anyone else except the Burtons being registered as proprietors of the Fell. On the one hand, while the appellants had standing to make the application to correct the mistake in the Register, they did not have, or even claim to have, title to the Fell. On the other hand, the Crown, which in the submission of the appellants and in the view of the Deputy Judge has a valid title to the Fell, showed (and still shows) no sign of asserting title against the Burtons, or wishing to engage in this dispute. In those circumstances it was a relevant consideration that the Fell should be owned by someone rather than left in limbo with continuing uncertainty about title to it.

105 ... [T]here was relevant credible evidence from Mr Burton that, since entering in possession of the Fell, he had invested time, effort and money on improving the Fell and its management, had discouraged harmful practices, such as tipping waste and use of motorised vehicles, had used the property as an amenity and had entered into commitments on which they and others relied. The Burtons had entered into grazing licensing agreements from October 2005 onwards and a sporting rights agreement for a 10 year term and had spent money on gates and posts, for which invoices were produced.

The ruling in *Walker v Burton* (contrast *Parshall v Hackney*) is surely correct. If somebody, albeit as a result of a good faith mistake, gets registered as proprietor of a parcel of land which would otherwise be ownerless, and spends money/time/effort managing that land, it is just that they should remain owner.

16.3 The Effect of Rectification on Priorities

Under Schedule 4 paragraph 8 the court and Registrar have the power to 'alter the register, so far as relating to rectification, extend to changing for the future the priority of any interest affecting the registered estate or charge concerned'. From the wording of this provision it appears that the effect of rectification is to alter the future priority of interests, and consequently does not operate retrospectively in relation to the earlier mistake.

The Court of Appeal in *Gold Harp Properties Ltd v Macleod* [2014] EWCA Civ 1084 considered whether rectification of the register which involved restoring an interest which has been removed would take priority over an interest which had been granted at a date between removal and restoration. In this case a notice of lease which had been removed from the register of title was held to have been done so by mistake. The Court of Appeal had to consider whether the earlier restored lease took priority over a subsequently registered lease. Underhill LJ concluded:

> 93. The primary effect of paragraph 8 is to confirm that the power of the Court or Registrar in that situation is not limited to restoring interest A to the Register but 'extends' to changing what would otherwise be the priority as between it and interest B—in other words, to giving it the priority which it should have had but for the mistake. The words 'for the future' no doubt qualify that power—the question being in what way—but that is the context in which they fall to be interpreted . . .
>
> 95. It is worth recalling that Schedule 4 is concerned with 'correcting' mistakes in the Register, and it is established by the decisions to which I have referred that the power to do so extends to correcting the consequences of such mistakes. It should be noted that that power is in some circumstances a duty: see paragraph 3 (3) . . .
>
> 96. . . . What paragraph 8 permits (for the future) is 'changing the priority' of an interest. What an interest having priority means is that the owner can exercise the rights which he enjoys by virtue of that interest to the exclusion of any inconsistent rights of the owner of the competing interest. The concept of priority thus bites at the moment that those rights are sought to be enjoyed. Once that is appreciated the effect of the words 'for the future' seems to me straightforward. *They mean that the beneficiary of the change in priority—that is, the person whose interest has been restored to the Register—can exercise his rights as owner of that interest, to the exclusion of the rights of the owner of the competing interest, as from the moment that the order is made, but that he cannot be treated as having been entitled to do so up to that point.* [Emphasis added]

Significantly this judgment not only restores the interest which was removed from the register by mistake but also reinstates the priority of that interest over the new interest which was registered at a later date. The court in this case not only dealt with the issue of restoring a mistake but also the consequences of having restored the interest. Rectification had, '. . . "retrospective effect" in relation to the priorities of competing interests affecting the registered estate, so that henceforth the priorities which previously subsisted, and which would otherwise have continued to subsist but for the rectification, are changed—albeit for the future only rather than this effect being "backdated" as such.' (Ruoff & Roper, at 46.018)

16.4 Indemnity

16.4.1 Indemnity for a Registered Proprietor Where Rectification is Granted

This is governed by Sch 8 LRA 2002. In practice, rectifications of the register are not that common, and that is something which everyone concerned thinks should remain the case. As Templeman J pointed out in *Epps v Esso*, the whole purpose of land registration is to guarantee titles by making them secure.

In those cases where rectification is ordered, Sch 8 LRA 2002 operates. Prima facie, a registered proprietor against whom rectification is granted is entitled to indemnity, that is, compensation. The registered proprietor will get the value of the estate or interest they lose, valued as at the date of rectification (see Sch 8 para 6(a) LRA 2002).

A registered proprietor who is rectified against, will however get no indemnity whatsoever if the rectification is to give effect to an overriding interest (*Re Chowood* [1933] Ch 574). This is clearly logical. A proprietor is in any event bound by an overriding interest. The proprietor thus loses nothing when the register is rectified against them. In *Re Chowood*, an adverse possessor had gained title to part of a piece of land of which Chowood Ltd was registered proprietor. The adverse possessor obtained rectification of the register. Chowood Ltd was held not to be entitled to any indemnity. The adverse possessor had an overriding interest under s70(1)(f) LRA 1925 and Chowood lost nothing as a result of the rectification.

Contrast this with a situation where the person is a victim of forgery and who has an overriding interest, then following *Swift 1st Ltd v Chief Land Registrar* [2014] All ER (D) 12 (February) there is a loss which will be indemnified.

A registered proprietor who is rectified against, will also get no indemnity whatsoever if he falls foul of what is now Sch 8 para 5(1):

> *Land Registration Act 2002*
>
> Schedule 8 Indemnities
>
> Claimant's fraud or lack of care
>
> 5. (1) No indemnity is payable under this Schedule on account of any loss suffered by a claimant—
>   (a) wholly or partly as a result of his own fraud; or
>   (b) wholly as a result of his own lack of proper care.

What then if the error which led to the rectification was partly as a result of a lack of proper care by the registered proprietor and partly the fault of someone else (perhaps the Registry)? This is covered by para 5(2):

> *Land Registration Act 2002*
>
> Schedule 8 Indemnities
>
> Claimant's fraud or lack of care
>
> 5. (2) Where any loss is suffered by a claimant partly as a result of his own lack of proper care, any indemnity payable to him is to be reduced to such extent as is fair having regard to his share in the responsibility for the loss.

There is here an analogy with the law of tort. Prior to 1945, a victim of (say) a road accident partly caused by the defendant's negligence but the victim was also partly to blame, could not recover any damages. The Law Reform (Contributory Negligence) Act 1945 allows the court to award such a victim an appropriate percentage of the damages they could have recovered if they had been innocent of all blame.

thinking point 16.7

Suppose the facts of Re 139 Deptford High Street *occur again today, except it is established that both the purchaser of number 139 and the Registry were negligent in not spotting the discrepancy in the documents of title. What would the court decide on an application by the railway for rectification of the register?*

1   It would rectify the register under the 'negligent proprietor in possession' rule.

2   It would award the purchaser of number 139 indemnity based on the current value of the land.

3   However, that indemnity would be reduced by whatever percentage the court considered appropriate, bearing in mind what may be called the purchaser's contributory negligence.

16.4.2 Indemnity for a Person Who is Refused Rectification

Schedule 8 para 1(b) LRA 2002 (formerly s83(2) LRA 1925) is designed to provide for the payment of indemnity where the restrictive provisions regarding rectification against a proprietor in possession in Sch 4 para 3(2) led to rectification being refused despite some error in the Registry. This form of indemnity is supposed to protect somebody like *Epps* (see section 16.2.4 under the heading 'Rectification Where it Would be Unjust Not to Rectify'). However, as Mr Justice Templeman realized in *Epps v Esso* there were two drawbacks for Mr Epps, or anybody in a similar situation:

- the land 'lost' is valued at the date the error occurred (in *Epps v Esso* this would be 1959, not 1973). This is still the law under the 2002 Act, see Sch 8 para 6(b); and

- by what was s83(11) LRA 1925, this kind of claim for indemnity had to be brought within six years of the error in the register occurring. Epps did not bring his claim until 1971, so he was too late to claim any compensation. Epps was out of time!

However, by Sch 8 para 8(b) LRA 2002, re-enacting a change first made by s2 Land Registration Act 1997, the six-year time limit now only starts running against a person in Epps's position from the date they knew or ought to have known that they had a claim against the Registry. But the land 'lost' is still valued as of the date the error in the Registry occurred.

Suppose the 2002 Act rule had been in force at the time of *Epps v Esso*. Epps only knew of his claim in 1968, when the Registry refused to register him as owner of the strip. His claim for indemnity, brought in 1971, would therefore have been 'in time' under the new law. But the 'error' by the Registry occurred in 1959, so he would have received only the 1959 value of the strip.

Concluding Remarks

It does seem that a rectification of the register for reasons other than adverse possession is a relatively rare occurrence. This is fortunate. If rectifications were frequent, much of the purpose and value of registration of title would be lost. The whole purpose of land registration is to guarantee the security of titles. It is therefore not surprising that both Parliament and the courts (*Epps v Esso*, also *Norwich and Peterborough Building Society v Steed* [1993] Ch 116, Court of Appeal) have reinforced the policy of limiting claims for rectification.

It may also be seen as encouraging that the Land Registry faces relatively few claims for indemnity. This is at least partly due to the efficiency of the Registry. But the rules regarding the award of indemnity used to be too restrictive. Epps rightly lost his claim for rectification; but it was tough that he did not get any compensation either. The changes to the indemnity rules made by the Land Registration Act 1997 and now incorporated into the 2002 Act are therefore very welcome.

Summary

Situations where Rectification is Likely to be Claimed:

- where there has been double conveyancing;
- where a registered proprietor has obtained registration by fraud;
- where a (perhaps negligent) mistake by the Registry and/or landowner(s) has resulted in the wrong person being registered.

Rectification Against a Registered Proprietor in Possession

This will only be granted if:

- the registered proprietor has been fraudulent; or
- the registered proprietor was negligent; or
- it is for some other compelling reason unjust not to rectify the register.

Indemnity where Rectification is Ordered

- The registered proprietor will normally get full compensation—the value of the land at the date of rectification.
- The registered proprietor will get no compensation if he has been fraudulent, or if the Registry's error was entirely caused by his negligence.
- If the Registry's error was partly the registered proprietor's fault, he will get reduced compensation.

Indemnity where Rectification is Refused Despite an Error at the Registry

The victim who has 'lost' land will be compensated, but only at the value of the land when the error occurred.

Reference

Ruoff & Roper: *Registered Conveyancing, Vol 2*, London: Sweet & Maxwell

Further Reading

Cooke, E, *The New Law of Land Registration*, Oxford: Hart, 2003
For a highly critical analysis of the current position, see Chapter 6.

Dixon, M, 'Proprietary rights and rectifying the effect of non-registration' [2005] Conv 447
Considers the effect of non-registration and what happens if a party subsequently applies for alteration of the register.

Lees, W, 'Title by registration: rectification, indemnity and mistake and the Land Registration Act 2002' (2013) 76(1) MLR 62
Explores the courts' interpretations of Sch 4 and where there is a mistake the availability of an indemnity.

Matthews, P, 'Registered land, fraud and human rights' (2008) 124 LQR 351
A short discussion about problems of identity theft and registered land.

Questions

The Aberconwy District (Llandudno, Conwy, Llanrwst, etc) became an area of compulsory registration of title on 1 December 1988.

In early 1988, Geoffrey purchased a small piece of land 'Lomasacre' situated in Aberconwy. Lomasacre formed a small part of the vast 'Brooke Estate' owned by John. Geoffrey did his own conveyancing; as a result no endorsement referring to the sale of Lomasacre was placed on the deeds to the Brooke Estate. Geoffrey has only visited Lomasacre on one occasion since he purchased it; on that occasion he dumped some rusting railings on part of the land.

Last week John sold the whole of the Brooke Estate to Malcolm; Malcolm believes that Lomasacre is part of the land he has purchased. He has successfully applied for registration as proprietor of the whole of the Brooke Estate.

Discuss.

Part 9

Easements

17

The Essential Characteristics of Easements

Introduction

This chapter provides an explanation of the essential characteristics of easements. In it we will be considering the question, 'What kinds of rights does the law recognize as easements?'

Where there is a claim for an easement over another person's land, it is necessary to first establish whether the right claimed has fulfilled the essential characteristics for an easement. Any alleged easement (whether it is of a new type or one of the existing, well-recognized categories) must comply with the four characteristics of an easement provided in the judgment in *Re Ellenborough Park* [1956] Ch 131. Once you are satisfied that the right claimed complies with the characteristics of an easement, you need to consider whether this right has in fact been created. There are a number of ways in which an easement can be created and these will be considered in Chapters 18 and 19.

17.1 Preliminary Considerations

point on terminology

You may come across the following terms when reading cases:

'hereditament' is a property right that is capable of being inherited.

'incorporeal hereditament' is an intangible property right such as an easement, profit, or rentcharge, which is capable of being inherited.

REVIEW QUESTION Re-read 1.3.3 on easements. Also re-read 1.2.2 on leases, 1.3.2 on restrictive covenants, and 1.3.4 on profits à prendre. Can you identify the differences between these rights? You should note that quite a wide variety of rights can exist as easements, but be careful not to confuse easements with either leases, restrictive covenants, or profits.

In 1.3.3 we provided a loose definition of an easement. An easement allows one landowner to make use of another nearby piece of land for the benefit of their own land. The benefit in this context could mean that the landowner will gain from the convenience of having this right. For example, a right of way over a neighbour's land to get to the main road may be more convenient than crossing a field to get to the main road. The types of easements that exist over another person's land are not restricted to rights of way but also include: right of support, right of light, and many others.

In continental legal systems the concept equivalent to easements is 'servitudes'. Modern continental systems, such as those in France and Germany, have a clear list of types of servitude, and no new types of servitude can be recognized. English law is more flexible. There is no exhaustive list of types of easement, and since the Second World War new types of easement have been recognized. In particular:

- the right of the occupants of one flat to use the toilet in a neighbouring flat: *Miller v Emcer Products* [1956] Ch 304; compare the right to use a neighbour's kitchen for washing: *Heywood v Mallalieu* (1883) 25 Ch D 357;

- the right of owners of houses situated around a 'private square' to use the private garden in the middle of the square for relaxation purposes: *Re Ellenborough Park* [1956] Ch 131; more recently applied in *Jackson v Mulvaney* [2003] 1 WLR 360;

- the right to emit a noise, ie the transmission of sound waves over the servient land, is capable of being an easement. This was acknowledged in *Coventry v Lawrence* [2014] UKSC 13 where the noise was from a speedway and stock-car stadium;

- the right of owners of a factory to use a neighbouring airfield. The easement allowed visitors to the factory to fly their private aircraft in and out of the airfield: *Dowty Boulton Paul v Wolverhampton Corporation (No 2)* [1973] 2 All ER 491.

Courts do not have a completely free hand to recognize (some would say 'invent') new easements. In *Phipps v Pears* [1964] 2 All ER 35, the Court of Appeal refused to accept as an easement the (alleged) right of one building to be protected from the weather by another building.

17.2 Characteristics of an Easement: *Re Ellenborough Park*

There are four characteristics of an easement and these can be found in the leading authority *Re Ellenborough Park* [1956] Ch 131. In 1855, Ellenborough Park and the surrounding property was an open and unbuilt-on piece of land. The owners of the land sold some of the plots surrounding the park to property developers and included in the conveyance was the right to enjoy the park subject to the payment of a fair and just proportion of the costs to maintain the park. Many years later, after the developed plots had been sold, which included in the conveyances the right to enjoy Ellenborough Park subject to maintenance payments, the case came before the courts questioning whether the purchasers of those plots of land (and their successors) had any enforceable rights to use Ellenborough Park.

The Court of Appeal held the purchasers (and their successors) of the plots had easements over the collective garden. The right to use Ellenborough Park as a private pleasure ground is a recognized easement in law. Sir Raymond Evershed MR said:

> The substantial question raised in this appeal is whether the respondent, or those whom he has been appointed to represent, being the owners of certain houses fronting upon, or, in some few cases, adjacent to, the garden or park known as Ellenborough Park in Weston-super-Mare, have any right known to the law, and now enforceable by them against the owners of the park, to the use and enjoyment of the park to the extent and in the manner later more precisely defined . . .
>
> It is clear from our brief recital of the facts that, if the house owners are now entitled to an enforceable right in respect of the use and enjoyment of Ellenborough Park, that right must have the character and quality of an easement as understood by, and known to, our law . . .
>
> For the purposes of the argument before us [counsel for the appellants] and [counsel for the defendants] were content to adopt, as correct, the four characteristics formulated in

Dr. Cheshire's Modern Real Property (7th edn.), p. 456 *et seq*. They are (i) There must be a dominant and a servient tenement: (ii) an easement must accommodate the dominant tenement: (iii) dominant and servient owners must be different persons: and (iv) a right over land cannot amount to an easement unless it is capable of forming the subject-matter of a grant.

The court in this case endorsed Cheshire's four characteristics of an easement:

- there must be a dominant and a servient tenement;
- the easement must accommodate the dominant land;
- the easement must be owned or occupied by different people;
- 'An easement must be capable of forming the subject matter of a grant'.

For a right claimed to be an easement all four characteristics must exist. If any one of those is missing then the right is not an easement.

17.3 There Must Be a Dominant and a Servient Tenement

As explained at 1.3.3, an easement can exist only if it is attached to ('appurtenant to') the dominant tenement. Tenement simply means land. In 1.3.3 we used the following example: Andy, current owner of High Farm, has the right to use a track across Jack's Low Field in order to get from the public road to and from High Farm (see Diagram 17.1).

Diagram 17.1
High Farm and Low Field

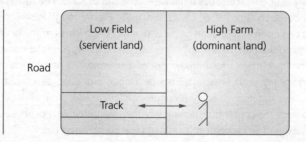

An easement can only exist if the 'easement' is 'appurtenant' to High Farm: High Farm is the dominant land; Low Field is the servient land. The dominant land has the benefit of the easement, in our example Andy gains the benefit of crossing Low Field. The servient land bears the burden of the easement.

Consider the following example, where the easement is not attached to the dominant land. Despo owns Wideviews Farm, situated in rural Derbyshire. She executes a deed in favour of Elena (a keen walker) granting Elena the right to use a path which crosses the farm. Elena owns no land whatsoever. Though the right granted by the deed will give Elena a lot of pleasure, it is certainly not an easement. Why? The facts state that Elena does not own any land. For an easement to exist Elena must own the dominant land on the date of the purported grant of the easement. As a result of this, the right granted to her by Despo is not attached for the benefit of another piece of land. It is not possible for an easement to exist in 'gross' (ie independently or unattached to land).

The right in this example is most likely a licence (permission) to cross the farm. Peter Gibson LJ explained why an easement cannot exist in 'gross' in *London & Blenheim Estates Ltd v Ladbroke Retail Parks Ltd* [1994] 1 WLR 31:

> If one asks why the law should require that there should be a dominant tenement before there can be a grant, or a contract for the grant, of an easement sufficient to create an interest in land binding successors in title to the servient land, the answer would appear to lie in the policy against encumbering land with burdens of uncertain extent. As was said by Fox L.J. in *Ashburn Anstalt v. Arnold* [1989] Ch. 1, 26, 'In matters relating to the title to land, certainty is of prime importance.' A further related answer lies in the reluctance of the law to recognise new forms of burden on property conferring more than contractual rights. Thus in *Ackroyd v. Smith* (1850) 10 C.B. 164, 188, Cresswell J., giving the judgment of the judges of the Court of Common Pleas, after referring to the impossibility of a grant of a right of way in gross said 'nor can the owner of the land render it subject to a new species of burden, so as to bind it in the hands of an assignee. 'Incidents of a novel kind cannot be devised, and attached to property, at the fancy or caprice of any owner:' *per* Lord Brougham L.C., in *Keppell v. Bailey* (1834) 2 Myl. & K. 517.' A right intended as an easement and attached to a servient tenement before the dominant tenement is identified would in my view be an incident of a novel kind.

This passage shows the reluctance of courts to acknowledge an easement in gross since it would burden the land to an 'uncertain extent'. This use of the term uncertain extent would suggest that the operational scope of the easement could be uncertain and unclear; the right claimed may be more than what is expected of an easement. Such an easement which has no clear limits could burden the servient land with excessive use. This is because the easement in gross is not restricted by the needs of the dominant land. Sturley (1980, at p 563) notes that '[w]ere an easement in gross to pass to a corporation or large group of people the problem would be more acute. Could the holder of a [right of] way in gross assign his right to the public at large, thus effectively creating a highway when an exclusive [right of] way had been intended?' That could be a real possibility!

An easement attached to the land provides certainty for any potential purchaser. If an easement was to exist in gross it may be viewed as a 'clog on title', where it may be difficult to discover who owns the easement (see Sturley, 1980, at pp 564–565). This will then depend on how the right is protected, and currently under the Land Registration Act 2002 (LRA 2002) there is no scope for protecting an easement in gross. Identifying who holds such rights may not be easy and may deter a purchaser from buying the property. This could make the land inalienable running contrary to the aims and objectives of the 1925 reform. Arguably, the right claimed may lie in a different right altogether, for example a restrictive covenant, lease, or a profit.

17.4 The Easement Must Accommodate the Dominant Tenement

A right to be an easement must 'accommodate' the dominant land; it must have some direct beneficial impact on the dominant land itself. It must not merely be for the grantee's personal benefit. Let us suppose that in the Wideviews Farm example Elena actually owns a house, but that house is situated in London, 150 miles away. The right to use the path across Wideviews is expressed to be for the benefit of Elena's London house. Can Elena's right be an easement? It will not be an easement.

For an easement to accommodate the dominant land it is not essential that the dominant and servient land be adjacent to each other, although they must be sufficiently near each other for the easement to be of direct benefit to the dominant land. In *Pugh v Savage* [1970] 2 All ER 353, there was a 'right of way' over one field to get to another field, but a third field lay between the servient and dominant fields. The right of way was held to be a valid easement.

In *Re Ellenborough Park* the houses were built around and near Ellenborough Park. Some of the properties were adjacent to the park and others were nearby. All of the owners of these properties were granted a right to enjoy the use of the park. The court had to consider whether there was sufficient connection between the right of full enjoyment of the park and the enjoyment of the residential property.

(To make the following passage from Evershed MR easier to read, we have added additional paragraphs and emphasized certain key sentences. The reader should also remember that Mr Cross, counsel for the appellants, was contending that the right to use the garden was *not* a valid easement.)

Evershed MR said:

> We pass, accordingly, to a consideration of the first of Dr. Cheshire's conditions—that of the accommodation of the alleged dominant tenements by the rights as we have interpreted them. For it was one of the main submissions by Mr. Cross on behalf of the appellant that the right of full enjoyment of the park, granted to the purchaser by the conveyance of December 23, 1864, was insufficiently connected with the enjoyment of the property conveyed, in that it did not subserve some use which was to be made of that property; and that such a right accordingly could not exist in law as an easement. In this part of his argument Mr. Cross was invoking a principle which is, in our judgment, of unchallengeable authority, expounded, in somewhat varying language, in many judicial utterances, of which the judgments in *Ackroyd v. Smith* [1850] 10 CB 164 are, perhaps, most commonly cited. We think it unnecessary to review the authorities in which the principle has been applied; for the effect of the decisions is stated with accuracy in Dr. Cheshire's Modern Real Property, 7th ed., at p. 457.
>
> > After pointing out that 'one of the fundamental principles concerning easements is that they must be not only appurtenant to a dominant tenement, but also connected with the normal enjoyment of the dominant tenement' and referring to certain citations in support of that proposition the author proceeded: 'We may expand the statement of the principle thus: a right enjoyed by one over the land of another does not possess the status of an easement unless it accommodates and serves the dominant tenement, and is reasonably necessary for the better enjoyment of that tenement, for if it has no necessary connexion therewith, although it confers an advantage upon the owner and renders his ownership of the land more valuable, it is not an easement at all, but a mere contractual right personal to and only enforceable between the two contracting parties.' ...
>
> Can it be said, then, of the right of full enjoyment of the park in question, which was granted by the conveyance of December 23, 1864, and which, for reasons already given, was, in our view, intended to be annexed to the property conveyed to Mr. Porter, that it accommodated and served that property? It is clear that the right did, in some degree, enhance the value of the property, and this consideration cannot be dismissed as wholly irrelevant. It is, of course, a point to be noted; but we agree with Mr. Cross's submission that it is in no way decisive of the problem; it is not sufficient to show that the right increased the value of the property conveyed, unless it is also shown that it was connected with the normal enjoyment of that property. *It appears to us that the question whether or not this connexion exists is primarily one of fact, and depends largely on the nature of the alleged dominant tenement and the nature of the right granted* ... [Emphasis added]

As appears from the map, the houses, which were built upon the plots around and near to Ellenborough Park, varied in size, some being large detached houses and others smaller and either semidetached or in a row. We have already stated that the purchasers of all the plots, which actually abutted on the park, were granted the right to enjoy the use of it, as were also the purchasers of some of the plots which, although not fronting upon the park, were only a short distance away from it. As to the nature of the right granted, the conveyance of 1864 shows that the park was to be kept and maintained as a pleasure ground or ornamental garden, and that it was contemplated that it should at all times be kept in good order and condition and well stocked with plants and shrubs; and the vendors covenanted that they would not at any time thereafter erect or permit to be erected any dwelling-house or other building (except a grotto, bower, summer-house, flower-stand, fountain, music-stand or other ornamental erection) within or on any part of the pleasure ground.

On these facts Mr. Cross submitted that the requisite connexion between the right to use the park and the normal enjoyment of the houses which were built around it or near it had not been established. *He likened the position to a right granted to the purchaser of a house to use the Zoological Gardens free of charge or to attend Lord's Cricket Ground without payment. Such a right would undoubtedly, he said, increase the value of the property conveyed but could not run with it at law as an easement, because there was no sufficient nexus between the enjoyment of the right and the use of the house.* [Emphasis added] It is probably true, we think, that in neither of Mr. Cross's illustrations would the supposed right constitute an easement, for it would be wholly extraneous to, and independent of, the use of a house as a house, namely, as a place in which the householder and his family live and make their home; and it is for this reason that the analogy which Mr. Cross sought to establish between his illustrations and the present case cannot, in our opinion, be supported.

A much closer analogy, as it seems to us, is the case of a man selling the freehold of part of his house and granting to the purchaser, his heirs and assigns, the right, appurtenant to such part, to use the garden in common with the vendor and his assigns. In such a case, the test of connexion, or accommodation, would be amply satisfied; for just as the use of a garden undoubtedly enhances, and is connected with, the normal enjoyment of the house to which it belongs, so also would the right granted, in the case supposed, be closely connected with the use and enjoyment of the part of the premises sold.

Such, we think, is in substance the position in the present case. The park became a communal garden for the benefit and enjoyment of those whose houses adjoined it or were in its close proximity. Its flower beds, lawns and walks were calculated to afford all the amenities which it is the purpose of the garden of a house to provide; and, apart from the fact that these amenities extended to a number of householders, instead of being confined to one (which on this aspect of the case is immaterial), we can see no difference in principle between Ellenborough Park and a garden in the ordinary signification of that word. *It is the collective garden of the neighbouring houses, to whose use it was dedicated by the owners of the estate and as such amply satisfied, in our judgment, the requirement of connexion with the dominant tenements to which it is appurtenant.* [Emphasis added]

The result is not affected by the circumstance that the right to the park is in this case enjoyed by some few houses which are not immediately fronting on the park. The test for present purposes, no doubt, is that the park should constitute in a real and intelligible sense the garden (albeit the communal garden) of the houses to which its enjoyment is annexed. But we think that the test is satisfied as regards these few neighbouring, though not adjacent, houses. We think that the extension of the right of enjoyment to these few houses does not negative the presence of the necessary 'nexus' between the subject-matter enjoyed and the premises to which the enjoyment is expressed to belong . . .

For the reasons which we have stated, we are unable to accept the contention that the right to the full enjoyment of Ellenborough Park fails *in limine* [at the outset] to qualify as a legal easement for want of the necessary connexion between its enjoyment and the use of the properties comprised in the conveyance of 1864, and in the other relevant conveyances.

The conclusion in *Ellenborough Park* that the right to use the communal garden was a valid easement should be contrasted with *Hill v Tupper* (1863) 159 ER 51 which provides a good example of a right which is personal in nature and not an easement. The Basingstoke Canal Company owned the canal and some land on the banks of the canal. They leased the land on the banks of the canal to Hill for the purposes of a boatyard. The lease included a clause granting Hill the exclusive right to put pleasure boats on the canal. Tupper nevertheless started placing his pleasure boats on the canal.

Hill sued Tupper, claiming that his 'pleasure boat monopoly' was actually an easement. If the court had accepted that claim, it would have meant that the pleasure boat monopoly was a property right which could be protected by suing anybody who interfered with it. The court, however, held that the pleasure boat monopoly was not an easement. The monopoly did not 'accommodate' the land leased to Hill; rather it was only for the benefit of Hill's business. Hill's only remedy was to sue the canal company for breach of contract. Commenting on this case Evershed MR in *Re Ellenborough Park* said:

> It is clear that what the plaintiff was trying to do was to set up, under the guise of an easement, a monopoly which had no normal connexion with the ordinary use of his land, but which was merely an independent business enterprise. So far from the right claimed sub-serving or accommodating the land, the land was but a convenient incident to the exercise of the right.

thinking point 17.1

Imagine that in Hill v Tupper, *the lease from the canal company granted Hill a right to cross the canal to get to and from his boatyard, but that right was being obstructed by Tupper's boats. Would Hill have been able to sue Tupper?*

Yes, Hill will be able to sue Tupper. The right to cross the canal would be a right of way (albeit over water), and therefore Hill would have an easement, a property right which can be protected by suing anybody who interferes with it.

In contrast, *Moody v Steggles* (1879) 12 Ch D 261 involved a claim by the dominant owner to have the right to advertise his pub on the defendant's house. The claimant's pub was situated behind the defendant's house and the sign provided directions to the pub. The court in this case acknowledged that though this easement did not physically relate to the land, the easement was connected with the manner in which the claimant used his property. It was the *nature* of the right which the court thought was more significant than the physical connection between the dominant and servient land. The dominant owner used the property as a pub and the sign was a means of communicating to the public the location of the pub. It was held that the claimant had an easement which benefited the dominant land. The easement in this case supported the business run on the dominant land, whereas in contrast in *Hill* the easement claimed was based on a personal/commercial advantage rather than benefiting the dominant land.

17.5 The Easement Must be Owned or Occupied by Different People

An easement allows one landowner to make use of another nearby piece of land for the benefit of his own land. Put simply, an easement is essentially a right exercised over another person's land. By definition, for an easement to exist the land must be owned or occupied by a different person.

It is not possible for a person to grant an easement to him or herself because there is no diversity of ownership or occupation. In this situation it could be possible to have what is known as a quasi-easement. Where the plots of land are in common ownership a quasi-easement will not be binding until it has met all the *Re Ellenborough Park* characteristics, for example the tenements must not be owned or occupied by the same person and, there must be a dominant and servient tenement.

Where a property has been leased, the landlord remains the owner of the property and the tenant occupies the property. This situation would fulfil the requirement of diversity of occupation. The tenant can be granted an easement over land belonging to the landlord but not included in the lease (*Borman v Griffith* [1930] 1 Ch 493).

17.6 Case Study—Apple Tree Farm

Tara owns Apple Tree Farm. Apple Tree Farm includes Daisyfield. To get to Daisyfield from the public road, Tara drives her tractor along a track across Greenfield, which is also part of her farm (see Diagram 17.2). Clearly, in this situation there is no question of there being an easement. A landowner such as Tara cannot have an easement over her own land!

Tara leases Daisyfield to Martin for ten years. The lease includes a clause that Martin shall have a right of way across Greenfield to gain access to Daisyfield. This clause will create a (leasehold) easement. The two fields are, of course, still owned (in fee simple) by the same person, but they are not occupied by the same person.

Diagram 17.2
Apple Tree Farm

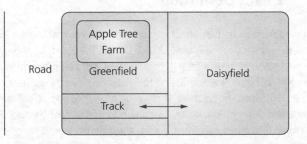

545

17.7 'An Easement Must Be Capable of Forming the Subject Matter of a Grant'

An easement is a property right and is capable of existing as a legal interest (see s1(2) Law of Property Act 1925 (LPA 1925)). For an easement to exist it has to be *capable* of being granted by deed even if it has not been granted by deed. In order to comply with this provision there are a number of subsidiary rules which will need to be considered in order to determine whether this characteristic has been complied with:

• there must be a capable grantor and capable grantee;
• an easement must be capable of reasonably exact definition;

- the easement ought to be within the general categories of established easements;
- an easement must not involve any expenditure by the servient owner;
- an easement must not be so extensive as to deprive the servient owner of possession.

17.7.1 There Must be a Capable Grantor and Capable Grantee

The person conveying the property right (ie the **grantor**) must be competent to grant an easement. A freehold owner of a property would be able to grant an easement, by virtue of the fact that the freehold owner has a legal estate of land and is capable of granting a legal easement.

A tenant for years is a capable grantor but the tenant's grant will only bind their leasehold estate (*Simmons v Dobson* [1991] 1 WLR 720). This simply means the person granting the easement must have a legal estate in land, if they do not then that person is not a capable grantor. This follows the maxim '*nemo dat quod non habet*' (no one can give a better title than he has).

Likewise, the **grantee** must be in a position to acquire the property right, that is, a capable grantee. Certain grantees are not in a position to acquire easements, for example a licensee of the servient land or a tenant who does not have the power to bind the leasehold.

17.7.2 An Easement Must be Capable of Reasonably Exact Definition

For an easement to be capable of forming the subject matter of a grant, it must be clearly defined. In *Harris v De Pinna* (1886) 33 Ch D 238, the court, applying this principle, held that there could be no easement for a general flow of air to a timber-drying shed. This was viewed by the court as being 'too vague and too indefinite'. Similarly, there cannot be an easement for 'a beautiful view' nor is there 'a privilege of wandering at will over all and every part of another's field or park' (known as '*jus spatiandi*': see *Re Ellenborough Park*). The consequence of having an ill-defined easement is that it will be unclear as to whether there has been an interference with the enjoyment of the easement.

An easement of light, under which a dominant building is entitled to natural light coming across the servient land, is not an exception to the rule that an easement must be capable of reasonably exact definition. There is no general easement of light over the whole land. An easement of light can only exist where it is sufficiently definite and this would only apply where the light comes through specific points in a building, for example a window. Where a dominant building has an easement of light over servient land, the dominant building is not entitled to an unlimited amount of natural light coming across the servient land. The House of Lords made this point clear in *Colls v Home and Colonial Stores* [1904] AC 179, where it was held that where there is an easement of light, 'The light reaching the windows [of the dominant building] must be such as is sufficient according to the usual notions of mankind for the comfortable enjoyment of the building, bearing in mind the type of the building and its locality.'

The existence of an easement of light over a piece of land restricts the kind of buildings which can be placed on that land. Putting a building upon the servient land does not infringe the easement of light provided the natural light which remains once the building is erected is still sufficient to satisfy the test laid down in the *Colls* case. In *Colls v Home and Colonial Stores Ltd* [1904] AC 179, the Earl of Halsbury LC commented:

> ... Light, like air, is the common property of all, or, to speak more accurately, it is the common right of all to enjoy it, but it is the exclusive property of none. If the same proposition against which I am protesting could be maintained in respect of air the progressive building of any town would be impossible. The access of air is undoubtedly interfered with by the buildings which are being built every day round London. The difference between the town and country is very appreciable to the dweller in cities when he goes to the open country, or to the top of a mountain, or even a small hill in the country; but would the possessor for twenty years of a house on the edge of a town be at liberty to restrain his neighbour from building near him because he had enjoyed the free access of air without buildings near him for twenty years? No doubt this is an extreme case, but it is one of the extreme cases which tries the principle.

17.7.3 The Easement Ought to be Within the General Categories of Established Easements

When the courts are considering a claim for a new type of easement not previously recognized there is a tendency to take a rather cautious approach towards such a claim. The categories of easements that exist are not contained in a closed list. It is possible to have a new type of easement. This reflects the need to modify the categories given the changes which take place in the socio-economic make-up of society over time. This was recognized by *Dyce v Lady Hay* (1852) 1 Macq 305 where Lord St Leonards LC noted that '[w]here new inventions come into use they may have the benefit of servitudes and easements; the law accommodating its practical operation to the varying circumstances of mankind'.

Apart from considering whether the right claimed is sufficiently definite, the court may also consider whether a new alleged easement is analogous to any established easement. In the 'right to use a toilet' case at 17.1 the Court of Appeal was influenced by *Heywood v Mallalieu* (1883) which had decided that a right to use a neighbour's kitchen could amount to an easement. An easement to park a car anywhere in a defined area has been acknowledged (see later, *London and Blenheim Estates Ltd v Ladbroke Retail Parks Ltd* [1992] 1 WLR 1278).

Easements are classified as either positive easements, or negative easements. The essence of a positive easement is that the benefits of the easement are enjoyed by occupants of the dominant land performing some activity such as walking across the servient land or, in *Miller v Emcer Products* [1956] Ch 304, using the toilet. Easements such as rights of way or rights to use an airfield are positive.

The law is very cautious when it comes to a claim for a new type of negative easement. A negative easement arises where dominant land (or building) just sits there and passively enjoys the light or support it gets 'from' the servient land or building. The right to light is a negative easement. The effect of a negative easement is often severely to hamper the development of the servient land. The law is thus reluctant to recognize new types of negative easements. This was a major reason why the Court of Appeal in *Phipps v Pears* [1965] 1 QB 76 refused to accept as an easement the (alleged) right of one building to be protected from the weather by another building. In this case a house was demolished, leaving a wall of a neighbouring house exposed which had not been built to withstand the weather. When frost began to cause cracks to appear in the wall the owner of the exposed house brought an action against his neighbour, claiming an easement of protection from the weather.

The Court of Appeal held there was no such right known to the law, and none should be recognized. Lord Denning MR said:

> The case, so put, raises the question whether there is a right known to the law to be protected—by your neighbour's house—from the weather. Is there an easement of protection?
>
> There are two kinds of easements known to the law: positive easements, such as a right of way, which give the owner of land a right himself to do something on or to his neighbour's land: and negative easements, such as a right of light, which gives him a right to stop his neighbour doing something on his (the neighbour's) own land. The right of support does not fall neatly into either category. It seems in some way to partake of the nature of a positive easement rather than a negative easement. The one building, by its weight, exerts a thrust, not only downwards, but also sideways on to the adjoining building or the adjoining land, and is thus doing something to the neighbour's land, exerting a thrust on it, see *Dalton* v. *Angus* [(1881) 6 App Cas 740], *per* Lord Selborne L.C. ibid. 793. But a right to protection from the weather (if it exists) is entirely negative. It is a right to stop your neighbour pulling down his own house. Seeing that it is a negative easement, it must be looked at with caution. Because the law has been very chary of creating any new negative easements.
>
> Take this simple instance: Suppose you have a fine view from your house. You have enjoyed the view for many years. It adds greatly to the value of your house. But if your neighbour chooses to despoil it, by building up and blocking it, you have no redress. There is no such right known to the law as a right to a prospect or view, see *Bland* v. *Moseley* (1587) cited in 9 Co. Rep. 58a cited by Lord Coke in *Aldred's* case (1610) 9 Co. Rep. 57b. The only way in which you can keep the view from your house is to get your neighbour to make a covenant with you that he will not build so as to block your view. Such a covenant is binding on him by virtue of the contract. It is also binding in equity on anyone who buys the land from him with notice of the covenant.

The House of Lords in *Hunter v Canary Wharf Ltd* [1997] AC 655, considered whether there was an easement giving the right to receive uninterrupted radio or TV signals. The claim failed because it did not come within the established categories of negative easements. Lord Hope of Craighead said:

> The presumption however is for freedom in the occupation and use of property. This presumption affects the way in which an easement may be constituted. A restraint on the owners' freedom of property can only be effected by agreement, by express grant or—in the case of the easement of light—by way of an exception to the general rule by prescription. The prospective developer should be able to detect by inspection or by inquiry what restrictions, if any, are imposed by this branch of the law on his freedom to develop his property. He should be able to know, before he puts his building up, whether it will constitute an infringement.
>
> The presumption also affects the kinds of easement which the law will recognise. When the easements are negative in character—where they restrain the owners' freedom in the occupation and use of his property—they belong to certain well known categories. As they represent an anomaly in the law because they restrict the owners' freedom, the law takes care not to extend them beyond the categories which are well known to the law. It is one thing if what one is concerned with is a restriction which has been constituted by express grant or by agreement. Some elasticity in the recognised categories may be permitted in such a case, as the owner has agreed to restrict his own freedom. But it is another matter if what is being suggested is the acquisition of an easement by prescription. Where the easement is of a purely negative character, requiring no action to be taken by the other proprietor and effecting no change on the owner's property which might reveal its existence, it is important to keep to the recognised categories. A very strong case would require to be made out if they were to be extended. I do not think that that has been demonstrated in the present case.
>
> There is no reported case where an easement against the interruption of the receipt of radio or television signals has yet been recognised. The closest analogy is with uninterrupted

prospect, which cannot be acquired by prescription, but only by agreement or by express grant. Unless restricted by covenant the owner is entitled to put up whatever he chooses on his own land, even though his neighbour's view is interrupted. The interruption of view will carry with it various consequences. It may reduce amenity generally, or it may impede more particular things such as the transmission of visual signals to the land from other properties. That may be highly inconvenient and it may even diminish the value of the land which is affected. But the proprietor of the affected land has nevertheless no actionable ground of complaint. He must make other arrangements if he wishes to continue to receive these signals on his own property. Radio and television signals seem to me to fall into the same general category. They may come from various directions over a wide area as they cross the developer's property. They may be of various frequencies, more or less capable of interruption by tall or metal-clad structures. Their passage from one point to another is invisible. It would be difficult, if not impossible, for the developer to become aware of their existence before he puts up the new building. If he were to be restricted by an easement from putting up a building which interfered with these signals, he might not be able to put up any substantial structures at all. The interference with his freedom would be substantial. I do not think that it would be consistent with principle for such a wide and novel restriction to be recognised.

cross-reference
See Chapter 20 on restrictive covenants.

As Lord Hope indicates in the second paragraph of the passage just quoted, the most appropriate solution where the dominant owner is seeking to restrict the servient owner's use of the land (eg to stop the servient owner from building) lies in a restrictive covenant between the parties.

A restrictive approach was adopted by the House of Lords in *Hunter v Canary Wharf* in relation to television reception; however in contrast, the Supreme Court has recently recognized the right to emit a noise as an easement. In *Coventry v Lawrence* [2014] UKSC 13 the claimants lived approximately half a mile from a speedway and stock-car stadium and a motocross track. Due to the high levels of noise from the stadium and track the claimants complained to their local council that this amounted to a nuisance. Lord Neuberger concluded:

33. ...the right to carry on an activity which results in noise, or the right to emit a noise, which would otherwise cause an actionable nuisance, is capable of being an easement. The fact that the noise from an activity may be heard in a large number of different properties can fairly be said to render it an unusual easement, but...whether or not there is an easement is to be decided between the owner of the property from which the noise emanates and each neighbouring property-owner. Equally, as Lewison LJ said at [*Coventry v Lawrence*] [2012] 1 WLR 2127, para 88 [in the Court of Appeal], the fact that a right is only exercisable at specified times does not prevent it from being an easement. As he also pointed out at para 89, one can characterise a right to emit noise in relatively conventional terms in the context of easements, namely as 'the right to transmit sound waves over' the servient land. Lord Parker of Waddington clearly assumed that the right to emit noise could be an easement in *Pwllbach* [1915] AC 634, 646, referring to *Lyttleton Times Co Ltd v Warners Ltd* [1907] AC 476. Furthermore, where there is an express grant, it should normally be reasonably easy to identify the level of permitted noise, the periods when it may be emitted, and the activities which may produce the noise.

The first sentence of the quote is significant in that it recognizes that 'the right to carry on an activity which results in noise, or the right to emit a noise, which would otherwise cause an actionable nuisance, is capable of being an easement'. Lord Neuberger acknowledges that this type of easement is somewhat unusual since it has the ability to affect a large number of properties and at varying times depending when the racing takes place. Furthermore, the characteristic of this easement is described as a 'right to transmit sound waves' over land. This attempts to provide some form of clarity to its definition, however as Dixon observes 'the exact scope of this easement presumably depends on the scope of the grant by which it is created, although one might suggest that an alleged right which is too indeterminate might still not qualify as an easement—in much the same way that not all rights to park are capable of being easements' [at p80]. Lord Neuberger aware of the potential vagueness of this right concluded:

> 38. ...The precise extent of a right to transmit sound waves obtained by prescription must be highly fact-sensitive, and may often depend not only on the amount and frequency of the noise emitted, but also on other factors including the character of the neighbourhood ...

17.7.4 An Easement Must Not Involve Any Expenditure by the Servient Owner

Lord Justice Browne-Wilkinson in *Rance v Elvin* (1985) 49 P & CR 65 stated that 'It is an essential feature of an easement that it merely requires the owner of the servient tenement to suffer something to be done on the servient tenement: a positive obligation on the owner of the servient tenement to do something is inconsistent with the existence of such an easement.' This statement acknowledges that there can be no positive obligation on the servient owner of land. An easement of this kind, that is, involving expenditure or other positive action, would not be recognized.

There appears to be one exception to this general rule. In rural areas you may come across the 'spurious easement' of fencing. Under this 'easement' the dominant farmer has the right to insist that the servient farmer maintain the boundary fence between their properties. Courts have repeatedly stressed that this fencing 'easement' is anomalous, and that no other exceptions to the 'no expenditure rule' will be tolerated. Support for this can be found in *Crow v Wood* [1971] 1 QB 77, where Lord Denning MR stated:

> The question is, therefore, whether a right to have a fence or wall kept in repair is a right which is capable of being granted by law. I think it is because it is in the nature of an easement. It is not an easement strictly so called because it involves the servient owner in the expenditure of money. It was described by Gale [*Easements*, 11th edn (1932), p 432] as a 'spurious kind of easement.' But it has been treated in practice by the courts as being an easement. Professor Glanville Williams on *Liability for Animals* (1939), says, at p. 209: 'If we put aside these questions of theory and turn to the practice of the courts, there seems to be little doubt that fencing is an easement.' In *Jones* v. *Price* [1965] 2 Q.B. 618, 633, Willmer L.J. said: 'It is clear that a right to require the owner of adjoining land to keep the boundary fence in repair is a right which the law will recognise as a quasi-easement.' Diplock L.J., at p 639, points out that it is a right of such a nature that it can be acquired by prescription which imports that it lies in grant, for prescription rests on a presumed grant.
>
> It seems to me that it is now sufficiently established—or at any rate, if not established hitherto, we should now declare—that a right to have your neighbour keep up the fences is a right in the nature of an easement which is capable of being granted by law so as to run with the land and to be binding on successors.

The easement of support is not an exception to the rule that an easement must not involve expenditure by the servient owner. Easements of support are, of course, common, often existing where there are semi-detached or terraced buildings. Where an easement of support exists, it is the right of the dominant building not to have support from the servient building deliberately withdrawn. Thus, if the servient owner knocks down the servient building, with the result that the dominant building collapses, the dominant owner's rights have been infringed.

What if the servient building simply falls down because of neglect by the servient owner?

The dominant owner has no claim for infringement of his easement. He can, however, enter the servient land and, at his own expense, reconstruct the support he was getting (Jones v Pritchard [1908] 1 Ch 630).

The servient owner is under no obligation to undertake repairs or maintenance so that the dominant owner can continue to enjoy the benefit of an easement, for example where a private right of way exists, the servient owner is under no liability to maintain the way. However, the dominant owner has the right to carry out repair works. Lord Scott of Foscote stated in *Transco Plc v Stockport MDC* [2004] 2 AC 1:

> It is well established that a servient owner has, in general, no positive obligation to repair or keep in good condition the servient land. Entitlement to the easement carries with it the subsidiary right of the dominant owner to carry out any necessary repairs to the servient land: see generally Gale on Easements, 17th ed (2002), pp 51–52, para 1–86. A deliberate act by the servient owner in damaging the servient land and thereby interfering with the enjoyment of the easement would be actionable in nuisance. In principle I can see no reason why a servient owner should not owe a duty of care to the dominant owner not to damage the servient land so as to interfere with the enjoyment of the easement. *But it would, it seems to me, be contrary to principle to hold a servient owner liable to the dominant owner for damage to the servient land, or for any other interference with the easement, caused neither by a negligent act nor by an intentional act of the servient owner.* [Emphasis added]

In brief, the only obligation that the servient landowner is under is to avoid doing anything which could interfere with the dominant owner's enjoyment of the easement.

REVIEW QUESTION You own Mill Lodge. Appurtenant to Mill Lodge is a right to drive vehicles along a private road across Long Meadow to get to and from Mill Lodge.

The surface of the private road is now in very poor condition, and your vehicles often get 'stuck in the mud'. How do you solve the problem?

17.7.5 An Easement Must Not be so Extensive as to Give the Dominant Owner Sole or Joint Possession of the Servient Land

The essence of an easement is that it is a right to make use of somebody else's land, not a claim to joint or exclusive possession of that land. This principle was stated clearly in *Reilly v Booth* (1892) 44 Ch D 12, where Lopes LJ stated 'There is no easement known to law which gives exclusive and unrestricted use of a piece of land.' Despite this clear statement, resolving disputes in this area is not without difficulty.

In *Copeland v Greenhalf* [1952] Ch 488 the alleged servient property was a long strip of land about 150 feet long and 20 feet wide. The servient owners used the strip to gain access to their orchard. The alleged dominant owners were 'wheelwrights', that is, vehicle repairers. For many years they parked vehicles awaiting repair on the strip. These vehicles often occupied a large part of the strip, but the wheelwrights were always careful to leave a gap through which the 'servient owners' could pass to get to their orchard.

The wheelwrights eventually claimed that they had a prescriptive easement to park their vehicles on the strip. Upjohn J emphatically rejected the claim to an easement:

> ...I think that the right claimed goes wholly outside any normal idea of an easement, that is, the right of the owner or the occupier of a dominant tenement over a servient tenement. *This claim ... really amounts to a claim to a joint user of the land by the defendant.* Practically, the defendant is claiming the whole beneficial user of the strip of land on the south-east side of the track there; he can leave as many or as few lorries there as he likes for as long as he likes; he may enter on it by himself, his servants and agents to do repair work thereon. In my judgment, that is not a claim which can be established as an easement. It is virtually a claim to possession of the servient tenement, if necessary to the exclusion of the owner; or, at any rate, to a joint user, and no authority has been cited to me which would justify the conclusion that a right of this wide and undefined nature can be the proper subject-matter of an easement. [Emphasis added]

The claim was rejected because the wheelwrights were in effect claiming, not a right against someone else's land, but joint possession of the strip of land. Such a claim was too extensive (or 'too big') to be an easement. The right claimed reflected a claim for ownership in land either in the form of a lease or freehold.

In contrast, in *Wright v Macadam* [1949] 2 KB 744 the claimant leased the top-floor flat to the defendant and gave her permission to use the shed in the garden to store coal. The claimant's lease had been renewed but there was no reference to the use of the shed in the lease agreement. The defendant later demanded payment from the claimant to use the shed. The Court of Appeal held that the claimant had the right to store coal in the shed and this amounted to an easement. This case has been criticized on the basis that storing coal in a shed would surely amount to exclusive possession. The servient owner is effectively excluded from using the shed until the coal has been used up.

The apparent conflict between *Wright v Macadam* [1949] and *Copeland v Greenhalf* was highlighted in *Grigsby v Melville* [1972] 1 WLR 1355.

In *Grigsby v Melville*, applying *Copeland v Greenhalf*, an alleged right to store goods in a cellar was held not to be an easement. The claim failed because it amounted virtually to an exclusive right of user so extensive over a confined space (in this case a cellar) on the servient land. Brightman J in his judgment referred to counsel for the defendant's argument that there was an inconsistency in the outcome of the judgments in *Copeland v Greenhalf* and *Wright v Macadam*. Mr Justice Brightman said:

> I am not convinced that there is any real inconsistency between the two cases. The point of the decision in *Copeland* v. *Greenhalf* [1952] Ch. 488, was that the right asserted amounted in effect to a claim to the whole beneficial user of the servient tenement and for that reason could not exist as a mere easement. The precise facts in *Wright* v. *Macadam* [1949] 2 K.B. 744, in this respect are not wholly clear from the report and it is a little difficult to know whether the tenant had exclusive use of the coal shed or of any defined portion of it. To some extent a problem of this sort may be one of degree.

The court suggested, in this case, that the assessment of whether there is excessive use depends on the degree or extent of exclusion of the servient owner. This assessment is based on the facts of each case. This was the approach adopted in *London & Blenheim Estates Ltd v Ladbroke Retail Parks Ltd* [1992] 1 WLR 1278 where Judge Paul Baker QC said on the issue of exclusive user that '[t]he matter must be one of degree. A small coal shed in a large property is one thing. The exclusive use of a large part of the alleged servient tenement is another.'

In *Miller v Emcer Products* [1956] Ch 304 (the right to use a toilet case), the Court of Appeal approved of, but distinguished, *Copeland v Greenhalf*. Romer LJ stated:

> In my judgment the right had all the requisite characteristics of an easement. There is no doubt as to what were intended to be the dominant and servient tenements respectively, and the right was appurtenant to the former and calculated to enhance its beneficial use and enjoyment. It is true that during the times when the dominant owner exercised the right, the owner of the servient tenement would be excluded, but this in greater or lesser degree is a common feature of many easements (for example, rights of way) and does not amount to such an ouster of the servient owner's rights as was held to be incompatible with a legal easement in *Copeland v Greenhalf*.

The claimant in *Jackson v Mulvaney* [2003] 1 WLR 360 argued that she had a right to use the communal garden for recreational and amenity purposes and to cultivate a flower bed. She succeeded in her claim. The Court of Appeal did not view the cultivation of a flower bed as exclusive possession of a particular area on the land; cultivating a flower bed was merely evidence that the claimant was exercising her right to use the communal garden for recreational and amenity purposes. The defendants in this case, by removing the flower bed without informing the claimant, had interfered with her rights. If the defendants had consulted with the claimant and given her the opportunity to move the flower bed, her rights to exercise the easement to use the communal garden for recreational and amenity purposes would not have been interfered with.

From the line of cases discussed so far the courts focus on whether the right claimed as an easement in fact amounts to a 'joint user' or 'exclusive possession'. Whether the servient owner has been barred from using their land is dependent on the extent to which the servient owner has been excluded; this is a matter of degree. If the servient owner is excluded from enjoying their land, there can be no easement.

Can There Ever be an Easement to Park Vehicles?

A slightly different analysis was used by the courts in assessing whether there is an easement to park vehicles, namely, whether the right claimed substantially interferes with the servient owner's use of the land.

In *London & Blenheim Estates Ltd v Ladbroke Retail Parks Ltd* [1992] 1 WLR 1278, the Deputy High Court Judge, Paul Baker QC (in obiter dicta) accepted that there could be an easement to park vehicles on a piece of (servient) land provided the servient land was sufficiently large, that is, the car should not take up too much space on the land. (The issue of whether a car parking easement could exist was not considered when the case went to the Court of Appeal.) Judge Paul Baker QC said:

> In the present case the right [easement to park a car] on its true construction is dependent upon the continued existence of car parking facilities for other persons. That leaves the main point under this head, whether the right to park cars can exist at all as an easement. I would not regard it as a valid objection that charges are made, whether for the parking itself or the general upkeep of the park. *The essential question is one of degree. If the right granted in relation to the area over which it is to be exercisable is such that it would leave the servient owner without any reasonable use of his land whether for parking or anything else, it could not be an easement, though it might be some larger or different grant.* The rights sought in the present case do not appear to approach anywhere near that degree of invasion of the servient land. If that is so—and I emphasise that I have not gone into the facts—I would regard the right claimed as a valid easement. [Emphasis added]

The court is clear in its suggested analysis of parking easements. The right claimed must be consistent with the nature of an easement. A parking easement will exist if the servient owner continues to have 'reasonable use' of their land and the right claimed must not amount to an 'invasion of the servient land'. The level of interference of the easement is a matter of degree. This requires an assessment of the facts of each individual case.

Consider Diagram 17.3. The issue of the extent to which the parked car takes over the plot of land is a question of degree. Where the parked car is on the small plot of land, the right claimed substantially interferes with the servient owner's reasonable use of the land. This would not amount to an easement.

Diagram 17.3
Small plot and large plot

If the plot of land is large and the parked car only takes a small part of that plot then that could amount to an easement. This is because the servient owner can still have reasonable use of their plot of land.

This obiter dictum from *London & Blenheim Estates Ltd v Ladbroke Retail Parks Ltd* has been accepted as correct in later cases, notably in *Batchelor v Marlow* [2003] 1 WLR 764. In that case the defendant garage owner claimed a (prescriptive) easement to park up to six cars on the servient land on Mondays to Fridays from 8.30 a.m to 6 p.m. Six cars would cover the whole of the servient land. The Court of Appeal, applying *Copeland v Greenhalf*, held that there could be no easement. The court considered an ingenious argument for the defendant, which was in effect, 'I only want to use this land for 47 and a half hours of the week, the claimant can have it for the other one hundred and 20 and a half.' In response to this argument Tuckey LJ stated:

> After that short diversion I return to the question which has to be answered in this case. Does an exclusive right to park six cars for 9½ hours every day of the working week leave the plaintiff without any reasonable use of his land, whether for parking or anything else?
>
> [Counsel for the claimant] emphasised the fact that the right asserted is exclusive of all others, including the plaintiff. Car parking over the whole of the land is highly intrusive because no other use can be made of it when cars are parked on it. In practice it prevents the plaintiff from making any use of his land and makes his ownership of it illusory. Not so, said [counsel for the defendants]. Mathematically the defendants only have use of the land for 47½ hours per week, whereas the plaintiff has 120½ hours. He suggested various uses which the plaintiff could make of the land. He could sell it to the defendants or charge them for using it outside business hours, if that is what they wanted. Outside those hours he could park on the land himself or charge others for doing so. He would be able to concrete over the surface of the land without interfering with the right.
>
> I think these suggestions demonstrate the difficulties which [counsel for the defendants] faces. Sale to the defendants would amount to a recognition that the rights they asserted had given them in practice a beneficial interest and no doubt the price would reflect this fact.

> The plaintiff could of course park himself at night or the weekends but the commercial scope for getting others to pay for doing so must be very limited indeed. I cannot see how the plaintiff would benefit from concreting over the land, although this would certainly enhance the defendants' right.
>
> If one asks the simple question: 'Would the plaintiff have any reasonable use of the land for parking?' the answer, I think, must be 'No'. He has no use at all during the whole of the time that parking space is likely to be needed. But if one asks the question whether the plaintiff has any reasonable use of the land for any other purpose, the answer is even clearer. His right to use his land is curtailed altogether for intermittent periods throughout the week. Such a restriction would, I think, make his ownership of the land illusory.

In considering the facts, Tuckey LJ concluded that the use of the land for parking left the claimant servient owner without any reasonable use of the land for any other purpose. The defendant failed in his claim for a parking easement.

Moncrieff v Jamieson—The Final Word on Car Parking?

The House of Lords considered an appeal from the Scottish Court of Session on, amongst other things, whether the right to park amounted to an easement in *Moncrieff v Jamieson* [2007] 1 WLR 2620.

The claimant ('pursuer') had a right of way over a strip of land 150 yards long to gain access to their house, which was wedged between the servient land and the sea. In practice, the dominant owners parked their cars (even overnight) on a wider part of the strip adjacent to their property. It was physically impossible to park the car on the dominant tenement because the only access to the dominant land was through a gate and down some steep steps.

In holding that the claimants did have a servitude (an easement) to park their vehicles, the Law Lords referred to the English cases of *Copeland v Greenhalf; Batchelor v Marlow*; and *London & Blenheim Estates Ltd v Ladbroke Retail Parks Ltd*. Their Lordships were of the view:

- that on the relevant issues, the English law of easements and the Scots law of servitudes were the same;
- that both legal systems did recognize an easement/servitude to park vehicles on servient land; and
- that in the view of the House of Lords a right is only too extensive to be an easement if the exercise of the right would deprive the servient owner of possession of his property.

Lord Scott in his judgment considered the issue of 'reasonable use' of the servient owner as discussed in *London & Blenheim Estates Ltd v Ladbroke Retail Parks Ltd* where there was a claim for a car parking easement. This, according to Judge Paul Baker QC in *London & Blenheim Estates Ltd v Ladbroke Retail Parks Ltd*, depended on the degree with which the right claimed was consistent with the nature of an easement. This was determined by whether the servient owner has reasonable use of the land. Lord Scott called this the 'ouster' principle having been influenced by an article written by Alexander Hill-Smith, 'Rights of parking and the ouster principle after *Batchelor v Marlow*' [2007] Conv 223. The ouster principle prevents the creation of an easement where the right claimed 'would prevent any reasonable use being made of the servient land by the servient owner' (per Lord Scott, at 47B).

In his assessment of the case law to which the ouster principle has been applied, Lord Scott noted that there are inconsistencies with the decisions, notably *Copeland v Greenhalf* and *Wright v Macadam*. Lord Scott made several observations on the manner in which the case law in this area may be interpreted. In considering *Wright v Macadam* his Lordship noted that there is a difference between 'sole' use and 'exclusive possession'.

In Lord Scott's view:

> [s]ole user, as a concept, is quite different from, and fundamentally inferior to, exclusive possession. Sole use of a coal shed for the storage of coal does not prevent the servient owner from using the shed for any purposes of his own that do not interfere with the dominant owner's reasonable use for the storage of coal.

Therefore, sole use would not be inconsistent with the nature of an easement.

If sole use amounted to the exclusion of the servient owner, for example if the dominant owner has the only set of keys to the coal shed, the servient owner is barred from entering the shed, this would show not only sole use on the part of the dominant owner but that dominant owner also has possession and control over the land. This would not amount to an easement. Lord Neuberger agreeing with Lord Scott said 'a right can be an easement notwithstanding that the dominant owner effectively enjoys exclusive occupation, on the basis that the essential requirement is that the servient owner retains possession and control'.

This approach of assessing whether the servient owner retains possession and control of land was considered in relation to the facts of *Batchelor v Marlow*. In a passage, which has the support of his colleagues, Lord Scott of Foscote said:

> 59. In my respectful opinion the test formulated in the *London & Blenheim Estates* case [1992] 1 WLR 1278 and applied by the Court of Appeal in *Batchelor v Marlow* [2003] 1 WLR 764, a test that would reject the claim to an easement if its exercise would leave the servient owner with no 'reasonable use' to which he could put the servient land, needs some qualification. It is impossible to assert that there would be no use that could be made by an owner of land over which he had granted parking rights. He could, for example, build above or under the parking area. He could place advertising hoardings on the walls. Other possible uses can be conjured up. And by what yardstick is it to be decided whether the residual uses of the servient land available to its owner are 'reasonable' or sufficient to save his ownership from being 'illusory'? It is not the uncertainty of the test that, in my opinion, is the main problem. It is the test itself. I do not see why a landowner should not grant rights of a servitudal character over his land to any extent that he wishes. The claim in *Batchelor v Marlow* for an easement to park cars was a prescriptive claim based on over 20 years of that use of the strip of land ... I can think of no reason why, if an area of land can accommodate nine cars, the owner of the land should not grant an easement to park nine cars on the land. The servient owner would remain the owner of the land and in possession and control of it. The dominant owner would have the right to station up to nine cars there and, of course, to have access to his nine cars. How could it be said that the law would recognise an easement allowing the dominant owner to park five cars or six or seven or eight but not nine? *I would, for my part, reject the test that asks whether the servient owner is left with any reasonable use of his land, and substitute for it a test which asks whether the servient owner retains possession and, subject to the reasonable exercise of the right in question, control of the servient land* ... [Emphasis added]

From this quotation Lord Scott emphatically rejected the 'reasonable use' test (referred to earlier as 'substantial interference') from *London & Blenheim Estates Ltd v Ladbroke Retail Parks Ltd*. The approach to be used towards parking (and presumably other) easements appears to have changed to whether the servient owner retains possession and control of the land, despite the reasonable exercise of the right claimed.

It is worth bearing in mind that where parking easements are concerned the right claimed may restrict the servient owner's use of the land, but this is not the same as exclusive possession. Lord Scott noted that in law the dominant owner's rights only go as far as giving them the right to park their cars on the land. The servient owner is entitled to do what they like with the land as long as the servient owner does not interfere with the dominant owner's right to park their cars.

Although the opinions given by Lord Scott and Lord Neuberger on the issue are technically obiter (because an appeal arose from the Scottish courts), it seems that the result in *Copeland v Greenhalf* would still be the same today, but both Lord Scott and Lord Neuberger expressed doubt as to whether *Batchelor v Marlow* was correctly decided. Nevertheless, recent cases continue to assert that *Batchelor v Marlow* remains good law (*Polo Woods Foundation v Shelton Agar* [2010] 1 P & CR 12; *Kettel v Bloomfold* [2012] EWHC 1422).

thinking point 17.3

1   *You take a lease of one office in a large block, and that lease gives you the exclusive possession of a numbered parking space in the basement car park. Could this parking right be an easement?*

    Clearly not, as you have 'exclusive possession' of the numbered space you therefore have a lease of the space.

2   *A lease granted you 'exclusive use' of a numbered parking space. Could this parking right be an easement?*

Applying Moncrieff v Jamieson, *this right would be an easement if it can be said that the freeholder (landlord) retains possession and control of the space.*

17.8 Access to Neighbouring Land Act 1992

This Act should be briefly mentioned. It is perfectly possible for an easement to exist granting the owners of the dominant property a right to go on the servient land in order to carry out maintenance and repairs to the dominant property. Such an easement is particularly useful where a building is constructed right up to the boundary with the servient property.

Unfortunately, such easements for 'access for repairs' are not particularly common. Until recently a building owner who wanted to go on to neighbouring land to carry out repairs to his own building had (in the absence of an easement) to rely on getting permission from the neighbour. Some neighbours can be extremely unreasonable.

The 1992 Act was designed to solve this problem, but it must be stressed that it does not create a statutory form of easement. Rather, it allows a landowner, who needs access to a neighbour's land to carry out maintenance/repair work on their own property, to get a County Court order authorizing the landowner to go on to the neighbour's land. There is, however, no automatic right to an order for access. The court hearing an application may decide that making an order will cause too much hardship to the neighbour.

If the court does make an access order, then the court can (and probably will) impose conditions as to days/times, and as to other matters such as insurance.

Concluding Remarks

The 1992 Act is a rare statutory intervention in an area of law which has otherwise been left to be developed by the courts.

The common law has not drawn up a fixed list of easements. This has the disadvantage of uncertainty, but has the great advantage of flexibility. The English law of easements can react to new technology, such as aircraft and computer cables, without the need to invoke the slow processes of the legislature.

Summary

Common Easements

- rights of way;
- rights of light;
- rights of support;
- rights to run drains or cables under adjoining land.

Less Common Easements

- right to use a neighbour's toilet;
- right to use a garden for relaxation purposes;
- right to park a car;
- right to emit noise.

Characteristics of an Easement

Re Ellenborough Park:

- *There must be a dominant and a servient tenement.* The dominant land must be benefited by the easement. Mere personal or business benefit (*Hill v Tupper*) is not sufficient.
- *The easement must accommodate the dominant land.*
- *The easement must be owned or occupied by different people.*
- *'An easement must be capable of forming the subject matter of a grant'.* An easement is a subsidiary right against somebody else's land. An easement cannot give a right to (joint) possession of the servient land. An easement to park a vehicle can exist provided the servient owner still retains 'possession' of the land parked upon.

The Access to Neighbouring Land Act 1992

This creates a statutory right between neighbours. This right is not an easement.

Reference

Dixon, M, 'The Sound of Silence' [2014] Conv 79

Further Reading

Baker, A, 'Recreational privileges as easements: law and policy' [2012] Conv 37
Baker discusses not only the right to use a communal garden, but what he calls 'pure recreational easements', such as the right to use a communal tennis court.

Gray, K, and Gray, SF, *Elements of Land Law*, 5th edn, Oxford: OUP, 2008
For a discussion of excessive user, see pp 621–627.

Haley, M, 'Easements, exclusionary use and elusive principles—the right to park' [2008] Conv 244
Case comment on *Moncrieff v Jamieson*.

Hill-Smith, A, 'Rights of parking and the ouster principle after *Batchelor v Marlow*' [2007] Conv 223
Discussion prior to *Moncrieff* of when and whether an easement of parking will be legally recognized.

Luther, P, 'Easements and exclusive possession' (1996) 16 Legal Studies 51
Critique of the courts' usage of 'exclusive possession' and 'substantial interference' as means of analysing the nature of easements.

Lyall, A, 'What are easements attached or appurtenant to' [2010] Conv 300
Discusses the Court of Appeal's judgment in *Wall v Collins* which concluded that easements are attached to land. This has subsequently been considered in the Law Commission's Consultation Paper, *Easements, Covenants and Profits à Prendre*.

Slessinger, E, 'Easing the way for easements' [2009] Conv 441
Considers the drafting of the grants of easements to meet modern problems.

Spark G, 'Easements of parking and storage: are easements non-possessory interests in land? [2012] Conv 6
Spark argues that a right can be an easement even if it gives *joint* possession of the servient land, but not if it gives exclusive possession.

Sturley, M, 'Easements in gross' (1980) 96 LQR 557
An interesting discussion of whether easements can exist in gross, see in particular pp 562–565.

Thompson, MP, 'Communal gardens' [2002] Conv 571
Case comment on *Jackson v Mulvaney* though cited as *Mulvaney v Gough*.

## 18

Creation of Express and Implied Grant of Easements

Introduction

In this chapter we consider the rules on the creation of an easement. Some (arguably rather strange) rules have developed under which a vendor (or lessor) of land create easements over land they retain in their possession even though those easements are not expressly mentioned in the conveyance (or lease). You may recall from contract law that the court may imply terms into a contract. In land law there is a similar approach where the courts are trying to give effect to the parties' intentions.

The greater part of this chapter will consider the possible means by which an easement can be created or acquired. It is important at the outset to determine whether an easement has been granted or whether it has been reserved. The reason for this is that certain rules governing the creation of easements apply only to grants and not to reservations. Issues relating to the protection of easements through registration will be discussed at the end of the chapter.

18.1 Creation of Easements (and Profits)—Legal or Equitable?

An easement or a profit is a legal interest in land provided that:

- it is created (expressly or impliedly) by deed (s52(1) Law of Property Act 1925 (LPA 1925)), by statute, or by prescription; and
- its duration is of a fee simple absolute in possession or a term of years absolute (s1(2) LPA 1925).

Where an easement has been created after 12 October 2003 by express grant or reservation by a registered proprietor the interest must be registered to be a legal easement. Section 27(2)(d) Land Registration Act 2002 (LRA 2002) requires the registration of registrable dispositions where the servient land is registered title. If the new dominant owner fails to register their new easement or profit, that new easement or profit will only be equitable despite being created by deed, and will only be a minor interest.

cross-reference
The registration of express and implied easements is dealt with in 18.9.

If the servient land is unregistered title, a legal easement will bind everyone, whereas an equitable easement will need to be registered as a land charge to bind purchasers.

18.2 Express Grant of Easements (and Profits)

A grant of an easement occurs where the servient owner gives a right over his/her land when the servient owner sells part of his/her property. Whether it is a freehold or leasehold estate the deed of transfer will expressly state that there is an easement over the servient owner's land. An easement created in this way is legal (though in registered land the easement must be registered to have effect in law).

Consider Diagram 18.1 where we provide an example of how an easement can be granted. Rajiv owns a mansion with several acres of land. He decides to sell the mansion, but not the area of land which runs alongside the main road to Chetsham. The only route to the mansion is by a road which runs through Rajiv's land. Dale buys the mansion. Rajiv, in his deed of transfer, has included a clause which gave Dale the right to drive over Rajiv's land to get to and from the mansion.

Diagram 18.1
Rajiv grants Dale an easement

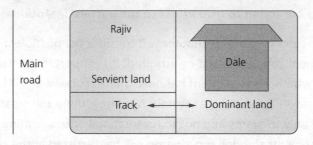

REVIEW QUESTION Is Dale's easement legal or equitable?

(Refer back to 18.1 and 18.2.)

REVIEW QUESTION Xanthia owns Northacre. Yolanda owns neighbouring Southacre. Xanthia executes a deed granting to Yolanda 'for her lifetime' the right to cross Northacre on foot to get to and from Southacre.

Xanthia is contemplating selling Northacre to Zaheer, and Yolanda is anxious that her right should be binding on Zaheer.

Advise Yolanda.

(Refer back to 18.1.)

18.3 Express Reservation of Easements (and Profits)

An 'express reservation' of an easement arises where the vendor sells part of their land and reserves (or keeps) an easement over the land sold. If the vendor wishes to reserve an easement then the vendor must do so expressly in the deed of transfer of the freehold or leasehold. The courts are reluctant to imply a reservation. The reason for this lies in the general principle that the grantor cannot derogate from the terms of their grant. Put simply 'you can't give with one hand and take away with the other'. It is for the parties under these circumstances to expressly agree to a reservation.

To put this in a practical context consider the following. Originally Clint owned a house with a large garden. He sold the front part of the garden, which faces the main road, to Mel. Clint retained the house and a small part of the garden for himself (see Diagram 18.2). To enable Clint to continue to use the pathway which runs through the whole of the garden to the main road, Clint included a clause in the conveyance retaining ('reserving') an easement of way over Mel's plot to get to and from the house to the main road.

Diagram 18.2
Clint retains the right to cross Mel's plot

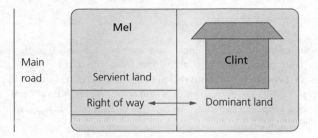

If the clause reserving Clint's right is vague in some way the court will construe this in Clint's favour as the dominant owner (*Johnstone v Holdway* [1963] 1 QB 601). This may strike you as rather odd. The basic rule that applies here is that where there is an ambiguity or doubt the clause should be interpreted against the servient owner, because the seller cannot derogate from his grant.

Under the pre-1926 legislation, if the dominant owner wanted to retain an easement the dominant owner had to reserve this right in the conveyance. There was a corresponding obligation on the servient owner to execute a conveyance regranting the easement to the dominant owner. In our example, Clint reserved the easement over the garden (servient land) and Mel regranted the easement to Clint. Since 1925, s65(1) LPA 1925 operates in such a way that the servient owner no longer needs to execute the conveyance regranting the easement to the dominant owner, but the servient owner is treated as having granted the easement to the dominant owner.

The interpretation of express reservations of easements sometimes gives rise to difficulties. In *St Edmundsbury Board of Finance v Clark (No 2)* [1975] 1 WLR 468 the Church of England originally owned a church and churchyard, and the adjoining rectory and rectory grounds. In 1945, the Church of England sold the rectory and its grounds to Clark.

The only access to the church building was across the rectory grounds, so the conveyance to Clark included an express reservation of an easement of way along an existing track across the rectory grounds to and from the church. Unfortunately, this reservation did not make it clear whether this right of way was 'on foot only', or whether vehicles could use the track. Clark, to the great inconvenience of weddings, funerals, etc, insisted that the right of way was 'on foot only'.

Evidence established that in 1945 there had been at the churchyard end of the track two solid gateposts only about four feet apart. This fact proved fatal to the Church's claim. The Court of Appeal held:

1 When interpreting an express grant or reservation of an easement, the physical circumstances of the pieces of land at the time of the grant or reservation had to be taken into account.

2 If, but only if, the doubts were not resolved by looking at the physical circumstances, the court should give the benefit of the doubt to the dominant owner and construe the grant in favour of the dominant owner.

The court (applying rule (1) from the previous list) concluded that the narrow gap through the gateposts which existed back in 1945 meant that the right of way was on foot only. In view of the physical facts in 1945, rule (2) (which the Church was trying to invoke) was not applicable. The court reaffirmed the principle that where the dominant owner reserves an easement, the law effectively recognizes that the servient owner has regranted the right to the dominant owner. Where there is some ambiguity in the construction of the reservation it is to be construed in favour of the dominant owner and against the servient owner.

Sir John Pennycuick observed:

> [Counsel for the parochial church council] relied, above all, on the undoubted facts that the disputed strip is wide enough—9 feet from tree root to tree root—for cars, including lorries, to drive along it without difficulty and that its surface in 1945 was sufficiently firm and even for them to do so. This is an important factor, but far from conclusive. One may well have a strip land capable of being used by cars but not adapted or appropriate for the passage of cars.
>
> [Counsel for the parochial church council] relied on another factor which seemed to us of importance, namely, that from time to time building materials would have to be taken to the church and there was no other route available. One would certainly expect the parties to have had this consideration in mind in 1945, when the church was in rather a dilapidated condition. They could not, of course, have foreseen the 1968 fire.
>
> We mention at this point, in order to avoid misunderstanding, that if there is no right of way for vehicles over the disputed strip, the church authorities may have a vehicular right of way of necessity to the church for the purpose of taking up building materials and the like. This possibility does not arise on the pleadings; but if there be such, it is open to Mr. Clark to select any reasonably convenient line, and he has in fact offered a longer vehicular way round to the north of the church for the repairs.
>
> There was some evidence as to the use of a small part of the disputed strip by hearses. But this did not, we think, turn out to be a factor of much importance. No serious difficulty arises in carrying a coffin over this short stretch and it would in any event be met at the entrance to the churchyard and carried into the church. Nor did any point arise as to weddings. In a parish of this size, neither weddings nor funerals are of frequent occurrence. The ordinary churchgoer, arriving by car or on foot, would be negligibly inconvenienced by a few yards extra walk.
>
> [Counsel for the parochial church council] sought to discount the gate at the churchyard end by pointing out its poor condition in 1945. This is a valid point so far as it goes. Obviously a broken-down wooden gate is of less significance than, for instance, a solid iron barrier. But the gate remains, to our mind, a factor of the first importance.

Applying the rule that in interpreting a grant one must consider the physical circumstances at the time of the grant, his Lordship concluded that the narrow gateway was fatal to the Church's claim.

18.4 Implied Grant of Easements (and Profits)

An easement over the servient land may be created by being inferred or implied into the deed of conveyance or lease. This would normally occur where the original dominant and servient tenements were in common ownership; the dominant land is then sold off (or leased). It is important to remember that to be recognized as an easement it must at the outset fulfil the criteria in *Re Ellenborough Park*, and the next stage is to consider whether the easement has been created. There are four ways in which an implied easement can be created:

- necessity;
- common intention;
- *Wheeldon v Burrows*; and
- s62 LPA 1925.

When an easement is implied into a deed of conveyance, the easement acquires legal status. The key point to note is that where a deed has been used the easement will be legal; if the document of transfer does not comply with the requirements of a deed (s52(1) LPA 1925, s1 Law of Property (Miscellaneous Provisions) Act 1989 (LP(MP)A 1989)), then the easement will only be recognized in equity (this does not apply to s62 easements, see 18.4.4)

Easements of necessity and common intention can be created by a grant or reservation. By contrast, implied easements under *Wheeldon v Burrows* and s62 can only arise by grant, and not by reservation. The law is more willing to infer the grant of an easement rather than infer the reservation of an easement. This is simply because an implied reservation is usually unfair. An implied reservation involves selling a plot of land but tacitly keeping an easement over that land. This runs counter to the principle that the grantor should not derogate from the grant.

18.4.1 Ways of Necessity

Such an easement would arise on the sale of a 'landlocked' parcel of land, that is, a vendor sells a part of their land which has no direct access to the public highway system. Otherwise, without the easement the land in question would be inaccessible. This test for necessity is a strict one. It involves determining whether the land can be used at all without the easement (see *Union Lighterage Co v London Graving Dock* [1902] 2 Ch 557 at 573; *Walby v Walby* [2012] EWHC 3089 at para 32). Necessity is based on the implied common intention of the parties, that is, both parties intended for there to be an easement but have not included it in the conveyance (*Nickerson v Barraclough* [1980] Ch 325).

Lord Oliver in *Manjang v Drammeh* (1990) 61 P & CR 194 lists the criteria for there to be an easement of necessity:

> There has to be found, first, a common owner of a legal estate in two plots of land. It has, secondly, to be established that access between one of those plots and the public highway can be obtained only over the other plot. Thirdly, there has to be found a disposition of one of the plots without any specific grant or reservation of a right of access.

This passage highlights three factors to consider for an easement of necessity: at one stage the plots were in common ownership; access between plots can only be obtained over one of the plots; one of the plots has been sold and the conveyance does not mention a grant or reservation of an easement.

A further factor to take into account is whether there is an alternative access route. If an alternative route exists, no matter how inconvenient it is for the dominant owner, this can be fatal to a claim for an easement of necessity. For example, in *Manjang v Drammeh* access to the land was possible but only by crossing a very wide River Gambia.

Where the criteria for an easement of necessity have been fulfilled the purchaser of the isolated 'landlocked' plot acquires an implied easement to cross the vendor's retained land. The vendor (servient owner) can fix the route of the easement, but it must be a reasonably convenient route (*Pearson v Spencer* (1861) 1 B & S 571), and once selected it cannot be varied (*Deacon v South Eastern Railway* (1889) 61 LT 377).

The way of necessity can be used only for those purposes for which the dominant land was being used at the time the necessity arose (ie at the time the land became isolated). In *Corporation of London v Riggs* (1880) 13 Ch D 798, Riggs acquired a 'landlocked' piece of farmland in the middle of Epping Forest. Epping Forest was (and still is) the property of the City of London. Riggs started building 'tea rooms' on his land. It was not disputed that Riggs had a 'way of necessity' to and from his land. However, he could use the way for farming purposes only. Neither contractors building the tea rooms, nor his future clientele, could use the way. Lord Jessel MR considered the scope of necessity:

> What does the necessity of the case require? The object of implying the re-grant, as stated by the older Judges, was that if you did not give the owner of the reserved close some right of way or other, he could neither use nor occupy the reserved close, nor derive any benefit from it. But what is the extent of the benefit he is to have? Is he entitled to say, I have reserved to myself more than that which enables me to enjoy it as it is at the time of the grant? And if that is the true rule, that he is not to have more than necessity requires, as distinguished from what convenience may require, it appears to me that the right of way must be limited to that which is necessary at the time of the grant; that is, he is supposed to take a re-grant to himself of such a right of way as will enable him to enjoy the reserved thing as it is.
>
> That appears to me to be the meaning of a right of way of necessity. If you imply more, you reserve to him not only that which enables him to enjoy the thing he has reserved as it is, but that which enables him to enjoy it in the same way and to the same extent as if he reserved a general right of way for all purposes: that is—as in the case I have before me—a man who reserves two acres of arable land in the middle of a large piece of land is to be entitled to cover the reserved land with houses, and call on his grantee to allow him to make a wide metalled road up to it. I do not think that is a fair meaning of a way of necessity: I think it must be limited by the necessity at the time of the grant; and that the man who does not take the pains to secure an actual grant of a right of way for all purposes is not entitled to be put in a better position than to be able to enjoy that which he had at the time the grant was made.

From *Riggs* it is clear that the scope of necessity is not wide. The court in *Riggs* adopted a narrow interpretation limiting it 'by the necessity at the time of the grant' which was only for farming purposes. The courts will assess the extent of necessity at the date of transfer and not some time in the future.

thinking point 18.1

Two years ago Alfredo bought 'Grove Mansion' from Busrat. Grove Mansion is a pleasant country house situated in the middle of Busrat's large country estate. The conveyance of Grove Mansion made no mention of easements.

Alfredo originally intended to live in Grove Mansion, but he quickly realized that would be too expensive. He is now thinking of converting it into a small hotel.

Advise Busrat who complains to you 'I do not want Alfredo's guests wandering all over my farmland.'

Applying Riggs, there is a way of necessity to/from Grove Mansion, but for private residential purposes only. Hotel guests will not be able to use the right of way.

18.4.2 Intended Easements

The second situation where an easement may be implied into a conveyance is based on the common intention of the parties. There is an overlap between easement of necessity and intended easements, in both of these cases necessity is a requirement. The broader scope of an intended easement was noted in *Pwllbach Colliery Co Ltd v Woodman* [1915] AC 634, where Lord Parker of Waddington stated that '[t]he law will readily imply the grant or reservation of such easements as may be necessary to give effect to the common intention of the parties to a grant of real property, with reference to the manner or purposes in and for which the land granted or some land retained by the grantor is to be used'.

To illustrate this point: if the dominant land was granted for a particular purpose known to the grantor, any easement over land retained by the grantor which is absolutely essential in order for that purpose to be carried out is implied into the grant in favour of the grantee. The leading modern case involved a situation where the dominant land was leased for a particular purpose, but the principle would equally apply where land was sold for a specific purpose known to the grantor. A common intention easement is not limited to a consideration of whether the property is inaccessible or unusable. When compared to necessity, where an alternative route is fatal to a claim, an intended easement is broader in its scope.

In *Wong v Beaumont Property Trust* [1965] 1 QB 173 a landlord had granted a lease of the basement of premises it owned to Blackaby. Blackaby covenanted:

- to run the premises as a 'popular restaurant';
- to comply with the Public Health Regulations; and
- to eliminate 'all noxious smells'.

Blackaby's attempts to run the premises as an English restaurant were a miserable failure. He assigned the lease to Wong, who converted the restaurant to Chinese food, with resounding success. However, the tenant upstairs complained about the dreadful 'noxious smells' coming from the basement. Public health officers were called in. They told Wong that unless a ventilation shaft was run from the basement up the back of the above-ground floors of the building, Wong would have to close down.

The landlord refused to let Wong put up the ventilation shaft, so Wong commenced proceedings, claiming that he had an easement entitling him to put up a shaft. The County Court judge found as a fact that, at the time the lease was granted to Blackaby, a ventilation shaft was necessary for the restaurant to function successfully and eliminate smells. The fact that neither of the original parties realized this need was irrelevant. It was held therefore that Wong was entitled to his ventilation shaft. The Court of Appeal affirmed this conclusion. Lord Denning MR said:

> The whole question in the case now is: Is the tenant entitled to put up this duct outside the building without the landlords' consent? The Midland Bank readily consent because they dislike very much the odours and smells which come up. The public health inspector says it is absolutely essential, if the business is to be carried on at all, that this ventilation duct should be put in. But the landlords object. It is difficult to see any good reason for the landlords' refusal. The judge has found that the duct would hardly make any appreciable difference to the landlords at all. Of course, it would be unsightly for a big duct to be put up on the back wall; but the back of these premises is unsightly anyway. It faces a back street and is hardly seen by anyone . . .
>
> The question is: Has the tenant a right to put up this duct without the landlords' consent? If he is to have any right at all, it must be by way of easement and not merely by way of implied contract. He is not the original lessee, nor are the defendants the original lessors. Each is a

successor in title. As between them, a right of this kind, if it exists at all, must be by way of an easement. In particular, an easement of necessity. The law on the matter was stated by Lord Parker of Waddington in *Pwllbach Colliery Co. Ltd v Woodman* [1915] AC 634, where he said (at p. 646), omitting immaterial words:

> The law will readily imply the grant or reservation of such easements as may be necessary to give effect to the common intention of the parties to a grant of real property, with reference to the manner or purposes in and for which the land granted...is to be used...But it is essential for this purpose that the parties should intend that the subject of the grant...should be used in some definite and particular manner. It is not enough that the subject of the grant...should be intended to be used in a manner which may or may not involve this definite and particular use.

That is the principle which underlies all easements of necessity...

...Here was the grant of a lease to the lessee for the very purpose of carrying on a restaurant business. It was to be a popular restaurant, and it was to be developed and extended. There was a covenant not to cause any nuisance; and to control and eliminate all smells; and to comply with the food hygiene regulations. That was 'a definite and particular manner' in which the business had to be conducted. It could not be carried on in that manner at all unless a ventilation system was installed by a duct of this kind. In these circumstances it seems to me that, if the business is to be carried on at all—if, in the words of Rolle's Abridgment, the lessee is to 'have any benefit by the grant' at all—he must of necessity be able to put a ventilation duct up the wall. It may be that in Mr Blackaby's time it would not have needed such a large duct as is now needed in the tenant's time; but nevertheless a duct of some kind would have had to be put up the wall. The tenant may need a bigger one. That does not matter. A man who has a right to an easement can use it in any proper way, so long as he does not substantially increase the burden on the servient tenement. In this case a bigger duct will not substantially increase the burden.

There is one point in which this case goes further than the earlier cases which have been cited. It is this. It was not realised by the parties, at the time of the lease, that this duct would be necessary. But it was in fact necessary from the very beginning. That seems to me sufficient to bring the principle into play. In order to use this place as a restaurant, there must be implied an easement, by the necessity of the case, to carry a duct up this wall. [Emphasis added]

A more recent example of an intended easement arose in *Donovan v Rana* [2014] EWCA Civ 99. Mrs Donovan sold a building plot with an express right to pass over a small plot of land which connected the building plot to the road 'for all purposes connected with the use and enjoyment of the property but not for any other purpose...'. The owners of the building plot fell into financial difficulties and sold it to Mr and Mrs Rana. In order to connect the utilities' main services from the road to their building plot, Mr and Mrs Rana allowed workmen to dig up the connecting plot, owned by Mrs Donovan, between the Rana's building plot and the road. The Court of Appeal, in giving judgment in favour of the Ranas, held that an easement was necessary for the parties' intended purpose ie for a dwelling house to be built on the plot with the necessary connections to the main utilities.

thinking point 18.2

Carlos recently sold to Davinder 'Glebe Cottage', a derelict house without mains electricity. At the time of the sale, Carlos knew that Davinder intended to renovate Glebe Cottage, and install all modern comforts.

It now appears that the only possible route for electric cables to Glebe Cottage is under White Land, a parcel of land retained by Carlos.

Advise Carlos.

Applying the intended easements rules, Davinder clearly has an implied easement for electric cables underneath White Land.

18.4.3 The Rule in *Wheeldon v Burrows*

The two rules for implied grant of easements discussed at 18.4.1 and 18.4.2, involve creating an easement as if 'out of thin air'. Before the sale (or lease) of the dominant land there is not the slightest sign of there being an easement in favour of the dominant land. Remember that in *Wong v Beaumont*, before and at the time of the original lease, nobody had even dreamed of a ventilation shaft down to the basement.

The rule in *Wheeldon v Burrows* (1879) 12 Ch D 31 operates in a very different way. Before we examine this rule it is worth briefly recapping on what is a quasi-easement.

A quasi-easement arises where the two plots are in common ownership. The common owner exercises over one plot for the benefit of the other plot, a right which could have been an easement had the two plots been in separate ownership.

For example, in Diagram 18.3 Farmer Giles owns two fields, Closefield and Awayfield. Whenever he needs to go to Awayfield, he gains access to it by using a worn track across Closefield. In this situation there is no easement because there is no dominant and servient tenement, Farmer Giles owns both plots.

Diagram 18.3

Two plots owned by the same person

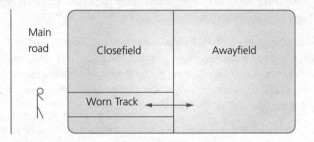

Or take another example. Bloggs owns a house and a large front garden to the south of his house. Underneath the garden there are drains, pipes, and cables, all leading out to the road. Bloggs also enjoys lovely sunshine streaming in over his garden to the windows of his house.

The rule in *Wheeldon v Burrows* requires that before the dominant land was sold (or leased) by the person who originally owned both pieces of land, a quasi-easement already existed in favour of what becomes the dominant land. If certain conditions are fulfilled then, on the sale or lease taking place, the quasi-easement is converted into an easement. This rule was explained by Thesiger LJ:

> ...on the grant by the owner of a tenement or part of that tenement as it is then used and enjoyed, there will pass to the grantee all those continuous and apparent easements (by which, of course, I mean *quasi* easements), or, in other words, all those easements which are necessary to the reasonable enjoyment of the property granted, and which have been and are at the time of the grant used by the owners of the entirety for the benefit of the part granted.
>
> ...in the case of a grant you may imply a grant of such continuous and apparent easements or such easements as are necessary to the reasonable enjoyment of the property conveyed, and have in fact been enjoyed during the unity of ownership, but that, with the exception which I have referred to of easements of necessity, you cannot imply a similar reservation in favour of the grantor of land.

You ought to have noticed from the quotation, this rule does not apply to implied reservations. It only applies on a grant in favour of the grantee. This follows the principle that we have mentioned previously: the grantor cannot derogate from their grant.

The Court of Appeal in *Kent v Kavanagh* [2007] Ch 1 confirmed that, prior to the transfer of the dominant land, the owner of the land must have owned *and occupied* both pieces of land.

The Almost Magical Conversion of Quasi-Easements into Easements

Under the rule in *Wheeldon v Burrows*, three conditions must all be satisfied before a quasi-easement is converted by implied grant into an easement upon the sale (or lease) of the dominant land:

1 Immediately prior to the transfer (sale or lease), the quasi-easement was used for the benefit of what becomes the dominant land.

2 The quasi-easement was 'continuous and apparent'.

3 The quasi-easement must be 'necessary for the reasonable enjoyment' of the (alleged) dominant land.

With respect to point (2), a quasi-easement is 'continuous and apparent' provided that it is regularly used and provided there is physical evidence on the plot of land involved of the existence of the right. For example, there might be a worn track leading across the 'servient' land towards the 'dominant' land. Even such matters as drains could be 'apparent' if there were such things as gratings and manhole covers on the 'servient' land.

The simplest illustration of *Wheeldon v Burrows* is *Borman v Griffith* [1930] 1 Ch 49. In that case, James owned a sizeable country estate. The estate included a mansion leased to Griffith for the purposes of a school. Running across the estate from the mansion to the main road was a properly made-up private driveway. On that private driveway was a smaller house known (somewhat confusingly) as 'The Gardens'.

In 1923, James agreed to lease The Gardens to Borman, a poultry farmer. This agreement said nothing about access to The Gardens. However, at the time of the agreement James was constructing an alternative access route to The Gardens. In wet weather this alternative route proved impassable for the lorries which served Borman's business. The lorries therefore used the main driveway, despite opposition from Griffith.

cross-reference
For a discussion on Wong v Beaumont, *see 18.4.2.*

The judge held, applying *Wheeldon v Burrows*, that an easement to use the driveway was to be implied into the 1923 agreement. He held that the three elements of the rule were satisfied. You should note in particular that for element (3), Borman had to show only that a right to use the driveway was 'necessary for the reasonable or convenient enjoyment' of the dominant land. He did not have to show the stricter standard of 'absolute necessity' which is required for an easement to arise under the 'intended easements' rule applied in *Wong v Beaumont*.

Maugham J said:

> ...In my view, the principles laid down in...*Wheeldon v Burrows* (1879) 12 ChD 31...are applicable. Without going through all those cases in detail, I may state the principle as follows—namely, that where, as in the present case, two properties belonging to a single owner and about to be granted are separated by a common road, or where a plainly visible road exists over the one for the apparent use of the other, and that road is necessary for the reasonable enjoyment of the property, a right to use the road will pass with the quasi-dominant tenement, unless by the terms of the contract that right is excluded: and in my opinion, if the present position were that the plaintiff was claiming against the lessor specific performance of the agreement of October 10 1923, he would be entitled to be given a right of way for all reasonable purposes along the drive, including the part that passes the farm on the way to the orchard.

> It is true that the easement, or, rather, quasi-easement, is not continuous. But the authorities are sufficient to show that a grantor of property, in circumstances where an obvious, i.e., visible and made road is necessary for the reasonable enjoyment of the property by the grantee, must be taken *prima facie* to have intended to grant a right to use it.

You should also note that Borman had only an agreement for a lease (ie an equitable lease) over The Gardens. Fortunately for him, this did not matter. The rule in *Wheeldon v Burrows* is applicable not only to conveyances and legal leases, but also to contracts for sale and equitable leases.

All Three Conditions Must Be Satisfied for an Easement to Arise under *Wheeldon v Burrows*

In *Wheeler v Saunders* [1996] Ch 20 and *Millman v Ellis* (1996) 71 P & CR 158 two almost simultaneous decisions of separate divisions of the Court of Appeal confirmed that for an easement to arise under *Wheeldon v Burrows*, all three conditions must be fulfilled.

In both cases the (alleged) dominant owners bought a property in the country, and claimed an implied grant of a right of way across land retained by the vendor. In both cases there was an alternative means of access to the property. Both cases were 'quasi-easement' cases where prior to the sale the vendor had used the quasi-easement to gain access to the property. In both cases the 'right' (prior to the sale) was continuous and apparent. Both cases therefore turned on the 'necessary for reasonable or convenient enjoyment' point.

Although this requirement has not been defined by the courts, it is clear that the term 'necessary' is not to be interpreted in the same vein as easement of necessity.

REVIEW QUESTION Can you remember what is an easement of necessity?

(If not, refer back to 18.4.1.)

In *Wheeler v Saunders* [1996] Ch 20, the alternative route was virtually just as convenient as the one being claimed by implied grant. The court rejected the claim to an implied easement. Peter Gibson LJ stated:

> But to my mind it is tolerably clear from Thesiger L.J.'s introduction of the test of necessity by the words 'or, in other words' that he was treating the first requirement as synonymous with the second. It is plain that the test of what is necessary for the reasonable enjoyment of land is not the same as the test for a way of necessity.

In *Millman v Ellis* (1996) the alternative route was dangerous and would involve making a detour. A court presided over by Sir Thomas Bingham MR held that a claim for an easement succeeded under *Wheeldon v Burrows* because it was necessary to avoid using the dangerous alternative route. Moreover, the claim succeeded even though the dangerous alternative route was by virtue of an easement expressly granted by the vendor, in the conveyance of the dominant property, over other land which he retained.

thinking point 18.3

For many years Eli owned both Holly House and adjoining meadow. The meadow is semi-derelict land, with a rough stony surface. Eli always parked his car on the meadow, the exact place varied from day to day.

Last week Eli sold Holly House to Francesca. No mention was made of easements. Francesca insists that she has a right to park her car on the meadow. 'Holly House has no place to park whatsoever' she complains. Eli replies 'Holly House is on a frequent bus route'.

Advise Francesca.

It is suggested that Francesca has acquired an easement under Wheeldon v Burrows.

- The quasi-easement was regularly exercised prior to the sale of Holly House.
- It was 'continuous and apparent', the car was there for everybody to see.
- In modern conditions, most people would accept that a place to park a car is reasonably necessary, even if public transport is available.

18.4.4 Section 62 Law of Property Act 1925

Law of Property Act 1925

62. General words implied in conveyances

(1) A conveyance of land shall be deemed to include and shall by virtue of this Act operate to convey, with the land, all buildings, erections, fixtures, commons, hedges, ditches, fences, ways, waters, watercourses, liberties, privileges, easements, rights, and advantages whatsoever, appertaining or reputed to appertain to the land, or any part thereof, or, at the time of conveyance, demised, occupied, or enjoyed with or reputed or known as part or parcel of or appurtenant to the land or any part thereof.

...

(4) This section applies only if and as far as a contrary intention is not expressed in the conveyance, and has effect subject to the terms of the conveyance and to the provisions therein contained.

(5) This section shall not be construed as giving to any person a better title to any property, right, or thing in this section mentioned than the title which the conveyance gives to him to the land or manor expressed to be conveyed, or as conveying to him any property, right, or thing in this section mentioned, further or otherwise than as the same could have been conveyed to him by the conveying parties.

The crucial part of s62 LPA 1925 reads:

A conveyance of land shall be deemed to include...all...liberties, privileges, easements, rights and advantages whatsoever, appertaining or reputed to appertain to the land...or enjoyed with...the land

This statutory provision first appeared in the Conveyancing Act 1881. It is very probable that Parliament did not intend it to be a rule under which new easements could be created. Almost certainly the original purpose behind what is now s62 was simply to reaffirm the common law rule that where a parcel of land is 'dominant' to an existing easement or profit, a conveyance of that dominant land automatically passes the right to enjoy the easement or profit to the new owner.

privilege
a licence (permission) to enter the land. This is revocable at will.

The courts have, however, given s62 a strange interpretation, under which a conveyance or lease of land may convert an existing **privilege** type of 'nebulous right' into a full easement.

The best illustration of how s62 operates to create an easement is the decision of the Court of Appeal in Wright v Macadam [1949] KB 744.

The case of *Wright v Macadam* concerned an apparently trivial matter which gave rise to a very important point of law. The defendant leased a top-floor flat to Mrs Wright. While this first lease was still running, Macadam gave Mrs Wright permission to store her coal in a coal shed situated in the garden to the small block of flats.

When Mrs Wright's first lease ran out, it was renewed for a further period. At the time of renewal nothing was said about the coal shed. Later, during the running of the second lease, Macadam demanded that Mrs Wright pay one shilling and sixpence (7.5p) per week for the use of the coal shed. She refused.

The Court of Appeal held that, on the renewal of the lease to Mrs Wright, there was implied into the renewed lease an easement to store coal in the coal shed. The crucial point (fatal from Macadam's point of view) was the existence of the privilege (ie permission to store coal), at the time the lease was renewed. The statutory magic of s62 therefore converted Mrs Wright's privilege into a full easement.

If, on the expiry of Mrs Wright's first lease, Macadam had leased the flat not to Mrs Wright but to a third party, s62 would have created an easement in favour of that third party.

Jenkins LJ considered the scope of s62 LPA 1925:

> The question in the present case, therefore, is whether the right to use the coal shed at the date of the letting of August 28 1943, was a liberty, privilege, easement, right or advantage appertaining, or reputed to appertain, to the land, or any part thereof, or, at the time of the conveyance, demised, occupied or enjoyed with the land—i.e., the flat—or any part thereof. It is enough for the tenants' purposes if they can bring the right claimed within the widest part of s. 62(1), i.e., if they can show that the right was at the time of the material letting demised, occupied or enjoyed with the flat or any part thereof.
>
> The predecessor of s. 62 of the Act of 1925, in the shape of s. 6 of the Act of 1881, has been the subject of a good deal of judicial discussion, and I think the effect of the cases can be thus summarised. First, the section is not confined to rights which, as a matter of law, were so annexed or appurtenant to the property conveyed at the time of the conveyance as to make them actual legally enforceable rights. Thus, on the severance of a piece of land in common ownership, the *quasi* easements *de facto* enjoyed in respect of it by one part of the land over another will pass although, of course, as a matter of law, no man can have a right appendant or appurtenant to one part of his property exercisable by him over the other part of his property. Secondly, the right, in order to pass, need not be one to which the owner or occupier for the time being of the land has had what may be described as a permanent title. A right enjoyed merely by permission is enough. The leading authority for that proposition is the case of *International Tea Stores Co. v. Hobbs* [1903] 2 Ch 165.

The court in *Wright v Macadam* followed the reasoning in *International Tea Stores Co v Hobbs* [1903] 2 Ch 165 where a permission had been granted, and on the conveyance of a fee simple the permission was converted to an easement. The facts in this case involved a landlord who owned two houses adjacent to each other. The landlord occupied one property and the tenant the other. The landlord gave the tenant permission to use a short cut across his land. The tenant purchased the house from the landlord. The conveyance did not include any reference to a right of way across the yard. The court held that the permission to cross the yard was by virtue of s6 Conveyancing Act 1881 (now s62 LPA 1925) now a right of way which passed to the claimant at the date of the conveyance. It was previously a privilege that had been enjoyed with the property prior to the conveyance.

thinking point 18.4

What if Macadam had sold the flat in fee simple to a third party?

The third party would have acquired an easement (in fee simple!) to store coal in the coal shed. Macadam would have been very unhappy at such a result.

The Breadth of the Section 62 Principle

It should be stressed that for s62 to convert a 'privilege' into an easement, all that is necessary is that the 'privilege' exists at the time of the relevant conveyance (or lease). Under the s62 rule there is no requirement that the 'privilege' be 'continuous and apparent'. Neither is there any requirement that the privilege be 'necessary for the reasonable or convenient enjoyment' of the dominant land.

We have already considered *International Tea Stores Co v Hobbs* where a licence had been given and this was converted to an easement. Similarly, the case of *Goldberg v Edwards* [1950] Ch 247 involved a 'privilege'.

Edwards owned a main building, together with an annex at the back of the main building. He leased the annex to Goldberg. That lease included an express grant of a right of way permitting all visitors to the annex to gain access using an open yard at the side of the main building. While this first lease was still in force, Edwards gave permission for visitors to the annex to pass through the hallway of the main building. (That way, they did not get wet!)

The first lease expired, but Goldberg was granted a new lease, with the same express clause regarding using the open yard at the side. The new lease made no express mention of the hallway, but Goldberg claimed that the new lease impliedly granted him an easement to use the hallway.

Goldberg's claim under *Wheeldon v Burrows* failed, because the Court of Appeal ruled that a right to use the hallway, while it had its advantages, was not 'necessary for the reasonable or convenient enjoyment' of the annex.

Despite losing on the *Wheeldon v Burrows* issue, Goldberg won the case; he was held to have acquired (on the renewal of his lease) an implied easement to use the hallway under s62!

thinking point 18.5

What is the moral for landlords of cases such as Wright v Macadam *and* Goldberg v Edwards?

- *Do not ever give your tenants any friendly permissions to make use of land you retain in your possession.*

- *If you have been so foolish as to give such a friendly permission, revoke it (in writing) preferably before the lease expires. Otherwise, insert a clause in the conveyance making it very clear that no permission has been given to use the land (see s62(4) LPA 1925 discussed previously).*

    Either way, there will then be no 'privilege' on which s62 LPA 1925 can work its statutory magic. (See also 18.6.)

cross-reference
For rules excluding implied grants of easements, see 18.6.

The Limits on s62 LPA 1925

Although s62 appears as a rule very dramatic in its effects, there are four important limitations upon its scope.

- *The right claimed must satisfy the characteristics of an easement.* The right claimed, by its nature, must be capable of being an easement. In *International Tea Stores Co v Hobbs* the court was satisfied that the use of a short cut across the landlord's land was a right of way.

- *Section 62 can operate only where there is a 'conveyance'.* A legal lease counts as a 'conveyance', but neither an equitable lease nor a contract for sale are 'conveyances' for the purposes of s62 LPA 1925. It is important to remember that a legal lease, apart from a lease of less than three years, is created by deed or registered disposition.

- *There must be a competent grantor.* Section 62 only operates where the claimed right existed at the time of the conveyance. The claimed right must be capable of being transferred by a competent grantor.
- *Section 62 applies only to convert 'privileges' into easements.* Unlike *Wheeldon v Burrows*, s62 cannot apply to 'quasi-easements', because prior to the conveyance there would be no diversity of ownership or occupation. Following the House of Lords' judgment in *Sovmots Investments v Secretary for the Environment* [1979] AC 144, approving *Long v Gowlett* [1923] Ch 177, s62 will only operate where there is prior to the conveyance diversity of occupation, that is, the dominant and servient land must be occupied by two different people.

In *Sovmots Investments v Secretary for the Environment* a London borough council made a compulsory purchase order of a number of maisonettes in the centre of London (a complex called Centre Point). The council argued that certain ancillary rights (water, electricity, and sewage) passed on conveyance of the land, and these must be taken to have passed with the maisonettes, otherwise it would not be possible to use these maisonettes for residential purposes. From the time the maisonettes were built to the date of the compulsory order, these maisonettes were not occupied. The House of Lords held that the ancillary rights did not automatically pass with the maisonettes. Lord Wilberforce, in this case, explained why 'quasi-easements' do not come within the scope of s62:

> ...section 62 does not fit this case. The reason is that when land is under one ownership one cannot speak in any intelligible sense of rights, or privileges, or easements being exercised over one part for the benefit of another. Whatever the owner does, he does as owner and, until a separation occurs, of ownership or at least of occupation, the condition for the existence of rights, etc, does not exist: see *Bolton* v *Bolton* (1879) 11 Ch D 968, per Fry J, and *Long* v *Gowlett* [1923] 2 Ch 177, in my opinion a correct decision.
>
> A separation of ownership, in a case like the present, will arise on conveyance of one of the parts (e.g. the maisonettes), but this separation cannot be projected back to the stage of the compulsory purchase order so as, by anticipation, to bring into existence rights not existing in fact.

Lord Edmund-Davies agreed with Lord Wilberforce and went on to note:

> ...the section cannot operate unless there has been some diversity of ownership or occupation of the quasi-dominant and quasi-servient tenements prior to the conveyance: see *Long* v. *Gowlett* [1923] 2 Ch. 177. It is true that in *Broomfield* v. *Williams* [1897] 1 Ch. 602 the contrary was held in the case of a claim to light, but, as Megarry and Wade, The Law of Real Property, 4th ed. (1975), p. 838, points out 'easement is an exception to many rules'.

There are two possible exceptions to the diversity of occupation rules under s62 LPA 1925. The first, noted in the previous extract, where this does not apply to easements of light.

The other exception is perhaps a little more tenuous. It would only arise, according to Peter Gibson LJ in the Court of Appeal in *P&S Platt Ltd v Crouch* [2004] 1 P & CR 242, when 'the rights were continuous and apparent, and so it matters not that prior to the sale . . . there was no diversity of occupation of the dominant and servient [land]'. Currently, there is uncertainty with regards to the status of this statement, though Patten LJ in *Alford v Hannaford* [2011] EWCA Civ 1099 suggested approval of this statement albeit in obiter, and whether the courts will follow it.

The High Court in *Wood v Waddington* [2014] EWHC 1358 appears to endorse the approach adopted by *Platt* and *Alford* in determining that prior diversity of occupation is not a strict requirement under s62. The reasoning of the court rests on its interpretation of 'easements, rights, and advantages . . . *enjoyed with* . . . *the land*' [emphasis added].

Morgan J. explained:

> 110. ... It is clear that section 62 can operate to create an easement or a right which did not exist, because of unity of ownership, before the relevant conveyance. So the reference in section 62 to 'easements' and 'rights' is not necessarily to pre-existing easements and rights. In explaining the operation of section 62 in a case where it is claimed that the section has converted something which was not a pre-existing easement or right into an easement or right, I find it easier to concentrate on the word 'advantage' and to consider what is meant by an 'advantage enjoyed with' the land conveyed. The use of the word 'enjoyed' imposes a requirement that the advantage in question has actually been enjoyed within a reasonable period of time before the conveyance. The word 'with' is important. It shows that the advantage must have been enjoyed with the land conveyed. This word must be considered in its context. The effect of section 62, where it operates, is to create an easement for the benefit of a dominant tenement and which is a burden on a servient tenement. The land conveyed will be the dominant tenement and the land retained will be the servient tenement. The use of the word 'with' suggests that before the conveyance, there must have been a relationship between the land to be conveyed and the land to be retained so that it can properly be said that the advantage in question was enjoyed with the land to be conveyed.

Morgan J focuses on the word 'with' to indicate that the focus should be on the relationship between the land conveyed and the land retained in order to ascertain whether the 'advantage' was enjoyed.

Having examined the pre-1881 authorities, Morgan J continues:

> 119. These authorities on general words in conveyances before the 1881 Act do not support the proposition that there is an absolute rule that section 62 can never apply to a claimed right of way unless there has been diversity of occupation before the relevant conveyance. They do support an approach, to be derived from the wording of section 62 itself, to the effect that, before the relevant conveyance, the advantage must have been enjoyed 'with' the land to be conveyed rather than as part of the rights of ownership of all of the land then in common ownership so that it can be, after the conveyance, an easement appurtenant to the land conveyed as the dominant tenement.

Morgan J by examining the older case law casts seeds of doubt as to whether the approach adopted in *Sovmots*, and approved in *Payne v Inwood* (1996) 74 P & CR 42, is to be regarded as an absolute rule ie there must be diversity of occupation before the relevant conveyance in order for s62 to operate and create an easement. However, Morgan J was of the opinion that *Long v Gowlett* [1923] 2 Ch 177 did not expressly lay down an absolute rule that an easement could not be granted under s62 where there had not been prior diversity of occupation. He asserted that the reasoning in both *Platt* and *Alford* focused on the fact that the right had to be continuous and apparent for the 'advantage' to pass under s62.

Morgan J concluded:

> **(7) 'Continuous and apparent' in the context of section 62**
>
> 132. The cases before the 1881 Act concerning the general words and claims to rights of way gave examples of facts which would allow the court to hold that the advantage claimed was 'enjoyed with' the land conveyed. The language used in those cases varied as to the necessary connection between the advantage claimed and the land conveyed. In *Long v Gowlett*, Sargant J commented that the case before him did not involve a continuous and apparent means of communication. Megarry & Wade at para. 28-033 uses the test of 'continuous and apparent' to determine whether the advantage is 'enjoyed with' the land conveyed. This approach has been adopted in the more recent decisions of the Court of Appeal to which

I have referred. It may be that a test of 'continuous and apparent' is not an improvement on the statutory wording of 'enjoyed with'. The reference to an easement being 'continuous and apparent' appears to be taken from the case law dealing with the implication of easements: see *Wheeldon v Burrows* (1879) 12 Ch D 31 . . . However, in that context, the phrase 'continuous and apparent' does not stand alone as it operates in conjunction with a requirement that the right claimed is necessary for the reasonable enjoyment of the land conveyed. This further requirement helps to identify the relationship of dominance and servience between the land conveyed and the land retained. Further, the phrase 'continuous and apparent' on its own has been considered to be lacking in clarity: see *Dalton v Angus* (1881) 6 App Cas 740 at 821 per Lord Blackburn. If the phrase 'continuous and apparent' is to be used as a proxy for the statutory words 'enjoyed with', then (in the context of section 62) what must be apparent is that the advantage claimed is enjoyed with the land to be conveyed rather than enjoyed as part of the common ownership of both the land to be conveyed and the land to be retained.

(8) Conclusions as to the operation of section 62

133. I will now summarise my understanding of the legal position. There is no absolute rule that a right of way cannot be claimed under section 62 where there has not been diversity of occupation before the relevant conveyance. The ultimate question is whether the advantage in question was, on the facts, 'enjoyed with' the land conveyed. Those words require two things to be shown. The advantage must have been 'enjoyed' in the period before the conveyance. Further, the advantage must have been enjoyed 'with' the land conveyed so that, after the conveyance, it will be appurtenant to the land conveyed as the dominant tenement. For these purposes, a consideration of how the advantage was actually used and whether it was apparently for the benefit of the land conveyed and apparently a burden on the land retained will be of great importance. The cases on the general words before the 1881 Act show, for example, that where there was a driveway leading across the land retained to serve the land conveyed it is possible to hold that the advantage of the use of the driveway was enjoyed with the land conveyed. I do not suggest that this example is the only possible case where a right of way would pass under the general words.

577

This approach adopted by Morgan J suggests a wider scope for s62. As with *Platt* and *Alford* the significance of this is yet to be determined and the case is currently subject to appeal.

thinking point 18.6

Why was s62 LPA 1925 of no help to Borman in Borman v Griffith?

You ought to have identified two reasons. First, Borman had only an equitable lease. Secondly (though this point is not expressly mentioned in the judgment), the case clearly involved a quasi-easement, to which s62 was thought to be inapplicable.

Section 62 and Profits à Prendre

Unlike the other three forms of implied grant which we have been discussing, it appears that s62 could apply so as to imply a profit into a conveyance (or lease) (*White v Williams* [1922] 1 KB 727).

This is illustrated by the following example:

Liam owns a house and an adjoining meadow. He leases the house to Teresa for ten years. Teresa is a keen horsewoman, and when Liam discovers that fact he says to her, 'Seeing we are now good friends you can pasture your horse in my meadow.' Teresa accepts the invitation.

When the lease of the house runs out, Liam sells the fee simple in the house to Pandya. The conveyance makes no mention of horses, but Pandya now produces his horse and says to Liam, 'I have got the right to put my horse in your meadow.' It would appear that Pandya is correct in this assertion. He has a fee simple profit to pasture one horse in the adjoining meadow.

18.5 Implied Reservation of Easements

REVIEW QUESTION What is an express reservation?

In 18.3 we discussed the express reservation of an easement. You may recall that this would arise where the vendor sells part of their land and reserves (or keeps) an easement over the land sold. An implied reservation, in contrast, is inferred by the courts. The courts are reluctant to impliedly reserve an easement simply because the person who wants to retain the claim right must do so expressly. Section 62 LPA 1925 and *Wheeldon v Burrows* cannot operate 'in reverse' to create easements by implied reservation. It is only possible to impliedly reserve an easement where it is a 'way of necessity' and an 'intended easement'.

18.5.1 Necessity

In *Union Lighterage Co v London Graving Dock Co* [1902] 2 Ch 557, Stirling LJ provided the clearest explanation of an implied reservation by necessity: 'an easement of necessity...means an easement without which the property retained cannot be used at all, and not one merely necessary to the reasonable enjoyment of that property'. This is a very strict interpretation of necessity. According to this quotation the only situation where this type of easement would be inferred by the courts would be where the land is landlocked. The easement of necessity must exist at the date of the reservation. If there is an alternative route then this will defeat the claim for an easement of necessity. For example, Matt owns Nearacre and Faracre. He foolishly sells Nearacre, with the result that Faracre becomes 'landlocked'. Matt is lucky. He will have a 'way of necessity' over Nearacre to get to Faracre.

REVIEW QUESTION Can you remember the principle in *Corporation of London v Riggs* at 18.4.1?

The case of *Sweet v Sommer* [2004] 2 P & CR DG24 shows a more relaxed approach being adopted to an easement of necessity. The issue in this case revolved around vehicular access to a property which was, in theory, landlocked. At the time of the grant there was an alternative means of access to the claimant's property but this would involve the demolition of a workshop by the claimant. Hart J implied a vehicular right of way. It is worth noting that this case was considered by the High Court. The Court of Appeal did not address this specific issue.

18.5.2 Intended Easements

thinking point 18.7

Wang owns a building which includes a basement. He leases the above-ground floors to Zoe on a 50-year lease, but he retains the basement. He opens a restaurant in the basement. The tenant of the upper floors complains, and the environmental health officers say that the restaurant has to have a ventilation shaft up the back of the above-ground floors. Can Wang claim an easement?

It would seem that Wang will be able to claim an easement for a ventilation shaft by implied reservation only if he can show that at the time the 50-year lease was granted Zoe knew that Wang intended to run a restaurant in the basement (Re Webb's Lease [1951] Ch 808). The Court of Appeal in Peckham v Ellison (2000) 79 P & CR 276 emphasized that in considering whether to imply a reservation each case will be assessed on the facts.

(18.6) Exclusion of the Rules Providing for Implied Grant and Reservation

The rules for implied grant and reservation which we have just discussed at some length depend upon 'the presumed agreement of the parties'.

It is perfectly permissible and indeed quite common for solicitors drafting contracts for sale (and contracts for leases) to include a clause in the contract excluding the rules relating to implied grant. Thus, in particular, a vendor or lessor of land who retains other land in the vicinity can, by careful drafting, avoid being saddled with easements which would otherwise arise 'by implication'.

Graham v Philcox [1984] QB 747 provides a useful illustration of what may happen if permission is not revoked before the land is sold.

The material facts of the case were that L owned a large garden with a house at one end of that garden. In 1960, L leased the house to T. This lease included an express grant to T of a right of way over the garden for the duration of the lease. In 1975 (while T's lease was still running), L sold the fee simple reversion in the house to G. The 1975 conveyance made no mention of a right of way. The Court of Appeal held that s62 implied into the 1975 conveyance the grant to G of a fee simple easement of way over the garden.

The practical effect of this case appears to be that if the landlord of Blackacre grants to a lessee of Blackacre a full easement over Retainedacre for the duration of the lease, and then the landlord sells the freehold to Blackacre, there will be implied into the conveyance of Blackacre a freehold easement over Retainedacre! In this case L found himself saddled with a fee simple easement of way over the garden he retained. What should L's solicitor have done to avoid that result?

L's solicitor should have included in the contract for sale of the house in 1975 a clause to the effect, 'On the conveyance of the house, no easements over the garden shall be implied under s62, 'the rule in *Wheeldon v Burrows*' or any other rule.' Out of extreme caution, a similar clause should also be included in the conveyance itself.

18.7 Compulsory Purchase and the Rules for Implied Grant

In *Sovmots Investments v Secretary for the Environment* [1979] AC 144, the House of Lords held that as the rules for implied grant and reservation of easements are founded on 'presumed agreement', the rules can have no application to land acquired under a compulsory purchase order.

18.8 Simultaneous Sales or Bequests

Alex owns Greenacre and Blueacre. He simultaneously grants or leaves by his will Greenacre to Brad and Blueacre to Chesney. It appears that *Wheeldon v Burrows* can operate in favour of Brad and/or Chesney, but the other rules of implied grant, such as s62, can have no application.

18.9 Express or Implied Easements?— Legal or Equitable?—Overriding or Minor?

The implied easement which arose in *Borman v Griffith* was (in effect) an implied term of the equitable lease which existed between James and Borman. The easement in that case was therefore only equitable.

In that respect, *Borman v Griffith* was an unusual case. Usually, when an implied easement (or profit) arises, that easement (or profit) is an implied term of a deed either transferring the legal freehold estate or granting a legal lease. Where (as in *Millman v Ellis, Wong v Beaumont*, and *Goldberg v Edwards*) an implied easement arises as an implied term of a deed, that easement will be legal.

18.9.1 Unregistered Servient Land

If a legal express or implied easement arises against unregistered servient land, that easement will of course be automatically binding on the whole world.

However, if an equitable implied easement arises against unregistered land, that easement will be registrable as a land charge, Class D(iii).

cross-reference
See 6.5.2 on easements under the LRA 2002.

18.9.2 Registered Servient Land

Express Easements

Where there is a new express grant of an easement to ensure that it will bind successors in title it must be registered (s27(2)(d) LRA 2002). If a dominant owner of an easement expressly granted or profit fails to register their right against the servient land, the easement or profit will take effect only as an equitable interest. The equitable easement would need to be registered as a notice (s32 LRA 2002) otherwise it will not bind successors in title (s29(1) LRA 2002).

Implied Easements Prior to the Commencement of the Land Registration Act 2002

If a legal implied easement arises prior to the commencement of the 2002 Act, that easement is undoubtedly an overriding interest within s70(1)(a) Land Registration Act 1925.

If an equitable implied easement arises prior to the commencement of the 2002 Act, that too will be overriding, assuming the decision in *Thatcher v Douglas* [1996] 146 NLJ 282 to be correct.

Implied Easements After the Commencement of the Land Registration Act 2002

If a legal implied easement is created after the commencement of the 2002 Act, it will normally be an overriding interest, but subject to the rules set out in Sch 3 para 3 LRA 2002:

- the purchaser had 'actual knowledge' of the easement or profit on the date of the land transfer in his favour;

  or

- the existence of the right would have been apparent 'on a reasonably careful inspection of the land over which the easement or profit is exercisable' (eg a worn track leading to the dominant land);

  or

- if the easement or profit has been exercised at least once in the year prior to the land transfer.

If an equitable implied easement is created after the commencement of the 2002 Act on 13 October 2003, that easement cannot be an overriding interest. The equitable easement must be registered as a notice (s32 LRA 2002). If it is not registered then it will not be binding (s29(1) LRA 2002).

 # Concluding Remarks

This whole chapter could be concluded in seven words: 'Make sure you draft your documents correctly.' As the Church of England discovered in *St Edmundsbury v Clark*, even an expressly created easement may prove to be incorrectly drafted.

The strange magic-like rules of implied grant benefit people such as Wong, Borman, Wright, and Goldberg, quite possibly in ways they did not really anticipate. Equally, people like Beaumont, Griffith (no doubt worried about the safety of his pupils), and the owners of the garden in *Graham v Philcox* find that they have 'impliedly granted' easements which may substantially depreciate the value of their land. Careful drafting of contracts, leases, and conveyances would have avoided such disasters.

The Law Commission, in its Report No 327, *Making Land Work: Easements, Covenants and Profits à Prendre*, recommends the abolition of implied grant under the ways of necessity, *Wheeldon v Burrows*, and intended easements rules.

Instead (recommendation 8.3):

> We recommend that an easement shall be implied as a term of a disposition where it is necessary for the reasonable use of the [dominant] land at that date [of disposition], bearing in mind:
> (1) the use of the land at the time of the grant;
> (2) the presence on the servient land of any relevant physical features;
> (3) the intention for the future use of the land, known to both parties at the time of the grant;
> (4) so far as relevant, the available routes for the easement sought; and
> (5) the potential interference with the servient land or inconvenience to the servient owner.

The magical transformation of 'privileges' (the Commission call them 'precarious rights') into full easements under s62 would also be abolished. However the Law Commission recommends 'that section 62…should continue to be able to convert easements, but not profits, from leasehold to freehold interests' (recommendation 8.5). Put another way, the *Wright v Macadam, Goldberg v Edwards* line of cases would be overruled by statute, but the decision in *Graham v Philcox* (see 18.6) would be retained.

Implied grant of profits (currently possible under s62) would be abolished.

Summary

Easements Expressly Granted or Reserved

Where an easement is expressly granted or reserved it is crucial that the exact nature of the right is spelt out in the deed creating the easement. If there is doubt about the scope of an easement, the court can consider the physical features of the relevant land at the time of the grant/reservation.

Four Forms of Implied Grant of Easements

All four have one common feature. Both the dominant and servient land must originally have been in common ownership.

- *A way of necessity* arises where a landowner sells part of their land, with the result that either the land sold or the land retained is 'landlocked'. The way can only be used for those purposes for which the dominant land was being used at the time the land became isolated.

- *An intended easement* arises where land is granted for a specific purpose, and the easement is absolutely essential if that purpose is to be carried out.

- *Wheeldon v Burrows* (1879) converts quasi-easements to easements when part of the land is sold or leased. There are several factors to consider for the rule in *Wheeldon v Burrows* to apply:

  - prior to the conveyance the plots were owned or occupied by the same person;

  - it is necessary to consider the grantor's use before the land was divided and sold. Did the owner of the land have the benefit of a quasi-easement? This rule only applies where the dominant land is sold first. To convert a 'quasi-easement' into a full easement the following must be satisfied:

  - immediately prior to the sale of part of the land the 'quasi-easement' was being used for the benefit of the part sold; and

– the 'quasi-easement' was continuous and apparent; and

– the right is reasonably necessary for the proper enjoyment of the part which has been sold.

- *Section 62 of the Law of Property Act 1925.* A privilege enjoyed by a tenant (such as Mrs Wright's licence to store coal) is converted into a full easement when a new lease is granted (or when the dominant land is sold). The following conditions must be fulfilled for s62 LPA 1925 to operate:

  – the right claimed must satisfy the characteristics of an easement;

  – section 62 can operate only where there is a 'conveyance';

  – there must be a competent grantor; and

  – section 62 applies only to convert 'privileges' into easements.

Implied grant depends on the presumed common intention of the parties. So a carefully drafted lease/conveyance can exclude the operation of the implied grant rules.

Table 18.1 usefully summarizes the different methods of acquiring an easement.

Table 18.1

Comparison of the methods of acquiring an easement

	Necessity	Intended easements	Wheeldon v Burrows	s62 LPA 1925
Grant	✓	✓	✓	✓
Reservation	✓	✓	✗	✗
When does it apply?	Necessity arises where there is no alternative route (landlocked)	Common intention of the parties in relation to the manner or purpose in and for which the land was granted	Prior to the conveyance: common ownership	Prior to the conveyance: diversity of ownership or occupation (note: the High Court in *Wood v Waddington* took a slightly different view)
	Necessity arises at the time of the grant	Common intention of the parties at the time of the grant	Quasi-easement	Privilege, licence
	Alternative route will defeat the claim		Quasi-easement: 'continuous and apparent' and reasonably necessary for the proper enjoyment of the land	Satisfy characteristics of an easement Competent grantor Conveyance
	Strict interpretation by the courts	Broader interpretation by the courts	Either conveyance or a contract Applies only to easements	Must have conveyance Applies to easements and profits
Legal	✓	✓	✓	✓
Equitable	✓	✓	✓	✗ Converts easement only on a conveyance of land

Further Reading

Adams, JE, 'Section 62 LPA again—ripe for reconsideration' [2000] Conv 293
Short discussion of the application of s62 to an easement of right of way.

Editor, 'Land registration, easements and overriding interests' [2005] Conv 545
Case comment on *Sweet v Sommer*.

Pulleyn, S, 'Equitable easements revisited' [2012] Conv 387
Considers how equitable easements may arise in modern law.

Tee, L, 'Metamorphoses and section 62 of the Law of Property Act 1925' [1998] Conv 115
Critical analysis of the operation of s62 LPA 1925.

West, J, '*Wheeldon v Burrows* revisited' [1995] Conv 346
This article considers the application of *Wheeldon v Burrows* in *Millman v Ellis*.

Questions

Last month Finn, owner of Manor Farm and White Tops, two neighbouring farms, sold and conveyed Manor Farm to Aya. The conveyance contained no provision relating to easements and profits.

Advise Aya regarding the following:

1 The only direct access to Manor Farm is a narrow footpath insufficiently wide to accommodate motor traffic. Aya wishes to make use of the private driveway which runs from Manor Farm through White Tops and leads into the adjoining public highway.

2 Some drains run from Manor Farm under White Tops. Aya wishes to make use of those drains.

19

Prescription for Easements (and Profits)

Introduction

The basic concept of prescription is not too difficult; an easement is acquired where the user has for a long period of time enjoyed the claimed right. As long as there is evidence to show long use, the court will then assume that the servient owner has at some stage agreed to this use a long time ago.

To illustrate what we have said, let us suppose that Jason owns Stable House, situated next to Largefield, which is owned by Kwame. The road from Stable House to the nearest shops is very circuitous. Jason has used a short cut across Largefield very regularly and in broad daylight for over 20 years. Jason has not got permission to do this from Kwame and he is a trespasser. Kwame has made no attempt to stop Jason. Jason has enjoyed this right of way for over 20 years, and based on the rules on prescription Jason acquires an easement to cross Largefield. He ceases to be a trespasser, and Kwame cannot stop him from enjoying this right. Put simply, Jason's use of the short cut (as a trespasser) for 20 years creates for himself (and for Stable House) an easement of way across Largefield.

This example, though a good way to start the discussion, rather oversimplifies the law of prescription. It would be easier if the law was simply that '20 years' user gives you a prescriptive easement (or profit)'! But that is not the case. Unfortunately, there are no less than three forms of prescription for easements and profits:

- common law prescription;
- lost modern grant; and
- the Prescription Act 1832.

If somebody (such as Jason in the previous example) is claiming a prescriptive easement (or profit) he will succeed only if:

- he can satisfy certain important rules which are common for all three forms of prescription;

  and

- he can satisfy the specific rules governing any one of the three forms of prescription.

19.1 Rules Common to All Three Forms of Prescription

19.1.1 User, to be Prescriptive, Must Be 'As of Right'

Hopefully, you noticed that in the Stable House example in the Introduction it said that Jason crossed Largefield openly, and without either permission or opposition from Kwame. Jason was acting in a manner as if he was 'rightfully entitled' to use the path (per Parker B, *Bright v Walker* (1834) 1 Cr M & R 221). Those things were said so as to ensure that Jason's user was 'as of right'. User is only 'as of right' if it is 'without force, without secrecy and without permission' (in Latin this is *nec vi, nec clam, nec precario*).

The Supreme Court in *R (Lewis) v Redcar & Cleveland Borough Council* [2010] 2 AC 70 considered the scope of 'as of right'. The case concerned a prescriptive claim by the local inhabitants for informal recreation over private land. The land in question was a golf course, and local inhabitants would walk their dogs and children would play games on the land. The local inhabitants would not interfere with or interrupt play by the golfers. They would wait until play had passed or for golfers to wave them by.

Lord Walker commented that use 'as of right' is reflected in the tripartite test: not by force, nor stealth, and without permission. The deference showed by the local inhabitants when the golfers were playing did not affect use 'as of right'. Lord Walker concluded:

> ...I have great difficulty in seeing how a reasonable owner would have concluded that the residents were not asserting a right to take recreation on the disputed land, simply because they normally showed civility (or, in the inspector's word, deference) towards members of the golf club who were out playing golf. It is not as if the residents took to their heels and vacated the land whenever they saw a golfer. They simply acted (as all the members of the court agree, in much the same terms) with courtesy and common sense. But courteous and sensible though they were (with occasional exceptions) the fact remains that they were regularly, in large numbers, crossing the fairways as well as walking on the rough...A reasonably alert owner of the land could not have failed to recognise that this user was the assertion of a right and would mature into an established right unless the owner took action to stop it (as the golf club tried to do, ineffectually, with the notices erected in 1998).

Allowing the golfers to play whilst they waited did not negate local inhabitants' use of the land 'as of right'.

The burden of proving use 'as of right' rests with the person claiming the right.

Without Force (*Nec Vi*)

If in the Stable House example Jason had had to force his way across Largefield, his user would not have been prescriptive.

In this context, 'force' has been given a very wide meaning, and the courts have ruled that user, to be prescriptive, must not be contentious in any way. Thus, physical violence, the breaking down of barriers, and the climbing over of fences are all 'forcible' user and therefore not prescriptive.

The courts have also held that user in face of express oral or written protests from the alleged servient owner should be deemed to be 'forcible', even though there is no actual violence.

Thus, if Kwame constantly wrote to Jason saying, 'Get off my land!', Jason could not acquire a prescriptive easement.

Without Secrecy (*Nec Clam*)

User, to be prescriptive, must be open; such that a reasonable person in the position of the alleged servient owner, diligent in the protection of his interests, would have a reasonable opportunity of discovering the right asserted (*Union Lighterage Co v London Graving Dock Co* [1902] 2 Ch 557).

In *Lloyds Bank v Dalton* [1942] 1 Ch 466, Dalton owned the servient building, which was a large dye-works. The dominant building was a small outhouse which claimed a prescriptive easement of support against the dye-works. The outhouse had, for well over 20 years, leant against a wall of the dye-works. That wall was a blank wall without any windows. The outhouse could therefore not be seen from the works, neither could it be seen from the public road.

The court nevertheless rejected Dalton's contention that there was 'secret' user. A reasonable owner would surely go around his premises from time to time. A reasonable owner would therefore at some stage have discovered the outhouse.

Bennett J said:

> ... It was not suggested that the plaintiffs' predecessors in title, in executing their works, had acted secretly. The defendant rested his case exclusively on the fact proved that in March 1939, the yard and the outbuilding were not visible from the dye-works or from a highway or other public place.
>
> It is clear law, I think, that an easement of support cannot be acquired unless the owner of the servient tenement has knowledge that his land or his building is in fact supporting the dominant tenement ...
>
> The question of the extent of the knowledge or means of knowledge on the part of the owner of the servient tenement was also considered by the Court of Appeal in *Union Lighterage Co.* v *London Graving Dock Co.* [1902] 2 Ch 557 Romer LJ stated the principle in these terms: '... on principle, it appears to me that a prescriptive right to an easement over a man's land should only be acquired when the enjoyment has been open—that is to say, of such a character that an ordinary owner of the land, diligent in the protection of his interests, would have, or must be taken to have, a reasonable opportunity of becoming aware of that enjoyment.'
>
> In the present case the dominant tenement had in fact been supported by the servient tenement for more than forty years before March 1939. The two tenements were on the slope of this hill. They were contiguous, and the defendant's tenement was below the plaintiffs' tenement. The buildings on the slope were close to one another. There was an open passage leading from Castle Terrace on to the plaintiffs' yard. Once in the plaintiffs' yard, it must have been obvious that the north-east end of that yard and of the outbuilding were supported by the dye-works, and the south-west wall of the dye-works. Lastly, the defendant was not called to give evidence at the trial. *It is notorious that the owners of land and buildings are interested in their boundaries, and, in my judgment, the facts proved at the trial of this case lead irresistibly to the conclusion that the successive owners of the dye-works, assuming them to have been reasonable persons, diligent in the protection of their interests, either must have known or must be taken to have had reasonable opportunity of becoming aware of the fact that the dye-works were supporting the north-east part of the plaintiffs' yard and of the outbuilding standing thereon.* [Emphasis added] For these reasons, the plea of claim, in my judgment, fails.

Lloyds Bank v Dalton should be contrasted with *Liverpool Corporation v Coghill* [1918] 1 Ch 307. Coghill ran a chemical factory which worked 24 hours a day. For many years Coghill poured borax effluent into the corporation's sewers. Coghill always did so in the 'wee small hours'. This was not out of any deliberate intent to conceal what it was doing. Discharging effluent at night suited its 'production cycle'.

The court held that Coghill could not claim a prescriptive right. Its user was in law 'secret', even though there was no deliberate attempt at concealment. Eve J stated:

> ...how can this intermittent use, or rather misuse, of surface and rain water gullies and drains wholly upon and within the limits of the defendants' premises be made the foundation of a legal right to pour a poisonous waste liquor (for such *ex hypothesi* it must be, or no necessity for asserting the easement would exist) into the plaintiffs' sewers, unless notice is brought home to the plaintiffs of what the defendants were doing? There has been no assertion by conduct or otherwise on the part of the defendants that they claimed to do these things as of right, nor have they produced any evidence to prove any notice of their acts to the corporation or their predecessors, or established the existence of any state of things from which such notice could legitimately be inferred. On the contrary, I am quite satisfied on the evidence of Mr Everett, who covers the period between 1879 and 1895, fortified by the resolution of July 30 1873, that the plaintiffs' predecessors had no knowledge of the facts. No attempt has been made to fix the corporation with notice since 1895, and when the matter of injury to the farm was taken up by their responsible officials in 1908 their whole course of conduct was quite inconsistent with their having any notice of what was going on inside the defendants' works. If, then, the methods adopted by the defendants could in any circumstances have been made the foundation of a prescriptive right, a point upon which I express no opinion, *I am satisfied that in the circumstances here disclosed the enjoyment has not been of such a character as to establish any such right. It has throughout been secret, not surreptitious or actively concealed from, but unknown to and unsuspected by the plaintiffs and their predecessors, and incapable, therefore, of being relied upon as the foundation of rights to their prejudice.* [Emphasis added] As Thesiger LJ says in the course of the judgment of the Court of Appeal in *Sturges* v *Bridgman* [1879] 11 ChD 852, 'Consent or acquiescence of the owner of the servient tenement lies at the root of prescription, and of the fiction of a lost grant, and hence the acts or user, which go to the proof of either the one or the other, must be in the language of the civil law, *nec vi, nec clam, nec precario*; for a man cannot, as a general rule, be said to consent or acquiesce in the acquisition by his neighbour of an easement through an enjoyment of which he has no knowledge, actual or constructive'.

thinking point 19.1

Suzie owns The Forge. For the last 25 years she has driven her four-wheel drive car across Ed's Stonehill Meadow to get to and from The Forge. However, those journeys have always been made at about 2 a.m. Is Suzie's user 'as of right'?

Suzie's user is in effect 'secret' and therefore will not be user as of right.

Without Permission (*Nec Precario*)

User does not depend on permission or consent. Even an oral permission is sufficient to negate prescription. Making periodic payments can also be viewed as permission. Normally, once a user is permissive, it will always be permissive, that is, a permission to use is normally regarded as lasting indefinitely. If, however, a permission were revoked but user still continued, the continued user would be 'as of right'.

In *London Tara Hotel v Kensington Close Hotel* [2012] P & CR 271 a private road separating the two hotels was part of the claimant hotel's land. In 1973 the then owners of the two hotels signed a written agreement of indefinite duration under which, in consideration for a charge of £1 a year (which was never collected), the private road could be used for access to the Kensington Close Hotel. The agreement was described as a 'personal licence'.

The ownership of the defendant hotel changed in 1980, but guests, staff, etc of the Kensington Close Hotel continued to use the private road until disputes arose in 2006. The Court of Appeal held that the personal licence, because it was *personal*, expired when the original licensee ceased to own the Kensington Close Hotel. It followed that the user since 1980 was *as of right* and the claim for a prescriptive easement succeeded.

Where the servient owner knows that user (ie by the dominant owner) is going on, and simply tolerates such user without ever giving express permission, then that user is 'as of right' (*Mills v Silver* [1991] Ch 271; *London Tara Hotel v Kensington Close Hotel* [2012] P & CR 271). In *Mills v Silver* the defendant purchased in 1986 a derelict farm set some distance from a public road. The defendant relied upon an old statutory declaration which indicated that the previous owner of the farm had for many years regularly and openly used a particular track to gain access to the farm. The defendant proceeded to use the track for passage on foot and by motor vehicle. The plaintiff objected to the use of vehicles, particularly when the defendant laid down 700 tons of stone along the track, to make a solid road. They sought an injunction and damages for trespass against the defendant.

The Court of Appeal held that the previous owner of the 'servient' land had not given permission for the previous owner of the 'dominant' land to use the track, nor had he objected to the use of it. He had merely 'tolerated' or acquiesced in the use of the track. Nevertheless, this did not defeat the defendant's claim that an easement had been acquired by prescriptive user 'as of right'. The defendants would be able to pass and repass, with or without vehicles, over the track. However, the laying of 700 tons of stone was an excessive exercise of the right to a right of way.

The issue of whether mere tolerated user was sufficient to amount to prescriptive user was the central issue in *Mills v Silver*. Earlier case law suggested that a mere tolerated user could not be user as of right. This view was firmly rejected by the Court of Appeal, Parker LJ said:

> In *Sturges* v. *Bridgman*, (1879) 11 Ch.D. 852 , 863, Thesiger L.J. giving the judgment of the court said:
>
> > 'the law governing the acquisition of easements by user stands thus: Consent or acquiescence of the owner of the servient tenement lies at the root of prescription, and of the fiction of a lost grant, and hence the acts or user, which go to the proof of either the one or the other, must be, in the language of the civil law, *nec vi, nec clam, nec precario*; for a man cannot, as a general rule, be said to consent to or acquiesce in the acquisition by his neighbour of an easement through an enjoyment of which he has no knowledge, actual or constructive, or which he contests and endeavours to interrupt, or which he temporarily licenses.'

This passage is in my judgment of prime importance in the determination of the present appeal for it makes plain (i) that consent or acquiescence to the user asserted as giving rise to the easement is an essential ingredient of the acquisition of the easement and (ii) that it is the nature of the acts of user which has to be examined in order to see whether the easement is established.

Unless the acts of user are of the requisite character, consent or acquiescence is irrelevant. If they are then consent or acquiescence is essential.

In *Hollins* v. *Verney*, (1884) 13 Q.B.D. 304, 315, Lindley L.J. giving the judgment of the court said:

> 'no actual user can be sufficient to satisfy the statute, unless during the whole of the statutory term…the user is enough at any rate to carry to the mind of a reasonable

person who is in possession of the servient tenement, the fact that a continuous right to enjoyment is being asserted, and ought to be resisted if such right is not recognised, and if resistance to it is intended.'

This shows clearly that the crucial matter for consideration is whether for the necessary period the use is such as to bring home to the mind of a reasonable person that a continuous right of enjoyment is being asserted. If it is and the owner of the allegedly servient tenement knows or must be taken to know of it and does nothing about it the right is established. It is no answer for him to say, 'I "tolerated" it.' If he does nothing he will be taken to have recognized the right and not intended to resist it. He will have consented to it or acquiesced in it.

19.1.2 Presumed Acquiesence

It is often said that prescription depends on presumed acquiescence by the servient owner. But 'presumed acquiescence' is not a separate element of prescription which must be proved in addition to user as of right. This is made clear at the beginning of the passage from *Mills v Silver* quoted in the previous section. In *London Tara Hotel Ltd v Kensington Close Hotel Ltd* [2012] P & CR 271 at 287, Lewison LJ said, after referring to Lord Kerr in *R v Cleveland and Redcar* [2010] 2 AC 70:

> 74 In my judgment there is clear authority at the highest level that if use satisfies the tripartite test (not by force, nor stealth, nor the licence of the owner,) then a prescriptive right will be established. There is no further criteria that must be satisfied. As Lord Kerr put it, once those three criteria are established it is *ipso facto* reasonable to expect the landowner to challenge the use. In other words, *once these three criteria are established the owner is taken to have acquiesced in the use.* It follows, in my judgment that unless the use by KCL was forcible, stealthy or permissive, a right of way will have been established. [Emphasis added]

thinking point 19.2

The Strauss family own and live in Crescendo House. For the last 25 years they have been crossing Jim's Wide Field to get to and from Crescendo House. Jim tells you 'I have not spoken to the Strauss family in 25 years. They are really noisy, playing music all night. I have just put up with what they have been doing'. Is the Strauss family user capable of giving rise to an easement?

Jim has neither consented to nor forbidden the crossing of Wide Field. He has simply put up with it; he has 'acquiesced'. The Strauss family have prescriptive user as of right of a right of way.

19.1.3 User Which is a Criminal Offence

As is shown in the Stable House and Largefield example in the Introduction, the user as of right which eventually gives rise to a prescriptive easement will (until the easement is acquired), usually constitute the civil tort of trespass to land. Trespass to land is not normally a criminal offence.

If the alleged prescriptive user necessarily involves the commission of a criminal offence, then a prescriptive easement cannot arise. However, the (very welcome) decision of the House of Lords in the test case of *Bakewell Management Ltd v Brandwood* [2004] 2 WLR 955 should be noted.

In that case the defendants, owners of houses on the edge of a common, had been for many years driving across the common to get from the public road to their homes. Section 193(4) Law of Property Act 1925 (LPA 1925) makes it an offence to drive across a common 'without lawful authority'. The claimants, the owners of the common, argued that the defendants' 'criminal' conduct could not give rise to a prescriptive easement.

The House of Lords ruled in favour of the defendants. The defendant home-owners' conduct was not necessarily criminal; it would be perfectly lawful if they had had authority from the servient owners to drive across the servient land. Further, the whole essence of prescription is that if the appropriate conditions regarding user as of right exist, the law conclusively presumes that the servient owner has granted the dominant owner authority to use the servient land!

19.1.4 User Must Be Continuous

The claimant (user) must show that the claimed easement is being continually enjoyed. Parker LJ in *Mills v Silver* said the 'crucial matter for consideration is whether for the necessary period the use is such as to bring home to the mind of a reasonable person that a continuous right of enjoyment is being asserted'.

What amounts to continuously enjoyed? In *Hollins v Verney* (1884) 13 QB 304, the alleged dominant owner had used the right of way only three times in the previous 20 years. The Court of Appeal rejected the claim for a prescriptive easement. It held that user must be sufficiently regular so that a reasonable servient owner would know some right was being asserted. (You should note that this is in effect much the same rule as is applied in 'secrecy' cases.)

19.1.5 User Must Be By or on Behalf of a Fee Simple Against a Fee Simple

The easement can only be acquired by the dominant owner of the fee simple ('user') or someone who is acting on behalf of the fee simple owner, and it can only be acquired against a fee simple estate. This is a peculiar rule which has become firmly embedded into English common law as demonstrated in *Simmons v Dobson* [1991] 1 WLR 720. Fox LJ stated:

> Now, in relation to common law prescription generally, user had to be by or on behalf of a fee simple owner against a fee simple owner. An easement can be granted expressly by a tenant for life or tenant for years so as to bind their respective limited interests, but such rights cannot be acquired by prescription . . .
>
> . . . as a matter of authority, it is established that one tenant cannot acquire an easement by prescription at common law against another tenant holding under the same landlord . . .
>
> While, therefore, there appears to be no case which directly decides that there can be no lost modern grant by or to a person who owns a lesser estate than the fee, the *dicta* are to the contrary and are very strong and of long standing. I take them to represent settled law . . .
>
> As to any departure from that state of the law, there are, I think, difficulties of principle. It is clear that common law prescription and prescription under the 1832 Act are, as a matter of decision, not available by or to owners of less estates than the fee. Lost modern grant is merely a form of common law prescription. It is based upon a fiction which was designed to meet, and did meet, a particular problem. It would, I think, be anomalous to extend the fiction further by departure, in relation to lost modern grant, from the fundamental principle of common law prescription . . .

In this case the claimant was the tenant of one property and the defendant was tenant of an adjoining property. Freehold title to both properties was held by the same landlord.

The claimant sought to show that, according to the doctrine of lost modern grant, they had the right to use a passageway over the defendant's premises. The Court of Appeal held that the tenant could not claim an easement by the doctrine of lost modern grant. The doctrine gave rise to a form of common law prescription, which could only apply between freeholders.

Prescriptive Easements are Only in Fee Simple

English law insists that a prescriptive easement or profit can be only of fee simple duration, that is, perpetual. This apparently simple rule creates complications where either:

- the person carrying out the user as of right is a lessee rather than a fee simple owner;

or

- the servient land has at any time been leased (or settled).

Five consequences flow from this rule:

1 However long a tenant carries on user as of right against their own landlord, the tenant cannot gain a prescriptive easement. For example, Lorenzo owns the fee simple in two warehouses: Large Warehouse and Small Warehouse. He leases Small Warehouse to Tamsin for 999 years. Tamsin immediately starts to cross through Large Warehouse using a passageway to get to Small Warehouse. She and the successors to her lease continue to do so 'as of right' for hundreds of years. A prescriptive easement cannot arise.

2 A tenant cannot acquire an easement against another tenant of the same landlord. See *Simmons v Dobson*.

3 If a tenant prescribes 'as of right' against a third party freehold owner, an easement is created for the benefit of the landlord's fee simple. Santos owns Large Field. Dylan owns neighbouring Small Field, which he leases for 50 years to Tariq. Tariq for 50 years crosses as of right Large Field to get to Small Field. A prescriptive easement can arise, which will benefit Dylan's fee simple.

4 A period of user entirely against a lessee or life tenant of the servient land cannot normally be prescriptive. However, if user commences against a fee simple owner in actual possession, it does not matter if the servient land is subsequently leased.

5 The Court of Appeal has held in *Williams v Sandy Lane (Chester) Ltd* [2007] 1 P & CR 27, that a period of user as of right which was entirely against a tenant gave rise to an easement in fee simple provided:

- the owner of the fee simple at some stage knew of the user; and

- (as will normally be the case) the owner of the fee simple had been able (during the user) to take proceedings to stop the user, but did not do so.

thinking point 19.3

Consider the old case of Palk v Shinner *(1852) 118 ER 215, which illustrates points (3) and (4) in the previous list. Palk leased his land to various tenants. From 1820 onwards, the tenants crossed Shinner's land 'as of right' to reach the land leased to them. From 1821 onwards, Shinner's land was leased to X. User as of right by the tenants continued until the dispute broke out in about 1850. What do you think was the result of the case?*

The court gave judgment for Palk, holding that his tenants were to be regarded as acting on his behalf (point (3)). Palk thus acquired a fee simple easement. Moreover, as the user as of right had commenced against Shinner personally (a fee simple owner in actual possession) it did not matter that the servient land had subsequently been leased (point (4)).

thinking point 19.4

What would be the position if Shinner had leased his land to X in 1818? The claim to a prescriptive easement would fail, as the user as of right would have been entirely against a lessee, unless Shinner at some stage knew of the user and was in a position to stop the user (Williams v Sandy Lane (Chester) Ltd).

19.1.6 User Must Be Against a Servient Owner Capable of Granting an Easement

In *Housden v Conservators of Wimbledon and Putney Commons* [2008] 1 WLR 1172, the claimants claimed a prescriptive right of way across a part of Wimbledon Common to gain access to their house. They and their predecessors had been cutting across the common 'as of right' for over 100 years. The claim failed at first instance as the defendant statutory body was held to have (under the legislation which was set up in 1891) no power to grant easements over the common. On appeal the Court of Appeal [2008] 3 All ER 1038 gave a wide interpretation to the 1891 Act and held that an easement was acquired by prescription as the defendants did have the power to grant an easement.

19.2 Prescription at Common Law

For reasons which will quickly become apparent, a claim for an easement or a profit by 'prescription at common law' is very rarely successful. The theory of this form of prescription is that a long time ago a deed was executed by the then servient owner in favour of the then dominant owner, granting the relevant easement or profit. However, this deed was granted so long ago that its execution is 'outside the scope of legal memory'.

Unfortunately, legal memory is elephantine, and stretches back to 1189 (called 'time immemorial' the year of the accession of Richard I). In effect, if you claim a prescriptive easement (or profit) at common law, you have boldly to assert that you and your predecessors have been exercising the right ever since 1189.

Fortunately, you do not have to produce evidence of user covering the whole of the last 800 or so years. If 20 years' user is proved, user right back to 1189 will be presumed. But the presumption can be rebutted by showing any of the following facts:

- at some time since 1189 the right was not exercised;

  or
- at some time since 1189 the right could not have been exercised;

  or
- at some time since 1189 dominant and servient plots were in common ownership.

Thus, a servient owner faced with a claim for prescription at common law will look round for rebutting evidence from elderly inhabitants or ancient records. The current owner of West Plot is claiming at common law a prescriptive easement of way over neighbouring East Plot. The owner of East Plot will be delighted if they can find some very senior citizen who says something like, 'When I was a little girl my mum worked at West Plot and nobody got to it by crossing East Plot. They always used the track across North Plot.' Or perhaps it will be, 'When I was a little boy East Plot was very swampy and impossible to cross. I remember because I once fell in; dad told me off.'

Ancient records will be just as effective. Proof that for a few years *circa* (say) 1400 the same person owned both West Plot and East Plot, will be enough to defeat the common law claim.

19.3 Prescription by Lost Modern Grant

The utility of common law prescription is largely destroyed by the absurd '1189 rule'. However, the old, pre-1875 courts invented a legal doctrine called 'lost modern grant'. This doctrine was designed to allow prescription for easements and profits where there was strong evidence of at least 20 years' 'user as of right' but it was clear that user had commenced 'in modern times'. 'Modern times' was any date after 1189!

Lost modern grant is a 'legal fiction'. A legal fiction occurs where the court 'finds as a fact' something everyone knows is really not true, and then decides the case on the basis of that 'fact'. The essence of 'lost modern grant' is that the court 'finds as a fact' that a deed was executed 'in modern times' granting the easement (or profit) claimed, but that deed has been lost.

In the days when civil cases (including land disputes) were tried by juries, 'lost modern grant' caused judges (particularly trial judges) a lot of trouble. Cockburn CJ in *Bryant v Foot* (1867) LR 2 QB 161, described the reality of what trial judges told juries:

> Juries were first told that from user, during living memory, or even during twenty years, they might presume a lost grant or deed; next they were recommended to make such presumption; and lastly, as the final consummation of judicial legislation, it was held that a jury should be told, not only that they might, but also that they were bound to presume the existence of such a lost grant, although neither judge nor jury, nor any one else, had the shadow of a belief that any such instrument had ever really existed.

Some nineteenth-century juries, sworn to 'well and truly try' the case, were understandably worried by this approach. Nevertheless, in 1881 the House of Lords in *Dalton v Angus* (1881) 6 App Cas 740, reaffirmed the validity of the lost modern grant rule.

Two developments in the twentieth century have greatly improved the situation. First, land law disputes are no longer tried by jury; they are tried by a judge alone. Secondly, this area of law has been much simplified by two relatively modern Court of Appeal decisions, *Tehidy Minerals v Norman* [1971] 2 QB 528 and *Oakley v Boston* [1976] QB 270.

Tehidy Minerals involved a claim for a prescriptive profit of grazing on a part of Bodmin Moor. In January 1920, a group of farmers started grazing their sheep on the servient land. They continued to do so 'as of right' until October 1941, when the land was requisitioned by the War Office for military training. The farmers continued to graze their sheep on the land, but it was conceded that this post-1941 grazing was by permission. (Permission came first from the War Office and then, after the land had been derequisitioned, from the servient owners.)

The farmers successfully claimed under 'lost modern grant' a prescriptive profit of pasture on the basis of their 1920 to 1941 user. The Court of Appeal held that a 'presumption' of lost modern grant arose where the claimant produced strong evidence of 20 years' user as of right. If there is such evidence then 'the deed which has got lost' is assumed to have been executed:

1 at the earliest, immediately before user as of right commenced; and

2 at the latest, 20 years before user as of right ceased.

The court held that it is not sufficient to rebut the 'presumption' of lost modern grant for the servient owner to show that the grant never in fact took place. The presumption of lost modern grant can be rebutted (and the claim for the profit or easement therefore defeated) only by showing that throughout the period (1) to (2), ('the relevant period') the grant was legally impossible. There would be 'legal impossibility' if, say, throughout 'the relevant period' the land had been requisitioned, or vested in a person who had no power to grant profits or easements.

In *Tehidy Minerals,* the relevant period for the presumed grant was January 1920 to October 1921. During those 21 months there was no question of a grant being legally impossible. Hence the farmers' victory. Buckley LJ said:

> No defendant has sought to prove any actual grant of common rights: at the trial the defendants relied on common law prescription, on the Prescription Act, 1832, and on the doctrine of lost modern grant...
>
> The co-existence of three separate methods of prescribing is, in our view, anomalous and undesirable, for it results in much unnecessary complication and confusion. We hope that it may be possible for the Legislature to effect a long-overdue simplification in this branch of the law.
>
> ...
>
> In our judgment *Angus* v. *Dalton* (1877) 3 Q.B.D. 85; (1878) 4 Q.B.D. 162; (1881) 6 App.Cas. 740 decides that, where there has been upwards of 20 years' uninterrupted enjoyment of an easement, such enjoyment having the necessary qualities to fulfil the requirements of prescription, then unless, for some reason such as incapacity on the part of the person or persons who might at some time before the commencement of the 20-year period have made a grant, the existence of such a grant is impossible, the law will adopt a legal fiction that such a grant was made, in spite of any direct evidence that no such grant was in fact made.
>
> If this legal fiction is not to be displaced by direct evidence that no grant was made, it would be strange if it could be displaced by circumstantial evidence leading to the same conclusion, and in our judgment it must follow that circumstantial evidence tending to negative the existence of a grant (other than evidence establishing impossibility) should not be permitted to displace the fiction. Precisely the same reasoning must, we think, apply to a presumed lost grant of a profit à prendre as to an easement.
>
> In the present case, if we are to presume lost grants, we must do so in respect of each of the four farms, Higher and Lower Hill, Cabilla and Pinsla Park. Each of the presumed grants must be supposed to have been made between January 20, 1920, and October 5, 1921, and to have been since lost in circumstances of which no one now has any recollection. This combination of circumstances seems to us to be exceedingly improbable, and we feel sympathy for the view expressed by Farwell J., in *Attorney-General* v. *Simpson* [1901] 2 Ch. 671, 698:
>
> > 'It cannot be the duty of a judge to presume a grant of the nonexistence of which he is convinced, nor can he be constrained to hold that such a grant is reasonably possible within the meaning of the authorities.'
>
> In view, however, of the decision in *Angus* v. *Dalton* (1877) 3 Q.B.D. 85; (1878) 4 Q.B.D. 162; (1881) 6 App.Cas. 740 we consider that it is not open to us in the present case to follow this line...
>
> For these reasons we think that grants of common rights of grazing over Tawna Down must be presumed to have been made since January 19, 1920, and before October 6, 1921, in respect of each of the four farms at present under consideration.
>
> We are therefore of opinion that prescriptive rights to grazing on the down must be regarded as having been in force at the date of the requisition in respect of all seven farms under discussion. What ensued thereafter can only have had the effect of suspending these rights unless it can be said that any of the claimants or any predecessor in title of his has abandoned

his grazing rights. For the plaintiffs it is contended that the arrangement of October 1960 amounted to abandonment by the commoners of their rights over Tawna Down. We do not agree. For reasons which we have already indicated we think that that arrangement was of a temporary and terminable character. Abandonment of an easement or of a profit à prendre can only, we think, be treated as having taken place where the person entitled to it has demonstrated a fixed intention never at any time thereafter to assert the right himself or to attempt to transmit it to anyone else. The fact that the commoners are content for the time being to subject the management of the grazing on the down to the control of the association is not, in our view, a circumstance which gives rise to any such conclusion. The commoners may well find it more advantageous for the time being to subject themselves to the control of the association in order to obtain the benefits of the fencing and maintenance by the association of the grazing on the down than to exercise their common rights. It does not at all follow from this that if at some time in the future the arrangement should come to an end, the commoners might not wish to reassert their common rights. We do not think that any abandonment has been shown to have taken place.

In the later case of *Oakley v Boston*, a differently constituted Court of Appeal applied the rules in *Tehidy Minerals*, but held against the claimant for an easement. The evidence was that there had been user as of right of an alleged right of way from 1914 to 1962. After that there had been insufficient user.

thinking point 19.5

In Oakley v Boston, *what was 'the relevant period' at some time during which the presumed grant would supposedly have taken place?*

Applying Tehidy Minerals v Norman, *the presumed grant would be some time between 1914 and 1942.*

There was, however, one crucial fact in *Oakley v Boston* which has not yet been mentioned. The alleged servient land had been, until 1952, 'glebe land'. Glebe land is land vested in the local vicar (of the Church of England) not in their personal capacity but in their official capacity as an 'ecclesiastical corporation sole'.

The Court of Appeal first held (interpreting some very obscure nineteenth-century legislation governing the Church) that a vicar owning land in his official capacity as an 'ecclesiastical corporation sole' had no power to grant easements.

thinking point 19.6

What, therefore, was the result of the case?

As throughout 'the relevant period' when the supposed grant could have taken place it was 'legally impossible', the claim for a prescriptive easement invoking lost modern grant failed.

 19.4 # Prescription Under the Prescription Act 1832

Sections 1 and 2 of the Prescription Act 1832 are complex. The sections have been set out in the following extract, but do not (yet) try to make sense of them.

Prescription Act 1832

1. Claims to right of common and other profits à prendre, not to be defeated after thirty years enjoyment by merely showing the commencement; after sixty years enjoyment the right to be absolute, unless had by consent or agreement

…No claim which may be lawfully made at the common law, by custom, prescription, or grant, to any right of common or other profit or benefit to be taken and enjoyed from or upon any land of our sovereign lord the King…or any land being parcel of the duchy of Lancaster or the duchy of Cornwall, or of any ecclesiastical or lay person, or body corporate, except such matters and things as are herein specially provided for, and except tithes, rent, and services, shall, where such right, profit, or benefit have been actually taken and enjoyed by any person claiming right thereto without interruption for the full period of thirty years, be defeated or destroyed by showing only that such right, profit, or benefit was first taken or enjoyed at any time prior to such period of thirty years, but nevertheless such claim may be defeated in any other way by which the same is now liable to be defeated; and when such right, profit, or benefit shall have been so taken and enjoyed as aforesaid for the full period of sixty years, the right thereto shall be deemed absolute and indefeasible, unless it shall appear that the same was taken and enjoyed by some consent or agreement expressly made or given for that purpose by deed or writing.

2. In claims of rights of way or other easement the periods to be twenty years and forty years

…No claim which may be lawfully made at the common law, by custom, prescription, or grant, to any way or other easement, or to any watercourse, or the use of any water, to be enjoyed or derived upon, over, or from any land or water of our said lord the King…or being parcel of the duchy of Lancaster or of the duchy of Cornwall, or being the property of any ecclesiastical or lay person, or body corporate, when such way or other matter as herein last before mentioned shall have been actually enjoyed by any person claiming right thereto without interruption for the full period of twenty years, shall be defeated or destroyed by showing only that such way or other matter was first enjoyed at any time prior to such period of twenty years, but nevertheless such claim may be defeated in any other way by which the same is now liable to be defeated; and where such way or other matter as herein last before mentioned shall have been so enjoyed as aforesaid for the full period of forty years, the right thereto shall be deemed absolute and indefeasible, unless it shall appear that the same was enjoyed by some consent or agreement expressly given or made for that purpose by deed or writing.

You will surely agree that these provisions are very badly drafted. The House of Lords came to that conclusion in *Flight v Thomas* (1841) 8 ER 91, but nothing has ever been done to reform or repeal the Act.

The complexity of the 1832 Act is to be contrasted with the relative simplicity of the 'lost modern grant' rule as restated in *Tehidy Minerals*. We would like to be able to say, 'Forget the Prescription Act, rely on lost modern grant.' But we cannot say that for two reasons:

cross-reference
See 19.3 for a discussion of Tehidy Minerals.

- the courts have repeatedly held that lost modern grant, being a 'legal fiction', can be relied upon only if the other forms of prescription (common law and the 1832 Act) fail; and

- the complexities of the Act produce the result that there are quite a few situations which the Act covers which are not covered by the other two forms of prescription.

19.4.1 Shorter and Longer Periods Under the Act

If you study ss 1 and 2 of the Act, you will eventually realize that the Act makes some kind of distinction between 'shorter periods' and 'longer periods'.

- Shorter periods: 20 years' user as of right for easements, and 30 years for profits.

- Longer periods: 40 years' user as of right for easements, and 60 years for profits.

Where a claim for an easement or a profit is based on 20 or 30 years' user as of right, the claim will not 'be defeated or destroyed by showing only that such right, profit, or benefit was first taken or enjoyed at any time prior to such period of [twenty] thirty years, but such claim may be defeated in any other way by which the same is now liable to be defeated' (s1 Prescription Act 1832).

Where a claim for an easement or a profit is based on 40 or 60 years' user as of right, 'the right thereto shall be deemed absolute and indefeasible' (s2 Prescription Act 1832).

We will return to the differences between the shorter and longer periods at 19.4.3. For the moment it is sufficient to say that most cases will be covered by the shorter periods. It will be relatively rare that a dominant owner will want to rely on the longer periods.

19.4.2 The 'Next Before Action' and 'Without Interruption' Rules

Section 4 of the 1832 Act introduces for the purposes of the Act (but not for the other forms of prescription) two very strange rules: the 'next before action' and 'without interruption' rules.

The 'Next Before Action' Rule

> Prescription Act 1832
>
> 4. Before mentioned periods to be deemed those next before suits
>
> Each of the respective periods of years hereinbefore mentioned shall be deemed and taken to be the period next before some suit or action wherein the claim or matter . . . be brought into question.

What this really means is that the period of 'user as of right' relied on by the dominant owner must be a period ending when the dispute between the parties arises. The dispute 'arises' when the writ or claim form in the court case is issued. It does not matter whether it is the servient owner suing as claimant claiming that there is no easement or profit or the dominant owner suing as claimant claiming a prescriptive easement or profit.

If there is a period (however long) of 'user as of right' followed by a gap when there is no user, and then after this gap the writ or claim form is issued, the Prescription Act 1832 is no help to the dominant owner. The dominant owner will have to rely on one of the other forms of prescription.

This point is illustrated by the facts of *Oakley v Boston*. The judge found as a fact that regular user as of right ceased in 1962. The writ in the case was not issued until 1972. Because of the ten-year gap in activity the alleged dominant owner had no chance under the 1832 Act. Similarly, in *Mills v Silver*, the dominant owners could rely only on lost modern grant, since the user as of right had been from 1922 to 1981 but the writ was not issued until 1987. (See also para 29 of Lord Scott's speech in *Bakewell Management v Brandwood*.)

---

pause for thought

Now study ss 1 and 2 of the 1832 Act in the previous extract and try to discern if there is some kind of pattern linking the two sections.

cross-reference

See 19.3 for a discussion on *Oakley v Boston*.

The 'Without Interruption' Rule

This rule always reminds one of the children's riddle, 'When is a door not a door? When it's ajar.' The riddle now posed to you is, 'When is an interruption not an interruption?' The answer is 'When we are dealing with the Prescription Act 1832 and the interruption has lasted less than a year.'

thinking point 19.7

In 1986, Tom, the owner of Greenland, started (as of right) to cross Fayola's Redland to get to and from Greenland. In 2006, for about six months, the path across Redland was blocked by Fayola. Fayola then removed the blockage and Tom recommenced his user as of right. Fayola has once again blocked the path. If Tom immediately issues a claim form claiming a prescriptive easement, will he win the case?

Yes, he will succeed. He will be able to show some 30 years' user 'next before action'. The six months' interruption is not an interruption for the purposes of the 1832 Act. (The result would be different if back around 2006, Fayola had blocked the path for 15 months.)

In thinking point 19.7 it was indicated that Tom immediately issued a claim when his path was blocked a second time. This was to avoid the (fatal for the dominant owner) gap between user as of right and commencement of legal proceedings.

Actually the immediate issue of a claim form is not essential. The 'without interruption' rule in effect creates an exception to the 'next before action' rule. Provided legal proceedings are commenced within a year of the date when the interruption first actually occurred, a dominant owner will be able to rely on user as of right continuing up to that date of actual interruption. In our Tom and Greenland example, Tom would lose if he delayed more than a year before issuing his claim.

Interruption of User as of Right in the Twentieth Year

The strange quirks of s4 were demonstrated as early as 1841 in the House of Lords' case of *Flight v Thomas* (1841) 8 ER 91. In that case the dominant owner had enjoyed his easement as of right for 19 years and 11 months. He was then interrupted by an obstruction. He waited a few months before issuing his writ. Thus 20 years had elapsed from the commencement of his user as of right, but he had not yet been 'interrupted' for one year. The Lord Chancellor provided an explanation of an interruption:

> ...The words of the fourth section of the Act are positive that no interruption for less than one year shall be deemed an interruption within the meaning of this Act—the meaning and purpose of the Act being to give 20 years' enjoyment the effect of absolute right—that no interruption of the enjoyment of that right for less than one year shall have effect for the purposes of the Act.

thinking point 19.8

What do you think was the result of the case?

The dominant owner was held to have a prescriptive easement. The practical result of this decision is that enjoyment for 19 years and a bit (even one day) will be sufficient to give a prescriptive easement under the 1832 Act, provided that the dominant owner times the issue of his claim form correctly. Similar principles would apply where one of the longer periods of prescription was being relied on and the interruption occurred in the thirtieth, fortieth, or sixtieth year of user as of right.

thinking point 19.9

In January 1997, Daiki started to cut across Manor Gardens to get to Primrose Hill, and has done so ever since. It is now March 2016. What should Shane, the owner of Manor Gardens, do to stop Daiki gaining an easement?

Shane should immediately issue a claim form against Daiki. Daiki will have only 19 years' (and a bit) user 'next before action', and therefore any claim for a prescriptive easement is bound to fail.

thinking point 19.10

If in March 2016, Shane does not issue a claim form but instead puts up a fence barring Daiki's way. What should Daiki do?

Daiki should 'lie low' until February 2017, and then issue a claim form claiming that he has a prescriptive easement. He should win, as the claim will be more than 20 years after user as of right commenced, but the 'interruption' will not have lasted one year.

19.4.3 Differences between Longer and Shorter Periods Under the Prescription Act 1832

Oral Permissions

When enacting the longer periods of prescription, the 1832 Act (ss 1 and 2) states that after 40 or 60 years' user, 'The right thereto [to the easement or profit] shall be deemed absolute and indefeasible, unless it shall appear that the same was taken and enjoyed by some consent or agreement expressly made or given for that purpose by deed or writing.'

User, to be prescriptive under the Prescription Act 1832, must (in principle) be 'as of right'. Thus the reference to 'consent...by deed or writing' seems very confusing. It would appear (though this has never been firmly decided by the courts) that for the longer periods of prescription the strange wording of the statute creates a small exception to the general rule that user to be prescriptive must be 'as of right'. It seems that if there has been 40 (or 60) years' user originally based on a purely oral permission, but that permission has not been renewed in the last 40 or 60 years, the user is prescriptive.

Consider the following example: in 1971, Stephen, the owner of Bluefield, gave oral permission to Dora, the owner of Redfield, allowing Dora to cross Bluefield to get to Redfield. That permission has never been renewed and Dora has been crossing Bluefield for the last 40-something years. Although normally a permission lasts indefinitely (see section 19.1.1 under the heading 'Without Permission (*Nec Precario*)'), an oral permission given more than 40 years ago is ignored. Thus Dora acquires a prescriptive easement of way under the longer period.

If Stephen had renewed the oral permission at any time in the last 40 years (say in 1984) Dora would lose her claim for a prescriptive easement: *Gardner v Hodgson's Kingston Brewery* [1903] AC 229 and *Healey v Hawkins* [1968] 3 All ER 836.

Periods Excluded from Computation by s7 of the 1832 Act

Section 7 of the 1832 Act applies only with respect to the shorter (20- or 30-year) prescription periods:

> *Prescription Act 1832*
>
> 7. Proviso for infants, etc
>
> Provided also, that the time during which any person otherwise capable of resisting any claim to any of the matters before mentioned shall have been or shall be an infant, idiot, non compos mentis, feme covert, or tenant for life, or during which any action or suit shall have been pending, and which shall have been diligently prosecuted, until abated by the death of any party or parties thereto, shall be excluded in the computation of the periods herein-before mentioned, except only in cases where the right or claim is hereby declared to be absolute and indefeasible.

This section creates a special rule designed to protect servient owners who are under a disability. In effect a period of user against a person under one of the disabilities listed in s7 is not to count towards the 20 (30) years. The disabilities are mental illness, being under age, and being a life tenant. Being a 'feme covert' (married woman) was a disability until 1882!

thinking point 19.11

In 1990, Wayne commenced user as of right of a pathway over Julia's land. From 1997 to 2005, Julia suffered from a mental illness. Wayne (if he continues the user as of right) does not acquire any right under the Act until . . .?

The answer is 2018. One way of looking at this is to say that the eight years of the mental illness has to be added to the normal prescription period of 20 years to produce a total period of 28 years.

What if between 1999 and 2003 (while Julia suffered from a mental illness) user as of right was prevented by a barbed wire fence? Wayne's claim for a prescriptive easement will fail. Section 7 is purely for the protection of servient owners. An 'interruption' occurring during the period of the disability cannot be ignored!

Periods Excluded from Computation by s8 of the 1832 Act

This provision applies only to the 40-year period of prescription for easements. It has no application to profits.

To try to help make sense of the provision, the section has been split into three parts in the following extract. You will also see that the word 'easement' has been added in the second line, although in the official edition of the 1832 Act the word used is 'convenient'. The word 'convenient' makes no sense: it is thought that it is a misprint for 'easement'.

> *Prescription Act 1832*
>
> 8. What time to be excluded in computing the term of forty years appointed by this Act
>
> Provided always, that when any land or water upon, over, or from which any such way or other [easement] watercourse or use of water shall have been or shall be enjoyed or derived hath been or shall be held under or by virtue of any term of life, or any term of years exceeding three years from the granting thereof,
>
> the time of enjoyment of any such way or other matter as hereinbefore mentioned, during the continuance of such terms, shall be excluded in the computation of the said period of forty years,
>
> in case the claim within three years after the end or sooner determination of such term be resisted by any person entitled to any reversion expectant on the determination thereof.

Section 8 operates in a way somewhat similar to s7 (see the previous section). However, notice carefully:

1 that the 'disabilities' are that either the servient land has been leased for a period of more than three years, or that the servient owner was a life tenant (see the last words of the first part of the section); and

2 that a servient owner can invoke the special protection given them by s8 only if proceedings disputing the easement are commenced within three years of the lease or life tenancy expiring. (See the third part of the section.)

thinking point 19.12

Airell commenced user as of right of a path over Sunny Meadow in 1970 and has continued ever since. From June 1973 to June 2013, the servient land was subject to a strict settlement under which Leon was the life tenant.

What is the position under the 1832 Act if in March 2016 either Airell commences an action claiming an easement, or the (new) servient fee simple owner commences proceedings against Airell?

The servient owner would win in proceedings based on the 1832 Act; he would be able to invoke the protection of s8, and therefore a claim under the longer 40-year period would fail.

thinking point 19.13

What if legal proceedings (begun by Airell or the servient owner) were not commenced until July 2016?

The servient owner would be too late to invoke the protection of s8, as more than three years would have elapsed since the expiry of the life tenancy. Airell would win under the longer period provided by the 1832 Act.

The Requirement that User be 'Against a Fee Simple' Does Not Apply to the Longer Periods of Prescription

(See 19.1.5 for the general rule.)

thinking point 19.14

Continue the example just discussed in the previous thinking point. The servient land was settled from June 1963 to June 2013 and that Airell's user as of right commenced (as before) in 1970. It is now March 2017, and Airell has just issued a claim form claiming a prescriptive easement under the 40-year period. Will he win?

Normally, the fact that user as of right commenced against a life tenant or lessee is fatal to a claim for a prescriptive easement. But when dealing with the 40-year period under the 1832 Act, the usual rule about 'user [commencing] against a fee simple' does not apply. So Airell will succeed in a claim under the 40-year period despite commencing his user against a life tenant.

thinking point 19.15

Use the same example in the previous thinking point, except that the servient (fee simple) owner issued a claim form against Airell sometime in 2016. Who will win this case?

Provided he issued his claim form before June 2016, the servient owner will win, as he will be protected by s8. If the servient owner delayed to the latter half of 2016 he would lose, as he would be outside the three-year period for 'resisting' given by the last part of s8.

19.4.4 Prescription for Easements of Light

This is governed by s3 Prescription Act 1832. Section 3 was designed to make it easier to acquire a prescriptive easement for light. Unfortunately, it is, if anything, now too easy for a building to acquire a prescriptive easement of light over an adjoining vacant plot of land. The rules under s3 differ quite substantially from the normal rules governing prescription.

> *Prescription Act 1832*
>
> 3. Claim to the use of light enjoyed for 20 years
>
> When the access and use of light to and for any dwelling house, workshop, or other building shall have been actually enjoyed therewith for the full period of twenty years without interruption, the right thereto shall be deemed absolute and indefeasible, any local usage or custom to the contrary notwithstanding, unless it shall appear that the same was enjoyed by some consent or agreement expressly made or given for that purpose by deed or writing.

User Under s3 Need Not Be As of Right

This was established in *Morgan v Fear* [1907] AC 425. The only aspect of user as of right applicable to s3 cases is that a *written* permission will debar a claim. Thus, if a dominant owner kept on demolishing obstructions to their light which appeared on the servient land, the dominant owner could acquire a prescriptive easement! The dominant owner would, however, be liable for trespassing on the servient land when carrying out demolition work.

The case of *G and S Brough Ltd v Salvage Wharf* [2010] Ch 11 should be noted. The claimants proved enjoyment as of right of an (alleged) easement of light since 1951. In 1999 they had agreed with the servient owners that, notwithstanding this easement, the servient owners could develop the servient land in a way which would (to some extent) infringe their right to light.

In 2004, further developments of the servient land were proposed, but in May 2007 the claimants sought a declaration that they had a prescriptive easement of light. This claim succeeded.

The Court of Appeal held that the 1999 agreement was not a written 'consent or agreement' within the proviso to s3. Put another way, agreeing to the development in 1999 did not deprive them of their easement.

The Normal Rules about User 'By or on Behalf of a Fee Simple Against a Fee Simple' Do Not Apply

Under s3 of the 1832 Act, a tenant can acquire an easement against their own landlord, or against a fellow tenant of their own landlord. Yet apparently any easement which arises under s3 is in fee simple!

Rights of Light Act 1959

In 1959, there were still some wartime bomb sites which had not been redeveloped. It was suddenly realized that it had been nearly 20 years since 'the Blitz', and that if there was not special legislation, prescriptive rights of light would be acquired over bomb sites. Such rights of light would severely limit redevelopment.

The 1959 Act included temporary provisions which are now only of historic interest. The prescription period was extended to 27 years if the action related to an infringement occurring before 1 January 1963.

The Act also included permanent provisions (of an almost comical nature) which remain in force today.

Prior to the Second World War, if you owned land over which there was a risk that a neighbour would acquire a prescriptive easement of light, you erected enormous hoardings on your land to block out his light. With the advent of modern planning law, this is no longer possible.

The 1959 Act creates a procedure for erecting imaginary buildings on one's land (this applies to servient land). You do not need planning permission to erect your imaginary building, and you should make your imaginary building very large!

You, 'the potential servient owner', register an imaginary obstruction on your land in the local land charges register kept by the district council. Registration is equivalent to an obstruction acquiesced in for one year, and the registration lasts only one year. This effectively prevents the acquisition of an easement.

thinking point 19.16

To be safe, how often should you register under the 1959 Act?

To be on the safe side, you should make a registration every 19 years. In that way your neighbour can never acquire a prescriptive easement of light.

If an imaginary obstruction is erected under the 1959 Act, the dominant owner may want to claim that they already have an easement of light and that the 'obstruction' has come too late. The 1959 Act allows him to sue as if his light were actually obstructed!

The (potential) operation of the 1959 Act is illustrated by the facts of *G and S Brough Ltd v Salvage Wharf* [2010] Ch 11. On 12 June 2006 the servient owners registered a (huge) imaginary obstruction on their land. The claimants issued their claim form for a declaration that they had a prescriptive easement on 2 May 2007, and won their case.

Had the claimants delayed and not issued their claim form until 12 June 2007 they would not have been able to show 20 years' 'uninterrupted' user as of right 'next before action'. (See para 48 of the judgment of Jackson LJ.)

REVIEW QUESTION It is often said that it is far too easy to acquire prescriptive easements of light, and that such easements prevent the redevelopment of derelict land. Why are such statements made?

19.4.5 Reform of Easements of Light

The practical effect of an easement of light on the servient land is similar to that of a restrictive covenant limiting the types of building (particularly their height), which can be erected on the servient land. In recent years there have been cases where the dominant owner to an easement of light has been able to either totally prevent a desirable development or say, 'I will only agree to the development if you buy out my right for £x00,000.'

In response to this problem the Law Commission in February 2013 issued a consultation paper on Rights to Light. Provisionally, the Law Commission makes three main proposals.

1 Prescription for Easements of Light should (prospectively) be abolished. No new prescriptive easements of light could arise, whether at Common Law, under lost modern grant or under s3 of the 1832 Act. Easements of Light could still arise by express or implied grant, but that (in practice) would be unlikely.

2 Easements for Light (including those in existence at the date of the new legislation) would become subject to s 84(1) of the Law of Property Act 1925, a provision discussed at 21.5 which hitherto has only applied to Restrictive Covenants. (Basically, an out of date easement for light could be cancelled by the Lands Chamber of the Upper Tribunal.)

3 A servient owner, fearing that a dominant owner might (perhaps belatedly) seek an injunction blocking his development plans, will be able to serve a notice on the dominant owner. The procedure is set out at paras. 6.12 and 6.13 of the consultation.

6.12 The procedure would provide that where an impending development will obstruct a dominant owner's light, the developer may serve on the dominant owner a Notice of Proposed Obstruction ('NPO'). The NPO would provide the dominant owner with information about the extent of the proposed obstruction and ask whether the claimant proposed to seek an injunction. The dominant owner would then have a period of time in which to seek professional advice and, if he or she wanted an injunction, the dominant owner would be obliged either to serve on the developer a counter-notice specifying whether he or she objected to the proposed obstruction, or to issue proceedings. If a counter-notice was served stating that the dominant owner objected to the proposed obstruction then the parties would then have a period of time in which to negotiate; if agreement could not be reached then the dominant owner would be required to issue proceedings.

6.13 If the dominant owner failed to object to the proposed obstruction by a counternotice (or failed to issue proceedings) when he or she was required to do so then an injunction would no longer be available as a remedy, although he or she could still (if able to establish an actionable interference at trial) be awarded damages.

In short, the dominant owner would have a stipulated period of time (say three months) in which to object to a proposed development and seek an injunction. If the dominant owner did not seek an injunction within the stipulated period, he/she would not be able to claim an injunction, but would still be able to claim damages.

Prescriptive Easements and Profits as Legal Interests

19.5

Every prescriptive easement or profit which arises under the rules discussed in this chapter is:

- of fee simple duration; and
- deemed to be created by deed.

It therefore follows that all prescriptive easements and profits are legal interests. Consequently, if the servient land is unregistered title, a prescriptive easement or profit will be good against the whole world. It will automatically be binding on a purchaser, whether or not that purchaser knew of the easement or profit.

If a prescriptive easement or profit arises prior to the commencement of the Land Registration Act 2002 (LRA 2002), it was always an overriding interest under s70(1)(a) Land Registration Act 1925 and remains one under Sch 3 para 3 LRA 2002.

If, however, a prescriptive easement or profit first arises after the commencement of the LRA 2002, it will usually, but not always, be an overriding interest subject to the rules discussed at 6.5.2.

Extinguishment of Easements

19.6

Extinguishment of easements is a short but not unimportant topic. In reading this section, keep in mind the facts of the following scenario.

Case Study—West House

In 1975 Johann purchased West House, and became registered proprietor. With the purchase of West House he also acquired a legal easement to walk across Eastacre to get to and from West House.

Eastacre has been derelict since about 1965. In 1970 it was acquired by ABC Ltd. Recently ABC Ltd sold Eastacre to XYZ Plc, which has planning permission to redevelop the land. These plans are in effect blocked by Johann's easement which cuts straight across the middle of Eastacre.

Johann admits 'I don't really need this easement. I only use it perhaps once or twice a year. But I will not give it up unless they pay me half a million pounds.'

This scenario may seem far-fetched, but it does illustrate a problem which is not uncommon. Land is ripe for (re)development, but an 'old' easement is preventing the development.

As we shall see in Chapter 21, there is a statutory procedure which private landowners can invoke in certain circumstances to remove 'old' (often outdated) restrictive covenants. But there is (currently) nothing similar for easements (or profits).

A public body which compulsorily purchases servient land will be able to cancel any easement which gets in the way of its plans, and compensation will be payable to the dominant owner. See, for example, ss 237 and 237A of the Town and Country Planning Act 1990.

At common law, there are only two ways of discharging an easement; either express release by the dominant owner or implied release.

19.6.1 Express Release

For there to be an express release the dominant owner must execute a deed giving up the easement. So if, in our case study, XYZ Plc really did think it was worth half a million pounds to get rid of Johann's easement, Johann and XYZ could execute a deed cancelling the easement across the centre of Eastacre. The deed (if desired) could also grant a new easement by an alternative route around the side of the proposed new development.

19.6.2 Implied Release

This can come about in two different ways:

1 abandonment;

2 radical change in the nature of the dominant land.

Abandonment

It was once thought that 20 years' NON-user of an easement raised a presumption that the easement had now been abandoned. But the 1993 Court of Appeal decision in *Benn v Hardinge* (1993) 66 P & CR 246 came as a shock to servient landowners.

In *Benn v Hardinge* (1993) the owners of Hackhurst Farm had in 1818 been granted a right of way over a made-up track across the servient land to get to and from two fields forming part of Hackhurst Farm. This right of way had never been used. The owners of Hackhurst Farm had always used an alternative route.

One hundred and seventy-five years later Benn, the current owner of Hackhurst Farm, wanted to use the made-up track, as he was finding that, in wet weather, his modern tractors were getting bogged down when using the alternative route. His claim succeeded!

The defendant's argument that the easement had been abandoned failed. After reviewing old authorities, the Court of Appeal concluded that an easement was only abandoned if the servient owner could prove:

1 at least 20 years' non-use

   AND

2 an intention on the part of the dominant owner to abandon the easement.

Dillon LJ, in giving the leading judgment, said:

> [In *Gotobed v Pridmore* (1971)] ... Buckley L.J. then says:
>
> > We differ in this way from the learned Judge because we are impressed by the ease with which the physical state of affairs could have been altered so as to restore the use of the right of way to the owner of the Curate's Allotment, just as the use of the right of way along the lane in *Cook v. Mayor and Corporation of Bath* was re-assumed by the plaintiff in that case by unbricking and restoring his back door. The facts do not in our judgment justify an inference that F. B. Chapman at any time resolved to give up the right of way altogether. The right of way although it was of no particular significance to him for the time being, was nevertheless a piece of property of potential value. Had he wished to part with some part of the southern portion of the Curate's Allotment, or should any successor of his at any time wish to do so, access by way of Cowbit Drove might well have been or become of great importance. Its abandonment should not be lightly inferred and, in our judgment the facts in the present case are insufficient to support such an inference.

That is a case in which there had been no user of the way, at least from 1919, when F. B. Chapman bought the Curate's Allotment, until the time when the dispute came about, over 50 years later. It seems therefore that it is not possible to say in any categoric way, as seems to be suggested in the passage in Megarry and Wade, that 20 years of non-user will usually suffice. That seems to stem from the view of Littledale J. in *Moore v. Rawson* which, so far as easements of way are concerned at any rate, is inconsistent with *Ward v. Ward* and the authorities in which *Ward v. Ward* has been applied.

I take the law to have been laid down in clear terms by the judgment of the court in *Gotobed v. Pridmore*. In view of that and the many expressions of high authority in the cases to which I have referred, to the effect that there must be an intention to abandon, I do not feel that it is open to us in this court to say that the way must be presumed to have been abandoned merely because it was not used because no one had occasion to use it, even for so long as 175 years. It is important in this context that the photographs show such a rural and unchanged situation on the servient owner's side of the boundary line. This is not an area where there has been great change and the plaintiff's land is used for farming sheep rather than for any matter which could not have been in contemplation at the time of the enclosure.

See also the older cases of *Moore v Rawson* (1824) 3 B & C 332; *Ward v Ward* (1852) 7 Ex 838; *Gotobed v Pridmore* (1971) Estates Gazette 75. More recently, an accessway which had not been used for 40 years was not considered to be abandoned by the Court of Appeal in *Dwyer v Westminster City Council* [2014] EWCA Civ 153.

In its 2009 consultation on *Easements, Covenants and Profits à Prendre*, the Law Commission comments pithily:

> There is conspicuous reluctance on the part of the courts to find that an easement has been extinguished. A striking aspect of the current law is that it is so out of step with prescriptive acquisition. It seems anomalous that it is possible to acquire a right after 20 years user as of right, while 175 years of non-user did not necessarily amount to abandonment.

Radical Change in the Dominant Tenement

Alterations to the dominant land which make the exercise of the easement impossible clearly indicate that the easement has been abandoned and therefore discharged. Suppose that North House enjoys an easement of support as against adjoining South House. The dominant North House is demolished. The easement of support is consequently extinguished.

thinking point 19.17

The West Art Studios enjoyed an easement of light over adjoining East Spaceacre. The art studios have just been demolished, while you have acquired East Spaceacre for redevelopment. Do you need to worry about the easement of light?

You need not worry. The easement has been extinguished. An easement of light relates to specific windows, and those have gone.

thinking point 19.18

In Benn v Hardinge *(1993) it was accepted by everyone that the easement was to be used only in connection with agriculture. What if Benn had covered the two dominant fields with houses?*

Clearly, the radical change in the dominant land would mean that the easement was discharged.

thinking point 19.19

What if in our case study, Johann had, shortly before XYZ bought Eastacre, erected a high wooden fence on his land blocking his access to the route across Eastacre?

It is submitted that the easement would NOT be extinguished. Johann could remove the fence at any time, and re-commence his occasional use of the right of way.

19.6.3 Extinguishment by Operation of Schedule 3 Paragraph 3 Land Registration Act 2002

Though the Law Commission seems to have overlooked this point in its 2009 consultation on the law of easements, Sch 3 para 3 provides (in effect) a new way in which easements created after 12 October 2003 can be extinguished. Remember that Sch 3 para 3, which applies to implied or prescriptive legal easements, makes overriding:

> (1) A legal easement or profit à prendre, except for an easement, or profit à prendre … which at the time of the disposition—
>
>   (a) is not within the actual knowledge of the person to whom the disposition is made, and
>
>   (b) would not have been obvious on a reasonably careful inspection of the land over which the easement or profit is exercisable.
>
> (2) The exception in sub-paragraph (1) does not apply if the person entitled to the easement or profit proves that it has been exercised in the period of one year ending with the day of the disposition.

It follows that if a registered title is servient land to an easement created on or after 13 October 2003, that easement is not binding unless either:

1 it has been protected by an entry of a notice; or

2 the existence of the easement is known to the purchaser; or

3 it is obvious on a reasonably careful inspection (unlikely if the right is only occasionally exercised); or

4 it has been exercised within the last year before the disposition.

If none of these four conditions are satisfied the easement will not be binding on the registered proprietor. It will therefore be extinguished!

(Note that sub-para (2) makes it clear that the onus of proof is on the dominant owner to show that the right has been used within the last year.)

 # Concluding Remarks

It has to be said that the English law of prescription is extremely complex, and is clearly in need of simplification and reform. Yet Parliament has, with the LRA 2002, added yet another complication. Perhaps our only consolation when we consider the complexities of the law is that (especially with the 1832 and 1959 Acts) there are aspects which are faintly comical.

There have been suggestions that the whole law of prescription should be abolished. Why should somebody, by trespassing for a long enough time, acquire a property right to do something which previously was unlawful? On the other hand, if you have been doing something for a very long time totally unchallenged, do you not feel that you have the right to do it?

The Law Commission, in its Report No 327, *Making Land Work: Easements, Covenants and Profits à Prendre* (2011) recommends that all the existing forms of prescription should be abolished (see recommendation 8.6). Instead there would be a simple rule that 20 years' user as of right should give rise to a prescriptive easement (see recommendation 8.7). The (sometimes criticized) rule that user must be by and against a fee simple would be retained (recommendations 8.8 and 8.11).

Prescription for profits would be abolished.

With regard to extinguishment of easements and profits, recommendation 8.16 states: 'We recommend that where an easement or profit has not been used for a continuous period of 20 years, there should be a rebuttable presumption that it has been abandoned.' The law would (in effect) be restored to the position many thought it to be prior to the 1993 decision in *Benn v Hardinge* (see 19.6.2).

Under recommendation 8.52, the Upper Tribunal would have power to modify or cancel outdated easements or profits created *after* (sic) the coming into force of the new legislation.

Summary

To claim a prescriptive easement (or profit), the claimant must show a long period (usually 20 years) of user as of right which comes within one of the three types of prescription.

User as of Right

This means user which is open and is neither with the servient owner's express consent nor against his express objections. The user is exercising the claimed right in a manner as if he was the owner of the right.

'User as of right' only arises if the following have been satisfied:

- without force;
- without secrecy;
- without permission.

Prescription at Common Law

This is presumptively established if the claimant can show 20 years' user as of right. That presumption can usually easily be rebutted by showing that user has not been (or cannot have been) continuous since 1189.

Prescription under Lost Modern Grant

This is established if the claimant can show strong evidence of 20 years' user as of right—this user does not have to be 'next before action'. The presumption of lost grant can only be rebutted by showing that the grant was legally impossible (*Tehidy Minerals Ltd v Norman*).

Prescription under the Prescription Act 1832

This is (in principle) established if the claimant can show 20 years' user as of right (30 years for profits) without interruption which is 'next before action'.

Prescription for an Easement of Light

This is governed by s3 of the 1832 Act. The light must have been enjoyed for at least 20 years 'next before action'. Potential servient owners should invoke the procedure in the Rights of Light Act 1959 to prevent the acquisition of an easement of light.

Extinguishment of Easements

- Expressly by deed.
- Impliedly by deliberate abandonment or radical change in the dominant land.
- By operation of Sch 3 para 3 LRA 2002.

Further Reading

Battersby, G, 'Some thoughts on easements under the Land Registration Act 2002' [2005] Conv 195
For a discussion of the complex impact of the LRA 2002 on conveyancing.

Burns, FR, 'Prescriptive easements in England and legal "climate change" ' [2007] Conv 133
Evaluative article which discusses whether prescriptive easement can continue to survive in modern English land law.

Sara, C, 'Prescription—what is it for?' [2004] Conv 13
An interesting article which considers the rationale for prescriptive easements.

Questions

1 Last month Finnegan, owner of Blackacre and Whiteacre, two neighbouring farms, sold and conveyed Blackacre to Milligan. The conveyance contained no provision relating to easements and profits.

Advise Milligan regarding the following:

(a) The only direct access to Blackacre is a narrow footpath insufficiently wide to accommodate motor traffic. Milligan wishes to make use of the private driveway which runs from Blackacre through Whiteacre and leads into the adjoining public highway.

(b) Some drains run from Blackacre under Whiteacre. Milligan wishes to make use of those drains.

(c) Cyrus, the owner of Redacre, an adjoining farm, claims that he can continue to graze his sheep on a hillside forming part of Blackacre where sheep from Redacre have been grazed 'as long as anyone can remember'.

2   In 1993, Louise acquired the freehold to Grand House. Grand House adjoins West Field, the freehold to which was then owned by Nellie. Over the years Nellie has leased West Field to Olive for short periods.

On acquiring Grand House, Louise immediately leased it to Terry for 70 years. Soon after taking the lease, Terry started to pasture the five sheep he owned in West Field, and to take a short cut across West Field to get to the nearest station. He continued both of these activities until September 2015, without any objection from Nellie or Olive.

In September 2015, Gurinder acquired the freehold to West Field from Nellie, and immediately ordered Terry not to make any further use of West Field. Initially Terry complied with this demand, but now both he and Louise are threatening legal action.

It is now January 2016.

Advise Gurinder.

Part 10
Freehold Covenants: Restrictive and Positive Covenants

20

Freehold Covenants

Introduction

In this and the ensuing chapter, we cover a complicated area of law. Chapters 20 and 21 discuss freehold covenants; leasehold covenants have been considered in Chapters 12 to 14.

A covenant is a promise between landowners regulating the use of the land. This could involve two neighbouring landowners restraining the use of their properties for particular activities or for maintaining the ambience of a particular area in which they live. Consider the following example.

Case Study—Marchland Close

Agnese owns in fee simple two adjoining high class residences, numbers 23 and 24 Marchland Close. In 1990 Agnese decided to sell 24 Marchland Close to Barry and to retain 23 Marchland Close for her own home. Agnese wanted to maintain 'the tone of the area'. In the conveyance of the fee simple in 24 Marchland Close, Agnese induced Barry to covenant (see Diagram 20.1):

1 that he will keep 24 Marchland Close in good repair, and repaint every five years;

2 not to carry on any business in 24 Marchland Close; and

3 to pay a proportion of the costs of the common private driveway between 23 Marchland Close and 24 Marchland Close.

Diagram 20.1
23 and 24 Marchland Close

23 Marchland Close (Agnese)	D R I V E W A Y	24 Marchland Close (Barry)

The most common issues which arise in relation to freehold covenants are whether covenants can be enforced against successors in title to the servient land (24 Marchland Close in the case study) and whether successors in title to the dominant land (23 Marchland Close in the case study) can enforce the covenants. Any purchaser of 24 Marchland Close will want to know whether the covenants can be enforced against them. Any purchaser of 23 Marchland Close will want to know whether they acquire the right to enforce the covenants.

Put another way, the central issues discussed in this chapter are:

• Does the burden of the covenant 'run' with the servient land so as to be a permanent burden on the servient land?

- Does the benefit of the covenant 'run' with the dominant land so that the successor in title can enjoy that benefit?

This chapter will first consider the fundamental difference between restrictive and positive covenants. Nineteenth-century case law firmly established that while restrictive covenants could be a permanent burden on servient land the burden of a positive covenant (eg a promise to repair) could not be enforced against a successor in title to the servient land. Consequently restrictive covenants are property rights in land; positive covenants are not.

Modern case law has focused on identifying the dominant land and (crucially) which dominant owners can enforce covenants.

In line with the historical development of the law, we will first consider the conditions which must be fulfilled before a covenant can be enforced against a successor in title to the servient land. We will then consider the rules regarding who can enforce covenants as dominant owners.

point on terminology

Since Agnese's property benefits from this covenant she is known as the 'covenantee'. Barry who agrees to the covenant and has the burden of complying with it is called the 'covenantor'.

20.2 Restrictive and Positive Covenants Distinguished

The difference between a positive and restrictive (or negative) covenant is hopefully apparent from the example given previously. A positive covenant involves positive action, in our example Barry covenants to repaint the building every five years. A negative covenant involves refraining from doing something, for example not opening a public house in your house.

You may be asking yourself 'why is it necessary to distinguish between them?' The reason is very simple. It is necessary because it helps to determine whether the benefit and burden of a covenant run with the land (ie whether the covenant has passed to the successor in title).

20.3 Does the Burden or Benefit Run with the Land?

To illustrate the 'running of covenants' we will consider the Marchland Close case study and some developments which have since occurred. Ciaran recently purchased 23 Marchland Close from Agnese. Ciaran wants to know if the benefits of the covenants are enforceable in the event of a breach. Barry sold 24 Marchland Close to Daria and she would like to know whether she must fulfil her obligations under the covenants (see Diagram 20.2).

Diagram 20.2
Do the benefits and burdens of the covenants run with the land?

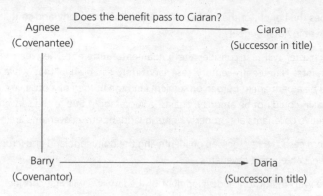

Does the burden pass to Daria?

In advising Ciaran and Daria, we need to consider the rules which govern the passing of the burden and benefit. These rules are governed by common law and equity. We will be considering these in detail in the following sections.

As a preliminary point, there is one simple rule which ought to be remembered at the outset: if a covenant cannot run under the common law rules then it is necessary to establish whether the covenant will pass in equity. It is important to remember that where the burden of a covenant passes, the corresponding benefit must pass as well. For example, if the burden of a covenant passes in equity, then it will still only be enforceable if the benefit of the covenant has passed in equity to somebody entitled to enforce the covenant.

20.4 Common Law: Does the Burden of a Covenant Run with the Land?

We shall be addressing the following question: 'when the property was transferred, did the covenant entered into by the original covenantor bind the successor in title?' If we continue to consider the Marchland Close case study, we shall be addressing the issue of whether the burdens of the covenants pass to Daria (see Diagram 20.3 at the end of 20.5 for the final summary).

The answer in common law is straightforward. The burden of a covenant, whether it is positive or negative, does not run with the land. Our advice to Daria, so far, is that she is not bound by either positive or negative covenants at common law, therefore, these covenants cannot be enforced against her. The leading authority is *Austerberry v Corporation of Oldham* (1885) 29 Ch D 750. In this case the claimant's predecessor conveyed to trustees land which was to be used as a road. The trustees covenanted that they would build the road and at all times keep it in repair and the public were permitted to use this road on payment of a toll. The road was built and created an access point for the claimant. Later the claimant sold his land to Austerberry and the trustees sold their land to the defendant. The main question in the case was whether Austerberry could enforce the repairing covenant against the defendant. The Court of Appeal held that the covenant was unenforceable. This was because the covenant was a 'positive covenant', that is, one which imposed a positive burden on the owner of the servient land. The court was of the opinion that if the parties wanted to burden the land, they should have created a rentcharge.

cross-reference
For a discussion of possible ways of making positive covenants burden the land, see 20.10.

This rule on the passing of the burden of a covenant in *Austerberry* was affirmed in the House of Lords in *Rhone v Stephens* [1994] 2 AC 310. Lord Templeman simply stated that 'as between persons interested in land...the benefit of a covenant may run with the land at law but not the burden: see the *Austerberry* case'.

(The Contracts (Rights of Third Parties) Act 1999 does not apply to the burden of a covenant.)

We noted previously that the burden of a restrictive or positive covenant will not pass at common law. This does not mean that the covenantee will have no redress in the event of a breach of a covenant. Equity has developed rules which deal with the passing of a burden. It is worth reiterating at this point that where the burden of a covenant passes in equity, the claimant must also show that the corresponding benefit has run in equity.

More often than not, when considering whether freehold covenants pass to successors in title you will need to consider the rules in equity for the transmission of the benefit since the common law rules do not permit the burden from passing.

20.5 Equity: Does the Burden of a Restrictive Covenant Run with the Land?

In contrast to the common law approach, equity took a different view to the burden passing to the successor in title. This point was considered in *Rhone v Stephens*.

In this case a property was divided into two separate dwellings, a house and a cottage, and it was done in such a way that the roof of the house was above one of the bedrooms in the cottage. The owner of the house covenanted with the purchaser of the cottage to maintain the roof which lies above the cottage. There was also a clause in the conveyance which contained mutual rights and obligations of support for the house and the cottage. A number of years later the condition of the roof had deteriorated and water leaked into the cottage bedroom. The owner of the cottage, who was a successor in title to the original covenantee, brought an unsuccessful action against the current owner of the house attempting to enforce the positive covenant to maintain the roof over the cottage.

Lord Templeman in explaining the approach taken in equity towards the passing of the burden stated:

> ...equity supplements but does not contradict the common law. When freehold land is conveyed without restriction, the conveyance confers on the purchaser the right to do with the land as he pleases provided that he does not interfere with the rights of others or infringe statutory restrictions. The conveyance may however impose restrictions which, in favour of the covenantee, deprive the purchaser of some of the rights inherent in the ownership of unrestricted land. In *Tulk* v *Moxhay* (1848) 2 Ph. 774, a purchaser of land covenanted that no buildings would be erected on Leicester Square. A subsequent purchaser of Leicester Square was restrained from building. The conveyance to the original purchaser deprived him and every subsequent purchaser taking with notice of the covenant of the right, otherwise part and parcel of the freehold, to develop the square by the construction of buildings. Equity does not contradict the common law by enforcing a restrictive covenant against a successor in title of the covenantor but prevents the successor from exercising a right which he never acquired.

Equity did not allow the owner of Leicester Square to build because the owner never acquired the right to build without the consent of the persons (if any) from time to time entitled to the benefit of the covenant against building . . .

Equity can thus prevent or punish the breach of a negative covenant which restricts the user of land or the exercise of other rights in connection with land. Restrictive covenants deprive an owner of a right which he could otherwise exercise. Equity cannot compel an owner to comply with a positive covenant entered into by his predecessors in title without flatly contradicting the common law rule that a person cannot be made liable upon a contract unless he was a party to it. Enforcement of a positive covenant lies in contract; a positive covenant compels an owner to exercise his rights. Enforcement of a negative covenant lies in property; a negative covenant deprives the owner of a right over property . . .

For over 100 years it has been clear and accepted law that equity will enforce negative covenants against freehold land but has no power to enforce positive covenants against successors in title of the land. To enforce a positive covenant would be to enforce a personal obligation against a person who has not covenanted. To enforce negative covenants is only to treat the land as subject to a restriction.

From this passage, we can draw two conclusions. In equity:

- restrictive covenants can run with the land; and
- positive covenants will not run with the land.

You would have noticed that in the previous passage in *Rhone v Stephens* Lord Templeman refers to *Tulk v Moxhay* (1848) 2 Ph 774 in support of his argument. *Tulk v Moxhay* is regarded as the leading case on the application of equity to the situation involving a covenant in a conveyance. The case involved a fee simple owner of land in Leicester Square, London who sold the land to Mr Elms. Elms covenanted in the conveyance, for himself, his heirs, and assigns that he would 'keep and maintain the said piece of ground . . . uncovered with any buildings, in neat and ornamental order'. The land was later sold by Elms to the defendant. That conveyance did not recite the covenant, but the defendant admitted that he had actual notice of it in any event. The defendant intended to build on the land. The court granted an injunction against the defendant to restrain a breach of the covenant. Lord Cottenham LC said:

That this court has jurisdiction to enforce a contract between the owner of land and his neighbour purchasing a part of it that the purchaser shall either use or abstain from using the land purchased in a particular way is what I never knew disputed. Here there is no question about the contract. The owner of certain houses in the square sells the land adjoining, with a covenant from the purchaser not to use it for any other purpose than as a square garden. It is now contended, not that the vendee could violate that contract, but that he might sell the piece of land, and that the purchaser from him may violate it without this court having any power to interfere. If that were so, it would be impossible for an owner of land to sell part of it without incurring the risk of rendering what he retains worthless. It is said that, the covenant being one which does not run with the land, this court cannot enforce it, but the question is not whether the covenant runs with the land, but *whether a party shall be permitted to use the land in a manner inconsistent with the contract entered into by his vendor, with notice of which he purchased.* Of course, the price would be affected by the covenant, and nothing could be more inequitable than that the original purchaser should be able to sell the property the next day for a greater price, in consideration of the assignee being allowed to escape from the liability which he had himself undertaken. [Emphasis added]

The central question for the court has been emphasized previously. The defendant's intended action of building on the land would have been inconsistent with the contract, and unconscionable even though he was not the promisor. This intervention by equity alleviated the harshness of the strict common law approach. This case laid the foundation for what is known as the 'rule in *Tulk v Moxhay*'.

In order for the burden of restrictive covenants to run with the land four conditions must be fulfilled before the obligation to observe the burden of a restrictive covenant will pass to a successor in title to the servient land:

1 the covenant must be negative in substance;
2 the covenant must, at the date of the covenant, be made to benefit the dominant land retained by the covenantee;
3 the covenant must touch and concern the dominant land; and
4 the covenant must be made with an intent to burden the servient land.

20.5.1 The Covenant Must Be Negative in Substance

The test is that the observance of the covenant must not necessitate expenditure on the part of the servient owner (*Haywood v Brunswick Permanent Benefit Building Society* (1881) 8 QBD 403). The substance of a covenant 'not to allow this building to fall into disrepair' is of course positive, and not a restrictive covenant. On the other hand, a covenant 'to keep Xacre as an open space uncovered by buildings' (the covenant involved in the 1847 case of *Tulk v Moxhay* (1848) 2 Ph 774, which in effect invented this whole area of law) is a restrictive covenant.

20.5.2 The Covenant Must, at the Date of the Covenant, be Made to Benefit the Dominant Land Retained by the Covenantee

In *London County Council v [Mrs] Allen* [1914] 3 KB 642 the LCC sold a large amount of land to Mr Allen, a builder. With respect to one small part of the land, Mr Allen covenanted not to build upon it. This small parcel was intended as an open space for the local residents. The LCC retained no other land in the vicinity.

Mr Allen sold the small parcel to his wife, who commenced building work. The LCC sought an injunction against Mrs Allen, which was refused. The council had no dominant land, so it could not claim it had the benefit of a restrictive covenant. (Nowadays the council would use town planning law to curb Mr and Mrs Allen's activities.)

Buckley LJ said:

> The reasoning of Lord Cottenham's judgment in *Tulk* v. *Moxhay* (1848) 2 Ph 774 is that if an owner of land sells part of it reserving the rest, and takes from his purchaser a covenant that the purchaser shall use or abstain from using the land purchased in a particular way, that covenant (being one for the protection of the land reserved) is enforceable against a sub-purchaser with notice. The reason given is that, if that were not so, it would be impossible for an owner of land to sell part of it without incurring the risk of rendering what he retains worthless. If the vendor has retained no land which can be protected by the restrictive covenant, the basis of the reasoning of the judgment is swept away. In *Haywood* v. *Brunswick Permanent Benefit Building Society* (1881) 8 QBD 403 the Court of Appeal declined to extend the doctrine of *Tulk* v. *Moxhay* (1848) 2 Ph 774 to covenants other than restrictive covenants. They rejected the doctrine that, inasmuch as the defendants took the land with notice of

the covenants, they were bound in equity to perform them. That therefore is not the principle upon which the equitable doctrine rests. In the present case we are asked to extend the doctrine of *Tulk* v. *Moxhay* (1848) 2 Ph 774 so as to affirm that a restrictive covenant can be enforced against a derivative owner taking with notice by a person who never has had or who does not retain any land to be protected by the restrictive covenant in question. In my opinion the doctrine does not extend to that case. The doctrine is that a covenant not running with the land, but being a negative covenant entered into by an owner of land with an adjoining owner, binds the land in equity and is enforceable against a derivative owner taking with notice. *The doctrine ceases to be applicable when the person seeking to enforce the covenant against the derivative owner has no land to be protected by the negative covenant. The fact of notice is in that case irrelevant.* [Emphasis added]

It follows that a restrictive covenant cannot exist 'in gross', that is, independently of *dominant* land. For the *burden* of a restrictive covenant to run with the servient land there must be a dominant tenement at the date of the covenant.

20.5.3 The Covenant Must Touch and Concern the Dominant Land

In order for a restrictive covenant to run with the land, it must touch and concern the land. That is, it must benefit the dominant land.

The land benefiting from the covenant must be sufficiently near to the servient land. This is simply to ensure that the restriction on the servient land does benefit the dominant land.

In *Newton Abbot Co-operative Society Ltd v Williamson and Treadgold* (1952) Ch 286, Mrs Mardon originally owned two shops in the small central Devon town of Bovey Tracey. The shops were about 50 yards apart on opposite sides of the street.

In 1923, Mrs Mardon sold one of the shops. In the conveyance of that shop there was imposed a restrictive covenant which said that no ironmongery was to be sold from the shop. The restrictive covenant did not identify the dominant land. However, the shop across the road retained by Mrs Mardon sold...ironmongery!

The judge held that there was a valid restrictive covenant which bound a subsequent purchaser of the shop sold by Mrs Mardon in 1923. Although the dominant land was not expressly identified in the conveyance which contained the restrictive covenant, it could be identified by examining the geography of the locality. That, in the view of the judge, was sufficient, despite the fact that the covenant was devised to prevent a competing ironmongery business from opening up in the shop sold by Mrs Mardon. The business on the dominant land benefited from the restrictive covenant.

The court has shown a willingness to consider the physical proximity of the dominant land to the servient land. What sort of distance would be outside the scope of the requirement of touching and concerning the land? In *Kelly v Barrett* [1924] 2 Ch 379, Pollock MR suggested that 'land at Clapham would be too remote and unable to carry a right to enforce...covenants in respect of...land at Hampstead' (five miles the other side of central London).

REVIEW QUESTION What would have been the legal position if the shops in *Newton Abbot Co-operative Society Ltd v Williamson and Treadgold* had been 500 yards apart in a large city?

20.5.4 The Covenant Must Be Made with an Intent to Burden the Servient Land

The nineteenth-century lawyers who 'invented' restrictive covenants drew a distinction between:

- a covenant intended to bind only the covenantor;

 and

- a covenant intended to throw a continuing burden on the land itself and thereby bind all subsequent owners of the land.

Only the latter type of covenant is a valid restrictive covenant.

Nineteenth-century covenants usually included phraseology like, 'I Charley Farns-Barns covenant on behalf of myself and my heirs and assigns...' This long-winded phraseology is no longer necessary. Restrictive covenants created after 1925 are now covered by a 'word-saving' provision, s79(1) Law of Property Act 1925 (LPA 1925).

> *Law of Property Act 1925*
>
> 79. Burden of covenants relating to land
>
> (1) A covenant relating to any land of a covenantor or capable of being bound by him, shall, unless a contrary intention is expressed, be deemed to be made by the covenantor on behalf of himself his successors in title and the persons deriving title under him or them, and, subject as aforesaid, shall have effect as if such successors and other persons were expressed.
>
> This subsection extends to a covenant to do some act relating to the land, notwithstanding that the subject-matter may not be in existence when the covenant is made.
>
> (2) For the purposes of this section in connection with covenants restrictive of the user of land 'successors in title' shall be deemed to include the owners and occupiers for the time being of such land.
>
> (3) This section applies only to covenants made after the commencement of this Act.

Section 79(1) in effect provides that covenants which relate to the covenantor's land are deemed to be made on behalf of his/her successors in title unless the contrary appears from the terms of the covenant. Thus, anybody who makes a covenant about the use of his/her land is presumed to intend that the covenant will be a permanent burden on the land irrespective of its ownership.

In the unlikely event that it is desired that the covenant should bind only the original covenantor and not his/her successors, this will have to be expressly stated.

thinking point 20.1

- *In the case study at 20.1 have you identified which of the covenants are positive and negative?*
- *What advice can you give Daria with regard to the burden of the covenants?*

The covenants:

1 *to keep 24 Marchland Close in good repair and repaint every five years; POSITIVE*

2 *not to carry on any business in 24 Marchland Close; NEGATIVE*

3 *to pay a proportion of the costs of the common private driveway between 23 Marchland Close and 24 Marchland Close. BOTH POSITIVE AND NEGATIVE.*

Common law

Both negative and positive covenants at common law do not run with the servient land.

Equity

- Positive covenants will not run with the land.

- Negative covenants will only pass to successors in title if the conditions in Tulk v Moxhay are fulfilled.

Diagram 20.3
Equity: do the burdens of the covenants pass to Daria?

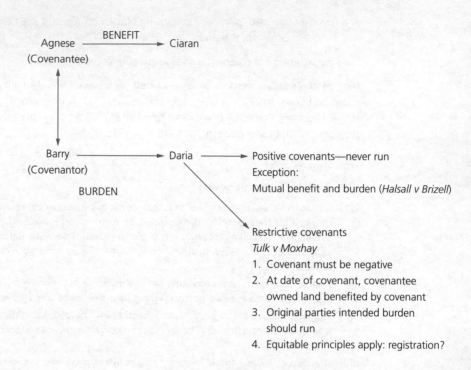

Agnese (Covenantee) — BENEFIT → Ciaran

Barry (Covenantor) → Daria

BURDEN

→ Positive covenants—never run
Exception:
Mutual benefit and burden (*Halsall v Brizell*)

→ Restrictive covenants
Tulk v Moxhay
1. Covenant must be negative
2. At date of covenant, covenantee owned land benefited by covenant
3. Original parties intended burden should run
4. Equitable principles apply: registration?

20.6 Does a Covenant Bind the Original Parties?

A covenant, whether positive or negative, is always enforceable between the original parties (privity of contract).

20.6.1 The Benefit of Restrictive Covenants—Identifying the Original Covenantees

It is perfectly possible to enter into a restrictive covenant for the benefit of a number of original covenantees. For example, a restrictive covenant can be entered into in favour of several landowners all with land adjacent to the servient land.

Ethan owned two adjoining houses, Centre House and East House. Centre House also neighbours West House, owned by William and North House owned by Neil.

Ethan sells Centre House to Celine. In the conveyance of Centre House, Celine covenants, for the benefit of East House, North House, and West House, that Centre House will not be used for business or professional purposes. Thus, clearly, there are intended to be three dominant houses and three original covenantees.

Prior to the Conveyancing Act 1881 there was a problem with the kind of arrangement just described. There was an old common law rule that only people who actually executed a deed could claim benefits under the deed. In our example only Celine and Ethan would execute the deed containing the restrictive covenant. Thus, at common law only Ethan could claim to be an original covenantee and only East House was dominant land. This, of course, was contrary to what Ethan and Celine intended.

The inconvenient old common law rule was abolished by what is now s56 LPA 1925. Under that section, any person identifiable at the time the deed is executed and intended to have the benefit of a covenant is an original covenantee, whether or not they executed the deed containing the covenant.

Law of Property Act 1925

56. Persons taking who are not parties . . .

(1) A person may take an immediate or other interest in land or other property, or the benefit of any condition, right of entry, covenant or agreement over or respecting land or other property, although he may not be named as a party to the conveyance or other instrument.

Put simply:

A person may take . . . the benefit of any . . . covenant . . . over or respecting land . . . although he may not be named as a party to the conveyance or other instrument.

In effect, under s56(1) LPA 1925 the reach of privity of contract is no longer limited to the original parties but is marginally widened to encompass a category of persons who did not formally enter into the original contract.

In principle, s56(1) LPA 1925 gives the right to a third party to enforce a covenant if it is purported to be made *with* that third party as a covenantee. The third party has been given the benefit of that covenant, and is treated as though they were an original covenantee. This approach was elucidated in *Re Ecclesiastical Commissioners for England's Conveyance* [1936] Ch 430 where Luxmoore J suggested in the assessment of who can enforce a covenant:

[w]hat is necessary to consider is the true construction of the conveyance . . . in order to ascertain whether any persons, not parties thereto, are described therein as the covenantees, and whether such covenants are expressed to affect any and what hereditaments. To determine what is the true construction of that document it is necessary to consider the surrounding circumstances as they existed at the date when it was executed.

In *White v Bijou Mansions* [1937] Ch 610, Simmonds J also considered the scope of s56:

. . . under s. 56 of [the LPA 1925] only that person can call it in aid who, although not named as a party to the conveyance or other instrument, is yet a person to whom that conveyance or other instrument purports to grant some thing or with which some agreement or covenant is purported to be made. To give it any other meaning appears to me to open the door to claims or assertion of rights which cannot have been contemplated by the Legislature, for if that be not the limitation which must be imposed on this section it appears to me that there is no limit and it will be open to anybody to come into Court and say: 'Here is a covenant which if enforced will redound to my advantage, therefore I claim the benefit of the section. I claim that this covenant or condition is one which should be enforced in my favour because it is for my benefit, whether intended for my benefit or not intended for my benefit would not appear to matter.' I cannot give to the section any such meaning as that. I interpret it as a section which can be called in aid only by a person in whose favour the grant purports to be made or with whom the covenant or agreement purports to be made.

From these extracts it can be seen that the ambit of s56(1) LPA 1925 allows a third party to enforce the benefit of the covenant(s). That third party must be identifiable and in existence at the time when the covenant was made.

thinking point 20.2

In our example, under the modern law, who are the original covenantees, and what is/are the dominant land(s)?

It is hoped you deduced that Ethan, Neil, and William, are all original covenantees. East House, North House, and West House are separate pieces of dominant land.

If a covenant is purported to be made with a generic class of persons (eg 'with the owners for the time being of houses in Blogtown Street') only those persons who are in existence and identifiable at the date of the covenant can make a claim based on s56(1) LPA 1925.

To illustrate this point, in 1995 Becky purchased number 1 Chessingham Close. She covenanted 'with the owners for the time being of numbers 2–6 Chessingham Close' to use number 1 for residential purposes only. Davinder, who owned number 5 in 1995 can enforce the covenant relying simply on s56(1).

If in 2010, Davinder sold number 5 to Edmund, Edmund will only be able to enforce the covenant if the benefit of the covenant has passed in equity under the rules of annexation, assignment, or building scheme discussed later. Edmund is not within the scope of s56(1).

20.6.2 Relaxing the Rules on Privity of Contract

All covenants entered into after 11 May 2000 are subject to the Contracts (Rights of Third Parties) Act 1999. The 1999 Act dispensed with the requirement that a claimant seeking to enforce the benefit of a covenant must be in existence at the time of the covenant. Section 1(1)–(3) relaxed the rules on privity of contract in the land law context.

Contracts (Rights of Third Parties) Act 1999

1. Right of third party to enforce contractual term.

(1) Subject to the provisions of this Act, a person who is not a party to a contract (a 'third party') may in his own right enforce a term of the contract if—
  (a) the contract expressly provides that he may, or
  (b) subject to subsection (2), the term purports to confer a benefit on him.

(2) Subsection (1)(b) does not apply if on a proper construction of the contract it appears that the parties did not intend the term to be enforceable by the third party.

(3) The third party must be expressly identified in the contract by name, as a member of a class or as answering a particular description but need not be in existence when the contract is entered into.

The third party can enforce a covenant if:

- the contract expressly states that the third party can enforce it, or the term purports to confer a benefit on him/her and is intended to be enforced by the third party. There is clearly no longer any need to consider whether the covenant has been purportedly made with the covenantee or for the benefit of the covenantee as required by s56(1) LPA 1925; and

- the third party is identified in the contract by name, as a member of a class or as answering a particular description. The third party does not need to be in existence at the time the contract was made. The effect of this provision is to dispense with the need to identify a specific individual and that they should be in existence at the time of the contract; the requirement is sufficiently broad and would catch 'successors in title' as used in the previous section.

20.7 Does the Benefit of a Covenant Run with Land?

Think back to the law of easements for a moment. If an easement is appurtenant (ie attached) to a parcel of dominant land, then that easement automatically 'runs' with the dominant land. This means that anybody who acquires the dominant land can automatically enjoy the benefit of the easement.

It would be wonderful if a similar statement could be made about the benefit of covenants. Unfortunately, that is impossible. The law as to when a successor to dominant land acquires the right to enforce a covenant benefiting that land is extremely complex.

The rules of common law regarding the running of benefit of covenants are of rather limited significance today. The rules operative today are largely derived from equity and were originally developed in the nineteenth and early twentieth centuries.

Until the Second World War the rules (though already quite complex) were clear and strictly enforced. Their strict enforcement sometimes meant that a purchaser of dominant land did not get the benefit of an existing covenant intended to benefit that land. But the law had the great merit of certainty.

That certainty was destroyed by some decisions of the courts, most notably the Court of Appeal decision in *Federated Homes Ltd v Mill Lodge Properties Ltd* [1980] 1 WLR 594. Those decisions showed a trend to change the old rules in favour of persons claiming to be dominant owners.

This trend made life very difficult for servient owners generally. If a person owns land which is subject to a restrictive covenant, it is sometimes very difficult to work out who the dominant owners are and thus who, if anyone, is entitled to sue if the covenant is broken. However, the Court of Appeal decision in *Crest Nicholson v McAllister* [2004] 1 WLR 2409, makes life easier for servient owners.

20.8 Common Law: Does the Benefit of a Covenant Run with Land?

The benefit of a covenant, whether positive or negative, unlike the burden, will pass to successors in title of the original covenantee, if the following conditions are satisfied:

1 the covenant must 'touch and concern' the land;

2 at the date of the covenant, the original covenantee held a legal estate in land;

3 the successor in title must derive their title from or under the original covenantee; and

4 at the date of the covenant, the benefit must have been intended to run with the land.

If we go back to the Marchland Close case study, if Daria has not complied with the covenants and is in breach, the issue we are addressing at this point is whether Ciaran is entitled to claim the benefit of the covenants and enforce them against Daria? (See Diagram 20.4.)

Diagram 20.4
Can Ciaran claim the benefit of the covenants and enforce them against Daria?

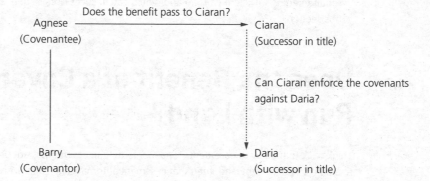

20.8.1 Covenant must 'Touch and Concern' the Land

The covenant must not be personal, it must benefit the land, or, using easements as an analogy the covenant must 'accommodate' the land. In *Smith v River Douglas Catchment Board* [1949] 2 KB 500, the covenant involved maintaining and improving river banks to prevent flooding. Tucker LJ said that the covenant:

> must either affect the land as regards mode of occupation, or … the value of the land … In this case the deed shows that its object was to improve the drainage of land liable to flooding and prevent future flooding … It affects the value of the land per se and converts it from flooded meadows to land suitable for agriculture.

The benefit must be associated with the land and Tucker LJ gives the examples of affecting the mode of occupation and adding value to the land. The court in *P & A Swift Investments v Combined English Stores Group* [1989] AC 632 formulated a test to determine whether the covenant touches and concerns the land:

1 the covenant must be of benefit to the covenantee who owns the land. The benefit to the owner ends when ownership of the land ceases;

2 the covenant must affect the nature, quality, mode of use, or value of the benefited land; and

3 the covenant must not be expressed as a personal covenant. This simply means that the covenant must not be addressed to a specific person.

20.8.2 At the Date of the Covenant, the Original Covenantee Held a Legal Estate in Land

The original covenantee must hold either one of the recognized legal estates: fee simple absolute in possession or a term of years absolute (s1(1) LPA 1925). If the original covenantee holds an equitable interest then the benefit will not run under the common law rules.

20.8.3 The Successor in Title Must Derive their Title From or Under the Original Covenantee

The requirement for pre-1926 covenants is that the successor in title to the original covenantee must hold the same legal estate as the original covenantee. However, for post-1925 covenants s78(1) LPA 1925 applies, and the person enforcing the covenant only needs to hold a legal estate, that is, either a fee simple absolute in possession or a term of years absolute (s1(1) LPA 1925).

20.8.4 At the Date of the Covenant, the Benefit Must Have Been Intended to Run with the Land

Where a pre-1926 covenant was created, the parties had to show that they intended that the benefit of a covenant passes to successors in title. Covenants created after the commencement of the LPA 1925 are governed by s78(1).

> *Law of Property Act 1925*
>
> 78. Benefit of covenants relating to land
>
> (1) A covenant relating to any land of the covenantee shall be deemed to be made with the covenantee and his successors in title and the persons deriving title under him or them, and shall have effect as if such successors and other persons were expressed.
>
> For the purposes of this subsection in connexion with covenants restrictive of the user of land 'successors in title' shall be deemed to include the owners and occupiers for the time being of the land of the covenantee intended to be benefited.

This simply means that the intention that the benefit should run is inferred.

Once the four conditions have been satisfied, the current owner can at common law sue for breach of a covenant (subject to the rules on the burden running with the land being satisfied). If any one of these conditions is not satisfied then the claimant may have to turn to equity to obtain satisfaction.

thinking point 20.3

Does the benefit pass to Ciaran in common law?

Applying the common law to the passing of the benefit to the case study scenario, we can summarize the position as shown in Diagram 20.5.

Diagram 20.5
Common law: passing of the benefit of positive and negative covenants

Test: *P & A Swift Investments* v *Combined English Stores Group* [1989]:

Covenant must benefit covenantee

Touch and concern the land → Must affect nature, quality, mode of use or value of benefited land

Must not be expressed as personal

BENEFIT

Agnese (Covenantee) → Ciaran (Positive and negative covenants)

At date of covenant, original covenantee held legal estate in land

Successor in title must derive their title from or under the original covenantee

At date of covenant, benefit intended to run with the land

Barry (Covenantor)   Daria (Successor in title)

BURDEN

20.9 Equity: Does the Benefit of a Covenant Run with the Land?

cross-reference
See 20.5.3 for the requirement of touching and concerning the land.

Under the common law rules we noted that the burden of a restrictive or positive covenant does not run with the land. The court in equity has shown a willingness to allow the burden of a restrictive covenant to pass subject to the conditions in *Tulk v Moxhay* being satisfied.

In equity, for the benefit of a covenant to pass, certain conditions must be satisfied. The restrictive covenant must, of course, 'touch and concern' the land.

REVIEW QUESTION What does 'touch and concern' the land mean?

(Refer back to 20.5.3.)

In addition to the requirement that the covenant touches and concerns the covenantee's land, the court in *Renals v Cowlishaw* (1879) 9 Ch D 125, set out three alternative methods by which the benefit of a covenant can pass to successors in title:

- annexation;
- assignment; and
- 'building scheme'.

20.9.1 Annexation

The essence of annexation is easy to follow. If the benefit of a restrictive covenant is annexed to Blackacre then the right to enforce the covenant passes on to all successors in title to Blackacre. Gray and Gray (2009, at p 272) provide a useful explanation of annexation:

> Annexation is the process by which the benefit of a restrictive covenant is metaphorically 'nailed' to a clearly defined area of land belonging to the covenantee, in such a way that the benefit passes with any subsequent transfer of the covenantee's interest in that land.

cross-reference
Section 78 is set out later in this section under the heading 'Federated Homes and "Statutory Annexation"'.

A controversial interpretation of s78(1) LPA 1925 was introduced into this area of the law by the judgment of the Court of Appeal in *Federated Homes Ltd v Mill Lodge Properties Ltd* [1980] 1 WLR 594, but the more recent decisions in *Roake v Chadha* [1984] 1 WLR 40 and *Crest Nicholson Residential (South) Ltd v McAllister* [2004] 1 WLR 2409 have largely limited the wide interpretation given by *Federated Homes*.

In any event, *Federated Homes* (as it was interpreted between 1980 and 2004) could not apply to covenants entered into pre-1926. This was confirmed by the decision in *Sainsburys v Enfield Borough Council* [1989] 2 All ER 817. We must first consider express annexation as applied to pre-1926 covenants. We must then explain the effect of *Federated Homes* as it was interpreted between 1980 and 2004, and finally consider how *Crest Nicholson* has restored greater certainty to this area of law.

Express Annexation

Express annexation is regarded as the traditional method of annexation. Express annexation can be achieved only by drafting the document containing the restrictive covenant to express an intention to benefit a defined piece of land, rather than merely to benefit the original covenantee.

633

To illustrate this, to achieve express annexation, drafting using one of the following methods should be employed (we will assume that Blackacre will benefit from the covenant):

- 'This covenant is entered into for the benefit of Blackacre.'
- 'This covenant is entered into for the benefit of Jones in his capacity as owner of Blackacre.'
- 'This covenant is entered into with Jones and his successors in title to Blackacre.'

By making direct reference to the dominant land, this indicates that the parties intend the benefit of the covenant should pass to successors in title. The traditional approach to annexation is best exemplified by *Renals v Cowlishaw* (1879) 11 Ch D 866. The conveyance of the servient land said that the restrictive covenant was entered into for the benefit of the vendors, 'their heirs, administrators and assigns'. That phrase implied the existence of dominant land, but the conveyance did not identify any dominant land. That omission was fatal. The Court of Appeal held that there had been no annexation. In contrast, the court in *Rogers v Hosegood* [1900] 2 Ch 388 upheld a claim for annexation where the covenant was expressed 'with the intent that the covenant may enure to the benefit of the vendors [who were the covenantees in this case] their successors and assigns and others claiming under them to all or any of their lands adjoining'.

A modern case, *Jamaica Mutual Life Assurance v Hillsborough* [1989] 1 WLR 1101, also involved a situation where the dominant land was not expressly identified.

In this case the owners of land sold plots to various parties, subject to a covenant against subdivision of the plots and prohibiting the use of the plots for the carrying on of any trade or business. The instruments of transfer of the plots did not expressly identify the land which the covenants were intended to benefit. One of the owners of the plots applied to the Supreme Court of Jamaica for a declaration as to the extent to which they were bound by the restrictive covenants contained in the instrument of transfer.

The Privy Council was applying Jamaican (not English) law, and held that in Jamaica annexation can be achieved only by an express clause in the document creating the restrictive covenants.

Lord Jauncey of Tullichettle said:

> ... There were in the instrument of transfer to Maurice William Facey no words stating that the restrictions therein were intended for the benefit of any land retained by Dunn and others. ...
>
> In *Renals* v *Cowlishaw* [1878] 9 ChD 125, 130, Hall V-C said:
>
>> that in order to enable a purchaser as an assign (such purchaser not being an assign of all that the vendor retained when he executed the conveyance containing the covenants, and that conveyance not shewing that the benefit of the covenant was intended to enure for the time being of each portion of the estate so retained or of the portion of the estate of which the plaintiff is assign) to claim the benefit of a restrictive covenant, this, at least, must appear, that the assign acquired his property with the benefit of the covenant, that is, it must appear that the benefit of the covenant was part of the subject-matter of the purchase.
>
> In *Rogers* v *Hosegood* [1900] 2 Ch 388, 407–408, Collins LJ said:
>
>> When, as in *Renals* v *Cowlishaw*, there is no indication in the original conveyance, or in the circumstances attending it, that the burden of the restrictive covenant is imposed for the benefit of the land reserved, or any particular part of it, then it becomes necessary to examine the circumstances under which any part of the land reserved is sold, in order to see whether a benefit, not originally annexed to it, has become annexed to it on the sale, so that the purchaser is deemed to have bought it with the land ...
>
> Both *Renals* v *Cowlishaw* and *Rogers* v *Hosegood* were referred to with approval in *Reid* v *Bickerstaff* [1909] 2 Ch 305 where Cozens-Hardy MR in the context of a submission that the benefit of a covenant was annexed to adjoining lands of the vendors said, at p. 321:
>
>> As to the second proposition the plaintiffs have a more plausible case, but I think they fail in establishing it. It is plain that they are not assignees of the covenant, of the existence of which they were not aware. It is equally plain that there is nothing in the deed of 1840, or in any document prior or subsequent thereto, to indicate that the covenant was entered into for the benefit of the particular parcels of which the plaintiffs are now owners. I cannot hold that the mere fact that the plaintiffs' land is adjacent and would be more valuable if the covenant were annexed to the land suffices to justify the court in holding that it was so annexed as to pass without mention by a simple conveyance of the adjacent land.
>
> Applying the principles to be derived from these three cases to the matters to which their Lordships have just referred their Lordships consider that Carey JA was mistaken in concluding that the covenant in the applicant's title was annexed to any land. ...

Annexation to the Whole or to Each and Every Part?

On the traditional view of the law, a restrictive covenant which is annexed to Blackacre is presumptively annexed only to the whole of Blackacre. This presumption can be rebutted if the conveyance includes some phrase such as 'this covenant is annexed to Blackacre and each and every part thereof'.

When drafting a restrictive covenant for the benefit of a large piece of land, the solicitor acting for the dominant owner needs to decide whether:

- to annex the covenant only to the whole of the dominant land;

  or

- to annex the covenant to 'each and every part of the dominant land'.

Each alternative has its advantages and disadvantages.

The Disadvantages of Annexation Only to the Whole of the Dominant Land—The 'Small Plot–Big Plot' Situation

Any annexation only to the whole may be ineffective if the servient land is small and the dominant land is (relatively) very large. This is because the dominant owner must prove that the whole of the large dominant land benefits from the covenant. The leading case is *Re Ballard's Conveyance* [1937] Ch 473 (see Diagram 20.6).

Diagram 20.6
The dominant and servient land in Re Ballard's Conveyance

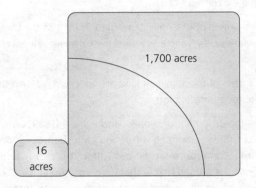

The then owners of the Childwickbury Estate sold 16 acres on the edge of the estate, but subject to a restrictive covenant that the land sold should be used for agricultural purposes only. This covenant was expressed to be for the benefit of 'the whole of the Childwickbury Estate'. Childwickbury extended to 1,700 acres. Clauson J in *Re Ballard's Conveyance* [1937] Ch 473 said:

I...hold that the land for the benefit of which the covenant was taken was the land (about 1,700 acres) now vested in Childwickbury Stud, Ltd, by conveyance from Mr Joel, and that the fact that it claims by virtue of a purchase from Mrs Ballard would not affect its title to sue.

That brings me to the remaining question, namely: Is the covenant one which, in the circumstances of the case, comes within the category of a covenant the benefit of which is capable of running with the land for the benefit of which it was taken? A necessary qualification, in order that the covenant may come within that category, is that it concerns or touches the land with which it is to run: see *per* Farwell J, in *Rogers* v *Hosegood* [1900] 2 Ch 388, at p. 395. That land is an area of some 1,700 acres. It appears to me quite obvious that, while a breach of the stipulations might possibly affect a portion of that area in the vicinity of Mr Wright's land, far the largest part of this area of 1,700 acres could not possibly be affected by any breach of any of the stipulations.

Counsel for the respondent company asked for an adjournment in order to consider whether it would call evidence (as I was prepared to allow it to do) to prove that a breach of the stipulations, or of some of them, might affect the whole of this large area. However, ultimately no such evidence was called.

The result seems to me to be that I am bound to hold that, while the covenant may concern or touch some comparatively small portion of the land to which it has been sought to

> annex it, it fails to concern or touch far the largest part of the land. I asked in vain for any authority which would justify me in severing the covenant, and treating it as annexed to or running with such part of the land as is touched by or concerned with it, though, as regards the remainder of the land, namely, such part as is not touched by or concerned with the covenant, the covenant is not, and cannot be, annexed to it, and accordingly does not, and cannot, run with it.

The judge held that there was no valid annexation. For annexation to be valid, the current owners of Childwickbury would have to have proved that all 1,700 acres were benefited by the 'agriculture only' covenant. In the judge's view, those parts of Childwickbury close to the 16 acres were benefited, but those further away were not (see Diagram 20.6).

If the covenant had been entered into 'for the benefit of Childwickbury and each and every part thereof', there would have been a valid annexation to any part of Childwickbury which would benefit from the covenant.

Where the issue of a large plot of land is concerned as long as the covenant is expressed for the benefit of 'the whole or each and every part' the covenant will pass on a sale of the whole of the dominant land.

More importantly, if parts of the dominant land are later sold off then the benefit will pass to any of the owners of these smaller plots.

This approach was adopted in *Marquess of Zetland v Driver* [1939] Ch 1, where the Marquess of Zetland was successful in preventing a fish and chip shop being opened. The court distinguished *Re Ballard's Conveyance* on the basis that 'it is clearly distinguishable from the present case, if only on the ground that in that case the covenant was expressed to run with the whole estate, whereas in the present case no such difficulty arises because the covenant is expressed to be for the benefit of the whole or any part or parts of the unsold settled property'.

cross-reference
Federated Homes v Mill Lodge Properties Ltd *will be discussed in more detail later in this section under the heading* 'Federated Homes *and "Statutory Annexation"'.*

The advantage of express annexation using 'each and every part' lies in the fact that the benefit will pass to each plot of land sold off from the dominant land. Moreover, a broader interpretation of the passing of the benefit of restrictive covenants was given in *Federated Homes Ltd v Mill Lodge Properties Ltd* [1980] 1 WLR 594. Brightman LJ said 'if the benefit of a covenant is, on a proper construction of a document, annexed to the land, prima facie it is annexed to every part thereof, unless the contrary clearly appear'. This simply means that once the benefit of a covenant is annexed to the land, it is presumed that it is annexed to each and every part.

The Modern Trend in 'Small Plot–Big Plot' Cases

Despite the court's approach in *Re Ballard's Conveyance* requiring evidence that the covenant benefits the whole area of land, in the last 50 years the courts have been much more willing to find as a fact that a covenant on a very small piece of land does benefit the whole of a large plot. Such findings of fact were made in *Marten v Flight Refuelling* [1961] 2 All ER 696 at 706, *Earl of Leicester v Wells-next-the-Sea UDC* [1972] 3 All ER 89, and in *Wrotham Park Estate v Parkside Homes* [1974] 1 WLR 798.

In *Wrotham Park Estate v Parkside Homes*, a covenant over 47 acres was annexed to the whole of a large estate extending to 4,000 acres. Was that annexation valid? The claimant called expert evidence from surveyors that the covenant over 47 acres could benefit all 4,000 acres. The defendant called expert evidence that the covenant could not possibly benefit all 4,000 acres. Judges from earlier generations would have probably dismissed the claimant's evidence and found that there was no valid annexation, and the issue of remedies discussed at 20.12 would not have arisen. However Brightman J held:

> There can be obvious cases where a restrictive covenant clearly is, or clearly is not, of benefit to an estate. Between the two extremes there is inevitably an area where the benefit to the estate is a matter of personal opinion where responsible and reasonable persons can have divergent views. In my judgment, in such cases, it is not for the court to pronounce which is the correct view. I think that the court can only decide whether a particular view is one which can reasonably be held.
>
> If a restriction is bargained for at the time of sale with the intention of giving the vendor a protection which he desires for the land he retains, and the restriction is expressed to be imposed for the benefit of the estate so that both sides are apparently accepting that the restriction is of value to the retained land, I think that the validity of the restriction should be upheld so long as an estate owner may reasonably take the view that the restriction remains of value to his estate, and that the restriction should not be discarded merely because others may reasonably argue that the restriction is spent.

In other words, if there is conflicting evidence as to whether the whole of the large plot benefits from the covenant, the decision should go in favour of annexation to the whole of the large piece of land. Thus, the owners of Wrotham Park got the benefit of the doubt. The covenant was held to be validly annexed to the whole of their land and they could enforce the covenant.

Annexation Destroyed on Subdivision of the Dominant Land

Where there is a valid annexation to only the whole of a dominant piece of land, then that annexation is destroyed on the subdivision of the dominant land (ie where the land is sold off in plots). In *Russell v Archdale* [1964] Ch 38, a company owned certain land which it conveyed to the defendant, the company retaining other land in the neighbourhood. The defendant purchaser entered into various restrictive covenants 'so as to…benefit and protect the vendor's adjoining and neighbouring land'. Some years later the plaintiffs bought *part* of the company's retained land. The conveyance was expressed to include the benefit of the covenants entered into by the defendants.

The court held that the annexation of the covenants to 'the vendor's adjoining and neighbouring land' was an annexation to the *whole* of the vendor's adjoining and neighbouring land and not to *each and every part* of it. Accordingly, as the plaintiffs had acquired a part only of the land, they could not enforce the benefit of the covenant by virtue of annexation.

Buckley J commenting on annexation said:

> No doubt every case of this kind, being one of construction, must be determined on the facts and the actual language used, but…I cannot see that the mere fact that the land intended to be benefited is described by such an expression as 'the land retained by the vendor', is sufficient to enable the court to come to the conclusion that the covenant is intended to benefit each and every part of that land…That being so, it must follow that the plaintiffs cannot enforce the covenant merely by reason of its annexation to the 'adjoining and neighbouring land' of the vendors under the conveyance of July 6 1938, since they [the claimants] have acquired part only of that land.

You should understand this principle if you consider Diagram 20.7 and the accompanying example.

Diagram 20.7
Annexation destroyed where dominant land subdivided

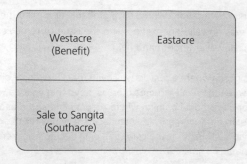

The owner of Eastacre enters into a restrictive covenant expressed to be for the benefit of only the whole of Westacre. While Westacre remains all in one piece there is no problem; successive owners of Westacre can enforce the covenant. But if Wayne, the current owner of Westacre, sells the southern half of the plot to Sangita, the right to enforce the covenant will not pass by virtue of annexation to Sangita.

If Wayne then sold the northern half of Westacre to Nadia, Nadia would not get the benefit of the covenant by virtue of annexation either. As has been said before, the division of the land by selling off a part or parts destroys the annexation.

thinking point 20.4

Consider what the position would be if the annexation had been to 'Westacre and each and every part thereof'.

The splitting of the land would not have been fatal to annexation. Both Nadia and Sangita would acquire the right to enforce the covenant.

The Disadvantage of Annexation to Each and Every Part

When the dominant land is subdivided, the number of owners entitled to enforce the covenant is bound to increase; with a large dominant area the number of dominant owners could initially be one, but later be enormous. Consider the situation represented by Diagram 20.8.

Diagram 20.8
Annexation to each and every part of Bigpots Estate

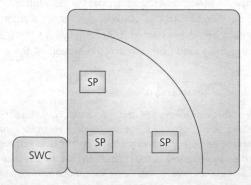

The Duke of Endswell owns the huge Bigpots Estate. He sells off 'south-west corner' (SWC), subject to a restrictive covenant banning building on the land. The covenant is annexed 'to the Bigpots Estate and each and every part thereof'. Subsequently, the Duke sells off other small pieces of land (SP) near to south-west corner.

Maks, the current owner of south-west corner, asks the Duke to cancel the 'no building' covenant. The Duke agrees to do so 'for a consideration of £20,000'. Maks obtains planning permission, but the purchasers of the other small pieces near to south-west corner have acquired the right to enforce the covenant! Any one of them could enforce the covenant against Maks.

Federated Homes and 'Statutory Annexation'

In *Federated Homes Ltd v Mill Lodge Properties Ltd* [1980] 1 WLR 594, Mackenzie Hill Ltd owned a large amount of development land. This land was divided into three areas called red land, green land, and blue land. Mackenzie Hill had outline planning permission to develop the land with 1,250 houses. It sold part of that land (blue land) to Mill Lodge. The conveyance included a restrictive covenant:

> In carrying out the development of the ... land [the purchaser] shall not build at a greater density than a total of 300 dwellings so as not to reduce the number of units [ie houses] which the vendor might eventually erect on the retained land under the existing planning consent.

Mackenzie Hill sold red and green land. Both red and green land were later sold to Federated Homes through various parties. The conveyance of red land did not contain the benefit of the covenant in the defendant's conveyance. The conveyance of green land did contain the defendant's covenant. The defendant obtained new planning permission to build 300 houses on blue land and obtained additional permission to build 32 houses. The claimants also applied for planning permission to build on red and green land, but found that the defendants' additional permission to build 32 houses adversely affected the claimants' development of blue land. The claimants applied for an injunction to prevent the defendant from building more than 300 houses.

The Court of Appeal had (*inter alia*) to decide whether the clause effected an annexation so that on the sale of red and green land the right to enforce the covenant passed automatically to Federated Homes. The Court in *Federated Homes* held that the clause quoted achieved a valid annexation.

Following the express annexation rules, nineteenth-century judges would have decided otherwise. They would have held, 'No annexation. The covenant was not correctly drafted. The dominant land was not clearly identified.' Many modern lawyers argued that that should have been the decision in 1980 (eg Newsom (1981) 97 LQR 32).

How did the court reach its conclusion? The Court of Appeal (led by Brightman LJ) considered how s78(1) LPA 1925 operated. This provision provides:

> *Law of Property Act 1925*
>
> 78.   Benefit of covenants relating to land
>
> (1)   A covenant relating to any land of the covenantee shall be deemed to be made with the covenantee and his successors in title and the persons deriving title under him or them, and shall have effect as if such successors and other persons were expressed ...

The court rejected the commonly held view that s78(1) LPA 1925 was (like the adjoining s79 considered at 20.5.4) a 'word-saving' provision not designed to change substantive law. Brightman LJ explained:

> If, as the language of s. 78 implies, a covenant relating to land which is restrictive of the user thereof is enforceable at the suit of (1) a successor in title of the covenantee, (2) a person deriving title under the covenantee or under his successors in title, and (3) the owner or occupier of the land intended to be benefited by the covenant, it must, in my view, follow that the

639

covenant runs with the land, because ex hypothesi every successor in title to the land, every derivative proprietor of the land and every other owner and occupier has a right by statute to the covenant. In other words, if the condition precedent of s. 78 is satisfied, that is to say, there exists a covenant which touches and concerns the land of the covenantee, that covenant runs with the land for the benefit of his successors in title, persons deriving title under him or them and other owners and occupiers.

Brightman LJ also stated that 'if the benefit of a covenant is, on a proper construction of a document, annexed to the land, *prima facie* it is annexed to every part thereof, unless the contrary clearly appears'. According to Brightman LJ, for 'statutory annexation' to take place the covenant must touch and concern the land or put another way, the covenant must relate to the covenantee's land. The issue of how the dominant land is identified is left unclear by Brightman LJ. But once there is statutory annexation, the benefit of the covenant passes on a sale of the whole or part of the dominant land.

The Practical Effect of *Federated Homes* Between 1980 and 2004

The decision in *Federated Homes* apparently meant that whenever a restrictive covenant had been entered into after 1925, that covenant was automatically annexed to each and every part of all land which the covenantee retained in the vicinity of the servient land.

A consequence of Brightman LJ leaving open the issue of identifying the benefited land is that it was not clear in what manner the dominant land should be identified. For example, should the land be identifiable from the covenant, the conveyance, or evidence from surrounding circumstances?

In order for the benefit of a covenant to pass automatically under statutory annexation there must be nothing in the covenant which excludes its application. Brightman LJ stated that 'a covenantee may expressly or by necessary implication retain the benefit of a covenant wholly under his own control, so that the benefit will not pass unless the covenantee chooses to assign'. Consequently, the benefit will not pass by statutory annexation if it is clear that it should only pass through express assignment.

Federated Homes apparently greatly simplified the law on restrictive covenants but it is not without criticism and problems. Goo (2002, at p 696) provides a useful critique of this case:

> First, it is said that if the decision is correct, then there will be no need for the devise of express assignment and express or implied annexation. Secondly, the Law of Property Act 1925 is a consolidation Act, which does not normally change the law unless the words clearly constrain the court to do so. If the words are capable of more than one construction, then the court should give effect to the construction which does not change the law. This is a strong argument with a narrow view. If Parliament intended to change the law, one would expect this to be expressed in unambiguous terms . . .
>
> Thirdly, in *Federated Homes*, the defendant was the original covenantor. It was a case between the original covenantor and the successors in title of the original covenantee. The benefit could have run at common law, and there is no need for the court to consider the running of the benefit in equity. Therefore, any subsequent court may treat the dictum of Brightman LJ regarding statutory annexation under s. 78 as merely *obiter dicta*.

thinking point 20.5

Consider the facts of the Newton Abbot Co-operative Society Ltd v Williamson and Treadgold *case set out at 20.5.3. That case, as we shall see at 20.9.2 under the heading 'Exceptions to the Rule that There Must Be an Express Assignment Clause', was decided on 'assignment' not 'annexation' principles. But try to apply the* Federated Homes *rule to the facts of* Newton Abbot Co-operative Society.

On the facts of Newton Abbot Co-operative Society *there would be an annexation to the ironmongers across the road (and each and every part of it), even though those premises were not even hinted at in the restrictive covenant.*

Drafting of Restrictive Covenants in the Light of *Federated Homes*

In *Roake v Chadha* [1984] 1 WLR 40, the judge specifically upheld the effectiveness of a clause (drafted in 1934) which made it clear that the benefit of a set of restrictive covenants was not to pass by annexation, but only by express assignment. The judge rejected an argument that the benefit of the covenants had nevertheless been annexed by virtue of s78(1) LPA 1925. He held that careful drafting had excluded the effect of s78(1) LPA 1925. Judge Paul Baker QC said:

[Counsel for the claimants] method of applying [s78 LPA 1925] is simplicity itself. The *Federated Homes* case [1980] 1 W.L.R. 594 shows that section 78 of the Act of 1925 brings about annexation, and that the operation of the section cannot be excluded by a contrary intention. As I have indicated, he supports this last point by reference to section 79, which is expressed to operate 'unless a contrary intention is expressed,' a qualification which, as we have already noticed, is absent from section 78. [Counsel for the claimants] could not suggest any reason of policy why section 78 should be mandatory, unlike, for example, section 146 of the Act of 1925, which deals with restrictions on the right to forfeiture of leases and which, by an express provision 'has effect notwithstanding any stipulation to the contrary.'

I am thus far from satisfied that section 78 has the mandatory operation which [counsel for the claimants] claimed for it. But if one accepts that it is not subject to a contrary intention, I do not consider that it has the effect of annexing the benefit of the covenant in each and every case irrespective of the other express terms of the covenant. I notice that Brightman L.J. in the *Federated Homes* case did not go so far as that, for he said, at p. 606:

'I find the idea of the annexation of a covenant to the whole of the land but not to a part of it a difficult conception fully to grasp. I can understand that a covenantee may expressly or by necessary implication retain the benefit of a covenant wholly under his own control, so that the benefit will not pass unless the covenantee chooses to assign; but I would have thought, if the benefit of a covenant is, on a proper construction of a document, annexed to the land, prima facie it is annexed to every part thereof, unless the contrary clearly appears.'

So at least in some circumstances Brightman L.J. is considering that despite section 78 the benefit may be retained and not pass or be annexed to and run with land. In this connection, I was also referred by [counsel for the defendants] to *Elphinstone's Covenants Affecting Land* (1946), p. 17, where it is said in a footnote:

'but it is thought that, as a covenant must be construed as a whole, the court would give due effect to words excluding or modifying the operation of the section...'

The true position as I see it is that even where a covenant is deemed to be made with successors in title as section 78 requires, one still has to construe the covenant as a whole to see whether the benefit of the covenant is annexed. Where one finds, as in the *Federated Homes* case, the covenant is not qualified in any way, annexation may be readily inferred; but where, as in the present case, it is expressly provided:

'this covenant shall not enure for the benefit of any owner or subsequent purchaser of any part of the vendor's Sudbury Court Estate at Wembley unless the benefit of this covenant shall be expressly assigned...'

one cannot just ignore these words. One may not be able to exclude the operation of the section in widening the range of the covenantees, but one has to consider the covenant as a whole to determine its true effect. When one does that, then it seems to me that the answer is plain and in my judgment the benefit was not annexed. That is giving full weight to both the statute in force and also what is already there in the covenant.

Roake v Chadha confirmed that the potential effects of *Federated Homes* could be avoided by careful drafting of covenants. But *Roake v Chadha* was of little comfort to competent draftsmen who found the meaning of their pre-1980 drafts seemingly changed retrospectively by the Court of Appeal.

cross-reference
For more on Jamaica Mutual Life, *see 20.9.1 under the heading 'Express Annexation'.*

cross-reference
Building schemes are discussed at 20.9.3.

The Privy Council and the Crucial Importance of Identifying Dominant Owners

Two modern Privy Council decisions applied Jamaican and Trinidadian law respectively. They made no reference either to s78 LPA 1925 or *Federated Homes*. However, both these cases were decided on policy grounds totally overlooked by *Federated Homes*. It is submitted that the reasoning in these two cases undermined *Federated Homes* as it was understood between 1980 and 2004.

The first case is *Jamaica Mutual Life Assurance Society v Hillsborough Ltd* [1989] 1 WLR 1101, where the Privy Council held that, in Jamaica, annexation can be achieved only by an express clause identifying the dominant land. It seems that one of the reasons for the Privy Council's decision was the policy consideration that a person entering into a restrictive covenant ought from the outset to know for certain the identity of the dominant land(s). *Federated Homes* totally overlooked this enormously important consideration.

In *Emile Elias v Pine Groves* [1993] 1 WLR 305, the case concerned an alleged building scheme. The Privy Council (advising through Lord Browne-Wilkinson) reaffirmed a long-standing principle first stated in 1909, that for a valid scheme the area of land covered by the scheme must be fixed before any land is sold off by the common vendor: 'In order to create a valid building scheme, the purchasers of all the land within the area of the scheme must know what that area is.'

Thus, in a building scheme, owners of land know the full extent of the dominant land. By contrast, somebody who buys land subject to restrictive covenants annexed under the *Federated Homes* principle would be guessing at the identity of the dominant land.

Federated Homes Emasculated—*Crest Nicholson v McAllister*

Crest Nicholson v McAllister [2004] 1 WLR 2409 made further inroads into *Federated Homes* automatic annexation. In this case two brothers bought land at Claygate in Surrey. Over a period from 1928 to 1936 they sold the land off in plots. Each conveyance was subject to a restrictive covenant in effect 'not more than one house per plot'. The conveyances did not identify any dominant land. There was certainly not a building scheme.

McAllister, who had acquired part of the land conveyed in 1936, claimed to be able to enforce the restrictive covenants in the earlier conveyances. He relied on the broad reading of the *Federated Homes* decision set out at the earlier heading 'The Practical Effect of *Federated Homes* Between 1980 and 2004'. He argued 'Under *Federated Homes* there is annexation to each and every part of all land which the covenantee retains in the vicinity. That land does not have to be identified in the covenant.'

The Court of Appeal rejected this wide reading of *Federated Homes* which had been adopted by most commentators since 1980. Rather, it held that for there to be a valid statutory annexation under s78, the dominant land must be either clearly spelt out in the conveyance itself, or the dominant land must be mentioned in the conveyance itself and 'easily ascertainable' from looking at the surrounding circumstances.

Crucially, like the Privy Council in *Jamaica Mutual Life v Hillsborough* [1989] 1 WLR 1101, the Court of Appeal stressed that the law must be such as to make it reasonably easy for servient owners to work out who the dominant owners are. At para 34 Chadwick LJ says:

> It is obviously desirable that a purchaser of land burdened with a restrictive covenant should be able not only to ascertain, by inspection of the entries on the relevant register, that the land is so burdened, but also to ascertain the land for which the benefit of the

covenant was taken—so that he can identify who can enforce the covenant. That latter object is achieved if the land which is intended to be benefited is defined in the instrument so as to be easily ascertainable. To require a purchaser of land burdened with a restrictive covenant, but where the land for the benefit of which the covenant was taken is not described in the instrument, to make inquiries as to what (if any) land the original covenantee retained at the time of the conveyance and what (if any) of that retained land the covenant did, or might have, 'touched and concerned' would be oppressive. It must be kept in mind that (as in the present case) the time at which the enforceability of the covenant becomes an issue may be long after the date of the instrument by which it was imposed.

Excluding statutory annexation by providing an express contrary intention in the covenant was approved by the court. Chadwick LJ said:

41. …it is impossible to identify any reason of policy why a covenantor should not, by express words, be entitled to limit the scope of the obligation which he is undertaking; nor why a covenantee should not be able to accept a covenant for his own benefit on terms that the benefit does not pass automatically to all those to whom he sells on parts of his retained land. As Brightman LJ [in *Federated Homes*] pointed out, in the passage cited by Judge Paul Baker QC, a developer who is selling off land in lots might well want to retain the benefit of a building restriction under his own control. Where, as in *Roake* v *Chadha* [1984] 1 WLR 40 and the present case, development land is sold off in plots without imposing a building scheme, it seems to me very likely that the developer will wish to retain exclusive power to give or withhold consent to a modification or relaxation of a restriction on building which he imposes on each purchaser; unfettered by the need to obtain the consent of every subsequent purchaser to whom (after imposing the covenant) he has sold off other plots on the development land. I can see no reason why, if original covenantor and covenantee make clear their mutual intention in that respect, the legislature should wish to prevent effect being given to that intention.

42. Second, it is important to keep in mind that, for the purposes of its application to restrictive covenants—which is the context in which this question arises where neither of the parties to the dispute were, themselves, party to the instrument imposing the covenant or express assignees of the benefit of the covenant—section 78 of the 1925 Act defines 'successors in title' as the owners and occupiers of the time being *of the land of the covenantee intended to be benefited*. In a case where the parties to the instrument make clear their intention that land retained by the covenantee at the time of the conveyance effected by the transfer is to have the benefit of the covenant only for so long as it continues to be in the ownership of the original covenantee, and not after it has been sold on by the original covenantee—unless the benefit of the covenant is expressly assigned to the new owner— *the land of the covenantee intended to be benefited* is identified by the instrument as (i) so much of the retained land as from time to time has not been sold off by the original covenantee and (ii) so much of the retained land as has been sold off with the benefit of an express assignment, but as not including (iii) so much of the land as has been sold off without the benefit of an express assignment. I agree with the judge in *Roake* v *Chadha* [1984] 1 WLR 40 that, in such a case, it is possible to give full effect to the statute and to the terms of the covenant.

The one point not covered by the *Crest Nicholson* case is whether the annexation is presumed to be to each and every part of the dominant land. It is submitted that, bearing in mind the problems of the multiplication of dominant owners set out at 'The Disadvantage of Annexation to Each and Every Part', annexation should be presumed to be to the whole of the dominant land unless the covenant expressly refers to 'each and every part'. This is contrary to what Brightman LJ said in *Federated Homes*.

20.9.2 Assignment of the Benefit of Restrictive Covenants

The Rules for a Valid Assignment

Although *Federated Homes* made the transmission of the benefit of a covenant in equity easier, assignment is now perhaps less important than it was, but it must still be considered in the light of decisions such as *Roake v Chadha* and *Crest Nicholson* which limit the scope of s78 and *Federated Homes*.

There are clear differences between assignment and annexation. This is shown in Table 20.1.

Table 20.1
Comparison between annexation and assignment

	Annexation	Assignment
What happens to the benefit?	Attaches the benefit to the land.	Transfers the benefit to a person (assignee).
Timing: when does it occur?	Attaches the benefit at the time the covenant was made.	Operates when the land is transferred (this could happen some years after the covenant was created).
What is the effect of this mode of transmission of the benefit?	The benefit will run with the land automatically with each transfer of land.	Each time there is a transfer of land, a new assignment of the benefit must be created.

The assignment rules are important in two types of situation:

- where the restrictive covenant has not been validly annexed to the dominant land; and
- where the restrictive covenant has been expressly annexed only to the whole of the dominant land, and that dominant land is subdivided. (Remember that the subdivision destroys the annexation: see 20.9.1 under the heading 'Annexation Destroyed on Subdivision of the Dominant Land'.)

Where assignment of the benefit of a restrictive covenant is under consideration, the rather elaborate rules in *Miles v Easter* [1933] Ch 611, especially at 632, apply. If a dominant owner is to be able to enforce a covenant under the assignment rules, four conditions must be satisfied:

1 *The covenant must be entered into for the benefit of 'ascertainable land'.* It must be possible to identify the dominant land from the terms of the document containing the covenant, or (as in *Newton Abbot Co-operative Society Ltd v Williamson and Treadgold*) from the surrounding circumstances.

2 *This 'ascertainable land' must actually be benefited by the existence of the covenant.* In *Marten v Flight Refuelling* [1961] 2 All ER 696 and *Earl of Leicester v Wells-next-the-Sea* [1972] 3 All ER 77 it seems to have been assumed that where the 'ascertainable land' is a large area, the whole of that area must be benefited for the rules to operate. In each of these cases the judge found that a very large area was benefited by the restrictive covenants.

3 *The assignee must have acquired at least part of the 'ascertainable land'.* In *Russell v Archdale* [1962] 2 All ER 305 and *Stilwell v Blackman* [1967] 3 All ER 514, it was held that a covenant annexed only to the whole of a piece of dominant land could be assigned on the sale of part of that dominant land.

4 *Simultaneous with the conveyance of the land, the assignee must have been assigned the benefit of the restrictive covenant.* The basic idea underlying this last rule is that every time the dominant land is conveyed (or transferred in any way), the conveyance or other transfer document should include an express clause assigning the benefit of the restrictive covenant.

thinking point 20.6

Robbie is contemplating buying Downacre. It appears that Downacre is dominant to a restrictive covenant over Slowacre, but that the covenant has not been annexed to Downacre. What will Robbie insist be put into the conveyance of Downacre?

He will insist that the conveyance to him of Downacre includes a special clause assigning him the benefit of the covenant.

If Robbie later sells Downacre to Priti, what will she insist Robbie put in the conveyance to her? She will, of course, insist that Robbie include in the conveyance to her a special clause assigning the benefit of the restrictive covenant.

Exceptions to the Rule that There Must Be an Express Assignment Clause

The courts have created two exceptions to the rule (see rule (4) in the previous list) that every time the land which is dominant to an unannexed covenant is sold, the covenant passes only if there is an express assignment clause.

The first exception was recognized in *Northbourne v Johnstone* [1922] 2 Ch 309. In that case the contract for sale of the dominant land included a special clause promising that the vendor would assign to the purchaser an unannexed restrictive covenant. Somebody forgot to include the special assignment clause in the conveyance itself. The court, nevertheless, held that the purchaser had acquired the right to enforce the covenant. It applied the maxim 'equity looks on as done that which ought to be done' to the contract. The contract transferred to the purchaser the right to enforce the covenant.

The *Northbourne* exception is clearly correct. The same cannot be said of the second exception, which was created by the *Newton Abbot Co-operative Society v Williamson and Treadgold* case. At one stage in the history of the dominant ironmongers the current owner died, but her will made no mention of the unannexed covenant. Nor did the 'assent' of the shop signed by her executors. There was, therefore, nothing which could be treated as an express assignment of the covenant to the person who had been left the shop. The judge nevertheless held that the current owners of the ironmongery could enforce the unannexed covenant.

In *Leicester v Wells-next-the-Sea* [1972] 3 All ER 77, the land dominant to the covenant was settled land. One life tenant died and was succeeded by another life tenant. The new vesting assent executed by the Settled Land Act trustees (the document required to transfer to him the legal estate) made no mention of the covenant, yet the new life tenant was held entitled to enforce the covenant.

The apparent effect of these two cases (on this point) is that if the dominant land devolves on death (rather than passing on sale) the new owner of the land can enforce the covenant without an express assignment in either the will, or the assent from the deceased's personal representatives.

These last two cases are an illustration of a trend mentioned at 20.7, that is, that modern courts tend 'to change the old rules in favour of persons claiming to be dominant owners'. You should note, too, that in these two cases the dominant owners in whose favour the rules were 'bent' were donees, not purchasers!

20.9.3 Building Schemes or Schemes of Development

If you go back to 1.3.2, you will see a modern example of what conveyancers have tradition-ally called 'a building scheme'. A building scheme arises where an area of land according to a plan is sold or leased in lots (commonly known as plots). When the lot is sold or leased the purchasers are subject to the benefit and burden of covenants which are mutually enforceable between the current owners. If a building scheme has been validly created then all properties within the scheme are both servient and dominant land.

The Conditions Required for a Valid Building Scheme

To establish a building scheme a number of conditions must be satisfied. These conditions were laid down in *Elliston v Reacher* [1908] 2 Ch 374, by Parker J at 384:

(1.) that both the plaintiffs and defendants derive title under a common vendor; (2.) that previously to selling the lands to which the plaintiffs and defendants are respectively entitled the vendor laid out his estate, or a defined portion thereof (including the lands purchased by the plaintiffs and defendants respectively), for sale in lots subject to restrictions intended to be imposed on all the lots, and which, though varying in details as to particular lots, are consistent and consistent only with some general scheme of development; (3.) that these restrictions were intended by the common vendor to be and were for the benefit of all the lots intended to be sold, whether or not they were also intended to be and were for the benefit of other land retained by the vendor; and (4.) that both the plaintiffs and the defendants, or their predecessors in title, purchased their lots from the common vendor upon the footing that the restrictions subject to which the purchases were made were to enure for the benefit of the other lots included in the general scheme whether or not they were also to enure for the benefit of other lands retained by the vendors. If these four points be established, I think that the plaintiffs would in equity be entitled to enforce the restrictive covenants entered into by the defendants or their predecessors with the common vendor irrespective of the dates of the respective purchases. I may observe, with reference to the third point, that the vendor's object in imposing the restrictions must in general be gathered from all the circumstances of the case, including in particular the nature of the restrictions. If a general observance of the restrictions is in fact calculated to enhance the values of the several lots offered for sale, it is an easy inference that the vendor intended the restrictions to be for the benefit of all the lots, even though he might retain other land the value of which might be similarly enhanced, for a vendor may naturally be expected to aim at obtaining the highest possible price for his land. Further, if the first three points be established, the fourth point may readily be inferred, provided the purchasers have notice of the facts involved in the three first points; but if the purchaser purchases in ignorance of any material part of those facts, it would be difficult, if not impossible, to establish the fourth point. It is also observable that the equity arising out of the establishment of the four points I have mentioned has been sometimes explained by the implication of mutual contracts between the various purchasers, and sometimes by the implication of a contract between each purchaser and the common vendor, that each purchaser is to have the benefit of all the covenants by the other purchasers, so that each purchase is in equity an assign of the benefit of these covenants. In my opinion the implication of mutual contract is not always a perfectly satisfactory explanation. It may be satisfactory where all the lots are sold by auction at the same time, but when, as in cases such as *Spicer* v. *Martin* 14 App Cas 12, there is no sale by auction, but all the various sales are by private treaty and at various intervals of time, the circumstances may, at the date of one or more of the sales, be such as to preclude the possibility of any actual contract. For example, a prior purchaser may be dead or incapable of contracting at the time of a subsequent purchase, and in any event it is unlikely that the prior and subsequent purchasers are ever brought into personal relationship, and yet the equity may exist between them. It is, I think, enough to say, using Lord Macnaghten's words in *Spicer* v. *Martin* 14 App Cas 12, that where the four points I have mentioned are established, the community of interest imports in equity the reciprocity of obligation which is in fact contemplated by each at the time of his own purchase.

To summarize:

- The claimant and the defendant derive title under a common vendor.
- The creator of the scheme (ie the developer) sells off the land in 'plots' (or known as 'lots') subject to restrictive covenants. The covenants must form part of an organized scheme for the whole area decided upon before selling commenced. The 'plots' may be empty sites ripe for development, or they may already have been built upon. (In the nineteenth century the developer would usually sell off vacant plots on which the purchasers would arrange for the construction of their houses in compliance with the covenants. In the twenty-first century the developers are usually firms like Wilson or Wimpey selling off houses they have already constructed.)
- The creator of the scheme must have intended the restrictions on each plot to be for the benefit of the other plots. They must have intended 'mutual enforceability'.
- The original purchasers from the creator of the scheme must have realized that the covenants were to be mutually enforceable between the purchasers.

A fifth condition was added to this list by the Court of Appeal in *Reid v Bickerstaff* [1909] 2 Ch 305. It requires, at the outset, the creator of a building scheme to set up a scheme for a defined area of land. Cozens-Hardy MR explained why this is important:

> What are some of the essentials of a building scheme? In my opinion there must be a defined area within which the scheme is operative. Reciprocity is the foundation of the idea of a scheme. A purchaser of one parcel cannot be subject to an implied obligation to purchasers of an undefined and unknown area. He must know both the extent of his burden and the extent of his benefit. Not only must the area be defined, but the obligations to be imposed within that area must be defined. Those obligations need not be identical. For example, there may be houses of a certain value in one part and houses of a different value in another part. A building scheme is not created by the mere fact that the owner of an estate sells it in lots and takes varying covenants from various purchasers. There must be notice to the various purchasers of what I may venture to call the local law imposed by the vendors upon a definite area.

The existence of this fifth condition is confirmed by the Privy Council in *Emile Elias & Co Ltd v Pine Groves Ltd* [1993] 1 WLR 305, which applied *Reid v Bickerstaff* acknowledging that merely defining the area of the scheme alone is not sufficient. Lord Browne-Wilkinson said 'This shows that it is not sufficient that the common vendor has himself defined the area. In order to create a valid building scheme, the purchasers of all the land within the area of the scheme must also know what that area is.'

It is clearly common sense that a purchaser would want to know the extent and content of the obligations. The courts have, however, since *Elliston v Reacher* taken a less prescriptive approach towards fulfilling the conditions set out in that case. Two cases are notable in this regard, as both cases did not comply with all four conditions.

In *Baxter v Four Oaks* [1965] Ch 816, there was a Victorian building scheme with one special feature. The common vendor had fixed the area of his scheme but had not divided his land into plots before commencing selling. Rather, he had sold each purchaser as much land as he (the purchaser) desired. In those days the purchaser took a vacant site and then built his own house. Cross J held that the special feature of the case did not prevent there being a building scheme. Cross J was of the view in this case that:

> In the early days it was not unusual for the common vendor to have prepared a deed of mutual covenant to be executed by each purchaser. If the various sales all took place at the same time—as they would, for instance, if all the land in question was put up for sale by auction in lots—then the various purchasers would, no doubt, be brought into direct contractual

relations with one another on signing the deed. But if the common vendor sold off different lots of land at intervals, it might well happen that by the time a later purchaser executed the deed, one of the earlier purchasers was dead. In such a case it would be difficult to found the right of the successors in title of the deceased earlier purchaser to enforce covenants against the later purchaser or his successors in title on any contract between the two original purchasers, even though each signed the deed.

The view taken by the courts has been rather that the common vendor imposed a common law on a defined area of land and that whenever he sold a piece of it to a purchaser who knew of the common law, that piece of land automatically became entitled to the benefit of, and subject to the burden of, the common law. With the passage in time it became apparent that there was no particular virtue in the execution of a deed of mutual covenant—save as evidence of the intention of the parties—and what came to be called 'building schemes' were enforced by the courts if satisfied that it was the intention of the parties that the various purchasers should have rights inter se, even though no attempt was made to bring them into direct contractual relations.

A statement of the law on this point which is often quoted is contained in Parker J.'s judgment in *Elliston* v. *Reacher* [1908] 2 Ch 374, 384 . . .

Cross J considered the four conditions in *Elliston v Reacher*:

The defendants naturally rely on Parker J's second requirement and argue that as Lord Clanrikarde did not lay out the part of his estate which faced Lichfield Road in lots before he began to sell it off, there could be no enforceable building scheme here, even though Lord Clanrikarde and the purchasers from him may have thought that there was.

It is, however, to be observed that *Elliston* v. *Reacher* [1908] 2 Ch 374 was not a case in which there was direct evidence afforded by the execution of the deed of mutual covenant that the parties in fact intended a building scheme. The question was whether one could properly infer that intention in all the circumstances. In such a case, no doubt the fact that the common vendor did not divide his estate into lots before beginning to sell it is an argument against there having been intention on his part and on the part of the various purchasers that there should be a building scheme, because it is, perhaps, prima facie unlikely that a purchaser of a plot intends to enter into obligations to an unknown number of subsequent purchasers. But I cannot believe that Parker J. was intending to lay down that the fact that the common vendor did not bind himself to sell off the defined area to which the common law was to apply in lots of any particular size but proposed to sell off parcels of various sizes according to the requirement of the various purchasers must, as a matter of law, preclude the court from giving effect to a clearly proved intention that the purchasers were to have rights inter se to enforce the provisions of the common law.

This passage indicates that the four criteria listed in *Elliston v Reacher* should not be treated as prescriptive. This is an indication that the courts were prepared to take a more flexible approach.

Re Dolphin's Conveyance [1970] 2 All ER 664 is a good example of a more relaxed attitude towards building schemes. In 1871, two sisters were tenants in common of the 30-acre 'Selly Hill Estate' on the then south-west edge of Birmingham. They started selling off sizeable parts of this estate. They then gave the remaining parts of Selly Hill to their nephew. He sold off further chunks of Selly Hill, until it had all gone by 1891.

As each chunk of Selly Hill was sold, restrictive covenants were imposed on the land. The purchasers promised to build only high-class housing; each house was to have a minimum of a quarter of an acre of grounds.

On each sale the vendors (the sisters or the nephew) covenanted that if they sold further parts of Selly Hill, the same restrictive covenants would be imposed. The judge inferred from this promise by the vendors a common intention that the covenants restricting the area to high-class housing were to be mutually enforceable. The judge went on to hold that although:

- there had been no scheme of restrictive covenants for the whole area decided upon before sale commenced; and
- the selling of the estate had been spread over 20 years;

there was nevertheless, in his view, a situation within the building scheme principle. Thus, current owners of large houses on Selly Hill could enforce the covenants against Birmingham Corporation, which had bought other parts of Selly Hill for high-density council housing. The decision in *Re Dolphin's Conveyance* is, however, very debatable. The decision contradicts the philosophy underlying both *Emile Elias* and *Crest Nicholson*. These cases stress that anybody who enters into a restrictive covenant is entitled to know, from the outset, the extent of the dominant land(s); that is, the owners of which parcels of land are entitled to enforce the covenants. It is suggested that *Re Dolphin's Conveyance* might well be overruled.

To sum up, the modern courts now focus on two conditions:

- the area of land covered by the building scheme must be identifiable; and
- the purchasers possess the necessary common intention to be bound by reciprocal obligations.

The Purchasers Possess the Necessary Common Intention to be Bound by Reciprocal Obligations

Lord Jauncey of Tullichettle stated in *Jamaica Mutual Life Assurance Society v Hillsborough Ltd* [1989] 1 WLR 1101 that the central prerequisite of a building scheme was:

> an acceptance by each purchaser of part of the lands from the common vendor that the benefit of the covenants into which he has entered will enure to the vendor and to others deriving title from him and that he correspondingly will enjoy the benefit of covenants entered into by other purchasers of part of the land. Reciprocity of obligations between purchasers of different plots is essential.

In effect, under a building scheme the purchasers must accept being bound by the common reciprocal obligations under the covenants. There is a common intention on the part of the purchasers to be bound. It is not sufficient to infer a scheme of development merely because there is a common vendor and common reciprocal covenants.

This common intention to be bound by mutually enforceable covenants can be demonstrated in a number of ways. For example, in *Elliston v Reacher* the intention that there was to be mutual enforceability was proved not by reference to documents, but by reference to the manner in which the original plots of land were advertised and sold.

In that case the building scheme was created in 1861. The plots were sold from an office in Ipswich, but the scheme itself was on ten acres of land at Felixstowe, 12 miles away on the Suffolk coast. Anybody entering the office in Ipswich would have seen on the wall a large plan of the scheme, with the restrictive covenants endorsed prominently on the plan. Potential purchasers of a plot could buy a copy of this plan (with the covenants listed). The covenants were of a kind designed to preserve the 'exclusive' nature of the area.

It was a natural inference from this advertising (drawn by all four judges who heard the case) that the creator of the scheme back in 1861 intended the covenants to be mutually enforceable.

The conclusion in *Elliston v Reacher* seems fair enough. But you should note that the dispute arose 45 years after the creation of the scheme; some of the original purchasers were still able to give evidence of what had happened. What if the dispute (which was over somebody wanting to build a hotel on one of the plots) had not arisen until 1990?

REVIEW QUESTION Which of the methods of passing the benefit would you suggest applies to Ciaran in our Marchland Close case study?

(Refer back to 20.8.)

In order to determine whether the rules in equity apply, go back and consider what we have said so far. The burden of a restrictive or positive covenant does not run at common law. It is then necessary to establish whether the covenant will pass in equity. In our advice to Ciaran he would need to establish which of the methods of transmission would apply to him (see Diagram 20.9).

Diagram 20.9
Does the benefit of the covenant pass to Ciaran in equity?

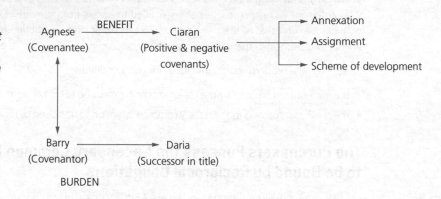

650

20.10 Possible Ways of Making Positive Covenants Run

20.10.1 Enlargement of Long Lease

Section 153 LPA 1925 allows for a very long lease (say 300 years) to be enlarged into a fee simple estate. The fee simple estate created by this method will be subject to the positive covenants contained in the lease and those covenants will bind future successors in title. This device is hardly, if ever, used.

20.10.2 Commonhold

One notable effect of the rule regarding the non-transmission of the burden of positive covenants is that it made it practically impossible to have freehold flats. A 'solution' to this problem, commonly adopted, is to grant a long lease of the flats (eg for 99 years) where the benefit and burden of the covenants will be enforceable through privity of estate.

cross-reference
For more details of commonhold, see 2.3.

People can now in theory (but rarely it seems in practice) use commonhold. The Commonhold and Leasehold Reform Act 2002 created a new tenure which allows a block of residential flats to be owned in fee simple by the commonhold association. The owners of the individual flats (known under the 2002 Act as units) will be subject to the Commonhold Community Statement which will contain details of positive and negative covenants delineating responsibility to either individual flat-owners or the commonhold association.

20.10.3 Indemnity Covenants

An indemnity covenant arises where the covenantor obtains from their successor in title a promise to pay damages in the event of a breach of a positive covenant. A chain of indemnity covenants is created on each subsequent sale; each purchaser agrees to indemnify *their* vendor should there be a breach of a positive covenant.

In the event of a breach of a covenant, the covenantee can sue the original covenantor for damages. Having paid up, that covenantor can make a claim from their successor in title, who will in turn claim from their successor in title (and so on). The problem with this is that this method is not infallible because as the chain increases in length there is a likelihood that this may break at some point. For example, what would happen if the original covenantor dies, or (if a limited company) goes into liquidation? The original covenantee will not be able to bring an action for damages against any of the subsequent successors in title because they were not parties to the original covenant.

20.10.4 Mutual Benefit and Burden

In *Halsall v Brizell* [1974] Ch 169, the purchasers of individual plots of a building estate were given the benefit of using various roads on the estate on the condition that they would contribute to the upkeep of the roads. Upjohn J referred to an ancient rule in his judgment: 'a man cannot take benefit under a deed without subscribing to the obligations thereunder'. Consequently, the court held that in equity since the purchasers enjoyed the benefit of using the roads, they must fulfil their obligation to pay towards maintenance costs.

cross-reference
See 20.5 for the facts of Rhone v Stephens.

How is this rule to apply? Should the mutual benefit and burden of covenants be connected to each other in some way or can they merely exist independently in the same document creating the covenants? The initial approach towards this question was answered in *Tito v Waddell (No 2)* [1977] Ch 106, where it was suggested that independent benefits and burdens of covenants in a transaction were to be treated as linked. This was called the 'pure principle of benefit and burden'. The effect of this would mean that all positive covenants in a transaction would run with the land. This was discredited in *Rhone v Stephens*, Lord Templeman said [at p322]:

> I am not prepared to recognise the 'pure principle' that any party deriving any benefit from a conveyance must accept any burden in the same conveyance ... It does not follow that any condition can be rendered enforceable by attaching it to a right nor does it follow that every burden imposed by a conveyance may be enforced by depriving the covenantor's successor in title of every benefit which he enjoyed thereunder. The condition must be relevant to the exercise of the right. In *Halsall v. Brizell* there were reciprocal benefits and burdens enjoyed by the users of the roads and sewers.

According to this statement, the benefit enjoyed and the corresponding burden must be intrinsically linked for that burden to be enforceable against a successor in title.

The Court of Appeal in *Thamesmead Town Ltd v Allotey* (2000) 79 P & CR 557 reviewed Lord Templeman's restrictive stance on the 'mutual benefit and burden' principle and identified two conditions which have to be met for a positive covenant to be enforceable under this rubric. Peter Gibson LJ summarized his findings:

> The reasoning of Lord Templeman suggests that there are two requirements for the enforceability of a positive covenant against a successor in title to the covenantor. The first is that the condition of discharging the burden must be relevant to the exercise of the rights which

enable the benefit to be obtained. In Rhone v. Stephens the mutual obligations of support was unrelated to, and independent of, the covenant to maintain the roof. The second is that the successors in title must have the opportunity to choose whether to take the benefit or having taken it to renounce it, even if only in theory, and thereby to escape the burden and that the successors in title can be deprived of the benefit if they fail to assume the burden.

According to Peter Gibson LJ the first condition requires a 'correlation between the burden and the benefit which the successor has chosen to take', such that where there is simply an incidental benefit this would not be sufficient for the enforcement of a burden by the successor in title. The second condition requires the successor in title to have the option as to whether they choose to accept the benefit and its correlative burden. Once these conditions have been satisfied it is only then that the positive covenant will be enforceable under the mutual benefit and burden principle.

In *Wilkinson v Kerdene Ltd* [2013] EWCA Civ 44 the principle in *Halzell v Brizell* was applied (and the reasoning in *Thamesmead Town Ltd v Allotey* followed) by the Court of Appeal to a holiday village complex in Cornwall. The complex had fallen into disrepair. Kerdene, the current owners of 'the common parts' (roads, paths, tennis courts etc.) were bringing things back into a good state, and were held entitled to recover the cost of these repairs from successors in title to the original owners of the holiday bungalows.

REVIEW QUESTION In the case study Barry originally covenanted 'to pay a proportion of the costs of the common private driveway between 23 Marchland Close and 24 Marchland Close'. Would this covenant come within the scope of the mutual benefit and burden rule?

(Consider the rule in *Halsall v Brizell*.)

20.10.5 Claim Under Mutual Benefit and Burden Not a Property Right

In *Elwood v Goodman* [2014] Ch 442 the defendants bought some industrial land which enjoyed the benefit of a private right of way. However, there was a reciprocal obligation on the owner of the industrial land to contribute to the upkeep of the private road.

The defendants used the private road, but refused to pay any contribution to its upkeep. They contended that as the obligation to contribute did not appear anywhere on the register of title, the obligation was not binding on them.

This contention was firmly rejected by the Court of Appeal. The right to claim contributions under the rule in *Halsall v Brizell* is not a property right which needs to be entered on the Land Register (by Notice or any other method).

At para 36 Patten,LJ said:

> 'I think that the judge was right to reject [counsel for the defendants'] argument on this point. The effect of registration under s 20(1) of the Land Registration Act 1925 is that the transferee takes the legal estate subject to registered incumbrances but otherwise free from all other estates and interests whatsoever. This, I think, confirms that to be registrable an incumbrance (such as the rights based on proprietary estoppel) must be capable of creating an estate or interest in the registered land. *Since the burden in equity of a positive covenant does not have this effect, it does not, in my judgment, require to be registered in order to bind successors in title of the original covenantor.*' [Emphasis added]

cross-reference
For brief explanation of rentcharges, see 1.3.5.

20.10.6 Estate Rentcharges

A rentcharge is the right to receive payment of a regular (usually annual) sum of money and often attached to this is a right of entry. Although we noted in 1.3.5 that no new rentcharges can be created, there is an exception for 'estate rentcharges', as defined by s2(3)–(5) Rentcharges Act 1977.

Estate rentcharges are rentcharges created for the purpose of making positive covenants enforceable against the owner for the time being of the land burdened by the rentcharge.

In *The Canwell Estate Co Ltd v Smith Brothers Farm Ltd* [2012] 2 All ER 1159 the defendant's predecessor in title had in 1990 bought a farm which had formed part of the much larger Canwell Estate. The amount payable under the 'estate rentcharge' varied according to a formula set out in the 1990 land transfer. This formula was in turn based on the amounts payable under covenants entered into by the predecessor in title to contribute a proportion of the claimant's costs of running the whole Canwell Estate (including in particular maintaining a private road).

The Court of Apppeal held that the 1990 land transfer had created a valid 'estate rentcharge', and gave judgment for arrears of rentcharge payments which had accumulated over seven years totalling £14,653.09.

20.11 Restrictive Covenants as Equitable Interests

Restrictive covenants were in effect first 'invented' in the mid-nineteenth century by the pre-1875 Court of Chancery. The common law courts never recognized them. Thus, historically, all restrictive covenants are equitable interests, and this was confirmed by s1 LPA 1925. The restrictive covenant affecting the servient land is subject to the following requirements:

- *Unregistered title*
  - pre-1926 restrictive covenant is still subject to the doctrine of notice and will bind everyone except the bona fide purchaser for value of a legal estate without notice;
  - post-1925 restrictive covenant is registrable as a Class D(ii) land charge (s2(5)(ii) Land Charges Act 1972).
- *Registered title*, the restrictive covenant must be protected by entry on the register of a notice (s32 Land Registration Act 2002).

20.12 Remedies to Enforce a Breach of a Covenant

Once a breach of a covenant has been established the usual remedy at common law is an award of damages. This would be available to the original covenantor and original covenantee. The successor in title of the original covenantee can claim damages from the original covenantor. To illustrate this, consider the case study in 20.1, where Agnese sold 23 Marchland Close to Ciaran. Barry had not complied with the covenants and was in breach. In this scenario we said that Ciaran was entitled to claim the benefit of the covenants and sue Barry for damages.

The fact that a restrictive covenant only runs with the land in equity means that the principal remedy to enforce a restrictive covenant against a successor in title to the servient land is an injunction; there is no automatic right to damages.

In restrictive covenant cases the court has discretion as to the remedy it can grant. The court may award damages instead of or in addition to an injunction. The principles guiding the courts in their assessment of whether to award damages instead of an injunction were stated in *Shelfer v City of London Electric Lighting Co* (1895) 1 Ch 287 by AL Smith LJ:

(1) If the injury to the plaintiff's legal rights is small,

(2) And is one which is capable of being estimated in money,

(3) And is one which can be adequately compensated by a small money payment,

(4) And the case is one in which it would be oppressive to the defendant to grant an injunction:—then damages in substitution for an injunction may be given.

These provide a useful benchmark for the assessment of a situation in an objective manner.

Recently, the Supreme Court in *Coventry v Lawrence* [2014] UKSC 13 was critical over how the *Shelfer* four stage test had since been applied by the courts. There was a tendency for the courts to apply it as an exhaustive test which did not give sufficient discretion to the courts in their broader considerations of the appropriate remedy. The Supreme Court observed that the application of the test should not be undertaken in a mechanical manner nor should the award of damages be simply limited to 'very exceptional circumstances'. Lord Neuberger was of the opinion that:

120. The court's power to award damages in lieu of an injunction involves a classic exercise of discretion, which should not, as a matter of principle, be fettered, particularly in the very constrained way in which the Court of Appeal has suggested in *Regan* and *Watson*. And, as a matter of practical fairness, each case is likely to be so fact-sensitive that any firm guidance is likely to do more harm than good.

121. ... this does not prevent the courts from laying down rules as to what factors can, and cannot, be taken into account by a judge when deciding whether to exercise his discretion to award damages in lieu. Indeed, it is appropriate to give as much guidance as possible so as to ensure that, while the discretion is not fettered, its manner of exercise is as predictable as possible. I would accept that the *prima facie* position is that an injunction should be granted, so the legal burden is on the defendant to show why it should not. And, subject to one possible point, I would cautiously (in the light of the fact that each case turns on its facts) approve the observations of Lord Macnaghten in *Colls* [1904] AC 179, 193, where he said:

'In some cases, of course, an injunction is necessary—if, for instance, the injury cannot fairly be compensated by money—if the defendant has acted in a high-handed manner—if he has endeavoured to steal a march upon the plaintiff or to evade the jurisdiction of the Court. In all these cases an injunction is necessary, in order to do justice to the plaintiff and as a warning to others. But if there is really a question as to whether the obstruction is legal or not, and if the defendant has acted fairly and not in an unneighbourly spirit, I am disposed to think that the Court ought to incline to damages rather than to an injunction. It is quite true that a man ought not to be compelled to part with his property against his will, or to have the value of his property diminished, without an Act of Parliament. On the other hand, the Court ought to be very careful not to allow an action for the protection of ancient lights to be used as a means of extorting money.'

123. Where does that leave A L Smith LJ's four tests? While the application of any such series of tests cannot be mechanical, I would adopt a modified version of the view expressed by Romer LJ in *Fishenden* 153 LT 128, 141. First, the application of the four tests must not be such as 'to be a fetter on the exercise of the court's discretion'. Secondly, it would, in the absence of additional relevant circumstances pointing the other way, normally be right to refuse an injunction if those four tests were satisfied. Thirdly, the fact that those tests are not all satisfied does not mean that an injunction should be granted.

124. As for the second problem, that of public interest, I find it hard to see how there could be any circumstances in which it arose and could not, as a matter of law, be a relevant factor. Of course, it is very easy to think of circumstances in which it might arise but did not begin to justify the court refusing, or, as the case may be, deciding, to award an injunction if it was otherwise minded to do so. But that is not the point. The fact that a defendant's business may have to shut down if an injunction is granted should, it seems to me, obviously be a relevant fact, and it is hard to see why relevance should not extend to the fact that a number of the defendant's employees would lose their livelihood, although in many cases that may well not be sufficient to justify the refusal of an injunction. Equally, I do not see why the court should not be entitled to have regard to the fact that many other neighbours in addition to the claimant are badly affected by the nuisance as a factor in favour of granting an injunction.

According to Lord Neuberger the *prima facie* remedy of an injunction should remain but qualified with a more contextual approach which will allow the courts to continue to use their discretion.

After *Coventry v Lawrence* whether or not an injunction is granted largely depends on whether it would be oppressive to the defendant. According to Nourse LJ in *Gafford v Graham* (1998) 77 P & CR 73 '[t]he essential prerequisite of an award of damages is that it should be oppressive to the defendant to grant an injunction'.

What amounts to oppression? That might arise where a mandatory injunction was sought to demolish a building, wall, or obstruction. The court can exercise its discretion and will take into account the circumstances of a case.

In *Wakeham v Wood* (1982) 43 P & CR 40, the land between the claimant's house and the sea was owned by the defendant subject to a restrictive covenant. This covenant stated '...that no building which shall be erected on the said land...shall be of sufficient height to obstruct the present view of the sea and beach from the property'. The defendant constructed a building despite protests from the claimant. The claimant sought an injunction to prevent the building being constructed any higher than had been reached and to have the building demolished.

Waller LJ in the Court of Appeal said:

> The authorities show that in the case of express negative covenants, that is where an agreement has been made that a particular thing is not to be done an injunction will be granted to restrain a breach. And where a defendant commits a breach of a negative covenant with his eyes open and after notice the court will grant a mandatory order, although there is and must be some limitation to this practice.

His Lordship considered *Shelfer v City of London Electric Lighting Co (No 1) (1894)* and the four requirements given previously. He went on to say:

> The present case does not in my view qualify in any particular with paragraphs (1) to (4) mentioned by A. L. Smith L.J. Here is a man who had been living in his house for 33 years with a view of the sea protected by a restrictive covenant. The defendant purchased the land subject to the restriction with knowledge of it at the time of purchase. He did not make any inquiry of the plaintiff either directly or indirectly, he did not inform his architect of the restriction, he took no notice

of his builder telling him of the plaintiff's objection and he put the roof trusses up in spite of letters from the plaintiff's solicitor. A more flagrant disregard of the plaintiff's rights it is difficult to imagine. As I have already indicated the judge concluded that there was a serious interference with the plaintiff's legal right to a view of the sea. I find it difficult to say that where one has a view protected by covenant the denial of that view is capable of being estimated in money terms and therefore it seems to me it cannot be adequately compensated by a small money payment. Indeed in this case the judge awarded a substantial money payment. It no doubt will be oppressive to the defendant if a mandatory injunction is granted against him, but that is entirely his own fault for proceeding with the construction in breach of the covenant after warning. This court has to consider the case at the time of the hearing before the judge. Thereafter the defendant knew that there was an appeal pending. Furthermore this is a case which falls foursquare within the last paragraph of the passage which I have quoted from A. L. Smith L.J.

In my judgment the judge in this case was in error in awarding damages in lieu of a mandatory injunction. The effect of so doing was to enable the defendant to buy his way out of his wrong. I have come to the conclusion that the only proper course for this court to take is to grant a mandatory injunction and I would allow this appeal.

This case is an example of a blatant breach of a restrictive covenant. In *Mortimer v Bailey* [2005] 2 P & CR 9 the Court of Appeal granted a mandatory injunction to demolish an extension to a house which had been built contrary to a restrictive covenant.

The courts have recognized that a mandatory injunction is not always the most appropriate remedy. The discretion which the court has on matters of remedies is well illustrated by the decision in *Wrotham Park Estate v Parkside Homes* [1974] 1 WLR 798.

In 1935, the Wrotham Park Estate, then owned by the Earl of Strafford, extended to about 4,000 acres. In that year the Earl sold 47 acres out of the estate. This land was subject to a restrictive covenant 'not to develop the . . . land for building purposes except in strict accordance with plans [approved by the owners of Wrotham Park Estate].' The covenant was expressed to be for the benefit of 'Wrotham Park Estate'. The claimant later acquired Wrotham Park Estate. The defendant, Parkside Homes Ltd, acquired a small part of the servient land.

The defendant obtained planning permission from the local authority to build 13 'middle class' houses on the land. It did not, however, submit its plans to the claimant for approval. It believed that the claimant was not entitled to enforce the covenant. In January 1972, the defendant started to lay the foundations.

On 14 February the claimant issued a writ claiming an injunction to restrain building. The claimant failed, however, to seek an 'interlocutory' (temporary) injunction to restrain development pending the full trial of the dispute. Parkside, accordingly, completed the building operations and the first residents moved into their new homes.

Brightman J held that the claimant was entitled to enforce the restrictive covenant but refused to order that the houses should be demolished. He said 'It would, in my opinion, be an unpardonable waste of much needed houses to direct that they be pulled down.' He thus exercised his 'discretion' to refuse a mandatory injunction to demolish the houses. But he also 'in his discretion' decided to award the claimant damages. He awarded the claimant damages equivalent to the 'price' it could reasonably have asked for releasing the covenant which amounted to 5 per cent of the defendant's profits on the houses which had been built.

Brightman J said:

I must now consider the relief to which the plaintiffs are entitled, that is to say a mandatory injunction or damages (both are not sought); if damages, whether substantial or nominal; or a declaration of the plaintiffs' rights as the sole relief. The plaintiffs made it abundantly clear at the outset of the case that the relief they primarily sought was a mandatory injunction. This did not stem from outraged feelings or from indifference to the welfare of those who have made the offending houses their homes. It sprang from the belief, sincerely held, that there was no other effective way of preserving the integrity of the planning restrictions imposed by the terms of the Blake conveyance. Quite apart from the benefit to the Wrotham Park Estate, the plaintiffs, as I have already said, take the view that they have a moral obligation towards the residents of the building estates to enforce the restrictive covenants so far as they are lawfully entitled to do so. I agree. The plaintiffs do not seek to bulldoze the occupiers out of their homes but are content that they shall have a period of two years in which to acquire other homes with the help of the £20,000 or so that will come to each of them under the indemnity assurance that has been arranged . . .

[Counsel for the claimant] submitted, and I accept, that it is no answer to a claim for a mandatory injunction that the plaintiffs, having issued proceedings, deliberately held their hand and did not seek the assistance of the court for the purpose of preserving the status quo. On the other hand, it is, in my view, equally true that a plaintiff is not entitled 'as of course' to have everything pulled down that was built after the issue of the writ. The erection of the houses, whether one likes it or not, is a fait accompli and the houses are now the homes of people. I accept that this particular fait accompli is reversible and could be undone. But I cannot close my eyes to the fact that the houses now exist. It would, in my opinion, be an unpardonable waste of much needed houses to direct that they now be pulled down and I have never had a moment's doubt during the hearing of this case that such an order ought to be refused. No damage of a financial nature has been done to the plaintiffs by the breach of the lay-out stipulation. The plaintiffs' use of the Wrotham Park Estate has not been and will not be impeded. It is totally unnecessary to demolish the houses in order to preserve the integrity of the restrictive covenants imposed on the rest of area 14. Without hesitation I decline to grant a mandatory injunction. But the fact that these houses will remain does not spell out a charter entitling others to despoil adjacent areas of land in breach of valid restrictions imposed by the conveyances. A developer who tries that course may be in for a rude awakening.

From this passage it is apparent that Brightman J considered the reality of the situation; demolishing the houses was not an option. In coming to this conclusion, Brightman J had examined the case law on the issue of awarding a mandatory injunction which indicated that this discretion applied by the courts should only be exercised in extreme cases or where very serious damage will occur. If the mandatory injunction was awarded to the claimant this would have been an oppressive measure against the defendant, something which the court in *Shelfer v City of London Electric Lighting Co (No 1) (1894)* was suggesting that ought to be avoided.

The award of damages by Brightman J in *Wrotham Park* was criticized in some quarters, but in *Jaggard v Sawyer* [1995] 1 WLR 269, the Court of Appeal approved it and applied it to a situation where a single house had been built in a garden in breach of a restrictive covenant. As in *Wrotham Park*, damages were awarded on the basis of what a reasonable dominant owner could have asked for releasing the covenant. The court went on to explain the reasoning for the award of damages instead of an injunction. Millett LJ said 'when the court awards damages in substitution for an injunction, it seeks to compensate the plaintiff for loss arising from future wrongs, that is to say, loss for which the common law does not provide a remedy'. Millett LJ confirmed that mandatory injunction should be used cautiously and that awarding damages did not amount to expropriation of the claimant's property. He stated:

It will be of small comfort . . . to be told that the jurisdiction [to award a mandatory injunction] is undoubted, though it is to be exercised with caution. What does need to be stressed, however, is that the consequences to which the plaintiff refers do not result from the judge's exercise of the statutory jurisdiction to award damages instead of an injunction, but from his refusal to grant an injunction. Lord Cairns's Act did not worsen the plaintiff's position but improved it. Thenceforth, if injunctive relief was withheld, the plaintiff was not compelled to wait until further wrongs were committed and then bring successive actions for damages; he could be compensated by a once and for all payment to cover future as well as past wrongs. Of course, the ability to do 'complete justice' in this way made it easier for the courts to withhold the remedy of an injunction, and it was therefore necessary for the judges to remind themselves from time to time that the discretion to withhold it, which had existed as well before 1858 as after it, was to be exercised in accordance with settled principles; that a plaintiff who had established both a legal right and a threat to infringe it was *prima facie* entitled to an injunction to protect it; and that special circumstances were needed to justify withholding the injunction.

Nevertheless references to the 'expropriation' of the plaintiff's property are somewhat overdone, not because that is not the practical effect of withholding an injunction, but because the grant of an injunction, like all equitable remedies, is discretionary. Many proprietary rights cannot be protected at all by the common law. The owner must submit to unlawful interference with his rights and be content with damages. If he wants to be protected he must seek equitable relief, and he has no absolute right to that. In many cases, it is true, an injunction will be granted almost as of course; but this is not always the case, and it will never be granted if this would cause injustice to the defendant.

Moreover, in *Gafford v Graham* (1998) 77 P & CR 73, the Court of Appeal refused an injunction which would have demolished a riding school built in breach of a restrictive covenant, and again granted only damages, basing its assessment on the value of a covenant release agreement.

The Chaotic State of the Law on the Running of Benefits of Covenants

The Law Commission in its 1984 Report No 127, *Restrictive Covenants*, summed up the situation at p 30:

A traveller in this area of the law, old though it is, walks on ground which is still shifting. Particularly striking examples come from the same two topics: the *Federated Homes* case has made radical and controversial changes in what was thought to be the law about annexation, and successive court decisions in recent years [in particular *Re Dolphin*] have altered the conditions thought to be essential for the establishment of a building scheme.

Shifts in the law as interpreted by the courts may be wholly beneficial so far as future covenants are concerned, but they must of course apply equally to existing covenants and here their effects are much more mixed. If a landowner sought legal advice periodically about the enforcement of a particular covenant, he would have to be told different things at different times; and his lot would not be a happy one if he had acted in good faith on advice given one year only to find it invalidated the next.

Before leaving the subject of uncertainty we would mention one particular instance in which the law...is productive of uncertainty in practice. There is at present no requirement that the instrument creating the covenant shall describe the benefited land clearly enough to enable it to be identified without extrinsic evidence.

It is submitted that what the Law Commission said in 1984 remains valid today, despite later developments, notably the decision in *Crest Nicholson*.

The Law Commission issued in 2008 a very extensive consultation concerning 'Easements, Profits à Prendre and Freehold Covenants'. In commenting about defects in the law of restrictive covenants, the Law Commission has this to say about the current position:

> 7.36 Most problems in practice appear to concern the difficulty in identifying who has the benefit of a restrictive covenant. This is due to two factors. First, there is no requirement that the instrument creating the covenant should describe the benefited land with sufficient clarity to enable its identification without extrinsic evidence. Secondly, there is no requirement or power for Land Registry to enter the benefit of an equitable interest such as a restrictive covenant on the register of title to the dominant land. The combination of these factors produces uncertainty. A vast number of covenants may fall into limbo as it is impossible to discover who (if anyone) is entitled to enforce them. It is, of course, impossible to negotiate a release from such covenants as it is not known with whom such negotiation should be initiated.

Crest Nicholson may have ameliorated the problems regarding identifying dominant owners, but the problems have certainly not disappeared.

20.13.1 'Land Obligations'

The Law Commission proposed back in 1984 to forbid the creation of new restrictive covenants. There would be a new type of right in land, 'land obligations'. Land obligations would either be negative or (subject to certain limits) positive.

The Law Commission, in its 2011 Report No 327, *Making Land Work: Easements, Covenants and Profits à Prendre*, refined its proposals for land obligations. The key recommendation is 8.24.

> We recommend that the owner of an estate in land shall be able to create positive and negative obligations that will be able to take effect (subject to the formal requirements for the creation of legal interests) as legal interests appurtenant to another estate in land, and therefore as registrable interests pursuant to the Land Registration Act 2002, provided that:
>
> (1) the benefit of the obligation touches and concerns the benefited land;
> (2) the obligation is either:
>   (a) an obligation not to do something on the burdened land;
>   (b) an obligation to do something on the burdened land or on the boundary (or any structure or feature that is treated as marking or lying on the boundary) of the burdened and benefited land; or
>   (c) an obligation to make a payment in return for the performance of an obligation of the kind mentioned in paragraph (b); and
> (3) the obligation is not made between lessor and lessee and relating to the demised premises.

Under the Commission's proposals in Report No 327, it will also be possible to create a land obligation burdening an unregistered title. Recommendation 8.29 states:

> We recommend that where title to the burdened land is unregistered, the burden of a land obligation be registrable as a land charge under the Land Charges Act 1972, and if not registered should be void against a purchaser of the burdened land or any interest in that land.

(If, as is to be hoped, this recommendation is enacted, we would have another example of a *legal* interest registrable as a land charge.)

Concluding Remarks

In this chapter you should have learnt about how freehold covenants can be enforced. It is important to identify the party against whom the action can be brought but also whether the benefit and burden pass to successors in title.

Legislation in the area of restrictive covenants (though desirable) is perhaps not essential. The Land Registration Act 2002, which has some effect on every other type of property right, has no impact on freehold covenants. What would be welcome would be cases in the Supreme Court which:

• overruled *Re Dolphin*;

• confirmed the Court of Appeal decision in *Crest Nicholson*; and

• made clear that annexation was presumed to be to the whole of the dominant land, unless the covenant expressly referred to 'each and every part'.

Summary

Enforcement of Covenants

• Original parties: always enforceable.

• Third parties:

  – s56(1) LPA 1925—the covenant must be purported to be made with a named person or a generic class of persons identifiable and in existence at the time of the covenant. Application: covenants created before May 2000;

  – s1 Contracts (Rights of Third Parties) Act 1999—contract expressly states third party can enforce it, or a term purports to confer a benefit on him and is intended to be enforced by the third party. Third party identified by name, as a member of a class or answering a particular description. Application: all covenants entered into after 11 May 2000.

Does the Burden of a Covenant Run with the Servient Land?

Common Law

• Positive covenants—No (see *Austerberry v Corporation of Oldham; Rhone v Stephens*):

  – exception: mutual benefit and burden (*Halsall v Brizell)*, requirement of reciprocity (*Rhone v Stephens*).

• Restrictive covenants—No.

Equity

• Positive covenants—No (see *Austerberry v Corporation of Oldham; Rhone v Stephens*).

• Restrictive covenants—apply the rule in *Tulk v Moxhay* (1848):

  – covenant must be negative in substance;

- covenant must, at the date of the covenant, be made to benefit the dominant land retained by the covenantee;
- touch and concern the dominant land; and
- covenant must be made with an intent to burden the servient land.

Passing of the Benefit—Restrictive Covenants

- annexation;
- assignment; and
- scheme of development (or building scheme).

A Restrictive Covenant is an Equitable Interest in Land

- Unregistered title:
  - pre-1926 restrictive covenant is still subject to the doctrine of notice and will bind everyone except the bona fide purchaser for value of a legal estate without notice;
  - post-1925 restrictive covenant is registrable as a Class D(ii) land charge (s2(5)(ii) Land Charges Act 1972).
- Registered title: the restrictive covenant is a minor interest which must be protected by entry on the register of a notice (s32 Land Registration Act 2002).

Remedy for a Breach of a Restrictive Covenant

The normal remedy for enforcing a restrictive covenant is an injunction. However, if a building has been completed in breach of covenant, the court is likely to award damages rather than order demolition of the premises (*Wrotham Park Estate v Parkside Homes*).

Further Reading

Cooke, E, 'To restate or not to restate. Old wine, New wineskins, old covenants, new ideas' [2009] Conv 448
Discusses the latest (late 2009) provisional thinking of the Law Commission on reforming the law of freehold covenants.

Gravells, N, 'Enforcement of positive covenants affecting freehold land' (1994) 110 LQR 346
Discusses positive covenants following the House of Lords decision in *Rhone v Stephens*.

Law Commission, *Restrictive Covenants* (Report No 127, 1984)
Although about 30 years old (and pre-dating *Crest Nicholson*) this remains very interesting and informative reading.

Law Commission, *Easements, Covenants and Profits à Prendre* (Consultation Paper No 186, 2008)
The Law Commission raised a number of issues for review and sought views from any persons interested.

Law Commission, *Making Land Law Work: Easements, Covenants and Profits à Prendre* (Report No 327, 2011)

Parts 5 and 6 discuss reform of covenants and the introduction of land obligations.

Newsom, GH, 'Universal annexation?' (1981) 97 LQR 32

A critical evaluation of *Federated Homes*.

Snape, J, 'The burden of positive covenants' (1994) 58 Conv 477

Discusses positive covenants following the House of Lords decision in *Rhone v Stephens*.

Stevens, R, 'The Contracts (Rights of Third Parties) Act 1999' (2004) 14 LQR 292

Provides an overview of why reform was necessary and how this Act applies.

Todd, PN, 'Annexation after *Federated Homes*' [1985] Conv 177

Discusses the decision in *Federated Homes*.

Watt, G, 'Building at risk of injunction' [2005] Conv 460

Discussion of *Mortimer v Bailey* and use of mandatory injunctions where the developer has ignored the restrictive covenant.

References

Goo, SH, *Sourcebook on Land Law*, 3rd edn, London: Cavendish Publishing, 2002.

Gray, K, and Gray, SF, *Elements of Land Law*, 5th edn, Oxford: OUP, 2009.

? Questions

In 1989, Adele owned two neighbouring properties, numbers 3 and 5 Abingdon Way. In June 1990, Adele decided to sell 3 Abingdon Way to Emilia, and included in the conveyance were a number of covenants. Emilia had covenanted:

1 to only use the property as a private dwelling house;

2 to pay a reasonable proportion towards the costs of the maintenance of the common private driveway between 3 and 5 Abingdon Way; and

3 to repaint the fence white every five years.

Adele sold 5 Abingdon Way to Tamir in November 2002. Earlier this year, Emilia sold 3 Abingdon Way to Raul. Raul is now planning to open a Spanish tapas bar; he has painted the fence red and yellow and he is refusing to pay £5,000 towards the costs of repairing the driveway.

Advise Tamir as to whether he can enforce the covenants against Raul.

## 21

Escaping from Restrictive Covenants

Introduction

If somebody buys a piece of land and obtains planning permission to develop it, their plans may still be obstructed by the existence of a restrictive covenant(s) burdening that land. The granting of planning permission does not authorize the breaching of restrictive covenants. The facts of *Re Dolphin's Conveyance* [1970] 2 All ER 664 (considered in Chapter 20 at 'The Conditions Required for a Valid Building Scheme') illustrate this point. The Corporation had planning permission for their council houses, but the restrictive covenants still prevented the development.

There are various courses of action open to the determined developer whose plans are obstructed by restrictive covenants. The main purpose of this chapter is to consider those various alternatives, inter alia, modification or discharge of a covenant. You will see that five alternatives are identified (at 21.1 to 21.5) but notice that they do to some degree overlap.

 21.1 ## Carry on Regardless

Some developers may boldly say, 'Let's ignore those restrictive covenants', and start work hoping that no 'dominant owner' will come along and object. In some types of situation there is little risk in doing this. In particular, you will sometimes come across 'building schemes' where the covenants to maintain the exclusivity of the area generally have been ignored.

thinking point 21.1

If a dominant owner in such an exclusive area tried to enforce the covenants by seeking an injunction, what do you think would probably happen?

The court would refuse an injunction, applying the maxim, 'He who comes to equity must come with clean hands.' In plain English, somebody who is in serious breach of the rules of the scheme is not entitled to enforce the rules against others.

thinking point 21.2

In contrast to thinking point 21.1, suppose you are a dominant owner, 'your hands are clean', and the developer has just moved the bulldozers on to the servient land. Think back to the facts of Wrotham Park, at 20.12. Consider what you should do.

Like the plaintiff in Wrotham Park you should issue a claim form (writ) without delay. But (unlike in Wrotham Park) you should immediately seek a temporary 'interim' injunction pending a full trial of the dispute.

Obtaining such an injunction is now relatively easy as you have to show to a judge only that you have an 'arguable case' that you are a dominant owner entitled to enforce the covenant. In view of the muddle and uncertainty in the law, it is not difficult for someone to put forward a plausible claim that they are a dominant owner.

21.2 'Doing a Parkside Homes'

This is merely a variant on the course of action already discussed at 21.1, and is often adopted. In the *Wrotham Park* case the defendants believed that nobody was entitled to enforce the covenant against them. They did, however, have nagging doubts. This is not an uncommon situation; it is yet another side effect of the chaotic law.

Parkside Homes thus commenced their building work, but took out an insurance policy to protect themselves (and the purchasers of their houses) should anyone succeed in a claim that the covenant could still be enforced. (See the end of the first paragraph of the extract from *Wrotham Park* set out at 20.12.) As we know, a claim to enforce the covenant did unexpectedly succeed. The £2,500 damages awarded by Brightman J was paid (as his Lordship well knew) by the insurers.

21.3 Attempt to Buy Out the Dominant Owners

You must first realize that if there are, for example, ten dominant owners, then all ten must be persuaded to give up their rights to enforce the covenant. If nine dominant owners say, 'OK, I will give up my rights', but the tenth says, 'Over my dead body, even ten million pounds would not persuade me!', then that is enough to exclude this course of action.

You must also appreciate that as a result of the chaos caused by modern cases such as *Federated Homes, Wrotham Park*, and *Re Dolphin's Conveyance* (see Chapter 20), it is often impossible to be certain that you have 'persuaded' every dominant owner. Dominant owners have a habit of turning up and convincing sympathetic judges that they have a valid claim. It may therefore be necessary to insure against the possibility of other dominant owners appearing.

21.4 Is the Freehold Subject to a Restrictive Covenant? What is the Scope of the Restrictive Covenant? Who Can Enforce It?

An application to the court for a declaration establishing whether the freehold land in question is or would be subject to a restrictive covenant, or where there is a restrictive covenant, the nature and extent of the covenant imposed is provided for in s84(2) Law of Property Act 1925 (LPA 1925). Importantly, for those concerned, the declaration will also include a conclusive list of all the dominant owners, which is binding on everybody in the whole world.

Law of Property Act 1925

84. Power to discharge or modify restrictive covenants affecting land

(2) The court shall have power on the application of any person interested—

(a) To declare whether or not in any particular case any freehold land is or would in any given event be affected by a restriction imposed by any instrument; or

(b) To declare what, upon the true construction of any instrument purporting to impose a restriction, is the nature and extent of the restriction thereby imposed and whether the same is or would in any given event be enforceable and if so by whom.

thinking point 21.3

Steve is a servient owner of Moss Deeping. He takes proceedings under s84(2) with respect to Moss Deeping. The court makes a declaration that Tom, Dan, and Hope (three close neighbours who were made parties to the court proceedings) are the dominant owners. Wanda (a slightly more distant neighbour) turns up after the court's decision and says, 'Hey, I am a dominant owner as well!' What will happen in any proceedings commenced by Wanda?

Wanda's claim must fail, even though she was not a party to the s84(2) proceedings.

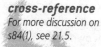

cross-reference
For more discussion on s84(1), see 21.5.

Because the effect of an order under s84(2) is to destroy possible claims (like that of Wanda) to be a dominant owner, the courts have laid down a special procedure to be adopted in s84(2) cases: *Re Sunnyfield* [1932] 1 Ch 79 at 93, and *Re 6, 8, 10 and 12 Elm Avenue, New Milton* [1984] 1 WLR 1398. The courts require that an applicant under s84(2) LPA 1925 (Steve in thinking point 21.3) circularizes all nearby owners, just in case any of them claim to be 'dominant'. The circular must tell the nearby owners that proceedings are pending, and that they have a right to join in as parties to those proceedings if they so wish. The circular will also warn that everyone is bound by the result of the proceedings whether or not they join in.

Having obtained a court order under s84(2) giving an exhaustive list of the dominant owners, the servient owner may well attempt to persuade those dominant owners to release their rights. If one or more refuse to be persuaded, then the servient owner may well then make an application to the Upper Tribunal under s84(1).

Emphasizing the care the court should take in s84(2) proceedings, Scott J said in the *Elm Avenue* case:

[This] brings me to consider the approach which ought to be adopted on an application for a declaration under section 84(2) of the Law of Property Act 1925, as amended (Law of Property Act 1969, section 28, Schedule 3). The subsection provides a means by which the owner of land, which may appear to be subject to restrictive covenants, can come to the court and ask for a declaration that it is not so subject. If the court makes that declaration it has an *in rem* [ie against the property] effect, and the property is not then so subject. The negative is established by the declaration sought. The position seems to me to be not in the least comparable to the situation which pertains where there is a list between somebody claiming to be entitled to the benefit of restrictions on the one hand and the owner of the property said to be subject to the restrictions and denying the entitlement of the plaintiff on the other hand. In such a case it is plain that the onus of establishing, on a balance of probabilities, that there is a scheme, and that the property for the benefit of which it is claimed is so entitled, lies on the person asserting those matters. But when an owner of land comes to the court for a declaration under section 84(2) it does not seem to me that he can claim to be entitled to the declaration simply on the basis that if there had been an opponent who had been arguing for the benefit of the restrictions that opponent would have failed on a balance of probabilities. That seems to me to be an erroneous approach. If there had been such a person, what inquiries and what case would have been made by such person is not able to be identified. It is the practice that, as a preliminary to bringing before the court a claim for a declaration under section 84(2), notice should be given to all persons in the area who might conceivably be interested in claiming the benefit of the restrictions. That has been done in this case. But it has been done in this case in the context of the wish of the council to construct its car park, and it is entirely possible that the overwhelming consents to the construction of the car park that have been received from persons living in the neighbourhood may be simply a reflection on the need of a car park in the area. I think I would be wrong in assuming that by giving those consents the persons giving them were acknowledging that they were not entitled to the benefit of the restrictions.

In *Re Dolphin's Conveyance*, Birmingham Corporation applied to the High Court for an order under s84(2). This application is the case which is reported and which we considered in chapter 20 at 'The Conditions Required for a Valid Building Scheme'. However, it is worth knowing that Birmingham Corporation, having established a (disappointingly long) list of dominant owners then applied to the Lands Tribunal for an order under s84(1) LPA 1925.

(Be wary of the confusing way in which the legislation is arranged. Section 84(2) is logically anterior to the rest of s84, including s84(1). Parliament, when amending s84 in 1969, should have removed s84(2) from its unnatural position and renumbered it s83A.)

21.5 Modification or Discharge of a Covenant Under s84(1)

The essence of s84(1) LPA 1925, is that it gives to the Upper Tribunal (until June 2009 the Lands Tribunal) the power to modify or discharge restrictive covenants (but not positive covenants) which are perhaps no longer desirable due to changes in the socio-economic make-up of the environment in which they exist. This may inhibit development of an area where it is no longer regarded as requiring the protection of the restrictive covenant.

The Upper Tribunal (as was also true of the Lands Tribunal) has currently no jurisdiction to decide disputes as to who is/are the dominant owners. Thus, unless an order has already been obtained from the court under s84(2) LPA 1925, an applicant under s84(1) to the Upper Tribunal has to concede even questionable claims by neighbours that they are dominant owners. In the case of *Re Bass* which we discuss at 21.5.1 under 'Public Interest', it was questionable whether some of the objecting local residents were dominant owners. To speed things up, the applicants did not dispute the claims of these residents to be dominant owners.

21.5.1 The Grounds for Discharge or Modification of Restrictive Covenants

Section 84(1) LPA 1925 was amended by s28 Law of Property Act 1969, to make it easier to get a restrictive covenant discharged or modified. This section provides:

Law of Property Act 1925

84. Power to discharge or modify restrictive covenants affecting land

(1) The Upper Tribunal shall (without prejudice to any concurrent jurisdiction of the court) have power from time to time, on the application of any person interested in any freehold

land affected by any restriction arising under covenant or otherwise as to the user thereof or the building thereon, by order wholly or partially to discharge or modify any such restriction on being satisfied—

(a) that by reason of changes in the character of the property or the neighbourhood or other circumstances of the case which the Upper Tribunal may deem material, the restriction ought to be deemed obsolete, or

(aa) that in a case falling within subsection (1A) below the continued existence thereof would impede some reasonable user of the land for public or private purposes or, as the case may be, would unless modified so impede such user; or

(b) that the persons of full age and capacity for the time being or from time to time entitled to the benefit of the restriction, whether in respect of estates in fee simple or any lesser estates or interests in the property to which the benefit of the restriction is annexed, have agreed, either expressly or by implication, by their acts or omissions, to the same being discharged or modified; or

(c) that the proposed discharge or modification will not injure the persons entitled to the benefit of the restriction:

[and an order discharging or modifying a restriction under this subsection may direct the applicant to pay to any person entitled to the benefit of the restriction such sum by way of consideration as the Tribunal may think it just to award under one, but not both, of the following heads, that is to say, either—

(i) a sum to make up for any loss or disadvantage suffered by that person in consequence of the discharge or modification; or

(ii) a sum to make up for any effect which the restriction had, at the time when it was imposed, in reducing the consideration then received for the land affected by it.]

Put simply, there are four grounds on which a restrictive covenant may be discharged or modified. These are as follows:

- restriction is obsolete (s84(1)(a));
- obstructs reasonable user of the land (s84(1)(aa));
- agreement to discharge or modify the restrictive covenant (s84(1)(b));
- no injury to persons who benefited from the restrictive covenant (s84(1)(c)).

Restriction is Obsolete

Ground (a) would be invoked where 'by reason of the changes of character of the property or neighbourhood or other circumstances' the covenant is obsolete, for example where there was a restrictive covenant for 'agricultural purposes only', but all the surrounding land had been built upon. Or suppose there was one house in a street which was subject to a 'residential purposes only' covenant, but all the other houses had been converted into offices.

In *Re Morningside (Leicester) Ltd's Application* [2014] UKUT 70 (LC) the land in question had been used as a doctor's surgery for around 25 years and had planning permission to use the land in this manner. This use was in breach of a covenant dating back to 1864 which restricted the use of the land to private dwelling houses. The Upper Tribunal held that covenant was obsolete because those who had the benefit of the covenant appeared to have acquiesced to the breach. The building had been modified to be used as a surgery and so the breach of the covenant was open and obvious.

Obstructs Some Reasonable User of the Land

This ground (aa) may strike you as alarmingly vague. What amounts to 'some reasonable user'? This is further defined by s84(1A). Under ground (aa), two elements must be satisfied, though the first element consists of two alternatives:

> *Law of Property Act 1925*
>
> 84. Power to discharge or modify restrictive covenants affecting land
>
> (1A) Subsection (1) (aa) above authorises the discharge or modification of a restriction by reference to its impeding some reasonable user of land in any case in which the Upper Tribunal is satisfied that the restriction, in impeding that user, either—
>
> > (a) does not secure to persons [dominant owner(s)] entitled to the benefit of it any practical benefits of substantial value or advantage to them; or
> >
> > (b) is contrary to the public interest;
>
> and that money will be an adequate compensation for the loss or disadvantage (if any) which any such person [dominant owner] will suffer from the discharge or modification.

The restrictive covenant can be modified or discharged if the continued existence of the restrictive covenant impedes 'some reasonable use of land for public or private purposes.' It must be proved that either the covenant does not secure any practical benefit of substantial value or advantage, or it is contrary to public interest. In either case, it must also be shown that any loss or disadvantage can be compensated adequately. In determining these issues, s84(1B) LPA 1925 provides that '…the Upper Tribunal shall take into account the development plan and any declared or ascertainable pattern for the grant or refusal of planning permissions in the relevant area…'

An applicant under this ground (aa) will argue that the 'public interest' requires this development. The applicant will make statements like 'much needed homes', or 'this factory if built will create X hundred jobs in an area of high unemployment', but this alone is not sufficient. An applicant under ground (aa) must also, however, always also show that 'money will be an adequate compensation for the loss or disadvantage'. So if the applicant's new factory, bus depot, or whatever, is going to make life unbearable for the dominant owner(s), the application should be refused.

It is also important not to misunderstand s84(1B). That provision is not referring to the fact that the applicant has (presumably) obtained planning permission to develop their individual plot of land; rather, it is telling the tribunal to consider the general planning picture for the area within which the applicant's plot is situated.

Town planners usually 'zone' areas for different purposes. One area may be zoned (ie designated) for housing, another for industry, a third for recreational activities, and so on. It is this 'zoning' which the Upper Tribunal has to take into account in applying s84(1B) LPA 1925.

What Does Practical Benefit Include?

The scope of practical benefit includes preserving a lovely view. In *Re Banks' Application* (1976) 33 P & CR 138, the servient land adjoined the sea. The dominant land was a row of seven houses inland from the servient land and on a higher level than the servient land. The restrictive covenant prohibited building on the servient land, thus preserving a lovely view over the sea from the dominant houses.

The servient owner obtained planning permission to build a bungalow which would impinge somewhat on the view from the dominant houses. The application failed under s84(1)(c) but succeeded under ground (aa). The restrictive covenant was modified so as to allow the bungalow to be built, but the servient owner had to pay £2,000 compensation to each of the five dominant owners who had objected.

In contrast, *Gilbert v Spoor* [1982] Ch 27 is another case dealing with the preservation of a magnificent landscape view, with a different outcome. The landscape view was visible from the land in the immediate vicinity but not from the objectors' properties who were subject to building scheme covenants. The applicant had obtained planning permission to build two houses on his land, and subsequently applied for the discharge or modification of the covenant to the Lands Tribunal which was refused because the restrictive covenant secured a 'practical benefit' to the defendants. The Court of Appeal refused to discharge or modify the covenant on appeal by the applicant. Eveleigh LJ said:

> The phrase 'any practical benefits of substantial value or advantage to them' is wide. The subsection does not speak of a restriction for the benefit or protection of land, which is a reasonably common phrase, but rather of a restriction which secures any practical benefits. The expression 'any practical benefits' is so wide that I would require very compelling considerations before I felt able to limit it in the manner contended for. When one remembers that Parliament is authorising the Lands Tribunal to take away from a person a vested right either in law or in equity, it is not surprising that the tribunal is required to consider the adverse effects upon a broad basis . . .
>
> In my judgment the tribunal was entitled to hold that the view was a benefit whether or not that benefit could be said to touch and concern the land. However, I am also of the view that the land of the objectors is, in each case, touched and concerned by the covenant. The covenant is intended to preserve the amenity or standard of the neighbourhood generally. The covenant is specifically aimed at density of housing. Extensive building can affect the amenity of a district in many ways. An estate can easily lose its character when buildings obstruct the views. It seems to me to be perfectly reasonable to say that the loss of a view just round the corner from the land may have an adverse effect upon the land itself for the loss of the view could prove detrimental to the estate as a whole. In my opinion, therefore, the tribunal was entitled to find as it did.

A wide interpretation was given to the concept 'practical benefit'; it involves taking into account the whole of the surroundings in which the application is intended to operate.

Public Interest

One approach to the question of public interest has been adopted by the Lands Tribunal in *Re Bass's Application* (1973) 26 P & CR 156. The Lands Tribunal evaluated s84(1)(aa) by considering its application through a seven-question analysis.

The applicants had bought some land in 'inner-city' Birmingham which was 'zoned' for industrial use. They obtained planning permission to establish on the land what they called 'a trunker park' (this means a large depot for long-distance beer lorries). It was estimated that some 250 lorries a day would come in and out of the depot. The land was, however, subject to a 'residential purposes only' restrictive covenant. Local residents, claiming to be the dominant owners to this covenant, defeated Bass's application under ground (aa) to have the covenant removed.

The tribunal analysed the issues raised by ground (aa) applications by considering seven questions:

1 Is the proposed user reasonable?

2 Do the covenants impede that user?

3 Does impeding the proposed user secure practical benefits to the objectors?

4 If the answer to the question is yes, are those benefits of substantial value or advantage?

5 Is impeding the proposed user contrary to the public interest?

6 If no to question 4, would money be adequate compensation?

7 If yes to question 5, would money be adequate compensation?

Applying these questions to the facts the tribunal concluded:

1 Is the proposed user reasonable?

Yes. Bass had obtained planning permission and the obtaining of such permission is usually conclusive proof that the user is a 'reasonable' one.

2 Do the covenants impede that user?

Clearly, yes!

3 Does impeding the proposed user secure practical benefits to the objectors?

Yes, the residents were spared all those lorries.

4 If the answer to the question is yes, are those benefits of substantial value or advantage?

Yes, for the same reason. (It is suggested that questions 3 and 4 will always go together.)

5 Is impeding the proposed user contrary to the public interest?

No! That was the crucial victory for the residents. Bass argued that if a landowner gets planning permission, this automatically proves that his plans are in the public interest. This argument was firmly rejected by the tribunal. The granting of planning permission merely indicates that the proposed development is not against the public interest. Mr JS Daniel QC noted the following in this regard:

> The question is whether impeding the proposal is contrary to the public interest. There is here more than a narrow nuance of difference; a planning permission only says, in effect, that a proposal will be allowed; it implies perhaps that such a proposal will not be a bad thing but it does not necessarily imply that it will be positively a good thing and in the public interest, and that failure of the proposal to materialise would be positively bad. Many planning permissions have got through by the skin of their teeth, and I think that the assistance derived from a planning permission at this stage of things is little more that the negative assistance of enabling it to be said that at any rate there was not a refusal.

Bass also argued that the establishment of their depot would benefit the economy of the area and create more jobs and that this was in the public interest. The tribunal accepted this was true, but these benefits had to be balanced against the noise and congestion the lorries would cause. In the tribunal's view, these disadvantages outweighed the economic advantages.

6 If no to question 4, would money be adequate compensation?

7 If yes to question 5, would money be adequate compensation?

The tribunal did not have to answer questions 6 and 7.

671

thinking point 21.4

If the tribunal had had to consider questions 6 and 7, what do you think the tribunal would have decided?

The tribunal would almost certainly have held that money was not adequate compensation for the residents for all the noise, stench, etc.

Agreement to Discharge or Modify the Restrictive Covenant

Ground (b) is virtually academic. If all the dominant owners agree to a restrictive covenant being discharged or modified, they will normally execute a deed to that effect. Applying to the tribunal in such a case would be a waste of time and money. The only possibility for a ground (b) case seems to be where the dominant owners indicated that they would agree to a discharge but then refused to execute the formal deed.

No Injury to Persons who Benefited from the Restrictive Covenant

Ground (c) cases are relatively rare. In one case there was a restrictive covenant on a shop that no alcohol should be sold from the premises. The purpose of such a covenant was to keep the area free from the evil of 'the demon drink'. The applicants, however, already had an off-licence a few doors away. They wanted to transfer that off-licence to the servient shop. The covenant was discharged under ground (c). The 'demon drink' was already in the area; moving the outlet would not make things worse for the dominant owners.

Modification: Rewriting the Covenant

> *Law of Property Act 1925*
>
> 84. Power to discharge or modify restrictive covenants affecting land
>
> (1C) It is hereby declared that the power conferred by this section to modify a restriction includes power to add such further provisions restricting the user of or the building on the land affected as appear to the Upper Tribunal to be reasonable in view of the relaxation of the existing provisions, and as may be accepted by the applicant; and the Upper Tribunal may accordingly refuse to modify a restriction without some such addition.

This makes it clear that 'modification' of a restrictive covenant includes removing one covenant and replacing it with a new one. Thus, for example, the Upper Tribunal could in appropriate circumstances remove a covenant saying 'agricultural purposes only' and replace it with one saying 'residential purposes only'.

21.6 Balancing Interests of the Parties—'Thin End of the Wedge'

It often happens that a purchaser of a plot on a building scheme applies to the Upper Tribunal to have one of the covenants removed from his plot. 'Removing the covenant from my plot will not damage the area as a whole', they argue. 'Thin end of the wedge', say other owners of plots on the scheme.

21.6.1 Case Study—The Firs

The Firs is a very exclusive building scheme consisting of 40 detached houses. The scheme covenants include an obligation not to use the houses for business, trade, or professional purposes.

Philpa buys a house in the scheme and intends to use the house as the base for her accountancy practice. She applies under s84(1)(aa) for a modification of the covenant. Some of her neighbours oppose the application, even though Philpa insists that her professional activities will not disturb the peace and quiet. The objectors argue that once she starts her accountancy activities that will set a precedent and others will want to follow.

In *McMorris v Brown* [1998] 3 WLR 971, the Privy Council was faced in a Jamaican appeal with an application to discharge a restrictive covenant prohibiting the subdivision of plots within a building scheme. Lord Hoffmann, in giving the advice of the Board, quoted the words of Judge Bernard Marder QC, the then president of the English Lands Tribunal.

> It is, however, legitimate in considering a particular application to have regard to the scheme of covenants as a whole and to assess the importance to the beneficiaries of maintaining the integrity of the scheme. . . . In so far as this application would have the effect if granted of opening a breach in a carefully maintained and outstandingly successful scheme of development, to grant the application would in my view deprive the objectors of a substantial practical benefit, namely the assurance of the integrity of the scheme.

Lord Hoffmann then added, 'Their lordships adopt that approach as correct in principle under the English and Jamaican statutes alike.' In the light of *McMorris v Brown*, Philpa's application should fail. The neighbours' desire for tranquil exclusivity should prevail.

Maintaining the Special Character of a Successful Building Scheme

In *Dobbin v Redpath* [2007] EWCA Civ 570, Briar Close was a building scheme of just five plots. The scheme (created in the early 1960s) included the usual covenant preventing the building of more than one house on each plot.

The applicant Dobbin had acquired the garden of number 1, and obtained planning permission to build a bungalow. He applied to the Lands Tribunal for appropriate modifications of the restrictive covenants. The application was refused by the Lands Tribunal, and that refusal was upheld by the Court of Appeal.

Bearing in mind Dobbin had planning permission, building a bungalow was a reasonable user of the servient land. But the one house per plot covenant still secured practical benefits of substantial value to the other owners within the building scheme. At para 8, Lawrence Collins LJ said:

> Despite its small size, the building scheme had achieved the creation of a pleasant, quiet cul de sac with low density residential development and the location of the proposed bungalow on that land would give that land a cramped, over-developed appearance.

Looking at the broader issues under s84(1)(aa) it is clear from *Dobbin v Redpath* (and cases cited by the Court of Appeal) that where there is a successful building scheme, the preservation of the existing environment is very likely to be ruled as 'practical benefits of substantial value', and therefore modification or removal of covenants will be refused.

21.6.2 Compensation for Dominant Owners

Where the Upper Tribunal discharges or modifies a restrictive covenant(s), it has discretion to award compensation to the dominant owner(s).

In practice, compensation is hardly ever awarded in cases succeeding under grounds (a), (b), and (c). However, the tribunal usually does award compensation in ground (aa) cases. When awarding compensation it has a choice between two alternative measures of compensation:

1 'a sum to make up for any loss or disadvantage suffered by [the dominant owner] in consequence of the discharge or modification'; or

2 'a sum to make up for any effect which the restriction had, at the time when it was imposed, in reducing the consideration then received for the land affected by it'.

The first alternative is the 'natural measure of compensation' and is the one normally used.

The second alternative recognizes the fact that when a covenant is placed upon a piece of land, that covenant depreciates the value of that land. Suppose that in 1965 Blackacre was sold for £20,000 subject to a covenant 'no buildings'. If that covenant had not been imposed the price for Blackacre would have been £25,000. The compensation payable under the second alternative will be £5,000.

thinking point 21.5

What are the practical objections to this 'second alternative' for assessing compensation?

If you are objecting, 'It is difficult to prove what the land would have been worth without the covenant, particularly if the covenant was imposed a long time ago', and 'This measure of damages is not inflation-proof', then you are right on both points. That is why the tribunal normally uses alternative (1) when awarding compensation (as it did in Re Banks' *Application (1976)).*

pause for thought

Restrictive covenants are a great nuisance to developers of land and bad for the economy of the country. They should all be abolished. We should trust the expertise of our town planners to protect us from undesirable developments. Do you agree with these sentiments?

Concluding Remarks

Many would not agree. There is (perhaps regrettably) widespread distrust of town planners and planning law. This stems in part from the fact (emphasized in *Re Bass's Application*) that planning permission for a development will be granted unless that development is contrary to the public interest. But there is also the widespread fear that town planners too often favour 'the public good' rather than the interests and anxieties of individuals who object to a particular development.

If you are a dominant owner in relation to a restrictive covenant banning or controlling development, you have a private law right which you can assert against the servient owner. You are not dependent for your protection on the whims of 'faceless' officials. However, in fairly limited circumstances, proceedings under s84(1) LPA 1925 may deprive you of your right.

From time to time there are suggestions that there should be further reforms to s84(1) to make it easier for servient owners to have awkward covenants removed or modified. There is some merit in this suggestion. At minimum, ground (aa) needs simplifying and the provisions for compensation need clarification.

But perhaps the oddest feature of s84(1) is the fact that the powers given by the provision are not given to the courts. This means that developers are often involved in wasteful duplicate litigation. Like Birmingham Corporation in *Re Dolphin's Conveyance*, they have to go first to the court under s84(2) and then to the Lands Tribunal (now the Upper Tribunal) under s84(1). A simple reform would be to give the High Court (and for less valuable properties, County Courts) jurisdiction to make orders under s84(1).

The Law Commission, in its 2011 Report No 327, *Making Land Work: Easements, Covenants and Profits à Prendre*, agrees that s84 LPA 1925 is confusingly laid out (see especially para 7.5 of the Report). Disappointingly, the Law Commission does not recommend any changes to the grounds for the discharge or modification of covenants (see para 7.14). It does however recommend that, to avoid wasteful duplicate litigation, the Upper Tribunal (Lands Chamber) should have jurisdiction to make orders under s 84(2) (see recommendation 8.54).

# Summary

Where a servient owner wants to carry out a development which would break a restrictive covenant, that owner has various options:

Carry on Regardless

This is possible where there seems little chance that the covenant will be enforced. Where there is a small risk of somebody enforcing the covenants, it may be possible to insure against that risk.

Buy Out Dominant Owners

The servient owner must be sure that he has bought out all possible claimants. If in doubt as to the identity of the dominant owners, he may take proceedings under s84(2) LPA 1925.

Modification or Discharge of the Covenants

Grounds for modifying or discharging covenants (s84(1) LPA 1925):

- obsolete;
- obstruction of some reasonable user;
- agreement;
- no injury.

Compensation for Dominant Owners

Usually awarded in obstruction of some reasonable user cases. Two alternatives:

1   Money awarded which covers loss or disadvantage suffered by the dominant owner(s).
2   Compensation awarded for the depreciation in value of the dominant land(s).

Further Reading

Martin, J, 'Remedies for breach of restrictive covenants' [1996] Conv 329
An overview of the remedies and deals with issues of enforcement.

Questions

In 1988, Lewis bought three adjoining properties in rural Barsetshire, and became registered proprietor of those three properties. The three properties were Hill Top Farm (500 acres), Riverview Farm (400 acres), and Coombe Manor. Coombe Manor consists of a 50-room mansion and a large ornamental garden.

In 1998, Lewis sold Coombe Manor to Sabina. The land transfer to Sabina included a restrictive covenant under which she promised not to use Coombe Manor for any business, commercial, or professional purposes. The covenant was expressed to be 'for the benefit of the land retained by Lewis'.

In 2008, Lewis sold Hill Top Farm to Raj. Neither the contract of sale nor the land transfer made any mention of the right to enforce the restrictive covenant over Coombe Manor.

In 2011, Lewis sold Riverview Farm to Tariq. The land transfer in Tariq's favour expressly included a special clause giving Tariq the right to enforce the restrictive covenant over Coombe Manor.

Earlier this year Dan bought Coombe Manor from Sabina. He has obtained planning permission to convert Coombe Manor into a hotel. However, both Raj and Tariq are threatening proceedings for an injunction. Raj has written saying, 'Your guests will trespass all over my fields', while Tariq has said, 'If you offer me enough money, I will release the covenant.'

Advise Dan.

Would your advice be different if, as a result of the development of a new city, Coombe Manor and the two farms are now on the edge of an urban area?

Part 11
Mortgages

The Creation of Mortgages

Introduction

pause for thought

Re-read 1.3.1 on mortgages. Note carefully the correct terminology. Remember, too, that it is borrowers who grant mortgages, not banks and building societies!

The English law of mortgages has been the product of a historical evolution spread over many hundreds of years. The modern mortgage has a specific meaning and this will be considered in 22.1. Despite some quite drastic changes made in 1925, there is still a large amount of law and terminology which is explicable only by reference to that long evolution.

Furthermore, because it is the product of a slow historical evolution, almost the whole of the law of mortgages has developed around mortgages of land which is unregistered title. There are, however, some important legal differences between mortgages of registered titles and mortgages of unregistered titles. Those differences particularly relate to 'formalities' and to 'priorities'.

22.1 What is a Mortgage?

In this section we will guide you through what amounts to a mortgage and explain the terminology used in this area.

Lindley LJ defined a mortgage in *Santley v Wilde* [1899] 2 Ch 474 as:

> a conveyance of land ... as a security for the payment of a debt or the discharge of some other obligation for which it is given. This is the idea of a mortgage: and the security is redeemable on the payment or discharge of such debt or obligation ...

cross-reference
For more discussion on the mortgagee's remedies, see Chapter 23.

This simply means that property is used as security for a loan and once the debt or obligation has been repaid the mortgage is discharged. The **mortgagee** (lender) is given a proprietary interest in the land subject to the right to redemption, and as a secured creditor can take priority over unsecured creditors. The **right to redeem** is the right to repay the loan on redemption; the proprietary interest given to the mortgagee is no longer valid, it is extinguished.

From the point of view of a lender, the great advantage of a mortgage is that the lender (mortgagee) is a secured creditor. If the loan is not repaid, the mortgagee can sell the property and recover his loan from the proceeds. If the **mortgagor** (borrower) is declared insolvent, the mortgagee has priority over the unsecured creditors, and (unless there is '**negative equity**') the mortgagee will get the money owed back.

thinking point 22.1

Asif's only asset is Greentrees Farm, worth £500,000. He mortgages the farm to Waterford Bank to secure a loan of £300,000. Asif is now declared bankrupt. His total debts are in the region of £1 million. Will Waterford Bank get all its money back?

The answer is 'yes'. The bank will recover the full amount of its loan from the proceeds of the sale of the farm. The other 'unsecured' creditors will not be so fortunate. They will only be paid a percentage of their debt.

So far we have considered what constitutes a mortgage. In contrast to a mortgage is a **charge**. A charge is technically different from a mortgage. A mortgage is a proprietary interest. A charge is a burden on land which gives the chargee (lender) legal rights over the land as security for the loan; such rights include possession and sale. Once the mortgage has been repaid, the charge is void.

The terms mortgage and charge are nowadays almost always used interchangeably, but it is important to note that they both have specific meanings.

mortgagee the lender who lends the money to the borrower in exchange for receiving a proprietary interest in land.

mortgagor the borrower who grants the lender a mortgage (an interest in the property).

charge burden on land which gives the chargee (lender) legal rights over the land as security for the loan.

right to redeem the right to repay the loan and have the mortgage (or charge) discharged.

'negative equity' a colloquial English expression for the situation where the amount of money owed by the borrower exceeds the value of the property on which the debt is secured.

22.2 Form of a Legal Mortgage of a Fee Simple before 1926

Before we examine modern law on mortgages, we will consider the development of mortgages over time to explain what was involved in the creation of a mortgage and the problems encountered with the 'old' type of mortgage. We hope that when we discuss mortgages post 1925 that you will understand the context within which mortgages operate, particularly why equity stepped in to alleviate the harshness of the common law.

The pre-1926 standard way of mortgaging a fee simple may strike you as rather surprising. The mortgagor conveyed to the mortgagee the whole fee simple in the land (ie the property), but subject to a proviso for redemption, that is, a clause in the mortgage deed that if the debt was redeemed (repaid) with the appropriate interest on a named date, the mortgagee was obliged to reconvey the fee simple to the mortgagor. This is known as the legal right to redeem.

It should be stressed that even with this 'old' form of mortgage, the mortgagor usually retained possession of the land. Remember that all a mortgagee normally requires is security for a loan. The mortgagee normally does not want the bother of managing the land on which the loan is secured.

legal redemption date

contractual date stipulated on the mortgage deed when the money borrowed should be repaid to the lender.

If the mortgagor duly redeemed on the date specified on the mortgage deed (called the legal redemption date) but the mortgagee did not reconvey the fee simple, the mortgagor could sue the mortgagee at common law for damages, or in equity for an order (of specific performance) that the property should be reconveyed.

What happened if the mortgagor failed to repay on the agreed **legal redemption date**? The approach of the common law was strict. The mortgagor lost all rights to the property, even if the property was worth far more than the debt owed, and even if the failure to repay on time was due to some kind of accident. To make matters worse for the mortgagor, the loan was still outstanding and had to be paid back.

cross-reference
*mortgagees' remedies
are discussed in
Chapter 23.*

22.2.1 Equitable Right to Redeem

Equity was much more sympathetic to mortgagors. The Court of Chancery ruled that if the mortgagor at any time after the legal redemption date repaid the loan with interest up to the date of actual repayment, the mortgagor was entitled to reclaim the land; if necessary equity would order (by a decree of specific performance) the reconveyance of the fee simple.

The equitable right to redeem allowed the mortgagor to retain the right to redeem continuing indefinitely after the legal redemption date. This was (and still is) the automatic right of every mortgagor; it can be terminated only by a foreclosure order, or by the mortgagee exercising his power of sale.

We now come to a point you may well find extremely strange. You may be thinking that the legal redemption date was (and is) fixed on the day when the parties anticipate that the loan will finally be repaid. So if Farns-Barnes borrowed £2,000 on 1 May 1900, the loan to be repaid in ten years' time, you might expect the legal redemption date in any mortgage to secure the loan to be 1 May 1910.

**equitable right to
redeem**

this arises where
the loan has not
been repaid on
the legal date of
redemption.

However, a very curious thing has happened to the legal redemption date. The **equitable right to redeem** has become all important and the legal redemption can now effectively be ignored. It has consequently long been the practice to set the legal redemption date at some nominal date, usually six months after the date of the mortgage. In the Farns-Barnes example, the legal redemption date would normally be fixed on 1 November 1900, though nobody really expected Farns-Barnes to repay on that date.

Despite the fact that it is of such fundamental importance, the equitable right to redeem was (and still is) not normally mentioned in the mortgage deed.

22.2.2 The Equity of Redemption

The equitable right to redeem must not be confused with 'equity of redemption'. The equity of redemption is the phrase used to represent the bundle of the mortgagor's rights with respect to the mortgaged land (and includes the right to redeem). The equitable right to redeem is by far the most important of those rights. Since 1925, a mortgagor owns both the legal estate and an 'equity of redemption'. Equity of redemption was described by Lord Hardwicke in an old case called *Casborne v Scarfe* (1738) 1 Atk 603:

> an estate in the land, for it may be devised, granted, or entailed with remainders...and there-fore cannot be considered as a mere right only...the person therefore intitled to the equity of redemption is considered as the owner of the land, and a mortgage in fee is considered as personal assets...The interest of the land must be some where, and cannot be in abeyance; but it is not the mortgagee, and therefore must remain in the mortgagor.

To put this passage into context, the legal estate is of no intrinsic value, but the value of the equity of redemption is the difference between the value of the property minus the total debt outstanding. Hence the expression, 'the equity in my house is £X,000'. The modern expression 'negative equity' arises where the amount of the debt exceeds the value of the property.

An equity of redemption can be disposed of like any other interest in land. It can be sold, settled, leased, etc. It can itself be mortgaged, so as to create a second mortgage. Prior to 1926, as a first legal mortgage was normally created by conveyance of the legal estate, the mortgagor retained only an equitable interest, and therefore second and subsequent (third, fourth, etc) mortgages were necessarily equitable. This is because they were created out of an equitable estate. The mortgagee, as they had the legal estate, had an automatic right to take possession of the deeds.

After 1925, a series of legal mortgages is a quite normal phenomenon, though with regards to the possession of the title deeds, a legal mortgagee has a statutory right to take possession of the title deeds, unless an earlier mortgagee has taken them. In practice, a first mortgagee normally exercises the right to take possession of the deeds.

22.2.3 Mortgagor Retaining Possession

It has long been the practice for mortgagees to allow mortgagors to remain in possession of the mortgaged property. Even today a mortgagee has the right to take possession. Mortgagees normally exercise that right only as a preliminary to enforcing their security by selling the property.

If a mortgagee did take possession, and held the property for a long period, equity would place on the mortgagee a strict duty to 'account on the basis of wilful default'; a phrase which means that there is a duty to get the maximum income from the land. This rule (which will be explained more fully in Chapter 23), coupled with the fact that the mortgagee does not normally want the responsibility of looking after the land, effectively makes it not worth the mortgagee's while taking possession unless the mortgagee wishes to enforce their security.

22.3 Legal Mortgages after 1925—Unregistered Land

The 1925 legislation no longer permitted the creation of the traditional form of mortgage, the conveyance of the fee simple with a provision for reconveyance on redemption. This type of mortgage was not compatible with the aims and objectives of the 1925 legislation, for example promoting the alienability of land. (Selling property subject to a mortgage under the traditional method was difficult because the mortgagee had the legal title and the mortgagor only an equitable interest.)

The legislators in 1925 recognized that in substance the mortgagor was the true owner of the property and that what the lender simply wanted was security for the loan. Under the 1925 legislation the mortgagor retained the fee simple, but granted the mortgagee as security for the loan either a very long lease, or a 'charge by way of legal mortgage'. In both cases a legal mortgage was created.

> *Law of Property Act 1925*
>
> 85. Mode of mortgaging freeholds
>
> (1) A mortgage of an estate in fee simple shall only be capable of being effected at law either by a demise for a term of years absolute, subject to a provision for cesser on redemption, or by a charge by deed expressed to be by way of legal mortgage;

These two ways of mortgaging a fee simple apply to unregistered titles.

22.3.1 Mortgage by Long Lease ('Mortgage by Demise')

Under s85(2) Law of Property Act 1925 (LPA 1925) the mortgagor granted to the mortgagee a lease for 3,000 years subject to a proviso for **cesser on redemption**, that is, a provision that on the debt being repaid on a named date the lease should automatically terminate. This named date was the legal redemption date and fixed usually at a nominal six months from the date of the creation of the mortgage. The equitable right to redeem would come into effect after the legal date of redemption had passed and so remained all important. Any attempt after 1925 to create a mortgage by conveyance of the fee simple was converted into a mortgage by demise.

Law of Property Act 1925

85. Mode of mortgaging freeholds

(2) Any purported conveyance of an estate in fee simple by way of mortgage made after the commencement of this Act shall (to the extent of the estate of the mortgagor) operate as a demise of the land to the mortgagee for a term of years absolute, without impeachment for waste, but subject to cesser on redemption, in manner following, namely:—

(a) A first or only mortgagee shall take a term of three thousand years from the date of the mortgage;

(b) A second or subsequent mortgagee shall take a term (commencing from the date of the mortgage) one day longer than the term vested in the first or other mortgagee whose security ranks immediately before that of such second or subsequent mortgagee:

and, in this subsection, any such purported conveyance as aforesaid includes an absolute conveyance with a deed of defeasance and any other assurance which, but for this subsection, would operate in effect to vest the fee simple in a mortgagee subject to redemption.

Any legal mortgage existing on 1 January 1926 which had been created by conveyance of the fee simple was automatically converted into a mortgage by demise for 3,000 years. The fee simple was automatically revested in the mortgagor.

Both parties were in a better position under this statutory provision. The mortgagee was granted an estate in land, a term of years absolute, which bound the mortgagor. The mortgagor retained the legal fee simple estate in land.

It is worth stressing that mortgages by long lease are virtually unknown today. Apart from the difficulty encountered in explaining how the mortgage would operate to a prospective borrower, that is, the mortgage creates a lease for 3,000 years, this method for creating mortgages no longer applies to registered titles after 12 October 2003.

22.3.2 Charge by Way of Legal Mortgage

The mortgagee has the same rights, powers, and remedies as if they had taken a mortgage by 3,000-year lease, although strictly speaking the mortgagee has no estate in the land, only a 'charge' which is a legal interest. The powers of the mortgagee are the same under both forms of mortgage and there is no distinction in treatment between them.

For a charge by way of legal mortgage a deed is necessary, identifying the land in question and expressly declaring it to be charged by way of legal mortgage (s87(1) LPA 1925).

A legal redemption date is not necessary, although one is usually inserted providing for repayment at a nominal six months. The charge by way of legal mortgage has become the most common type of mortgage created for both unregistered and registered land.

Law of Property Act 1925

87. Charges by way of legal mortgage

(1) Where a legal mortgage of land is created by a charge by deed expressed to be by way of legal mortgage, the mortgagee shall have the same protection, powers and remedies (including the right to take proceedings to obtain possession from the occupiers and the persons in receipt of rents and profits, or any of them) as if—

    (a) where the mortgage is a mortgage of an estate in fee simple, a mortgage term for three thousand years without impeachment of waste had been thereby created in favour of the mortgagee; and

    (b) where the mortgage is a mortgage of a term of years absolute, a sub-term less by one day than the term vested in the mortgagor had been thereby created in favour of the mortgagee.

(2) Where an estate vested in a mortgagee immediately before the commencement of this Act has by virtue of this Act been converted into a term of years absolute or sub-term, the mortgagee may, by a declaration in writing to that effect signed by him, convert the mortgage into a charge by way of legal mortgage, and in that case the mortgage term shall be extinguished in the inheritance or in the head term as the case may be, and the mortgagee shall have the same protection, powers and remedies (including the right to take proceedings to obtain possession from the occupiers and the persons in receipt of rents and profits or any of them) as if the mortgage term or sub-term had remained subsisting.

The power conferred by this subsection may be exercised by a mortgagee notwithstanding that he is a trustee or personal representative.

(3) Such declaration shall not affect the priority of the mortgagee or his right to retain possession of documents, nor affect his title to or right over any fixtures or chattels personal comprised in the mortgage.

(4) Subsection (1) of this section shall not be taken to be affected by section 23(1)(a) of the Land Registration Act 2002 (under which owner's powers in relation to a registered estate do not include power to mortgage by demise or sub-demise).

As a means of protecting the mortgagee's priority over other creditors, the mortgagee traditionally took possession of the title deeds of the property. If the mortgagor attempted to grant another mortgage to a different mortgagee then the absence of the title deeds would indicate that there was potentially another mortgage in place already. Section 85(1) LPA 1925 continues with the traditional approach and gives the mortgagee the right to take possession of the title deeds.

Law of Property Act 1925

85. Mode of mortgaging freeholds

(1) ...

Provided that a first mortgagee shall have the same right to the possession of documents as if his security included the fee simple.

For a discussion on a puisne mortgage, see 4.7.4 'Class C(i) Puisne Mortgage'.

Once the mortgage has been redeemed, that is, the loan has been repaid, the mortgagor is entitled to have their title deeds returned to them (s96(2) LPA 1925).

If the title deeds were not deposited with the mortgagee, for example if there was a second or third mortgage and there are no title deeds to hand over, then the puisne mortgage is registrable as a land charge (Class C(i)).

Legal Mortgages after 1925—Unregistered Land

Where title is unregistered a first 'protected legal mortgage' triggers compulsory first registration of the mortgagor's estate (ss 4(1)(g) and 6(2)(a) Land Registration Act 2002 (LRA 2002)). A protected legal mortgage has been defined in s4(8) LRA 2002:

> *Land Registration Act 2002*
>
> 4. When title must be registered
>
> (8) For the purposes of subsection (1)(g)—
>
>   (a) a legal mortgage is protected if it takes effect on its creation as a mortgage to be protected by the deposit of documents relating to the mortgaged estate, and
>
>   (b) a first legal mortgage is one which, on its creation, ranks in priority ahead of any other mortgages then affecting the mortgaged estate.

Thus, a 'protected legal mortgage' arises where a mortgage deed has been executed and the title deeds have been deposited with the mortgagee, and will rank in priority ahead of any other subsequent mortgages. The estate will undergo first registration and once this has been completed the mortgage will be registered as a registered charge on the register of title. If registration of the mortgage is not completed within two months of the disposition then the mortgage will take effect as an equitable charge (s7(2)(b) LRA 2002).

thinking point 22.2

In what circumstances would it be possible for a new puisne mortgage of an unregistered title to be created today?

Where an unregistered title was mortgaged prior to 1997, that mortgage is still outstanding, and the owner of the fee simple now creates a second mortgage.

22.4 Legal Mortgages of Registered Land

Prior to 13 October 2003, in registered land the mortgage could be created by using either one of the unregistered forms, namely mortgage by demise or charge by way of legal mortgage, or by registered charge. The latter was the most commonly used method. The registered charge had to be created by deed and registered to take effect at law. The land must be identified by reference to the register. (In practice the title number(s) is given.) While a nominal legal redemption date is not necessary for a mortgage by registered charge, old practices die hard, and one usually is inserted.

The charge was registered in the charges register of the register of title, with the chargee being named as the owner of the charge. The chargee was issued with a charge certificate, and the land certificate was deposited at the Land Registry.

Since 13 October 2003, it is no longer possible to create a legal mortgage of registered land by demise or sub-demise (sub-lease) (s87(4) LPA 1925). Section 23(1) LRA 2002 only permits the creation of a legal mortgage, whether freehold or leasehold, by a registered charge.

Form 22.1
Land Registry Form CH1 for
registering a legal charge

Land Registry
Legal charge of a registered estate

CH1

This form should be accompanied by either Form AP1 or Form FR1

If you need more room than is provided for in a panel, and your software allows, you can expand any panel in the form. Alternatively use continuation sheet CS and attach it to this form.

Conveyancer is a term used in this form. It is defined in rule 217A, Land Registration Rules 2003 and includes persons authorised under the Legal Services Act 2007 to provide reserved legal services relating to land registration and includes solicitors and licensed conveyancers.

Leave blank if not yet registered.	1	Title number(s) of the property:
Insert address including postcode (if any) or other description of the property, for example 'land adjoining 2 Acacia Avenue'.	2	Property:
	3	Date:
Give full name(s).	4	Borrower:
Complete as appropriate where the borrower is a company.		For UK incorporated companies/LLPs Registered number of company or limited liability partnership including any prefix: For overseas companies (a) Territory of incorporation: (b) Registered number in the United Kingdom including any prefix:
Give full name(s).	5	Lender for entry in the register:
Complete as appropriate where the lender is a company. Also, for an overseas company, unless an arrangement with Land Registry exists, lodge either a certificate in Form 7 in Schedule 3 to the Land Registration Rules 2003 or a certified copy of the constitution in English or Welsh, or other evidence permitted by rule 183 of the Land Registration Rules 2003.		For UK incorporated companies/LLPs Registered number of company or limited liability partnership including any prefix: For overseas companies (a) Territory of incorporation: (b) Registered number in the United Kingdom including any prefix:
Each proprietor may give up to three addresses for service, one of which must be a postal address whether or not in the UK (including the postcode, if any). The others can be any combination of a postal address, a UK DX box number or an electronic address.	6	Lender's intended address(es) for service for entry in the register:

Place 'X' in any box that applies.

Add any modifications.

7	The borrower with
	☐ full title guarantee
	☐ limited title guarantee
	charges the property by way of legal mortgage as security for the payment of the sums detailed in panel 9

Place 'X' in the appropriate box(es).

You must set out the wording of the restriction in full.

Standard forms of restriction are set out in Schedule 4 to the Land Registration Rules 2003.

8	☐ The lender is under an obligation to make further advances and applies for the obligation to be entered in the register
	☐ The borrower applies to enter the following standard form of restriction in the proprietorship register of the registered estate:

Insert details of the sums to be paid (amount and dates) and so on.

9	Additional provisions

The borrower must execute this charge as a deed using the space opposite. If there is more than one borrower, all must execute. Forms of execution are given in Schedule 9 to the Land Registration Rules 2003. If a note of an obligation to make further advances has been applied for in panel 8 this document must be signed by the lender or its conveyancer.

10	Execution

WARNING

If you dishonestly enter information or make a statement that you know is, or might be, untrue or misleading, and intend by doing so to make a gain for yourself or another person, or to cause loss or the risk of loss to another person, you may commit the offence of fraud under section 1 of the Fraud Act 2006, the maximum penalty for which is 10 years' imprisonment or an unlimited fine, or both.

Failure to complete this form with proper care may result in a loss of protection under the Land Registration Act 2002 if, as a result, a mistake is made in the register.

Under section 66 of the Land Registration Act 2002 most documents (including this form) kept by the registrar relating to an application to the registrar or referred to in the register are open to public inspection and copying. If you believe a document contains prejudicial information, you may apply for that part of the document to be made exempt using Form EX1, under rule 136 of the Land Registration Rules 2003.

© Crown copyright (ref: LR/HO) 10/11

> *Land Registration Act 2002*
>
> 23. Owner's powers
>
> (1) Owner's powers in relation to a registered estate consist of—
>
>   (a) power to make a disposition of any kind permitted by the general law in relation to an interest of that description, other than a mortgage by demise or sub-demise, and
>
>   (b) power to charge the estate at law with the payment of money.

cross-reference
Mortgages of leases will be discussed in 22.6.

A legal mortgage by registered charge must be created by deed (ss 52(1) and 205(ii) LPA 1925), and more specifically it must be created as a 'registered charge'. Section 25(1) LRA 2002 provides that the registrable charge will only take effect if it 'complies with such requirements as to form and content as rules may provide'. There are no rules on the content of the mortgage deed but the Land Registration Rules 2003 provide an example of a form (see Form 22.1, Form CH1). Normally lenders will have their own form which sets out the same information as the CH1 form from the Land Registry.

Under s27(2)(f) LRA 2002 the mortgage, a registrable disposition, to take effect at law must be registered on the register of title. Once the registration requirements have been met, the mortgage is now a legal charge. Registration of the mortgage is important, because the failure to do so would lead the mortgage relegated to only being recognized in equity.

Under the LRA 2002 charge certificates are no longer issued. Some people may be surprised by this, but it is a logical corollary to the abolition of Land Certificates. Mortgagees will have to rely on the accuracy of the Registry's records.

22.5 Types of Mortgages

It should be borne in mind that the law of mortgages has largely developed around what is sometimes called the 'classic mortgage'. A classic mortgage is one where it is envisaged that the whole debt will be repaid in one lump sum, for example John borrowed £5,000, to be repaid in ten years' time on 23 March 2026.

Many modern mortgages are, of course, instalment mortgages, where it is envisaged that regular payments are made in instalments over a long period of time. The time period is usually 25 years, but there is no legal rule requiring that the period be 25 years. The general law of mortgages applies to instalment mortgages. It will in practice follow one of the following two patterns:

1 The borrower covenants to repay the whole debt on a nominal redemption date (say six months); there are then clauses providing for repayment by instalments if there is no repayment on the redemption date.

2 There is no nominal redemption date; the borrower covenants to repay by instalments and there is a proviso that if they are a stated period in arrears (eg two months) the whole capital debt becomes repayable. Thus there is a 'floating' legal redemption date.

In practice there are two main types of mortgages available from banks and building societies: repayment and interest-only mortgages.

The mortgagor who has a repayment mortgage is required to pay capital and interest in instalments to the mortgagee. The instalments are paid on a monthly basis for usually up to 25 years. Once the capital and interest have been repaid to the mortgagee, the mortgage is discharged and the property is wholly owned by the mortgagor.

The interest-only mortgage (commonly known as the endowment mortgage) requires the mortgagor to pay the interest only to the mortgagee (usually in instalments). During the period of the mortgage the capital is not repaid. When the mortgage was created the mortgagor would have taken out an investment policy (commonly known as an endowment assurance policy) which will mature at the end of the duration of the mortgage, usually 25 years, or on the mortgagor's earlier death. The money obtained from this matured policy is used to repay the mortgagee. This type of mortgage has caused considerable controversy in recent years because, when assessing the value of the investment policy, it has been known for the policy to fall short of the predicted value, leaving mortgagors having to meet the shortfall from other financial resources.

If you are a mortgagor, it may at this stage be both interesting and useful to study the terms of 'your' mortgage. But be warned, in 1904, one of the greatest judges of the day, Lord Macnaghten, commented, 'No one...by the light of nature ever understood an English mortgage of real estate.' Despite the changes made in 1925, this remains true.

22.6   **Mortgages of Leases**

22.6.1   Pre 1926

cross-reference
for the discussion
on privity of estate
see 13.2.

Where the mortgagor had a leasehold estate there were two methods by which a legal mortgage was created either:

1 by assignment of the whole term of years with a proviso for reassignment on redemption. In this situation the mortgagee would come into privity of estate with the landlord and therefore be liable for the rent and to perform other covenants entered into by the tenant; or

cross-reference
for the discussion
on the burden of
covenants running with
freehold land, see 20.3.

2 by sub-lease with a proviso for cesser on redemption. The mortgagee's sub-lease was one day shorter than the mortgagor's lease. This was the most favoured method used before 1926 because it avoided the rules under privity of estate. Liability stemming from covenants contained in the head lease could potentially be avoided by the mortgagee. Whether the covenants were enforceable against the mortgagee depended on whether the burden of the covenants passed to the mortgagee.

22.6.2   Post 1925

The assignment of the lease (option 1 in the previous list) was no longer possible under s86(1) LPA 1925. A legal mortgage of a lease, whether unregistered or registered land, could only take the form of either:

• a sub-lease with a proviso for cesser on redemption;

   or

• a charge by way of legal mortgage.

If any attempt was made to mortgage a lease by assignment it was converted into a mortgage by sub-lease, the sub-lease to run out ten days before the lease mortgaged expires. This is provided for in s86(2), which also provides rules on second and subsequent mortgages in paras (a) and (b).

Where a charge by way of legal mortgage is used the mortgagee is in the same position, that is, the same right and remedies, as if they had taken a mortgage by sub-lease to run out one day before the term mortgaged (see s87(1)(b) LPA 1925).

22.7 Equitable Mortgages of Legal Estates

22.7.1 Equitable Mortgage by Deposit of Deeds—Unregistered Land

Equity treated any transaction (other than one by deed) carried through with intent to create a mortgage as a contract for a mortgage, and therefore as an equitable mortgage. In particular, if a borrower deposited title deeds with a lender with intent that the property to which they related should be security for the loan, the depositing of the deeds was sufficient to create an equitable mortgage even though no new document was executed (*Russel v Russel* (1783) 1 Bro CC 269).

The following scenario used to be quite common. Bloggs goes to his bank manager to see whether he can arrange an overdraft. 'What security can you offer us?' asks the manager. Bloggs produces the title deeds to his house. The manager looks at them: '35 Blogtown Way; that must be worth at least £90,000', he murmurs. 'Hand these deeds over to us and you can have an overdraft up to £70,000.' Bloggs hands over the deeds and the manager immediately authorizes the overdraft. Before anything has been signed Bloggs has created an equitable mortgage.

Before 27 September 1989, depositing the title deeds as security for a loan was a valid method of creating an equitable mortgage. The deposit of the deeds under s40(2) LPA 1925 was construed as part performance of a contract to create a mortgage. The mere deposit of deeds alone is not sufficient; it must be coupled with an intention that these deeds are to be used as security for the loan. Thus, in practice an equitable mortgage 'by deposit of title deeds' was almost always immediately followed by a document recording the terms of the loan (interest rates, length of time for repayment, etc). This written evidence would be sufficient to prove the parties' intention. Moreover, because of the rules governing mortgagees' statutory powers and rights the document was usually a deed, referred to as a 'memorandum under seal'.

In *United Bank of Kuwait Plc v Sahib* [1997] Ch 107, Chadwick LJ summarized the law in this area:

> it was not the mere deposit of title deeds which gave rise to an equitable mortgage or charge; it was necessary to establish that the deeds were deposited for the purpose of securing an obligation. In most cases there would be evidence of something said, written or done from which that purpose could be established and the obligation identified. But in some cases there would be no evidence other than that the depositor and the depositee were, or were about to become, debtor and creditor. In those cases the court could infer the purpose and identify the obligation from that fact alone. But the basis of the rule, as explained in *Coote on Mortgages*, was that the equitable charge arose because the court was satisfied from whatever evidence there was that the parties had made an agreement (expressly or by implication) that the debtor should grant security for an obligation which the court could identify, that the agreement was (or, but for the provisions of section 40 of the Law of Property Act 1925, would have been) specifically enforceable, and that the deposit of the title deeds was treated as an act of part performance sufficient to take the case out of section 40 and so enable the agreement to be enforced notwithstanding the absence of any memorandum in writing capable of satisfying subsection (1) of that section. In other words, the equitable charge which arose upon the deposit of title deeds was contract-based.

cross-reference
For a discussion of s2 LP(MP)A 1989, see 3.9.2.

Since 27 September 1989 it is no longer possible to create an equitable mortgage by deposit of deeds. This is because under s2(1) Law of Property (Miscellaneous Provisions) Act 1989 (LP(MP)A 1989) a contract to create an interest in land must be in writing. An equitable mortgage by deposit of deeds is technically such a contract.

Law of Property (Miscellaneous Provisions) Act 1989

2. Contracts for sale etc. of land to be made by signed writing

(1) A contract for the sale or other disposition of an interest in land can only be made in writing and only by incorporating all the terms which the parties have expressly agreed in one document or, where contracts are exchanged, in each.

Chadwick LJ following on from his reasoning in the extract, stated that 'the rule that a deposit of title deeds for the purpose of securing a debt operated, without more, as an equitable mortgage or charge, then it is difficult to see how the rule can have survived section 2 of the Act of 1989'. According to Phillips LJ in the same case, the intention 'of section 2 of the Law of Property (Miscellaneous Provisions) Act 1989 is to introduce certainty in relation to contracts for the disposition of interests in land where uncertainty existed before'.

It is now no longer sufficient to have an oral transaction, such as a deposit of deeds, followed by a memorandum recording the transaction. Any post-1989 mortgages in this form are void; *United Bank of Kuwait v Sahib* (which actually involved a purported mortgage of a registered title by deposit of the land certificate) confirms this point.

22.7.2 Equitable Mortgage of a Registered Title by Deposit of the Land Certificate

So far we have considered the position in unregistered titles. Under the Land Registration Act 1925 (LRA 1925) title to land is evidenced in the register of title and not title deeds. Section 66 LRA 1925 allowed for the creation of a charge by deposit of the land certificate or charge certificate, which was the same as an equitable mortgage by the deposit of title deeds. However, this is no longer a method that can be used because of the decision in *United Bank of Kuwait Plc v Sahib* [1997] Ch 107 which reinforced the requirement of a written contract to create an equitable mortgage, and because there is no equivalent to a mortgage by deposit of the land certificate in the LRA 2002.

In *Sahib*, the United Bank of Kuwait obtained judgment against Sahib for a debt he owed to the bank. Sahib then confirmed in writing to Société Générale Alsacienne de Banque SA ('Sogenal'), the third defendant, that the land certificate to his land (he held the freehold jointly with his wife) was being held on behalf of Sogenal as security for a loan made by Sogenal.

The United Bank of Kuwait obtained a charging order against Sahib's interest in the land. Did Sogenal have a valid equitable mortgage which took priority over the bank's charging order?

The Court of Appeal held that as a result of s2 LP(MP)A 1989 there was not a valid equitable mortgage. There was no document in writing and signed by both parties which amounted to a specifically enforceable contract.

Peter Gibson LJ initially considered the application of s2 LP(MP)A 1989:

> Since 1783 a deposit of title deeds relating to a property by way of security has been taken to create an equitable mortgage of that property without any writing not with standing section 4 of the Statute of Frauds 1677 (29 Car. 2, c. 3) and its successor, section 40 of the Law of Property Act 1925. The main question that arises on this appeal is whether this much criticised but well established rule has survived the coming into force of section 2 of the Law of Property (Miscellaneous Provisions) Act 1989.
>
> . . .
>
> **The section 2 point**
>
> Section 2 of the Act of 1989 was enacted to give effect to the substance of that part of the Law Commission's Report, Transfer of Land: Formalities for Contracts for Sale etc. of Land (Law Com. No. 164) (1987) which recommended the repeal of section 40 of the Law of Property Act 1925 and the abolition of the doctrine of part performance and proposed new requirements for the making of a contract for the sale or other disposition of an interest in land. The material parts of section 2 are:
>
> > '(1) A contract for the sale or other disposition of an interest in land can only be made in writing and only by incorporating all the terms which the parties have expressly agreed in one document or, where contracts are exchanged, in each. (2) The terms may be incorporated in a document either by being set out in it or by reference to some other document. (3) The document incorporating the terms or, where contracts are exchanged, one of the documents incorporating them (but not necessarily the same one) must be signed by or on behalf of each party to the contract. . . . (5) . . . nothing in this section affects the creation or operation of resulting, implied or constructive trusts. (6) In this section—'disposition' has the same meaning as in the Law of Property Act 1925; 'interest in land' means any estate, interest or charge in or over land or in or over the proceeds of sale of land. . . . (8) Section 40 of the Law of Property Act 1925 (which is superseded by this section) shall cease to have effect.'

'Disposition' in section 205(1)(ii) of the Law of Property Act 1925 includes a conveyance, and 'conveyance' includes a mortgage or charge. Section 40…contained provisions less stringent than the Act of 1989 governing formalities relating to contracts for the sale or other disposition of land or any interest in land, and by subsection (2) had preserved the law relating to part performance.

The effect of section 2 of the Act of 1989 is, therefore, that a contract for a mortgage of or charge on any interest in land or in the proceeds of sale of land can only be made in writing and only if the written document incorporates all the terms which the parties have expressly agreed and is signed by or on behalf of each party. In the present case it is not suggested that there is any such written document.

Peter Gibson LJ then went on to consider the application of s2 LP(MP)A 1989 in relation to an equitable mortgage by deposit of deeds:

(1) [Counsel for Sogenal] submitted that there is nothing in the Act of 1989 which expressly or by necessary implication repeals the provisions of the Act of 1925 and later legislation recognising and extending the scope of a security by deposit of title deeds. He relied on four statutory provisions to the following effect…

[Counsel for Sogenal] submitted that it was significant that none of those provisions was referred to in the Act of 1989 as having been repealed or otherwise affected by section 2. He drew attention to the fact that some commentators have concluded from this that section 2 was not intended to repeal the rule relating to the creation of security by deposit of title deeds: see *Snell's Equity*, 29th ed. (1990), p. 445, *Cheshire and Burn's Modern Law of Real Property*, 15th ed. (1994), p. 679 and Bently and Coughlan, 'Informal dealings with land after section 2' (1990) 10 L.S. 325, 341.

I differ with reluctance from such distinguished property lawyers, but I am not persuaded that their views on this point are correct…In any event, earlier legislative references to rights or interests created by the deposit of title deeds must now be read in the light of the Act of 1989. The new formalities required by section 2 govern the validity of all dispositions of interests in land. I cannot see that the references relied on by [Counsel for Sogenal] in the earlier legislation can displace what otherwise is the plain meaning and effect of section 2 on contracts in whatever form to mortgage land.

(2) [Counsel for Sogenal] pointed to the fact that there is nothing in the Law Commission's report which initiated the reforms effected by the Act of 1989 to suggest that security by deposit of title deeds was intended to be affected or was even considered…

But the intention of the Law Commission to include in its proposals contracts to grant mortgages was made plain (see paragraph 4.3 of the report), and, as a deposit of title deeds by way of security takes effect as an agreement to mortgage, in logic there is no reason why the creation of security by deposit of title deeds should have been excepted from the proposals. This is all the more likely when one considers the part played by the doctrine of part performance in the recognition by equity judges of the *Russel v. Russel*, 1 Bro.C.C. 269 doctrine: see further (5) below. In any event, if the wording of section 2 is clear, as I think it is, the absence from the Law Commission's report of a reference to security by deposit of title deeds cannot alter the section's effect.

(3) …

(4) [Counsel for Sogenal] then said that the rule that a deposit of title deeds by way of security creates a mortgage is not dependent on any actual contract between the parties, though, if there is one, that contract will govern the parties' rights; if there is an actual contract, it must comply with section 2; but that does not affect the legal presumptions or inferences which arise when there is a mere deposit.

I accept that there need not be an express contract between the depositor of the title deeds and the person with whom they are deposited for an equitable mortgage to arise (subject to section 2). But I have already stated why it is clear from the authorities that the deposit is treated as rebuttable evidence of a contract to mortgage. Oral evidence is admissible to establish whether or not a deposit was intended to create a mortgage security, whether or not the original deposit was intended at the outset to be security for further advances, whether or not it was agreed subsequently that that deposit should be security for further advances and whether or not any memorandum of agreement accurately stated the terms of the contract or was complete. To allow inquiries of this sort after the Act of 1989 in order to determine whether an equitable mortgage has been created and on what terms seems to me to be wholly inconsistent with the philosophy of section 2, requiring as it does that the contract be made by a single document containing all the terms of the agreement if it is to be valid.

(5) ...It is clear that the rule relating to the creation of an equitable mortgage by deposit proceeded on the footing that the act of deposit constituted a sufficient act of part performance of the presumed agreement to mortgage...

...To the extent that part performance is an essential part of the rationale of the creation of an equitable mortgage by the deposit of title deeds, that too is inconsistent with the new philosophy of the Act of 1989...

(6) [Counsel for Sogenal] then submitted that in other situations equity treats void dispositions, for example void leases and void mortgages, as agreements to dispose of what the disponor can dispose. He said that there was nothing in the Law Commission's report or in the problems there addressed to suggest that section 2 was intended to affect such agreements.

I have already referred to the express reference in the Law Commission's report to the intention to include in its proposals contracts to grant mortgages. In the same paragraph, paragraph 4.3, it was made clear that contracts to grant leases were also to be included. In my judgment, for the like reasons to those given in (2) above, the absence from the report of express mention of the effect of void dispositions as agreements to dispose cannot alter the effect of section 2.

(7) [Counsel for Sogenal] submitted that, although equity will presume to infer an agreement from the deposit of title deeds, it does not follow that for all purposes the parties' rights are to be treated as if they lie in contract. He sought to derive support for this proposition from the remarks of Hoffmann J. in *Spiro v. Glencrown Properties Ltd.* [1991] Ch. 537, 544. There Hoffmann J. was considering how, for the purposes of the Act of 1989, an option to buy land should be characterised. He pointed out that an option was neither an offer nor a conditional contract, not having all the incidents of the standard form of either of those concepts, and said that each analogy is in the proper context a valid way of characterising the situation created by an option. He continued: 'The question in this case is not whether one analogy is true and the other false, but which is appropriate to be used in the construction of section 2...' He concluded not that the option fell outside the scope of section 2 but that it came within it. In the present case, for the reasons already given, it seems to me clear that the deposit of title deeds takes effect as a contract to mortgage and as such falls within section 2.

695

Despite the arguments put forward by counsel for Sogenal which were thorough and examined every aspect which could potentially provide a loophole to the application of s2 LP(MP)A 1989, they were not sufficiently convincing.

22.7.3 Comparison of Legal and Equitable Mortgages pre 1989

REVIEW QUESTION Refer back to 3.7, regarding the creation of equitable interests in land. Consider how that section may be applied to informal mortgages.

With both a legal and an equitable mortgage the usual position was that a new deed was executed and the mortgagee took the existing title deeds to the property (unregistered land) or the land certificate (registered land). With a legal mortgage, the new deed was executed with the intent that it should create the mortgage; the existing title deeds or land certificate were handed over for other reasons. These reasons were to facilitate enforcement of the security should that be necessary, and to preserve the 'priority' of the mortgage. With an equitable mortgage, the new deed made it clear that it merely recorded a mortgage already created by deposit of the existing title deeds.

22.7.4 Comparison of Legal and Equitable Mortgages after 1989

An equitable mortgage may arise out of two situations:

* the parties intended to create a legal mortgage but there has been a failure to comply with the necessary formalities of a deed. For example, in *Bank of Scotland Plc v Waugh* [2014] EWHC 2117 the legal charge had not be attested according to s1(3) Law of Property (Miscellaneous Provisions) Act 1989 but was nevertheless valid as an equitable mortgage. If the transaction has complied with s2 LP(MP)A 1989 and can be enforced by specific performance, then following the maxim 'Equity treats as done that which ought to be done' and *Walsh v Lonsdale*, it will be treated as a contract for a mortgage enforceable in equity; or

* the parties have a contract to create a legal mortgage. The contract must fulfil the requirements under s2 LP(MP)A 1989, and following *Walsh v Lonsdale* if the court is able to grant specific performance as a remedy, then equity will treat this mortgage as an equitable one.

In both of these two situations, for the remedy of specific performance to be available, the mortgage money must have been advanced because equity will not force a person to make a loan.

To create an equitable mortgage after 26 September 1989, a written document will be required, signed by both parties, contracting to create or actually creating the mortgage. Thus, after 26 September 1989:

* a legal mortgage must be by deed:
  - requirements of a deed are found in s1 LP(MP)A 1989; and

* an equitable mortgage must be by a written document. This document will not be a deed, but must fulfil the requirements under s2 LP(MP)A 1989, that is:
  - in writing;
  - be signed by both parties; and
  - include all the terms of the mortgage.

22.7.5 Mortgages of Equitable Interests

Where the mortgagor has only an equitable interest, for example a life interest under a strict settlement, then it is not possible to grant a legal mortgage. The method of creating a mortgage for this type of trust interest is based on the pre-1926 rules on assignment of the whole equitable interest to the mortgagee, on the proviso that when the mortgage has been repaid the interest will be re-transferred to the mortgagor. The requirements for such a transfer must comply with s53(1)(c) LPA 1925 which require the transfer to be made in writing or by will.

22.7.6 Protecting an Equitable Mortgage

If the mortgagor's land is unregistered title an equitable mortgage would need to be registered as a Class C(iii) general equitable charge. This would only apply where the mortgagee does not take the title deeds to the property mortgaged. Where there is an equitable mortgage and the mortgagee takes the title deeds there is no requirement to register the land charge.

In registered land the equitable mortgage which is referred to as an equitable charge must be registered as a notice on the mortgagor's register of title (s32 LRA 2002). This will give the details of the chargee (the lender) as the proprietor of a charge on the registered estate (s59(2) LRA 2002). This ensures that any subsequent mortgagees know that there is already an equitable charge on the property.

Concluding Remarks

It is hoped that you are already beginning to appreciate the emphasis placed on historical evolution in the introduction to this chapter. Historical evolution explains why, even after 1925, the form of a legal mortgage with its legal redemption date and (unstated) equitable right to redeem, defies common sense and 'the light of nature'.

As will be confirmed by later chapters, the legal evolution of the law of mortgages most certainly did not end in 1925. Indeed, as we have just seen, Parliament made quite a drastic change to equitable mortgages in 1989. In the next chapter we will see further modern contributions to the evolution, not just from Parliament, but also from the courts.

Summary

It is no longer possible to mortgage land by a conveyance of the freehold.

Legal Mortgages post 1925

These invariably take the form of a charge by way of legal mortgage. Such 'charges' usually still include a nominal 'legal redemption date' requiring repayment after only six months.

Nobody expects repayment on the nominal date. Once that date is past, the mortgagor has an 'equitable right to redeem' which continues indefinitely.

The 'equity of redemption' is the phrase used to cover all the rights which the mortgagor enjoys pending repayment of the mortgage.

Unregistered Land

Legal Mortgage of a Fee Simple post 1925

Two methods, by which a legal mortgage can be created are:

- mortgage by demise (long lease); and
- charge by way of legal mortgage.

First Mortgage Triggers First Registration

- Compulsory registration of the mortgagor's estate (ss 4(1)(g) and 6(2)(a) LRA 2002).
- Mortgage will be registered as a charge on the mortgagor's register of title—must be done within two months of disposition.

Mortgages of Leases post 1925

- Sub-lease with a proviso for cesser on redemption.
- Charge by way of legal mortgage.

Equitable Mortgages

There are two situations where an equitable mortgage of a legal estate may arise (note: deposit of deeds—no longer available; this form of mortgage was abolished by s2 LP(MP)A 1989):

- transaction intended as mortgage not by deed but complying with s2 LP(MP)A 1989;
- contract to create a legal mortgage complying with s2.

Protecting an Equitable Mortgage

- Registration as Class C(iii) land charge—applies only if mortgagee does not take the title deeds.
- If mortgagee has taken title deeds no need to register.

Registered Land

Legal Mortgage of a Fee Simple—LRA 1925

Two methods, by which a legal mortgage can be created, are:

- unregistered forms of mortgage: mortgage by demise; charge by way of legal mortgage; and
- most popular: registered charge.

Legal Mortgage of a Fee Simple—LRA 2002

- registered charge.

Mortgages of Registered Leases post 1925

- sub-lease with a proviso for cesser on redemption;
- registered charge. (The only form available after 2003.)

Equitable Mortgages—pre-1989

There were two main situations by which an equitable mortgage may arise:

- deposit of land certificate or charge certificate;
- contract to create a legal mortgage.

Equitable Mortgages—post 1989

- contract to create a legal mortgage;
- transaction not by deed but intended as a mortgage and complying with s2 LP(MP)A 1989.

Protecting an Equitable Mortgage

- referred to as an equitable charge—must be registered as a notice (s32 LRA 2002) on mortgagor's register of title.

 # Further Reading

Robinson, M, 'In the Chancery adventure playground' (1997) 113 LQR 533
Case comment on *United Bank of Kuwait v Sahib*.

23

The Remedies of Mortgagees

Introduction

In this chapter we meet another area of law, steeped in history, but ill-adapted to the economic realities of the twenty-first century. The continued existence of foreclosure can be explained only by history. The same is true of the mortgagee's, more or less automatic, right to take possession of the mortgaged property. As you read through this chapter you may well be surprised (perhaps indeed worried) by an apparent pro-mortgagee bias in the law. But the big 'institutional' lenders (banks, building societies, etc) will argue that they need to have means of enforcing their security quickly and cheaply. They will argue that stricter limits on mortgagees' remedies might benefit individual mortgagors, but would be against the economic interests of the country as a whole, in particular the mortgagee would be less willing to lend to any borrower who is viewed (in any way) as a risk.

Further, there is a lesson to be learnt from the (worldwide) banking crisis of autumn 2008. Put bluntly, this shows that if a bank cannot quickly recover money it has lent out, then that bank will itself be in financial difficulty.

 ## 23.1 Remedies of Legal Mortgagees—An Overview

Where the mortgagor has defaulted on the mortgage terms the mortgagee has a number of remedies available to them for enforcing the security:

- action on mortgagor's covenant to repay;
- taking possession;
- sale;
- appointing a receiver; and
- foreclosure.

The remedies of foreclosure and taking possession stem from the fact that (pre 1926) the mortgagee held the fee simple in the land subject to the mortgagor's equitable right to redeem. By contrast, the remedies of sale and appointing a receiver were originally conferred by express provision in the mortgage deed, but are now conferred on mortgagees by statutory provisions. Moreover, these remedies (unlike foreclosure and possession) can be exercised without taking court proceedings. However, mortgagees who want to sell the property will, in modern economic conditions, almost certainly want to sell with vacant possession. They may therefore need a court order giving vacant possession before putting the property on the market. Nevertheless, it should be stressed that it is possible for a mortgage lender to sell the property while it is still occupied by the borrower (or his/her tenants).

A mortgagee can exercise any or all of the remedies, including an action in contract, in combination, provided the total amount recovered does not exceed the total capital and interest owed.

23.2 Action on a Mortgagor's Covenant to Repay

Where a mortgagor has defaulted on the repayments of the loan, the mortgagee has the option to sue in contract to recover the debt owed. In the mortgage contract there will be a specific personal covenant where the mortgagor promises to repay the loan. This remedy is available to the mortgagee even if the mortgagee chooses to exercise their right to use any one of the other remedies.

This remedy is normally used in cases where there is negative equity (ie where the debt owed exceeds the value of the property). The mortgagee would be seeking to recover the outstanding amount still owed following the sale of the property. In this type of situation the mortgagor may be insolvent and the mortgagee merely becomes an unsecured creditor for the money outstanding.

Under s20(1) Limitation Act 1980, the mortgagee must bring their action to recover capital within 12 years from the date of the right to receive the money accrued. If the mortgagee seeks to claim arrears of interest, they are statute barred after six years (s20(5) Limitation Act 1980).

23.3 Mortgagees Taking Possession

pause for thought

'... the right of the mortgagee to possession in the absence of some contract has nothing to do with default on the part of the mortgagor. The mortgagee may go into possession before the ink is dry on the mortgage unless there is something in the contract, express or by implication, whereby he has contracted himself out of that right' (per Harman J in Four Maids Ltd v Dudley Marshall (Properties) Ltd [1957] Ch 317).

Why does a mortgagee have the right to take possession immediately the mortgage is made?

You should remember that in the past (pre-1926) a mortgagee had an estate in the mortgaged land, while nowadays a mortgagee's 'charge by way of legal mortgage' gives the mortgagee rights equivalent to an estate. The mortgagee can assert those rights at any time and say, 'give me control of what is (in effect) my land', subject to any agreement to the contrary. Similarly under s87(1) Law of Property Act 1925 (LPA 1925) the legal chargee in registered land also has this right.

The Court of Appeal has reaffirmed the validity of the principle that a mortgagee is entitled to possession at any time he chooses. This includes taking possession before the legal date of redemption has passed and importantly, before any default on the part of the mortgagor. In *Ropaigealach v Barclays Bank Plc* [2000] QB 263, Clarke LJ said:

> ...in the absence of a provision to the contrary in the mortgage, a mortgagee has a right of immediate possession (as the ink dries on the document). Although I suspect that many mortgagors would be astonished to discover that a bank which had lent them money to buy a property for them to live in could take possession of it the next day...if a mortgagee chooses to take possession and moreover to do so by using reasonable force to remove the mortgagor there is nothing that the mortgagor can do about it.

Furthermore, in two cases a mortgagee was held entitled to assert its immediate right to possession of the mortgaged property, notwithstanding substantial counterclaims for unliquidated damages brought by the mortgagors which, if valid, would totally extinguish the mortgagors' debts: *Ashley Guarantee v Zacaria* [1993] 1 All ER 254; *National Westminster Bank plc v Skelton* [1993] 1 All ER 242.

In practice, of course, mortgagees are content to allow the mortgagor to keep possession, and will take possession only if things start going wrong. The usual reason for taking possession is in order to sell with vacant possession and recoup the capital. The desirability of selling with vacant possession is so great that if a mortgagee's court proceedings for possession are in some way delayed, the sale is (speaking from a practical point of view) also delayed.

Where the mortgaged property is let, because of the priority of the lease over the mortgage or consent to letting the property was granted by the mortgagee, the mortgagee cannot take physical possession but the mortgagee will take possession in the sense that they will continue to receive the rent to fulfil arrears. In this situation the mortgagee would normally appoint a receiver to manage the property.

23.3.1 Court Proceedings for Possession Brought by a Mortgagee

As we have mentioned previously, as a general principle the mortgagee's right to possession is not in any way dependent on default by the mortgagor. It flows from the fact that a mortgagee has an estate in the land mortgaged, or rights equivalent to an estate. Despite the fact that the mortgagee has the right to possession, the mortgagee will not (in reality) seek possession whenever they choose. In the normal course of events, the mortgagee will only initiate possession proceedings if the mortgagor has defaulted on their payments.

At common law the mortgagee can take physical possession of the property without resorting to a possession order from the court if this can be achieved without the use or threat of violence (*Ropaigealach v Barclays Bank Plc* [2000]). This would normally only happen where the property is unoccupied. Where the mortgagor is still in possession it is rare that the mortgagee will use peaceable re-entry for fear of criminal or civil liability. For example, under s6(1) Criminal Law Act 1977, it is an offence for any person without lawful authority to use or threaten violence for the purpose of securing entry into premises if they know that there is someone present who opposes their entry.

A mortgagee seeking possession in practice always seeks a court possession order. Prior to 1970 proceedings were normally brought in the Chancery Division. As a general principle the court's inherent jurisdiction to adjourn proceedings or deny an order for possession is very limited. Nowadays, unless the mortgaged property is a house within Greater London, a mortgagee's possession proceedings must be brought in the County Court. This rule, which applies irrespective of the value of the house, is designed to avoid a provincial house-owner from having their case dealt with in London.

The court has inherent jurisdiction to grant temporary relief to the mortgagor. In *Birmingham Citizens Permanent Building Society v Caunt* [1962] Ch 883, the court allowed the application for possession proceedings to be adjourned for a short period of time (28 days) to allow the mortgagor to pay off the entire debt. The court went on to say that if there is no reasonable prospect of the whole debt being paid then the court will not adjourn proceedings. In the context of residential mortgages, mortgagors would find it virtually impossible to pay off the whole debt within 28 days.

23.3.2 Mortgagee Taking Possession of a Dwelling House

The court's inherent jurisdiction used in *Birmingham Citizens Permanent Building Society v Caunt* provided a limited amount of relief for mortgagors during possession proceedings. Parliament introduced s36 Administration of Justice Act 1970 (AJA 1970) in response to a review undertaken by the Payne Committee in 1969.

Section 36 AJA 1970 gives the court a wide discretion to adjourn possession proceedings, or to make a possession order but suspend its operation. The aim is to give mortgagors time to find the money and also, in the meantime, protect the mortgagors in their homes. Section 36 was very much a response to a social problem in the late 1960s. Less reputable mortgagees had taken possession of houses (with a view to selling with vacant possession), even though there had been no default (or no serious default) by the mortgagor.

Administration of Justice Act 1970

36. Additional powers of court in action by mortgagee for possession of dwelling-house

(1) Where the mortgagee under a mortgage of land which consists of or includes a dwelling-house brings an action in which he claims possession of the mortgaged property, not being an action for foreclosure in which a claim for possession of the mortgaged property is also made, the court may exercise any of the powers conferred on it by subsection (2) below if it appears to the court that in the event of its exercising the power the mortgagor is likely to be able within a reasonable period to pay any sums due under the mortgage or to remedy a default consisting of a breach of any other obligation arising under or by virtue of the mortgage.

(2) The court—

 (a) may adjourn the proceedings, or

 (b) on giving judgment, or making an order, for delivery of possession of the mortgaged property, or at any time before the execution of such judgment or order, may—

  (i) stay or suspend execution of the judgment or order, or

  (ii) postpone the date for delivery of possession, for such period or periods as the court thinks reasonable.

(3) Any such adjournment, stay, suspension or postponement as is referred to in subsection (2) above may be made subject to such conditions with regard to payment by the mortgagor of any sum secured by the mortgage or the remedying of any default as the court thinks fit.

Under s36, the power to adjourn or suspend exists if it appears to the court that it is likely that the mortgagor will be able to repay within a 'reasonable period', 'any sums due under the mortgage' (ie the whole capital debt). The adjournment or suspension can be made on conditions, for example 'the possession order is made but suspended for one year on condition that the mortgagor repays the debt at X pounds per month'; or 'I adjourn the proceedings for six months provided you repay half the debt in two months' time and the other half before the six months is up'.

The jurisdiction of s36 only extends to mortgagees applying for a possession order. Clarke LJ reluctantly acknowledged in *Ropaigealach v Barclays Bank Plc* [2000] QB 263 that the exercise of the common law right of possession by peaceable re-entry did not come within the scope of s36 AJA 1970. Clarke LJ said:

> I agree, although I must confess that I do so with considerable reluctance. The effect of construing section 36 of the Administration of Justice Act 1970 (as extended by section 8 of the Administration of Justice Act 1973) in the manner proposed is that there is what appears to me to be a curious anomaly in the powers of the court to afford relief to mortgagors against mortgagees who wish to take possession of mortgaged dwelling houses. It is not in dispute that, where a mortgagee takes proceedings for possession, the court has power under section 36 in some circumstances to stop the mortgagee from taking possession. Those circumstances are where it appears to the court that if it exercises its power the mortgagor is likely within a reasonable period to pay the sums due under the mortgage or to remedy a relevant default under the mortgage, as the case might be.

The fact that s36 only applies where the mortgagee takes possession proceedings was highlighted by Briggs J in *Horsham Properties Group v Clark* [2009] 1 WLR 1295.

The defendant mortgagors (borrowers) fell into arrears with their repayments. The lenders (acting through a receiver) exercised their power of sale under s101 LPA 1925 without taking proceedings for possession of the house. They sold the house at auction to purchasers who then sold the property on to Horsham Properties Group. These sales took place with the defendant borrowers still living in the house.

Horsham sued to evict the defendants as trespassers. Their claim succeeded. Briggs J held:

1 That applying s101 LPA 1925 the sale by auction overreached the defendants' rights (their equity of redemption) and that the defendants were therefore trespassers vis-à-vis the purchasers.
2 This result was unaffected by the Human Rights Act 1998 and the guarantee in the First Protocol to the European Convention on Human Rights of 'free enjoyment of possessions'. The mortgagee's power of sale, with or without vacant possession, is part of the bargain struck when the mortgage is entered into, so the mortgagor cannot complain when that part of the bargain is invoked.

The practical result of *Horsham Properties* is worrying. The mortgagee can avoid the protections provided by ss34–36 AJA 1970 if the mortgagee can find a purchaser who is willing to buy without vacant possession. On completion, the purchaser can evict the mortgagor(s) as trespasser(s). However, it appears that institutional lenders are not taking advantage of the *Horsham Properties* decision.

A Further 'Reform' in 1973

Section 36 originally proved rather ineffective, because judges, even in instalment mortgage cases, initially interpreted the phrase 'any sums due' to mean the whole capital debt. In *Halifax Building Society v Clark* [1973] Ch 307, the mortgagor failed to pay two consecutive monthly instalment payments and his arrears amounted to £100. The mortgage agreement contained a clause which required the repayment of the entire loan in the event of missing two consecutive payments. The amount outstanding was £1,420. The court did not take advantage of the discretion to adjourn possession proceedings due to two reasons. First, the interpretation of 'any sums due' by the court meant the whole debt, and not the instalments that were due. Secondly, there was no likelihood of the mortgagor or his wife being able to pay the entire debt 'within a reasonable period'.

This defect was rectified by the enactment of s8 Administration of Justice Act 1973, which operates where the mortgage in question is an instalment mortgage. Under s8, an adjournment of possession proceedings or a suspended possession order can be granted if it is likely that within a reasonable period the mortgagor will be able to pay off arrears of instalments (if any) and meet any further instalments which fall due within that reasonable period.

> *Administration of Justice Act 1973*
>
> 8. Extension of powers of court in action by mortgagee of dwelling-house
>
> (1) Where by a mortgage of land which consists of or includes a dwelling-house, or by any agreement between the mortgagee under such a mortgage and the mortgagor, the mortgagor is entitled or is to be permitted to pay the principal sum secured by instalments or otherwise to defer payment of it in whole or in part, but provision is also made for earlier payment in the event of any default by the mortgagor or of a demand by the mortgagee or otherwise, then for purposes of section 36 of the Administration of Justice Act 1970 (under which a court has power to delay giving a mortgagee possession of the mortgaged property so as to allow the mortgagor a reasonable time to pay any sums due under the mortgage) a court may treat as due under the mortgage on account of the principal sum secured and of interest on it only such amounts as the mortgagor would have expected to be required to pay if there had been no such provision for earlier payment.
>
> (2) A court shall not exercise by virtue of subsection (1) above the powers conferred by section 36 of the Administration of Justice Act 1970 unless it appears to the court not only that the mortgagor is likely to be able within a reasonable period to pay any amounts regarded (in accordance with subsection (1) above) as due on account of the principal sum secured, together with the interest on those amounts, but also that he is likely to be able by the end of that period to pay any further amounts that he would have expected to be required to pay by then on account of that sum and of interest on it if there had been no such provision as is referred to in subsection (1) above for earlier payment.

cross-reference
See example (2) at 22.5 which illustrates this point.

Section 8(1) defines 'any sums due under the mortgage' as the amounts the mortgagor would have to pay if there had been no provision requiring the entire debt to be paid in the event of default in payments. Consequently, any clause making the whole capital debt repayable if instalments are in arrears is to be ignored when applying s8 of the 1973 Act.

Under s8(2) the court will only adjourn possession proceedings where the mortgagor is likely to be able to pay within a reasonable period the outstanding amounts due (ie outstanding instalments) and the interest. It is also clear that the court will take into account whether it is likely that the mortgagor will be able to continue to meet the repayments.

thinking point 23.1

Could you express this point in another (perhaps clearer) way?

The mortgagee will not get an order for immediate possession if the mortgagor can show that he is (within a reasonable period) likely to catch up with the instalments.

Reasonable Period

But what is a 'reasonable' period for the court to allow the mortgagor to catch up with the instalments? The period of time must be fixed and the date when the 'reasonable period' ends must be specified (*Royal Trust Co of Canada v Markham* [1975] 1 WLR 1416).

A relaxed interpretation of 'reasonable period' was first shown in *Cheltenham and Gloucester Building Society v Grant* (1994) 26 HLR 703. The Grants purchased a property with the assistance of a mortgage. At the time, Grant was working in the building trade. His wife left him. To look after their son, Grant had to give up work. Although he claimed income support it was not sufficient to meet his mortgage payments. He defaulted on his payments and the claimants commenced possession proceedings. Grant claimed that he would return to work when his son was older. The district judge suspended possession proceedings for one year to give Grant the opportunity to 'get on his feet again'. The Court of Appeal noted that although Grant's prospects of obtaining employment within the year were 'extremely unspecific', it did not justify interfering with the discretion used by the district judge.

The district and county court judges at first did not have specific guidance on what amounted to a 'reasonable period' of time, or as to factors to be taken into account when considering whether the mortgagor can pay the arrears and current instalments. Until 1996, the time period that tended to be given to allow the mortgagor to catch up with their arrears was 'a year, two or three years at most'. The decision of the Court of Appeal in *Cheltenham and Gloucester Building Society v Norgan* [1996] 1 WLR 343 thus came as a considerable surprise.

In *Cheltenham and Gloucester Building Society v Norgan* the Court of Appeal held that with an instalment mortgage a 'reasonable period' means the full remaining period of the mortgage. In *Norgan*'s case the mortgage was an instalment mortgage created in 1986 and repayable over 22 years. The court in effect held that Mrs Norgan would be entitled to the protection of s8 provided she could show that she would have caught up with her instalments by 2008. To put it mildly, this case represented a considerable shift in the law in favour of mortgagors.

The court, in effect, restructured the payment schedule in order to keep the mortgage alive. The court took into consideration the policy document adopted by the lenders published by the Council of Mortgage Lenders (CML). This document provided guidance to members on the devices available to them in the event of mortgage arrears and possession cases, for example the term of the loan can be extended for repayment mortgages and the interest to be paid on the mortgage can be deferred for a period if the mortgagor has a shortfall in income. Included in this policy document was a statement that lenders would only take possession as a last resort.

Waite LJ adopted a purposive interpretation of the legislation saying:

> it does seem to me that the logic and spirit of the legislation require, especially in cases where the parties are proceeding under arrangements such as those reflected in the C.M.L. statement, that the court should take as its starting point the full term of the mortgage and pose at the outset the question: 'Would it be possible for the mortgagor to maintain payment-off of the arrears by instalments over that period?'

Waite LJ went on to say:

> ...I would acknowledge, also, that this approach will be liable to demand a more detailed analysis of present figures and future projections than it may have been customary for the courts to undertake until now. There is likely to be a greater need to require of mortgagors that they should furnish the court with a detailed 'budget' of the kind that has been supplied by the mortgagor in her affidavit in the present case...There may also be cases, as [counsel for the claimant] points out, in which it is less obvious than in this case that the mortgagee is adequately secured—and detailed evidence, if necessary by experts, may be required to see if and when the lender's security will become liable to be put at risk as a result of imposing postponement of payments in arrear. Problems such as these—which I suspect will arise only rarely in practice although they will undeniably be daunting when they do arise—should

not however be allowed, in my judgment, to stand in the way of giving effect to the clearly intended scheme of the legislation.

There is another factor which, to my mind, weighs strongly in favour of adopting the full term of the mortgage as the starting point for calculating a 'reasonable period' for payment of arrears. It is prompted by experience in this very case. The parties have been before the court with depressing frequency over the years on applications to enforce, or further to suspend, the warrant of possession, while Mrs. Norgan and her husband have struggled, sometimes with success and sometimes without, to meet whatever commitment was currently approved by the court. Cheltenham has (in exercise of its power to do so under the terms of the mortgage) added to its security the costs it has incurred in connection with all these attendances … It is an experience which brings home the disadvantages which both lender and borrower are liable to suffer if frequent attendance before the court becomes necessary as a result of multiple applications under section 36 of the Act of 1970 … One advantage of taking the period most favourable to the mortgagor at the outset is that, if his or her hopes of repayment prove to be ill-founded and the new instalments initially ordered as a condition of suspension are not maintained but themselves fall into arrear, the mortgagee can be heard with justice to say that the mortgagor has had his chance, and that the section 36 powers (although of course capable in theory of being exercised again and again) should not be employed repeatedly to compel a lending institution which has already suffered interruption of the regular flow of interest to which it was entitled under the express terms of the mortgage to accept assurances of future payment from a borrower in whom it has lost confidence …

In view of the long history of this litigation, and the anxiety it has involved, in particular for Mrs. Norgan and her family, it would have been the wish of this court to determine all outstanding issues for ourselves, so that each side might have left this court knowing exactly where they stood. But, as Evans L.J. made clear to the parties at the hearing, there are too many matters unresolved, on evidence which is still not wholly complete, to enable us to do so. I would therefore allow the appeal and remit the case to the county court for (1) a determination of the disputed items and a finding as to what precisely is now, or (as the case may be) will at the expiry of the mortgage term be, due from the mortgagor on capital and interest instalment account respectively—including in the latter account a precise figure for the current interest in arrear; (2) a calculation of (a) the instalments which the mortgagor would be required to pay if the arrears so found were to be made payable by instalments over the whole of the remaining period of the mortgage term and (b) the instalments of interest currently due under the mortgage; (3) a determination of the question whether, in the light of the court's findings as to the current and prospective ability of the mortgagor to discharge the instalments under (2)(a) and (b), there are any unusual circumstances justifying a departure from the remaining term of the mortgage as the period that is prima facie 'reasonable' for the purposes of section 36 of the Act of 1970 and section 8 of the Act of 1973; (4) a determination of the question whether, in the light of its conclusions under (1) (2) and (3), this would be a suitable case in which to exercise the court's discretion to suspend the warrant of possession for any and if so what period.

Waite LJ in reaching his conclusion suggested that mortgagors would need to provide evidence of a detailed financial plan which could be analysed to determine the viability of the mortgagor's payment schedule. There was a warning for mortgagors who have already defaulted once and had their payments restructured. If they default again, the mortgagee is justified to say 'the mortgagor has had his chance' and the court may be less willing to entertain another adjournment of possession proceedings. The court has taken this stance because in the court's view, they have exercised a wide discretion by using the full remaining term of the mortgage as a starting point for restructuring mortgage payments.

Evans LJ persuaded by the Council of Mortgage Lenders policy document on 'Alleviating Arrears Problems' said '[g]iven these statements of policy, I do not see how the plaintiffs can properly say that it is not appropriate to take account of the whole of the remaining part of the original term when assessing a "reasonable period" for the payment of arrears'. Evans LJ also provided guidance on the type of considerations that are likely to be relevant in determining 'reasonable period', these include:

> (a) How much can the borrower reasonably afford to pay, both now and in the future? (b) If the borrower has a temporary difficulty in meeting his obligations, how long is the difficulty likely to last? (c) What was the reason for the arrears which have accumulated? (d) How much remains of the original term? (e) What are relevant contractual terms, and what type of mortgage is it, i.e. when is the principal due to be repaid? (f) Is it a case where the court should exercise its power to disregard accelerated payment provisions (section 8 of the Act of 1973)? (g) Is it reasonable to expect the lender, in the circumstances of the particular case, to recoup the arrears of interest (1) over the whole of the original term, or (2) within a shorter period, or even (3) within a longer period, i.e. by extending the repayment period? Is it reasonable to expect the lender to capitalise the interest or not? (h) Are there any reasons affecting the security which should influence the length of the period for payment? In the light of the answers to the above, the court can proceed to exercise its overall discretion, taking account also of any further factors which may arise in the particular case.

From this passage it is clear that the court will not exercise its discretion if there is no realistic likelihood of the arrears and current instalments being paid. It is crucial that mortgagors show evidence that they have a realistic ability to meet the payments which include current instalments, arrears, interest, and other sums that come within the scope of the mortgage. It is only under those circumstances that the court will effectively rewrite the payment schedule for possibly the remaining length of the mortgage. It is worth noting that the payment schedule for paying off the arrears can be a shorter period of time than the remaining length of the mortgage. This is illustrated by *Bank of Scotland Plc v Zinda* [2012] 1 WLR 728, where the County Court had postponed possession for nine and a half years even though the mortgage had 23 years to run. This approach was not questioned by the Court of Appeal.

Possibly surprisingly, no building society or other institutional lender has tried to challenge *Norgan* in the House of Lords or Supreme Court. This is probably because *Norgan* does have one advantage for institutional lenders. *Norgan* forces borrowers who get into difficulties to consider their position long term. The borrower who wants to invoke the Administration of Justice Acts to prevent the mortgagee taking possession must now come to court armed with long-term financial plans.

REVIEW QUESTION In the light of *Norgan*, do you think *Grant* would have been decided in the same way today? What factors would the court take into consideration in deciding whether to exercise their discretion?

Can the Mortgagor Sell the Property to Pay Off the Mortgage Debt?

A situation may arise where there is substantial positive equity in a house, the mortgagor is in arrears with instalments and will not be able to catch up within a reasonable time, and the mortgagor wants to sell the property. The mortgagor may well be able to get a higher price than the mortgagee who is selling a repossessed property under a forced sale. In this situation the County Courts are willing to make a suspended possession order against the mortgagor, thus enabling them to conduct a sale during the period of the suspension. It seems that the suspension is likely to be between three and 12 months, depending on the exact circumstances of the case.

In the Court of Appeal decision in *National and Provincial Building Society v Lloyd* (1996) 28 HLR 459 it was held that, where the mortgagor wishes to sell, possession proceedings could be adjourned or suspended for a 'reasonable period' of six or nine months or a year. Neill LJ said:

> It is true that both at common law (see the decision of Russell J. in *Caunt*...), and in the passages to which I have referred in the more recent cases since the enactment of section 36 of the Administration of Justice Act 1970, it has been said that in the case of the sale of mortgaged property the adjournment or suspension which will be allowed will only be allowed if a sale will take place within a short period of time... if there were, in a hypothetical case, clear evidence that the completion of the sale of a property, perhaps by piecemeal disposal, could take place in six or nine months or even a year, I see no reason why a court could not come to the conclusion in the exercise of its discretion under the two sections that, to use the words of the section, 'the mortgagor was likely to be able within a reasonable period to pay any sums due under the mortgage.' The question of a 'reasonable period' would be a question for the court, in the individual case.

In this case, the defendant had fallen into arrears but was optimistic that he would be able to sell some smallholdings to cover the arrears. The principle in *Norgan* of giving the mortgagor 'a proper opportunity of making good their default' and that of respecting the interests of both parties was also considered by the court. Despite the defendant's optimism towards the sale of the smallholdings, the court did not feel that there was sufficient realistic evidence of a likely sale and declined to suspend possession.

Are the courts willing to entertain a prolonged postponement? This was an issue that the court in *Bristol and West Building Society v Ellis* (1997) 73 P & CR 158 had to consider. Ellis had arrears amounting to £16,000 and the outstanding capital sum of £60,000. In evidence to the court she could pay a lump sum of £5,000 and an additional £10 per month towards the arrears. It was her intention to discharge her debt by selling the house after her children had completed their university education which she anticipated to be three to five years. She produced two estate agents' valuations of her property which indicated that if she was to sell, the proceeds from sale would be sufficient to cover her mortgage debt. Possession was suspended and she was ordered to pay the additional £10 per month towards the arrears. The building society appealed claiming that it would take Ellis 98 years to pay off the arrears and that suspending possession for three to five years was not reasonable in terms of s36 AJA 1970.

Auld LJ:

> Mr Duggan, on behalf of the building society sought to extract from [*Lloyd*] a principle that a year is about the maximum period that a court could consider reasonable for this purpose. Whilst that may be a likely maximum in many cases, I do not read Neill L.J.'s words as establishing it as a rule of law or as a matter of general guidance. It all depends on the individual circumstances of each case, though the important factors in most are likely to be the extent to which the mortgage debt and arrears are secured by the value of the property and the effect of time on that security.
>
> Where the property is already on the market and there is some indication of delay on the part of the mortgagor, it may be that a short period of suspension of only a few months would be reasonable. Where there is likely to be considerable delay in selling the property and/or its value is close to the total of the mortgage debt and arrears so that the mortgagee is at risk as to the adequacy of the security, immediate possession or only a short period of suspension may be reasonable. Where there has already been considerable delay in realising a sale of the property and/or the likely sale proceeds are unlikely to cover the mortgage debt and arrears or there is simply no sufficient evidence as to sale value, the normal order would be for immediate possession...

Having explained the law, Auld LJ then applied the law to the facts.

…As to the time of sale, all that the district judge had was her statement in her affidavit that she anticipated selling within three to five years when her children completed their education. As to value, the evidence was not compelling: two estate agents' estimates of between £80,000 and £85,000 as against the redemption figure at the time of just over £77,000 plus costs. As a result of Mrs Ellis's payment of the lump sum ordered by the district judge and subsequent payments, the total figure of indebtedness is now about £70,000, including about £10,000 arrears of interest. Given the inevitable uncertainty as to the movement of property values over the next few years and the reserve with which the courts should approach estate agents' estimates of sale prices [see *Clothier* [1994] 1 All ER 439 at 455, per Nolan LJ] no court could be sanguine about the adequacy, now or continuing over that period, of the property as a security for the mortgage debt and arrears. In my view, the evidence was simply insufficient to entitle the district judge to contemplate, behind the order he made, a likelihood that the house would or could be sold at a price sufficient to discharge Mrs Ellis's overall debt to Bristol & West within any reasonable period, and certainly not one of up to three to five years.

In situations where the mortgagor wishes to make the sale, the suspension of possession proceedings for the sale of the property for the duration of the remaining mortgage term is clearly out of the question.

A Possible Lifeline to Mortgagors with Negative Equity?

In the previous section we considered the situation where mortgagors want to sell their property to pay off the mortgage debt. In some cases this has been possible where there has been sufficient positive equity in the property and there is a realistic prospect of a purchaser buying the property. The issue we are now considering is the approach adopted by the courts towards mortgagors wishing to sell where there is negative equity.

The mortgagor may apply for an order of sale to the High Court under s91 LPA 1925.

Law of Property Act 1925

91. Sale of mortgaged property in action for redemption or foreclosure

(1) Any person entitled to redeem mortgaged property may have a judgment or order for sale instead of for redemption in an action brought by him either for redemption alone, or for sale alone, or for sale or redemption in the alternative.

(2) In any action, whether for foreclosure, or for redemption, or for sale, or for the raising and payment in any manner of mortgage money, the court, on the request of the mortgagee, or of any person interested either in the mortgage money or in the right of redemption, and, notwithstanding that—

(a) any other person dissents; or

(b) the mortgagee or any person so interested does not appear in the action;

and without allowing any time for redemption or for payment of any mortgage money, may direct a sale of the mortgaged property, on such terms as it thinks fit, including the deposit in court of a reasonable sum fixed by the court to meet the expenses of sale and to secure performance of the terms.

In *Palk v Mortgage Services Funding plc* [1993] Ch 330 the Palks owned a house encumbered with a debt amounting to £358,000. They had found a prospective purchaser willing to pay just £283,000, and they wanted to sell the property and make up the difference out of their personal resources.

The mortgagee refused to agree to this, and took proceedings for possession. It was the mortgagee's intention not to sell the house until 'the market improved', and in the meantime to let the house to a tenant. It was clear that the rent obtainable would be substantially less than the interest continuing to accrue. Thus the amount owed by the Palks would steadily increase, as would the amount of 'negative equity'.

The Palks thus faced an ever-increasing debt and (presumably) eventual bankruptcy. They therefore applied for and obtained an order of sale under s91(2) LPA 1925, a hitherto little known provision of the 1925 Act which gives the court a discretion to order the sale of mortgaged property. In making the order for sale the Court of Appeal stressed that a mortgagee must not exercise its various powers in a manner wholly unfair to the mortgagor.

Sir Donald Nicholls V-C said:

A new problem

So far as I am aware, foreclosure actions are almost unheard of today and have been so for many years. Mortgagees prefer to exercise other remedies. They usually appoint a receiver or exercise their powers of sale. Take the present case: the security is inadequate, but Mortgage Services is not seeking to foreclose, nor is it seeking to sell at once. It is seeking to hold on to the house, preferably without becoming accountable as a mortgagee in possession, with a view to exercising its own power of sale at some future date. It is seeking to do this despite the income shortfall mentioned above. The 19th century cases were not concerned with this situation. The principle applied in those cases does not address the problem which has now arisen.

Underlying the present case is not merely a disagreement between a mortgagor and a mortgagee about the likely future trend of house prices. I suspect that probably another feature is a difference in their attitudes towards taking risks. We were told that Mortgage Services has many properties in a similar situation and that this case raises an important question of principle for the company. A substantial lender may be prepared to take risks that would be imprudent for a householder with limited financial resources.

There is also the further feature that the interests of the mortgagor and the mortgagee do not march hand in hand in all respects. The security afforded by the house is not the only remedy possessed by Mortgage Services: the company also has a personal claim against Mrs. Palk. If the property market does not improve as Mortgage Services hopes, and so the shortfall ultimately becomes larger than it is now, the company can have recourse against Mrs. Palk for the increased shortfall. Hence, it is said, Mortgage Services is intent on speculating at Mrs. Palk's expense. If its gamble on property prices fails, the company can still go against Mrs. Palk . . .

The thrust of Mortgage Services' answer is that, in exchange for the loan, it acquired a security and several remedies. The company may choose which remedy it wishes to pursue and when, so long as it acts in good faith and not for some collateral purpose. It may choose the time of sale, however disadvantageous this may be for the mortgagor. If it decides to sell, it must exercise reasonable care to obtain the proper market value, but it is under no duty to exercise its power of sale. Mr. Lightman relied on the observations of Lord Templeman in *China and South Sea Bank Ltd. v. Tan Soon Gin* [alias George Tan] [1990] 1 A.C. 536, 545:

> 'If the creditor chose to exercise his power of sale over the mortgaged security he must sell for the current market value but the creditor must decide in his own interest if and when he should sell.'

Thus, he submitted, if the mortgagee decides to postpone a sale indefinitely, there is no occasion for the court to intervene . . .

A duty to be fair

The first observation I make on this argument is to emphasise that a mortgagee does owe some duties to a mortgagor. As Lord Templeman noted in the *China and South Sea Bank* case, at p. 545, a mortgagee can sit back and do nothing. He is not obliged to take steps to realise his security. But if he does take steps to exercise his rights over his security, common law and equity alike have set bounds to the extent to which he can look after himself and ignore the mortgagor's interests. In the exercise of his rights over his security the mortgagee must act fairly towards the mortgagor. His interest in the property has priority over the interest of the mortgagor, and he is entitled to proceed on that footing. He can protect his own interest, but he is not entitled to conduct himself in a way which unfairly prejudices the mortgagor. If he takes possession he might prefer to do nothing and bide his time, waiting indefinitely for an improvement in the market, with the property empty meanwhile. That he cannot do. He is accountable for his actual receipts from the property. He is also accountable to the mortgagor for what he would have received but for his default. So he must take reasonable care to maximise his return from the property. He must also take reasonable care of the property. Similarly if he sells the property: he cannot sell hastily at a knock-down price sufficient to pay off his debt. The mortgagor also has an interest in the property and is under a personal liability for the shortfall. The mortgagee must keep that in mind. He must exercise reasonable care to sell only at the proper market value . . .

Sir Donald Nicholls V-C had no difficulty with the mortgagee's duties of obtaining a proper market rent and, if selling, a proper market price where there was positive equity. Concern was raised over situations involving negative equity, because 'the borrower is in the mortgagee's hands'. Sir Donald Nicholls V-C continued:

Whether in that situation a mortgagee is at liberty to exercise his rights of leasing and sale in a way that in all likelihood will substantially increase the burden on the borrower or guarantor beyond what otherwise would be the case is not a question I need decide on this appeal, for a reason I shall mention later. That he can act in such a cavalier fashion is not a proposition I find attractive. That is a question which may call for careful examination on another occasion. For present purposes it is sufficent to note that, quite apart from section 91(2), there is a legal framework which imposes some constraints of fairness on a mortgagee who is exercising his remedies over his security.

In the present case Mortgage Services is exercising its rights over the house . . . If the situation had been that the rental would exceed or equal or at least approach the interest she would save if the house were sold, it might have been reasonable for the company to decide to postpone the sale and to let the house for the time being. In the long run property prices can be expected to recover, so postponing the sale would be in the company's interest and would be unlikely to be prejudicial to Mrs. Palk. That is not the situation. Mortgage Services intends to let the property, despite the income shortfall: the rentals to be credited to Mrs. Palk will fall significantly short of the interest she would save if the house were sold. This is an important feature of this case. Unless good fortune shines on the parties, she is bound to suffer financially by a postponement of the sale . . . [Mortgage services] commercial judgment is that it is likely to do better by waiting. In other words, it hopes that house prices will not merely rise but that they will do so at a rate which will compensate for the financial disadvantage suffered by postponing receipt of the proceeds of sale . . .

However, and this is my second observation on the mortgagees' argument, whether in these circumstances Mortgage Services is in breach of any duty it owes to Mrs. Palk is not a crucial question on this appeal, for this reason: an exercise by the court of its statutory power to direct a sale even against the wishes of Mortgage Services is not dependent on there first having been a breach of duty by the company. The discretion given to the court by section 91(2) is not hedged about with preconditions. The question on this appeal is how ought the court to exercise its discretion under the statute in the particular circumstances and against the background that a mortgagee owes at least some duties in law to a mortgagor when exercising his rights over the mortgaged property. That Mortgage Services is not, or may not be, in breach of any duty it owes Mrs. Palk is only one of the circumstances to be taken into account.

The court's discretion

I turn therefore to the question of discretion. As to this, the features which strike me most forcibly are, first, the unfairness of Mrs. Palk being compelled to participate in and underwrite the risk Mortgage Services wishes to take. If Mortgage Services wishes to chance its arm, and run the risk involved in waiting to see what happens to house prices, it should be free to do so. In common fairness, however, it ought not to be able to saddle Mrs. Palk with that risk and a rising debt against her wishes...The second notable feature is that the primary objective of the company can be achieved without Mrs. Palk being compelled to become an unwilling risk-taker. If Mortgage Services takes over the property at current market value, it can obtain for itself the benefit of any improvement in house prices. This result would strike a fair balance between the interests of the parties.

Section 91(2) gives the court a discretion in wide terms. The discretion is unfettered. It can be exercised at any time. Self-evidently, in exercising that power the court will have due regard to the interests of all concerned. The court will act judicially. But it cannot be right that the court should decline to exercise the power if the consequence will be manifest unfairness.

In my view this is a case in which a sale should be directed even though there will be a deficiency. It is just and equitable to order a sale because otherwise unfairness and injustice will follow.

The injustice in this case would have left the Palks in an intolerable position. If the mortgagees went into possession and leased the property the mortgage would still have been alive. The Palks would obviously have to find alternative accommodation and meet the costs of that, and the interest on the mortgage in the meantime would continue to accrue. In the event of the mortgagee selling the property if the proceeds from the sale did not cover the mortgage debt, the Palks could be sued under the personal covenant to repay. Either way, the Palks were in an unfortunate position.

Palk's case, which was decided during the property recession of the early 1990s, received wide publicity, and was warmly welcomed. But the facts of the case, a mortgagee seeking possession of a house but not intending to sell, were unusual. *Palk*'s case was, moreover, distinguished in *Cheltenham and Gloucester Building Society v Krausz* [1997] 1 WLR 1558.

The Limits on *Palk*—The Judgment in *Krausz's Case*

In *Cheltenham and Gloucester Building Society v Krausz* [1997] 1 WLR 1558, the defendants defaulted on a loan of £58,300 from the claimant building society which was secured by a mortgage on their home. Following the issue of a warrant for possession which fell due for execution on 12 June 1995, the defendants negotiated a sale of the property for £65,000. However, by that time the mortgage debt amounted to some £83,000 and the claimant refused to agree to the sale on the ground that a higher price could be obtained. The defendants thereafter applied to the County Court for an order suspending possession on the ground that they had found a purchaser and gave notice of their intention to apply to the High Court for an order for sale pursuant to s91 LPA 1925. The District Judge dismissed their application. The County Court judge allowed the defendants' appeal and ordered a stay of the warrant for possession pending determination of the application under s91. The claimant appealed.

The Court of Appeal held that the County Court had no power under s36 AJA 1970 (as amended by s8 Administration of Justice Act 1973) to suspend a warrant for possession of mortgaged property in order to enable the mortgagor to make an application for sale under s91 LPA 1925 where the proceeds of sale would not discharge the mortgage debt fully, unless other funds were available to the mortgagor to make up the shortfall.

Phillips LJ said:

Palk's case established, for the first time, that the court has power under section 91(2) to make an order for sale on the application of a mortgagor, notwithstanding that the proceeds of sale will be insufficient to discharge the mortgage debt.

In *Palk's* case the issue was simply whether or not the property should be sold. No issue arose as to the terms on which it should be sold. As to that matter, section 91(2) empowers the court to direct a sale 'on such terms as it thinks fit.' . . .

Barrett v. Halifax Building Society (1995) 28 H.L.R. 634 marks the next development in this area of the law, and one which demonstrates the importance of the present appeal. In that case the plaintiffs had mortgaged their home and then defaulted on their repayment obligations. The situation was one of negative equity—the mortgage debt substantially exceeded the value of their home. By the time that their [the mortgagee's] action came on for hearing they [mortgagor's] had negotiated a sale of the property, subject to contract. They [mortgagor's] sought an order that they be permitted to proceed with that sale and to remain in possession until completion . . .

The mortgagees resisted the order sought. They did not contend that they would be able to obtain a better price but urged that if the sale went ahead it would break their established policy not to permit borrowers with negative equity themselves to conduct the sale of their property without also at the same time making proposals for the repayment of any resulting deficit. The judge held that this was not a material circumstance which he ought to take into account when exercising his discretion . . .

[The judge] proceeded to grant the plaintiffs the order that they sought. Just as in *Palk's* case [1993] Ch. 330 the report does not suggest that in *Barrett's* case, 28 H.L.R. 634 any challenge was made by the mortgagees to the order suspending possession pending the plaintiffs' application to the Chancery court.

The consequences of the procedure followed in *Barrett's* case appear to me to be far reaching. In any case in which there is negative equity it will be open to the mortgagor to resist an order for possession on the ground that he wishes to obtain a better price by remaining in possession and selling the property himself. In not every case will the primary motive for such an application be the wish to obtain a better price than that which the mortgagee is likely to obtain on a forced sale. Often the mortgagor will be anxious to postpone for as long as possible the evil day when he has to leave his home . . . There will be a danger, if the mortgagee does not obtain possession, that the mortgagor will delay the realisation of the property by seeking too high a price, or deliberately procrastinating on completion. At present there is a simple procedure for seeking possession in the county court and the issue tends to be whether there are arrears and whether the mortgagor is likely to be able to discharge these in a reasonable time. If possession is to be suspended whenever this appears reasonable in order to give mortgagors the opportunity to sell the property themselves, the courts are going to have to enter into an area of difficult factual inquiry in order to decide in the individual case whether or not this course will be to the common benefit of mortgagor and mortgagee. Furthermore there will be obvious practical difficulties for mortgagees in monitoring the negotiations of mortgagors who are permitted time to market their properties. For these reasons it seems to me that the procedure followed and the decision reached in the *Barrett* case tend fundamentally to undermine the value of the mortgagee's entitlement to possession. Having touched on the implications of the issue raised in this case I turn to consider whether, in law, the county court has jurisdiction to suspend possession in such circumstances.

. . .

Before the decision in *Palk's* case it seemed that section 36 of the Act of 1970 and section 91 of the Act of 1925 were complementary. An application under section 91 would only be contemplated where the proceeds of sale were expected to exceed the mortgage debt. In these circumstances section 36 gave the court the power to suspend possession in order to enable an application for sale under section 91 to be made. It is, however, quite clear that section 36 does not empower the court to suspend possession in order to permit the mortgagor to sell the mortgaged premises where the proceeds of sale will not suffice to discharge the mortgage debt, unless of course other funds will be available to the mortgagor to make up the shortfall. A mortgagor seeking relief in the circumstances of *Palk's* case is thus unable to invoke any statutory power to suspend the mortgagee's right to enter into possession . . .

In my judgment the very specific delimitation of the power given by section 36 makes it clear that the legislature did not intend that the court should have any wider jurisdiction to curtail the mortgagee's right to possession. That right enables the mortgagee to exercise his power of sale in the manner he chooses and in the confidence that he can offer a purchaser vacant possession.

Krausz curtailed the apparent wide scope of the judgment in *Palk* in situations involving negative equity. One of the problems that may arise as highlighted by Phillips LJ is that the mortgagor who may be selling the property may prevaricate in order to stay in the property longer. It is clear from the previous passage that s91(2) LPA 1925 should only be used where the proceeds of the sale will cover the outstanding debt, or in the situation where, if there is a potential shortfall in the proceeds of sale, there are additional funds available to meet the outstanding debt.

Krausz stands for the, arguably obvious, proposition that where the mortgagee in a negative equity situation is seeking possession of the property to sell with vacant possession, then an application by the mortgagor for an order of sale under s91(2) will be refused, and the mortgagee will be able to obtain possession and sell the property.

Protection for Persons Deriving Title from the Mortgagor

A person deriving title from the mortgagor of a dwelling house can ask the court to adjourn or suspend possession proceedings (s39 AJA 1970). In particular, this will include a spouse or civil partner of the mortgagor with rights of occupation under the Family Law Act 1996.

thinking point 23.2

Who else would count as 'deriving title' for the purposes of this legislation?

A cohabitee who had a constructive trust interest would certainly derive title.

Contributions to mortgage payments by the spouse or civil partner, who is entitled to occupy the property as a home right, will be treated as though they have been made by the mortgagor (s30(3) Family Law Act 1996).

However, the mortgagee is under no obligation to notify the spouse or civil partner of the mortgagor's default. Mrs Goddard, in *Hastings and Thanet Building Society v Goddard* [1970] 3 All ER 954, found out about her husband's arrears only when it was far too late for her to do anything about them. If the mortgagee seeks possession and the spouse or civil partner has registered their right of occupation, then the mortgagee must serve notice of the possession proceedings on the spouse or civil partner (s56 Family Law Act 1996).

Under s55 Family Law Act 1996, any connected person to the mortgagor may be made party to the possession proceedings if the court is satisfied that:

- the connected person will be able to meet the mortgagor's liabilities under the mortgage;
- the court finds no special reason against the connected person being made a party to the action; and

- the court is satisfied that the connected person may be expected to make payments or do such other things that might affect the outcome of the possession proceedings.

Section 54(5) defines 'connected person' as 'that person's spouse, former spouse, civil partner, former civil partner, cohabitant, or former cohabitant'. In the case of joint mortgagors, the possession proceedings are brought against both parties.

23.3.3 Duty of Mortgagee in Possession to Account Strictly

The rules are based in equity and apply only in those cases where a mortgagee takes possession on a long term basis.

A mortgagee who takes long-term possession must use any income gained from the land (eg in particular rents from tenants) to pay off the interest on the debt. Any surplus income is (at the mortgagee's option) either paid to the mortgagor, or put to reducing the capital debt. The mortgagee is not permitted to benefit financially over and above what is due to him from having taken possession from the mortgagor.

One rule we have already mentioned at 22.2.3 must now be explained more fully: if a mortgagee takes possession on a long-term basis, the mortgagee must account 'on the basis of wilful default'. This means that the mortgagee must manage the property to get the maximum income obtainable by reasonable means. If the mortgagee fails to get that maximum income, they will nevertheless be deemed to have received it. (The amount owed by the mortgagor will thus be reduced by the amount of extra income the mortgagee should have obtained.)

The leading case on this point is still *White v City of London Brewery* (1889) 42 Ch D 237. Before we consider this case, it is worth putting this type of case into some sort of context. Many of the cases concerning mortgage law arose around the turn of the nineteenth/twentieth century, and quite a few of them involved public houses. When considering these cases, remember that in some respects economic conditions were different over a century ago; in particular, interest rates were generally lower.

In *White v City of London Brewery* (1889) 42 Ch D 237 a pub, originally a 'free' house, was mortgaged to a brewery; rather surprisingly the mortgage did not contain a tie clause. The brewery took possession and leased the pub as a 'tied house'.

In those days a tied house was confined to one brewery's products and fetched a lower rent than a 'free' house, which can sell whatever brands of beer it wishes. The pub was later sold and the claimant brought an action for the mortgagee to account for the rents and profits of the mortgaged premises. In finalizing the amount which White owed the brewery, the court ruled that the brewery had to account on the basis of the higher rent of £60 per year which a 'free house' would then have commanded. At the time the actual rent received was £20 per year. (The tie in the lease was to the mortgagees, but that is irrelevant.)

The Mortgagee's Statutory Power of Sale

The mortgagee usually opts to sell the property in the event of the mortgagor defaulting on their mortgage payments. This remedy is used in conjunction with the right to possession because *usually* the mortgagee wants to sell the property with vacant possession to attract a higher price and quicker sale.

Prior to 1926 the mortgage would normally expressly state that in the event of default of payment, the mortgagee had power to sell the property. After 1925 the mortgagee is given the statutory power to sell the property under ss101(1) and 103 LPA 1925. The relevant statutory provisions draw a distinction between the statutory **power of sale** 'arising' and the statutory power becoming 'exercisable'. We will consider the significance of this distinction in the following section.

cross-reference
For a discussion on possession orders, see 23.3.1.

power of sale
the statutory right to sell mortgaged property and recoup what is owed from the proceeds.

23.4.1 When Does the Statutory Power Arise?

Law of Property Act 1925

101. Powers incident to estate or interest of mortgagee

(1) A mortgagee, where the mortgage is made by deed, shall, by virtue of this Act, have the following powers, to the like extent as if they had been in terms conferred by the mortgage deed, but not further (namely):

(i) A power, when the mortgage money has become due, to sell, or to concur with any other person in selling, the mortgaged property, or any part thereof, either subject to prior charges or not, and either together or in lots, by public auction or by private contract, subject to such conditions respecting title, or evidence of title, or other matter, as the mortgagee thinks fit, with power to vary any contract for sale, and to buy in at an auction, or to rescind any contract for sale, and to re-sell, without being answerable for any loss occasioned thereby;

...

(4) This section applies only if and as far as a contrary intention is not expressed in the mortgage deed, and has effect subject to the terms of the mortgage deed and to the provisions therein contained.

The mortgagee's right to sell arises when the three conditions under s101(1) LPA 1925 are satisfied:

1 the mortgage must be by deed;

   and

2 the mortgage debt must be due, that is, the legal redemption date must be passed or in the case of instalment mortgages when the instalment is due and has not been paid (*Payne v Cardiff RDC* [1932] 1 KB 241;

   and

3 the mortgage deed does not expressly exclude the power of sale.

23.4.2 When Does the Statutory Power become Exercisable?

Law of Property Act 1925

103. Regulation of exercise of power of sale

A mortgagee shall not exercise the power of sale conferred by this Act unless and until—

(i) Notice requiring payment of the mortgage money has been served on the mortgagor or one of two or more mortgagors, and default has been made in payment of the mortgage money, or of part thereof, for three months after such service; or

(ii) Some interest under the mortgage is in arrear and unpaid for two months after becoming due; or

(iii) There has been a breach of some provision contained in the mortgage deed or in this Act, or in an enactment replaced by this Act, and on the part of the mortgagor, or of some person concurring in making the mortgage, to be observed or performed, other than and besides a covenant for payment of the mortgage money or interest thereon.

The power, having first arisen, becomes exercisable if any one of the following three conditions is satisfied:

1 notice has been served on the mortgagor requiring repayment and three months have elapsed without the mortgagor repaying the whole debt;

or

2 interest is at least two months in arrears;

or

3 there has been a breach of a term of the mortgage other than one relating to repayment of capital and interest.

23.4.3 Protection for Purchasers in Good Faith from Mortgagees

If a mortgagee attempts to convey the property before the power of sale has even arisen, this will result in the transfer of the mortgage only. The purchaser simply acquires the rights of the mortgagee and not the property.

Once the power has arisen, a mortgagee can convey a good title to a purchaser free of the mortgagor's rights, that is, the equitable right to redeem, whether or not the power has become exercisable.

A purchaser in good faith from a mortgagee need satisfy themselves only that the power of sale has arisen; the purchaser is under no duty to enquire whether the power has become exercisable (*Bailey v Barnes* [1894] 1 Ch 25).

thinking point 23.3

What do you think is the rationale underlying the rule that has just been stated?

The rule is eminently sensible from the point of view of the purchaser from the mortgagee. It is relatively easy for a purchaser to check if the power of sale has arisen; it would be very difficult for them to check whether the power has become exercisable and would slow down the process of sale.

It follows from this that if a mortgagee were to sell after the power had arisen but before it became exercisable, the mortgagor's only redress would be a claim for damages against the mortgagee (s104(2) LPA 1925). Exceptionally, if a purchaser had actual knowledge of the fact that a power of sale had not become exercisable the purchaser would not be immune, as they would not be a purchaser in good faith.

Law of Property Act 1925

104. Conveyance on sale

(2) Where a conveyance is made in exercise of the power of sale conferred by this Act, or any enactment replaced by this Act, the title of the purchaser shall not be impeachable on the ground—

(a) that no case had arisen to authorise the sale; or

(b) that due notice was not given; or

(c) where the mortgage is made after the commencement of this Act, that leave of the court, when so required, was not obtained; or

(d) whether the mortgage was made before or after such commencement, that the power was otherwise improperly or irregularly exercised;

and a purchaser is not, either before or on conveyance, concerned to see or inquire whether a case has arisen to authorise the sale, or due notice has been given, or the power is otherwise properly and regularly exercised; but any person damnified by an unauthorised, or improper, or irregular exercise of the power shall have his remedy in damages against the person exercising the power.

23.4.4 Mortgagee's Duties on Selling the Property

cross-reference
For a discussion on possession proceedings, see 23.3.1.

Before we go on to consider how the courts have dealt with these issues, it is worth reminding you at this point, that in the case of owner-occupied properties the mortgagee normally obtains possession of the property before the sale goes ahead. It is more attractive to potential purchasers to sell the property with vacant possession rather than with the mortgagor who is in situ and refusing to move. (The purchaser would have to seek a possession order from the court.)

thinking point 23.4

By contrast, if the mortgagee is selling a block of flats or a block of offices, the last thing the mortgagee wants is the block to be empty. They want the block to be full of tenants paying good rents. Why?

The mortgagee will want to sell the block as an attractive investment.

A mortgagee can sell either by auction or by 'private treaty' (by 'private treaty' is meant negotiating with buyers individually). There is no need to obtain a court order to sell the property. Regarding the conduct of the sale by the mortgagee, the legislators of the 1925 Act had envisaged that there may be potential problems in this area. This is exemplified by s104(2) which allows any person who suffers a loss due to 'unauthorised, or improper, or irregular exercise of the power' to claim damages. Other than that, there is no further guidance for mortgagees about their conduct during the sale process.

It is important in such a situation that the conduct of the mortgagee in selling the property is fair. There is no specific code of conduct for mortgagees though the courts have attempted to strike a balance for both parties since they both have a vested interest in the outcome. The mortgagor, on the one hand, wants the property to be sold at the best price to ensure that the debt is covered by the sale. The mortgagee, on the other hand, wants the funds tied up in the property to be released as quickly as possible.

In dealing with a sale there are a number of issues that arise, for example when selling a property is the mortgagee acting primarily in their own interest or in the interest of the mortgagor?

Who decides what is the best time to sell? If the market is depressed could the sale be postponed until 'things are better'? What is the best price for the property? etc.

Whose Interests Should the Mortgagee Take into Account when Selling the Property?

The mortgagee has certain obligations towards the mortgagor and the issue is what is the nature and extent of these obligations. The courts have acknowledged that the nature of this relationship does not come within the strict confines of a fiduciary nature (ie trustee and beneficiary relationship). If it did then the trustee would have to act in the interests of the beneficiary when selling the property, but the reality is that the mortgagee is acting primarily in their own interest to recover the funds which are tied up in the property. The Court of Appeal in *Cuckmere Brick Co v Mutual Finance Co* [1971] Ch 949 considered whether the mortgagee was a trustee of the power of sale and acted for the best interests of the beneficiary (the mortgagor). Salmon LJ said:

> ...It is well settled that a mortgagee is not a trustee of the power of sale for the mortgagor. Once the power has accrued, the mortgagee is entitled to exercise it for his own purposes whenever he chooses to do so. It matters not that the moment may be unpropitious and that by waiting a higher price could be obtained. He has the right to realise his security by turning it into money when he likes. Nor, in my view, is there anything to prevent a mortgagee from accepting the best bid he can get at an auction, even though the auction is badly attended and the bidding exceptionally low. Providing none of those adverse factors is due to any fault of the mortgagee, he can do as he likes. If the mortgagee's interests, as he sees them, conflict with those of the mortgagor, the mortgagee can give preference to his own interests, which of course he could not do were he a trustee of the power of sale for the mortgagor.

A notable element of this passage is that the court has endorsed the primacy of the mortgagee's interests over the mortgagor's. The court in *Palk v Mortgage Services Funding Plc* [1993] Ch 330 elaborated on this point, Nicholls V-C emphasized that:

> a mortgagee does owe some duties to a mortgagor. As Lord Templeman noted in the *China and South Sea Bank* case [[1990] 1 AC 536, PC], at p. 545, a mortgagee can sit back and do nothing. He is not obliged to take steps to realise his security. But if he does take steps to exercise his rights over his security, common law and equity alike have set bounds to the extent to which he can look after himself and ignore the mortgagor's interests. In the exercise of his rights over his security the mortgagee must act fairly towards the mortgagor. His interest in the property has priority over the interest of the mortgagor, and he is entitled to proceed on that footing. He can protect his own interest, but he is not entitled to conduct himself in a way which unfairly prejudices the mortgagor.

The mortgagee can act in their own interests though these may be in conflict with the mortgagor. However, it is clear from the passage quoted that in dealing with the power of sale the mortgagee must act fairly (ie in good faith). That alone is not sufficient; the mortgagee must act with reasonable care. According to Salmon LJ in *Cuckmere Brick Co v Mutual Finance Co* [1971]:

> there are other dicta which suggest that in addition to the duty of acting in good faith, the mortgagee is under a duty to take reasonable care to obtain whatever is the true market value of the mortgaged property at the moment he chooses to sell it...The proposition that the mortgagee owes both duties, in my judgment, represents the true view of the law.

There was considerable debate as to whether the duty owed by the mortgagee to the mortgagor was based in tort or in equity. In *Cuckmere Brick Co v Mutual Finance Co* it was suggested that because of the proximity of the relationship between the mortgagee and the mortgagor they were 'neighbours' implying a tortious relationship. In this case, a property company owned a sizeable vacant site on the edge of Maidstone. The company had planning permission to develop the site for houses or flats. The mortgagees exercised their power of sale. They sold by auction. The adverts for the auction mentioned that there was planning permission for houses, but not the permission for flats. Because of this omission the site did not fetch as high a price as it should have. The Court of Appeal held that the mortgagee could choose when to sell the property, but the mortgagee had failed to take reasonable care to obtain a proper price.

The court in *Parker-Tweedale v Dunbar Bank Plc* [1991] Ch 12, clarified the position and stated that the duty owed by the mortgagee to the mortgagor was not based in tort but 'recognised in equity as arising out of the particular relationship between them' (per Nourse LJ). In this case the matrimonial home was held by the wife on trust for sale for herself and her husband. The claimants defaulted in repaying a loan to the defendant bank. The mortgage was secured against the matrimonial home, the bank took possession and sold the house. The house was sold to a development company for £575,000 and one week later it was sold on to another company for £700,000. The husband brought this present action against the bank, claiming that the bank had owed him a duty of care to obtain a proper price upon sale of the property. The Court of Appeal held that the duty of care owed by the bank to the mortgagor (the wife) did not extend to the husband, whose only interest in the house was a beneficial interest under a trust for sale. Nourse LJ said:

> It was settled by the decision of this court in *Cuckmere Brick Co. Ltd v Mutual Finance Ltd* [1971] Ch 949 that a mortgagee, although he may exercise his power of sale at any time of his own choice, owes the mortgagor a duty to take reasonable care to obtain a proper price for the mortgaged property at that time. But there is no support, either in the authorities or on principle, for the proposition that where the mortgagor is a trustee, even a bare trustee, of the mortgaged property a like duty is owed to a beneficiary under the trust of whose interest the mortgagee has notice.

> In seeking to support that proposition the plaintiff...relied on the following passage in the judgment of Salmon LJ in *Cuckmere Brick Co. Ltd v Mutual Finance Ltd* [1971] Ch 949 at 966:

>> Approaching the matter first of all on principle, it is to be observed that if the sale yields a surplus over the amount owed under the mortgage, the mortgagee holds this surplus in trust for the mortgagor. If the sale shows a deficiency, the mortgagor has to make it good out of his own pocket. The mortgagor is vitally affected by the result of the sale but its preparation and conduct is left entirely in the hands of the mortgagee. The proximity between them could scarcely be closer. Surely they are 'neighbours'. Given that the power of sale is for the benefit of the mortgagee and that he is entitled to choose the moment to sell which suits him, it would be strange indeed if he were under no legal obligation to take reasonable care to obtain what I call the true market value at the date of the sale.

> This reference to 'neighbours' has enabled the plaintiff to argue that the duty is owed to all those who are within the neighbourhood principle, i.e. to adapt the words of Lord Atkin [*Donoghue (or M'Alister) v Stevenson* [1932] AC 562], to all persons who are so closely and directly affected by the sale that the mortgagee ought reasonably to have them in contemplation as being so affected when he is directing his mind to the sale. Further support for the application of the neighbourhood principle in this context can be gained from the judgment of Lord Denning MR in *Standard Chartered Bank Ltd v Walker* [1982] 1 WLR 1410 at 1415, where it was held that the duty to take reasonable care to obtain a proper price was owed to a surety for the mortgage debt as well as to the mortgagor himself.

> In my respectful opinion it is both unnecessary and confusing for the duties owed by a mortgagee to the mortgagor and the surety, if there is one, to be expressed in terms of the tort of

negligence. The authorities which were considered in the careful judgments of this court in *Cuckmere Brick Co. Ltd v Mutual Finance Ltd* demonstrate that the duty owed by the mortgagee to the mortgagor was recognized by equity as arising out of the particular relationship between them. Thus Salmon LJ himself said at 967:

> It would seem, therefore, that many years before the modern development of the law of negligence, the courts of equity had laid down a doctrine in relation to mortgages which is entirely consonant with the general principles later evolved by the common law.

The duty owed to the surety arises in the same way. In *China and South Sea Bank Ltd v Tan* [1990] 2 WLR 56 at 58 Lord Templeman, in delivering the judgment of the Privy Council, having pointed out that the surety in that case admitted that the moneys secured by the guarantee were due, continued:

> But the surety claims that the creditor owed the surety a duty to exercise the power of sale conferred by the mortgage and in that case the liability of the surety under the guarantee would either have been eliminated or very much reduced. The Court of Appeal [in Hong Kong] sought to find such a duty in the tort of negligence but the tort of negligence has not yet subsumed all torts and does not supplant the principles of equity or contradict contractual promises ... Equity intervenes to protect a surety.

Once it is recognised that the duty owed by the mortgagee to the mortgagor arises out of the particular relationship between them, it is readily apparent that there is no warrant for extending its scope so as to include a beneficiary or beneficiaries under a trust of which the mortgagor is the trustee.

Nourse LJ noted that despite the reference used in *Cuckmere* to the 'neighbour principle', Salmon LJ had acknowledged in his judgment that the duty between mortgagor and mortgagee lay in equity.

When Should the Mortgagee Sell?

Once the power to sell becomes exercisable the court in *Cuckmere Brick Co v Mutual Finance Co* said that in deciding the timing of the sale the mortgagee is entitled to consult their own interests to the total exclusion of the mortgagor's interests, but this is subject to obtaining the 'true market value'. Salmon LJ said:

> Given that the power of sale is for the benefit of the mortgagee and that he is entitled to choose the moment to sell which suits him, it would be strange indeed if he were under no legal obligation to take reasonable care to obtain what I call the true market value at the date of the sale. Some of the textbooks refer to the 'proper price', others to the 'best price'. Vaisey J in *Reliance Permanent Building Society v Harwood-Stamper* [1944] 2 All ER 75, seems to have attached great importance to the difference between these two descriptions of 'price'. My difficulty is that I cannot see any real difference between them. 'Proper price' is perhaps a little nebulous, and 'the best price' may suggest an exceptionally high price. That is why I prefer to call it 'the true market value'.

> ...I accordingly conclude, both on principle and authority, that a mortgagee in exercising his power of sale does owe a duty to take reasonable precaution to obtain the true market value of the mortgaged property at the date on which he decides to sell it. No doubt in deciding whether he has fallen short of that duty, the facts must be looked at broadly and he will not be adjudged to be in default unless he is plainly on the wrong side of the line.

The court took the pragmatic approach of letting the mortgagee decide when to sell.

A mortgagee can sell at a time when the market for the type of property comprised in the mortgage is depressed. This point is confirmed by the Privy Council in *China and South Sea*

Bank v Tan [1990] AC 295. In this case a surety had guaranteed the repayment of a loan which the claimant bank had made to a company. The company defaulted on the loan at a time when the shares in the company were adequate security for the loan. However, the bank did not enforce its security (by selling the shares) until the shares were virtually worthless. The bank sought repayment of the loan under the guarantee given by the surety. The surety, in his defence, argued that the bank owed him a duty to have sold the shares at the time when the proceeds would have been sufficient to pay off the loan. The Privy Council held that the surety was obliged to pay off the company's debt to the bank and the bank had not acted in bad faith.

Lord Templeman observed that:

> ...If the creditor does nothing and the debtor declines into bankruptcy the mortgaged securities become valueless and if the surety decamps abroad the creditor loses his money. If disaster strikes the debtor and the mortgaged securities but the surety remains capable of repaying the debt then the creditor loses nothing. The surety contracts to pay if the debtor does not pay and the surety is bound by his contract. If the surety, perhaps less indolent or less well protected than the creditor, is worried that the mortgaged securities may decline in value then the surety may request the creditor to sell and if the creditor remains idle then the surety may bustle about, pay off the debt, take over the benefit of the securities and sell them. No creditor could carry on the business of lending if he could become liable to a mortgagee and to a surety or to either of them for a decline in value of mortgaged property, unless the creditor was personally responsible for the decline. Applying the rule as specified by Pollock CB in *Watts v Shuttleworth* (1860) 5 H & N 235 at 247–248, 157 ER 1171 at 1176, it appears to their Lordships that in the present case the creditor did no act injurious to the surety, did no act inconsistent with the rights of the surety and the creditor did not omit any act which his duty enjoined him to do. The creditor was not under a duty to exercise his power of sale over the mortgaged securities at any particular time or at all.

Similarly there is no duty on the mortgagee to wait for a likely increase in the value of the property (*Silven Properties v Royal Bank of Scotland* [2004] 1 WLR 997).

What Amounts to the 'True Market Value'?

In *Silven Properties v Royal Bank of Scotland* [2004] 1 WLR 997, the receiver in acting on behalf of the mortgagee had made a quick sale of a portfolio of mortgaged properties rather than wait:

- for the possible granting of planning permission applications relating to certain properties; and
- for two vacant properties to be re-let.

The mortgagees were held not liable for the alleged shortfall in the price obtained. What amounts to the 'true market value' was explained by Lightman J:

> When and if the mortgagee does exercise the power of sale, he comes under a duty in equity (and not tort) to the mortgagor (and all others interested in the equity of redemption) to take reasonable precautions to obtain 'the fair' or 'the true market' value of or the 'proper price' for the mortgaged property at the date of the sale...If the period of time between the dates of the decision to sell and of the sale is short, there may be no difference in value between the two dates and indeed in many (if not most cases) this may be readily assumed. But where there is a period of delay, the difference in date could prove significant. The mortgagee is not entitled to act in a way which unfairly prejudices the mortgagor by selling hastily at a knock-down price sufficient to pay off his debt: *Palk v Mortgage Services Funding plc* [1993] Ch 330, 337–338, per Sir Donald Nicholls V-C. He must take proper care whether by fairly and properly exposing the property to the market or otherwise to obtain the best price reasonably

> obtainable at the date of sale. The remedy for breach of this equitable duty is not common law damages, but an order that the mortgagee account to the mortgagor and all others interested in the equity of redemption, not just for what he actually received, but for what he should have received: see *Standard Chartered Bank Ltd v Walker* [1982] 1 WLR 1410, 1416b.

This case illustrates the pragmatic approach towards considering the 'true market value'. This is a recognition that the market value of the property can vary and can be difficult to estimate. The court reinforces the importance of taking reasonable care to sell the property and obtaining the best price reasonably obtainable, but that does not involve the court mathematically fixing an appropriate sale price for the property (see *Michael v Miller* [2004] 2 EGLR 151, and confirmed in *Aodhcon LLP v Bridgeco Ltd* [2014] EWHC 535).

In *Meah v GE Money Home Finance Ltd* [2013] EWHC 20 the property was advertised at a grossly inadequate value, however the court found that the property had been sufficiently exposed to the market and there was no evidence that the price obtained for the property was less than the best price reasonably achievable. The mortgagee had not breached its duty.

If the mortgagee fails to obtain the true market value, he will have to account for the difference. Salmon LJ explained the consequences of a surplus and deficit on the sale of the mortgaged property in *Cuckmere Brick Co v Mutual Finance Co*:

> Approaching the matter first of all on principle, it is to be observed that if the sale yields a surplus over the amount owed under the mortgage, the mortgagee holds this surplus in trust for the mortgagor. If the sale shows a deficiency, the mortgagor has to make it good out of his own pocket. The mortgagor is vitally affected by the result of the sale but its preparation and conduct is left entirely in the hands of the mortgagee.

The mortgagee will have to account for a shortfall in the price if the property was sold quickly at a low price (see the earlier extract from *Silven Properties v Royal Bank of Scotland* where Lightman J refers to *Palk v Mortgage Services Funding plc*). The onus of proving that the mortgagee is in breach of this duty of care is on the mortgagor.

Mode of Sale

To comply with the requirement of obtaining the 'true market value' there are several factors that the mortgagee will need to consider. For example:

- Advertisements—'fairly and properly exposing the property to the market or otherwise to obtain the best price reasonably obtainable at the date of sale' (per Lightman J, *Silven Properties v Royal Bank of Scotland* [2004]).
  - Provide a full description of the property. In *Cuckmere Brick Co v Mutual Finance Co* the property was advertised without including details of planning permission which had been granted.
- It is for the mortgagee, subject to any restrictions in the mortgage deed, to decide on the mode of sale, ie by private treaty or public auction. The mortgagee can decide how the sale should be advertised and for how long the property should be left on the market (*Michael v Miller* [2004]).
- The mortgagee can sell the property in the condition that it is in. There is no obligation to undertake improvements or to increase its value (per Lightman J, *Silven Properties v Royal Bank of Scotland*).
- The mortgagee can investigate whether the value of the mortgaged property can be increased by a lease or applying for planning permission (or even apply for planning

permission). The mortgagee is free to stop this investigation at any time and proceed with the sale (per Lightman J, *Silven Properties v Royal Bank of Scotland*).

- The mortgagee should not necessarily accept the first offer to buy the mortgaged property. In *Bishop v Blake* [2006] EWHC 831, the mortgagee and the mortgagor's tenants colluded prior to the sale of the property, it was sold at an undervalue, and had not been advertised properly. The purchasers (the mortgagor's tenants) had to pay the difference to the mortgagor.

- At an auction the mortgagee can accept the best obtainable bid despite the auction being poorly attended or bidding being exceptionally low (per Salmon LJ, *Cuckmere Brick Co v Mutual Finance Co*).

REVIEW QUESTION Consider whether a mortgagee should be placed under a duty to take care as to the timing of sale.

Remember, in particular, what was said in the Introduction to this chapter.

23.4.5 Can a Mortgagee Sell to Their 'Friends'?

Mortgagees cannot sell to themselves or to nominees in trust for themselves, or to their agents (*Martinson v Clowes* (1882) 21 Ch D 857). Any attempt to do so will render the sale void.

A less rigid approach is taken where the mortgagee sells to a company in which they have a substantial shareholding. If the sale is challenged by the mortgagor, the onus of proof is on the mortgagee to show that reasonable efforts were made to obtain the best price.

In *Tse Kwong Lam v Wong Chit Sen* [1983] 1 WLR 1349, the mortgagee sold the mortgaged property by public auction. The mortgagee had instructed the auctioneer prior to the auction that the reserve price was to be $1.2 million. This was announced to the persons present. The only bidder at the auction was the mortgagee's wife who matched the reserve price. The mortgagee's wife was acting on behalf of a company of which both the mortgagee and his wife were directors. The Privy Council held that if the sale is challenged by the mortgagor the onus of proof will be on the mortgagee to show that the sale was undertaken in good faith and that reasonable efforts had been taken to obtain the best price at the time of the sale. On the facts, there was a conflict of duty due to the closeness of the relationship the mortgagee had with the purchasing company. Furthermore, the mortgagee failed to show 'that in all respects he acted fairly to the borrower and used his best endeavours to obtain the best price reasonably obtainable for the mortgaged property' (per Lord Templeman).

REVIEW QUESTION How, then, should the mortgagees have conducted themselves in *Tse Kwong Lam*?

Consider carefully what was discussed throughout 23.4.4.

23.4.6 Position of Purchasers and the Question of Price

A purchaser from the mortgagee is under no duty to pay the best price. Provided they act in good faith they will get a good title, even though the mortgagee should have obtained a higher price by taking greater care. It is not bad faith for a purchaser to consider that they have got a good bargain. It would be bad faith if the mortgagee and the purchaser conspired so that a deliberately low price was charged to the purchaser.

23.4.7 The Effect of Sale

The mortgagor's equity of redemption is destroyed as soon as the contract of sale is made. This is the point at which the mortgagee has exercised their power of sale. If the mortgagee has contracted to sell, the mortgagor cannot prevent completion by paying off the debt (*Lord Waring v London and Manchester Assurance Co Ltd* [1935] Ch 310).

The conveyance by the mortgagee conveys the fee simple previously vested in the mortgagor free from the rights of the mortgagor and all subsequent mortgagees. These rights are all overreached (s2(1)(ii) LPA 1925). It is hoped you noticed that we have here an exception to the ancient principle **nemo dat quod non habet** ('you cannot give what you have not got'). The conveyance is in principle subject to any mortgages having priority over that of the vendor, although an earlier mortgagee may permit a later mortgagee to sell free from the earlier mortgage.

Suppose that Messyacre is worth approximately £130,000. It is subject to a first mortgage for £70,000 in favour of Freya, and to a second mortgage for £50,000 in favour of Sean. Any sale by Sean would be (in principle) subject to Freya's first mortgage. Thus Sean is unlikely to get more than £60,000 on such a sale. Freya might, however, allow the sale to take place free from her rights. Sean would obviously then get a price in the region of £130,000. Freya (under the rules which are about to be discussed) would still get 'first dip' into the proceeds of sale.

23.4.8 Destination of Proceeds of Sale

The mortgagee has always been regarded as 'trustee of the proceeds of sale'. Proceeds in the hands of a mortgagee must be applied in a particular order set out in s105 LPA 1925, which provides the following order:

1 paying off the total debt (capital and interest) owed to any mortgagee earlier in priority who permitted the property to be sold free from his mortgage (Freya in the example at 23.4.7);

2 discharging any costs of sale and any attempted sale;

3 discharging the total debt (capital and interest) owed to the mortgagee;

4 the balance (if any) must be paid to the mortgagee next in order of priority or, if none, to the mortgagor.

> *Law of Property Act 1925*
>
> 105. Application of proceeds of sale
>
> The money which is received by the mortgagee, arising from the sale, after discharge of prior incumbrances to which the sale is not made subject, if any, or after payment into court under this Act of a sum to meet any prior incumbrance, shall be held by him in trust to be applied by him, first, in payment of all costs, charges, and expenses properly incurred by him as incident to the sale or any attempted sale, or otherwise; and secondly, in discharge of the mortgage money, interest, and costs, and other money, if any, due under the mortgage; and the residue of the money so received shall be paid to the person entitled to the mortgaged property, or authorised to give receipts for the proceeds of the sale thereof.

If there is a mortgagee later in priority than the one selling, but the seller pays the balance to the mortgagor, then the seller is in principle liable for any loss suffered by a later mortgagee.

There will be no such liability if the seller had no notice of the later mortgage. If the later mortgage has been registered as a land charge or entered on the register of title, the seller will automatically be fixed with notice of the later mortgage. A mortgagee should therefore search the land charges register or the register of title (depending on whether the land is unregistered or registered) before paying surplus proceeds to the mortgagor.

If a later mortgagee receives surplus proceeds of sale from an earlier mortgagee, the later mortgagee must apply them as if they were proceeds of a sale effected by him/her.

23.5 Power to Appoint a Receiver

The mortgagee is given the power to appoint a **receiver** under s109 LPA 1925. This remedy is in practice usually exercised where the mortgaged land is subject to leases, and the mortgagee wishes to intercept rent payable under those leases. It is a particularly attractive remedy where the mortgaged property is a block of flats or offices, or a row of shops. The mortgagee, rather than taking possession and being subject to the strict accounting rules discussed in 23.3.3, may well opt to appoint a receiver who will be responsible for collecting rents.

. . . .

receiver

broadly defined, a receiver is appointed to take control and management of a property. In the narrow context of land law, a receiver is either:

- appointed by the mortgagee to take control of the mortgaged land; or
- in the context of leases—appointed by the court or the First Tier Tribunal to take control of premises which the landlord has allowed to fall into disrepair.

Receivers of insolvent companies have a much wider role; they take over the whole running of the company.

. . . .

cross-reference
See 23.4 for a discussion on the power of sale.

Where a mortgagee appoints a receiver, the rents payable by the tenants must be paid by them to the receiver and not to the mortgagor. The power to appoint a receiver arises when the power of sale arises; it becomes exercisable when the power of sale becomes exercisable. If there were a purported appointment of a receiver before the power arose, any payment of rent to the receiver would not discharge the tenants' obligations.

thinking point 23.5

Bearing in mind what was said at 23.4.3, what do you think would be the position if a receiver were appointed after the power to appoint had arisen but before it had become exercisable? Would rent paid to the receiver discharge the tenant's obligations?

If the power to appoint has arisen, any payments by the tenant to the receiver are valid, whether or not the power has become exercisable.

Any money received by the receiver must be applied in the following order:

1 to pay rents, rates, etc payable with respect to the mortgaged estate;

2 to pay interest on any mortgages having priority over the appointor's mortgage;

3 to pay the receiver's commission (usually 5 per cent of the gross receipts);

4 to pay insurance on the property;

5 to pay for repairs on the property, if the mortgagee so directs;

6 to pay the interest due to the appointing mortgagee; and

7 if the mortgagee so directs, to reduce the capital debt (otherwise any surplus goes to the mortgagor).

In practice it is heads (6) and (7) which really matter from the mortgagee's point of view.

23.5.1 Receiver Deemed to be the Mortgagor's Agent

The mortgagee, exercising the power to appoint a receiver given by s109(1) LPA 1925, can choose whoever they think fit to act as a receiver. The mortgagee does not have to choose a professional person such as an accountant or surveyor. Yet the receiver is deemed to be the mortgagor's agent. Section 109(2) states that 'the mortgagor shall be solely responsible for the receiver's acts or defaults unless the mortgage deed otherwise provides'.

A consequence of s109(2) LPA 1925 is that, as the Court of Appeal confirmed in *Medforth v Blake* [2000] Ch 86, where a receiver takes over management of a mortgaged property, the receiver owes a duty of care to the mortgagor to take care in looking after the property. More specifically, Sir Richard Scott V-C with regard to the duty of care said '[t]he origin of the receiver's duty, like the mortgagee's duty, lies...in equity'. He stated:

> In my judgment, in principle and on the authorities, the following propositions can be stated. (1) A receiver managing mortgaged property owes duties to the mortgagor and anyone else with an interest in the equity of redemption. (2) The duties include, but are not necessarily confined to, a duty of good faith. (3) The extent and scope of any duty additional to that of good faith will depend on the facts and circumstances of the particular case. (4) In exercising his powers of management the primary duty of the receiver is to try and bring about a situation in which interest on the secured debt can be paid and the debt itself repaid. (5) Subject to that primary duty, the receiver owes a duty to manage the property with due diligence. (6) Due diligence does not oblige the receiver to continue to carry on a business on the mortgaged premises previously carried on by the mortgagor. (7) If the receiver does carry on a business on the mortgaged premises, due diligence requires reasonable steps to be taken in order to try to do so profitably.

thinking point 23.6

If a receiver defaults by, say, running off to Latin America with the rents they have collected, who bears the loss?

The mortgagor takes the risk of the receiver's dishonesty or incompetence. This is to be contrasted with the very strict 'wilful default' rule which operates if the mortgagee personally takes long-term control of the land (see 23.3.3).

In *Downsview v First City Corporation* [1993] 3 All ER 626, the Privy Council held that while the power to appoint a receiver must be exercised in good faith only for the purposes of enforcing the mortgagee's security, the mortgagee owes the mortgagor no duty to be careful in selecting the receiver appointed.

It is therefore not surprising that mortgagees rarely take long-term personal possession of mortgaged property. In cases where the capital of the debt is well secured but there have been problems with interest payments, appointing a receiver is a much more attractive remedy!

There is, however, one (arguable) advantage if a mortgagee takes personal possession of unregistered land rather than appointing a receiver. If a mortgagee personally takes possession of an unregistered title and remains in possession for 12 years without either acknowledging the mortgagor's title or receiving any payment from the mortgagor towards capital or interest, the mortgagor's rights are extinguished by the Limitation Acts. The mortgagee acquires an unencumbered title by virtue of adverse possession. If a receiver's appointment lasts more than 12 years (or even 112 years), this cannot affect the mortgagor's title.

The receiver is agent of the mortgagor, and therefore cannot be in adverse possession against the mortgagor.

In the case of registered title there will be no possibility of a mortgagee who has appointed a receiver being registered as owner under Sch 6 Land Registration Act 2002.

23.6 Foreclosure

It should be stressed that the word 'foreclosure' is being used here in its narrow technical sense. Sometimes the word is used by non-lawyers to mean any action taken by the mortgagee to enforce their security. Understanding the concept of foreclosure is important to your understanding of the law of mortgages as a whole, even though, in modern conditions, foreclosures are relatively rare.

In *Palk* v *Mortgage Services Funding Plc* [1993] Ch 330 Sir Donald Nicholls V-C commenting on the use of foreclosure as a remedy said that 'foreclosure actions are almost unheard of today and have been for many years'. Why is this the case? The reason for this lies in the draconian outcome of foreclosure proceedings.

The effect of a foreclosure order absolute before 1926 was that the legal estate already vested in the mortgagee was freed from the mortgagor's equitable right to redeem, which was destroyed by the order. The mortgagee became the legal owner of the property.

Since 1925, if a foreclosure order absolute is made the mortgagee becomes the legal owner of the estate and the equitable right to redeem is extinguished. Thus, the effect of a **foreclosure** order is that the mortgagee becomes an outright owner. The mortgagee, in that case, recoups the money owed and in cases of positive equity will gain from the surplus left as a result of the value of the property exceeding the value of the debt. The mortgagee gets everything!

foreclosure
a process under which a mortgagee of land enforces their security by obtaining a court order which makes them outright owner of the mortgaged land.

23.6.1 The Foreclosure Process

Foreclosure is only available on application to the High Court once the legal redemption date has passed. The equitable right to redeem arises after this date; the foreclosure procedure enables the mortgagee to extinguish the mortgagor's equitable right to redeem the property, and become the legal and equitable owner.

The foreclosure process will probably strike you as long and cumbersome, but the reason for the complexities is the desire to protect the mortgagor. Once a foreclosure order has been granted by the court, that is, a *foreclosure absolute*, the mortgagor loses all their rights. A foreclosure order is made in two stages:

1 An order for a *foreclosure nisi* directs the preparation of accounts setting out exactly how much is owed. It further provides that if the money owed is not repaid within a specified

period (usually six months) after the account has been drawn up, the foreclosure shall become *absolute*.

2 The order for a *foreclosure absolute* vests the property in the mortgagee. At the discretion of the court, even a foreclosure order absolute may be 'reopened' in exceptional circumstances, and the equity of redemption thereby revived. In *Campbell v Holyland* (1877) 7 Ch D 166, Jessel MR provided a list of circumstances which would enable the court to exercise its discretion in equity to 'reopen' the foreclosure:

- promptness of the mortgagor's application to reopen foreclosure;
- an accident which prevented the mortgagor from raising the money from a particular source;
- disparity between the outstanding debt and the value of the property; and
- property holds a special value, for example an old family estate which has a special value not quantifiable in money.

The court, also in that case, showed a willingness to reopen the foreclosure absolute if the property had been sold within 24 hours and it transpired that the value of the property was more than the amount of mortgage debt. Under those circumstances the court indicated that it would be willing to perhaps return the property to the mortgagor.

23.6.2 Judicial Sale in Foreclosure Proceedings

Hopefully you are already beginning to appreciate why foreclosure is not very common today. You may, however, be thinking, 'Despite it being a long-drawn-out affair, foreclosure will be attractive where the mortgaged property is worth substantially more than the total debt.'

You would be wrong in thinking in this way. The mortgagee or mortgagor (or any persons deriving title through any one of them, such as a second mortgagee or the owner of a constructive trust interest) may apply to the court for an order of judicial sale in place of foreclosure (s91(2) LPA 1925). Although there is discretion, a sale will generally be ordered where the value of the property is noticeably greater than the mortgage debt. This route is particularly beneficial to the mortgagor, as once the money from the sale has been used to discharge the mortgage debt and any additional costs incurred, any money that remains belongs to the mortgagor. Hopefully, you can now see why foreclosure is rarely used nowadays.

thinking point 23.7

Foreclosure is occasionally resorted to in 'negative equity situations'. Why?

Although foreclosure is a slow process, where the value of the property is less than the mortgage debt there is seemingly no risk of an order for judicial sale. The mortgagee gets the property, and can sit and hope that (perhaps because of an improvement in the economy) the property will increase in value.

23.6.3 Foreclosure and Dwelling Houses

If the mortgaged property is or includes a dwelling house, there is a further safeguard protecting the mortgagor. The court may adjourn foreclosure proceedings if the mortgagor is likely to be able within a reasonable time to pay 'any sums' due under the mortgage. This flows from s8(3) Administration of Justice Act 1973, which extended to foreclosure the rules restricting a mortgagee taking possession of a dwelling house.

23.7 Remedies of an Equitable Mortgagee or Chargee

23.7.1 Taking Possession

It seems that an equitable mortgagee has no right to take possession of the property, unless the memorandum under seal (or other document) gives the mortgagee the right, which it usually does. It is usually wise to seek a court order for possession.

An equitable chargee does not have a legal estate in land nor a contract for an estate in land (eg a contract for a lease) and so, cannot take possession.

23.7.2 Sale and Appointing a Receiver

A pre-1989 equitable mortgage by deposit of title deeds accompanied by a memorandum under seal was 'made by deed' for the purposes of the statutory power of sale (s101(1) LPA 1925) and other statutory powers, such as the power to appoint a receiver.

Where an equitable mortgage is not 'made by deed' there will be no statutory powers of sale or appointing a receiver. The mortgagee can apply to the court for an order of judicial sale (s91 LPA 1925), or for the court to appoint a receiver.

Section 2 Law of Property (Miscellaneous Provisions) Act 1989 in effect requires all equitable mortgages to be made by a formal document. To incorporate the statutory powers of sale and appointing a receiver, that document will have to be a deed!

cross-reference
See 23.6 for a discussion on foreclosure.

23.7.3 Foreclosure

Nowadays this remedy operates exactly as with a legal mortgage. The only difference is that once an order for foreclosure absolute has been given, the court grants an order for the mortgagor to convey the property to the mortgagee, and so the mortgagee will have the legal title to the property.

Concluding Remarks

The decisions of the Court of Appeal in *Norgan*, *Palk*, *Krausz*, and *Lloyd* all demonstrate that modern judges are striving valiantly to shape the law to fit in with current economic realities.

It is very easy to advocate statutory reform, but it is far more difficult to agree what those reforms should be. Most critics agree that nothing valuable would be lost if foreclosure were abolished and the mortgagee's right to possession restricted to cases where the mortgagor is in serious default. But other questions are more difficult. For example:

- Should the mortgagee be under a duty as to the timing of sale?
- Should (in the light of *Downsview*) restrictions be placed on who can be appointed a receiver?
- Should (strengthening the rule in *Palk*) a mortgagor who has negative equity have an automatic right to cut his losses by having the property sold?
- What, if anything, should be done about the problem highlighted by *Horsham Properties*?

In considering these questions, remember that mortgagees (including the big institutional lenders) will argue that restrictions on their remedies to enforce mortgages will reduce their willingness to lend amounts up to almost the full value of the mortgaged property. If loans secured by a mortgage cease to be readily available, the whole economy of the country will suffer.

Summary

Action on Mortgagor's Covenant to Repay

- Sue in contract.
- Normally used in negative equity cases—mortgagee seeks to recover outstanding amount owed following sale of the property at less than the amount owed.

Sale

- Once the power of sale has arisen, the mortgagee can sell at any time, even when the market is depressed.
- The mortgagee will be liable to the mortgagor if they sell before the power of sale has become exercisable, or if they are negligent in the way the sale is conducted.
- If allegations are made that the sale has been conducted negligently, the onus of proof is on the mortgagor.
- If a mortgagee sells to 'an associated person', the onus will be on the mortgagee to prove they got the best price.

Possession

- Possession is exercised as a preliminary to selling the property:
    - unoccupied premises—common law peaceable re-entry;
    - dwelling house—Administration of Justice Acts restrictions apply.
- Possession proceedings:
    - mortgagor will be able to prevent possession if they can show that they can catch up with their repayments within 'a reasonable time'. Reasonable time means the full duration of the mortgage;
    - negative equity—mortgagor wants to cut their losses by selling, the court may delay a mortgagee's claim to possession for up to a year, at most.

Appoint a Receiver

- This is only relevant where the mortgaged property is leased out to tenants.
- Anybody can be appointed as a receiver, and any losses caused by the receiver are born by the mortgagor:
  - the mortgagor can sue the receiver for negligence.
- The rent collected by the receiver is used to pay off interest owed.
- Any rent remaining after interest has been paid goes to the mortgagor, unless the mortgagee asks for it to be used to reduce the capital debt.

Foreclosure

- Mortgagor's rights are destroyed by court order, and the mortgagee becomes outright owner.
- If there is any positive equity and the mortgagee seeks foreclosure, the mortgagor should ask for a court order of sale.

 # Further Reading

Bently, L, 'Mortgagee's duties on sale—no place for tort?' [1990] Conv 431
Article which examines three cases which curtail the apparent use of the 'neighbour principle' in *Cuckmere*.

Dixon, M, 'Combating the mortgagee's right to possession: new hope for the mortgagor in chains?' (1998) 18(3) *Legal Studies* 279
Extensive critique which examines *Palk v Mortgage Services* in the light of *Cheltenham and Gloucester v Krausz*.

Dixon, M, 'Mortgages duties and commercial transactions' [2006] Conv 278
Case comment which explores the mortgagee's duties when selling a property.

Dixon, M, 'Mortgagees' powers and duties, mortgages, repossession' [2008] Conv 474
Discussion in the light of the 2008–9 credit crisis.

Dixon, M, 'Editor's notebook. Mortgagees powers and duties' [2010] Conv 111
Discusses possible reforms of mortgagees' remedies.

Haley, M, 'Mortgage default: possession, relief and judicial discretion' (1997) 17(3) *Legal Studies* 483
This provides a good discussion on the courts' use of discretion on overriding the mortgagee's right to possession.

Kenny, A, 'No postponement of the evil day' [1998] Conv 223
Evaluation of the courts' approach towards postponement of possession by the mortgagee following *Cheltenham and Gloucester v Krausz*.

Thompson, MP, 'Back to square two' [1996] Conv 118
Case comment on the impact of *Norgan*.

❓ Questions

In 2008, Ketna borrowed £60,000 from the Doorway Building Society. The loan is secured by a first legal mortgage of Ketna's freehold house 'Arkwrite Towers'.

In 2010, Ketna borrowed a further £30,000 from Princewest Finance Ltd secured by a second legal mortgage on Arkwrite Towers. The interest on this loan is 15 per cent, and Ketna has fallen into arrears with her repayments to Princewest.

1 Explain whether it will be possible for Princewest to take possession of and sell Arkwrite Towers, and how such a sale would affect the position of the Doorway Building Society.

2 If Princewest sells Arkwrite Towers at less than its open market value, consider whether Ketna would have any remedy against either:

   (a) Princewest, or

   (b) the purchaser from Princewest.

3 How must Princewest apply the proceeds of any sale of Arkwrite Towers?

The Operation of Mortgages

24

Introduction

The main focus of this chapter will be the position of the mortgagor. The courts have recognized that where the parties are in an unequal bargaining position there is potential for oppression and coercion. We will initially consider the mortgagor's rights and also consider grounds on which a transaction can be set aside. Finally, we will cover redemption of a mortgage and insurance.

Much of the law discussed in this chapter dates from the first 40 years of the twentieth century. This is true not just for the relevant legislation, which is still largely in its 1925 form, but also for much of the case law. Consequently, a law, developed for the economic conditions which prevailed at the beginning of the twentieth century, has to be applied to the very different conditions (in particular the usually higher interest rates) which prevail at the beginning of the twenty-first century.

24.1 Rights of the Mortgagor

In the previous chapter we considered the rights and remedies afforded to the mortgagee in the event of the mortgagor defaulting on the repayment of his loan. The harshness of some of the remedies has been arguably alleviated by the courts, where they have strived to balance the interests of both parties to ensure fairness, but also taken into account the fact that a contract exists, and one party has not met its obligations. In this type of a situation, we discussed the options available to the mortgagee, that is, end the agreement altogether and recover the capital or keep the agreement alive and give the mortgagor another chance.

Equity takes on a protective role towards the mortgagor. This is because a mortgage transaction should simply involve the property being used as security for a loan, and once the debt or obligation has been repaid the mortgage is discharged. That is all. Due to the nature of the transaction and the imbalance of the parties, the mortgagee may attempt to take advantage of the mortgagor by excluding or restricting the equitable right to redeem the mortgage, or persuade the mortgagor to agree to terms which are unfair. In this regard equity protects the mortgagor in the following ways:

- protects the equitable right to redeem from being restricted;
- collateral advantages;
- restraint on trade.

24.1.1 The Rules of Equity Protecting the Equitable Right to Redeem

The equitable right to redeem cannot be excluded by the terms of the mortgage, otherwise if it was excluded this would amount to a 'clog' or 'fetter' on the right to redeem. Lindley MR in *Santley v Wilde* [1899] 2 Ch 474 explained:

> Any provision inserted to prevent redemption on payment or performance of the debt or obligation for which the security was given is what is meant by a clog or fetter on the equity of redemption and is therefore void. It follows from this, that 'once a mortgage always a mortgage'…A 'clog' or 'fetter' is something which is inconsistent with the idea of 'security': a clog or fetter is in the nature of a repugnant condition…If I give a mortgage on a condition that I shall not redeem, that is a repugnant condition.

A clog or fetter is an intolerable restriction of the rights of the mortgagor. The right to redemption is regarded as inviolable. In *Browne v Ryan* [1901] 2 IR 653 Walker LJ said:

> Where a transaction appears, or has been declared to be a mortgage…the mortgagor is entitled to get back his property as free as he gave it, on payment of principal, interest, and costs, and provisions inconsistent with the right cannot be enforced. The equitable rules 'once a mortgage always a mortgage' and that the mortgagee cannot impose any 'clog or fetter on the equity of redemption' are merely concise statements of the same rule.

The approach of not permitting any clog or fetter must be treated with caution. These passages seem to assume at the outset that the mortgagor is the vulnerable party. Is that always the case? That may be so when considering residential mortgages, but can the same be said about commercial mortgages where the parties to the contract are at the same level, that is, both are businesses and have equal bargaining strength. Where businesses are concerned they ought to be able to have the freedom to contract and the clog and fetter analysis seems to inhibit this freedom. The issue to consider whilst reading sections 24.1.2 to 24.1.5 is whether the clog and fetter analysis still holds true today.

To escape from the clog and fetter rule, attempts have been made, from time to time, to disguise a mortgage as some other transaction. However, equity treats any transaction which in substance is the grant of security for a loan, as a mortgage. For example, suppose Andrea conveys Greenacre to Betty for £w, but Betty immediately grants Andrea an option to repurchase the property in x years' time for £y. £y appears to be £w plus interest for x years. This transaction would be regarded as unfair because Betty has become the legal owner of Greenacre and the right to redeem has been circumvented. Equity will examine the substance of the transaction and consider the intention of the parties at the time of the agreement. In our scenario equity will treat this transaction as a mortgage, with an equitable right to redeem continuing after x years have expired.

24.1.2 No Irredeemable Mortgages

The equitable right to redeem becomes effective when the legal date of redemption has passed. If the mortgage includes a term which excludes the equitable right then it is void. Consequently, a mortgage cannot be made irredeemable.

It is important to remember that the essence of a mortgage is that by having repaid the debt the mortgagor must get the property back free from all rights of the mortgagee. As the older cases say, there must be no 'fetters' or 'clogs' on redemption. One consequence of this is that it is impossible to include, as a term of the mortgage, a provision giving the mortgagee an option to purchase the mortgaged property. But if, after the land has been mortgaged, the mortgagor as a completely separate transaction grants an option to the mortgagee, the option is valid.

The House of Lords in *Samuel v Jarrah Timber and Wood Paving Corporation Ltd* [1904] AC 323 considered whether an option to purchase granted to the mortgagee exercisable within 12 months of granting the mortgage was void. The House of Lords did not consider the option as being disadvantageous to the mortgagor even though its effect was to exclude the right to redeem. The House, having taken into account the legal authorities in this area, concluded the option was void despite the view that this agreement amounted to a fair bargain. Lord Macnaghten said:

> Speaking for myself, I should not be sorry if your Lordships could see your way to modify it so as to prevent its being used as a means of evading a fair bargain come to between persons dealing at arms' length and negotiating on equal terms. The directors of a trading company in search of financial assistance are certainly in a very different position from that of an impecunious landowner in the toils of a crafty money-lender. At the same time I quite feel the difficulty of interfering with any rule that has prevailed so long . . .

The House of Lords recognized that the principle against clogs or fetters on the right to redeem was not without problems, particularly in the commercial context. As this passage says, the parties were regarded as being at arm's length and negotiating on equal terms. The parties had entered into the contract with their 'eyes open'.

The harshness of this decision in the commercial context was lessened somewhat by *Reeve v Lisle* [1902] AC 461, where the option to purchase was granted ten days after the mortgage. The option was treated as a separate and independent transaction and its validity upheld.

In *Lewis v Frank Love Ltd* [1961] 1 WLR 264 the court considered two transactions which were created on the same day: mortgage and an option to purchase. The court focused on the substance of the documents and whether they formed part of the same transaction. The court concluded that the option was a clog on the equitable right to redeem.

Jonathan Parker LJ in *Warnborough Ltd v Garmite* [2003] EWCA Civ 1544 explained the approach adopted by the courts in situations where there is a transaction involving a mortgage and an option to purchase for the mortgagee and said that it is:

> glaringly clear from the authorities that the mere fact that, contemporaneously with the grant of a mortgage over his property, the mortgagor grants the mortgagee an option to purchase the property does no more than raise the question whether the rule against 'clogs' applies: it does not begin to answer that question. As has been said over and over again in the authorities, in order to answer that question the court has to look at the 'substance' of the transaction in question: in other words, to inquire as to the true nature of the bargain which the parties have made. To do that, the court examines all the circumstances, with the assistance of oral evidence if necessary.

Whatever the position regarding options granted to mortgagees, it would appear that, as a completely separate transaction, a mortgagor can sell or lease the land to the mortgagee (*Alec Lobb (Garages) Ltd v Total Oil* [1985] 1 All ER 303).

24.1.3 Postponement of Redemption

Occasionally a mortgage is created which deliberately postpones the legal redemption date from the traditional six months, and in effect provides that the debt cannot be repaid until *x* years have run. Most mortgagees are, of course, very pleased when the debt is repaid, so you may well be asking, 'Why should a mortgagee want to postpone the right to redeem?' There are two possible answers to this question. In some cases the mortgagee, who is in effect investing their money in the loan, may want to be sure that their investment continues for a long period. The mortgagee may not want the bother of finding a new investment if the mortgage debt is repaid.

The second answer lies in the well-known fact that when a brewery lends money to a publican, the mortgage will include a tie clause tying the publican's pub to the brewery. (A similar thing happens, of course, with petrol companies and filling stations.) By postponing the right to redeem, the brewery (or petrol company) hopes to prolong the duration of the tie as long as possible.

A postponement of redemption is valid only if on all the facts the postponement is not 'unconscionable or oppressive' to the mortgagor. If the postponement is void under this rule, the mortgagor can redeem at any time.

Where there is a mortgage of a lease, and the postponement is so long that the right to redeem is of very little value, the postponement is undoubtedly void. In *Fairclough v Swan Brewery Ltd* [1912] AC 565, a lease of a hotel with 17 years to run was mortgaged to a brewery, redemption being postponed until there was just six weeks to run on the lease. (The mortgage of course included a 'tie' to the brewery.) The Privy Council having considered the substance of the mortgage agreement had no difficulty holding the postponement invalid because had the lease been redeemed on the date of redemption it would be valueless. Lord Macnaghten said:

> ...a mortgage cannot be made irredeemable. That is plainly forbidden. Is there any difference between forbidding redemption and permitting it, if the permission be a mere pretence? Here the provision for redemption is nugatory. The encumbrance on the lease the subject of the mortgage according to the letter of the bargain falls to be discharged before the lease terminates, but at a time when it is on the very point of expiring, when redemption can be of no advantage to the mortgagor even if he should be so fortunate as to get his deeds back before the actual termination of the lease. For all practical purposes this mortgage is irredeemable. It was obviously meant to be irredeemable. It was made irredeemable in and by the mortgage itself.

Where there is a mortgage of a fee simple there is no set rule that a postponement for greater than *x* years is void, but for less than *x* years is valid. Whether the postponement is oppressive or unconscionable depends on the circumstances of each case. The relative economic strengths of the parties are all important.

In *Knightsbridge Estates v Byrne* [1939] Ch 441 a London property company mortgaged land to an insurance company (both parties were of equal bargaining strength). A postponement of redemption for 40 years was held to be valid. It was in all the circumstances perfectly fair that the insurance company stipulate that the mortgage continue as a long-term investment. Sir Wilfrid Greene MR said:

> The first argument was that the postponement of the contractual right to redeem for forty years was void in itself, in other words, that the making of such an agreement between mortgagor and mortgagee was prohibited by a rule of equity. It was not contended that a provision in a mortgage deed making the mortgage irredeemable for a period of years is necessarily void. The argument was that such a period must be a 'reasonable' one, and it was said that the period in the present case was an unreasonable one by reason merely of its length. This argument was not the one accepted by the learned judge.
>
> Now an argument such as this requires the closest scrutiny, for, if it is correct, it means that an agreement made between two competent parties, acting under expert advice and presumably knowing their own business best, is one which the law forbids them to make upon the ground that it is not 'reasonable.' If we were satisfied that the rule of equity was what it is said to be, we should be bound to give effect to it... A decision to that effect would, in our view, involve an unjustified interference with the freedom of business men to enter into agreements best suited to their interests and would impose upon them a test of 'reasonableness' laid down by the Courts without reference to the business realities of the case.

...The property was subject to a mortgage at a high rate of interest and this mortgage was liable to be called in at any time. In these circumstances the respondents were, when the negotiations began, desirous of obtaining for themselves two advantages: (1.) a reduction in the rate of interest, (2.) the right to repay the mortgage moneys by instalments spread over a long period of years. The desirability of obtaining these terms from a business point of view is manifest, and it is not to be assumed that these respondents were actuated by anything but pure considerations of business in seeking to obtain them...The resulting agreement was a commercial agreement between two important corporations experienced in such matters, and has none of the features of an oppressive bargain where the borrower is at the mercy of an unscrupulous lender. In transactions of this kind it is notorious that there is competition among the large insurance companies and other bodies having large funds to invest, and we are not prepared to view the agreement made as anything but a proper business transaction.

But it is said not only that the period of postponement must be a reasonable one, but that in judging the 'reasonableness' of the period the considerations which we have mentioned cannot be regarded; that the Court is bound to judge 'reasonableness' by a consideration of the terms of the mortgage deed itself and without regard to extraneous matters. In the absence of clear authority we emphatically decline to consider a question of 'reasonableness' from a standpoint so unreal. To hold that the law is to tell business men what is reasonable in such circumstances and to refuse to take into account the business considerations involved, would bring the law into disrepute ...

Assuming therefore, without in any way deciding, that the period during which the contractual right of redemption is postponed must be a 'reasonable' one (a question which we will now proceed to examine), we are of opinion that the respondents have failed to establish (and the burden is on them) that there is anything unreasonable in the mere extension of the period for forty years in the circumstances of the present case.

But in our opinion the proposition that a postponement of the contractual right of redemption is only permissible for a 'reasonable' time is not well-founded. Such a postponement is not properly described as a clog on the equity of redemption, since it is concerned with the contractual right to redeem. It is indisputable that any provision which hampers redemption after the contractual date for redemption has passed will not be permitted. Further, it is undoubtedly true to say that a right of redemption is a necessary element in a mortgage transaction, and consequently that, where the contractual right of redemption is illusory, equity will grant relief by allowing redemption. This was the point in the case of *Fairclough v. Swan Brewery Co.* [1912] AC 565 ...

Moreover, equity may give relief against contractual terms in a mortgage transaction if they are oppressive or unconscionable, and in deciding whether or not a particular transaction falls within this category the length of time for which the contractual right to redeem is postponed may well be an important consideration. In the present case no question of this kind was or could have been raised.

But equity does not reform mortgage transactions because they are unreasonable. It is concerned to see two things—one that the essential requirements of a mortgage transaction are observed, and the other that oppressive or unconscionable terms are not enforced. Subject to this, it does not, in our opinion, interfere. The question therefore arises whether, in a case where the right of redemption is real and not illusory and there is nothing oppressive or unconscionable in the transaction, there is something in a postponement of the contractual right to redeem, such as we have in the present case, that is inconsistent with the essential requirements of a mortgage transaction? Apart from authority the answer to this question would, in our opinion, be clearly in the negative. Any other answer would place an unfortunate restriction on the liberty of contract of competent parties who are at arm's length—in the present case it would have operated to prevent the respondents obtaining financial terms which for obvious reasons they themselves considered to be most desirable. It would, moreover, lead to highly inequitable results. The remedy sought by the respondents and the only remedy which is said to be open to them is the establishment of a right to redeem at any time on the ground that the postponement of the contractual right to redeem is void ...

The court in *Knightsbridge Estates v Byrne* resisted any variation on the approach adopted by the courts so far in evaluating an agreement according to whether the postponement was reasonable or not. The court indicated a marked reluctance to interfere with bargains agreed between two equal parties and viewed the mortgage agreement as 'a proper business transaction'. Equity would only grant relief where the terms are oppressive or unconscionable and not simply because they are unreasonable, though as the court said it may be a consideration. The focus remains the same and in the court's evaluation of oppression and unconscionability they found nothing which would suggest otherwise. The parties were after all at arm's length.

collateral advantage
a mortgagee stipulates in return for their loan they shall get as well as a normal rate of interest, some other additional benefit.

24.1.4 Collateral Advantages

The modern approach of the courts towards collateral advantages differs considerably from cases stemming from the seventeenth and eighteenth centuries. At that time collateral advantages were viewed with suspicion and as a means of exploiting the borrower. They were also perceived as a means of circumventing the usury laws. The usury laws limited the rate of interest which the mortgagee could charge. The usury laws were repealed in 1854. The House of Lords in *G & C Kreglinger v New Patagonia Meat and Cold Storage Co Ltd* [1914] AC 25 took a completely different view from hitherto and Lord Parker of Waddington declared:

> there is now no rule in equity which precludes a mortgagee ... from stipulating for any collateral advantage, provided such collateral advantage is not either (1.) unfair and unconscionable, or (2.) in the nature of a penalty clogging the equity of redemption, or (3.) inconsistent with or repugnant to the contractual and equitable right to redeem.

These principles form the basis of the courts' assessment of collateral advantages.

The most common example of a collateral advantage is, as you may have guessed, a 'tie' (known as a solus agreement) to a mortgagee brewery or petrol company. Examples of other kinds of more unusual collateral advantages include index-linked capital repayments and very high interest rates.

Collateral advantages give rise to two distinct problems:

- validity of the advantage while the loan remains outstanding; and
- validity of the advantage after redemption of the mortgage.

Validity While the Mortgage Subsists

A collateral advantage is in principle valid as long as the mortgage remains unredeemed. It is void only if it is oppressive or unconscionable in nature.

'Ties' are generally not oppressive or unconscionable, nor it seems are they in unreasonable restraint of trade, provided they cease on redemption and the right to redeem is not postponed beyond the traditional six months.

In *Multi-Service Bookbinding v Marden* [1979] Ch 84, there was a rather unusual 'collateral advantage'. In September 1966, the claimant company mortgaged its premises to the defendant private investor, who lent £36,000. The mortgage was entered into at a time of quite high inflation, and at a time when the pound was depreciating against other major currencies. The defendant was anxious to preserve the real value of his investment—to make it inflation-proof.

Clause 6 of the mortgage, called 'the Swiss franc uplift', provided for the capital and interest repayments to increase proportionate to the decrease in value of the pound sterling against the Swiss franc. In modern terminology, the repayments were index-linked to the Swiss franc.

In September 1966 one pound sterling was worth a little over 12 Swiss francs. Ten years later (when the litigation commenced) the pound had slumped to be worth a little over four Swiss francs. Thus, if clause 6 was valid, the repayments in pounds sterling would be about three times greater than the original figures. The company sought a declaration that clause 6 was invalid.

Clause 6 was upheld, it was neither oppressive nor unconscionable. But note that the lender in this case was a private individual anxious to preserve his capital investment. An unscrupulous firm of moneylenders might well not receive such sympathetic treatment.

Browne-Wilkinson J said:

> I turn then to the question whether the mortgage is unconscionable or unreasonable. The plaintiffs' starting point on this aspect of the case is a submission that a lender on mortgage is only entitled to repayment of principal, interest and costs. If the lender additionally stipulates for a premium or other collateral advantage the court will not enforce such additional stipulation unless it is reasonable. Then it is submitted that clause 6, providing for the payment of the Swiss franc uplift in addition to the nominal amount of capital and interest, is a premium which in all the circumstances is unreasonable. Alternatively it is said that the terms of the mortgage taken together are unreasonable. In my judgment the argument so advanced is based on a false premise. Since the repeal of the usury laws there has been no general principle that collateral advantages in mortgages have to be 'reasonable' . . .
>
> I therefore approach the second point on the basis that, in order to be freed from the necessity to comply with all the terms of the mortgage, the plaintiffs must show that the bargain, or some of its terms, was unfair and unconscionable; it is not enough to show that, in the eyes of the court, it was unreasonable. In my judgment a bargain cannot be unfair and unconscionable unless one of the parties to it has imposed the objectionable terms in a morally reprehensible manner, that is to say, in a way which affects his conscience.
>
> The classic example of an unconscionable bargain is where advantage has been taken of a young, inexperienced or ignorant person to introduce a term which no sensible well-advised person or party would have accepted. But I do not think the categories of unconscionable bargains are limited; the court can and should intervene where a bargain has been procured by unfair means.
>
> . . . considering the mortgage bargain as a whole, in my judgment there was no great inequality of bargaining power as between the plaintiffs and the defendant. The plaintiff company was a small but prosperous company in need of cash to enable it to expand: if it did not like the terms offered it could have refused them without being made insolvent . . . The defendant is not a professional moneylender and there is no evidence of any sharp practice of any kind by him. The borrowers were represented by independent solicitors of repute. Therefore the background does not give rise to any pre-supposition that the defendant took an unfair advantage of the plaintiffs.
>
> . . . The defendant made a hard bargain. But the test is not reasonableness. The parties made a bargain which the plaintiffs, who are businessmen, went into with their eyes open, with the benefit of independent advice, without any compelling necessity to accept a loan on these terms and without any sharp practice by the defendant. I cannot see that there was anything unfair or oppressive or morally reprehensible in such a bargain entered into in such circumstances.

The court in this case discarded the notion of 'reasonableness' of the bargain as the applicable test. The focus is on whether the bargain is unfair or unconscionable, and imposed on the mortgagor in a manner which is viewed as 'morally reprehensible'. There was nothing to suggest that that was the case here. The bargaining powers of the parties were found to be equal and the mortgagor had sought independent advice.

In contrast to this case, in *Cityland & Property (Holdings) Ltd v Dabrah* [1968] Ch 166, the court struck down an unfair mortgage term. The mortgagor had borrowed £2,900 to purchase a property. The loan included a large premium payable on the repayment of the capital and when added to the loan the total sum to be repaid at the end of six years was £4,553. A year later the borrower defaulted on the loan. The mortgagee claimed payment of all the money owed, that is, £4,553 minus what had been paid. The court in this case evaluated the premium added to the loan at 57 per cent, which was equivalent to 19 per cent interest to be paid per annum. This was out of proportion to the prevailing investment rates at the time. An interest rate of 7 per cent was substituted. In this case the strength of the parties was imbalanced and there was no justification for such a high premium.

In *Davies v Directloans Ltd* [1986] 2 All ER 783, the terms of a loan granted to a cohabiting couple to enable them to buy a house were held valid, even though the rate of interest charged was 21.6 per cent at a time when the market rate was approximately 17 per cent. The couple's income was very uncertain (they were artists by profession), and they were therefore unable to borrow from institutional lenders. The higher rate of interest in the court's view reflected that given the precarious state of their finances and having had legal advice, the interest rate charge was not extortionate.

Collateral Advantages after Redemption

The types of collateral advantages that are under consideration in this section are usually solus agreements. The solus agreement or tie is a sole distribution agreement, for example a brewery in return for having provided the finance for a loan to a pub landlord would require the pub to sell only the brewery's beer and other products. According to *Biggs v Hoddinott* [1898] 2 Ch 307 this type of agreement is perfectly valid as long as it is not an oppressive or unconscionable bargain.

The difficult issue is whether the solus agreement can continue beyond the redemption of the mortgage. However, the basic principle is that where a collateral advantage is inserted in a mortgage, it ceases to have effect on the redemption of a mortgage even though it was intended that the advantage should continue after redemption.

thinking point 24.1

What happens, on redemption of the mortgage, to a 'tie clause' tying the borrower to the lender's beer, petrol, or whatever?

The answer to this was explained by the House of Lords in Noakes v Rice *[1902] AC 24.*

In *Noakes v Rice* there was a solus tie between a brewery and pub landlord. The effect of this agreement was such that the pub prior to the mortgage was a free house, but if the mortgage was redeemed it would continue to be a 'tied house'. The House of Lords confirmed that the solus tie clause in a mortgage must cease on redemption. The Earl of Halsbury LC explained:

> ...it appears to me that undoubtedly this was a mortgage, and that the equity of redemption is clogged and fettered here by the continuance of an obligation which would render this house less available in the hands of its owner during the whole period and beyond the whole period of the term, apart from the realization of the security. Under those circumstances, as a matter of the merest and simplest reasoning, I am wholly unable to come to any other conclusion than that there is a clog and fetter here which the law will not permit.

This orthodox approach was unsuccessfully challenged in *Bradley v Carritt* [1903] AC 253. The mortgagor was the controlling shareholder of a tea company and mortgaged his shares to a tea broker. The mortgage included a collateral advantage under which the mortgagor promised that the mortgagee should always remain broker to the company or pay commission to him if he loses his tea brokerage in the company.

The House of Lords by a majority held that the mortgagor, having paid off the mortgage, was released from this promise of permanent employment for the mortgagee and the collateral advantage became void. Had the collateral advantage continued to be valid, the mortgagor would have never been free to dispose of his shares. He would have had to have kept them. Lord Davey said:

> ...In the present case the agreement is that the appellant W M Bradley will, 'as a shareholder,' use his best endeavours to secure the sale of the company's teas to the respondent or his firm, and in the event of the teas being sold through another broker will pay to the respondent the amount of the commission which he or his firm might have earned. In other words, he agrees to use the voting power attached to his shares in a particular way for the respondent's benefit. Now, what is a share? It is but a bundle of rights, of which the right of voting at meetings of the company is not the least valuable. My Lords, can it be said that the mortgagee does not retain a hold upon the shares which form the mortgaged property, or that the mortgagor has full redemption of it, when the latter is not free to exercise an important right in such manner as he may think most conducive to his own interests? He may think it advantageous to the company to employ another broker, or that the change would produce a better return on his shares, but if he gives effect to his opinion he incurs what is in effect a heavy penalty. Again, the appellant could not part with or otherwise deal with his shares without losing the influence in the company's counsels which might enable him to secure the performance of the first part of the agreement, or running a serious risk of liability under the second part...

(This rule regarding collateral advantages as a fetter on the equitable right to redeem applies whether the collateral advantage (tie clause or whatever) is contained in the mortgage deed, or in some other document contemporaneous to the mortgage.)

A Collateral Advantage as an Independent Agreement

The House of Lords in *Kreglinger v New Patagonia Meat Co* [1914] AC 25 took a slightly different view of collateral advantages. A collateral advantage appearing in a mortgage deed may on occasion be treated as an independent agreement separate from the mortgage. If a collateral advantage is held to be an independent agreement it has continuing validity after redemption of the mortgage.

In *Kreglinger v New Patagonia Meat Co* the meat company were mortgagors, while the mortgagees were a firm of woolbrokers. The mortgage contained a provision that for the next five years the company should not sell any sheepskins to any other person without first offering them to the woolbrokers at the best price obtainable elsewhere.

The idea of this clause was, in effect, to guarantee to the woolbrokers (the mortgagees) a supply of sheepskins for the next five years. The woolbrokers accepted a slightly reduced rate of interest in return for this guarantee (2.5 per cent instead of 2.75 per cent). The mortgagor repaid the debt after only two years. The House of Lords held that the 'sheepskins clause' remained valid for the full five years, even though the mortgagors had redeemed the mortgage. Viscount Haldane LC said:

> The result is that a collateral advantage may now be stipulated for by the mortgagee provided that he has not acted unfairly or oppressively, and provided that the bargain does not conflict with the third form of the principle. This is that a mortgage...cannot be made irredeemable, and that any stipulation which restricts or clogs the equity of redemption is void. It is obvious that the reason for the doctrine in this form is the same as that which gave rise to the other forms. It is simply an assertion in a different way of the principle that once a mortgage always a mortgage and nothing else.
>
> ...it is inconsistent with the objects for which they were established that these rules should crystallize into technical language so rigid that the letter can defeat the underlying spirit and purpose. Their application must correspond with the practical necessities of the time. The

rule as to collateral advantages, for example, has been much modified by the repeal of the usury laws and by the recognition of modern varieties of commercial bargaining...Unless such a bargain is unconscionable it is now good. But none the less the other and wider principle remains unshaken, that it is the essence of a mortgage that in the eye of a Court of Equity it should be a mere security for money, and that no bargain can be validly made which will prevent the mortgagor from redeeming on payment of what is due, including principal, interest, and costs...But whenever a right to redeem arises out of the doctrine of equity, he is precluded from fettering it. This principle has become an integral part of our system of jurisprudence and must be faithfully adhered to.

...the question in the present case is whether the right to redeem has been interfered with. And this must, for the reasons to which I have adverted in considering the history of the doctrine of equity, depend on the answer to a question which is primarily one of fact. What was the true character of the transaction? Did the appellants make a bargain such that the right to redeem was cut down, or did they simply stipulate for a collateral undertaking, outside and clear of the mortgage, which would give them an exclusive option of purchase of the sheepskins of the respondents? The question is in my opinion not whether the two contracts were made at the same moment and evidenced by the same instrument, but whether they were in substance a single and undivided contract or two distinct contracts. Putting aside for the moment considerations turning on the character of the floating charge, such an option no doubt affects the freedom of the respondents in carrying on their business even after the mortgage has been paid off. But so might other arrangements which would be plainly collateral, an agreement, for example, to take permanently into the firm a new partner as a condition of obtaining fresh capital in the form of a loan. The question is one not of form but of substance, and it can be answered in each case only by looking at all the circumstances, and not by mere reliance on some abstract principle...

The distinction drawn by the House of Lords in *Kreglinger* between advantages which 'form part of the terms of the mortgage' and advantages which are 'independent agreements' is often criticized as being very artificial. The 'independent agreement' rule is in reality a convenient way of distinguishing collateral advantages such as 'ties' imposed by the unequal bargaining strengths of the parties, from fair advantages agreed to by parties of equal bargaining strength. *Kreglinger* was a case falling into the latter category.

24.1.5 Restraint on Trade

Under contract law any agreement which unreasonably restricts the freedom to trade is void on grounds of public policy. The courts have shown a willingness to consider mortgage agreements within the context of a restraint on trade. In *Esso Petroleum Co Ltd v Harper's Garage (Stourport) Ltd* [1968] AC 269, the respondents owned two garages and entered into two separate solus agreements with Esso. The respondent agreed to buy petrol from Esso. The first agreement was to last for four years and five months. The second agreement was to last for 21 years. In relation to the second garage the respondents received a loan from Esso to be repaid in instalments over 21 years and not redeemable before the end of that period. Included in the mortgage agreement was a covenant to keep the garage open during normal working hours and to purchase all fuel from Esso.

The House of Lords accepted that the tie in for four years and five months was reasonable and valid. However, the 21-year solus tie was an unreasonable restraint on trade. Lord Reid explained there had to be some economic justification to permit a long tie-in period, '...I would think that there must at least be some clearly established advantage to the producing company—something to show that a shorter period would not be adequate—before so long a period could be justified. But in this case there is no evidence to prove anything of the kind.'

The House of Lords also disapproved of the prolonged length of time redemption period. Lord Hodson said:

> The mortgage was irredeemable for 21 years and was part and parcel of the tying agreement and the compulsory trading agreement, so that unless ties contained in a mortgage are outside the doctrine of restraint of trade the period of 21 years is so long as to be unreasonable in the absence of evidence to justify it. I see no reason why a tie in a mortgage is to be treated in a special way. The point was considered in *Horwood v. Millar's Timber & Trading Co. Ltd.* [1917] 1 KB 305 although this was not a case of mortgage of land, and the court held that a covenant in restraint of trade contained in a mortgage deed was bad. Reliance was placed on *Knightsbridge Estates Trust Ltd. v. Byrne* [1939] Ch 441 for the proposition of Sir Wilfrid Greene M.R. that 'equity does not reform mortgage transactions because they are unreasonable. It is concerned to see … that oppressive or unconscionable terms are not enforced.' The Master of the Rolls was not dealing with covenants in restraint of trade. These must be tested by the same criterion, whether they are contained in mortgages or not, unless there is some exception in relation to land. I have already expressed the view that there is no such exception. I agree, therefore, with the opinion of the Court of Appeal that the tying covenant and the compulsory trading covenant are unenforceable. These are so closely linked with the provision that the mortgage is to be irredeemable for 21 years that I would hold that they all fall together, so that the respondents are entitled to redeem.

(Solus ties could potentially come within the scope of Article 101 of the Treaty on the Functioning of the European Union as being an anti-competitive agreement (*Crehan v Inntrepreneur Pub Co (CPC)* [2007] 1 AC 333).)

24.1.6 Statutory Regulation of Mortgages

The vast majority of residential mortgages, which are first mortgages, are regulated by the Financial Services and Markets Act 2000.

Mortgages such as second mortgages and other credit agreements are regulated under the Consumer Credit Act 2006. The 2006 Act repeals and replaces ss 137–140 Consumer Credit Act 1974. The new provisions apply to all loans taken out by an individual on or after 6 April 2007. Rather controversially the Act also applies retrospectively to existing loan agreements from April 2008.

The old concept of 'extortionate credit bargain' which had not in practice provided much protection for borrowers, has been replaced by the broader concept of an 'unfair credit relationship'. If there is such an unfair credit relationship, the court will be able to intervene and protect the borrower, if necessary by varying or rewriting the terms of the agreement.

Under the Consumer Credit Act 2006, in determining whether there is an unfair credit relationship, the court must consider all the circumstances, including:

> *Consumer Credit Act 2006*
>
> 19. Unfair relationships between creditors and debtors
>
> After section 140 of the 1974 Act insert—
>
> 140A. Unfair relationships between creditors and debtors
>
> 1. (a) any of the terms of the agreement or of any related agreement;
>   (b) the way in which the creditor has exercised or enforced any of his rights under the agreement or any related agreement;
>   (c) any other thing done (or not done) by, or on behalf of, the creditor (either before or after the making of the agreement or any related agreement).

Note that the court is not just concerned with the original terms of the agreement, but also how those terms (eg as to variable interest rates) have been operated by the creditor. It is suggested that the 2006 Act is unlikely to create problems for big institutional lenders lending money secured by mortgages, but may well be used against less scrupulous lenders such as some of the smaller finance houses.

24.2 Leasing of the Mortgaged Property

24.2.1 Leases Prior to the Mortgage

The basic principle with leases granted before the creation of the mortgage is that the mortgagee will be bound by the lease.

If the freehold title is registered title then it must be remembered that legal leases for more than seven years must be substantively registered. If a new lease by deed for more than seven years is not entered onto the register, then it will not be binding on a subsequent mortgagee.

If the freehold title is unregistered, then existing legal leases are good against the whole world, and are therefore binding on a subsequent mortgagee.

24.2.2 Leases Subsequent to the Mortgage

Under s99 Law of Property Act 1925 (LPA 1925), a mortgagor in possession has a statutory power to grant certain kinds of leases that will bind the mortgagee. This includes: a lease for 50 years for agricultural or occupation purposes, or building leases for 999 years (s99(3)(i)–(ii) LPA 1925).

This statutory power belongs to the mortgagee if they have taken possession, or if the mortgagee has appointed a receiver; otherwise the power belongs to the mortgagor. In practice, modern mortgages usually exclude the mortgagor's power to grant leases, but not the mortgagee's.

thinking point 24.2

Why do you think that modern mortgages usually exclude the mortgagor's statutory power to grant leases?

Because, despite the restrictions set out in the following text, mortgagees fear that mortgagors will lease the property on terms which (particularly as to rent) will reduce the value of their security.

In the relatively rare cases where the statutory power to grant a lease applies, the following restrictions are imposed (s99 LPA 1925):

- no mining or forestry leases are allowed;
- building leases may be granted for up to 999 years; otherwise the lease must not exceed 50 years;
- the lease must take effect in possession within 12 months;
- the lease must be at the best rent reasonably obtainable. A premium ('fine') must not be charged;

- the tenant must covenant to pay the rent. There must be a forfeiture clause for non-payment of rent if the rent is 30 days in arrear (a lesser period of grace may be fixed); and

- the lease need not be by deed. The tenant, however, should execute a counterpart (ie copy of the lease), but failure to do so does not invalidate the lease.

24.2.3 Unauthorized Leases

Mortgagees commonly exclude the mortgagor's statutory power to grant leases by including in the mortgage deed a prohibition on granting leases. If the mortgagor remains in possession of the mortgaged property and grants an unauthorized lease, the lease will not bind the mortgagee and will be void against the mortgagee (*Dudley and District Benefit Building Society v Emerson* [1949] Ch 707). This lease will nevertheless still bind the mortgagor and the tenant. In this situation a tenancy by estoppel has been created (*Iron Trades Employers Insurance Association Ltd v Union Land and House Investors Ltd* [1937] Ch 313).

A tenant who has an unauthorized lease is in a weak position. There are two reasons for this. First, the tenant may be viewed by the mortgagee as a trespasser. The mortgagee can in that case exercise their legal right to take possession by evicting the tenant. In *Iron Trades Employers Insurance Association Ltd v Union Land and House Investors Ltd* [1937] Ch 313, Farwell J explained:

> The mortgagee as soon as he ascertained that the mortgagor had granted a lease to a third party was entitled to take steps to evict the tenant, to treat him as a trespasser, and, subject to the tenant's right to redeem, the mortgagee could evict him and recover possession of the property. On the other hand, he might, if he desired, confirm what had been done, but if, knowing the facts, he stayed his hand and did nothing, he might find himself in danger of being held to have acquiesced in and thereby confirmed the lease and, therefore, not entitled to oust the tenant.

Mortgagees need to be careful not to lose their right to evict the unauthorized tenant. Merely knowing there is a tenant in the mortgaged property is not in itself sufficient to imply that the mortgagee has consented to the tenant being there (*Taylor v Ellis* [1960] Ch 368). The mortgagee could, however, be estopped from claiming that the lease is not binding on them. The mortgagee could use words or conduct which would indicate to a reasonable person in the position of the tenant that the mortgagee does regard the tenant's rights as binding upon them.

Appointing a receiver does not give rise to an estoppel, as the receiver is deemed to be the mortgagor's agent. However, creating the impression that the mortgagee is now the landlord and the receiver is their agent would raise the estoppel. For example, in *Chatsworth Properties v Effiom* [1971] 1 All ER 604 the mortgagee wrote to the tenants saying, 'Do not pay your rent to your *former* landlord, but to the receiver we have appointed.' The mortgagee was held to be estopped, and bound by the tenants' leases.

The second reason for the weakness of the tenant's position is that the tenant may only find out about the mortgagor's (landlord) financial problems when formal notification of possession proceedings is made (*Britannia Building Society v Earl* [1990] 1 WLR 422). To alleviate the potential problems of the tenant having to find a new place to live in a short period of time, the Mortgage Repossession (Protection of Tenants etc) Act 2010 provides protection for tenants who have unauthorized leases. This Act gives the tenant of a dwelling house one opportunity to apply to the court to postpone possession. Postponement can only be granted for a period of up to two months. Mortgagees are now under an obligation to send a notice to the property warning of a proposed possession order being executed.

Vitiating Factor—Undue Influence

In the previous section we have considered the position of the mortgagor desperate for a loan who has been placed under unfair pressure by the mortgagee. In this section we are considering the situation where a third party pressurizes the mortgagor into cooperating in the granting of a mortgage so that the third party can get a loan from a lending organization.

More specifically, the third party may have exerted undue influence or made misrepresentations and this has led the spouse, cohabitee, relative, or friend to agree to a mortgage of co-owned property. The mortgage is to secure a loan which the third party will use for their own purposes. For example, consider the fact scenario: H and W (who may or may not be married) jointly own their home. H wants to raise money, usually to finance a business enterprise. H wants to be able to mortgage the house to secure a bank loan, but to do that he needs W's agreement. H puts emotional pressure on W to execute the deed, and she, wanting to please her husband (or partner), signs. The business venture fails, and the bank, which did not actually know of the pressure H had put on W, wants to enforce its mortgage.

In this situation what W really wants is for the court to rule that H's undue influence (albeit not known to the bank) makes the mortgage void against the bank.

In an attempt, on the one hand, to provide safeguards for a person who has been subject to undue influence or misrepresentation and, on the other, to protect the mortgagee from losing its security, the courts have developed specific guidelines to ensure that the interests of both parties are balanced. Both undue influence and misrepresentation are treated in the same manner by the courts. In general there are three factors that will need to be considered where it is alleged that a transaction is vitiated by undue influence:

- the surety or mortgagor must establish undue influence, that is, he or she was induced into agreeing to the loan;
- factual circumstances which should lead the lender to believe that there is a possibility of undue influence; and
- the steps the bank needs to take in the event of a possibility of undue influence arising.

The two notable House of Lords decisions *O'Brien* and *Etridge* considered these issues and they will form the basis of our discussions. In cases concerning undue influence, you will come across the term 'surety'. Almost invariably, in this context, this concept involves (primarily) W agreeing to the mortgage of the co-owned home.

24.3.1 What is Undue Influence According to *O'Brien*?

What amounted to undue influence was considered in the House of Lords in *Barclays Bank v O'Brien* [1994] 1 AC 180.

Mrs O'Brien, the claimant, was surety for a loan made by the bank to her husband. Mr O'Brien's business had been struggling and the loan was taken out to resolve some of its financial problems. The loan was secured by a mortgage on the matrimonial home, in which Mrs O'Brien had an equitable interest. No one at the bank explained the mortgage documents to her nor was she advised to seek legal advice. Mrs O'Brien signed the mortgage documents at the bank without reading them and without taking independent legal advice.

In due course Mr O'Brien defaulted in repayment of the loan and the bank sought to enforce its security by taking possession of the matrimonial home. Mrs O'Brien claimed that the mortgage should be set aside, alleging that Mr O'Brien had assured her that the loan was of £60,000 only. It was, in fact, a loan of £135,000. The House of Lords held the mortgage was void against the wife. The bank had constructive notice of Mrs O'Brien's equity and could not enforce its later equity by taking possession of the matrimonial home.

In this case the House of Lords adopted the classification of undue influence devised by the court in *Bank of Credit and Commerce International v Aboody* [1990] 1 QB 180. Undue influence arises in two ways. First, actual undue influence where there is obvious pressure or coercion used. Secondly, undue influence is presumed; it is presumed by the relationship between the parties—the vulnerable partner due to the nature of the relationship may be taken advantage of by the stronger partner. Lord Browne-Wilkinson explained:

Undue influence

A person who has been induced to enter into a transaction by the undue influence of another ('the wrongdoer') is entitled to set that transaction aside as against the wrongdoer. Such undue influence is either actual or presumed. In *Bank of Credit and Commerce International S.A. v. Aboody* [1990] 1 Q.B. 923, 953, the Court of Appeal adopted the following classification.

Class 1: Actual undue influence

In these cases it is necessary for the claimant to prove affirmatively that the wrongdoer exerted undue influence on the complainant to enter into the particular transaction which is impugned.

Class 2: Presumed undue influence

In these cases the complainant only has to show, in the first instance, that there was a relationship of trust and confidence between the complainant and the wrongdoer of such a nature that it is fair to presume that the wrongdoer abused that relationship in procuring the complainant to enter into the impugned transaction. In Class 2 cases therefore there is no need to produce evidence that actual undue influence was exerted in relation to the particular transaction impugned . . . Such a confidential relationship can be established in two ways, viz.,

Class 2(A)

Certain relationships (for example solicitor and client, medical advisor and patient) as a matter of law raise the presumption that undue influence has been exercised.

Class 2(B)

Even if there is no relationship falling within Class 2(A), if the complainant proves the de facto existence of a relationship under which the complainant generally reposed trust and confidence in the wrongdoer, the existence of such relationship raises the presumption of undue influence. In a Class 2(B) case therefore, in the absence of evidence disproving undue influence, the complainant will succeed in setting aside the impugned transaction merely by proof that the complainant reposed trust and confidence in the wrongdoer without having to prove that the wrongdoer exerted actual undue influence or otherwise abused such trust and confidence in relation to the particular transaction impugned.

Lord Browne-Wilkinson then applied this analysis to the husband and wife relationship:

. . . although the concept of the ignorant wife leaving all financial decisions to the husband is outmoded, the practice does not yet coincide with the ideal. In a substantial proportion of marriages it is still the husband who has the business experience and the wife is willing to follow his advice without bringing a truly independent mind and will to bear on financial decisions. The number of recent cases in this field shows that in practice many wives are still subjected to, and yield to, undue influence by their husbands. Such wives can reasonably look to the law for some protection when their husbands have abused the trust and confidence reposed in them.

On the other hand, it is important to keep a sense of balance in approaching these cases. It is easy to allow sympathy for the wife who is threatened with the loss of her home at the suit of a rich bank to obscure an important public interest viz., the need to ensure that the wealth currently tied up in the matrimonial home does not become economically sterile. If the rights secured to wives by the law renders vulnerable loans granted on the security of matrimonial homes, institutions will be unwilling to accept such security, thereby reducing the flow of loan capital to business enterprises. It is therefore essential that a law designed to protect the vulnerable does not render the matrimonial home unacceptable as security to financial institutions.

Lord Browne-Wilkinson concluded that although Class 2(A) did not include the presumption of undue influence as between husband and wife, a wife would more likely come within the presumed undue influence category of Class 2(B) 'by her husband than by others because, in practice, many wives do repose in their husbands trust and confidence in relation to their financial affairs. Moreover the informality of business dealings between spouses raises a substantial risk that the husband has not accurately stated to the wife the nature of the liability she is undertaking, i.e., he has misrepresented the position, albeit negligently.'

Class 2(B) was not to be confined to a heterosexual marriage but also included the emotional relationship between cohabitees (heterosexual or homosexual).

Is the Lender Aware of the Possibility of Undue Influence?

Having found that Mrs O'Brien came within a class of persons who could set aside the transaction, Lord Browne-Wilkinson went on to consider whether Mrs O'Brien could have her transaction set aside against the bank due to the wrongdoing on the part of her husband.

There were two routes for the House of Lords to consider: Mrs O'Brien's husband was acting as an agent for the bank or the bank had notice (actual or constructive) of the undue influence exercised by her husband. The former approach was eliminated since Mr O'Brien was acting on his own behalf and not as an agent of the bank. Lord Browne-Wilkinson preferred to adopt the doctrine of notice in his evaluation of the case.

A wife who has been induced to stand as a surety for her husband's debts by his undue influence, misrepresentation or some other legal wrong has an equity as against him to set aside that transaction. Under the ordinary principles of equity, her right to set aside that transaction will be enforceable against third parties (e.g. against a creditor) if either the husband was acting as the third party's agent or the third party had actual or constructive notice of the facts giving rise to her equity. Although there may be cases where, without artificiality, it can properly be held that the husband was acting as the agent of the creditor in procuring the wife to stand as surety, such cases will be of very rare occurrence. The key to the problem is to identify the circumstances in which the creditor will be taken to have had notice of the wife's equity to set aside the transaction.

The doctrine of notice lies at the heart of equity. Given that there are two innocent parties, each enjoying rights, the earlier right prevails against the later right if the acquirer of the later right knows of the earlier right (actual notice) or would have discovered it had he taken proper steps (constructive notice). In particular, if the party asserting that he takes free of the earlier rights of another knows of certain facts which put him on inquiry as to the possible existence

> of the rights of that other and he fails to make such inquiry or take such other steps as are reasonable to verify whether such earlier right does or does not exist, he will have constructive notice of the earlier right and take subject to it.

Lord Browne-Wilkinson's reference to the doctrine of notice is potentially rather confusing. The notice referred to in *O'Brien* is very different from the doctrine of notice encountered in the High Chimneys case study in Chapter 4. In that chapter we were concerned with an issue of property law—whether an equitable property interest existing against land which is unregistered title can bind somebody who subsequently acquires the land or rights in the land, for example was Mrs Tizard's constructive trust interest binding on the later mortgagee, Kingsnorth Finance? That doctrine of notice (which in principle applies only to unregistered land) should perhaps now be referred to as 'proprietary doctrine of notice'.

The notice referred to in *O'Brien* focuses on the bank being put on inquiry to determine whether there is undue influence where a wife acts as a surety for her husband's debts. Put on inquiry, according to Lord Browne-Wilkinson, would arise by a combination of two factors: first, if the transaction was on the face of it financially disadvantageous for the wife and, secondly, if there was a substantial risk that the husband had exerted undue influence towards the wife. The lender, to avoid being fixed with constructive notice of the wife's equity to have the transaction set aside, would need to take certain preventative steps (considered in 24.3.2). In *O'Brien*, the purpose of the loan was to provide financial support for Mr O'Brien's failing company and there was no benefit for Mrs O'Brien. Under these circumstances, the bank was put on inquiry and ought to have taken precautionary measures to avoid being fixed with constructive notice.

The House of Lords in *CIBC Mortgages v Pitt* [1994] 1 AC 200 came to a different result from that in *O'Brien*. Mr and Mrs Pitt jointly owned the matrimonial home. Mr Pitt wanted to borrow money using the house as security to buy shares on the stock market. Mrs Pitt was unhappy, nevertheless she agreed to this to avoid further arguments. Mr and Mrs Pitt applied for a loan of £150,000. They stated that the purpose of the loan was to purchase a holiday home and to discharge the existing mortgage on the house. A legal charge was executed to provide security for the loan. Mr Pitt bought shares and was successful with his investments until the stock market crashed. He fell into arrears with his mortgage payments and the bank sought a possession order. Mrs Pitt argued that the transaction be set aside. Her signature was procured by reason of undue influence and that she had not understood the nature of the obligation or the amount involved.

The House of Lords acknowledged that Mrs Pitt had established actual undue influence. The case then turned on whether the lenders were put on inquiry. Lord Browne-Wilkinson said:

> What, then, was known to the plaintiff that could put it on inquiry so as to fix it with constructive notice?
>
> So far as the plaintiff was aware, the transaction consisted of a joint loan to husband and wife to finance the discharge of an existing mortgage on 26 Alexander Avenue, and as to the balance to be applied in buying a holiday home. The loan was advanced to both husband and wife jointly. There was nothing to indicate to the plaintiff that this was anything other than a normal advance to husband and wife for their joint benefit.

Despite the fact that there was evidence of actual undue influence, the House of Lords held that because this was a joint venture there was nothing to indicate to the bank that this loan was for anything else but their joint benefit. Lord Browne-Wilkinson distinguished cases of joint benefit from surety cases such as *O'Brien*, where there was a substantial risk of undue influence where the loan is not for the benefit of the surety.

What Steps Should the Bank Take to Avoid being Fixed with Constructive Notice?

Lord Browne-Wilkinson in *O'Brien* said:

> What, then are the reasonable steps which the creditor should take to ensure that it does not have constructive notice of the wife's rights, if any? Normally the reasonable steps necessary to avoid being fixed with constructive notice consist of making inquiry of the person who may have the earlier right (i.e. the wife) to see whether such right is asserted. It is plainly impossible to require of banks and other financial institutions that they should inquire of one spouse whether he or she has been unduly influenced or misled by the other. But in my judgment the creditor, in order to avoid being fixed with constructive notice, can reasonably be expected to take steps to bring home to the wife the risk she is running by standing as surety and to advise her to take independent advice. As to past transactions, it will depend on the facts of each case whether the steps taken by the creditor satisfy this test. However for the future in my judgment a creditor will have satisfied these requirements if it insists that the wife attend a private meeting (in the absence of the husband) with a representative of the creditor at which she is told of the extent of her liability as surety, warned of the risk she is running and urged to take independent legal advice. If these steps are taken in my judgment the creditor will have taken such reasonable steps as are necessary to preclude a subsequent claim that it had constructive notice of the wife's rights.

From this passage it is clear that Lord Browne-Wilkinson did not envisage asking the wife direct questions regarding undue influence as a practical option. The focus lies on the lender explaining the implications and the risks involved in the transaction. Practically this would involve the lender having a meeting with the wife, without the husband being present. She would also be advised to seek independent legal advice. If these steps are not taken, the lender will be fixed with constructive notice.

24.3.2 Undue Influence—Reconsidered

The decision in *O'Brien* gave rise to a flood of litigation on the kind of precautions banks should take to avoid having constructive notice of H's undue influence. Put another way, what exactly should a bank do to ensure that its mortgage is valid and cannot be challenged by W on the grounds that she was pressured into signing?

This question is answered by the House of Lords decision in a group of eight cases usually referred to as *Royal Bank of Scotland v Etridge (No 2)* [2002] 2 AC 773.

What is Undue Influence According to *Etridge*?

Etridge dispenses with the formal classification system of undue influence originally devised by *Aboody* and approved in *O'Brien*. The Law Lords found this unhelpful and instead retained the basic distinction between actual and presumed undue influence. The burden of proving undue influence lies with the person who is asserting the claim, and the evidence required to prove this depends on the circumstances. Actual undue influence includes overt exertion of pressure or coercion.

In the event that actual undue influence cannot be proven then the complainant may seek to show presumed undue influence. If a person falls within the scope of categories of relationship which the 'law presumes, irrebuttably, that one party had influence over the other' (per Lord Nicholls), the complainant only needs to prove the existence of this relationship, for example parent and child. Excluded from this category of relationship is that of a husband and wife.

Where the person making the claim of undue influence does not fall within the established categories of relationship where undue influence is presumed, then the complainant must prove that:

- the complainant placed trust and confidence in the other party; and
- the transaction cannot be readily explained by the relationship of the parties.

Irrespective of the nature of the relationship between the parties in dispute, it is apparent from the judgment in *Etridge* that the party seeking to have the transaction set aside must be able to satisfy the evidential burden of a 'transaction which calls for explanation'. Lord Nicholls said:

> On proof of these two matters the stage is set for the court to infer that, in the absence of a satisfactory explanation, the transaction can only have been procured by undue influence. In other words, proof of these two facts is prima facie evidence that the defendant abused the influence he acquired in the parties' relationship. He preferred his own interests. He did not behave fairly to the other. So the evidential burden then shifts to him. It is for him to produce evidence to counter the inference which otherwise should be drawn.

The House of Lords addressed the problematic question of what amounts to a 'manifest disadvantage' for the complainant. This issue originated from the House of Lords in *National Westminster Bank Plc v Morgan* [1985] AC 686 where Lord Scarman stated:

> the transaction ... must constitute a disadvantage sufficiently serious to require evidence to rebut the presumption that in the circumstances of the relationship between the parties it was procured by the exercise of undue influence.

The label 'manifest disadvantage' was attached to this test to encapsulate what was required; however, according to Lord Nicholls this label was misleading and had led to confusion in its application. He suggested discarding this label of 'manifest disadvantage' and adhering to the original test (outlined in the previous passage) which requires the court to examine the nature of the transaction and the factual circumstances surrounding it.

This test has one particular merit as it may act as a filter to dismiss applications concerning transactions which raise complaints of undue influence but where the factual circumstances do not satisfy the evidential burden. That is, the complainant has failed to produce sufficient evidence that the transaction is so disadvantageous to him/her that the onus is shifted to the lender to prove that the transaction is not vitiated by undue influence.

When is the Lender Put on Inquiry?

The use of the doctrine of notice in *O'Brien* was clarified in *Etridge*. In *O'Brien* where the wife stood as surety for her husband's debts, the bank was put on inquiry. The bank, in order to avoid being fixed with constructive notice of the wife's rights, would have to fulfil certain requirements to ensure that the wife's agreement had been properly obtained. Lord Nicholls, commenting on this approach, regarded constructive notice as a 'misnomer' because the bank was not actually required to make inquiries.

The use of the terminology of the bank being 'put on inquiry' continues to prevail though without the association with the doctrine of notice. Instead Lord Nicholls set a low threshold for the lender to be put on inquiry. The lender is 'put on inquiry' whenever a person stands as surety for another's debts, these include:

- spouse;

- 'unmarried couples, whether heterosexual or homosexual, where the bank is aware of the relationship...Cohabitation is not essential' (per Lord Nicholls);
- where the money is being advanced jointly but the bank is aware that the money is solely for the husband's purposes, and not for their joint purposes; and
- a spouse becomes surety for the debts of a company whose shares are held either by the husband or wife. The bank is put on inquiry even if the spouse is a director or secretary of the company.

This list predominantly focuses on the husband–wife relationship. The House of Lords explained that in the wider context, there are numerous relationships which would put the bank on inquiry. An exhaustive list of relationships which could be regarded as being at substantial risk of undue influence could not be feasibly drawn up since each case would be dealt with on its merits. Lord Nicholls considered the broad application of the bank 'being put on inquiry':

> ...if a bank is not to be required to evaluate the extent to which its customer has influence over a proposed guarantor, the only practical way forward is to regard banks as 'put on inquiry' in every case where the relationship between the surety and the debtor is non-commercial. The creditor must always take reasonable steps to bring home to the individual guarantor the risks he is running by standing as surety. As a measure of protection, this is valuable. But, in all conscience, it is a modest burden for banks and other lenders. It is no more than is reasonably to be expected of a creditor who is taking a guarantee from an individual. If the bank or other creditor does not take these steps, it is deemed to have notice of any claim the guarantor may have that the transaction was procured by undue influence or misrepresentation on the part of the debtor.
>
> Different considerations apply where the relationship between the debtor and guarantor is commercial, as where a guarantor is being paid a fee, or a company is guaranteeing the debts of another company in the same group. Those engaged in business can be regarded as capable of looking after themselves and understanding the risks involved in the giving of guarantees.

What Steps Should the Bank Take?

The House of Lords in *Etridge* reconsidered the approach suggested by Lord Browne-Wilkinson in *O'Brien*. Comprehensive guidelines were provided by the House of Lords in *Etridge* to ensure that the risks of standing as surety would be brought home to him/her in a meaningful way. This is important because standing as surety usually involves agreeing that family-owned property is mortgaged to secure the loan. The bank, in cases arising after *Etridge*, 'satisfies these requirements if it insists that the wife attend a private meeting with a representative of the bank at which she is told of the extent of her liability as surety, warned of the risk she is running and urged to take independent legal advice. In exceptional cases the bank, to be safe, has to insist that the wife is separately advised' (per Lord Nicholls).

In practice, experience has shown, post *O'Brien*, that the banks were reluctant to have a private meeting with the surety (usually the wife), because the banks thought that they could stand to lose more than they gained by giving advice to the surety. Instead the banks preferred this task being undertaken by a solicitor. This was accepted by the House of Lords as the preferred course of action for giving advice.

Lord Nicholls outlined the steps the bank should take when it has been put on inquiry and 'for its protection is looking to the fact that the wife has been advised independently by a solicitor':

> 79 (1)...Since the bank is looking for its protection to legal advice given to the wife by a solicitor who, in this respect, is acting solely for her, I consider the bank should take steps to check directly with the wife the name of the solicitor she wishes to act for her. To this end, in

future the bank should communicate directly with the wife, informing her that for its own protection it will require written confirmation from a solicitor, acting for her, to the effect that the solicitor has fully explained to her the nature of the documents and the practical implications they will have for her. She should be told that the purpose of this requirement is that thereafter she should not be able to dispute she is legally bound by the documents once she has signed them. She should be asked to nominate a solicitor whom she is willing to instruct to advise her, separately from her husband, and act for her in giving the necessary confirmation to the bank. She should be told that, if she wishes, the solicitor may be the same solicitor as is acting for her husband in the transaction. If a solicitor is already acting for the husband and the wife, she should be asked whether she would prefer that a different solicitor should act for her regarding the bank's requirement for confirmation from a solicitor.

The bank should not proceed with the transaction until it has received an appropriate response directly from the wife.

(2) Representatives of the bank are likely to have a much better picture of the husband's financial affairs than the solicitor. If the bank is not willing to undertake the task of explanation itself, the bank must provide the solicitor with the financial information he needs for this purpose. Accordingly it should become routine practice for banks, if relying on confirmation from a solicitor for their protection, to send to the solicitor the necessary financial information. What is required must depend on the facts of the case. Ordinarily this will include information on the purpose for which the proposed new facility has been requested, the current amount of the husband's indebtedness, the amount of his current overdraft facility, and the amount and terms of any new facility. If the bank's request for security arose from a written application by the husband for a facility, a copy of the application should be sent to the solicitor. The bank will, of course, need first to obtain the consent of its customer to this circulation of confidential information. If this consent is not forthcoming the transaction will not be able to proceed.

(3) Exceptionally there may be a case where the bank believes or suspects that the wife has been misled by her husband or is not entering into the transaction of her own free will. If such a case occurs the bank must inform the wife's solicitors of the facts giving rise to its belief or suspicion.

(4) The bank should in every case obtain from the wife's solicitor a written confirmation to the effect mentioned above.

Lord Nicholls identifies a problem that may arise in obtaining legal advice for the wife in these circumstances. Should the solicitor only act for the wife? The benefit to the wife would rest largely on the fact that she would perhaps feel less inhibited about discussing the financial aspects of the transaction with the solicitor, than if the solicitor was also representing the husband. Lord Nicholls thought that a solicitor could act for the husband or bank provided that the solicitor was satisfied this was in the wife's best interests and did not give rise to a conflict of interest. In the event that there was a conflict of interest the solicitor would cease to act for her. In reaching this conclusion he was aware of the financial reality of obtaining legal advice. Lord Nicholls said:

A requirement that a wife should receive advice from a solicitor acting solely for her will frequently add significantly to the legal costs. Sometimes a wife will be happier to be advised by a family solicitor known to her than by a complete stranger. Sometimes a solicitor who knows both husband and wife and their histories will be better placed to advise than a solicitor who is a complete stranger.

The House of Lords has recognized that increasing the costs and burden on the party seeking the loan was not a viable option. Faith was placed in the legal profession in providing independent legal advice and it was felt that the bank could justifiably rely on the 'professional competence and propriety of the solicitor in providing proper and adequate advice to the wife notwithstanding that he, the solicitor, is acting also for the husband' (per Lord Scott).

Lord Nicholls provided specific guidance on the role of the solicitor in the provision of advice:

> 64 ...As a first step the solicitor will need to explain to the wife the purpose for which he has become involved at all...The solicitor will need to obtain confirmation from the wife that she wishes him to act for her in the matter and to advise her on the legal and practical implications of the proposed transaction.
>
> 65 ...Typically, the advice a solicitor can be expected to give should cover the following matters as the core minimum. [1] He will need to explain the nature of the documents and the practical consequences these will have for the wife if she signs them. She could lose her home if her husband's business does not prosper. Her home may be her only substantial asset, as well as the family's home. She could be made bankrupt. [2] He will need to point out the seriousness of the risks involved. The wife should be told the purpose of the proposed new facility, the amount and principal terms of the new facility, and that the bank might increase the amount of the facility, or change its terms, or grant a new facility, without reference to her. She should be told the amount of her liability under her guarantee. The solicitor should discuss the wife's financial means, including her understanding of the value of the property being charged. The solicitor should discuss whether the wife or her husband has any other assets out of which repayment could be made if the husband's business should fail. These matters are relevant to the seriousness of the risks involved. [3] The solicitor will need to state clearly that the wife has a choice. The decision is hers and hers alone. Explanation of the choice facing the wife will call for some discussion of the present financial position, including the amount of the husband's present indebtedness, and the amount of his current overdraft facility. [4] The solicitor should check whether the wife wishes to proceed. She should be asked whether she is content that the solicitor should write to the bank confirming he has explained to her the nature of the documents and the practical implications they may have for her, or whether, for instance, she would prefer him to negotiate with the bank on the terms of the transaction. Matters for negotiation could include the sequence in which the various securities will be called upon or a specific or lower limit to her liabilities. The solicitor should not give any confirmation to the bank without the wife's authority.
>
> 66 The solicitor's discussion with the wife should take place at a face-to-face meeting, in the absence of the husband. It goes without saying that the solicitor's explanations should be couched in suitably non-technical language. It also goes without saying that the solicitor's task is an important one. It is not a formality.
>
> 67 The solicitor should obtain from the bank any information he needs. If the bank fails for any reason to provide information requested by the solicitor, the solicitor should decline to provide the confirmation sought by the bank.
>
> 68 ...the advice which a solicitor can be expected to give must depend on the particular facts of the case. But I have set out this 'core minimum' in some detail...

In summary, when the bank is put on inquiry in the event of a person acting as surety for another person's debt, the bank must comply with the following steps:

- Bank to communicate with the surety—inform the surety written confirmation is required from a solicitor stating that the solicitor has fully explained the nature of the documents and the practical implications. The surety will be asked to nominate a solicitor.

- Bank must receive an appropriate response from the surety before it can proceed.

- Provision of financial information—bank must obtain permission from its client to allow disclosure of its client's financial information to the surety's solicitor. The bank will need to seek permission from their client to provide the following confidential information to the solicitor which will include: the purpose of the loan, the current debt owed to the bank, the amount of the current overdraft facility, and the amount and terms of any new facility; and where applicable a written application by the client for a loan. If the client does not give permission for disclosure the transaction will not be able to proceed.

- Meeting with solicitor:
  - solicitor should obtain all the necessary information from the bank. In the event the relevant information is not provided, the solicitor can refuse to give confirmation that legal advice has been given to the surety;
  - face-to-face meeting without the bank's client (usually the husband) being present;
  - explanation of the purpose of the meeting; confirmation is required that the surety wants the solicitor to act on behalf of the surety. Core minimum advice to surety includes:
    - explanation of the nature of the documents and the practical consequences if the surety signs them. Explanations should be given in non-technical language;
    - highlight the seriousness of the risks involved. The surety to be told the purpose of the loan, the amount, and principal terms of the loan, and surety's liability under guarantee;
    - explanation that the decision rests solely with the surety and that he or she has a choice in the matter;
    - check whether the surety wishes to proceed. Confirmation from the surety that the solicitor may proceed to confirm to the bank that all the relevant information has been explained and discussed.

Are the Banks Taking Note of the Etridge Guidelines?

The simple answer to this question is, it appears 'Yes'. In *Hewett v First Plus Financial Group Plc* [2010] EWCA Civ 312 the bank conceded that it had not complied with the guidelines set out in *Etridge* in a case which involved a married couple re-mortgaging their property to pay off the husband's credit card debts. This case is noteworthy because the Court of Appeal considers the scope of undue influence where the husband has not disclosed a material fact to the wife prior to agreeing to a joint re-mortgage.

Mr Hewett persuaded his wife to agree to jointly re-mortgage the property because of his credit card debts. At that time Mrs Hewett was unaware her husband was having an affair. They later divorced. Mr Hewett's debts increased to £40,000 and he became bankrupt. Mrs Hewett acquired her former husband's beneficial interest in the property from the trustee in bankruptcy for £1 but could not pay the mortgage instalments. First Plus sought possession of the property.

The Court of Appeal held that Mr Hewett's conduct amounted to undue influence.

Mrs Hewett had sufficient trust and confidence in her husband which gave rise to an obligation of candour and fairness. On this latter point, Briggs J noted that undue influence is not confined to cases where 'the wife meekly follows her husband's directions without question'. As far as the judge was concerned 'the purpose of an obligation of candour is that the wife should be able to make an informed decision (with or without the benefit of independent advice) properly and fairly appraised of the relevant circumstances'. There is a clear obligation to inform the other party of material facts so that an *informed decision* can be made.

Consequently, Mr Hewett was under an obligation of candour and fairness to disclose his extramarital affair because at the time when Mrs Hewett undertook her decision to agree to the re-mortgage it was based on the assumption that Mr Hewett was committed to their marriage and family life. Mr Hewett had not discharged his obligation of candour and fairness.

24.4 Redemption of Mortgages

24.4.1 When May Redemption Take Place?

A mortgage may be redeemed:

1 on the legal redemption date;
2 at any other time expressly permitted by the terms of the mortgage;
3 on the expiry of six months' notice of intention to repay; or
4 at any time, without notice, if the mortgagee is demanding repayment or attempting to enforce the security, or if the loan was intended to be temporary.

Notice, therefore, that unless situations (1), (2), or (4) apply, a mortgagor is not entitled as a matter of law suddenly to turn up at the mortgagee's door and say, 'Here is all the money I owe you.' Unless one of those situations apply, the mortgagee is entitled to six months' notice, or six months' interest in lieu of notice.

In practice, institutional lenders such as banks and building societies are usually flexible in their approach to redemption, and are usually happy to accept repayment at less than six months' notice.

24.4.2 Who May Redeem?

The original mortgagor may redeem, together with any persons who derive title through the mortgagor.

> **thinking point 24.3**
>
> *What sort of people 'derive title' through a mortgagor?*
>
> *Undoubtedly this concept covers a spouse and civil partner with home rights under the Family Law Act 1996, or anybody (eg a cohabitee) with a constructive trust interest in the property (ss35 and 36 Family Law Act 1996).*

24.4.3 The Effect of Redemption

If a mortgage is repaid by the mortgagor him or herself, it is simply discharged. If it is repaid by a third party entitled to redeem, then the mortgage is transferred to that third party; that (in effect) means that the third party assumes the role of mortgagee.

24.4.4 Machinery of Redemption—Unregistered Land

Where a mortgage is redeemed, the parties could execute a new deed discharging or transferring the mortgage (as the case may be). However, it is the normal practice to invoke s115 LPA 1925 under which the mortgagee endorses on or annexes to the mortgage deed a receipt for the debt, indicating who is paying the money. If the person named is the mortgagor, the mortgage is simply discharged; if the person named is a third party, the receipt will transfer the mortgage to him.

On redemption the title deeds should be handed back to the mortgagor or handed to the transferee (as the case may be). If the loan is repaid by the mortgagor, then before handing the title deeds back the mortgagee must search the land charges register. If the mortgagee thereby discovers a subsequent mortgagee, the mortgagee must hand the title deeds to that subsequent mortgagee.

24.4.5 Machinery of Redemption—Registered Land

In registered land where the mortgage is redeemed, the registered charge entered onto the register of title must be removed. A form from the Land Registry must be completed and executed by deed.

24.4.6 Consolidation of Mortgages

Consolidation of mortgages occurs where a mortgagee has two mortgages created by the same mortgagor, and insists that if one mortgage is redeemed the other mortgage is redeemed as well. This right of consolidation is of practical value where the mortgagor proposes to repay a well-secured loan, but to leave a poorly secured loan outstanding. For example, Bloggs owns Blackacre and Whiteacre, both worth £50,000 and both mortgaged to the Muggtown Bank. The debt secured on Blackacre is £70,000; the debt secured on Whiteacre is only £15,000. Bloggs proposes to repay the £15,000 secured on Whiteacre.

The following conditions must be satisfied for consolidation to be effected:

1 At least one of the two mortgages must confer a right of consolidation. (Modern mortgages always include a clause entitling the mortgagee to consolidate.)
2 The legal redemption date on each mortgage must be passed.
3 Both mortgages must have been made by the same mortgagor.
4 At some point of time (however long or short) both mortgages were in common ownership, and both equities of redemption were in common ownership.

Consider the following examples of condition (4) (assuming the first three conditions are satisfied):

(i) X mortgages Brownacre to A and Greenacre to B. C acquires both mortgages. C is entitled to consolidate. C would no doubt wish to do so if the loan secured on Greenacre was for £70,000 but Greenacre is now worth only £50,000, while Brownacre is worth considerably more than the loan secured on Brownacre.

(ii) C would still be entitled to consolidate if subsequently the equity of redemption in Brownacre was sold to Y, and the equity in Greenacre was sold to Z. If (say) Y was compelled to pay off the mortgage on Greenacre, Y would take the mortgage on Greenacre by transfer (for what it's worth!).

(iii) If (say) X had sold the equity in Blackacre to Y before C had acquired both mortgages, there could be no consolidation by C.

This consolidation rule is often criticized, and should perhaps be abolished. The consolidation rule is a major reason why, in modern conditions, people are reluctant to buy a property subject to a mortgage which will not be discharged out of the proceeds of sale.

thinking point 24.4

Why is consolidation a risk to somebody who buys an equity of redemption, that is, a property subject to an outstanding mortgage?

A person who buys land subject to a mortgage always runs the risk that the mortgage on his land will be consolidated with a mortgage of which he has never even heard. (Y, in our recent example, may never have heard of Greenacre.)

24.5 Fire Insurance of the Mortgaged Property

A mortgagee whose mortgage is 'made by deed' has a statutory power (ss 101 and 108 LPA 1925) to take out fire insurance on the mortgaged property and add the premiums to the capital debt. The policy must be for an amount specified in the mortgage deed, but in the absence of a specific provision the amount must not exceed two-thirds of the cost of restoring the building in the event of total destruction.

The statutory power is excluded if:

1 the mortgage deed specifically provides that there shall be no fire insurance;
2 the mortgagor maintains a policy in accordance with the express terms of the deed; or
3 the mortgage deed says nothing about fire insurance, but the mortgagor with the mortgagee's consent keeps up a policy for at least two-thirds of the cost of restoration in the event of total destruction.

As you may already have guessed, the statutory power relating to insurance is totally inadequate for modern conditions.

thinking point 24.5

How do institutional lenders such as banks and building societies deal with this problem?

Institutional lenders invoke exclusion (2). Most modern mortgages specifically require the mortgagor to maintain insurance cover (against all catastrophes, not just fire) to the full value of the property. Alternatively, they provide that the mortgagee will insure the property for its full value and add the premiums to the mortgage debt.

○ Concluding Remarks

In the Introduction to this chapter it was stressed that the law has not kept pace with economic realities. Hopefully, however, you have noticed that some of these rules, for example those relating to insurance and leasing, can and often are avoided by careful drafting of the mortgage. The parties 'contract out' of the awkward rules.

The parties cannot (of course) contract out of the rules regarding undue influence. Nor can the parties contract out of the arguably outmoded and largely judge-made rules regarding delaying redemption and collateral advantages. In an era when the phrase 'consumer protection' had not even been thought of, the judges realized that borrowers needed protection from oppressive terms which lenders might otherwise impose.

However, as the *Kreglinger* case perhaps demonstrates, these judge-made rules lack the flexibility of modern legislation such as the Consumer Credit Act or the Unfair Contract Terms Act. Moreover, these judge-made rules apply to all borrowers, whatever their wealth or status. As with many other aspects of land law, reform of the law of mortgages is urgently required to make it suitable for the social and economic conditions of the twenty-first century.

 # Summary

Rights of the Mortgagor

Rules in Equity which Protect Equitable Right to Redeem

- No irredeemable mortgages.
- Postponement of redemption; must not, in all the circumstances including the relative economic strengths of the parties, be unconscionable and oppressive.

Collateral Advantages

Benefits to the mortgagee going beyond the usual right to payment of capital and interest:

- validity of the collateral advantage while the loan remains outstanding:
  - is the bargain unfair or unconscionable?
- validity of the collateral advantage after redemption of the mortgage:
  - traditional approach—the solus tie or other collateral advantage ceases on redemption of the mortgage (*Noakes v Rice; Bradley v Carritt*);
  - a collateral advantage could be treated as an independent agreement. It is necessary to examine the substance of the bargain to determine whether it is an independent agreement (*Kreglinger v New Patagonia Meat Company*).

Restraint on Trade

A collateral advantage will be void if it is an unreasonable restraint of trade.

Leasing Mortgaged Property

- Lease granted *before* mortgage has been created—binds mortgagee.
- Lease granted *after* mortgage has been created—does not bind mortgagee except if the mortgagee agrees to the continuation of the lease, by words or conduct.

Vitiating Factor—Undue Influence

- *Actual undue influence*—overt exertion of pressure or coercion.
- *Presumed undue influence*—consider the relationship between the parties and whether the transaction requires an explanation:

- relationship between the parties:
  - certain categories of persons where the law presumes pressure may be exerted over a vulnerable party;
  - relationships where there is in fact trust and confidence;
- transaction which calls for explanation:
  - 'the transaction…must constitute a disadvantage sufficiently serious to require evidence to rebut the presumption that in the circumstances of the relationship between the parties it was procured by the exercise of undue influence' (per Lord Scarman, *National Westminster Bank Plc v Morgan*).

- *When is the lender 'put on inquiry'?* Whenever a person stands as surety for another's debts, these include:
  - spouse;
  - unmarried couples (includes heterosexual or homosexual), cohabitees, or where the bank is aware of the relationship;
  - where the money is being advanced jointly but the bank is aware that the money is solely for the husband's purposes, and not for their joint purposes;
- *Bank is put on inquiry:* the Bank must comply with the following steps:
  - Bank to communicate with the surety—inform the surety that written confirmation is required from a solicitor chosen by the surety stating that the solicitor has fully explained the nature of the documents and the practical implications. Bank must receive an appropriate response from the surety before it can proceed;
  - provision of financial information—Bank must obtain permission from its client to allow disclosure of its client's financial information to the surety's solicitor;
  - *meeting with surety's solicitor:*
    - solicitor has face-to-face meeting with surety. Bank's client (usually the husband) should not be present;
    - *core minimum* advice to surety includes: clear explanation in non-technical language of the nature of the documents and the practical consequences if the surety signs them; highlight the seriousness of the risks involved. The surety to be told the purpose of the loan, the amount and principal terms of the loan, and the extent of the surety's liability; check that the surety, at his/her free choice, wishes to proceed. Confirmation from the surety that the solicitor may tell the Bank that all the relevant information has been explained and discussed.

Redemption of Mortgages

- The right to redeem belongs not just to the mortgagor, but also any person deriving title from the mortgagor.
- Unless the mortgagee is pressing for repayment, anybody intending to redeem a mortgage may have to give six months' notice or pay six months' interest in lieu of notice.
- If someone other than the mortgagor redeems the mortgage, then (normally) the mortgage is transferred to that person.
- Consolidation of mortgages is a possible trap for mortgagors. The mortgagor wanting to pay off one loan may find themselves having to pay off two loans.

Fire Insurance and Leasing of Mortgaged Property

The LPA 1925 contains quite elaborate rules on these issues, but the parties can (and usually do) 'contract out' of these rules.

# Further Reading

Brown, S, 'The Consumer Credit Act 2006; a real additional mortgagor protection?' [1990] Conv 431

Considers the extent to which mortgagees are subject to this legislation.

Harpum, C, and Dixon, M, 'Fraud, undue influence and mortgages of registered land' [1994] Conv 421

A response to Thompson's 1994 article on the issue of the use of the doctrine of notice in *O'Brien*.

Omar, PJ, 'Equitable interests and the secured creditor: determining priorities' [2006] Conv 509

Considers the issue of the priority of equitable interests if the property is sold.

Thompson, MP, 'The enforceability of mortgages' [1994] Conv 140

Case note on *O'Brien* with a commentary on the doctrine of notice.

Thompson, MP, 'Wives, sureties and banks' [2002] Conv 174

This article provides a critical evaluation of *O'Brien* following *Etridge (No 2)*.

Index

Introductory Note

References such as '178–9' indicate (not necessarily continuous) discussion of a topic across a range of pages. Wherever possible in the case of topics with many references, these have either been divided into sub-topics or only the most significant discussions of the topic are listed. Because the entire work is about the 'land law', the use of this term (and certain others which occur constantly throughout the book) as an entry point has been minimized. Information will be found under the corresponding detailed topics.

Revision & study guides from the **No.1** legal education publisher

When you're aiming high, reach for credible, high quality revision and study guides that will help you consolidate knowledge, focus your revision, and maximise your potential.

Oxford's **Concentrate** series

When you're serious about success

Oxford's **Q&A** series

Don't just answer the question: nail it

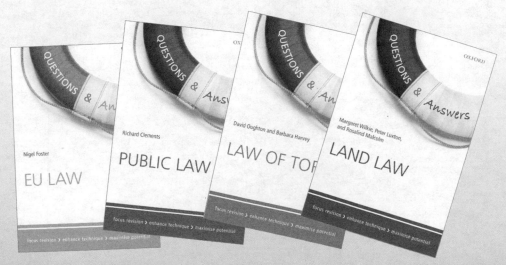

These titles and more available from your campus bookshop or direct from **www.oup.com**.